The International League

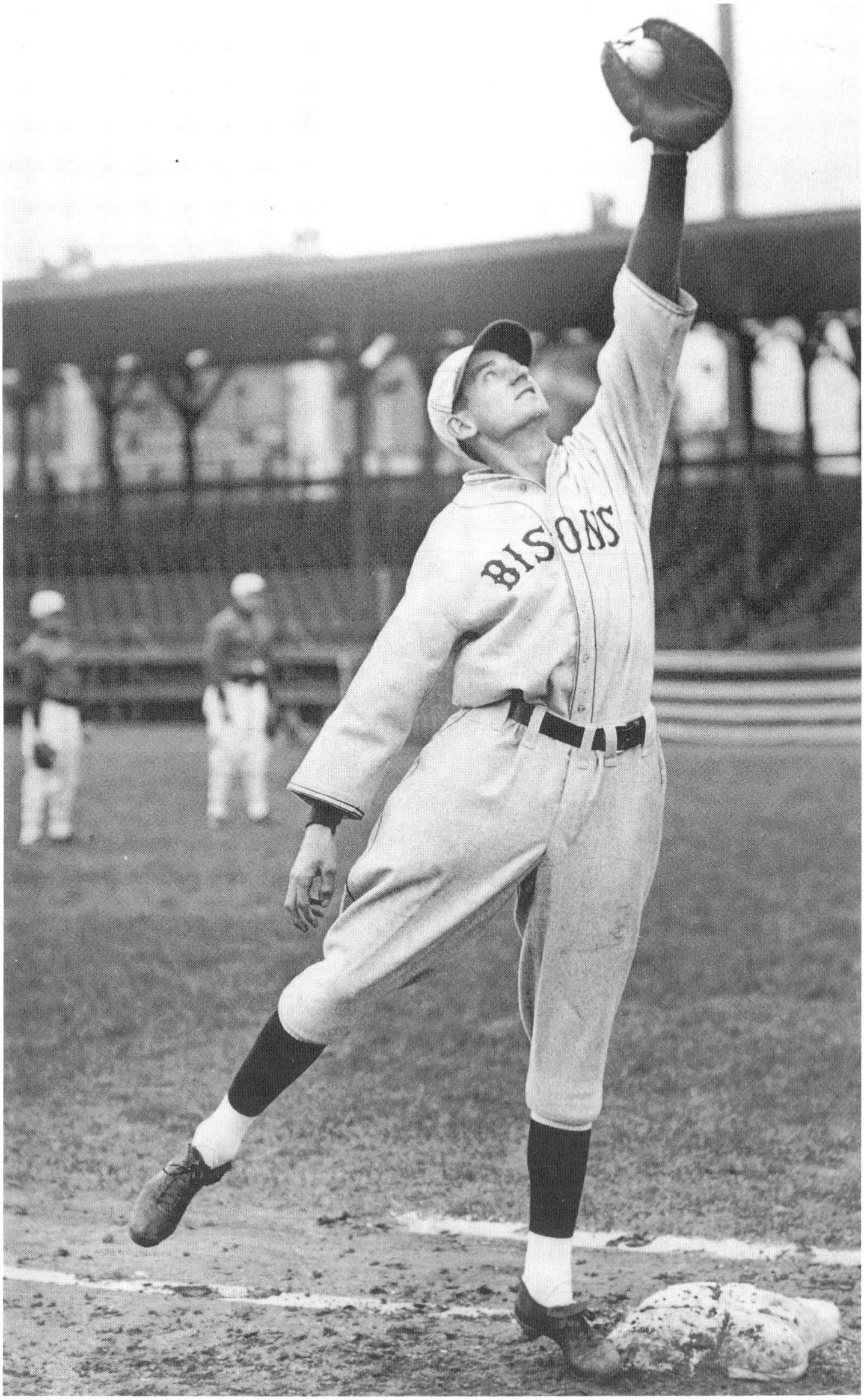
BISONS

The International League

Year-by-Year Statistics, 1884–1953

BY

MARSHALL D. WRIGHT

McFarland & Company, Inc., Publishers

Jefferson, North Carolina, and London

Frontispiece: Baxter Jordan, a first baseman for Buffalo
(1929), Newark (1930, 1931), Baltimore (1932, 1939) and
Syracuse (1939)

British Library Cataloguing-in-Publication data are available

Library of Congress Cataloguing-in-Publication data are available

Library of Congress Catalog Card Number 97-075784

ISBN 0-7864-0458-2 (library binding; 50# alkaline paper)

Manufactured in the United States of America

McFarland & Company, Inc., Publishers
  Box 611, Jefferson, North Carolina 28640

To Karen

TABLE OF CONTENTS

ACKNOWLEDGMENTS

It is a simple fact that a book cannot be completed without the help of others. This is certainly true about the pages to follow. With this in mind, I would like to thank the following colleagues and friends who helped greatly with this project.

On a professional level, I would like to thank Howe Sportsdata International for granting me access to their vast collection of <u>Spalding</u> and <u>Reach</u> guides. I would also like to thank Ray Nemec for providing the hard-to-find statistics missing from the guides, and player's names. For the text portion, I relied almost exclusively on the fine efforts of my colleagues in the Society for American Baseball Research. Thanks also to Gary Austin for supplying background information on the 1890 International League. Also, the Baseball Research Library in Cooperstown, New York, was very helpful in filling several holes in the data.

On a personal level, I would like to thank Jay Virshbo and my friends and associates at Howe Sportsdata International.

Lastly, I would like to thank my family, especially my wife, Jane, for her patience, kindness, and love, as well as her keen editing eye, and my father, Robert Wright, for his help with the text. And a special thanks to my son Denny, whose cheerful companionship keeps me fresh and alert—constantly aware of the important things in life.

INTRODUCTION

For many years, the statistics of the major leagues have been made available to the public in a variety of ways. Reference works such as Macmillan's *Baseball Encyclopedia* and Viking's *Total Baseball* series give major league players complete statistical coverage. With the major leagues so thoroughly chronicled, it is time to turn our attention to the vast world of minor league baseball, which has been too long ignored by reference works such as the ones just mentioned. This book opens a new world of statistical data, a whole league's worth—the International League.

The International League and its cohorts, the American Association and the Pacific Coast League, have ruled minor league baseball for many years. Each has filled its own unique niche in the minors. The American Association is noted for its stability; for fifty years the league's franchises remained unchanged. The Pacific Coast League's independence has set it apart. For the International League, the defining characteristic has been longevity. For over 100 years this circuit has graced the world of the minors—the longest by far of any league.

The league that we now call the International League was formed as the Eastern League in 1892, changing its name to the International League in 1912. Until 1935, the circuit traced its lineage back to the Eastern League's 1892 formation. In the mid-thirties, however, the books suddenly began claiming that the league had its beginnings with the Eastern League of 1884 , another organization entirely. The books then traced the league's path through several different organizations and name changes before linking it with the 1892 group. It is not this book's role to dispute this lineage, merely to point out its tangled path. That is why 1884 has been chosen as this volume's starting point.

For many years, the International League was a stable organization. True, many franchises came and went, but 1953 saw a different type of franchise shift, the first of its kind. Immediately following the 1953 campaign, one of the league's most successful franchises, the Baltimore Orioles, was booted out of Baltimore in favor of an incoming major league team, in this case the St. Louis Browns. This was not a simple relocation of one minor league franchise to another city; this was encroachment of the highest level—one league moving in on another's territory.

For many years leading up to 1953, most, if not all, minor league teams had working relationships with the major leagues, if they were not owned outright by major league clubs. These relationships naturally kept minor league rosters in a state of flux as players were sent up and down from one level to another. In the International League, this practice was prevalent, as this top minor league served as a direct conduit to the majors. As a part of this process, a major league team occasionally felt it necessary to relocate one of its minor league clubs to another city. But in 1953 a line was crossed. Not content to dictate the location of the International League's players and teams, the major leagues moved a minor league franchise so that an incoming major league team could have a clear field. This action did not spell the demise of the International League; the league prospered and continued much as it had before. But this different kind of encroachment serves as a clear dividing line between two eras. And that is why 1953 has been chosen as this book's ending point.

In the volume that follows is the statistical history of the International League's first 70 years. The book is arranged chronologically, and then by team within each year. For each team several categories are listed: wins, losses, winning percentage, place in the standings, games behind, and manager or managers. Within each team, complete batting and pitching statistics are included. For each batter, twelve statistical categories are used: games, at bats, runs, hits, runs batted in, doubles, triples, home runs, bases on balls, strikeouts, stolen bases, and batting average. For each pitcher twelve categories are also included: wins, losses, winning percentage, games, games started, complete games, shutouts, innings pitched, hits allowed, bases on balls allowed, strikeouts, and earned run average. On each team, the batters are arranged with the top eight positional players listed first (1b, 2b, ss, 3b, 3 of, and c) followed by all of the other hitters in order of most games played. The team's roster of pitchers is placed in order of most wins.

For most years, several players played on more than one team. These men are listed at the end of each year in the multi-team player category. Occasionally, a multi-team batter will have played most of his games for one team—enough to be included in that team's top eight. In those cases, that player is listed with that club as well as in the multi-player section.

League and team leaders in all categories are in boldface type. Multi-team leaders are marked with an asterisk as well.

The statistics used in this book came from the printed sources available. Those sources include the *Spalding* and *Reach* guides, *Players' League Guide*, *Sporting Life*, and the *Sporting News*. For several years some of the information was not extant in these sources. To access this missing information, I turned to one of the founding members of the Society for American Baseball Research, Mr. Ray Nemec.

Mr. Nemec generously supplied me with the following information based on painstaking game-by-game research performed by himself and others. Researchers and the seasons they researched include Ray Nemec (1888, 1889, 1890, 1918 International; 1891, 1892, 1894, 1895, 1898, 1899 Eastern); Vern Luse (1884, 1885, 1886, 1893, 1896, 1897 Eastern; 1887 International); C.R. Howard (1885 New York State); and Eves Raja (1885 Canadian). I am indeed grateful and indebted to them for allowing me to include their work. In addition, Mr. Nemec supplied all the material on players participating in fewer than ten games per year from 1934 through 1953, and a great deal of information on hard-to-find first names of players up until 1917. A direct result of this research by Mr. Nemec and others has been the rewriting of the International League record book. In several instances, additional information has altered a champion's record, causing him to lose his title. In other cases, data previously uncompiled, such as pitchers earned averages before 1916, have resulted in new record holders. In every case, any uprooted champion or new record holder has been carefully chronicled.

Despite this outpouring of research support, some gaps remain in the statistical work. For several years, entire statistical categories are unavailable. In addition, a few team batting totals are not extant. Some of the players' first names remain missing as well. In the case of missing data, the category regrettably is left blank. In the future, an intrepid researcher will have to plug the holes.

In a few cases, the International League record book shows a particular league leader whose record has not been corroborated in the extant material. If this leader pertains to a team mentioned in the text, his record is noted.

For many years the International League was not known by that name. During the course of the narrative, reference will be made to the six different names used. "The League" will serve as a general term for the family of leagues that made up the Interna-tional's history.

In the nineteenth century, some seasons and teams were unstable. In several cases, teams dropped out or disbanded in the middle of the season. Sometimes, an offending team's record was dropped from the league records. Sometimes it was not. In a few instances, a disbanded team's record would have placed it at or near the top of the standings—but since it didn't finish the season, it was relegated to the bottom of the heap. To remain consistent, I have included all available teams' statistics. In addition, I have placed the teams in order of their actual winning percentage, regardless of whether they finished the season.

The International League is baseball's longest running minor league—113 years and still going strong. For its first 70 years, meandering through the nineteenth century, enduring three wars, thriving in boom times and surviving poverty, until its change at the hands of major league intrusion, the International League had engaging stories to tell.

PRELUDE
BASEBALL BACK EAST

The cities of America's Eastern Seaboard have witnessed many of the important events in baseball's history. When the rules of baseball were codified in the 1840s, the very first games were played in New York City and Hoboken, New Jersey. In the 1850s and 1860s, when the first teams (such as the Mutuals, Eckfords, and the Olympics) were organized, they were located in cities like New York, Brooklyn, and Washington, D.C. In the 1870s the first professional leagues, the National Association in 1871 and the National League in 1876, encompassed these same cities. When more locales clamored for teams, a need arose for auxiliary leagues. When formed, these circuits also had a distinctly eastern flavor.

The first of these additional, or minor, leagues sprang forth in 1877. In that year two loosely formed conglomerates, the League Alliance and the International Association, started play in several eastern (as well as midwestern and Canadian) cities. The League Alliance consisted of thirteen teams, while the International Association comprised seven teams. In 1877, the Red Cap club from St. Paul finished with the most wins (28) in the League Alliance, while the Tecumseh club from Canada won the International Association honors with a record of 13-4.

Teams from both the International Association and the League Alliance did well against major league opponents in 1877. For instance, the League Alliance's Syracuse Star team finished with a 12-12 record, while the London team from the International Association won 10 of 21.

Nevertheless, both leagues faltered. Because both lacked the authority to set schedules, discipline members, or keep teams from playing in more than one league, numerous problems arose. As a result, both the International Association and the League Alliance sputtered and died after the 1878 season.

During the next few years, other eastern, non–major league organizations surfaced. In 1881, the Eastern Championship Association began play with six mostly independent teams in New York, Philadelphia, and Washington, D.C. This league filled a need because, surprisingly enough, none of the three cities fielded a team in the National League. During the 1881 season, the Metropolitans of New York were considered the top club as they won 32 contests against Association opponents. In a partial 1882 season, the Metropolitans also were considered the champions.

Also in 1881 and 1882, the Metropolitans played a full slate of games against other teams. In contests against non–Association teams, the Metropolitans won 81 matches during the course of the year, including 18 against major league opponents. In 1882, the Metropolitans improved to 101 wins, 29 at the expense of National League nines.

The Eastern Championship Association folded after the 1882 season, their demise due to the defection of two of their members: The Athletics of Philadelphia left in 1882, and the Metropolitans were planning a jump to the American Association, a new major league, in 1883.

To fill the void, in 1883, a new minor baseball league formed in several cities located in New York, New Jersey, Pennsylvania, and Delaware. Called the Interstate Association, it enjoyed modest success as six of the seven teams finished the season intact. The top team in the Interstate proved to be the Brooklyn Grays, who finished with a mark of 44-28, just ahead of the Harrisburg club.

Before the 1884 season, the Interstate Association disbanded, then reorganized and took a new name. Honoring the history of baseball in its region, the group chose an appropriate title. It would be simply known as the Eastern League.

1884
UNSTABLE BEGINNINGS

In September 1883, several members of a mid–Atlantic baseball minor league, the Interstate Association, were approached about forming a new and larger league. Under the direction of Henry Diddlebock, a Philadelphia sportswriter, this new league was to be called the Union League and would consist of franchises in Reading, Trenton, Harrisburg, and Wilmington. In January 1884, the new organization changed its name to the Eastern League to avoid confusion with the new major league Union Association also set to start play in 1884. By opening day on May 1, four more clubs had been added: Newark, Allentown, Baltimore, and Richmond.

The Eastern League dropped into a crowded baseball world. Three separate major leagues were operating, as well as a half-dozen minor league circuits. Many of the Eastern League teams were being operated in major league territory—some in the same cities. With such competition, casualties were bound to occur. Three weeks after the season began, the Baltimore franchise, in competition with two major league teams, packed it in. A team from Lancaster was allowed to take its place. However, the bleeding continued. In early July, the Harrisburg club was forced to cease operations. A team from Brooklyn was admitted in its stead, but was promptly expelled after two games for failing to pay guarantees to the visiting team. In mid-July, a team from York, Pennsylvania, was pasted onto the league structure, restoring the eight-team format. Alas, a few weeks later, the Reading club went belly-up, reducing the total to seven.

The poor Eastern League's woes continued, this time from outside sources. On August 4, the Richmond club left to join the American Association. One week later, Wilmington jumped ship to join the Union Association, leaving only five teams.

On the field, the Quicksteps of Wilmington were the class of the league, winning 50 of 62 decisions. But since they failed to finish their season, the pennant was awarded to second-place Trenton. The rest of the teams finished in the following order: Reading, Richmond, Lancaster, Newark, Allentown, Harrisburg, York, Baltimore, and Brooklyn. Newark's John Coogan won the batting title (.375), while Thomas Burns of Wilmington hit the most home runs (11). From the pitching box, Con Murphy from Trenton and Newark won the most games (21), while Ed Dugan of Richmond struck out the most batters (260). Pat Friel of Reading and Allentown posted the lowest earned run average (1.23).

Despite all its trials, the Eastern League managed to finish its season, bloodied but not broken. The next year the revitalized league would resume its progress—but it would not become an ancestor to the International League. The evolutionary ladder was about to divide.

WILMINGTON Quicksteps

1st   50-12   .806   Joe Simmons

BATTERS	POS-GAMES	GP	AB	R	H	BI	2B	3B	HR	BB	SO	SB	BA
Redleg Snyder	1B62,OF1	63	255	48	47		6	6	3				.184
Charles Bastian	2B63	63	266	75	90		19	12	5				.338
Thomas Burns	SS51,P12,3B2	61	288	107	97		9	15	11				.337
Jim Say	3B54	54	250	47	66		10	4	1				.264
Dennis Casey	OF57,SS4	57	270	63	100		16	6	2				.370
Thomas Lynch	OF49,C15,1B1	63	278	93	89		10	9	7				.320
William McCloskey	OF20,C21,3B2,SS2	42	179	34	47		4	4	1				.263
Tony Cusick	C31,SS9,OF9,3B6	59	240	66	58		7	3	0				.242
Edward Nolan	P24,OF8	31	141	32	46		6	3	2				.326
Dan Casey	P14,OF1	18	73	12	16		2	0	1				.219
Henry Murphy	P10,OF3,SS2,3B1	15	62	15	17		2	1	0				.274

PITCHERS	W	L	PCT	G	GS	CG	SH	IP	H	BB	SO	ERA
Edward Nolan	18	5	.783	24	23	22	0	203	165	55	150	1.40
Dan Casey	10	2	.833	14	13	12	0	113	107	19	73	1.91
Henry Murphy	8	2	.800	10	9	9	4	88	63	13	55	1.32
Thomas Burns	7	2	.778	12	9	8	1	86	72	8	49	1.47

TRENTON Trentonians

2nd   46-39   .541   -11.5   Pat Powers

BATTERS	POS-GAMES	GP	AB	R	H	BI	2B	3B	HR	BB	SO	SB	BA
John Shetzline	1B43,3B40,2B4,OF1	87	404	105	127		13	9	0				.314
Henry Myers	2B44	44	190	48	42		3	4	3				.221
Leo Smith	SS87	87	356	57	83		6	2	1				.233
Bill Schenck	3B	(see multi-team players)											
James Brouthers	OF55,1B39,2B11,SS1	87	342	51	71		12	6	0				.208
Wash Williams	OF	(see multi-team players)											
John Reccius	OF	(see multi-team players)											
George Stone	C	(see multi-team players)											
E. Doyle	2B28,P4	31	127	41	51		13	3	3				.402
John Fox	C13,OF10,1B3,3B2	24	111	14	24		3	0	0				.216
Bill Keinzil	OF18	18	77	20	22		3	1	3				.286
Thomas Daly	C4,OF2	5	19	1	7		0	0	0				.368
John McCabe	P5	5	19	3	3		1	1	0				.158
Michael Dorsey	P2	2	8	1	2		0	0	0				.250
Bryan Sweeney	P	2	7	0	1		0	0	0				.143
Henry McCormick	P2,OF1	2	5	1	1		0	0	0				.200

PITCHERS	W	L	PCT	G	GS	CG	SH	IP	H	BB	SO	ERA
John Fox	7	5	.583	13	13	11	0	105	103	18	47	1.89
John McCabe	3	2	.600	5	5	5	0	46	47	3	13	2.56
E. Doyle	1	1	.500	4	1	1	0	22	22	5	10	1.64
Henry McCormick	1	1	.500	2	2	1	0	12	13	5	6	1.50
Bryan Sweeney	0	2	.000	2	2	2	0	17	21	4	2	1.59
Michael Dorsey	0	2	.000	2	2	2	0	16	25	10	4	8.44

READING Actives

3rd   28-27   .509   -18.5   Frank Helfer

BATTERS	POS-GAMES	GP	AB	R	H	BI	2B	3B	HR	BB	SO	SB	BA
Henry Boyle	1B33	33	157	40	45		9	4	1				.287
Bernard McLaughlin	2B39,SS5,P5,OF1	46	222	53	64		16	3	3				.288
Charles Gagus	SS45,P5,2B3,C1	52	229	43	54		3	2	1				.236
James Halpin	3B55	55	231	41	63		5	3	0				.273
Frank Helfer	OF14,1B6,2B1	23	101	16	31		3	0	1				.307
John Grady	OF	(see multi-team players)											
Pat Friel	OF	(see multi-team players)											
John Cullen	C	(see multi-team players)											
Peter Meegan	P31,OF6,2B2,1B1,SS1	38	147	19	30		1	1	0				.204
John Schappert	P5,OF1	6	27	4	6		3	0	0				.222
Yeager	OF1	3	13	3	2		0	0	0				.154
Perkins	OF2,C1	2	8	1	0		0	0	0				.000
Keifer	OF1	1	5	2	2		0	0	0				.400

READING (cont.)
Actives

BATTERS	POS-GAMES	GP	AB	R	H	BI	2B	3B	HR	BB	SO	SB	BA
Ressler	OF1	1	4	1	2		0	0	0				.500
Yetzer	OF1	1	4	1	1		0	0	0				.250

PITCHERS		W	L	PCT	G	GS	CG	SH	IP	H	BB	SO	ERA
Peter Meegan		15	14	.517	31	29	28	0	252	248	67	198	2.07
Bernard McLaughlin		2	0	1.000	5	4	3	0	36	48	11	19	1.75
Charles Gagus		2	2	.500	5	3	3	0	35	33	4	30	1.80
John Schappert		1	4	.200	5	5	4	0	43	47	8	25	2.09

RICHMOND
Virginias
4th 30-30 .500 -19 Ted Sullivan - Abner Powell

BATTERS	POS-GAMES	GP	AB	R	H	BI	2B	3B	HR	BB	SO	SB	BA
James Powell	1B61,OF1	61	266	30	67		12	3	2				.252
Terry Larkin	2B24	24	97	18	22		3	2	0				.227
E. Ford	SS			(see multi-team players)									
William Nash	3B60,P2	60	256	71	86		14	11	1				.336
Ed Glenn	OF56	61	276	67	73		7	2	3				.264
Dick Johnston	OF56,SS6	60	271	57	77		6	9	2				.284
W. Stratton	OF30,2B7	36	136	17	25		0	2	0				.184
Bill Dugan	C33,OF7,2B2,SS2,3B1	47	184	39	40		4	5	1				.217
Ed Dugan	P32,SS3,2B1	36	135	29	34		3	1	1				.252
Henry Morgan	C23,OF7,2B4,SS2	32	120	20	22		0	0	0				.183
Bill Smiley	2B24,SS7,3B1	31	141	30	31		1	2	0				.220
John Doyle	P23,SS3,OF1	30	114	18	24		5	3	0				.211
Lewis Hardie	SS4,C4,2B1,3B1,OF1	11	49	6	11		2	2	0				.224
Ted Sullivan	P2,OF2	3	9	0	0		0	0	0				.000
Ed Scharf	SS2	2	9	0	1		0	0	0				.111
James Devine	P2	2	8	1	3		0	0	0				.375
Myron Allen	OF1,P1	2	8	2	2		0	0	0				.250
Hetcher	OF1,P1	1	4	1	4		0	0	0				1.000

PITCHERS		W	L	PCT	G	GS	CG	SH	IP	H	BB	SO	ERA
Ed Dugan		20	12	.625	32	29	28	5	266	251	19	260	1.76
John Doyle		9	12	.429	23	23	21	0	208	212	42	116	2.16
Ted Sullivan		1	0	1.000	2	2	1	0	14	14	4	3	1.29
Myron Allen		0	1	.000	1	0	0	0	1	5	0	0	27.00
James Devine		0	2	.000	2	2	2	0	17	21	5	2	3.71
William Nash		0	0	----	2	0	0	0	6	7	4	1	0.00
Hetcher		0	0	----	1	1	0	0	7	7	2	3	2.57

LANCASTER
Ironsides
5th 30-31 .492 -19.5 Robert Clark

BATTERS	POS-GAMES	GP	AB	R	H	BI	2B	3B	HR	BB	SO	SB	BA
Jacob Goodman	1B60	60	261	52	90		24	2	2				.345
William Higgins	2B62	62	274	46	66		9	2	0				.241
Phil Tomney	SS			(see multi-team players)									
James Donald	3B39,SS21	61	251	27	48		3	5	0				.191
Jim McTamany	OF48,1B1,SS1,P1	50	224	30	61		9	5	1				.272
Ed Green	OF20	20	80	13	18		3	0	0				.225
Henry Bradley	OF			(see multi-team players)									
David Oldfield	C40,OF16,1B2	55	237	45	65		9	3	0				.274
Harry Pyle	P39,OF8,2B1	43	163	22	28		3	0	0				.172
Gene Derby	C13,OF9,2B2	37	156	22	38		3	2	0				.249
Frank Foreman	P15,OF2	26	102	16	22		1	0	0				.216
Williamson	P3,OF3,1B1	7	26	4	2		0	0	0				.077
J. Hamilton	OF5	5	21	2	2		0	0	0				.095
Heisler	SS1	1	5	2	2		0	0	0				.400
William Zecher	OF	1	5	1	2		0	0	0				.400
Renia	2B1	1	4	3	1		0	0	0				.250
Bill Hyndman	P1	1	3	1	1		0	0	0				.333
Succor	OF1	1	3	0	2		0	0	0				.667

LANCASTER (cont.)
Ironsides

PITCHERS		W	L	PCT	G	GS	CG	SH	IP	H	BB	SO	ERA
Harry Pyle		19	17	.528	39	36	35	2	329	345	30	196	2.19
Frank Foreman		5	9	.357	15	15	14	0	121	131	29	60	2.24
Bill Hyndman		1	0	1.000	1	1	1	1	9	3	3	6	0.00
Williamson		1	2	.333	3	3	2	0	23	36	6	5	4.70
Jim McTamany		0	0	----	1	1	-	0	5	8	1	0	5.40

NEWARK   6th   40-43   .482   -20.5   David Pierson
Domestics

BATTERS	POS-GAMES	GP	AB	R	H	BI	2B	3B	HR	BB	SO	SB	BA
P. McDonald	1B	(see multi-team players)											
Ed Pierson	2B84	84	380	78	100		10	1	0				.263
George Weigand	SS58,OF12,1B10,P2	84	342	54	82		7	1	0				.240
Gil Hatfield	3B	(see multi-team players)											
John Coogan	OF69,3B14	84	341	95	**128**		17	8	2				**.375**
Charles Gaunt	OF43,C22,3B5,1B2,2B1	73	298	58	60		6	2	0				.201
Charles Hollenbeck	OF30,SS1	30	138	20	34		3	5	0				.246
Ed Cramer	C31,OF6,3B4	44	153	23	32		8	0	2				.209
Levi Hickman	P31,OF2	36	129	17	26		3	0	1				.202
Andrew Swan	1B33,3B1,P1	34	133	22	28		4	2	0				.211
Charles George	C20,OF4,3B1	29	107	13	22		1	0	0				.206
Latham	P14,OF7	21	83	8	23		2	0	0				.277
Oberle	OF11,C3	12	47	8	13		2	0	0				.277
Laughlin	3B11	11	44	5	8		3	0	0				.182
Ed Knouff	P10,OF3	10	30	2	3		0	0	0				.100
David Pearson	OF7,P1	8	29	4	3		0	0	0				.103
Dick Burns	C3,OF2,2B2	6	24	1	4		0	0	0				.167
James Donnelly	P4	4	14	1	4		0	0	0				.286
Charles Parsons	P2,OF2	3	10	2	1		0	0	0				.100
Charles Jones	3B2	2	9	1	3		0	0	0				.333
Collins	P2,OF1	2	8	0	1		0	0	0				.125
Fletcher	OF1	2	8	0	0		0	0	0				.000
Charlie Sweasy	OF2	2	8	0	0		0	0	0				.000
Kelley	P1	1	4	0	0		0	0	0				.000
Maidhoff	P1	1	3	1	0		0	0	0				.000
Joe Reilly	C1	1	3	0	0		0	0	0				.000
Eakin	C1	1	3	0	0		0	0	0				.000

PITCHERS		W	L	PCT	G	GS	CG	SH	IP	H	BB	SO	ERA
Levi Hickman		14	12	.538	31	30	28	0	261	228	46	219	2.07
Latham		8	5	.615	14	13	12	2	120	129	8	54	2.93
Ed Knouff		4	5	.444	10	10	7	1	78	91	16	34	2.87
Dave Pearson		1	0	1.000	1	1	1	0	11	9	3	6	2.45
James Donnelly		1	3	.250	4	4	4	0	38	46	1	8	3.08
Charles Parsons		0	1	.000	2	2	1	0	15	17	4	5	1.80
Kelley		0	1	.000	1	1	1	0	9	14	6	4	2.00
Maidhoff		0	1	.000	1	1	1	0	8	22	1	4	5.63
George Weigand		0	0	----	2	0	0	0	9	9	0	0	3.00
Collins		0	0	----	1	0	0	0	2	3	1	0	0.00
Andrew Swan		0	0	----	1	0	0	0	1	1	0	1	0.00

ALLENTOWN   7th   31-44   .413   -25.5   Dutch Dehlman -
Dukes   K. Debelle

BATTERS	POS-GAMES	GP	AB	R	H	BI	2B	3B	HR	BB	SO	SB	BA
Dutch Dehlman	1B69	69	277	47	61		6	1	1				.220
Denny Mack	2B41,SS1	42	167	37	41		4	1	2				.246
Franklin Lang	SS75	75	294	51	68		9	6	0				.231
Charles Alcott	3B57,1B3,2B3,P3,OF2	75	305	62	87		10	10	2				.285
John Galligan	OF74	74	323	54	69		3	3	0				.214
William Devinney	OF33	36	145	22	37		7	0	1				.255
Sam Landis	OF	(see multi-team players)											
Ernest Smith	C23,OF5,2B1,3B1	31	112	13	18		0	1	0				.161
Tom Healey	P23,OF8,2B3	30	110	26	24		2	2	0				.218
Meaney	P24,OF5	27	96	10	17		0	0	1				.177
John Conner	C14,2B1,OF1	17	60	10	8		1	0	0				.133
E. Ward	P3,OF1	5	19	2	1		0	0	0				.053
W. Gould	C3,OF2	5	18	2	3		1	0	0				.167

ALLENTOWN (cont.)
Dukes

BATTERS	POS-GAMES	GP	AB	R	H	BI	2B	3B	HR	BB	SO	SB	BA
O'Brien	2B3	3	11	0	3		0	0	0				.273
Geary	C1	1	4	1	2		0	0	0				.500
Swift	C1	1	4	1	1		0	1	0				.250

PITCHERS		W	L	PCT	G	GS	CG	SH	IP	H	BB	SO	ERA
Tom Healey		10	9	.526	21	20	18	0	170	183	21	74	2.17
Meaney		7	18	.280	25	25	21	1	204	255	27	56	2.82
E. Ward		0	3	.000	3	3	3	0	27	40	5	5	0.67
Charles Alcott		0	0	----	3	0	0	0	8	12	0	1	1.13

HARRISBURG   8th   16-25   .390   -29.5   Robert Sturgeon
Olympics

BATTERS	POS-GAMES	GP	AB	R	H	BI	2B	3B	HR	BB	SO	SB	BA
Barth	1B19	19	70	6	11		2	1	0				.157
John Farrell	2B29,1B9	38	160	18	46		10	3	0				.288
Joe Lufberry	SS	(see multi-team players)											
John Bell	3B13,2B9	22	84	15	20		0	0	0				.238
Ed Dailey	OF22,P8,3B2,OF2	32	138	30	41		6	4	0				.297
John Reccius	OF	(see multi-team players)											
Gil Hatfield	OF	(see multi-team players)											
John Munyan	C12,OF2,3B1	14	51	6	5		0	0	0				.098
John Heintzman	1B10,P6,OF2	19	73	11	21		2	2	1				.288
Ed Sales	OF7,P3,2B1	13	50	5	11		3	2	0				.220
William Rush	OF8,SS1	8	30	3	3		0	0	1				.100
Cliff Roecker	SS3	4	15	4	2		0	0	0				.133
George Smith	OF1	3	14	3	3		0	0	0				.214
George Cummins	P2,OF1	3	9	1	1		0	0	0				.111
Stine	P1	2	7	1	0		0	0	0				.000
Clint Caswell	OF1	1	4	2	0		0	0	0				.000
James Wilson	OF1	1	4	1	1		0	0	0				.250
Skinner	SS1	1	4	0	1		0	0	0				.250
Keener	OF1	1	3	1	0		0	0	0				.000

PITCHERS		W	L	PCT	G	GS	CG	SH	IP	H	BB	SO	ERA
Ed Dailey		5	0	1.000	8	8	4	0	52	63	16	25	2.87
Stine		1	0	1.000	1	1	1	0	9	8	3	2	3.00
Ed Sales		0	1	.000	3	1	1	0	20	27	2	6	2.70
George Cummins		0	2	.000	2	2	2	0	19	27	10	2	1.89
George Smith		0	2	.000	2	1	1	0	15	16	9	0	4.20
John Heintzman		0	6	.000	6	6	5	0	45	72	29	18	4.00

YORK   9th   10-21   .323   -25.5   John Murphy
White Roses

BATTERS	POS-GAMES	GP	AB	R	H	BI	2B	3B	HR	BB	SO	SB	BA
Louis Smith	1B33	33	135	20	28		3	1	1				.207
George Pierce	2B33	33	152	30	51		10	3	1				.336
Ed Green	SS31,P1	32	134	13	22		2	2	0				.164
Louis Carl	3B33	33	151	41	51		5	1	0				.338
David Cain	OF30	30	129	32	41		7	2	0				.318
Thomas McKee	OF18	18	73	12	15		3	0	0				.205
Dick Conway	OF14,P17	31	119	19	23		0	0	1				.193
William Betz	C15,SS1,OF1	24	94	11	12		0	0	1				.128
William Avery	P15,OF2,SS1	20	74	10	9		1	1	0				.122
Henry Zieber	OF10,C10	19	71	8	12		1	1	0				.169
Eugene Vadeboncoeur	C8,OF7	15	64	13	17		2	1	0				.266
H. King	OF8	8	31	4	4		1	0	0				.129
Dyer	C1	1	4	1	2		0	0	0				.500

PITCHERS		W	L	PCT	G	GS	CG	SH	IP	H	BB	SO	ERA
William Avery		6	8	.429	15	15	15	1	138	157	17	36	1.30
Dick Conway		4	12	.250	17	17	17	0	153	187	29	56	1.47
Ed Green		0	1	.000	1	1	1	0	9	15	3	5	0.00

BALTIMORE Monumentals

BALTIMORE Monumentals | 10th | 3-10 | .231 | -22.5 | Harrison Spence

BATTERS	POS-GAMES	GP	AB	R	H	BI	2B	3B	HR	BB	SO	SB	BA
John Munce	1B	(see multi-team players)											
Gil Hatfield	2B	(see multi-team players)											
Joe Lufberry	SS	(see multi-team players)											
Harrison Spence	3B12	12	45	11	11		4	0	0				.244
Daniel Erek	OF10	10	37	7	6		1	0	0				.162
Stewart Denham	OF	(see multi-team players)											
Sam Landis	OF	(see multi-team players)											
John Brill	C	(see multi-team players)											
William Rittenhouse	P5,OF3	8	30	5	6		1	0	0				.200
John Hanna	C5,OF1	6	23	3	3		0	0	0				.130
James McElroy	P6	6	21	2	5		0	0	0				.238

PITCHERS	W	L	PCT	G	GS	CG	SH	IP	H	BB	SO	ERA
James McElroy	2	4	.333	6	6	6	0	54	36	20	35	1.00
William Rittenhouse	1	4	.200	5	5	5	0	45	84	10	18	3.00

BROOKLYN Greys

BROOKLYN Greys | 11th | 0-2 | .000 | -20 | Endler

BATTERS	POS-GAMES	GP	AB	R	H	BI	2B	3B	HR	BB	SO	SB	BA
McGurk	1B2	2	8	2	1		0	0	0				.125
Dooley	2B2	2	8	0	1		0	0	0				.125
Simmons	SS2	2	9	4	3		1	0	0				.333
Bonney	3B2	2	7	3	4		1	1	0				.571
Kelly	OF2	2	8	0	1		1	0	0				.125
Stoltz	OF1,P1	1	4	0	0		0	0	0				.000
Jones	OF1	1	5	0	1		0	0	0				.200
Art Thompson	C2	2	7	2	3		1	0	0				.429
John Holzberger	P2	2	7	0	2		0	0	0				.286
Higgins	OF1	1	3	1	1		0	1	0				.333
Kerwin	OF1	1	3	0	0		0	0	0				.000

PITCHERS	W	L	PCT	G	GS	CG	SH	IP	H	BB	SO	ERA
John Holzberger	0	2	.000	2	2	1	0	13	22	2	4	2.77
Stoltz	0	0	----	1	0	0	0	4	2	0	0	0.00

MULTI-TEAM PLAYERS

BATTERS	POS-GAMES	TEAMS	GP	AB	R	H	BI	2B	3B	HR	BB	SO	SB	BA
P. McDonald	1B43,OF20,3B20,C5	NE-AL	84	346	68	101		10	7	2				.292
Gil Hatfield	3B58,2B12,1B10,OF10	B-H-N	82	345	62	88		8	5	0				.235
Joe Lufberry	SS67,OF9,2B1	BA-HA-NE	77	339	46	83		5	0	0				.245
John Reccius	OF76,P1	HAR-TRE	76	329	85	92		18	13	3				.280
John Grady	OF43,C27,OF6,2B1	REA-TRE	71	314	66	80		16	7	2				.255
Henry Bradley	OF36,3B30,P4	HAR-LAN	69	321	50	68		3	1	0				.212
Pat Friel	OF25,P20,1B18,SS1	RE-AL	65	287	47	80		6	5	1				.279
George Stone	C38,OF11	TRE-NEW	64	271	40	54		6	2	0				.199
Sam Landis	OF37,P27	BAL-ALL	58	240	48	69		8	2	0				.288
Wash Williams	OF47,P10,1B1,2B1,C1	TR-RI	57	243	35	55		9	7	1				.226
Jacob Knowdell	C41,OF13,SS2,3B2	HAR-TRE	57	210	29	52		7	2	0				.248
John Cullen	C31,OF24,2B3	REA-WIL	55	261	51	82		14	4	2				.314
Bill Schenck	3B47,SS9	TRE-RIC	55	238	37	59		4	4	1				.248
Marsh Quinton	OF35,C23,1B1	TRE-RIC	54	237	33	69		17	3	1				.291
Phil Tomney	SS43,OF10,P1	REA-LAN	53	231	49	57		12	8	0				.247
Harry Jacoby	OF25,2B14,P1	RE-WI-AL	53	214	43	52		6	7	1				.243
Con B. Murphy	P40,OF13	TRE-NEW	50	198	28	43		7	2	0				.217
Joe Miller	1B23,P23,OF6	WIL-TRE	46	191	24	41		5	1	0				.215
Gus Alberts	2B20,OF12,SS4,1B1,3B1	R-A	44	178	34	48		9	3	2				.270
Gus Weidel	P32,OF6,SS4	HAR-TRE	43	145	25	19		1	0	0				.131
J. Guehrer	C30,2B4,1B1	ALL-LAN	39	146	17	29		5	0	0				.199
John Munce	OF28,1B12	BAL-WIL	39	161	35	47		5	0	1				.292
Peter Kilroy	P24,OF15	NEW-ALL	37	136	19	32		1	0	0				.235
E. Ford	SS22,3B1,1B1	RIC-NEW	27	112	8	18		3	2	0				.161
Joseph Kappel	C14,OF5	BAL-ALL	23	96	12	24		5	0	0				.250
John Brill	C17,OF3	BAL-HAR	23	85	7	18		0	0	0				.212

MULTI-TEAM PLAYERS (cont.)

BATTERS	POS-GAMES	TEAMS	GP	AB	R	H	BI	2B	3B	HR	BB	SO	SB	BA
Marty Creegan	C14,OF5	REA-ALL	19	69	9	12		2	0	0				.174
Stewart Denham	OF11,3B5	BAL-NEW	18	67	10	10		0	0	0				.149
Charles Ingraham	P8,OF1	TRE-LAN	17	69	12	14		0	0	0				.203
Jimmy Ryan	C9,OF8,P2	TRE-ALL	15	57	10	2		1	0	0				.036
E. Shay	C5,OF3,1B1	RIC-LAN	7	22	3	4		0	0	0				.182
Ed Morris	P3,OF2	NEW-ALL	3	13	2	3		0	0	0				.231

PITCHERS		TEAMS	W	L	PCT	G	GS	CG	SH	IP	H	BB	SO	ERA
Con B. Murphy		TRE-NEW	21	14	.600	40	39	36	0	333	296	53	144	1.51
Gus Weidel		TRE-HAR	14	17	.452	32	32	28	0	260	311	54	135	2.98
Pat Friel		REA-ALL	11	6	.647	20	19	17	0	161	136	30	88	**1.23**
Joe Miller		WIL-TRE	11	10	.524	23	19	16	0	174	160	43	74	1.71
Sam Landis		BAL-ALL	11	12	.478	27	22	21	2	212	242	19	73	2.25
Peter Kilroy		NEW-ALL	10	12	.455	23	20	20	1	183	206	42	89	2.41
Charles Ingraham		TRE-LAN	5	3	.625	8	8	6	0	67	91	20	27	3.49
Wash Williams		TRE-RIC	2	4	.333	10	7	5	0	64	72	23	30	1.55
Henry Bradley		HAR-LAN	1	1	.500	4	1	0	0	15	23	3	4	1.20
Ed Morris		NEW-ALL	0	1	.000	3	2	1	0	15	28	6	5	6.00
Jimmy Ryan		TRE-ALL	0	1	.000	2	1	1	0	13	11	1	7	1.38
Phil Tomney		REA-LAN	0	0	----	1	0	0	0	3	4	0	0	9.00
John Reccius		HAR-TRE	0	0	----	1	0	0	0	2	2	0	0	0.00

TEAM BATTING

TEAMS	GP	AB	R	H	BI	2B	3B	HR	BB	SO	SB	BA
WILMINGTON	63	2486	**648**	726		95	**63**	35				**.292**
TRENTON	87	3325	610	**813**		119	58	14				.245
READING	55	2178	433	588		87	37	11				.270
RICHMOND	61	2283	427	570		61	45	10				.250
LANCASTER	62	2370	384	564		79	26	3				.238
NEWARK	86	3139	519	760		79	24	5				.242
ALLENTOWN	75	2740	485	642		64	33	11				.234
HARRISBURG	40	1410	239	336		45	17	4				.238
YORK	33	1231	214	287		35	12	4				.233
BALTIMORE	12	419	61	95		11	1	0				.227
BROOKLYN	2	69	12	17		4	2	0				.246
	288	21650	4032	5398		579	318	97				.249

TEAM PITCHING

TEAMS	W	L	PCT	G	GS	CG	SH	IP	H	BB	SO	ERA
WILMINGTON	**50**	12	**.806**	63	63	58	5	560	467	112	354	1.62
TRENTON	46	39	.541	**87**	**87**	76	0	764	776	146	325	1.59
READING	28	27	.509	55	55	50	0	484	479	114	344	1.84
RICHMOND	30	30	.500	61	61	54	5	547	558	91	294	2.06
LANCASTER	30	31	.492	62	62	55	3	545	608	82	281	2.41
NEWARK	40	43	.482	**87**	**87**	79	4	777	813	135	431	2.43
ALLENTOWN	31	**44**	.413	75	75	68	3	672	767	76	226	2.24
HARRISBURG	16	25	.390	40	40	35	0	349	437	118	157	3.09
YORK	10	21	.323	33	33	33	1	300	359	49	97	**1.35**
BALTIMORE	3	10	.231	12	21	12	0	107	135	33	55	2.02
BROOKLYN	0	2	.000	2	2	1	0	17	24	2	4	2.12
	284	284	.500	576	576	521	21	5122	5423	958	2568	2.12

1885
ALTERNATE LINEAGE

The 1885 Eastern League started much as it had the year before. Reorganized, it fielded eight franchises, all of which had played in the 1884 Eastern. However, though it used the same name and included many of the same teams, the 1885 Eastern League is not located under the International League's umbrella.

Up until 1934, the International League was thought to have originated with the formation of an "Eastern League"—different from the 1884 group—that formed in 1892. In 1935, league officials suddenly decided to push its lineage back to the 1884 Eastern League. But according to that 1935 decision, the International traced its path in another direction in 1885—through a small organization in upper New York state.

The New York State League, as this organization was known, started the season by fielding teams in six cities: Syracuse, Rochester, Utica, Binghamton, Oswego, and Albany. Like all too many circuits of its day, the New York State couldn't finish its season intact. On July 27, with a record of 24-20, the Albany club called it quits. (Earlier, a team from Elmira had played briefly in the league, losing all nine of its decisions from July 6 through July 16). The league promptly threw out all the Albany and Elmira games from the standings, with their accompanying statistics, leaving the remaining quintet to finish the season.

The New York State League's first season ended with Syracuse on top followed by Rochester, Utica, Binghamton, and Oswego. The leading batter was Doc Kennedy of Rochester, who struck the ball at a .387 clip. The top pitcher came from Syracuse: James Devine, who finished with a 0.76 earned run average. (Note: for this year, and a few other nineteenth century seasons, earned run averages were computed on an earned runs per game basis, rather than per inning as they are done today.)

At first glance, the International League's 1935 decision to include the New York State in its genealogy appears to be sound. At that time, two New York State League members, Syracuse and Rochester, had been part of the International League scene for many years. But neither played in the Eastern League in 1884. Newark did play in the 1884 Eastern, and they were also a member of the International in 1935.

It was probably a matter of continuance. Rochester and Syracuse had been members of all the different organizations constituting the International League from 1885 forward. Newark had a more spotty existence in these leagues. In the end, it was consistency rather than age that determined the lineage. However, it wasn't a total dead end for the Eastern League. In a couple of years, they would become a significant branch of the International League's family tree.

SYRACUSE Stars

1st   45-32   .584   Henry Ormsbee - John Humphries

BATTERS	POS-GAMES	GP	AB	R	H	BI	2B	3B	HR	BB	SO	SB	BA
Jay Faatz	1B50	50	211	39	57								.270
Thomas Kearns	2B57	57	225	41	56								.249
Frank Spill	SS77	77	299	62	68								.227
Hobart Van Alstyne	3B77	77	283	40	65								.230
Charles Osterhout	OF73,2B	73	322	74	77								.239
Hart Oberland	OF64	64	263	46	64								.243
M. Griffin	OF55,2B21,1B	77	321	67	91								.283
John Humphries	C44,1B,OF	49	184	25	62								.337
Dell Darling	C29,1B	36	132	29	34								.258
James Devine	P29,OF	30	107	11	15								.140
John Tickner	1B20	20	77	4	11								.143
Malcolm McArthur	P16	16	55	6	5								.091

PITCHERS	W	L	PCT	G	GS	CG	SH	IP	H	BB	SO	ERA
James Devine				29					239			**0.76**
Malcolm McArthur				16					132			0.94

ROCHESTER Flour Cities

2nd   40-36   .526   -4.5   James Jackson

BATTERS	POS-GAMES	GP	AB	R	H	BI	2B	3B	HR	BB	SO	SB	BA
Doc Kennedy	1B43	43	191	50	74								**.387**
Hayes	2B61	61	248	38	62								.250
Tom Callahan	SS64,C,OF	69	286	46	72								.252
Charles Whitney	3B70	70	292	63	89								.305
Farrow	OF70,C	71	267	31	61								.228
Glasser	OF39,1B,SS	39	161	35	37								.230
O'Connor	OF34,1B,P	47	183	36	53								.290
Jim Toy	C41,OF,SS	49	196	34	57								.291
John Schappert	P36,1B,2B,OF	36	128	16	30								.234
Stephen Toole	P26,OF,2B,1B	33	141	36	46								.326
Joe Visner	C15,OF	27	119	32	43								.361

PITCHERS	W	L	PCT	G	GS	CG	SH	IP	H	BB	SO	ERA
John Schappert				**36**					320			1.36
Stephen Toole				26					215			0.88

UTICA Pentups

3rd   41-38   .518   -5   David Dischler - Dick Dwyer

BATTERS	POS-GAMES	GP	AB	R	H	BI	2B	3B	HR	BB	SO	SB	BA
Richard Dwyer	1B61,2B	61	276	54	84								.304
Emery Hengle	2B63,SS	65	276	66	87								.315
Louis Say	SS48	48	188	37	40								.213
John Messitt	3B39,1B,OF	44	180	37	44								.244
Sandy Griffin	OF75	75	287	52	80								.279
Simons	OF68	68	270	52	85								.315
Ed Shattuck	OF65,SS	78	317	59	71								.224
David McKeough	C39,OF,2B	44	158	30	37								.234
John Pendergrass	P36,OF	39	144	15	28								.194
Jim Say	3B36	36	144	26	43								.249
George McKeough	P31,OF	33	116	14	16								.138
Mike Lawlor	C29	29	102	2	9								.088

PITCHERS	W	L	PCT	G	GS	CG	SH	IP	H	BB	SO	ERA
John Pendergrass				**36**					292			1.06
George McKeough				31					279			1.35

BINGHAMTON   4th   36-42   .462   -9.5   Leonard Baldwin
Bingoes

BATTERS	POS-GAMES	GP	AB	R	H	BI	2B	3B	HR	BB	SO	SB	BA
Maurice Bresnahan	1B		(see multi-team players)										
James Curry	2B46	46	176	21	28								.159
Gus Alberts	SS55,OF,P,C,3B	55	220	46	65								.295
Pat Larkin	3B72	72	298	60	84								.282
Joseph McGuckin	OF75,P,SS	76	313	68	80								.256
Tom Sexton	OF38,SS,2B,3B	42	166	20	37								.223
J. Morrison	OF23	24	93	20	35								.376
O'Rourke	C44,OF,2B,SS	58	226	27	43								.190
John Holzberger	P33,OF,1B,2B	50	175	19	38								.217
Bones Ely	P17,OF	29	110	16	27								.245
John McGuinness	1B21	21	98	19	22								.224
Dick Buckley	C15,OF,1B	21	85	9	18								.212
McFarland	SS,C,OF	20	87	12	19								.218
Al Maul	P,1B,OF	20	70	14	20								.286
Grayson Pierce	2B17	17	76	13	20								.263

PITCHERS	W	L	PCT	G	GS	CG	SH	IP	H	BB	SO	ERA
John Holzberger				33					306			0.94
Bones Ely				17					167			1.29

OSWEGO   5th   32-46   .410   -13.5   Michael Gill -
Sweegs   M. Gorman - Salladin

BATTERS	POS-GAMES	GP	AB	R	H	BI	2B	3B	HR	BB	SO	SB	BA
Corcoran	1B		(see multi-team players)										
Frank Olin	2B49	49	207	52	79								.382
John Shoupe	SS26	26	104	11	24								.231
James McDonald	3B66	66	276	32	66								.239
Mike Mansell	OF59	59	225	45	54								.240
Milt West	OF39,SS,1B,2B	58	250	46	73								.292
William Avery	OF21,P19	41	129	25	20								.155
Charles Faatz	C20,OF,1B,SS	27	104	11	21								.202
William Sweeney	P21,2B15,OF	50	197	43	57								.289
Ed Fusselbach	C18,SS,OF	36	149	22	36								.242
James Harmon	OF	34	140	31	36								.257
Marsh Quinton	C16,SS,OF	24	97	12	30								.309
Robert Callaghan	OF18,C	23	96	10	20								.208
Jersey Bakely	P15,OF	22	68	9	16								.235
Peter Carrigan	P,OF,SS,3B,2B	16	69	6	21								.304

PITCHERS	W	L	PCT	G	GS	CG	SH	IP	H	BB	SO	ERA
William Sweeney				21					193			1.33
William Avery				19					181			0.89
Jersey Bakely				15					132			1.07

MULTI-TEAM PLAYERS

BATTERS	POS-GAMES	TEAMS	GP	AB	R	H	BI	2B	3B	HR	BB	SO	SB	BA
Corcoran	1B78,OF	UTI-OSW	82	308	53	67								.218
Maurice Bresnahan	1B69,P	ROC-BIN	69	293	57	76								.259
John Mansell	OF32,SS,1B,P,3B	BIN-ROC	46	194	49	48								.247
William Betz	C25,OF,2B	OSW-BIN	40	133	18	24								.180
Jack Owens	C,2B,1B	UTI-OSW	15	60	9	11								.183

TEAM BATTING

TEAMS	GP	AB	R	H	BI	2B	3B	HR	BB	SO	SB	BA
SYRACUSE	77	2736	481	660								.241
ROCHESTER	75	2687	**526**	**735**								**.274**
UTICA	**79**	2735	480	678								.248
BINGHAMTON	77	2690	439	636								.236
OSWEGO	78	**2818**	451	685								.244
	193	13666	2377	3394								.248

1886
NORTHERN AID

To stay in existence, the five-team New York State League needed an infusion of teams. First it turned to another city in upper New York state: Buffalo, which joined the league early in 1886. Next came teams from north of the border. In 1885, a small five-team circuit called the Canadian League operated in Ontario. Its members included clubs in Toronto, Hamilton, London, and Guelph. In March 1886, its two largest teams, the Hamilton Clippers and the Toronto Canucks, jumped to fill the seventh and eighth slots in the New York State League. Reflecting the influence from Canada, the league renamed itself the International League.

Utica proved to be the best team of this revamped grouping as they glided to an easy first-place showing, five and one-half games over Rochester. The two Canadian entries, Toronto and Hamilton, finished in the next two spots, followed by Buffalo, Syracuse, Binghamton, and Oswego. The most remarkable point of the 1886 season was not the placement of teams; it was the fact that they all finished the season, playing a schedule of nearly 100 games. Not one team dropped out, went bankrupt, or had to be replaced.

Jonathan Morrison from Toronto finished with the highest batting average (.346), while Rochester's Joe Visner and Buffalo's John Fields hit the most home runs (8). Bill Serad, from pennant-winning Utica, dominated the pitching statistics as he won the pitcher's Triple Crown. Serad finished the season with the most wins (30), most strikeouts (260), and best earned run average (1.02)

The influx of teams from Canada proved to be the New York (now International) League's saving grace. They provided stability in 1886 to a shaky organization and allowed it to finish the year intact. But Canadian influence didn't end here. From the late nineteenth century through the present day, teams from Canada have been an integral part of the International League—an influence which goes far beyond a change in name.

UTICA
Pentups

1st   62-34   .646   Emory Hengle

BATTERS	POS-GAMES	GP	AB	R	H	BI	2B	3B	HR	BB	SO	SB	BA
George Latham	1B58	58	235	27	59		6	0	0			7	.249
Emery Hengle	2B93	93	402	82	109		16	3	0			22	.271
James Halpin	SS76,P1	76	329	42	84		17	2	0			23	.255
Bill Shindle	3B96	96	417	80	129		20	15	3			25	.309
Mike Griffin	OF96	96	404	86	116		18	8	1			34	.287
John Carroll	OF90,2B3,C1	93	386	82	99		18	9	1			42	.256
Sandy Griffin	OF74,1B20	94	401	87	120		22	9	0			6	.299
David McKeough	C53,1B1	54	200	18	32		2	0	0			11	.160
Bill Serad	P47,OF1	48	184	19	23		4	0	0			2	.125
Joseph Hofford	C40,OF1	41	152	28	36		2	0	1			2	.237
John Pendergrass	P39,SS1	39	153	18	32		7	0	0			1	.209
Mike Moynahan	SS20,OF2	22	93	20	28		9	2	0			1	.301
Ed Shattuck	OF21	21	95	19	21		3	0	0			2	.221
Otto Schomberg	1B17	17	70	17	25		5	0	1			2	.357
George Wetzel	P5	5	19	2	2		0	0	0			0	.105
Mike Mattimore	P5	5	16	2	2		0	0	0			4	.125
John Fields	OF2	2	6	1	1		1	0	*0			0	.167
Jim Toy	C1	1	4	0	1		0	0	0			1	.250

PITCHERS	W	L	PCT	G	GS	CG	SH	IP	H	BB	SO	ERA
Bill Serad	30	17	.638	47	47	47	1	416	346	82	260	1.02
John Pendergrass	27	12	.692	39	39	38	2	347	372	29	92	1.97
Mike Mattimore	4	*1	.800	5	5	5	1	42	34	10	23	0.86
George Wetzel	1	4	.200	5	5	5	0	41	55	24	23	3.95
Jim Halpin	0	0	----	1	0	0	0	0	0	0	0	0.00

ROCHESTER
Maroons

2nd   56-39   .589   -5.5   Frank Bancroft - Alonzo Knight

BATTERS	POS-GAMES	GP	AB	R	H	BI	2B	3B	HR	BB	SO	SB	BA
Doc Kennedy	1B95	95	399	79	136		32	6	5			13	.341
Walter Hackett	2B79	79	316	34	72		8	1	2			11	.228
Ed McKean	SS75,2B1	76	318	62	97		7	1	1			29	.305
Charles Whitney	3B86	86	326	49	74		12	1	1			15	.227
Alonzo Knight	OF91,1B2,C1	92	374	50	97		12	6	2			11	.259
Joe Visner	OF69,C28,2B1,3B1	94	413	87	129		22	10	8			12	.312
Bill Keinzil	OF59	59	222	46	42		8	5	6			6	.189
Ed Warner	C45,OF9,2B1	52	188	27	28		6	1	0			3	.149
Jersey Bakely	P35,OF3	36	114	17	22		4	2	0			2	.188
Franklin Gardner	OF30,2B2	31	107	17	20		5	0	1			4	.187
William Horner	P22,OF9	30	116	13	27		4	1	0			5	.233
George Harter	C18,OF12	28	107	4	23		1	0	0			1	.215
Charles Parsons	P26,OF2	27	98	7	17		0	0	0			0	.173
Ed Caskins	SS15	15	60	10	15		3	1	1			1	.250
Bob Blakiston	3B5,2B4,SS1	10	38	3	15		1	0	0			2	.395
Miah Murray	C9,OF1	10	34	5	8		1	0	0			0	.235
Bob Barr	P6,OF3	9	32	5	8		2	1	0			0	.250
Frank Parker	2B5,OF3	8	29	4	3		1	0	0			1	.103
Norm Baker	OF4,P4	8	26	2	7		1	1	0			0	.269
George Bradley	SS4,P2,3B1	7	25	5	5		0	0	0			4	.200
Ed Seward	OF2,P2	4	18	3	2		0	0	0			5	.111
Dan Corcoran	3B4	4	15	0	4		1	0	0			1	.267
Al Maul	P2	2	6	0	1		1	0	0			0	.167
Marsh Quinton	OF1,C1	1	4	0	0		0	0	0			0	.000
Wood	2B1	1	4	0	0		0	0	0			0	.000
Jerry Moore	OF1,C1	1	3	1	1		0	0	0			0	.333
Joe Gunson	C1	1	3	0	0		0	0	0			0	.000
John Hofford	P1	1	3	0	0		0	0	0			0	.000
Pat Murphy	C1	1	1	1	0		0	0	0			0	.000

PITCHERS	W	L	PCT	G	GS	CG	SH	IP	H	BB	SO	ERA
Jersey Bakely	18	13	.581	35	32	31	2	293	244	80	156	1.37
Charles Parsons	15	10	.600	26	26	25	1	233	198	27	139	1.12
William Horner	14	8	.636	22	21	19	1	187	157	52	106	1.59
Bob Barr	4	2	.667	6	6	6	1	53	37	11	35	0.85
John Hofford	1	0	1.000	1	1	1	0	7	6	3	5	0.00
George Bradley	1	1	.500	2	2	2	0	18	27	2	12	4.50
Al Maul	1	1	.500	2	2	2	0	17	17	6	13	2.40
Ed Seward	1	1	.500	2	2	2	0	17	20	3	9	1.20
Norm Baker	1	3	.250	4	4	4	0	35	24	9	20	0.51

TORONTO Canucks

3rd	53-41	.563	-8	John Humphries		

BATTERS	POS-GAMES	GP	AB	R	H	BI	2B	3B	HR	BB	SO	SB	BA
Jay Faatz	1B93	93	396	81	121		18	1	2			33	.306
Fred Macklin	2B34	34	132	20	29		0	0	0			19	.220
Frank Spill	SS42,3B38,OF1,P1	77	311	43	72		10	4	1			19	.232
William Smith	3B54,OF2,P1	56	237	52	75		14	3	3			12	.316
Jonathan Morrison	OF94	94	407	108	141		20	9	5			11	.346
Charles Osterhout	OF88	88	381	64	85		13	6	1			32	.223
Joseph McGuckin	OF45,3B1	46	181	20	35		5	1	0			11	.171
Dell Darling	C52,SS9,OF8	69	262	39	56		11	0	3			16	.214
Gus Alberts	SS38,OF27,2B21,3B7	92	390	81	93		13	8	2			18	.238
William Veach	P40,OF17,1B2	59	231	36	54		9	2	2			12	.234
John Humphries	C43,1B1,OF1	44	180	27	33		1	0	0			5	.183
Hugh Weir	3B26,SS7	33	126	18	29		1	0	0			20	.230
Bob Emslie	P27,OF3	30	122	21	30		3	0	0			0	.246
John Davis	P23,OF1,SS1	24	88	9	16		1	0	0			4	.182
James Curry	2B15	15	53	2	8		1	0	0			0	.151
James McKinley	P5	5	16	1	3		0	0	0			0	.188

PITCHERS	W	L	PCT	G	GS	CG	SH	IP	H	BB	SO	ERA
William Veach	20	19	.513	40	40	40	1	353	334	113	205	1.73
John Davis	16	7	.696	23	23	22	1	204	198	39	120	1.59
Bob Emslie	14	12	.538	27	27	27	0	239	297	76	70	2.30
James McKinley	3	2	.600	5	5	5	1	41	32	8	21	1.10
William Smith	0	0	----	1	0	0	0	3	2	0	1	3.38
Frank Spill	0	0	----	1	0	0	0	1	0	3	0	0.00

HAMILTON Clippers

4th	52-43	.547	-9.5	Charles Collins - Thomas Crooks		

BATTERS	POS-GAMES	GP	AB	R	H	BI	2B	3B	HR	BB	SO	SB	BA
Michael Jones	1B88,P10	94	377	46	87		4	1	2			19	.231
Charles Collins	2B81,1B4	81	337	63	78		10	2	0			45	.231
Nat Kellogg	SS81,2B11,P1	92	370	60	90		16	1	1			11	.243
John Rainey	3B96	96	408	77	123		21	7	1			25	.301
William Wright	OF92,2B3	93	378	78	103		15	6	1			23	.272
William Andrus	OF75,SS15,2B4	93	392	81	96		7	3	3			28	.245
Joseph Knight	OF64,P15	78	321	47	91		21	6	1			6	.277
Andrew Sommers	C56,OF3	59	223	29	58		7	1	1			6	.260
Mike Morrison	P29,OF13,1B2,2B1	41	150	16	28		1	4	1			2	.187
John Morrison	C30,1B5,OF2,2B1	37	120	20	20		4	1	0			4	.167
Joseph McGuckin	OF31	31	125	19	19		6	1	0			4	.152
Peter Wood	P21,OF8,1B1	30	120	12	38		5	2	1			3	.317
John Thompson	C13,OF3,1B1	17	63	13	18		1	2	1			3	.286
Malcolm McArthur	P16	16	54	3	2		0	0	0			1	.037
John Hibbard	P3	3	11	4	5		0	1	0			1	.455
George Mallory	P3,OF1	3	9	1	2		0	0	0			0	.222
James Reardon	P2	2	8	2	1		0	0	0			0	.125
William Farrell	P2	2	6	0	1		1	0	0			0	.167

PITCHERS	W	L	PCT	G	GS	CG	SH	IP	H	BB	SO	ERA
Peter Wood	14	7	.667	21	21	21	2	191	159	29	120	1.65
Mike Morrison	13	13	.500	29	28	25	0	237	191	91	190	1.37
Jonas Knight	11	3	.786	15	15	14	3	134	160	36	53	2.62
Malcolm McArthur	5	10	.333	16	16	16	0	183	132	58	80	1.24
Michael Jones	4	3	.571	10	6	6	0	69	66	12	23	0.91
John Hibbard	2	1	.667	3	3	3	0	27	33	12	11	2.00
James Reardon	1	0	1.000	2	2	2	0	18	14	5	6	2.00
George Mallory	1	2	.333	3	3	2	0	23	26	10	3	3.91
William Farrell	0	2	.000	2	2	2	0	17	15	10	6	3.71
Nat Kellogg	0	0	----	1	0	0	0	3	6	1	0	9.00

BUFFALO Bisons

5th	50-45	.526	-11.5	John Chapman	

BATTERS	POS-GAMES	GP	AB	R	H	BI	2B	3B	HR	BB	SO	SB	BA
Stephen Dunn	1B51	51	225	36	71		8	2	0			2	.316

BUFFALO (cont.)
Bisons

BATTERS	POS-GAMES	GP	AB	R	H	BI	2B	3B	HR	BB	SO	SB	BA
Frank Grant	2B48,P4	49	192	38	66		13	7	2			12	.344
Hugh Weir	SS57	57	224	33	62		4	1	1			2	.277
John McGlone	3B99,P1	**99**	421	77	105		17	4	5			46	.249
James Brouthers	OF83,2B17,SS1	98	413	72	110		16	3	4			11	.266
Daniel Connors	OF76,P1	76	335	56	98		9	4	3			2	.293
John Remsen	OF47	47	176	43	45		6	5	5			4	.256
Ernest Smith	C55,OF9,3B2,SS2	62	214	26	33		6	1	0			15	.154
John Fields	C28,OF20,SS11,2B6	63	244	50	77		11	8	*8			10	.316
Tom Callahan	SS23,2B18,OF11,C6	53	207	46	55		5	5	2			8	.266
Mike Walsh	P51	51	185	23	31		2	3	0			1	.168
Mike Firle	1B35,OF11,P2,3B1	46	183	25	37		7	2	2			3	.202
Peter Wood	P18,OF3	19	66	10	21		3	0	0			2	.318
Frank Brill	P13,OF6	18	73	8	19		0	1	0			1	.260
P. McDonald	1B14	14	55	12	22		4	2	3			2	.400
Fred Jevne	OF14	14	51	4	4		0	0	0			15	.078
Charles Calhoun	C11,2B3	12	43	6	7		0	0	0			0	.163
Knight	2B10	10	36	6	5		0	1	0			1	.139
John Holzberger	OF7	7	24	4	4		1	0	1			0	.167
Allen	OF6	6	23	0	6		0	0	0			0	.261
George Bradley	SS6	6	22	3	3		1	1	0			0	.136
Fred Wood	C6,OF1,SS1	6	21	4	4		1	0	0			0	.190
William Murray	OF5	5	18	1	4		0	0	0			0	.222
Al Sheppard	P3,OF1	3	12	1	2		0	0	0			0	.167
James Becannon	P5,OF1	5	18	1	3		0	0	0			0	.167
A. Clarke	P5	5	18	1	2		1	0	0			0	.111
Dave Eggler	OF2	2	8	0	1		0	0	0			0	.125
Hutchings	2B2	2	4	1	1		0	0	0			0	.250
Dan Flynn	P1	1	4	0	1		0	0	0			0	.250
John Foley	2B1,P1	1	4	0	0		0	0	0			0	.000
B. Carr	P1	1	3	0	0		0	0	0			0	.000

PITCHERS	W	L	PCT	G	GS	CG	SH	IP	H	BB	SO	ERA
Mike Walsh	27	21	.563	**51**	51	51	7	451	430	117	206	1.58
Frank Brill	8	4	.667	13	12	12	0	110	126	31	31	2.29
Peter Wood	6	11	.353	18	18	16	0	148	176	47	81	2.19
A. Clarke	3	2	.600	5	5	5	0	44	65	13	11	4.09
James Becannon	3	2	.600	5	5	4	0	38	42	11	16	1.18
Frank Grant	2	1	.667	4	2	1	0	29	36	10	11	2.17
Al Sheppard	1	2	.333	3	3	2	0	23	24	7	9	1.58
B. Carr	0	1	.000	1	1	1	0	9	15	5	6	1.00
Dan Flynn	0	1	.000	1	1	1	0	9	20	5	1	5.00
M. Firle	0	0	----	2	1	0	0	4	6	1	2	9.00
Daniel Connors	0	0	----	1	0	0	0	4	7	0	1	4.50
John McGlone	0	0	----	1	0	0	0	4	5	2	1	0.00
John Foley	0	0	----	1	0	0	0	1	2	0	0	0.00

SYRACUSE　　　　　6th　　46-47　　.491　　-14.5　　Henry Ormsbee -
Stars　　　　　　　　　　　　　　　　　　　Frank Olin - James Gifford

BATTERS	POS-GAMES	GP	AB	R	H	BI	2B	3B	HR	BB	SO	SB	BA
Charles W. Householder	1B50,C5	55	240	24	55		4	1	0			6	.229
Harry Jacoby	2B56,OF28,SS11	94	371	80	90		18	5	5			22	.243
Phil Tomney	SS83,P1	83	326	58	80		14	3	2			30	.245
Charles Alcott	3B57	57	229	33	60		11	1	0			6	.262
Henry Simon	OF91,3B4,SS3	95	407	66	107		18	13	4			22	.263
Hart Oberlander	OF77	77	298	48	67		12	0	1			15	.225
Frank Olin	OF37,2B29	66	278	51	91		13	5	0			22	.327
Dick Buckley	C44,1B1,OF1	46	179	28	39		9	1	0			6	.218
Doug Crothers	P43,OF1	44	159	19	28		3	1	0			7	.176
William McCloskey	C29,1B5,3B4,OF1	38	143	17	25		3	0	0			8	.175
Bill Harbridge	1B34,P1	34	120	23	29		1	0	0			3	.242
James Green	OF26,SS1	26	110	14	25		6	2	0			8	.227
John Gladman	3B25	25	97	12	24		4	0	0			4	.247
John Schappert	P24	24	85	9	16		2	0	0			1	.188
James Devine	P15,OF1	15	54	4	5		1	0	0			2	.093
Joe Crotty	C7,OF6	12	40	7	8		1	1	0			3	.200
Henry Bittman	2B10	10	39	4	13		2	0	0			5	.333
Charles Marr	OF10	10	42	10	14		3	2	0			5	.333
Henry Kappel	3B7	7	28	5	8		2	1	0			4	.286
B. Taylor	C6,OF1	7	27	3	5		1	0	0			2	.185

SYRACUSE (cont.)
Stars

BATTERS	POS-GAMES	GP	AB	R	H	BI	2B	3B	HR	BB	SO	SB	BA
Ed Glenn	OF7	7	25	4	7		1	0	0			3	.280
James Devlin	P6	6	21	5	4		0	0	0			0	.190
Cal Broughton	C4,OF1	5	18	1	1		0	0	0			0	.056
Walter Andrews	1B4	4	14	2	4		1	0	0			1	.286
Ed Knouff	P3	3	11	0	0		0	0	0			0	.000
Charles Sweeney	P2,1B1,OF1	3	8	4	1		0	0	0			0	.125
Buttercup Dickerson	3B1,OF1	2	5	0	1		0	0	0			0	.200
Gus Meehan	C1	1	4	0	1		0	0	0			0	.250
Baker	P1	1	4	0	0		0	0	0			0	.000

PITCHERS		W	L	PCT	G	GS	CG	SH	IP	H	BB	SO	ERA
Doug Crothers		27	16	.628	43	43	43	3	386	381	121	143	1.56
John Schappert		10	14	.417	25	25	25	1	225	229	79	84	2.00
James Devine		6	9	.400	15	15	14	1	129	150	39	45	2.23
James Devlin		2	4	.333	6	6	6	0	52	42	14	30	1.05
Ed Knouff		1	1	.500	3	3	3	0	28	14	6	28	0.32
Baker		0	1	.000	1	1	1	0	9	10	2	2	0.00
Charles Sweeney		0	2	.000	2	2	1	0	13	20	6	5	4.85
Bill Harbridge		0	0	----	1	0	0	0	5	6	5	2	0.00
Phil Tomney		0	0	----	1	0	0	0	5	6	0	1	1.80

BINGHAMTON   7th   37-58   .389   -24.5   C. McCormack -
Crickets   David Sullivan

BATTERS	POS-GAMES	GP	AB	R	H	BI	2B	3B	HR	BB	SO	SB	BA
Al Maul	1B26,P17,OF4	45	160	24	28		6	0	1			6	.175
Charles Jones	2B39,3B7,P1	46	176	32	39		5	2	0			15	.222
F. Friss	SS34,3B1	35	124	21	27		8	2	2			1	.218
Hobart Van Alstyne	3B22	22	95	14	19		6	0	0			7	.200
Robert Gilks	OF61,SS15,3B8,P1	85	386	51	103		15	4	0			23	.268
Joseph Kappel	OF52,2B21,C16,SS2,3B1	90	370	70	108		15	5	3			8	.292
John Lavin	OF51,1B1	52	201	27	41		8	1	1			3	.204
Jim Roxburgh	C49,OF6,3B2	53	192	25	34		6	0	0			13	.177
John Munyan	C36,OF35,3B6,SS4,P1	76	317	51	80		16	2	1			10	.253
Ed Toohey	OF48	48	195	33	45		6	3	3			10	.231
Ed Seward	P25,OF13	37	145	22	41		6	0	0			5	.283
John Troy	2B36	36	152	31	44		9	2	0			9	.289
Clarence Cross	SS29	29	122	16	33		2	0	1			0	.270
Ed Sales	P23,OF10,3B2,2B1	29	122	13	30		3	1	0			0	.246
Richard Dwyer	1B24	24	105	16	21		4	0	0			19	.200
Charles Levis	1B24	24	94	16	23		8	2	0			3	.245
George Bradley	3B13,1B6	19	74	9	16		3	0	0			1	.216
Dan Corcoran	3B19	19	73	8	11		4	0	0			0	.151
James Becannon	P14,OF2,SS1	17	64	7	17		1	1	0			4	.266
Dan Stearns	1B15	15	56	12	14		2	1	1			2	.250
Chris Hassett	SS10,OF2	12	45	5	6		1	0	0			5	.133
Gene Moriarity	OF10	10	37	5	11		2	0	1			4	.297
W. Dilworth	P8	8	31	1	1		0	0	0			0	.032
J. Morrison	3B8	8	26	1	1		0	0	0			1	.038
Bob Blakiston	3B8	8	25	1	3		0	0	0			0	.120
Charles Dooley	P6	6	25	0	1		0	0	0			0	.040
James McLaughlin	OF4,P2	6	22	2	4		1	0	0			2	.182
John Driscoll	3B3	3	9	0	1		0	0	0			0	.111
Michael Redigan	SS1	1	4	1	1		0	0	0			0	.250
Robert Gamble	P1	1	4	0	1		0	0	0			0	.250

PITCHERS		W	L	PCT	G	GS	CG	SH	IP	H	BB	SO	ERA
Ed Seward		10	14	.417	25	24	24	0	220	188	51	156	1.19
Al Maul		9	6	.600	17	17	15	0	136	149	30	83	1.39
Ed Sales		7	12	.368	23	22	17	1	183	208	39	70	2.45
W. Dilworth		3	5	.375	8	8	8	0	70	67	11	61	2.06
Charles Dooley		2	4	.333	6	6	6	0	54	65	24	16	3.67
James Becannon		2	12	.167	14	14	14	0	123	143	46	60	2.27
Robert Gilks		1	2	.333	7	2	1	0	31	36	18	19	2.03
Robert Gamble		1	0	1.000	1	1	1	0	9	8	2	5	0.00
John Munyan		0	1	.000	1	0	0	0	2	3	1	1	4.50
James McLaughlin		0	2	.000	2	2	2	0	17	22	12	11	3.18
Charles Jones		0	0	----	1	0	0	0	1	0	2	0	0.00

OSWEGO Starchboxes	8th	23-72	.242	-38.5	Milt West - Henry Ormsbee

BATTERS	POS-GAMES	GP	AB	R	H	BI	2B	3B	HR	BB	SO	SB	BA
Tom Morrissey	1B65	65	264	43	69		11	0	1			8	.261
Joe Ardner	2B89,P2	89	352	40	84		12	1	0			21	.239
John Shoupe	SS31,OF23,C1	55	202	42	52		3	0	0			21	.257
Pat Larkin	3B83,OF1,P1	84	347	41	71		8	2	0			7	.205
Milt West	OF78,2B5,1B5,SS3,3B1	91	404	66	118		25	3	3			21	.292
H. Chrisman	OF39,C37,SS8,3B3	81	303	21	51		5	3	0			19	.168
Woods	OF34,C2	35	149	21	50		13	1	0			1	.336
Harry Parker	C27,1B5,3B1,SS1	32	118	11	24		1	0	0			3	.203
Ed Green	P31,SS10,3B4,OF3,2B2	46	146	12	22		3	0	0			7	.151
Mike Mattimore	P39,OF3	41	140	16	26		3	0	0			4	.186
Jim Toy	C22,1B6,SS4,3B3,OF3	38	143	12	31		3	4	0			1	.217
James Collins	SS29,OF3,C3	34	129	17	27		2	2	0			4	.209
Charles F. Householder	1B14,OF8	23	89	4	15		2	0	0			0	.169
John Richmond	SS12,OF6,3B1	18	70	10	14		1	1	0			0	.200
James Green	OF14,SS1	15	60	7	14		2	0	0			3	.233
Walter Walker	OF12,C2	14	52	8	10		1	0	0			2	.172
Hart Oberlander	OF13	13	48	6	13		2	0	0			2	.271
Joe Flynn	OF12	12	49	7	8		0	0	0			1	.163
Joseph McGuckin	OF11	11	39	6	5		1	0	0			3	.128
Joe Walsh	OF10	10	41	2	4		2	0	0			1	.098
William Horner	OF6,P6	10	38	2	3		0	0	0			0	.079
M. Schell	P10,OF1	10	33	2	3		0	0	0			0	.091
William Sweeney	P3,OF1	5	22	2	3		0	0	0			1	.136
Ed Shattuck	OF5	5	19	1	2		0	0	0			2	.105
Al Warner	P5,OF1	5	16	3	3		0	0	0			0	.188
Burroughs	2B2,C2	4	14	1	5		1	0	0			1	.357
Sayer	OF4,C1	4	14	1	1		0	0	0			0	.071
Charles Robinson	OF1,C1	2	7	0	1		0	0	0			0	.143
John Greening	P2	2	6	0	0		0	0	0			0	.000
Thomas Callahan	SS1,C1	1	4	0	1		0	0	0			0	.250
Callendar	C1	1	4	1	0		0	0	0			0	.000
Lou Galvin	P1	1	4	2	0		0	0	0			0	.000
George McKeough	P1	1	4	0	0		0	0	0			0	.000
Bill Crossley	C1	1	3	0	0		0	0	0			0	.000
Grennell	P1	1	3	0	0		0	0	0			0	.000
Ed Clark	P1	1	2	0	0		0	0	0			0	.000

PITCHERS	W	L	PCT	G	GS	CG	SH	IP	H	BB	SO	ERA
Mike Mattimore	12	*26	.316	39	38	37	0	334	326	86	182	1.62
Ed Green	6	22	.214	32	28	25	0	242	246	99	118	1.79
Al Warner	2	3	.400	5	5	4	0	40	54	6	17	3.38
William Sweeney	1	2	.333	3	3	3	0	27	46	14	14	4.00
William Horner	1	5	.167	6	6	4	0	46	46	16	26	1.57
M. Schell	1	8	.111	10	9	8	0	79	88	37	28	1.59
Ed Clark	0	1	.000	1	1	1	0	8	6	5	6	3.38
Lou Galvin	0	1	.000	1	1	1	0	8	11	9	7	0.00
Grennell	0	1	.000	1	1	1	0	9	12	3	3	2.00
George McKeough	0	1	.000	1	1	1	0	8	10	8	6	3.38
John Greening	0	2	.000	2	2	1	0	13	18	15	6	2.77
Joe Ardner	0	0	----	2	0	0	0	6	4	2	3	0.00
Pat Larkin	0	0	----	1	0	0	0	7	4	1	6	2.57

TEAM BATTING

TEAMS	GP	AB	R	H	BI	2B	3B	HR	BB	SO	SB	BA
UTICA	96	**3566**	**630**	**919**		**150**	48	7			**187**	.258
ROCHESTER	96	3395	534	853		132	37	27			125	.251
TORONTO	95	3513	622	880		120	34	19			178	.251
HAMILTON	96	3480	571	860		120	39	13			186	.247
BUFFALO	**99**	3522	587	899		115	**50**	**36**			125	.255
SYRACUSE	95	3382	531	818		130	36	12			162	.242
BINGHAMTON	96	3451	514	804		137	26	14			135	.233
OSWEGO	95	3432	407	731		110	17	4			118	.213
	384	27741	4396	6764		1014	287	132			1216	.244

TEAM PITCHING

TEAMS	W	L	PCT	G	GS	CG	SH	IP	H	BB	SO	ERA
UTICA	**62**	34	**.646**	96	96	**95**	4	846	707	145	398	1.44
ROCHESTER	56	39	.589	96	96	92	6	860	730	193	**495**	**1.29**
TORONTO	53	41	.563	95	95	94	3	840	863	239	417	1.83
HAMILTON	52	43	.547	96	96	91	5	857	802	264	492	1.74
BUFFALO	50	45	.526	**99**	**99**	93	**7**	**874**	**954**	253	376	2.00
SYRACUSE	46	47	.491	95	95	93	5	851	858	272	340	1.73
BINGHAMTON	37	58	.389	96	96	88	1	845	889	235	482	1.97
OSWEGO	23	**72**	.242	95	95	86	0	827	861	**301**	422	1.86
	379	379	.500	768	768	732	31	6800	6664	1902	3422	1.73

1887
CONSOLIDATION

Before the 1886 season, what was then the New York State League added some strong teams from another league to boost its own chances for the upcoming season. Prior to the 1887 campaign, this same league, now called the International League, did much the same. The organization they turned to was a familiar friend: the Eastern League.

The Eastern League had stumbled through the 1886 season with only five of its eight members finishing. When the Eastern collapsed after the end of the 1886 season, the International plucked its two strongest members, Newark and Jersey City, to join them as the circuit's ninth and tenth franchises.

As the 1887 season unfolded, the stability of 1886 was soon forgotten. At the end of May, with only three wins to show for their efforts, the Oswego club folded. A team from Scranton was admitted in its stead with the provision that it would not have to inherit Oswego's woeful mark. Six weeks later, in mid–July, the Utica club was purchased by Wilkes-Barre. They too wanted to start with a clean slate, with all the Utica games thrown out. But the newcomers, Newark and Jersey City, balked at such a proposal. Both had lost several wins when the Oswego games had been tossed, and they didn't want their 6-0 marks against Utica wiped from the official record. Newark and Jersey City's votes prevailed, and the Wilkes-Barre team took over where Utica left off. Finally, on August 19, the Binghamton Crickets disbanded and withdrew from the league.

The final outcome saw Toronto edging Buffalo by three games, with Syracuse and Newark shortly behind. Hamilton and Jersey City each won more than they lost, while Rochester, Binghamton, Wilkes-Barre, Scranton, Utica, and Oswego finished in arrears. The batting title was won by Ed Crane of Toronto with a lofty total of .428. (Note: in 1887 only, walks counted as hits, contributing to Crane's and others' high totals. In later years, the walk-hits were expunged from the official records. But since no official walk totals were ever kept, the "official" batting leader remains unknown.) Frank Grant, from Buffalo, hit the most home runs (11). Two pitchers tied at 33 for the most wins: George Stovey of Newark and Ed Crane from Toronto. The best earned run average was tabulated by Syracuse Star Con Murphy (2.19), calculated on an earned runs per game basis.

The incoming New Jersey franchises brought strength to the International League in 1887, and pulled the remnants of the league's founding father, the Eastern League, into the fold. Although neither would remain long with the International in the nineteenth century, both Newark and Jersey City would hold vital roles during the league's twentieth century years.

TORONTO Canucks

1st	65-36	.643			Charles Cushman		

BATTERS	POS-GAMES	GP	AB	R	H	BI	2B	3B	HR	BB	SO	SB	BA
Jay Faatz	1B99	99	433	96	138		17	7	4			47	.313
Thomas Kearns	2B104	104	424	58	127		16	9	3			32	.300
Gus Alberts	SS103	103	504	111	184		18	14	1			60	.365
Chris Rickley	3B49	49	222	42	69		5	5	1			16	.310
Mike Slattery	OF100	100	475	**134**	167		**31**	8	8			**112**	.352
Jim McCormick	OF67,3B29	96	400	69	133		21	7	5			15	.328
Pit Gilman	OF54	54	233	49	63		11	5	2			34	.270
Bill Traffley	C45	45	190	34	58		8	2	2			21	.307
Ed Decker	OF45,C25	99	450	88	151		5	9	4			31	.335
Ed Crane	P47,OF35	87	376	83	161		30	8	6			21	**.428**
Al Sheppard	P28	29	117	24	38		3	1	0			6	.325
James McKinley	P8	8	32	3	8		0	0	0			0	.250
John Davis	P7	7	27	2	6		0	0	0			0	.222
George Stallings		1	4	0	1		0	0	0			0	.250

PITCHERS	W	L	PCT	G	GS	CG	SH	IP	H	BB	SO	ERA
Ed Crane	33	13	.719	47					540	**141**		2.49
Al Sheppard	17	12	.586	28					314	55		2.75
James McKinley	4	3	.571	8	8	7		69	93	22	19	2.74
John Davis	4	3	.571	7	7	7		62	93	13	23	3.19

BUFFALO Bisons

2nd	63-40	.611	-3		John Chapman		

BATTERS	POS-GAMES	GP	AB	R	H	BI	2B	3B	HR	BB	SO	SB	BA
Mike Lehane	1B103,P2	103	452	110	177		27	11	9			16	.392
Frank Grant	2B105	105	459	81	162		26	10	11			40	.366
Henry Easterday	SS97	97	409	66	133		13	5	1			32	.325
John Reidy	3B86,C16	102	438	68	146		17	1	1			12	.333
Charles Hamburg	OF96	96	437	87	151		20	3	5			35	.345
John Remsen	OF95	95	422	83	165		19	9	5			24	.391
John Galligan	OF63	63	291	43	97							10	.333
Dan Dugdale	C	(see multi-team players)											
John Fanning	P50	50	206	35	48		11	0	1			15	.233
Mike Walsh	P37	37	149	17	23		4	0	0			3	.164
James Purvis	C18	18	85	9	38		5	2	0			7	.447
Harry Zell	OF10,P5	17	80	15	18		1	0	0			6	.225
Tom Callahan	C12	12	50	10	14		3	0	0			4	.280
Tom O'Rourke	C12	12	47	4	14		3	0	0			3	.300
William Husted	P5	6	19	2	6		0	0	0			1	.316
George Knowlton	P4	4	14	0	1		0	0	0			0	.071
W. Mooney		4	13	0	2		0	0	0			0	.154
W. Reilly		1	4	0	1		0	0	0			0	.250
Charles Miller		1	4	0	0		0	0	0			0	.000

PITCHERS	W	L	PCT	G	GS	CG	SH	IP	H	BB	SO	ERA
John Fanning	28	**21**	.571	50					645	103		3.82
Mike Walsh	27	9	**.750**	37					446	84		2.35
George Knowlton	3	1	.750	4	4	4		36	52	12	2	2.00
William Husted	2	3	.400	5	5	4		43	67	11	14	4.60
Mike Lehane	1	0	1.000	2	0	0		5	6	3	0	0.00
Harry Zell	1	3	.250	5	5	4		41	73	19	7	3.51

SYRACUSE Stars

3rd	61-40	.604	-4		James Gifford - Joseph Simmons		

BATTERS	POS-GAMES	GP	AB	R	H	BI	2B	3B	HR	BB	SO	SB	BA
Thomas Lynch	1B82	82	338	80	117		17	5	2			31	.357
Henry Bittmann	2B99	99	409	75	121		15	3	0			51	.296
Oliver Beard	SS103	103	477	90	176		26	2	0			30	.356
Joe Battin	3B51	51	224	24	53		5	1	0			14	.237
Henry Simon	OF109	**109**	490	106	179		21	12	4			74	.365
Harry Jacoby	OF96	96	510	114	189		28	10	3			35	.371
Charles Marr	OF89,3B14	103	**517**	131	185		24	6	0			83	.358
Al Schellhase	C56	56	184	25	36		2	0	0			23	.196

SYRACUSE (cont.)
Stars

BATTERS	POS-GAMES	GP	AB	R	H	BI	2B	3B	HR	BB	SO	SB	BA
Ed Dundon	P40	58	200	29	65		11	3	2			10	.325
Dick Buckley	C50	50	198	35	66		13	4	1			5	.333
Robert Higgins	P29,OF13	41	164	26	48		7	3	0			28	.294
George Strief	3B30	30	156	29	61		5	3	0			8	.391
Con B. Murphy	P27	27	168	23	60		5	1	0			15	.357
Duke Jantzen	C12	12	52	8	9		0	0	0			4	.173
J. Haley		1	2	0	0		0	0	0			0	.000

PITCHERS	W	L	PCT	G	GS	CG	SH	IP	H	BB	SO	ERA
Robert Higgins	20	7	.741	29					317	67		2.90
Ed Dundon	20	15	.571	40					430	75		2.45
Con B. Murphy	17	8	.680	27					292	53		**2.19**
Charles Marr	1	1	.500	5	0	0		27	29	8	8	3.33

NEWARK   4th   59-39   .602   -4.5   Charles Hackett -
Little Giants   Lawrence Murphy

BATTERS	POS-GAMES	GP	AB	R	H	BI	2B	3B	HR	BB	SO	SB	BA
James Field	1B96,P1	96	413	84	141		19	7	2			37	.341
Tom McLaughlin	2B100	100	381	52	120		11	3	1			46	.315
Leo Smith	SS104	104	401	54	97		11	2	0			38	.242
John Irwin	3B102,P1	102	431	79	135		10	6	1			104	.313
John Coogan	OF100	100	448	65	162		11	7	2			31	.361
William Annis	OF98	98	434	78	134		13	17	1			79	.309
Art Stuart	OF37	44	189	28	56		5	0	0			10	.296
Fleet Walker	C65	69	254	44	67		6	2	1			36	.264
George Stovey	P48	54	208	25	53		7	1	0			16	.255
Mike Hughes	P42	48	154	12	46		8	1	1			4	.299
Gene Derby	C25	27	114	17	35		4	0	1			6	.307
Bart Cantz	C14	22	78	14	21		6	0	0			7	.269
Robert Miller	P3	3	12	1	3		0	0	0			1	.250
John Cuff		2	5	0	1		0	0	0			0	.200

PITCHERS	W	L	PCT	G	GS	CG	SH	IP	H	BB	SO	ERA
George Stovey	33	14	.702	48				424	538	119	107	2.46
Mike Hughes				42					452	127		2.45
Robert Miller	3	0	1.000	3	3	3		27	38	13	8	1.00
James Fields	0	0	----	1	0	0		3	10	4	0	24.00
John Irwin	0	0	----	1	0	0		1	3	1	0	0.00

HAMILTON   5th   57-42   .575   -7   George Stroud -
Hams   Charles Collins -Peter Wood

BATTERS	POS-GAMES	GP	AB	R	H	BI	2B	3B	HR	BB	SO	SB	BA
William McQuery	1B		(see multi-team players)										
Charles Collins	2B58,3B11	69	296	54	92		10	1	0			51	.311
Marr Phillips	SS99,P1	100	420	60	141		24	8	4			45	.336
John Rainey	3B70	70	330	63	115		12	3	1			34	.348
William Wright	OF100	100	464	92	198		16	4	2			73	.427
Mike Mansell	OF100	100	457	109	157		15	16	1			74	.344
Joseph Knight	OF100	100	442	86	148		24	8	5			41	.335
Ed Warner	C53	61	228	26	55		6	3	1			13	.241
Wood	P39,2B27	59	269	41	96		13	5	2			22	.371
Jerry Moore	C36,1B11	51	195	28	55		8	1	0			17	.282
Michael Jones	P33	42	159	17	40		6	1	1			13	.252
William Horner	P26	35	138	20	43		3	0	0			14	.312
Hugh Weir	3B17	17	71	11	21		2	0	0			14	.296
John Morrison	C15	15	65	10	24		3	0	0			3	.369

PITCHERS	W	L	PCT	G	GS	CG	SH	IP	H	BB	SO	ERA
Wood	21	13	.618	39					421	39		2.62
Michael Jones	18	12	.600	33					362	77		2.54
William Horner				26					313	42		3.23
Marr Phillips	0	0	----	1	0	0		7	10	5	0	6.43

JERSEY CITY Skeeters

		6th	48-49	.494	-15	Pat Powers

BATTERS	POS-GAMES	GP	AB	R	H	BI	2B	3B	HR	BB	SO	SB	BA
Tom O'Brien	1B71,OF10	71	378	101	159		21	10	6			63	.421
John McCabe	2B44	44	199	26	57		2	3	1			13	.286
Franklin Lang	SS99	99	401	84	103		8	5	0			87	.257
John Corcoran	3B73,C21,P5	97	421	71	134		22	8	0			59	.318
Len Sowders	OF95	95	432	85	161		15	11	5			31	.373
Pat Friel	OF93	93	415	85	163		13	13	2			85	.393
Joe Brown	OF45	45	193	32	61		6	3	0			18	.316
Pat Murphy	C46	46	197	21	56		6	1	0			19	.284
John Hiland	2B41,OF37	78	348	73	119		9	2	0			57	.342
Mike Muldoon	3B28,2B12	44	170	26	58		9	2	1			9	.341
Sam Shaw	P38	39	156	13	39		2	2	0			15	.250
Ledell Titcomb	P34	34	140	10	20		2	0	0			3	.143
Stephen Brady	1B20	20	90	22	24		2	0	0			13	.267
John Huston	OF17	17	103	17	37		6	0	0			4	.359
William Daley	P11	14	50	3	9		0	0	0			3	.180
Charles Helfer		7	30	1	11		0	0	0			0	.367
Beadle	P1	1	5	1	1		0	0	0			0	.200
John Schafer	P1	1	5	1	1		0	0	0			0	.200
Willard Holland		1	2	0	1		0	0	0			0	.500

PITCHERS	W	L	PCT	G	GS	CG	SH	IP	H	BB	SO	ERA
Sam Shaw	17	19	.472	38					510	89		2.68
Ledell Titcomb	18	14	.563	34					347	81		2.32
William Daley	7	5	.583	11					143	49		2.64
John Corcoran	2	1	.667	5	2	2		34	41	9	12	1.85
John Schafer	1	0	1.000	1	1	1		9	20	5	1	10.00
John Huston	0	6	.000	10	7	6		66	120	36	22	4.64
Beadle	0	0	----	1	1	0		4	15	2	1	18.00

ROCHESTER Maroons

		7th	49-52	.485	-16	John Humphries

BATTERS	POS-GAMES	GP	AB	R	H	BI	2B	3B	HR	BB	SO	SB	BA
Doc Kennedy	1B91	91	403	79	151		27	2	4			12	.375
James Knowles	2B87,P1	87	440	85	163		22	15	8			54	.370
John Cline	SS63,P2	63	317	57	114		10	5	2			29	.360
John McGlone	3B85	85	375	81	136		16	4	3			63	.363
Daniel Connors	OF99	99	424	64	134		12	5	2			15	.316
Fred Lewis	OF82	82	377	87	153		27	7	4			16	.406
Jonathan Morrison	OF67	67	312	47	89		7	4	1			8	.282
Charles Zimmer	C64	64	272	50	90		18	5	6			22	.331
Joe Visner	OF41,SS17,C13	81	368	59	114		15	12	1			22	.310
Jersey Bakely	P41	46	173	21	50		4	0	0			4	.288
John Humphries	C18	28	112	13	31		1	0	0			5	.276
Charles Parsons	P23	23	95	18	18		0	0	0			2	.189
J. Creegan		12	47	3	9		0	0	0			0	.191
W. Heberling	SS10	10	31	2	5		1	0	0			2	.161
J. Dooley	P1	9	36	3	6		1	0	0			0	.167
Bob Barr	P5	5	22	2	6		0	0	0			0	.273
John Tickner		2	6	0	1		0	0	0			0	.167
T. Grover	P1	1	5	0	0		0	0	0			0	.000
Laydon	P1	1	5	0	0		0	0	0			0	.000
Coyle		1	4	0	1		0	0	0			0	.250
O. Visner		1	3	1	3		0	0	0			0	1.000

PITCHERS	W	L	PCT	G	GS	CG	SH	IP	H	BB	SO	ERA
JerseyBakely	21	21	.500	41					471	98		2.56
Charles Parsons	13	9	.591	23					260	24		2.39
Bob Barr	3	2	.600	5	5	5		44	53	15	6	1.62
T. Grover	0	1	.000	1	1	1		12	21	8	2	4.50
Laydon	0	1	.000	1	1	0		3	16	2	0	18.00
John Cline	0	0	----	2	0	0		5	12	2	0	3.38
J. Dooley	0	0	----	1	0	0		2	7	2	0	4.50
James Knowles	0	0	----	1	0	0		1	2	1	0	0.00

BINGHAMTON Crickets

	8th	27-46	.369	-24	Henry Ormsbee - Alonzo Knight

BATTERS	POS-GAMES	GP	AB	R	H	BI	2B	3B	HR	BB	SO	SB	BA
Joseph Straub	1B	(see multi-team players)											
Bones Ely	2B44,OF28,P10	84	349	75	123		25	6	2			8	.352
Phil Tomney	SS	(see multi-team players)											
Robert Gilks	3B50,OF24,P1	75	362	68	121		19	0	1			29	.325
Milt West	OF54	54	254	48	88		18	0	4			4	.346
Harry Lyons	OF	(see multi-team players)											
Joseph Kappel	OF	(see multi-team players)											
Thomas Quinn	C30	30	119	16	37		6	0	0			5	.311
John Fowler	2B32,P2	34	157	42	58		12	1	0			23	.350
Anthony Madigan	P19	20	67	3	13		0	0	0			1	.191
Alonzo Knight		9	38	2	6		0	0	0			0	.158
Peter McShannic		7	28	2	3		1	0	0			0	.107
Eugene Bagley		6	26	8	8		2	0	0			2	.308
Renfroe	P6	6	25	7	8		0	1	0			0	.320
George Keefe	P5	5	19	2	2		0	0	0			0	.105
Clarence Childs		3	13	1	7		2	0	0			0	.538
Daniel Alexander	P3	3	11	1	2		0	0	0			0	.182
William McCloskey		2	8	0	1		0	0	0			0	.125

PITCHERS	W	L	PCT	G	GS	CG	SH	IP	H	BB	SO	ERA
Anthony Madigan	6	12	333	19					266	59		3.45
Bones Ely	3	4	.429	10					110	27		3.70
George Keefe	2	3	.400	5	5	5		45	60	14	17	3.60
Renfroe	2	4	.333	6	6	4		46	70	18	4	5.24
Robert Gilks	0	1	.000	1	1	1		9	18	1	1	7.00
Daniel Alexander	0	3	.000	3	3	2		19	54	23	5	10.73
John Fowler	0	0	----	2	1	0		10	16	2	2	4.50

WILKES-BARRE Coal Barons

	9th	14-36	.280	-26.5	William Hoover - Fergy Malone - Denny Mack

BATTERS	POS-GAMES	GP	AB	R	H	BI	2B	3B	HR	BB	SO	SB	BA
Charles W. Householder	1B48	48	184	16	41		3	0	1			3	.223
Jerry O'Brien	2B44	44	175	18	47		10	1	0			7	.269
Ed Sales	SS49,P3	51	207	35	62		15	3	2			14	.299
Robert Pettit	3B16	16	79	12	35		6	2	1			14	.443
Charles Kelly	OF48	50	222	36	59		8	4	1			20	.266
Wiliam Hoover	OF45	45	230	56	81		13	3	3			28	.368
John McKee	OF17	17	77	10	19		4	2	1			8	.248
Bill Hallman	C28	38	147	19	49		8	1	0			10	.333
Frank Brill	P21	31	123	13	28		4	0	0			10	.228
Mike Cody	C10	19	70	6	19		2	0	0			0	.271
John Schweitzer	3B14,P1	14	53	5	13		0	0	0			2	.245
John Roach	P11	16	60	3	14		3	0	0			1	.233
J. Fitzsimmons	C12	12	45	3	10		1	0	0			1	.222
Al Warner	P8	9	35	3	13		3	0	0			0	.351
James Becannon		6	22	1	6		1	0	0			0	.273
Bill Campion	P2	3	12	0	2		0	0	0			0	.167
George Staltz	P2	2	8	0	2		0	0	0			0	.250
Hathaway		1	4	0	1		0	0	0			0	.250
Louis Renner		1	4	0	0		0	0	0			0	.000
McGovern	P1	1	3	0	0		0	0	0			0	.000

PITCHERS	W	L	PCT	G	GS	CG	SH	IP	H	BB	SO	ERA
Frank Brill	8	13	.381	21					273	38		3.52
John Roach	3	8	.273	11					147	20		4.18
Al Warner	2	5	.286	8	8	7		65	122	29	18	4.57
Bill Campion	0	1	.000	2	1	1		9	22	1	3	10.00
McGovern	0	1	.000	1	1	1		9	12	2	0	6.00
Ed Sales	0	2	.000	3	2	0		13	37	8	7	8.31
George Staltz	0	2	.000	2	2	2		17	31	0	2	2.65
John Schweitzer	0	0	----	1	0	0		5	7	3	1	3.60
Charles W. Householder	0	0	----	1	0	0		2	6	1	1	9.00

SCRANTON
Indians

10th   19-55   .256   -32.5   Denny Mack - Chris
Meisel - Fergy Malone

BATTERS	POS-GAMES	GP	AB	R	H	BI	2B	3B	HR	BB	SO	SB	BA
Thomas McGuirk	1B38	38	161	16	52		7	1	0			8	.317
Steiner Simmons	2B37	37	142	16	32		3	0	0			0	.225
John Shoupe	SS43	43	180	27	52		6	2	1			28	.289
Charles Jones	3B27	27	127	24	47		3	1	0			24	.370
Ed Burke	OF39,3B17	56	265	61	103		13	9	2			41	.388
Charles Osterhout	OF38	39	178	22	44		8	1	0			15	.247
Peter Hasney	OF34	34	131	13	28		0	0	1			7	.214
Bill Crossley	C36,OF10	47	181	30	55		11	2	1			13	.304
William Schriver	C31,3B23	56	253	30	66		8	4	2			7	.281
Bill Gleason	P13,OF10	23	99	13	30		7	2	0			1	.303
Sam Crane	2B21	21	85	12	19		2	2	0			1	.224
Maurice Bresnahan	1B15	15	62	5	12		1	0	0			1	.194
Jouett Meekin	P12	14	54	9	14		3	0	0			7	.259
George Backer	P11	12	45	7	11		1	1	0			0	.244
John Holzberger		7	30	1	4		1	1	0			0	.133
Ed Cramer		3	15	2	5		0	0	1			0	.333
Joseph O'Brien		2	8	2	3		1	0	0			0	.375
James Dee		1	4	1	2		1	0	0			0	.500
Egan		1	4	0	0		0	0	0			0	.000
William Devinney		1	4	0	0		0	0	0			0	.000

PITCHERS		W	L	PCT	G	GS	CG	SH	IP	H	BB	SO	ERA
Hart Oberlander		5	18	.217	24					295	84		2.37
Jouett Meekin		4	7	.364	12					177	39		3.75
George Backer		4	7	.364	11					147	20		3.82
Bill Gleason		1	12	.071	12					159	41		3.67

UTICA
Pentups

11th   12-39   .235   -28   David Dischler

BATTERS	POS-GAMES	GP	AB	R	H	BI	2B	3B	HR	BB	SO	SB	BA
George Latham	1B44	44	182	21	51		2	0	0			13	.280
Emery Hengle	2B51,P1	51	236	46	87		9	2	0			23	.369
James Halpin	SS21	21	89	10	20		0	1	0			4	.225
Jim Say	3B50,P1	50	227	40	77		15	4	2			14	.340
John Carroll	OF47	47	244	61	81		12	3	1			27	.332
Sandy Griffin	OF	(see multi-team players)											
James Brouthers	OF	(see multi-team players)											
Joseph Hofford	C	(see multi-team players)											
Fleischmann	SS18	26	122	20	42		4	2	0			5	.344
John Hofford	P19	19	94	14	39		10	1	0			3	.415
John Pendergrass	P16	18	51	3	15		2	0	0			1	.234
Charles F. Householder	OF12,P1	12	48	4	15		3	1	0			0	.312
Delahanty	P6	7	30	3	6		0	0	0			0	.200
George Bausewine	P2	5	16	1	0		0	0	0			0	.000

PITCHERS		W	L	PCT	G	GS	CG	SH	IP	H	BB	SO	ERA
John Hofford		6	12	.333	19					316	62		5.32
Delahanty		2	3	.400	6	5	5		47	69	8	7	3.64
John Pendergrass		1	15	.063	16					241	22		3.91
George Bausewine		0	2	.000	2	2	2		17	31	10	1	4.24
Emery Hengle		0	0	----	1	0	0		8	16	3	1	9.00
Jim Say		0	0	----	1	0	0		7	15	4	0	5.14
Charles F. Householder		0	0	----	1	0	0		5	5	3	0	1.80

OSWEGO
Starchboxes

12th   3-23   .115   -25.5   Wes Curry -
Mike Gill

BATTERS	POS-GAMES	GP	AB	R	H	BI	2B	3B	HR	BB	SO	SB	BA
Louis Grawley	1B18	23	99	11	29		3	0	0			2	.293
James Humphries	2B,P1	15	71	9	32		2	0	0			9	.451
Jim Deasley	SS14	21	100	16	30		3	1	1			4	.300
William Farmer	3B,C12	25	103	12	22		3	0	0			7	.214
Harry Lyons	OF	(see multi-team players)											
John Lavin	OF	(see multi-team players)											

OSWEGO (cont.)
Starchboxes

BATTERS	POS-GAMES	GP	AB	R	H	BI	2B	3B	HR	BB	SO	SB	BA
Hart Oberlander	OF	(see multi-team players)											
David Oldfield	C	(see multi-team players)											
Ed Fusselbach	SS14	14	96	15	33		5	2	0			13	.354
Jake Virtue	P5	10	35	3	10		2	0	0			2	.286
Jim Hyndman	P4	6	26	1	6		0	0	0			1	.231
Randolph Jackson	P1	5	20	0	4		2	0	0			0	.200
Lawrence James	P5	5	20	2	1		0	0	0			3	.050
Charles Hilsey	P3	3	12	1	3		0	0	0			0	.250
Frank Olin		2	8	1	3		0	0	0			1	.375
Helfer		1	5	3	3		0	0	0			0	.600
Frank Madigan		1	4	1	0		0	0	0			0	.000
Daniel Alexander	P1	1	4	0	0		0	0	0			0	.000
Lloyd		1	3	0	0		0	0	0			0	.000

PITCHERS		W	L	PCT	G	GS	CG	SH	IP	H	BB	SO	ERA
Jake Virtue		1	4	.200	5	4	2		32	57	18	6	2.53
Daniel Alexander		0	1	.000	1	1	1		8	16	2	1	3.38
Charles Hilsey		0	2	.000	3	3	1		12	30	13	2	7.50
Jim Hyndman		0	3	.000	4	3	3		28	60	15	6	7.07
Lawrence James		0	5	.000	5	5	5		43	94	16	10	7.74
Randolph Jackson		0	0	----	1	0	0		6	12	7	1	1.50
James Humphreys		0	0	----	1	0	0		5	11	3	1	0.00

MULTI-TEAM PLAYERS

BATTERS	POS-GAMES	TEAMS	GP	AB	R	H	BI	2B	3B	HR	BB	SO	SB	BA
William McQuery	1B102	SYR-HAM	102	421	71	168		29	6	4			38	.399
Phil Tomney	SS98	BIN-SCR	98	403	66	129		13	5	3			19	.320
Sandy Griffin	OF94	UTI-BUF	94	433	98	162		21	12	2			12	.374
Joseph Straub	1B87	BIN-SCR	93	421	68	135		22	2	1			12	.321
Dennis Casey	OF90	BIN-NEW	90	400	66	128		12	2	1			41	.320
Joseph Hofford	C70	UTI-JC	70	282	32	99		10	2	0			30	.351
David Oldfield	C50,OF15	OSW-TOR	66	278	41	98		6	3	0			7	.353
James Brouthers	OF63	OS-UT-WB	63	296	37	92		8	3	1			6	.311
Joseph Kappel	OF44,C29	BIN-BUF	63	277	63	102		22	6	4			26	.368
Harry Lyons	OF51	OSW-BIN	58	266	52	77		7	3	2			22	.289
John Henry	OF27,P13	NEW-SCR	47	221	47	78		6	2	2			38	.394
Ed Green	P36	BI-BU-WB	47	172	21	42		2	1	0			8	.244
Dan Dugdale	C44	ROC-BUF	44	182	25	55		5	1	0			5	.302
Hart Oberlander	P24,OF19	OSW-SCR	43	159	28	69		9	0	1			6	.355
Ed Sixsmith	C40	UTI-BUF	40	168	17	50		2	0	0			5	.298
John Lavin	OF37	OSW-SCR	39	162	16	45		11	0	2			2	.278
James Gray	3B31	SYR-BUF	31	126	14	41		9	0	2			11	.325
George Hayes	P30	OSW-ROC	30	120	8	28		1	0	0			0	.233
Ed Williams	C20	BIN-SCR	28	114	19	29		3	1	0			6	.254
Alexander Jacobs	P25	JC-BI-SC	25	82	8	17		3	1	0			8	.207
Norm Baker	P24	ROC-TOR	24	97	13	23		1	0	2			4	.237
Stephen Dunn	OF14	ROC-UTI	21	72	10	26		5	0	1			6	.278
Doug Crothers	P19	SYR-HAM	20	80	13	19		2	0	0			11	.237
Charles Whitney	3B13	BIN-SCR	13	57	6	18		1	1	0			5	.316
Jeremiah Reardon	P11	UTI-SCR	11	48	6	10		1	0	0			4	.208
Frank Cox		UTI-SCR	11	46	4	11		1	0	0			6	.261

PITCHERS		TEAMS	W	L	PCT	G	GS	CG	SH	IP	H	BB	SO	ERA
Ed Green		BI-BU-WB	16	18	.471	36					438	72		3.25
Norm Baker		ROC-TOR	14	11	.560	24					302	78		3.04
George Hayes		OSW-ROC	8	12	.400	30					370	56		3.50
Alexander acobs		JC-BI-SC	6	19	.240	25					320	26		2.92
Doug Crothers		SYR-HAM	5	11	.313	19					238	45		3.63
John Henry		NEW-SCR	3	5	.375	13					192	40		3.85
Jeremiah Reardon		UTI-SCR	3	8	.273	11					169	22		6.55

TEAM BATTING

TEAMS	GP	AB	R	H	BI	2B	3B	HR	BB	SO	SB	BA
TORONTO	104	4101	833	1384							414	.337
BUFFALO	105	4130	830	1382							229	.335
SYRACUSE	**109**	**4232**	**840**	**1465**							431	**.346**
NEWARK	104	3811	611	1170							456	.307
HAMILTON	100	3904	676	1340							448	.343
JERSEY CITY	99	3905	701	1269							**498**	.325
ROCHESTER	99	4004	676	1315							265	.328
BINGHAMTON	77	3128	540	952							179	.304
WILKES-BARRE	49	1807	245	515							124	.285
SCRANTON	64	2753	394	795							195	.291
UTICA	51	2076	316	677							126	.326
OSWEGO	25	1128	154	341							73	.302
	493	38959	7016	12605							3338	.324

1888
SYRACUSE STARS

Out of the rubble of the 1887 season, only five teams remained to carry on the fight in 1888. One of this quintet, the Syracuse Stars, would rise during the year to become the International's first dominant team.

The Syracuse Stars entered the International League picture with the New York State League of 1885, where they won the pennant. Next followed a lackluster sixth place, before a close third in 1887. The Stars' fortunes seemed to be on the rise.

Before the campaign started, three new teams were added to take the place of the Newark, Jersey City, Wilkes-Barre, and Scranton teams. New clubs were added from Albany and Troy, as well as a new Canadian franchise from London, Ontario. This new alignment was given a slightly altered name, the International Association.

The Syracuse Stars jumped out of the gate quickly, pursued closely by the defending champions from Toronto. The two pulled away from the pack as they raced through the summer. In the end, Syracuse bested Toronto by five and one-half games, as they won 81 of 111 decisions. Far behind were Hamilton, Rochester, London, Buffalo, and Troy in third through seventh place. Below this group was last-place Albany, which won only 19 games, finishing a whopping 59 games behind the leaders. Their .181 win percentage ranks as an all-time International League low.

The Stars ended up with a league best .280 batting average, boosted by three of the circuit's top ten hitters: Oliver Beard (.350), William Wright (.349), and Charles Marr (.342). Syracuse also boasted the best pitcher as Con Murphy finished with the stingiest earned run average (1.27), computed on an earned runs per game basis. The only honors not garnered by a Star were batting laurels taken by London's Patsy Donovan (.359) and the strikeout crown won by Toronto's Al Atkinson (307).

After 1888, the Syracuse Stars went on to several first division finishes, culminating with another pennant in the late 1890s. Shortly thereafter, the team dropped out of the league, only to reappear after World War I. After another brief hiatus the Syracuse team reentered the International League during the 1930s, this time to stay.

Though they have been a strong member of the circuit for many years, fielding many strong teams, their pennant success has been dismal. Following the final nineteenth century Star pennant, Syracuse would have to wait more than 70 years for another.

The Syracuse Stars of 1888 stack up well against the all-time great clubs of the International League. In more than 100 years of International League baseball (for teams that played full schedules), Syracuse's .730 winning percentage has only been bested once.

SYRACUSE
Stars

1st   81-30   .730   Charles Hackett

BATTERS	POS-GAMES	GP	AB	R	H	BI	2B	3B	HR	BB	SO	SB	BA
William McQuery	1B112	**112**	470	77	145							24	.309
William Higgins	2B71	71	295	46	69							27	.234
Oliver Beard	SS112	**112**	**497**	100	174							60	.350
Joe Battin	3B110	110	434	52	85							31	.196
Charles Marr	OF111	**112**	485	111	164							83	.342
William Wright	OF110	110	464	**143**	162							40	.349
Bones Ely	OF101	**112**	493	98	140							47	.284
Fleet Walker	C77	77	283	38	48							34	.170
Con B. Murphy	P49	55	222	37	46							20	.207
Al Schellhase	C35	36	132	32	36							40	.273
Robert Higgins	P24	25	102	17	23							9	.225
Long	2B19	19	73	10	15							6	.205
Ed Dundon	P18	18	74	9	19							4	.257
Clarence Childs	2B	9	37	4	11		1	0	0			1	.297

PITCHERS	W	L	PCT	G	GS	CG	SH	IP	H	BB	SO	ERA
Con B. Murphy				49					360	**108**	169	**1.27**
Robert Higgins				24					215	40	98	2.56
Ed Dundon				18					182	29	54	2.76

TORONTO
Canucks

2nd   75-35   .682   -5.5   Charles Cushman

BATTERS	POS-GAMES	GP	AB	R	H	BI	2B	3B	HR	BB	SO	SB	BA
Patrick Hartnett	1B110	110	445	63	105							25	.236
Thomas Kearns	2B110	111	440	95	126							71	.286
Tom McLaughlin	SS106	107	437	82	108							50	.247
Chris Rickley	3B94	94	400	69	112							53	.280
Ed Burke	OF106	111	473	95	112							107	.237
Dennis Connors	OF101	101	444	69	121							50	.273
Mike Mansell	OF	(see multi-team players)											
David Oldfield	C56	56	314	47	61							4	.194
Ed Decker	C54,OF27	79	383	65	120							37	.313
Al Atkinson	P48	48	178	22	39							15	.219
Al Sheppard	P36	36	137	23	41							13	.299
Lewis	OF22	22	94	22	24							5	.255

PITCHERS	W	L	PCT	G	GS	CG	SH	IP	H	BB	SO	ERA
Al Atkinson				48					349	79	**307**	1.36
Al Sheppard				36					249	71	127	2.19

HAMILTON
Mountaineers

3rd   66-44   .600   -14.5   Harry Fisher

BATTERS	POS-GAMES	GP	AB	R	H	BI	2B	3B	HR	BB	SO	SB	BA
ThomasLynch	1B51	51	219	41	53							24	.242
Wilman Andrus	2B109	110	481	102	115							89	.239
Marr Phillips	SS101	101	402	69	121							54	.301
John Rainey	3B111	111	490	100	140							74	.286
Joseph Knight	OF111	111	496	99	148							64	.298
Ed Swartwood	OF77,1B32	109	428	81	127							73	.297
Peter Wood	OF25,P51,1B15	96	410	65	132							27	.322
JoeVisner	C64,OF38	107	462	68	138							41	.298
Ed Thayer	C43,OF16	65	235	32	49							33	.209
Michael Jones	P28	33	124	15	25							5	.202
Ed Green	P27	31	121	14	23							15	.190

PITCHERS	W	L	PCT	G	GS	CG	SH	IP	H	BB	SO	ERA
Peter Wood				51					414	56	163	1.80
Michael Jones				28					250	46	90	2.07
Ed Green				27					272	47	110	2.59

ROCHESTER   4th   62-45   .579   -14.5   Henry Leonard
Jingoes

BATTERS	POS-GAMES	GP	AB	R	H	BI	2B	3B	HR	BB	SO	SB	BA
Doc Kennedy	1B104	104	406	52	120							18	.296
Charles Collins	2B105	105	423	84	110							85	.260
Fred Miller	SS87	87	242	39	68							23	.199
Ezra Sutton	3B50	50	210	34	61							31	.289
Henry Simon	OF106	106	436	91	156							61	.358
Sandy Griffin	OF93	93	410	90	127							19	.310
John Peltz	OF50	50	207	23	52							6	.251
Jim Toy	C65	75	279	42	58							5	.205
Bob Barr	P48	50	175	28	37							0	.211
Will Calihan	P30	44	162	21	39							17	.241
John McHale	C20,OF18	40	174	16	34							4	.291
David McKeough	C21	28	98	11	11							7	.112
George Hayes	P15	15	74	4	6							1	.081
Stephen Toole		15	57	8	12							2	.211

PITCHERS	W	L	PCT	G	GS	CG	SH	IP	H	BB	SO	ERA
Bob Barr				48					354	67	216	1.58
Will Calihan				30					257	59	170	1.83
George Hayes				15					130	21	64	2.48

LONDON   5th   53-53   .500   -25   Philip Powers
Tecumsehs

BATTERS	POS-GAMES	GP	AB	R	H	BI	2B	3B	HR	BB	SO	SB	BA
Walter Prince	1B32	32	135	26	44							5	.326
Buttercup Dickerson	2B93	98	405	64	140							29	.346
John Howe	SS57	57	246	34	62							27	.292
Frank Scheibeck	3B45,SS45	92	387	84	118							81	.305
Patsy Donovan	OF103	103	460	115	165							80	**.359**
Len Sowders	OF52,1B26	78	295	73	94							28	.319
J. Quinn	OF45	48	199	31	53							19	.266
Thomas Kinslow	C79	81	325	46	65							16	.200
Emil Geiss	P29	57	200	16	32							12	.160
Sam LaRoque	OF32	38	145	33	42							17	.290
Louis Renner	1B22	31	94	20	28							23	.298
William Husted	P29	30	116	7	10							1	.086
Lawrence Corcoran	OF23	28	109	17	21							26	.193
William Crowley	OF24	24	102	6	20							4	.196
Charles Alcott	3B18	18	69	11	13							2	.159

PITCHERS	W	L	PCT	G	GS	CG	SH	IP	H	BB	SO	ERA
Emil Geiss				29					296	28	68	2.79
Willaim Husted				29					257	65	124	2.72

BUFFALO   6th   48-62   .436   -32.5   John Chapman
Bisons

BATTERS	POS-GAMES	GP	AB	R	H	BI	2B	3B	HR	BB	SO	SB	BA
Mike Lehane	1B106	106	464	83	149							16	.321
Frank Grant	2B53,OF31	84	347	95	120							23	.346
Jim Flynn	SS55	65	240	39	53							11	.221
John Reidy	3B70,C17	89	375	44	83							15	.220
Charles Hamburg	OF76	100	436	115	136							34	.312
Cliff Carroll	OF68	68	287	60	87							27	.282
John Remsen	OF51	51	208	29	53							10	.255
Jim Welch	C35	38	149	16	31							4	.212
Joseph Kappel	OF36,C31	66	235	37	50							9	.213
Henry Bittmann	2B49	49	193	29	49							9	.254
William Hart	OF27,P18	45	182	24	33							8	.181
John Fanning	P39	39	139	15	30							3	.258
Cazenovia Gibbs	P27	29	109	10	18							2	.165
Frank Graves	C16	16	51	4	10							4	.196

BUFFALO (cont.)
Bisons

PITCHERS	W	L	PCT	G	GS	CG	SH	IP	H	BB	SO	ERA
John Fanning				39					354	58	119	2.87
Cazenovia Gibbs				27					268	17	52	3.22
William Hart				18					185	38	65	3.72

TROY   7th   29-79   .268   -50.5   Ted Sullivan - L. Burkett -
Trojans   Mort Hackett - P. Werden

BATTERS	POS-GAMES	GP	AB	R	H	BI	2B	3B	HR	BB	SO	SB	BA
Phil Baker	1B83	83	350	54	79							42	.226
John Troy	2B62	62	269	49	79							41	.294
Walter Hackett	SS70	73	280	27	61							15	.218
Art Stuart	OF99	99	391	42	106							37	.271
George Haddock	OF80,P31	107	402	60	91							51	.226
Fred Seering	OF44,P32	74	231	68	49							5	.212
James Manning	C42,SS20,OF19	79	293	31	48							14	.164
Patrick Dealey	C34,OF21,SS15	73	316	66	76							39	.240
Perry Werden	2B26,OF15	46	178	11	33							17	.185
George Keefe	P38	46	172	17	32							3	.186
Hiram Wright	C23	45	152	9	15							6	.099

PITCHERS	W	L	PCT	G	GS	CG	SH	IP	H	BB	SO	ERA
George Keefe				38					274	95	184	3.47
Fred Seering				32					301	68	67	3.13
George Haddock				31					301	66	120	3.36

ALBANY   8th   19-86   .181   -59   Tom York
Governors

BATTERS	POS-GAMES	GP	AB	R	H	BI	2B	3B	HR	BB	SO	SB	BA
Stephen Dunn	1B81	99	385	40	93							18	.239
James Dee	2B28	28	117	17	28							14	.239
John Nelson	SS	(see multi-team players)											
James Halpin	3B106	106	412	39	91							34	.221
William Hoover	OF79,2B19	101	406	90	114							63	.222
James Roseman	OF41	41	180	30	55							12	.306
Frank Foreman	OF35,P35	75	291	26	58							14	.199
Thomas Quinn	C67	74	291	25	60							25	.206
Pete Weckbecker	C42,OF24	69	260	31	51							46	.198
Allen	OF26	39	146	14	30							7	.205
Emory Nusz	SS20	20	77	8	15							8	.195
Downey		19	69	5	15							3	.217
Graff	P26	19	62	9	12							3	.194
A. Wilson	1B16	16	64	7	14							2	.219

PITCHERS	W	L	PCT	G	GS	CG	SH	IP	H	BB	SO	ERA
Frank Foreman				35					346	67	127	3.09
Graff				16					185	22	44	3.93

MULTI-TEAM PLAYERS

BATTERS	POS-GAMES	TEAMS	GP	AB	R	H	BI	2B	3B	HR	BB	SO	SB	BA
John Nelson	SS98	BUF-ALB	100	386	60	107							26	.275
Mike Mansell	OF100	HAM-TOR	100	371	53	88							70	.237
Richard Knox	OF56,2B27	ROC-ALB	83	322	41	61							19	.189
John Messitt	2B20,OF19,3B15	LO-TO-TR	67	284	59	67							57	.237
Gillespie	OF50	TRO-ALB	50	225	30	72							17	.320
T. Calihan	3B49	ROC-TOR	49	198	30	51							14	.258
Nat Kellogg	SS18	BUF-HAM	32	125	11	23							4	.184
W. Bishop	P32	LON-SYR	32	109	15	14							5	.129

PITCHERS		TEAMS	W	L	PCT	G	GS	CG	SH	IP	H	BB	SO	ERA
W. Bishop						32					270	66	98	1.90

TEAM BATTING

TEAMS	GP	AB	R	H	BI	2B	3B	HR	BB	SO	SB	BA
SYRACUSE	**112**	**4171**	**789**	**1157**							435	**.280**
TORONTO	108	4104	708	1047							479	.255
HAMILTON	110	4099	709	1122							**531**	.274
ROCHESTER	106	3831	601	907							305	.237
LONDON	103	3856	660	1021							422	.265
BUFFALO	106	3856	646	979							194	.254
TROY	107	3706	538	872							348	.235
ALBANY	106	3548	461	845							313	.210
	429	31171	5112	7950							3027	.255

1889
STOLEN BASE

The stolen base statistic was first compiled at the major and minor league level in 1886. Designed to account for a baserunner's speed and daring on the basepaths, it soon became an essential statistic. However, for the first few years of its tabulation, the stolen base statistic wasn't all it appeared.

In 1886 the International League recorded 1,217 stolen bases, with the leader claiming 46 thefts. In 1887, the league total jumped to 3,338, with the individual best total at 112. In 1888, the league total remained high at 3,027, while six different players each stole more than 80. By modern standards, these totals seem absurdly high. For instance, the 1996 International League recorded 1,107 stolen bases, one-third the total of the 1887 numbers. Was yesteryear's baseball star that much more fleet of foot? The answer lies in the definition of a stolen base.

Today, a stolen base occurs when a runner advances while the pitcher is attempting to pitch. In the nineteenth century, that was only one of the ways to steal a base. If a baserunner went from first to third on a single, he was given credit for a steal; likewise, if he advanced on an out. Virtually any legerdemain on the part of the runner was rewarded with a stolen base added to his column. With such an encompassing definition, it was easy for nineteenth century teams and players to rack up huge stolen base numbers.

The makeup of the 1889 International Association differed slightly from the previous year. Dropped from the rolls were Troy and Albany. Taking their places were teams from Toledo and Detroit.

The Detroit Wolverines, fresh from the roster of the 1888 National League, romped to an easy International League pennant in 1889. The Syracuse Stars stepped back to second, while Rochester and Toledo rounded out the first division. The bottom four rungs were taken by Toronto, London, Buffalo, and Hamilton. Batting honors were grabbed by Toledo's Perry Werden, who batted .394, and by Toronto's William Hoover, who poled 10 home runs. On the pitching side, Bob Barr from Rochester won the most games (29), while Toronto hurler Ledell Titcomb finished with the lowest earned average (1.29), gauged on an earned runs per game basis. His teammate Tom Vickery and Toledo's Ed Cushman each fanned a league high 194. True to the era, stolen base totals remained high as the league was credited with 2,717, with Toronto's Ed Burke (97) leading the way.

During the early 1890s, the liberal interpretation of the stolen base rule continued. In 1898, the criteria narrowed to define a stolen base as we know it today. As a result, we most likely will never see the huge stolen base totals pile up again. Mike Slattery's record performance in 1887—112 stolen bases—is likely to last.

DETROIT Wolverines

	1st	72-39	.649		Robert Leadley

BATTERS	POS-GAMES	GP	AB	R	H	BI	2B	3B	HR	BB	SO	SB	BA
Jake Virtue	1B107	107	382	80	120		16	11	6			40	.314
William Higgins	2B112	112	513	79	134		11	16	7			37	.261
Bobby Wheelock	SS112	112	483	130	136		20	5	4			89	.281
James Donnelly	3B80	89	369	85	105		22	1	1			64	.284
George Rooks	OF112	112	455	109	138		17	15	4			50	.303
Count Campau	OF111	112	442	111	126		14	11	5			69	.285
George Shaffer	OF110	110	436	99	131		14	5	8			38	.300
Mike Goodfellow	C56	57	210	43	67		1	4	1			8	.319
Jacob Wells	C49	53	200	30	45		4	2	0			15	.225
Frank Knauss	P40	40	147	17	35		5	1	1			5	.238
Edgar Smith	P27	33	100	28	29		3	0	1			8	.290
Lev Shreve	P27	27	97	17	20		2	3	0			4	.206
Harry Zell		16	58	9	17		2	1	1			4	.293

PITCHERS		W	L	PCT	G	GS	CG	SH	IP	H	BB	SO	ERA
Frank Knauss		27	13	.675	40					297	145	193	1.65
Edgar Smith		18	8	**.692**	27					225	85	81	2.55
Ledell Shreve		18	9	.667	27					233	94	56	2.07

SYRACUSE Stars

	2nd	63-44	.589	-7	John Chapman

BATTERS	POS-GAMES	GP	AB	R	H	BI	2B	3B	HR	BB	SO	SB	BA
William McQuery	1B104	104	438	70	131		30	4	0			20	.299
Clarence Childs	2B105	105	425	79	145		21	12	1			53	.341
Bernard McLaughlin	SS105	105	389	58	101		15	5	2			21	.259
Joe Battin	3B106	107	419	44	70		11	1	0			15	.167
D. Connors	OF107	107	452	67	121		11	7	0			44	.267
William Wright	OF107	107	423	107	131		11	9	1			29	.309
Bones Ely	OF103	107	455	68	111		19	9	5			39	.244
Fleet Walker	C50	50	171	29	37		1	1	0			18	.216
Grant Briggs	C45	53	182	22	46		9	1	1			4	.252
Con B. Murphy	P46	47	173	21	36		8	2	0			11	.208
John Keefe	P39	40	150	18	36		6	1	0			0	.240

PITCHERS		W	L	PCT	G	GS	CG	SH	IP	H	BB	SO	ERA
Con B. Murphy		28	18	.609	46					399	153	131	1.85
John Keefe		24	15	.615	39					204	114	138	1.84

ROCHESTER Jingoes

	3rd	60-49	.550	-11	Henry Leonard - Pat Powers

BATTERS	POS-GAMES	GP	AB	R	H	BI	2B	3B	HR	BB	SO	SB	BA
William O'Brien	1B93	95	375	53	119		18	3	4			15	.317
Thomas O'Brien	2B43	43	175	18	47		8	1	1			12	.268
Marr Phillips	SS108	108	433	54	116		24	8	1			37	.290
James Knowles	3B44	44	178	32	45		7	8	1			15	.253
Sandy Griffin	OF109	111	456	101	134		22	17	5			45	.294
John Peltz	OF109	109	408	61	91		14	11	3			19	.242
Henry Simon	OF102	102	385	71	107		12	13	2			56	.278
David McKeough	C71	72	242	34	33		2	0	1			19	.136
Jim Toy	C25,3B19	51	187	25	32		8	1	1			4	.171
Bob Barr	P47	47	160	14	25		2	0	0			2	.156
T. Calihan	3B44	44	172	15	27		4	0	0			11	.156
Stephen Toole	P25	38	135	16	25		1	5	0			12	.185
J. Fitzgerald	P18	18	45	11	13		1	0	0			0	.288
Dan Burke	C17	17	59	3	12		4	0	0			1	.203

PITCHERS		W	L	PCT	G	GS	CG	SH	IP	H	BB	SO	ERA
Bob Barr		29	18	.617	47					385	129	169	1.68
J. Fitzgerald		10	7	.588	18					160	83	77	2.38
S. Toole		9	16	.360	25					195	104	132	1.60

TOLEDO
Black Pirates

4th   54-51   .514   -15   Charles Morton

BATTERS	POS-GAMES	GP	AB	R	H	BI	2B	3B	HR	BB	SO	SB	BA
Perry Werden	1B104	109	424	107	**167**		32	11	2			58	**.394**
Taylor Shafer	2B66	80	287	46	68		8	3	0			45	.237
Thomas Nicholson	SS87	87	361	52	109		18	7	0			39	.302
William Alvord	3B52	52	224	33	69		12	4	0			11	.308
Bill Van Dyke	OF106	106	424	64	108		16	8	1			69	.254
John Sneed	OF95	95	337	74	92		14	9	0			35	.273
William Bottenus	OF70	70	269	48	61		10	6	2			37	.226
Harry Sage	C71	71	235	22	46		7	2	0			5	.196
Sam Barkley	2B30,3B16	50	197	26	49		11	3	2			1	.248
Frederick Smith	P38	43	153	24	35		6	2	0			1	.224
Ed Cushman	P32	32	110	7	18		2	0	0			0	.163
Arthur Sunday	OF31	31	128	32	51		12	8	1			4	.398
Bill Joyce	3B30	30	110	27	18		3	0	5			11	.163
George Stallings	C22	28	91	12	24		3	1	0			8	.263
William Wehrle	P22	26	87	8	9		1	2	0			0	.103
Joe Quest		21	81	9	16		1	0	0			0	.197
Emmett Rogers	C15	15	55	9	14		0	0	0			3	.254

PITCHERS		W	L	PCT	G	GS	CG	SH	IP	H	BB	SO	ERA
Frederick Smith		21	16	.568	38					346	138	117	2.05
Ed Cushman		18	14	.563	32					284	89	194	2.09
William Wehrle		9	13	.409	22					189	48	64	1.90

TORONTO
Canucks

5th   56-55   .505   -16   Charles Cushman

BATTERS	POS-GAMES	GP	AB	R	H	BI	2B	3B	HR	BB	SO	SB	BA
Patrick Hartnett	1B89	89	373	50	104		14	9	0			15	.279
Tom McLaughlin	2B65,SS43	108	391	72	77		10	7	1			90	.197
Robert Pettit	SS36	41	179	47	50		7	3	0			18	.279
Chris Rickley	3B91	91	339	46	75		12	4	0			18	.207
William Hoover	OF110	110	483	114	161		16	12	**10**			72	.333
Ed Burke	OF106	109	476	102	150		19	8	7			**97**	.315
George McMillan	OF106	106	385	80	95		12	3	0			65	.247
Deacon McGuire	C93	93	354	72	100		30	5	7			20	.282
John Grim	1B23,2B22,C20	83	334	52	87		10	4	1			52	.260
Tom Vickery	P44	44	158	31	42		4	1	0			12	.264
Bill Serad	P35	36	123	20	24		3	1	0			4	.194
Ledell Titcomb	P27	29	106	8	18		0	1	0			1	.169
Swift	2B27	27	98	9	14		1	0	0			5	.146

PITCHERS		W	L	PCT	G	GS	CG	SH	IP	H	BB	SO	ERA
Tom Vickery		20	22	.476	44					394	171	194	2.39
Bill Serad		19	16	.543	35					317	112	70	2.11
Ledell Titcomb		14	13	.519	27					225	95	125	**1.29**

LONDON
Tecumsehs

6th   51-55   .481   -18.5   Philip Powers - Dude
Esterbrook - Wally Fessenden

BATTERS	POS-GAMES	GP	AB	R	H	BI	2B	3B	HR	BB	SO	SB	BA
Ellis	1B39	39	171	31	48		8	6	2			10	.280
Pat Pettee	2B47,SS29	76	312	39	72		11	0	1			18	.230
Frank Scheibeck	SS78,3B28	108	416	104	113		19	8	3			53	.271
John Campana	3B31	31	119	15	30		11	1	0			1	.252
Joseph Knight	OF108	108	472	81	165		28	15	3			41	.349
Patsy Donovan	OF53	53	224	45	60		8	1	1			27	.268
Pat Friel	OF41	41	176	45	58		6	7	1			26	.329
Thomas Kinslow	C58	72	274	45	94		11	9	1			9	.343
Sam LaRoque	3B30,OF28	68	243	40	51		9	8	0			27	.209
Michael Jones	P36	46	167	14	31		2	2	0			2	.185
Miah Murray	C40	44	150	21	33		6	3	1			8	.220
Dude Esterbrook	1B39	39	160	30	44		12	3	1			16	.275
John Hiland	OF37	37	147	37	45		10	1	0			21	.306
Cain	P31	34	116	7	18		4	0	0			2	.155
Buttercup Dickerson	2B27	31	131	16	33		8	2	0			3	.251

LONDON (cont.)
Tecumsehs

BATTERS	POS-GAMES	GP	AB	R	H	BI	2B	3B	HR	BB	SO	SB	BA
Emil Geiss	P15	31	106	7	17		2	0	0			4	.160
Peter Wood		29	117	14	37		6	0	0			5	.313
D. Coughlin	C15	21	73	12	17		0	0	1			3	.233
Walter Prince	1B19	19	71	7	14		1	1	1			0	.197

PITCHERS		W	L	PCT	G	GS	CG	SH	IP	H	BB	SO	ERA
Michael Jones		19	16	.543	36					335	92	99	2.19
Cain		11	20	.355	31					298	114	134	2.45
Emil Geiss		9	6	.600	15					141	31	37	2.46

BUFFALO   7th   41-65   .387   -28.5   John Rowe - Jim
Bisons   White - Will White

BATTERS	POS-GAMES	GP	AB	R	H	BI	2B	3B	HR	BB	SO	SB	BA
Mike Lehane	1B109	109	445	66	134		29	11	7			11	.301
Charles Collins	2B		(see multi-team players)										
John Rainey	SS65,3B43	108	452	91	138		26	14	1			36	.305
John Reidy	3B53	70	267	31	62		10	4	0			7	.232
Charles Hamburg	OF109	109	413	74	116		16	6	3			40	.278
Al Sheppard	OF86	92	345	59	92		12	9	1			29	.266
William Andrus	OF72,2B37	109	450	88	114		22	18	0			45	.253
Patrick Dealey	C51,OF18	71	258	33	44		8	2	1			20	.170
Ed Thayer	C47	52	181	27	44		10	4	2			10	.243
Jim Whitney	P24	29	95	12	20		4	0	0			1	.210
Will White	P18	20	68	5	10		0	2	0			1	.147
John Fanning	P16	16	54	7	9		1	0	1			3	.166

PITCHERS		W	L	PCT	G	GS	CG	SH	IP	H	BB	SO	ERA
Jim Whitney		13	11	.542	24					244	30	78	2.66
John Fanning		7	9	.438	16					161	57	73	3.71
Will White		6	12	.333	18					160	56	38	2.50

HAMILTON   8th   35-74   .321   -36   Ed Swartwood -
Hams   Abner Powell

BATTERS	POS-GAMES	GP	AB	R	H	BI	2B	3B	HR	BB	SO	SB	BA
William Phillips	1B82	82	302	26	74		19	1	0			9	.245
Frank Ward	2B47	50	201	34	62		5	1	0			37	.308
Ed Sales	SS104	104	451	70	119		20	4	5			20	.264
Peter McShannic	3B54	54	267	21	40		3	0	0			24	.187
Steve Brodie	OF104	111	467	87	141		17	21	1			50	.302
Ed Swartwood	OF85	105	427	69	121		21	10	3			36	.283
McCann	OF38	38	161	20	26		3	0	1			18	.161
David Oldfield	C41	43	150	13	30		5	2	0			2	.200
W. Blair	P52	65	241	31	66		9	4	0			5	.273
Harry Spies	C34	43	156	14	28		3	1	0			5	.179
Abner Powell	OF27	40	149	30	48		5	4	1			26	.322
Mark Polhemus	OF19	19	79	18	18		0	1	0			0	.228

PITCHERS		W	L	PCT	G	GS	CG	SH	IP	H	BB	SO	ERA
W. Blair		24	28	.462	52					521	112	140	2.42

MULTI-TEAM PLAYERS

BATTERS	POS-GAMES	TEAMS	GP	AB	R	H	BI	2B	3B	HR	BB	SO	SB	BA
Thomas Kearns	2B77,3B33	HAM-LON	109	438	70	123		38	7	0			41	.280
Charles Collins	2B103	ROC-BUF	103	379	93	110		8	3	0			81	.277
Joe Lufberry	SS41,2B27	BUF-ROC	68	275	24	49		3	3	0			4	.178
John McGlone	3B31,SS22	DET-TOR	53	204	37	45		3	2	1			39	.220
James Banning	C34	HAM-DET	47	163	26	28		1	2	0			11	.171

MULTI-TEAM PLAYERS (cont.)

BATTERS	POS-GAMES	TEAMS	GP	AB	R	H	BI	2B	3B	HR	BB	SO	SB	BA
Art Stuart	OF43	BUF-HAM	44	186	18	38		4	1	1			8	.204
Will Calihan	P39	ROC-BUF	41	135	24	28		7	0	0			4	.200
Cazenovia Gibbs	P31	BUF-HAM	40	143	14	30		4	0	0			2	.209
Joseph Hofford	C16	SYR-ROC	16	47	6	13		1	1	0			1	.276

PITCHERS		TEAMS	W	L	PCT	G	GS	CG	SH	IP	H	BB	SO	ERA
Will Calihan		ROC-BUF	20	19	.513	39					373	140	159	1.74
Cazenovia Gibbs		BUF-HAM	8	23	.258	31					371	64	63	3.70

TEAM BATTING

TEAMS	GP	AB	R	H	BI	2B	3B	HR	BB	SO	SB	BA
DETROIT	**111**	4074	**876**	**1133**							453	**.278**
SYRACUSE	107	3825	601	897							263	.234
ROCHESTER	108	3821	607	963							312	.252
TOLEDO	106	3635	609	932							342	.256
TORONTO	108	3941	734	931							**495**	.235
LONDON	107	3991	462	1017							278	.254
BUFFALO	107	3613	588	942							241	.260
HAMILTON	108	**4129**	593	946							333	.229
	431	31029	5070	7761							2717	.250

1890
THE JIG IS UP

In 1884, the International League's founding organization, the Eastern League, butted heads with three separate major leagues. Despite the stiff competion and the shedding of several franchises, the Eastern staggered to the end of the campaign more or less intact. In 1890 much the same thing happened. However, this time the final outcome was not nearly as favorable.

Before starting the 1890 season, the International League (changed from Association) first had to find enough teams to even have a league. The Syracuse, Rochester, and Toledo clubs had jumped to the majors—the American Association—leaving the International with only five teams. A team jointly represented by Saginaw and Bay City, Michigan, was hastily cobbled onto the league structure to make a workable six-team league.

The real trouble started once the season began. Competing against three different major leagues, the International was frequently the odd man out. On June 2, with a Players' League team as a rival, Buffalo shifted its franchise to Montreal. Nine days later, the team transferred to Grand Rapids, Michigan. Montreal was not out of the league for long as the beleaguered Hamilton franchise landed there on June 23.

By early July, the International League as a whole was in serious straits. None of the franchises were in robust health, as evidenced by the frequent changes in locale. Several teams had even sold their better players to raise cash. But it was not enough. On July 7, league owners gave up the ghost and called it a season. On July 8, the *Detroit Free Press* simply but eloquently summed up the issue, stating, "The Jig Is Up."

Detroit was declared the winner of the truncated season by percentage points over Saginaw–Bay City, and by one game over Toronto. The Hamilton/Montreal franchise came next, followed by Buffalo/Montreal/Grand Rapids and London. The leading batter, William Andrus (.339), came from the Buffalo/Montreal/Grand Rapids team, while four players tied for the home run derby with a modest total of three.

Despite this failure, the International League would rebound the next year with a new organization and a new name. The mid-season termination of 1890 would prove to be an isolated incident. During the International's next 100 years—which included many lean ones—the league always managed to finish its campaign. The year 1890 remains the sole exception to the International League's otherwise perfect completion record.

DETROIT Wolverines

1st 31-19 .620 Robert Leadley

BATTERS	POS-GAMES	GP	AB	R	H	BI	2B	3B	HR	BB	SO	SB	BA
Jake Virtue	1B	49	176	28	52		13	1	0			11	.295
William Higgins	2B	39	172	21	42		6	1	0			10	.244
Bobby Wheelock	SS,2B	49	214	42	54		6	1	0			21	.252
George Rhue	3B,OF	29	106	19	16		4	0	1			11	.151
Count Campau	OF,3B	39	158	29	49		5	4	3			18	.310
Edgar Smith	OF,P	30	122	19	35		2	4	1			6	.287
Bill Hulin	OF		(see multi-team players)										
Mike Goodfellow	C,OF	39	152	14	40		3	1	1			2	.263
J. McCarthy	P	19	65	11	14		1	0	0			1	.215
Jacob Wells	C,3B,OF	17	54	7	13		4	0	0			2	.241
James Donnelly	3B,OF	16	58	15	15		5	0	0			4	.259
Frank Knauss	P	15	48	7	11		1	1	0			0	.229
Miller	SS,2B,3B	12	46	6	6		0	0	0			3	.130
Connor	OF	12	45	3	11		2	0	0			0	.244
Joe Banning	3B,C	12	40	4	8		1	0	0			4	.200
Harris	3B	10	42	2	10		1	1	0			0	.238
F. O'Neill	C,OF	6	20	2	7		1	0	0			0	.350
Cazenovia Gibbs	P	1	3	1	1		0	0	0			0	.333

PITCHERS		W	L	PCT	G	GS	CG	SH	IP	H	BB	SO	ERA
J. McCarthy													
Frank Knauss													
Edgar Smith													
Cazenovia Gibbs													

SAGINAW - BAY CITY Hyphens

2nd 32-20 .615 -0 Malcolm McArthur

BATTERS	POS-GAMES	GP	AB	R	H	BI	2B	3B	HR	BB	SO	SB	BA
Robert Hamilton	1B	44	181	40	53		6	0	2			5	.293
Frank Day	2B	46	199	39	52		13	1	1			23	.261
Doyle	SS		(see multi-team players)										
Joe Battin	3B	26	96	16	20		2	0	2			2	.208
Milt West	OF	46	193	28	58		8	1	2			4	.301
Al Sheppard	OF,P	42	168	23	45		4	0	0			3	.268
Nichol	OF	19	75	12	19		3	1	0			2	.253
John Arundel	C	27	92	5	14		2	0	0			2	.152
Harry Zell	P,OF	28	100	13	20		7	0	0			4	.200
Brown	C,1B,SS	27	100	10	25		2	1	0			2	.250
Peter McShannic	3B	20	78	11	16		0	0	1			1	.205
Fred Craves	OF	19	75	7	8		1	0	0			4	.107
Stein	P	19	67	4	7		1	0	0			1	.104
Hugh Weir	SS	9	29	5	4		0	0	0			4	.138
Spindler	OF	2	7	0	0		0	0	0			0	.000

PITCHERS		W	L	PCT	G	GS	CG	SH	IP	H	BB	SO	ERA
Stein													
Al Sheppard													
Harry Zell													

TORONTO Canucks

3rd 30-20 .600 -1 Charles Collins

BATTERS	POS-GAMES	GP	AB	R	H	BI	2B	3B	HR	BB	SO	SB	BA
Peter Wood	1B,P	51	218	26	50		6	0	0			6	.226
Tom McLaughlin	2B	51	175	24	38		2	1	0			22	.217
Albert Ike	SS	51	183	31	38		7	3	1			8	.208
Chris Rickley	3B	51	183	27	43		3	1	0			15	.235
Dan Connor	OF	51	203	28	46		6	1	1			18	.227
William Bottenus	OF	49	195	42	48		7	5	0			26	.246
Coleman	OF,P,1B	49	189	28	53		7	4	1			6	.280
John Grim	C,OF	50	203	28	46		6	1	1			18	.227
Jack Newman	OF,C,1B	23	76	9	26		3	0	0			3	.342
Ledell Titcomb	P,OF	22	77	4	11		0	1	0			1	.143
Bill Serad	P	12	44	3	11		1	0	0			2	.250
William Atkinson	P,OF	1	3	2	1		1	0	0			0	.333

TORONTO (cont.)
Canucks

PITCHERS	W	L	PCT	G	GS	CG	SH	IP	H	BB	SO	ERA
Ledell Titcomb												
Bill Serad												
Coleman												
William Atkinson												
Peter Wood												

HAMILTON / MONTREAL   4th   24-26   .480   -7   Jimmy Dean
Mountaineers / Canadiens

BATTERS	POS-GAMES	GP	AB	R	H	BI	2B	3B	HR	BB	SO	SB	BA
Ed Cartwright	1B	51	206	45	50		10	5	2			25	.243
Joseph Dowie	2B	51	189	24	32		6	1	1			17	.169
Ed Sales	SS	50	200	26	47		9	0	0			10	.235
Frank Foulkrod	3B	51	203	20	40		3	0	2			17	.197
Don Casey	OF	51	212	33	68		8	1	0			19	.321
Abner Powell	OF,P	44	181	30	45		2	0	0			34	.249
Chris Fulmer	OF,C	32	118	28	28		6	0	0			24	.237
James Tuohey	C	30	105	15	27		2	0	1			6	.257
Charles Petty	P	22	67	5	10		0	1	0			1	.149
T. Miller	OF,SS	21	85	12	19		3	1	0			4	.224
A. LaTouche	P	17	58	7	15		3	0	0			1	.259
O. Sprogell	P	17	59	7	10		0	0	0			4	.169
Harry Spies	C,OF·	10	32	2	3		0	0	0			1	.094

PITCHERS	W	L	PCT	G	GS	CG	SH	IP	H	BB	SO	ERA
Charles Petty												
A. LaTouche												
O. Sprogell												
Abner Powell												

BUFFALO Bisons
MONTREAL Canadiens   5th   14-29   .326   -13.5   Davis Bacon
GRAND RAPIDS Shamrocks

BATTERS	POS-GAMES	GP	AB	R	H	BI	2B	3B	HR	BB	SO	SB	BA
Dan Quinn	1B		(see multi-team players)										
Pat Pettee	2B	26	108	12	29		5	1	0			6	.269
W. McMahon	SS	19	64	8	11		4	0	1			2	.172
David Coughlin	3B		(see multi-team players)										
William Andrus	OF	41	174	39	59		5	2	1			18	.339
John Burke	OF	41	166	26	44		6	1	0			3	.265
Newman	OF	19	74	12	19		5	1	0			4	.257
Emil Smith	C,1B	16	50	5	11		1	0	0			0	.220
Arthur Sippi	2B,3B	17	72	11	18		6	0	1			3	.250
George Meister	3B	17	66	7	19		3	1	0			1	.288
John Whalen	C,1B	15	58	3	10		2	0	1			0	.172
David Oldfield	C	15	49	8	10		0	0	0			1	.204
Andrew Dunning	P	12	40	7	8		3	0	1			0	.200
William Schellerman	P	12	39	2	3		0	1	0			0	.077
Jack McMahon	C,1B	8	37	1	8		0	1	0			0	.216
Bert Inks	P	7	22	2	5		1	0	1			0	.227
Joseph Hart	OF,P	6	22	5	3		2	0	0			0	.136
Frank Killen	P	4	13	3	2		0	0	0			0	.154
Ed Egan	2B	2	9	4	5		1	0	0			0	.556
James Purvis	1B2	2	9	3	3		0	0	0			0	.333
D. Moore	OF	2	9	2	1		0	0	0			0	.111
Nick Ivory	C,OF	2	8	2	1		0	0	0			0	.125
Dick Conway	P	1	4	0	2		0	0	0			0	.500

PITCHERS	W	L	PCT	G	GS	CG	SH	IP	H	BB	SO	ERA
William Schellerman												
Andrew Dunning												
Bert Inks												
Frank Killen												
Dick Conway												

LONDON   6th   15-32   .319   -14.5   Wally Fessenden
Tecumsehs

BATTERS	POS-GAMES	GP	AB	R	H	BI	2B	3B	HR	BB	SO	SB	BA
Charles Lutenberg	1B,P	48	183	14	38		6	1	0			15	.208
Pat Wright	2B	48	182	20	43		7	2	0			14	.236
William Parks	SS,2B	26	102	11	21		3	0	3			6	.206
John Reidy	C,3B	36	139	10	31		3	0	0			3	.223
Pat Friel	OF	48	194	30	57		3	4	1			23	.294
John Leighton	OF	47	175	33	46		4	3	0			20	.263
John Hiland	OF	47	168	39	35		4	0	0			17	.208
Con D. Murphy	C	19	63	3	5		0	0	0			3	.079
Michael Jones	P	20	65	3	9		6	0	0			0	.138
Fred DeMarris	P	18	53	5	8		0	0	0			2	.151
Porter	P	8	31	1	3		0	0	0			0	.097
Myers	P,SS	3	9	0	0		0	0	0			0	.000
Colfer	C,3B	2	5	1	0		0	0	0			0	.000
Sweeney	C1	1	1	0	0		0	0	0			0	.000

PITCHERS	W	L	PCT	G	GS	CG	SH	IP	H	BB	SO	ERA
Michael Jones												
FredDeMarris												
Porter												
Myers												
Charles Lutenberg												

MULTI-TEAM PLAYERS

BATTERS	POS-GAMES	TEAMS	GP	AB	R	H	BI	2B	3B	HR	BB	SO	SB	BA
Bill Hulin	OF,3B	DET-H/M	46	176	27	39		6	3	0			12	.222
David Coughlin	3B	B/M/GR-LO	44	172	32	34		6	0	0			15	.198
James Connor	SS	B/M/GR-LO	44	168	21	56		10	2	2			9	.333
George Rooks	OF	B/M/GR-DE	43	178	27	39		10	2	1			5	.219
Doyle	SS,OF	LO-SA/BC	43	171	33	51		7	0	3			7	.298
Dan Quinn	1B,OF	B/M/GR-DE	38	144	17	31		5	0	3			10	.215
D. Roche	C,OF,SS	H/M-LON	15	56	9	13		0	0	1			10	.232
Maguire	P	H/M-SA/BC	11	40	1	6		1	0	0			0	.150
William O'Neill	P	B/M/GR-DE	8	23	1	3		0	0	0			0	.132

PITCHERS	TEAMS	W	L	PCT	G	GS	CG	SH	IP	H	BB	SO	ERA
Maguire	LO-SA/BC												
William O'Neill	B/M/GR-DET												

1891
LES GERMAN

The International League pitching record for most wins in a season has proved elusive. The official league record book says that in 1887, George Stovey finished with an all-time best 35 wins. However, further research has reduced his win total to 33. To date, the most reliable candidate for the most-wins-in-a-season record has been a pitcher named Les German.

In 1891, from the major league Baltimore Orioles, Les German joined the staff of the Buffalo Bisons, where he commenced to have a superb year. Starting quickly, German won his first nine decisions. After a loss, he then whipped off seven more wins in a row. At season's end, Les German was credited with 35 wins, leading his Bisons to an easy pennant.

Out of the ruins of the 1890 International League, a whole new organization was formed. Only one 1890 city, Buffalo, was represented in this new circuit, yet the International League claims it as an ancestor. Joining Buffalo were Albany, Lebanon, New Haven, Providence, Rochester, Syracuse, and Troy. This new league billed itself the Eastern Association. The word International was dropped from the title because no Canadian cities were present in the league structure.

As the 1891 Eastern Association campaign unfolded, a familiar trend manifested itself: bankruptcy. Between August 11 and 25, Providence, New Haven, Rochester, and Syracuse went belly-up. Undaunted, the remaining four franchises, Albany, Buffalo, Lebanon, and Troy, played a second season from late August to September 26. The statistics generated during this month-long extra season would count for the individual players, but the wins and losses for each team would not. (Note: the won-loss records for these four teams in their second season are noted in the tables.)

Buffalo won both sections with ease, compiling the third best record in International League history. Behind the Bisons finished Albany, Syracuse, New Haven, Troy, Lebanon, Rochester, and Providence. Milt West from Syracuse was the circuit's top batter (.339), while New Haven's Dan Lally hit the most home runs (5). Pitchers A. Gilliland from New Haven and Tony Fricken from Albany carried off the best earned run average (0.89) and strikeout (197) titles.

After his stellar performance, Les German bounced back to the majors, staying for a five-year stretch in the 1890s. But is he the true record holder? Originally, German was credited with 34 wins in 1891, but further research indicated that his total should read 35. Whether he is the true record holder is still in doubt as not all nineteenth century records have been fully analyzed. Until they are, Les German's 35-win season will reign supreme.

BUFFALO 1st 72-27 .727 Pat Powers
Bisons *1st* *17-8* *.680*

BATTERS	POS-GAMES	GP	AB	R	H	BI	2B	3B	HR	BB	SO	SB	BA
James Field	1B123,P2	123	480	101	122		19	14	3			45	.254
Joe Mack	2B117,P1	118	503	108	147		31	5	2			38	.292
Leo Smith	SS122	123	445	69	87		10	3	0			28	.195
James Knowles	3B125	125	520	115	146		17	5	2			77	.281
Harry Lyons	OF124	124	551	83	166		17	5	2			41	.301
Ted Scheffler	OF123,SS1	123	522	156	153		23	17	4			82	.293
Joe Hornung	OF1171B2,P2,2B1,SS1,	121	501	117	139		30	10	2			48	.277
Pete Weckbecker	C71,SS2,2B2,1B1,OF1	77	293	39	63		6	1	0			29	.215
Les German	P51,OF3	51	181	31	57		6	0	2			5	.314
Bob Barr	P	34	118	19	26		4	1	0			4	.220
Pat Murphy	C31,2B2	33	128	18	26		2	3	0			4	.203
David McKeough	C26	31	106	21	25		2	2	0			10	.236
Will Calihan	P25,OF4,3B1	30	102	16	22		1	2	1			7	.216
Herb Goodall	P16	17	59	9	14		1	0	0			0	.237
William Schellerman	P2	2	9	3	4		0	0	0			1	.444
John Carroll	OF2	2	6	1	1		0	0	0			2	.167
William Daley	P2	2	5	2	2		0	0	0			0	.400

PITCHERS		W	L	PCT	G	GS	CG	SH	IP	H	BB	SO	ERA
Les German		35	11	.761	51	46	42	1	404	382	161	124	1.38
Bob Barr		26	9	.743									
Wil Calihan		16	6	.727	25	25	8	0	216	191	106	66	1.25
Herb Goodall		8	7	.533	16	16	14	2	129	126	50	66	1.67
William Schellerman		2	0	1.000	2	2	2	0	18	16	5	7	1.00
Joe Hornung		1	0	1.000	2	1	1	0	13	14	4	1	2.08
William Daley		1	1	.500	2	2	1	0	13	10	13	11	0.00
James Fields		0	1	.000	2	1	1	0	13	10	4	1	2.77
Joe Mack		0	0	----	1	0	0	0	2	1	0	1	4.50

ALBANY 2nd 57-41 .582 -14.5 Joe Gerhardt
Senators *2nd* *15-8* *.652* *-1*

BATTERS	POS-GAMES	GP	AB	R	H	BI	2B	3B	HR	BB	SO	SB	BA
Doc Kennedy	1B119	119	444	85	138		41	6	2			10	.311
Joe Gerhardt	2B106	106	346	55	83		14	5	1			14	.240
William Hanrahan	SS117	117	415	71	102		14	7	2			37	.246
Henry Kappel	3B120	120	405	76	94		26	3	0			40	.232
Charles Brady	OF121,2B1	122	514	87	121		5	5	1			61	.235
Herman Bader	OF121	121	456	111	107		4	7	0			106	.234
John Gunshannon	OF69	69	262	38	65		10	6	1			15	.248
Thomas Hess	C63,OF8,1B2,SS2	77	297	38	77		17	4	0			11	.259
Marsh Brown	C42,OF8	52	190	31	52		8	1	0			5	.274
Tony Fricken	P40,OF3	42	152	24	43		5	2	0			4	.283
James Devlin	P42	42	136	21	30		2	1	0			5	.220
Charles Willis	OF31,P4	34	138	18	33		5	1	0			11	.239
Daniel Roche	C21,OF4	25	96	18	18		3	1	0			6	.187
Dan Casey	P13	13	34	3	11		3	0	0			0	.324
Robert Murphy	P11	11	36	1	10		2	0	0			1	.278
Bruton	2B8	8	28	6	5		0	0	0			2	.179
O. Sprogell	P6	6	18	0	3		1	0	0			0	.167
Michael Kilroy	P6,OF1	6	17	1	2		0	0	0			1	.118
Mike O'Rourke	P5	5	13	1	2		0	0	0			1	.154
Tom Miller	SS1	1	4	1	1		1	0	0			0	.250
Frank White	P1	1	2	0	1		0	0	0			0	.500

PITCHERS		W	L	PCT	G	GS	CG	SH	IP	H	BB	SO	ERA
James Devlin		26	14	.650	42	40	40	3	368	361	70	117	1.91
Tony Fricken		25	15	.625	40	39	38	2	352	326	148	197	1.41
Dan Casey		7	5	.583	13	11	9	1	97	111	33	18	2.51
Michael Kilroy		5	1	.833	6	6	5	0	49	24	9	13	0.92
Mike O'Rourke		3	1	.750	5	5	4	0	37	32	20	4	1.46
Robert Murphy		2	8	.200	11	8	7	0	82	100	49	35	2.41
Frank White		1	0	1.000	1	1	1	0	9	8	8	1	1.00
O. Sprogell		1	1	.500	6	5	2	0	38	54	16	16	2.61
Charles Willis		1	3	.250	4	4	4	0	36	44	22	10	2.00

SYRACUSE Stars

	3rd	56-42	.571	-15.5	George Frazier

BATTERS	POS-GAMES	GP	AB	R	H	BI	2B	3B	HR	BB	SO	SB	BA
Jay Faatz	1B75	75	263	53	68		14	3	0			33	.259
Tom McLaughlin	2B89,OF1	90	334	54	94		12	2	0			40	.281
Tom Miller	SS94,OF1	94	358	51	73		9	3	0			32	.210
Ed Doyle	3B34	34	120	15	25		6	1	0			1	.208
Henry Simon	OF97	97	408	82	119		20	11	1			38	.292
Pat Friel	OF96,3B1	97	418	92	109		13	4	0			35	.261
Milt West	OF64,1B22,3B2,2B1	86	369	49	125		23	3	2			16	**.339**
Thomas Quinn	C50,3B23,OF1	73	253	39	52		3	1	0			7	.206
George Myers	C40,3B8,2B5,OF5,1B3	60	222	20	52		9	5	0			11	.234
William Coughlin	P42,OF10	52	184	23	49		8	3	1			11	.266
Michael Kilroy	P13,3B8,OF8,2B2	31	112	6	19		3	0	0			1	.170
Alex Ferson	P23,OF4	27	90	9	22		1	0	2			3	.244
Fred Link	P18,OF1	18	44	2	4		0	0	0			0	.091
William Smalley	3B11	11	40	4	9		0	0	0			1	.225
David Coughlin	3B9	9	33	4	5		1	0	0			0	.152
John Gallagher	P8	8	25	4	7		0	0	1			0	.280
Joseph Doyle	OF5,SS2	7	27	7	6		0	0	0			0	.222
John McCormick	2B1,1B1	2	10	1	2		0	0	0			0	.200
Ed Green	P2,3B1	2	6	0	1		1	0	0			0	.167
Spears	3B2	2	6	0	0		0	0	0			0	.000
Mike Morrison	P2,OF1	2	4	1	1		0	0	0			0	.250
Joe Battin	3B1	1	4	1	1		0	0	0			0	.250
Treat	OF1	1	4	0	0		0	0	0			0	.000
John Leighton	OF1	1	3	0	0		0	0	0			0	.000
Harry Lemon	P1	1	1	0	0		0	0	0			0	.000

PITCHERS	W	L	PCT	G	GS	CG	SH	IP	H	BB	SO	ERA
William Coughlin	28	12	.700	42	41	40	3	367	310	97	168	1.05
Alex Ferson	15	6	.714	23	21	17	0	184	146	79	85	1.18
Fred Link	8	7	.533	18	15	14	1	136	122	50	44	0.99
John Gallagher	3	3	.500	8	8	5	0	53	64	27	20	2.55
Michael Kilroy	3	8	.273	13	11	11	1	92	79	32	35	1.66
Ed Green	0	1	.000	2	1	1	0	12	20	5	5	1.50
Harry Lemon	0	1	.000	1	0	0	0	3	7	6	2	9.00
Mike Morrison	0	2	.000	2	1	0	0	5	3	3	2	0.00

NEW HAVEN Nutmegs

	4th	48-39	.552	-18	Walt Burnham

BATTERS	POS-GAMES	GP	AB	R	H	BI	2B	3B	HR	BB	SO	SB	BA
Sid Farrar	1B87	87	343	67	107		17	9	1			40	.312
Pat Pettee	2B87	87	368	44	95		15	2	1			12	.260
Ed Sales	SS		(see multi-team players)										
Con Doyle	3B50	50	192	46	53		3	3	0			27	.276
Dan Lally	OF84	84	353	56	98		20	8	5			16	.278
James Sommer	OF72,3B12	84	312	53	73		14	0	2			28	.234
James Cudworth	OF		(see multi-team players)										
Thelson	C27,OF10,1B1	37	136	18	40		7	1	1			12	.294
George Wilson	C26,OF11,3B1	37	133	27	37		11	3	2			4	.278
Franklin Lang	SS37	37	116	23	23		2	1	0			16	.198
William Horner	P32,OF3	35	127	13	24		3	1	0			5	.189
Ed Decker	C21,OF10,3B2	31	119	9	25		3	1	0			6	.210
Art Clarkson	P30,OF1	30	104	12	19		2	1	0			4	.188
John Carroll	OF17,SS1	17	73	12	15		2	2	0			9	.205
A. Gilliland	P14	14	54	6	6		1	1	0			1	.111
John Doran	P13,OF1	14	49	8	10		3	0	0			4	.204
Louis Guinasso	C9,OF1	10	36	5	9		4	0	0			0	.250
Joseph Hofford	C10	10	33	5	7		3	1	0			0	.212
Condoff	P2	2	5	0	1		1	0	0			0	.200
Mike Morrison	P1	1	5	1	1		0	0	0			1	.200
John Henry	OF1	1	5	1	0		0	0	0			0	.000
John Lyston	P1	1	4	1	1		1	0	0			0	.250

PITCHERS	W	L	PCT	G	GS	CG	SH	IP	H	BB	SO	ERA
Art Clarkson	16	12	.571	30	27	25	5	239	198	90	132	1.54
William Horner	16	14	.533	32	32	29	0	267	274	95	96	2.12
A. Gilliland	9	4	.692	14	13	13	0	121	89	69	83	**0.89**
John Doran	5	7	.429	13	11	9	0	103	93	58	71	1.92
John Lyston	1	0	1.000	1	1	1	0	9	5	2	2	0.00

NEW HAVEN (cont.)
Nutmegs

PITCHERS	W	L	PCT	G	GS	CG	SH	IP	H	BB	SO	ERA
Ed Sales	1	0	1.000	1	0	0	0	5	4	1	0	1.80
Condoff	0	1	.000	2	2	1	0	13	21	2	9	1.38
Mike Morrison	0	1	.000	1	1	1	0	8	8	5	7	2.25

TROY		5th	46-58		.442		-28.5		David Mahoney			
Trojans		*4th*	*5-19*		*.208*		*-11.5*					

BATTERS	POS-GAMES	GP	AB	R	H	BI	2B	3B	HR	BB	SO	SB	BA
Robert Hamilton	1B57	57	194	32	53		6	1	0			7	.273
Frank Day	2B59,OF6	62	250	47	63		4	3	1			33	.252
Marr Phillips	SS107,2B9	118	452	72	135		20	7	0			37	.299
Charles Jones	3B46	46	191	25	38		4	0	0			14	.199
Count Campau	OF121,P4	122	471	86	111		18	10	3			45	.236
John Henry	OF85	85	361	49	88		13	3	0			46	.244
John Messitt	OF58,2B39,1B9,3B3,C2	111	421	104	90		14	8	1			84	.214
Jacob Wells	C91,1B7,OF3,3B1	92	330	50	84		8	8	0			21	.255
William McQuery	1B44	44	179	25	50		13	1	0			2	.279
Henry Lynch	OF32,SS5,3B3,2B1	40	157	25	32		3	1	0			7	.204
Pat Shea	P31,OF9	38	124	28	35		2	0	1			3	.282
Thomas Brahan	P31OF5	35	111	9	15		0	2	0			4	.135
William Mooney	3B23,SS7,2B2	32	119	18	23		5	3	0			8	.193
Peter Eagan	OF27	27	119	14	23		4	0	0			12	.193
Dan Murphy	C12,2B11,OF4,3B1	27	104	12	24		1	0	0			0	.231
Elmer Cleveland	3B24,SS2	26	96	11	22		4	1	0			1	.229
James Maguire	P26	26	77	9	11		1	0	0			1	.143
Richard Knox	OF20	20	79	14	20		6	1	1			5	.253
Henry Cote	C16,1B1,OF1	18	59	9	16		5	2	0			2	.271
William Day	P10,OF4	15	60	2	13		1	0	0			0	.217
Edwin Bligh	C9,OF1	10	33	2	5		0	0	0			0	.152
James Tuohey	1B6,C2	8	31	5	10		1	1	0				.322
John Doran	P9	9	22	0	3		0	0	0			1	.136
John Taylor	P8	8	26	3	4		2	0	0				.154
William Collins	C5	5	18	1	3		0	1	0			0	.167
Mike O'Rourke	P4,1B1	5	8	1	1		0	0	0			0	.125
Mike Sullivan	P4	4	8	0	2		0	0	0			0	.250
Gene Derby	C3	3	7	0	1		0	0	0			0	.143
William Carey	P3	3	2	1	0		0	0	0			0	.000
James Burns	P2	2	8	0	0		0	0	0			0	.000
William Parks	SS1	1	4	2	2		0	0	0			0	.500
Geary	P1	1	3	1	0		0	0	0			0	.000
Andrew Weidman	C1	1	3	0	0		0	0	0			0	.000
Robert Miller	P1	1	2	0	0		0	0	0			0	.000
Foley	P1	1	1	0	0		0	0	0			0	.000

PITCHERS	W	L	PCT	G	GS	CG	SH	IP	H	BB	SO	ERA
Thomas Brahan	9	15	.375	31	23	23	2	229	220	78	103	1.88
Pat Shea	15	15	.500	31	27	20	0	235	216	125	94	1.72
James Maguire	10	13	.435	26	24	21	1	208	218	81	73	2.12
John Taylor	4	3	.571	8	7	7	0	64	52	29	18	0.98
John Doran	4	4	.500	9	8	8	1	75	56	26	35	2.40
William Day	3	7	.300	10	10	8	0	83	98	58	36	2.00
John Staib	3	9	.250	12	12	11	0	104	110	41	23	2.94
Mike Sullivan	1	1	.500	4	3	1	0	17	17	10	7	3.17
Mike O'Rourke	1	2	.333	4	3	2	0	26	15	7	4	1.73
Foley	0	1	.000	1	1	0	0	3	6	4	0	6.00
Count Campau	0	2	.000	4	2	1	0	22	24	12	1	1.64
James Burns	0	2	.000	2	2	2	0	17	12	10	7	2.65
William Carey	0	0	----	3	1	0	0	7	9	2	6	3.86
Geary	0	0	----	1	0	0	0	6	3	4	0	0.00
Robert Miller	0	0	----	1	1	0	0	4	4	2	0	0.00

LEBANON		6th	37-60		.381		-34		James Randall			
Cedars		*3rd*	*11-13*		*.458*		*-5.5*					

BATTERS	POS-GAMES	GP	AB	R	H	BI	2B	3B	HR	BB	SO	SB	BA
John McCormick	1B68,2B8,OF3	78	304	31	83		10	5	1				.273
Ben Conroy	2B69,3B2,SS2	71	281	38	61		7	4	0			11	.217

LEBANON (cont.)
Cedars

BATTERS	POS-GAMES	GP	AB	R	H	BI	2B	3B	HR	BB	SO	SB	BA
Monte Cross	SS117,3B1	118	451	57	108		21	10	2			29	.239
Ed Doyle	3B48	48	182	19	35		3	1	0			4	.192
George Staltz	OF115,2B1	115	452	77	113		12	12	1			28	.250
John Petrie	OF58	58	212	35	58		18	3	0			14	.274
Alex Donahue	OF52,3B18,2B10,SS1	82	339	48	78		9	3	0			33	.230
Doc Bushong	C	(see multi-team players)											
Charles McCaffrey	C48,2B9,OF2	58	211	22	44		7	1	0			3	.208
Joseph Fitzgerald	P40,OF12,2B10,1B1	58	197	17	35		7	2	1			7	.178
James Tuohey	3B20,C18,OF6, 2B2,SS1	47	168	21	36		2	0	0				.214
John Peltz	OF40	40	176	24	43		6	1	1			5	.244
James Daly	OF40	40	170	28	42		3	7	0			1	.247
Thomas O'Brien	1B38	40	162	14	32		4	1	0			4	.198
David Anderson	P29,OF5,2B2,SS1	34	120	15	24		2	4	0			3	.200
John Coleman	OF21,1B7,P1	28	109	12	23		4	2	0			1	.211
Herb Goodall	P28	28	92	6	23		3	0	0			0	.250
Belden Hill	3B20,2B1	20	72	6	8		2	0	0			4	.111
John Taylor	P20,OF2	20	57	7	7		0	0	0				.123
Joe Jones	OF19	19	72	13	14		3	0	0			2	.194
M. Kurtz	C17,OF1	18	66	5	8		2	0	0			4	.111
Henry Sage	C16,1B4	18	60	4	10		1	0	0				.167
Edward Tate	1B9,C8	15	54	6	17		3	0	0			1	.315
William Clymer	2B10,SS1	11	39	6	5		0	0	0			4	.128
F. Cooke	3B10,SS1	11	38	8	10		0	0	0			1	.263
Joseph Neal	P11	11	35	3	6		0	0	0				.171
Bayne	P10	10	30	3	3		0	0	0			0	.100
William Greenwood	2B7	7	16	3	3		0	0	0			0	.188
John Meister	2B3	3	9	0	0		0	0	0			0	.000
Feen	P2	2	6	0	1		0	0	0			0	.167
Ira Davis	2B1	1	4	0	0		0	0	0			0	.000
Henry Smith	P1	1	0	0	0		0	0	0			0	----

PITCHERS	W	L	PCT	G	GS	CG	SH	IP	H	BB	SO	ERA
Joseph Fitzgerald	12	17	.414	40	33	25	1	303	283	78	123	1.81
Herb Goodall	12	12	.500	28	25	24	2	237	217	86	62	1.41
David Anderson	10	14	.417	29	23	22	1	223	201	79	78	1.74
Joseph Neal	6	5	.556	11	11	9	0	86	88	28	23	1.36
John Taylor	5	14	.263	20	18	12	0	131	127	39	60	1.92
Henry Smith	0	1	.000	1	1	0	0	1	2	2	0	0.00
Feen	0	2	.000	2	2	2	0	16	18	5	2	3.94
Bayne	0	9	.000	10	9	7	0	72	85	31	18	1.98
John Coleman	0	0	----	1	0	0	0	8	7	2	1	2.25

ROCHESTER   7th   36-60   .375   -34.5   Thomas Power -
Hop Bitters   Kerstein

BATTERS	POS-GAMES	GP	AB	R	H	BI	2B	3B	HR	BB	SO	SB	BA
Thomas Power	1B81,SS11,OF2	92	337	53	74		13	9	2			25	.220
Ed McDonald	2B38,1B1,OF1	39	137	26	38		10	0	0			17	.277
Peter Sweeney	SS74,3B8,OF3,1B2	87	353	66	85		16	10	5			32	.269
William Mooney	3B55	55	204	14	37		6	0	0				.181
Joseph Knight	OF95	95	394	75	118		27	11	0			25	.299
Robert Gilks	OF58,3B11,2B2,SS1	71	318	38	67		10	1	0			7	.211
Joe Visner	OF48,SS1	49	197	31	65		8	10	4			6	.330
William Urquhart	C44,3B24,1B10,OF5	82	312	29	59		12	1	0			7	.189
Fred Roberts	OF47,1B1	49	166	29	27		1	4	0			10	.163
Henry Reitz	2B31,SS6	37	138	15	25		4	1	0			10	.181
William Bowman	C32,1B2	34	137	24	37		10	1	3			6	.270
Henry Blauvelt	P24,OF8,2B1	31	95	10	18		1	0	0			3	.174
Ed Cushman	P25,OF1	27	91	2	13		1	0	0			1	.143
Thomas McDermott	2B22	22	92	18	18		2	3	0				.190
Phil Begy	OF21,2B1,SS1	21	91	10	18		2	0	0			6	.197
Joseph Neal	OF3	16	55	4	6		1	0	0				.109
Lev Shreve	P14,SS1,OF1	15	53	2	8		1	0	0			0	.151
Charles McCullough	P15	15	50	1	3		1	0	0			0	.060
Henry Sage	C14	14	49	4	6		2	0	0				.122
William Collins	C10	10	32	1	7		1	0	0			1	.219
James Sullivan	P4,OF2	6	12	1	1		0	0	0			2	.083
Franklin Lang	SS5	5	18	1	3		0	1	1			0	.167
Sam Shaw	P4	4	10	0	1		0	0	0			1	.100
Nolan	P4,OF1	4	8	1	1		0	0	0			1	.125

ROCHESTER (cont.)
Hop Bitters

BATTERS	POS-GAMES	GP	AB	R	H	BI	2B	3B	HR	BB	SO	SB	BA
Tierney	P2	2	7	1	2		0	0	0			0	.286
Ledell Titcomb	P2	2	6	0	0		0	0	0			0	.000
Heberling	2B1	1	3	0	0		0	0	0			0	.000
Charles Morton	OF1	1	4	1	2		0	0	0			0	.500
Patrick Mays		1	4	1	1		0	0	0			1	.250
Charles Smith	2B1	1	4	0	0		0	0	0			0	.000
A. Moore	2B1	1	4	0	0		0	0	0			0	.000

PITCHERS		W	L	PCT	G	GS	CG	SH	IP	H	BB	SO	ERA
Henry Blauvelt		9	11	.450	24	19	17	0	173	165	57	84	1.77
Ed Cushman		7	16	.304	25	23	22	4	203	177	58	92	1.46
Lev Shreve		6	7	.462	14	13	12	0	110	109	80	34	1.39
Joseph Neal		6	7	.462	13	13	13	1	115	107	35	35	2.43
Charles McCullough		5	9	.357	15	14	14	0	124	134	56	65	1.82
Sam Shaw		2	2	.500	4	4	3	1	34	25	11	10	1.06
James Sullivan		1	3	.250	4	4	3	0	32	34	28	7	1.97
Ledell Titcomb		0	2	.000	2	2	1	0	14	13	14	8	3.86
Tierney		0	2	.000	2	2	1	0	14	22	15	6	2.57
Nolan		0	1	.000	4	2	0	0	19	30	13	11	3.79

PROVIDENCE
Clamdiggers

8th 29-54 .349 -35 Bill McGunnigle

BATTERS	POS-GAMES	GP	AB	R	H	BI	2B	3B	HR	BB	SO	SB	BA
Patrick Hartnett	1B73	73	294	32	84		13	1	0			9	.286
William Higgins	2B48	48	187	18	44		6	2	1			7	.235
Henry Easterday	SS83	83	307	45	68		10	6	1			19	.214
James Hanivan	3B64	64	232	34	66		11	0	0			15	.284
Thomas Kearns	OF78,3B2	83	312	56	77		14	1	2			24	.247
Mike Mansell	OF74	74	244	53	63		13	6	1			26	.258
William Annis	OF	(see multi-team players)											
Dan Murphy	C53,2B16,3B2	70	270	31	67		14	1	0			19	.248
Dan Burke	C33,OF4,1B2,3B1	40	135	14	32		4	2	0			5	.237
Mike Sullivan	P32,OF1	32	100	8	14		1	0	0			4	.140
Charles Jones	3B21	21	85	8	21		6	0	0				.247
Thomas McDermott	2B11,OF6	17	71	9	13		3	0	0				.183
John Lyston	OF2	14	40	1	3		1	0	0			1	.075
Daniel Ryan	P7,1B2,OF2	11	37	7	11		3	2	0			3	.297
William Tuckerman	P7	7	21	0	3		0	0	0			0	.143
Foley	P7	7	14	1	3		1	1	0			0	.214
Morse	P6	6	16	2	0		0	0	0			0	.000
Louis Guinasso	OF4	4	13	2	3		0	0	0			0	.231
William Sullivan	P3	3	6	1	0		0	0	0			0	.000
James Maguire	P2	2	5	0	1		1	0	0			0	.200
Bill McGunnigle	OF1	1	4	0	1		0	0	0			0	.250
William Schellerman	P1	1	4	0	1		0	0	0			0	.250
Pat Shea	P1	1	4	0	1		0	0	0			0	.250
Ledell Titcomb	P1	1	0	0	0		0	0	0			0	----

PITCHERS		W	L	PCT	G	GS	CG	SH	IP	H	BB	SO	ERA
Mike Sullivan		11	17	.393	32	27	22	1	250	222	146	146	1.55
John Lyston		6	7	.462	14	14	11	0	106	99	39	33	2.12
John Staib		6	9	.400	17	15	14	1	141	144	56	41	2.55
William Tuckerman		3	1	.750	7	4	4	0	46	45	14	16	2.15
Daniel Ryan		2	4	.333	7	6	6	0	52	45	30	33	0.35
William Sullivan		1	1	.500	3	3	2	0	18	14	8	5	0.50
William Schellerman		0	1	.000	1	1	1	0	9	8	1	1	0.00
Pat Shea		0	1	.000	1	1	1	0	9	9	5	2	5.00
Ledell Titcomb		0	1	.000	1	1	0	0	1	5	2	1	18.00
James Maguire		0	2	.000	2	2	2	0	16	16	5	13	1.13
Morse		0	4	.000	6	5	2	0	43	43	27	11	2.51
Foley		0	5	.000	7	3	2	0	33	33	18	15	3.00

MULTI-TEAM PLAYERS

BATTERS	POS-GAMES	TEAMS	GP	AB	R	H	BI	2B	3B	HR	BB	SO	SB	BA
Ed Sales	SS56,3B43,OF17	TR-SY-NH	112	352	79	108		17	5	2			24	.307
James Cudworth	OF61,1B4	NH-PRO	66	248	53	53		6	2	1			30	.214
William Annis	OF54	NH-PRO	54	220	24	44		4	2	0			28	.200
John Staib	P29,OF1	PRO-TRO	30	105	6	17		0	0	0			3	.162
Doc Bushong	C29,1B1	LEB-SYR	29	106	11	17		0	0	0			4	.160

1892
SPLIT AND FRAGMENTED

Most of the Eastern Association of 1891 returned intact for the 1892 campaign. Only Lebanon had withdrawn. To the seven existing teams were added three others: Binghamton, Elmira, and Philadelphia. The name was altered from the Eastern Association to the Eastern League.

As the season started, a new wrinkle formed. The Eastern League, copying their major league brethren in the National, announced that they would be adopting a split-season schedule to generate more fan interest. The first half was scheduled to end in late July, with the second continuing on to September. Afterward, a post-season series would be played to determine the champion.

Despite the split format, the same old bugaboo raised its ugly head in the Eastern League: Not enough fans were attending the games. Just before the close of the first half, Philadelphia and New Haven folded. When the first half ended, Syracuse found itself unable to start the second. Utica was brought in to finish the Syracuse schedule, but when Elmira withered as well, luckless Utica was dropped, leaving a total of six teams to complete the second half.

Providence won the first half by a single game over Albany, while Binghamton won the second half by three over Buffalo. Binghamton went on to dust Providence four games to two to win the league title.

In the composite totals, first-half participant Elmira had the best winning percentage, followed by Rochester, New Haven, Binghamton, Troy, Albany, Providence, Buffalo, Syracuse/Utica, and Philadelphia. Of the teams that completed both halves, Rochester had the best mark. Joseph Knight, who shared time with Binghamton and Syracuse/Utica, was the best batsman at .358. (Note: In league records the batting titlist is Binghamton's Willie Keeler at .373. Further research has revised Keeler's total to .354.) Milt West and William Hoover of Albany and Rochester shared the home run title with five. A bevy of pitchers finished the year with earned run averages under one; the lowest of these was turned in by James Sullivan of Providence (0.81). Henry Fournier, pitching for New Haven, Buffalo, and Syracuse/Utica, won the most games (30), while William Daley from Buffalo and Albany struck out a league-best 207.

The 1892 season represented the ultimate in chaos in a league already known for its instability. Only six of ten teams could even finish the season. But this would be the last time such problems would be present in the International League family tree. Stability was just a season away.

ELMIRA Gladiators

1st   33-27   .556   -2.5   Bobby Wheelock

BATTERS	POS-GAMES	GP	AB	R	H	BI	2B	3B	HR	BB	SO	SB	BA
Doc Kennedy	1B	60	239	43	84		18	3	0			4	.351
William Delaney	2B	50	190	26	31		2	2	0			9	.163
Bobby Wheelock	SS	60	227	64	60		10	1	0			*32	.264
James Knowles	3B	60	240	43	68		14	2	1			20	.283
Henry Simon	OF	60	244	42	63		8	4	0			18	.258
Henry Lynch	OF	60	221	45	75		7	5	1			20	.339
William Heine	OF	28	110	24	32		5	0	0			8	.291
Frank Boyd	C	57	210	30	50		9	4	1			7	.238
Dick Johnston	OF	22	93	11	19		2	0	0			3	.204
Tony Fricken	P19	19	57	8	13		2	0	0			1	.228
John Dolan	P18	18	60	7	8		2	1	0			1	.133
Con B. Murphy	P17	17	59	9	13		0	2	0			1	.220
Vince Dailey	OF	16	61	6	12		0	0	0			4	.197
O. Sprogell	P9	9	32	1	3		0	0	0			0	.094
James McGarr	2B	7	26	1	7		1	0	0			2	.269

PITCHERS	W	L	PCT	G	GS	CG	SH	IP	H	BB	SO	ERA
Tony Fricken	11	6	.647	19	19	17	1	157	156	57	44	2.18
John Dolan	10	7	.588	18	17	16	0	152	146	63	55	1.78
Con B. Murphy	10	7	.588	17	15	15	3	150	155	55	30	1.68
O. Sprogell	2	7	.222	9	9	9	0	79	70	39	23	1.82

ROCHESTER Hop Bitters

2nd   68-57   .544   Sam Wise

BATTERS	POS-GAMES	GP	AB	R	H	BI	2B	3B	HR	BB	SO	SB	BA
Jay Faatz	1B	50	190	31	46		6	0	0			10	.242
Sam Wise	2B,1B,SS	110	454	90	143		20	*15	2			30	.315
Jim Sullivan	SS,3B	50	152	17	41		3	2	0			10	.214
Harry Morelock	3B,SS,OF	66	224	39	47		5	0	0			9	.210
William Hoover	OF	113	451	81	127		23	9	*5			39	.282
Jim McTamney	OF	107	418	78	92		16	5	3			27	.220
Ed Swartwood	OF	93	375	68	108		22	5	1			25	.288
David McKeough	C	98	348	39	53		7	2	1			14	.152
Bobby Wheelock	SS	51	211	38	50		12	2	1			*13	.237
James McGarr	3B,2B	49	193	30	54		11	2	2			19	.280
George Myers	C,1B,3B,OF	38	150	15	39		7	2	0			1	.260
George Meakim	P31	31	106	19	20		1	0	0			4	.189
Will Calihan	P26	29	94	10	15		1	0	0			0	.160
Jumbo Schoeneck	1B	28	115	10	28		2	0	0			1	.243
John Dolan	P21,OF	26	88	6	13		3	1	1			5	.148
Herb Goodall	P26	26	78	7	10		3	1	0			4	.128
Joe Sommers	OF	24	94	11	17		0	0	0			5	.181
Ed Flanagan	1B	23	100	10	23		6	0	0			3	.230
David Coughlin	SS,OF	16	60	8	8		1	1	0			2	.133
Ralph Johnson	OF	15	55	4	15		4	1	0			4	.273
William Coughlin	P7,OF	13	48	3	5		1	0	0			2	.104
William Alvord	SS,3B	11	43	3	9		0	0	0			4	.188
George Townsend	C	9	37	3	8		0	0	0			0	.216
Maurice Sullivan	P7,OF	9	23	3	4		0	1	0			0	.174
McNamara	C,OF,1B	8	21	2	2		1	0	0			0	.095
Andrew Costello	SS,2B	7	24	2	6		1	0	0			0	.250
John Shearon	OF,P2	7	23	3	6		2	0	0			1	.261
Parke Swartzel	P7	7	21	3	2		1	0	0			1	.095
William Darnbrough	P6	6	15	2	5		1	0	0			2	.333
Al Atkinson	P5	5	17	0	1		0	0	0			0	.059
Dennis Fitzgerald	2B,SS	5	12	0	1		0	0	0			0	.083
John McGlone	3B	4	11	2	1		0	0	0			2	.091
John Meister	2B	3	13	1	3		1	0	0			0	.231
Henry Blauvelt	P2,OF	3	10	0	1		0	0	0			0	.100
Pete Weckbecker	C	3	8	2	3		0	0	0			0	.375
Herman Bader	OF	2	9	1	4		0	0	0			0	.444
Martin Duke	P2	2	8	0	2		0	0	0			0	.250
Peter Eagan	OF	1	4	1	1		0	0	0			1	.250
William Watkins	OF	1	4	0	1		0	0	0			0	.250
William Fagan	OF	1	4	0	0		0	0	0			0	.000

PITCHERS	W	L	PCT	G	GS	CG	SH	IP	H	BB	SO	ERA
George Meakim	22	8	.733	31	30	27	3	260	214	78	114	1.04

ROCHESTER (cont.)
Hop Bitters

PITCHERS	W	L	PCT	G	GS	CG	SH	IP	H	BB	SO	ERA
John Dolan	14	6	.700	21	19	18	3	176	169	64	54	2.10
Will Calihan	14	9	.609	26	21	18	0	210	184	75	76	1.63
Herb Goodall	10	12	.455	26	23	18	1	181	161	77	59	1.74
Parke Swartzel	3	2	.600	7	5	5	0	49	50	16	10	1.29
William Coughlin	2	4	.333	7	6	6	0	56	79	18	17	4.82
Martin Duke	1	1	.500	2	2	2	0	18	30	8	9	1.50
Al Atkinson	1	3	.250	5	5	4	0	42	39	12	9	2.79
Henry Blauvelt	0	1	.000	2	1	1	0	14	18	10	6	3.86
John Shearon	0	2	.000	2	2	2	0	18	19	15	1	1.50
William Darnbrough	0	3	.000	6	4	2	0	30	29	17	9	3.56
Maurice Sullivan	0	5	.000	7	5	4	0	42	58	19	9	3.86

NEW HAVEN
Nutmegs
3rd   20-17   .541   -4   Dan Shannon

BATTERS	POS-GAMES	GP	AB	R	H	BI	2B	3B	HR	BB	SO	SB	BA
Tom Morrissey	1B	18	75	7	17		4	1	0			4	.227
Dan Shannon	2B	31	131	18	32		1	2	0			6	.244
Monte Cross	SS	21	82	10	16		3	0	0			7	.195
James Donnelly	3B	38	137	29	33		6	1	0			16	.241
Ed Beecher	OF	38	158	23	33		4	2	0			11	.209
Sandy Griffin	OF	38	149	20	45		15	0	0			10	.302
Phil Blansfield	OF	36	134	13	30		5	1	0			4	.224
Jacob Wells	C	38	139	21	34		6	0	0			9	.245
Ed Flanagan	1B	20	81	10	20		4	0	0			3	.247
Henry Fournier	P20	20	67	8	17		3	1	2			0	.254
Henry Gruber	P18,OF	19	66	7	10		3	0	0			2	.152
Lawrence Murphy	OF	18	73	13	22		4	1	0			4	.301
Ed Cassian	OF,P3,3B	13	46	5	11		4	0	0			0	.239
Dick Johnston	OF	1	2	0	0		0	0	0			1	.000

PITCHERS	W	L	PCT	G	GS	CG	SH	IP	H	BB	SO	ERA
Henry Fournier	*13	6	.684	*20	*19	*17	0	*163	*144	57	62	1.88
Henry Gruber	6	9	.400	18	17	16	0	151	143	37	40	2.03
Ed Cassian	1	1	.500	3	2	2	0	23	19	5	5	1.17

BINGHAMTON
Bingoes
4th   60-52   .536   -1.5   Mike Lehane

BATTERS	POS-GAMES	GP	AB	R	H	BI	2B	3B	HR	BB	SO	SB	BA
Mike Lehane	1B	105	431	43	98		22	3	2			10	.227
Charles Bastian	2B,P1	63	263	54	60		6	2	1			8	.228
William Hanrahan	SS	64	273	52	71		15	4	4			12	.260
Willie Keeler	3B,SS,P1	93	373	92	132		20	11	1			10	.354
Mike Slattery	OF	101	408	78	111		16	10	2			12	.272
William Moran	OF,2B,SS	57	209	30	42		4	0	0			29	.201
Joseph Knight	OF	46	197	45	*74		*22	6	3			6	*.376
William Heine	C,OF	39	150	25	43		7	4	0			16	.287
John Fitzgerald	P41,SS,OF	48	158	16	25		1	0	0			2	.134
Henry Lynch	OF,SS,2B	37	151	30	41		5	2	1			6	.272
George Townsend	C	33	117	13	25		3	1	0			2	.214
George Staltz	OF	32	129	21	33		5	1	2			8	.256
Bert Inks	P29,OF	30	108	19	28		3	2	0			3	.259
John Irwin	3B	28	104	12	19		3	0	0			6	.183
John Meister	2B	21	85	9	24		7	1	0			3	.282
George Wilson	C	18	67	8	14		2	0	1			1	.209
Con D. Murphy	C,OF	15	56	5	11		1	0	0			4	.196
Martin Duke	P13,OF	14	38	1	7		1	0	0			0	.184
Victor Wilber	2B,OF,SS	12	42	1	13		1	0	0			3	.310
William Coughlin	P8,OF	12	40	6	8		0	0	0			1	.200
Herman Pitz	C,2B,SS,OF	12	28	1	4		0	0	0			1	.143
John Carroll	OF,2B	11	44	5	6		1	0	0			2	.136
Dan Casey	P10	10	34	2	5		1	0	0			0	.147
F. Barnett	P8,OF	9	33	3	6		1	0	0			0	.182
Sam Wise	2B	8	39	11	14		4	*3	1			1	.359
John McGlone	OF	8	32	5	8		1	1	0			1	.250
Phil Blansfield	OF,2B,C	8	34	6	11		1	0	0			2	.324

BINGHAMTON (cont.)
Bingoes

BATTERS	POS-GAMES	GP	AB	R	H	BI	2B	3B	HR	BB	SO	SB	BA
Henry Cote	C,OF	8	25	10	8		1	0	0			0	.320
Marsh Brown	OF,C	6	23	6	6		2	0	0			5	.261
Fred Evans	P5	5	15	3	5		3	1	0			0	.333
Frank Wilson	P2,2B	4	14	2	4		0	0	0			0	.267
John Rainey	3B	4	14	2	4		0	0	0			0	.286
Charles Baldwin	P1	1	5	1	1		0	0	0			0	.200
Fred Tenney	OF	1	4	0	1		0	0	0			0	.250
Herm Doscher	SS	1	4	0	0		0	0	0			0	.000
W. Nevens	P1	1	2	0	0		0	0	0			0	.000

PITCHERS	W	L	PCT	G	GS	CG	SH	IP	H	BB	SO	ERA
Bert Inks	20	8	.714	29	28	25	1	235	211	114	126	1.88
John Fitzgerald	14	20	.412	41	34	32	1	313	329	115	136	2.07
F. Barnett	6	2	.750	8	7	7	0	62	53	22	39	2.32
Martin Duke	5	7	.417	13	12	10	1	97	78	36	64	1.76
Dan Casey	4	5	.444	10	10	7	0	79	70	39	27	1.94
William Coughlin	3	5	.375	8	8	8	0	73	88	19	27	2.96
Frank Wilson	2	0	1.000	2	2	1	0	18	15	5	5	5.50
Charles Baldwin	1	0	1.000	1	1	1	0	9	8	7	5	1.00
Fred Evans	1	3	.250	5	4	2	0	28	37	12	7	4.82
Willie Keeler	0	1	.000	1	1	1	0	9	18	2	0	5.00
W. Nevens	0	1	.000	1	0	0	0	6	5	1	1	1.50
Charles Bastian	0	0	----	1	0	0	0	2	1	1	0	0.00

TROY   5th   62-57   .521   -3   Joe McGlone
Trojans

BATTERS	POS-GAMES	GP	AB	R	H	BI	2B	3B	HR	BB	SO	SB	BA
Thomas Power	1B	69	257	30	60		10	2	0			9	.233
John Pickett	2B	68	283	37	73		12	3	1			8	.258
Marr Phillips	SS	**117**	**490**	65	124		28	4	1			15	.253
Thomas Cahill	3B95	95	398	59	107		19	1	0			26	.269
Ted Scheffler	OF,3B,P1	116	469	**114**	128		29	7	1			28	.273
William Johnson	OF	112	442	54	120		10	6	3			18	.271
Henry Simon	OF	52	192	23	46		9	2	1			11	.240
Art Clark	C,3B,OF,2B	86	339	53	86		16	1	0			25	.254
Ed McDonald	3B,2B,OF	65	225	38	48		8	0	0			16	.213
Ed Breckenridge	1B	50	177	27	41		12	4	2			0	.232
Art Clarkson	P45	49	168	25	24		1	0	0			3	.143
John McGlone	3B	37	132	17	22		2	0	0			17	.167
John Freeman	OF,P13	31	123	17	29		7	0	0			1	.236
Mickey Welch	P31	31	103	9	15		3	0	0			1	.146
Charles McCaffrey	C,2B,OF	24	83	7	13		2	0	0			0	.157
Tony Fricken	P20	20	71	8	14		1	0	0			4	.197
Frank Bird	C,OF	10	37	4	9		1	0	0			2	.243
Mike Sullivan	P10	10	34	2	3		1	0	0			0	.088
Thomas Kearns	OF	7	26	6	8		1	0	1			2	.304
John Messitt	OF,2B	6	22	2	5		2	0	0			0	.227
Peter Gilbert	2B	6	22	0	1		0	0	0			0	.045
Con D. Murphy	C,OF	6	18	1	2		0	0	0			0	.111
Dan Shields	2B	3	12	4	3		0	0	0			2	.250
Wilson	P2,OF	3	12	2	2		0	0	0			0	.167
George Meakim	P2,OF	3	10	0	0		0	0	0			0	.000
Charles Ahearn	C	1	4	0	1		0	0	0			0	.250
Pat Pettee	2B	1	4	0	0		0	0	0			0	.000
Al Lawson	OF	1	3	0	0		0	0	0			1	.000

PITCHERS	W	L	PCT	G	GS	CG	SH	IP	H	BB	SO	ERA
Art Clarkson	24	19	.558	45	44	43	3	390	317	161	179	0.97
Mickey Welch	16	14	.533	31	30	29	3	268	225	111	120	0.87
Tony Fricken	12	7	.632	20	19	19	0	175	132	51	60	1.34
John Freeman	4	7	.364	13	12	12	1	110	102	64	29	1.88
Mike Sullivan	3	7	.300	10	10	10	0	89	80	52	32	1.11
Wilson	1	1	.500	2	2	2	0	18	21	8	4	1.00
George Meakim	1	1	.500	2	2	2	0	17	21	6	6	2.65
Ted Scheffler	0	0	----	1	0	0	0	5	6	1	0	1.80

ALBANY
Senators

6th   60-58   .509   -4.5   James Field

BATTERS	POS-GAMES	GP	AB	R	H	BI	2B	3B	HR	BB	SO	SB	BA
James Field	1B,P3	**117**	473	79	107		17	9	4			17	.226
William Eagan	2B,OF,SS,P1	96	371	64	97		11	6	2			21	.261
Franklin Lang	SS	107	354	50	61		9	2	0			21	.172
Charles Jones	3B	63	259	38	45		3	0	0			6	.174
Milt West	OF	57	234	35	74		11	2	5			10	.316
Charles Brady	OF,SS,2B	49	201	23	37		3	1	1			8	.184
Joe Visner	OF,2B	45	170	29	48		10	5	1			8	.284
Thomas Hess	C	63	233	29	50		10	1	0			5	.215
Ed Beecher	OF,2B	50	193	40	53		14	1	1			16	.275
Ed Sales	3B,2B	50	183	24	43		12	0	1			8	.235
Richard Knox	OF	45	159	27	33		8	1	1			10	.208
Con D. Murphy	C,OF,3B	37	141	15	39		5	1	0			7	.277
James Devlin	P29,OF	35	125	18	35		2	1	0			1	.280
John Taylor	P28,OF	33	109	10	21		0	1	1			6	.193
Herman Bader	OF	31	115	21	23		2	1	0			19	.200
Joe Sommers	OF,2B,SS	27	103	16	29		5	1	0			5	.282
John Hayes	C,2B,OF	26	98	6	27		1	0	0			1	.276
George Staltz	OF	23	91	16	26		2	2	0			6	.286
William Daley	P22,OF	22	86	11	18		1	0	1			3	.209
John Doran	P22	22	80	10	15		2	0	1			3	.188
Marsh Brown	C,OF	18	66	8	12		1	0	0			0	.182
Bill Van Dyke	OF	16	67	9	19		1	1	0			4	.284
John Shearon	P8,OF,1B	13	47	4	10		3	0	0			2	.213
Mike Sullivan	P8,OF	9	26	3	10		1	0	2			0	.385
Joe Gerhardt	2B	4	13	2	1		1	0	0			0	.077
Con B. Murphy	P4	4	13	3	1		0	0	0			1	.077
James Knowles	3B	2	9	2	3		0	1	0			0	.333
John Dolan	P2	2	6	0	0		0	0	0			0	.000
Pat Shea	P1	1	4	1	1		0	0	0			0	.250

PITCHERS	W	L	PCT	G	GS	CG	SH	IP	H	BB	SO	ERA
John Doran	14	6	.700	22	19	19	2	179	144	63	77	0.86
John Taylor	14	13	.519	28	28	25	4	229	192	44	119	2.27
James Devlin	14	14	.500	29	29	27	1	258	273	63	77	2.02
William Daley	10	*12	.455	22	21	19	2	183	201	*104	*100	2.51
Mike Sullivan	4	4	.500	8	7	7	0	68	54	23	27	2.25
John Shearon	3	3	.500	8	7	5	2	60	53	22	24	2.10
Con B. Murphy	1	3	.250	4	3	3	0	27	37	14	4	4.00
John Dolan	0	1	.000	2	2	1	0	12	12	6	4	3.75
Pat Shea	0	1	.000	1	1	1	0	9	10	7	2	4.00
James Field	0	0	----	3	0	0	0	12	16	3	3	0.73
Bill Eagan	0	0	----	1	0	0	0	2	0	0	0	0.00

PROVIDENCE
Clamdiggers

7th   57-59   .491   -6.5   Walt Burnham

BATTERS	POS-GAMES	GP	AB	R	H	BI	2B	3B	HR	BB	SO	SB	BA
Sid Farrar	1B	108	419	88	119		23	8	2			31	.284
Joe Mack	2B	76	304	58	77		16	2	2			11	.253
Leo Smith	SS	114	430	59	96		16	2	1			17	.223
Robert Pettit	3B	107	438	93	126		13	4	0			41	.288
Pat Friel	OF,P1	109	443	98	123		13	4	3			39	.278
John Leighton	OF	89	352	42	87		14	3	1			17	.247
Joe Hornung	OF,3B	70	285	50	85		15	0	4			19	.298
John Ryan	C	82	293	28	65		10	0	1			12	.222
Mike Kilroy	P51	53	181	14	24		0	0	0			2	.133
William Grey	C,2B,3B,1B,OF	48	185	30	42		8	2	1			9	.227
James Knowles	3B	35	139	18	31		2	0	0			10	.223
James Cooney	2B,OF	25	106	13	27		2	1	0			2	.255
John Stafford	P16	17	62	8	9		3	0	0			1	.145
James Sullivan	P17	17	60	4	11		2	1	0			3	.183
Bob Barr	P12,1B	14	43	5	9		3	0	0			1	.209
Pat Murphy	C	14	43	4	8		1	0	0			1	.186
Dennis Sullivan	P13	13	42	4	3		0	0	0			1	.071
John Messitt	OF,1B	13	41	5	13		1	0	0			3	.317
Frank Knauss	P12	12	31	4	6		0	0	0			0	.194
James Collopy	3B	10	40	7	11		2	0	0			2	.275
Fred Lake	C,OF,1B	9	33	5	10		1	1	1			3	.303
William Hoover	OF	6	26	5	7		1	0	*0			4	.269
Ed McDonald	OF	5	21	4	4		1	0	0			2	.190

PROVIDENCE (cont.)
Clamdiggers

BATTERS	POS-GAMES	GP	AB	R	H	BI	2B	3B	HR	BB	SO	SB	BA
Alex Ferson	P4	4	14	0	0		0	0	0			0	.000
Ed Cassian	P2	2	8	3	3		0	1	0			1	.375
Goff	OF	1	4	0	1		0	0	0			0	.250
Magill	OF	1	4	1	0		0	0	0			0	.000
James Hanivan	OF	1	4	0	0		0	0	0			0	.000
Casey	P1	1	2	0	0		0	0	0			0	.000
Peckham	P1	1	0	0	0		0	0	0			0	----

PITCHERS	W	L	PCT	G	GS	CG	SH	IP	H	BB	SO	ERA
Mike Kilroy	25	22	.532	51	45	42	5	415	374	170	151	1.73
James Sullivan	7	10	.412	17	16	16	1	144	133	34	57	0.81
Dennis Sullivan	6	2	.750	13	12	9	1	98	101	49	32	1.57
Frank Knauss	6	6	.500	12	11	8	1	82	78	46	31	1.21
Bob Barr	5	5	.500	12	12	10	1	92	102	30	29	2.84
John Stafford	4	11	.267	16	16	14	0	136	144	62	80	1.99
Ed Cassian	1	0	1.000	2	1	0	0	10	14	6	4	5.40
Alex Ferson	1	3	.250	4	4	4	1	35	48	15	6	2.83
Peckham	0	1	.000	1	0	0	0	2	3	2	0	4.50
Robert Pettit	0	0	----	2	0	0	0	4	4	1	0	0.00
Casey	0	0	----	1	1	0	0	5	10	3	2	9.00
Pat Friel	0	0	----	1	0	0	0					

BUFFALO   8th   53-60   .469   -9   Dan Stearns -
Bisons   Dan Shannon

BATTERS	POS-GAMES	GP	AB	R	H	BI	2B	3B	HR	BB	SO	SB	BA
Dan Stearns	1B,SS	47	182	27	40		7	2	0			16	.220
Dan Shannon	2B	74	310	54	84		10	4	1			12	.271
Monte Cross	SS,3B	94	344	59	92		18	5	3			20	.267
James Donnelly	3B	78	316	58	76		7	2	0			23	.241
James Daly	OF,1B,2B	104	445	60	127		21	5	2			10	.279
Sandy Griffin	OF	57	223	29	74		10	0	1			6	.332
John Messitt	OF,1B	31	119	18	25		3	1	0			4	.210
William Urquhart	C,1B,OF,2B	40	153	17	30		3	0	1			1	.196
William Schellerman	P34,OF	51	177	17	38							4	.214
Frank Boyd	C,OF	41	154	18	29		7	1	0			1	.188
Doc Kennedy	1B	34	132	13	29		5	0	1			2	.220
Bill Van Dyke	OF,SS	32	129	15	21		1	0	0			7	.163
Henry Fournier	P22,OF	32	116	14	28		5	1	0			0	.241
Henry Kappel	3B	32	114	10	27		1	0	0			10	.237
William Daley	P22,OF	24	77	5	18		1	0	1			3	.234
Pat Pettee	2B	23	96	8	29		2	0	0			2	.302
Lawrence Murphy	OF	21	85	10	15		1	1	0			4	.176
Patrick Dealey	C,1B,OF,SS	21	79	7	13		0	0	0			0	.165
Jacob Wells	C,1B	20	73	7	13		1	0	0			2	.178
Pete Weckbecker	C,1B	19	62	8	17		2	0	0			2	.274
John Rowe	2B,SS,1B	18	67	17	20		4	0	0			0	.299
Joe Hornung	OF,P1	17	71	13	18		3	0	0			0	.254
John Fields	OF	16	62	6	14		0	0	0			1	.226
Al Maul	OF,P6	15	57	8	10		2	1	0			2	.175
F. Barnett	P12,OF	14	50	4	13		0	1	0			1	.260
John Burke	OF	12	45	8	16		0	0	0			2	.356
James Conway	P11,OF	11	37	1	5		0	0	0			0	.135
Frank Foreman	P5,OF	9	30	8	8		2	0	0			0	.267
Andrew Weidman	C,OF	7	26	1	8		0	0	0			0	.308
Poodles Bahen	C,OF	7	22	2	5		1	0	0			2	.185
William Bowman	C	5	16	1	4		0	0	0			0	.250
Dennis Casey	OF	4	16	3	1		0	0	0			0	.063
George Hodson	P4	4	14	0	1		0	0	0			0	.071
James Maloney	P4	4	13	1	0		0	0	0			0	.000
Dennis Conners	OF	3	11	0	1		0	0	0			0	.091
George Sharrott	P2	2	7	0	1		0	0	0			0	.143
James Collins	2B,OF	1	4	0	2		0	0	0			0	.500
Baker	C	1	4	0	1		0	0	0			0	.250
Dave Jones	1B	1	4	0	0		0	0	0			0	.000
Cannon	OF	1	3	0	0		0	0	0			0	.000

PITCHERS	W	L	PCT	G	GS	CG	SH	IP	H	BB	SO	ERA
William Schellerman	19	12	.613	34	31	31	3	290	234	57	140	1.43
Henry Fournier	*14	8	.636	*22	*22	*19	3	*184	*179	56	52	1.66

BUFFALO (cont.)
Bisons

PITCHERS	W	L	PCT	G	GS	CG	SH	IP	H	BB	SO	ERA
William Daley	8	*14	.364	22	22	17	1	177	159	*107	*107	2.24
F. Barnett	4	6	.400	12	10	10	0	103	92	45	63	2.10
Frank Foreman	3	2	.600	5	5	5	0	44	54	16	13	2.25
James Conway	3	7	.300	11	11	10	0	94	117	18	14	2.87
George Sharrott	1	1	.500	2	2	2	0	17	13	3	8	0.00
Al Maul	1	4	.200	6	5	4	0	43	58	14	13	4.81
George Hodson	0	3	.000	4	3	3	0	33	40	11	10	3.55
James Maloney	0	2	.000	4	2	2	0	29	39	7	15	3.41
Joe Hornung	0	0	----	1	0	0	0	1	5	2	0	13.50

SYRACUSE / UTICA   9th   24-36   .400   -11.5   Jay Faatz
Stars

BATTERS	POS-GAMES	GP	AB	R	H	BI	2B	3B	HR	BB	SO	SB	BA
Jay Faatz	1B	61	242	36	65		11	0	0			15	.269
William Higgins	2B	36	144	11	29		3	0	0			2	.201
Tom Miller	SS	55	220	30	47		10	1	0			12	.214
Con Doyle	3B	59	242	37	62		6	0	0			17	.256
Joseph Knight	OF	61	259	48	*84		*17	1	0			9	*.324
Mike Mansell	OF	36	126	17	26		3	1	0			6	.206
William Wolf	OF27	27	117	16	24		4	0	0			4	.205
George Myers	C,OF,3B	42	159	21	38		8	0	0			5	.239
William Urquhart	OF,C,3B	48	182	23	43		3	2	0			3	.236
Ed Beecher	OF	24	100	12	29		6	2	0			4	.290
Ed Sales	2B,3B,OF,SS	23	91	9	19		3	0	0			3	.209
William Coughlin	P22	22	78	9	13		2	1	0			2	.167
Bob Barr	P17	17	59	7	16		1	0	0			1	.271
Henry Fournier	P13,SS,OF	14	48	5	11		0	0	0			0	.229
Mike Sullivan	P9	9	33	4	10		0	0	0			0	.303
John Thornton	OF,P3,3B	6	21	2	6		1	1	0			1	.286
Ed McDonald	2B,OF	5	20	1	3		0	0	0			0	.150
Tim Shinnick	2B	4	17	3	4		0	0	0		1	2	.235
John Gallagher	P3	3	5	0	0		0	0	0			0	.000
Herman Bader	OF	2	10	0	1		0	0	0			0	.100
Frank Goodyear	3B,OF	1	4	0	1		0	0	0			0	.250
Rogers	3B	1	4	0	1		0	0	0			0	.250
Calthorp	3B	1	1	0	0		0	0	0			0	.000

PITCHERS	W	L	PCT	G	GS	CG	SH	IP	H	BB	SO	ERA
William Coughlin	14	8	.636	22	21	20	3	194	174	45	70	1.39
Bob Barr	4	12	.250	17	16	14	0	146	163	51	50	2.40
Mike Sullivan	3	6	.333	9	9	9	1	80	69	39	44	1.13
Henry Fournier	*3	8	.273	*13	*11	*10	0	*93	*114	37	39	2.52
John Thornton	0	1	.000	3	3	1	0	17	19	12	3	1.56
John Gallagher	0	1	.000	3	1	1	0	13	18	4	6	2.08

PHILADELPHIA   10th   12-26   .316   -12.5   Harry Lyons
Reserves

BATTERS	POS-GAMES	GP	AB	R	H	BI	2B	3B	HR	BB	SO	SB	BA
Thomas Golden	1B	35	136	18	33		4	1	0			12	.245
Charles Bastian	2B,C	34	123	20	28		5	0	0			2	.232
William Hanrahan	SS	33	127	17	29		8	2	0			9	.228
Ed Sales	3B	31	120	15	26		3	0	0			4	.217
Harry Lyons	OF	34	145	23	38		7	2	0			13	.262
Andrew Costello	OF,P1	34	123	7	24		6	0	0			2	.195
John Messitt	OF,C,1B,2B	25	94	14	23		8	1	0			11	.245
George Wilson	C	19	68	7	15		3	0	0			5	.221
William Grey	C,3B,OF,SS,2B	24	94	10	23		7	0	0			6	.245
James Devlin	P14,OF	16	51	3	6		0	0	0			0	.118
Al Maul	P13,OF	14	45	2	9		2	0	0			0	.200
Sumner Bowman	P5,OF	8	28	2	4		0	0	0			0	.143
Joseph Kappel	OF	3	12	3	5		0	0	0			0	.417
Charles McCaffrey	C	3	11	0	1		0	0	0			0	.091
James Darragh	1B	2	8	2	1		0	0	0			0	.125
Ed Green	P2	2	6	1	0		0	0	0			1	.000
Matt Kilroy	P2,OF	2	6	0	0		0	0	0			0	.000

PHILADELPHIA (cont.)
Reserves

BATTERS	POS-GAMES	TEAMS	GP	AB	R	H	BI	2B	3B	HR	BB	SO	SB	BA
George Ulrich	C		1	4	1	1		0	0	0			0	.250
Carmody	P1,OF		1	4	0	1		0	0	0			0	.250

PITCHERS	W	L	PCT	G	GS	CG	SH	IP	H	BB	SO	ERA
James Devlin	6	7	.463	14	14	14	2	118	102	33	42	1.14
Al Maul	4	8	.333	13	12	11	1	105	105	43	57	2.05
Sumner Bowman	2	3	.400	5	5	4	0	42	46	26	13	2.79
Matt Kilroy	0	1	.000	2	1	1	0	12	12	10	5	0.75
Carmody	0	1	.000	1	1	0	0	5	9	0	4	0.00
Ed Green	0	2	.000	2	2	2	0	18	19	6	4	2.00
Andrew Costello	0	0	----	1	0	0	0	4	5	5	2	4.50

TEAM BATTING

TEAMS	GP	AB	R	H	BI	2B	3B	HR	BB	SO	SB	BA
ELMIRA	60	2069	360	538		80	24	3			130	**.260**
ROCHESTER	**125**	**4311**	642	**1014**		161	49	16			**238**	.235
NEW HAVEN	38	1340	184	320		62	9	2			77	.239
BINGHAMTON	112	3749	617	962		159	**52**	**18**			154	.257
TROY	119	4156	604	984		**174**	39	19			188	.233
ALBANY	118	4029	593	938		134	39	19			188	.233
PROVIDENCE	118	4053	**650**	997		147	29	16			232	.246
BUFFALO	113	3945	527	953		117	24	10			137	.242
SYRACUSE/UTICA	61	2182	291	532		78	9	1			86	.244
PHILADELPHIA	38	1205	145	267		53	6	0			65	.222
	451	31039	4613	7505		1165	271	95			1496	.242

1893
STABILITY

From 1884 to 1892, the various leagues comprising the International League had known little stability. One problem was in-season insolvency: For over half the years, at least one club fizzled out before season's end. Another problem was lack of continuity. The leagues had been reorganized at least three times, used five different names, and seen seven different men holding the post of league president. With the constant changes in league structure and titles, there was no consistent thread tying things together from one year to another. This was soon to change.

Following the 1892 season, a man named Pat Powers was elected president of the Eastern League. Powers was no newcomer to the league, having served as manager of the 1884 Trenton club and the 1891 Buffalo team. For the 1892 season, Pat Powers served as manager for the major league New York Giants before being asked to take the reins of the Eastern League.

Powers' first task in 1893 was to find enough teams to fill out the league. Nearly half of the 1892 teams had bailed out in midstream, but five of the ten—Albany, Binghamton, Buffalo, Troy, and Providence—wanted back in. To reach the optimum eight-team level, Powers recruited three more clubs: Erie, Springfield, and Wilkes-Barre.

At the end of the 1893 season, two of the new teams, Erie and Springfield, finished a close first and second, followed immediately by third-place Troy. Buffalo, Albany, Providence, Binghamton, and Wilkes-Barre sat on the remaining rungs. Wilkes-Barre's Frank Bonner hit 16 home runs (the league's highest to date) while Joseph Knight from Binghamton won the batting title (.389). (Note: League records indicate the batting titlist was Buffalo's Frank Drauby at .379; further research has placed his total at .363.) In pitching, first-place Erie boasted the top winner, William Clarke (31), and earned run average leader, George Nicol (1.80). Strikeout leader Bert Inks (139) pitched for both Binghamton and Springfield.

Pat Powers' immediate achievement for the 1893 season was stability. For the first time since 1889, all the league's teams had finished their campaigns. However, Powers' overall legacy would prove to be his longevity. For the next 14 years, Powers served as the Eastern League president. He stepped down in 1906, only to return in 1907 to serve an additional four years. The league prospered under his tutelage. True, there were a few franchise failures and relocations in the years of his tenure. But these small bumps were nothing compared to the epidemic of failures in the 1880s and early 1890s. Those days of chaos were now behind.

ERIE Blackbirds

	1st	63-41	.606		Charles Morton

BATTERS	POS-GAMES	GP	AB	R	H	BI	2B	3B	HR	BB	SO	SB	BA
John Fields	1B,P	102	394	77	105		10	14	7			5	.264
Thomas Nicholson	2B	103	398	93	118		17	7	5			57	.296
Frank Scheibeck	SS,3B	101	415	121	126		33	2	7			39	.304
William Kuehne	3B	91	375	61	106		16	7	3			6	.283
John Shearon	OF	103	428	92	142		28	17	4			31	.332
Bill Van Dyke	OF	98	379	84	106		16	7	3			35	.280
Dan Lally	OF	82	339	79	113		25	6	7			14	.333
John Berger	C,SS,OF,1B	77	281	51	70		17	3	4			8	.249
William Clarke	P46,OF,SS	49	165	24	41		9	1	1			6	.248
Albert Mays	P23,OF	43	147	27	39		3	0	0			5	.265
George Nicol	P23	23	81	9	17		6	0	0			6	.210
James Peoples	C,OF	22	71	17	25		6	1	2			4	.342
Ed Zinran	C,OF,SS	19	67	8	16		2	0	0			0	.239
James Maguire	3B,SS	12	42	10	10		0	3	0			2	.238
Hank O'Day	P7	7	18	3	3		0	0	0			1	.167
Charles DeWald	P6	6	21	8	7		2	1	2			0	.333
Ed Cushman	P4	4	2	0	1		0	0	0			0	.500
John Healey	P3,OF	3	12	1	2		1	1	0			0	.167

PITCHERS	W	L	PCT	G	GS	CG	SH	IP	H	BB	SO	ERA
William Clarke	31	14	**.689**	46	**45**	**41**		388	407	108	80	2.62
George Nicol	13	9	.591	23	23	21		200	157	89	84	**1.80**
Albert Mays	8	9	.471	23	16	14		173	192	66	31	4.05
Charles DeWald	5	1	.833	6	6	6		54	50	12	18	2.01
John Healey	1	2	.333	3	3	2		18	25	13	2	3.00
Ed Cushman	0	1	.000	4	2	0		10	11	9	0	3.60
John Fields	0	0	----	1	0	0		5	9	3	1	0.00

SPRINGFIELD Ponies

	2nd	64-44	.593	-1	Thomas Burns

BATTERS	POS-GAMES	GP	AB	R	H	BI	2B	3B	HR	BB	SO	SB	BA
Mike Lehane	1B	103	450	89	147		23	8	2			10	.327
Thomas Burns	2B	65	257	57	76		7	5	1			6	.296
Frank Shannon	SS	103	425	126	116		9	10	2			38	.273
Peter Gilbert	3B	99	411	123	154		14	13	7			32	.375
William Bottenus	OF	103	424	101	142		20	17	7			22	.335
Emmett Seery	OF	103	426	132	125		14	16	4			32	.293
Henry Lynch	OF,2B,3B	93	394	114	126		19	17	5			56	.320
John Ryan	C,OF,1B	91	368	80	118		16	10	6			4	.321
Thomas Leahy	OF,C	35	137	29	40		7	6	2			22	.292
William Coughlin	P30,OF	31	122	18	37		4	1	0			4	.303
Mike Bradley	2B	30	131	29	44		9	4	1			4	.363
Hebry Stevens	P8	8	24	4	4		1	0	0			0	.167
Philip Corcoran	P6	6	20	2	4		0	0	0			0	.200
Eugene O'Connor	C,OF	6	10	2	2		0	0	0			0	.200
Tom Vickery	P4	4	9	1	1		1	0	0			0	.111
Ed Crane	P3	3	8	0	0		0	0	0			0	.000
Ed Cassian	P1,OF	2	6	2	4		0	0	0			1	.667
Ash	P2	2	1	0	0		0	0	0			0	.000
Kelley	P1	1	1	0	0		0	0	0			0	000

PITCHERS	W	L	PCT	G	GS	CG	SH	IP	H	BB	SO	ERA
William Coughlin	19	11	.633	30	30	30		271	248	94	70	3.52
Philip Corcoran	4	1	.800	6	4	3		34	60	23	11	2.09
Tom Vickery	3	1	.750	4	4	4		35	34	16	16	1.80
Hebry Stevens	2	4	.333	8	5	5		55	78	25	14	2.80
Ed Crane	1	2	.333	3	3	2		19	32	21	2	3.32
Ed Cassian	0	1	.000	1	1	1		9	14	4	4	3.00
Kelley	0	1	.000	1	1	0		1	4	5	0	0.00
Ash	0	0	----	2	0	0		3	4	2	0	6.00

TROY Trojans

	3rd	67-50	.573	-2.5	J. Maloney

BATTERS	POS-GAMES	GP	AB	R	H	BI	2B	3B	HR	BB	SO	SB	BA
Ed Breckenridge	1B	(see multi-team players)											

TROY (cont.)
Trojans

BATTERS	POS-GAMES	GP	AB	R	H	BI	2B	3B	HR	BB	SO	SB	BA
John Prickett	2B	98	408	91	123		22	4	3			19	.301
Marr Phillips	SS	73	301	54	88		8	1	0			14	.292
James Donnelly	3B	103	406	84	129		17	2	1			39	.318
Henry Simon	OF	113	470	58	157		21	9	2			27	.349
William Johnston	OF	113	445	97	140		15	9	3			16	.315
Ted Scheffler	OF,SS	111	450	138	143		30	10	9			34	.318
Thomas Cahill	C,SS,OF,3B	94	403	76	111		17	5	1			29	.276
Dan Murphy	C,3B,1B,2B,SS,OF,P	63	220	24	43		5	0	0			6	.195
Henry Gruber	P43,OF,1B	50	157	27	45		9	0	2			0	.297
James Devlin	P40,OF	41	132	14	34		2	0	0			2	.258
Charles Dooley	1B	19	68	13	22		6	1	0			1	.324
Seth Sigsby	P	11	32	6	7		1	0	0			0	.219
Fred Schmidt	P	1	3	0	1		0	0	0			0	.333

PITCHERS		W	L	PCT	G	GS	CG	SH	IP	H	BB	SO	ERA
Henry Gruber		22	17	.564	43	37	34		345	392	135	51	2.64
James Devlin		21	15	.583	40	35	31		307	327	108	58	2.81
Seth Sigsby		6	3	.667	11	11	8		88	99	25	28	3.68
Fred Schmidt		0	1	.000	1	1	1		9	22	6	1	9.00
Dan Murphy		0	0	----	1	0	0		4	8	4	0	0.00

BUFFALO   4th   61-50   .550   -5.5   John Chapman
Bisons

BATTERS	POS-GAMES	GP	AB	R	H	BI	2B	3B	HR	BB	SO	SB	BA
Dan Stearns	1B111,2B	114	470	119	161		35	9	7			8	.343
John Rowe	2B	110	465	113	158		22	9	3			15	.340
James Collins	SS,3B,OF	76	296	49	88		15	2	1			7	.297
Jacob Drauby	3B,P7,SS,OF	106	421	115	153		40	8	11			16	.363
William Wolf	OF,SS	114	470	94	161		34	5	3			18	.343
James Daly	OF,3B	112	480	125	155		29	7	6			15	.317
Sandy Griffin	OF	83	330	78	113		26	7	2			9	.342
William Urquhart	C,OF,3B,1B	72	270	54	83		15	2	1			7	.307
Frank Boyd	C,1B,2B,SS,OF	39	142	30	43		13	0	0			7	.306
Chauncey Fisher	P37	36	130	18	28		3	0	0			2	.215
Ed Daley	SS	28	115	28	35		9	1	0			4	.304
William Schellerman	P9,OF	9	35	10	11		1	0	1			1	.314
William Hoffer	P9	9	26	7	4		0	0	0			0	.154
Matthew Gagen	P6	6	17	3	2		1	0	0			0	.118
Robert Cargo	SS	5	21	3	3		0	0	1			1	.143
James Meakim	P5	5	12	0	1		0	0	0			0	.083
Asa Priest	P4	4	12	2	2		0	0	0			0	.167
Harry Mack	P2	2	5	2	2		0	0	0			0	.400
Phil Reccius	P1	2	3	0	1		0	0	0			0	.333
Reimes	P1	1	5	2	2		0	0	1			0	.400
Thomas Higgins	P1	1	4	0	2		0	0	0			0	.500
James Kilroy	P1	1	2	0	0		0	0	0			0	.000

PITCHERS		W	L	PCT	G	GS	CG	SH	IP	H	BB	SO	ERA
Chauncey Fisher		17	17	.500	37	33	29		301	317	143	116	2.36
William Schellerman		6	3	.667	9	9	8		77	98	25	24	3.51
Jacob Drauby		4	1	.800	7	4	3		45	59	22	15	2.20
Matthew Gagen		3	1	.667	6	5	3		48	61	21	10	3.38
William Hoffer		3	4	.429	9	8	6		67	72	23	19	2.82
Asa Priest		2	2	.500	4	3	3		34	42	22	13	3.44
Harry Mack		1	1	.500	2	2	1		10	21	12	0	5.40
Reimes		1	0	1.000	1	1	1		9	9	2	4	1.00
James Meakim		1	2	.333	5	3	2		26	34	11	2	3.46
Thomas Higgins		0	0	----	1	0	0		8	9	6	3	5.63
James Kilroy		0	0	----	1	0	0		4	4	1	3	2.25
Phil Reccius		0	0	----	1	1	0		1	4	1	0	40.50

ALBANY Senators
5th 54-62 .466 -15 L. Fassett

BATTERS	POS-GAMES	GP	AB	R	H	BI	2B	3B	HR	BB	SO	SB	BA
Lew Whistler	1B	36	144	44	49		3	4	4			4	.340
William Eagan	2B	113	454	137	152		23	9	5			58	.335
William Hanrahan	SS	109	439	94	134		30	7	7			12	.305
Dan Minnehan	3B,OF	83	354	71	109		28	5	3			5	.308
Joe Visner	OF	107	455	94	138		30	9	12			16	.303
Richard Knox	OF,P5	97	360	85	102		25	7	13			22	.283
Charles Willis	OF,P1	28	123	24	36		8	0	0			2	.293
Thomas Hess	C,1B,OF,SS,3B	93	370	63	106		23	3	4			2	.286
George Wilson	C,1B	66	256	53	81		23	5	7			3	.314
Harley Payne	P41,OF	63	237	33	65		13	2	1			1	.274
Will Calihan	P38,OF,2B	46	153	23	35		5	1	0			3	.229
George Bausewine	P24,1B,OF	31	109	18	23		6	1	1			0	.211
James Knowles	3B,1B	28	115	24	36		9	3	0			3	.313
Doc Kennedy	1B	22	89	14	25		2	0	1			1	.284
William Hoover	OF	22	87	12	22		2	0	1			1	.253
Pete Weckbecker	OF,C,1B	11	42	2	13		0	0	0			0	.310
Henry Kappel	3B	10	41	13	10		4	0	0			4	.244
Thomas McGuirk	1B	6	21	2	5		0	0	0			0	.238
Joe Gerhardt	1B	4	14	3	1		1	0	0			1	.071
C. Hendricks	OF,C	3	12	3	3		2	0	0			0	.250
William Daley	P3	3	6	1	3		0	0	0			0	.500
Thomas Smith	P2	2	5	0	2		0	0	0			0	.400
Sullivan	P	1	3	0	1		0	0	0			0	.333
McCahill	P	1	1	0	0		0	0	0			0	.000

PITCHERS	W	L	PCT	G	GS	CG	SH	IP	H	BB	SO	ERA
Will Calihan	18	20	.474	38	38	36		334	323	120	73	3.43
Thomas Payne	17	22	.436	41	38	38		337	373	124	112	3.87
George Bausewine	12	11	.522	24	22	22		201	250	81	59	3.54
Richard Knox	3	2	.600	5	3	2		37	56	27	13	4.17
William Daley	1	0	1.000	3	3	1		11	9	7	5	2.38
Thomas Smith	1	0	1.000	2	1	1		10	12	9	5	2.38
Charles Willis	0	1	.000	1	1	1		8	10	5	1	5.63
Sullivan	0	1	.000	1	1	1		8	15	4	0	6.75
McCahill	0	0	----	1	1	0		0	0	4	0	

PROVIDENCE Clamdiggers
6th 47-67 .412 -21 Walt Burnham

BATTERS	POS-GAMES	GP	AB	R	H	BI	2B	3B	HR	BB	SO	SB	BA
James Rogers	1B	57	242	46	82		18	5	1			18	.339
Robert Pettit	2B,P	104	427	84	115		13	3	3			43	.269
James Cooney	SS	90	384	60	93		19	4	0			37	.236
Charles Bassett	3B,OF	97	380	74	107		21	0	5			26	.282
Pat Friel	OF	109	453	88	145		20	4	2			41	.320
Joe Hornung	OF,1B,3B	55	230	56	65		12	1	3			16	.283
Harry Lyons	OF,3B	49	212	42	75		7	3	0			25	.354
David McKeough	C,OF,3B,2B,SS	108	359	56	92		8	7	0			28	.256
James Sullivan	P47	59	195	22	34							7	.174
William Campion	1B	50	183	46	57		10	7	2			34	.311
Ed Swartwood	OF	40	142	41	45		15	1	1			18	.317
Frank Rudderham	P22,OF	24	74	8	12		1	0	0			1	.162
Dennis Sullivan	P15	17	45	4	11							2	.244
John Whalen	C,OF,1B,2B	15	53	7	13		1	2	0			3	.234
Andrew Dunning	P6,OF	8	27	2	4		1	0	0			0	.148
Doyle	P3,OF,2B	5	16	1	0		0	0	0			0	.000
J. Martin	3B,P1,SS	4	14	6	3		0	0	1			1	.214
Charles Jones	P3,OF	4	13	3	3		0	0	0			1	.231
William Alvord	3B	3	12	0	3		0	0	0			0	.250
Weidman	P2,OF	3	7	1	1		0	0	0			0	.143
William Sullivan	P1,OF	1	4	1	0		0	0	0			0	.000
Laven	P1	1	1	1	0		0	0	0			0	.000
Mike Kilroy	P1	1	0	0	0		0	0	0			0	----

PITCHERS	W	L	PCT	G	GS	CG	SH	IP	H	BB	SO	ERA
James Sullivan				47								
Frank Rudderham	10	8	.556	22	19	18		169	196	38	60	2.93
Dennis Sullivan				15								

PROVIDENCE (cont.)
Clamdiggers

PITCHERS	W	L	PCT	G	GS	CG	SH	IP	H	BB	SO	ERA
Charles Jones	1	2	.333	3	2	2		23	25	15	9	1.57
Doyle	0	1	.000	3	2	1		10	11	13	3	2.70
Mike Kilroy	0	1	.000	1	1	0		2	5	3	0	9.00
Weidman	0	2	.000	2	2	1		12	24	2	1	5.25
Andrew Dunning	0	5	.000	6	5	4		45	59	22	15	2.20
Robert Pettit	0	0	----	3	0	0		9	11	4	0	2.08
Laven	0	0	----	1	0	0		5	9	3	2	5.40
J. Martin	0	0	----	1	0	0		4	4	4	1	2.25
William Sullivan	0	0	----	1	1	0		4	3	2	1	6.75

BINGHAMTON   7th   41-61   .402   -21   A. Patton
Bingoes

BATTERS	POS-GAMES	GP	AB	R	H	BI	2B	3B	HR	BB	SO	SB	BA
Clarence Conley	1B	92	359	64	67		12	6	2			7	.187
Charles M. Smith	2B	96	393	112	127		20	14	4			35	.323
Franklin Lang	SS	95	347	86	93		15	3	1			41	.268
F. Shea	3B		(see multi-team players)										
Joseph Knight	OF	94	437	110	**170**		28	**17**	2			26	**.389**
A. Stanhope	OF,SS	36	157	30	45		15	2	0			7	.283
Mike Slattery	OF		(see multi-team players)										
Grant Briggs	C,3B,OF,2B,SS,1B	75	313	61	80		25	4	4			4	.256
Dan Sweeney	C,OF	56	231	22	52		8	4	0			4	.225
John Barnett	P37,OF	39	133	39	43		7	6	0			4	.293
James Duryea	P14,OF	20	81	13	16		2	2	1			2	.198
Willie Keeler	3B	15	68	9	17		2	2	1			1	.250
William Carey	P15	15	59	11	19		2	1	0			1	.322
Jessie Allen	C,OF	12	48	5	11		2	1	0			1	.229
Dan Mahoney	C,OF	8	34	10	12		3	0	0			1	.353
Dennis Casey	OF	8	32	6	10		0	0	0			3	.313
Gus Moran	1B	8	25	6	4		1	0	0			0	.160
Victor Wilber	OF	6	22	2	3		1	0	0			0	.136
John Rafferty	3B	5	16	3	3		0	2	0			0	.188
O'Hara	2B,OF	4	18	1	4		1	0	0			0	.222
Dan Casey	P3	3	14	3	4		0	0	0			0	.286
Tom Miller	3B	1	4	1	2		1	0	0			0	.500
Walter Plock	2B	1	4	1	1		1	0	0			0	.250
Martin	SS	1	4	0	1		0	0	0			0	.250
Mulroy	3B	1	3	0	1		0	0	0			0	.333

PITCHERS	W	L	PCT	G	GS	CG	SH	IP	H	BB	SO	ERA
John Barnett	19	17	.528	37	35	32		287	334	135	99	3.13
James Duryea	7	6	.538	14	13	13		113	129	38	35	3.02
William Carey	5	7	.417	15	13	11		122	151	58	35	3.92
Dan Casey	2	1	.667	3	3	3		27	31	11	8	3.67

WILKES-BARRE   8th   41-63   .394   -22   Dan Shannon
Coal Barons

BATTERS	POS-GAMES	GP	AB	R	H	BI	2B	3B	HR	BB	SO	SB	BA
John Irwin	1B,3B,OF,P1	62	262	47	76		7	5	2			7	.290
Tim Shinnick	2B	63	253	44	59		5	3	3			14	.233
Frank Bonner	SS,OF,3B	92	409	92	154		22	15	**16**			18	.377
Ed Sales	3B,P1	104	422	81	128		25	8	3			13	.303
George Henry	OF74	75	310	52	78		9	5	3			27	.252
George Staltz	OF,2B,SS	63	255	49	81		8	6	6			18	.318
Candy LaChance	OF,C,1B,2B,SS	70	319	77	113		26	8	12			19	.354
Fred Lake	C,OF,SS,1B	98	388	88	102		19	11	12			24	.263
M. McLaughlin	P45,OF	48	173	27	40		2	1	2			4	.231
George Wood	OF	38	170	34	54		9	5	1			4	.316
Herb Goodall	P28,1B,OF	37	121	16	34		7	3	0			3	.281
Bobby Wheelock	2B	27	114	16	30		3	2	1			7	.263
Count Campau	OF,SS	20	86	15	28		6	6	1			3	.326
Mark Polhemus	OF	17	71	12	25		1	2	2			2	.352
Otis Stocksdale	P14	15	49	9	14							5	.286
John Freeman	P6,OF	9	36	8	13		2	1	1			2	.361
George Shaffer	OF,1B	9	31	4	8		0	1	0			1	.258

WILKES-BARRE (cont.)
Coal Barons

BATTERS	POS-GAMES	GP	AB	R	H	BI	2B	3B	HR	BB	SO	SB	BA
George Ulrich	2B,OF	5	20	2	2		1	0	0			0	.100
Fred Betts	OF	4	21	4	5		0	0	0			0	.238
Marty Bergen	C,3B	3	10	2	1		0	0	0			0	.100
John Roach	P2	2	10	2	2		0	1	0			0	.200
Kelly	P2	2	4	0	0		0	0	0			0	.000

PITCHERS		W	L	PCT	G	GS	CG	SH	IP	H	BB	SO	ERA
M. McLaughlin		16	22	.421	45	36	32		335	424	110	107	3.95
Otis Stocksdale		7	4	.636	14	12	9		98	113	42	30	3.66
Herb Goodall		7	16	.304	28	25	18		196	249	138	41	4.22
John Roach		1	1	.500	2	2	2		17	32	7	2	6.35
John Freeman		0	5	.000	6	5	4		43	60	40	7	4.19
Kelly		0	2	.000	2	2	2		17	22	8	4	5.29
Ed Sales		0	0	----	1	0	0		2	3	0	0	0.00
John Irwin		0	0	----	1	0	0		1	4	0	0	18.00

MULTI-TEAM PLAYERS

BATTERS	POS-GAMES	TEAMS	GP	AB	R	H	BI	2B	3B	HR	BB	SO	SB	BA
Ed Breckenridge	1B	TRO-WB	109	391	102	120		19	14	10			10	.307
William Heine	OF,SS,2B,3B,C	BU-BI-PR	95	350	68	94		11	5	0			50	.269
Mike Slattery	OF	WB-PR-BI	83	342	84	104		26	10	2			21	.315
F. Shea	3B	BIN-ALB	73	308	66	100		23	6	4			15	.325
Thomas Dowse	C,OF,1B,2B,SS	BUF-WB	65	239	46	76		15	1	2			11	.305
Edward Deady	OF,1B,2B,3B,P1	PRO-BIN	60	260	59	83		17	7	2			36	.319
Bert Inks	P39	BIN-SPR	40	133	29	48		5	1	2			4	.361
Monte Cross	SS	BUF-TRO	37	126	24	24		2	0	2			19	.206
William Campfield	P32,OF	BIN-WB	34	128	23	37		2	3	4			5	.289
Bob Barr	P34	BUF-PRO	34	122	18	27		6	3	2			0	.221
John Messitt	OF,1B	ALB-PRO	27	84	21	22		0	1	0			0	.262
Mike Madden	P22,OF	PRO-ERI	27	73	15	16		1	0	0			5	.213
Tony Fricken	P24,2B,OF	WB-TR-AL	26	82	8	20		3	0	0			3	.244
Henry Fournier	P19,OF	AL-BU-BI	23	87	10	26		6	1	1			0	.253
Harry Morelock	3B,2B,OF,SS	AL-TR-BU	21	77	16	21		0	1	1			3	.273
Robert Miller	P21	TRO-SPR	21	69	11	13		1	0	0			1	.188
Jud Smith	SS,OF,3B	BIN-WB	18	77	16	22		1	0	0			4	.286
John Fitzgerald	P18,OF	WB-PRO	18	51	11	10		1	1	0			6	.196
John Ruckle	P16,OF	BIN-WB	17	66	8	17		3	1	0			2	.258
George Meakim	P17	BUF-TRO	17	56	15	13		2	0	0			4	.232
Harry Burrell	P7	SPR-WB	7	23	5	4		0	1	0			0	.174
James Gannon	P4	ER-PR-SP	4	14	5	1		0	0	0			1	.071
Thomas Donovan	P4	TRO-ALB	4	9	1	1		0	0	0			0	.111

PITCHERS		TEAMS	W	L	PCT	G	GS	CG	SH	IP	H	BB	SO	ERA
Bert Inks		BIN-SPR	23	15	.605	39	36	33		317	333	150	139	2.50
Bob Barr		BUF-PRO	18	14	.563	34	29	28		277	319	92	70	2.14
William Campfield		BIN-WB	16	13	.552	32	29	27		254	275	117	84	2.80
Tony Fricken		WB-TR-AL	12	6	.667	24	20	13		169	226	82	13	3.42
George Meakim		BUF-TRO	9	7	.563	17	17	15		139	162	61	35	2.46
Robert Miller		TRO-SPR	9	8	.529	21	18	15		157	235	45	30	4.54
Mike Madden		PRO-ERI	7	8	.467	22	18	9		134	183	74	47	4.22
John Ruckle		BIN-WB	5	10	.333	16	15	15		135	167	45	34	3.46
Harry Burrell		SPR-ALB	3	2	.600	7	7	2		44	45	54	9	3.86
Henry Fournier		AL-BU-BI	2	15	.118	19	17	15		151	225	79	29	5.17
James Gannon		ER-PR-SP	1	1	.500	4	3	2		27	38	18	4	4.33
Thomas Donovan		TRO-ALB	0	2	.000	4	3	1		18	18	23	5	2.50
John Fitzgerald		WB-PRO	0	12	.000	18	11	8		112	162	73	20	4.25
Edward Deady		PRO-BIN	0	0	----	1	0	0		5	6	2	1	1.80

TEAM BATTING

TEAMS	GP	AB	R	H	BI	2B	3B	HR	BB	SO	SB	BA
ERIE	104	3768	789	1078								.286
SPRINGFIELD	103	3810	989	1185								.311
TROY	117	4035	846	1214								.299

TEAM BATTING (cont.)

TEAMS	GP	AB	R	H	BI	2B	3B	HR	BB	SO	SB	BA
BUFFALO	114	4082	930	**1326**								**.324**
ALBANY	117	**4122**	891	1246								.301
PROVIDENCE	112	3925	647	1087								.276
BINGHAMTON	101	3853	840	1157								.300
WILKES-BARRE	104	3774	763	1155								.306
	436	31369	6695	9448								.301

1894
FIREPOWER

Before the 1893 season, baseball rule-makers decided to "fix" the alarming decline in batting averages, which had been hovering near the .250 level in virtually every league. Their solution was to move the distance between the pitcher and batter back 10 feet, from 50 to 60. This, rule-makers argued, would allow batters, to have more time to see and to hit the ball, resulting in higher averages. They were correct.

In 1893, in both the major and minor leagues, batting averages soared. The Eastern League saw its league average hit .301, as 21 regular players topped .320. In 1894, this level would climb still further.

With the stable success of 1893 fresh in its memory, the Eastern League's 1894 campaign would prove somewhat disappointing. Before the season commenced, the Albany franchise was replaced by one from Syracuse. During the season, on July 26, the Troy club found itself unable to continue. A team from Scranton was added as a replacement. On August 16, Binghamton surrendered its franchise, and a team from Allentown took its place with the stipulation that their home games would be played in Yonkers.

At season's end, the Providence Clamdiggers were the champions, double-digit games ahead of the rest of the pack, which finished as follows: Troy, Erie, Syracuse, Springfield, Buffalo, Wilkes-Barre, Allentown, Binghamton, and Scranton. Joseph Knight, playing for Wilkes-Barre and Providence, led the batting with a .371 mark. Buffalo's Jacob Drauby extended the league record while swatting 21 home runs.

Joseph Knight was one of 32 Eastern League regulars (75 or more games) who batted over .320. Seven of the ten teams to participate in 1894 batted over .300, with Buffalo (.323) leading the way. In all, the league pushed its average up to the .308 mark. A corollary to the high averages was the sheer amount of runs scored. Buffalo scored over 1,000 runs, averaging nearly nine per game, while the league averaged over seven.

For the next several years, Eastern League averages remained high as pitchers struggled to find an extra ten feet on their fastball. The "fix" instituted by baseball in 1893 certainly yielded its desired effect: more offensive firepower. Unfortunately for pitchers of the mid–1890s, this firepower was seemed to be directed solely at them.

PROVIDENCE Clamdiggers

PROVIDENCE Clamdiggers	1st	78-34	.696	William Murray

BATTERS	POS-GAMES	GP	AB	R	H	BI	2B	3B	HR	BB	SO	SB	BA
James Rogers	1B109	112	492	97	167		21	12	8			37	.339
John Stricker	2B108	108	436	88	123		16	6	1			52	.282
James Cooney	SS98	98	422	68	119		27	6	2			28	.282
C.harles Bassett	3B108	109	484	125	178		36	6	6			32	.368
Harry Lyons	OF108	108	511	131	171		30	14	6			37	.335
William Murray	OF108	109	430	80	112		10	11	2			68	.260
Joseph Knight	OF	(see multi-team players)											
Ed Dixon	C63	80	320	58	109		10	6	2			33	.340
Pat McCauley	C53	53	197	33	50		4	2	2			27	.254
James Sullivan	P39	40	155	23	37		4	1	1			10	.239
John Egan	P30	35	105	25	26		3	2	0			9	.248
Frank Rudderham	P30	30	105	7	17		1	0	0			2	.162
Thomas Lovett	P16	16	62	7	15		2	0	0			0	.242

PITCHERS	W	L	PCT	G	GS	CG	SH	IP	H	BB	SO	ERA
James Sullivan				39								
John Egan				30								
Frank Rudderham				30								
Thomas Lovett				16								

TROY Trojans

TROY Trojans	2nd	43-32	.573	-16.5	Thomas Cahill

BATTERS	POS-GAMES	GP	AB	R	H	BI	2B	3B	HR	BB	SO	SB	BA
Ed Breckenridge	1B	(see multi-team players)											
John Pickett	2B71	71	304	54	98		11	6	3			12	.322
Leo Smith	SS	(see multi-team players)											
James Donnelly	3B	(see multi-team players)											
William Johnson	OF	(see multi-team players)											
Henry Simon	OF	(see multi-team players)											
Ted Scheffler	OF	(see multi-team players)											
Thomas Cahill	C	(see multi-team players)											
Dan Murphy	C24	29	116	11	30							1	.258
Marr Phillips	SS	15	59	8	10							1	.169

PITCHERS	W	L	PCT	G	GS	CG	SH	IP	H	BB	SO	ERA
(see multi-team players)												

ERIE Blackbirds

ERIE Blackbirds	3rd	57-49	.538	-18	Charles Morton

BATTERS	POS-GAMES	GP	AB	R	H	BI	2B	3B	HR	BB	SO	SB	BA
James Field	1B109	109	436	71	150		24	12	6			16	.344
Thomas Nicholson	2B105	105	453	115	151		24	7	6			71	.333
Charles M. Smith	SS106	108	432	102	115		15	7	5			19	.266
William Kuehne	3B106	106	427	64	109		16	7	4			13	.255
Dan Lally	OF108	108	458	78	152		19	7	8			8	.331
Bill Van Dyke	OF108	108	434	66	120		15	8	5			36	.276
John Shearon	OF103	103	445	108	158		30	19	9			23	.355
John Berger	C58	67	255	50	80		9	8	8			3	.314
Joe Gunson	C54	64	261	40	78		9	1	1			2	.299
Joe Herndon	P46	47	159	21	29		3	1	2			1	.182
John Healey	P34	37	137	21	37		5	2	4			0	.270
Gus McGinnis	P27	27	89	11	24		2	0	0			1	.269

PITCHERS	W	L	PCT	G	GS	CG	SH	IP	H	BB	SO	ERA
Joe Herndon				46								
John Healey				34								
Gus McGinnis				27								

SYRACUSE Stars   4th   63-56   .529   -18.5   Jay Faatz

BATTERS	POS-GAMES	GP	AB	R	H	BI	2B	3B	HR	BB	SO	SB	BA
Clarence Conley	1B62	62	247	30	71		4	3	1			9	.287
William Eagan	2B111	111	435	97	129		17	9	1			30	.297
Monte Cross	SS69	69	247	62	73		9	3	4			34	.296
Dan Minnehan	3B111	115	504	95	182		24	6	2			11	.361
Curt Welch	OF108	108	422	111	125		22	4	2			31	.296
Sandy Griffin	OF			(see multi-team players)									
Wiliam Hoover	OF			(see multi-team players)									
Thomas Hess	C89	98	381	64	114		16	5	2			6	.299
George Bausewine	P41	44	146	28	45		8	3	2			4	.308
Matt Kilroy	P25	30	98	22	33		14	2	0			8	.337
George Wilson	C20	27	104	18	30							1	.288
Jay Faatz	1B25	25	102	15	30							0	.294

PITCHERS			W	L	PCT	G	GS	CG	SH	IP	H	BB	SO	ERA
George Bausewine						41								
Matt Kilroy						25								

SPRINGFIELD Ponies   5th   57-54   .514   -20.5   Thomas Burns

BATTERS	POS-GAMES	GP	AB	R	H	BI	2B	3B	HR	BB	SO	SB	BA
Mike Lehane	1B			(see multi-team players)									
Thomas Burns	2B36	36	146	27	45		9	2	3			1	.308
Frank Shannon	SS109	109	493	115	158		13	13	6			15	.320
Henry Lynch	3B87,2B20	110	469	127	158		30	14	3			44	.337
William Bottenus	OF110	110	440	111	147		31	11	6			22	.334
Phil Nadeau	OF85	110	469	128	162		24	**21**	7			30	.345
Pat Friel	OF			(see multi-team players)									
Thomas Leahy	C95	101	423	96	116		12	10	7			30	.274
William Coughlin	P45	49	178	26	41		4	1	1			1	.230
T. Sheehan	OF32	32	144	31	60		10	4	0			2	.416
John Messitt		32	112	20	25							2	.223

PITCHERS			W	L	PCT	G	GS	CG	SH	IP	H	BB	SO	ERA
William Coughlin						45								

BUFFALO Bisons   6th   64-61   .512   -20.5   John Chapman

BATTERS	POS-GAMES	GP	AB	R	H	BI	2B	3B	HR	BB	SO	SB	BA
Jacob Drauby	1B46,OF37	97	436	126	153		32	5	**21**			12	.351
John O'Brien	2B60	60	276	77	91		15	6	1			14	.330
Ed Lewee	SS71	71	262	56	87		15	5	7			3	.332
Thomas Dowse	3B			(see multi-team players)									
James Collins	OF125	**125**	562	126	**198**		57	13	9			18	.352
James Daly	OF82	82	336	82	103		15	10	1			7	.307
William Clymer	OF61,2B54	121	523	97	176		27	16	3			36	.337
William Urquhart	C83	101	402	80	126		18	4	8			7	.313
Frank Boyd	C61	82	330	76	105		18	2	9			10	.318
William Hoffer	P57,OF19	76	282	63	91		14	2	7			5	.323
Abe Johnson	SS49	51	213	31	55		11	1	0			13	.258
Jud Smith	2B13	24	96	14	35		6	3	0			3	.365
Albert Weddige	3B14	21	86	19	29		5	0	2			1	.337
William Bott	P18	18	66	11	18							2	.272
Chauncey Fisher	P17	17	60	5	13							3	.217

PITCHERS			W	L	PCT	G	GS	CG	SH	IP	H	BB	SO	ERA
William Hoffer						57								
William Bott						18								
Chauncey Fisher						17								

WILKES-BARRE Coal Barons

7th 54-56 .495 -23 Dan Shannon

BATTERS	POS-GAMES	GP	AB	R	H	BI	2B	3B	HR	BB	SO	SB	BA
Brown	1B54	54	233	28	67		13	2	3			2	.288
Dan Shannon	2B77	77	347	77	121		14	12	4			21	.349
John McMahon	SS90	90	393	43	97		9	6	3			4	.247
John Gillen	3B106	106	417	89	139		19	15	6			17	.333
Fred Betts	OF107	107	463	114	155		22	11	11			21	.335
Abe Lizotte	OF63	78	336	63	108		21	15	5			8	.321
John Hess	OF	(see multi-team players)											
John Warner	C97	97	387	71	118		14	8	7			17	.305
John Keenan	P38	47	175	24	50		0	3	0			1	.286
William Campfield	P29	29	94	20	32		3	5	3			1	.340
Milt West	1B	14	68	19	24		5	0	0			3	.312

PITCHERS	W	L	PCT	G	GS	CG	SH	IP	H	BB	SO	ERA
John Keenan				38								
William Campfield				29								

ALLENTOWN (YONKERS) Buffalos

8th 8-16 .333 -26 King Kelly

BATTERS	POS-GAMES	GP	AB	R	H	BI	2B	3B	HR	BB	SO	SB	BA
King Kelly	1B12	15	61	11	23		3	0	0			2	.377
Sam Wise	2B20	20	80	14	20		1	0	0			7	.250
W. Sweeney	SS20	20	74	7	16		2	3	0			2	.216
Joe Mulvey	3B22	22	92	13	36		8	2	0			2	.391
Wood	OF22	22	86	21	29		4	1	0			2	.337
P. Sweeney	OF17	21	86	21	32		6	2	0			3	.372
Costello	OF13	22	86	9	18		1	1	0			1	.209
Kilroy	C,1B	19	64	10	12		0	0	0			4	.188
John Milligan	C,1B	11	39	4	8		1	0	1			1	.205

PITCHERS	W	L	PCT	G	GS	CG	SH	IP	H	BB	SO	ERA
	(see multi-team players)											

BINGHAMTON Bingoes

9th 18-62 .225 -44 Herm Doscher

BATTERS	POS-GAMES	GP	AB	R	H	BI	2B	3B	HR	BB	SO	SB	BA
Thomas Power	1B	(see multi-team players)											
Joe Mack	2B66	66	272	62	76		12	7	2			10	.278
William Hanrahan	SS	(see multi-team players)											
Milt Whitehead	3B	(see multi-team players)											
George Gore	OF48	48	191	46	61		17	1	1			5	.319
Edward Lytle	OF	(see multi-team players)											
Harley Payne	OF	(see multi-team players)											
Lohbeck	C42	42	160	20	29		4	1	0			7	.181
Sweeney	1B23	27	116	21	40							0	.344
Harry Raymond	3B22	22	92	23	33		5	3	1			4	.359
Connors	OF19	19	75	12	14		2	0	0			1	.187
Marshall	P13	17	62	10	19							0	.206
Franklin Lang	SS16	16	60	19	11		3	1	1			7	.183
Carr	OF15	15	71	13	24		6	3	2			2	.338
O'Brien	3B15	15	61	9	22							0	.361

PITCHERS	W	L	PCT	G	GS	CG	SH	IP	H	BB	SO	ERA
Marshall				13								

SCRANTON Miners

10th 8-31 .205 -33.5 Thomas Cahill

BATTERS	POS-GAMES	GP	AB	R	H	BI	2B	3B	HR	BB	SO	SB	BA
Mike Lehane	1B	(see multi-team players)											
Thomas Cahill	2B	(see multi-team players)											

SCRANTON (cont.)
Miners

BATTERS	POS-GAMES	GP	AB	R	H	BI	2B	3B	HR	BB	SO	SB	BA
Leo Smith	SS	(see multi-team players)											
Phelan	3B20	26	103	20	26		4	0	0			8	.252
Rogers	OF18	21	82	10	21		3	1	0			1	.256
William Johnson	OF	(see multi-team players)											
William Hoover	OF	(see multi-team players)											
William Patchen	C32	32	135	15	53		10	4	0			5	.393

PITCHERS		W	L	PCT	G	GS	CG	SH	IP	H	BB	SO	ERA
		(see multi-team players)											

MULTI-TEAM PLAYERS

BATTERS	POS-GAMES	TEAMS	GP	AB	R	H	BI	2B	3B	HR	BB	SO	SB	BA
Henry Simon	OF114	TRO-SYR	114	485	123	143		16	14	3			22	.295
Joseph Knight	OF113	WB-PRO	113	493	108	183		8	10	1			34	**.371**
Ed Breckenridge	1B113	TRO-SPR	113	440	98	146		26	17	9			11	.331
William Johnson	OF111	TRO-SCR	111	463	111	155		27	24	1			14	.333
Ted Scheffler	OF111	TRO-SPR	111	459	**138**	150		28	15	2			29	.327
Leo Smith	SS108,3B16	TRO-SCR	108	421	67	97		10	5	2			1	.230
Sandy Griffin	OF106	BUF-SYR	106	465	103	167		41	2	2			14	.359
Edward Lytle	OF	WB-BIN	101	479	115	162		26	3	4			39	.338
Mike Lehane	1B99	SPR-SCR	99	386	67	110		17	11	3			5	.283
Thomas Cahill	C51,2B28	SCR-TRO	91	402	73	132		23	10	1			26	.328
Thomas Dowse	3B67	BI-BU-TR	88	355	76	126		23	9	4			5	.354
James Donnelly	3B83	TRO-SPR	83	361	91	104		22	7	0			15	.288
William Hoover	OF83	SYR-SCR	83	344	74	105		19	4	6			21	.305
Thomas Power	1B79	BIN-SYR	79	328	72	116		16	3	0			15	.353
Robert Pettit	OF57	PRO-WB	78	368	65	106		11	4	1			12	.288
John Hess	OF74	WB-SCR	78	348	72	105		17	11	0			8	.301
Dan Stearns	1B76	WB-BUF	76	307	76	87		14	3	1			14	.283
Pat Friel	OF60	BI-SC-SP	60	251	58	81		24	12	6			17	.323
William Hanrahan	SS54	BIN-SYR	54	221	36	67		8	2	0			4	.303
Tom Vickery	P52	BUF-SPR	54	199	47	70		19	5	6			8	.356
James Duryea	P40	BIN-ALL	53	190	24	56		3	2	0			6	.295
Harley Payne	OF47,P18	SYR-BIN	52	197	37	65		13	1	0			5	.329
James Delaney	P50	BIN-SCR	51	188	35	53		6	4	1			6	.281
William Heine	SS35	BIN-BUF	50	203	35	60							8	.295
Henry Gruber	P45	TRO-SPR	45	151	33	40		5	0	1			0	.284
John Rafter	C43	BIN-SYR	43	184	31	67		14	4	1			14	.364
J. Barnett	P42	BIN-SYR	42	132	23	40		9	2	0			2	.303
George Meakim	P39	TRO-WB	39	135	28	30		1	4	0			4	.222
William Quarles	P35	WB-SCR	35	127	16	26		4	1	0			2	.204
Gene DeMontreville	SS39	BU-BI-SC	36	146	31	45		2	5	6			4	.308
Thomas Donovan	P34	SC-TR-AL	34	121	12	29		1	0	0			4	.239
Milt Whitehead	3B30	BIN-SCR	30	131	28	39		3	2	0			8	.297
James Dolan	P25	BIN-SPR	25	84	12	21							0	.250
C. Blackburn	P18	WB-SCR	18	66	9	13		0	0	2			0	.196

PITCHERS		TEAMS	W	L	PCT	G	GS	CG	SH	IP	H	BB	SO	ERA
Tom Vickery		BUF-SPR				52								
James Delaney		BIN-SCR				50								
Henry Gruber		TRO-SPR				45								
John Barnett		BIN-SYR				42								
James Duryea		BIN-ALL				40								
George Meakim		TRO-WB				39								
William Quarles		WB-SCR				35								
Thomas Donovan		SC-TR-AL				34								
James Dolan		BIN-SCR				25								
Harley Payne		SYR-BIN				18								
C. Blackburn		WB-SCR				18								

TEAM BATTING

TEAMS	GP	AB	R	H	BI	2B	3B	HR	BB	SO	SB	BA
PROVIDENCE	112	4210	842	1306		**267**	73	31			365	.310
TROY	75	2775	588	821		111	54	24			97	.295

TEAM BATTING (cont.)

TEAMS	GP	AB	R	H	BI	2B	3B	HR	BB	SO	SB	BA
ERIE	107	4018	751	1214		154	74	51			194	.302
SYRACUSE	119	4092	811	1260		181	48	21			186	.307
SPRINGFIELD	111	4004	942	1268		221	**130**	42			184	.316
BUFFALO	125	**4630**	**1022**	**1500**		261	74	**79**			154	**.323**
WILKES-BARRE	110	3949	773	1196		166	107	51			136	.302
ALL. (YONKERS)	24	735	118	220		28	11	2			28	.288
BINGHAMTON	80	3018	585	919		163	60	19			128	.304
SCRANTON	39	1269	200	372		60	25	2			154	.293
	451	32700	6632	10076		1612	656	322			1626	.308

1895
SPRINGFIELD PONIES

In the midst of the hard-hitting 1890s, a team trotted to the fore of the Eastern League. Located in the shadow of the Berkshires, this team excelled in all facets of the game. The city was Springfield, Massachusetts, and the team was called the Ponies.

Springfield was a relative newcomer to the league, having joined the roster of the Eastern in 1893. After a strong second-place showing during their inaugural season, the Ponies slumped to fifth in 1894. Not much was expected of the club in 1895.

Joining the Springfield Ponies in the 1895 Eastern League were three new entries. Gone were the Erie, Allentown, and Binghamton teams. In their stead arrived Toronto, Rochester, and Providence—three old friends who had graced the circuit before.

As the season progressed, Springfield and its closest follower, Providence, proved to be the league's elite duo. At season's close, Springfield held a six-game lead over their Rhode Island rivals. Wilkes-Barre and Syracuse finished third and fourth, while Buffalo, Scranton, Rochester, and Toronto finished fifth through eighth.

Springfield's first pennant was won on the strength of hitting and pitching as it ranked first in both categories. The team batted a robust .319, led by such stalwarts as Henry Lynch (.350), Joe Gunson (.346), James Donnelly (.332), Frank Shannon (.328), and Ted Scheffler (.315). A young outfielder, Fielder Jones, also contributed by batting .424 over a 50-game period. From the pitching slab, the Ponies enjoyed the services of the Eastern League's top winner (James Callahan with 30) and the earned run average champion (William Coughlin at 1.87). All said, a most powerful team—one of the strongest of the decade.

Among the honors not garnered by Springfield players was the batting title won by Scranton's Frank Ward (.372). (Note: Jud Smith from Toronto was originally listed as the winner at .373; further research has placed his total at .355. However, Mr. Smith did walk away with the home run crown, knocking out a league-best 14.) Hurler George Harper from Rochester struck out the most batters (233).

After its 1895 pennant, Springfield bounced back to the second division, where it resided until drifting out of the league in 1900. Fifty years later the city would return for a brief four-year stay. But 1895 would prove to be the Ponies' high-water mark in the International League. It was easily their most powerful entry, resulting in their sole title.

SPRINGFIELD Ponies

SPRINGFIELD   1st   79-36   .687   Thomas Burns

BATTERS	POS-GAMES	GP	AB	R	H	BI	2B	3B	HR	BB	SO	SB	BA
Peter Gilbert	1B98,3B15,2B1	113	492	97	144		22	10	4			27	.293
Ed McDonald	2B112,3B1	113	443	93	115		17	9	2			24	.260
Frank Shannon	SS108	108	464	126	152		28	6	1			39	.328
James Donnelly	3B94	94	398	112	132		19	8	1			21	.332
Ted Scheffler	OF112	112	476	93	150		21	12	4			41	.315
Henry Lynch	OF98,3B4,SS4,2B1	105	454	111	159		20	15	3			52	.350
Fielder Jones	OF51	51	227	58	95		6	5	3			21	.424
Joe Gunson	C75,1B1	77	312	43	108		13	4	0			2	.346
Thomas Leahy	C42,OF19,1B2	62	237	60	69		12	4	3			24	.291
James Callahan	P42,1B,OF5	52	202	42	60		7	9	3			11	.297
Henry Gruber	P36,1B8,OF1	45	173	27	56		7	5	2			2	.324
William Coughlin	P33	34	118	19	35		3	0	1			4	.297
John Chesbro	P7	7	15	5	6		1	2	0			0	.400
George McKillop	P6	6	19	2	4		1	0	0			0	.211

PITCHERS		W	L	PCT	G	GS	CG	SH	IP	H	BB	SO	ERA
James Callahan		**30**	9	**.769**	42	40	37	0	352	388	77	91	2.48
William Coughlin		24	8	.750	33	31	27	2	270	266	56	48	**1.87**
Henry Gruber		18	15	.545	36	35	32	0	304	379	82	64	3.02
John Chesbro		2	1	.667	7	2	1	0	32	39	22	6	2.81
George McKillop		2	3	.400	6	5	5	0	48	56	5	9	3.75

PROVIDENCE Grays

PROVIDENCE   2nd   74-44   .627   -6.5   William Murray

BATTERS	POS-GAMES	GP	AB	R	H	BI	2B	3B	HR	BB	SO	SB	BA
James Rogers	1B111,3B1,SS1	112	481	86	159		31	8	4			31	.331
John Stricker	2B82	92	368	72	90		6	2	1			57	.245
James Cooney	SS117	117	499	64	151		16	4	1			29	.303
Charles Bassett	3B116	116	515	103	146		25	7	4			21	.283
Harry Lyons	OF118	118	528	122	186		31	7	5			40	.352
Joseph Knight	OF118	118	507	99	180		33	10	3			17	.355
William Murray	OF116,1B2	117	464	102	154		23	12	2			**71**	.332
Pat McCauley	C98	91	335	73	106		20	10	4			30	.316
Ed Dixon	C32,2B24,1B5,SS1,3B1,OF1	70	259	43	70		11	6	4			13	.270
Thomas Lovett	P38	39	136	21	37		3	2	1			3	.272
Frank Rudderham	P35	35	119	20	20		2	1	0			1	.168
George Hodson	P29,OF2	31	107	17	14		2	0	0			3	.131
John Egan	P22,1B1	24	78	16	18		2	3	0			1	.231

PITCHERS		W	L	PCT	G	GS	CG	SH	IP	H	BB	SO	ERA
Thomas Lovett		24	13	.649	38	37	35	3	328	356	112	72	2.61
Frank Rudderham		21	11	.656	35	32	31	1	286	312	86	104	2.64
George Hodson		20	8	.714	29	29	26	0	251	255	108	69	2.33
John Egan		8	9	.471	22	19	18	1	169	209	69	31	3.09

WILKES-BARRE Coal Barons

WILKES-BARRE   3rd   61-49   .555   -15.5   Dan Shannon

BATTERS	POS-GAMES	GP	AB	R	H	BI	2B	3B	HR	BB	SO	SB	BA
Howard Earl	1B111	111	486	82	159		20	16	7			24	.327
Dan Shannon	2B74	73	334	73	111		19	7	2			20	.332
John McMahon	SS91	91	372	48	85		10	5	0			11	.228
Charles A. Smith	3B107	107	444	61	123		21	7	2			13	.277
Edward Lytle	OF108,SS3	111	477	114	166		25	12	2			33	.348
Abe Lizotte	OF107,C4	111	484	110	164		31	**29**	5			9	.339
Sandy Griffin	OF	(see multi-team players)											
William Diggins	C85,OF3,SS1	87	361	50	105		13	8	2			8	.291
Fred Betts	OF41,P24,3B3	68	276	57	79		17	3	4			13	.286
Frank Bonner	2B37,SS16	53	231	47	75		18	6	0			5	.325
John Keenan	P46,2B1	46	148	23	35		8	1	0			5	.236
Thomas Colcolough	P23	23	81	12	15		0	1	1			2	.185
William Campfield	P12	16	61	13	10		3	2	1			1	.164
George Bausewine	P3	3	7	0	1		0	0	0			0	.143
McGroarty	P1	1	3	0	0		0	0	0			0	.000
William Wynne	P1	1	2	1	1		1	0	0			0	.500

WILKES-BARRE (cont.)
Coal Barons

PITCHERS	W	L	PCT	G	GS	CG	SH	IP	H	BB	SO	ERA
John Keenan	29	11	.725	46	38	36	0	365	425	102	60	3.13
Fred Betts	11	10	.526	24	22	21	2	196	249	60	29	2.37
Thomas Colcolough	10	11	.476	23	21	18	2	188	222	77	70	3.12
William Campfield	7	9	.438	16	16	13	0	130	190	40	27	4.37
George Meakim	4	5	.444	12	9	7	0	72	91	44	16	2.63
George Bausewine	1	2	.333	3	3	2	0	20	23	6	1	4.05
McGroarty	0	1	.000	1	1	1	0	8	20	3	2	11.25
Wynne	0	0	----	1	1	0	0	4	11	1	1	4.15

SYRACUSE   4th   62-53   .539   -17   Sandy Griffin
Stars

BATTERS	POS-GAMES	GP	AB	R	H	BI	2B	3B	HR	BB	SO	SB	BA
Thomas Power	1B116	116	498	96	165		21	9	3			21	.335
William Eagan	2B116	116	471	93	131		16	2	0			35	.278
Charles Moss	SS116	116	464	83	142		23	6	1			18	.306
Dan Minnehan	3B116	116	492	90	166		30	10	10			11	.337
Henry Simon	OF116	116	496	106	179		32	6	7			11	.361
Curt Welch	OF89	89	354	87	81		7	0	0			21	.229
Dan Sweeney	OF81	81	344	64	94		20	5	3			14	.273
Thomas Hess	C83,1B3,2B1,SS1,3B1,OF4	92	348	60	115		20	4	4			11	.330
Matt Kilroy	P,OF30	58	313	39	85		17	1	1			10	.399
John Rafter	C45,OF1	46	168	31	47		6	4	0			6	.280
John Barnett	P45	45	147	30	37		3	2	0			3	.252
James Gannon	P21	21	64	10	9		3	1	0			0	.141
William Day	P19,OF1	19	63	10	7		2	0	0			2	.111
Martin McQuaid	OF6	6	23	4	12		2	0	0			2	.522
Frank Lathrop	P3	3	9	0	1		0	0	0			1	.111
Henry Killeen	P1	1	5	2	2		0	2	0			0	.400

PITCHERS	W	L	PCT	G	GS	CG	SH	IP	H	BB	SO	ERA
John Barnett	20	19	.513	45	40	37	0	362	416	138	79	2.16
Matt Kilroy	14	9	.609	31	20	16	0	209	287	73	42	3.10
Joseph Delaney	11	4	.733	16	16	13	1	131	163	32	40	2.89
William Day	9	8	.529	19	19	15	1	146	191	45	17	2.96
James Gannon	9	10	.474	21	19	15	0	157	209	64	44	3.66
Henry Killeen	0	1	.000	1	1	1	0	9	16	7	3	2.00
Frank Lathrop	0	2	.000	3	2	2	0	20	31	14	4	4.50

BUFFALO   5th   63-61   .508   -20.5   Charles Morton
Bisons

BATTERS	POS-GAMES	GP	AB	R	H	BI	2B	3B	HR	BB	SO	SB	BA
James Field	1B124,P1	124	513	101	152		34	11	5			5	.296
Sam Wise	2B106,SS7	111	480	80	152		26	21	4			20	.317
Ed Lewee	SS120	120	477	85	128		32	3	4			17	.268
Jacob Drauby	3B116	116	494	102	146		35	10	2			7	.296
William Clymer	OF125	125	535	108	165		28	6	8			25	.308
John Shearon	OF122,P1	122	519	131	182		41	18	7			27	.351
William Bottenus	OF112	112	464	111	139		29	9	9			18	.300
William Urquhart	C91,1B1	93	373	62	100		14	4	6			4	.268
Thomas Dowse	C37,OF16,2B20,3B12	81	335	62	112		23	2	1			4	.334
Joe Herndon	P33,OF	40	128	24	29		3	1	1			3	.227
William Wadsworth	P34	34	124	16	24		1	2	0			2	.194
Gus McGinnis	P23	23	79	7	17		1	0	0			1	.215
Tom Vickery	P22	22	74	8	21		4	0	0			2	.284
Henry Lampe	P11,OF1	12	49	8	11		0	0	0			2	.224
Mike Kilroy	P4	4	12	1	1		0	0	0			1	.083

PITCHERS	W	L	PCT	G	GS	CG	SH	IP	H	BB	SO	ERA
Joe Herndon	19	11	.633	33	30	26	0	258	360	83	70	3.80
William Wadsworth	17	14	.548	34	32	31	1	290	369	117	128	2.70
Gus McGinnis	8	12	.400	23	22	18	1	181	231	47	50	3.03
Tom Vickery	8	13	.381	22	22	19	0	184	204	80	47	2.99
Henry Lampe	6	3	.667	11	9	9	0	93	127	37	55	3.68

BUFFALO (cont.)
Bisons

PITCHERS	W	L	PCT	G	GS	CG	SH	IP	H	BB	SO	ERA
Henry Fournier	3	5	.375	9	7	6	0	77	104	22	17	4.68
Mike Kilroy	1	2	.333	4	3	3	0	31	43	16	9	2.61
George Meakim	0	0	----	1	0	0	0	2	5	1	0	9.00
John Shearon	0	0	----	1	0	0	0	2	3	3	1	0.00
James Field	0	0	----	1	0	0	0	4	8	2	0	9.00

SCRANTON   6th   44-72   .379   -35.5   Billy Barnie
Coal Heavers

BATTERS	POS-GAMES	GP	AB	R	H	BI	2B	3B	HR	BB	SO	SB	BA
Dan Stearns	1B70,SS3,OF11,2B1	85	325	64	86		18	10	1			11	.265
Frank Ward	2B96,OF4	104	419	93	156		23	5	1			26	.372
Paul Radford	SS36,2B20,OF2	57	226	52	34		7	2	0			12	.150
John Huston	3B54,SS25,P5,OF2	81	315	51	89		22	4	0			15	.283
Peter Eagan	OF75	75	324	59	105		22	4	0			6	.324
Pat Meaney	OF48,P30	76	311	51	104		10	8	1			4	.334
William Johnson	OF41	41	169	22	38		8	4	0			2	.225
Emmett Rogers	C49,OF5,SS1	54	203	23	60		10	2	0			5	.296
Alex Smith	C36,OF27,1B10	70	289	49	85		11	6	2			15	.294
Charles Brady	3B29,OF29	58	230	29	49		10	1	0			10	.213
Tom Bannon	OF35,SS13	47	198	44	69		11	3	0			24	.348
William Schriver	C32,OF4,3B3	38	147	29	44		12	3	1			3	.299
William Clarke	1B35	35	143	26	55		7	4	2			4	.385
Thomas Johnson	P33,OF2	34	105	16	25		3	1	0			4	.238
William Sweeney	SS25,OF1	31	117	16	27		5	0	1			3	.231
Frank Butler	OF25	25	104	21	27		5	1	0			2	.260
John Luby	P10,OF6	16	49	3	9		2	0	0			0	.184
Robert Miller	P8,OF7	14	42	4	10		1	1	0			1	.238
Dennis Houle	OF13	13	50	8	9		3	2	0			1	.180
Charles Brown	P11	11	36	3	9		2	0	0			0	.250
J. Brodie	P6,OF3,2B1	10	33	4	6		1	0	0			0	.273
William Quarles	P7	7	21	1	5		2	0	0			0	.238
Frank Winkelman	3B2,OF2	4	14	2	4		0	1	0			1	.286
William Patchen	C2	2	7	1	1		0	0	0			0	.143
Pat Fox	P2	2	5	0	0		0	0	0			0	.000
Hickey	C1	1	2	0	0		0	0	0			0	.000
James Nolan	P1	1	1	0	0		0	0	0			0	.000
Frank Knauss	P1	1	0	0	0		0	0	0			0	----

PITCHERS	W	L	PCT	G	GS	CG	SH	IP	H	BB	SO	ERA
Thomas Johnson	12	14	.462	33	28	23	0	247	293	121	79	2.18
Pat Meaney	12	16	.429	30	25	25	0	240	309	88	60	3.15
Joseph Delaney	10	10	.500	24	19	14	0	169	221	57	49	2.61
John Luby	4	5	.444	10	10	7	0	78	88	32	17	3.15
Charles Brown	2	6	.250	11	9	9	0	89	105	44	25	2.63
John Huston	1	2	.333	5	2	2	0	35	53	33	8	4.37
J. Brodie	1	4	.200	6	5	5	0	49	84	22	4	4.56
William Quarles	1	5	.167	7	7	5	1	54	72	21	8	3.86
Robert Miller	1	6	.143	8	8	5	0	61	104	11	10	4.13
Frank Knauss	0	1	.000	1	1	0	0	4	4	3	0	6.75
Pat Fox	0	2	.000	2								
James Nolan	0	0	----	1	0	0	0	0	0	3	0	0.00

ROCHESTER   7th   47-82   .364   -38.5   John Chapman - Tim Shinnick
Browns   Pete Sweeney - John Berger

BATTERS	POS-GAMES	GP	AB	R	H	BI	2B	3B	HR	BB	SO	SB	BA
Ed Breckenridge	1B88	88	347	76	110		24	6	7			8	.317
Charles Hamburg	2B40,OF46,1B34	120	500	89	139		27	6	2			30	.278
Joseph Keenan	SS38,P,2B1	44	173	26	42		6	4	2			8	.243
John O'Brien	3B81,OF22,2B7	110	469	83	161		20	10	4			7	.343
James Daly	OF129	129	552	110	191		20	13	6			5	.346
William Lush	OF98	98	404	105	140		11	28	8			22	.347
James Garry	OF		(see multi-team players)										
John Berger	C76,SS4,OF4,3B2,2B1,P1	84	315	57	93		11	7	2			5	.295
Frank White	C40,OF22,SS3	63	238	23	54		8	4	0			4	.227
George Harper	P48,OF2	50	180	31	42		2	1	2			8	.233

ROCHESTER (cont.)
Browns

BATTERS	POS-GAMES	GP	AB	R	H	BI	2B	3B	HR	BB	SO	SB	BA
John Tighe	2B34	34	150	23	42		6	2	1			4	.280
James Duryea	P29,OF5	34	114	20	35		3	3	3			0	.307
John Warner	SS11,1B9,C3	23	88	8	18		0	4	0			1	.205
Mark Baldwin	P16,OF1	19	66	6	9		1	1	1			0	.136
William Hanrahan	SS16	16	62	13	19		2	1	0			2	.306
Franklin Lang	SS14	14	49	2	10		1	0	0			1	.204
Dan Pfenninger	SS6,3B5	11	41	5	14		2	0	0			1	.341
John McPartlin	P11	10	32	4	2		0	0	0			0	.063
Charles Hewitt	P8	8	27	3	5		0	0	0			1	.185
Francis Donahue	P6,OF2	8	25	4	8		2	0	0			0	.320
John Walters	OF6	6	24	3	3		0	0	0			1	.125
Michael Hickey	SS2,3B2	4	16	3	4		1	0	0			0	.250
George Henry	OF3	3	10	0	2		1	0	0			0	.200
Robinson	P3	3	9	2	2		0	0	0			0	.222
Stevens	P2	2	8	1	3		1	0	0			0	.375
Oldfield	P2	2	5	0	0		0	0	0			0	.000
Heckman	SS1	1	6	1	0		0	0	0			0	.000
Kenzie	SS1	1	4	2	0		0	0	0			2	.000
Johnson	P1	1	1	0	0		0	0	0			0	.000
David Gore	C1	1	1	0	0		0	0	0			0	.000
Reardon	SS1	1	0	0	0		0	0	0			0	----

PITCHERS	W	L	PCT	G	GS	CG	SH	IP	H	BB	SO	ERA
George Harper	24	21	.533	48	45	43	0	395	461	146	233	2.26
James Duryea	7	18	.280	29	27	24	0	227	324	64	72	4.35
Mark Baldwin	6	9	.400	16	15	14	0	126	156	52	44	3.21
Charles Hewitt	4	4	.500	8	6	5	0	58	83	13	10	4.19
Ed Crane	2	6	.250	9	9	7	0	61	78	32	20	3.54
John McPartlin	2	8	.200	11	10	8	0	87	114	35	23	2.91
Francis Donahue	1	5	.167	6	6	6	0	53	88	16	11	5.60
James Garry	0	1	.000	1	1	1	0	0	6	1	1	108.00
Meakim	0	1	.000	1	1	1	0	4	7	2	2	4.16
Harley Payne	0	2	.000	2	2	1	0	12	20	2	7	6.00
Stevens	0	2	.000	2	2	2	0	18	34	20	4	3.00
Robinson	0	2	.000	3	2	2	0	22	38	9	7	4.50
Joseph Keenan	0	4	.000	4	4	4	0	32	62	14	6	6.19
Oldfield	0	0	----	2	0	0	0	8	14	18	2	5.67
Johnson	0	0	----	1	0	0	0	5	6	0	0	1.80
John Berger	0	0	----	1	0	0	0	5	6	2	0	0.00

TORONTO   8th   43-76   .361   -38   Charles Maddock -
Canucks   John Chapman

BATTERS	POS-GAMES	GP	AB	R	H	BI	2B	3B	HR	BB	SO	SB	BA
Charles Lutenberg	1B110,OF1	111	464	90	134		24	2	4			17	.289
Tim Shinnick	2B	(see multi-team players)											
Gene DeMontreville	SS118	118	492	91	146		20	11	3			27	.297
Jud Smith	3B117	118	484	114	172		21	12	14			18	.355
John Freeman	OF104	104	447	101	150		28	19	6			17	.336
John Meara	OF71	71	290	42	78		3	3	0			21	.269
James Casey	OF68,C29,2B2	100	375	50	85		11	2	1			10	.227
Fred Lake	C92,OF8,1B1	102	395	65	130		17	6	5			9	.329
George Gray	P46,OF1	47	154	22	37		2	3	0			4	.240
John Deitrich	OF45	45	192	31	50		9	6	1			3	.260
Arthur Sippi	2B38	38	162	22	37		4	1	1			7	.228
William Congalton	OF13	13	47	10	8		2	1	0			3	.170
Sam Shaw	P10	10	42	6	10		0	0	0			0	.238
Bill Dinneen	P6	6	18	1	3		1	0	0			0	.167
Jeff Blakely	1B4,OF1	5	18	3	4		0	0	0			0	.222
Brunneman	P5	5	14	2	2		0	0	0			0	.143
Bernard McGarry	P4,1B1	5	12	0	3		0	0	0			0	.250
Charles Hastings	P3	3	9	0	1		0	0	0			0	.111
Al Sheppard	1B1	1	5	0	0		0	0	0			0	.000
Frank Southard	P1	1	1	0	1		0	0	0			0	1.000

PITCHERS	W	L	PCT	G	GS	CG	SH	IP	H	BB	SO	ERA
George Gray	15	27	.357	46	40	36	1	354	447	142	88	3.00
Harley Payne	10	9	.526	19	19	18	0	163	205	44	54	3.20
Ed Crane	7	18	.280	29	26	23	1	236	261	111	79	2.40
Sam Shaw	4	6	.400	10	10	9	0	84	119	48	17	3.86

TORONTO (cont.)
Canucks

PITCHERS	W	L	PCT	G	GS	CG	SH	IP	H	BB	SO	ERA
William Whitrock	3	4	.429	7	7	7	0	59	69	36	9	3.66
Brunneman	2	2	.500	5	5	3	0	37	50	20	3	3.89
Charles Hastings	1	1	.500	3	2	2	0	21	25	11	3	2.14
Bernard McGarry	1	2	.333	4	2	1	0	17	20	14	3	2.65
Henry Fournier	0	2	.000	2	2	2	0	17	34	5	4	6.88
Bill Dinneen	0	4	.000	6	5	4	0	38	55	20	10	4.74
Frank Southard	0	0	----	1	0	0	0	2	2	2	1	0.00

MULTI-TEAM PLAYERS

BATTERS	POS-GAMES	TEAMS	GP	AB	R	H	BI	2B	3B	HR	BB	SO	SB	BA
Tim Shinnick	2B115,3B6	ROC-TOR	120	472	87	112		12	11	0			20	.237
Sandy Griffin	OF100	SYR-WB	100	416	79	128		23	12	1			19	.308
James Garry	OF91,P	SPR-ROC	91	378	63	112		15	6	0			13	.296
Harley Payne	OF55,P,C1	ROC-TOR	78	291	44	82		11	4	3			4	.282
Peter Sweeney	OF12,SS31,2B8	SCR-ROC	53	210	37	59		7	2	1			7	.281
Milt Whitehead	3B49	ROC-SCR	49	196	31	53		5	3	0			3	.270
John Wente	C47,OF1	ROC-WB	48	179	27	45		8	1	3			6	.251
Joseph Delaney	P,OF4	SCR-SYR	44	144	25	36		7	2	1			0	.250
Ed Crane	P,OF5	TOR-ROC	43	136	20	44		8	3	1			0	.324
Charles M. Smith	3B13,2B5,OF,1B2	RO-PR-TO	23	91	11	19		4	0	2			1	.209
George Meakim	P,OF,1B1	WB-RO-BU	16	44	3	5		1	0	0			0	.114
William Heine	SS10,1B2	ROC-SCR	12	48	7	6		0	1	0			1	.125
Henry Fournier	P	BUF-TOR	12	38	1	9		4	0	0			0	.237
John Lawler	OF9	SP-SY-RO	9	31	11	5		0	1	0			1	.161
William Whitrock	P	TOR-PRO	8	30	3	4		0	1	1			0	.133
Joseph Corbett	SS1,3B1	SCR-TOR	2	8	0	3		0	0	0			0	.375
James Corbett	1B2	SCR-TOR	2	8	0	2		0	0	0			0	.250

TEAM BATTING

TEAMS	GP	AB	R	H	BI	2B	3B	HR	BB	SO	SB	BA
SPRINGFIELD	113	4289	937	1355		187	95	27			279	.319
PROVIDENCE	118	4411	830	1335		205	72	29			317	.303
WILKES-BARRE	111	4227	774	1223		202	109	27			162	.289
SYRACUSE	117	4299	839	1320		208	56	29			168	.307
BUFFALO	125	4691	907	1388		275	87	47			138	.296
SCRANTON	116	4181	714	1184		206	66	10			154	.283
ROCHESTER	130	4729	826	1342		177	101	42			126	.284
TORONTO	118	4294	759	1229		163	78	40			153	.286
	474	35121	6586	10376		1623	664	251			1497	.295

1896
STEINERT CUP

Immediately after the 1895 season, the two top teams in the Eastern League, the first-place Springfield Ponies and the second-place Providence Grays, squared off in a six-game playoff to claim possession of the Steinert Cup. Donated by Steinert and Sons of Providence, this "elegant silver cup" was to reward the victor of this post-season matchup.

The Steinert Cup was modeled after the Temple Cup, its major league equivalent, which had first been played for in 1894. The Steinert Cup, like the Temple Cup, called for an after-season matchup between the first- and second-place teams. The rules governing the Temple Cup stated that the first three-time winner of the cup would gain its possession. The Steinert Cup donors altered this equation, requiring three *consecutive* victories for permanent appurtenance.

The 1895 Steinert Cup playoffs started on September 16 with the first of three scheduled games in Springfield. The Ponies proceeded to sweep the trio on their homeground before traveling to Providence. There, the Grays won the first two before bowing 9-6 in the final match, allowing Springfield to claim the first Steinert Cup.

As the Eastern League 1896 campaign unfolded, the Toronto club found itself in a financial morass. In July, the club transferred to Albany in hopes of greener pastures. When these hopes proved unfounded, the club moved back to Toronto, where it finished the season.

The Providence Grays claimed the title in 1896, moving up a notch from second. Buffalo and Rochester finished close behind, with Toronto, Syracuse, Springfield, Wilkes-Barre, and Scranton much farther back. The batting title fell to Abe Lizotte of Wilkes-Barre, who hit .390 (originally .404). Jacob Drauby from Providence hit the most home runs (18).

The 1896 Steinert Cup featured first-place Providence facing off against the second-place Buffalo Bisons. Once again, the first-place team was victorious as the Grays polished off the Bisons posting 4-1, 17-13, 16-7, and 11-4 victories. Buffalo managed only two wins, 7-5 and 8-2.

No team had the opportunity to take permanent hold of the Steinert Cup, as there was only one more tilt (in 1897) for the prize. But the idea of a post-season playoff tournament didn't die with the demise of the Steinert Cup. It would be resurrected, albeit in a much different form, after the turn of the century.

PROVIDENCE
Grays

1st   71-47   .602   William Murray

BATTERS	POS-GAMES	GP	AB	R	H	BI	2B	3B	HR	BB	SO	SB	BA
Jacob Drauby	1B111	111	493	96	162		35	11	18			9	.329
James Canavan	2B118	118	500	123	170		35	20	7			64	.340
James Cooney	SS109	109	471	83	143		18	8	1			28	.304
Charles Bassett	3B118	118	519	109	154		17	6	6			29	.297
Joseph Knight	OF118	118	519	112	193		32	6	2			21	.372
Harry Lyons	OF117,SS	117	555	108	173		22	10	3			50	.312
William Murray	OF111,SS	111	432	97	130		26	8	3			75	.301
Ed Dixon	C91,1B,SS,OF	95	357	74	105		26	6	6			28	.294
George Hodson	P43	45	154	14	23		3	0	1			3	.149
William Friel	P18,SS,OF	30	101	15	20		4	1	0			2	.198
Frank Rudderham	P25	28	86	12	19		1	0	0			2	.221
Pat Dolan	P16,OF,SS	22	80	10	17		0	1	0			6	.329
John Knorr	P14	14	44	7	8		1	1	0			0	.182
Edward Lewis	P	9	31	3	6		2	0	0			1	.194
M. Bryant	PH	1	1	0	0		0	0	0			0	.000

PITCHERS	W	L	PCT	G	GS	CG	SH	IP	H	BB	SO	ERA
George Hodson				43								
Frank Rudderham				25								
William Friel				18								
Pat Dolan				16								
John Knorr				14								
Edward Lewis												

BUFFALO
Bisons

2nd   70-53   .569   -3.5   John Rowe

BATTERS	POS-GAMES	GP	AB	R	H	BI	2B	3B	HR	BB	SO	SB	BA
James Field	1B121	121	497	108	159		33	11	4			18	.320
Sam Wise	2B77	77	323	76	112		22	12	6			18	.347
Claude Ritchey	SS89,3B,OF	101	389	65	98		24	4	1			12	.252
Ed Gremminger	3B90,2B	90	374	59	108		17	2	1			11	.289
Charles Stahl	OF121,P	121	515	130	173		24	23	5			34	.336
William Goodenough	OF114	114	469	81	139		18	3	1			31	.296
William Clymer	OF107,2B13	120	513	116	140		27	7	5			46	.273
Harry Smith	C68	68	264	39	73		14	7	4			8	.277
Ed Lewee	SS37,2B32,3B19,OF	91	330	57	82		14	5	0			9	.248
William Urquhart	C59,OF14,3B,1B,2B	83	331	54	97		12	4	3			9	.293
John Wadsworth	P38	38	118	17	34		3	3	2			1	.288
James Gannon	P35	36	105	16	19		5	3	0			11	.181
George Gray	P23	23	79	14	17		3	0	0			1	.215
John Ruhland	OF,3B	9	40	9	12		4	0	0			2	.300
John Roach	P	2	3	0	1		0	0	0			0	.333
George Gaffney	P	1	2	0	1		0	0	0			0	.500
Ralph Bottenus	P	1	0	0	0		0	0	0			0	----

PITCHERS	W	L	PCT	G	GS	CG	SH	IP	H	BB	SO	ERA
John Wadsworth				38								
James Gannon				35								
George Gray				23								
John Roach												
George Gaffney												
Ralph Bottenus												
Charles Stahl												

ROCHESTER
Browns

3rd   68-58   .543   -7   Dan Shannon

BATTERS	POS-GAMES	GP	AB	R	H	BI	2B	3B	HR	BB	SO	SB	BA
Charles Dooley	1B124	124	526	95	173		46	18	3			15	.329
Dan Shannon	2B77	79	347	63	112		17	10	1			11	.323
Oliver Beard	SS126	126	553	106	192		35	4	1			20	.347
Joe Mulvey	3B112	112	468	82	133		29	8	0			20	.284
William Johnson	OF128	128	516	102	151		17	14	2			17	.293
William Bottenus	OF124	124	508	121	154		29	10	1			24	.303
James Daly	OF113	113	508	98	173		31	13	0			12	.341

ROCHESTER (cont.)
Browns

BATTERS	POS-GAMES	GP	AB	R	H	BI	2B	3B	HR	BB	SO	SB	BA
Frank Boyd	C126,1B,2B	128	491	72	127		20	4	1			18	.259
Dan McFarlan	P42	44	152	25	36		10	3	0			2	.237
Will Calihan	P19,3B	20	63	7	10		3	0	0			3	.159
Arthur Herman	P16	16	52	5	11		5	0	0			0	.212
Gus Weyhing	P	12	39	6	8		0	0	0			1	.205
William Zimmer	2B,C,3B	11	40	4	10		0	0	0			1	.250
Kelley	3B,C	6	23	0	1		0	0	0			0	.043
Cohen	3B	6	21	2	5		1	0	0			1	.238
William Day	P	6	20	3	5		1	0	0			0	.250
Seibel	OF	5	21	4	3		1	0	0			0	.143
Dan Sweeney	2B,C	4	12	1	4		0	0	0			0	.333
John Barry	2B,3B	2	11	0	4		0	0	0			1	.364
J. McDermott	P	2	5	2	1		0	0	0			0	.200
Tull	P	2	3	0	0		0	0	0			0	.000

PITCHERS	W	L	PCT	G	GS	CG	SH	IP	H	BB	SO	ERA
Dan McFarlan				42								
Will Calihan				19								
Arhtur Herman				16								
Gus Weyhing												
William Day												
J. McDermott												
Tull												

TORONTO (ALBANY)   4th   59-57   .509   -11   Al Buckenberger
Maple Leafs (Senators)

BATTERS	POS-GAMES	GP	AB	R	H	BI	2B	3B	HR	BB	SO	SB	BA
Charles Lutenberg	1B108	108	433	61	112		12	8	0			16	.259
Richard Padden	2B60	60	247	59	68		9	2	2			18	.275
Tom Delahanty	SS83	99	383	86	94		10	5	2			40	.245
Jud Smith	3B110	110	415	79	134							37	.323
John Freeman	OF114	114	445	86	135		26	14	8			25	.303
Thomas O'Brien	OF108	108	438	73	126		22	11	9			10	.288
Joseph Wright	OF88	88	361	70	104		18	9	4			37	.288
James Casey	C66,OF18,SS	95	361	85	116		16	7	1			37	.321
Harry Truby	2B31	38	139	22	37							3	.266
Sam Moran	P24,OF	38	91	9	25		0	4	0			1	.275
Bill Dinneen	P27	31	84	8	16		2	0	0			1	.190
Jack Dunn	P27	30	97	14	20		2	1	0			5	.206
Henry Staley	P24	24	81	11	21		2	0	1			0	.259
Albert Wagner	SS20,OF	20	79	12	20		2	0	1			5	.253
Joe Sugden	C	14	55	5	13		1	0	0			4	.236
Elmer Horton	P,OF	14	43	9	11		0	1	0			3	.259
William Stuart	SS	13	49	11	15		4	0	0			2	.306
Edward Boyle	C	13	44	4	7		0	0	0			1	.159
Bill Smink	C	2	8	1	0		0	0	0			0	.000
John Linnehan	C	2	7	0	0		0	0	0			0	.000
Stuart Sanford	OF	1	4	0	0		0	0	0			0	.000
James Dean	P	1	2	0	1		0	0	0			0	.500

PITCHERS	W	L	PCT	G	GS	CG	SH	IP	H	BB	SO	ERA
Bill Dinneen				27								
Jack Dunn				27								
Sam Moran				24								
Henry Staley				24								
Elmer Horton												
James Dean												

SYRACUSE   5th   59-62   .488   -13.5   Charles Reilly - George Kuntzsch
Stars

BATTERS	POS-GAMES	GP	AB	R	H	BI	2B	3B	HR	BB	SO	SB	BA
George Carey	1B122	122	492	76	149		22	5	4			11	.303
William Eagan	2B106,P	106	403	114	127		21	4	1			51	.315

SYRACUSE (cont.)
Stars

BATTERS	POS-GAMES	GP	AB	R	H	BI	2B	3B	HR	BB	SO	SB	BA
Charles Moss	SS	(see multi-team players)											
Dan Minnehan	3B73,OF49	111	447	76	138		30	8	2			17	.309
James Garry	OF109	109	452	76	123		15	4	0			19	.272
John Shearon	OF68	98	344	62	105							19	.305
Tom Bannon	OF54	54	217	48	71		12	1	1			25	.327
John Ryan	C61,OF18	91	364	49	91		18	9	1			11	.250
Joseph Delaney	P43,1B,2B,OF	49	139	20	36		6	0	0			4	.259
Ernest Mason	P48,OF	48	141	19	33		4	1	0			2	.234
Thomas Hess	C44,OF	44	161	24	34		5	1	1			3	.211
Alex Whitehill	P35	35	111	7	30		3	0	0			1	.270
Joe Harrington	3B16,SS,2B	30	122	18	28		2	4	1			4	.230
Fred Zahner	C19	20	65	4	18		2	1	0			1	.277
Vic Willis	P17	17	49	7	11		1	1	0			1	.224
George Treadway	OF	13	53	7	19		6	0	0			1	.358
George Ulrich	2B	10	41	3	10		0	0	0			4	.244
Oscar Hill	OF	7	23	2	3		0	0	0			2	.130
George Keck	C	4	12	0	2		0	0	0			0	.167
Henry Lampe	P	1	4	1	1		0	0	0			0	.250
John Rafter	C	1	1	0	0		0	0	0			0	.000
David Barber	C	1	1	0	0		0	0	0			0	.000

PITCHERS		W	L	PCT	G	GS	CG	SH	IP	H	BB	SO	ERA
Ernest Mason					48								
Joseph Delaney					43								
Alex Whitehill					35								
Vic Willis					17								
Henry Lampe													
William Eagan													

SPRINGFIELD   6th   54-64   .458   -17   Thomas Burns
Ponies

BATTERS	POS-GAMES	GP	AB	R	H	BI	2B	3B	HR	BB	SO	SB	BA
Dan Brouthers	1B50	50	204	41	77		16	9	3			10	.377
Henry Lynch	2B	(see multi-team players)											
William Fuller	SS75	74	321	65	88		6	4	1			47	.274
Peter Gilbert	3B61,2B29,1B23	111	471	91	155		31	9	0			34	.329
Ted Scheffler	OF118	118	492	120	170		31	18	3			52	.346
Richard Harley	OF65	65	257	58	87		7	6	3			18	.339
Oliver Smith	OF	(see multi-team players)											
Thomas Leahy	C58,OF37,2B	102	402	70	101		10	5	4			60	.251
William Coughlin	P42,OF,1B,SS	43	151	10	24		2	0	0			5	.159
Dan Sweeney	OF33	33	134	33	36		8	3	0			8	.269
William Shannon	SS17,3B,OF	29	109	20	24		5	0	0			4	.220
John Stricker	2B23	23	98	26	27		5	2	0			9	.276
John Leighton	OF23	23	93	12	26		2	3	0			10	.280
Ed McDonald	2B23	23	87	10	22		3	2	0			2	.253
Joe Werrick	2B,3B	14	57	7	17		3	0	0			3	.298
Fred Tenney	1B,OF,P	13	59	9	22		2	0	1			1	.386
James Duncan	C,1B,OF	12	50	8	19		2	2	1			4	.380
James Seymour	P,OF,2B	12	39	5	11		3	0	0			0	.282
Marvin Hawley	P,2B	9	23	2	7		2	0	0			0	.304
Henry Killeen	P	7	24	4	8		3	0	1			0	.333
Thomas Smith	P	7	22	2	5		0	0	0			0	.227
John McDougall	P	6	20	0	2		0	0	0			0	.100
James Collopy	2B	5	22	1	4		3	0	0			0	.182
William Inks	1B,OF	4	10	0	2		0	1	0			0	.200
Thomas Donovan	P	2	8	0	3		0	0	0			0	.375
Frank Sexton	P	1	6	1	3		1	0	0			0	.500
Thomas Burns	2B	1	5	0	2		0	0	0			0	.400
Ira Davis	2B	1	4	0	0		0	0	0			0	.000
James Brennan	1B	1	3	0	0		0	0	0			0	.000
W. Brumeyer	P	1	3	0	0		0	0	0			0	.000
McElroy	P	1	1	0	0		0	0	0			0	.000

PITCHERS		W	L	PCT	G	GS	CG	SH	IP	H	BB	SO	ERA
William Coughlin					42								
James Seymour													
Marvin Hawley													

SPRINGFIELD (cont.)
Ponies

PITCHERS	W	L	PCT	G	GS	CG	SH	IP	H	BB	SO	ERA
Henry Killeen												
Thomas Smith												
John McDougall												
Thomas Donovan												
Frank Sexton												
W. Brumeyer												
McElroy												
Fred Tenney												

WILKES-BARRE   7th   49-66   .426   -20.5   John Chapman -
Coal Barons   Howard Earl

BATTERS	POS-GAMES	GP	AB	R	H	BI	2B	3B	HR	BB	SO	SB	BA
Howard Earl	1B87,SS	93	407	50	100		18	4	0			16	.246
Frank Bonner	2B106,SS	107	476	82	162		33	13	4			6	.340
John McMahon	SS105	105	425	62	89		7	4	3			9	.209
Charles A. Smith	3B113	114	494	62	123		14	5	1			10	.249
Abe Lizotte	OF112	112	500	97	**195**		33	18	3			13	**.390**
Edward Lytle	OF110,2B	110	495	98	138		19	5	1			36	.279
Fred Betts	OF105,P	113	491	87	173		39	10	3			23	.352
William Diggins	C62,OF,2B,SS	77	315	38	98		12	6	0			4	.311
John Wente	C53,1B,OF	61	240	33	59		6	4	2			6	.246
John Keenan	P42,OF	44	152	20	35		6	3	0			8	.230
Howard Luckey	P32,OF	35	112	16	31		3	1	1			4	.277
Thomas Colcolough	P26	27	84	14	21		3	1	0			3	.250
William Goeckel	1B22	22	91	19	32		3	2	0			9	.352
William Yerrick	P17	18	62	10	13		2	1	0			0	.210
William Vaught	2B	4	16	3	4		1	0	0			2	.250

PITCHERS	W	L	PCT	G	GS	CG	SH	IP	H	BB	SO	ERA
John Keenan				42								
Howard Luckey				32								
Thomas Colcolough				26								
William Yerrick				17								
Fred Betts												

SCRANTON   8th   44-67   .396   -23.5   Michael McDermott -
Miners   Sandy Griffin

BATTERS	POS-GAMES	GP	AB	R	H	BI	2B	3B	HR	BB	SO	SB	BA
William Massey	1B40	40	172	19	57		9	2	0			0	.331
Frank Ward	2B	(see multi-team players)											
James Maguire	SS63,3B46	109	441	63	128		22	5	3			12	.290
Arlie Latham	3B44	44	178	49	46		1	2	0			39	.258
Pat Meaney	OF106,P	106	452	91	154		19	7	4			13	.341
Peter Eagan	OF101	101	431	91	145		26	8	3			39	.336
John O'Brien	OF	(see multi-team players)											
John Berger	C49,3B,OF	50	188	23	45		4	2	0			7	.239
Ed Hutchinson	1B36,2B15,C	78	304	60	73		10	4	2			11	.240
Thomas Johnson	P34,1B,2B,OF	39	127	10	22		4	0	0			0	.173
Richard Brown	P30,OF	30	109	15	22		3	0	0			0	.202
William Keister	2B17,3B,OF	27	117	13	22		1	2	0			4	.188
Edward Rafferty	C23,OF	25	92	15	29		4	0	0			1	.315
Charles Flack	OF,SS	21	76	12	18		0	0	0			2	.237
James Outcalt	P18,C	21	68	10	14		0	1	0			1	.206
William Horner	P,1B,OF	19	63	7	13		0	0	0			0	.206
Frank Bowerman	C,1B	14	41	4	12		2	1	0			3	.293
George Harper	P,OF	12	48	4	15		2	0	0			1	.308
Pearce Childs	1B,OF	9	39	14	16		3	3	3			1	.410
Michael Hickey	2B,OF,SS	8	28	6	9		2	0	0			1	.321
Joseph Corbett	P,OF	7	23	1	4		1	2	0			0	.174
John Hess	1B,C	6	24	4	4		0	1	0			0	.167
John Dietrich	3B,SS	4	14	1	2		1	0	0			0	.143
Edward Herr	P,1B	4	13	2	3		2	0	0			0	.231
Williams	1B,C	3	12	0	2		0	0	0			0	.167
Ed Bradley	OF	3	9	2	2		0	0	0			1	.222
Sam Vigneaux	C	2	7	1	1		0	0	0			1	.143

SCRANTON (cont.)
Miners

BATTERS	POS-GAMES	GP	AB	R	H	BI	2B	3B	HR	BB	SO	SB	BA
Joseph Otten	C	2	7	0	0		0	0	0			0	.000
Arch Stimmel	P	1	1	1	1		0	0	1			0	1.000
George Zeigler	P	1	1	0	0		0	0	0			0	.000

PITCHERS			W	L	PCT	G	GS	CG	SH	IP	H	BB	SO	ERA
Thomas Johnson						34								
Richard Brown						30								
James Outcalt						18								
William Horner														
George Harper														
Joseph Corbett														
Edward Herr														
Pat Meaney														
Arch Stimmel														
George Zeigler														

MULTI-TEAM PLAYERS

BATTERS	POS-GAMES	TEAMS	GP	AB	R	H	BI	2B	3B	HR	BB	SO	SB	BA
Charles Moss	SS114	SYR-SCR	114	430	58	108		16	3	0			19	.251
Frank Ward	2B83,1B14,OF	SCR-TOR	104	409	83	126		24	7	2			27	.308
Henry Lynch	2B39,SS31,OF22	SPR-ROC	92	380	94	102		18	7	1			44	.268
Charles Reilly	3B86	SYR-SPR	86	343	55	95		19	6	3			23	.277
John O'Brien	OF,2B,3B,1B	ROC-SCR	82	335	66	101		15	11	3			10	.301
Oliver Smith	OF79,P	SYR-SPR	79	317	80	102		18	7	2			23	.322
Dan Coogan	C46,1B17,2B,SS,OF	SP-PR	79	277	55	73		8	5	0			15	.264
Joe Gunson	C61,1B,2B	SPR-SCR	63	243	25	72		7	2	1			2	.296
Thomas Dowse	C26,2B13,1B,3B,OF	TO-RO	51	182	26	47		4	4	0			11	.258
Henry Gruber	P25,1B14	SPR-BUF	40	130	24	30		3	1	1			1	.231
Sandy Griffin	OF	WB-SCR	39	152	22	42		5	1	3			5	.276
Joe Herndon	P36	BUF-ROC	38	103	17	15		1	0	1			3	.146
John Easton	P24,1B,OF	SPR-ROC	32	105	14	33		5	2	0			6	.314
Harry Raymond	SS27,2B,3B	SYR-ROC	30	124	17	29		5	1	0			3	.234
Thomas Gillen	P24,OF	ROC-SCR	26	91	13	21		2	0	0			1	.231
Thomas Lovett	P25	ROC-SCR	25	95	10	24		2	1	0			0	.222
Frank McPartlin	P24	TOR-SPR	24	78	10	20		3	1	0			1	.256
Tom Startzell	P	BUF-ROC	9	21	4	9		2	0	0			1	.429
William Reidy	P	SYR-SPR	7	27	5	3		1	1	0			1	.111
Jordan	P	SYR-SPR	6	15	11	4		0	0	0			0	.267
William Milligan	P	SPR-BUF	5	13	2	5		0	2	0			0	.385
Ed Crane	P	PRO-SPR	4	15	1	5		0	0	0			0	.333
McNerney	P	SPR-BUF	2	4	1	1		0	1	0			0	.250

PITCHERS		TEAMS	W	L	PCT	G	GS	CG	SH	IP	H	BB	SO	ERA
Joe Herndon		BUF-ROC				36								
Thomas Lovett		ROC-SCR				25								
Henry Gruber		SPR-BUF				25								
Frank McPartlin		TOR-SPR				24								
John Easton		SPR-ROC				24								
Thomas Gillen		ROC-SCR				24								
Oliver Smith		SYR-SPR													
Tom Startzell		BUF-ROC													
William Reidy		SYR-SPR													
Jordan		SYR-SPR													
William Milligan		SPR-BUF													
Ed Crane		PRO-SPR													
McNerney		SPR-BUF													

TEAM BATTING

TEAMS	GP	AB	R	H	BI	2B	3B	HR	BB	SO	SB	BA
PROVIDENCE	118	4486	898	1361		227	81	47			298	.303
BUFFALO	123	4482	863	1293		225	86	32			178	.288
ROCHESTER	128	4794	877	1421		264	91	12			158	.296
TORONTO (ALB.)	117	4165	745	1133		158	80	34			212	.272
SYRACUSE	124	4385	711	1185		185	53	14			181	.270

TEAM BATTING (cont.)

TEAMS	GP	AB	R	H	BI	2B	3B	HR	BB	SO	SB	BA
SPRINGFIELD	119	4389	814	1299		193	86	23			**313**	.296
WILKES-BARRE	114	4386	691	1280		200	77	18			127	.292
SCRANTON	111	4065	692	1142		162	60	24			156	.281
	477	35152	6291	10114		1614	614	204			1623	.288

1897
DAN BROUTHERS

One of the Eastern League's most cherished records—highest batting average for a season—was set in 1897. It was not set by a dewy-cheeked phenom, nor by a player in the prime of his career. The record holder's name is Dan Brouthers. A week after the 1897 season started, Brouthers celebrated his thirty-ninth birthday.

Dan Brouthers broke into professional baseball in 1879 for the Troy National League club. After a few games in the minors, Brouthers landed with the big-league Buffalo Bisons in 1881. During the next sixteen major league years, playing for Buffalo, Detroit, three different Boston teams, Brooklyn, Baltimore, Louisville, and Philadelphia, Brouthers never once batted lower than .300. Along the way he won five batting titles, finishing with a .342 lifetime batting mark—good for eighth on the all-time major league list. In short, Dan Brouthers was one of the most talented and most feared batting stars of the nineteenth century.

During the 1896 season, the Philadelphia Phillies released Dan Brouthers. Almost immediately, he signed on with the Eastern League's Springfield Ponies. Here he batted a healthy .377 over the season's final 50 games. As it turned out, Brouthers was merely fine-tuning his game for the next year.

In 1897, Brouthers posted his finest season. Playing in nearly all of the Ponies games, Dan Brouthers rapped out 208 hits, 44 doubles, while hitting an astonishing .415 average—the best the league had ever seen or would ever see. (Note: Ed Crane hit .428 in 1887. That total included walks, which counted as hits for that year alone. The walk-hits were later discarded from the record.) Brouthers certainly had proved he wasn't washed up at 39.

Brouther's exploits could lead Springfield no higher than fourth. Above resided Syracuse, Buffalo, and Toronto. Below lay Providence, Scranton, Rochester/Montreal (on July 16, the Rochester ballpark burned, necessitating a transfer to Montreal), and Wilkes-Barre. The home run title was collected by John Freeman of Toronto with a total of 20. Pitcher John Malarkey from Syracuse won the most games (27).

After 1897, Dan Brouthers spent another two years in the Eastern League. Later he joined the Hudson River League, where he won another batting title, before finally retiring at the age of 48. His phenomenal season in 1897 remains a testament to the fact that veteran skills can frequently overcome limitations imposed by age. In this case, those limitations were not just overcome—they were stomped flat.

SYRACUSE
Stars

1st 83-50 .624 Al Buckenberger

BATTERS	POS-GAMES	GP	AB	R	H	BI	2B	3B	HR	BB	SO	SB	BA
Howard Earl	1B113	113	422	59	119		15	10	4			21	.282
William Eagan	2B135	135	493	128	151		29	6	1			50	.306
Frank Scheibeck	SS121,OF	122	420	61	100		9	7	2			13	.238
Jud Smith	3B134	134	517	120	162		27	10	6			36	.313
James Garry	OF135	135	534	94	156		19	4	1			24	.292
Abe Lizotte	OF130,1B,C	136	548	90	177		40	9	5			21	.324
Tom Bannon	OF	(see multi-team players)											
John Ryan	C80,OF	87	308	51	91		19	4	3			14	.296
Al Shaw	C62,3B,SS	63	187	24	48		12	3	1			4	.257
John Malarkey	P46,OF	46	136	17	30		2	0	0			3	.221
Henry Lampe	P38,OF	43	132	21	37		2	1	0			4	.280
Vic Willis	P40	40	120	11	23		0	0	0			0	.192
Bill Kissinger	P18,OF	19	66	5	11		0	0	0			0	.167
Ed Breckenridge	1B	13	55	6	8		3	1	0			0	.145
William Gallagher	SS	11	45	7	5		0	1	0			3	.111
James Grove	OF	9	35	4	7		2	1	0			1	.200
Elmer Horton	P,1B,2B,OF	7	19	3	4		0	0	0			1	.211
Ernest Mason	P	4	8	0	0		0	0	0			0	.000
Daniel Crough	C	3	9	1	2		1	0	0			0	.222
Thomas Dowse	C	2	6	2	1		1	0	0			0	.167

PITCHERS	W	L	PCT	G	GS	CG	SH	IP	H	BB	SO	ERA
John Malarkey	27	14	.659	46								
Henry Lampe	22	13	.629	38								
Vic Willis	21	16	.568	40								
Bill Kissinger	11	4	.733	18								
Elmer Horton												
Ernest Mason												

TORONTO
Maple Leafs

2nd 75-49 .605 -3.5 Art Irwin

BATTERS	POS-GAMES	GP	AB	R	H	BI	2B	3B	HR	BB	SO	SB	BA
Dan McGann	1B128	128	543	128	192		32	20	5			32	.354
Wallace Taylor	2B116	116	449	65	143		27	8	0			11	.319
Albert Wagner	SS88,3B	101	406	77	132		28	7	6			23	.325
Harvey Smith	3B85,2B	85	332	74	100		12	5	4			16	.301
John Freeman	OF124	124	513	107	183		32	10	20			37	.357
Robert McHale	OF118	118	520	108	152		27	5	0			50	.302
John White	OF113,3B	118	506	103	158		16	7	5			50	.312
James Casey	C90,OF	108	431	84	123		19	5	2			41	.285
William Lush	SS33,3B22,OF29,2B	91	348	128	111		15	13	9			70	.319
Frank Snyder	C37,1B,P	39	144	35	49		3	7	2			9	.340
W. Williams	P37	37	134	30	36							2	.269
Bill Dinneen	P34	34	104	11	19		2	0	0			1	.183
Elisha Norton	P27	27	72	9	16		2	1	0			3	.222
Welcome Gaston	P23	23	67	11	20		1	1	0			1	.299
Henry Staley	P19	20	57	7	14		1	0	0			1	.246
Weithoff	P	7	18	1	3		0	0	0			0	.167
George Ulrich	2B	5	22	2	2		0	0	0			0	.091
Charles Moss	SS	3	10	0	1		0	1	0			0	.100
John McDougall	P	3	10	0	0		0	0	0			0	.000

PITCHERS	W	L	PCT	G	GS	CG	SH	IP	H	BB	SO	ERA
Bill Dinneen	19	9	.679	34								
W. Williams	17	15	.531	37								
Elisha Norton	15	5	.750	27								
Welcome Gaston	12	8	.600	23								
Henry Staley	9	5	.643	19								
Weithoff												
John McDougall												
Frank Snyder												

BUFFALO Bisons

3rd 74-57 .565 -8 John Rowe

BATTERS	POS-GAMES	GP	AB	R	H	BI	2B	3B	HR	BB	SO	SB	BA
James Field	1B130	130	512	100	141		31	11	5			17	.275
Sam Wise	2B122	122	486	94	164		33	5	1			22	.338
Suter Sullivan	SS		(see multi-team players)										
Ed Gremminger	3B133	133	510	92	140		30	6	8			13	.286
Rome Grey	OF133	133	563	118	174		29	11	2			19	.309
Lawrence Gilboy	OF132	132	574	110	201		42	3	2			26	.350
William Clymer	OF130	130	543	104	146		33	4	7			26	.269
William Urquhart	C67	70	253	31	76		12	7	1			8	.319
James Brown	P42	42	127	18	27		5	2	1			0	.213
George Gray	P40	40	147	14	38		4	3	1			0	.259
Halle Souders	P27	27	93	6	13		0	0	0			0	.157
Harry Smith	C25	25	89	13	26		5	0	1			7	.292
William Wadsworth	P	10	29	4	6		0	1	1			0	.207
Les German	P	3	11	1	2		0	0	0			0	.182
Andrew Reid	C,2B	2	5	1	0		0	0	0			0	.000
R. Gregory	P	1	2	0	0		0	0	0			0	.000
Harvey Bailey	P	1	1	0	0		0	0	0			0	.000
Page	P	1	1	0	0		0	0	0			0	.000
Rockwell	P	1	1	0	0		0	0	0			0	.000

PITCHERS	W	L	PCT	G	GS	CG	SH	IP	H	BB	SO	ERA
George Gray	22	13	.629	40								
James Brown	19	17	.528	42								
Halle Souders	16	10	.615	27								
William Wadsworth												
Les German												
R. Gregory												
Harvey Bailey												
Page												
Rockwell												

SPRINGFIELD Ponies

4th 68-55 .553 -10 Thomas Burns

BATTERS	POS-GAMES	GP	AB	R	H	BI	2B	3B	HR	BB	SO	SB	BA
Dan Brouthers	1B126	126	501	112	208		44	13	15			21	.415
James Rogers	2B69	69	277	52	74		17	0	3			9	.267
William Fuller	SS119	120	500	100	126		16	2	0			29	.252
Peter Gilbert	3B119,OF,1B,2B	127	515	79	157		24	4	5			16	.305
Danny Green	OF124	124	529	134	159		28	17	6			45	.301
Oliver Smith	OF81	81	296	51	76		9	2	2			18	.257
Ted Scheffler	OF78	79	316	69	93		20	8	2			42	.294
James Duncan	C105,1B	106	372	48	95		15	0	4			8	.255
Walter Woods	OF31,P31,3B,C	70	265	50	97		20	1	0			10	.366
Robert Moore	2B58	58	214	24	50		6	0	0			2	.234
James Bannon	OF55	55	235	64	86		15	7	3			36	.366
Art Nichols	C27,OF,1B	40	139	29	35		6	0	0			14	.252
James Korwan	P26	27	81	8	15		1	2	0			1	.185
Pat Dolan	P15	18	60	14	17		4	0	0			1	.283
John Cavanaugh	SS	7	31	6	5		0	0	0			3	.161
Charles McGinnis	P	7	19	2	3		1	0	0			0	.158
George Magoon	3B,SS	6	25	3	6		1	0	0			1	.240
Scott Stratton	OF	6	20	3	5		1	0	0			1	.250
James Toft	C	3	7	0	2		0	0	0			0	.286
Richard Sullivan	C	3	3	0	0		0	0	0			0	.000
McFarland	P	1	4	1	1		0	0	0			0	.250
George Moore	SS	1	4	1	1		0	0	0			0	.250
Gildea	P	1	4	0	1		0	0	0			0	.250

PITCHERS	W	L	PCT	G	GS	CG	SH	IP	H	BB	SO	ERA
Walter Woods	16	11	.593	31								
James Korwan	14	11	.560	26								
Pat Dolan	9	4	.692	15								
Charles McGinnis												
McFarland												
Gildea												

PROVIDENCE Grays

| PROVIDENCE Grays | 5th | 68-60 | .521 | -12.5 | William Murray |

BATTERS	POS-GAMES	GP	AB	R	H	BI	2B	3B	HR	BB	SO	SB	BA
Jacob Drauby	1B101,OF	104	413	71	121		20	7	10			7	.293
Curtis Weigand	2B108,3B26	134	590	114	167		23	14	11			40	.283
James Cooney	SS126	126	480	70	129		17	1	0			14	.269
Charles Bassett	3B104,1B25	129	507	63	129		21	3	6			7	.255
Harry Lyons	OF131	131	570	91	173		17	3	1			33	.304
Joseph Knight	OF128	128	528	100	177		36	9	0			13	.335
William Murray	OF65	65	235	33	59		9	2	0			17	.254
Ed Dixon	C103,OF,1B,SS	120	465	77	129		21	5	6			18	.299
William Braun	P45,OF	57	166	21	47		6	1	2			2	.283
Dan Coogan	C25,OF	50	153	23	34		1	1	0			5	.222
George Hodson	P41	41	118	16	23		2	0	0			1	.195
John Egan	P33,OF	34	101	11	12		1	0	0			4	.119
Charles Abbey	OF30	30	113	25	31		3	0	0			9	.274
John O'Brien	2B25	25	91	18	24		0	1	1			11	.264
Frank Rudderham	P23	23	70	6	12		1	0	0			0	.172
George Yeager	OF,1B	11	35	7	10		2	0	0			0	.286
William Friel	OF	10	37	4	9		2	1	0			2	.243

PITCHERS	W	L	PCT	G	GS	CG	SH	IP	H	BB	SO	ERA
George Hodson	23	14	.622	41								
William Braun	22	18	.550	45								
John Egan	17	14	.548	33								
Frank Rudderham	8	13	.381	23								

SCRANTON Miners

| SCRANTON Miners | 6th | 53-60 | .469 | -20 | Sandy Griffin |

BATTERS	POS-GAMES	GP	AB	R	H	BI	2B	3B	HR	BB	SO	SB	BA
William Massey	1B114	114	463	69	145		23	10	3			14	.313
Frank Bonner	2B118	118	492	83	177		28	10	2			14	.360
Oliver Beard	SS		(see multi-team players)										
James Maguire	3B118	118	448	48	98		16	4	0			4	.219
Peter Eagan	OF98	98	420	77	127		21	2	5			14	.302
John Walters	OF83	83	349	67	119		17	4	0			3	.341
Jack O'Brien	OF		(see multi-team players)										
Frank Boyd	C75,1B,OF	81	274	26	50		13	2	0			10	.201
Joe Gunson	C48,OF	57	197	20	45		1	5	0			9	.229
Sandy Griffin	OF41	43	165	23	58		9	3	1			1	.352
Thomas Gillen	P34	34	112	15	16		1	1	0			2	.143
George Harper	P31	31	105	13	21		3	1	0			2	.200
Charles Morse	P24	25	88	7	14		3	1	0			0	.165
Thomas Johnson	P11	11	39	3	4		1	0	0			0	.103
Stan Yerkes	P	2	8	1	1		0	0	0			0	.125

PITCHERS	W	L	PCT	G	GS	CG	SH	IP	H	BB	SO	ERA
Thomas Gillen	15	16	.484	34								
George Harper	13	14	.481	31								
Charles Morse				24									
Thomas Johnson	5	6	.454	11								
Stan Yerkes													

ROCHESTER / MONTREAL Blackbirds / Royals

| ROCHESTER / MONTREAL Blackbirds / Royals | 7th | 45-76 | .372 | -32 | Dan Shannon - George Weidman - Charles Dooley |

BATTERS	POS-GAMES	GP	AB	R	H	BI	2B	3B	HR	BB	SO	SB	BA
Charles Dooley	1B122	122	519	80	155		27	13	6			14	.299
Dan Shannon	2B		(see multi-team players)										
Frank Shannon	SS124	124	519	114	156		20	9	4			31	.301
Joe Mulvey	3B58	58	234	29	63		8	4	0			10	.269
John Richter	OF101,2B,3B	121	500	78	153		21	8	6			21	.306
William Bottenus	OF		(see multi-team players)										
John Shearon	OF		(see multi-team players)										
McNamara	C32	35	126	19	32							4	.254

ROCHESTER / MONTREAL (cont.)
Blackbirds / Royals

BATTERS	POS-GAMES	GP	AB	R	H	BI	2B	3B	HR	BB	SO	SB	BA
Henry Lynch	OF83,2B	94	365	87	110		14	4	2			38	.301
Edward Henry	3B39,2B33	72	281	39	91		11	1	4			8	.324
William Yerrick	P35	35	110	13	11		2	0	0			0	.100
John Berger	OF16,C,2B	33	116	14	26		4	0	0			1	.224
James Gannon	P33,OF	33	99	9	17		2	3	0			0	.172
Dan McFarlan	P32,OF	32	111	24	35		6	2	5			0	.315
Ralph Frary	C28	28	103	19	30		8	2	2			2	.291
W. McFarland	P19	19	58	7	19		1	0	0			0	.328
Edward Lytle	OF17	17	70	12	19		3	1	0			2	.271
Richard Butler	C,2B,OF	16	67	15	19		3	3	3			2	.284
Robert Becker	P16	16	54	3	10		0	0	0			1	.185
John O'Neill	C15	15	51	4	13		3	1	0			2	.241
Charles Vaught	2B	11	47	8	9		1	0	1			2	.191
Pat McCauley	C	5	21	2	6		1	0	0			0	.286
George Weidman	OF	5	17	3	2		0	0	0			0	.118
Phil Geier	2B	5	15	2	6		2	0	0			0	.400
Van Patterson	C	4	17	1	3		0	0	0			0	.176
Belcourt	P	4	14	2	7		0	0	0			0	.500
Joe Herndon	P	4	12	2	3		0	0	0			0	.250
Cotton	P	3	5	2	2		0	0	0			0	.400
Gallagher	P	2	2	0	0		0	0	0			0	.000
Williams	P	1	5	0	1		0	0	0			0	.200
O'Brien	OF	1	4	0	1		0	0	0			0	.250
Charles Carr	C	1	4	0	1		0	0	0			0	.250
Buckheart	C	1	4	0	1		0	0	0			0	.250
James Corbett	1B	1	4	0	0		0	0	0			0	.000
Mark Mason	P	1	3	0	1		0	0	0			0	.333

PITCHERS	W	L	PCT	G	GS	CG	SH	IP	H	BB	SO	ERA
William Yerrick	16	16	.500	35								
Dan McFarlan	12	12	.500	32								
James Gannon	8	21	.276	33								
W. McFarland	6	8	.429	19								
Robert Becker	4	12	.250	16								
Belcourt												
Joe Herndon												
Cotton												
Gallagher												
Williams												
Mark Mason												

WILKES-BARRE
Coal Barons

8th   30-85   .261   -44   Abner Powell - Dan Shannon

BATTERS	POS-GAMES	GP	AB	R	H	BI	2B	3B	HR	BB	SO	SB	BA
William Goeckel	1B118,P10,SS	118	491	71	162		20	3	1			22	.330
Dan Shannon	2B	(see multi-team players)											
John McMahon	SS79	79	297	24	72		12	2	0			12	.243
Charles Atherton	3B53	53	196	28	64		16	7	5			8	.327
Fred Betts	OF119,P	120	485	83	142		28	4	5			11	.293
Frederick Odwell	OF,P30	72	258	39	74		4	5	4			16	.287
Pat Meaney	OF	(see multi-team players)											
William Diggins	C81,1B,SS,OF	81	324	30	92		14	0	2			3	.284
John Gonding	C49,OF,3B	63	224	27	54		2	1	2			9	.241
John Keenan	P38,2B	38	130	7	20		3	0	0			8	.154
Charles Prowse	SS31	31	113	9	26		3	1	0			3	.230
John Sharrott	OF29	29	109	29	27		3	2	1			14	.248
Abner Powell	OF27	27	110	17	24		3	0	0			9	.218
Sam Mills	2B26	26	104	13	30		3	1	0			7	.289
Charles Sholta	2B21	21	82	13	18		3	0	0			3	.220
J. Brott	OF,3B	11	47	7	13		3	0	0			2	.277
Thomas Colcolough	P	11	37	5	8		1	0	0			1	.216
Case Patten	P	10	33	0	5		1	0	0			0	.152
Lucien Smith	P	10	17	2	3		0	0	0			0	.176
Sheehan	P	9	28	2	3		0	0	0			0	.107
John Roach	P	6	18	1	5		0	1	0			0	.278
Manville	P	6	18	2	2		0	0	0			1	.111
Johnson	P	3	10	2	0		0	0	0			1	.000
William Ritchie	3B	3	9	1	1		0	0	0			1	.111
Charles Collare	OF	2	6	0	1		0	0	0			0	.167

WILKES-BARRE (cont.)
Coal Barons

PITCHERS	W	L	PCT	G	GS	CG	SH	IP	H	BB	SO	ERA
John Keenan	10	26	.278	38								
Frederick Odwell	7	22	.241	30								
William Goeckel	6	4	.600									
Thomas Colcolough												
Case Patten												
Lucien Smith												
Sheehan												
John Roach												
Manville												
Johnson												
Fred Betts												

MULTI-TEAM PLAYERS

BATTERS	POS-GAMES	TEAMS	GP	AB	R	H	BI	2B	3B	HR	BB	SO	SB	BA
William Bottenus	OF115	R/M-WB	115	453	87	114		15	7	1			16	.263
Suter Sullivan	SS112	BUF-SCR	113	413	74	123		21	6	8			12	.298
John Shearon	OF110	SYR-R/M	111	467	89	133		25	5	4			16	.285
Jack O'Brien	OF108,SS,1B	SCR-SYR	111	435	93	136		17	5	1			31	.313
Tom Bannon	OF105	SYR-R/M	111	401	78	110		18	9	3			38	.274
Dan Shannon	2B104	ROC-WB	106	452	66	118		15	3	2			6	.261
Pat Meaney	OF88,P	SCR-WB	93	362	60	113		16	4	1			13	.312
Oliver Beard	SS84	SCR-SYR	84	362	59	118		19	6	2			11	.326
John Barry	SS59,OF	BUF-SCR	80	295	47	78		11	1	4			21	.264
Charles A. Smith	3B70	WB-R/M	71	274	25	70		10	0	1			6	.255
Fred Zahner	C57,OF,1B	R/M-BUF	59	192	26	51		5	4	1			5	.266
Willard Mains	P43	SPR-TOR	45	133	19	40		6	0	1			0	.301
James Daly	OF41	SCR-WB	41	151	21	45		9	2	0			5	.298
William Baker	C27,OF	TOR-R/M	37	119	18	38		4	0	0			0	.319
William Wellner	P23	SCR-WB	23	73	5	19		2	0	0			1	.260
Frank McPartlin	P23	TOR-BUF	23	71	7	14		2	2	1			0	.197
Bert Inks	P16	SPR-BUF	16	46	3	11		2	0	0			0	.239
William Coughlin	P15	SPR-WB	15	47	7	10		1	0	0			2	.213
Alex Whitehill	P,OF	SYR-SPR	7	15	0	2		0	0	0			0	.133
Fallon	P	SCR-SPR	2	6	0	0		0	0	0			0	.000

PITCHERS		TEAMS	W	L	PCT	G	GS	CG	SH	IP	H	BB	SO	ERA
Willard Mains		SPR-TOR	20	14	.588	43								
Frank McPartlin		BUF-TOR	11	7	.611	23								
Bert Inks		SPR-BUF	6	7	.462	16								
William Wellner		WB-SCR	6	16	.273	23								
William Coughlin		SPR-WB	3	7	.300	15								
Alex Whitehill		SYR-SPR												
Fallon		SCR-SPR												

1898
WAR FEVER

Baseball's coexistence with the two major wars of the twentieth century is well chronicled. Both World War I and World War II had a profound influence on the game, both on and off the field. What is not so well chronicled is another conflict that occurred just before the turn of the nineteenth century. Looking back, this war appears as a mere snag in the tapestry of American History. But to the people of 1898 it appeared as big as life.

In February 1898, the United States battleship *Maine* exploded in Havana, Cuba. Spain, which was in control of the island, was blamed for the tragedy. The American outcry was swift and angry; the public wanted Spain to pay. The United States government responded by declaring war on Spain in April 1898.

As the war against Spain progressed through the spring and summer of 1898, "war fever" gripped the country. This fever combined the excitement of potential conflict with the fear of actual participation. Americans were genuinely concerned about such issues as the draft and possible Spanish invasion. Activities like baseball were put on the back burner.

The Spanish-American War's effect on baseball was manifested in a variety of ways. Baseball owners were required to pay a war tax. Several minor leagues, such as the Texas and Southern leagues, were forced to dissolve because of lack of interest. And several ballplayers signed up for active duty.

The Eastern League of 1898 managed to stagger through the season relatively unscathed. Before the season, Montreal, which had finished up for Rochester the year before, replaced the Scranton franchise. However, once again, Rochester couldn't finish the season as they moved to Ottawa in mid–July. At the conclusion of the season, the new team, Montreal, surprisingly found itself in first place by three games over Wilkes-Barre. The rest of the teams, all clustered within 18 games of Montreal, finished in the following order: Buffalo, Providence, Syracuse, Springfield, and Rochester/Ottawa. The leading batter, John Freeman (.347), graced the roster of the Toronto Maple Leafs.

The United States' war with Spain was wrapped up rather quickly during the summer of 1898. Decisive American victories in Cuba, Puerto Rico, and the Philippines caused the Spanish to sue for peace in August. The war's long-term effect on baseball proved negligible as matters returned to normal the next year. However, the events of 1898 showed that baseball could exist in a country at war, although on an altered, less-important level. This proved a good lesson to remember as America faced much more formidable wars in the decades to follow.

MONTREAL Royals   1st   68-48   .586   Charles Dooley

BATTERS	POS-GAMES	GP	AB	R	H	BI	2B	3B	HR	BB	SO	SB	BA
Charles Dooley	1B95	95	375	54	119							15	.317
John O'Brien	2B	(see multi-team players)											
Frank Scheibeck	SS116	116	450	79	113							24	.251
Edward Henry	3B115	115	406	50	102							14	.252
Tom Bannon	OF119	119	491	87	141							42	.287
John Shearon	OF116	116	455	79	134							16	.295
John Barry	OF78,1B18	112	428	88	140							26	.327
Richard Butler	C57,OF20	78	255	31	63							12	.247
Fred Jacklitsch	C50	66	211	29	48							11	.228
Dan McFarlan	P47	56	184	27	42							3	.228
Miller	2B39	39	149	20	30							9	.201
Halle Souders	P36	36	104	15	19							2	.183
Bert Abbey	P25	25	71	3	11							1	.155

PITCHERS		W	L	PCT	G	GS	CG	SH	IP	H	BB	SO	ERA
Dan McFarland					47								
Halle Souders					36								
Bert Abbey					25								

WILKES-BARRE Coal Barons   2nd   62-48   .564   -3   Dan Shannon

BATTERS	POS-GAMES	GP	AB	R	H	BI	2B	3B	HR	BB	SO	SB	BA
William Goeckel	1B103	103	446	96	134							40	.301
Charles Atherton	2B101	101	402	60	116							22	.289
Suter Sullivan	SS68	68	283	47	85							6	.300
William Coughlin	3B47	47	171	21	53							5	.310
Bill Halligan	OF99	101	416	73	123							9	.296
William Wright	OF58	58	210	57	78							4	.371
John Richter	OF54,3B44	98	386	63	115							17	.298
Harry Smith	C72	76	271	30	61							7	.225
John Gonding	C41	80	279	42	73							8	.262
Frederick Odwell	OF50	53	216	29	66							10	.306
Case Patten	P40	40	117	7	14							1	.120
John McMahon	SS34	34	123	14	26							5	.211
Bill Duggleby	P26	28	94	6	18							1	.191
Jamison	P24	24	75	6	14							2	.187
John Keenan	P19	19	60	4	13							1	.217

PITCHERS		W	L	PCT	G	GS	CG	SH	IP	H	BB	SO	ERA
Case Patten					40								
Bill Duggleby					26								
Jamison					24								
John Keenan					19								

TORONTO Maple Leafs   3rd   64-55   .538   -5.5   Art Irwin

BATTERS	POS-GAMES	GP	AB	R	H	BI	2B	3B	HR	BB	SO	SB	BA
Ben Beaumont	1B53	53	210	30	55							5	.262
Wallace Taylor	2B121	121	468	58	139							6	.297
Frank Gatins	SS112	118	467	83	136							9	.291
James Casey	3B71,C34	122	516	**123**	169							**66**	.328
John Freeman	OF122	122	496	112	172							24	**.347**
Rome Grey	OF122	122	**543**	110	**174**							21	.320
Jim Hannivan	OF	(see multi-team players)											
Frank Snyder	C62	62	226	30	59							10	.261
Fox	3B49	54	199	45	53							17	.267
W. Williams	P37	41	128	21	39							2	.305
Welcome Gaston	P32	37	134	16	29							0	.216
Jack Carney	1B30	32	139	20	43							3	.309
Kirtley Baker	P30	30	90	16	21							0	.233
McFarland		17	38	5	11							0	.290

TORONTO (cont.)
Maple Leafs

PITCHERS	W	L	PCT	G	GS	CG	SH	IP	H	BB	SO	ERA
W. Williams				37								
Welcome Gaston				32								
Kirtley Baker				30								

BUFFALO 4th 62-60 .508 -9 John Rowe
Bisons

BATTERS	POS-GAMES	GP	AB	R	H	BI	2B	3B	HR	BB	SO	SB	BA
William Urquhart	1B69,C21	100	389	56	102							6	.262
Sam Wise	2B123	123	497	77	144							16	.290
Frank Shannon	SS80	80	333	56	90							32	.270
Ed Gremminger	3B122	122	467	74	126							11	.270
John White	OF123	124	524	91	144							30	.275
Ed Householder	OF71,1B31	102	413	56	129							9	.312
James Garry		(see multi-team players)											
William Diggins	C105	107	385	46	107							8	.278
James Brown	P44	48	146	14	31							1	.212
James Toman	SS42	42	162	19	26							2	.161
George Gray	P37	38	134	20	30							1	.224
Morris Amole	P25	25	84	9	19							0	.226

PITCHERS	W	L	PCT	G	GS	CG	SH	IP	H	BB	SO	ERA
James Brown				44								
George Gray				37								
Morris Amole				25								

PROVIDENCE 5th 58-60 .492 -11 William Murray
Clamdiggers

BATTERS	POS-GAMES	GP	AB	R	H	BI	2B	3B	HR	BB	SO	SB	BA
Jacob Drauby	1B57	57	233	41	68							10	.292
E. Canavan	2B37,1B44	119	484	103	142							50	.293
James Cooney	SS100	100	371	46	89							11	.240
John Cassidy	3B57	67	218	45	84							13	.385
Henry Lynch	OF106	106	423	105	113							66	.267
Harry Lyons	OF77	77	334	48	82							13	.246
John Walters	OF	(see multi-team players)											
Pat Crisham	C83,OF23	109	444	69	126							22	.284
Thomas Leahy	C33,OF25,SS16	80	278	56	71							27	.255
William Braun	P34	40	121	23	28							4	.231
William Murray	OF38	39	142	15	41							24	.289
John Egan	P39	39	109	19	22							1	.202
Tom Stouch	2B37	37	138	15	33							8	.239
George Noblit	OF33	34	132	19	29							5	.220
Tom News	1B16	19	74	12	19							2	.257
Frank Rudderham	P18	18	55	4	10							1	.182
George Hodson	P16	16	41	5	6							0	.146
Roy Evans	P15	15	55	1	10							0	.182

PITCHERS	W	L	PCT	G	GS	CG	SH	IP	H	BB	SO	ERA
John Egan				39								
William Braun				34								
Frank Rudderham				18								
George Hodson				16								
Roy Evans				15								

SYRACUSE 6th 52-63 .452 -15.5 George Kuntzsch
Stars

BATTERS	POS-GAMES	GP	AB	R	H	BI	2B	3B	HR	BB	SO	SB	BA
Howard Earl	1B66	66	243	36	69							8	.284
George Smith	2B42	42	161	22	33							5	.205

SYRACUSE (cont.)
Stars

BATTERS	POS-GAMES	GP	AB	R	H	BI	2B	3B	HR	BB	SO	SB	BA
James Maguire	SS25	25	82	6	15							6	.183
Jud Smith	3B76	76	306	56	91							20	.297
Jack O'Brien	OF96	110	440	71	148							27	.336
Abe Lizotte	OF84,1B29	115	442	47	121							16	.274
James Hannivan	OF	(see multi-team players)											
Frank Burrell	C61,1B22	87	306	31	73							3	.239
Bob Becker	P30	45	141	23	37							1	.262
John Malarkey	P39	42	134	15	20							4	.149
Fred Lake	C33	36	118	16	24							2	.203
William Eagan	2B24	24	88	15	20							4	.227
Al Shaw	C23	23	77	7	15							1	.195
George Blackburn	P19	23	71	10	15							2	.211
George Bone	SS22	22	78	2	11							1	.141

PITCHERS		W	L	PCT	G	GS	CG	SH	IP	H	BB	SO	ERA
John Malarkey					39								
Bob Becker					30								
George Blackburn					19								

SPRINGFIELD   7th   48-63   .432   -17.5
Ponies

BATTERS	POS-GAMES	GP	AB	R	H	BI	2B	3B	HR	BB	SO	SB	BA
William Massey	1B	(see multi-team players)											
Harry Gleason	2B50,SS20	72	267	28	53							7	.199
Charles Reilly	SS73	79	295	42	72							9	.244
Peter Gilbert	3B44	44	175	15	44							3	.252
Danny Green	OF87	87	356	66	115							27	.323
Pat Dolan	OF78,P16	96	376	62	116							14	.309
James Bannon	OF	(see multi-team players)											
Art Nichols	C86,3B19	107	438	94	136							42	.311
George Hemming	OF36,P21	59	207	29	60							2	.290
John Pappalau	P36	37	123	11	18							0	.146
James Korwan	P33	33	91	9	12							0	.132
Tom Hernon	OF26	26	105	20	36							8	.343
James Rogers	2B24	24	93	6	24							0	.258
William Friel		24	76	12	20							2	.263
Callopy	3B20	20	76	4	10							0	.132
Shea	C19	19	67	3	12							0	.179
David Pickett	OF15	15	63	7	19							0	.302

PITCHERS		W	L	PCT	G	GS	CG	SH	IP	H	BB	SO	ERA
John Pappalau					36								
James Korwan					33								
George Hemming					21								
Pat Dolan					19								

ROCHESTER / OTTAWA   8th   53-70   .431   -18.5   William Clymer -
Patriots / Wanderers   Sandy Griffin

BATTERS	POS-GAMES	GP	AB	R	H	BI	2B	3B	HR	BB	SO	SB	BA
Michael Kelley	1B63	63	252	42	71							10	.282
Frank Bonner	2B104	120	490	72	146							12	.298
Joseph Bean	SS101	101	368	58	88							12	.239
William Keister	3B93	95	398	66	128							14	.322
William Clymer	OF103,2B19	122	455	75	120							29	.264
Robert McHale	OF88	92	388	57	110							6	.284
Joseph Knight	OF	(see multi-team players)											
Frank Boyd	C86	97	334	30	64							6	.192
Joe Gunson	C35	45	169	17	41							3	.243
Elmer Horton	P31	35	118	13	19							4	.161
George Harper	P30	30	98	5	10							2	.102
Charles Morse	P18	22	83	7	11							0	.133
James Gannon	P15	22	69	9	14							0	.203

ROCHESTER / OTTAWA (cont.)
Patriots / Wanderers

BATTERS	POS-GAMES	GP	AB	R	H	BI	2B	3B	HR	BB	SO	SB	BA
Joe Herndon	P16	16	50	5	11							3	.220
Stan Yerkes	P15	15	47	4	9							0	.191

PITCHERS		W	L	PCT	G	GS	CG	SH	IP	H	BB	SO	ERA
Elmer Horton					31								
George Harper					30								
Charles Morse					18								
Joe Herndon					16								
Stan Yerkes					15								
James Gannon					15								

MULTI-TEAM PLAYERS

BATTERS	POS-GAMES	TEAMS	GP	AB	R	H	BI	2B	3B	HR	BB	SO	SB	BA
John Walters	OF119	R/O-PRO	119	501	96	143							25	.286
Jim Hannivan	OF69,SS45	SYR-TOR	114	477	91	157							16	.329
William Massey	1B113	SPR-R/O	113	471	71	142							16	.302
John O'Brien	2B113	SYR-MON	113	431	63	104							26	.241
Curtis Weigand	3B80,2B18	SPR-R/O	111	403	60	101							28	.251
Sandy Griffin	OF105	R/O-BU-WB	105	429	70	138							12	.322
James Bannon	OF94	SPR-MON	104	438	87	122							35	.279
James Garry	OF94	SYR-BUF	94	440	75	117							24	.266
William Lush	3B43,SS21,2B16	SPR-SYR	92	340	87	93							53	.274
Joseph Knight	OF90	WB-R/O	90	358	62	121							8	.338
Mike Lawrence	OF75	BUF-SYR	89	332	39	84							9	.253
James Field	1B55	BUF-R/O	56	231	29	60							6	.260
Dan Brouthers	1B50	SPR-TOR	50	189	42	63							2	.333
James Duncan	C32	SPR-TOR	32	114	23	31							1	.272
Lawrence Gilboy	OF26	BUF-SYR	26	112	12	29							7	.259
Peter Eagan	OF24	R/O-BUF	24	92	9	23							3	.251
Elsey		MON-R/O	21	78	12	19							7	.244
Bill Smink	C18	MON-SPR	20	63	13	23							4	.365
Henry Vorhees	P17	SYR-MON	19	53	5	10							0	.189
Sheehan	OF18	TOR-BUF	18	69	13	25							2	.362

PITCHERS		TEAMS	W	L	PCT	G	GS	CG	SH	IP	H	BB	SO	ERA
Henry Vorhees		SYR-MON				17								

1899
FROM THE ASHES

On July 16, 1897, Rochester's Eastern League ballpark burned to the ground. The team, sometimes known as the Browns (named for the Kodak Brownie camera; Kodak's headquarters were located in Rochester) was forced to relocate to Montreal for the rest of the season. In 1898, bad luck continued to dog the team as financial troubles forced the team to seek greener pastures in July—this time in Ottawa. Undaunted, Rochester decided to give baseball another try, reorganizing a new team for 1899.

Joining Rochester in the 1899 Eastern League were two new entries. Worcester and Hartford took the places of Wilkes-Barre and Buffalo. To christen its new team, Rochester chose a new name. No longer would they known as the Browns, Blackbirds, Patriots, or any one of the half-dozen names used previously. From now on they would be called the Rochester Bronchos.

As 1899 unfolded, for the first time in several years, all eight Eastern League teams finished the season intact and in their original locations. But the big surprise of the campaign proved to be the play of the revived Rochester club. In the two previous years, with teams that finished the season in other locales, the team had finished seventh in 1897 and eighth in 1898. This trend was turned on its head in 1899 as the Bronchos roared to the pennant by a comfortable margin over Montreal. The newcomers from Worcester finished a strong third, while Toronto, Springfield, and Hartford were clustered around the .500 mark. Providence and Springfield finished in the last two spots. The league's best batting total was turned in by Toronto's James Bannon (.341).

Rochester's last-to-first accomplishment was the first of its kind in the league, a feat to be repeated only a handful of times in the years to come. But the most important fact is that after two years of disruption, this 1899 Rochester team finished the season in one piece. This started a remarkable legacy. From 1899 to the present day, in each and every year, a Rochester team has played in the International League, completing every season. This is an achievement no other city or team can come close to matching.

ROCHESTER
Bronchos

1st   72-43   .626   Al Buckenberger

BATTERS	POS-GAMES	GP	AB	R	H	BI	2B	3B	HR	BB	SO	SB	BA
Harry O'Hagen	1B102	112	428	78	121							42	.283
George Smith	2B113	113	459	75	133							39	.290
Joseph Bean	SS103	103	358	55	105							23	.296
James Burke	3B113	113	398	60	117							33	.294
Count Campau	OF113	113	462	92	129							36	.279
George Barclay	OF89	92	362	60	105							31	.290
Cavelle	OF	(see multi-team players)											
Bill Smink	C108	110	413	72	128							27	.310
Charles Morse	P35	35	113	13	24							4	.212
Bob Becker	P32	34	101	14	22							1	.218
Bert Conn	P31	31	93	14	22							1	.237
Ed Householder	OF27	27	100	20	35							1	.350
Coogan		24	78	11	13							3	.167
C. Bowen	P24	24	76	10	14							1	.184

PITCHERS	W	L	PCT	G	GS	CG	SH	IP	H	BB	SO	ERA
Charles Morse				35								
Bob Becker				32								
Bert Conn				31								
C. Bowen				24								

MONTREAL
Royals

2nd   61-50   .554   -9   Charles Dooley

BATTERS	POS-GAMES	GP	AB	R	H	BI	2B	3B	HR	BB	SO	SB	BA
Charles Dooley	1B116	116	459	72	131							18	.285
Abbie Johnson	2B118	118	458	76	122							28	.266
Frank Scheibeck	SS114	114	462	80	105							29	.227
Edward Henry	3B115	115	419	53	117							5	.279
Tom Bannon	OF117	117	464	82	127							64	.274
John Shearon	OF82	82	340	44	85							15	.250
George Bannon	OF78	78	280	35	73							26	.261
Fred Jacklitsch	C91	102	340	59	99							32	.291
Pat Moran	C34	51	150	31	40							8	.267
Bill Duggleby	P42	42	121	16	32							1	.264
Halle Souders	P41	41	108	19	26							3	.241
Harry Felix	P35	38	112	13	27							4	.241
Frederick Odwell	OF34	34	130	15	28							6	.215
John Richter	OF21	30	111	14	24							3	.216

PITCHERS	W	L	PCT	G	GS	CG	SH	IP	H	BB	SO	ERA
Bill Duggleby				42								
Halle Souders				41								
Harry Felix				35								

WORCESTER
Farmers

3rd   58-51   .532   -11   Frank Leonard

BATTERS	POS-GAMES	GP	AB	R	H	BI	2B	3B	HR	BB	SO	SB	BA
Charles Carr	1B88	94	376	59	121							8	.322
Martin McQuaid	2B44	44	154	26	26							3	.169
Joe Harrington	SS41	67	265	39	70							4	.264
Charles Kuhns	3B91,SS22	113	485	84	158							17	.326
Joseph Rickert	OF112	112	454	111	133							39	.292
Charles Frisbee	OF74	74	304	72	110							26	.362
John Sharrott	OF67	67	272	62	72							17	.265
George Yeager	C63	90	326	61	103							11	.316
Kitty Bransfield	C57,OF19	89	330	58	104							17	.315
Elmer Horton	P31	39	131	23	30							6	.229
Henry Lampe	P31	38	116	17	34							1	.293
Fred Klobedanz	P32	37	111	17	27							2	.243
Gus Klopf	SS27	27	103	10	22							2	.214
Jim Smith		23	83	17	24							4	.289
Miller		23	78	9	20							0	.256

WORCESTER(cont.)
Farmers

PITCHERS	W	L	PCT	G	GS	CG	SH	IP	H	BB	SO	ERA
Fred Klobedanz				32								
Henry Lampe				31								
Elmer Horton				31								

TORONTO   4th   55-55   .500   -14.5   Wallace Taylor
Maple Leafs

BATTERS	POS-GAMES	GP	AB	R	H	BI	2B	3B	HR	BB	SO	SB	BA
Ben Beaumont	1B114	114	438	53	117							20	.267
Frederick Roat	2B67	71	274	24	66							4	.241
Al Wagner	SS63,OF22	93	372	69	112							25	.301
Jud Smith	3B107	107	430	78	134							24	.312
Rome Grey	OF112	112	458	90	145							33	.317
Jim Hannivan	OF111	113	443	84	132							29	.298
James Bannon	OF48,SS22,2B21	111	454	112	155							44	**.341**
Jack Rothfuss	C67	77	275	35	65							6	.237
W. Williams	P35	43	129	13	28							1	.217
J. Brown	OF23	36	117	18	31							6	.265
A. Alloway	P31	31	86	17	18							2	.209
John Sutthoff	P30	30	92	12	14							0	.152
Richard Butler	C26	27	91	14	22							4	.242
Wallace Taylor	2B15	18	65	12	25							1	.385
Harry Bemis		17	61	7	12							2	.197
Davis		16	62	6	15							2	.242

PITCHERS	W	L	PCT	G	GS	CG	SH	IP	H	BB	SO	ERA
W. Williams				35								
A. Alloway				31								
John Sutthoff				30								

SPRINGFIELD   5th   52-56   .481   -16.5   Thomas Brown
Ponies

BATTERS	POS-GAMES	GP	AB	R	H	BI	2B	3B	HR	BB	SO	SB	BA
George Hemming	1B75	95	384	69	122							4	.318
Walt Curley	2B73	77	313	54	98							22	.313
Frank Shannon	SS113	113	434	82	120							26	.277
Burt Myers	3B109	109	395	57	109							21	.276
Thomas Campbell	OF112	112	458	75	139							12	.304
Pat Dolan	OF108	113	447	80	132							21	.295
Thomas Brown	OF108	108	402	65	90							22	.224
Ed Phelps	C86	86	298	45	74							13	.248
JohnPappalau	P40	40	127	13	26							3	.205
Joe Gunson	C22	29	94	12	26							4	.277
Harry Gleason	2B25	26	87	14	20							4	.230
Kirtley Baker	P20	20	62	11	13							0	.215
Charles Pittinger	P15	18	59	4	10							7	.169

PITCHERS	W	L	PCT	G	GS	CG	SH	IP	H	BB	SO	ERA
John Pappalau				40								
Kirtley Baker				20								
Charles Pittinger				15								

HARTFORD   6th   50-56   .472   -17.5   Billy Barnie
Indians

BATTERS	POS-GAMES	GP	AB	R	H	BI	2B	3B	HR	BB	SO	SB	BA
Michael Kelley	1B58	58	224	37	74							15	.330
William Stuart	2B	(see multi-team players)											
Frank Gatins	SS97	97	365	52	107							36	.293
Bill Shindle	3B106	108	439	89	136							24	.310
George Turner	OF56	56	230	59	77							9	.335

HARTFORD (cont.)
Indians

BATTERS	POS-GAMES	GP	AB	R	H	BI	2B	3B	HR	BB	SO	SB	BA
Matt Kilroy	OF49	50	195	34	48							6	.247
Louis Lippert	OF48	48	189	34	58							16	.307
William Urquhart	C86	94	355	35	98							13	.276
Phil Knell	P30,OF18	48	172	16	38							3	.221
William Massey	1B47	47	186	37	67							4	.360
Wilson		27	94	10	25							2	.266
Lou Sockalexis	OF24	24	91	8	18							2	.198
Duke Esper	P23	23	65	9	12							1	.185
T. Johnson	P21	21	60	2	7							0	.117
George Hodson	P19	20	67	6	10							0	.149
McCarthy	OF18	18	69	5	13							5	.188
Frank Boyd	C16	16	53	8	20							1	.377
Reisling		15	51	7	10							2	.196

PITCHERS	W	L	PCT	G	GS	CG	SH	IP	H	BB	SO	ERA
Phil Knell				30								
Duke Esper				23								
T. Johnson				21								
George Hodson				19								

PROVIDENCE   7th   54-62   .466   -18.5   William Murray
Clamdiggers

BATTERS	POS-GAMES	GP	AB	R	H	BI	2B	3B	HR	BB	SO	SB	BA
Al Davis	1B110	110	445	88	151							29	.339
John Cassidy	2B73	73	295	58	89							11	.302
James Cooney	SS83	83	318	46	87							11	.274
Charles Nyce	3B113	113	442	74	128							15	.290
John Walters	OF120	**120**	**491**	100	**160**							28	.326
Tom Hernon	OF66	66	273	52	76							13	.278
William Murray	OF53	53	183	28	39							11	.214
Thomas Leahy	C102	111	426	65	130							35	.306
Pete Lamar	OF51,C18	76	272	43	70							16	.257
William Braun	P34	50	142	30	37							1	.260
Roy Evans	P42	42	129	3	13							1	.101
Dave Dunkle	P36	36	121	16	28							0	.231
Tom Stouch	2B34	34	129	13	32							5	.248
Clancy	SS28	28	101	10	20							3	.198
Donovan	OF17	23	89	6	16							5	.180

PITCHERS	W	L	PCT	G	GS	CG	SH	IP	H	BB	SO	ERA
Roy Evans				**42**								
Dave Dunkle				36								
William Braun				34								

SYRACUSE   8th   39-68   .364   -29   Lew Whistler - Sandy Griffin
Stars

BATTERS	POS-GAMES	GP	AB	R	H	BI	2B	3B	HR	BB	SO	SB	BA
James Field	1B37	37	142	18	31							2	.218
Henry Lynch	2B	(see multi-team players)											
Mike Woodlock	SS51	51	188	27	46							10	.245
Charles A. Smith	3B35	35	131	16	43							3	.328
Sandy Griffin	OF69	69	256	32	61							4	.238
Abe Lizotte	OF55,1B18	73	300	50	91							12	.303
Winters	OF	(see multi-team players)											
O'Neill	C36	38	123	11	30							2	.244
D. Williams	C35	57	195	20	50							6	.257
P. Shannon	OF33	33	125	17	29							10	.232
John Calhoun	1B33	33	123	15	34							5	.276
William Hargrove	OF33	33	120	23	35							11	.292
George Wrigley	SS31	31	125	14	34							8	.272
Robert McKinney	3B23	29	116	20	41							7	.353
Murray Steelman		29	100	15	30							5	.300

SYRACUSE (cont.)
Stars

BATTERS	POS-GAMES	GP	AB	R	H	BI	2B	3B	HR	BB	SO	SB	BA
Gus Dundon	3B23	24	86	13	21							11	.244
Mazena	2B22	22	86	4	17							2	.198
Cross		20	69	8	12							0	.174
Kennedy	OF18	18	71	17	24							4	.339
John Keenan	P18	18	59	11	12							2	.203
John Malarkey	P15	17	59	3	11							1	.186
Croft		16	64	15	12							2	.188
George Villeman	P16	16	57	8	12							0	.210
Lew Whistler	1B16	16	56	4	9							2	.160
Dixon		15	50	2	16							1	.320

PITCHERS	W	L	PCT	G	GS	CG	SH	IP	H	BB	SO	ERA
John Keenan				18								
George Villeman				16								
John Malarkey				15								

MULTI-TEAM PLAYERS

BATTERS	POS-GAMES	TEAMS	GP	AB	R	H	BI	2B	3B	HR	BB	SO	SB	BA
Henry Lynch	2B62,OF38	PRO-SYR	100	419	90	118							48	.282
Cavelle	OF83	ROC-HAR	84	310	43	86							21	.277
Winters	OF80	SYR-MON	80	321	36	83							7	.259
William Stuart	2B69	SPR-HAR	69	251	39	48							9	.191
William Lush	OF52	SYR-ROC	55	188	41	43							25	.229
Dan Brouthers	1B45	SPR-ROC	45	170	27	40							2	.235
Bob McHale	OF33	ROC-HAR	39	145	14	26							5	.179
Mike McDermott	P30	SPR-SYR	31	106	10	26							6	.245

PITCHERS	TEAMS	W	L	PCT	G	GS	CG	SH	IP	H	BB	SO	ERA
Mike McDermott	SPR-SYR				30								

1900
BALL AND GLOVE

Baseball's batting statistics have been widely chronicled almost since the beginning of organized teams in the 1850s. Another set of statistics, existing side-by-side with batting, has been kept nearly as long. These other statistics, called fielding statistics, keep track of the defensive part of the game.

Fielding statistics were designed to measure a player's ability to catch and throw the ball accurately. The categories included are total chances accepted (how many times the ball is handled), assists (how many times a throw is made for a putout), putouts (how many batters or runners are retired via a catch, base touched, or runner tagged), errors (how many errant throws or dropped balls), and fielding percentage (errors divided by total chances). Fielding percentage is probably the most important statistic of the group.

As baseball was originally intended, the main confrontation of the game was the batters on one side versus the fielders on the other. The pitcher's job was to put the ball in play so that the fielders could catch the ball or throw the runner out. Only later did the pitcher's role change into the batter-versus-pitcher game we know today.

Providence jumped to the front of the pack during the 1900 campaign, pursued closely by Rochester, with Hartford and Worcester also figuring in the picture. At season's end, Providence had prevailed by five games over Rochester, nine over Hartford, and sixteen over Worcester. Springfield, Toronto, Montreal, and Syracuse finished in the last four spots. The batting titlist came from Worcester as Kitty Bransfield batted .371.

Fielding in 1900 was typical of the era. Fielding averages were in the range of .920 for catchers, .940 for outfielders, .975 for first basemen, .950 for second basemen, and .910 for third basemen. The shortstops, usually seeing the most chances finished with a percentage of .890. These numbers are significantly higher than those of 20 years before. In the 1870s, entire leagues struggled to reach the .900 level.

Through the years, league fielding averages have climbed to the .975 level in the International League. The low fielding averages for the early years are explained by two factors. One, ballfields 100 years ago weren't the manicured lawns they are today. Two, basket-sized gloves weren't the norm in the nineteenth century. As a matter of fact, until the late 1880s, most players wore no gloves at all.

PROVIDENCE   1st   84-52   .618   William Murray
Clamdiggers

BATTERS	POS-GAMES	GP	AB	R	H	BI	2B	3B	HR	BB	SO	SB	BA
John Cassidy	1B137	138	569	96	179							33	.315
Jim Connor	2B136	136	553	87	157							14	.284
Fred Parent	SS133	137	541	94	155							23	.287
Jud Smith	3B		(see multi-team players)										
Al Davis	OF134	135	549	108	182							70	.332
Jim Walters	OF121	121	479	85	143							20	.299
James Stafford	OF88,3B36	133	506	65	136							32	.269
Thomas Leahy	C97	97	341	40	101							16	.296
William Braun	P35	48	137	20	25							2	.182
Dave Dunkle	P41	41	134	5	33							2	.246
Pat McCauley	C37	40	135	20	34							5	.252
Roy Evans	P39	39	128	10	28							3	.219
Dan Friend	P31	35	118	12	22							4	.186
George Noblitt	OF27	27	109	13	23							4	.211
Frank Corridon		17	52	8	11							3	.212
John Clements	C	13	37	3	12								.324

PITCHERS		W	L	PCT	G	GS	CG	SH	IP	H	BB	SO	ERA
Dave Dunkle					41								
Roy Evans					39								
William Braun					35								
Dan Friend					31								

ROCHESTER   2nd   77-56   .579   -5.5   Al Buckenberger
Bronchos

BATTERS	POS-GAMES	GP	AB	R	H	BI	2B	3B	HR	BB	SO	SB	BA
Harry O'Hagan	1B138	138	534	102	154							47	.288
George Smith	2B125	125	506	93	138							38	.273
Frank Bonner	SS138	138	548	89	173							25	.316
Ed Gremminger	3B116	116	427	59	117							7	.274
Ed Householder	OF130	131	519	71	153							14	.295
Count Campau	OF130	130	507	70	127							25	.251
William Lush	OF122	124	477	102	136							46	.285
Ed Dixon	C57	57	199	14	45							2	.227
Ed Murphy	P47	52	150	15	39							3	.260
Charles Morse	P35	37	119	9	24							0	.202
Frank McPartlin	P36	36	106	9	19							2	.179
Deal	C26	32	107	6	22							1	.206
Cy Bowen	P32	32	96	7	16							0	.167
Walker		16	41	2	11							0	.268

PITCHERS		W	L	PCT	G	GS	CG	SH	IP	H	BB	SO	ERA
Ed Murphy					47								
Frank McPartlin					36								
Charles Morse					35								
Cy Bowen					32								

HARTFORD   3rd   68-55   .553   -9.5   Billy Barnie -
Indians   Bill Shindle

BATTERS	POS-GAMES	GP	AB	R	H	BI	2B	3B	HR	BB	SO	SB	BA
William Massey	1B127	127	472	70	122							7	.259
Burt Myers	2B82,SS33	122	483	55	137							20	.284
Frank Gatins	SS102	102	386	56	108							17	.280
Bill Shindle	3B119	119	486	75	133							9	.274
George Turner	OF116	116	464	86	131							7	.282
Thomas Fleming	OF95	95	360	48	91							23	.253
Scott Stratton	OF77	77	262	32	75							5	.286
Morris Steelman	C111	113	384	44	99							9	.258
Bill Donovan	P40	65	223	30	65							6	.292
George Hemming	OF38,P23	61	248	27	59							1	.238
Frank Ward	2B36	48	185	34	44							12	.238
Ralph Miller	P32	32	102	8	23							0	.225
William Urquhart	C20	32	102	8	20							3	.196
Pat Flaherty	P25	26	89	16	26							3	.292

HARTFORD (cont.)
Indians

PITCHERS		W	L	PCT	G	GS	CG	SH	IP	H	BB	SO	ERA
Bill Donovan					40								
Ralph Miller					32								
Pat Flaherty					25								
George Hemming					23								

WORCESTER   4th   62-63   .496   -16.5   Frank Leonard
Farmers

BATTERS	POS-GAMES	GP	AB	R	H	BI	2B	3B	HR	BB	SO	SB	BA
Kitty Bransfield	1B122	122	501	115	186							40	.371
Frank Connaughton	2B100	100	393	52	103							13	.262
Joseph Bean	SS	(see multi-team players)											
James Delehanty	3B55,SS25	80	317	55	89							18	.281
Joseph Rickert	OF126	126	520	112	145							59	.279
John Sharrott	OF118	118	469	96	145							37	.309
Harry Blake	OF71	71	278	56	68							27	.245
Mal Kittridge	C127	127	483	66	145							32	.300
Fred Klobedanz	P41	50	158	13	31							3	.196
Tom Sheehan	3B30	39	131	14	27							6	.206
Bill Magee	P35	36	116	11	18							2	.155
Elmer Horton	P33	33	104	14	27							1	.260
Charles Pittinger	P21	21	71	4	10							0	.155
Raidy	SS17	18	65	6	11							1	.169
Foster		17	51	6	12							5	.235

PITCHERS		W	L	PCT	G	GS	CG	SH	IP	H	BB	SO	ERA
Fred Klobedanz					41								
Bill Magee					35								
Elmer Horton					33								
Charles Pittinger					21								

SPRINGFIELD   5th   61-63   .492   -17   Thomas Burns
Ponies

BATTERS	POS-GAMES	GP	AB	R	H	BI	2B	3B	HR	BB	SO	SB	BA
Tommy Tucker	1B126	126	476	59	133							7	.259
Walt Curley	2B125	125	486	75	122							18	.251
Frank Shannon	SS111	111	436	71	106							19	.244
Frank Eustace	3B	(see multi-team players)											
Pat Dolan	OF125	126	514	86	169							15	.329
Julius Knoll	OF88	88	363	57	105							8	.289
George Shoch	OF88	88	345	51	105							8	.304
James Toft	C78	78	269	31	61							6	.227
Charles Cargo	SS28,3B21	49	192	26	46							6	.240
Walter Woods	P38	47	147	19	28							0	.191
John Pappalau	P38	38	134	19	30							1	.224
Thomas Campbell	OF35	35	136	16	29							3	.287
Harry Gleason	3B26	26	99	10	23							1	.232
Pete McBride	P19	21	73	12	20							1	.274
Frank Foreman	P17	17	57	3	8							1	.140

PITCHERS		W	L	PCT	G	GS	CG	SH	IP	H	BB	SO	ERA
John Pappalau					38								
Walter Woods					38								
Pete McBride					19								
Frank Foreman					17								

TORONTO   6th   63-67   .485   -18   Ed Barrow
Maple Leafs

BATTERS	POS-GAMES	GP	AB	R	H	BI	2B	3B	HR	BB	SO	SB	BA
Charles Carr	1B118	118	490	70	160							11	.326

TORONTO (cont.)
Maple Leafs

BATTERS	POS-GAMES	GP	AB	R	H	BI	2B	3B	HR	BB	SO	SB	BA
Wallace Taylor	2B	(see multi-team players)											
William Clymer	SS75	87	317	45	89							9	.281
Robert Schaub	3B127	127	463	73	142							10	.307
James Bannon	OF131	131	538	99	163							31	.303
Rome Grey	OF89	89	356	66	104							18	.292
Jim Hannivan	OF	(see multi-team players)											
Harry Bemis	C82	82	283	41	85							10	.300
Mike Roach	C57	63	227	25	52							9	.229
Lou Bruce	SS21	60	171	23	47							3	.275
W. Williams	P37	41	122	17	34							0	.279
A. Alloway	P34	34	94	11	13							0	.138
Bill Duggleby	P29	29	101	7	22							0	.218
Jim Cockman	3B17	17	63	11	10							1	.159

PITCHERS		W	L	PCT	G	GS	CG	SH	IP	H	BB	SO	ERA
W. Williams					37								
A. Alloway					34								
Bill Duggleby					29								

MONTREAL   7th   53-71   .427   -25   Charles Dooley
Royals

BATTERS	POS-GAMES	GP	AB	R	H	BI	2B	3B	HR	BB	SO	SB	BA
Charles Dooley	1B96	96	348	47	95							3	.279
Abbie Johnson	2B115	117	470	60	116							18	.247
Frank Scheibeck	SS127	127	497	78	113							24	.227
Edward Henry	3B131	131	512	53	139							7	.272
Abe Lizotte	OF127	127	522	67	140							8	.268
Frederick Odwell	OF117	117	464	75	133							26	.287
Tom Bannon	OF	(see multi-team players)											
Bill Moran	C85	88	299	47	83							4	.278
Tom Raub	1B30,C26,OF22	79	282	35	71							8	.252
Joseph Delehanty	OF51	54	206	22	51							2	.247
Halle Souders	P36	43	126	30	31							0	.246
Dan McFarlan	P35	38	125	13	19							0	.152
Harry Felix	P35	35	119	14	20							3	.168
George Cross	P30	30	105	8	28							1	.267
James Garry	OF22	22	88	5	24							2	.273

PITCHERS		W	L	PCT	G	GS	CG	SH	IP	H	BB	SO	ERA
Halle Souders					36								
Dan McFarlan					35								
Harry Felix					35								
George Cross					30								

SYRACUSE   8th   43-84   .339   -36.5   Art Irwin
Stars

BATTERS	POS-GAMES	GP	AB	R	H	BI	2B	3B	HR	BB	SO	SB	BA
G. Stafford	1B50	50	195	22	47							6	.241
William Gilbert	2B82,SS33	116	440	74	105							42	.300
Charles Kuhns	SS	(see multi-team players)											
George Wrigley	3B	(see multi-team players)											
William Hargrove	OF122	122	453	74	120							22	.265
John White	OF63,2B35	100	393	59	103							26	.262
Henry Lynch	OF	(see multi-team players)											
Bill Smink	C	(see multi-team players)											
Nick Altrock	P46	57	174	22	37							2	.213
John Calhoun	1B25	50	183	22	44							6	.241
George Pfanmiller	P30	39	124	12	16							0	.153
Weaver	1B26	38	145	14	35							6	.241
Lewis Wiltse	P32	36	114	14	27							1	.237
Cliff Latimer	C26	27	91	8	20							0	.220
Brown	OF26	26	102	12	35							4	.337

SYRACUSE (cont.)
Stars

BATTERS	POS-GAMES	GP	AB	R	H	BI	2B	3B	HR	BB	SO	SB	BA
Tom Messitt	C19	21	72	4	14							2	.194
Bishop	P17	17	49	1	10							0	.204
Pete Lamar	C16	16	45	9	13							2	.289

PITCHERS	W	L	PCT	G	GS	CG	SH	IP	H	BB	SO	ERA
Nick Altrock				46								
Lewis Wiltse				32								
George Pfanmiller				30								
Bishop				17								

MULTI-TEAM PLAYERS

BATTERS	POS-GAMES	TEAMS	GP	AB	R	H	BI	2B	3B	HR	BB	SO	SB	BA
Charles Kuhns	3B53,SS42,OF28	SY-WO	125	501	61	137							23	.274
Tom Bannon	OF125	MON-TOR	125	490	93	140							28	.304
Henry Lynch	OF74,2B52	SYR-TOR	125	471	92	142							31	.302
George Wrigley	2B53,SS48	SYR-WOR	123	443	56	111							21	.250
Jud Smith	3B119	PRO-WOR	119	424	74	120							21	.283
Joseph Bean	SS59,2B19,3B16	WOR-ROC	111	416	56	113							22	.272
Jim Hannivan	OF96	SYR-TOR	103	395	47	100							18	.253
Bill Smink	C86	SYR-ROC	100	368	36	93							9	.254
Ed Phelps	C94	SP-MO-RO	94	318	41	76							7	.239
Jack Rothfuss	OF50,1B36	SYR-TOR	86	336	42	73							9	.217
Frank Eustace	3B71	SPR-SYR	72	266	42	56							7	.211
Wallace Taylor	2B69	SY-TO-MO	72	258	21	69							0	.268
Buckley	OF44	SPR-ROC	44	170	20	54							4	.318
Homer Smoot	OF32	SYR-PRO	42	149	17	42							3	.282
GusDundon		SYR-TOR	26	98	11	23							0	.235
George Bannon	P23	SYR-SPR	23	73	9	16							0	.219
John Richter	OF16	MO-HA-WO	21	64	6	12							1	.188

PITCHERS	TEAMS	W	L	PCT	G	GS	CG	SH	IP	H	BB	SO	ERA
George Bannon	SYR-SPR				23								

1901
CHARTER MEMBER

Through the nineteenth century, the major and minor leagues coexisted in relative peace. The National Agreement, hammered out in 1883, served as the basis for the relationship. The treaty, signed by the National League and American Association from the majors, and the Northwestern League from the minors, solidified the link between the top baseball leagues and those residing on lower tiers. The basic tenets of the National Agreement stated that no league would encroach into another league's territory, or tamper with its players.

By century's cusp, this agreement, rewritten and modified, was starting to fray. The key point of dissension was the battle between the National League and the upstart American League. The American League, recently a minor league, disobeyed two of the tenets, moving into an existing National League city (Chicago) as well as annulling many existing player contracts. Fed up, the National League terminated its agreement with minor leagues, leaving them to stand alone.

Before the 1901 Eastern League season, Buffalo took the place of Springfield. During the season, on July 25, Syracuse was transferred to Brockton, Massachusetts. In addition, the Hartford team closed up shop two weeks early on September 10. Rochester returned to the top roost by a goodly amount over Toronto and Providence. Hartford, Worcester, and Montreal clustered together in the middle, all significantly ahead of Syracuse/Brockton and Buffalo. Homer Smoot, from Worcester, took home the batting prize (.356), while Rochester's Rome Grey swatted the most home runs (12). On the mound John Malarkey (Rochester) and Dave Dunkle (Providence) each won 26.

Realizing their vulnerability as independent organizations, several minor leagues acted. In September 1901, representatives from seven leagues met and formed the National Association of Professional Baseball Leagues, whose primary duties included protecting members from player tampering, and serving as arbiter in all disputes including territorial questions. The National Association also organized the minor leagues into classifications, ranking teams according to age and city size. This assured that each league would see even competition. One of the National Association's seven charter members was the Eastern League.

As minor league baseball moved through the twentieth century, new minor leagues were put under the National Association's umbrella. The organization was able to monitor placement of teams so that existing teams were not compromised. Now operating under the guidance of the major leagues, and with modifications, it is the same organization that governs minor league today. The National Association is an organization that allows the majors and minors to coexist, each with its own role.

ROCHESTER Hustlers
1st 89-49 .645 Al Buckenberger

BATTERS	POS-GAMES	GP	AB	R	H	BI	2B	3B	HR	BB	SO	SB	BA
Harry O'Hagen	1B136	136	520	113	166		27	11	3			51	.320
George Smith	2B133	133	536	111	169		26	13	7			33	.315
Joseph Bean	SS137	137	555	113	173		17	3	2			39	.312
Ed Gremminger	3B128	128	467	85	160		29	14	10			13	.343
George Barclay	OF139	139	573	112	194		25	6	3			46	.339
William Lush	OF132	132	491	137	152		27	22	7			50	.310
Rome Grey		(see multi-team players)											
Ed Phelps	C92	93	328	58	95		11	3	4			18	.290
Ed Dixon	C44	55	175	20	36		7	3	2			4	.206
John Malarkey	P37	37	115	17	18		5	0	1			5	.157
Frank McPartlin	P35	35	109	11	26		1	1	1			4	.239
Cy Bowen	P31	31	92	10	16		0	0	1			0	.174

PITCHERS		W	L	PCT	G	GS	CG	SH	IP	H	BB	SO	ERA
John Malarkey		26	11	.702	37			3					
Frank McPartlin		22	10	.687	35			3					
Cy Bowen		16	12	.571	31			3					

TORONTO Maple Leafs
2nd 74-52 .587 -9 Ed Barrow

BATTERS	POS-GAMES	GP	AB	R	H	BI	2B	3B	HR	BB	SO	SB	BA
Charles Carr	1B108	108	444	56	135		20	4	6			18	.304
Frank Bonner	2B129	129	529	104	180		36	12	10			16	.340
Lou Bruce	SS80	101	357	62	115		10	7	0			10	.322
Robert Schaub	3B127	127	458	65	119		15	2	2			21	.260
James Bannon	OF130	130	520	125	177		24	13	7			34	.340
William Hargrove	OF111	111	411	53	101		17	4	5			17	.245
G. Brown	OF103	103	427	72	135		17	6	1			19	.316
Harry Bemis	C81	89	293	49	90		17	2	6			9	.307
W. Williams	P34	53	173	21	44		4	3	2			1	.255
Nick Altrock	P34	34	98	2	13		2	0	1			0	.133
G. Sullivan	P24	25	80	9	25		0	1	0			0	.313
Lew Carr	3B19	19	64	13	25		3	2	0			3	.391

PITCHERS		W	L	PCT	G	GS	CG	SH	IP	H	BB	SO	ERA
W. Williams		19	13	.593	34			4					
Nick Altrock		16	13	.571	34			2					
G. Sullivan		11	11	.500	24			2					

PROVIDENCE Clamdiggers
3rd 73-58 .558 -12.5 William Murray

BATTERS	POS-GAMES	GP	AB	R	H	BI	2B	3B	HR	BB	SO	SB	BA
John Cassidy	1B99	116	463	79	144		29	11	1			25	.311
Jim Connor	2B121	121	452	47	115		16	2	2			5	.254
Suter Sullivan	SS99,3B18	119	449	62	143		17	1	0			13	.318
Edward Henry	3B119	119	438	60	121		18	1	1			6	.276
John Walters	OF132	132	543	96	174		23	1	0			13	.320
James Stafford	OF132	132	505	77	134		20	5	5			20	.265
John Flournoy	OF102	102	404	68	115		21	2	8			36	.285
Pat McCauley	C87	88	299	49	59		12	2	0			5	.198
Dan Friend	P35,OF21	57	200	21	66		16	1	0			6	.330
Dave Dunkle	P44	44	153	17	38		9	1	0			2	.248
Thomas Leahy	C23,1B16	40	147	13	49		12	1	1			3	.333
Albert Wagner	SS37	37	157	29	47		5	7	1			4	.299
Frank Corridon	P35	35	123	7	27		6	1	0			0	.220
Fred Brown		20	70	5	20							0	.286

PITCHERS		W	L	PCT	G	GS	CG	SH	IP	H	BB	SO	ERA
Dave Dunkle		26	13	.667	44			2					
Frank Corridon		17	13	.564	35			3					
Dan Friend		17	14	.548	35			2					

HARTFORD   4th   58-56   .509   -19   Bill Shindle
Wooden Nutmegs

BATTERS	POS-GAMES	GP	AB	R	H	BI	2B	3B	HR	BB	SO	SB	BA
William Massey	1B115	115	438	59	122		21	13	3			6	.279
Lou Bierbauer	2B				(see multi-team players)								
George Shoch	SS53,OF59	114	429	54	136		20	2	0			7	.317
Bill Shindle	3B121	121	491	70	139		24	3	1			14	.283
Charles Kuhns	OF85,SS33	118	480	73	144		23	8	1			16	.300
James Garry	OF79	79	324	40	81		5	0	1			1	.250
George Turner	OF				(see multi-team players)								
Morris Steelman	C87	90	298	29	87		6	2	1			8	.292
Frank Gatins	SS41	41	155	18	42		6	0	2			7	.271
William Urquhart	C32	41	133	16	26		8	1	1			0	.195
Thomas Fleming	OF36	36	151	14	38		1	1	0			5	.252
George Hemming	P29	36	110	10	20		5	0	1			0	.195
Ralph Miller	P27	29	102	13	22		2	0	0			0	.216
Eugene McCann	P19	21	69	5	14		2	1	0			1	.203
Jim Gardner	P18	21	65	6	15		3	2	0			0	.231

PITCHERS	W	L	PCT	G	GS	CG	SH	IP	H	BB	SO	ERA
Ralph Miller	13	12	.520	27			0					
George Hemming	12	11	.521	29			5					
Jim Gardner	11	7	.611	18			3					
Eugene McCann	9	6	.600	19			1					

WORCESTER   5th   62-64   .492   -21   Mal Kittridge
Quakers

BATTERS	POS-GAMES	GP	AB	R	H	BI	2B	3B	HR	BB	SO	SB	BA
Slater	1B				(see multi-team players)								
George Wrigley	2B120	120	483	62	146		26	10	7			20	.302
Frank Shannon	SS80	80	264	35	66		9	1	0			8	.250
Robert Unglaub	3B110	110	441	62	109		19	8	7			12	.247
Homer Smoot	OF120	120	486	81	173		37	5	4			16	**.356**
Joseph Rickert	OF112	112	467	87	135		27	8	4			32	.289
Pat Carney	OF53	63	261	45	87		13	6	2			3	.333
John Clements	C61	61	220	41	68		19	2	7			3	.309
O'Reilly	SS51	61	246	31	46		5	2	0			5	.187
Tom Doran	C55	55	198	22	62		9	3	0			3	.309
Fred Klobedanz	P43	43	138	19	26		7	0	0			0	.188
Griffin	P27	41	143	18	38		11	1	0			0	.265
John Pappalau	P34	35	121	14	37		5	0	0			0	.306
Bill Magee	P33	33	106	11	21		4	1	2			0	.198
John Sharrott	OF25	26	101	16	29		5	0	1			2	.287
Morrison	OF26	26	98	7	21		6	0	0			1	.214
Larry McLean	C21	21	82	10	19		3	0	1			2	.232

PITCHERS	W	L	PCT	G	GS	CG	SH	IP	H	BB	SO	ERA
Fred Klobedanz	19	16	.543	43			2					
John Pappalau	16	16	.500	34			2					
Bill Magee	15	15	.500	33			0					
Griffin	11	13	.458	27			0					

MONTREAL   6th   64-66   .492   -21.5   Charles Dooley
Royals

BATTERS	POS-GAMES	GP	AB	R	H	BI	2B	3B	HR	BB	SO	SB	BA
Charles Dooley	1B98	98	359	48	107		21	2	9			13	.298
Abbie Johnson	2B134	134	477	58	117		19	2	1			14	.245
Lawrence Quinlan	SS125	126	435	30	105		19	2	0			6	.241
Tom Sheehan	3B131	131	460	76	112		17	6	3			11	.243
Frederick Odwell	OF125	126	480	74	143		33	6	3			35	.298
John Shearon	OF119	119	471	59	127		29	7	1			29	.270
Joseph Delahanty	OF118	131	517	78	151		34	16	5			19	.292
Tom Raub	C46,1B23	85	333	58	95		22	3	11			15	.285
Wilson	C17	74	291	41	87		12	3	0			6	.299
Halle Souders	P36	40	121	12	21		4	0	1			0	.174

MONTREAL (cont.)
Royals

BATTERS	POS-GAMES	GP	AB	R	H	BI	2B	3B	HR	BB	SO	SB	BA
Michael O'Neill	P23	38	120	14	31							0	.258
Harry Felix	P36	37	125	14	25		3	2	2			1	.200
Gordon	C17	17	54	6	9		1	0	2			1	.167

PITCHERS		W	L	PCT	G	GS	CG	SH	IP	H	BB	SO	ERA
Harry Felix		22	14	.611	36			1					
Halle Souders		16	17	.484	36			3					
Michael O'Neill		11	10	.523	23			2					

SYRACUSE / BROCKTON   7th   40-73   .354   -36.5   Frank Leonard
Stars / B's

BATTERS	POS-GAMES	GP	AB	R	H	BI	2B	3B	HR	BB	SO	SB	BA
Duff Cooley	1B55	55	227	27	77		13	1	2			8	.340
Burt Myers	2B		(see multi-team players)										
Art Madison	SS		(see multi-team players)										
Jud Smith	3B98	98	401	47	106		24	7	1			6	.264
Tom Bannon	OF114	114	459	76	109		17	5	3			25	.238
Harry Blake	OF88	88	337	41	82		14	3	4			10	.244
Mike Lynch	OF39	44	161	23	43		6	1	0			9	.267
Mike Roach	C57	70	235	31	56		6	3	0			10	.238
Walter Woods	P32,2B17,OF	88	293	39	62		6	1	3			8	.212
Frank McManus	C	71	263	27	65		12	2	1			3	.247
George Pfanmiller	P28	39	121	15	34		6	3	0			2	.281
John Barnett	P25	26	87	7	17		4	2	0			1	.195
Lee DeMontreville	SS24	24	89	16	20		1	1	0			4	.225
Heine	2B24	24	86	6	17							3	.198
Ed MacGamwell	OF22	23	86	9	24		4	1	1			1	.279
John White	OF22	22	85	12	24		2	0	2			6	.282

PITCHERS		W	L	PCT	G	GS	CG	SH	IP	H	BB	SO	ERA
Walter Woods		11	17	.392	32			1					
George Pfanmiller		9	15	.375	28			1					
John Barnett		9	16	.360	25			1					

BUFFALO   8th   45-87   .341   -41   George Carey - Thomas Burns - Walt Burnham - Jim Franklin - Joe Franklin
Pan Ams

BATTERS	POS-GAMES	GP	AB	R	H	BI	2B	3B	HR	BB	SO	SB	BA
George Carey	1B134	134	532	76	168		37	5	8			5	.316
Charles Atherton	2B40,SS25	71	281	41	85		12	0	5			8	.303
William Hayward	SS47	51	208	24	48		4	1	0			6	.231
Jay Andrews	3B127	127	492	56	138		27	4	1			13	.281
Bill Halligan	OF133	133	518	79	142		29	5	1			21	.274
Jake Gettman	OF97	99	403	76	119		20	10	3			39	.295
William Clymer	OF67,2B52	132	550	93	134		34	5	6			26	.244
Kid Speer	C117	117	409	45	117		15	0	1			12	.286
William Hooker	P43	49	149	11	31		3	0	0			2	.208
Morris Amole	P37	40	135	8	27		4	1	1			0	.200
Doc Kennedy	C25	37	114	13	25		5	0	0			0	.219
Harry Fisher	SS23	26	95	6	19		1	0	0			3	.200
Harley Parker	P	24	75	6	23		1	1	0			1	.307
Dan Kerwin	P	21	73	7	19		2	2	0			1	.260
Wiley		17	69	12	19		3	1	0			2	.275
Hopper	OF16	16	67	9	16		6	1	0			1	.239

PITCHERS		W	L	PCT	G	GS	CG	SH	IP	H	BB	SO	ERA
William Hooker		12	25	.324	43			2					
Morris Amole		11	25	.305	37			1					
Dan Kerwin		6	6	.500									
Harley Parker		1	7	.125									

MULTI-TEAM PLAYERS

BATTERS	POS-GAMES	TEAMS	GP	AB	R	H	BI	2B	3B	HR	BB	SO	SB	BA
Rome Grey	OF124	BUF-ROC	124	473	72	145		18	11	12			36	.307
Lou Bierbauer	2B106	BUF-HAR	109	390	39	94		10	0	0			1	.261
Art Madison	SS80,2B25	TOR-S/B	105	388	48	99		11	2	0			2	.255
Slater	1B102	TO-WO-S/B	104	385	45	89		18	1	5			8	.231
Pat Crisham	1B59,C25	PRO-WOR	84	311	32	80		15	3	0			4	.257
George Turner	OF83	HAR-TOR	83	331	63	94		16	2	2			9	.284
James Toft	C58,1B17	TOR-HAR	75	248	30	64		8	1	0			3	.258
Ike Francis	SS24	ROC-S/B	54	207	33	53		8	4	2			1	.265
Pat Flaherty	P27,OF22	S/B-TOR	54	156	23	37		5	2	2			6	.237
Dan McFarlan	P40	MON-ROC	48	159	15	37		3	2	1			4	.233
Bert Conn	P24	ROC-PRO	48	142	22	46		8	0	0			5	.324
Charles Hastings	P36	BUF-HAR	40	116	13	30		2	3	0			0	.259
Fred McFall	P35	TOR-S/B	38	111	8	25		0	2	0			1	.225
Burt Myers	2B34	HAR-S/B	34	133	12	28		5	0	0			4	.211

PITCHERS		TEAMS	W	L	PCT	G	GS	CG	SH	IP	H	BB	SO	ERA
Dan McFarlan		MON-ROC	20	12	.625	40			1					
Pat Flaherty		S/B-TOR	15	16	.483	27			1					
Charles Hastings		BUF-HAR	14	17	.451	36			1					
Fred McFall		TOR-S/B	13	17	.433	38			1					
Bert Conn		ROC-PRO	7	12	.368	24			1					

TEAM BATTING

TEAMS	GP	AB	R	H	BI	2B	3B	HR	BB	SO	SB	BA
ROCHESTER						196	90	53				
TORONTO						180	60	40				
PROVIDENCE						211	38	19				
HARTFORD						158	36	13				
WORCESTER						211	49	39				
MONTREAL						227	56	30				
SYR/BROCK						147	36	21				
BUFFALO						220	40	29				
						1550	405	244				

1902
NO GAMES BEHIND

During the first 20 years of the International League's family of circuits, over half a dozen pennant races were decided by less than five games. Of particular note were the races in 1893, when Erie was victorious by one game, and in 1890, when Detroit and Saginaw–Bay City finished scant percentage points apart. In 1902, 1890's close finish would be duplicated—a finish with no games separating the first two teams.

One of the most popular methods used to measure success in a given league is determining how many games behind the leader a particular team resides. The formula runs as follows: Add the difference between two teams' wins and losses, and divide by two. For example, if team A has a 6-3 record, while team B is 3-6, team B is considered three games behind (3 wins ahead + 3 losses behind divided by 2). For teams playing an unequal number of games, the same formula is used. If team A is 6-3, while team B is 3-5, team B is two and one-half games behind (3 wins ahead + 2 losses behind divided by 2).

As the 1902 season got underway, two teams jumped to the front. The Toronto Maple Leafs and Buffalo Bisons put on a battle royal during the summer. The final six weeks of the race rarely saw more than a game or two separating the teams. When all was finished, Toronto's record stood at 85-42, while Buffalo with six more decisions was 88-45. As each team was 43 games over .500, they finished deadlocked in the games-behind department. If this had happened today, there would have been a one-game playoff. But in 1902, games ahead or behind weren't crucial in deciding pennant winners; winning percentage was the criterion. In that department, Toronto came out on top, .669 to .662.

Following the Maple Leafs and Bisons, the rest of the pack (Jersey City, Worcester, Providence, Rochester, Montreal, and Newark) finished far to the rear. (Jersey City and Newark replaced Syracuse and Hartford.) Jersey City's Bill Halligan won the batting title (.351), Pop Foster from Montreal and Baltimore hit the most home runs (14), while Frank Corridon of Providence won the most games (28).

The pennant races of 1890 and 1902 were the closest the league had seen to that date, but it took modern research to determine this fact. As originally compiled, the standings showed Detroit with a one-game lead in 1890, and Buffalo one-half game behind in 1902. Further investigation altered virtually all of the 1890 and 1902 teams' win-loss records. Saginaw–Bay City gained five wins in 1890, while 1902 Buffalo dropped one of their losses. Though these pennant races were as close as could be, at the time nobody realized that future generations would tighten them further.

TORONTO Maple Leafs

TORONTO   1st   85-42   .669   Ed Barrow

BATTERS	POS-GAMES	GP	AB	R	H	BI	2B	3B	HR	BB	SO	SB	BA
William Massey	1B128	128	521	77	162		31	10	5				.311
James Miller	2B93	93	381	55	97								.255
Jim Downey	SS119	119	465	62	127		13	2	1				.273
Lew Carr	3B96	108	377	61	92		10	5	0				.244
John White	OF119	119	461	80	118		16	6	2				.256
James Bannon	OF62,2B34,3B31	127	516	90	150		10	12	1				.291
William Hargrove	OF59	59	219	36	55								.251
James Toft	C110	112	354	45	91		10	1	1				.257
Lou Bruce	OF55,P20	88	316	56	99		17	5	2				.313
Brennan	OF23,C20	43	144	12	30		2	0	0				.208
Jim Jones	OF42	42	165	30	48								.230
Herb Briggs	P29	29	86	13	22		2	0	0				.256
Jim Gardner	P23	23	75	10	15		1	0	0				.200
Ed Scott	P18	18	56	8	10								.179
Duke Esper	P13	13	44	7	7								.179
Yance Weidensaul		12	37	4	15								.405

PITCHERS	W	L	PCT	G	GS	CG	SH	IP	H	BB	SO	ERA
Herb Briggs	20	8	.714	29								
Jim Gardner	19	4	.826	23								
Lou Bruce	18	2	**.900**	20								
Ed Scott	8	9	.471	18								
Duke Esper	5	8	.385	13								

BUFFALO Bisons

BUFFALO   2nd   88-45   .662   -0   George Stallings

BATTERS	POS-GAMES	GP	AB	R	H	BI	2B	3B	HR	BB	SO	SB	BA
Jack Law	1B68	79	290	43	67								.231
Charles Atherton	2B96	100	378	59	102		31	7	2				.270
William Nattress	SS66	66	247	28	62		14	1	0				.251
Dave Brain	3B128	130	537	**127**	178		25	6	5				.331
Jake Gettman	OF117	117	489	121	166		21	7	8				.339
Bill Milligan	OF95	96	367	60	113								.308
Jack Lynch	OF93	117	442	72	138		14	1	2				.312
Al Shaw	C103	103	352	56	88		11	4	2				.250
Myron Grimshaw	OF68,1B66	135	561	97	178		24	8	4				.317
Al Ferry	P31	34	107	17	34		8	2	0				.318
William Hooker	P33	33	111	12	20		2	0	0				.180
Louis LeRoy	P20	29	85	9	21		1	0	0				.247
Morris Amole	P28	28	96	15	18		2	2	0				.187
Lou Bevier	C23	24	78	9	21								.269
George Gray	P18	18	46	6	12								.261
Pink Hawley	P14	15	44	7	12								.273

PITCHERS	W	L	PCT	G	GS	CG	SH	IP	H	BB	SO	ERA
William Hooker	22	9	.710	33								
Al Ferry	20	5	.800	31								
Morris Amole	14	12	.538	28								
Louis LeRoy	11	5	.687	20								
George Gray	8	7	.533	18								
Pink Hawley	6	8	.429	14								

JERSEY CITY Skeeters

JERSEY CITY   3rd   72-65   .526   -18   Thomas Reilly - Lew Carr

BATTERS	POS-GAMES	GP	AB	R	H	BI	2B	3B	HR	BB	SO	SB	BA
Charles Carr	1B100	100	415	75	139		21	10	3				.335
Stephen Griffin	2B	(see multi-team players)											
Mickey Doolan	SS125	125	490	72	114		14	5	1				.233
Bill Shindle	3B132	132	531	84	153		16	3	3				.269
Bill Halligan	OF138	**138**	518	110	**182**		32	14	4				**.351**
George Shoch	OF129	137	487	67	121		14	3	1				.248
Wally Clement	OF74	74	323	64	103		5	2	1				.319
Frank McManus	C71	84	327	45	88		8	2	3				.269

JERSEY CITY (cont.)
Skeeters

BATTERS	POS-GAMES	GP	AB	R	H	BI	2B	3B	HR	BB	SO	SB	BA
Walter Woods	2B32,OF26,P13	92	342	42	79		7	1	3				.231
John Butler	C62	67	236	27	69		7	5	1				.292
George Pfanmiller	P36	39	120	8	21		3	1	0				.175
Eugene McCann	P34	35	113	13	19		3	1	0				.168
Clarence Childs	2B33	33	138	29	40								.290
Donahue	OF31	31	130	15	39								.231
John Barnett	P26	26	78	7	9		0	1	0				.115
Connors		14	53	7	12								.226

PITCHERS		W	L	PCT	G	GS	CG	SH	IP	H	BB	SO	ERA
Eugene McCann		21	12	.636	34								
George Pfanmiller		17	19	.472	36								
John Barnett		11	14	.440	26								
Walter Woods		8	4	.667	13								
Burns		1	2	.333									
John Luby		1	5	.167									

WORCESTER   4th   68-65   .511   -20   Frank Leonard
Hustlers

BATTERS	POS-GAMES	GP	AB	R	H	BI	2B	3B	HR	BB	SO	SB	BA
Bill Clancy	1B126	126	538	98	157		21	7	9				.292
George Wrigley	2B125	127	482	70	138		21	7	3				.286
Frank Connaughton	SS		(see multi-team players)										
Joseph Delahanty	3B135	135	545	86	151		19	12	8				.277
Joseph Rickert	OF127	127	507	75	138		19	4	3				.272
Charles Frisbee	OF115	115	470	93	152		14	6	2				.323
James Sebring	OF99	103	416	71	136								.327
Morris Steelman	C66	69	246	20	60		5	2	0				.244
George Merritt	OF35,P21	64	239	38	68		12	2	1				.285
Art Madison	SS56	56	211	30	58		6	3	0				.275
Pat Crisham	C37	56	210	26	59		12	3	0				.281
Fred McFall	P34	34	112	13	32		3	0	0				.286
Cy Falkenberg	P29	30	96	10	15		1	2	0				.156
Charles Hastings	P27	28	85	11	12		3	0	0				.141
John Sharrott		13	59	8	18								.305
Ike Van Zandt		11	43	5	12		3	2	0				.279
O'Reilly		10	29	3	8								.277

PITCHERS		W	L	PCT	G	GS	CG	SH	IP	H	BB	SO	ERA
Cy Falkenberg		18	11	.621	29								
Fred McFall		14	16	.467	34								
Charles Hastings		13	12	.520	27								
George Merritt		11	10	.524	21								
Gokey		3	0	1.000									
Griffin		1	2	.333									

PROVIDENCE   5th   67-67   .500   -21.5   William Murray
Grays

BATTERS	POS-GAMES	GP	AB	R	H	BI	2B	3B	HR	BB	SO	SB	BA
John Cassidy	1B124	126	476	85	153		27	3	2				.321
Jim Connor	2B129	130	463	44	107		12	2	1				.231
Joseph Bean	SS80	80	292	60	99		20	1	0				.339
Suter Sullivan	3B127	127	496	83	143		26	2	3				.288
Albert Wagner	OF70,SS47	124	463	93	133		23	9	0				.269
Harry Armbruster	OF67	67	245	25	62		8	0	0				.253
Dan Friend	OF51,P	59	219	21	57								.260
John Dillon	C		(see multi-team players)										
Frank Corridon	P44,OF23	82	275	24	72		9	0	0				.262
Bert Conn	P22	52	173	20	39		4	2	1				.225
George Hildebrand	OF44	44	171	29	40								.234
McMahon	OF44	44	169	22	52		5	3	0				.308
Fred Brown	P13	39	133	19	33		3	0	2				.248
G. Sullivan	P37	38	125	14	30		8	2	0				.240

PROVIDENCE (cont.)
Grays

BATTERS	POS-GAMES	GP	AB	R	H	BI	2B	3B	HR	BB	SO	SB	BA
Smith		16	59	3	17								.288
Dolan		15	46	2	7								.152
Moore		12	50	3	10								.200
Pete Lamar		12	40	3	10								.250

PITCHERS		W	L	PCT	G	GS	CG	SH	IP	H	BB	SO	ERA
Frank Corridon		28	15	.651	44								
G. Sullivan		11	12	.478	37								
Bert Conn		9	13	.409	22								
Stackpole		4	4	.500									
Fred Brown		4	7	.364									
Dan Friend		1	5	.167									

ROCHESTER   6th   57-74   .435   -30   Ed McKean -
Bronchos   Harold O'Hagan

BATTERS	POS-GAMES	GP	AB	R	H	BI	2B	3B	HR	BB	SO	SB	BA
Ed McKean	1B77	78	293	31	92								.314
Lee DeMontreville	2B42	42	85	10	18								.212
Gus Ziemer	SS71	71	263	26	61		5	0	2				.232
Edward Henry	3B64,2B38	103	379	34	85		13	0	0				.224
Harry Blake	OF123	127	501	98	149		22	8	5				.297
Jack Hayden	OF122	122	513	95	167		16	3	8				.326
Rome Grey	OF46	46	196	30	49								.250
Ed Phelps	C91	91	357	64	91								.255
Elmer Horton	P31	46	136	16	31								.228
Dan McFarlan	P30	45	160	21	43		7	0	3				.269
Harry O'Hagen	1B38	38	139	19	40		1	0	0				.288
Dennis	OF35	35	122	9	28		0	1	0				.230
Bob Becker	P28	29	85	10	18		0	1	0				.212
Marshall		15	54	18	17								.315
Freck		14	47	9	5								.106
Cates	P12	14	40	7	9								.225
Frank		13	48	4	10								.208
Coogan		10	26	6	4								.154

PITCHERS		W	L	PCT	G	GS	CG	SH	IP	H	BB	SO	ERA
Dan McFarlan		15	15	.500	30								
Bob Becker		12	16	.429	28								
Elmer Horton		12	18	.400	31								
Cy Bowen		3	3	.500									
Al Mattern		1	2	.333									
Cates		0	9	.000	12								

MONTREAL   7th   58-78   .426   -31.5   Charles Dooley
Royals

BATTERS	POS-GAMES	GP	AB	R	H	BI	2B	3B	HR	BB	SO	SB	BA
Charles Dooley	1B102	102	381	34	96		11	2	2				.252
Abbie Johnson	2B82	82	274	19	63								.230
Lawrence Quinlan	SS117	117	419	22	91		8	1	0				.217
James Stafford	3B102	124	486	73	126		22	2	1				.259
John Shearon	OF135	135	557	85	163		22	5	2				.293
J. Kelly	OF132	132	507	57	131		21	6	1				.258
Frederick Odwell	OF69	69	276	48	79								.286
Tom Raub	C54,1B37	109	434	83	120		22	7	13				.276
Charles Fuller	C40	51	179	30	37		5	2	0				.207
Halle Souders	P38	45	136	9	15		1	1	0				.110
William Diggins		18	60	6	10								.167
William Mills	P18	18	57	4	8								.140
Stroh		18	50	2	7								.140
Hill		17	54	5	12								.222
Tom Sheehan		16	59	9	13								.220
O'Hara		15	52	4	6								.115
Langton		15	36	3	8								.222
J. Raub	P13	14	46	1	5		0	0	0				.109

MONTREAL(cont.)
Royals

PITCHERS	W	L	PCT	G	GS	CG	SH	IP	H	BB	SO	ERA
Halle Souders	16	21	.432	38								
William Mills	6	12	.333	18								
Dunleavy	5	1	.833									
J. Raub	5	8	.385	13								
Langton	3	9	.250	14								
Johnston	1	3	.250									

NEWARK　　8th　　39-98　　.285　　-51　　Walt Burnham
Sailors

BATTERS	POS-GAMES	GP	AB	R	H	BI	2B	3B	HR	BB	SO	SB	BA
Ed MacGamwell	1B52	52	189	21	52		6	7	2				.275
Art Devlin	2B52	52	203	23	43								.212
Daly	SS63	82	295	36	63								.214
William Hayward	3B		(see multi-team players)										
Joseph Schrall	OF120	120	441	70	111								.252
John Weaver	OF68	68	255	30	71		11	6	2				.278
Matty McIntyre	OF		(see multi-team players)										
Harry Jope	C70	82	262	17	48		3	2	0				.183
Tim Jordan	1B25	42	153	16	42								.274
George Hemming	P27	40	150	14	39		6	0	0				.260
Edwin Moriarity	P37	38	113	10	21		1	0	0				.186
Thackera	C37	37	113	13	23								.204
James Garry	OF28	28	115	18	29								.252
Larry Hesterfer	P24	25	81	1	15		1	0	0				.183
Wright	1B24	24	100	15	31								.310
Schultz	OF23	23	86	9	31		3	0	2				.360
Henry		23	83	3	16								.193
Lou Bierbauer		18	69	0	8								.116
Matthews		18	60	4	11								.183
Charles Wagner		16	60	7	12		0	0	0				.200
Drauby		14	57	5	14								.246
Grant		14	53	5	6								.113
Cameron		14	48	2	8								.167
Elmer Stricklett	P11	11	34	4	5								.147
George Cross	P11	11	34	1	5								.146
Culver		10	36	3	8								.222
Otis Stocksdale	P	10	34	2	7								.206
Wadsworth	P	10	31	5	8								.258

PITCHERS	W	L	PCT	G	GS	CG	SH	IP	H	BB	SO	ERA
Edwin Moriarity	12	21	.364	37								
George Hemming	11	15	.423	27								
Larry Hesterfer	6	13	.316	24								
Elmer Stricklett	3	6	.333	11								
George Cross	2	9	.182	11								
Wadsworth	1	2	.333									
Fredericks	1	3	.250									
Fred Applegate	1	5	.167									
Henry Fox	0	3	.000									
Charles Parkins	0	3	.000									
Otis Stocksdale	0	4	.000									

MULTI-TEAM PLAYERS

BATTERS	POS-GAMES	TEAMS	GP	AB	R	H	BI	2B	3B	HR	BB	SO	SB	BA
Matty McIntyre	OF138	BUF-NEW	138	500	75	128		21	6	6				.256
Stephen Griffin	2B68,3B64	JC-NEW	132	484	68	139		18	3	0				.287
Pop Foster	OF98,2B23	PRO-MON	129	465	72	117		19	6	14				.252
William Hayward	3B79,SS29	NEW-JC	127	501	54	128		16	2	3				.255
Ike Francis	SS75,3B51	ROC-BUF	127	499	71	143		17	2	3				.287
Frank Connaughton	SS117	BUF-WOR	119	448	52	118		17	6	1				.264
John Dillon	C41	ROC-PRO	58	196	19	49		2	0	0				.204
John McAleese	OF38,P16	ROC-NEW	55	191	21	45		3	1	1				.236
Pat McCauley	C54	PR-WO-NE	54	166	20	17		0	0	0				.102
Kellogg	2B36	ROC-NEW	36	127	13	26								.205
M. Kelly	C22	WOR-PRO	34	113	5	20		1	0	0				.177

MULTI-TEAM PLAYERS (cont.)

BATTERS	POS-GAMES	TEAMS	GP	AB	R	H	BI	2B	3B	HR	BB	SO	SB	BA
Jake Thielman	P34	RO-NE-JC-TO	34	96	13	19								.198
Edward Fertsch	P31	PRO-JC	31	94	10	12		0	0	0				.128
Bill Magee	P29	MON-BUF	30	105	15	20		2	0	0				.190
John Pappalau	P27	WOR-TOR	27	81	3	14		0	0	0				.169
Watty Lee	P24	MON-TOR	25	74	6	14								.189
Walsh		TOR-NEW	17	54	8	11								.204
Clark		NEW-JC	13	45	5	13								.289
Lovell		MON-PRO	11	41	2	11								.268
Robert Blewett	P10	MON-TOR	10	25	0	1								.040

PITCHERS	TEAMS	W	L	PCT	G	GS	CG	SH	IP	H	BB	SO	ERA
Bill Magee	MON-BUF	18	11	.621	29								
Edward Fertsch	PRO-JC	17	11	.607	31								
Jake Thielman	RO-NE-JC-TO	16	18	.471	34								
John Pappalau	WOR-TOR	12	12	.500	27								
Watty Lee	MON-TOR	9	12	.429	24								
John McAleese	ROC-NEW	8	7	.533	16								
Joe Yeager	TOR-MON	2	4	.333									
Robert Blewett	MON-TOR	1	7	.125									
Maurice Wolfe	JC-MON	0	3	.000									

1903
JERSEY CITY SKEETERS

In 1903, one of the Eastern League's newest members made a name for itself. In only its second year, this team rewrote the league's record book, permanently etching its name in a place reserved for the elite. That name was the Jersey City Skeeters.

Jersey City's first foray into the league structure came in 1887, as the Skeeters along with Newark joined the International League. After a mediocre sixth-place finish, Jersey City dropped out after only one year. In 1902, the team (again with Newark) rejoined the league and finished a strong third. This success would prove to be a mere prelude.

There was one new entry in the Eastern League structure of 1903. The city of Baltimore, for many years a major league town, was granted a franchise. Montreal was eased aside to make room for the Maryland city. However, Montreal was not out of the league for long. When Worcester failed in mid–July, the team was moved to Montreal to finish the season.

As the 1903 season began, the Skeeters quickly made a mockery of the quest for first, ripping off a 16-game win streak to start the season. Only Buffalo remained close as summer turned to fall. Near the end of the campaign, Jersey City erased all doubt with another long win skein—this time 24 in a row. At season's end, the Skeeters had racked up 92 wins and an 11-game bulge over Buffalo and Toronto. Far back in the distance finished the also-rans: Baltimore, Newark, Providence, Worcester/Montreal, and Rochester.

As one would expect, Jersey City players dominated the statistical charts. The batters were paced by batting champion Harry McCormick (.362), John Halligan (.313), and John Cassidy (.311). The moundsmen featured a trio of 20-game winners: George Pfanmiller with his league-best 28, Eugene McCann with 26, and Jake Thielman with 23. The only accolades not won by Jersey City were the home run crown taken home by Ed Atherton of Buffalo (9) and the strikeout title carried off by Toronto's Herb Briggs (205).

Although the 1903 Skeeters won more of their games than any other league team to date, their 92 wins were nowhere near the most ever won by an Eastern or International League team. Jersey City's all-time record reflects another fact about its remarkable season: The team's 92 wins came in only 125 games. Other teams may have won more games, but they all played many more contests to accomplish the feat. Jersey City's .736 winning percentage still tops the list for any International League champion.

JERSEY CITY Skeeters

| | | 1st | 92-33 | | .736 | | | | | | | | William Murray | |

BATTERS	POS-GAMES	GP	AB	R	H	BI	2B	3B	HR	BB	SO	SB	BA
John Cassidy	1B116	116	457	88	142		25	4	2			45	.311
Mickey Doolan	2B122	122	456	78	131		25	11	3			24	.287
Joseph Bean	SS126	126	484	112	139		25	1	0			44	.287
Walter Woods	3B116	116	399	57	107		21	3	1			17	.268
Harry McCormick	OF121	122	474	105	172		24	15	5			25	.362
Bill Halligan	OF120	120	432	86	135		20	8	4			21	.313
Wally Clement	OF110	110	464	86	123		8	3	2			30	.265
Frank McManus	C81,1B5	84	287	36	68		8	4	2			18	.239
John Dillon	C57	57	188	14	34							3	.181
Jake Thielman	P,1B5,3B4	42	115	20	29							5	.252
George Pfanmiller	P	40	115	20	19							4	.164
Eugene McCann	P	37	120	18	30							6	.250
John Barnett	P	20	76	8	12							1	.158

PITCHERS	W	L	PCT	G	GS	CG	SH	IP	H	BB	SO	ERA
George Pfanmiller	28	9	.757						253	57	126	
Eugene McCann	26	11	.724						271	78	126	
Jake Thielman	23	5	.821						164	63	80	
John Barnett	11	7	.611						153	40	42	

BUFFALO Bisons

| | | 2nd | 79-43 | | .648 | | -11.5 | | | | | George Stallings | |

BATTERS	POS-GAMES	GP	AB	R	H	BI	2B	3B	HR	BB	SO	SB	BA
Myron Grimshaw	1B70,OF21	91	364	52	108		16	9	0			10	.297
Frank LaPorte	2B47,C17	66	275	35	66		8	6	2			8	.240
William Nattress	SS124	124	477	84	108		14	7	3			38	.242
Fred Hartman	3B111	111	446	63	131		21	5	2			15	.294
Matty McIntyre	OF121	121	447	93	153		21	11	4			32	.342
John Shearon	OF92	92	357	39	82		10	3	2			11	.230
Jake Gettman	OF91	91	359	96	120		17	7	4			20	.334
Al Shaw	C75	75	255	38	63		9	4	0			12	.247
Ed Atherton	OF51,2B40,1B18	110	426	81	133		22	3	9			11	.312
Bill Milligan	OF25,P	53	154	36	43		9	2	4			1	.279
Al Ferry	P,OF9	46	120	21	28							1	.233
Charles Luskey	C29,2B2	31	99	10	23							2	.232
Bill Magee	P	26	77	8	13							3	.169
George Carey	1B24	24	90	8	23							0	.257
William Hooker	P	21	57	7	12							3	.211
Louis LeRoy	P	18	45	1	11							0	.244
Ed MacGamwell	1B16	16	53	13	14							2	.264
Lew McAllister	2B9,C4	14	55	10	17							3	.309
Lane		4	15	4	3							0	.200

PITCHERS	W	L	PCT	G	GS	CG	SH	IP	H	BB	SO	ERA
Bill Milligan	21	6	.778						212	47	113	
Al Ferry	20	8	.714						215	90	92	
Bill Magee	14	9	.610						189	62	61	
William Hooker	10	5	.667						111	28	43	
Louis LeRoy	7	7	.500						105	20	46	
Laroy	6	4	.600						81	24	55	

TORONTO Maple Leafs

| | | 3rd | 82-45 | | .646 | | -11 | | | | | James Gardner - Art Irwin | |

BATTERS	POS-GAMES	GP	AB	R	H	BI	2B	3B	HR	BB	SO	SB	BA
William Massey	1B121	121	461	66	139		31	5	3			19	.302
James Miller	2B115	115	418	56	104		11	7	0			18	.247
Jim Downey	SS114	114	426	49	104		7	2	1			16	.244
Lew Carr	3B71	71	235	20	55		6	3	0			6	.234
John White	OF125	125	492	79	154		11	8	0			36	.313
Lou Bruce	OF94,P	100	337	64	120		9	3	2			15	.356
Yance Weidensaul	OF66	66	251	39	64		4	7	0			12	.255
James Toft	C100	100	334	26	79		10	2	0			5	.233
Charles Kuhns	3B45,OF36,SS33,2B15	117	460	66	119		13	9	0			12	.259

TORONTO (cont.)
Maple Leafs

BATTERS	POS-GAMES	GP	AB	R	H	BI	2B	3B	HR	BB	SO	SB	BA
Herb Briggs	P	36	123	10	20							1	.163
Golden	OF30	30	111	13	29							3	.261
Maurice Wolfe	P	25	70	4	9							1	.129
Charles Kisinger	P	18	59	3	15							1	.254
Jim Murray	OF11	11	43	5	12							3	.279
Lewis Rapp	3B10	11	34	11	5							5	.148

PITCHERS		W	L	PCT	G	GS	CG	SH	IP	H	BB	SO	ERA
Herb Briggs		26	8	.765						234	83	205	
Lou Bruce		12	4	.750						111	20	52	
Maurice Wolfe		12	13	.480						195	76	93	
Charles Kisinger		11	7	.611						107	29	119	

BALTIMORE   4th   71-54   .568   -21   Wilbert Robinson -
Orioles   Hugh Jennings

BATTERS	POS-GAMES	GP	AB	R	H	BI	2B	3B	HR	BB	SO	SB	BA
Tom Jones	1B90,2B37	127	511	78	171		24	11	3			17	.335
Louis Castro	2B86,1B9	111	454	65	149		16	21	0			19	.328
Hugh Jennings	SS32	32	122	26	40							9	.328
Stephen Griffin	3B	(see multi-team players)											
Jack Hayden	OF121	121	478	90	166		20	13	2			29	.349
John Kelly	OF101	101	378	59	118		19	13	4			22	.312
Walt McCreedie	OF74	74	275	39	92		6	1	0			19	.335
Wilbert Robinson	C75	75	241	15	64		5	2	3			2	.266
Thomas Dowd	OF55	55	215	30	49							15	.228
Ahearn	C40,3B3	43	130	18	38		4	4	1			6	.292
Lewis Wiltse	P	40	118	40	35		7	5	1			2	.305
Fred Burchell	P	32	90	8	23							2	.256
Lyons	3B30,SS10,2B7	30	110	18	24							7	.218
Lawrence Quinlan	SS23	25	77	4	15							5	.195
Fox	2B19	19	69	10	14							3	.203
Merle Adkins	P	18	57	5	12							0	.211
Curtis	3B6,SS2	10	29	7	9							0	.310
Woods		8	26	6	2							3	.193
Bill Pounds	P	8	20	1	7							0	.350
Halle Souders	P	7	18	2	3							0	.166

PITCHERS		W	L	PCT	G	GS	CG	SH	IP	H	BB	SO	ERA
Lewis Wiltse		19	12	.613						201	34	117	
Fred Burchell		17	9	.727						199	77	109	
Merle Adkins		11	5	.687						122	32	58	
Rutherford		2	2	.500						33	15	21	
Bill Pounds		2	4	.333						49	8	8	
Halle Souders		2	4	.333						74	12	13	

NEWARK   5th   74-63   .540   -24   Walt Burnham
Sailors

BATTERS	POS-GAMES	GP	AB	R	H	BI	2B	3B	HR	BB	SO	SB	BA
Harry O'Hagen	1B132	132	461	80	117		15	8	2			35	.253
Wallace Taylor	2B96,SS2	98	335	33	91		14	0	3			6	.272
Charles Wagner	SS110,3B5,OF3	120	469	66	113		10	8	2			19	.241
Art Devlin	3B127	127	460	71	132		15	9	1			51	.287
John Lawlor	OF140	140	460	64	130		13	4	1			24	.283
Pat Dillard	OF127,1B9	136	294	52	118		22	7	2			19	.239
James Bannon	OF107,SS21,3B3	110	402	48	81		22	2	4			12	.201
John Shea	C93	93	298	20	61		9	3	0			7	.205
O'Brien	2B56	56	177	16	43		5	2	0			11	.244
Larry Hesterfer	P	35	99	12	10							1	.101
Edwin Moriarity	P	34	93	9	15							3	.161
Albert Pardee	P	32	91	5	10							1	.110
Walsh	P,OF8	28	70	6	15							4	.214
John Burke	P	21	88	13	20							0	.227
Flanagan	OF17	17	54	8	16							4	.296

NEWARK (cont.)
Sailors

BATTERS	POS-GAMES	GP	AB	R	H	BI	2B	3B	HR	BB	SO	SB	BA
Flanagan		15	45	6	11							1	.244
Ira Thomas	C14	14	31	2	8							1	.258
Larkin	SS9,3B2	10	39	5	10							1	.256

PITCHERS		W	L	PCT	G	GS	CG	SH	IP	H	BB	SO	ERA
Larry Hesterfer		17	12	.586						205	87	140	
Edwin Moriarity		15	17	.469						227	65	80	
Albert Pardee		13	14	.481						250	66	114	
John Burke		11	8	.579						151	61	69	
Walsh		9	5	.643						70	28	77	
Newenham		5	1	.833						52	11	16	

PROVIDENCE   6th   45-86   .344   -50   Richard Cogan
Grays

BATTERS	POS-GAMES	GP	AB	R	H	BI	2B	3B	HR	BB	SO	SB	BA
Pat Crisham	1B132	137	**530**	44	137		20	10	6			14	.257
Jim Connor	2B112	112	410	58	107		12	4	0			16	.261
Roy Rock	SS48	48	106	13	34							3	.320
James Stafford	3B130	130	472	52	109		18	3	3			23	.224
Harry Armbruster	OF131	131	467	68	120		14	5	2			20	.257
Albert Wagner	OF110,2B8,3B2	120	468	66	113		10	8	2			19	.241
Bert Conn	OF71,P	89	290	33	70		16	7	4			19	.241
William Diggins	C74	74	232	6	39							6	.168
Richard Cogan	OF54	54	197	26	53							6	.267
Sylvester	SS37	41	143	10	24							3	.167
Leon Viau	P,OF3	40	115	16	15							1	.130
Daniel Duggan		38	128	6	21							1	.164
Stan Yerkes	P	37	113	15	26							0	.230
Frank Shannon	SS34	34	128	6	21							9	.164
Westlake	C12	12	47	3	3							0	.081
Farmer		11	32	3	7							3	.219
McLaughlin	OF4	4	15	2	3							1	.200

PITCHERS		W	L	PCT	G	GS	CG	SH	IP	H	BB	SO	ERA
Leon Viau		12	19	.387						303	62	77	
Stan Yerkes		9	24	.273						**306**	59	97	
Bert Conn		5	10	.333						150	43	40	
Gray		2	6	.250						96	23	11	
Frank McPartlin		2	8	.200						94	25	10	
Clement		1	5	.167						58	12	8	

WORCESTER / MONTREAL   7th   37-93   .285   -57.5   George Wrigley - Bill Clancy
Riddlers / Royals   Gene DeMontreville

BATTERS	POS-GAMES	GP	AB	R	H	BI	2B	3B	HR	BB	SO	SB	BA
Bill Clancy	1B105	105	442	69	140		15	5	5			16	.317
Tom Sheehan	2B46,3B21	68	234	19	57		6	4	0			5	.244
Frank Connaughton	SS110,2B4	123	476	58	121		23	7	0			19	.254
Hurst	3B35,OF28	63	215	16	54		3	1	1			2	.250
H. Kellackey	OF,1B17,C13	111	412	47	93		13	5	0			9	.227
Rome Grey	OF56	56	226	25	70		9	3	0			1	.310
Steve Brodie	OF	(see multi-team players)											
Pat McCauley	C67	67	233	33	56							12	.240
Gene Demontreville	2B40,SS3	45	117	20	45							9	.254
Schroeder	OF20,3B20	44	210	11	32							4	.147
Joseph Delahanty	OF30	40	165	24	33							6	.261
George Wrigley	2B30,3B9	39	163	21	44							13	.269
Joseph Rickert	OF35	35	130	25	40							14	.307
Luyster		33	72	8	21							1	.292
John Pappalau	P	26	77	8	19							0	.246
Lave Winham	P	22	65	4	10							0	.154
Charles Frisbee	OF14	20	85	12	21							2	.247
Fred Applegate	P	13	43	4	13							0	.288
John Sharrott	OF11	11	47	6	11							0	.235
Fred McFall		10	34	4	9							0	.265

WORCESTER / MONTREAL(cont.)
Riddlers / Royals

PITCHERS	W	L	PCT	G	GS	CG	SH	IP	H	BB	SO	ERA
John Pappalau	9	13	.409						219	42	87	
Lave Winham	7	12	.368						143	75	71	
Fred Applegate	5	4	.556						52	47	32	

ROCHESTER   8th   34-97   .260   -61   Art Irwin - Abbie
Bronchos   Johnson - George Smith

BATTERS	POS-GAMES	GP	AB	R	H	BI	2B	3B	HR	BB	SO	SB	BA
Pete LePine	1B128,OF6	133	442	64	138		15	11	2			10	.312
Abbie Johnson	2B90,1B2,SS2	96	348	29	58		6	0	0			6	.167
Art Madison	SS	(see multi-team players)											
Burt Myers	3B	(see multi-team players)											
Joseph Schrall	OF129	129	487	72	121		21	9	0			13	.248
John Tuohey	OF47	47	183	11	38							6	.202
Howard	OF43	43	174	15	30							7	.176
Charles Fuller	C	(see multi-team players)											
Harry Blake	3B26,OF22	48	174	28	38							6	.218
Frank Leary	P	37	94	3	12							0	.128
Hardt	OF31	31	117	14	33							3	.291
Frank Scheibeck	SS31	31	114	14	22							3	.193
George Smith	3B17	28	76	10	20							3	.263
Bob Becker	P	26	85	7	19							0	.223
Lilly	C24	25	85	8	18							5	.212
Lovell	3B20	20	67	8	17							2	.253
Evers	C12	12	38	3	10							1	.269

PITCHERS	W	L	PCT	G	GS	CG	SH	IP	H	BB	SO	ERA
Bob Becker	11	12	.478						211	44	81	
Frank Leary	8	29	.286						245	84	111	

MULTI-TEAM PLAYERS

BATTERS	POS-GAMES	TEAMS	GP	AB	R	H	BI	2B	3B	HR	BB	SO	SB	BA
Art Madison	SS90,3B20	W/M-ROC	110	421	43	107		12	7	0			9	.254
Steve Brodie	OF102	BAL-W/M	103	389	34	97		12	1	0			15	.255
Morris Steelman	C100	W/M-ROC	100	326	21	72		9	0	2			7	.221
Jack Thiery	OF84,C8	NEW-BUF	89	286	58	69		7	6	1			8	.241
Stephen Griffin	3B82	JC-BAL	82	281	41	87		16	3	0			2	.306
Charles Fuller	C74,1B5	BA-RO-TO	79	263	30	65		10	5	0			14	.247
Burt Myers	3B53,2B21	BA-TO-RO	76	252	40	63							4	.250
Charles Gettig	OF21,SS17,3B10,P	BAL-ROC	71	234	26	54		4	1	2			5	.231
George Merritt	OF94,3B5,2B3	JC-W/M	60	222	34	57		8	4	0			11	.257
Green	3B53,SS11	BAL-TOR	53	186	21	47							16	.253
Brennan	C46	TOR-W/M	46	158	15	43		7	1	0			3	.272
John McAleese	1B28,OF5,P	ROC-BAL	46	157	23	51		9	2	0			7	.325
Ike Francis	2B30,SS14	PRO-BUF	44	159	23	43							2	.270
George Hemming	OF20,P	TOR-W/M	43	151	15	46		3	3	1			6	.305
Spiesman	C39	W/M-ROC	39	113	12	19							3	.168
William Mills	P	ROC-TOR	38	120	4	14							0	.116
Alex Jones	P	PRO-BUF	21	76	5	13							2	.173
Cy Falkenberg	P	W/M-TOR	20	62	7	13							0	.210
Dan McFarlan		ROC-PRO	18	60	8	18							5	.300
Hardy	P	TOR-BUF	18	58	5	11							0	.190
Morris Amole	P	BUF-PRO	18	57	6	11							0	.193
Edward Fertsch	P	JC-ROC												
Brown	C13	PRO-JC	13	47	7	13							1	.277
Henry Vorhees	P	BAL-BUF	11	25	2	5							0	.200

PITCHERS		TEAMS	W	L	PCT	G	GS	CG	SH	IP	H	BB	SO	ERA
William Mills		ROC-TOR	19	19	.500						289	87	151	
Alex Jones		PRO-BUF	9	9	.500						153	45	64	
Hardy		TOR-BUF	8	8	.500						142	37	58	
Morris Amole		BUF-PRO	8	10	.444						132	43	51	
Cy Falkenberg		W/M-TOR	7	7	.500						86	39	81	
Edward Fertsch		JC-ROC	6	8	.429						165	58	49	
Gettig		BAL-ROC	6	10	.375						122	50	33	

MULTI-TEAM PLAYERS (cont.)

PITCHERS	TEAMS	W	L	PCT	G	GS	CG	SH	IP	H	BB	SO	ERA
George Hemming	TOR-W/M	6	12	.333						174	17	40	
John McAleese	ROC-BAL	4	5	.444						74	18	34	
Henry Vorhees	BAL-BUF	3	6	.333						76	17	19	

TEAM BATTING

TEAMS	GP	AB	R	H	BI	2B	3B	HR	BB	SO	SB	BA
JERSEY CITY	128	4198	759	1179								.281
BUFFALO	124	4237	718	1186								.279
TORONTO	129	4286	554	1133								.264
BALTIMORE	124	4274	611	1217								.285
NEWARK	141	4478	548	1066								.238
PROVIDENCE	132	4292	440	955								.223
WOR/MONTREAL	130	4534	524	1102								.243
ROCHESTER	131	4307	466	1020								.237
	520	34606	4620	8858								.256

1904
POST-SEASON PLAY

During the 1890s, the Eastern League experimented with a post-season championship series. Dubbed the Steinert Cup, this series pitted the first- and second-place teams against one another. The Steinert Cup playoffs were discontinued after only two years. After the 1904 season another playoff series was unveiled. This series would expand beyond the boundaries of the league.

In 1902, a rival to the Eastern League had sprung up in the midwest. Calling itself the American Association, it soon proved every bit the Eastern's equal, drawing from the same talent base. This rivalry-in-the-making took a turn when the presidents of both leagues proposed a post-season matchup between their pennant winners. The first of these matchups was to take place after the 1904 season.

The Eastern League entered 1904 with only one minor change. The Montreal Royals, who had taken the place of Worcester halfway through the 1903 season, would now be Worcester's permanent replacement.

The Buffalo Bisons put together a strong squad and walked away with the bunting. Baltimore, Jersey City, and Newark finished in the first division, while Montreal, Toronto, Providence, and Rochester finished in the second. Montreal's Joe Yeager won the batting title with a .332 mark, while Frank LaPorte of Buffalo hit the most home runs (9). Mal Eason from Jersey City pitched his team to the most wins (26), and Toronto's Cy Falkenberg rang up the most strikeouts (175).

The inaugural test between the Eastern League and the American Association was scheduled to start immediately at season's end. Waiting in the wings to face the Buffalo Bisons was the American Association champion St. Paul Saints. The first two games were scheduled at the Bisons' home park. In the first of the twain, Buffalo whitewashed the Saints 7-0. Buffalo also prevailed in game two, needing 10 innings for the 5-4 decision. After several delays due to bad weather, and while en route to St. Paul, the third game was played in Columbus, Ohio. Here the Saints finally bested the Bisons 4-2. After further weather-related delays, the rest of the series was canceled, leaving Buffalo the victor, two games to one.

This inaugural tilt between the Eastern League and American Association was not given a name until it was resumed two years later, when it was dubbed the Little World Series. This series was played off and on until just after World War I, when it became an annual event for more than 50 years. During its tenure, the Little World Series (later called the Junior World Series) served as a showcase highlighting the two best teams from two of the best minor league circuits in the land.

BUFFALO Bisons

| | | | 1st | 88-46 | | .657 | | | | | | George Stallings | | |

BATTERS	POS-GAMES	GP	AB	R	H	BI	2B	3B	HR	BB	SO	SB	BA
Myron Grimshaw	1B138	138	544	98	177		31	14	2			22	.325
Frank LaPorte	2B124	124	457	60	129		21	11	9			22	.282
William Nattress	SS127	127	408	53	102		18	7	1			29	.250
Ed Courtney	3B138	138	528	94	148		20	11	1			37	.280
Joseph Delahanty	OF129	132	475	77	134		31	11	1			33	.282
Otis Clymer	OF125	126	504	97	148		18	8	0			56	.293
Jake Gettman	OF60	60	233	47	60		11	2	0			13	.258
Lew McAllister	C81,SS14	114	394	60	100		13	3	0			20	.254
Al Shaw	C64	64	215	23	56		12	1	1			8	.260
Lew Brockett	P	40	106	11	26		2	1	0			0	.245
Charles Kisinger	P	39	113	9	29		6	3	0			1	.257
Ernie Greene	P	35	100	15	25		3	1	1			3	.250
Bill Magee	P	25	75	5	7		1	0	0			0	.093
Alex Jones	P	23	76	4	13		4	0	0			0	.171
Stan Yerkes	P	18	46	3	7		4	0	0			0	.152
Bill Matthews	P	9	22	2	1		0	0	0			0	.045

PITCHERS	W	L	PCT	G	GS	CG	SH	IP	H	BB	SO	ERA
Charles Kisinger	24	11	.686						258	55	132	
Bill Magee	15	8	.652						158	60	51	
Lew Brockett	14	11	.560						216	57	62	
Alex Jones	12	8	.600						168	69	51	
Stan Yerkes	10	3	.769						118	30	32	
Ernie Greene	8	3	.727						97	30	38	
Bill Matthews	5	1	.833						54	10	30	

BALTIMORE Orioles

| | | | 2nd | 78-52 | | .600 | | -8 | | | | Hugh Jennings | | |

BATTERS	POS-GAMES	GP	AB	R	H	BI	2B	3B	HR	BB	SO	SB	BA
Tim Jordan	1B132	132	471	91	133		15	16	6			23	.282
Hugh Jennings	2B78,SS15	92	332	65	97		21	0	1			23	.292
Phil Lewis	SS122	123	470	69	110		17	7	0			30	.294
Stephen Griffin	3B124	124	418	53	114		13	2	0			40	.273
John Kelly	OF133	133	479	63	142		21	2	0			39	.296
Herm McFarland	OF130	130	483	82	124		14	12	3			39	.257
Jack Hayden	OF123	123	517	87	146		22	12	1			42	.282
Hugh Hearne	C56	56	172	22	43		9	2	1			6	.250
Charles Loudenslager	2B61,3B10	85	281	32	72		8	8	0			8	.256
Bill Byers	C55	55	181	15	45		2	2	0			5	.243
Lewis Wiltse	P	46	124	20	33		1	4	1			2	.266
Fred Burchell	P	45	136	9	31		5	1	0			0	.228
Merle Adkins	P	39	97	8	27		3	0	0			0	.278
Wilbert Robinson	C32	32	93	8	22		3	0	0			3	.236
Del Mason	P	25	74	5	18		1	0	0			0	.243

PITCHERS	W	L	PCT	G	GS	CG	SH	IP	H	BB	SO	ERA
Merle Adkins	22	9	.709						257	48	99	
Lewis Wiltse	20	8	.714						226	57	95	
Del Mason	16	7	.696						180	37	99	
Fred Burchell	16	17	.485						287	105	106	

JERSEY CITY Skeeters

| | | | 3rd | 76-57 | | .571 | | -11.5 | | | | William Murray | | |

BATTERS	POS-GAMES	GP	AB	R	H	BI	2B	3B	HR	BB	SO	SB	BA
John Cassidy	1B97	97	371	55	110		14	3	0			33	.296
Mickey Doolan	2B70,SS62	132	491	65	130		21	13	2			37	.265
Joseph Bean	SS67	67	240	43	59		7	0	0			17	.246
Walter Woods	3B122	122	410	45	91		16	3	1			11	.222
Bill Halligan	OF133	134	451	77	136		31	11	0			33	.302
William Keister	OF128	134	530	79	145		25	6	2			53	.274
Wally Clement	OF99	99	389	64	123		14	10	1			36	.316
John Dillon	C45	45	157	20	32		2	0	0			2	.204
George Merritt	OF39,1B36	92	322	49	97		13	6	2			24	.301

JERSEY CITY (cont.)
Skeeters

BATTERS	POS-GAMES	GP	AB	R	H	BI	2B	3B	HR	BB	SO	SB	BA
Harry Pattee	2B44	44	168	25	44		5	3	0			14	.261
Mal Eason	P	42	125	10	21		4	0	0			2	.168
George Vandegrift	C40	40	135	9	30		3	1	0			8	.222
Jake Thielman	P	35	104	11	25		3	3	1			0	.240
George Pfanmiller	P	32	86	10	21		2	2	0			2	.244
Carrisch	C24	24	84	10	24		3	0	0			2	.286
Eugene McCann	P	23	60	7	12		2	1	1			1	.206
O'Neil	C22	22	75	11	23		4	0	0			1	.307
Art Mueller	P	21	57	5	15		1	0	0			0	.263
John Barnett	P	16	38	5	5		0	0	0			2	.132
Tom Stankard	2B14	14	54	10	12		1	0	0			3	.222

PITCHERS	W	L	PCT	G	GS	CG	SH	IP	H	BB	SO	ERA
Mal Eason	26	11	.703						265	66	131	
George Pfanmiller	15	11	.577						188	45	65	
Eugene McCann	12	9	.571						158	49	62	
Jake Thielman	10	11	.476						185	74	69	
Art Mueller	8	8	.500						132	23	60	
John Barnett	4	6	.400						105	36	49	

NEWARK   4th   77-59   .566   -12   Walt Burnham
Sailors

BATTERS	POS-GAMES	GP	AB	R	H	BI	2B	3B	HR	BB	SO	SB	BA
Harry O'Hagen	1B110	110	418	74	107		10	4	0			28	.256
Charles Wagner	2B82	82	292	32	61		7	1	3			15	.209
Frank Gatins	SS136	136	447	50	108		18	6	1			51	.242
Jim Cockman	3B138	138	522	60	130		12	2	2			32	.249
James Bannon	OF137	142	532	63	132		24	8	3			32	.248
Pat Dillard	OF129	132	504	63	130		24	9	2			16	.258
Jim Jones	OF120	132	470	53	121		21	7	0			30	.257
John Shea	C99	99	284	28	60		6	2	0			14	.211
William Mahling	2B55	84	254	44	60		3	2	1			28	.236
Larry Hesterfer	P	45	127	6	17		1	0	0			0	.134
Lynch	C42	42	135	21	31		3	0	1			5	.230
John Burke	P	33	98	7	18		5	0	0			1	.184
Albert Pardee	P	32	79	12	15		1	1	0			0	.190
Stafford	1B30	30	109	11	20		3	1	0			8	.183
Breckenridge	P	21	54	5	4		0	0	0			1	.073
Edwin Moriarity	P	13	41	3	12		0	0	0			1	.293
Mitchell	OF12	12	43	6	9		2	0	0			2	.209

PITCHERS	W	L	PCT	G	GS	CG	SH	IP	H	BB	SO	ERA
Larry Hesterfer	23	16	.590						275	105	148	
Albert Pardee	19	11	.633						200	59	94	
Breckenridge	10	6	.625						135	50	84	
Edwin Moriarity	7	3	.700						92	18	34	
John Burke	7	7	.500						120	40	55	
Wenig	1	2	.333						48	19	12	

MONTREAL   5th   67-62   .519   -18.5   Charles Atherton - Ed Barrow
Royals

BATTERS	POS-GAMES	GP	AB	R	H	BI	2B	3B	HR	BB	SO	SB	BA
Bill Clancy	1B119	123	497	87	154		12	21	0			25	.308
William Dyer	2B59	68	247	19	60		9	3	0			12	.243
Joe Yeager	SS118	124	440	81	146		26	13	2			38	.332
Fred Hartman	3B101	101	359	47	97		22	1	3			24	.270
Michael Joyce	OF118	130	464	61	118		6	7	1			48	.254
J. Walters	OF101	101	388	61	110		14	3	0			13	.283
Harry Hoffman	OF39	45	152	23	33		5	2	0			9	.217
George Gibson	C72	80	269	29	55		7	3	0			9	.204
Frank McManus	C53	66	215	22	53		5	2	0			15	.247
Reuben Adams	P,OF18	47	135	16	36		1	2	0			0	.266
Archibald McCarthy	P	35	99	6	17		1	0	0			0	.172

MONTREAL (cont.)
Royals

BATTERS	POS-GAMES	GP	AB	R	H	BI	2B	3B	HR	BB	SO	SB	BA
John Pappalau	P	35	96	11	18		2	0	0			1	.188
Louis LeRoy	P	33	91	7	22		3	0	0			0	.242
J. Kelly	OF19	20	69	8	13		2	1	0			2	.190
Luyster	OF17	18	64	4	10		0	0	0			1	.156
Tom Doran		10	37	2	7		1	0	0			0	.189

PITCHERS	W	L	PCT	G	GS	CG	SH	IP	H	BB	SO	ERA
John Pappalau	18	14	.563						266	76	77	
Archibald McCarthy	16	17	.485						247	76	131	
Louis LeRoy	14	10	.583						207	57	87	
Reuben Adams	13	10	.565						186	55	77	

TORONTO   6th   67-71   .486   -23   Art Irwin -
Maple Leafs   Richard Harley

BATTERS	POS-GAMES	GP	AB	R	H	BI	2B	3B	HR	BB	SO	SB	BA
Lewis Rapp	1B95	104	364	47	101		10	10	2			28	.277
Roy Parker	2B61	61	212	27	48		6	2	0			8	.226
Ike Francis	SS65	66	235	31	55		8	3	1			6	.234
Lew Carr	3B135	135	419	60	91		14	3	0			25	.217
John White	OF134	134	509	70	141		26	11	1			29	.277
Richard Harley	OF127	133	503	74	127		10	6	1			35	.253
Jim Murray	OF122	135	494	75	125		19	14	4			46	.253
Charles Fuller	C83	89	300	31	72		9	2	0			19	.240
Yance Weidensaul	2B56,SS49	119	419	70	108		16	4	0			24	.258
Tom Raub	C64,1B26	100	332	45	93		13	12	0			22	.280
Cy Falkenberg	P	40	115	7	19		2	2	0			0	.165
Clarence Currie	P	35	98	12	22		1	3	1			3	.224
Fred Applegate	P	34	101	3	13		2	2	0			0	.129
William Massey		24	79	7	19		3	1	0			3	.241
Clark	2B16	18	56	4	7		1	0	0			0	.125
Lou Bruce	P	16	41	3	7		1	0	0			0	.171
Jim Gardner	P	9	22	4	3		0	1	0			0	.136

PITCHERS	W	L	PCT	G	GS	CG	SH	IP	H	BB	SO	ERA
Clarence Currie	18	10	.643						253	90	79	
Cy Falkenberg	18	17	.514						249	**119**	**175**	
Fred Applegate	12	16	.429						190	86	131	
Lou Bruce	4	3	.571						67	14	19	
Jim Gardner	2	3	.400						70	18	29	

PROVIDENCE   7th   52-81   .391   -35.5   Thomas Daly
Grays

BATTERS	POS-GAMES	GP	AB	R	H	BI	2B	3B	HR	BB	SO	SB	BA
Thomas Daly	1B125	127	481	45	124		22	1	2			20	.258
Jim Connor	2B104	104	366	35	82		16	1	0			17	.227
Roy Rock	SS135	135	461	33	106		12	1	1			7	.230
Harry Aubrey	3B109,2B20	129	432	45	111		13	1	1			24	.257
Bert Conn	OF130	132	488	62	124		22	4	3			21	.254
Ernest Vinson	OF76	76	272	53	98		12	6	1			7	.360
Albert Wagner	OF74	80	296	45	70		10	3	2			18	.237
Ira Thomas	C63	66	225	20	55		8	3	0			2	.244
Bill Milligan	OF33,P	65	228	31	46		13	2	2			13	.202
Harry Armbruster	OF40	45	151	16	41		2	1	0			11	.272
Jim Fairbank	P	39	117	12	22		3	0	0			0	.189
Hickman	3B21	32	106	7	19		4	0	0			5	.179
Morris Amole	P	24	68	3	17		2	0	0			1	.250
Monte Beville	C19	19	69	7	19		3	1	0			1	.275
Harris	OF11	13	47	2	14		0	2	0			3	.298
James Callahan	P	13	35	7	8		0	0	0			0	.229
Daniel Duggan	C10	12	29	4	2		0	1	0			0	.069

PITCHERS	W	L	PCT	G	GS	CG	SH	IP	H	BB	SO	ERA
Jim Fairbank	14	17	.452						249	105	112	

PROVIDENCE (cont.)
Grays

PITCHERS	W	L	PCT	G	GS	CG	SH	IP	H	BB	SO	ERA
Morris Amole	8	11	.421						157	47	31	
James Callahan	7	6	.538						94	53	25	
Bill Milligan	7	12	.368						188	54	69	
Ambrose Puttman	6	1	.857						49	14	29	
Al Kellogg	2	3	.400						47	33	27	
Jackson	1	2	.333						36	12	10	
Jerry Nops	1	4	.200						24	8	12	
Swanson	0	4	.000						36	4	11	
William Hooker	0	5	.000						55	12	10	

ROCHESTER   8th   28-105   .211   -59.5   George Smith
Bronchos

BATTERS	POS-GAMES	GP	AB	R	H	BI	2B	3B	HR	BB	SO	SB	BA
George Carey	1B134	134	517	45	142		23	4	2			5	.275
George Smith	2B69,SS49	126	510	46	122		25	4	1			13	.239
Art Madison	SS35	35	114	10	38		5	2	0			4	.333
Charles Kuhns	3B	(see multi-team players)											
Ed DeGroff	OF133	133	482	54	107		16	8	1			43	.222
Pete LePine	OF84	84	308	55	79		6	5	6			19	.257
John Flournoy	OF47	49	174	26	43		10	3	0			7	.247
Pat McCauley	C52	52	174	16	44		8	1	0			5	.253
Nichols	2B47,C27	93	320	25	68		10	2	0			13	.212
Collins	OF30	58	193	20	45		4	1	1			3	.233
George Schultz	P	48	159	12	19		2	0	0			1	.120
Edward Fertsch	P	35	98	8	16		3	1	0			2	.163
Harry Barton		31	112	7	25		2	0	0			2	.223
Curtin	3B14	29	107	5	22		0	1	0			0	.206
Summers	C13	28	95	5	22		1	0	0			1	.232
Oliver Faulkner	P	28	71	6	10		1	2	0			0	.141
J. S. Kennedy	3B25	25	88	6	21		5	0	0			2	.239
Charles Gettig	3B13	19	56	6	7		0	0	0			0	.125
J. Kennedy	C17	17	63	3	17		2	0	0			0	.270
Lawton		15	46	4	14		3	2	0			0	.304
Joe Wall	C13	14	26	4	9		0	1	0			1	.346
Fitzhenry	OF10	11	44	3	11		0	1	0			3	.250

PITCHERS	W	L	PCT	G	GS	CG	SH	IP	H	BB	SO	ERA
Edward Fertsch	8	21	.276						266	95	80	
Oliver Faulkner	6	13	.316						184	62	94	
George Schultz	6	22	.214						245	102	94	
Harry Kane	2	5	.286						68	43	39	
James Cleary	1	4	.200						50	16	12	
Bob Becker	1	7	.125						74	14	12	

MULTI-TEAM PLAYERS

BATTERS	POS-GAMES	TEAMS	GP	AB	R	H	BI	2B	3B	HR	BB	SO	SB	BA
Ed Atherton	2B62,OF58	BUF-MON	131	495	77	139		23	6	1			26	.281
Charles Kuhns	3B54,SS31	TOR-MON	85	322	33	71		6	0	0			10	.216
Elmer Bliss	OF37,P	MON-ROC	65	211	15	55		7	4	1			2	.261
Tom Barry	OF45	BUF-MON	52	174	27	36		3	1	0			12	.207
James Toft	C43	TOR-PRO	44	142	8	22		2	0	0			2	.155
Jack Thoney	3B22	ROC-MON	36	138	20	47		9	3	2			12	.346
William Mills	P	TO-RO-BA	35	90	6	11		1	1	0			0	.122
Maurice Wolfe	P	TOR-MON	35	73	9	18		1	0	0			0	.247
Frank Leary	P	ROC-TOR	26	73	5	13		3	2	0			2	.179
Leon Viau		MON-PRO	23	66	4	12		1	1	0			0	.182
D. Walters	P	ROC-BAL	19	51	7	10		0	0	0			0	.190
Jim Limerick	P	BUF-ROC	11	21	1	0		0	0	0			0	.000

PITCHERS	TEAMS	W	L	PCT	G	GS	CG	SH	IP	H	BB	SO	ERA
Maurice Wolfe	TOR-MON	10	13	.435						182	82	79	
William Mills	TO-RO-BA	9	20	.310						281	88	94	
Frank Leary	ROC-TOR	7	14	.333						204	71	78	

MULTI-TEAM PLAYERS (cont.)

PITCHERS	TEAMS	W	L	PCT	G	GS	CG	SH	IP	H	BB	SO	ERA
Elmer Bliss	MON-ROC	4	9	.308						132	25	53	
D. Walters	BAL-ROC	4	13	.235						154	44	77	
Jim Limerick	BUF-ROC	2	5	.286						62	29	40	

TEAM BATTING

TEAMS	GP	AB	R	H	BI	2B	3B	HR	BB	SO	SB	BA
BUFFALO	135	4598	711	1233							251	.269
BALTIMORE	129	4393	635	1187							246	.270
JERSEY CITY	132	4424	616	1185							299	.268
NEWARK	137	4508	561	1064							279	.233
MONTREAL	127	4265	357	1096							257	.257
TORONTO	138	4478	590	1087							248	.243
PROVIDENCE	133	4330	459	1006							145	.232
ROCHESTER	133	4559	431	1038							138	.228
	532	35555	4360	8896							1863	.250

1905
PROVIDENCE CLAMDIGGERS

In the final decade of the nineteenth century, many new teams first saw service in the Eastern League. One of the strongest of this group hailed from Providence, Rhode Island.

Providence's foray into organized baseball began at a high level. The city's first team appeared in 1878 in the National League, where they remained for eight years. After winning two pennants, accompanied by several first division finishes, Providence left the National League after the 1885 season. When the Eastern Association was organized following the 1890 season, Providence was a natural invitee. The city joined the league in time for the start of the 1891 season.

Success came quickly to the Clamdiggers (sometimes called the Grays) as they won four pennants in their first nine years. For the next three years, the Clamdiggers wallowed in the second division, winding up in seventh place in 1904. This, however, would prove a temporary residence.

In 1905, Providence hired a new player-manager. Jack Dunn brought a spark that rekindled the team's fire. As the 1905 season unfolded, Providence found itself in a dogfight for the lead. After a spirited battle with Baltimore, the Clamdiggers claimed the prize by a slim half-game margin. Jersey City finished a close third, followed by Newark, Buffalo, Montreal, Rochester, and Toronto.

Providence's flag was earned by fine batting performances from Herm McFarland (.319), Ira Thomas (.311), and Jack Dunn himself (.301). Their pitching teammate, Jack Cronin, finished with the circuit's most wins (29). League honors not garnered by the Rhode Island crew included the batting title (Buffalo's Frank LaPorte, .331), home run title (Jim Murray of Buffalo/Toronto, 9), and the strikeout crown (Walt Clarkson of Jersey City, 195).

After 1905, the team slid into mediocrity, turning in three tail-end finishes in a row. The team rebounded to claim another flag in the years leading up to the First World War before leaving the league in 1917. In the mid–1920s, Providence returned for a curtain call, serving as a mid-season replacement. Following this brief tenure, the team left the International League for good.

For nearly 30 years, Providence was an integral part of the International family of leagues. The team's demise left a void in the league's structure in southern New England. Some 60 years later, this void was filled by Providence's nearby neighbor, Pawtucket, who remains with the International League to this day.

PROVIDENCE Clamdiggers

| | | 1st | 83-47 | | .638 | | | | Jack Dunn | | |

BATTERS	POS-GAMES	GP	AB	R	H	BI	2B	3B	HR	BB	SO	SB	BA
Bert Conn	1B130	130	461	75	125		14	14	2			25	.271
Jack Dunn	2B127	135	521	73	157		18	5	0			19	.301
Roy Rock	SS135	135	464	71	126		11	8	0			12	.272
James Morgan	3B63	63	226	38	66		7	1	0			10	.292
Steve Brodie	OF134	134	500	45	135		12	3	0			18	.270
Herm McFarland	OF114	114	420	91	134		19	9	3			33	.319
Harry Ball	OF84	86	322	49	73		9	6	2			19	.227
Ira Thomas	C83	85	286	42	89		15	6	2			13	.311
Phil Poland	3B53,OF21	83	291	36	71		6	3	2			15	.244
Fred Jacklitsch	C59	62	191	28	60		8	6	1			5	.314
Jack Cronin	P42	42	124	14	30		4	3	2			1	.242
Ed Poole	P37	37	115	10	30		2	2	0			2	.261
Jerry Nops	P35	35	104	15	23		1	3	0			1	.221
Ambrose Puttmann	P16	16	50	2	12		3	2	1			0	.240
George Josslyn	P16	16	50	7	11		4	0	1			0	.220
Kelly		11	34	2	4		0	0	0			0	.118

PITCHERS		W	L	PCT	G	GS	CG	SH	IP	H	BB	SO	ERA
Jack Cronin		29	12	.707	42				338	266	71	190	
Ed Poole		21	12	.636	37				298	271	66	126	
Jerry Nops		17	12	.586	35				281	259	39	105	
George Josslyn		9	6	.600	16				138	126	28	58	
Ambrose Puttmann		6	5	.545	16				121	98	39	73	

BALTIMORE Orioles

| | | 2nd | 82-47 | | .636 | | -0.5 | | Hugh Jennings | | |

BATTERS	POS-GAMES	GP	AB	R	H	BI	2B	3B	HR	BB	SO	SB	BA
Tim Jordan	1B130	130	493	77	154		26	10	1			22	.312
James Mullen	2B66	66	222	33	58		10	1	1			13	.261
Hugh Jennings	SS56	56	179	24	45		8	0	0			3	.251
Offa Neal	3B47,SS79	124	493	69	138		20	7	2			17	.280
John Kelly	OF128	128	472	85	126		21	1	0			42	.267
John McAleese	OF119	119	459	80	131		15	3	0			33	.285
Claude Rothgeb	OF63	63	238	36	64		10	3	0			7	.269
Bill Byers	C90	91	295	38	96		15	5	1			3	.325
Charles Loudenslager	2B62,3B30,OF13	105	368	39	98		14	6	1			18	.266
Hugh Hearne	C70	74	202	21	61		12	2	0			8	.302
Jack Hayden	OF46	46	186	31	44		5	7	1			9	.237
Fred Burchell	P41	44	126	16	28		1	0	1			4	.222
Del Mason	P35	35	101	11	20		5	0	0			1	.198
John McNeal	P33	33	87	8	13		2	0	0			0	.149
Merle Adkins	P32	32	99	1	15		0	1	0			1	.152
Lynch	3B21	21	60	7	14		2	0	0			0	.233
Sylvester	3B19	19	54	6	9		1	1	1			0	.167
Lewis Wiltse	P16	16	38	2	6		1	0	0			0	.158
Bill O'Hara	OF11	14	50	9	18		3	1	1			1	.360
Bill Hallman		13	50	2	8		1	0	0			0	.160
Stephen Griffin	3B11	11	33	2	11		1	1	0			0	.333

PITCHERS		W	L	PCT	G	GS	CG	SH	IP	H	BB	SO	ERA
Fred Burchell		24	10	.706	41				295	241	83	145	
John McNeal		18	9	.667	33				243	184	71	105	
Merle Adkins		18	9	.667	32				262	239	48	81	
Del Mason		18	11	.621	35				266	259	76	134	
Lewis Wiltse		3	5	.375	16				73	81	10	26	

JERSEY CITY Skeeters

| | | 3rd | 81-49 | | .623 | | -2 | | William Murray | | |

BATTERS	POS-GAMES	GP	AB	R	H	BI	2B	3B	HR	BB	SO	SB	BA
John Cassidy	1B79	79	274	51	73		19	4	1			19	.266
Harry Pattee	2B88	89	313	42	93		9	7	1			20	.297
Joseph Bean	SS97	97	358	64	104		10	0	0			14	.291
Walter Woods	3B127	127	454	45	95		12	1	2			17	.209
Wally Clement	OF134	134	559	85	155		20	9	1			59	.277

JERSEY CITY (cont.)
Skeeters

BATTERS	POS-GAMES	GP	AB	R	H	BI	2B	3B	HR	BB	SO	SB	BA
Bill Halligan	OF130	130	443	84	124		21	8	2			24	.280
William Keister	OF126	134	520	71	151		22	6	3			**68**	.290
Pat McCauley	C80	80	247	24	55		14	4	0			23	.223
George Merritt	2B45,1B31,SS29	113	411	62	105		15	2	4			29	.255
George Vandegrift	C56,1B27	92	304	25	74		11	3	0			4	.243
Walt Clarkson	P33	33	96	8	13		0	2	0			3	.135
Viv Lindaman	P33	33	93	11	18		4	0	0			3	.193
Jake Thielman	P17	31	85	8	18		4	1	1			2	.212
George Pfanmiller	P26	30	70	8	12		2	0	0			4	.171
Fred Olmstead	P26	26	71	3	15		0	1	0			1	.211
Eugene McCann	P12	13	32	3	5		0	0	0			0	.156
Charles Cargo	SS10	10	29	3	8		1	0	0			4	.276
George McQuillan	P9	9	17	0	1		0	0	0			0	.059

PITCHERS		W	L	PCT	G	GS	CG	SH	IP	H	BB	SO	ERA
Viv Lindaman		24	7	.774	33				266	243	48	116	
Walt Clarkson		17	12	.586	33				263	210	72	**195**	
George Pfanmiller		10	9	.526	26				188	174	45	90	
Fred Olmstead		8	12	.400	26				187	159	74	103	
Eugene McCann		7	1	.875	12				74	63	22	33	
Jake Thielman		7	3	.700	17				119	95	60	53	
George McQuillan		5	2	.714	9				54	42	14	30	

NEWARK   4th   69-62   .527   -14.5   Walt Burnham
Sailors

BATTERS	POS-GAMES	GP	AB	R	H	BI	2B	3B	HR	BB	SO	SB	BA
Harry O'Hagen	1B113	119	435	62	109		19	4	0			27	.251
William Mahling	2B115	121	389	68	95		11	5	0			35	.244
Frank Gatins	SS114	114	395	50	94		17	2	3			36	.238
Jim Cockman	3B132	132	478	53	111		11	6	1			31	.232
Jim Jones	OF131	131	470	55	114		19	6	1			32	.243
Ed Swander	OF115	115	428	50	107		13	8	0			20	.250
Murphy	OF110	110	382	35	92		17	4	0			27	.241
John Shea	C78	78	237	8	42		4	1	0			1	.177
Joe Connor	C40,1B18	61	173	23	43		3	0	0			12	.249
Charles Wagner	2B16,SS14	49	139	16	31		6	1	1			8	.223
Larry Hesterfer	P39	39	106	12	23		1	0	0			2	.217
Edwin Moriarity	P32	35	92	11	20		1	1	0			0	.217
Albert Pardee	P33	33	83	7	12		0	0	0			0	.145
McLane	P14	22	44	4	10		3	2	1			1	.227
Foster	OF15	15	48	13	22		8	0	3			6	.458
John Skopec	P8	8	19	1	3		2	0	0			0	.158

PITCHERS		W	L	PCT	G	GS	CG	SH	IP	H	BB	SO	ERA
Albert Pardee		19	11	.633	33				268	220	53	85	
Larry Hesterfer		19	17	.528	39				305	266	**100**	133	
Edwin Moriarity		15	13	.536	32				256	220	48	101	
McLane		3	7	.300	14				85	59	29	34	
John Skopec		2	4	.333	8				51	38	29	34	
Bonno		1	2	.333					19	18	12	6	

BUFFALO   5th   63-74   .460   -23.5   George Stallings
Bisons

BATTERS	POS-GAMES	GP	AB	R	H	BI	2B	3B	HR	BB	SO	SB	BA
Ed Murphy	1B116	116	439	43	106		14	6	2			21	.242
Frank LaPorte	2B111,SS10	120	447	75	148		**39**	11	8			24	**.331**
William Nattress	SS113	122	421	60	104		12	4	4			22	.247
Lew Brockett	3B82,2B12	110	399	44	91		14	3	0			21	.228
Jake Gettman	OF137	137	558	84	152		27	10	2			16	.272
Joseph Delahanty	OF89,1B12	104	396	50	124		22	9	5			18	.313
W. Miller	OF78	78	285	33	62		9	2	0			12	.218
Frank McManus	C71	71	242	26	60		8	0	0			11	.248

BUFFALO (cont.)
Bisons

BATTERS	POS-GAMES	GP	AB	R	H	BI	2B	3B	HR	BB	SO	SB	BA
Lew McAllister	C51,3B36,SS12	105	380	42	89		10	5	0			10	.234
Bill Milligan	P36,OF10	48	139	19	41		11	2	1			1	.295
Ernie Greene	P20	44	132	11	27		2	1	0			0	.205
Hugh Hill	OF42	42	161	20	35		5	2	1			11	.217
Charles Kisinger	P39	39	122	9	20		5	1	1			4	.164
Stan Yerkes	P35	35	94	2	12		2	0	0			1	.128
Brown	3B22	24	81	7	18		2	2	0			0	.222
Alex Jones	P19	19	48	2	9		1	0	0			1	.188
Bob Woods	C18	18	71	7	24		3	1	0			0	.338

PITCHERS		W	L	PCT	G	GS	CG	SH	IP	H	BB	SO	ERA
Charles Kisinger		20	15	.574	39				317	289	82	157	
Bill Milligan		19	16	.543	36				282	268	73	117	
Stan Yerkes		13	19	.406	35				263	303	49	85	
Ernie Greene		8	8	.500	20				141	123	41	75	
Alex Jones		3	11	.214	19				135	142	37	39	

MONTREAL   6th   56-80   .412   -30   James Bannon
Royals

BATTERS	POS-GAMES	GP	AB	R	H	BI	2B	3B	HR	BB	SO	SB	BA
Candy LaChance	1B117	117	430	38	117		12	4	0			21	.272
James Miller	2B93	95	320	44	57		5	0	0			18	.178
L. Hartmann	SS80	85	276	19	48		6	2	0			10	.174
Fred Hartman	3B77	77	279	30	63		12	2	3			12	.226
Michael Joyce	OF138	138	491	66	129		8	2	0			36	.263
Patrick Meaney	OF119	129	480	52	111		16	2	1			23	.231
James Bannon	OF98,3B28	134	484	68	124		22	7	0			32	.256
Tom Raub	C74,1B17	103	351	34	103		11	5	5			33	.293
Yance Weidensaul	2B46,OF22,SS17	91	332	50	95		16	2	1			12	.286
William Dyer	SS32,3B11	43	160	9	32		7	1	0			1	.200
George Gibson	C41	41	131	7	38		6	1	0			8	.290
John Pappalau	P35	35	101	6	18		2	0	0			0	.178
Frank Barber	P28	32	102	3	16		1	0	0			0	.157
Louis LeRoy	P32	32	89	0	12		2	0	0			0	.135
Archibald McCarthy	P28	28	77	5	13		1	0	0			0	.169
Charles Kuhns	3B15	24	80	10	20		5	0	0			2	.250
James		12	38	2	4		0	0	0			0	.105
Charles Clancy	P11	11	29	3	5		0	0	0			0	.172
Harry Felix	P11	11	28	1	5		2	0	0			0	.179
Ferry		11	28	4	4		0	0	0			1	.143
Buss	C10	10	30	0	5		0	0	0			0	.167

PITCHERS		W	L	PCT	G	GS	CG	SH	IP	H	BB	SO	ERA
Louis LeRoy		18	12	.600	32				250	198	63	166	
Archibald McCarthy		14	11	.560	28				232	226	44	111	
John Pappalau		13	20	.394	35				290	310	59	124	
Frank Barber		7	17	.292	28				224	225	71	81	
Clancy		3	4	.429	11				68	80	18	21	
Harry Felix		1	9	.100	11				85	85	20	31	

ROCHESTER   7th   51-86   .372   -35.5   Al Buckenberger
Bronchos

BATTERS	POS-GAMES	GP	AB	R	H	BI	2B	3B	HR	BB	SO	SB	BA
Bill Clancy	1B69	69	266	26	77		1	5	1			10	.289
Amby McConnell	2B80	80	287	23	73		4	3	1			9	.254
George Smith	SS87,2B50	139	550	65	138		13	8	0			25	.251
James O'Brien	3B86,SS38	124	424	42	90		13	6	0			16	.212
John Manning	OF121	124	475	57	120		3	2	0			24	.253
Hogan Yancey	OF113	113	426	56	101		14	12	3			28	.237
George Barclay	OF108	108	421	56	103		6	4	0			27	.245
Morris Steelman	C85	89	274	26	61		5	3	0			8	.223
Fred Payne	C67,OF14	86	254	17	66		8	6	2			5	.260
George Carey	1B43	43	167	11	42		8	0	0			2	.252
J. S. Kennedy	3B35	36	125	14	26		5	4	1			6	.208

ROCHESTER (cont.)
Bronchos

BATTERS	POS-GAMES	GP	AB	R	H	BI	2B	3B	HR	BB	SO	SB	BA
James Cleary	P35	36	96	1	11	1	0	0			1	.115
Oliver Faulkner	P35	35	103	1	13	3	2	0			0	.126
George Schultz	P35	35	98	6	16	0	1	0			1	.163
D. Walters	P32	32	92	4	19	1	0	0			0	.206
Leonard Burrell	3B15,2B14	30	95	9	29	6	2	0			2	.305
Rothfuss	OF27	27	86	12	23	3	2	1			4	.240
Jim Wallace	OF11	11	36	2	7	0	1	0			2	.194
Owens	SS10	10	30	4	5	0	0	0			0	.167

PITCHERS	W	L	PCT	G	GS	CG	SH	IP	H	BB	SO	ERA
George Schultz	13	21	.382	35				260	261	93	102	
James Cleary	11	17	.393	35				249	229	73	117	
Oliver Faulkner	11	18	.379	35				287	263	83	128	
D. Walters	11	18	.379	32				244	232	73	124	
Frank McLean	2	2	.500					39	39	13	11	
Schitzer	0	3	.000					28	37	13	12	

TORONTO   8th   48-88   .353   -38   Richard Harley -
Maple Leafs   Ed Barrow

BATTERS	POS-GAMES	GP	AB	R	H	BI	2B	3B	HR	BB	SO	SB	BA
O'Brien	1B71,3B49	126	456	34	98		10	10	1			9	.215
Gus Soffel	2B136	136	482	60	112		12	11	6			28	.232
George Magoon	SS104	109	374	38	84		11	2	0			8	.225
Lew Carr	3B44,SS26	70	232	23	44		8	2	1			10	.190
John White	OF137	137	515	64	142		13	14	1			33	.278
Richard Harley	OF	(see multi-team players)											
Jim Murray	OF	(see multi-team players)											
James Toft	C92,1B11	103	299	28	71		9	1	0			7	.237
Lewis Rapp	1B49,OF20	69	264	35	73		7	4	2			21	.276
Sullivan	C57	57	157	8	34		3	1	0			3	.217
William Cristall	P32,OF18	53	143	10	27		3	3	0			2	.189
Clarence Currie	P45	51	143	13	24		6	1	1			5	.168
Ed Zimmerman	3B44	44	149	11	28		4	1	0			3	.188
Cy Falkenberg	P23	23	68	7	16		0	1	1			0	.235
Bill Magee	P13	13	33	2	6		0	0	0			0	.182
Long	P9	11	30	1	6		0	0	0			0	.200
Art Mueller	P11	11	24	0	0		0	0	0			0	.000
Fred Applegate	P8	8	23	2	4		0	1	0			0	.174
Ralph Caldwell	P7	7	18	2	7		0	0	0			0	.389

PITCHERS	W	L	PCT	G	GS	CG	SH	IP	H	BB	SO	ERA
Clarence Currie	16	19	.457	45				303	262	77	114	
Cy Falkenberg	11	10	.524	23				190	141	58	146	
William Cristall	7	17	.292	32				212	224	76	71	
Bill Magee	4	5	.444	13				97	106	27	25	
Fred Applegate	3	4	.429	8				62	45	28	38	
Long	2	6	.250	9				57	70	15	17	
Ralph Caldwell	1	5	.167	7				43	42	9	19	
Art Mueller	1	9	.100	11				76	68	19	23	

MULTI-TEAM PLAYERS

BATTERS	POS-GAMES	TEAMS	GP	AB	R	H	BI	2B	3B	HR	BB	SO	SB	BA
Richard Harley	OF131	TOR-PRO	132	495	53	122		12	4	0			32	.246
Jim Murray	OF77	BUF-TOR	83	321	57	81		14	8	9			20	.252
Ben Houser	OF53,1B26	ROC-TOR	79	301	29	87		7	11	0			8	.289
Pat Dillard	OF63,3B10	NE-TO-PRO	77	264	24	54		9	2	1			8	.205
Cliff Latimer	C28	NEW-MON	30	84	5	17		1	0	0			0	.202
John McPherson	P25	NEW-TOR	25	66	3	10		0	1	0			0	.152
Edward Fertsch	P24	NEW-ROC	24	60	3	8		2	0	0			0	.133
Tom Bird	C14	BUF-MON	20	48	10	13		0	0	0			2	.271
Harry Aubrey		PRO-MON	11	34	2	6		0	0	0			1	.176

MULTI-TEAM PLAYERS (cont.)

PITCHERS	TEAMS	W	L	PCT	G	GS	CG	SH	IP	H	BB	SO	ERA
Edward Fertsch	NEW-ROC	9	10	.474	24				176	176	48	57	
John McPherson	TOR-NEW	6	13	.316	25				189	209	57	47	

TEAM BATTING

TEAMS	GP	AB	R	H	BI	2B	3B	HR	BB	SO	SB	BA
PROVIDENCE	134	4284	645	**1195**							130	**.279**
BALTIMORE	131	4280	**697**	1179							169	.270
JERSEY CITY	136	**4493**	614	1153							**311**	.252
NEWARK	132	4118	490	974							240	.237
BUFFALO	137	4467	569	1155							187	.259
MONTREAL	138	4299	470	1060							209	.241
ROCHESTER	**139**	4490	460	1080							180	.241
TORONTO	137	4288	441	1013							176	.231
	542	34719	4386	8809							1602	.254

1906
LOWEST HIGH

When baseball moved the pitching distance back 10 feet in 1893, hitters began to rule the game. In 1893, more than 40 Eastern League regular players batted over .300. By 1895, the number rose, as more than 50 players chalked up .300-plus averages. As the decade progressed, the halcyon hitting days in the Eastern League leveled off. By 1900, the Eastern League had only 15 hitters with averages of .300 or more. In 1905, the number had dropped to seven. In the next year, the number would sink further still.

Several reasons for the drop in averages have been postulated. One theory suggests that pitchers, after several years, finally got used to the longer distance. A second theory credits the pitchers' more frequent use of trick pitches, such as the spitter, shine-ball, and emery-ball. In any event, by the first decade of the twentieth century, pitchers were back in control of the game.

In 1906, after a one-year absence, Buffalo returned to the Eastern League's top seat. Jersey City, Baltimore, and Rochester finished second through fourth, while Newark, Providence, Montreal, and Toronto finished fifth through eighth.

On the roster of the last-place Toronto Maple Leafs was an outfielder named Jack Thoney. Thoney enjoyed a solid season in 1906, finishing with 173 hits, 32 doubles, 41 stolen bases, and a .294 batting average. His hit and double totals led the league, but more surprisingly, so did his batting average, as not one single player in the Eastern League cracked .300.

Other Eastern League leaders included Jim Murray from Buffalo (7 home runs), pitcher Del Mason from Baltimore (26 wins), and fellow Oriole Fred Burchell (183 strikeouts).

Jack Thoney's .294 was the lowest batting average ever to lead the league. But the Eastern League was not the only circuit to lack a .300 leader in at least one season. For three straight years (1908–1910) the Pacific Coast League's batting leader fell short of the mark. The Southern Association's hitting leader fell shy in 1909.

Pitchers would remain in control for many more seasons (until trick pitches were outlawed after World War I), though there would always be at least one .300 hitter in the league. Mr. Thoney took care of things himself the very next year as he led the Eastern for the second straight season, this time with an average worthy of a champion.

BUFFALO Bisons
1st   85-55   .607   George Stallings

BATTERS	POS-GAMES	GP	AB	R	H	BI	2B	3B	HR	BB	SO	SB	BA
George McConnell	1B132	132	501	55	118		20	9	1			10	.236
George Smith	2B140	140	527	67	146		16	4	0			23	.277
William Nattress	SS142	142	510	95	125		24	2	2			37	.245
Hunter Hill	3B63	63	224	23	45		2	4	1			14	.201
Jim Murray	OF136	136	529	68	150		23	13	7			38	.284
Jake Gettman	OF127,1B9	136	516	90	150		22	7	1			22	.291
John White	OF	(see multi-team players)											
Lew McAllister	C67	86	277	35	73		15	2	0			12	.264
Mickey Corcoran	3B55	66	301	32	69		6	6	1			15	.229
Frank McManus	C55	55	198	18	38		6	4	0			2	.192
Lew Brockett	P37	44	141	25	41		4	2	3			5	.291
Bill Milligan	OF20,P16	41	160	16	40		4	4	3			3	.250
Charles Kisinger	P38	38	120	6	18		0	1	0			4	.150
Bill Tozer	P24	24	72	10	19		1	1	0			7	.264
Ernie Greene	P8	11	29	3	7		0	2	0			3	.241
John Vowinkel	P8	8	16	1	4		0	0	0			1	.250

PITCHERS		W	L	PCT	G	GS	CG	SH	IP	H	BB	SO	ERA
Charles Kisinger		23	12	.657	38				319	273	61	171	
Lew Brockett		23	13	.639	37				313	275	87	122	
Bill Tozer		16	6	.727	24				195	139	41	64	
Bill Milligan		8	8	.500	16				151	145	34	66	
Ernie Greene		2	4	.333	8				56	49	26	20	
John Vowinkel		2	5	.286	8				53	45	21	14	
Bill Thomas		1	0	1.000					9	13	5	2	

JERSEY CITY Skeeters
2nd   80-57   .584   -3.5   William Murray

BATTERS	POS-GAMES	GP	AB	R	H	BI	2B	3B	HR	BB	SO	SB	BA
John Cassidy	1B129	129	504	54	131		10	5	5			21	.260
William Keister	2B109,OF8	118	418	40	105		15	5	2			27	.251
Joseph Bean	SS113,2B12	125	441	55	97		9	2	0			20	.220
Edward Grant	3B75,2B9	86	307	45	99		7	9	1			8	.322
Wally Clement	OF133	133	546	75	149		16	7	1			46	.271
Charles Hanford	OF116	116	428	68	108		8	3	4			30	.252
Bill Halligan	OF82	82	269	26	67		11	8	2			9	.249
John Butler	C91	91	302	24	63		10	4	0			7	.209
George Merritt	OF70,P5	90	316	44	80		7	3	2			23	.222
Walter Woods	3B67	75	252	31	57		9	2	1			9	.226
George Vandegrift	C48	48	152	12	35		5	0	0			1	.230
Lew Moren	P34	34	80	3	10		1	0	0			1	.125
Bill Foxen	P33	33	90	6	13		0	1	0			2	.144
William Moskiman	P32	32	93	8	18		2	2	0			0	.194
Mack	P31	31	76	6	10		1	0	0			2	.132
Eugene McCann	P14	14	45	6	12		0	2	0			1	.267

PITCHERS		W	L	PCT	G	GS	CG	SH	IP	H	BB	SO	ERA
Bill Foxen		18	12	.600	33				261	210	93	99	
Lew Moren		16	13	.552	34				251	191	96	123	
Mack		15	9	.625	31				224	153	68	96	
William Moskiman		15	13	.536	32				255	204	76	102	
Eugene McCann		9	5	.643	14				109	69	34	41	
George Pfanmiller		5	0	1.000	5				40	17	6	11	
George Merritt		1	4	.200	5				43	27	11	23	
Jake Thielman		0	1	.000					20	23	9	5	

BALTIMORE Orioles
3rd   76-61   .555   -7.5   Hugh Jennings

BATTERS	POS-GAMES	GP	AB	R	H	BI	2B	3B	HR	BB	SO	SB	BA
Frederick Hunter	1B115	115	404	68	97		20	9	3			15	.240
James Mullen	2B120	120	426	58	125		15	8	2			26	.293
Hugh Jennings	SS51,2B24	75	242	24	60		9	1	0			2	.248
Mike Mowery	3B68	68	230	29	61		9	6	2			6	.265
John Kelly	OF138	138	531	75	151		16	6	3			63	.284

BALTIMORE (cont.)
Orioles

BATTERS	POS-GAMES	GP	AB	R	H	BI	2B	3B	HR	BB	SO	SB	BA
Bill O'Hara	OF134	137	513	93	128		16	12	3			37	.250
Bob Hall	OF102,3B23	125	470	73	112		13	9	0			28	.239
Bill Byers	C94	94	305	20	76		16	6	0			5	.249
Hugh Hearne	C67,1B24	95	300	42	92		15	6	1			9	.307
McDonnell	SS51	51	175	19	37		6	0	0			3	.211
Del Mason	P38	39	130	8	30		2	1	0			0	.231
Fred Burchell	P38	38	126	7	21		3	0	0			4	.167
Ray Demmitt	OF36	36	123	20	37		5	2	0			6	.301
Merle Adkins	P33	33	99	2	14		2	0	0			0	.141
J. S. Kennedy	3B10	26	45	4	8		0	0	0			0	.178
Hatfield	3B22	22	68	5	14		3	0	0			0	.206
John McNeal	P21	21	57	7	9		0	1	0			0	.158
Conrad Starkell	P7	7	18	4	4		0	0	0			0	.222

PITCHERS		W	L	PCT	G	GS	CG	SH	IP	H	BB	SO	ERA
Del Mason		26	9	.743	38				324	266	83	162	
Fred Burchell		20	18	.526	38				332	269	105	183	
Merle Adkins		16	15	.516	33				268	204	42	102	
John McNeal		9	12	.429	21				166	167	65	62	
Ramsay		2	0	1.000					27	22	8	12	
Conrad Starkell		2	4	.333	7				48	52	11	11	

ROCHESTER   4th   77-62   .554   -7.5   Al Buckenberger
Bronchos

BATTERS	POS-GAMES	GP	AB	R	H	BI	2B	3B	HR	BB	SO	SB	BA
Bill Clancy	1B141	141	549	73	151		17	12	3			36	.275
Charles Loudenslager	2B142	142	507	60	128		20	10	1			29	.252
Charles Moran	SS125	125	437	32	81		7	1	0			11	.185
Leonard Burrell	3B108	108	401	37	91		5	2	0			19	.227
John Duffy	OF107	107	426	53	97		4	5	3			22	.228
James Barrett	OF73	74	289	42	80		10	7	0			4	.277
George Barclay	OF69	69	263	25	50		7	0	0			8	.190
Morris Steelman	C82	84	257	18	44		6	1	0			5	.171
Fred Carisch	C57	57	194	16	44		4	3	0			9	.227
Frank McLean	P37	37	107	9	14		2	2	0			2	.131
Charles Case	P29	29	102	2	12		1	0	0			0	.108
Ed Lennox	3B28	28	104	12	28		5	3	0			7	.270
D. Walters	P24	24	74	3	9		0	0	0			2	.122
Weldon Henley	P22	22	68	4	7		2	0	0			3	.103
James Cleary	P20	20	68	4	12		0	1	0			0	.176
Jim Flanagan	OF10	10	43	5	14		1	0	0			1	.326

PITCHERS		W	L	PCT	G	GS	CG	SH	IP	H	BB	SO	ERA
Charles Case		17	9	.654	29				264	197	53	94	
Frank McLean		16	19	.457	37				309	264	61	113	
D. Walters		14	9	.609	24				203	172	87	81	
Welden Henley		11	9	.550	22				194	139	72	87	
James Cleary		10	10	.500	20				177	140	57	75	
Hughes		4	0	1.000					37	25	11	11	
Nelson		2	0	1.000					36	26	32	12	
George Schultz		1	0	1.000					14	13	10	13	
Oliver Faulkner		1	2	.333					24	25	8	5	
Leo Hafford		0	1	.000					15	15	9	8	

NEWARK   5th   66-71   .482   -17.5   Walt Burnham
Sailors

BATTERS	POS-GAMES	GP	AB	R	H	BI	2B	3B	HR	BB	SO	SB	BA
Art Brown	1B136	136	498	37	117		9	5	1			16	.235
William Mahling	2B78	78	264	38	69		3	2	1			17	.261
Frank Gatins	SS69,OF18	90	329	31	78		11	1	4			15	.237
Jim Cockman	3B136	136	512	75	121		24	8	3			38	.236
Jim Jones	OF130	130	474	59	121		27	1	5			20	.255
Clyde Engle	OF87,2B30	125	449	51	97		13	1	0			23	.216

NEWARK (cont.)
Sailors

BATTERS	POS-GAMES	GP	AB	R	H	BI	2B	3B	HR	BB	SO	SB	BA
Charles Malay	OF		(see multi-team players)										
John Shea	C64	64	194	12	31		3	0	0			2	.160
Charles Wagner	SS63,2B33	98	339	30	80		4	6	1			23	.236
Pat McCauley	C43	43	140	9	24		3	0	1			7	.171
Albert Pardee	P35	35	88	6	11		1	1	0			0	.125
Oscar Stanage	C31	31	113	2	17		5	1	0			1	.150
Bill Carrick	P31	31	85	5	8		2	1	0			1	.094
Edward Fertsch	P27	27	79	5	11		1	0	0			2	.139
Edwin Moriarity	P23	23	74	3	20		6	0	0			0	.270
Larry Hesterfer	P17	17	46	4	4		0	0	0			0	.087

PITCHERS		W	L	PCT	G	GS	CG	SH	IP	H	BB	SO	ERA
Bill Carrick		17	11	.607	31				242	210	58	69	
Albert Pardee		15	18	.455	35				294	222	69	102	
Larry Hesterfer		11	4	.733	17				135	121	64	29	
Edward Fertsch		11	14	.440	27				244	216	65	68	
Edwin Moriarity		8	13	.381	23				210	167	54	56	
Charles Roy		2	4	.333	6				48	40	11	7	
McCoy		1	3	.250					25	28	15	5	
Charles Clancy		0	1	.000					14	17	6	2	
Williams		0	1	.000					8	11	3	3	
Fitzhenry		0	1	.000					7	8	6	0	
Schultz		0	1	.000					1	4	2	1	

PROVIDENCE   6th   65-75   .464   -20   Jack Dunn
Grays

BATTERS	POS-GAMES	GP	AB	R	H	BI	2B	3B	HR	BB	SO	SB	BA
Candy LaChance	1B133	133	479	43	124		11	4	0			7	.259
Jack Dunn	2B124	124	461	46	122		8	5	0			20	.265
Roy Rock	SS141	141	482	40	109		11	5	1			12	.226
Alan Storke	3B50	57	214	27	62		11	2	1			4	.290
Richard Harley	OF115	115	430	55	110		6	2	1			25	.256
Kip Selbach	OF74	74	268	28	69		11	4	0			7	.258
Phil Poland	OF63,3B45	119	457	69	117		9	10	1			24	.256
Harry Barton	C67,OF13,2B12	93	317	31	82		7	4	1			8	.259
Jack Cronin	P37	37	114	7	23		5	0	1			2	.202
Cooper	C29	32	100	5	15		0	0	0			1	.150
Harry Hardy	P26	26	78	3	8		0	0	0			0	.103
John McCloskey	P25	25	77	4	15		2	0	0			1	.192
George Josslyn	P25	25	76	7	15		1	0	0			0	.197
Ed Poole	P24	24	76	2	10		1	0	0			0	.132
Krueger	3B21	21	66	2	11		0	0	0			2	.167
Offa Neal	3B19	19	75	7	19		2	1	0			2	.253
William Higgins	C19	19	63	3	19		1	0	0			1	.302
Chester Crist	C10	10	37	3	12		2	0	0			0	.324
Thornhill	3B9	9	33	4	8		1	0	0			1	.242
Breckendorf	C9	9	21	0	1		0	0	0			0	.048

PITCHERS		W	L	PCT	G	GS	CG	SH	IP	H	BB	SO	ERA
Jack Cronin		16	19	.457	37				241	273	91	122	
John McCloskey		15	9	.625	25				190	156	29	69	
Ed Poole		14	10	.583	24				193	162	64	68	
Harry Hardy		11	13	.458	26				208	165	55	77	
George Josslyn		10	11	.476	25				203	195	38	58	
Mulvey		0	1	.000					17	10	9	3	
Cooper		0	1	.000					21	25	6	9	
Frazer		0	1	.000					9	19	7	2	
Beisel		0	1	.000					8	14	5	1	
Wiener		0	1	.000					7	10	5	4	
Brown		0	1	.000					6	12	5	0	
Claude Elliott		0	3	.000					27	27	4	9	
Jerry Nops		0	4	.000					32	43	6	1	

MONTREAL Canucks

7th	57-83	.407	-28	James Bannon - Mal Kittridge

BATTERS	POS-GAMES	GP	AB	R	H	BI	2B	3B	HR	BB	SO	SB	BA
Joe Connor	1B85,C25	113	413	39	108		10	4	1			20	.262
James Connors	2B	(see multi-team players)											
L. Hartman	SS118	119	392	36	80		10	3	0			13	.204
Albert Wagner	3B101	104	408	50	100		14	8	0			27	.248
Michael Joyce	OF116	16	435	64	87		8	5	1			27	.200
Frank Huelsman	OF113	113	389	55	104		21	7	5			21	.267
James Bannon	OF	(see multi-team players)											
John Dillon	C60	62	216	13	38		3	0	0			2	.176
George Bannon	OF27,SS22,2B15,P	87	294	25	68		16	3	3			8	.231
Tom Raub	OF36,C28,1B11	75	265	20	63		7	6	2			12	.238
William Massey	1B50	50	178	15	36		4	0	0			8	.202
George Simmons	2B36	36	133	6	23		5	2	0			1	.173
Andrew Herbst	OF22,P10	32	118	4	26		4	3	0			7	.220
Jimmy Whalen	P30	30	94	5	14		0	1	0			1	.149
John Pappalau	P29	29	91	11	17		3	1	1			0	.187
Ruhland	3B23	23	79	0	9		2	0	0			4	.114
Mal Kittridge	C21	21	69	8	13		1	0	0			0	.189
Louis LeRoy	P21	21	65	5	12		0	0	0			0	.185
Robert Keefe	P13	13	39	2	5		0	1	0			0	.129
Al Mattern	P12	12	29	1	2		0	0	0			0	.069
John Phelan	OF10	10	30	7	8		1	0	2			2	.267
McMahon	3B8	8	31	3	8		0	0	0			1	.258

PITCHERS	W	L	PCT	G	GS	CG	SH	IP	H	BB	SO	ERA
John Pappalau	15	13	.536	29				260	208	73	75	
Jimmy Whalen	12	17	.414	30				246	333	53	71	
Robert Keefe	7	6	.538	13				108	99	30	56	
Louis LeRoy	6	14	.300	21				177	177	53	87	
Andrew Herbst	4	6	.400	10				95	94	25	21	
Cy Barger	2	2	.500					31	24	14	11	
Joe Stanley	2	3	.400					34	15	21	20	
Al Mattern	2	9	.182	12				96	99	41	40	
Deering	1	1	.500					9	12	15	2	
George Bannon	1	2	.333					22	19	15	2	
Dubois	0	2	.000					14	15	8	3	

TORONTO Maple Leafs

8th	46-88	.343	-36	Ed Barrow

BATTERS	POS-GAMES	GP	AB	R	H	BI	2B	3B	HR	BB	SO	SB	BA
John Flynn	1B95	95	340	33	70		12	3	1			11	.206
Yance Weidensaul	2B	(see multi-team players)											
Edwin Frank	SS66	74	256	25	64		3	4	2			6	.250
James Frick	3B107	107	385	30	80		11	8	0			17	.278
Jack Thoney	OF141	141	**589**	83	**173**		32	12	6			41	**.294**
Rip Cannell	OF81	81	304	23	78		6	8	0			6	.257
Jim Wallace	OF	(see multi-team players)											
Bob Wood	C	(see multi-team players)											
Tamsett	SS47	47	150	13	28		3	1	0			10	.187
Fred Mitchell	P29	39	119	12	26		2	2	0			7	.219
Charles McCafferty	P34	34	92	3	12		1	1	0			3	.130
Jim McGinley	P33	33	97	9	19		3	2	0			1	.196
Jack Slattery	C31	31	125	11	29		2	1	0			3	.232
James Toft	C30	30	86	4	13		1	1	0			1	.151
Archibald McCarthy	P26	26	72	2	6		1	0	0			1	.083
Meek	1B24	24	93	9	26		3	0	0			4	.279
Ronan	OF9,2B7	23	90	8	16		3	1	0			5	.177
Long	2B21	21	77	3	19		2	0	0			3	.247
McGovern	C20	21	57	3	8		2	0	0			1	.140
Wotell	OF15	20	65	8	16		3	3	0			3	.246
William Yale	1B15	15	50	5	9		1	0	0			3	.180
Riggs	OF12	12	44	3	13		1	0	0			4	.297
Williams	P8	8	23	2	5		2	0	0			0	.217

PITCHERS	W	L	PCT	G	GS	CG	SH	IP	H	BB	SO	ERA
Jim McGinley	15	13	.536	33				292	240	68	113	
Fred Mitchell	11	15	.423	29				239	196	87	91	
Charles McCafferty	11	19	.367	34				263	215	**107**	87	
Williams	3	4	.429	8				60	55	30	17	

TORONTO (cont.)
Maple Leafs

PITCHERS	W	L	PCT	G	GS	CG	SH	IP	H	BB	SO	ERA
Archibald McCarthy	2	21	.087	26				225	235	61	108	
Owens	0	4	.000					17	18	6	5	
Drennan	0	5	.000					37	35	11	8	

MULTI-TEAM PLAYERS

BATTERS	POS-GAMES	TEAMS	GP	AB	R	H	BI	2B	3B	HR	BB	SO	SB	BA
John White	OF131	TOR-BUF	131	472	59	122		12	6	1			21	.258
Yance Weidensaul	2B85,OF11	MON-TOR	113	398	42	101		11	5	0			16	.254
Steve Brodie	OF112	PRO-NEW	112	387	41	110		14	4	0			10	.284
James Bannon	OF104	MON-ROC	110	411	65	103		12	6	1			29	.249
Charles Malay	OF102	NEW-ROC	103	382	49	98		12	7	0			11	.257
James O'Brien	2B40,3B29,SS28	ROC-TOR	97	304	40	69		7	4	0			16	.227
Jim Wallace	OF91	ROC-TOR	92	333	49	80		8	0	1			11	.241
Bob Wood	C66	BUF-TOR	66	231	20	59		7	2	1			5	.253
James Connors	2B54	MON-TOR	54	196	19	35		4	0	0			3	.179
Grubb	SS25,3B18,P	BA-TO-RO	49	167	13	36		2	4	0			9	.215
Hogan Yancey	OF45	ROC-TOR	45	186	18	42		5	5	0			7	.226
Clarence Currie	P31	TOR-BUF	32	88	6	13		2	1	0			1	.148
Tom Doran	C26	TOR-ROC	28	95	6	15		2	1	0			1	.158
John Burke	P12	NEW-MON	13	47	2	10		4	0	0			0	.213

PITCHERS		TEAMS	W	L	PCT	G	GS	CG	SH	IP	H	BB	SO	ERA
Clarence Currie		TOR-BUF	14	15	.483	31				250	205	93	93	
John Burke		NEW-MON	5	7	.417	12				131	114	48	34	
Grubb		BA-TO-RO	1	3	.250					34	24	17	10	

TEAM BATTING

TEAMS	GP	AB	R	H	BI	2B	3B	HR	BB	SO	SB	BA
BUFFALO	**143**	**4826**	**621**	**1225**		**163**	65	**26**			207	**.254**
JERSEY CITY	137	4154	483	1024		110	53	18			199	.247
BALTIMORE	138	4320	568	1078		152	**70**	14			**209**	.250
ROCHESTER	**143**	4487	492	1004		108	50	8			184	.224
NEWARK	139	4066	474	907		148	38	22			201	.223
PROVIDENCE	141	4311	446	1061		107	43	6			132	.246
MONTREAL	142	4747	458	1104		132	51	16			187	.233
TORONTO	141	3683	396	826		123	64	10			184	.224
	562	34594	3938	8229		1043	434	120			1503	.238

1907
TORONTO MAPLE LEAFS

One Eastern League team suffered a see-saw existence during the opening decade of the twentieth century. The team won a flag during this period, but also finished sixth twice and eighth twice. This team was the Toronto Maple Leafs.

The city of Toronto joined the International family in 1886 when the Canadian League melded with the New York State League to form the International League. During its five-year stay, the team did well, finishing third twice, second once, and winning the pennant in 1887. After the chaotic year of 1890, the Maple Leafs dropped out of the league.

In 1895, Toronto was readmitted. After a series of so-so entries, the team pushed to the fore and captured the prize in 1902. After this success, they faced obscurity, bottoming with a duo of last-place finishes in 1905 and 1906. To the surprise of all, the team rebounded the very next year.

Toronto, Buffalo, Newark, and Jersey City proved to be the contending quartet of teams during the Eastern League's 1907 crusade. During the summer, Newark and Jersey City were shed from the group. In the race's latter stages, Buffalo went into a slump, leaving the Maple Leafs to claim the laurels. They had accomplished what few other league teams could do: They had vaulted from last to first in one year.

Only three Torontonians reached the .300 plateau—batting champion Jack Thoney, .341; Bill Carrigan, .319; and Joe Kelley, .322—but the team led the Eastern League in hitting (.260). Their best pitcher was Jim McGinley with a record of 22–10.

Behind Toronto and Buffalo, in the overall pennant race, Providence made a late-season surge to finish third. Newark, Jersey City, and Baltimore finished around .500, while Rochester and Montreal ended up seventh and eighth. Bill Abstein and William Nattress, from Providence and Buffalo respectively, hit the most home runs (7), while Jersey City pitcher Joe Lake finished with the most wins (25) and strike-outs (187).

As the years unfolded, the Toronto Maple Leafs continued their up-and-down ways. They won their share of pennants (9) before leaving the league in 1967, but they also finished last a number of times (6), including three times in a row just before World War II.

The Toronto Maple Leafs of 1907 weren't the city's strongest entry in the league. On at least two other occasions, a Maple Leaf team finished with a better record. But for another reason, the 1907 team stands alone. No other team, in all the annals of the International League, has exceeded their 37-game jump from last to first. Certainly a notable achievement.

TORONTO   1st   83-51   .619   Joe Kelley
Maple Leafs

BATTERS	POS-GAMES	GP	AB	R	H	BI	2B	3B	HR	BB	SO	SB	BA
John Flynn	1B98	99	339	47	73		8	9	4			23	.215
Larry Schlafly	2B68,SS26	94	333	61	93		11	10	4			30	.279
James Frick	SS111	112	376	50	91		6	2	2			15	.245
William Phyle	3B121	121	445	54	104		16	9	2			24	.234
Mike Wotell	OF121	125	419	49	98		14	9	2			21	.234
Yance Weidensaul	OF99	125	458	57	118		11	9	1			20	.258
Jack Thoney	OF94	102	413	**93**	136		20	7	5			35	**.329**
Bill Carrigan	C82	86	291	46	93		10	8	0			12	.319
Joe Kelley	1B33,OF28,2B10	91	314	32	101		10	8	1			15	.322
Pat Hurley	C52	54	155	20	29		6	2	0			2	.187
Fred Mitchell	2B20,P14	44	125	12	32		4	1	0			2	.256
Jim McGinley	P35	35	84	7	12		2	2	0			0	.143
Dick Rudolph	P31	32	81	12	22		3	0	0			1	.271
Larry Hesterfer	P30	30	70	10	18		1	1	0			0	.257
Tim Flood	2B20	29	116	20	31		7	2	0			10	.267
Elmer Moffitt	P25	25	50	7	12		0	3	0			0	.240
Crooks	OF21	23	87	8	20		1	3	0			3	.230
Fred Applegate	P23	23	61	2	12		1	0	0			1	.197
Welch		17	46	4	10		0	0	0			0	.217
John Hoey	OF15	15	48	9	16		0	1	0			0	.333
Connor		14	34	6	12		1	1	0			0	.353
Bob Wood		11	30	5	11		2	1	0			0	.367
Albert Jacobson	P5	5	13	1	2		0	0	0			0	.154

PITCHERS	W	L	PCT	G	GS	CG	SH	IP	H	BB	SO	ERA
Jim McGinley	22	10	.688	35				256	225	51	111	
Larry Hesterfer	16	11	.593	30				219	188	67	60	
Dick Rudolph	13	8	.619	31				223	190	47	82	
Elmer Moffitt	11	6	.647	25				150	126	48	70	
Fred Applegate	9	9	.500	23				168	156	53	85	
Fred Mitchell	6	3	.667	14				100	68	42	45	
Albert Jacobson	2	2	.500	5				36	34	9	15	

BUFFALO   2nd   73-59   .553   -9   Lew McAllister
Bisons

BATTERS	POS-GAMES	GP	AB	R	H	BI	2B	3B	HR	BB	SO	SB	BA
George McConnell	1B132	133	503	57	147		28	7	2			15	.292
George Smith	2B128	128	499	48	119		17	2	0			24	.239
William Nattress	SS134	134	508	91	130		17	3	7			26	.256
Hunter Hill	3B	(see multi-team players)											
John White	OF114	116	425	67	123		13	6	0			25	.289
Jim Murray	OF114	115	430	57	117		19	7	5			30	.272
Jake Gettman	OF95	95	348	49	96		16	8	1			15	.276
Jack Ryan	C81,3B16	104	337	27	81		9	1	1			5	.240
George Schirm	OF75	78	258	41	54		3	1	1			24	.209
Lew McAllister	C55	73	222	16	56		7	0	0			4	.252
Bill Milligan	P30	44	105	6	24		2	0	0			1	.229
Charles Kisinger	P34	34	98	9	23		1	1	0			3	.235
Bill Tozer	P33	33	90	7	10		1	0	0			2	.111
John Vowinkel	P31	31	79	7	11		3	0	0			1	.139
Ernie Greene	P18	18	39	5	10		2	0	0			0	.256
Clarence Currie	P13	13	19	2	1		0	0	0			0	.053
Ralph Parrott		10	30	1	4		1	0	0			0	.133

PITCHERS	W	L	PCT	G	GS	CG	SH	IP	H	BB	SO	ERA
Bill Tozer	21	10	.677	33				253	209	55	64	
Bill Milligan	17	12	.586	30				246	215	62	91	
Charles Kisinger	15	10	.600	34				254	205	63	113	
John Vowinkel	14	12	.538	31				235	219	46	76	
Clarence Currie	4	4	.500	13				56	67	26	24	
Ernie Greene	2	5	.286	18				105	101	40	37	
Levi Knapp	0	3	.000	3				27	23	13	19	

PROVIDENCE Grays

3rd   72-63   .533   -11.5   Hugh Duffy

BATTERS	POS-GAMES	GP	AB	R	H	BI	2B	3B	HR	BB	SO	SB	BA
Bill Abstein	1B135	136	519	56	145		18	12	7			31	.279
Amby McConnell	2B129	129	494	79	158		16	5	2			50	.320
Forrest Crawford	SS109	109	375	39	84		14	3	0			16	.224
Harry Lord	3B134	136	515	72	143		11	9	0			26	.278
Phil Poland	OF131	136	498	68	143		20	8	2			30	.287
Chet Chadbourne	OF118	128	464	70	138		12	7	2			21	.294
John Phelan	OF		(see multi-team players)										
Bob Peterson	C82	91	279	20	64		9	4	0			4	.229
Donovan	C52	86	154	6	27		1	0	0			2	.175
Clinton	OF21,P17	42	128	11	28		2	2	1			3	.219
Jack Cronin	P33	36	96	6	22		4	1	0			2	.229
Hugh Duffy	OF17	35	73	9	22		1	0	0			5	.301
George McQuillan	P31	31	82	12	19		0	0	1			5	.232
Joe Harris	P25	25	77	7	17		2	3	0			0	.221
Edward Barry	P22	23	49	3	5		0	1	1			0	.102
Stevens	P20	20	47	3	6		0	0	0			0	.128
Dooin	OF11	19	62	5	10		0	0	0			0	.161
Killian	P15	16	32	5	8		2	0	0			0	.250
Rebel Oakes	OF14	15	49	2	10		0	0	0			1	.204

PITCHERS		W	L	PCT	G	GS	CG	SH	IP	H	BB	SO	ERA
George McQuillan		19	7	.731	31				225	197	58	105	
Joe Harris		16	9	.640	25				205	161	55	130	
Jack Cronin		16	15	.516	33				257	214	63	97	
Stevens		7	8	.466	20				134	112	56	47	
Edward Barry		7	10	.412	22				145	92	56	109	
Clinton		3	6	.333	17				102	107	50	55	
Killian		2	7	.222	15				88	79	48	41	

JERSEY CITY Skeeters

4th (T)   67-66   .504   -15.5   Joseph Bean

BATTERS	POS-GAMES	GP	AB	R	H	BI	2B	3B	HR	BB	SO	SB	BA
George Merritt	1B108	121	394	60	104		7	9	1			44	.264
William Keister	2B89	90	311	38	78		10	4	0			23	.251
Joseph Bean	SS132	132	472	50	108		10	2	1			26	.229
Walter Woods	3B67,2B19	89	281	29	59		6	2	1			7	.210
Charles Hanford	OF137	137	494	73	123		16	5	2			31	.249
Wally Clement	OF133	133	563	66	160		10	11	4			35	.284
Bill Halligan	OF104	107	369	37	87		9	9	0			6	.236
George Vandegrift	C66,1B28	98	303	31	72		6	3	0			8	.238
Paul Sentell	3B67,2B11	81	283	22	61		6	0	1			15	.215
Joe Lake	P44	57	154	21	42		5	6	1			2	.272
Frank McManus	C42	46	145	7	30		3	0	0			3	.207
Bill Foxen	P33	33	91	7	15		1	1	0			2	.165
George Pfanmiller	P31	32	87	5	18		2	3	0			3	.207
Curtis	OF26	29	102	9	23		0	0	0			3	.225
John Butler	C24	24	78	9	25		5	0	0			0	.320
Jesse Whiting	P18	20	51	2	5		0	0	0			0	.098
Matt Fitzgerald	C17	19	56	2	13		3	2	0			2	.232
Earl Moore	P10	10	22	1	4		0	0	0			0	.182
Del Mason	P7	7	23	0	3		0	0	0			0	.130
Deegan	P6	6	13	0	1		0	0	0			0	.077

PITCHERS		W	L	PCT	G	GS	CG	SH	IP	H	BB	SO	ERA
Joe Lake		25	14	.641	44				344	261	60	187	
George Pfanmiller		17	10	.629	31				243	212	45	70	
Bill Foxen		8	18	.308	33				237	176	88	133	
Del Mason		6	1	.857	7				63	40	8	31	
Jesse Whiting		5	10	.333	18				130	125	39	32	
Earl Moore		3	6	.333	10				78	58	31	35	
Deegan		2	4	.333	6				39	27	8	16	

NEWARK   4th (T)   67-66   .504   -15.5   Walt Burnham
Sailors

BATTERS	POS-GAMES	GP	AB	R	H	BI	2B	3B	HR	BB	SO	SB	BA
Bud Sharpe	1B122	125	453	36	95		10	6	2			15	.210
James Mullen	2B130	131	462	64	114		17	10	2			35	.247
William Mahling	SS110,OF12	128	466	57	111		10	2	2			27	.238
Jim Cockman	3B125	125	436	38	101		19	1	0			25	.232
Jim Jones	OF132	132	471	47	115		12	4	4			24	.244
Elmer Zacher	OF128	128	445	44	106		19	3	0			21	.238
Clyde Engle	OF106,SS21	130	486	75	109		19	4	6			33	.224
Oscar Stanage	C72,1B13	86	284	19	57		14	2	0			5	.201
Archibald McCarthy	P36	56	129	11	36		5	0	1			2	.279
John Shea	C50	50	131	5	26		3	1	0			3	.199
Albert Pardee	P40	40	102	9	6		0	1	0			0	.059
Paul Krichell	C24	30	70	4	18		1	0	0			1	.257
LaBelle	P25	28	66	3	9		0	0	0			1	.136
Bill Carrick	P20	20	57	5	8		2	0	0			1	.140
Lewis Wiltse	P6	13	33	5	7		0	0	0			1	.212
McDonald		11	32	4	10		1	0	0			0	.313
Charles McCafferty	P11	11	23	4	2		0	0	0			1	.087
Charles Roy	P7	7	15	0	2		0	0	0			0	.133
John Frill	P6	6	14	0	0		0	0	0			0	.000

PITCHERS	W	L	PCT	G	GS	CG	SH	IP	H	BB	SO	ERA
Albert Pardee	21	17	.553	40				337	291	69	98	
Archibald McCarthy	18	12	.600	36				258	193	59	121	
Bill Carrick	9	10	.474	20				170	149	32	52	
LaBelle	7	10	.412	25				162	138	57	51	
Charles McCafferty	3	5	.375	11				74	90	26	24	
John Frill	2	3	.400	6				53	38	13	22	
Lewis Wiltse	2	3	.400	6				51	41	12	18	
Charles Roy	2	4	.333	7				43	42	13	14	

BALTIMORE   6th   68-69   .495   -16.5   Jack Dunn
Orioles

BATTERS	POS-GAMES	GP	AB	R	H	BI	2B	3B	HR	BB	SO	SB	BA
Frederick Hunter	1B98	98	312	46	72		6	7	1			29	.231
Jack Dunn	2B98	99	351	29	78		4	1	0			16	.222
H. Beach	SS70	70	217	21	56		3	0	0			11	.258
Leonard Burrell	3B140	140	465	35	102		11	1	1			19	.219
Bill O'Hara	OF132	132	484	65	124		12	3	0			57	.256
Ray Demmitt	OF119	123	422	72	114		18	10	1			33	.270
John Kelly	OF76	76	275	36	60		7	2	1			31	.218
Hugh Hearne	C86	97	290	34	87		8	8	0			19	.300
Bob Hall	2B45,SS30,OF23	114	398	62	97		15	7	0			34	.244
Lewis Rapp	1B44,OF44	91	300	29	60		8	4	3			18	.200
Bill Byers	C61	70	221	30	72		12	3	0			11	.326
Harry Hardy	P40	44	110	5	25		4	1	0			2	.227
Merle Adkins	P39	39	96	7	23		1	0	0			1	.240
James	SS34	34	118	4	23		4	1	0			1	.195
Fred Burchell	P34	34	92	4	18		0	1	0			5	.196
John McCloskey	P33	33	93	7	11		1	0	0			4	.118
Hambacher	OF11	17	54	8	16		3	0	0			6	.296

PITCHERS	W	L	PCT	G	GS	CG	SH	IP	H	BB	SO	ERA
Merle Adkins	20	11	.645	39				283	250	61	109	
Harry Hardy	15	15	.500	40				273	260	76	105	
Fred Burchell	15	17	.469	34				265	233	90	114	
John McCloskey	14	15	.483	33				250	195	90	125	

ROCHESTER   7th   59-76   .437   -24.5   Al Buckenberger
Bronchos

BATTERS	POS-GAMES	GP	AB	R	H	BI	2B	3B	HR	BB	SO	SB	BA
Bill Clancy	1B115	115	438	59	126		13	10	0			24	.287
Charles Loudenslager	2B92	92	348	52	100		5	5	2			20	.287
Charles Moran	SS77,2B19	97	315	26	75		7	1	0			5	.238

ROCHESTER (cont.)
Bronchos

BATTERS	POS-GAMES	GP	AB	R	H	BI	2B	3B	HR	BB	SO	SB	BA
Ed Lennox	3B136	136	456	40	110		11	11	2			10	.241
Jack Hayden	OF122	126	462	48	109		14	11	0			16	.236
Jim Flanagan	OF109,1B21	131	482	66	147		25	9	5			22	.305
James Bannon	OF87	114	418	59	97		15	2	0			26	.232
Tom Doran	C86	89	287	16	47		4	0	0			5	.164
Charles Malay	OF68,2B10	104	322	46	73		9	4	1			8	.227
Sundheim	SS42,2B16	58	206	23	47		5	2	0			5	.228
Alex Bannister	P40	41	99	5	15		0	0	0			1	.151
William Higgins	C35	40	106	9	31		6	1	0			3	.292
Frank McLean	P36	36	105	6	14		1	0	0			0	.133
John Pappalau	P36	36	92	2	10		1	0	0			1	.109
Weldon Henley	P21	23	53	7	9		1	0	0			0	.170
Jim Byrnes	C20	22	67	3	13		1	1	0			1	.194
D. Walters	P16	16	34	1	8		0	0	0			1	.235
Kelly		10	35	3	3		0	0	0			0	.086

PITCHERS		W	L	PCT	G	GS	CG	SH	IP	H	BB	SO	ERA
Frank McLean		15	17	.469	36				295	278	69	107	
John Pappalau		14	19	.424	36				294	327	67	111	
Alex Bannister		12	20	.375	40				299	297	81	84	
Weldon Henley		11	8	.579	21				154	151	79	76	
D. Walters		4	8	.333	16				96	109	31	28	

MONTREAL
Royals

	8th	46-85	.351	-35.5	Mal Kittridge - James Morgan

BATTERS	POS-GAMES	GP	AB	R	H	BI	2B	3B	HR	BB	SO	SB	BA
Art Brown	1B132	132	481	51	115		12	5	2			18	.239
David Shean	2B110	115	384	33	89		13	2	1			10	.232
Mickey Corcoran	SS		(see multi-team players)										
James Morgan	3B118	122	416	43	91		20	4	4			13	.219
Michael Madigan	OF115	117	402	40	85		8	3	6			16	.211
Michael Joyce	OF87	90	306	47	74		5	1	0			24	.242
Snowden	OF43	43	140	13	24		3	2	0			7	.171
William Clarke	C42	42	122	13	27		5	2	0			0	.221
Andrew Herbst	P26,OF17	45	131	13	24		5	2	0			2	.183
Mal Kittridge	C40	40	121	5	26		5	1	0			2	.215
Lew Brockett	OF26,P7	36	125	7	18		1	1	2			0	.144
Tom Hughes	P34	36	92	4	17		2	1	0			2	.184
Connors	C29	34	97	6	21		2	1	0			3	.216
Joe Stanley	P33	33	88	3	9		0	0	0			0	.102
Waters	C29	30	93	3	12		1	0	0			2	.129
Doc Newton	P17	18	43	5	6		0	0	0			2	.139
Robert Keefe	P18	18	43	2	5		0	0	0			0	.116

PITCHERS		W	L	PCT	G	GS	CG	SH	IP	H	BB	SO	ERA
Tom Hughes		14	17	.452	34				262	215	96	131	
Doc Newton		9	8	.529	17				143	94	44	55	
Joe Stanley		7	21	.250	33				259	221	133	126	
Andrew Herbst		5	16	.238	26				199	210	54	55	
Lew Brockett		4	3	.571	7				58	47	25	24	
Robert Keefe		4	13	.235	18				131	127	45	56	

MULTI-TEAM PLAYERS

BATTERS	POS-GAMES	TEAMS	GP	AB	R	H	BI	2B	3B	HR	BB	SO	SB	BA
Mickey Corcoran	SS71,3B54	BUF-MON	125	458	50	114		18	7	1			28	.244
John Phelan	OF112	MON-PRO	112	366	58	95		11	2	1			37	.259
George Needham	OF58,SS38	MON-BUF	107	398	36	92		12	1	2			9	.231
Hunter Hill	3B63,SS24,2B15	MON-BUF	102	357	28	86		9	0	0			13	.241
Toren	P25	BAL-TOR	25	50	3	8		0	0	0			1	.154
Cy Barger	P16	MON-ROC	20	47	6	15		0	2	0			2	.319

MULTI-TEAM PLAYERS (cont.)

PITCHERS	TEAMS	W	L	PCT	G	GS	CG	SH	IP	H	BB	SO	ERA
Toren	BAL-TOR	5	7	.417	25				130	115	38	47	
Cy Barger	MON-ROC	3	10	.231	16				113	110	48	41	

TEAM BATTING

TEAMS	GP	AB	R	H	BI	2B	3B	HR	BB	SO	SB	BA
TORONTO	137	**4417**	**554**	**1149**		137	**88**	**21**			216	**.260**
BUFFALO	134	4406	536	1100		**149**	38	20			191	.250
PROVIDENCE	136	4393	525	1145		123	59	17			204	.261
JERSEY CITY	137	4373	473	1043		99	57	11			214	.239
NEWARK	134	4228	437	944		132	34	17			194	.223
BALTIMORE	**141**	4413	499	1056		118	49	7			**300**	.239
ROCHESTER	137	4384	475	1040		118	57	10			153	.237
MONTREAL	132	4150	385	902		120	33	16			151	.217
	544	34764	3884	8379		996	415	119			1623	.241

1908
LAYING ONE DOWN

In the nineteenth century, the first professional baseball leagues kept track of only a few batting statistics. Some of these are familiar today: games played, at bats, runs, hits, and stolen bases (added in 1886). A category added in 1890, however, has largely been forgotten. This category is the sacrifice hit.

The sacrifice hit statistic was designed to reward the unselfish batter who "sacrifices" himself (is called out) so a teammate can move up a base. Originally, a player was given a sacrifice hit when he advanced a runner via a bunt, ground out, or fly out. After 1894, only a bunted ball was called a sacrifice hit. Also beginning the same year, to reward the chivalrous player, a sacrifice hit was no longer counted as an at bat against him.

In 1908, Baltimore rose to the top to claim its first flag. In a spirited race, the Orioles bested Providence by two games, and Newark by two and one-half. Buffalo finished a close fourth, followed by Montreal, Toronto, Jersey City, and Rochester. M. Jones from Montreal won the batting crown (.309), while William Phyle of Toronto popped the most home runs (16). From the mound, Baltimore's Merle Adkins won a league-best 29, while Tom Hughes from Newark struck out a total of 161.

In 1908, a new category was added to the sacrifice hit department. Now, if a runner scored on a fly ball out, the batter received credit for a sacrifice hit. This new feature bumped the 1908 totals up 10 percent as the league finished with over 1,500 sacrifice hits, led by Newark (218). Individually, Buffalo's George Schirm had 42 successful sacrifice hits to lead the league. (Later, the fly ball out portion of the statistic was put in a new category and given its own title, the sacrifice fly.)

If these totals seem high, it's because they are. Baseball, during the early years of the twentieth century, was played on a station-to-station basis. Runners were advanced one base at a time, quite often by means of a sacrifice hit. Games were frequently low-scoring affairs, with every run held dear. To baseball strategists, moving the runner over by means of a sacrifice hit was often the best option. The International League's record was set in this era, when a player named Cliff Brady was credited with an astounding 64 sacrifice hits in 1923.

Today, though the sacrifice hit is still kept as an official statistic, it is not widely used; the 1996 International League's total was 410. The downturn of this statistic's use can be attributed to the changing nature of the game. Since the 1920s, because of increased hitting game-wide, baseball has not been played on a base-to-base level. Strategists claim that a runner in scoring position with one out (via a sacrifice hit) is not as desirable as a potential home run two batters later—a base advancement where no one is sacrificed.

BALTIMORE Orioles
1st   83-57   .593   Jack Dunn

BATTERS	POS-GAMES	GP	AB	R	H	BI	2B	3B	HR	BB	SO	SB	BA
John Cassidy	1B68	68	234	32	66		5	2	0			5	.282
Jack Dunn	2B90	92	294	34	72		9	1	1			11	.245
John Knight	SS121,3B19	140	495	62	113		10	12	9			16	.228
Bob Hall	3B89,SS21	125	437	68	117		13	7	4			33	.268
Bill O'Hara	OF141	143	532	87	150		13	3	3			3	.282
Chet Chadbourne	OF99	103	372	51	95		5	3	0				.255
Francis Pfeffer	OF51,P7	58	196	23	59		10	2	1			7	.301
Bill Byers	C68	74	246	20	63		8	4	1			3	.256
Sam Strang	2B53,OF24,3B17	103	379	78	100		15	9	3			36	.264
Hugh Hearne	C51	66	200	21	52		4	3	0			5	.260
Frederick Hunter	1B49	51	143	27	35		4	1	2			16	.245
Merle Adkins	P45	45	113	9	17		2	0	0			0	.150
Frank Dessau	P38	38	96	8	18		5	0	0			3	.188
John McCloskey	P35	35	107	7	22		1	0	0			3	.206
Monte Pfyl	1B30	30	104	10	28		2	3	1			4	.269
Wilbert Robinson	C29	30	103	9	22		2	3	0			0	.213
A. Pearson	P23	27	66	5	11		1	0	0			1	.167
Art Brouthers	3B16	21	66	5	6		0	0	0			4	.091
Harry Hardy	P19	19	47	1	11		2	0	1			2	.234
Schmitt	P11	12	29	1	3		0	0	0			0	.103

PITCHERS		W	L	PCT	G	GS	CG	SH	IP	H	BB	SO	ERA
Merle Adkins		29	12	.707	45				326	263	75	139	
Frank Dessau		15	13	.536	38				270	218	87	137	
John McCloskey		15	14	.517	35				272	240	77	119	
A. Pearson		9	6	.600	23				155	147	43	65	
Hardy Hardy		8	6	.571	19				131	109	41	45	
Schmitt		5	1	.833	11				73	55	21	23	
Francis Pfeffer		3	3	.500	7				54	63	11	16	

PROVIDENCE Grays
2nd   79-57   .581   -2   Hugh Duffy

BATTERS	POS-GAMES	GP	AB	R	H	BI	2B	3B	HR	BB	SO	SB	BA
Bill Abstein	1B145	145	545	78	148		17	19	5			26	.272
Donahue	2B115,SS18	133	471	70	111		7	9	0			23	.236
Roy Rock	SS127	131	442	41	111		4	6	0			5	.251
Harry Arndt	3B137	137	523	63	152		19	11	5			20	.295
Harry Hoffman	OF134	135	519	86	145		13	11	2			32	.279
James Barrett	OF74	82	306	55	73		9	4	0			7	.239
Jim McHale	OF55,2B15	70	250	24	55		5	4	0			12	.220
Bob Peterson	C97	98	293	26	64		8	1	1			6	.218
Phil Poland	OF45	50	180	20	56		7	3	0			6	.311
Sam Frock	P47	48	122	14	23		1	1	2			0	.189
Hugh Duffy		37	57	10	19		5	2	1			5	.333
Jack Cronin	P32	33	88	6	19		2	0	0			1	.216
William Sline	P33	33	70	8	9		2	0	0			0	.129
Ralph Glaze	P24	29	68	9	14		0	2	1			1	.206
Harry Ostdick	C26	27	84	11	21		5	0	0			0	.250
Edward Barry	P26	26	64	7	10		0	1	0			0	.156
Clark	C20	20	67	8	16		3	0	0			1	.239
Friel	P13	14	30	3	5		1	0	0			6	.167
Eaton		12	31	1	3		0	0	0			1	.094
Logan		10	26	3	8		1	0	0			1	.308

PITCHERS		W	L	PCT	G	GS	CG	SH	IP	H	BB	SO	ERA
Sam Frock		24	14	.632	47				325	266	111	149	
Jack Cronin		18	10	.643	32				247	199	45	111	
Ralph Glaze		14	6	.700	24				181	136	34	97	
Edward Barry		14	10	.583	26				187	146	63	115	
William Sline		8	11	.421	33				220	206	46	94	
Friel		1	3	.250	13				87	68	51	32	

NEWARK   3rd   79-58   .577   -2.5   George Stallings
Indians

BATTERS	POS-GAMES	GP	AB	R	H	BI	2B	3B	HR	BB	SO	SB	BA
Bud Sharpe	1B128	**146**	**559**	56	151		19	9	0			16	.270
James Mullen	2B141	141	506	56	112		12	6	0			31	.221
William Mahling	SS138	138	449	56	120		14	9	0			20	.267
Clyde Engle	3B141	141	532	69	138		18	7	1			41	.259
Josh Devore	OF139	140	518	91	150		15	8	0			48	.290
Henry McIlveen	OF78	83	310	36	76		6	4	1			13	.245
John Kelly	OF	(see multi-team players)											
Oscar Stanage	C103	107	355	30	70		10	0	4			9	.197
Delos Drake	OF34,1B18	66	231	22	47		4	6	0			7	.203
Art Mueller	P33	35	84	5	17		1	0	0			1	.202
Tom Hughes	P30	30	86	4	10		1	1	0			1	.116
John Frill	P27	27	76	10	12		1	0	0			1	.158
Baerwald	OF20	26	90	8	23		1	1	0			6	.256
Carrisch	C21	25	61	3	8		0	0	0			2	.131
Paul Krichell	C22	24	56	5	11		1	0	0			1	.196
Lew Brockett	P21	23	70	4	15		4	0	0			1	.214
Miller	P16	20	35	2	5		0	0	0			0	.143
Roy Beecher	P14	18	48	11	13		0	2	0			6	.271
Thomas Philbin	C15	17	45	5	10		2	0	0			1	.222
Albert Pardee	P17	17	42	1	3		0	0	0			0	.071
Doc Newton	P10	10	24	1	1		0	0	0			0	.042

PITCHERS	W	L	PCT	G	GS	CG	SH	IP	H	BB	SO	ERA
Art Mueller	18	7	**.720**	33				227	187	52	103	
Tom Hughes	16	9	.640	30				247	170	61	**161**	
John Frill	13	10	.565	27				218	171	53	97	
Lew Brockett	11	7	.611	21				181	128	50	93	
Roy Beecher	7	3	.700	14				111	97	7	27	
Albert Pardee	7	6	.538	17				121	118	25	41	
Miller	2	5	.286	16				79	55	40	38	
Doc Newton	2	5	.286	10				73	63	26	42	

BUFFALO   4th   75-65   .536   -8   George Smith
Bisons

BATTERS	POS-GAMES	GP	AB	R	H	BI	2B	3B	HR	BB	SO	SB	BA
Bill Clancy	1B	(see multi-team players)											
George Smith	2B120	120	421	34	95		12	3	0			21	.226
William Nattress	SS124	124	465	68	110		23	2	1			15	.239
Hunter Hill	3B116	116	379	32	70		6	3	0			9	.185
George Schirm	OF140	140	501	83	134		14	6	1			61	.267
John White	OF135	137	457	59	135		16	6	6			35	.293
Jim Murray	OF122	122	448	47	103		17	8	4			27	.230
James Archer	C82	82	255	17	53		7	1	2			2	.208
William Keister	2B23,OF20,3B18	85	244	29	60		8	4	0			23	.246
Jack Ryan	C39,1B23	72	217	19	40		5	1	0			6	.184
George McConnell	P30,1B12	44	136	12	29		6	1	1			1	.213
Lew McAllister	C32	44	120	15	32		5	0	0			3	.267
Bill Milligan	P17	38	69	10	18		4	3	1			0	.261
John Vowinkel	P36	37	86	8	23		7	0	0			0	.267
Charles Kisinger	P34	34	91	6	11		2	0	0			1	.121
Levi Knapp	P18	29	59	2	16		3	1	0			4	.271
Bill Tozer	P20	21	45	5	8		0	0	0			0	.178
Bill Malarkey	P5	5	14	2	2		0	0	0			1	.143

PITCHERS	W	L	PCT	G	GS	CG	SH	IP	H	BB	SO	ERA
John Vowinkel	19	13	.594	36				258	243	57	58	
George McConnell	17	12	.586	30				242	183	94	134	
Charles Kisinger	16	14	.533	34				256	193	61	117	
Bill Tozer	10	7	.588	20				137	126	33	41	
Levi Knapp	6	6	.500	18				121	99	53	59	
Bill Milligan	5	6	.455	17				131	109	43	46	
Bill Malarkey	2	3	.400	5				45	37	7	24	

MONTREAL Royals

	5th	64-75	.461	-18.5	James Casey

BATTERS	POS-GAMES	GP	AB	R	H	BI	2B	3B	HR	BB	SO	SB	BA
Steve Evans	1B141	141	510	85	149		25	6	5			20	.292
Mike Corcoran	2B133	133	508	51	122		15	6	4			15	.240
William Louden	SS124	125	407	50	80		13	8	1			19	.197
James Casey	3B132	133	497	64	116		13	3	6			22	.233
Michael Joyce	OF141	141	570	76	130		14	3	0			26	.241
Jim Jones	OF134	135	517	67	**160**		18	5	5			30	**.309**
Michael O'Neill	OF117	117	441	55	128		14	6	1			16	.290
William Clarke	C62	65	173	12	30		5	3	0			3	.173
George Needham	OF26,SS18,2B12,3B12	82	270	24	46		3	4	0			15	.170
Frank McManus	C41	42	136	8	29		4	1	0			5	.213
Jim Ball	C48	48	144	9	20		1	2	0			1	.139
Joe Stanley	P36	37	96	5	15		2	0	0			1	.156
Elijah Jones	P36	36	104	3	12		0	0	0			3	.114
Bob Wicker	P29	32	82	9	23		2	1	0			1	.280
Robert Keefe	P32	32	75	4	11		1	0	0			1	.147
Francis Donahue	P11	14	43	1	8		3	0	1			0	.186
Ray Tift	P7	7	24	1	7		1	0	0			0	.292

PITCHERS		W	L	PCT	G	GS	CG	SH	IP	H	BB	SO	ERA
Elijah Jones		19	14	.576	36				296	250	67	116	
Bob Wicker		15	11	.577	29				225	202	48	103	
Robert Keefe		15	12	.556	32				240	184	72	112	
Joe Stanley		11	21	.344	36				253	201	133	100	
Francis Donahue		3	7	.300	11				94	99	27	26	
Ray Tift		0	4	.000	7				60	56	26	21	

TORONTO Maple Leafs

	6th	68-69	.495	-16.5	Michael Kelley - Larry Schlafly

BATTERS	POS-GAMES	GP	AB	R	H	BI	2B	3B	HR	BB	SO	SB	BA
Mert Whitney		(see multi-team players)											
Larry Schlafly	2B74,OF19	105	325	43	72		12	6	1			23	.222
James Frick	SS79	79	279	22	60		3	1	0			11	.215
Jim Cockman	3B121,SS15	136	485	45	112		9	6	2			17	.231
Yance Weidensaul	OF96,2B29	128	462	47	114		10	1	0			13	.247
Jake Gettman	OF85,1B30	115	462	50	117		13	2	6			8	.253
Ben Caffyn	OF70	78	292	33	63		9	4	4			16	.216
Sam Brown	C54	65	186	11	43		6	0	0			2	.231
William Phyle	2B36,OF21,3B16,SS12	87	310	36	84		6	4	**16**			13	.271
Sam Mertes	OF56	60	219	28	48		6	1	2			8	.229
Dick Rudolph	P36	51	130	13	28		3	0	0			2	.215
William Pearce	C36	42	128	10	32		3	1	0			1	.250
Fred Mitchell	P21	35	105	7	15		2	0	1			0	.143
Jim McGinley	P34	34	90	4	19		6	0	0			0	.211
Michael Kelley	1B31	32	113	6	27		4	0	1			2	.239
Fred Applegate	P28	30	74	7	14		1	1	0			0	.189
Keenan	SS26	29	94	7	15		0	1	0			3	.160
Thielman	OF13	19	60	7	14		1	1	0			3	.233
Myron Grimshaw	1B16	18	67	7	14		2	2	0			2	.209
Elmer Moffitt	P18	18	45	1	5		0	0	0			0	.111
Kilroy	P14	15	32	2	5		0	0	0			0	.156
Hickey	P12	12	38	0	0		0	0	0			0	.000

PITCHERS		W	L	PCT	G	GS	CG	SH	IP	H	BB	SO	ERA
Dick Rudolph		18	12	.600	36				262	243	48	117	
Jim McGinley		15	16	.484	34				256	236	53	92	
Fred Applegate		8	12	.400	28				192	158	81	82	
Elmer Moffitt		6	7	.461	18				138	109	43	50	
Fred Mitchell		6	10	.375	21				166	134	55	59	
Hickey		3	6	.333	12				98	98	44	26	
Kilroy		2	8	.200	14				97	85	40	33	
Cobean		0	3	.000					30	43	20	4	

JERSEY CITY Skeeters

JERSEY CITY Skeeters	7th	58-79	.423	-23.5	Joseph Bean - Eugene McCann

BATTERS	POS-GAMES	GP	AB	R	H	BI	2B	3B	HR	BB	SO	SB	BA
George Merritt	1B124	124	417	40	97		10	3	3			28	.233
Ike Rockenfield	2B68	71	220	22	57		12	4	1			5	.259
Joseph Bean	SS127	136	512	52	104		11	1	1			28	.203
Shaw	3B59	59	225	27	53		3	1	2			12	.236
Ed DeGroff	OF139	142	513	74	131		12	11	12			36	.253
Wally Clement	OF96	96	388	51	103		12	5	3			24	.265
Charles Hanford	OF95	110	399	53	107		17	6	4			19	.268
Matt Fitzgerald	C60	73	226	18	55		4	2	3			2	.243
Gastmeyer	2B53,3B25,SS19,OF11	108	347	18	61		5	3	0			10	.176
Walter Woods	C34,3B26,2B11	82	269	17	58		5	4	1			4	.216
Jack Fox	OF55	57	220	27	59		9	4	2			10	.268
Del Mason	P39	45	132	7	25		2	0	1			0	.189
Harry Gleason	3B35	36	120	8	29		6	0	0			6	.242
Ed Lafitte	P33	35	105	9	19		2	0	0			1	.181
Chester Crist	C29	33	103	3	16		2	1	0			0	.156
Earl Moore	P30	30	90	6	10		1	1	0			0	.111
George Pfanmiller	P14	22	48	4	6		4	1	0			0	.125
Vernon Manser	P18	19	47	4	7		0	0	0			1	.149
Lewis Wiltse	P10	13	33	4	4		1	0	0			0	.121
Young	P9	9	23	1	2		0	0	0			0	.087
Plank	P6	6	16	1	2		0	0	0			0	.125

PITCHERS	W	L	PCT	G	GS	CG	SH	IP	H	BB	SO	ERA
Del Mason	16	19	.457	39				323	278	65	111	
Earl Moore	13	12	.520	30				245	191	102	155	
Ed Lafitte	12	19	.387	33				269	214	81	154	
George Pfanmiller	7	3	.700	14				89	81	28	16	
Vernon Manser	3	11	.214	18				128	124	36	55	
Lewis Wiltse	2	4	.333	10				77	66	25	31	
Young	2	7	.222	9				74	67	17	44	
Plank	1	2	.333	6				39	26	17	10	

ROCHESTER Bronchos

ROCHESTER Bronchos	8th	55-82	.415	-26.5	Al Buckenberger - John Ganzel

BATTERS	POS-GAMES	GP	AB	R	H	BI	2B	3B	HR	BB	SO	SB	BA
Ross Erwin	1B50,C46	106	335	33	81		10	3	2			4	.242
Charles Loudenslager	2B132	132	505	51	126		14	6	1			22	.250
Ed Holly	SS118	123	456	47	110		18	7	0			19	.219
Ed Lennox	3B123	124	409	49	112		25	5	2			26	.274
Jim Flanagan	OF134	137	499	62	129		15	7	4			20	.259
Ed Anderson	OF117	124	432	63	96		5	3	0			21	.222
W. McAvoy	OF84	85	310	31	80		20	3	2			7	.258
Pat Hurley	C57	58	173	7	29		0	1	0			1	.168
Emil Batch	OF53,SS26,3B24,2B11	134	503	51	131		15	7	0			18	.260
Cy Barger	P32,1B15	63	167	13	36		1	1	1			0	.216
Weldon Henley	P29	34	101	7	18		1	1	0			1	.178
Bill Duggleby	P32	32	89	3	15		4	0	0			0	.157
Alex Bannister	P31	31	77	5	16		0	1	0			0	.208
Campbell		15	36	1	5		0	0	0			1	.139
Maroney	P14	14	32	1	3		0	0	0			0	.094
Wall		10	31	2	5		0	0	0			0	.161
F. Snyder	P7	9	22	1	6		1	1	0			0	.273
Edmund Minahan	P9	9	19	0	4		0	0	0			0	.211
Crowley	P6	6	12	0	1		1	0	0			0	.083

PITCHERS	W	L	PCT	G	GS	CG	SH	IP	H	BB	SO	ERA
Weldon Henley	14	13	.519	29				256	188	102	102	
Cy Barger	13	13	.500	32				248	212	75	102	
Bill Duggleby	12	15	.444	32				258	261	63	58	
Alex Bannister	9	15	.375	31				227	228	52	72	
Pembroke Finlayson	2	1	.667					24	13	10	11	
Maroney	2	7	.222	14				90	101	44	33	
Crowley	1	3	.250	6				34	32	13	12	
F. Snyder	1	6	.143	7				58	57	22	12	
Edmund Minahan	0	6	.000	9				50	61	24	25	

MULTI-TEAM PLAYERS

BATTERS	POS-GAMES	TEAMS	GP	AB	R	H	BI	2B	3B	HR	BB	SO	SB	BA
Mert Whitney	1B132	BUF-TOR	132	481	44	114		11	9	2			10	.237
Ray Demmtt	OF114	BAL-NEW	118	418	68	113		11	4	1			14	.270
John Phelan	OF113	TOR-PRO	117	397	63	98		7	3	3			26	.247
John Kelly	OF111	BAL-NEW	112	464	73	121		12	3	1			30	.261
George Vandegrift	C78,1B11	JC-TOR	98	327	21	63		5	4	0			3	.193
Bill Clancy	1B87	BUF-ROC	87	336	43	85		10	6	1			18	.253
John Butler	C54	JC-ROC	57	173	14	47		9	1	0			2	.272
John Neuer	P9	NEW-TOR	9	23	1	6		0	1	0			1	.261

PITCHERS		TEAMS	W	L	PCT	G	GS	CG	SH	IP	H	BB	SO	ERA
John Neuer		NEW-TOR	1	6	.143	9				59	45	44	41	

TEAM BATTING

TEAMS	GP	AB	R	H	BI	2B	3B	HR	BB	SO	SB	BA
BALTIMORE	144	4590	597	1132		120	55	26			239	.247
PROVIDENCE	145	4575	**610**	**1167**		115	**78**	20			178	**.255**
NEWARK	**146**	**4786**	572	1162		124	59	8			**247**	.243
BUFFALO	140	4447	489	1046		146	48	15			222	.235
MONTREAL	141	4607	523	1094		135	51	23			181	.237
TORONTO	140	4487	417	1001		104	41	**35**			135	.223
JERSEY CITY	142	4596	459	1031		121	49	33			181	.224
ROCHESTER	142	4640	476	1109		**149**	49	13			145	.238
	570	36728	4143	8742		1014	430	173			1528	.238

1909
IRON MAN

Major league veteran Joe McGinnity had pitched nearly 10 years in the big leagues. Following a career that long, most players would be content to wind down their playing time after a few more seasons. Not Joe McGinnity. His career wasn't even halfway done.

Joe McGinnity broke into baseball in 1893 with the Montgomery club in the Southern League. After one more season, at Kansas City, McGinnity dropped out of organized baseball for several years. He resurfaced in Peoria in 1898, compiling a 10–3 record. This mark got him noticed, and Joe McGinnity joined the major leagues with Baltimore in 1899. For the next ten years, he pitched at the major league level, mostly for the New York Giants. Highlights included his two 30-win seasons (1903 and 1904) and his doubleheader wins in 1903, where McGinnity pitched both games of three twin bills. It was the latter feat that garnered him the name "Iron Man", though McGinnity would claim it was from his offseason work in an iron foundry. After the 1908 season, where McGinnity went 11–7 at the age of 38, the New York Giants released him. As it turned out, McGinnity had a few innings left.

In 1909, Joe McGinnity joined the Eastern League's Newark Indians, to bolster their pitching and to serve as manager. He soon proved himself one of the Eastern's elite as he led the league in wins (29), games (55), innings pitched (422), shutouts (11), and strikeouts (195). Iron Man McGinnity had certainly delivered the goods.

Rochester became the second Eastern League team in two years to jump from the basement to the attic as it claimed the 1909 pennant. McGinnity's heroics led the Newark squad to second, over Providence in third and Toronto in fourth. Buffalo, Montreal, Baltimore, and Jersey City rounded out the standings. The batting title was claimed by Toronto's Myron Grimshaw (.309), while the leading home run hitter hailed from Rochester—George Simmons with a total of eight.

Joe McGinnity went on to pitch four seasons in the league, highlighted by a 30-win season. For the next few years, he pitched on the West Coast, mostly with Tacoma of the Northwestern League. After a four-year hiatus following World War I, McGinnity resurrected his career in the I.I.I. League with Danville. Joe McGinnity's career finally came to an end in 1925 with Dubuque of the Mississippi Valley League, where he compiled a 6–6 record. He was 54 years old.

Joe McGinnity's stay in the Eastern League, a mere blip in his career, saw him set two key records. His 422 innings pitched in 1909, and his 11 shutouts have never been matched. Overall, Joe McGinnity, during his nearly 30 years in baseball, won 482 games while losing 357—numbers reflecting his Iron Man career.

ROCHESTER Hustlers

| | 1st | 90-61 | .596 | | John Ganzel |

BATTERS	POS-GAMES	GP	AB	R	H	BI	2B	3B	HR	BB	SO	SB	BA
John Ganzel	1B114	119	429	42	131		30	3	1			11	.305
Harry Pattee	2B155	155	564	70	141		15	4	3			37	.250
Ed Holly	SS149,OF5	154	583	58	131		25	9	1			28	.225
George Simmons	3B92,1B24,OF18	137	472	59	141		28	9	8			12	.299
Ed Anderson	OF134	136	477	76	96		8	9	0			34	.201
William Maloney	OF125	125	438	51	102		8	5	0			38	.233
Emil Batch	OF98,3B34,SS9	145	492	56	124		19	3	0			27	.252
Ross Erwin	C87,1B12	102	338	25	93		10	2	6			7	.275
John Butler	C75	76	253	16	50		9	0	0			3	.198
Fred Osborn	OF64	64	238	39	71		13	4	4			5	.298
Cy Barger	P45	50	130	9	32		2	0	0			1	.246
Jim Holmes	P39	39	86	7	7		0	0	0			0	.081
Roy Beecher	P34	37	66	6	17		2	0	0			1	.258
Weldon Henley	P23	23	63	4	13		1	0	1			0	.206
F. Snyder	P22	22	42	6	8		1	1	0			0	.190
Bill Chappelle	P21	21	52	4	9		0	1	1			0	.173
Pat Ragan	P9	9	23	0	0		0	0	0			0	.000
Joe Kustus	OF7	7	25	0	6		1	1	0			0	.240
Monte Beville		2	2	1	1		0	0	0			0	.500

PITCHERS		W	L	PCT	G	GS	CG	SH	IP	H	BB	SO	ERA
Cy Barger		23	13	.639	45				328	254	82	128	
Jim Holmes		16	11	.593	39				235	198	78	118	
Roy Beecher		10	6	.625	34				173	183	21	55	
Weldon Henley		10	9	.526	23				169	141	75	59	
Bill Chappelle		9	12	.429	21				138	144	30	51	
Pat Ragan		6	2	.750	9				70	48	11	35	
F. Snyder		6	4	.600	22				116	104	34	48	

NEWARK Indians

| | 2nd | 86-67 | .562 | -5 | Harry Wolverton - Joe McGinnity |

BATTERS	POS-GAMES	GP	AB	R	H	BI	2B	3B	HR	BB	SO	SB	BA
Bud Sharpe	1B156	156	569	65	137		22	4	1			16	.241
Larry Schlafly	2B150	150	521	65	109		20	3	1			36	.209
William Louden	SS147	149	545	67	116		16	4	1			29	.213
Harry Wolverton	3B108	108	390	37	102		16	6	5			9	.262
John Kelly	OF156	156	581	79	161		37	4	3			40	.277
Benny Meyer	OF156	156	519	69	130		15	10	2			37	.250
Jake Gettman	OF149	149	561	78	162		30	8	6			16	.289
Joe Crisp	C64	74	213	13	39		7	1	1			11	.183
Art Mueller	P40,SS12,3B7	65	149	12	19		3	0	0			6	.128
Joe McGinnity	P55	56	130	7	30		3	0	0			4	.231
Lapp	C41	51	148	12	37		6	2	0			2	.250
Ed Zimmerman	3B46	46	178	20	47		2	4	1			7	.264
Walter Blair	C38	42	127	7	23		5	1	1			3	.181
John Frill	P34	34	80	4	11		2	0	0			0	.138
Jack Flater	P29	33	60	4	11		4	0	0			1	.182
Brady	P22	26	70	3	12		1	0	0			1	.170
Charles Parkins	P26	26	57	3	5		0	0	0			0	.088
Charles Loudenslager	2B5	8	28	1	4		0	0	0			0	.143
White	OF5	7	19	2	2		0	0	0			1	.105
Larkins		2	6	1	2		1	0	0			0	.333
Wilson		2	4	0	0		0	0	0			0	.000
Thomas Philbin		2	2	0	1		0	0	0			0	.500
Heuser		2	2	1	0		0	0	0			0	.000

PITCHERS		W	L	PCT	G	GS	CG	SH	IP	H	BB	SO	ERA
Joe McGinnity		29	16	.644	55				422	297	78	195	
Art Mueller		16	11	.593	40				242	204	88	123	
John Frill		16	13	.552	34				248	213	58	105	
Brady		10	8	.556	22				160	162	34	82	
Jack Flater		8	9	.470	29				155	148	46	48	
Charles Parkins		6	8	.429	26				155	129	38	49	

PROVIDENCE   3rd   80-70   .533   -9.5   Hugh Duffy
Clamdiggers

BATTERS	POS-GAMES	GP	AB	R	H	BI	2B	3B	HR	BB	SO	SB	BA
John Anderson	1B113,OF12	127	467	47	122		21	2	2			26	.261
Claude Ritchey	2B62	62	219	16	52		6	1	0			2	.237
Lena Blackburne	SS121	121	444	52	121		10	7	0			32	.273
Harry Arndt	3B80,2B33,1B23	139	530	51	135		16	11	2			18	.255
John Phelan	OF151	151	549	88	113		13	8	3			46	.206
Harry Hoffman	OF150	154	575	68	**164**		14	11	0			32	.285
Herb Moran	OF149	154	571	**92**	153		19	1	0			**58**	.268
Matt Fitzgerald	C77	84	264	15	59		7	7	1			4	.223
Bob Peterson	C76,2B12,1B7	104	309	28	73		5	4	1			6	.236
Roy Rock	2B38,SS29,3B26	91	305	24	67		6	1	0			6	.220
Ed Courtney	3B29,1B17	54	156	11	32		10	1	1			2	.205
Frank Barberich	P37	39	108	8	23		1	0	0			0	.213
James Lavender	P35	35	97	4	13		0	0	0			0	.134
Ed Lafitte	P33	34	89	8	23		4	0	0			0	.258
Jack Cronin	P33	33	77	5	11		2	0	0			1	.143
Edward Barry	P32	32	79	5	17		2	0	0			1	.215
Shaw	3B15,2B14	30	108	14	27		2	2	0			4	.250
Wilson	C6	9	24	2	3		0	0	0			0	.125
Harry Hardy	P9	9	15	0	3		0	0	0			0	.200
William Sline	P7	7	15	1	1		1	0	0			0	.067
Harris		2	4	0	1		0	0	0			0	.250
Rivard		1	2	0	1		1	0	0			0	.500

PITCHERS	W	L	PCT	G	GS	CG	SH	IP	H	BB	SO	ERA
Frank Barberich	20	11	.645	37				289	216	67	108	
Jack Cronin	16	8	**.667**	33				260	185	50	112	
James Lavender	14	17	.452	35				244	223	94	103	
Ed Lafitte	13	11	.542	33				232	197	48	100	
Edward Barry	11	13	.458	32				213	154	53	102	
William Sline	3	2	.600	7				46	43	16	23	
Harry Hardy	1	5	.167	9				44	53	17	13	

TORONTO   4th   79-72   .523   -11   Joe Kelley
Maple Leafs

BATTERS	POS-GAMES	GP	AB	R	H	BI	2B	3B	HR	BB	SO	SB	BA
Ben Houser	1B150	151	567	82	161		17	8	6			15	.284
James Mullen	2B130	132	479	53	113		16	5	1			31	.236
William Mahling	SS123,OF7	135	472	56	119		14	3	1			20	.252
James Frick	3B103,SS10	118	380	34	79		13	5	0			13	.208
Yance Weidensaul	OF124,3B14	138	482	52	106		14	1	1			27	.220
Myron Grimshaw	OF109,2B10	124	482	56	149		20	10	3			12	**.309**
Joe Kelley	OF95	107	357	49	96		23	1	1			11	.269
Fred Mitchell	C92	109	342	24	101		12	6	1			15	.295
George Vandegrift	C69	74	231	17	52		12	0	0			5	.225
Dick Rudolph	P42	42	116	11	22		5	0	0			3	.190
Jim McGinley	P40	41	108	7	18		4	1	1			4	.167
Goode	OF37	38	141	14	33		7	0	1			6	.234
Watty Lee	OF22,P12	38	104	12	30		5	0	1			1	.288
Robert Vaughn	SS23	25	81	6	15		2	1	0			3	.185
Doc Newton	P25	25	62	5	11		2	3	0			1	.177
Al Kellogg	P18	18	42	1	4		0	0	0			0	.095
William Phyle	3B12	12	45	1	11		0	0	0			0	.244
Elmer Moffitt	P9	9	14	0	1		0	0	0			0	.071
Thomas	OF5	5	19	2	3		0	0	0			0	.158
Bull Durham	P5	5	13	1	2		0	0	0			0	.154
Moore		4	14	0	1		0	0	0			0	.071
Carl Lundgren		4	8	0	1		0	0	0			0	.125
Greene		2	6	0	2		0	0	0			0	.333

PITCHERS	W	L	PCT	G	GS	CG	SH	IP	H	BB	SO	ERA
Dick Rudolph	23	14	.622	42				326	261	50	116	
Jim McGinley	22	13	.629	40				327	284	62	105	
Doc Newton	12	10	.545	25				172	132	66	97	
Watty Lee	4	3	.571	12				86	76	14	23	
Al Kellogg	4	10	.286	18				120	88	73	53	
Elmer Moffitt	1	4	.200	9				45	53	11	10	
Bull Durham	0	4	.000	5				37	52	15	9	

BUFFALO   5th   72-79   .477   -18   George Smith
Bisons

BATTERS	POS-GAMES	GP	AB	R	H	BI	2B	3B	HR	BB	SO	SB	BA
Bill Clancy	1B127	128	476	58	115		14	11	1			20	.242
George Smith	2B124	127	434	37	108		10	3	1			20	.249
William Nattress	SS107	108	384	50	79		11	3	1			20	.206
Dave Brain	3B131,1B20	151	556	60	130		27	15	2			23	.234
John White	OF	153	568	72	159		17	12	2			20	.280
George Schirm	OF139	139	521	72	123		17	6	1			51	.236
Jim Flanagan	OF			(see multi-team players)									
Lew McAllister	C64,OF8	81	257	14	59		6	3	0			7	.230
Alva Williams	C34,2B5,OF5	51	149	15	35		1	3	0			6	.235
John Vowinkel	P42	47	122	11	21		3	0	0			2	.172
Charles Kisinger	P44	44	109	6	14		3	0	0			3	.129
Collins	OF31	31	109	8	32		1	1	0			7	.294
Bill Malarkey	P31	31	72	4	6		0	0	0			0	.083
Luther Taylor	P39	40	91	2	7		0	1	0			0	.077
Bill Hessler	OF27	27	90	8	15		0	0	1			5	.167
Fred Burchell	P19	26	66	7	15		0	1	0			1	.227
Levi Knapp	OF9,P5	16	43	5	5		0	0	0			2	.116
Mack Allison	P13	13	20	2	2		0	0	0			0	.100
Bill Klinck	2B11	12	36	3	9		0	0	0			0	.250
A. Marcan		3	7	0	1		0	0	0			0	.143

PITCHERS	W	L	PCT	G	GS	CG	SH	IP	H	BB	SO	ERA
Charles Kisinger	18	19	.486	44				309	271	74	125	
John Vowinkel	16	16	.500	42				304	287	79	71	
Luther Taylor	16	18	.470	39				313	250	81	161	
Bill Malarkey	13	11	.542	31				229	193	49	80	
Fred Burchell	6	9	.400	19				145	105	60	70	
Mack Allison	2	3	.400	13				70	82	19	18	

MONTREAL   6th   68-83   .450   -22   James Casey
Royals

BATTERS	POS-GAMES	GP	AB	R	H	BI	2B	3B	HR	BB	SO	SB	BA
George Cockill	1B141	141	523	52	129		15	4	3			27	.247
Mickey Corcoran	2B149	149	561	61	139		25	7	2			36	.248
Joe Yeager	SS128	128	490	59	137		25	8	0			14	.280
James Casey	3B106,OF8	118	398	44	96		9	1	0			10	.241
Michael O'Neill	OF154	154	554	52	133		17	14	1			17	.240
Michael Joyce	OF152	152	566	74	121		13	5	2			27	.214
Jim Jones	OF134	135	484	32	119		23	1	2			16	.246
Paul Krichell	C			(see multi-team players)									
Colvin	3B38,SS29	76	232	11	38		5	1	2			0	.164
George Winter	P35,3B10,OF7	60	160	11	30		3	3	0			1	.187
William Clarke	C40	40	129	11	23		3	0	0			2	.178
Robert Keefe	P38	38	85	7	10		4	0	0			0	.117
Smith	P37	37	89	7	11		1	0	0			0	.124
Bob Wicker	P29	36	89	6	17		1	0	0			1	.191
Ralph Savidge	P26	28	84	4	13		2	0	0			0	.155
Buelow	C19	19	46	4	8		1	0	0			0	.174
Elijah Jones	P9	9	27	3	7		1	0	0			0	.259
Egan		7	12	3	4		1	1	0			0	.333
Rogers	P5	5	3	2	1		0	0	0			0	.333

PITCHERS	W	L	PCT	G	GS	CG	SH	IP	H	BB	SO	ERA
George Winter	15	12	.556	35				253	204	41	71	
Smith	15	14	.517	37				274	219	119	94	
Robert Keefe	13	18	.419	38				271	226	60	122	
Bob Wicker	11	14	.440	29				234	235	69	79	
Ralph Savidge	11	15	.423	26				260	217	50	95	
Elijah Jones	3	6	.333	9				82	62	16	33	
Rogers	1	2	.333	5				20	24	12	8	

BALTIMORE Orioles

7th   67-86   .438   -24   Jack Dunn

BATTERS	POS-GAMES	GP	AB	R	H	BI	2B	3B	HR	BB	SO	SB	BA
John Cassidy	1B85	86	310	29	83		7	3	0			10	.268
Jack Dunn	2B83,OF11	100	319	34	57		8	4	0			9	.179
Phil Lewis	SS98,2B28	126	447	32	103		8	3	0			14	.230
Bob Hall	3B136	136	507	64	139		14	6	2			23	.274
James Jackson	OF134	137	475	68	125		17	15	3			23	.263
James Slagle	OF115	115	411	69	110		12	3	2			21	.268
Phil Poland	OF97,3B6	100	362	37	92		10	3	1			20	.255
Bill Byers	C94	104	340	26	91		12	4	0			4	.268
Sam Strang	OF63,2B34	107	351	54	101		15	13	2			2	.288
Charles Schmidt	1B56,P8	66	221	20	54		4	2	0			5	.244
Monte Cross	SS62	62	205	13	37		1	2	0			11	.180
Hugh Hearne	C27,1B20	59	156	8	39		5	0	0			3	.250
Merle Adkins	P48	48	110	10	19		3	0	0			1	.172
Frank Dessau	P44	44	130	7	17		2	0	1			1	.131
Harry Cheek	C43	43	130	12	29		1	0	0			3	.223
James Catiz	3B17,2B13	37	108	11	27		3	1	0			5	.250
Clarke	OF35	35	134	21	34		5	3	1			4	.253
A. Pearson	P29	32	65	2	9		1	0	0			1	.138
Joe Stanley	P27	27	41	3	8		3	0	0			0	.195
John McCloskey	P25	25	62	4	9		1	0	0			1	.145
Michael Bills	P10	16	39	8	14		0	2	0			1	.359
Maroney	P5	6	12	0	2		0	0	0			0	.167
Conn		3	10	3	5		1	0	0			1	.500
Reilly		2	8	1	2		1	0	0			0	.250

PITCHERS		W	L	PCT	G	GS	CG	SH	IP	H	BB	SO	ERA
Merle Adkins		21	19	.525	48				337	320	75	132	
Frank Dessau		18	17	.514	44				359	333	136	189	
A. Pearson		8	13	.381	29				175	161	50	62	
John McCloskey		7	11	.389	25				171	187	59	56	
Charles Schmidt		3	2	.600	8				51	53	18	10	
Michael Bills		3	3	.500	10				59	66	11	21	
Joe Stanley		3	14	.176	27				134	127	47	64	
Maroney		0	4	.000	5				35	46	9	16	

JERSEY CITY Skeeters

8th   63-87   .420   -26.5   Eugene McCann - John Calhoun - Jack Ryan

BATTERS	POS-GAMES	GP	AB	R	H	BI	2B	3B	HR	BB	SO	SB	BA
John Calhoun	1B146	146	538	45	126		17	1	0			11	.234
Earl Gardner	2B95	95	326	37	95		11	5	0			9	.291
Ed Foster	SS148	148	536	50	130		14	10	6			37	.242
Jack Hannifan	3B74,2B39,OF31	150	533	48	114		19	3	5			25	.214
Dan Moeller	OF152	152	591	80	146		6	7	7			42	.247
Charles Hanford	OF143	143	527	59	125		13	12	6			37	.237
Fred Eley	OF105	106	388	52	82		5	5	6			15	.211
Lawrence Spahr	C72	78	222	20	51		8	2	4			4	.230
Jim Esmond	3B72,2B8	85	285	21	61		7	2	0			8	.214
George Merritt	P30,3B10,1B8,OF7	58	168	11	34		1	1	0			3	.202
Russ Ford	P32	34	92	4	11		3	1	0			0	.119
Carl Sitton	P30	31	86	3	14		1	1	0			0	.163
Vernon Manser	P27	29	84	4	11		1	0	0			0	.131
Ed McDonough	C22	22	63	4	8		0	0	0			0	.127
Bill Milligan	P14	21	50	2	12		2	1	1			0	.240
Waller	P20	20	56	1	6		0	0	1			0	.107
William Zimmerman	OF15	16	54	3	9		0	0	0			0	.167
Goetell	P12	13	30	1	5		0	0	0			0	.167
Jack Wanner	2B11	11	39	2	7		0	1	0			1	.179
J. Londrigan	2B9	9	37	7	12		2	1	2			1	.324
Jack Ferry	P7	9	17	1	5		0	0	0			0	.294
Gray	OF7	8	25	0	4		0	1	0			0	.160
O'Hara	SS7	7	25	3	5		0	0	0			0	.200
Chester Crist		3	7	2	0		0	0	0			1	.000
Del Mason		3	4	0	0		0	0	0			0	.000

PITCHERS		W	L	PCT	G	GS	CG	SH	IP	H	BB	SO	ERA
George Merritt		14	14	.500	30				233	183	49	118	
Russ Ford		13	13	.500	32				276	172	78	189	
Carl Sitton		11	13	.458	30				219	173	77	89	

JERSEY CITY (cont.)
Skeeters

PITCHERS	W	L	PCT	G	GS	CG	SH	IP	H	BB	SO	ERA
Vernon Manser	10	13	.435	27				216	157	69	83	
Waller	6	14	.300	20				162	136	42	68	
Bill Milligan	5	8	.385	14				115	106	41	45	
Goettell	3	3	.500	12				72	60	28	20	
Jack Ferry	1	5	.167	7				38	29	7	16	

MULTI-TEAM PLAYERS

BATTERS	POS-GAMES	TEAMS	GP	AB	R	H	BI	2B	3B	HR	BB	SO	SB	BA
Jim Flanagan	OF106	ROC-BUF	117	399	41	98		11	3	0			20	.246
Jack Ryan	C82,1B11	BUF-JC	99	309	21	62		7	2	0			2	.201
Eddie McDonald	3B58,OF23,2B13	ROC-TOR	98	356	48	89		15	4	0			13	.250
Walter Woods	3B51,SS41,2B11,1B6	BU-JC	98	315	26	64		7	2	0			13	.203
Paul Krichell	C82	NEW-MON	89	261	18	68		7	1	0			7	.261
Francis Pfeffer	OF38,P31	BAL-TOR	75	220	18	50		12	1	0			7	.227
George Starnagle	C54,1B15	TOR-MON	68	204	8	38		2	0	0			2	.186
Fallon	OF41	MON-TOR	46	156	8	26		3	1	0			8	.167
Joe Knotts	C26	BUF-JC	36	102	9	29		2	2	0			1	.285
George McConnell	P15,1B12	ROC-JC	25	84	9	22		6	1	1			0	.262

PITCHERS		TEAMS	W	L	PCT	G	GS	CG	SH	IP	H	BB	SO	ERA
Francis Pfeffer		BAL-TOR	14	10	.583	31				211	173	76	100	
George McConnell		ROC-JC	9	3	.750	13				106	72	22	74	

TEAM BATTING

TEAMS	GP	AB	R	H	BI	2B	3B	HR	BB	SO	SB	BA
ROCHESTER	154	**5076**	**559**	1231		184	52	26			210	.243
NEWARK	**156**	5038	555	1178		**192**	47	22			221	.234
PROVIDENCE	154	5013	539	1216		143	56	10			**238**	.243
TORONTO	154	5063	542	**1247**		185	49	17			187	**.246**
BUFFALO	153	4925	511	1107		131	**65**	9			216	.225
MONTREAL	154	5021	473	1129		156	46	12			160	.225
BALTIMORE	**156**	5073	544	1232		143	**65**	13			176	.243
JERSEY CITY	154	5039	476	1108		115	55	**38**			194	.220
	618	40248	4199	9448		1249	435	147			1602	.235

1910
NO HITS, NO WALKS, NO ERRORS

The goal of any pitcher is to pitch a no-hitter, where no opponent reaches first by means of a safe hit. A further achievement would be to prevent the opponent from reaching base by any means—hit, walk, or error. This ultimate accomplishment is known as a perfect game.

The first no-hitter thrown in the league happened in 1884—the very first year of operation—when Richmond's Ed Dugan bested Newark 9–1. During the next 25 years, nearly 20 more no-hitters were twirled, including three in 1909 alone. However, no league pitcher was able to break through to the next level and pitch a perfect game. That feat would have to wait until 1910, when a Buffalo Bison pitcher accomplished the task.

Chester Carmichael joined the roster of the Eastern League Buffalo squad, after a brief two-game cup of coffee with the major league Cincinnati Reds, in 1909. In Buffalo, Carmichael toiled for a mediocre team as the club's number two starting pitcher. In August, however, his season took a sudden turn for the better.

On August 10, Carmichael was scheduled to face the seventh-place Jersey City Skeeters in what appeared to be a meaningless game. At game's end, however, the result was far from insignificant. Carmichael had won the game 1–0, pitching nine innings without allowing a single opposing baserunner via a hit, walk, or error. In short, Chester Carmichael had thrown the league's first perfect game.

For the second straight year, Rochester claimed the Eastern League flag over the bridesmaid Newark Indians. Baltimore and Toronto finished over .500 in third and fourth, while Montreal, Buffalo, Jersey City, and Providence finished in the final four spots. Toronto's Jack Slattery paced the hitters with a .310 mark, while fellow Maple Leaf Al Shaw knocked a league-best 11 home runs. Once again, Joe McGinnity pitched the most victories (30), while Lefty Russell of Baltimore struck out the most batters (219).

Chester Carmichael finished the 1910 season with a 13–12 record—not a bad mark for a sixth-place team. After only one year, he drifted out of the league for good. Although he was only 21 when he pitched his masterpiece, Carmichael never again reached the major leagues.

In two years' time, another league pitcher would toss a perfect game, although it was tainted by being only seven innings long. The league waited another 40 years for another nine-inning perfecto. When it happened again in 1952, it happened in much the same way as 1910. The 1952 perfect game pitcher was an average hurler for a mediocre team located in the city of Buffalo.

ROCHESTER Hustlers

ROCHESTER   1st   92-61   .601   John Ganzel

BATTERS	POS-GAMES	GP	AB	R	H	BI	2B	3B	HR	BB	SO	SB	BA
Chester Spencer	1B136	139	489	47	117		10	7	1			8	.239
Charles Alperman	2B89,3B59	149	534	70	138		19	16	2			18	.258
Bert Tooley	SS123	138	486	71	122		13	3	1			43	.251
Joe Ward	3B45	45	159	18	48		7	2	0			6	.302
Fred Osborn	OF144	156	582	75	176		25	10	0			18	.302
Emil Batch	OF100,3B30	134	480	64	135		15	5	2			20	.281
Dan Moeller	OF	(see multi-team players)											
Walter Blair	C145	146	481	44	124		24	6	0			16	.258
Ed Anderson	OF34	48	123	14	17		0	1	0			4	.138
George McConnell	P36	45	126	15	42		7	3	2			1	.333
Ed Lafitte	P42	43	110	4	15		1	3	0			0	.136
George Simmons	3B25	36	118	20	32		10	4	1			4	.271
Pat Ragan	P33	35	100	2	14		3	1	0			0	.140
Jim Holmes	P33	33	87	2	7		0	0	0			0	.080
Ralph Savidge	P31	31	76	3	10		2	0	0			1	.132
Herb Moran	OF28	29	103	18	30		1	1	0			7	.291
John Ganzel		29	49	4	11		3	0	0			2	.224
Roy Beecher	P10	18	26	1	7		0	0	0			2	.269
Leon Martel	C13	16	37	2	7		1	0	0			1	.189
John Castle	OF10	11	28	2	10		0	0	0			4	.263
George Starnagle	C10	11	22	2	3		0	0	0			1	.136

PITCHERS	W	L	PCT	G	GS	CG	SH	IP	H	BB	SO	ERA
Ed Lafitte	23	14	.622	42				317	236	79	201	
George McConnell	19	12	.613	36				294	200	76	165	
Jim Holmes	17	10	.630	33				233	181	95	101	
Pat Ragan	16	11	.593	33				291	241	58	160	
Ralph Savidge	13	12	.520	31				225	201	45	75	
Roy Beecher	2	1	.667	10				40	44	4	7	

NEWARK Indians

NEWARK   2nd   88-66   .571   -4.5   Joe McGinnity

BATTERS	POS-GAMES	GP	AB	R	H	BI	2B	3B	HR	BB	SO	SB	BA
Joe Agler	1B144	144	418	46	84		8	1	0			15	.201
Larry Schlafly	2B137,1B10	142	484	51	108		18	1	2			24	.223
William Louden	SS142	142	500	59	118		17	4	5			41	.236
Ed Zimmerman	3B155	156	602	86	146		20	12	2			32	.243
John Kelly	OF144	145	551	70	160		29	6	2			29	.290
Jake Gettman	OF121,1B13	132	485	54	130		19	7	2			24	.268
Bob Ganley	OF100	114	382	35	90		8	3	0			17	.236
Hugh Hearne	C74	94	236	25	61		10	1	0			3	.258
Benny Meyer	OF65,2B35	119	347	49	91		14	3	0			22	.262
Joe McGinnity	P61	64	141	14	28		6	0	0			1	.199
Joe Crisp	C60	60	179	12	31		5	3	2			3	.173
Browne	OF37	40	128	18	32		1	1	0			12	.250
Charles Parkins	P30	31	41	4	5		2	0	0			0	.122
Holtz	C11	28	41	4	11		1	0	0			0	.268
Robert Holmes	P20	20	29	0	4		0	0	0			0	.138
Charles Loudenslager		19	72	3	14		1	0	0			2	.194
Rube Waddell	P15	15	28	1	3		0	0	0			1	.107
Egan	P14	14	14	1	2		0	1	0			0	.143
Bob Spade	P10	13	16	1	6		0	1	0			0	.375
Steve Brodie	OF	11	28	2	6		0	0	0			0	.214
James Cleary		10	13	1	2		0	0	0			0	.154

PITCHERS	W	L	PCT	G	GS	CG	SH	IP	H	BB	SO	ERA
Joe McGinnity	30	19	.612	61				408	325	71	132	
Charles Parkins	11	5	.688	30				145	112	47	49	
Rube Waddell	5	3	.625	15				97	73	41	53	
James Cleary	3	2	.600					40	33	21	21	
Robert Holmes	3	9	.250	20				103	98	35	35	
Egan	1	4	.200	14				53	51	22	11	
Bob Spade	1	4	.200	10				46	47	17	11	

BALTIMORE Orioles

BALTIMORE Orioles	3rd	83-70	.544	-9	Jack Dunn

BATTERS	POS-GAMES	GP	AB	R	H	BI	2B	3B	HR	BB	SO	SB	BA
Bill Clancy	1B107	107	426	55	103		12	7	2			12	.242
Sam Strang	2B59	61	202	24	49		5	2	2			4	.243
Simon Nicholls	SS124	124	455	59	116		13	5	2			27	.257
Bob Hall	3B79,2B22	106	347	30	70		7	5	0			13	.202
James Slagle	OF146	146	540	89	145		15	3	2			26	.269
James Walsh	OF133	140	481	70	129		17	7	5			18	.268
Wilbur Good	OF118	130	504	76	151		9	12	7			22	.300
Ben Egan	C101	106	319	31	74		12	5	5			6	.232
Charles Schmidt	1B49,OF17,P	85	253	29	74		4	3	2			4	.292
Bill Byers	C69	79	213	13	52		8	1	1			1	.244
Jack Dunn	2B55,3B12	76	241	34	62		7	1	0			11	.257
James Frick	3B37,SS21	69	219	26	57		6	1	1			5	.260
Rube Vickers	P55	55	127	8	24		1	3	1			1	.189
Lefty Russell	P44	47	126	18	33		5	3	1			0	.262
William Heitmuller	OF39	39	127	15	42		5	4	1			3	.331
Merle Adkins	P37	37	81	1	10		1	0	0			0	.123
Ed Donnelly	P34	34	61	5	10		0	0	0			0	.164
Morrie Rath	2B19	28	107	18	37		0	2	1			7	.346
Alex Malloy	P28	28	49	8	11		0	0	0			0	.224
James Catiz	3B22	22	78	8	13		2	0	0			3	.167
James Seymour	OF12	15	53	6	15		3	0	0			0	.283
Murray	C12	13	14	1	0		0	0	0			0	.000
Maroney	P11	11	23	2	1		0	0	0			0	.043

PITCHERS		W	L	PCT	G	GS	CG	SH	IP	H	BB	SO	ERA
Rube Vickers		25	24	.510	55				364	333	112	214	
Lefty Russell		24	14	.649	44				337	215	135	219	
Merle Adkins		12	16	.429	37				246	224	54	111	
Ed Donnelly		11	4	.733	34				173	153	43	81	
Alex Malloy		5	7	.419	28				142	118	54	73	
Maroney		4	3	.571	11				69	62	33	35	
Charles Schmidt		1	2	.333					55	51	20	20	

TORONTO Maple Leafs

TORONTO Maple Leafs	4th	80-72	.526	-11.5	Joe Kelley

BATTERS	POS-GAMES	GP	AB	R	H	BI	2B	3B	HR	BB	SO	SB	BA
Jack Slattery	1B83,C11	100	365	32	113		17	4	0			5	.310
James Mullen	2B138	138	516	64	124		10	7	2			21	.241
Robert Vaughn	SS128	128	403	41	87		5	2	1			23	.216
Eddie McDonald	3B97,OF17	128	407	58	99		10	4	1			22	.243
Joseph Delahanty	OF136	144	522	60	150		29	10	2			10	.287
Al Shaw	OF134	139	517	79	146		22	13	11			27	.282
Bill O'Hara	OF118	122	442	60	116		15	4	2			18	.262
George Vandegrift	C63	64	184	19	43		6	0	0			0	.234
Ed Fitzpatrick	3B67,SS30,2B16	119	381	38	87		6	2	4			14	.228
Myron Grimshaw	1B35,OF26	62	223	24	64		8	4	3			10	.287
Charles Tonneman	C45	51	145	10	42		6	1	0			3	.290
Joe Kelley	OF28	46	110	13	31		5	2	0			4	.282
Dick Rudolph	P41	44	106	13	25		4	2	0			7	.236
Jim McGinley	P41	41	81	4	10		1	0	0			1	.123
Doc Newton	P37	37	90	6	16		2	1	0			0	.178
Dick Carroll	P26	27	54	3	8		0	0	0			1	.148
Smith	P20	20	43	2	6		0	0	0			0	.140
Corey	P20	20	28	4	7		0	0	0			1	.250
Ed Killian	P	10	27	0	8		2	0	0			0	.296
Carl Lundgren	P10	10	15	0	2		1	0	0			0	.133

PITCHERS		W	L	PCT	G	GS	CG	SH	IP	H	BB	SO	ERA
Dick Rudolph		23	15	.603	41				304	242	69	125	
Doc Newton		17	14	.548	37				263	230	120	138	
Jim McGinley		16	19	.457	41				256	222	54	86	
Dick Carroll		9	7	.563	26				159	151	37	40	
Smith		6	3	.667	20				125	112	76	41	
Corey		4	3	.571	20				82	71	24	31	
Ed Killian		2	6	.250					69	48	20	34	
Carl Lundgren		1	4	.200	10				47	51	18	14	

MONTREAL Royals

MONTREAL Royals	5th	71-80	.470	-20	Ed Barrow

BATTERS	POS-GAMES	GP	AB	R	H	BI	2B	3B	HR	BB	SO	SB	BA
George Cockill	1B121	132	463	36	93		9	5	2			16	.201
William Nattress	2B74,SS66	149	489	50	104		16	3	0			19	.213
Ed Holly	SS	(see multi-team players)											
Joe Yeager	3B134	145	560	41	141		21	1	1			17	.252
Jim Jones	OF143	147	552	47	128		20	1	3			11	.232
Ray Demmitt	OF130	130	483	62	121		20	11	5			14	.251
Albert Jube	OF55	55	215	24	48		4	0	0			8	.223
Paul Krichell	C88	102	281	29	70		14	0	0			12	.249
Harry Curtis	C49	70	203	18	45		5	1	0			7	.222
Robert Keefe	P42	42	91	5	10		1	1	0			1	.110
George Winter	P25	36	85	9	17		3	0	0			2	.200
Jim Wiggs	P35	35	71	5	9		1	1	0			1	.127
Elijah Jones	P34	34	71	5	13		1	0	0			2	.183
Jack Hardy	C16	31	97	7	32		2	3	0			7	.330
Michael Joyce	OF22	27	85	12	16		0	0	0			5	.188
J. Bailey	OF18	21	69	9	12		2	0	0			2	.174
Hunter	OF10	17	52	6	10		0	0	1			5	.192
Madden	OF10	13	48	8	9		0	0	0			6	.188

PITCHERS	W	L	PCT	G	GS	CG	SH	IP	H	BB	SO	ERA
Robert Keefe	22	12	.647	42				291	194	81	120	
Elijah Jones	13	12	.520	34				233	204	68	83	
Jim Wiggs	8	16	.333	35				225	163	95	139	
George Winter	2	10	.167	25				175	160	32	50	

BUFFALO Bisons

BUFFALO Bisons	6th	69-81	.460	-21.5	William Smith

BATTERS	POS-GAMES	GP	AB	R	H	BI	2B	3B	HR	BB	SO	SB	BA
Ed Sabrie	1B118	118	392	32	105		13	3	0			7	.268
George Smith	2B	(see multi-team players)											
Charles Starr	SS92	93	312	33	85		5	1	0			12	.272
Mickey Corcoran	3B	(see multi-team players)											
Noah Henline	OF149	151	577	84	158		26	10	1			45	.274
John White	OF138	148	487	58	133		13	5	0			25	.273
Art McCabe	OF116	117	439	36	105		14	5	0			15	.239
Alva Williams	C84,1B15	117	355	27	83		11	6	0			10	.234
Walter Woods	C40,SS17,3B13	73	231	24	44		3	2	0			6	.190
Chester Carmichael	P29	40	96	7	21		2	0	0			0	.219
John Vowinkel	P40	40	87	6	15		2	0	1			2	.172
George Schirm	OF29	38	108	13	32		3	1	0			6	.296
Luther Taylor	P34	34	77	3	11		2	1	0			0	.143
Dave Brain	3B31	31	122	16	28		5	0	0			4	.230
Mike Konnick		30	82	5	20		3	2	0			1	.244
Wheeler Johnston	OF13,1B11	29	88	11	18		1	2	0			6	.205
Bill Malarkey	P20	20	54	7	14		2	0	0			0	.259
George Speer	P10	10	21	1	3		0	0	0			1	.143

PITCHERS	W	L	PCT	G	GS	CG	SH	IP	H	BB	SO	ERA
Luther Taylor	16	16	.500	34				257	201	63	106	
Chester Carmichael	13	12	.520	29				217	193	16	92	
John Vowinkel	12	17	.414	40				240	247	50	55	
Bill Malarkey	10	6	.625	20				161	159	29	69	
George Speer	3	3	.500	10				61	68	21	25	

JERSEY CITY Skeeters

JERSEY CITY Skeeters	7th	66-88	.429	-26.5	Jack Ryan

BATTERS	POS-GAMES	GP	AB	R	H	BI	2B	3B	HR	BB	SO	SB	BA
Bill Abstein	1B118	118	425	57	111		16	7	4			27	.261
Jack Hannifan	2B114,SS36	153	548	39	113		15	4	2			21	.206
Johnson	SS120,1B11	140	462	72	103		14	12	9			41	.223
Jim Esmond	3B157	157	573	66	139		16	8	4			34	.242
Charles Hanford	OF128	133	477	57	116		19	9	4			31	.243
Wally Clement	OF110	122	456	65	120		13	13	4			20	.263

JERSEY CITY (cont.)
Skeeters

BATTERS	POS-GAMES	GP	AB	R	H	BI	2B	3B	HR	BB	SO	SB	BA
Otto Deininger	OF	(see multi-team players)											
Chester Crist	C66	66	195	7	34		3	2	0			4	.174
John Butler	C59	65	180	7	36		5	0	0			3	.200
George Wheeler	OF41	48	176	15	46		4	5	0			6	.261
Vernon Manser	P36	38	92	7	13		1	0	0			1	.141
Jack Ferry	P26	35	88	9	20		0	1	0			2	.227
Harry Camnitz	P31	31	73	4	12		1	0	0			0	.164
Carl Sitton	P31	31	67	3	8		1	0	0			1	.119
Lawrence Spahr	C25	29	73	5	14		0	2	0			1	.192
J. Londrigan	OF19	27	79	6	16		1	2	0			2	.203
Bartley	P23	23	39	1	1		0	0	0			0	.036
Crooks	1B20	21	77	8	16		0	0	0			5	.208
John Frill	P19	19	52	2	3		0	0	0			0	.058
Jack Ryan	C13	18	46	2	7		1	0	0			0	.152
Walsh		17	43	5	9		1	1	1			0	.209
Bill Milligan		11	11	0	1		0	0	0			0	.091
O'Hara		10	34	1	6		1	0	0			1	.176

PITCHERS	W	L	PCT	G	GS	CG	SH	IP	H	BB	SO	ERA
Vernon Manser	12	19	.387	36				266	246	71	133	
Carl Sitton	9	14	.391	31				198	186	57	48	
John Frill	8	5	.615	19				153	130	37	73	
Jack Ferry	8	11	.421	26				203	183	45	99	
Harry Camnitz	6	16	.273	31				205	187	76	77	
Bill Bartley	5	10	.333	23				119	111	33	32	

PROVIDENCE
8th 61-92 .399 -31 James Collins
Grays

BATTERS	POS-GAMES	GP	AB	R	H	BI	2B	3B	HR	BB	SO	SB	BA
Ed Courtney	1B75	78	271	28	59		9	3	1			10	.218
Jake Atz	2B101,SS25	129	429	53	109		10	1	0			18	.254
Roy Rock	SS125	125	421	28	102		10	6	0			7	.242
James Collins	3B117	121	438	35	98		11	4	1			12	.224
Curt Elston	OF145	148	548	52	137		23	11	3			11	.250
Harry Hoffman	OF130	137	514	63	136		18	6	2			19	.265
John Phelan	OF99	101	374	46	68		11	0	0			22	.182
Matt Fitzgerald	C84	95	314	19	74		7	4	0			0	.236
Harry Arndt	1B42,3B36,2B26	120	407	40	103		21	6	2			11	.253
Bob Peterson	C73,2B17	102	316	19	54		6	2	0			8	.171
Lyndon Welday	OF67	85	290	30	69		5	1	0			3	.238
Sullivan	1B30,2B17	47	158	6	23		4	2	0			0	.146
James Lavender	P45	45	108	2	7		2	0	0			0	.065
William Sline	P39	39	89	3	13		2	0	0			0	.146
Elmer Steele	P35	36	106	4	27		7	2	0			0	.255
Baberich	P21	24	60	4	7		0	0	0			0	.117
Martini		23	71	7	19		2	1	1			1	.268
Wilson	P11	13	20	0	1		0	0	0			0	.050

PITCHERS	W	L	PCT	G	GS	CG	SH	IP	H	BB	SO	ERA
Elmer Steele	19	11	.633	35				294	237	43	101	
James Lavender	15	22	.405	45				314	248	96	147	
William Sline	11	19	.367	39				278	266	65	141	
Barberich	5	12	.294	21				148	133	47	58	
Wilson	1	5	.167	11				43	46	18	17	

MULTI-TEAM PLAYERS

BATTERS	POS-GAMES	TEAMS	GP	AB	R	H	BI	2B	3B	HR	BB	SO	SB	BA
Dan Moeller	OF157	JC-ROC	158	625	96	168		15	14	6			47	.269
Otto Deininger	OF138	ROC-JC	154	583	88	172		24	13	7			42	.295
George Smith	2B141	MON-BUF	145	499	47	132		16	2	0			18	.265
Ed Holly	SS124	ROC-MON	129	438	37	98		18	4	2			14	.223
Mickey Corcoran	3B95,OF23	MON-BUF	128	489	65	133		19	6	5			38	.272
Harry Pattee	2B65,SS45	ROC-BUF	124	417	56	92		9	3	0			24	.221

MULTI-TEAM PLAYERS (cont.)

BATTERS	POS-GAMES	TEAMS	GP	AB	R	H	BI	2B	3B	HR	BB	SO	SB	BA
Lew McAllister	C96	BU-TO-MO-NE	110	344	34	88		10	5	1			8	.256
Walter East	2B61	MON-BUF	73	238	18	55		6	3	0			6	.231
Watty Lee	P38	TOR-NEW	72	154	12	41		8	0	4			0	.266
Jean Dubuc	P30	BUF-MON	58	116	17	39		6	4	2			4	.336
Deal	1B56	TO-MO-BU	56	199	16	37		3	0	3			13	.186
Art Mueller	P35	NEW-TOR	45	106	9	22		2	1	0			2	.208
Fred Burchell	P37	BUF-MON	41	81	3	8		1	0	0			0	.098
George Merritt	P25	JC-BUF	40	107	7	19		0	0	0			1	.178
Charles Kisinger	P34	JC-BUF	34	78	8	9		1	0	0			1	.115
Jack Cronin	P18	PRO-BUF	19	44	3	9		2	1	0			0	.205
Crowley	P16	PRO-MON	16	35	0	7		0	0	0			0	.200

PITCHERS	TEAMS	W	L	PCT	G	GS	CG	SH	IP	H	BB	SO	ERA
Watty Lee	TOR-NEW	22	10	.688	38				280	237	68	83	
Charles Kisinger	BUF-JC	16	7	.696	34				237	172	68	110	
George Merritt	JC-BUF	15	9	.625	25				207	178	43	94	
Fred Burchell	BUF-MON	15	13	.536	37				234	186	101	138	
Jean Dubuc	BUF-MON	9	13	.409	30				201	175	74	80	
Crowley	PRO-MON	4	6	.400	16				93	95	21	32	
Jack Cronin	PRO-BUF	4	9	.308	18				117	112	45	38	

TEAM BATTING

TEAMS	GP	AB	R	H	BI	2B	3B	HR	BB	SO	SB	BA
ROCHESTER	**159**	**5194**	609	**1289**		167	76	14			210	.248
NEWARK	156	5055	568	1213		173	48	20			227	.240
BALTIMORE	156	5108	**632**	1286		132	64	34			171	**.252**
TORONTO	155	4975	569	1265		153	59	28			191	.254
MONTREAL	154	4920	467	1114		163	36	17			173	.226
BUFFALO	153	4892	506	1203		137	49	7			196	.246
JERSEY CITY	157	5105	543	1166		136	80	**36**			**254**	.228
PROVIDENCE	156	5052	448	1134		150	50	10			122	.224
	545	40301	4342	9670		1211	462	166			1544	.240

1911
HUSTLERS' TRIO

In the first decade of the twentieth century, the Rochester franchise reached a nadir. Since their first-place finish in 1901, the Bronchos had finished last three times, including one (1905) which ranked as the league's second worst record of the twentieth century. After another visit to the cellar in 1908, Rochester's fortunes were about to turn.

John Ganzel had been a major league player for ten years. Normally used as a first baseman, in 1908 he also served as manager for the major league Cincinnati Reds. Late in the season, he was approached by Rochester manager C.T. Chapin and offered a similar position with the Eastern League club. Intrigued, Ganzel accepted and was soon busy assembling his team. To put a new stamp on the club, they were rechristened the Rochester Hustlers.

In 1909, Rochester rose from the doldrums to win their first pennant in eight years, with manager Ganzel himself playing first. In 1910, the team duplicated the feat with an even better record. There was ample reason to expect the same in 1911.

The Rochester Hustlers ended the inaugural week of the 1911 season in first place. After a dip to third during the latter days of April, the Hustlers regained the lead the next week. From there, the team never fell from the top perch as they rode to their third straight flag, finishing with the best record of their three-year run.

The Baltimore Orioles and Toronto Maple Leafs, in second and third, finished ahead of the .600 mark. No other Eastern League team was close as Buffalo, Montreal, Jersey City, Newark, and Providence all failed to cross the .500 barrier. Providence's Hank Perry won the batting title (.343), while Tim Jordan poled the most home runs (20). Pitcher Rube Vickers, from Baltimore, won the most games (32). His teammate, Jim Dygert, struck out the most batters (218).

John Ganzel's Rochester Hustlers twice finished second before he resigned midway through the 1915 season. Ganzel's success stemmed from his expertise in assembling talent. Former major leaguers such as George McConnell and Emil Batch were infused into the club along with newcomers like George Simmons to make a formidable unit. Also helping significantly were the deep pockets of owner C.T. Chapin, who spent freely to acquire the best players.

From 1909 to 1911, the Rochester Hustlers accomplished what no other league team had to this point. Twenty years before, the Detroit Wolverines had won two pennants in a row. This record was equaled, then shattered by the Hustlers' trio of flags.

ROCHESTER Hustlers

| | | 1st | 98-54 | | .645 | | | | | John Ganzel | | |

BATTERS	POS-GAMES	GP	AB	R	H	BI	2B	3B	HR	BB	SO	SB	BA
Chester Spencer	1B149	149	514	71	137		9	6	2	34	45	21	.267
Charles Alperman	2B109	111	388	46	95		10	11	5	12	24	12	.245
Ed Foster	SS140	140	532	95	153		21	10	2	60	31	37	.288
Joe Ward	3B121	125	460	53	142		31	10	0	21	34	15	.309
Herb Moran	OF152	152	585	109	169		25	9	0	77	50	43	.289
Fred Osborn	OF152	152	568	76	165		16	7	2	56	29	18	.290
Dan Moeller	OF99	101	353	65	102		14	12	3	27	68	30	.298
Fred Mitchell	C86	88	264	32	77		12	0	0	22	28	5	.292
George Simmons	2B57,3B33	110	352	57	110		17	10	2	28	34	18	.312
Emil Batch	OF81	96	265	43	74		21	2	0	36	34	9	.279
Fred Jacklitsch	C78	80	226	21	54		12	5	2	43	38	5	.239
Tom McMillan	SS24	50	93	22	26		4	0	0	7	10	11	.279
George McConnell	P43	47	132	18	38		8	3	1	3	8	0	.285
Jim Holmes	P46	46	94	7	15		4	0	0	4	27	2	.159
Irvin Wilhelm	P39	40	70	7	19		1	1	0	3	9	0	.271
Vernon Manser	P30	33	69	9	6		0	0	0	4	27	2	.087
Frank Dessau	P31	31	53	8	10		2	0	0	8	13	1	.189
Tom Hughes	P28	28	80	6	13		2	0	0	2	23	3	.162

PITCHERS		W	L	PCT	G	GS	CG	SH	IP	H	BB	SO	ERA
George McConnell		30	8	.789	43				317	236	75	193	
Jim Holmes		16	10	.615	46				262	242	103	147	
Tom Hughes		15	12	.556	28				217	201	62	132	
Irvin Wilhelm		14	7	.667	39				208	201	35	62	
Vernon Manser		14	9	.609	30				201	207	68	70	
Frank Dessau		9	7	.563	31				148	160	48	65	

BALTIMORE Orioles

| | | 2nd | 95-58 | | .621 | | -3.5 | | | Jack Dunn | | |

BATTERS	POS-GAMES	GP	AB	R	H	BI	2B	3B	HR	BB	SO	SB	BA
Charles Schmidt	1B142	142	546	74	159		26	11	6	35	76	12	.291
Morrie Rath	2B112,3B27	142	536	108	182		10	3	2	70	22	25	.340
Fritz Maisel	SS95	102	344	50	80		8	5	0	30	38	22	.233
Mickey Corcoran	3B115,OF23	144	588	92	175		20	19	5	35	59	34	.298
James Walsh	OF149	151	529	88	140		15	15	5	75	81	29	.265
James Seymour	OF103	112	436	63	129		24	10	2	39	28	14	.296
William Heitmuller	OF86	88	339	37	87		12	6	1	23	16	23	.257
Ben Egan	C129	135	535	53	119		24	7	1	16	84	10	.274
Fred Parent	SS55,2B39,OF22	121	446	68	118		19	8	0	52	26	21	.265
Rube Vickers	P57	57	143	12	33		4	1	0	6	26	0	.231
Jim Dygert	P51	51	128	7	26		2	0	1	2	21	0	.204
Merle Adkins	P47	47	96	7	18		4	0	0	2	14	2	.187
Bill Byers	C33	43	85	6	14		1	0	0	6	9	0	.165
Sam Frock	P32	32	72	9	16		4	3	1	2	32	0	.222
Jack Dunn		20	49	5	15		0	1	1	5	8	0	.306
Tom Atkins	P14	14	24	3	8		1	0	0	2	8	0	.333
Chester Emerson	OF13	13	44	7	13		1	1	0	3	3	0	.295
Fred Payne	C10	13	41	7	13		3	2	0	6	1	2	.312
Gantt	P11	11	15	0	1		0	0	0	3	3	0	.067

PITCHERS		W	L	PCT	G	GS	CG	SH	IP	H	BB	SO	ERA
Rube Vickers		32	14	.696	57				369	313	105	169	
Jim Dygert		25	15	.625	51				319	258	139	218	
Merle Adkins		16	14	.533	47				288	263	64	127	
Sam Frock		14	8	.636	32				194	199	30	184	
Tom Atkins		5	2	.714	14				76	70	35	48	
Gantt		1	2	.333	11				50	55	20	24	

TORONTO Maple Leafs

| | | 3rd | 94-59 | | .614 | | -4.5 | | | Joe Kelley | | |

BATTERS	POS-GAMES	GP	AB	R	H	BI	2B	3B	HR	BB	SO	SB	BA
Tim Jordan	1B152	152	552	107	182		33	5	20	90	52	30	.330
Ed Fitzpatrick	2B108	110	345	47	86		11	7	4	35	35	16	.249
Robert Vaughn	SS117	119	387	49	105		11	3	0	43	37	24	.271

TORONTO (cont.)
Maple Leafs

BATTERS	POS-GAMES	GP	AB	R	H	BI	2B	3B	HR	BB	SO	SB	BA
William Bradley	3B139	139	531	79	156		30	13	8	28	35	25	.294
Bill O'Hara	OF147	147	568	103	145		15	7	1	61	86	38	.255
Al Shaw	OF145	145	546	107	150		25	4	16	76	**100**	40	.275
Joseph Delahanty	OF125	125	472	69	125		19	10	5	40	47	11	.265
Ed Phelps	C93	96	310	43	84		8	8	2	45	31	13	.271
Brad Kocher	C60	64	205	23	50		8	2	1	14	28	6	.244
James Mullen	2B60	62	220	22	57		9	6	0	15	24	10	.259
T. Smith	SS36	55	164	21	39		5	4	1	31	15	11	.237
John Lush	P36	51	118	14	30		8	3	1	19	10	3	.254
Art Mueller	P38	47	111	12	26		0	1	0	3	6	1	.234
Dick Rudolph	P40	43	106	17	27		6	1	0	10	16	5	.255
Dave Rowan	OF24	40	96	21	29		5	1	0	12	4	3	.302
Willie Keeler	OF38	39	155	26	43		7	0	0	9	2	4	.278
Jeff Tesreau	P35	35	75	5	15		1	0	0	5	17	2	.200
Lester Backman	P24	27	57	6	15		2	0	0	2	14	1	.263
Jim McGinley	P23	23	46	4	7		1	1	0	6	14	0	.152
Jack Slattery		15	35	5	12		0	1	0	1	2	0	.343
Ted Cather	P14	14	21	3	4		0	0	0	1	3	0	.190
Ed Killian	P9	10	29	5	5		0	0	0	4	4	1	.172

PITCHERS	W	L	PCT	G	GS	CG	SH	IP	H	BB	SO	ERA
Dick Rudolph	18	11	.621	40				276	266	64	136	
John Lush	18	12	.600	36				264	244	71	103	
Art Mueller	17	8	.680	38				223	201	71	104	
Jeff Tesreau	14	9	.609	35				213	181	96	152	
Lester Backman	10	5	.667	24				141	120	41	39	
Jim McGinley	10	7	.588	23				129	132	29	37	
Ed Killian	4	3	.571	9				67	70	26	35	
Ted Cather	3	4	.429	14				69	66	14	27	

BUFFALO   4th   74-75   .497   -22.5   George Stallings
Bisons

BATTERS	POS-GAMES	GP	AB	R	H	BI	2B	3B	HR	BB	SO	SB	BA
Bud Sharpe	1B100	102	377	47	106		15	5	0	21	23	17	.281
Frank Truesdale	2B144	144	520	63	130		12	5	0	52	57	40	.250
Charles Starr	SS112	115	402	56	100		10	2	0	62	26	28	.249
Eddie McDonald	3B91	91	309	83	63		12	5	1	41	56	8	.204
Art McCabe	OF143	145	555	67	160		25	11	2	28	43	25	.288
George Schirm	OF118	132	473	86	128		12	4	2	66	63	40	.271
John White	OF82	105	312	38	85		17	5	0	36	26	9	.272
William Killefer	C99	103	331	29	83		8	1	0	9	30	10	.251
Jim Murray	OF75	81	302	47	99		14	12	5	17	41	17	.328
Hugh Miller	1B52	70	239	22	58		10	0	1	14	29	14	.243
Erve Wratten	3B44	44	136	20	34		4	0	0	13	22	4	.250
Ralph Stroud	P37	37	74	5	11		4	1	0	4	27	0	.149
Bill Malarkey	P35	35	53	3	6		2	0	0	5	25	1	.113
George Merritt	P34	34	79	7	17		2	0	2	4	12	1	.215
Frank Corridon	P32	32	68	7	19		1	0	1	2	13	5	.279
Ad Brennan	P25	25	55	12	15		0	1	0	3	8	1	.272
Wallace Shultz	P24	24	58	2	16		0	0	0	0	4	1	.276
Henry Groh	SS22	22	78	16	26		3	3	1	7	8	0	.333
Henry Beckendorf	C12	12	32	1	6		0	0	0	1	12	1	.188
Jim Riley	2B10	10	34	4	6		0	0	0	3	6	0	.176

PITCHERS	W	L	PCT	G	GS	CG	SH	IP	H	BB	SO	ERA
Ad Brennan	14	8	.636	25				170	140	40	105	
Ralph Stroud	12	9	.571	37				232	214	73	135	
Frank Corridon	11	8	.579	32				168	173	49	62	
Wallace Shultz	11	8	.579	24				149	155	54	73	
George Merritt	8	11	.421	34				183	179	42	98	
Bill Malarkey	7	12	.368	35				175	200	44	68	

MONTREAL Royals   5th   72-80   .474   -26   Ed McCafferty

BATTERS	POS-GAMES	GP	AB	R	H	BI	2B	3B	HR	BB	SO	SB	BA
Chick Gandil	1B138	138	520	78	158		13	14	11	38	43	30	.304
Charles French	2B112	112	469	70	115		19	8	2	48	38	22	.245
Ed Holly	SS108	108	389	41	106		10	3	1	20	47	21	.321
Joe Yeager	3B134	134	539	85	167		29	9	1	25	37	20	.310
Ward Miller	OF156	**156**	576	97	**191**		23	10	4	75	46	**63**	.330
Ray Demmitt	OF153	153	543	73	146		29	16	6	68	59	28	.269
Charles Hanford	OF139	156	497	105	141		26	18	11	50	62	29	.284
Harry Curtis	C84	84	268	24	56		4	3	0	15	27	7	.209
William Nattress	2B46,SS18,3B14	88	265	54	62		7	8	1	41	38	7	.234
Frank Roth	C72	72	217	18	55		12	2	1	10	23	5	.254
Jack Hardy	C26,1B14	54	128	19	41		2	2	2	14	8	3	.320
Jean Dubuc	P38	54	119	12	25		4	1	2	10	19	3	.210
B. Purtell	SS44	50	167	16	39		7	1	0	17	24	3	.233
William Burke	P43	47	100	5	20		0	1	0	8	26	1	.200
J. Bailey	OF25	41	110	6	23		3	2	1	6	27	4	.209
Frank Barberich	P33	33	88	5	15		1	0	0	0	16	0	.170
Dick Carroll	P33	33	81	2	14		0	0	0	1	24	0	.173
Fred Burchell	P26	26	45	1	2		0	0	0	2	12	0	.044
William Parson	P15	15	35	2	3		0	0	0	0	4	0	.086
Carl Sitton	P10	11	15	3	4		1	1	0	3	2	0	.267
George LaClaire	P10	10	7	0	1		0	0	0	0	1	0	.143

PITCHERS	W	L	PCT	G	GS	CG	SH	IP	H	BB	SO	ERA
Jean Dubuc	21	11	.656	38				264	230	114	126	
William Burke	16	17	.485	43				288	251	**153**	135	
Frank Barberich	11	14	.440	33				230	242	83	81	
Dick Carroll	10	10	.500	33				212	220	55	45	
Fred Burchell	4	10	.286	26				130	143	58	41	
William Parson	3	8	.273	15				92	109	39	34	
George LaClaire	1	2	.333	10				29	36	14	10	
Carl Sitton	0	2	.000	10				43	54	29	17	

JERSEY CITY Skeeters   6th   63-88   .417   -34.5   Jack Ryan

BATTERS	POS-GAMES	GP	AB	R	H	BI	2B	3B	HR	BB	SO	SB	BA
Bill Abstein	1B151	153	588	62	145		20	13	4	31	46	25	.247
Richard Breen	2B156	**156**	591	65	138		7	4	0	48	21	39	.233
Roxy Roach	SS109	109	387	41	98		7	5	3	21	42	12	.263
Alvin Dolan	3B144	146	530	79	138		14	13	7	53	87	52	.260
Otto Deininger	OF155	155	**623**	82	171		18	13	5	51	91	21	.274
George Wheeler	OF140	142	509	61	143		22	14	2	36	76	12	.281
Jake Gettman	OF	(see multi-team players)											
Charles Tonneman	C69	87	221	17	42		9	3	1	27	29	4	.190
Robert Wells	C40,OF24	81	207	25	53		4	2	0	28	19	8	.256
John Butler	C63	67	191	12	31		1	3	2	12	36	2	.162
John Frill	P40	40	89	3	12		0	0	0	2	15	0	.135
Elijah Jones	P39	39	92	4	19		0	0	0	6	9	0	.207
Walter Justus	P37	37	76	3	12		1	2	0	2	10	0	.158
Charles Kisinger	P35	36	57	2	11		2	0	0	3	5	2	.193
Jack Thoney	OF34	34	134	11	35		4	4	0	8	12	1	.261
Del Mason	P29	29	64	3	13		0	1	0	3	8	0	.203
Jack Doscher	P20	20	46	3	10		0	0	0	1	14	0	.217
Jack Ryan		16	28	0	5		2	0	0	0	2	0	.179
Kessler	P10	12	23	3	7		1	0	1	1	5	0	.304
Myers		12	19	4	4		0	0	0	1	4	1	.211
Bill Bartley	P11	11	17	2	4		0	1	1	3	6	0	.235

PITCHERS	W	L	PCT	G	GS	CG	SH	IP	H	BB	SO	ERA
Elijah Jones	16	13	.552	39				270	246	79	97	
John Frill	16	17	.485	40				276	267	65	148	
Del Mason	8	9	.471	29				189	183	42	89	
Charles Kisinger	7	13	.350	35				182	179	53	93	
Walter Justus	7	19	.269	37				240	232	90	50	
Jack Doscher	4	10	.286	20				135	129	33	47	
Bill Bartley	3	3	.500	11				56	60	29	21	
Kessler	2	4	.333	10				58	68	32	18	

NEWARK Indians
7th   57-95   .375   -41   Joe McGinnity

BATTERS	POS-GAMES	GP	AB	R	H	BI	2B	3B	HR	BB	SO	SB	BA
Joe Agler	1B140	140	471	68	122		10	12	0	82	78	25	.259
George Smith	2B98	99	353	34	74		11	0	0	19	28	8	.210
William Louden	SS90,3B54	139	452	62	137		22	7	3	52	59	31	.303
Reams	3B46	49	111	11	19		1	1	0	12	39	7	.171
John Kelly	OF152	152	583	73	153		20	8	10	41	64	25	.261
Jack Dalton	OF118	126	458	49	147		17	5	0	32	59	25	.322
Harry Bailey	OF81	88	307	40	78		7	12	0	29	57	14	.254
Hick Cady	C114,1B10	136	439	42	114		16	7	1	21	52	12	.260
Benny Meyer	2B35,OF16,SS10	120	301	31	75		9	7	0	23	45	17	.249
Lew McCarty	C60	75	176	12	38		8	1	0	9	16	3	.216
Robert Fisher	SS60,2B11	71	264	20	82		13	2	0	5	16	10	.312
Watty Lee	P42	70	124	7	21		4	1	0	25	26	0	.169
Thomas Mee	3B24,2B22	57	164	23	34		3	2	0	21	28	7	.207
Joe McGinnity	P43	43	89	5	14		0	0	0	2	5	0	.157
Collins	OF41	42	148	20	32		5	4	0	9	18	9	.216
Robert Holmes	P37	37	69	1	5		0	0	0	3	16	0	.078
Browne	OF28	34	104	10	23		1	3	0	7	7	3	.221
James Frick	3B26	28	75	8	15		0	0	0	6	6	3	.200
Shontz	P23	25	25	1	6		0	0	0	1	7	1	.240
C. Smith	P24	24	52	5	8		1	1	0	4	18	0	.153
Boice	P23	23	30	2	3		0	0	0	0	9	0	.100
Swayne	OF14	20	51	6	11		0	0	0	2	2	3	.216
Ed Zimmerman	3B11	11	41	7	15		0	0	0	1	3	1	.366
Charles Parkins	P11	11	10	1	3		0	0	0	0	0	0	.300
Tom Cantwell	P	10	23	1	6		0	0	0	1	5	1	.261

PITCHERS	W	L	PCT	G	GS	CG	SH	IP	H	BB	SO	ERA
Watty Lee	15	19	.441	42				279	318	64	80	
Robert Holmes	12	15	.444	37				214	220	67	78	
Joe McGinnity	12	19	.387	43				278	269	53	77	
C. Smith	10	10	.500	24				160	145	21	94	
Shontz	2	3	.400	23				80	107	25	39	
Boice	2	12	.167	23				104	129	39	38	
Charles Parkins	1	5	.167	11				41	41	10	10	

PROVIDENCE Grays
8th   54-98   .355   -44   James Collins - Jake Atz

BATTERS	POS-GAMES	GP	AB	R	H	BI	2B	3B	HR	BB	SO	SB	BA
Robert Tarleton	1B143	143	532	55	119		28	10	1	14	85	23	.224
Jake Atz	2B118,SS13	130	485	70	138		15	3	2	50	23	12	.284
Roy Rock	SS140	140	496	45	126		12	3	0	33	23	5	.254
James Gillespie	3B110	110	398	37	112		10	8	2	17	55	10	.281
Hank Perry	OF140	140	539	82	185		33	21	3	56	59	21	.343
George Anderson	OF126	126	501	77	119		16	9	0	51	69	20	.238
Curt Elston	OF123	123	438	66	135		27	14	6	44	38	14	.306
Bob Peterson	C86	86	260	19	62		8	2	0	19	32	5	.238
John Phelan	OF71	94	264	40	60		4	4	0	25	37	16	.273
Frank McDermott	3B31,2B13	78	234	24	55		10	5	5	30	17	9	.235
Henri Rondeau	C56	56	164	21	44		1	4	0	11	28	6	.268
James Lavender	P49	49	121	7	23		5	0	0	5	45	1	.190
William Sline	P35	35	86	3	13		3	0	0	2	24	0	.151
Hugh Bedient	P35	35	62	2	9		1	0	0	6	28	0	.145
Sheehan	C34	34	101	8	24		5	1	0	7	23	2	.237
Matt Fitzgerald	C27	27	84	2	19		6	1	0	3	10	0	.226
George Nill	2B22	22	80	7	17		1	1	0	7	14	3	.213
Ralph Pond	OF21	21	53	2	10		0	1	0	7	14	0	.189
Joe Doyle	P14	14	21	0	3		0	0	0	2	3	0	.143
Fred Sherry	P13	13	29	3	5		2	0	0	0	8	0	.172
Maroney	P13	13	28	2	1		0	0	0	0	14	0	.036
McLeod	P11	11	20	3	4		0	0	0	0	1	0	.200

PITCHERS	W	L	PCT	G	GS	CG	SH	IP	H	BB	SO	ERA
James Lavender	19	22	.463	49				340	339	150	163	
William Sline	12	17	.414	35				258	247	73	106	
Hugh Bedient	8	11	.421	35				191	153	48	118	
McLeod	3	2	.600	10				49	66	18	13	
Fred Sherry	3	6	.333	13				75	81	19	25	
Joe Doyle	2	7	.222	14				75	77	23	50	
Maroney	1	8	.111	13				75	76	26	36	

MULTI-TEAM PLAYERS

BATTERS	POS-GAMES	TEAMS	GP	AB	R	H	BI	2B	3B	HR	BB	SO	SB	BA
Jake Gettman	OF119	JC-BAL	123	487	54	124		14	9	1	33	47	14	.255
Noah Henline	OF81	BAL-BUF	94	315	41	72		4	4	2	27	47	19	.229
F. Fullerton	SS39,OF22,3B12	BAL-JC	90	252	32	59		6	1	0	14	22	8	.234
Lew McAllister	C64	MON-BUF	83	212	20	39		3	1	1	17	17	7	.184
Bob Hall	SS27	NEW-BUF	41	121	11	25		2	0	0	19	14	7	.206
George Pierce	P29	BUF-PRO	30	59	5	12		0	0	0	5	14	2	.203
Luther Taylor	P30	BUF-MON	30	40	1	6		0	0	0	3	13	0	.150
John Vowinkel	P11	BUF-NEW	12	12	0	1		0	0	0	0	4	0	.083

PITCHERS	TEAMS	W	L	PCT	G	GS	CG	SH	IP	H	BB	SO	ERA
Luther Taylor	BUF-MON	6	10	.375	30				133	130	36	58	
George Pierce	BUF-PRO	2	13	.133	29				169	168	97	118	
John Vowinkel	BUF-NEW	1	2	.333	11				38	48	9	16	

TEAM BATTING

TEAMS	GP	AB	R	H	BI	2B	3B	HR	BB	SO	SB	BA
ROCHESTER	152	5076	751	1387		204	94	18			211	**.273**
BALTIMORE	151	**5113**	728	1389		176	92	25			193	.272
TORONTO	154	5062	**786**	1372		191	68	**57**			216	.271
BUFFALO	154	5067	625	1267		149	54	17			**238**	.250
MONTREAL	156	5182	721	**1395**		207	103	44			236	.269
JERSEY CITY	**157**	4998	530	1222		130	82	26			195	.244
NEWARK	155	5016	552	1235		153	72	15			211	.246
PROVIDENCE	155	4989	589	1291		186	87	18			146	.259
	617	40563	5282	10558		1396	652	220			1646	.260

1912
NEW LOOK

During its first few years, the International League was known by many names. It was first called the Eastern League in 1884; then the name changed to the New York State League in 1885. After absorbing Canadian franchises in 1886, the league became the International Association, reflecting the circuit's dual-nation status. The word international remained in the league's title until 1890, when the league disbanded mid-season.

When the league was resurrected in 1891 it was renamed the Eastern Association. The word international was not used in the circuit's title because there were no longer any Canadian teams present. The title was changed to Eastern League before the 1892 season and remained the same for 20 years, although the league makeup changed.

In 1895, Canada once again entered the league, placing a team from Toronto. In 1897, Montreal joined, followed by Ottawa in 1898. From then, at least one Canadian team had been present in the circuit. Still, the name Eastern League remained; but change was in the air.

After 1910, the Eastern League's first president, Pat Powers, stepped down. His replacement was a man named Ed Barrow. Barrow was a good fit for the job, having served as an Eastern League manager for several years. One of the first items on his agenda was addressing the inaccurate league title. After a year of lobbying, Barrows convinced the Eastern League that a change was necessary. Before the 1912 season, to honor the Canadian contributions and continuing company in the league, the title Eastern League was changed to the more fitting International League.

In 1912, Rochester nearly won its fourth straight flag. Instead, the Hustlers were overtaken by a hard-charging Toronto club during the race's latter stages. Behind Rochester, Newark and Baltimore placed third and fourth. Buffalo, Montreal, and Jersey City placed next. Providence, for the third straight year, finished dead last. Eddie Murphy from Baltimore finished as the best batter (.361), and Tim Jordan of Toronto won his second consecutive home run title (19). Pitching laurels were attained by Toronto's Dick Rudolph for most wins (25) and Providence's Bill Bailey for most strikeouts (169).

The 1912 change to the title of International League has held for more than 80 years. This steadiness shows that the league outgrew its need to change identities every few years. But more importantly, the name change honored Canada's contribution.

TORONTO
Maple Leafs
1st 91-62 .591 Joe Kelley

BATTERS	POS-GAMES	GP	AB	R	H	BI	2B	3B	HR	BB	SO	SB	BA
Tim Jordan	1B155	**155**	548	109	171		26	10	**19**	**105**	60	29	.312
Amby McConnell	2B127	127	433	83	139		18	10	0	62	49	31	.321
Ed Holly	SS138	138	486	55	126		16	5	0	22	37	29	.259
William Bradley	3B145	145	531	81	155		23	17	3	34	47	19	.292
Bill O'Hara	OF146	146	560	91	170		16	13	2	50	85	38	.304
Al Shaw	OF135	135	463	96	146		27	6	15	64	76	29	.315
Henry Myers	OF134	134	467	89	160		25	11	5	68	52	48	.343
Harry Bemis	C	(see multi-team players)											
Jack Dalton	OF110	110	348	62	102		15	4	0	50	40	23	.293
Ed Fitzpatrick	2B44,3B28,SS18	95	275	49	75		11	9	1	40	32	33	.273
George Graham	C45	45	141	11	33		4	2	0	11	13	3	.234
Dick Rudolph	P42	42	111	11	26		8	1	0	3	13	4	.234
Art Mueller	P31,SS11	42	73	12	11		1	2	0	3	8	6	.151
John Lush	P36	40	91	14	32		6	2	1	10	8	2	.352
Bert Maxwell	P35	35	83	11	22		1	1	1	10	17	1	.265
Bill Fischer	C34	34	92	12	19		0	0	0	7	12	0	.207
Louis Drucke	P26	31	52	7	16		5	4	0	8	16	1	.308
Johnston	OF19	19	33	4	7		0	0	0	5	4	2	.212
Lester Backman	P13	16	24	3	7		1	1	0	3	3	2	.292
William Steele	P12	15	24	1	8		0	1	0	1	1	0	.333
Gaspar	P12	12	25	3	6		0	0	0	1	4	0	.240
Maury Kent	P11	11	20	3	4		0	0	1	1	3	0	.200

PITCHERS		W	L	PCT	G	GS	CG	SH	IP	H	BB	SO	ERA
Dick Rudolph		**25**	10	**.714**	42				299	295	63	137	
Bert Maxwell		19	14	.576	35				264	249	53	80	
John Lush		17	9	.654	36				241	223	52	100	
Louis Drucke		8	6	.571	26				138	161	53	64	
Art Mueller		6	7	.462	31				144	154	68	67	
Lester Backman		5	3	.625	13				59	62	14	8	
Maury Kent		5	3	.625	11				62	63	17	18	
Gaspar		4	3	.571	12				79	108	15	32	
William Steele		0	1	.000	12				37	46	16	16	

ROCHESTER
Hustlers
2nd 86-67 .562 -5 John Ganzel

BATTERS	POS-GAMES	GP	AB	R	H	BI	2B	3B	HR	BB	SO	SB	BA
Joe Ward	1B99,3B21	120	414	51	112		22	8	7	24	28	7	.271
Johnson	2B153	153	550	84	145		31	13	8	56	101	21	.264
Tom McMillan	SS113	113	441	88	132		16	6	0	57	31	57	.299
Alvin Dolan	3B120	120	494	99	175		12	15	11	40	39	78	.354
Fred Osborn	OF145	145	513	59	149		26	12	3	52	59	20	.290
Wid Conroy	OF132,3B22	154	574	85	160		27	8	6	74	60	45	.279
John Lelivelt	OF125	125	478	78	168		33	14	3	37	31	23	.351
Walter Blair	C115	115	379	41	104		18	4	1	36	42	7	.274
Emil Batch	OF67	86	205	24	52		10	4	0	22	23	6	.254
Chester Spencer	1B85	85	260	34	60		9	9	1	28	33	11	.231
Irvin Wilhelm	P58	60	73	8	18		2	1	0	5	13	0	.247
Fred Jacklitsch	C53	53	144	25	41		7	3	0	32	27	2	.285
Ed Klepfer	P37	37	73	4	6		1	0	0	2	21	0	.082
Tom Hughes	P35	36	93	7	20		4	1	1	1	20	1	.215
Jack Martin	SS34	34	122	19	34		4	1	0	11	19	4	.279
F. Smith	OF22	22	95	15	35		7	1	0	2	5	2	.368
Jones	P21	21	31	1	4		0	1	0	0	5	0	.129
John Quinn	P13	16	46	6	17		1	0	0	1	6	1	.370
Benny Kauff	OF13	13	12	5	3		0	1	0	3	1	2	.250
John Ganzel	1B11	11	12	0	5		0	0	0	0	2	0	.417
Robert Keefe	P10	10	30	2	4		0	0	0	4	12	0	.133

PITCHERS		W	L	PCT	G	GS	CG	SH	IP	H	BB	SO	ERA
Tom Hughes		17	10	.630	35				239	239	74	122	
Irvin Wilhelm		16	10	.615	58				222	225	39	80	
Ed Klepfer		13	9	.591	37				200	201	73	86	
John Quinn		8	4	.667	13				108	94	14	44	
Robert Keefe		7	3	.700	10				82	63	18	32	
D. Martin		3	1	.750	10				42	50	34	20	
Jones		3	8	.273	21				104	113	39	19	

NEWARK Indians

	3rd	80-72	.527	-10.5		Joe McGinnity

BATTERS	POS-GAMES	GP	AB	R	H	BI	2B	3B	HR	BB	SO	SB	BA
Harry Swacina	1B151	151	609	73	193		35	15	1	13	27	14	.317
Enos Kirkpatrick	2B119	119	463	91	141		20	10	5	55	50	33	.305
Robert Vaughn	SS123	123	423	55	103		7	2	1	35	40	20	.243
Ed Zimmerman	3B153	153	547	76	155		15	10	5	48	45	19	.283
John Collins	OF141	148	588	104	162		27	15	0	27	47	40	.276
William Zimmerman	OF129	129	462	63	145		24	11	2	40	37	37	.314
James Seymour	OF124	124	454	59	139		21	7	0	30	18	18	.306
Harry Smith	C68	68	178	23	58		8	5	0	10	10	6	.326
Curtis Bernard	OF111	111	316	35	86		10	2	0	26	24	11	.272
Lew McCarty	C62	62	143	18	26		5	1	0	15	14	1	.182
Watty Lee	P50	53	101	11	29		5	1	1	11	14	0	.287
Elliott Dent	P42	43	54	0	4		0	0	0	2	13	0	.074
John Enzmann	P36	40	59	7	7		4	1	0	4	30	1	.119
Joe McGinnity	P37	39	94	10	19		2	1	0	2	10	1	.202
Prince Gaskell	P36	36	49	2	8		1	0	0	6	11	1	.163
Ed Gagnier	2B31	31	108	15	26		4	1	0	6	5	2	.241
Bert Tooley	SS29	29	114	18	25		0	1	0	6	13	8	.219
George Bell	P18	19	44	4	15		1	0	0	2	6	0	.341
Bill Schardt	P13	13	14	1	1		0	0	0	1	5	0	.071
Coulson	OF10	10	10	1	0		0	0	0	2	5	0	.000

PITCHERS	W	L	PCT	G	GS	CG	SH	IP	H	BB	SO	ERA
Joe McGinnity	16	10	.615	37				261	293	43	62	
Watty Lee	16	19	.457	50				292	320	55	64	
Elliott Dent	13	12	.520	42				198	205	28	49	
John Enzmann	10	4	.714	36				177	165	50	49	
George Bell	10	4	.714	18				123	127	18	43	
Prince Gaskell	7	13	.350	36				170	182	55	61	
Bill Schardt	3	6	.333	13				60	79	23	28	

BALTIMORE Orioles

	4th	74-75	.497	-15		Jack Dunn

BATTERS	POS-GAMES	GP	AB	R	H	BI	2B	3B	HR	BB	SO	SB	BA
Charles Schmidt	1B151	151	577	88	158		28	14	2	34	63	27	.274
Fred Parent	2B146	149	558	64	171		18	13	2	42	27	23	.306
Fritz Maisel	SS107,3B22	129	446	64	123		12	6	1	58	52	58	.276
Mickey Corcoran	3B132,OF14	146	590	103	188		28	16	3	31	53	38	.319
James Walsh	OF117	117	438	96	155		22	20	2	49	40	35	.354
Eddie Murphy	OF115	122	510	108	184		14	15	7	34	36	34	.361
Jake Gettman	OF94	94	349	57	120		26	19	3	28	40	10	.344
Bill Bergen	C	(see multi-team players)											
Fred Payne	C50,OF12	62	177	31	51		11	6	0	22	16	7	.288
Rube Vickers	P43	43	85	7	20		5	0	0	2	16	1	.236
Robert Shawkey	P41	41	119	15	29		5	1	0	5	18	1	.244
Dave Danforth	P37	37	78	11	18		0	2	0	7	17	0	.231
W. Smith	P33	33	56	6	12		1	0	1	2	12	0	.214
Lord	OF31	31	123	14	34		9	2	0	6	10	3	.277
Claud Derrick	SS23	30	112	21	30		6	3	0	11	10	2	.267
George Maisel	OF16	21	79	9	20		1	0	0	4	7	3	.253
Walker	P18	18	36	2	9		2	0	0	2	8	0	.250
Ben DeMott	P13	17	34	3	11		0	0	0	0	4	0	.324
Unglaub	OF16	16	45	5	11		3	0	0	2	9	1	.244
Braggo Roth	P13	13	36	3	3		1	1	0	3	18	0	.083
George Twombly		12	35	8	11		3	1	0	5	3	2	.315
Claude Cooper	OF11	11	41	3	17		1	0	0	5	2	2	.415
Merle Adkins	P11	11	9	2	4		0	0	0	2	0	0	.444

PITCHERS	W	L	PCT	G	GS	CG	SH	IP	H	BB	SO	ERA
Robert Shawkey	17	18	.486	41				317	290	128	168	
Rube Vickers	13	14	.481	43				215	244	101	95	
Dave Danforth	12	10	.545	37				221	197	59	116	
W. Smith	11	8	.579	33				143	127	87	85	
Braggo Roth	7	2	.778	13				96	76	29	50	
Walker	5	8	.385	18				97	117	37	54	
Ben DeMott	3	3	.500	13				61	57	17	24	
Merle Adkins	0	1	.000	11				27	44	12	9	

BUFFALO Bisons

5th **71-78** **.477** **-18** George Stallings

BATTERS	POS-GAMES	GP	AB	R	H	BI	2B	3B	HR	BB	SO	SB	BA
Fred Beck	1B123,OF14	141	473	66	149		23	7	6	35	43	14	.315
Frank Truesdale	2B153	153	597	120	162		13	9	1	88	78	43	.271
Milt Stock	SS111	111	352	46	91		8	3	0	38	31	27	.259
Art Bues	3B154	154	568	77	160		19	17	9	51	62	19	.282
Art McCabe	OF143	144	559	81	174		19	11	5	28	35	19	.311
Jim Murray	OF138	138	518	88	161		20	24	15	52	86	21	.311
George Schirm	OF104	104	352	62	110		15	2	1	49	41	25	.313
Fred Mitchell	C82	82	259	22	60		6	1	0	29	25	4	.232
Wally Schang	C48	48	138	24	46		5	10	2	12	33	3	.334
Ralph Stroud	P40	40	89	7	9		0	0	0	10	28	0	.101
Fred Beebe	P38	38	98	14	25		2	2	1	6	18	0	.255
Bill Jones	1B35	35	93	16	24		6	2	1	15	14	3	.259
Charles Jamieson	P31	33	82	7	13		1	1	0	8	12	1	.159
Phifer Fullenweider	P24	24	44	2	7		0	1	0	2	8	0	.159
Ernest Gilmore	OF22	22	48	7	12		0	1	1	1	11	1	.250
Lew Brockett	P12	17	38	3	12		3	1	0	2	6	2	.316
Ennett Munsell	P14	14	21	3	4		0	0	0	2	3	0	.190
Bob Ewing	P12	12	26	4	7		1	0	0	1	9	0	.269
Charles Hightower	P12	12	17	2	4		1	0	0	0	5	0	.235

PITCHERS		W	L	PCT	G	GS	CG	SH	IP	H	BB	SO	ERA
Fred Beebe		16	10	.615	38				272	260	90	114	
Ralph Stroud		16	15	.516	40				260	265	104	145	
Charles Jamieson		13	7	.650	31				208	226	57	84	
Phifer Fullenwider		6	9	.400	24				135	149	59	57	
Bob Ewing		5	4	.556	12				83	98	15	35	
Lew Brockett		3	3	.500	12				76	90	27	12	
Ennett Munsell		3	4	.429	14				71	72	36	36	
Charles Hightower		2	4	.333	12				54	65	19	23	

MONTREAL Royals

6th **71-81** **.467** **-19.5** William Lush—Joe Yeager—Kitty Bransfield

BATTERS	POS-GAMES	GP	AB	R	H	BI	2B	3B	HR	BB	SO	SB	BA
Jack Fournier	1B60	60	217	39	67		12	8	3	19	23	13	.309
Bill Cunningham	2B102	102	383	44	109		16	9	6	30	78	14	.285
B. Purtell	SS118,2B22	140	470	58	115		11	5	1	54	47	18	.245
Joe Yeager	3B122	122	447	69	126		26	7	0	31	21	22	.282
Ray Demmitt	OF138	138	503	74	130		25	12	2	54	59	18	.258
Joe Connolly	OF127	127	459	28	145		18	9	6	56	41	27	.316
Charles Hanford	OF116	116	429	75	130		26	9	5	40	46	18	.303
Ed Burns	C52	52	143	19	39		8	3	0	20	8	5	.273
Russell	OF71	71	242	36	60		5	4	1	24	21	8	.247
Frank Smith	P32	40	85	10	22		5	1	1	7	15	0	.259
Frank Betcher	3B15,OF14	37	112	17	20		2	0	0	11	13	1	.179
Al Mattern	P35	35	92	6	18		1	0	0	4	13	0	.196
Luther Taylor	P30	30	47	3	4		1	0	0	3	7	0	.083
Chick Gandil	1B29	29	110	20	34		9	3	2	10	9	9	.309
Murphy	C28	28	91	2	17		3	3	0	1	11	4	.187
Francis Madden	C27	27	81	10	24		2	1	0	7	10	1	.296
Angermeier	C22	26	90	6	20		1	0	0	2	6	2	.222
Kitty Bransfield	1B24	24	90	4	20		3	1	0	8	6	0	.222
Pierce	C18	18	54	6	7		1	0	0	0	11	2	.130
Gunning	1B10	10	36	1	7		0	0	0	3	6	0	.194
Mickey Kelliher	1B16	16	56	4	10		0	0	0	6	10	3	.179
Charles French	2B15	15	43	6	8		0	0	0	7	3	5	.186
Averett	P11	12	11	1	1		0	0	1	0	3	0	.091
William Nattress	2B11	11	21	2	5		0	0	0	5	3	1	.238
Jim Esmond	2B10	10	29	7	3		3	0	0	10	5	0	.103
Gene Dale	P10	10	28	1	4		3	0	0	1	1	0	.143
William Burke	P	10	16	2	1		1	0	0	0	7	0	.063

PITCHERS		W	L	PCT	G	GS	CG	SH	IP	H	BB	SO	ERA
Al Mattern		17	10	.630	35				249	281	71	73	
Frank Smith		12	10	.545	32				202	171	35	105	
Luther Taylor		8	8	.500	30				158	181	45	49	
Gene Dale		4	6	.400	10				82	75	32	25	
Averett		2	3	.400	11				39	27	15	7	

JERSEY CITY Skeeters

	7th	70-85	.452	-22	Larry Schlafly		

BATTERS	POS-GAMES	GP	AB	R	H	BI	2B	3B	HR	BB	SO	SB	BA
John Knight	1B78	78	257	33	54		10	7	1	25	34	9	.210
Richard Breen	2B145	145	569	108	149		30	7	2	59	40	38	.262
Hal Janvrin	SS75,3B38,OF19	132	488	65	142		17	8	3	26	31	23	.291
William Purtell	3B112,SS12,2B11	141	512	64	142		12	11	3	31	14	24	.277
Roland Barrows	OF122	122	433	83	139		30	9	4	61	43	30	.321
Jack Thoney	OF84	84	346	41	88		10	5	4	10	47	9	.255
Otto Deininger	OF	(see multi-team players)											
Robert Wells	C99	102	290	41	91		10	7	1	35	20	10	.314
Henri Rondeau	C74,OF10	90	257	23	80		9	4	0	14	30	2	.311
Larry Schlafly	OF13,1B10,2B10	62	145	14	38		1	5	1	15	17	5	.262
Martin McHale	P43	45	79	8	14		1	3	0	3	25	0	.177
Joe Agler	1B40	40	131	26	33		1	2	0	28	18	9	.252
Jack Doscher	P37	37	73	1	16		1	0	0	1	20	1	.219
Del Mason	P33	33	63	4	9		1	0	0	1	11	1	.143
George Wheeler	OF17	17	57	7	17		2	3	0	8	8	2	.298
Meyer	SS17	17	61	8	14		3	0	0	0	5	1	.230
Alex Main	P11	13	25	4	9		1	1	1	1	3	0	.360
Casey Hageman	P11	11	18	2	4		0	0	0	3	5	0	.222

PITCHERS		W	L	PCT	G	GS	CG	SH	IP	H	BB	SO	ERA
Martin McHale		12	17	.414	43				231	237	92	117	
Jack Doscher		10	11	.476	37				223	238	98	153	
Del Mason		9	12	.429	33				192	202	78	80	
Alex Main		4	4	.500	11				63	76	20	22	
Casey Hagemann		2	5	.286	11				60	71	37	22	

PROVIDENCE Grays

	8th	63-87	.420	-26.5	Fred Lake - Bill Donovan		

BATTERS	POS-GAMES	GP	AB	R	H	BI	2B	3B	HR	BB	SO	SB	BA
Charles Lathers	1B138	138	549	85	172		5	14	1	31	26	21	.313
Jake Atz	2B155	155	533	85	139		25	5	2	74	36	19	.261
David Shean	SS111	111	441	64	127		16	13	1	36	35	14	.288
James Gillespie	3B90,OF27	117	400	24	95		5	2	0	15	51	5	.238
Delos Drake	OF122	122	476	69	139		21	13	4	30	36	15	.292
Curt Elston	OF112	112	363	55	115		21	17	1	51	26	7	.317
Hank Perry	OF66	66	242	42	62		11	5	2	26	24	10	.256
Boss Schmidt	C132	132	462	63	158		25	18	5	26	14	5	.342
Clarence Mitchell	OF55,P21	80	226	24	65		10	4	1	26	33	4	.288
Frank McDermott	3B67,SS12	79	279	47	75		13	5	3	38	31	14	.269
Paddy Baumann	3B44,SS10	54	172	26	54		6	5	1	15	15	6	.314
Ed Lafitte	P42	49	123	10	33		6	1	0	3	16	0	.268
Bill Bailey	P43	48	82	7	16		1	1	0	14	22	1	.195
William Sline	P41	41	83	3	15		2	0	0	6	24	0	.181
Gabby Street	C32	32	106	10	24		4	1	0	4	4	2	.227
Al Platte	OF24	24	94	16	25		1	3	0	10	13	2	.266
Guy Tutwiler	OF23	23	87	9	16		3	0	0	8	16	2	.184
Henry Beckendorf	C19	19	43	5	10		3	1	0	9	6	0	.233
Covington	P15	16	40	5	4		0	0	0	4	13	0	.100
Alex Remneas	P15	15	28	4	7		1	0	0	2	8	0	.250
Sheckard	OF11	11	26	2	4		0	0	0	1	7	1	.153
Frank Bruggy	C10	10	34	6	9		1	2	0	2	4	1	.265
Duggan	OF10	10	31	4	7		0	0	0	7	10	1	.226

PITCHERS		W	L	PCT	G	GS	CG	SH	IP	H	BB	SO	ERA
William Sline		15	15	.500	41				259	269	78	120	
Ed Lafitte		15	17	.469	42				295	288	98	153	
Bill Bailey		14	18	.438	43				254	280	130	169	
Clarence Mitchell		7	6	.538	21				109	117	43	59	
Covington		3	11	.214	15				107	116	60	53	
Alex Remneas		1	5	.167	15				77	96	20	31	

MULTI-TEAM PLAYERS

BATTERS	POS-GAMES	TEAMS	GP	AB	R	H	BI	2B	3B	HR	BB	SO	SB	BA
Otto Deininger	OF140	JC-BUF	140	512	86	149		26	12	3	52	59	20	.291
John Kelly	OF115	NEW-JC	115	395	47	95		15	4	3	26	36	18	.240
Bill Bergen	C99	NEW-BAL	99	234	27	62		11	1	0	26	40	6	.265
Harry Bemis	C98	TOR-JC	98	316	37	103		11	13	1	12	31	7	.326
Bob Higgins	C95	TOR-NEW	95	283	21	74		2	2	0	26	16	2	.261
A. McCrone	OF81	JC-BAL	88	266	45	80		10	5	1	30	39	23	.301
Roxy Roach	SS66,3B18	JC-BAL	84	292	27	75		11	4	2	31	22	15	.257
Charles Hartman	SS66	MON-NEW	81	244	34	56		7	6	0	27	28	12	.230
Monroe Stark	SS78	NEW-BUF	78	264	30	62		14	2	0	20	31	10	.235
Lew McAllister	C68	BUF-BAL	68	182	24	46		9	1	1	16	15	3	.253
Roy Rock	SS52	PRO-BAL	52	170	11	40		5	0	0	17	16	3	.235
Jim Holmes	P46	ROC-BUF	47	91	5	14		3	0	0	4	24	0	.154
Frank Roth	C46	MON-BUF	46	130	13	39		4	0	1	9	10	6	.301
William McTigue	P32,OF10	BUF-MON	42	99	15	31		4	5	0	3	17	0	.313
John Frill	P37	JC-BUF	37	83	3	12		0	0	0	3	16	0	.145
Vernon Manser	P35	ROC-JC	37	56	6	12		0	0	0	0	15	3	.214
Harry Curtis	C35	MO-TO-JC	35	91	7	21		0	1	0	7	12	1	.231
Viebahn	P34	MON-JC	34	84	7	14		1	1	0	1	19	1	.167
Jerry Akers	P30	MON-ROC	30	64	6	7		0	0	0	2	22	2	.109
R. Wilson	C26,1B11	TOR-PRO	26	70	8	9		2	1	0	2	13	9	.129
Dick Carroll	P25	MON-JC	25	53	3	9		1	2	0	1	10	0	.170
Jim Dygert	P17	BAL-PRO	17	24	3	2		1	0	0	3	7	0	.083
Frank Barberich	P12	MO-NE-PR	12	14	0	2		0	0	0	0	2	0	.143
Thomas	P11	PRO-ROC	11	11	1	1		0	0	0	1	4	0	.091

PITCHERS		TEAMS	W	L	PCT	G	GS	CG	SH	IP	H	BB	SO	ERA
John Frill		JC-BUFF	17	8	.680	37				215	226	61	95	
Jim Holmes		ROC-BUF	15	18	.455	46				273	284	85	98	
William McTigue		BUF-MON	11	12	.478	32				172	167	92	145	
Viebahn		MON-JC	10	18	.357	34				241	260	83	75	
Vernon Manser		ROC-JC	9	11	.450	35				154	168	64	43	
Dick Carroll		MON-JC	8	8	.500	25				138	150	50	37	
Jerry Akers		MON-ROC	6	17	.261	30				185	194	45	66	
Jim Dygert		BAL-PRO	3	5	.375	17				66	80	43	34	
Thomas		PRO-ROC	0	2	.000	11				37	49	26	15	
Frank Barberich		MO-NK-PR	0	3	.000	12				36	53	13	12	

TEAM BATTING

TEAMS	GP	AB	R	H	BI	2B	3B	HR	BB	SO	SB	BA
TORONTO	**158**	5262	**856**	**1540**		215	109	**49**	**591**	600	**292**	**.293**
ROCHESTER	154	5174	745	1466		**229**	101	39	491	578	276	.283
NEWARK	153	5176	702	1439		189	88	15	385	453	215	.278
BALTIMORE	155	**5295**	781	1532		221	**123**	21	425	561	266	.289
BUFFALO	154	5148	752	1435		183	100	44	494	**645**	204	.279
MONTREAL	153	4969	679	1282		197	88	31	470	581	188	.258
JERSEY CITY	156	5036	689	1367		179	95	28	415	535	222	.271
PROVIDENCE	155	5197	685	1413		187	109	22	471	513	139	.272
	619	41257	5889	11474		1600	813	249	3742	4466	1802	.278

1913
THE GOLDEN AGE

Before World War I, minor league baseball on and off the field was vastly different from the game of today. Games were played on grass and dirt, usually in less than two hours. No furry mascot interrupted the proceedings. None of a team's good players were plucked from the roster in midseason to satisfy the whims of another club further up the food chain. Probably for these reasons, many consider this era immediately before World War I the golden age of baseball. Baseball had grown up in its first fifty years; its rules were now stable and firm. Yet it was uncorrupted by many of the practices that draw complaints today. What may seem golden to us looking back, however, was not quite as shiny to those actually participating at the time.

Minor league players and teams of yesteryear didn't always have it easy. In the first fifteen years of the twentieth century, at least eight players died from injuries inflicted during a ballgame. Most if not all of these injuries could have been prevented with modern equipment such as batting helmets. During the same period, more than three dozen minor league teams folded or were uprooted during the course of a season, sending their players scrambling for further employment. Finally, for a whole race of people—African Americans—playing baseball in a National Association league (like the International) was an unattainable dream, as they were simply not allowed to participate.

The 1913 International League crowned a new champion. The Newark Indians, after 11 years of futility, claimed their first prize, beating second-place Rochester by four games. Baltimore, Buffalo, and Montreal finished clustered in the middle, followed by Providence, Toronto, and Jersey City grouped at the back. George Simmons from Rochester finished with the highest batting average (.339), while fellow Hustler Del Paddock hit the most home runs (8). Pitchers Watty Lee of Newark and Braggo Roth of Baltimore each won 22 games, while Bill Bailey of Providence struck out a league-best 188.

Fed up with many of the modern aspects of the game, many of today's fans long for a simpler, more innocent time, when baseball was played for the joy of the sport. In truth, baseball was a simpler game before World War I, unencumbered with extraneous trappings. But as noted above, it was not perfect, and certainly not entirely innocent.

NEWARK Indians   1st   95-57   .625   Harry Smith

BATTERS	POS-GAMES	GP	AB	R	H	BI	2B	3B	HR	BB	SO	SB	BA
Harry Swacina	1B141	141	530	64	172		21	7	1	16	21	18	.325
Gus Getz	2B135	137	491	49	135		17	4	1	6	21	35	.275
Ed Gagnier	SS117,2B21	138	515	61	118		15	3	0	27	39	14	.229
Ed Zimmerman	3B149	149	510	55	117		15	10	5	49	55	23	.229
William Zimmerman	OF153	153	572	89	149		16	13	1	55	50	24	.260
Henry Myers	OF126	127	445	49	129		16	7	1	10	27	25	.290
Jack Dalton	OF113	115	413	63	131		14	4	1	71	49	15	.317
Bob Higgins	C94	94	296	38	78		7	5	0	29	21	20	.264
John Collins	OF72,1B12	92	331	61	99		16	17	0	26	30	28	.299
Bert Tooley	SS39	58	178	26	43		5	0	0	17	22	9	.242
Lew McCarty	C40	40	128	13	46		7	1	0	2	1	0	.359
Harry Smith	C35	38	93	8	22		3	0	0	5	10	1	.237
Watty Lee	P36	38	84	9	18		5	1	0	15	12	0	.214
Cy Barger	P31	37	107	12	31		4	1	0	2	19	2	.290
George Bell	P31	31	65	3	9		1	0	0	0	16	0	.138
Raleigh Aitchison	P29	29	83	4	14		1	0	0	8	19	1	.169
Al Schacht	P23	23	34	0	4		1	0	0	2	11	0	.118
John Enzmann	P19	20	42	6	7		1	1	0	2	15	1	.167

PITCHERS	W	L	PCT	G	GS	CG	SH	IP	H	BB	SO	ERA
Watty Lee	22	9	.710	36				262	266	49	62	
Raleigh Aitchison	21	5	.808	29				237	195	69	83	
Cy Barger	17	9	.674	31				248	197	72	80	
John Enzmann	11	4	.733	19				131	99	46	55	
George Bell	10	11	.476	31				203	199	42	70	
Al Schacht	4	6	.400	23				115	99	41	38	
Ed Donnelly	2	3	.400	7				31	32	17	15	
Cliff Curtis	2	3	.400	5				39	29	18	24	
Prince Gaskell	0	2	.000	5				19	19	7	8	

ROCHESTER Hustlers   2nd   92-62   .597   -4   John Ganzel

BATTERS	POS-GAMES	GP	AB	R	H	BI	2B	3B	HR	BB	SO	SB	BA
Charles Schmidt	1B123	123	471	67	151		26	8	0	40	33	22	.321
George Simmons	2B125,1B25	150	545	99	185		28	12	6	76	43	25	.339
Jack Martin	SS131	131	493	81	145		17	7	1	53	44	20	.294
John Priest	3B52,OF42,SS22	128	515	73	148		11	8	4	53	49	30	.287
F. Smith	OF112	117	450	58	122		15	2	1	26	29	4	.271
Guy Zinn	OF102	110	408	68	117		16	8	4	37	40	19	.287
Del Paddock	OF95,3B43	125	489	71	132		17	13	8	47	72	12	.270
Fred Jacklitsch	C84	84	222	26	65		17	7	1	53	44	20	.294
Wid Conroy	OF83,3B11	112	359	57	98		21	4	2	54	29	11	.273
Robert Williams	C73	73	240	17	58		5	2	1	24	26	1	.242
Tom McMillan	3B25,2B21	66	206	28	45		3	2	0	29	16	5	.218
Irvin Wilhelm	P44	46	100	7	17		3	1	1	7	23	0	.170
John Quinn	P38	44	110	11	25		3	2	1	12	27	3	.227
Robert Keefe	P35	35	89	5	11		2	0	1	10	35	0	.124
Tom Hughes	P32	32	84	4	16		1	1	0	0	23	2	.190
D. Martin	P29	29	69	2	8		0	0	0	8	2	0	.116
Chet Hoff	P27	28	47	4	11		2	0	0	0	3	1	.234
Art Devlin		23	78	7	15		2	0	1	15	8	4	.192
Hal Irelan	3B21	22	66	8	17		2	0	1	16	8	1	.258
Charles McDonald	OF17	17	66	12	22		3	4	0	4	9	5	.333

PITCHERS	W	L	PCT	G	GS	CG	SH	IP	H	BB	SO	ERA
Robert Keefe	21	12	.636	35				273	262	78	99	
John Quinn	19	13	.594	38				268	261	62	153	
Irvin Wilhelm	18	7	.720	44				256	247	86	118	
Tom Hughes	15	13	.536	32				239	222	74	146	
D. Martin	13	10	.565	29				169	196	85	83	
Chet Hoff	7	3	.700	27				132	128	43	98	

BALTIMORE
Orioles
3rd 77-73 .513 -17 Jack Dunn

BATTERS	POS-GAMES	GP	AB	R	H	BI	2B	3B	HR	BB	SO	SB	BA
Ben Houser	1B154	154	539	64	168		22	2	0	66	38	24	.312
Fred Parent	2B61,OF10	79	269	35	72		7	2	0	36	14	15	.268
Claud Derrick	SS80	80	279	42	80		8	6	3	28	35	15	.287
Thomas Downey	3B47	47	175	23	43		13	4	0	22	15	16	.246
Claude Cooper	OF102	104	355	40	104		8	2	0	20	32	9	.293
George Twombly	OF93,2B15	116	369	51	94		14	5	3	49	55	26	.255
Mickey Corcoran	OF55,2B22,3B17	114	439	52	110		18	8	1	29	43	17	.251
Ben Egan	C138	138	429	63	120		16	7	4	19	55	7	.280
Fritz Maisel	SS66,3B45	111	421	**119**	119		16	2	4	56	73	**44**	.283
Neal Ball	2B57,SS11	71	245	43	72		6	6	0	25	58	17	.294
Dave Danforth	P53	55	90	9	13		2	2	0	10	34	3	.144
Braggo Roth	P39	44	99	6	29		4	2	0	5	27	2	.293
Ralph Capron	OF43	43	155	23	40		4	1	0	7	12	15	.258
Fred Payne	OF31	42	136	19	27		4	2	0	6	8	3	.198
Ezra Midkiff	3B41	41	157	25	56		3	4	1	8	7	10	.357
Bert Daniels	OF41	41	145	29	35		3	4	1	24	11	13	.241
George Maisel	OF10	35	92	10	23		3	0	0	4	19	6	.250
Bill Bergen	C35	35	82	3	16		3	1	0	6	9	2	.195
Ensign Cottrell	P32	32	62	5	13		0	1	0	3	9	0	.210
Gustave Gleichman	OF31	31	89	14	18		2	3	0	5	22	2	.202
Robert Shawkey	P26	27	72	7	20		5	1	0	3	10	1	.278
John Taff	P19	19	34	7	12		1	2	0	5	9	1	.353
Cad Coles	OF18	18	51	8	12		2	1	0	1	9	1	.235
William McTigue	P14	16	30	0	7		1	0	0	0	5	0	.233
Bill Morrisette	P16	16	29	1	5		0	0	0	0	11	0	.172
Allen Russell	P11	11	32	4	5		1	0	0	3	8	0	.156

PITCHERS		W	L	PCT	G	GS	CG	SH	IP	H	BB	SO	ERA
Braggo Roth		**22**	9	.710	39				258	277	78	155	
Dave Danforth		16	14	.533	**53**				304	288	96	150	
Ensign Cottrell		14	8	.636	32				183	160	86	105	
Robert Shawkey		9	11	.450	26				189	167	58	132	
William McTigue		8	5	.615	14				64	59	34	29	
John Taff		6	10	.375	19				108	132	52	50	
Bill Morrisette		4	3	.571	16				78	83	30	24	
Allen Russell		4	3	.571	11				60	53	32	35	
Johnson		1	2	.333	9				38	50	14	16	

BUFFALO
Bisons
4th 78-75 .510 -17.5 William Clymer

BATTERS	POS-GAMES	GP	AB	R	H	BI	2B	3B	HR	BB	SO	SB	BA
Fred Beck	1B85	93	321	32	77		12	5	2	14	42	5	.240
Frank Truesdale	2B155	155	574	98	150		18	14	1	113	65	30	.261
Roxy Roach	SS155	155	555	70	154		22	10	2	62	43	24	.277
Art Bues	3B	(see multi-team players)											
Jim Murray	OF119	119	436	53	131		21	16	6	22	73	19	.300
George Jackson	OF110	116	423	72	110		15	7	3	40	58	29	.260
Charles Hanford	OF	(see multi-team players)											
Hank Gowdy	C87,1B11	104	300	35	95		16	4	3	25	21	8	.317
Clarence Lehr	OF59	66	224	36	60		6	4	3	12	16	4	.268
Louis LaLonge	C60	60	170	18	42		6	1	0	19	18	5	.247
Charles Jamieson	P32,OF10	51	127	7	30		3	0	0	1	19	1	.236
Phifer Fullenweider	P35	37	99	5	12		0	0	0	0	19	0	.121
Jim Stephens	C34	34	82	5	17		2	0	0	8	5	0	.207
Fred Beebe	P29	33	53	8	17		3	0	0	2	11	1	.321
John Frill	P32	32	78	6	13		1	0	0	1	25	0	.167
Frank O'Rourke	3B13	19	44	5	8		1	0	0	2	7	0	.182
George Matteson	P11	13	11	0	1		0	0	0	2	6	0	.091
James Seymour	OF12	12	47	3	11		1	0	0	3	2	0	.234

PITCHERS		W	L	PCT	G	GS	CG	SH	IP	H	BB	SO	ERA
Phifer Fullenweider		20	12	.625	35				261	212	76	99	
Charles Jamieson		14	10	.583	32				204	212	91	62	
John Frill		12	15	.444	32				214	235	65	85	
Fred Beebe		11	14	.440	29				189	203	70	81	
Bert Morse		2	0	1.000	6				20	12	24	8	
George Matteson		1	1	.500	11				43	47	21	19	

BUFFALO (cont.)
Bisons

PITCHERS	W	L	PCT	G	GS	CG	SH	IP	H	BB	SO	ERA
Leon Cadore	1	2	.333	8				49	26	16	19	
Louis Gervais	0	1	.000	5				24	34	17	6	

MONTREAL Royals

5th 74-77 .490 -20.5 Kitty Bransfield

BATTERS	POS-GAMES	GP	AB	R	H	BI	2B	3B	HR	BB	SO	SB	BA
Hugh Miller	1B49	49	182	8	40		2	0	1	9	16	1	.220
Ed Lennox	2B86,1B37	129	440	66	141		27	9	5	68	41	7	.320
B. Purtell	SS116	120	371	36	78		5	2	0	38	27	9	.210
Joe Yeager	3B98	108	375	30	93		15	2	1	7	12	10	.248
Ray Demmitt	OF139	144	535	68	174		29	6	4	30	44	20	.325
William Allen	OF119	127	461	61	132		12	11	0	57	72	18	.286
Frank Gilhooley	OF117	117	458	74	150		13	3	0	58	14	36	.328
Ed Burns	C93	95	285	37	84		12	5	0	27	23	8	.295
Jim Esmond	2B57,SS53,3B16	125	442	52	105		9	4	1	39	41	7	.238
Francis Madden	C84	84	222	15	53		7	0	0	17	17	1	.239
Rafael Almeida	3B27,OF24	52	180	31	48		6	2	1	36	17	13	.267
Frank Smith	P51	52	121	16	28		4	0	4	6	35	0	.231
Howard McGraner	P40	43	87	17	26		2	1	0	16	3	2	.299
Art Griggs	1B40	40	144	21	42		7	4	0	7	15	5	.292
Gene Dale	P37	38	76	8	17		5	0	0	2	15	0	.224
Al Mattern	P35	35	82	0	10		0	0	0	1	18	0	.122
Bill Cunningham	2B34	34	112	10	19		5	0	0	9	27	1	.170
Del Mason	P31	31	69	3	10		1	0	0	0	13	0	.145
Mullin	P12	12	16	0	4		0	0	0	2	2	0	.250
Carlo	P11	11	18	2	2		0	0	0	2	7	0	.111

PITCHERS	W	L	PCT	G	GS	CG	SH	IP	H	BB	SO	ERA
Smith	21	16	.568	51				354	301	84	177	
Howard McGraner	16	13	.552	34				236	231	88	112	
Gene Dale	13	10	.565	37				192	172	83	87	
Del Mason	12	9	.571	31				224	189	59	79	
Al Mattern	12	14	.462	35				221	243	62	86	
Carlo	3	3	.500	11				59	52	22	13	
Clark	1	2	.333	6				22	15	18	12	
William Burke	0	2	.000	6				23	31	12	7	

PROVIDENCE Grays

6th 69-80 .463 -24.5 Bill Donovan

BATTERS	POS-GAMES	GP	AB	R	H	BI	2B	3B	HR	BB	SO	SB	BA
Ed Onslow	1B101	101	391	51	104		10	6	0	26	34	19	.266
David Shean	2B133	133	462	73	130		16	11	4	59	36	21	.281
Paddy Baumann	SS66	75	295	41	87		10	11	2	16	23	6	.295
Charles Deal	3B99	99	382	60	119		19	12	2	28	20	7	.312
Matty McIntyre	OF151	151	548	81	156		13	15	1	68	47	13	.285
Ray Powell	OF124	124	467	55	125		10	14	2	48	92	23	.268
Al Platte	OF120	120	441	83	135		8	8	3	81	77	32	.306
Brad Kocher	C91	91	295	46	74		4	13	3	16	44	8	.251
Jewel Ens	1B45,3B39,SS20,2B18	124	443	51	95		11	6	4	23	44	12	.214
Jack Onslow	C88	88	251	20	57		5	3	0	36	36	7	.227
Clarence Mitchell	OF35,P17	63	177	31	59		6	0	0	30	21	4	.333
Ed Lafitte	P38	47	117	16	35		3	2	1	8	18	1	.299
Bill Bailey	P43	43	123	7	13		3	0	0	12	24	1	.106
Jacob Reisigl	P40	40	90	9	22		1	4	0	3	12	1	.244
Ollie O'Mara	SS37	37	132	9	31		1	0	0	7	17	3	.235
Bunny Fabrique	SS20	35	139	19	36		6	0	0	4	26	6	.259
Frank McDermott	3B20	24	80	11	25		5	4	0	15	9	3	.313
William Sline	P18	18	46	5	9		0	0	0	3	10	0	.196
Harry Moran	P18	18	25	1	3		2	1	0	3	6	0	.120
Charles Wheatley	P17	17	26	2	3		0	0	0	2	8	0	.115
Bill Donovan	P9	15	24	5	7		0	1	0	4	8	0	.292
Wally Pipp	1B14	14	34	4	16		1	3	0	2	2	2	.444
Carl Zamloch	P11	11	25	1	2		0	0	0	3	3	2	.080

PROVIDENCE (cont.)
Grays

PITCHERS	W	L	PCT	G	GS	CG	SH	IP	H	BB	SO	ERA
Bill Bailey	19	15	.559	43				307	233	157	188	
Ed Lafitte	15	15	.500	38				242	271	103	89	
Jacob Reisigl	14	15	.483	38				257	244	76	103	
William Sline	8	7	.533	18				126	120	55	29	
Clarence Mitchell	4	5	.444	17				100	116	31	31	
Bill Donovan	3	2	.600	9				41	49	20	20	
Carl Zamloch	3	5	.375	11				68	71	31	23	
Charles Wheatley	3	6	.333	13				82	91	35	20	
Harry Moran	2	4	.333	17				78	75	23	37	

TORONTO   7th   70-83   .458   -25.5   Joe Kelley
Maple Leafs

BATTERS	POS-GAMES	GP	AB	R	H	BI	2B	3B	HR	BB	SO	SB	BA
Hugh Bradley	1B			(see multi-team players)									
Amby McConnell	2B127	127	426	54	106		11	3	3	62	31	19	.249
Ed Holly	SS124	124	440	43	101		12	2	0	29	30	29	.230
William Bradley	3B135	135	501	49	139		24	4	4	29	14	19	.277
Bill O'Hara	OF143	143	532	90	142		20	4	4	76	73	16	.267
Joe Schultz	OF74,1B27,SS19	124	451	60	135		22	4	2	26	50	24	.299
Charles Kroy	OF53	53	177	6	53		8	2	0	21	15	6	.299
George Graham	C99	99	319	23	65		11	0	0	28	17	7	.204
Fitzpatrick	2B61,OF10	75	288	34	71		14	4	1	24	17	21	.247
Harry Bemis	C65	69	202	12	51		10	2	0	4	22	1	.252
John Lush	P36	46	107	10	30		3	1	1	7	8	0	.280
George Gaw	P29	31	58	2	14		2	1	0	2	13	0	.241
C. Brown	P32	36	87	6	20		5	0	0	3	11	0	.230
Charles Pick	3B11,SS11	26	86	14	26		2	0	0	14	4	9	.302
Bunn Hearn	P34	34	78	5	8		3	0	0	0	18	0	.103
Bert Maxwell	P29	29	81	3	18		2	0	0	2	13	0	.222
D. Brown	C22	22	60	8	14		2	1	0	8	1	0	.233
Benny Meyer	OF20	21	45	4	9		0	1	0	9	9	0	.200
Leo Callahan	OF16	16	59	14	18		1	3	1	5	5	1	.305
R. Wilson	OF16	16	34	4	12		0	0	0	8	5	2	.353
Brandt	P16	16	26	2	4		1	0	0	0	5	0	.154
Ted Goulait	P12	16	19	3	4		0	0	0	0	5	0	.211
Irving Trout		13	23	3	3		0	0	0	0	2	0	.130
Kent	P10	10	22	2	6		1	0	0	2	3	0	.273

PITCHERS	W	L	PCT	G	GS	CG	SH	IP	H	BB	SO	ERA
John Lush	17	13	.567	36				255	296	67	92	
C. Brown	13	13	.500	32				228	248	94	80	
Bert Maxwell	13	14	.481	29				222	211	72	78	
Bunn Hearn	11	11	.500	34				222	214	41	97	
George Gaw	8	11	.421	29				173	174	62	71	
Maury Kent	4	4	.500	10				62	72	27	17	
Ted Goulait	3	5	.375	12				60	66	37	43	
Brandt	3	7	.300	16				79	66	47	58	
Fred Herbert	0	2	.000	8				33	37	6	9	
Schwab	0	2	.000	5				22	23	11	6	

JERSEY CITY   8th   53-101   .344   -43   Larry Schlafly -
Skeeters   William Purtell

BATTERS	POS-GAMES	GP	AB	R	H	BI	2B	3B	HR	BB	SO	SB	BA
Bill Calhoun	1B107	107	366	53	93		8	6	2	27	49	15	.254
John Knight	2B77	77	300	40	81		9	6	1	19	24	16	.270
Robert Vaughn	SS			(see multi-team players)									
William Purtell	3B95,SS34	134	503	42	154		18	12	3	21	13	10	.306
Al Shaw	OF112	112	492	65	109		19	11	7	47	56	10	.222
Art McCabe	OF101	106	398	41	101		14	3	1	19	31	12	.254
Jim Eschen	OF76	89	321	47	84		10	6	4	32	55	12	.262
Robert Wells	C64,OF14	97	279	25	70		2	7	1	37	16	1	.251
John Kelly	OF63	63	197	24	57		7	4	2	16	13	11	.289
Chick Brandom	P51	54	87	6	10		0	0	0	2	13	0	.115
Larry Schlafly	2B14	46	76	13	18		2	0	2	27	16	3	.237
Malcolm Barry	1B43	43	143	14	35		4	3	0	9	13	4	.245

JERSEY CITY (cont.)
Skeeters

BATTERS	POS-GAMES	GP	AB	R	H	BI	2B	3B	HR	BB	SO	SB	BA
Bernard Koehler	2B39	39	139	14	28		5	1	0	11	14	8	.201
Mike Donlin	OF36	36	136	17	37		2	5	1	5	12	9	.272
C. Thompson	P35	35	85	1	7		1	0	0	0	26	0	.082
Davis	P32	32	71	4	11		0	0	0	8	17	0	.155
Jack Doscher	P31	31	71	9	21		0	0	0	3	13	0	.296
Martin McHale	P28	31	58	8	12		1	2	0	2	16	0	.207
Courtney	SS19	26	87	10	27		1	3	1	9	15	3	.310
Vernon Manser	P19	21	39	2	11		2	0	0	1	8	0	.282
Andy Coakley	P16	21	35	5	11		0	0	0	5	6	0	.314
Joe Crisp	C19	19	60	4	15		1	1	1	2	9	2	.250
Irving	OF11	11	39	3	11		0	0	0	3	9	2	.282
Bradley	SS10	10	33	1	6		1	1	0	1	7	0	.182
Cooney	P10	10	12	0	1		0	0	0	0	3	0	.083

PITCHERS	W	L	PCT	G	GS	CG	SH	IP	H	BB	SO	ERA
Jack Doscher	11	12	.478	31				213	217	86	68	
Martin McHale	10	9	.526	28				165	144	40	70	
Davis	10	16	.385	32				208	215	96	109	
C. Thompson	8	10	.444	35				205	205	43	62	
Chick Brandom	8	16	.333	51				228	232	60	107	
Vernon Manser	5	7	.417	19				95	119	28	23	
Andy Coakley	3	8	.273	16				94	105	32	41	
Viebahn	1	2	.333	8				32	23	14	13	
John Verbout	1	6	.143	9				74	58	23	20	
Cooney	0	6	.000	10				36	53	25	8	

MULTI-TEAM PLAYERS

BATTERS	POS-GAMES	TEAMS	GP	AB	R	H	BI	2B	3B	HR	BB	SO	SB	BA
Robert Vaughn	SS79,3B68	JC-BUF	147	572	82	169		21	8	2	64	43	23	.296
Art Bues	3B140	BUF-JC	140	499	60	128		21	10	1	44	45	11	.257
Hub Northen	OF119	NEW-JC	127	430	59	127		23	7	7	61	51	18	.295
Charles Hanford	OF118	MON-BUF	123	464	67	132		22	7	6	38	53	19	.284
Otto Deininger	OF80,1B30	BUF-MON	123	448	53	116		20	9	5	36	69	10	.259
Hugh Bradley	1B108	JC-TOR	108	376	42	109		13	8	2	31	21	18	.290
Tim Jordan	1B102	TOR-BUF	102	349	40	92		15	3	1	73	33	9	.264
Walter Blair	C100	ROC-JC	100	322	15	66		6	4	0	21	30	2	.205
Hank Perry	OF92	BUF-JC	95	338	58	96		15	7	4	49	43	8	.284
Richard Breen	2B30	JC-ROC	37	106	9	27		1	2	0	5	2	2	.255
Jim Holmes	P37	BUF-NEW	37	83	6	13		2	0	0	5	18	1	.157
Alex Main	P27	JC-BUF	31	66	8	13		3	0	0	4	29	0	.197

PITCHERS	TEAMS	W	L	PCT	G	GS	CG	SH	IP	H	BB	SO	ERA
Alex Main	JC-BUF	15	9	.625	27				187	134	101	92	
Jim Holmes	BUF-NEW	14	8	.636	37				230	208	106	74	

TEAM BATTING

TEAMS	GP	AB	R	H	BI	2B	3B	HR	BB	SO	SB	BA
NEWARK	154	4909	613	1339		164	65	12	354	459	219	.273
ROCHESTER	156	5234	710	1434		192	78	34	595	584	169	.274
BALTIMORE	154	5007	659	1340		166	68	18	451	536	260	.268
BUFFALO	155	5134	563	1336		195	73	30	500	659	184	.260
MONTREAL	156	5155	588	1354		172	56	20	479	534	148	.263
PROVIDENCE	152	5041	684	1353		136	112	22	520	617	179	.268
TORONTO	155	5142	607	1337		196	48	27	489	482	195	.260
JERSEY CITY	157	5302	482	1330		146	96	29	252	489	149	.251
	620	40924	4906	10823		1367	596	162	3640	4360	1503	.264

1914
DISMANTLED

On August 15, 1914, Baltimore resided in the International League's top spot. With many of the league's best players, the Orioles seemed a cinch to win it all. Yet, when the season ended, they found themselves far from first. The reason is simple: The players who led them to the first division were no longer on the team.

The Baltimore Orioles were under the tutelage of Jack Dunn, who joined the team before the 1907 season. In Baltimore, Dunn assembled a strong team chock-full of major league veterans. Going into the 1914 season, Dunn's team looked particularly strong. Unfortunately for him, the International League was at war, and one of the key battlegrounds was the city of Baltimore.

In 1913, an outlaw minor league called the Federal League started in six midwestern cities. Before the 1914 season, the league announced that it would expand to eight teams, with one franchise located in Baltimore. They were also upgrading themselves to major league status. Worst of all, the Baltimore Federal ballpark would be located right across the street from the Orioles' home field.

On opening day, 1914, a paltry crowd of 1,500 watched a local pitcher named George Ruth make his professional debut for the Baltimore Orioles. On the same day, at the same time, the Baltimore Federals drew over 20,000. To the detriment of the Orioles, this trend continued. To keep his tottering team afloat, Dunn was forced to take ultimate action: He had to sell his best players to raise money. By August, he had sold eight, including all three of his starting outfielders and his two top pitchers.

George Ruth, one of the two pitchers sold by Dunn, led Providence to the 1914 International League flag. This hurler, later known as "Babe," joined the Grays in August and won 9 of 11 decisions, helping them to the pennant. Buffalo and Rochester tied for second, while Toronto and Newark finished fourth and fifth. The depleted Oriole squad finished sixth, ahead only of Montreal and Jersey City. David Shean, from Providence, won the batting title (.334), while Wally Pipp of Rochester knocked out the most home runs (15). Grays pitcher Carl Mays won a league-high 24 games, and Rochester's Tom Hughes struck out a league-best 182.

Federal League encroachment in Baltimore left the Orioles in tatters. As bad as that seemed at the time, the Federal League was not done toying with its minor league brethren. Very soon, not just Baltimore, but a significant portion of the International League would be feeling Federal tentacles sliding into their territories.

PROVIDENCE Grays

| | | 1st | 95-59 | .617 | | | | | Bill Donovan | | |

BATTERS	POS-GAMES	GP	AB	R	H	BI	2B	3B	HR	BB	SO	SB	BA
Ed Onslow	1B154	154	569	88	183		16	18	6	43	37	28	.322
David Shean	2B149	149	533	98	178		22	14	7	50	3	25	.334
Bunny Fabrique	SS147	147	485	73	118		6	2	2	67	34	22	.243
Paddy Baumann	3B137,OF6	143	518	81	146		13	11	2	35	40	36	.282
Al Platte	OF156	156	597	128	190		16	23	5	96	87	31	.318
Guy Tutwiler	OF148	148	544	74	161		21	29	5	54	78	8	.296
Ray Powell	OF142	142	496	78	137		8	15	2	45	69	34	.276
Jack Onslow	C91	91	290	32	76		8	3	3	36	47	4	.262
Brad Kocher	C79	79	244	34	61		9	7	3	24	32	3	.250
Carl Mays	P36	51	119	21	33		3	6	1	10	20	1	.277
Wright	3B21,SS15,2B4	40	118	12	23		2	1	0	14	11	4	.195
Wallace Shultz	P37	37	93	12	23		1	1	0	9	8	0	.247
Matty McIntyre	OF33	33	87	15	27		4	1	1	12	5	2	.310
Bill Bailey	P27	27	63	3	7		1	0	0	3	20	0	.111
John Oldham	P24	26	59	8	10		2	0	0	6	19	0	.169
Ralph Comstock	P24	24	62	4	9		1	0	0	2	14	0	.145
Bentley	P20	20	31	4	5		1	0	0	4	4	0	.161
Bill Donovan	P8	10	15	1	4		0	0	0	0	5	1	.267
Jewel Ens	3B5	5	19	4	4		0	2	0	1	1	0	.211

PITCHERS		W	L	PCT	G	GS	CG	SH	IP	H	BB	SO	ERA
Carl Mays		24	8	.750	36				273	249	73	129	
Wallace Shultz		19	12	.613	37				219	208	114	108	
John Oldham		14	7	.667	24				183	154	54	93	
Bill Bailey		11	8	.579	27				179	158	83	115	
Ralph Comstock		9	12	.429	24				172	180	56	79	
Bentley		6	4	.600	20				104	104	45	51	
Bill Donovan		0	1	.000	8				31	41	12	18	

BUFFALO Bisons

| | | 2nd | 89-61 | .593 | -4 | | | | William Clymer | | |

BATTERS	POS-GAMES	GP	AB	R	H	BI	2B	3B	HR	BB	SO	SB	BA
Ben Houser	1B63	63	240	26	59		2	2	0	18	10	5	.246
Joe McCarthy	2B146	146	537	63	143		25	11	4	34	53	27	.266
Roxy Roach	SS150	150	532	74	140		26	5	3	56	49	21	.263
Robert Vaughn	3B147	147	550	74	148		12	5	0	68	45	35	.269
Frank Gilhooley	OF142	142	562	116	174		13	15	0	79	25	62	.310
Lester Channell	OF138	138	517	87	155		27	12	5	72	50	20	.300
George Jackson	OF95	97	312	54	84		17	4	4	32	51	12	.269
Louis LaLonge	C92	92	293	25	80		7	1	0	30	18	6	.273
Charles Jamieson	OF40,P20	75	221	39	68		17	4	0	25	24	14	.308
Jim Stephens	C53	53	151	18	38		6	3	0	15	10	3	.252
George McConnell	P29	45	108	11	32		7	0	1	4	8	2	.296
Chick Brandom	P41	42	60	3	5		2	0	0	2	7	1	.083
Phifer Fullenweider	P36	36	93	7	8		2	1	0	3	17	0	.084
Fred Beebe	P35	35	100	6	16		2	0	0	3	22	1	.160
Lore Bader	P30	30	80	9	19		1	0	0	4	19	0	.238
Bill Wright	OF11	11	26	2	6		1	0	0	1	2	0	.231
Albert Tyson	P8	9	14	1	4		0	1	0	1	3	0	.286

PITCHERS		W	L	PCT	G	GS	CG	SH	IP	H	BB	SO	ERA
Fred Beebe		22	10	.688	34				267	244	90	151	
Phifer Fullenweider		19	14	.576	36				263	274	83	107	
Lore Bader		16	7	.696	30				224	214	79	101	
George McConnell		14	10	.583	29				235	195	56	120	
Chick Brandom		10	10	.500	41				187	179	62	85	
Charles Jamieson		3	8	.273	20				86	99	32	37	
Albert Tyson		1	0	1.000	8				39	41	16	18	

ROCHESTER Hustlers

| | | 3rd | 91-63 | .591 | -4 | | | | John Ganzel | | |

BATTERS	POS-GAMES	GP	AB	R	H	BI	2B	3B	HR	BB	SO	SB	BA
Wally Pipp	1B154	154	551	98	173		18	27	15	70	61	26	.312
John Priest	2B141,OF10	151	574	88	131		15	12	1	62	62	41	.228

ROCHESTER (cont.)
Hustlers

BATTERS	POS-GAMES	GP	AB	R	H	BI	2B	3B	HR	BB	SO	SB	BA
Tom McMillan	SS156	156	528	83	136		10	9	0	76	33	40	.258
Joe Schultz	3B155	155	576	95	182		33	10	1	50	35	30	.316
F. Smith	OF117	126	444	46	111		14	5	1	32	23	14	.250
Charles Messenger	OF104	104	390	59	99		14	3	3	52	42	20	.254
Chester Spencer	OF101	110	312	38	72		6	4	2	26	40	4	.231
Robert Williams	C146	146	484	29	122		13	5	0	40	47	5	.252
Leo Walsh	OF99,2B15	120	405	57	127		18	4	2	24	47	15	.314
Bill Upham	P51	52	83	8	17		5	0	0	5	26	0	.205
Chet Hoff	P42	43	89	7	13		0	0	0	6	14	0	.146
Lew McAllister	C33	33	33	2	8		2	1	0	5	5	0	.242
Tom Hughes	P33	35	89	8	16		0	2	0	5	21	2	.180
Robert Keefe	P30	30	81	7	9		2	0	0	7	21	2	.111
McMurray	C27	27	42	6	8		1	0	0	6	2	1	.190
Duchesnil	P19	22	31	3	4		1	0	0	1	10	0	.129
Manning	P18	20	20	1	2		0	0	0	2	2	1	.100
Herche	P17	17	45	5	8		2	0	1	2	11	0	.178
Meikle	P11	11	14	1	1		0	0	0	1	5	0	.071
Richard Breen	2B7	7	16	1	1		0	0	0	1	1	1	.063

PITCHERS	W	L	PCT	G	GS	CG	SH	IP	H	BB	SO	ERA
Bill Upham	21	12	.636	51				237	223	52	109	
Tom Hughes	17	9	.654	33				263	205	77	182	
Robert Keefe	17	10	.629	30				242	232	68	102	
Chet Hoff	15	14	.517	42				266	254	109	146	
Herche	7	8	.467	17				112	105	58	55	
Duchesnil	6	2	.750	19				97	103	26	33	
Manning	2	3	.400	18				61	57	31	24	
Meikle	2	4	.333	11				46	51	14	12	

TORONTO   4th   74-70   .514   -21   Joe Kelley
Maple Leafs

BATTERS	POS-GAMES	GP	AB	R	H	BI	2B	3B	HR	BB	SO	SB	BA
Tim Jordan	1B142	142	491	96	148		27	4	13	82	50	21	.301
Ed Fitzpatrick	2B140	140	523	105	136		22	6	3	69	33	44	.260
Robert Fisher	SS128	128	486	87	151		17	4	5	35	21	37	.311
Charles Pick	3B132	134	505	76	151		13	7	2	57	47	41	.299
Bill O'Hara	OF135	135	488	54	148		14	6	0	62	69	25	.303
R. Wilson	OF114	114	451	68	124		16	10	2	33	18	22	.275
John Sullivan	OF63	64	196	26	49		6	5	4	26	35	3	.250
William Kelly	C114	114	365	35	89		12	5	0	21	41	11	.244
Priest		96	258	32	66		4	5	1	42	63	7	.256
Charles Kroy	OF60	62	176	16	46		4	0	0	16	14	6	.261
Clint Rogge	P39	39	91	8	23		0	1	1	5	17	0	.253
Fred Herbert	P39	39	86	6	14		2	0	1	7	26	0	.163
Bunn Hearn	P37	37	94	13	21		2	2	2	0	24	1	.213
Johnson	P32	32	54	5	10		1	0	0	15	27	0	.185
William Wagner	P23	23	65	10	18		1	3	0	4	12	2	.277
Snell	C23	23	43	6	7		0	0	0	12	11	3	.163
Irving Trout	OF15	19	60	8	17		1	1	0	8	9	3	.283
Isaacs	3B14	14	48	9	15		1	0	1	12	7	2	.313
Emilio Palmero	P9	9	11	0	3		0	0	0	0	2	0	.273
William Ritter	P9	9	10	0	2		0	0	0	0	3	0	.200

PITCHERS	W	L	PCT	G	GS	CG	SH	IP	H	BB	SO	ERA
Clint Rogge	17	12	.586	38				254	238	89	108	
Fred Herbert	16	15	.516	37				231	238	60	55	
William Wagner	13	7	.650	22				165	192	69	48	
Bunn Hearn	13	13	.500	36				243	234	78	136	
Johnson	8	14	.364	32				183	188	67	102	
William Ritter	1	2	.333	9				34	36	14	27	
Emilio Palmero	0	3	.000	9				30	30	18	15	

NEWARK Indians   5th   73-77   .487   -20   Harry Smith

BATTERS	POS-GAMES	GP	AB	R	H	BI	2B	3B	HR	BB	SO	SB	BA
Clarence Kraft	1B96	96	342	60	95		11	15	9	37	60	14	.278
Gus Getz	2B107	107	401	40	116		16	1	0	9	21	28	.289
Ray Mowe	SS104	104	371	52	99		11	0	0	31	25	25	.267
Ed Zimmerman	3B148	148	519	68	139		23	8	3	36	38	32	.268
William Zimmerman	OF148	148	546	66	152		24	7	0	51	39	26	.278
Leo Callahan	OF125	129	450	80	141		9	16	4	56	20	24	.313
Leo Witterstatter	OF119	128	451	52	135		12	9	0	47	23	11	.299
Mike Hechinger	C97	97	266	23	64		11	3	0	44	41	1	.241
Bert Tooley	SS75,2B28,1B22,3B9	133	498	78	127		15	9	1	59	43	30	.255
Henry Myers	OF61	61	214	25	60		4	9	2	4	18	14	.280
Holmquist	OF25,1B24,P20	55	142	12	33		7	2	0	10	27	2	.232
Mack Wheat	C50	50	152	13	36		5	1	1	4	41	0	.237
Harry Smith	C34	34	77	10	18		2	1	0	5	11	2	.234
Collins	OF32	32	110	11	32		5	0	1	4	9	4	.291
Al Schacht	P31	32	60	4	11		1	0	0	5	14	0	.183
Cliff Curtis	P30	30	89	5	10		1	0	0	2	26	0	.112
S. Smith	P23	30	76	5	17		3	1	1	3	18	0	.224
Watty Lee	P26	28	69	4	14		4	0	1	6	13	1	.203
George Bell	P14	14	22	0	3		0	0	0	2	5	0	.136
Britton	P10	11	14	1	0		0	0	0	3	2	0	.000
Elmer Brown	P8	9	21	1	3		0	0	1	2	6	0	.143
O'Rourke	C8	8	28	3	9		2	0	0	1	5	0	.321

PITCHERS		W	L	PCT	G	GS	CG	SH	IP	H	BB	SO	ERA
Cliff Curtis		16	12	.571	30				248	218	102	100	
Al Schacht		12	10	.545	31				181	158	63	80	
Watty Lee		11	12	.478	26				182	199	46	107	
S. Smith		8	12	.400	23				185	174	58	79	
Holmquist		5	6	.455	20				97	104	32	38	
Elmer Brown		3	4	.429	8				55	46	32	34	
Britton		2	0	1.000	10				50	36	23	9	
George Bell		1	4	.200	14				61	72	19	37	

BALTIMORE Orioles   6th   72-77   .483   -20.5   Jack Dunn

BATTERS	POS-GAMES	GP	AB	R	H	BI	2B	3B	HR	BB	SO	SB	BA
Gustave Gleichman	1B127	133	459	63	132		10	15	1	45	78	17	.288
Neal Ball	2B149	149	561	84	157		26	7	1	49	92	28	.280
Fred Parent	SS90,3B9,OF9	108	371	41	104		16	3	1	48	27	14	.280
Ezra Midkiff	3B69	69	270	53	78		8	3	0	21	13	26	.289
Jack Dunn, Jr.	OF84	89	278	16	48		4	3	1	16	63	4	.173
William Cree	OF72	72	270	48	96		18	5	1	23	18	19	.356
Bert Daniels	OF66	66	259	45	84		11	9	3	22	23	21	.324
James McAvoy	C75	76	247	19	58		10	2	1	14	27	7	.235
John Murray	3B56,OF20	76	289	30	71		4	0	0	31	28	3	.246
Claud Derrick	SS66	66	232	42	71		8	5	2	23	23	19	.306
George Twombly	OF64	64	257	44	69		4	4	3	14	8	14	.268
Allen Russell	P47	55	116	12	22		1	0	1	16	37	6	.190
Carroll	OF45	45	158	10	35		8	0	0	8	59	4	.222
Ben Egan	C42	42	140	10	35		5	1	1	1	15	2	.250
Ross Erwin	OF23,1B17	40	122	9	36		4	2	0	10	6	1	.295
Kane	C24,1B11	35	98	3	21		1	0	0	7	13	2	.214
Dave Danforth	P32	32	64	4	8		1	0	1	1	29	0	.125
Ensign Cottrell	P26	26	68	6	11		0	1	0	0	14	1	.162
Davidson	P22	26	57	5	11		1	0	0	1	13	1	.193
Bill Morrisette	P21	23	54	6	14		2	2	2	1	13	1	.259
Ralph Capron	OF18	20	77	12	15		1	2	0	1	12	5	.195
Sandusky	OF16	18	51	7	13		1	2	0	7	12	1	.255
Frank Jarman	P16	16	47	1	5		1	0	0	5	15	0	.107
Ernest Shore	P10	11	21	2	5		0	0	0	1	4	0	.238
Pedone	OF7	7	19	1	2		0	0	0	1	6	0	.105
Howard	P5	5	6	0	1		0	0	0	0	3	0	.167

PITCHERS		W	L	PCT	G	GS	CG	SH	IP	H	BB	SO	ERA
Ensign Cottrell		13	7	.650	26				184	179	72	92	
Dave Danforth		12	15	.444	32				184	147	75	68	
Allen Russell		11	16	.407	47				286	248	143	164	

BALTIMORE (cont.)
Orioles

PITCHERS	W	L	PCT	G	GS	CG	SH	IP	H	BB	SO	ERA
Davidson	8	7	.533	22				118	100	133	89	
Bill Morrisette	7	10	.412	21				128	129	74	70	
Ernest Shore	5	3	.625	10				62	59	11	28	
Frank Jarman	4	9	.308	16				129	118	48	50	

MONTREAL   7th   60-89   .403   -32.5   Kitty Bransfield - Dan Howley
Royals

BATTERS	POS-GAMES	GP	AB	R	H	BI	2B	3B	HR	BB	SO	SB	BA
John Flynn	1B134	134	469	64	145		17	13	9	78	80	17	.309
Joe Yeager	2B63,3B21	88	306	26	71		8	2	1	19	18	3	.232
B. Purtell	SS153	153	535	64	104		14	3	0	78	51	12	.195
Jack Boyle	3B78	78	275	24	62		7	1	0	27	25	1	.225
George Whiteman	OF149	149	562	92	176		20	15	8	73	40	32	.313
Ed Kippert	OF134	134	458	73	110		23	7	3	82	67	24	.240
Otto Deininger	OF117	137	497	70	137		21	13	7	61	73	10	.276
Francis Madden	C79	79	253	22	56		3	1	0	23	25	1	.221
Paul Smith	OF83	83	254	34	78		5	1	0	30	39	11	.307
Halstein	2B40,3B24,1B11	76	265	16	57		3	2	1	14	15	6	.215
Dan Howley	C62	64	203	17	50		2	3	0	13	18	5	.246
Keller	2B25,3B19	44	167	18	34		5	0	0	23	17	4	.204
James Dowd	P30,3B7	44	87	13	21		1	1	1	11	14	1	.241
Gene Dale	P36	40	99	9	26		5	1	2	3	17	0	.263
J. Smith	C30	30	103	10	28		2	4	0	10	20	0	.272
Robert Couchman	P30	30	67	5	13		2	0	0	3	14	0	.194
Bill Cunningham	2B28	28	88	11	15		2	0	1	10	21	2	.170
Del Mason	P27	28	80	5	10		1	0	0	5	11	0	.125
Frank Miller	P26	27	72	3	12		1	0	1	2	28	0	.167
Malay	OF7	16	37	1	2		0	0	0	6	4	0	.143
Jay Cashion	P9	14	32	5	12		0	2	1	1	3	0	.375
Howard McGraner	P5	13	14	2	2		0	0	0	2	4	0	.143
Cogan	3B5	5	17	2	3		0	0	0	0	1	1	.176

PITCHERS	W	L	PCT	G	GS	CG	SH	IP	H	BB	SO	ERA
Robert Couchman	12	12	.500	30				214	222	58	56	
Del Mason	12	14	.462	27				216	225	55	98	
Gene Dale	10	17	.370	36				253	276	88	87	
Frank Miller	9	13	.409	26				188	181	69	120	
Jay Cashion	4	4	.500	9				60	58	42	20	
James Dowd	4	12	.250	30				159	188	48	56	
Howard McGraner	1	2	.333	5				28	32	12	10	

JERSEY CITY   8th   48-106   .312   -47   Rudy Hulswitt
Skeeters

BATTERS	POS-GAMES	GP	AB	R	H	BI	2B	3B	HR	BB	SO	SB	BA
Malcolm Barry	1B117	117	395	41	118		15	7	1	30	23	11	.299
Rudy Hulswitt	2B71	71	227	29	67		14	6	0	26	20	7	.295
Herbert Murphy	SS125,3B12	137	456	56	107		14	11	4	46	66	11	.235
Art Bues	3B130	130	508	53	142		19	15	4	29	26	22	.280
Taylor Farrell	OF62	63	219	25	45		3	0	1	31	34	6	.206
Jim Eschen	OF		(see multi-team players)										
W. Wright	OF		(see multi-team players)										
Bill Reynolds	C89	89	264	21	72		11	3	0	14	39	3	.273
Monte Pfyl	OF55,1B40	95	325	46	89		8	7	2	42	38	16	.274
Fred Tyler	C74	74	215	22	54		5	8	1	10	38	3	.251
Dolf Luque	2B29,P14,3B10	71	233	22	52		6	8	1	16	45	5	.223
Fisher	OF43	63	226	32	54		11	4	1	23	28	9	.239
John Kelly	OF51	51	192	29	55		7	3	0	27	22	15	.287
Robert Wells	C29,OF15	44	95	6	23		4	1	0	14	5	3	.242
Fred Bruck	P42	43	82	9	13		2	0	0	14	36	0	.159
Strait	OF36	39	128	15	30		4	4	2	21	13	2	.234
C. Thompson	P36	37	82	6	11		1	0	0	7	20	0	.134
Bernard Koehler	SS16,2B15	35	111	11	26		4	0	0	17	9	9	.234
Williams	P29	29	59	4	10		0	0	1	3	15	0	.169
Claude Cooper	OF26	26	88	12	23		2	0	1	6	8	2	.261
William Pearce	C13	13	44	3	9		1	0	1	2	5	0	.205

JERSEY CITY (cont.)
Skeeters

BATTERS	POS-GAMES	GP	AB	R	H	BI	2B	3B	HR	BB	SO	SB	BA
H. Pearce	SS12	12	42	4	11		1	1	0	2	9	2	.262
George Shears	P12	12	10	0	2		0	0	0	3	3	0	.200
Wiley Taylor	P11	11	16	1	1		0	0	0	1	1	1	.063
Meyers	1B9	9	29	5	6		1	0	0	8	5	2	.207
Joseph Harris	OF8	8	33	2	9		0	0	0	1	2	8	.273
Tee	C8	8	17	2	2		0	0	0	2	4	0	.118
Burr	P7	7	4	0	0		0	0	0	0	3	0	.000
T. Thompson	P7	7	2	0	1		0	0	0	0	0	0	.500
C. Reynolds	P6	6	8	0	1		0	0	0	1	2	1	.207
Al Shaw	1B5	5	15	3	3		1	0	0	0	2	0	.200
Rube Vickers	P5	5	12	0	3		1	0	0	0	5	0	.250

PITCHERS	W	L	PCT	G	GS	CG	SH	IP	H	BB	SO	ERA
Fred Bruck	14	19	.424	42				275	303	113	116	
C. Thompson	9	18	.333	36				243	296	54	66	
Williams	4	14	.222	29				168	211	69	57	
Rube Vickers	2	2	.500	5				23	40	11	8	
George Shears	2	5	.286	12				51	51	15	20	
Dolf Luque	2	10	.167	14				108	129	65	41	
C. Reynolds	1	1	.500	6				27	37	13	4	
Wiley Taylor	1	5	.167	11				52	55	12	26	
Burr	0	1	.000	7				19	12	20	9	
T. Thompson	0	3	.000	7				10	18	6	8	

MULTI-TEAM PLAYERS

BATTERS	POS-GAMES	TEAMS	GP	AB	R	H	BI	2B	3B	HR	BB	SO	SB	BA
Roland Barrows	OF138	ROC-BAL	140	484	80	138		24	15	5	69	64	13	.285
Jim Eschen	OF120	JC-BUF	120	431	53	111		18	4	5	27	76	24	.258
W. Wright	OF96	JC-TOR	97	392	71	117		20	4	3	34	30	19	.298
Clarence Lehr	2B59,1B32	JC-BUF	91	342	60	82		14	5	5	21	16	41	.240
Al Carlstrom	1B54,3B23	MON-BUF	77	279	35	72		12	5	1	20	29	5	.258
Paul Krichell	C65	BUF-TOR	65	191	31	66		12	0	0	29	19	15	.346
Babe Ruth	P35	BAL-PRO	46	121	22	28		2	10	1	9	26	4	.231
John Verbout	P36	JC-BUF	36	63	2	4		0	0	1	14	28	0	.063
Gilbert	P28	TOR-JC	34	59	3	12		1	0	0	1	16	1	.203
Al Mattern	P32	MON-NEW	33	64	6	13		1	0	0	1	17	0	.203
John Enzmann	P23	NEW-ROC	24	60	4	11		1	1	0	2	14	0	.183
Earl Richter	P23	MON-NEW	23	64	1	5		1	0	0	2	24	0	.078
John Frill	P19	JC-TOR	19	41	1	5		0	0	0	1	10	1	.122

PITCHERS		TEAMS	W	L	PCT	G	GS	CG	SH	IP	H	BB	SO	ERA
Babe Ruth		BAL-PRO	23	8	.742	35				245	210	101	139	
John Verbout		JC-BUF	12	12	.500	36				207	210	66	73	
John Enzmann		NEW-ROC	11	8	.579	23				164	109	36	62	
Al Mattern		MON-NEW	11	11	.500	32				206	217	54	63	
Earl Richter		MON-NEW	8	10	.444	23				175	174	96	83	
Gilbert		TOR-JC	7	10	.412	28				176	172	81	72	
John Frill		JC-TOR	6	7	.462	19				131	149	42	24	

TEAM BATTING

TEAMS	GP	AB	R	H	BI	2B	3B	HR	BB	SO	SB	BA
PROVIDENCE	155	4990	763	1409		136	137	36	523	549	218	.282
BUFFALO	152	5010	796	1340		194	69	20	497	514	220	.267
ROCHESTER	156	5077	602	1298		168	90	26	530	551	220	.256
TORONTO	146	4820	703	1328		154	60	36	543	571	246	.276
NEWARK	153	5012	627	1333		166	88	23	422	529	212	.266
BALTIMORE	149	4923	617	1307		156	80	24	393	698	190	.265
MONTREAL	153	5046	595	1231		141	70	35	591	607	128	.244
JERSEY CITY	156	5070	570	1264		174	85	30	459	691	169	.249
	610	39948	5273	10510		1289	679	230	3958	4710	1603	.263

1915
FEDERAL INVASION

In 1914, an irritant known as the Federal League made its presence known in International League circles. The Federal League, a third major league, jumped into two league cities, Baltimore and Buffalo, upsetting matters greatly. In 1915, the Federal irritant would turn into a threat.

Not content with their 1914 lineup of teams, the Federals turned their attention to other toothsome targets. Wanting a team in the New York metropolitan area, the Federals fastened their eyes on the biggest adjacent city: Newark, New Jersey. There, the Feds placed the Newark Peppers. This caused the International League Newark Bears to seek other climes. In early July, the Bears transferred their team to Harrisburg.

The Baltimore International team, after their terrific pounding at the gate in 1914, didn't even wait for the 1915 season to make a change. After the 1914 season, Baltimore management moved the team to Richmond.

In 1915, the International League had a measure of success against the Federals in a third field of competition: Buffalo. Here, the International League Bisons thrived, while fielding a contending team. During the season's final week, after a two-month stretch in second, Buffalo passed Providence to claim the flag. All the Buffalo Feds could manage was sixth.

In the International, behind Buffalo and Providence, Toronto, Rochester, and Montreal finished third, fourth, and fifth. The two displaced clubs finished next, Newark/Harrisburg in sixth and Richmond in seventh. Jersey City finished in the cellar. The leading batsman graced the roster of Toronto, Morrie Rath at .332. Montreal enjoyed the skill of George Whiteman, who hit a league-high 14 home runs. The star pitchers came from Buffalo and Richmond. Bison Fred Beebe won a league-best 27, while Richmond Climber Allen Russell whiffed 239 batters.

By 1916, the Federal threat had ended with the league's demise. However, it took a little while for the shaken International teams to settle back into their original roosts.

Soon another threat would engulf the International League. This threat would go far beyond the teams and players that a rival league could test. This new test involved men and nations—and the whole world.

BUFFALO Bisons

BUFFALO   1st   86-50   .632   Patsy Donovan

BATTERS	POS-GAMES	GP	AB	R	H	BI	2B	3B	HR	BB	SO	SB	BA
Joe Judge	1B140	140	493	68	158		19	15	0	58	55	28	.320
Joe McCarthy	2B135	135	515	71	137		24	5	0	38	70	17	.266
Walt Keating	SS138	138	436	57	92		11	2	1	70	87	27	.211
Al Carlstrom	3B139	140	500	59	123		6	8	3	39	80	21	.246
Charles Jamieson	OF138	138	522	82	160		28	9	0	50	54	16	.307
Lester Channell	OF130	130	458	62	139		22	13	5	60	29	11	.304
Frank Gilhooley	OF122	122	450	92	145		19	11	3	88	27	53	.322
Louis LaLonge	C73	76	219	27	63		11	1	0	25	35	3	.288
George Jackson	OF52	78	200	59	123		6	8	3	39	80	21	.246
Jack Onslow	C72	74	229	15	48		9	2	0	14	36	6	.210
Lore Bader	P48	51	122	15	30		4	1	0	9	16	1	.246
Fred Beebe	P35	38	106	9	23		2	0	0	10	26	1	.217
Phifer Fullenweider	P36	36	83	10	17		2	0	0	4	18	0	.205
George Gaw	P33	35	83	9	16		3	0	1	5	20	1	.193
Albert Tyson	P19	23	19	2	2		1	0	0	0	3	0	.105

PITCHERS		W	L	PCT	G	GS	CG	SH	IP	H	BB	SO	ERA
Fred Beebe		27	7	**.794**	35				301	282	110	118	
Lore Bader		20	18	.526	48				**334**	308	119	132	
Phifer Fullenweider		17	12	.586	36				242	256	83	93	
George Gaw		16	9	.640	33				233	203	74	84	
John Oldham		3	1	.750	5				45	39	15	11	
Albert Tyson		2	2	.500	18				63	68	21	15	

PROVIDENCE Grays

PROVIDENCE   2nd   85-53   .616   -2   David Shean

BATTERS	POS-GAMES	GP	AB	R	H	BI	2B	3B	HR	BB	SO	SB	BA
Ed Onslow	1B124	124	455	73	134		8	13	0	56	27	32	.295
David Shean	2B116	121	457	68	141		23	7	0	31	22	11	.309
Bunny Fabrique	SS137	137	521	71	136		11	6	0	47	44	15	.261
Mike McNally	3B105	106	388	60	98		12	3	1	45	29	26	.253
Chick Shorten	OF137	137	543	81	175		26	14	0	48	54	27	.322
Ray Powell	OF130	130	453	67	113		17	14	3	41	51	16	.249
Guy Tutwiler	OF72	76	284	32	85		12	15	0	23	34	9	.299
Joe Casey	C72	73	233	27	65		9	6	4	22	16	6	.278
Robert Gill	OF36,3B33,2B10	90	301	48	72		8	10	3	19	31	10	.239
Edwin Eayrs	OF26,P16	54	147	24	40		3	4	0	11	19	4	.272
Wallace Shultz	P38	47	118	13	34		5	1	1	14	10	0	.288
Joe Oeschger	P37	39	95	11	22		4	1	0	6	14	0	.232
Guy Cooper	P34	35	84	11	16		2	1	0	7	8	0	.190
Ralph Comstock	P25	25	59	3	8		0	0	0	2	17	0	.136
Walter Rehg	2B18	19	64	6	13		2	1	1	7	0	4	.203
Herb Pennock	P13	14	35	2	8		1	1	0	0	7	0	.229
Masterman		12	32	2	9		0	1	0	2	5	0	.281

PITCHERS		W	L	PCT	G	GS	CG	SH	IP	H	BB	SO	ERA
Joe Oeschger		21	10	.677	37				252	192	91	127	
Wallace Shultz		18	10	.643	38				291	253	93	77	
Ralph Comstock		15	6	.714	25				178	135	70	113	
Guy Cooper		13	13	.500	34				237	215	104	99	
Edwin Eayrs		7	6	.538	16				103	93	57	40	
Herb Pennock		6	4	.600	13				90	72	38	57	

TORONTO Maple Leafs

TORONTO   3rd   72-67   .518   -15.5   William Clymer

BATTERS	POS-GAMES	GP	AB	R	H	BI	2B	3B	HR	BB	SO	SB	BA
Dawson Graham	1B135	138	506	64	146		13	3	2	42	38	21	.289
Clyde Wares	2B65	76	238	30	62		12	1	2	34	22	10	.261
Neal Ball	SS		(see multi-team players)										
Morrie Rath	3B86,2B11	97	361	52	120		13	0	0	24	17	10	**.332**
G. Williams	OF89	90	340	57	97		15	9	8	25	44	31	.285
Larry Gilbert	OF68	68	243	38	79		9	5	4	36	11	16	.325
Thomas Daley	OF64	64	211	21	55		11	1	0	29	8	15	.261
Brad Kocher	C		(see multi-team players)										

TORONTO(cont.)
Maple Leafs

BATTERS	POS-GAMES	GP	AB	R	H	BI	2B	3B	HR	BB	SO	SB	BA
Irving Trout	OF62	80	250	29	57		4	1	2	29	17	1	.228
Dolf Luque	P31,2B18	73	196	20	43		5	4	0	19	22	8	.219
Hollander	3B42	54	194	26	48		2	6	0	30	24	10	.248
Roxy Roach	SS47	47	167	22	43		11	4	2	13	11	8	.257
William Kelly	C47	47	139	12	36		1	1	0	9	9	1	.259
Fred Herbert	P37	37	98	10	26		3	3	0	8	24	2	.265
W. Manning	P36	37	94	3	16		1	0	0	0	14	0	.170
William McTigue	P34	36	94	13	27		3	1	5	7	18	1	.287
Bill O'Hara	OF27	27	94	6	16		1	1	0	10	9	0	.170
Rollin Cook	P23	23	43	2	5		0	0	0	6	12	0	.116
Fred Parent	2B22	22	80	16	22		1	1	1	13	3	3	.275
Brown	OF13	19	65	7	15		3	1	0	4	9	3	.231
R. Wilson		16	58	4	14		0	0	0	5	3	0	.241
Eugene Cocreham	P16	16	27	3	7		1	2	0	4	9	0	.259
Sheehan	2B15	15	54	8	12		1	1	0	2	7	0	.222
Mike Konnick	C14	14	28	4	7		0	1	0	1	3	0	.250
Carroll		10	25	0	5		0	0	0	2	3	0	.200

PITCHERS	W	L	PCT	G	GS	CG	SH	IP	H	BB	SO	ERA
William McTigue	17	10	.630	34				241	213	90	152	
Fred Herbert	16	17	.485	37				275	251	72	91	
Dolf Luque	15	9	.625	31				225	190	100	133	
W. Manning	14	18	.438	36				263	265	72	94	
Rollin Cook	7	6	.538	23				129	113	36	33	
Eugene Cocreham	2	6	.250	16				88	98	31	51	

ROCHESTER   4th   69-69   .500   -18   John Ganzel -
Hustlers   Robert Williams

BATTERS	POS-GAMES	GP	AB	R	H	BI	2B	3B	HR	BB	SO	SB	BA
Walter Holke	1B142	142	542	71	153		14	11	1	34	42	26	.282
John Priest	2B103,3B20	128	461	47	116		14	12	0	29	42	31	.252
Thomas Stevenson	SS138	139	476	56	112		15	11	1	42	74	17	.235
Des Beatty	3B64	98	288	33	74		15	3	1	33	26	10	.257
Robert Clemens	OF132	140	552	81	150		23	6	5	55	76	35	.272
Charles Piez	OF114	117	430	49	111		10	7	2	36	33	17	.258
William Zimmerman	OF72	72	276	33	80		4	5	0	28	20	10	.290
Robert Williams	C119	122	377	28	98		18	0	3	37	43	6	.260
Art Kores	3B57,2B12	75	276	42	76		11	11	2	18	16	17	.275
Fred Hersche	P48	49	112	11	20		4	0	2	5	32	0	.179
Emilio Palmero	P41	46	105	16	23		1	2	0	10	20	0	.219
Ross Erwin	C29	38	81	8	18		0	1	0	10	5	4	.222
Walker	OF34	36	105	18	30		10	4	0	17	19	6	.286
Al Huenke	P35	35	67	5	15		0	0	0	2	9	0	.224
Eric Erickson	P31	31	82	6	18		1	1	0	1	18	0	.220
Chet Hoff	P26	29	69	8	28		4	1	0	4	4	2	.406
Wanamaker	C14	19	37	4	8		0	0	0	2	5	1	.219
Maurice Shannon	2B10	10	32	4	6		0	1	0	2	8	0	.188

PITCHERS	W	L	PCT	G	GS	CG	SH	IP	H	BB	SO	ERA
Emilio Palmero	19	16	.543	41				300	228	134	163	
Eric Erickson	14	8	.636	31				216	167	89	173	
Fred Hersche	13	16	.448	48				305	270	141	129	
Chet Hoff	12	10	.545	26				185	166	94	101	
Al Huenke	11	13	.458	35				211	200	89	84	
A. Williams	1	2	.333	5				12	11	11	6	

MONTREAL   5th   67-70   .489   -19.5   Dan Howley
Royals

BATTERS	POS-GAMES	GP	AB	R	H	BI	2B	3B	HR	BB	SO	SB	BA
John Flynn	1B128	128	478	64	138		13	6	13	45	61	7	.289
Hal Irelan	2B118	120	433	72	103		16	9	9	73	53	24	.238
Ken Nash	SS99,2B10	109	435	67	111		11	4	0	51	32	19	.255
Art Devlin	3B112,1B12	124	448	45	122		18	6	2	48	39	12	.272
George Whiteman	OF141	141	526	106	164		27	13	14	69	42	25	.312
William Holden	OF102	104	376	44	94		14	6	4	45	32	14	.250

MONTREAL (cont.)
Royals

BATTERS	POS-GAMES	GP	AB	R	H	BI	2B	3B	HR	BB	SO	SB	BA
Paul Smith	OF88	88	331	51	102		18	2	4	28	53	22	.308
Dan Howley	C85	88	287	34	71		6	0	7	20	27	9	.247
Rafael Almeida	OF42,3B17	81	227	38	60		8	4	4	48	28	18	.264
Francis Madden	C59	63	203	25	46		11	1	2	12	17	1	.227
Charles Fullerton	P34	43	129	12	29		3	1	0	5	18	1	.225
James Dowd	P34	35	92	11	15		3	0	2	9	16	1	.163
Leon Cadore	P29	30	83	7	15		1	1	0	4	23	0	.181
Frank Miller	P22	22	75	10	21		1	0	2	1	11	0	.280
Earl Richter	P19	19	49	2	10		1	0	1	2	18	0	.205

PITCHERS	W	L	PCT	G	GS	CG	SH	IP	H	BB	SO	ERA
Charles Fullerton	18	14	.563	34				275	281	124	105	
Frank Miller	15	6	.714	22				183	170	65	118	
James Dowd	14	9	.609	34				275	281	124	105	
Leon Cadore	10	14	.417	29				230	244	76	110	
Earl Richter	4	11	.267	19				136	119	65	46	
Fred Sherry	1	4	.200	5				45	41	12	13	

NEWARK / HARRISBURG   6th   61-76   .445   -25.5   Harry Smith
Indians / Senators

BATTERS	POS-GAMES	GP	AB	R	H	BI	2B	3B	HR	BB	SO	SB	BA
Clarence Kraft	1B137	140	505	90	155		25	24	11	52	80	22	.307
Bert Tooley	2B126	127	461	68	125		11	9	0	46	28	39	.271
Ray Mowe	SS111	115	405	55	90		9	2	1	47	24	23	.222
Ed Zimmerman	3B132	132	471	57	142		17	8	0	32	19	24	.301
Leo Witterstatter	OF125	135	492	52	151		17	2	1	24	15	16	.307
Ed Mensor	OF89	112	384	56	84		6	3	0	85	36	24	.219
Leo Callahan	OF75	78	272	43	71		11	10	0	31	23	19	.261
Mike Hechinger	C94	104	299	25	68		9	2	1	46	41	5	.227
Joseph Chabek	P37	46	81	9	13		4	0	0	7	20	1	.160
Snow	C32	44	127	7	25		2	1	0	10	17	0	.197
Al Schacht	P38	38	66	7	12		0	0	0	8	10	0	.182
Watty Lee	P28	31	71	4	13		1	0	0	16	10	0	.183
John Enzmann	P30	30	95	9	19		2	4	2	0	26	2	.200
Tierney	OF25	27	95	6	20		3	2	0	6	12	3	.211
Charles Schmutz	P12	11	23	2	7		2	2	0	2	5	0	.304

PITCHERS	W	L	PCT	G	GS	CG	SH	IP	H	BB	SO	ERA
John Enzmann	16	13	.552	30				262	241	73	84	
Al Schacht	13	13	.500	38				225	218	56	78	
Joseph Chabek	12	15	.444	37				229	217	64	80	
Watty Lee	10	14	.417	28				211	243	67	48	
Walt Smallwood	3	3	.500	7				47	47	20	15	
Charles Schmutz	2	4	.333	11				73	85	20	27	
Elmer Brown	0	3	.000	7				46	37	33	21	

RICHMOND   7th   59-81   .422   -29   Jack Dunn
Climbers

BATTERS	POS-GAMES	GP	AB	R	H	BI	2B	3B	HR	BB	SO	SB	BA
Tim Jordan	1B	(see multi-team players)											
Angel Aragon	2B63,OF36,SS24	131	488	59	143		14	9	2	42	25	18	.293
Sam Crane	SS97	97	362	60	93		10	4	3	39	63	9	.257
Charles Pick	3B85,2B17	102	375	71	109		19	11	0	58	25	27	.291
John Bates	OF141	141	476	87	141		27	9	6	106	42	32	.296
James Thompson	OF71	83	276	39	73		10	4	0	32	36	12	.264
Jack Dunn, Jr.	OF51	61	174	27	31		0	0	0	16	35	7	.178
Alex Schaufele	C77	77	239	23	41		3	3	0	26	66	5	.172
Allen Russell	P49	53	108	19	19		0	2	0	20	41	2	.176
George Twombly	OF20,2B19	52	191	32	57		3	4	0	21	6	15	.298
Bill Morrisette	P49	50	119	14	28		5	1	0	4	28	1	.235
Wilson Fewster	2B30,SS11	48	158	13	40		6	2	0	18	27	7	.253
Bill Bankston	OF41	41	137	15	33		1	2	0	12	19	4	.241
Mullin	1B39	39	143	25	53		6	4	0	13	15	8	.371

RICHMOND (cont.)
Climbers

BATTERS	POS-GAMES	GP	AB	R	H	BI	2B	3B	HR	BB	SO	SB	BA
Tom Healy	3B16,SS11	37	129	16	33		3	0	0	1	14	3	.256
Breckenridge	OF30	35	138	26	35		4	2	0	15	30	5	.254
Paul Krichell	C25	35	95	11	23		4	0	0	16	14	2	.242
Hoffman	OF25	34	114	13	33		2	7	2	22	12	3	.289
Sweeney	C	31	85	8	16		0	2	0	14	7	3	.188
Ensign Cottrell	P20	20	60	1	14		3	0	0	3	11	0	.233
Lee Meadows	P13	16	16	2	6		2	0	0	0	5	0	.375
Stertzer	P13	15	33	6	7		0	0	0	3	6	0	.212
O'Donnell	C10	13	37	1	10		1	0	0	2	5	0	.270

PITCHERS		W	L	PCT	G	GS	CG	SH	IP	H	BB	SO	ERA
Allen Russell		21	15	.583	49				317	276	164	239	
Bill Morrisette		16	26	.381	49				312	351	149	164	
Ensign Cottrell		7	11	.389	20				164	169	72	85	
Andrews		3	0	1.000	7				46	48	17	19	
Frank Jarman		2	2	.500	8				75	78	26	27	
Stertzer		2	7	.222	13				74	88	47	40	
Cram		1	3	.250	7				40	50	20	11	
Lee Meadows		0	2	.000	13				23	22	45	23	
Healy		0	3	.000	6				27	30	8	20	

JERSEY CITY   8th   52-85   .380   -34.5   George Wiltse -
Skeeters   Joe Yeager

BATTERS	POS-GAMES	GP	AB	R	H	BI	2B	3B	HR	BB	SO	SB	BA
Malcolm Barry	1B129	129	481	62	139		14	3	0	27	28	16	.289
Frank Truesdale	2B120	121	459	80	139		14	4	0	56	40	19	.303
B. Purtell	SS			(see multi-team players)									
Art Bues	3B130	130	476	66	133		18	10	3	49	32	16	.279
Ed Barney	OF62	62	230	29	77		12	1	0	25	28	7	.335
W. Wright	OF60	62	217	23	50		4	3	1	24	16	11	.230
Jim Thorpe	OF			(see multi-team players)									
Bill Reynolds	C			(see multi-team players)									
S. Manning	OF54	59	201	16	41		3	2	0	22	30	6	.204
Walt Tragresser	C47	53	157	16	39		4	3	0	13	25	4	.248
Joel Sherman	P30,OF15	49	120	11	24		1	1	0	10	20	3	.200
Gene Layden	OF41	47	143	13	41		4	2	0	26	24	10	.287
Blake	OF33	46	163	21	41		1	1	0	11	20	5	.251
John Verbout	P42	42	75	3	8		1	0	0	5	24	0	.107
Fred Bruck	P37	37	75	4	6		0	0	0	11	35	0	.080
Turner	SS36	38	125	12	25		3	2	0	7	15	5	.200
Jimmy Ring	P35	36	68	4	9		1	0	0	2	28	1	.132
Dick Crutcher	P25	33	77	7	9		2	0	0	7	24	0	.117
Pius Schwert	C22	31	84	8	18		3	0	0	8	14	4	.214
Archie Yelle	C23	27	74	7	18		2	1	1	6	10	1	.243
George Wiltse	P11	12	20	1	5		2	0	0	1	3	0	.250
C. O'Leary	SS10	10	33	3	8		1	0	0	2	1	1	.242

PITCHERS		W	L	PCT	G	GS	CG	SH	IP	H	BB	SO	ERA
Jimmy Ring		12	17	.414	35				212	210	117	120	
Joel Sherman		11	11	.500	30				204	189	54	58	
Dick Crutcher		9	9	.500	25				177	151	70	96	
Fred Bruck		9	20	.310	37				255	257	92	87	
John Verbout		8	20	.286	42				253	279	75	78	
George Wiltse		2	2	.500	11				46	38	6	20	
C. Thompson		1	2	.333	5				31	31	5	14	
Schorr		0	1	.000	5				11	15	4	4	

MULTI-TEAM PLAYERS

BATTERS	POS-GAMES	TEAMS	GP	AB	R	H	BI	2B	3B	HR	BB	SO	SB	BA
B. Purtell	SS133	MON-JC	133	451	57	97		9	5	1	76	61	19	.215
F. Smith	OF124	ROC-MON	127	441	48	108		15	4	1	52	27	16	.245
Neal Ball	SS81,2B33	RIC-TOR	114	377	47	87		13	4	1	42	74	23	.231
William Tamm	OF41,SS21,2B13,3B10	M-J-H	104	332	20	69		4	2	0	16	26	7	.208
Tim Jordan	1B102	TOR-RIC	102	351	51	99		20	6	2	74	35	12	.282

MULTI-TEAM PLAYERS (cont.)

BATTERS	POS-GAMES	TEAMS	GP	AB	R	H	BI	2B	3B	HR	BB	SO	SB	BA
Brad Kocher	C99	PRO-TOR	99	333	29	84		11	8	4	21	39	7	.252
Bill Reynolds	C78	JC-HAR	99	260	25	51		7	2	3	30	39	2	.196
Jim Thorpe	OF94	JC-HAR	96	370	51	112		13	7	2	19	63	22	.303
Ray Demmitt	OF67	TOR-JC	70	231	34	70		10	3	4	29	14	10	.303
Ted Cather	OF30,3B12,2B11	TOR-JC	59	204	21	58		11	2	1	20	27	6	.285
Joe Yeager	3B17,2B12,OF11	MON-JC	54	144	18	36		5	2	0	7	7	2	.250
Richard Goodbred	P20	RIC-HAR	20	44	4	4		1	0	0	4	9	2	.091
Charles Messenger	OF18	ROC-TOR	18	53	11	16		0	0	2	6	5	0	.302
O'Brien	P16	PRO-RIC	17	38	3	6		1	0	0	2	8	0	.158
Martin McHale	P14	MON-RIC	14	33	2	4		0	0	0	2	7	1	.121
Bentley	P10	PRO-JC	14	21	2	3		0	0	0	2	6	0	.143

PITCHERS	TEAMS	W	L	PCT	G	GS	CG	SH	IP	H	BB	SO	ERA
Richard Goodbred	RIC-HAR	8	7	.533	20				130	124	38	50	
O'Brien	PRO-RIC	5	6	.455	16				95	111	34	36	
Martin McHale	MON-RIC	4	9	.308	14				91	115	29	32	
Bentley	PRO-JC	1	2	.333	10				53	56	13	21	

TEAM BATTING

TEAMS	GP	AB	R	H	BI	2B	3B	HR	BB	SO	SB	BA
BUFFALO	140	4444	605	1218		176	66	14	486	587	196	.274
PROVIDENCE	138	4611	640	1263		152	105	16	403	429	176	.274
TORONTO	142	4497	549	1181		140	59	37	437	456	170	.263
ROCHESTER	141	4661	562	1200		148	79	18	419	536	189	.257
MONTREAL	141	4643	672	1213		165	57	65	522	520	176	.261
HARRISBURG	140	4428	543	1130		131	74	19	450	453	207	.255
RICHMOND	144	4605	656	1191		152	73	16	570	620	189	.259
JERSEY CITY	139	4408	509	1107		124	50	11	441	566	141	.251
	563	36297	4736	9503		1188	563	196	3728	4167	1444	.262

1916
URBAN SHOCKER

In 1885, in the New York State League, a new pitching statistic was introduced. Called "runs earned by opponent," it sought to measure a pitcher's worth by noting how many runs per game (excluding runs scored via error or catcher mistakes) he allowed. The statistic was kept sporadically through the 1892 season.

The statistic was reintroduced in 1916 as the "earned run average." There was a key difference between the nineteenth century version and the 1916 version. The early version measured earned runs per game for a pitcher, not taking into account how many innings were pitched. The new version rounded off each game to the nearest inning, using the following calculation: earned runs multiplied by nine (innings in a game) divided by innings pitched. Certainly this was a more accurate representation of a pitcher's record. The first achiever of the best earned run average in 1916, Urban Shocker, is also recognized by the International League as the all-time leader in this category.

Urban Shocker joined the International League in 1916, playing for the Toronto Maple Leafs. Pitching for a fifth-place club, Shocker compiled a nifty 15–3 record, while sporting a league-best 1.31 earned run average. No International League pitcher since has equaled the mark. However, there is evidence to dispute Shocker's record.

The International League saw two changes before the 1916 season. First, the Jersey City franchise was sold to Jack Dunn, who promptly moved it to Baltimore. Second, the Harrisburg team moved back to Newark. Buffalo won its second straight title over Providence, Montreal, Baltimore, Toronto, Richmond, Rochester, and Newark. Jim Smyth from Montreal was the top batter (.344), while Baltimore's George Twombly hit the most home runs (12). The top winning pitcher was Montreal's Leon Cadore (25), while the most strikeouts were chalked up by Toronto hurler William McTigue (187).

During the past 20 years, baseball researchers have gone over many of the league's nineteenth century pitching records, compiling earned run averages using the method started in 1916. As a result, several pitchers with lower marks than Urban Shocker's 1916 record have emerged. The lowest of these newfound records belongs to James Sullivan, who posted a 0.81 mark for Providence in 1892.

Late in the 1916 season, Urban Shocker joined the major leagues, embarking on a 13-year career. Although his earned run average record is in dispute, another record Shocker set in 1916 is not. During his fine season, Urban Shocker pitched 54 consecutive scoreless innings—a record that stands undisputed.

BUFFALO Bisons

1st 82-58 .586 Patsy Donovan

BATTERS	POS-GAMES	GP	AB	R	H	BI	2B	3B	HR	BB	SO	SB	BA
John Hummell	1B94,2B23	117	418	64	126		17	6	0	58	38	10	.301
James O'Neill	2B64,SS24	97	325	34	69		8	1	1	16	34	5	.212
Joe McDonald	SS119,3B18	140	464	54	125		19	5	1	53	54	12	.269
Al Carlstrom	3B124	139	525	84	149		22	11	5	44	38	12	.284
Merlin Kopp	OF137	137	497	109	144		14	6	2	88	95	59	.290
Lester Channell	OF121	128	465	83	153		27	4	6	54	32	14	.329
George Jackson	OF113	116	449	80	146		34	9	2	51	51	11	.325
Jack Onslow	C107	108	351	37	98		12	4	3	22	37	1	.279
Robert Gill	2B47,1B14	109	397	57	123		15	8	0	19	39	7	.310
Ray Haley	C32,1B29	63	210	24	58		13	0	1	18	16	6	.276
George Gaw	P41	48	99	12	16		0	0	0	6	17	1	.162
Albert Tyson	P29	39	97	13	28		1	4	0	5	8	0	.289
Lore Bader	P36	37	108	14	25		4	0	0	3	15	0	.231
Anderson	P24	24	33	2	4		0	0	0	3	10	0	.121
Joseph Engel	P19	21	42	4	10		3	0	0	2	11	0	.239
Herb Pennock	P15	17	44	3	7		1	0	0	0	7	0	.159
Fred Wilder	C17	17	40	5	14		3	0	1	1	4	1	.350
Ralph Burrill	P10	10	39	3	12		0	0	0			0	.308

PITCHERS	W	L	PCT	G	GS	CG	SH	IP	H	BB	SO	ERA
Lore Bader	23	8	.742	36				294	294	91	127	2.05
Albert Tyson	19	9	.697	37				251	247	125	62	2.15
George Gaw	16	13	.552	41				272	293	95	98	2.92
Joseph Engel	9	7	.563	19				120	108	65	59	2.55
Herb Pennock	7	6	.538	15				113	99	36	76	1.67
Chuck Anderson	4	7	.364	24				115	135	58	35	4.85
Vean Gregg	2	2	.500	4								

PROVIDENCE Grays

2nd 76-62 .551 -5 David Shean

BATTERS	POS-GAMES	GP	AB	R	H	BI	2B	3B	HR	BB	SO	SB	BA
Ed Onslow	1B103	108	414	59	129		12	4	1	26	21	34	.312
David Shean	2B133	133	482	53	137		19	4	2	74	21	17	.284
Bunny Fabrique	SS139	139	486	72	153		16	7	2	57	33	22	.315
Fred Brainard	3B124	125	457	54	110		11	7	2	27	54	28	.241
Walter Rehg	OF124,3B12	137	530	90	157		29	9	2	59	48	20	.296
Guy Tutwiler	OF102,1B17	119	436	75	136		19	20	6	44	34	9	.312
Edwin Eayrs	OF102,P11	113	377	52	107		11	10	1	50	44	7	.284
Archie Yelle	C84	91	284	32	54		6	2	2	28	27	6	.191
Earl Blackburn	C42,1B13	58	193	30	49		14	5	0	16	20	8	.254
Ray Powell	OF57	57	228	46	71		12	9	2	23	24	6	.311
Wallace Shultz	P38	51	109	12	26		4	3	1	12	12	0	.239
Ben Tincup	P33	45	96	12	24		3	1	1	8	14	3	.250
Frank Kane	OF35	40	110	14	22		8	0	1	7	26	3	.200
Stan Baumgartner	P34	39	93	7	11		2	1	0	10	22	2	.118
C. Peters	P32	32	81	3	14		2	1	0	4	20	1	.173
Harry Billiard	P30	30	59	3	6		0	0	0	7	17	1	.102

PITCHERS	W	L	PCT	G	GS	CG	SH	IP	H	BB	SO	ERA
C. Peters	19	10	.655	32				232	198	69	64	2.29
Ben Tincup	16	11	.593	33				227	225	90	112	2.50
Stan Baumgartner	15	12	.556	34				247	210	87	114	1.98
Wallace Shultz	13	14	.481	38				237	219	93	77	2.55
Harry Billiard	8	11	.421	30				171	160	112	70	2.90
Edwin Eayrs	4	1	.800	11				61	61	27	31	1.62
Schriever	1	0	1.000	3								
Dominic Mulrenan	0	1	.000	4								
Davis	0	2	.000	2								

MONTREAL Royals

3rd 75-64 .539 -6.5 Dan Howley

BATTERS	POS-GAMES	GP	AB	R	H	BI	2B	3B	HR	BB	SO	SB	BA
J. Slattery	1B127	127	467	69	139		19	23	4	58	44	7	.298
Jim Smythe	2B103	114	436	87	150		18	3	3	82	28	45	.344

MONTREAL (cont.)
Royals

BATTERS	POS-GAMES	GP	AB	R	H	BI	2B	3B	HR	BB	SO	SB	BA
Joseph Wagner	SS98,2B29	127	476	83	135		21	7	10	62	63	16	.284
Harry Damrau	3B141	141	524	74	159		30	7	4	64	78	14	.303
Herb Moran	OF133	133	538	115	146		26	1	0	109	43	33	.271
Paul Smith	OF103	107	419	91	135		14	4	4	45	54	44	.322
GeorgeMaisel	OF101	115	473	80	140		17	2	6	45	38	16	.296
Tom Madden	C71	73	245	28	61		10	0	1	29	22	6	.249
Ted Cather	OF75	83	277	49	76		14	3	6	34	37	4	.274
Dan Howley	C45	52	171	25	41		2	5	1	17	13	5	.240
Leon Cadore	P43	47	138	21	36		3	3	4	8	24	0	.261
Robert Wells	C32	44	141	18	36		3	1	0	19	14	2	.255
Charles Fullerton	P33	43	140	22	36		4	2	1	7	20	4	.257
Richard Goodbred	P37	37	90	4	20		3	1	0	8	15	0	.222
Colwell	P31	31	79	5	12		0	0	0	8	27	0	.152
Rafael Almeida	SS29	30	116	22	26		6	1	0	19	10	3	.224

PITCHERS	W	L	PCT	G	GS	CG	SH	IP	H	BB	SO	ERA
Leon Cadore	25	14	.641	43				334	352	78	145	3.10
Charles Fullerton	19	12	.613	33				258	283	102	90	3.56
Goodbred	14	14	.500	37				242	258	59	105	2.90
Colwell	10	12	.455	31				222	239	93	84	3.81
S. Smith	0	2	.000	9								

BALTIMORE   4th   74-66   .529   -8   Jack Dunn
Orioles

BATTERS	POS-GAMES	GP	AB	R	H	BI	2B	3B	HR	BB	SO	SB	BA
C. Russell	1B112	112	436	68	133		10	11	2	45	42	11	.305
Larry Kopf	2B75,SS65	140	513	91	150		19	6	2	90	33	26	.292
Sam Crane	SS62	63	221	30	49		6	1	0	17	25	14	.222
J. Ritter	3B	(see multi-team players)											
Bill Lamar	OF124	125	492	61	152		19	5	2	20	31	11	.309
John Bates	OF114	118	420	90	131		20	6	5	92	39	12	.312
Elmer Miller	OF79	79	308	61	104		20	8	9	34	15	22	.338
James McAvoy	C123	131	446	48	103		12	6	0	41	28	14	.231
George Twombly	OF74,2B30,1B21	131	504	83	158		21	10	12	51	27	24	.313
Turner Barber	OF25,3B24	49	192	34	54		8	5	1	15	13	5	.281
Roy Hartzell	2B28,3B18	47	177	25	57		7	7	2	13	14	5	.322
Winston	C20	43	111	9	24		4	0	0	6	6	1	.216
Bill Morrisette	P43	43	98	9	21		2	0	1	5	22	0	.214
Joel Sherman	P38	40	115	16	31		3	0	0	8	10	2	.270
Dan Tipple	P40	40	86	17	10		0	0	0	10	43	1	.116
Crowell	P27	28	67	4	10		1	0	0	3	9	1	.149
Wilson Fewster	SS13	16	49	7	9		0	0	0	11	10	1	.184
Jack Bentley	P11	16	41	6	10		1	1	2	0	10	0	.243
Herb Thormahlen	P14	16	31	2	8		3	0	0	3	9	0	.258

PITCHERS	W	L	PCT	G	GS	CG	SH	IP	H	BB	SO	ERA
Dan Tipple	20	12	.625	40				263	257	127	138	2.57
Joel Sherman	19	16	.543	38				265	302	53	92	2.89
Bill Morrisette	16	13	.552	43				261	259	123	118	3.11
Crowell	9	8	.529	27				181	175	103	63	3.13
Jack Bentley	7	3	.700	11				85	80	17	24	2.12
Lona Jaynes	1	0	1.000	4								
Tom Knowlson	1	2	.333	9				46	57	26	18	4.70
Herb Thormahlen	1	7	.125	14				69	71	28	32	3.65
Newton	0	5	.000	11				53	63	27	12	3.91

TORONTO   5th   73-66   .525   -8.5   Joe Birmingham - Lena Blackburne
Maple Leafs

BATTERS	POS-GAMES	GP	AB	R	H	BI	2B	3B	HR	BB	SO	SB	BA
Dawson Graham	1B140	140	558	65	164		14	7	2	36	38	27	.294
Frank Truesdale	2B143	143	559	74	160		19	3	1	81	53	44	.286
J. Smith	SS83	85	306	36	68		13	4	1	26	65	13	.222
Lena Blackburne	3B85,SS58,P3	143	523	66	146		28	4	0	49	31	22	.279

TORONTO (cont.)
Maple Leafs

BATTERS	POS-GAMES	GP	AB	R	H	BI	2B	3B	HR	BB	SO	SB	BA
John Murray	OF127	127	489	60	122		30	4	0	34	44	31	.249
Harry Thompson	OF93,P19	109	347	58	85		12	7	2	52	25	24	.245
Irving Trout	OF80,3B37	119	399	47	103		14	0	0	49	23	14	.258
William Kelly	C47	51	170	10	37		2	0	0	11	24	3	.217
William McTigue	P38,OF14	61	164	13	49		6	4	1	6	16	1	.299
Paul Krichell	C43	48	140	17	39		3	0	0	15	12	8	.278
Ray McKee	C39	44	139	17	45		5	1	3	16	10	4	.323
Jim Viox	OF42	42	144	18	45		8	2	0	20	9	6	.313
Fred Herbert	P37	38	88	4	16		1	0	0	4	29	0	.182
Joe Birmingham	OF28	37	116	6	29		5	0	0	5	21	0	.250
W. Manning	P28	35	77	4	16		4	0	0	1	5	2	.208
Hogan	3B25	29	97	9	18		3	0	0	4	11	0	.186
Burch	OF24	25	82	14	19		4	0	0	19	13	0	.232
Urban Shocker	P24	24	60	6	17		1	2	1	7	11	0	.283
Hayden	C16	16	54	8	15		2	0	0	4	4	1	.278

PITCHERS	W	L	PCT	G	GS	CG	SH	IP	H	BB	SO	ERA
William McTigue	16	15	.516	38				290	259	88	**187**	1.95
Fred Herbert	16	16	.500	37				247	263	57	59	2.99
Urban Shocker	15	3	**.833**	24				185	115	73	152	**1.31**
W. Manning	8	13	.381	28				174	176	51	73	3.00
Harry Thompson	7	4	.636	19				117	111	28	64	1.93
Brady	4	3	.571	11				70	64	34	30	2.05
Cliff Markle	4	6	.400	11				83	93	46	65	3.80
Russell	2	1	.667	13				46	48	33	14	2.93
Lena Blackburne	1	0	1.000	3								
Rollin Cook	0	1	.000	2								
I. Smith	0	1	.000	1								
Lyons	0	1	.000	1								
McQuillan	0	2	.000	8								

RICHMOND   6th   64-75   .460   -17.5   William Smith
Climbers

BATTERS	POS-GAMES	GP	AB	R	H	BI	2B	3B	HR	BB	SO	SB	BA
Hack Eibel	1B93,2B11	104	374	47	95		10	9	3	46	64	21	.254
John Priest	2B		(see multi-team players)										
Angel Aragon	SS82	84	300	44	95		16	6	0	28	15	14	.317
Frank McDermott	3B121	121	441	67	108		15	6	1	49	28	10	.245
Bill Bankston	OF140	140	511	74	**166**		23	10	3	51	41	13	.325
Tim Hendryx	OF115,3B21	135	489	88	157		29	6	5	85	51	16	.321
Robert Clemens	OF115	118	430	80	126		17	7	1	81	66	26	.293
Bill Reynolds	C104	113	351	33	88		11	4	3	29	40	2	.251
Mickey Kelliher	1B48,OF43	106	360	36	94		14	9	1	23	33	11	.262
O'Donnell	C47	60	169	13	22		3	2	0	16	21	0	.130
Samuel Ross	P38	38	95	13	18		0	2	0	8	15	0	.189
Albert Leake	P23	38	79	7	21		4	3	1			1	.266
Gene Steinbrenner	SS27	34	118	12	38		3	2	0	15	12	6	.322
H. Rhoades	P27	27	63	1	7		1	0	0	5	25	0	.111
Frank McKenry	P31	32	84	3	16		2	0	0	1	22	0	.190
Kircher	2B12	22	68	9	13		3	0	0	5	8	3	.191
Roche	2B20	21	54	6	11		0	0	0	6	7	2	.204
Moore	2B16	20	69	6	12		1	0	0	3	14	1	.174
Ray Keating	P12	12	33	1	8		0	1	0			0	.242
Lute Boone	SS11	11	34	5	9		1	0	0			3	.265

PITCHERS	W	L	PCT	G	GS	CG	SH	IP	H	BB	SO	ERA
Samuel Ross	15	13	.536	38				265	234	90	133	2.85
H. Rhoades	10	13	.435	27				192	185	91	86	3.99
Albert Leake	9	12	.429	23				165	161	63	72	2.62
Frank McKenry	8	11	.421	31				206	264	36	74	4.10
Al Humphries	6	3	.667	13				74	76	19	25	1.83
George Crable	5	5	.500	14				87	72	50	29	2.89
Frank Jarman	3	3	.500	9				59	77	27	22	4.10
Ray Keating	3	7	.300	12				82	81	40	37	3.51
Gleason	2	2	.500	8								
John Verbout	1	1	.500	4								
Mahaffey	0	1	.000	2								

ROCHESTER
Hustlers

7th   60-78   .435   -21   Thomas Leach

BATTERS	POS-GAMES	GP	AB	R	H	BI	2B	3B	HR	BB	SO	SB	BA
Walter Holke	1B121	122	477	81	164		16	5	2	38	52	24	.344
Wes Siglin	2B136	142	533	68	152		20	11	1	31	46	17	.285
Jim McAuley	SS136	136	461	58	118		13	4	0	75	75	24	.256
Art Devlin	3B74	82	289	24	78		9	1	0	31	19	7	.270
Merwin Jacobson	OF133	136	512	88	143		26	8	4	55	83	17	.279
Yale Sloan	OF101	112	434	52	130		15	4	0	30	31	29	.300
Thomas Leach	OF75,3B25	115	390	72	95		17	11	3	66	36	17	.244
George Hale	C85,1B12	105	326	33	86		13	5	0	18	13	9	.264
Taylor Farrell	OF51	55	203	23	47		11	3	0	19	20	7	.232
Charles Dooin	C32,OF12	49	161	16	32		3	1	0	7	10	4	.199
Des Beatty	3B28	38	103	12	24		7	0	0	9	10	0	.233
Fred Hersche	P36	37	81	11	21		4	0	1	3	14	1	.260
Cliff Hill	P35	35	80	9	19		4	1	1	6	19	0	.238
Joe Casey	C32	34	106	9	27		4	0	0	13	10	0	.255
Walt Leverenz	P25	34	90	8	27		2	0	0	1	26	0	.300
Kirmayer	P27	30	74	8	14		1	2	0	7	13	1	.189
William Ritter	P23	23	48	1	8		1	0	0	0	23	0	.167
Charles Babington	3B10	22	77	16	16		2	1	1	6	16	10	.208

PITCHERS		W	L	PCT	G	GS	CG	SH	IP	H	BB	SO	ERA
Cliff Hill		14	16	.467	35				258	227	98	129	1.92
Fred Hersche		11	14	.440	36				227	233	86	91	2.54
Walt Leverenz		9	13	.409	25				187	172	94	103	2.65
Kirmayer		8	9	.471	27				194	203	49	88	2.74
Way		7	6	.538	13				106	122	30	33	3.06
William Ritter		6	11	.353	23				143	135	48	92	2.39
Brown		2	0	1.000	3								
Kramer		2	4	.333	9								
Al Huenke		1	1	.500	4								
Sherman		0	1	.000	3								
Teste		0	3	.000	7								

NEWARK
Indians

8th   52-87   .374   -29.5   Fred Tenney

BATTERS	POS-GAMES	GP	AB	R	H	BI	2B	3B	HR	BB	SO	SB	BA
Art Durgin	1B124	126	469	56	132		23	2	2	44	48	23	.281
Hal Cable	2B123	124	494	56	132		11	1	0	47	48	30	.267
Tom Healy	SS60,OF27,P12	112	379	29	92		12	2	1	33	40	10	.243
Ed Zimmerman	3B		(see multi-team players)										
Leo Witterstatter	OF139	139	525	68	154		17	7	2	49	17	11	.293
Leo Callahan	OF92	101	356	45	110		17	5	3	29	21	10	.309
Horace Milan	OF		(see multi-team players)										
Ben Egan	C89	92	311	25	89		10	5	3	12	30	1	.286
Pius Schwert	C52	84	263	24	61		6	2	0	10	36	6	.232
Henry Stafford	SS23,OF18	41	148	16	34		4	0	0	15	18	8	.230
Walt Smallwood	P38	41	123	9	28		5	0	0	2	22	1	.228
John Enzmann	P34	37	79	10	16		6	2	0	2	16	0	.202
Kibler	3B34	36	136	11	34		2	0	0	16	11	4	.250
Jack Enright	P33	34	80	0	8		1	1	0	1	29	0	.100
Ray Mowe	SS26	26	80	5	20		0	0	0	7	8	2	.250
Chick Shorten	OF25	25	104	13	28		3	1	0	4	3	3	.269
Edwin Pieh	P23	23	53	3	9		1	0	0	4	8	0	.170
Aschenbacher	SS22	22	74	6	13		1	0	0	3	17	2	.176
Roy Wilkinson	P18	18	48	5	4		1	0	0	1	8	0	.083
Fred Tenney		16	22	0	7		0	0	0	1	1	0	.318
Schrier		13	34	5	8		0	0	0			0	.235

PITCHERS		W	L	PCT	G	GS	CG	SH	IP	H	BB	SO	ERA
John Enzmann		14	13	.519	34				226	237	55	105	3.02
Walt Smallwood		14	19	.424	38				304	337	79	79	2.99
Edwin Pieh		8	10	.444	23				152	158	74	50	3.73
Jack Enright		6	18	.250	33				222	193	121	91	3.29
Roy Wilkinson		4	12	.250	18				136	153	58	46	3.64
Mangen		2	1	.667	3				20	15	10	4	3.60
Al Schacht		2	6	.250	20				77	96	30	19	4.45
Tom Healy		1	2	.333	12				53	67	11	21	4.25
Jenkins		0	1	.000	1								
Tom Turner		0	1	.000	1								

NEWARK (cont.)
Bears

PITCHERS	W	L	PCT	G	GS	CG	SH	IP	H	BB	SO	ERA
Wood	0	1	.000	1								
Bressler	0	2	.000	2								

MULTI-TEAM PLAYERS

BATTERS	POS-GAMES	TEAMS	GP	AB	R	H	BI	2B	3B	HR	BB	SO	SB	BA
J. Ritter	3B108,OF19	BAL-NEW	128	468	44	121		20	1	2	23	77	18	.258
Horace Milan	OF102	NEW-ROC	105	390	54	98		10	5	2	47	49	21	.251
Ed Zimmerman	3B90	NEW-BAL	91	311	33	71		15	2	1	48	27	10	.228
John Priest	2B62,P6	MON-RIC	80	276	31	69		5	5	0	25	22	16	.250
Elmer Zacher	OF31	NEW-ROC	43	132	17	34		7	0	2	6	13	7	.258
Phifer Fullenweider	P24	BUF-RIC	24	58	7	14		0	1	0	0	7	1	.241

PITCHERS		TEAMS	W	L	PCT	G	GS	CG	SH	IP	H	BB	SO	ERA
Phifer Fullenweider		BUF-RIC	6	8	.429	24				150	173	45	50	4.08
Gittings		NEW-RIC	3	4	.429	11				56	67	40	17	3.85
Guy Cooper		BUF-RIC	2	6	.250	12				70	69	44	30	3.99
John Priest		MON-RIC	1	3	.250	6								

TEAM BATTING

TEAMS	GP	AB	R	H	BI	2B	3B	HR	BB	SO	SB	BA
BUFFALO	141	4747	693	1331		**194**	61	21	455	557	135	.280
PROVIDENCE	139	4592	621	1225		165	**86**	22	409	458	158	.267
MONTREAL	141	**4911**	**811**	**1366**		**194**	58	**47**	**639**	531	**193**	.278
BALTIMORE	140	4731	695	1329		183	62	40	492	467	152	**.281**
TORONTO	**143**	4696	550	1226		172	36	9	465	479	189	.261
RICHMOND	141	4585	591	1201		161	71	19	494	537	137	.262
ROCHESTER	142	4773	629	1284		173	61	14	451	**573**	183	.269
NEWARK	139	4602	475	1141		147	33	15	406	516	141	.248
	563	37637	5065	10103		1389	468	187	3811	4118	1288	.268

1917
FAREWELL TOUR

Baseball superstar Nap Lajoie had enjoyed a stellar major league career. Beginning in 1896, the second baseman had played in 21 major league seasons for four different teams. Along the way, Lajoie won four batting titles, including an American League record of .422 in 1901, leading to a .339 career average. He was a well-loved player—many say the best second baseman of all time. But as he neared the end of his major league stay, his play started to slip. When Lajoie batted a lackluster .246 for the Philadelphia Athletics in 1916, some thought his baseball career was over. As it turned out, Lajoie had one more good season left. But it wouldn't be in the majors; it would be on the fields of the International League.

In January 1917, the Toronto Maple Leafs announced they had enlisted the services of Nap Lajoie both to play and to manage the team. As the season started, throngs turned out to see the popular star one more time. Several International League teams staged "Lajoie Days" to honor him.

Toronto, after a dismal start, clawed their way into the International League race. By June, led by Lajoie's efforts, the team reached fourth. By August, they had climbed to the top. There, they held off the Providence Grays to cop the flag by a game and a half. Baltimore finished third, followed by Newark in fourth and Rochester in fifth. Buffalo, Montreal, and Richmond finished on the last three rungs. In the batting race, Lajoie proved himself still a star, winning the title with a lusty .380 average, the league's highest in 20 years. He also led the circuit in hits (221) and doubles (39). Not a bad season for someone whose career was nearing its end.

Other International League leaders in 1917 included Harry Damrau from Montreal, who hit the most home runs (16), and Toronto's Harry Thompson with 25 pitching wins. Vean Gregg of Providence won two honors as he sported a circuit-best 1.72 earned run average in addition to a strikeout crown (249).

In April 1918, after a salary dispute, Nap Lajoie was granted his release. He quickly joined the Indianapolis Indians of the American Association. Here he played and managed the club until the circuit disbanded in July because of World War I. It would be Lajoie's last season.

Nap Lajoie's triumphal tour through the International League proved a fitting tribute to one of baseball's finest. Here, fans had a chance to see him go out in style, winning a batting title as he led his team to the pennant—the only pennant Nap Lajoie won in his entire career.

TORONTO Maple Leafs

1st 93-61 .604 Nap Lajoie

BATTERS	POS-GAMES	GP	AB	R	H	BI	2B	3B	HR	BB	SO	SB	BA
Nap Lajoie	1B74,2B77	151	581	83	**221**		39	4	5			4	**.380**
Frank Truesdale	2B	(see multi-team players)											
W. Murray	SS47	47	173	16	35		5	2	0			4	.202
Lena Blackburne	3B101,SS48	154	564	46	150		23	5	3			21	.266
Merwin Jacobson	OF154	155	599	106	173		26	13	6			12	.289
George Whiteman	OF140	140	530	104	181		32	10	7			23	.342
Jesse Altenburg	OF80	80	314	64	96		8	3	1			20	.306
Louis LaLonge	C91	93	305	38	77		5	0	0			5	.252
Joe Schultz	3B55,OF49	105	412	52	129		18	7	3			19	.313
Harry Thompson	P38,OF25	79	210	26	60		13	2	0			7	.286
Dawson Graham	1B67	68	243	25	65		7	2	0			14	.267
William Kelly	C65	68	223	16	42		2	1	0			6	.188
Bunn Hearn	P37	40	123	9	29		4	0	3			0	.236
J. Smith	SS38	38	128	13	31		4	1	4			6	.242
Hal Justin	P31	31	66	5	5		2	0	0			1	.076
Irving Trout		18	57	8	8		0	0	0			3	.140
George Zabel	P16	17	46	2	10		1	0	0			0	.217
Dan Costello	1B16	16	62	9	13		1	1	0			2	.210
C. Allen	OF13	13	41	5	10		1	1	0			0	.243

PITCHERS	W	L	PCT	G	GS	CG	SH	IP	H	BB	SO	ERA
Harry Thompson	**25**	11	.694	38			5	318	289	85	123	2.46
Bunn Hearn	23	9	**.719**	37			4	310	292	62	133	2.03
George Zabel	10	5	.667	16			2	122	111	33	58	2.43
Hal Justin	10	10	.500	31			2	193	207	91	68	3.74
Al Gould	4	5	.444	9			1	73	59	26	37	2.71

PROVIDENCE Grays

2nd 90-61 .596 -1.5 Jack Egan

BATTERS	POS-GAMES	GP	AB	R	H	BI	2B	3B	HR	BB	SO	SB	BA
Guy Tutwiler	1B121,OF22	147	542	73	140		9	**17**	1			15	.258
Mike Massey	2B74	74	275	38	66		8	2	1			13	.240
James Cooney	SS134	137	522	73	146		11	7	1			26	.280
Fred Thomas	3B153	153	543	79	137		19	16	4			20	.252
Ed Onslow	OF117,1B27	144	543	81	146		15	9	2			29	.269
Ray Powell	OF77	77	307	55	84		7	14	1			12	.273
George Twombly	OF65	66	249	42	67		7	5	1			9	.269
Walter Mayer	C78	79	213	44	62		9	3	2			8	.291
Fred Brainard	2B63,OF31	101	396	84	116		21	9	12			35	.293
Edwin Eayrs	OF62,P21	87	266	35	65		10	2	0			10	.244
Walter Rehg	OF57	70	276	58	84		12	8	1			13	.304
Nick Allen	C63	65	223	25	53		6	2	0			2	.238
Frank Kane	OF40	46	142	26	43		5	3	1			3	.303
Wallace Shultz	P36	38	100	14	31		5	1	2			0	.310
C. Peters	P37	37	86	11	14		4	0	0			0	.163
S. Gregg	P31	31	90	3	21		1	1	1			1	.233
William McTigue	P21	31	64	11	20		2	5	1			0	.312
Norm McNeil	C13	24	55	5	17		0	0	0			1	.309
Frank Shellenback	P24	24	51	9	14		3	1	3			0	.274
Ed Reulbach	P19	19	36	7	10		1	0	0			0	.278

PITCHERS	W	L	PCT	G	GS	CG	SH	IP	H	BB	SO	ERA
S. Gregg	21	9	.700	31			4	267	193	76	**249**	**1.72**
Wallace Shultz	16	17	.485	36			1	277	271	93	98	2.89
C. Peters	15	10	.600	37			0	244	257	63	76	2.55
Ed Reulbach	10	5	.667	19			1	120	117	55	63	2.85
Frank Shellenback	9	6	.600	24			0	139	148	55	53	3.04
Edwin Eayrs	9	7	.563	21			0	129	112	71	76	3.63
William McTigue	7	4	.636	21			0	124	119	44	41	2.48

BALTIMORE Orioles

3rd 88-61 .591 -2.5 Jack Dunn

BATTERS	POS-GAMES	GP	AB	R	H	BI	2B	3B	HR	BB	SO	SB	BA
Alva Williams	1B84	85	309	56	86		16	3	3			11	.278

BALTIMORE (cont.)
Orioles

BATTERS	POS-GAMES	GP	AB	R	H	BI	2B	3B	HR	BB	SO	SB	BA
Wilson Fewster	2B72	97	331	49	99		7	0	1			16	.299
Maurice Shannon	SS95	95	344	47	86		14	6	3			5	.250
Art Bues	3B150	150	600	75	165		27	14	4			22	.275
Turner Barber	OF149	149	619	111	218		28	12	0			19	.352
Baldomero Acosta	OF144	144	557	119	153		28	13	1			27	.275
Bill Lamar	OF105	106	411	54	119		19	6	0			6	.290
James McAvoy	C110	123	418	47	131		25	1	6			12	.313
Jack Bentley	1B65,OF21	93	362	59	124		17	11	5			3	.342
Alex Schaufele	C52	54	145	19	32		1	2	0			1	.221
Herb Thormahlen	P46	46	117	8	23		4	0	0			1	.197
Cliff Hill	P41	43	112	16	28		3	2	0			2	.250
Sam Newton	P34	35	63	12	14		1	1	0			1	.222
Jim Parnham	P33	34	100	5	16		5	1	0			0	.160
Otis Lawry	OF26	29	101	20	40		1	0	1			9	.396
Joel Sherman	P14	19	41	7	10		2	0	0			0	.243

PITCHERS		W	L	PCT	G	GS	CG	SH	IP	H	BB	SO	ERA
Herb Thormahlen		25	12	.677	46			3	329	301	89	124	2.74
Cliff Hill		20	12	.625	41			2	278	259	117	118	3.02
Jim Parnham		16	9	.640	33			1	244	240	84	87	2.95
Sam Newton		8	9	.471	34			0	169	172	68	70	4.32
Joel Sherman		6	3	.667	14			0	83	94	37	32	4.93

NEWARK   4th   86-68   .558   -7   Thomas Needham
Bears

BATTERS	POS-GAMES	GP	AB	R	H	BI	2B	3B	HR	BB	SO	SB	BA
C. Russell	1B122	125	449	63	102		15	6	1			14	.227
Frank Fuller	2B157	157	646	95	163		28	5	1			20	.252
John Lewis	SS55,3B34,1B23	129	468	45	118		12	3	2			10	.252
Gus Getz	3B126	126	483	55	145		16	2	0			26	.300
Leo Callahan	OF143	147	544	81	170		19	5	2			23	.313
Ross Eldred	OF139	143	487	67	131		26	5	6			27	.269
Bruno Haas	OF129	132	497	52	127		20	8	5			18	.256
Ben Egan	C100	106	337	21	78		16	2	0			2	.231
E. Blackwell	C67	76	234	12	38		4	0	0			1	.162
E. Brandell	SS54	61	193	23	46		2	3	0			5	.238
Howard Camp	OF50	50	192	25	58		10	4	0			4	.302
Walt Smallwood	P45	50	105	7	18		3	2	1			0	.171
John Enzmann	P43	46	234	12	38		4	0	0			1	.162
Sam Ross	P36	46	96	15	20		2	0	0			0	.208
Ray Mowe	SS43	43	158	21	30		0	2	0			8	.190
Roy Wilkinson	P33	35	74	7	9		1	0	0			0	.121
Bob McGraw	P30	30	60	2	9		2	0	0			1	.150
George Pennington	P25	27	60	4	12		1	1	0			0	.200

PITCHERS		W	L	PCT	G	GS	CG	SH	IP	H	BB	SO	ERA
Walt Smallwood		21	15	.583	45			4	283	273	67	109	2.99
Sam Ross		17	12	.586	36			1	269	257	110	100	2.94
John Enzmann		17	15	.531	43			4	294	269	57	92	2.30
Roy Wilkinson		12	6	.667	33			3	222	177	105	81	2.39
George Pennington		11	10	.524	25			1	162	125	68	85	2.28
Bob McGraw		8	9	.471	30			0	182	162	94	98	3.17

ROCHESTER   5th   72-82   .468   -21   Mickey Doolan
Hustlers

BATTERS	POS-GAMES	GP	AB	R	H	BI	2B	3B	HR	BB	SO	SB	BA
Jose Rodriguez	1B139,2B16	155	615	70	155		18	7	0			33	.252
Robert Fisher	2B80,OF33	115	456	63	118		23	1	0			20	.259
Mickey Doolan	SS88,2B15	105	365	43	104		10	4	0			4	.285
J. Schepner	3B64,SS68	138	462	52	121		12	3	0			18	.262
Edgar Collins	OF119	125	441	42	91		8	5	0			14	.206
Taylor Farrell	OF107	107	363	63	105		11	9	2			12	.289
A. Schweitzer	OF89	90	323	45	90		8	1	1			9	.279

ROCHESTER (cont.)
Hustlers

BATTERS	POS-GAMES	GP	AB	R	H	BI	2B	3B	HR	BB	SO	SB	BA
Gus Sandberg	C97	107	316	27	72		8	2	2			5	.228
Ross Young	3B55,OF46,2B35	140	506	85	180		18	5	1			34	.356
Lew Wendell	C63,3B37	130	415	37	88		15	4	0			9	.212
C. Lohman	P41,OF10	57	159	12	34		3	0	0			2	.213
C. Causey	P39	47	113	7	16		0	0	0			2	.142
Al Schacht	P42	42	90	3	17		2	0	0			0	.189
Joseph Lotz	P32	36	84	9	16		4	0	0			0	.190
George Kelly	OF32	32	120	16	36		14	1	4			7	.300
G. Smith	P24	24	62	1	2		0	0	0			0	.032
LaRue Kirby	OF14	16	58	4	14		1	1	0			0	.241
L. Simmons	OF13	14	45	9	12		0	0	0			5	.267

PITCHERS	W	L	PCT	G	GS	CG	SH	IP	H	BB	SO	ERA
C. Lohman	24	15	.615	41			4	334	316	69	119	2.48
C. Causey	17	13	.567	39			1	292	257	118	122	2.40
Al Schacht	12	21	.364	42			2	268	296	97	81	4.00
G. Smith	8	11	.421	24			1	178	155	62	101	2.32
Joseph Lotz	7	14	.333	32			1	211	204	119	97	3.02

BUFFALO   6th   67-84   .444   -24.5   Patsy Donovan
Bisons

BATTERS	POS-GAMES	GP	AB	R	H	BI	2B	3B	HR	BB	SO	SB	BA
John Hummel	1B141	146	511	77	136		21	7	2			10	.266
Robert Gill	2B102,OF40	145	530	64	139		21	3	1			11	.262
Joe McDonald	SS137	142	502	69	124		19	7	6			7	.247
Al Carlstrom	3B140	146	545	76	134		19	8	0			9	.246
Merlin Kopp	OF149	150	577	101	169		10	12	3			57	.293
George Jackson	OF111	112	404	46	111		20	3	3			7	.275
Lester Channell	OF94	94											
Jack Onslow	C91	93	271	28	59		7	4	0			1	.218
Albert Tyson	P28	51	101	6	25		2	4	0			1	.247
Jack Steinfeldt	OF48	48											
Thomas Daly	C42	47	157	24	54		6	2	0			4	.344
Joseph Engel	P40	46	99	12	15		1	0	0			0	.152
John Tuman	OF14	42	115	11	24		1	1	0			5	.208
Dick McCabe	P38	38	83	3	10		1	0	0			0	.120
M. Killilea	2B24,3B10	36	129	7	27		5	0	0			1	.209
Hal Cable	2B13	27	68	8	12		0	0	0			6	.176
Joe Casey	C23	23	73	4	19		2	1	0			1	.260
Weldon Wyckoff	P20	22	52	6	10		2	1	0			0	.192
James O'Neill	2B10	15	39	3	9		2	1	0			0	.231

PITCHERS	W	L	PCT	G	GS	CG	SH	IP	H	BB	SO	ERA
Dick McCabe	15	13	.536	38			1	259	264	83	94	3.06
Joseph Engel	13	17	.433	40			1	269	278	126	108	3.68
Albert Tyson	12	13	.480	28			2	212	204	93	47	3.19
Weldon Wyckoff	6	11	.353	20			1	140	139	73	53	2.76
Jimmy Ring	4	2	.667	6			2	50	41	28	13	1.62

MONTREAL   7th   56-94   .373   -35   Dan Howley
Royals

BATTERS	POS-GAMES	GP	AB	R	H	BI	2B	3B	HR	BB	SO	SB	BA
J. Slattery	1B110	111	425	43	107		15	5	3			6	.252
H. Damrau	2B99,1B28	138	527	73	137		25	12	16			11	.260
Jim McAuley	SS120	120	476	71	123		13	6	0			19	.258
Ed Zimmerman	3B141	141	557	77	150		23	4	13			10	.269
Herb Moran	OF150	150	556	96	158		22	3	0			27	.289
Paul Smith	OF136	138	526	67	159		14	11	1			19	.302
William Holden	OF116	135	416	48	113		21	8	5			6	.272
Dan Howley	C79	85	276	36	67		12	0	5			3	.243
Ted Cather	OF61,2B15	87	321	46	77		9	1	8			8	.240
Tom Madden	C76	80	268	30	64		9	2	4			4	.238

MONTREAL (cont.)
Royals

BATTERS	POS-GAMES	GP	AB	R	H	BI	2B	3B	HR	BB	SO	SB	BA
B. Duffy	P33	51	137	16	45		8	6	1			0	.328
Ed Gerner	P41	46	145	14	26		4	2	2			1	.180
William Purtell	2B35	35	133	10	37		2	0	1			2	.278
Waite Hoyt	P28	28	83	5	16		0	1	0			1	.193
Oscar Major	SS24	24	90	5	19		3	0	0			1	.211

PITCHERS		W	L	PCT	G	GS	CG	SH	IP	H	BB	SO	ERA
Ed Gerner		20	20	.500	41			5	337	349	113	108	2.93
B. Duffy		9	17	.346	33			1	224	257	83	69	3.54
Waite Hoyt		7	17	.292	28			1	215	206	78	65	2.51

RICHMOND   8th   53-94   .361   -36.5   William Smith -
Virginians   Otto Knabe

BATTERS	POS-GAMES	GP	AB	R	H	BI	2B	3B	HR	BB	SO	SB	BA
Hack Eibel	1B109,P21	125	445	73	134		32	6	4			14	.301
Otto Knabe	2B82	88	278	40	80		8	2	2			9	.288
M. McGaffigan	SS84	84	342	47	92		9	3	1			26	.269
Frank McDermott	3B65	65	242	30	63		11	0	0			7	.260
Bill Bankston	OF131	131	507	59	152		21	16	2			18	.300
Charles Hanford	OF123	125	464	82	118		22	8	12			17	.254
Robert Clemens	OF116	116	435	69	126		19	8	9			20	.290
Bill Reynolds	C99	111	340	26	82		12	5	7			1	.241
George Distell	OF68,1B24,3B17	121	389	52	99		6	5	2			15	.254
Art Koehler	C38,1B29	84	247	30	63		11	0	5			4	.255
Sam McConnell	SS52	80	305	41	71		7	4	0			10	.233
William Conroy	3B59	60	219	28	54		3	1	0			6	.247
Edwin Mooers	2B21,SS11	44	148	8	24		2	1	0			0	.162
William Adams	P42	43	100	7	16		2	0	0			0	.160
William Donahue	P22	24	55	6	6		3	0	0			0	.109
Charles Young	P19	24	39	0	10		0	0	0			1	.256
John Kerr	C9	17	39	6	11		0	0	2			0	.282

PITCHERS		W	L	PCT	G	GS	CG	SH	IP	H	BB	SO	ERA
William Adams		11	19	.367	42			1	291	312	134	99	3.59
Hack Eibel		8	9	.471	21			1	145	163	56	46	3.73
Charles Young		6	7	.462	19			1	113	102	72	54	3.58
William Donahue		6	11	.353	22			0	136	157	67	43	3.84
Guy Hoffman		4	3	.571	14			0	71	79	25	28	4.82
L. Magalis		4	4	.500	12			0	63	68	34	25	4.14
William Stewart		2	2	.500	8			0	57	68	21	23	5.53

MULTI-TEAM PLAYERS

BATTERS	POS-GAMES	TEAMS	GP	AB	R	H	BI	2B	3B	HR	BB	SO	SB	BA
Frank Truesdale	2B152	BAL-TOR	152	618	102	170		15	5	1			28	.275
John Warhop	P36,SS10	BAL-TOR	55	160	16	33		8	3	1			2	.206
Jack Enright	P39	TOR-RIC	47	111	5	15		4	0	0			0	.135
Fred Hersche	P36	ROC-MON	39	114	13	29		5	0	2			0	.254
Sterling Stryker	P32	ROC-MON	33	60	3	9		0	0	0			0	.150
Albert Leake	P31	BUF-TOR	32	73	11	13		2	0	0			0	.179
Dan Tipple	P31	TOR-BAL	31	82	2	8		0	0	0			0	.097
Lona Jaynes	P30	MON-BUF	30	76	7	15		1	2	2			0	.198
Frank Lyons	P16	TOR-MON	16	37	1	5		0	0	0			0	.135
George Gaw	P15	BUF-PRO	15	33	1	9		0	0	0			0	.273

PITCHERS		TEAMS	W	L	PCT	G	GS	CG	SH	IP	H	BB	SO	ERA
John Warhop		BAL-TOR	15	10	.600	36			3	240	252	92	75	3.94
Albert Leake		BUF-TOR	13	12	.520	31			0	211	196	84	82	3.16
Fred Hersche		ROC-MON	13	18	.419	36			1	279	290	115	108	3.07
Dan Tipple		TOR-BAL	11	14	.440	31			1	228	200	125	91	3.16
Jack Enright		TOR-RIC	11	19	.367	39			2	270	260	**168**	89	3.33
Lona Jaynes		MON-BUF	8	14	.364	30			1	220	229	114	98	3.11
Sterling Stryker		ROC-MON	6	13	.316	32			1	157	169	88	58	3.95

MULTI-TEAM PLAYERS (cont.)

PITCHERS	TEAMS	W	L	PCT	G	GS	CG	SH	IP	H	BB	SO	ERA
George Gaw	BUF-PRO	5	6	.455	14			0	91	100	25	27	3.06
Frank Lyons	TOR-MON	1	9	.100	16			0	102	106	30	26	4.15

TEAM BATTING

TEAMS	GP	AB	R	H	BI	2B	3B	HR	BB	SO	SB	BA
TORONTO	156	5225	710	1479		**216**	54	33	495	452	201	**.283**
PROVIDENCE	153	5053	783	1353		158	**101**	35	**578**	459	**207**	.268
BALTIMORE	151	**5268**	**798**	**1491**		212	81	23	544	531	171	.283
NEWARK	**157**	5234	639	1310		182	48	18	489	578	159	.250
ROCHESTER	156	5137	610	1298		165	46	10	552	528	190	.253
BUFFALO	152	4956	626	1235		162	68	21	555	535	128	.249
MONTREAL	151	5187	666	1344		186	61	**62**	572	505	121	.259
RICHMOND	148	4913	622	1251		171	60	48	518	**606**	155	.255
	612	40973	5454	10761		1452	519	250	4303	4194	1332	.263

1918
SOLE SURVIVOR

By 1918, the United States was engaged in World War I. As a result, the 1918 baseball season was in jeopardy. Eventually, ten minor leagues decided to take the gamble and start the 1918 season. Of these ten, only one survived.

Because of the war, many International League executives wanted to discontinue the circuit after the 1917 season. Interest in baseball had lagged, and many players had joined the service or a war-related industry. After the 1917 campaign, the Buffalo franchise was bankrupt. When three other teams, Richmond, Providence, and Montreal, announced they would cease operations, the International League scrambled for replacements. Reorganizing itself, the league (temporarily using the title New International League) found new backers for the Buffalo team and placed new teams in Syracuse, Jersey City, and Binghamton.

To most Americans, World War I was a remote conflict on distant battlefields. However, the war was brought right to America's shores when German U-boats attacked just a few miles off the Massachusetts coast during the summer of 1918. In addition, Secretary of War Newton Baker issued his "work or fight" order. This edict, aimed squarely at businesses such as baseball, proved to be the death knell for the minor leagues. All but one closed up shop by mid–July.

The minor league's sole survivor was the International League. Despite lagging attendance, and fluctuating rosters as players left to join the war effort (Jersey City used over 60 players), the league completed its schedule with only one casualty: The Syracuse franchise moved to Hamilton in August. Toronto squeaked out the pennant over Binghamton on the season's last day, while Baltimore placed third. Newark, Rochester, Buffalo, Syracuse/Hamilton, and Jersey City rounded out the standings. Howard McLarry from Binghamton won the batting title (.385), while Toronto's Fred Lear won the home run crown with a total of five. Baltimore's Ralph Worrell won the most games (25), while Rochester's Harry Heitman and Godfrey Brogan boasted the lowest earned run average (1.32) and most strikeouts (157).

The International League had demonstrated impressive resilience. When all other minor leagues went down in flames, the International persevered and gave its fans much-needed entertainment for the duration.

TORONTO Maple Leafs   1st   88-39   .693   Dan Howley

BATTERS	POS-GAMES	GP	AB	R	H	BI	2B	3B	HR	BB	SO	SB	BA
Ed Onslow	1B100	100	358	61	114		9	6	2			33	.318
Fred Lear	2B80,1B18	99	345	76	119		14	8	5			27	.345
Joseph Wagner	SS83,2B13	96	348	63	89		16	3	2			26	.256
William Purtell	3B98	101	367	43	114		8	1	0			12	.311
Alex Reilley	OF65	65	258	54	72		3	0	0			27	.279
Leo Callahan	OF56,1B	60	208	45	66		14	2	1			15	.317
John Mokan	OF53	55	184	29	39		3	6	1			8	.212
Fred Fisher	C87	91	298	27	63		8	3	2			2	.211
Andy Anderson	2B31,OF26,SS16	77	284	22	75		15	3	0			8	.264
Fred Hersche	P29,OF18	58	180	28	40		5	1	0			3	.222
Dan Howley	C45,OF	50	163	14	26		3	0	0			3	.159
John Warhop	OF27,SS11,P7	49	177	16	36		4	0	0			8	.203
Loren Thrasher	OF38	41	162	10	33		11	1	0			7	.204
Hal Justin	P32	32	98	13	18		4	2	0			0	.184
Alex Peterson	P27	28	73	5	5		0	0	0			0	.069
Frank Dolan	OF,3B,SS,1B	22	81	12	21		2	1	1			4	.259
Fred Bailey	OF21	21	76	14	19		6	0	0			6	.250
Frederick Lied	OF18	18	77	9	23		3	2	0			2	.299
Eusebio Gonzales	SS11,3B	16	55	13	15		1	0	0			9	.272
Sam Lewis	P12	12	36	1	5		1	0	0			0	.139
George Crable	P7,OF	8	22		7		1	0	0			0	.318
Lore Bader	OF,P3	7	25		6		2	0	0			0	.240
Herb Thormahlen	P2	2	3		1		0	0	0			0	.333
Bannon	PH	1	1	0	0		0	0	0			0	.000

PITCHERS		W	L	PCT	G	GS	CG	SH	IP	H	BB	SO	ERA
Fred Hersche		21	6	.778	29	26	25		244	205	80	118	1.88
Hal Justin		19	10	.655	32	30	27		272	247	71	87	2.75
Alex Peterson		18	8	.692	27	25	23		236	190	59	115	2.06
Sam Lewis		7	2	.778	12	9	8		95	73	24	44	1.61
John Warhop		4	2	.667	7	6	6		41	46	16	27	3.73
Lore Bader		3	0	1.000	3	3	3		27	16	6	15	
George Crable		2	3	.400	7	6	5		52	57	29	33	4.50
Herb Thormahlen		0	1	.000	2	1	1		11	11	2	3	

BINGHAMTON Bingoes   2nd   85-38   .691   -1   Charles Hartman

BATTERS	POS-GAMES	GP	AB	R	H	BI	2B	3B	HR	BB	SO	SB	BA
Howard McLarry	1B103	103	335	51	129		**26**	7	4			15	**.385**
Charles Hartman	2B117	117	448	44	99		11	2	1			13	.221
Leo Hanley	SS113,OF	113	380	38	75		12	5	0			5	.197
Ed Zimmerman	3B86	86	323	66	72		12	2	1			16	.223
James Riley	OF115	115	424	62	126		18	7	0			21	.297
William Kay	OF88	90	339	61	110		16	12	1			9	.324
Fred Oakes	OF48	49	187	21	45		5	3	0			10	.241
William Fischer	C70,OF14	86	398	52	101		11	4	1			20	.254
Harry Hooper	3B37,OF23,2B	68	252	35	62		4	0	0			8	.246
John Haddock	C37	49	134	5	28		5	1	0			0	.209
Peter Knisely	OF41	41	146	28	54		9	5	0			9	.370
Festus Higgins	P32	32	72	9	20		3	1	0			0	.278
John Beckvermit	P25	29	74	7	21		2	0	0			2	.284
Sam Frock	P22	24	51	3	10		3	0	0			1	.196
Luther Barnes	P22	22	52	4	12		1	0	0			0	.230
John Verbout	P17,OF,2B	18	50	4	7		1	0	0			0	.140
James Smith	C10,1B	14	39	4	8		1	0	0			0	.205
Bill Haines	C10	13	32	3	4		2	0	0			0	.125
Webb	P6	13	25	2	8		1	0	0			0	.320
O'Rourke	SS11	11	39	5	11		2	1	0			3	.282
Pete Shields	1B	8	29		8		5	1	0			2	.276
Oscar Tuero	P8	8	23		2		0	0	0			0	.087
Michael Bills	P8	8	22		5		1	0	0			0	.227
Brennan	C,2B	7	21		3		2	0	0			0	.143
Earl Champion	P6	6	16		3		0	0	0			0	.188
Joe Gingras	P4	4	13		3		0	0	0			0	.231

PITCHERS		W	L	PCT	G	GS	CG	SH	IP	H	BB	SO	ERA
John Beckvermit		17	4	**.810**	25	22	16		177	123	59	104	1.48
Festus Higgins		15	4	.789	32	21	16		210	178	51	68	1.89

BINGHAMTON (cont.)
Bingoes

PITCHERS	W	L	PCT	G	GS	CG	SH	IP	H	BB	SO	ERA
Luther Barnes	13	4	.765	22	16	11		146	126	42	60	1.85
JohnVerbout	9	4	.692	17	12	10		117	107	24	33	1.61
Sam Frock	9	9	.500	22	15	14		143	117	29	75	1.88
Oscar Tuero	5	2	.714	8	8	6		62	54	15	40	1.89
Earl Champion	4	1	.800	6	5	3		47	38	14	16	1.72
Michael Bills	4	4	.500	8	7	6		68	65	22	15	2.39
Joe Gingras	3	0	1.000	4	3	2		34	22	11	12	
Webb	3	3	.500	6	5	5		44	53	19	12	2.54

BALTIMORE
3rd   74-53   .583   -14   Jack Dunn
Orioles

BATTERS	POS-GAMES	GP	AB	R	H	BI	2B	3B	HR	BB	SO	SB	BA
Francis Griffin	1B113	113	431	62	125		14	10	2			20	.290
Otis Lawry	2B111,SS	121	470	78	149		11	11	2			35	.317
Sam Crane	SS48	48	181	27	50		8	3	1			16	.276
Max Bishop	3B121,SS	125	465	59	121		15	2	0			8	.260
James Mulvey	OF128	128	486	81	149		24	9	2			17	.307
Sumpter Clarke	OF82	83	295	33	76		3	8	0			14	.258
Dutch Zwilling	OF44,1B	45	156	21	43		11	4	1			9	.276
Ben Egan	C105	105	366	37	98		14	5	2			9	.268
Bert Lewis	P32,OF15,SS,1B,2B	63	162	16	35		5	1	0			1	.216
Ralph Worrell	P,OF	48	143	8	25		5	0	0			1	.175
Jim Parnham	P,1B	47	129	13	32		5	2	3			0	.248
Clare McAlpin	SS45,3B	46	154	21	33		2	0	0			2	.214
Joe Shannon	OF43	44	170	28	57		10	2	3			5	.335
Allen Herbert	P20,OF	24	72	6	15		1	0	0			0	.208
Del Mason	P15	24	44	4	14		6	0	0			0	.318
Charles Dysert	OF21	21	78	14	15		2	0	0			1	.193
Parker	C20	20	69	5	18		2	0	1			3	.261
Blythe	OF19	19	70	6	13		3	0	0			0	.186
O'Keefe	SS13	14	45		8		0	0	0			0	.178
Rudolph Kneisch	P14	14	26	1	3		0	0	0			0	.115
Dawson Graham	OF,2B,1B	10	41	4	6		3	0	0			1	.146
A. Smith	SS,3B	9	32		7		2	0	0			2	.219
Charles Loudenslager	2B	7	26		12		2	2	0			0	.462
Refaumn	OF	6	20		3		0	0	0			1	.150
Whalen	OF	6	14		3		0	0	0			1	.214
Alex Schaufele	C	5	9		1		0	0	0			1	.111
Jack Dunn, Jr.	OF,P,2B	4	12		3		0	0	0			0	.250
Deinzer	P4	4	9		2		0	0	0			0	.222
Kelly	OF	3	9		1		0	0	0			0	.111
S. Herpsberger	P3	3	8	0	0		0	0	0			0	.000
Brown	OF	3	7	0	0		0	0	0			0	.000
Stroh	3B	2	4		1		0	0	0			0	.250
Connice	P1	1	2	0	0		0	0	0			0	.000
Monahan	P1	1	2	0	0		0	0	0			0	.000
Shutz	PH	1	1	0	0		0	0	0			0	.000
Rhuark	P1	1	0	0	0		0	0	0			0	----

PITCHERS	W	L	PCT	G	GS	CG	SH	IP	H	BB	SO	ERA
Ralph Worrell	25	10	.714	40	37	30		321	268	112	156	2.24
Jim Parnham	22	10	.688	34	27	22		259	202	98	138	2.15
Bert Lewis	12	12	.500	32	21	16		207	184	89	82	2.35
Allen Herbert	8	8	.500	20	16	10		142	143	60	59	3.23
Del Mason	4	3	.571	15	9	6		61	61	23	20	2.66
Rudolph Kneisch	2	6	.250	14	9	6		85	81	28	34	2.57
S. Herpsberger	1	1	.500	3	2	2		20	21	6	4	
Monahan	0	1	.000	1	1	0		6	5	4	2	
Deinzer	0	2	.000	4	2	1		25	29	18	13	
Connice	0	0	----	1	1	0		6	12	1	2	
Jack Dunn, Jr.	0	0	----	1	0	0		2	2	2	1	
Rhuark	0	0	----	1	0	0		0	0	1	0	

NEWARK
4th   64-63   .504   -24   Tom McCarthy
Bears

BATTERS	POS-GAMES	GP	AB	R	H	BI	2B	3B	HR	BB	SO	SB	BA
Adam Swigler	1B46,OF21,P12	78	267	29	64		8	5	1			7	.239

NEWARK (cont.)
Bears

BATTERS	POS-GAMES	GP	AB	R	H	BI	2B	3B	HR	BB	SO	SB	BA
Walter Shay	2B94,SS	104	413	59	102		11	1	1			19	.247
John Stansbury	SS27	27	106	8	26		2	1	0			4	.245
Thomas Downey	3B116	124	448	72	115		12	1	0			25	.257
Ted Cather	OF126	127	474	65	132		17	6	1			25	.278
John Jacobs	OF76,SS11	87	282	35	79		7	4	1			22	.280
Guy Zinn	OF	(see multi-team players)											
Tom Madden	C101	108	337	35	100		10	1	1			6	.297
Ed Rommel	P32,OF14,2B20,SS,1B	78	242	18	50		6	2	0			2	.206
Germany Schaefer	1B21,OF,SS	32	129	18	31		5	0	0			9	.240
Harry Leibold	OF25	25	82	5	14		0	0	0			0	.171
Ed Holly	SS24	24	89	15	27		6	0	0			3	.303
John Ross	P15,OF	24	75	4	18		1	2	0			2	.240
Fiedler	SS23	23	71	13	15		1	1	0			5	.211
Aicer Jensen	P20,OF	22	55	1	12		1	0	0			0	.218
Harry Damrau	SS	18	63	8	21		2	0	0			4	.333
John Ogden	P11	17	54	2	9		1	1	0			0	.167
Kelly	C14,OF	16	40	1	4		1	0	0			4	.100
O'Brien	C14	15	40	3	7		2	0	0			1	.175
Seymour	OF11	13	41	2	9		0	0	0			0	.219
Wilbert Hubbell	P11,OF	13	34	4	4		0	1	0			1	.118
Frank Bruggy	OF,C	11	43	9	16		3	0	1			5	.372
Frank Woodward	P6,OF	11	33	2	8		2	0	0			0	.242
Clyde Barfoot	P7,OF	10	27	1	3		0	0	0			0	.111
Waite Hoyt	P6,OF	7	24		5		0	0	0			0	.208
Burke	SS	3	9		1		0	0	0			0	.111
Kane	OF	1	4	0	0		0	0	0			0	.000
Corcoran	SS	1	3		1		0	0	0			0	.333
Jack McCarthy	PH	1	1		1		0	0	0			0	1.000
Jack Doscher	P1	1	0	0	0		0	0	0			0	----

PITCHERS	W	L	PCT	G	GS	CG	SH	IP	H	BB	SO	ERA
Ed Rommel	12	15	.444	32	27	25		235	213	62	80	2.22
John Ross	10	4	.714	15	14	11		124	112	45	67	2.32
Aicer Jensen	8	10	.444	20	17	15		158	126	40	64	2.11
Wilbert Hubbell	7	4	.636	11	11	11		92	77	15	32	1.57
Adam Swigler	6	4	.600	12	8	7		89	83	30	44	2.53
Clyde Barfoot	5	2	.714	7	7	6		56	56	13	17	1.29
John Ogden	5	5	.500	11	10	10		79	60	28	41	1.49
Frank Woodward	4	2	.667	6	5	5		51	26	23	22	1.41
Waite Hoyt	2	4	.333	6	6	6		51	37	11	27	2.29
McLaughlin	1	1	.500	3	2	2		21	26	11	6	
Jack Doscher	0	0	----	1	1	0		4	2	1	0	

ROCHESTER   5th   60-61   .496   -25   Art Irwin
Hustlers

BATTERS	POS-GAMES	GP	AB	R	H	BI	2B	3B	HR	BB	SO	SB	BA
Karl Kolseth	1B,P1	(see multi-team players)											
Robert Orr	2B30	30	104	10	22		3	0	1			6	.212
J. Brady	SS92	93	357	45	87		5	5	1			9	.244
J. Kost	3B85,2B,1B	89	324	27	72		7	1	0			9	.222
Ted Menze	OF114	114	411	62	103		14	11	1			14	.251
William Estes	OF98,1B21	122	456	71	131		19	7	1			30	.287
Norman Reeves	OF88,C,P1	95	327	30	95		10	2	0			12	.291
Earl Smith	C51,1B35,OF	94	335	51	120		24	14	1			19	.358
Gene Walsh	3B34,2B31	66	248	21	48		5	1	0			9	.193
Godfrey Brogan	P39,OF22	65	170	22	41		2	3	1			2	.241
Harry Heitman	P27,OF13	47	149	22	50		7	0	0			1	.336
Bernard Hungling	SS23,C,OF,3B	47	130	21	36		10	0	0			5	.277
Henry Hagen	P31,OF	40	100	5	15		1	0	0			1	.150
George Hogan	1B22,OF11	34	126	9	20		4	1	0			4	.159
Michael Flaherty	C17,OF,2B	25	73	4	15		1	0	0			0	.205
Alfred Grant	P19	20	35	2	5		0	0	0			1	.143
Dazzy Vance	P10,OF	13	33	3	8		1	0	0			0	.242
Whitrock	SS,OF	7	29		6		1	0	0			0	.207
Ryan	2B,SS	7	22		2		0	0	0			0	.091
Russell	P6	7	15		5		0	0	0			0	.333
Roy Wilkinson	P6	6	22		7		1	0	0			0	.318
Levie	OF	6	12		1		0	0	0			0	.083
Ross Erwin	1B	4	14		5		2	0	0			1	.357

ROCHESTER (cont.)
Hustlers

BATTERS	POS-GAMES	GP	AB	R	H	BI	2B	3B	HR	BB	SO	SB	BA
Ray Gordinier	P3	3	9		1		0	0	0			0	.111
Goldberg	OF	2	7		4		0	0	0			0	.571
G. Smith	P2	2	5	0	0		0	0	0			0	.000
Chief Manners	P2	2	1	0	0		0	0	0			0	.000
O'Keefe	P2	2	1	0	0		0	0	0			0	.000
Hartman	2B	1	4	0	0		0	0	0			0	.000
Kircher	1B	1	4		1		0	0	0			0	.250
Britt	OF	1	3	0	0		0	0	0			0	.000
Speigel	1B	1	2		0		0	0	0			0	.000
Pike	PH	1	1		1		0	0	0			0	1.000

PITCHERS		W	L	PCT	G	GS	CG	SH	IP	H	BB	SO	ERA
Harry Heitman		17	6	.739	27	21	20		204	137	61	89	**1.32**
Godfrey Brogan		16	**18**	.471	39	31	28		279	250	**123**	**157**	2.10
Henry Hagen		12	14	.462	31	27	21		235	212	86	128	2.41
Dazzy Vance		4	5	.444	10	9	8		81	93	23	34	3.88
Alfred Grant		4	7	.364	19	13	9		110	125	46	21	2.46
Roy Wilkinson		3	2	.600	6	6	5		55	47	27	24	1.64
Russell		2	3	.400	6	5	3		42	34	16	28	2.15
G. Smith		1	1	.500	2	2	1		16	11	6	5	
Norman Reeves		0	1	.000	1	1	0		2	4	5	0	
Karl Kolseth		0	1	.000	1	1	0		1	5	0	1	
Chief Manners		0	2	.000	2	2	0		5	6	7	0	
Ray Gordinier		0	3	.000	3	3	3		27	24	26	17	
O'Keefe		0	0	----	2	1	0		5	12	3	0	

BUFFALO
Bisons

| | 6th | 53-68 | .438 | -32 | George Wiltse |

BATTERS	POS-GAMES	GP	AB	R	H	BI	2B	3B	HR	BB	SO	SB	BA
George Wiltse	1B82,P4,OF	83	312	38	81		3	3	0			13	.260
Bucky Harris	2B66,SS20	85	320	51	77		11	7	0			4	.291
Herb Armstrong	SS94	95	337	30	70		12	3	0			5	.208
Stan Nowak	3B57	58	188	19	32		1	1	0			2	.170
Joe Schultz	OF90	91	318	29	67		6	3	0			8	.211
Mike Murphy	OF60,3B14,C,2B,1B	93	292	35	58		9	5	0			6	.199
Tom McCabe	OF39	39	149	10	32		2	3	1			9	.215
Benny Bengough	C62	65	220	16	49		8	0	0			14	.223
Lee Strait	1B38,OF28	68	244	30	86		15	7	1			11	.352
Chief Meyers	C59	65	204	28	67		14	1	0			2	.328
John Bates	OF37	37	129	29	37		3	4	0			9	.287
Don Donelson	OF35	36	128	13	36		4	1	0			4	.281
Harold DeVinney	P27,OF	35	95	6	15		1	1	0			0	.157
Guy Cooper	P19,OF,1B	35	89	9	26		1	0	0			0	.292
Frank Rose	P30,OF	32	91	9	19		2	0	1			1	.209
Mickey Corcoran	2B27	28	110	9	26		1	1	0			3	.236
Martin Murphy	OF21	22	65	14	11		0	0	0			7	.169
John Steffen	P19OF	21	45	6	9		0	0	0			0	.200
Mike Lynch	2B12,SS,3B	19	62	12	13		3	0	0			2	.210
Alphonse Thomas	P17	18	39	1	6		1	0	0			0	.154
Al Carlstrom	3B12,OF	14	46	9	12		1	0	0			2	.261
John Ondorchak	P7	8	16		4		0	0	0			1	.250
Alex Shields	P6,2B	7	17		2		0	0	0			0	.118
Manuel Baranda	OF,2B,1B	6	21		3		0	0	0			0	.143
Al Honeck	SS	4	13		1		0	0	0			0	.077
Poole	OF	4	12		3		0	0	0			1	.250
Tom Gallagher	P4	4	8		0		0	0	0			0	.000
Roy Conway	2B,OF	3	8		1		0	0	0			0	.125
Kessell	OF	2	6		1		0	0	0			0	.167
Jiminez	OF	2	2		0		0	0	0			0	.000
O'Brien	OF	2	2	0	0		0	0	0			0	.000
Jack Miller	P1	1	0	0	0		0	0	0			0	----

PITCHERS		W	L	PCT	G	GS	CG	SH	IP	H	BB	SO	ERA
Frank Rose		14	10	.583	30	25	19		229	236	71	68	3.19
Guy Cooper		9	6	.600	19	15	14		148	126	39	60	1.94
John Steffen		7	7	.500	19	14	12		120	123	27	38	2.32
Harold DeVinney		7	14	.333	27	19	17		210	180	54	76	2.36
Alphonse Thomas		5	10	.333	17	13	12		114	104	41	49	3.39
Tom Gallagher		2	1	.667	4	3	3		28	28	8	10	

BUFFALO (cont.)
Bisons

PITCHERS	W	L	PCT	G	GS	CG	SH	IP	H	BB	SO	ERA
George Wiltse	1	1	.500	4	2	1		17	14	6	7	
Brown	1	1	.500	3	2	2		20	29	6	9	
Alex Shields	1	4	.200	6	5	4		44	54	9	24	4.10
John Ondorchak	1	6	.143	7	7	4		43	63	31	8	
Jack Miller	0	0	.000	1	1	0		0	3	1	0	

SYRACUSE / HAMILTON   7th   38-76   .333   -43.5   Patsy Donovan
Stars / Tigers

BATTERS	POS-GAMES	GP	AB	R	H	BI	2B	3B	HR	BB	SO	SB	BA
Harold Weafer	1B67,2B25,OF	93	299	25	74		7	2	0			2	.247
William Paige	2B43,OF36	83	284	34	85		13	2	0			13	.299
J. Carroll	SS44,3B42,2B	86	313	39	82		15	4	1			17	.262
E. McHale	3B31,2B19,SS10	63	211	29	45		8	1	0			18	.213
Frank Eckstein	OF98,SS17	115	417	40	97		9	2	1			13	.233
Albert Ray	OF27,P18	44	140	15	31		6	1	0			2	.221
Bill Irving	OF		(see multi-team players)										
V. Hopper	C70,OF	78	242	24	48		7	4	0			4	.198
Dean Barnhardt	P32,OF21	58	159	20	36		2	6	0			0	.227
Raymond Dowd	2B18,SS17	43	168	19	49		3	1	0			13	.292
Joe Cobb	C26,OF,1B	37	111	13	22		7	1	0			6	.198
R. Turner	C14,OF,1B	27	90	3	12		3	0	1			0	.133
Pat Shea	P20	23	62	5	11		3	0	0			0	.177
Welch	OF22	22	83	4	15		0	0	0			4	.181
Sullivan	1B16,OF	21	63	7	9		0	0	0			3	.143
Leo Walker	P11,OF	14	35	2	6		1	0	0			0	.171
Robert Davis	SS13	13	47	7	16		1	0	0			4	.340
William Garvey	1B10,OF	13	42	4	6		0	0	0			0	.143
Darney	P6,OF	12	25	1	3		0	0	0			0	.120
Ringwood	OF,C	8	25		2		0	0	0			0	.040
Leo Gowkey	P7,OF	7	15		4		0	0	0			0	.267
Anderson	SS	4	14		7		2	0	0			1	.500
Wilson	C	4	11		3		0	0	0			0	.273
Tobin	SS	3	9		3		0	0	0			0	.333
Finlayson	3B	3	8		1		0	0	0			0	.125
Elliott	P2	2	1	0	0		0	0	0			0	.000
Doc Scanlan	P1	1	3		1		0	0	0			0	.333
C. DeLong	C	1	3	0	0		0	0	0			0	.000
Lewis	OF	1	3	0	0		0	0	0			0	.000
Muir	P1	1	3	0	0		0	0	0			0	.000
Furman	P1	1	0	0	0		0	0	0			0	----

PITCHERS	W	L	PCT	G	GS	CG	SH	IP	H	BB	SO	ERA
Dean Barnhardt	12	17	.414	32	24	22		248	238	75	90	2.54
Pat Shea	8	11	.421	20	17	15		149	165	50	62	3.08
Albert Ray	5	7	.417	18	14	12		122	160	54	32	3.76
Leo Walker	2	6	.250	11	10	8		81	82	25	29	3.22
Doc Scanlan	1	0	1.000	1	1	0		5	3	3	4	0.00
Leo Gowkey	1	4	.200	7	6	2		32	40	18	13	
Furman	0	1	.000	1	1	0		1	2	2	0	
Muir	0	1	.000	1	1	1		8	7	4	2	
Elliott	0	2	.000	2	1	0		5	15	3	1	
Darney	0	3	.000	6	3	2		32	32	10	18	

JERSEY CITY   8th   30-94   .242   -56.5   Harry Lord -
Skeeters   Dave Driscoll

BATTERS	POS-GAMES	GP	AB	R	H	BI	2B	3B	HR	BB	SO	SB	BA
Harvey Bluhm	1B51	53	203	21	59		10	4	2			9	.290
Phil Cooney	2B52,SS11	63	248	26	49		1	2	0			8	.198
Walter Barbare	SS40	48	183	26	67		8	2	0			12	.366
Charles Kromhaus	3B40,2B37,SS33	111	358	31	70		16	3	0			12	.196
Jacob Felz	OF115	118	425	47	116		16	4	0			10	.273
Richard Wheeler	OF84	87	315	33	74		5	6	1			14	.235
Brock	OF46	48	171	21	34		3	0	0			1	.199
William Carroll	C53	54	172	12	40		6	3	0			2	.233
Richard Breen	C39,1B	51	164	19	51		3	5	0			7	.311

JERSEY CITY (cont.)
Skeeters

BATTERS	POS-GAMES	GP	AB	R	H	BI	2B	3B	HR	BB	SO	SB	BA
John Fleiger	C21,1B,2B,OF	45	84	9	15		3	1	0			2	.179
J. Irving	SS23,3B10	33	130	11	33		3	3	0			8	.254
Menzel	OF31	31	108	7	17		1	1	0			2	.157
Joe LaBate	P14	31	83	12	19		0	1	0			5	.224
Bill Zitzmann	1B19,OF	25	89	14	32		3	5	0			4	.360
Joe Stapleton	2B22,1B	23	76	5	18		2	4	0			7	.237
Ververs	P20	22	49	7	10		1	0	0			0	.205
Norton	OF20	20	67		13		1	1	0			0	.194
Herman Hehl	P20	20	49	2	7		1	1	0			0	.143
Albert Waldbauer	P15,OF	19	51	1	12		0	0	0			1	.235
Hurley	1B16	17	49	2	5		1	0	0			1	.102
Dick McCabe	P10,OF	17	47	4	13		1	0	0			1	.277
Hanson Horsey	P17	17	38	1	2		0	0	0			0	.053
Morgan	SS15	15	57	5	13		2	2	0			1	.228
Adrian Lynch	P14	14	44	1	6		0	0	0			0	.136
Maude	P14	14	30	0	9		0	1	0			0	.300
O'Connor	1B,C	13	38		6		1	0	0			0	.158
Willard McGraw	C11	11	34	2	4		2	0	0			1	.118
McAllister	1B,C,OF,P1	10	22		2		0	0	0			0	.091
Martin	OF	5	11		0		0	0	0			0	.000
Jacob Pitler	2B	4	12		3		0	0	0			1	.250
Butler	SS,2B	3	12		3		0	0	0			0	.250
Harter	OF	3	11		3		0	0	0			0	.273
Clougher	C	3	8		3		0	0	0			0	.375
McFarland	P3	3	3		1		0	0	0			0	.333
Powell	P3	3	3		0		0	0	0			0	.000
Abbott	SS	2	8		2		1	0	0			0	.250
Sayre	3B,1B	2	8		1		0	0	0			1	.125
Clinton	P2	2	6		1		0	0	0			0	.167
Leonard	2B	2	6		0		0	0	0			0	.000
Miller	C	2	6	0	0		0	0	0			0	.000
Moran	3B	2	5		1		0	0	0			0	.200
Ryan	2B	2	4		1		0	0	0			0	.250
Bill Maloney	P2	2	4	0	0		0	0	0			0	.000
Chappelle	SS	2	2		1		0	0	0			0	.500
Lohr	OF	1	4		2		0	0	0			1	.500
Morris	SS	1	4		2		1	0	0			0	.500
Dwyer	OF	1	4	0	1		0	0	0			0	.250
Terhune	OF	1	4		1		0	0	0			0	.250
Huntley	P1	1	3		1		0	0	0			0	.333
DesJardin	P1	1	3	0	0		0	0	0			0	.000
Hoyle	P1	1	3	0	0		0	0	0			0	.000
McGarry	P1	1	3	0	0		0	0	0			0	.000
Slaughter	P1	1	3	0	0		0	0	0			0	.000
Weldon Wyckoff	P1	1	3	0	0		0	0	0			0	.000
Frank Truesdale	3B	1	3		0		0	0	0			0	.000
Smith	SS	1	2		0		0	0	0			0	.000
Walker	P1	1	2	0	0		0	0	0			0	.000
Roxey	P1	1	1		1		0	0	0			0	1.000
Edwards	PH	1	1	0	0		0	0	0			0	.000
Ladd	C	1	0	0	0		0	0	0			0	----
McCloskey	PR	1	0		0		0	0	0			0	----
O'Brien	2B	1	0	0	0		0	0	0			0	----
Quinlan	P1	1	0	0	0		0	0	0			0	----

PITCHERS	W	L	PCT	G	GS	CG	SH	IP	H	BB	SO	ERA
Adrian Lynch	9	5	.643	14	14	13		122	100	33	42	1.55
Whitehouse	3	3	.500	6	5	5		44	53	19	12	4.50
Joe LaBate	3	4	.429	14	7	7		87	84	23	24	2.58
Herman Hehl	3	15	.167	20	14	14		143	155	54	34	3.53
Ververs	3	15	.167	20	14	12		139	157	58	40	3.23
Clinton	2	0	1.000	2	2	2		18	9	6	11	
Maude	2	8	.200	14	13	9		89	101	41	40	3.53
Dick McCabe	2	8	.200	10	10	10		85	80	19	42	2.86
Hanson Horsey	2	11	.154	17	15	11		125	138	32	28	2.66
Waldbauer	1	13	.071	15	14	13		117	106	55	67	3.69
Hoyle	0	1	.000	1	1	1		8	5	4	2	
Huntley	0	1	.000	1	1	1		5	1	2	1	
McGarry	0	1	.000	1	1	1		9	5	5	4	
Slaughter	0	1	.000	1	1	1		10	5	3	5	
Weldon Wyckoff	0	1	.000	1	1	1		9	7	2	7	
DesJardin	0	1	.000	1	1	0		5	4	4	0	
Walker	0	1	.000	1	1	1		9	10	1	4	
Powell	0	2	.000	3	2	1		11	19	10	3	
Bill Maloney	0	2	.000	2	2	1		14	17	4	9	

JERSEY CITY (cont.)
Skeeters

PITCHERS	W	L	PCT	G	GS	CG	SH	IP	H	BB	SO	ERA
McFarland	0	0	----	3	0	0		9	11	8	2	
McAllister	0	0	----	1	0	0		4	5	2	1	
Quinlan	0	0	----	1	0	0		2	5	4	1	
Roxey	0	0	----	1	0	0		5	5	4	0	

MULTI-TEAM PLAYERS

BATTERS	POS-GAMES	TEAMS	GP	AB	R	H	BI	2B	3B	HR	BB	SO	SB	BA
Gil Whitehouse	OF94,P6	TOR-JC	105	383	49	105		12	8	3			16	.274
William McCarren	3B85,2B10,OF10	NE-JC-BU	105	363	54	97		11	4	1			17	.267
Bill Irving	OF102	BIN-S/H	104	393	60	107		17	4	1			16	.272
Louis Raymond	2B47,3B30,OF	S/H-ROC	87	304	30	89		11	6	0			11	.293
Karl Kolseth	1B74	NE-RO-BA	79	264	29	67		14	8	2			15	.254
William Buckley	OF71,SS	BIN-BUF	76	260	36	58		3	0	0			5	.223
Guy Zinn	OF68	NEW-JC	70	266	25	58		11	1	0			7	.218
George O'Neill	C58	TOR-ROC	58	186	20	45		4	0	0			10	.242
Bob Heck	P35,OF	S/H-TOR	50	120	14	27		2	0	2			1	.235
Elmari Bowman	1B16,3B,OF	TOR-JC	34	110	14	27		3	1	0			6	.245
Fred Achiele	P23,OF11	TOR-HAM	34	101	8	15		2	1	0			0	.149
Tom Brown	3B15,OF,P3	BUF-S/H	24	86	9	20		3	0	0			3	.233
Greene	1B21	BIN-S/H	22	77	9	17		2	0	0			2	.221
Fred Walker	P20	NEW-BIN	20	49	5	9		0	0	0			1	.184
Ed Miller	1B17,SS	NEW-ROC	19	62	14	15		1	2	0			4	.242
Henry Helfrich	P17,OF	BAL-BUF	19	54	3	11		2	0	0			0	.204
McLaughlin	OF,P3	ROC-NEW	11	35	2	6		0	0	0			0	.171
LaDestro	P8	S/H-NEW	8	16		1		0	0	0			0	.125
Joe Sargent	3B	NEW-JC	2	8		2		0	0	0			0	.250

PITCHERS	TEAMS	W	L	PCT	G	GS	CG	SH	IP	H	BB	SO	ERA
Bob Heck	S/H-TOR	17	16	.516	35	28	26		286	260	74	160	1.88
Fred Walker	NEW-BIN	8	9	.471	20	17	14		143	143	53	42	2.58
Fred Achiele	TOR-S/H	7	13	.350	23	17	16		166	185	60	47	2.98
Henry Helfrich	BAL-BUF	5	11	313	17	17	13		135	142	45	55	2.60
LaDestro	S/H-NEW	0	5	.000	8	5	3		48	53	8	10	3.56

TEAM BATTING

TEAMS	GP	AB	R	H	BI	2B	3B	HR	BB	SO	SB	BA
TORONTO	**129**	4161	**585**	1076		144	40	**17**	**466**	437	**213**	.259
BINGHAMTON	125	4030	562	1072		**156**	51	10	405	371	167	**.266**
BALTIMORE	**129**	**4214**	472	**1117**		148	**60**	16	352	451	161	.265
NEWARK	127	4019	474	985		110	34	5	335	354	176	.245
ROCHESTER	122	3955	466	1027		130	51	8	262	**469**	168	.260
BUFFALO	123	3988	470	953		109	40	6	393	448	126	.239
SYR/HAM	115	3653	375	854		110	30	6	347	**507**	130	.234
JERSEY CITY	126	4020	411	948		111	53	3	339	501	130	.233
	498	32040	3815	8032		1018	359	71	2899	3538	1271	.251

1919
ED ONSLOW

During the second two decades of the twentieth century, hundreds of players graced the fields of the International League. One particular first baseman met almost all of them, either as teammates or as opponents. His name was Ed Onslow.

Ed Onslow started his career with the Lansing club of the Southern Michigan League in 1911. After he hit .385 in his second year with the team, he joined the Detroit Tigers of the American League for a 35-game tryout, playing alongside his brother Jack. In 1913, Onslow joined the International League, latching on with Providence. He stayed with the Grays through the 1917 season. When the team left the league, Onslow joined the Toronto Maple Leafs for the 1918 season. Interspersed were two brief callups to the majors, one in 1913 with Detroit and another in 1918 for Cleveland.

During his first seven years in the International, Onslow proved himself a solid but not spectacular performer. He batted over .300 four times, the highest in 1914 (.322). He hit for a fair amount of power, occasionally reaching the double digits for home runs in a season. But he did show surprising speed for a first baseman, stealing more than 30 bases in five separate campaigns.

The 1919 International League welcomed one new member, Reading, which took the place of Syracuse. Baltimore won the pennant, completing its rise from the Federal League wars. Ed Onslow's Toronto squad finished second, well ahead of Buffalo in third and Binghamton in fourth. Newark, Rochester, Jersey City, and Reading finished fifth through eighth. Otis Lawry from Baltimore won the batting title (.364), while Rochester's George Kelly knocked out the most home runs (15). Oriole pitcher Jim Parnham took two league titles, winning 28 while striking out 187. Buffalo's Ray Jordan had the lowest earned run average (1.43).

In 1919, Ed Onslow had a typical season. He batted .303 with no home runs and 36 stolen bases. After 1919, his career took off. Playing for Toronto, Rochester, and Providence, Onslow batted no less than .311 for the next eight seasons, hitting a high-water mark of .347 in 1923. In 1928, Onslow enjoyed his fourth and final trip to the majors with a short stint with the Washington Senators. Afterwards, Ed Onslow rejoined the International for two more seasons, with Baltimore and Newark.

In all, Ed Onslow played 17 seasons in the International League, participating in 2,109 games. Both marks are all-time International League records. More importantly, Onslow was no journeyman player, artificially augmenting his career for longevity's sake. During his International League tenure, Onslow batted nearly .320, the result of 2,445 career hits—more hits than any other league player.

BALTIMORE Orioles

1st   100-49   .671   Jack Dunn

BATTERS	POS-GAMES	GP	AB	R	H	BI	2B	3B	HR	BB	SO	SB	BA
Jack Bentley	1B92	92	377	51	122		24	10	11			5	.324
Max Bishop	2B126	126	446	71	116		16	9	1			17	.260
Joe Boley	SS137	137	505	69	152		19	2	1			12	.301
Fritz Maisel	3B145	145	587	135	197		44	7	1			63	.336
Merwin Jacobson	OF149	149	578	115	203		36	13	4			37	.351
John Honig	OF133	133	513	82	164		26	10	6			16	.320
Otis Lawry	OF133	133	494	132	180		10	13	2			56	.364
Wade Lefler	C78	78	231	35	65		10	1	1			5	.282
Ben Egan	C71	71	238	32	63		7	1	3			8	.341
Alex Schaufele	C57	57	158	23	38		6	2	0			3	.241
Jim Parnham	P44	53	146	15	36		5	2	4			0	.247
Harry Frank	P48	48	95	9	14		0	0	0			0	.147
Ray Morgan	2B43	43	161	26	41		8	1	0			5	.255
Sumpter Clarke	OF31	31	91	11	23		3	0	0			1	.253
Rudolph Kneisch	P26	26	53	4	7		0	2	0			0	.132
Cliff Hill	P24	25	64	8	16		2	0	1			0	.250
Sam Newton	P20	20	39	2	9		1	0	0			0	.231
Ralph Seibold	P16	19	49	8	12		1	0	0			3	.245

PITCHERS	W	L	PCT	G	GS	CG	SH	IP	H	BB	SO	ERA
Jim Parnham	28	12	.700	44			2	350	297	107	187	2.44
Harry Frank	24	6	.800	48			0	255	273	55	77	2.78
Cliff Hill	12	3	.800	24			3	160	160	57	36	3.15
Ralph Seibold	10	5	.667	16			1	125	105	63	69	3.17
Rudolph Kneisch	10	9	.526	26			2	147	145	58	32	3.37
Sam Newton	6	8	.429	20			0	115	133	50	51	4.85
Harry Thompson	4	0	1.000	5			0	45	49	7	8	2.80
Ellis Johnson	2	2	.500	8			1	39	43	40	16	7.61
Allen Herbert	1	0	1.000	5			0	21	15	9	5	1.29

TORONTO Maple Leafs

2nd   92-57   .617   -8   George Gibson

BATTERS	POS-GAMES	GP	AB	R	H	BI	2B	3B	HR	BB	SO	SB	BA
Jack Onslow	1B141	141	488	69	148		28	6	0			36	.303
Andy Anderson	2B135	135	466	48	120		15	9	3			13	.258
Eusebio Gonzales	SS146	146	515	105	127		22	3	0			36	.247
William Purtell	3B109	109	369	47	104		7	1	0			16	.282
George Whiteman	OF149	149	592	102	179		39	9	4			25	.302
Clint Breckenridge	OF83	83	272	34	59		1	1	0			14	.217
Frank Schulte	OF		(se multi-team players)										
Gus Sandberg	C110	110	331	39	91		18	3	3			4	.275
Al McInnis	SS95	95	266	24	64		6	0	0			12	.241
B. Purtell	SS67	67	200	26	31		4	0	0			4	.155
Jake Deufel	C56	56	145	17	31		4	2	0			2	.214
Vern Spencer	OF46	46	174	31	56		13	2	0			11	.322
Fred Hersche	P34	39	81	6	16		3	1	1			0	.198
Alex Peterson	P36	38	71	3	9		0	0	0			1	.127
Hal Justin	P35	36	72	4	16		2	0	0			0	.222
Wilbert Hubbell	P35	35	85	6	14		1	1	1			1	.165
Bob Heck	P32	33	75	4	11		2	0	0			0	.147
John Jones	P32	32	72	5	13		2	0	0			0	.181

PITCHERS	W	L	PCT	G	GS	CG	SH	IP	H	BB	SO	ERA
Hal Justin	17	9	.654	35			3	203	214	58	56	3.11
Wilbert Hubbell	17	11	.607	35			5	260	215	48	91	1.91
Fred Hersche	16	5	.762	34			3	198	199	61	103	3.13
Bob Heck	15	10	.600	32			1	225	215	89	87	2.92
John Jones	14	10	.583	32			2	219	208	75	79	2.79
Alex Peterson	13	12	.520	36			2	223	207	81	83	2.39

BUFFALO Bisons

3rd   81-67   .548   -18.5   George Wiltse

BATTERS	POS-GAMES	GP	AB	R	H	BI	2B	3B	HR	BB	SO	SB	BA
George Wiltse	1B124	124	422	53	108		9	2	0			11	.256

BUFFALO (cont.)
Bisons

BATTERS	POS-GAMES	GP	AB	R	H	BI	2B	3B	HR	BB	SO	SB	BA
Bucky Harris	2B120	120	447	68	126		18	8	2			28	.282
Walt Keating	SS148	148	546	69	149		18	1	0			34	.273
William McCarren	3B139	139	479	72	131		27	10	2			15	.273
Don Donelson	OF148	148	582	88	145		21	7	3			19	.249
Ed Barney	OF148	148	559	91	153		10	5	2			35	.274
Lee Strait	OF119	119	430	72	147		36	7	7			16	.342
Benny Bengough	C103	103	351	37	97		17	4	1			4	.277
Joe Casey	C81	81	247	25	70		7	3	1			2	.283
Charley Loudy	2B60	60	193	17	52		2	5	0			4	.269
Al Carlstrom	OF38	38	140	15	37		2	0	0			6	.264
Alphonse Thomas	P36	37	92	8	17		3	0	0			1	.185
Fred Harcher	P28	35	93	9	27		7	0	1			0	.290
Harold DeVinney	P28	35	81	4	21		2	1	0			0	.259
Bill Ryan	P28	33	71	4	11		0	0	0			0	.155
Ray Jordan	P28	28	81	6	14		3	0	0			1	.173

PITCHERS		W	L	PCT	G	GS	CG	SH	IP	H	BB	SO	ERA
Bill Ryan		15	8	.652	28			2	205	188	75	87	1.80
Ray Jordan		15	10	.600	28			7	226	170	46	99	1.43
Alphonse Thomas		15	13	.536	36			2	262	222	94	107	1.99
Harold DeVinney		12	11	.522	28			1	188	193	61	74	2.12
Fred Harcher		11	13	.458	28			3	218	237	67	51	2.36
Ray Gordinier		7	3	.700	14			1	97	51	40	42	1.40
Cy Marshall		5	2	.714	10			1	64	80	16	19	1.27
Frank Rose		0	2	.000	5			0	24	25	10	5	4.88

BINGHAMTON
Bingoes

4th   75-71   .514   -23.5   Frank Schulte - Charles Hartman

BATTERS	POS-GAMES	GP	AB	R	H	BI	2B	3B	HR	BB	SO	SB	BA
Howard McLarry	1B140	140	478	85	156		26	13	3			21	.326
Charles Hartman	2B103	103	374	52	88		5	3	1			12	.235
Frank O'Rourke	SS141	141	571	91	166		27	9	2			34	.291
Frank Ellerbe	3B115	115	420	55	120		20	12	7			5	.286
James Riley	OF145	145	563	71	163		11	9	0			20	.290
Joe Shannon	OF140	140	512	63	143		32	15	1			17	.279
William Holden	OF		(see multi-team players)										
Harry Smith	C93	93	262	40	73		11	5	2			14	.279
Bill Fischer	C73	73	242	42	86		10	3	1			12	.355
Pat Gillespie	3B55	55	151	12	32		3	0	0			4	.212
Harry Donovan	P36	37	75	4	15		6	1	0			0	.200
Pete Shields	OF35	35	101	17	26		4	0	3			2	.257
Festus Higgins	P34	35	72	7	14		1	1	0			2	.194
Pat Martin	P27	27	82	7	19		4	0	0			0	.232
John Harper	P21	21	57	8	19		2	1	0			1	.333
Luther Barnes	P21	21	50	2	8		1	1	0			0	.160
John Beckvermit	P19	20	37	3	5		1	0	0			0	.135
Dan Costello	OF18	18	57	5	15		1	0	0			1	.263

PITCHERS		W	L	PCT	G	GS	CG	SH	IP	H	BB	SO	ERA
Pat Martin		17	6	.739	27			3	222	172	78	144	2.51
Festus Higgins		16	9	.640	34			0	226	215	99	59	2.87
Harry Donovan		11	15	.423	36			1	212	217	91	90	4.28
Luther Barnes		10	8	.556	21			4	149	147	34	46	2.90
John Harper		7	9	.438	21			1	143	139	51	67	2.77
John Beckvermit		5	8	.385	19			3	111	116	46	33	3.16
Joe Gingras		3	4	.429	11			0	65	72	34	16	4.57
Joe Faircloth		0	3	.000	6			0	20	29	4	4	6.75

NEWARK
Bears

5th   71-80   .470   -30   Patsy Donovan

BATTERS	POS-GAMES	GP	AB	R	H	BI	2B	3B	HR	BB	SO	SB	BA
Ed Miller	1B149	149	537	110	158		30	10	3			87	.294
Gene Walsh	2B		(see multi-team players)										
Joe Sargeant	SS124	124	429	42	102		25	8	2			11	.238

NEWARK (cont.)
Bears

BATTERS	POS-GAMES	GP	AB	R	H	BI	2B	3B	HR	BB	SO	SB	BA
Clare McAlpin	3B85	85	281	28	64		7	1	1			10	.228
Jack Jacobs	OF145	145	482	77	129		25	7	1			36	.268
Joe Letter	OF143	143	525	76	141		21	14	2			28	.269
Ted Cather	OF105	105	389	41	88		16	2	0			18	.226
Frank Bruggy	C126	126	417	57	145		26	5	2			44	.348
Tom Madden	C67	67	179	18	40		8	1	1			6	.223
Ed Rommel	P41	62	147	15	27		3	3	0			0	.184
Raymond Dowd	2B43	43	158	22	52		10	0	0			9	.329
Pat Shea	P37	37	85	7	8		2	0	0			0	.094
Pat Lyons	P34	34	59	3	11		2	0	0			0	.186
Bob Davis	3B32	32	80	8	17		2	2	0			1	.213
Walter Shay	2B29	29	102	10	16		0	0	0			8	.157
Hal Denke	OF29	29	79	9	21		3	0	0			3	.266
Sterling Stryker	P25	25	42	2	8		0	3	0			0	.190
Frank Powers	OF23	23	60	7	13		2	2	1			1	.216

PITCHERS		W	L	PCT	G	GS	CG	SH	IP	H	BB	SO	ERA
Ed Rommel		22	15	.595	41			7	309	293	72	85	2.48
Pat Shea		13	19	.406	37			3	267	253	77	85	2.93
Pat Lyons		9	9	.500	34			1	180	174	53	47	3.10
Sterling Stryker		5	10	.333	25			1	125	111	50	45	2.30
Aicer Jensen		2	4	.333	12			0	77	77	32	21	3.16
Terhune		1	2	.333	5			0	18	22	12	7	4.50

ROCHESTER   6th   67-83   .447   -33.5   Art Irwin
Hustlers

BATTERS	POS-GAMES	GP	AB	R	H	BI	2B	3B	HR	BB	SO	SB	BA
George Kelly	1B103	103	376	72	134		21	14	**15**			23	.356
Joe Nagle	2B141	141	511	41	135		15	6	1			13	.264
Jose Rodriguez	SS139	139	538	73	142		14	3	0			16	.264
J. Kost	3B75	75	267	32	62		6	5	0			7	.232
Charles See	OF78,P13	78	297	56	115		16	7	5			13	.387
Wid Matthews	OF57	57	206	24	46		2	1	0			13	.223
A. Schweitzer	OF			(see multi-team players)									
George O'Neill	C119	119	385	42	95		8	4	0			4	.288
Ed Carris	C60	60	223	20	49		9	0	0			6	.220
Walt Ralinger	OF56	56	180	18	41		5	2	0			7	.232
Manuel Cueto	OF46	46	163	27	57		11	2	0			10	.350
Harry Heitman	P21	46	131	10	32		1	3	0			0	.244
Bill Lamar	OF44	44	179	33	66		9	4	3			13	.369
Jose Acosta	P43	44	113	4	14		2	3	0			2	.124
Godfrey Brogan	P36	44	108	10	24		1	3	0			1	.222
Enoch Shinault	C41	41	97	10	22		1	1	1			2	.227
Tom Long	3B39	39	166	21	56		7	3	0			3	.337
Robert Orr	2B37	37	141	12	32		4	1	0			13	.227
John Clifford	P32	32	92	8	21		4	0	0			1	.228
John Ogden	P27	27	80	4	17		1	0	0			2	.213
Matt Donohue	1B25	25	70	8	19		4	0	0			0	.271
Clarence Pitt	OF24	24	83	6	21		3	0	0			5	.253
Herb Moran	OF22	22	88	15	18		1	1	0			1	.205

PITCHERS		W	L	PCT	G	GS	CG	SH	IP	H	BB	SO	ERA
Jose Acosta		17	14	.548	43			3	319	**372**	53	93	3.19
John Clifford		15	16	.484	32			3	256	275	70	86	2.39
Godfrey Brogan		11	20	.355	36			0	251	250	**131**	75	3.94
John Ogden		10	13	.435	27			2	190	199	73	98	2.37
Harry Heitman		7	11	.389	21			3	142	152	85	53	3.29
Charley See		5	6	.455	13			0	108	90	49	64	3.00
Walt Bernhardt		0	3	.000	5			0	30	32	17	12	4.20

JERSEY CITY   7th   56-93   .376   -44   Bill Donovan
Skeeters

BATTERS	POS-GAMES	GP	AB	R	H	BI	2B	3B	HR	BB	SO	SB	BA
Thomas DeNoville	1B98	98	368	33	92		11	5	0			4	.276

JERSEY CITY (cont.)
Skeeters

BATTERS	POS-GAMES	GP	AB	R	H	BI	2B	3B	HR	BB	SO	SB	BA
Paddy Baumann	2B136	136	520	74	156		20	4	1			22	.300
Ed Mooers	SS87	87	314	26	68		11	2	0			6	.217
Tom Fitzsimmons	3B69	69	268	22	69		6	2	0			6	.257
Frank Wigglesworth	OF148	148	537	64	154		22	15	1			9	.287
Frank Kane	OF88	88	297	36	82		6	6	3			20	.276
Bill Zitzmann	OF60	60	203	28	50		4	3	0			11	.246
Joe Cobb	C100	10	315	34	73		15	6	6			10	.232
Harry Biemiller	SS62,P19	82	247	19	38		8	2	2			4	.154
Joe Hyde	C56	56	154	21	33		4	1	1			1	.214
Reid Zellars	P38	45	117	10	32		5	2	0			1	.274
Al Schacht	P40	42	116	7	22		1	0	0			1	.190
Jim Sharp	2B31	31	101	9	21		3	1	0			1	.202
Lew Wendell	1B20	20	72	8	16		3	1	0			0	.222
John Russell	1B10,P10	20	45	2	11		2	1	0			0	.244
Bill Morrisette	P19	19	56	2	12		1	1	1			1	.214
Jack Berrigan	SS18	18	60	6	12		1	0	0			2	.200
Ben Kingston	OF16	16	30	4	9		1	0	0			0	.300

PITCHERS		W	L	PCT	G	GS	CG	SH	IP	H	BB	SO	ERA
Al Schacht		19	17	.528	40			9	318	296	59	98	1.95
Reid Zellars		13	23	.361	38			3	302	285	102	142	2.08
Harry Biemiller		6	6	.500	19			0	119	121	61	39	2.35
Bill Morrisette		5	12	.294	19			0	148	153	66	61	2.86
Walt DeVitalis		4	3	.571	8			1	60	60	20	24	2.10
Robert Tecarr		3	1	.750	10			0	55	56	21	24	0.98
George Miller		2	4	.333	9			0	49	58	31	26	3.86
Dan Tipple		2	8	.200	10			0	66	76	40	21	3.82
John Russell		1	7	.125	10			0	60	74	24	18	3.60
Bill Maloney		0	3	.000	5			0	29	34	16	7	4.37

READING   8th   51-93   .354   -46.5   Charles Dooin -
Coal Barons   Charles Kelchner

BATTERS	POS-GAMES	GP	AB	R	H	BI	2B	3B	HR	BB	SO	SB	BA
Mike Konnick	1B110	110	385	64	129		27	7	8			9	.335
John Hummel	2B122	122	433	64	135		25	5	2			8	.312
Jim Walsh	SS71	71	252	21	63		8	4	1			6	.250
Eugene Sheridan	3B140	140	496	54	136		22	8	2			9	.274
Joe Burns	OF134	134	524	72	148		22	8	1			21	.282
Harry Weiser	OF122	122	453	79	137		25	10	2			22	.302
Jesse Altenburg	OF99	99	386	51	125		13	12	2			24	.324
A. Cook	C			(see multi-team players)									
Myrl Brown	P46	48	107	6	25		0	2	0			1	.233
Frank Brower	1B47	47	167	21	53		10	4	1			7	.317
Dave Keefe	P34	43	98	7	15		3	1	0			0	.153
Dean Barnhardt	P21	42	86	8	19		4	1	0			1	.221
Charles Dooin	C38	38	110	10	24		3	0	0			4	.218
Sam Fishburn	SS35	35	138	14	38		8	0	0			4	.275
Phil Weinert	P35	35	76	5	13		3	0	0			0	.171
Frank Crossin	C34	34	112	13	35		12	1	1			1	.313
Ed Bariess	P23	31	48	5	10		2	0	0			0	.208
Ross Swartz	P8	28	74	11	15		0	1	0			1	.203
Harold Weafer	1B21	21	76	5	16		5	0	0			1	.211
Jesse Baker	SS18	18	67	5	7		2	1	0			1	.104

PITCHERS		W	L	PCT	G	GS	CG	SH	IP	H	BB	SO	ERA
Myrl Brown		18	21	.462	46			1	307	299	113	128	2.93
Dean Barnhardt		10	7	.588	21			1	138	158	34	54	3.60
Dave Keefe		10	17	.370	34			2	226	239	61	101	3.71
Phil Weinert		6	15	.286	35			2	202	206	101	98	4.68
Ross Swartz		2	0	1.000	8			0	33	32	26	17	4.10
Ed Bariess		2	11	.154	23			0	102	116	49	49	5.29
Norman Plitt		0	7	.000	9			0	58	73	30	25	5.28

MULTI-TEAM PLAYERS

BATTERS	POS-GAMES	TEAMS	GP	AB	R	H	BI	2B	3B	HR	BB	SO	SB	BA
Mickey Doolan	2B139	BAL-REA	139	496	49	149		27	6	3			10	.300
Frank Schulte	OF132	BIN-TOR	132	455	66	113		15	9	8			23	.248
A. Schweitzer	OF127	JC-ROC	127	415	50	117		20	3	2			15	.282
William Holden	OF110	TOR-BIN	110	387	57	109		23	10	7			12	.282
Gene Walsh	2B90	ROC-NEW	90	291	42	75		8	3	0			15	.258
F. Hudgins	C83	NE-BU-JC	83	249	15	55		5	2	0			2	.221
A. Cook	C77	NEW-REA	77	263	27	57		7	3	2			3	.217
Thomas Downey	3B40	NEW-JC	40	151	14	39		4	2	0			3	.258
Dick McCabe	P35	BIN-NEW	36	98	6	19		4	0	0			0	.194
John Haddock	C35	BIN-TOR	35	105	7	15		1	0	0			0	.143
Bill Donohue	P27	REA-BIN	27	59	6	15		3	1	1			0	.254
George Gaw	P24	BUF-NEW	25	50	4	7		1	0	0			0	.140
John Blake	OF16	BUF-ROC	16	52	3	12		0	0	0			3	.230

PITCHERS	TEAMS	W	L	PCT	G	GS	CG	SH	IP	H	BB	SO	ERA
Dick McCabe	BIN-NEW	15	16	.484	35			4	270	268	49	108	2.30
George Gaw	BUF-NEW	8	8	.500	24			0	166	176	35	40	2.71
Bill Donohue	REA-BIN	4	10	.286	27			2	151	160	85	50	4.29
Fred Bruck	BIN-JC	1	3	.250	6			0	23	27	13	7	5.09
Jack Enright	NEW-JC	0	3	.000	10			0	30	28	33	7	5.40

TEAM BATTING

TEAMS	GP	AB	R	H	BI	2B	3B	HR	BB	SO	SB	BA
BALTIMORE	149	5092	859	1524		231	83	37			241	.299
TORONTO	149	4760	631	1209		188	47	23			190	.254
BUFFALO	148	4924	656	1326		182	53	19			182	.269
BINGHAMTON	146	4724	640	1289		189	83	24			169	.273
NEWARK	151	4772	614	1201		198	67	11			279	.252
ROCHESTER	150	5025	601	1360		168	64	28			172	.271
JERSEY CITY	149	4797	489	1176		151	63	15			115	.245
READING	144	4771	588	1318		218	75	26			114	.276
	593	38865	5078	10403		1525	535	183			1462	.268

1920
TWO-HORSE RACE

Near the end of August 1920, the Toronto Maple Leafs had a one-game lead in the International League. The Leafs then proceeded to win 90 percent of their September games—an impressive feat. With that dandy run, it's a shame they finished where they did.

The International League had a slightly new look in 1920. Binghamton was out, replaced by Syracuse. Also, Newark was gone, with a team from Akron taking its place.

As the 1920 pennant race unfolded, two teams emerged from the pack: the Toronto Maple Leafs and the Baltimore Orioles. The two chased each other while all the other teams were chasing them. As the campaign entered its final month, only a few percentage points separated Baltimore and Toronto. The Maple Leafs then won 20 of their last 22 games. In any other year, this kind of winning skein would have sewn up the pennant. Unfortunately for the Leafs, the Orioles did them one better. Baltimore won their last 25 games in a row to win the flag by two and one-half games.

The rest of the teams finished far astern. Buffalo and Akron finished third and fourth, while Reading and Jersey City finished next. Rochester and Syracuse brought up the rear. Most of the league leaders came from the rosters of the two best teams. Baltimore claimed the top hitter (Merwin Jacobson, .404), the pitcher with the most wins (John Ogden, 27), and the pitcher with the lowest earned run average (Jack Bentley, 2.11). Toronto pitcher Pat Shea finished in a tie for the most wins (27). The honors not garnered by Baltimore and Toronto included the home run title (22), which was shared by two Reading batters, Frank Brower and Mike Konnick. The strikeout crown was nabbed by Rochester hurler Virgil Barnes (142).

The 1920 International League pennant race was a contest between two fine teams. Never before had two teams galloped down the stretch with such sparkling closing records. Despite their loss, Toronto can take a small measure of pride in their record. The Maple Leafs' .701 winning percentage ranks as an all-time high—for a second place team.

BALTIMORE
Orioles

1st   110-43   .719   Jack Dunn

BATTERS	POS-GAMES	GP	AB	R	H	BI	2B	3B	HR	BB	SO	SB	BA
Jack Bentley	1B125,P22	145	622	109	231		39	12	20			13	.371
Max Bishop	2B119	122	404	54	100		17	8	4			20	.248
Joe Boley	SS143	143	543	90	167		30	14	3			13	.308
Fritz Maisel	3B154	154	640	145	204		33	10	2			45	.319
Merwin Jacobson	OF154	154	581	161	235		35	16	7			18	.404
Otis Lawry	OF153	153	584	155	184		21	8	1			36	.315
William Holden	OF148	148	576	104	203		49	16	4			21	.352
Ben Egan	C81	81	287	32	95		13	5	8			2	.331
Wade Lefler	C38,1B36	94	280	39	94		13	3	4			2	.336
Nigel Marlette	2B42	74	217	28	52		10	1	1			3	.240
Harry Frank	P48	49	106	6	13		1	0	0			0	.123
John Ogden	P45	46	130	17	27		3	1	2			1	.208
Rudolph Kneisch	P36	38	67	7	13		2	1	0			1	.194
James Sullivan	P29	29	48	4	10		4	0	0			0	.208
William Styles	C24	25	97	15	28		5	4	0			3	.289
Jim Parnham	P15	23	33	6	7		0	0	1			0	.212
Lefty Grove	P19	19	49	4	4		0	0	0			0	.082
Sam Newton	P12	12											.095
Newt Fike	P10	10											.400

PITCHERS	W	L	PCT	G	GS	CG	SH	IP	H	BB	SO	ERA
John Ogden	27	9	.750	45		31	4	321	342	100	137	3.25
Harry Frank	25	12	.676	48		18	2	270	287	71	96	3.87
Jack Bentley	16	3	.842	22		15	5	167	149	29	97	2.11
Lefty Grove	12	2	.857	19		10	1	123	120	71	88	3.81
Rudolph Kneisch	11	4	.733	36		5	0	162	171	67	55	2.72
James Sullivan	7	11	.389	29		6	1	147	146	103	96	4.76
Jim Parnham	5	0	1.000	15		5	1	72	69	25	34	3.00
Sam Newton	5	2	.714	12		4	1	56	55	25	24	2.41
Newt Fike	2	0	1.000	10		2	0	39	35	11	27	5.08

TORONTO
Maple Leafs

2nd   108-46   .701   -2.5   Hugh Duffy

BATTERS	POS-GAMES	GP	AB	R	H	BI	2B	3B	HR	BB	SO	SB	BA
Ed Onslow	1B135	135	511	87	173		23	12	7			31	.339
Eusebio Gonzales	2B96,3B15	121	364	68	108		16	4	0			38	.297
Frank O'Rourke	SS148	148	615	130	201		37	11	4			37	.327
Lena Blackburne	3B133	150	545	91	171		19	7	1			34	.314
James Riley	OF145	148	562	100	173		19	11	5			24	.308
George Whiteman	OF126	128	458	74	124		27	6	6			18	.271
Benny Kauff	OF79	79	300	67	103		18	6	12			28	.343
Gus Sandberg	C79	96	320	36	81		10	8	2			7	.253
Andy Anderson	2B63,OF38	121	390	66	120		13	5	5			18	.308
Michael Devine	C71	76	232	40	70		5	6	2			8	.302
Vern Spencer	OF70	71	266	49	86		11	2	2			13	.323
Lore Bader	P39	46	92	11	26		3	1	0			0	.283
Pat Shea	P43	44	105	12	22		1	0	2			0	.210
Bill Ryan	P44	44	89	9	15		2	0	0			1	.169
Maurice Craft	P11	24	49	16	15		1	2	3			3	.306
Alex Peterson	P22	23	30	5	2		0	0	0			0	.067
Bill Snyder	P15	17	35	2	6		0	0	0			0	.171
Bob Heck	P17	17	32	5	10		2	0	0			0	.313
Bunn Hearn	P14	14											.216

PITCHERS	W	L	PCT	G	GS	CG	SH	IP	H	BB	SO	ERA
Pat Shea	27	7	.794	43		25	7	298	262	122	131	2.63
Bill Ryan	19	9	.679	44		21	4	261	240	119	113	2.73
Lore Bader	19	9	.679	39		15	3	229	217	77	94	2.91
Maurice Craft	8	0	1.000	11		5	1	66	49	22	33	2.18
Bill Snyder	8	1	.889	15		5	0	84	72	34	35	3.65
Bunn Hearn	8	4	.667	14		8	0	99	112	14	45	3.46
Alex Peterson	7	6	.538	22		6	0	97	110	54	29	5.37
Bob Heck	4	1	.800	17		3	0	76	71	30	17	2.96

BUFFALO Bisons

3rd   96-57   .627   -14   George Wiltse

BATTERS	POS-GAMES	GP	AB	R	H	BI	2B	3B	HR	BB	SO	SB	BA
Ed Miller	1B138	138	494	102	164		38	7	6			44	.332
Raymond Dowd	2B134	134	509	81	156		15	3	0			59	.306
Walt Keating	SS145	145	492	68	111		10	2	0			43	.226
Joe Sargent	3B83	117	368	62	112		29	4	8			19	.304
Frank Gilhooley	OF147	148	583	139	200		30	10	2			45	.343
Ed Barney	OF119	125	415	76	129		20	5	2			35	.311
Lee Strait	OF114,1B15	129	467	85	142		21	14	1			42	.304
Frank Bruggy	C70	85	253	36	87		14	2	1			16	.344
William McCarren	3B70,2B22	100	334	63	109		18	7	8			13	.326
John Jacobs	OF88	99	313	61	96		14	5	4			36	.307
Benny Bengough	C52	53	184	10	36		3	2	0			1	.196
Thomas Rogers	P32	38	110	16	28		1	1	3			2	.255
Dick McCabe	P37	37	89	12	22		5	2	0			2	.247
Alphonse Thomas	P28	30	58	9	17		2	1	0			1	.293
Pat Martin	P26	26	71	6	16		1	2	0			1	.226
Harry Heitman	P22	25	59	4	17		3	0	0			1	.288
Ray Gordinier	P23	24	57	5	15		1	0	1			1	.263
Frank Werre	P24	24	52	2	6		0	0	0			0	.115
Bob Carruthers	P17	17	23	1	3		0	0	0			0	.130

PITCHERS		W	L	PCT	G	GS	CG	SH	IP	H	BB	SO	ERA
Dick McCabe		22	6	.786	37		20	2	232	221	40	103	2.26
Thomas Rogers		14	15	.483	32		23	2	251	262	68	106	3.20
Pat Martin		13	9	.591	26		16	1	185	178	79	111	2.73
Frank Werre		10	3	.769	24		10	2	143	144	49	61	2.46
Alphonse Thomas		10	6	.625	28		9	0	148	162	59	67	4.01
Harry Heitman		10	6	.625	22		10	1	143	132	52	34	2.84
Ray Gordinier		7	7	.500	23		8	2	135	162	87	56	4.07
Bob Carruthers		5	3	.625	17		2	0	73	87	22	23	4.19

AKRON Buckeyes

4th   88-63   .583   -21   Dick Hoblitzell

BATTERS	POS-GAMES	GP	AB	R	H	BI	2B	3B	HR	BB	SO	SB	BA
Dick Hoblitzel	1B112	118	403	78	118		16	6	3			11	.293
Pete Shields	2B139	139	530	137	156		35	15	16			10	.294
William Webb	SS124	135	488	102	161		39	15	7			20	.330
William Purtell	3B143	143	516	77	162		26	4	4			4	.314
James Walsh	OF141	150	589	102	189		36	13	15			13	.321
Joe Shannon	OF130	131	509	91	174		33	15	11			17	.342
Jim Thorpe	OF126	128	522	102	188		28	15	16			22	.360
Harry Smith	C96	109	354	57	107		23	4	7			15	.302
John Walker	C59,1B36	107	385	60	130		28	1	10			3	.338
Bill Irving	OF56	65	179	29	43		10	1	1			1	.241
Ray Culp	SS24,P17	43	124	20	29		5	1	4			2	.234
Cliff Hill	P39	42	91	14	23		5	2	3			2	.253
Joseph Finneran	P39	40	95	9	21		2	2	0			1	.221
Luther Barnes	P34	34	87	11	22		7	1	2			0	.253
Pat Flaherty	P25	26	47	7	5		0	1	1			2	.106
Earl Mosely	P25	26	44	1	7		1	2	0			0	.159
Otis Lambeth	P12	12											.208
John Harper	P8	8											.187
Bill Fisher	P5	5											.111
Festus Higgins	P5	5											.286

PITCHERS		W	L	PCT	G	GS	CG	SH	IP	H	BB	SO	ERA
Joseph Finneran		20	11	.645	39		23	0	249	318	81	62	3.69
Luther Barnes		17	12	.586	34		17	1	230	247	99	101	3.21
Cliff Hill		14	11	.560	38		18	1	230	250	98	76	3.92
Pat Flaherty		12	5	.706	25		8	0	127	162	57	41	3.55
Earl Mosely		7	2	.778	25		6	0	122	115	70	67	4.43
Ray Culp		4	5	.444	17		5	0	88	91	33	31	2.76
Festus Higgins		2	1	.667	5		0	0	23	30	13	11	8.22
John Harper		2	4	.333	8		3	0	45	63	16	23	5.60
Otis Lambeth		2	5	.286	12		4	1	66	70	31	24	4.77
Bill Fisher		1	2	.333	5		2	0	27	20	16	12	4.34

READING
Marines

5th   65-85   .433   -43.5   John Hummell

BATTERS	POS-GAMES	GP	AB	R	H	BI	2B	3B	HR	BB	SO	SB	BA
Frank Brower	1B107	107	415	96	161		31	13	22			11	.388
Walter Oberc	2B74,OF36,3B16	130	460	66	143		23	5	7			6	.311
Eugene Sheridan	SS135	135	521	67	142		24	4	0			22	.273
Earl Marriott	3B118,2B23	142	532	80	172		32	13	6			17	.323
Joe Burns	OF151	151	605	122	197		35	8	1			29	.326
Jesse Altenburg	OF141	141	596	109	167		26	4	5			26	.280
John Hummel	OF67,2B46	118	426	78	136		33	2	6			9	.320
Mike Konnick	C122	135	506	94	170		33	11	22			13	.336
John Peters	OF52	65	178	21	50		11	2	1			5	.281
Francis Karpp	P39	40	72	5	10		2	0	0			0	.139
Myrl Brown	P39	39	80	3	10		0	0	0			0	.125
Dean Barnhardt	P36	38	90	11	16		1	3	0			1	.177
Elmari Bowman	1B35	35	135	20	40		12	2	5			2	.296
Fred Thomas	3B17,SS16	35	129	17	32		6	2	5			5	.248
Ross Swartz	P31	32	68	7	14		4	1	0			0	.206
Ed Bariess	P32	32	61	10	15		3	1	0			0	.246
Hal Justin	P23	23	50	5	5		1	1	0			0	.100
Yockey Holmes	P19	19	34	2	6		0	0	0			0	.176
Frank Crossin		17	47	9	11		1	1	0			0	.235

PITCHERS					W	L	PCT	G	GS	CG	SH	IP	H	BB	SO	ERA
Dean Barnhardt					14	12	.538	36		20	1	229	267	75	70	4.05
Myrl Brown					13	22	.371	39		17	0	223	249	100	109	4.84
Francis Karpp					12	13	.480	39		13	0	214	271	84	83	4.37
Ross Swartz					8	11	.421	31		14	0	180	183	80	79	3.85
Hal Justin					7	8	.467	23		9	0	132	163	49	43	4.71
Ed Bariess					6	11	.353	32		8	0	164	202	85	60	5.50
Yockey Holmes					3	3	.500	19		2	0	88	138	33	16	7.43

JERSEY CITY
Skeeters

6th   62-91   .405   -48   Bill Donovan

BATTERS	POS-GAMES	GP	AB	R	H	BI	2B	3B	HR	BB	SO	SB	BA
Thomas DeNoville	1B151	151	589	65	182		33	3	2			14	.309
Ed Mooers	2B59,3B59,SS15	142	546	80	155		19	9	1			19	.284
Bill Zitzmann	SS78,OF54,3B17	152	566	115	176		30	8	11			42	.311
Paddy Baumann	3B73	95	323	51	104		12	5	1			12	.322
Frank Wigglesworth	OF153	153	580	84	180		19	11	3			23	.310
Frank Kane	OF138	141	543	80	167		27	16	7			17	.308
William Zimmerman	OF93	93	322	56	100		13	1	0			12	.311
Otto Freitag	C103	107	304	35	72		11	5	0			1	.237
Emmett McCann	SS49,2B42	98	357	62	109		16	5	0			10	.305
Ed Gill	P31	55	112	21	27		1	0	1			7	.241
Harry Biemiller	P31	40	80	4	13		0	0	1			0	.162
Alex Ferguson	P35	39	100	8	26		0	1	0			0	.260
Ben Kingston	OF24	38	87	7	20		2	0	0			2	.230
Joe Hyde	C34	34	117	12	28		5	2	0			1	.239
Irvin Wilhelm	P34	34	85	7	16		1	0	0			1	.188
Albert Stark	2B26	33	105	14	26		2	0	0			1	.248
Ralph Carlson	P28	29	73	3	8		1	0	0			0	.110
William Grevell	P19	19	55	5	9		0	0	0			1	.164
Harry Hurley	C16	19	28	3	8		1	0	0			1	.286
Harry Vanderbach	C16	18	40	1	8		2	1	0			1	.200

PITCHERS					W	L	PCT	G	GS	CG	SH	IP	H	BB	SO	ERA
Alex Ferguson					21	13	.618	35		26	1	265	257	77	112	2.82
Irvin Wilhelm					12	12	.500	34		21	4	236	275	55	74	3.09
Ed Gill					9	15	.375	31		19	1	201	230	86	73	4.17
Ralph Carlson					8	13	.381	28		14	0	208	270	47	61	4.50
Harry Biemiller					6	17	.261	31		17	0	193	188	94	69	2.79
William Grevell					4	14	.222	19		10	0	136	154	78	55	4.37

ROCHESTER
Hustlers

7th 45-106 .298 -63.5 George Stallings

BATTERS	POS-GAMES	GP	AB	R	H	BI	2B	3B	HR	BB	SO	SB	BA
Jose Rodriguez	1B94	94	338	43	108		17	2	0			9	.320
William Hollahan	2B59,3B33,1B21	131	464	55	123		22	5	2			14	.265
Al White	SS133,2B18	151	565	71	148		20	17	2			5	.262
Henry Long	3B115,2B24	145	607	79	194		19	9	2			16	.320
Wid Matthews	OF150	150	539	79	161		13	10	1			27	.299
Robert Kinsella	OF124	130	454	62	143		21	10	4			19	.315
Emmons Bowen	OF93,2B47	149	530	78	155		30	5	1			19	.292
Fred Ross	C78	94	272	22	53		5	1	0			3	.195
Harry Manning	C54,1B24	79	284	20	61		4	3	0			7	.215
Eugene Foley	OF32	47	135	10	31		8	1	2			0	.230
Virgil Barnes	P41	45	122	8	23		0	3	0			1	.189
John Clifford	P32	33	77	8	16		1	0	0			0	.208
George Krahe		25	64	5	12		3	0	0			0	.187
Jose Acosta	P24	25	55	3	7		1	1	0			0	.127
Paul Beyers	C18	20	58	7	20		4	4	0			2	.345
Thomas Beck	P9	20	44	5	12		1	0	1			0	.273
Ken Sedgewick	P14	14											.298
Reynolds Kelly	P9	13											.158
Harry Burfeind	P11	11											.192
Dan Sherman	P11	11											.105
L. Seaman	P9	9											.000
Harry Snyder	P9	9											.143
Basil Workman	P8	8											.063
Jim Garton	P8	8											.059
Art Lintz	P8	8											.148

PITCHERS		W	L	PCT	G	GS	CG	SH	IP	H	BB	SO	ERA
Virgil Barnes		12	23	.343	41		25	1	303	371	79	142	4.28
Jose Acosta		11	9	.550	24		14	3	170	212	24	49	4.28
John Clifford		7	21	.250	32		18	3	211	217	62	56	4.10
Harry Snyder		3	2	.600	9		3	0	56	57	32	20	4.66
Art Lintz		3	5	.375	8		5	0	59	71	25	15	5.80
Basil Workman		2	4	.333	8		4	0	37	44	16	21	3.89
Ken Sedgewick		2	8	.200	12		8	0	95	119	46	20	5.69
Jim Garton		1	3	.250	8		2	0	51	64	26	14	5.64
Harry Burfeind		1	6	.143	11		4	0	64	74	47	22	6.47
Dan Sherman		0	4	.000	11		3	0	54	93	20	10	5.83
L. Seaman		0	4	.000	9		1	0	31	38	7	16	4.07
Thomas Beck		0	4	.000	9		2	0	36	43	26	9	9.54
Reynolds Kelly		0	6	.000	9		3	0	42	57	19	10	6.00

SYRACUSE
Stars

8th 33-116 .221 -75 Tony Cummings - Amby McConnell - John Engman - Tom Madden

BATTERS	POS-GAMES	GP	AB	R	H	BI	2B	3B	HR	BB	SO	SB	BA
Tim Jordan	1B69	69	238	34	61		16	3	5			2	.256
Al Carlstrom	2B		(see multi-team players)										
Joe Benes	SS92,OF32	133	458	51	120		10	3	4			6	.262
Clare McAlpin	3B142	142	528	50	111		15	3	2			9	.210
Leo Witterstatter	OF86	96	371	48	101		18	7	1			4	.272
Frank Schulte	OF39	39	151	18	37		8	0	4			5	.245
Don Donelson	OF		(see multi-team players)										
Tom Madden	C47	68	166	22	45		9	0	0			0	.271
Herb Armstrong	SS59,2B36	95	327	31	73		6	5	1			3	.223
Howard McGraner	OF28,P17	52	153	16	35		9	3	3			0	.229
Thomas Gildea	OF38	51	152	19	33		4	0	1			3	.217
Amby McConnell	2B33	33	138	25	49		5	4	0			1	.355
Ben Gaiser	OF29	29	119	8	25		4	3	0			1	.210
Ed Buckley	P13	27	89	5	16		3	0	0			0	.180
Raymond Werre	1B19	19	67	8	14		1	0	0			2	.109
John Enzmann	P13	19	61	9	24		4	2	1			0	.393
Lester Sell	P19	19	57	8	11		6	1	0			0	.193
Win Carlson	P17	18	45	4	8		0	0	0			0	.178
Dan Tipple	P17	17	41	1	7		1	0	0			0	.171
Joe Purtell	P6	7											.133
John Murphy	P5	5											.000
John Steffen	P5	5											.250

SYRACUSE (cont.)
Stars

PITCHERS	W	L	PCT	G	GS	CG	SH	IP	H	BB	SO	ERA
Howard McGraner	5	11	.313	18		12	0	127	190	59	23	6.31
John Enzmann	3	8	.273	13		10	0	105	130	43	43	5.91
Dan Tipple	3	10	.231	17		9	0	114	129	62	43	4.19
Lester Sell	3	12	.200	19		13	1	141	167	65	48	4.54
Ed Buckley	2	10	.167	13		8	1	104	125	45	28	5.02
John Steffen	1	4	.200	5		3	0	31	37	12	1	4.07
Win Carlson	1	10	.091	17		10	0	108	133	39	19	4.83
John Murphy	0	3	.000	5		2	0	25	28	8	6	4.68
Joe Purtell	0	4	.000	6		2	0	31	49	15	3	8.71

MULTI-TEAM PLAYERS

BATTERS	POS-GAMES	TEAMS	GP	AB	R	H	BI	2B	3B	HR	BB	SO	SB	BA
Don Donelson	OF147	BUF-SYR	147	570	89	149		25	10	4			17	.261
Al Carlstrom	2B58,1B53	JC-SYR	125	486	50	122		17	3	3			7	.251
Charles Niebergall	C78	SYR-BUF	92	277	32	67		9	2	2			5	.242
Joe Casey	C69	BA-BU-SY	85	258	28	75		16	0	4			4	.291
Fred Harscher	P23	SY-BU-JC	39	119	17	40		5	1	0			1	.336
Richard Cotter	C31	JC-REA	39	96	16	28		8	0	0			1	.291
Harry Donovan	P34	AKR-SYR	38	86	3	14		1	0	0			1	.163
Emmett Perryman	P34	SYR-AKR	34	89	4	14		2	1	0			0	.157
Lona Jaynes	P17	BUF-ROC	24	46	10	13		2	0	0			0	.283
Frank Quinn	P23	TOR-SYR	23	51	6	12		1	0	1			0	.235
A. Cook		REA-BUF	18	48	8	12		1	0	1			1	.250
Charles Connelly		SYR-ROC	16	39	6	8		2	0	0			0	.205
Cecil Dye	OF	TOR-SYR	3	9	0	1		0	0	0			0	.111

PITCHERS		TEAMS	W	L	PCT	G	GS	CG	SH	IP	H	BB	SO	ERA
Emmett Perryman		SYR-AKR	10	18	.357	34		19	1	249	263	80	103	4.23
Lona Jaynes		BUF-ROC	8	5	.615	17		5	0	97	129	29	31	5.57
Harry Donovan		AKR-SYR	7	15	.318	35		16	0	210	244	89	56	4.67
Frank Quinn		TOR-SYR	6	9	.400	23		8	0	141	170	67	51	4.89
Fred Harscher		SY-BU-JC	4	13	.235	23		16	0	151	201	57	41	5.54

TEAM BATTING

TEAMS	GP	AB	R	H	BI	2B	3B	HR	BB	SO	SB	BA
BALTIMORE	**155**	5363	**992**	**1706**		280	**100**	59			180	**.318**
TORONTO	154	5119	889	1523		212	82	53			262	.298
BUFFALO	154	5120	871	1524		236	69	37			**368**	.298
AKRON	152	5124	909	1572		**303**	**100**	**101**			125	.305
READING	151	5224	854	1561		287	75	80			151	.299
JERSEY CITY	153	5151	735	1461		200	68	27			157	.284
ROCHESTER	151	4985	598	1341		179	73	15			118	.269
SYRACUSE	150	5056	573	1232		196	53	33			68	.244
	610	41142	6421	11920		1893	620	405			1429	.290

1921
BALTIMORE ORIOLES

In the years following World War I, a monumental International League dynasty emerged. Located in the league's southernmost city, this dynasty would run off a pennant string unmatched in league annals. The team was the Baltimore Orioles.

The Baltimore Orioles joined the league in 1903. During their first few seasons, the Orioles finished in the first division several times, but couldn't push to the top. After the 1907 season, Jack Dunn, a former major league player, joined the team as its manager. Dunn was a shrewd judge of baseball talent, and he assembled a pennant winner in 1908. Shortly thereafter, Dunn bought the Baltimore Orioles. After a few more mid-range finishes, Dunn put together a strong club in 1914. Unfortunately, the Federal League war intervened, forcing Dunn to sell his players to remain afloat, and eventually forcing him to sell his team to Richmond.

Following the 1915 season, Jack Dunn purchased the moribund Jersey City club and moved it to Baltimore. Once again he began to assemble his team. By 1918, the Orioles were back in third. In 1919, they won the pennant with the first 100-win season in league history. In 1920 they duplicated the feat, with an impressive 25-game winning streak to end the season. Notable achievements certainly, but the 1921 Orioles were to be stronger yet.

The 1921 Orioles made a laughingstock of the pennant race as they finished 20 games ahead of second-place Rochester, and more ahead of the rest: Buffalo, Toronto, Newark (taking the place of Akron), Syracuse, Jersey City, and Reading. The Orioles won an astounding 119 games, scoring 1140 runs. The team batted a collective .313 behind the efforts of batting champion Jack Bentley's .412 average and leading 21 home run total. Other contributors included Otis Lawry (.352), Merwin Jacobson (.340), Fritz Maisel (.339), Max Bishop (.319), Joe Boley (.317), and William Holden (.302, 19 HR). As expected, pitching was strong, as evidenced by top winner John Ogden (31–8) and top strikeout man Lefty Grove (254). The only honor not received by an Oriole was the earned run average crown won by Rochester's John Enzmann (2.25).

The Baltimore Orioles, after their three-pennant run, went on to win another four in a row, establishing themselves as the greatest dynasty in league history. Not only did they win seven in a row, they did so in convincing fashion. During their seven-year run, the Orioles averaged 111 wins per season, 10 games per year over their second-place rivals. On four separate occasions, a second-place team won more than 100 games, only to be pushed aside by the Orioles juggernaut.

In all of minor league history, only one team (1934 Los Angeles) has beaten the 119-win mark of the 1921 Baltimore Orioles. For that reason alone, they are ranked among the league's elite, as one of the best minor league teams of all time.

BALTIMORE Orioles   1st   119-47   .717   Jack Dunn

BATTERS	POS-GAMES	GP	AB	R	H	BI	2B	3B	HR	BB	SO	SB	BA
Jack Bentley	1B129,P18	141	597	122	246		47	16	21			10	.412
Max Bishop	2B140	140	520	106	166		28	16	14			12	.319
Joe Boley	SS152	152	590	103	187		37	21	5			6	.317
Fritz Maisel	3B152	153	652	154	221		30	6	8			31	.339
Merwin Jacobson	OF166	167	632	163	215		38	14	12			26	.340
William Holden	OF128	129	490	104	148		23	10	19			8	.302
Otis Lawry	OF107	134	509	130	179		19	13	3			28	.352
Ben Egan	C91	95	319	35	86		18	1	5			1	.270
Wade Lefler	OF41,1B38,C27	115	396	71	125		19	5	3			3	.316
John Ogden	P42	60	166	13	34		2	2	1			1	.205
Lefty Grove	P47	47	113	14	19		4	1	1			0	.168
Cal Davis	C42	44	108	10	29		3	4	1			1	.269
Alphonse Thomas	P40	43	125	18	28		3	0	3			0	.224
Rufus Clarke	P29	38	94	11	27		5	1	0			0	.287
Harry Frank	P36	37	67	9	12		0	1	0			1	.179
James Lyston	OF21	33	74	5	14		2	0	0			0	.189
Matt Donahue	OF29	30	113	32	34		7	1	1			2	.301
Nigel Marlette		22	57	10	12		2	0	0			3	.211
Dick Porter	2B16	16	56	5	18		0	0	0			1	.321
William Styles		9											.290
James Matthews	P5	5											.000
Maxwell Owens		4											.091
James Aitcheson		3											.500
McComas		3											.200
Schuler		3											.600
Schimm		2											.500
Broadway Jones		2											.200
Rudolph Kneisch		1											.000
Robertson		1											.000
Ditman		1											.000
James Sullivan		1											.000

PITCHERS	W	L	PCT	G	GS	CG	SH	IP	H	BB	SO	ERA
John Ogden	31	8	.795	42		33	6	318	296	103	161	2.29
Lefty Grove	25	10	.714	47		26	1	313	237	179	254	2.56
Alphonse Thomas	24	10	.706	40		26	2	301	288	133	176	2.78
Harry Frank	13	7	.650	36		7	2	178	208	55	88	3.08
Jack Bentley	12	1	.923	18		11	1	119	90	33	71	2.35
Rufus Clarke	9	4	.692	29		8	0	143	170	79	48	4.97
James Matthews	1	1	.500	5		0	0	10	8	13	5	5.40

ROCHESTER Colts   2nd   100-68   .595   -20   George Stallings

BATTERS	POS-GAMES	GP	AB	R	H	BI	2B	3B	HR	BB	SO	SB	BA
Fred Merkle	1B153	163	636	132	216		45	20	4			29	.340
Harvey Hiller	2B112	114	433	74	130		24	1	2			20	.300
Walt Pearce	SS		(see multi-team players)										
Norm McMillan	3B156	161	619	124	197		22	23	6			46	.318
Homer Summa	OF166	166	655	142	218		36	21	13			20	.333
Maurice Archdeacon	OF163	164	622	166	202		17	10	3			53	.325
Bob Fothergill	OF141	143	582	114	197		34	23	12			23	.338
James Mattox	C100	103	320	49	110		15	12	2			13	.344
Ted Hauk	SS41,2B35	90	317	57	102		25	8	3			4	.322
Sam Post	1B19,P10	55	104	25	40		4	3	1			1	.385
Fred Blake	P42	42	115	13	38		5	3	0			1	.330
John Wisner	P42	42	114	12	29		2	1	0			0	.254
George Morgan	P34	34	84	13	24		4	4	2			0	.286
George Murray	P30	33	73	17	28		5	2	3			0	.384
William McCabe	OF18	30	96	18	23		4	2	0			3	.240
Elwood Wirts	C27	28	96	22	34		4	3	1			3	.354
Allan Conkwright	P21	21	31	2	1		1	0	0			0	.032
Joseph Murphy	C20	20	64	6	16		3	0	0			0	.250
James Keenan	P18	18	28	4	5		1	0	0			0	.179
Earl Brown	P17	18	21	4	4		1	0	0			0	.190
Ralph Knight	P15	15	28	1	4		1	0	0			0	.143
Fred Ross		14											.237
George Tyler	P8	12											.375
Charles Hargreaves		11											.241
Walter Keeley		11											.129
Melville Merritt		10											.130

ROCHESTER (cont.)
Colts

BATTERS	POS-GAMES	GP	AB	R	H	BI	2B	3B	HR	BB	SO	SB	BA
Edwin Krehmeyer		9											.258
Earl Johnson	P9	9											.154
Earl Clauser		8											.714
John Huber		6											.067
Enoch Shinault		4											.214
Godfrey Brogan		3											.200
Louis Cowan		3											.000
Walter Kimmick		2											.000
Alan Clarke		1											.000
Clyde Gatchel		1											.000
Jay O'Connor		1											.000
Robert Ware		1											.000

PITCHERS	W	L	PCT	G	GS	CG	SH	IP	H	BB	SO	ERA
John Wisner	22	11	.667	42		24	2	288	296	90	143	3.44
Fred Blake	21	13	.618	42		25	3	300	307	143	187	3.33
George Morgan	17	10	.630	34		18	0	214	236	98	73	4.04
George Murray	13	7	.650	30		11	0	169	211	77	80	3.67
James Keenan	9	0	1.000	18		7	0	73	69	34	53	2.84
George Tyler	4	1	.800	8		4	1	61	75	28	27	5.01
Earl Brown	3	1	.750	17		3	0	63	73	23	13	2.85
Sam Post	3	3	.500	10		1	0	42	48	28	12	4.50
Earl Johnson	3	3	.500	9		2	0	44	61	6	11	4.29
Allan Conkwright	3	6	.333	21		4	0	90	104	30	33	4.20
Ralph Knight	2	8	.200	15		4	0	78	73	51	33	2.42

BUFFALO
Bisons

3rd   99-69   .589   -21   George Wiltse

BATTERS	POS-GAMES	GP	AB	R	H	BI	2B	3B	HR	BB	SO	SB	BA
Ed Miller	1B138	139	498	92	141		27	10	5			28	.283
Raymond Dowd	2B161	162	516	79	174		35	5	2			54	.292
John Sheehan	SS89,3B39	127	486	103	120		18	8	1			29	.247
William McCarren	3B131	139	488	91	137		22	2	12			24	.281
Frank Gilhooley	OF164	164	641	131	201		28	17	1			55	.314
Ed Barney	OF132	136	438	92	144		40	12	8			36	.329
John Jacobs	OF122	126	436	72	115		31	8	6			35	.264
Benny Bengough	C95	101	363	47	100		23	5	1			7	.275
Don Donelson	OF93	115	327	54	93		9	5	2			14	.284
Walt Keating	SS83	90	284	41	69		6	1	1			27	.243
Walt Tragresser	C56	66	205	29	50		8	5	1			7	.244
Ed Tomlin	1B35,P23	61	163	18	51		3	3	1			5	.313
Harry Heitman	P41	54	128	11	27		5	1	0			0	.211
Dick McCabe	P41	41	93	13	21		5	1	0			1	.226
Ray Gordinier	P37	41	85	13	17		1	1	0			2	.200
Frank Werre	P32	32	74	3	9		1	1	0			1	.122
Pius Schwert	C20	29	65	10	17		2	1	0			1	.262
Thomas Rogers	P26	26	78	7	19		2	1	0			2	.244
Joseph Reddy	P19	20	28	2	3		2	0	0			0	.107
Howard Crandall	P19	19	42	7	13		1	0	0			0	.310
Joseph Thomas		4											.000
George Wiltse		4											.284
Carl Kies		1											.000

PITCHERS	W	L	PCT	G	GS	CG	SH	IP	H	BB	SO	ERA
Ray Gordinier	18	8	.692	37		18	1	223	221	120	118	3.56
Harry Heitman	17	12	.586	41		21	3	231	225	84	97	3.20
Dick McCabe	17	17	.500	41		25	3	283	310	54	114	2.42
Frank Werre	15	9	.625	32		11	3	206	179	79	73	2.62
Thomas Rogers	15	9	.625	26		19	1	191	204	59	112	3.11
Ed Tomlin	7	5	.583	23		8	0	99	112	34	27	3.46
Howard Crandall	6	5	.545	19		4	0	94	128	49	26	4.31
Joseph Reddy	4	4	.500	19		6	0	82	97	19	34	1.98

TORONTO Maple Leafs

4th   89-77   .536   -30   Larry Doyle - Lena Blackburne

BATTERS	POS-GAMES	GP	AB	R	H	BI	2B	3B	HR	BB	SO	SB	BA
Ed Onslow	1B139	140	524	92	176		32	5	12			25	.336
Eusebio Gonzales	2B128,3B37	160	581	107	175		28	6	0			60	.301
Ike Davis	SS157	157	566	88	132		22	5	3			33	.233
Lena Blackburne	3B136	136	461	56	128		14	9	5			17	.278
Vern Spencer	OF152	152	611	102	187		34	6	4			34	.306
Jesse Altenburg	OF148	148	537	106	186		18	14	9			27	.346
Andy Anderson	OF123	125	419	70	133		28	8	12			16	.317
James Riley	OF64,1B22	101	357	42	99		16	5	4			15	.277
Michael Devine	C94	101	333	48	112		20	5	3			7	.336
Harry Thompson	P31	51	94	17	25		1	0	3			2	.266
Gus Sandberg	C75	78	267	26	86		12	3	1			4	.322
William Snyder	P38	38	89	16	23		5	1	0			1	.258
Joseph Wagner	2B33	37	118	10	27		2	1	0			5	.229
Gary Fortune	P34	34	73	7	12		0	0	0			0	.164
Wid Matthews	OF27	32	97	20	31		4	1	0			8	.320
Curtis Fullerton	P29	29	76	6	14		2	2	0			0	.184
Ed Reis	P29	29	55	6	9		0	0	1			0	.164
John Enzmann	P25	27	60	2	12		1	0	0			1	.200
Jesse Winters	P21	21	61	2	13		2	0	0			1	.213
Larry Doyle		19	37	8	10		2	1	0			3	.270
Harry Purcell		18	27	7	5		0	2	0			0	.185
Joseph Boehling	P13	13											.174
William Taylor	P6	6											.200
Dewey Hill		5											.125
J. Brown		3											.000
Egan		1											.500
Edward Williams		1											.000

PITCHERS	W	L	PCT	G	GS	CG	SH	IP	H	BB	SO	ERA
Harry Thompson	15	9	.625	31		19	3	220	231	55	62	3.52
William Snyder	15	12	.556	38		19	3	246	249	87	82	3.62
Curtis Fullerton	14	10	.583	29		19	0	217	205	67	85	2.78
Gary Fortune	14	15	.483	34		15	3	219	207	122	120	3.62
Jesse Winters	11	8	.579	21		13	1	161	156	54	70	2.91
John Enzmann	10	10	.500	25		17	2	176	168	36	73	**2.25**
Ed Reis	7	5	.583	29		6	0	125	129	85	37	4.82
Joseph Boehling	2	5	.286	13		2	0	56	59	30	33	3.86
William Taylor	1	1	.500	6		0	1	15	18	13	8	5.40

NEWARK Bears

5th   72-92   .439   -46   James Walsh

BATTERS	POS-GAMES	GP	AB	R	H	BI	2B	3B	HR	BB	SO	SB	BA
Peter Krumenaker	1B144	144	533	63	149		23	15	4			11	.280
Joe Benes	2B	(see multi-team players)											
Maurice Shannon	SS82	121	488	86	156		23	19	4			26	.320
William Webb	3B121,SS22	148	550	86	170		30	18	5			20	.309
Frank McGowan	OF158	160	569	100	175		23	21	15			27	.308
James Walsh	OF122,1B19,3B15	153	581	106	209		39	16	2			29	.360
Pete Shields	OF112,2B44	153	591	129	159		38	8	5			21	.269
Frank Withrow	C102	108	350	31	76		16	2	3			11	.217
Thomas Ray	SS25,2B21	49	165	25	37		5	1	0			1	.226
Luther Barnes	P43	44	96	9	18		4	1	0			1	.188
John Singleton	P42	42	103	6	8		0	3	0			0	.078
Al Woods	SS19,OF16	39	135	13	41		4	3	1			1	.304
Lyle Bigbee	P21	30	58	8	14		2	2	1			1	.241
Joseph Finneran	P26	26	62	6	10		2	0	1			1	.161
Nicholas Mameo		15	32	6	10		2	0	0			1	.313
Emmett Perryman	P14	14											.107
Dan Tipple	P12	12											.250
John Harper	P7	8											.200
Albert Barsch	P7	7											.250
Albert Stark		7											.240
Robert David	P5	5											.375
F. Gosker		5											.083
Cliff Hill		5											.077
Howard Baldwin		3											.286
Ralph Carlson		3											.000
John Spatz		2											.500
Herbert Usilton		2											.143

NEWARK (cont.)
Bears

BATTERS	POS-GAMES	GP	AB	R	H	BI	2B	3B	HR	BB	SO	SB	BA
John Bailey		2											.000
Maurice Bahr		1											.333
Baier		1											.000
Harry Burfeind		1											.000
J. Dale		1											.000
Richard Durning		1											.000
Dan Fisher		1											.000
Gwynn		1											.000
Hanna		1											.000
Aicer Jensen		1											.333
Joseph Lane		1											.000
Price		1											.000
Rickard		1											.333
Clayton White		1											.500

PITCHERS		W	L	PCT	G	GS	CG	SH	IP	H	BB	SO	ERA
John Singleton		12	20	.375	42		24	2	275	306	95	116	2.94
Joseph Finneran		10	9	.526	26		15	0	162	203	57	33	3.83
Luther Barnes		10	19	.345	43		17	2	249	304	89	100	3.73
Lyle Bigbee		9	6	.600	21		10	0	121	104	77	74	2.60
Emmett Perryman		5	7	.417	14		4	0	82	98	30	34	3.40
Dan Tipple		4	0	1.000	12		0	0	39	37	31	24	4.62
John Harper		1	3	.250	7		2	0	35	29	15	11	2.83
Albert Barsch		1	3	.250	7		4	0	34	30	41	7	4.24
Robert David		0	2	.000	5		0	0	22	33	8	3	6.14

SYRACUSE   6th   71-96   .425   -48.5   Tom Madden -
Stars   Frank Shaughnessy

BATTERS	POS-GAMES	GP	AB	R	H	BI	2B	3B	HR	BB	SO	SB	BA
Leo Witterstatter	1B151	160	612	89	201		31	8	4			11	.328
Jim Esmond	2B60,OF30,3B19	118	427	59	125		26	4	6			7	.293
Earl Adams	SS163	164	655	124	174		26	5	0			23	.266
Jewel Ens	3B150	150	570	103	191		28	12	19			17	.335
Frank Schulte	OF155	159	589	117	182		35	12	16			15	.309
Art Smith	OF122	123	473	91	156		27	14	11			30	.330
Clarence Mueller	OF75	75	298	73	108		27	6	7			12	.362
Charles Niebergall	C97	111	369	52	106		17	6	3			6	.287
Frank Dodson	P33	54	145	17	39		8	2	1			1	.269
Lawrence Prediger	C47	52	146	19	30		1	5	1			0	.205
Art Olsen	P41	50	108	16	27		3	2	0			0	.250
Mike Kircher	P45	45	95	6	19		3	0	0			0	.200
Les Montgomery	P40	45	86	8	13		1	0	0			1	.151
Richard Simon	2B40	40	124	13	29		3	2	0			4	.234
Lester Sell	P40	40	77	5	15		0	1	0			0	.195
Frank Shaughnessy	1B15	29	62	4	16		3	0	0			1	.258
Al Carlstrom		23	82	9	16		1	0	0			0	.195
George Toporcer	2B21	21	71	15	24		4	1	0			4	.338
Ed Delaney	P7	14											.276
Clarence Wanner	P12	12											.200
Jake May	P9	11											.385
Tom Madden		11											.250
Eugene Caldera	P8	9											.154
Walt Schulz	P9	9											.211
Matt Kirley	P5	5											.167
Robert Unglaub		4											.444
Ed Bliss		4											.059
Leslie Kuhnart		3											.200
Kahoe		2											.333
George Dillon		1											.000
Harry Donovan		1											.000
Al Grabowski		1											.000
Hamilton		1											.000
Hobey Light		1											.000
William McCarron		1											.500
Roth		1											.000

PITCHERS		W	L	PCT	G	GS	CG	SH	IP	H	BB	SO	ERA
Art Olsen		14	14	.500	41		18	3	250	280	115	108	4.64
Frank Dodson		14	14	.500	33		21	0	252	273	131	85	4.36

SYRACUSE (cont.)
Stars

PITCHERS	W	L	PCT	G	GS	CG	SH	IP	H	BB	SO	ERA
Les Montgomery	12	12	.500	40		15	0	216	255	73	83	4.25
Mike Kircher	12	21	.364	45		21	1	250	317	59	88	4.21
Lester Sell	9	17	.346	40		14	0	221	255	99	79	4.60
Jake May	3	4	.429	9		4	0	57	79	27	42	5.36
Matt Kirley	2	1	.667	5		2	0	19	12	10	4	0.47
Walt Schulz	2	6	.250	9		4	0	50	81	33	24	7.38
Ed Delaney	1	0	1.000	7		0	0	33	48	16	5	6.82
Clarence Wanner	1	2	.333	12		1	0	42	49	17	14	6.21
Eugene Caldera	0	3	.000	8		2	0	37	42	21	15	3.89

JERSEY CITY   7th   59-106   .358   -59.5   Patsy Donovan
Skeeters

BATTERS	POS-GAMES	GP	AB	R	H	BI	2B	3B	HR	BB	SO	SB	BA
Thomas DeNoville	1B157	158	596	67	181		26	9	5			30	.304
Cliff Brady	2B79,3B59	150	543	104	163		21	14	2			32	.300
John Jones	SS79,2B17	95	360	41	111		26	9	1			14	.308
Harry Damrau	3B60	60	225	32	73		14	5	5			12	.324
Frank Kane	OF165	166	628	116	197		18	18	5			68	.314
Bill Zitzmann	OF126,SS17	143	519	106	144		19	7	9			20	.277
Frank Wigglesworth	OF76	78	302	33	89		8	9	0			9	.295
Otto Freitag	C106	111	296	29	76		13	4	3			2	.257
Jean Duval	2B71,OF51	138	443	80	101		10	9	3			33	.228
Earl Lucey	OF30,P22	81	137	20	26		4	1	1			4	.190
Norm McNeil	C75	80	199	26	54		7	4	2			4	.271
Edward Wurm	P37,OF15	75	125	21	28		5	2	1			1	.224
Harold Walker	3B30,SS22	58	176	19	46		5	5	1			3	.261
George Metivier	P34	54	86	12	23		1	1	1			0	.267
Joe Stapleton	OF27	50	130	18	27		5	1	0			5	.208
Robert Tecarr	P49	50	108	10	22		3	3	0			1	.204
John Clifford	P47	48	104	6	17		1	0	0			1	.173
Harry Biemiller	P44	45	85	4	12		1	0	0			1	.141
Matt Butler	SS26,3B16	44	147	20	34		2	0	0			3	.231
Julian Graveson	OF18	19	65	6	16		0	1	0			2	.246
Otto Scheck		14											.148
Vincent Haley	P5	5											.333
William Harris		3											.000
Stan Rees		3											.143
Frank Schwartz		2											.250
George Wright		2											.000
Fred Sawyer		1											.000

PITCHERS	W	L	PCT	G	GS	CG	SH	IP	H	BB	SO	ERA
Robert Tecarr	19	20	.487	49		28	0	306	336	99	103	3.27
Edward Wurm	11	14	.440	37		11	0	188	236	99	78	5.36
Harry Biemiller	11	20	.355	44		18	4	245	258	143	106	3.20
John Clifford	8	23	.258	47		21	1	277	345	103	87	4.64
George Metivier	6	15	.286	34		10	0	157	218	88	46	4.81
Earl Lucey	2	9	.182	22		2	0	75	80	57	28	4.68
Vincent Haley	0	0	----	5		0	0	12	16	14	2	3.75

READING   8th   56-110   .337   -63   Dick Hoblitzell
Aces

BATTERS	POS-GAMES	GP	AB	R	H	BI	2B	3B	HR	BB	SO	SB	BA
Dick Hoblitzel	1B124	126	473	82	166		25	9	8			22	.351
John Cavanaugh	2B64,SS63	132	407	40	94		17	4	2			5	.231
Walter Wolfe	SS63	73	240	33	59		4	2	1			8	.246
Fred Thomas	3B148,2B15	162	656	15	220		38	21	11			32	.335
Edwin Goebel	OF163	163	621	103	190		36	10	19			40	.306
Joe Burns	OF109	111	421	83	127		19	5	1			16	.302
James Peters	OF77	81	270	40	64		10	0	0			6	.237
Carl Johnson	C81	86	228	28	48		8	2	5			3	.211
Walter Oberc	OF66,2B36	116	419	51	108		24	4	5			7	.258
Frank Polan	OF73,C20	98	313	32	81		16	2	0			8	.259
Maurice Craft	1B33,P15	59	198	22	46		6	1	2			3	.232
Ross Swartz	P27	46	99	13	23		4	1	0			0	.232

READING (cont.)
Aces

BATTERS	POS-GAMES	GP	AB	R	H	BI	2B	3B	HR	BB	SO	SB	BA
Francis Karpp	P45	46	87	5	18		2	1	0			0	.207
Myrl Brown	P42	43	103	11	22		2	0	0			1	.214
Clarence Fisher	P41	41	97	8	14		2	0	0			0	.144
W. Mills	2B31	39	131	11	23		4	1	0			2	.175
Fred Carts	P28	29	71	10	19		1	3	0			1	.268
Richard Cotter	C26	27	93	8	24		5	1	0			0	.258
Virgil Flinn		24	49	4	7		1	0	1			0	.143
Joseph Carlin		19	68	5	12		2	0	0			1	.176
Elsworth Hughes	P10	10											.143
Aloysius Sarsfield	P8	8											.200
Charles Trader	P8	8											.538
John Herbst		8											.238
Cliff Prann		5											.375
Roy Keener		4											.250
Arthur Lentz		4											.000
Willard Poole		4											.000
Tex Irwin		2											.400
P. McKinstry		2											.000
Crosby		1											.000
Mike O'Brien		1											.000
T. Shanahan		1											.000

PITCHERS	W	L	PCT	G	GS	CG	SH	IP	H	BB	SO	ERA
Myrl Brown	17	14	.548	42		20	1	258	275	101	114	4.26
Fred Carts	10	12	.455	28		15	1	172	221	58	85	5.18
Francis Karpp	9	23	.281	45		18	0	235	261	103	69	4.40
Clarence Fisher	8	25	.242	41		18	3	245	285	112	99	4.82
Elsworth Hughes	4	2	.667	10		1	0	36	42	24	13	6.00
Maurice Craft	4	6	.400	15		6	0	89	121	37	37	4.35
Ross Swartz	2	13	.133	27		13	0	170	217	85	62	5.09
Aloysius Sarsfield	1	2	.333	8		1	0	37	52	8	13	7.30
Charles Trader	0	3	.000	8		1	0	30	61	10	4	7.80

MULTI-TEAM PLAYERS

BATTERS	POS-GAMES	TEAMS	GP	AB	R	H	BI	2B	3B	HR	BB	SO	SB	BA
Joe Benes	2B149	SY-RO-NE	149	524	71	154		29	5	6			14	.294
Walt Pearce	SS141	REA-ROC	141	463	75	116		18	8	2			22	.251
Harry Smith	C109	NEW-REA	109	305	41	80		12	5	2			12	.262
Eugene Madden	OF107	NEW-SYR	107	398	63	113		15	4	3			22	.284
Dean Barnhardt	P40,OF15	REA-NEW	69	146	14	35		5	0	1			0	.240
Harry Manning	C60	BU-BA-NE	60	162	18	38		2	1	0			1	.235
Paul Smith	OF40	SYR-ROC	58	154	33	40		5	3	0			3	.260
Curtis Daughton	OF48	NEW-BUF	57	159	16	38		3	1	0			8	.239
George Gilham	C56	ROC-SYR	56	144	16	33		9	2	1			1	.229
George Faulkner	SS25	ROC-SYR	28	90	9	21		2	2	0			3	.233
Bob Carruthers	P23	ROC-JC	23	28	1	2		0	1	0			0	.071
Atwood Gordy	P20	BAL-NEW	20	49	2	8		0	0	0			2	.163
James Murphy	P6	BAL-NEW	10											.100
William Stewart	P10	NEW-BAL	10											.308

PITCHERS		TEAMS	W	L	PCT	G	GS	CG	SH	IP	H	BB	SO	ERA
Dean Barnhardt		REA-NEW	10	17	.370	40		17	3	236	271	74	77	4.58
Atwood Gordy		BAL-NEW	8	8	.500	20		9	1	119	148	54	26	3.48
Bob Carruthers		ROC-JC	2	4	.333	23		1	0	74	105	39	18	4.74
William Stewart		NEW-BAL	0	2	.000	10		0	0	35	45	39	12	4.91
James Murphy		BAL-NEW	0	2	.000	10		0	0	32	43	20	7	4.78

TEAM BATTING

TEAMS	GP	AB	R	H	BI	2B	3B	HR	BB	SO	SB	BA
BALTIMORE	167	5843	1140	1831		293	112	102			144	.313
ROCHESTER	169	5795	1112	1803		277	148	55			237	.311
BUFFALO	168	5535	927	1523		271	87	41			325	.275
TORONTO	166	5845	840	1603		244	73	57			254	.292

TEAM BATTING (cont.)

TEAMS	GP	AB	R	H	BI	2B	3B	HR	BB	SO	SB	BA
NEWARK	164	5480	812	1524		250	120	48			180	.278
SYRACUSE	168	5789	943	1680		280	87	75			171	.290
JERSEY CITY	166	5359	774	1449		190	103	39			243	.270
READING	166	5556	763	1490		248	75	58			169	.268
	667	45202	7311	12903		2053	805	475			1723	.285

1922
JOHN OGDEN

During the glory days of the Baltimore Orioles, their star-studded hitting lineup featuring Merwin Jacobson, John Bentley, and Dick Porter got the most attention. However, their pitching staff, including the likes of Jim Parnham, Harry Frank, and Alphonse Thomas, was equally impressive. At least one other Oriole pitcher deserves mention. His name was John Ogden, and many consider him the best of the bunch.

John Ogden's baseball career started at a high level as he first briefly played for the National League's New York Giants in 1918. Later that same year he joined the International League, landing with the Newark club. In 1919, with Rochester, Ogden became a full-time starter, compiling a 10–13 record for the sixth-place team. Before the next year, fortune smiled on John Ogden as he was acquired by Jack Dunn's Baltimore Orioles—the best team in the International League. Ogden would soon reap the benefits.

In 1920, Ogden had his breakthrough season. Winning a league-best 27 games, he helped pitch the Orioles to the pennant. In 1921, Ogden performed even better as he won 31 games, easily the league's highest total.

In the 1922 International season, Baltimore once again swept to the pennant with its bevy of stars. Rochester, with a fine 105-victory campaign, finished a distant second. Buffalo and Jersey City finished in the first division's last two spots, while Toronto, Reading, Syracuse, and Newark filled the second division. Bob Fothergill, from Rochester, won the batting title (.383), while Toronto's Al Wingo set a new home run record as he blasted out 34.

A new hitting statistic was tabulated in 1922. Called "runs batted in," it measured how many runs scored from a given batter's hitting prowess. The first leader in this category was Fred Merkle from Rochester, who finished with 130.

John Ogden finished with fewer wins than the year before, but he still managed to lead the league with 24. Charles Bender from Reading had the lowest earned run average (2.41), while Oriole Lefty Grove racked up 205 strikeouts.

After 1922, John Ogden pitched five more seasons for the Orioles, winning an average 21 games per season. In 1928, he finally got a full-time shot in the majors, pitching a full season for the St. Louis Browns. After four major league campaigns, Ogden rejoined the International League for a brief curtain call in 1933 and 1934.

When John Ogden's stellar career in the International League was tallied, one record was undeniably his: 213 career wins. Remarkably, he took a relatively short time to accomplish the feat. John Ogden's International League stay was only a little over 11 years—quality years in which he averaged nearly 20 wins a season.

BALTIMORE Orioles

BALTIMORE 1st   115-52   .689   Jack Dunn
Orioles

BATTERS	POS-GAMES	GP	AB	R	H	BI	2B	3B	HR	BB	SO	SB	BA
Jack Bentley	1B141,P16	153	619	109	217	128	39	6	22	23	19	6	.351
Max Bishop	2B90,OF12	110	352	47	92	54	19	5	7	54	28	2	.261
Joe Boley	SS147,1B1,OF1	151	562	106	193	98	34	13	11	45	32	10	.343
Fritz Maisel	3B133	135	549	122	168	64	31	6	11	68	21	30	.306
James Walsh	OF163,2B2,1B1	164	636	131	208	106	47	9	5	64	31	10	.327
Otis Lawry	OF146	148	543	122	181	60	18	9	6	66	44	20	.333
Merwin Jacobson	OF124	124	451	84	137	71	18	5	6	62	31	18	.304
James McAvoy	C97,2B1	101	339	48	105	58	17	4	10	28	41	4	.310
William Styles	C52,OF40,1B36,2B12,SS7,3B1,P1	148	476	73	150	94	28	5	14	45	36	5	.315
Dick Porter	2B68,3B33,OF19,SS16	136	480	73	134	70	16	7	8	60	31	6	.279
John Ogden	P44,OF2	53	123	18	27		2	3	2			2	.220
Harry Frank	P45	46	98	12	13		1	0	1			1	.133
Alphonse Thomas	P42	42	92	5	14		0	1	2			0	.152
Lefty Grove	P41,1B1	42	77	3	13		2	0	0			0	.169
Joseph Barry	C31,OF2	38	103	6	25		2	0	0			0	.243
Jim Parnham	P36	38	108	19	34		6	2	6			1	.315
Sewell Dixon	OF23,3B4,2B3,SS1	31	87	9	15		1	1	1			0	.172
Max Owen	OF6,C4	12											.148
James Matthews	P4	4											.200
Jack Reid	P4	4											.067
Rufus Clarke	P2,1B1	3											.500
Edward Manley	C2	3											.000
Mike Roman	2B2	2											.167
Jack Dunn, Jr.	PH	1											.000

PITCHERS	W	L	PCT	G	GS	CG	SH	IP	H	BB	SO	ERA
John Ogden	24	10	.706	44		26	0	310	345	111	118	3.92
Harry Frank	22	9	.710	45		19	2	281	282	74	114	3.30
Lefty Grove	18	8	.692	41		11	3	209	146	152	205	2.80
Alphonse Thomas	18	9	.667	42		19	2	252	279	103	159	4.14
Jim Parnham	16	10	.615	36		23	4	250	274	78	119	4.39
Jack Bentley	13	2	.867	16		11	3	109	84	30	70	1.73

ROCHESTER Tribe

ROCHESTER 2nd   105-62   .629   -10   George Stallings
Tribe

BATTERS	POS-GAMES	GP	AB	R	H	BI	2B	3B	HR	BB	SO	SB	BA
Fred Merkle	1B163	163	631	145	219	130	41	10	7	72	55	26	.347
Cliff Brady	2B167	167	658	127	205	92	42	15	0	80	47	25	.312
Harold Gagnon	SS65	65	223	41	67	35	7	3	8	30	24	3	.300
Harry Lunte	3B95,SS18	116	411	42	129	66	20	5	0	17	16	4	.314
Maurice Archdeacon	OF163	163	628	151	202	44	20	8	5	118	58	55	.322
Thomas Connelly	OF159	160	603	117	195	99	28	7	3	80	68	23	.323
Bob Fothergill	OF101	101	397	75	152	79	35	12	4	28	15	7	.383
Harry Lake	C114	120	406	43	109	53	18	4	1	20	34	3	.268
Robert Murray	3B59,SS48,2B2	128	399	72	118	49	7	2	1	60	26	11	.296
David Hillis	SS23,3B22,OF11,1B5,2B1	72	200	24	53	39	7	5	1	12	34	3	.265
Plateau Cox	P44	49	102	15	23		0	0	0			0	.225
William Hughes	P43	43	97	10	16		4	0	0			0	.165
John Wisner	P41	42	94	17	22		0	1	0			0	.234
Fred Blake	P34,OF1	35	92	4	20		0	0	0			1	.217
James Keenan	P32	32	65	5	12		1	0	0			0	.185
James Allen	P30	30	64	9	19		1	2	1			0	.297
Edward Callahan	C9,OF6,P1	24	41	4	6		1	1	0			0	.146
John Mann	SS20	21	65	9	16		1	1	0			1	.246
Ken King	OF20	20	72	4	12		1	1	0			1	.167
Forrest Cobb	OF4	19	19	3	4		0	0	0			0	.211
Fred Leach	OF15,1B1	17	47	9	17		1	1	4			0	.362
Matt Donohue	OF8	8											.400
Frank Dodson	OF1,P1	3											.167
Burt Lewis	P3	3											.000
George Grey	P2	2											.000
Carl Meador	P2	2											.500
Louis Cowan	P2	2											.250
Ralph Judd	P2	2											.143
Louis Hall	PR	2											.000
Albert Irving	P2	2											.000
Bill Tierney	P2	2											.000
Norman Lehr	P1	1											.333
Carlisle Benson	P1	1											.000

ROCHESTER (cont.)
Tribe

BATTERS	POS-GAMES	GP	AB	R	H	BI	2B	3B	HR	BB	SO	SB	BA
William Bach	P1	1											.000
William Maloney	2B1	1											.000
Floyd Wheeler	P1	1											.000

PITCHERS	W	L	PCT	G	GS	CG	SH	IP	H	BB	SO	ERA
John Wisner	22	8	.722	41		17	2	256	270	75	100	3.20
William Hughes	18	16	.529	43		20	6	262	239	100	139	2.85
James Keenan	17	8	.680	32		10	2	181	171	72	78	2.54
Fred Blake	17	9	.654	34		23	1	241	252	104	122	2.76
Plateau Cox	15	9	.625	44		15	1	245	278	73	95	4.00
James Allen	10	7	.588	30		9	0	165	149	80	76	3.33

BUFFALO   3rd   95-72   .569   -20   George Wiltse
Bisons

BATTERS	POS-GAMES	GP	AB	R	H	BI	2B	3B	HR	BB	SO	SB	BA
William Kelly	1B89,OF4	115	377	61	115	54	23	10	12	35	65	4	.305
Art Butler	2B134	142	499	110	160	56	40	5	6	99	26	22	.321
John Sheehan	SS151	151	532	96	148	58	24	8	1	94	51	24	.278
Eugene Sheridan	3B151,SS15	166	590	63	148	64	22	6	0	41	34	16	.251
Frank Kane	OF164	164	600	118	164	88	26	14	14	90	73	32	.273
Cecil Dye	OF132	134	468	88	146	67	26	12	4	55	39	18	.312
Ed Rafferty	OF75	76	260	50	67		5	4	0			4	.258
Benny Bengough	C109	110	384	52	105	31	18	5	1	36	10	2	.273
Ed Miller	1B82,2B35,3B2,SS1	126	460	83	142	42	21	4	4	51	38	28	.309
Luke Urban	C56,3B10	72	214	26	64		10	0	1			5	.299
Joseph Burns	OF67	68	267	47	71		7	4	1			5	.266
Harry Heitman	OF32,P22	64	170	28	55		12	2	4			1	.324
Frank Werre	P42	42	68	3	8		2	0	0			0	.118
George Mohart	P41	41	92	10	13		1	0	1			0	.141
Clarence Fisher	P40	40	108	14	22		2	0	3			0	.204
Joseph Reddy	P37,3B1	38	86	9	17		3	0	0			1	.198
Ed Tomlin	P22,OF3	26	52	6	18		3	1	1			0	.346
Dick McCabe	P19	19	34	0	4		0	1	0			0	.118
Manley Llewellyn	P16	16	30	4	8		1	0	0			0	.267
Charles Cully	3B9	9											.219
John Weinecke	P9	9											.111
William Pierre	C3	4											.000
Murray Boland	P1	1											.000

PITCHERS	W	L	PCT	G	GS	CG	SH	IP	H	BB	SO	ERA
Clarence Fisher	21	10	.677	40		22	1	273	270	108	98	2.87
George Mohart	17	12	.586	41		19	3	269	297	88	81	3.85
Joseph Reddy	15	13	.536	37		22	2	252	317	63	115	4.18
Frank Werre	13	13	.500	42		11	2	204	231	87	62	4.68
Harry Heitman	9	4	.692	22		7	1	114	130	46	32	4.34
Edward Tomlin	8	4	.667	22		6	0	105	117	48	27	4.03
Manley Llewellyn	6	6	.500	16		7	1	86	111	44	35	6.07
Dick McCabe	4	7	.364	19		4	0	104	136	19	35	5.02

JERSEY CITY   4th   83-82   .503   -31   Ben Egan
Skeeters

BATTERS	POS-GAMES	GP	AB	R	H	BI	2B	3B	HR	BB	SO	SB	BA
James Holt	1B149	149	561	87	171	106	35	11	9	57	49	16	.305
Glenn Killinger	2B127,OF5,SS2	135	439	76	117	55	18	7	6	67	75	20	.267
Thomas Ray	SS		(see multi-team players)										
William McCarren	3B128,SS2	130	460	54	130	90	22	4	6	50	56	8	.283
John Jacobs	OF158	158	627	126	202	66	38	20	13	86	89	34	.322
Don Donelson	OF145	146	549	96	172	61	21	6	1	70	48	18	.313
Bill Zitzmann	OF113,3B14,SS12	139	476	111	142	62	26	8	5	82	55	18	.298
Otto Freitag	C120	121	366	47	93	31	18	1	0	72	47	9	.254
Harry Damrau	2B33,3B30,1B19	89	275	42	78	42	13	2	2	37	48	6	.284
Joseph Lucey	OF33,P23,1B3,2B1,SS1	69	179	27	40	27	9	2	6	10	30	2	.223
Julian Graveson	OF46	49	167	24	44	25	4	2	0	9	10	4	.263
Reid Zellars	P40,OF2	44	113	17	33		2	1	1			1	.292

JERSEY CITY (cont.)
Skeeters

BATTERS	POS-GAMES	GP	AB	R	H	BI	2B	3B	HR	BB	SO	SB	BA
George Metivier	P30	43	99	7	22		3	2	0			1	.222
Earl Hanson	P36,OF4	42	106	17	24		5	1	1			2	.226
Ben Egan	C41	41	116	8	26		4	1	0			0	.224
Edward Wurm	P31,OF2	40	79	9	17		6	0	0			0	.215
George Braun	SS33,2B1,3B1	36	118	18	27		3	0	1			9	.229
Robert Tecarr	P36	36	77	3	11		0	0	0			0	.143
Bob Carruthers	P32	32	50	1	5		3	0	0			0	.100
Frank Delaney	C20	21	48	3	12		4	0	0			2	.250
Mike Dunn	SS8,2B6,OF1	14											.137
William Knowlton	P4	5											.000
James Smith	SS4	4											.286
D'Arcy Flowers	SS3	3											.333
A. Wagner	2B1,SS1	2											.375
Norm Lutz	P1	1											.000

PITCHERS		W	L	PCT	G	GS	CG	SH	IP	H	BB	SO	ERA
George Metivier		18	7	.720	31		22	2	222	211	78	68	2.92
Reid Zellars		16	15	.516	40		22	0	257	270	144	87	2.59
Robert Tecarr		15	15	.500	36		22	3	251	321	52	51	3.76
Earl Hanson		15	16	.484	36		23	1	245	245	117	92	2.61
Edward Wurm		9	14	.391	31		10	2	169	206	125	50	4.89
Joseph Lucey		7	7	.500	23		9	0	128	131	101	53	3.87
Bob Carruthers		2	8	.200	32		6	0	144	164	55	35	3.06

TORONTO   5th   76-88   .463   -37.5   Ed Onslow
Maple Leafs

BATTERS	POS-GAMES	GP	AB	R	H	BI	2B	3B	HR	BB	SO	SB	BA
Ed Onslow	1B155	155	554	91	180	105	30	13	7	70	31	22	.325
Eusebio Gonzales	2B81,SS22,3B19	118	387	55	106	37	17	7	0	81	35	24	.274
John Jones	SS110	110	398	61	114	44	21	6	4	20	18	11	.286
Andy Anderson	3B112,OF23,2B16,SS9,1B1	158	551	97	167	100	33	13	14	95	58	23	.303
Al Wingo	OF160	160	623	119	199	122	29	10	34	70	82	15	.319
George Orme	OF136,1B4,2B4	146	535	91	145	52	19	5	3	91	57	25	.271
Joe Kelly	OF		(see multi-team players)										
Fred Fisher	C		(see multi-team players)										
Harry Stupp	2B72,3B22,1B3	106	342	49	99	34	22	1	2	36	31	13	.289
Harry Thompson	OF39,P24	76	204	32	58		5	2	1			4	.284
Sam Vick	OF46,1B1	50	172	30	40	31	7	4	2	28	23	4	.233
George Connally	P42,2B1	45	81	15	17		5	1	1			2	.210
William Taylor	P46,OF1	41	99	8	27		2	1	0			0	.273
Vincent Driscoll	C36	38	125	11	31		6	3	0			1	.248
Jewett Richardson	SS25,2B5,3B2	37	113	5	22		2	2	0			2	.195
John Enzmann	P37	37	64	6	14		3	1	1			0	.219
Ira Townsend	P29	29	61	1	8		1	0	0			0	.131
Stan Baumgartner	P21,OF6	27	64	7	14		2	0	0			0	.219
Cliff Best	P26	27	58	6	9		2	0	2			1	.155
John Ring	3B10	12											.400
Ed Reis	P11	11											.214
John Singleton	P9	9											.071
Cliff Hegedorn	SS5	5											.286
Jacob Miller	OF5	5											.250
Leo Johnson	P2	2											.000
Gary Fortune	P1	1											.000
Vic Keen	P1	1											.000
Frank Rapp	P1	1											.000

PITCHERS		W	L	PCT	G	GS	CG	SH	IP	H	BB	SO	ERA
William Taylor		18	15	.545	36		22	1	241	308	57	96	4.18
John Enzmann		10	9	.526	37		11	0	178	195	51	91	3.49
George Connally		10	12	.455	42		13	1	204	218	86	92	4.59
Cliff Best		9	8	.529	26		9	2	160	168	70	56	4.39
Stan Baumgartner		8	10	.444	21		14	0	143	153	42	36	3.21
Harry Thompson		7	9	.438	24		10	0	158	204	34	35	4.78
Ira Townsend		7	13	.350	29		12	2	170	196	65	60	4.08
Ed Reis		1	4	.200	11		1	0	38	50	15	23	5.69

READING
Aces

6th   71-93   .433   -42.5   Charles Bender

BATTERS	POS-GAMES	GP	AB	R	H	BI	2B	3B	HR	BB	SO	SB	BA
Sam Post	1B80	84	288	55	95	47	19	10	1	42	22	13	.330
Bill Barrett	2B59,1B17,SS4	80	281	42	89	40	23	8	2	16	48	3	.317
Fred Thomas	SS100,3B57	157	579	86	157	86	26	14	6	59	58	28	.271
Gus Getz	3B105.2B63	**167**	654	70	149	52	13	4	0	23	17	17	.228
Frank Gilhooley	OF164	164	636	124	**230**	64	35	13	0	107	25	22	.362
William Lightner	OF86	88	290	32	84	32	12	8	0	46	34	6	.299
Henry Haines	OF				(see multi-team players)								
Justin Clarke	C93	104	281	38	81	30	17	1	1	46	28	2	.288
Walt Tragresser	OF67,1B3	71	202	21	49	29	13	0	1	21	28	3	.243
Otto Pahlman	1B54	56	205	23	55	27	9	0	0	14	19	6	.268
Thomas Miller	OF50	53	177	28	53	30	7	0	4	11	24	5	.299
Walter Wolfe	SS42,2B6,1B3,3B1,OF1	53	164	12	26		5	0	0			7	.159
Francis Karpp	P34	43	86	9	20		1	1	0			1	.233
Fred Carts	P33	33	71	8	14		2	0	0			1	.197
James Durkin	SS21,3B8,2B1	32	87	14	20		3	2	0			5	.230
Charles Bender	P30,2B1	31	70	6	16		5	0	0			0	.229
Myrl Brown	P28	29	72	10	17		2	1	0			0	.236
Myles Thomas	P27	29	49	9	10		1	0	0			0	.204
Andrew Kotch	OF14	20	45	7	12		4	1	1			2	.267
John Scott	2B18	18	64	8	14		1	2	0			1	.219
Carl Johnson	C17	17	46	8	11		3	2	0			0	.239
Al Schacht	P16	16	34	3	4		1	0	0			0	.118
Harold Yordy	OF9	14											.353
Joe Conti	3B8	9											.143
Babe Herman	1B8	8											.258
Phil Weinert	P7	7											.200
Richard Niehaus	P7	7											.000
Joe Fitzgerald	C4	6											.200
Oliver Eyrich	P6	6											.182
Bernard Knauss	2B4	5											.308
James Kernan	C3,1B2	5											.000
Norm McNeil	C4	4											.500
William Murphy	OF1	4											.000
Ray Kennedy	C2	3											.500
James Driscoll	OF1	3											.400
William Harner	SS1,OF1	3											.200
James Haggerty	C2	2											.333
Harry Toppel	PH	2											.000
Reeve Hamilton	P2	2											.000
Ray Fedder	P2	2											.000
George Dickinson	P1	1											1.000
Elsworth Hughes	P1	1											.000
John Cavanaugh	SS1	1											.000
Drew Rader	P1	1											.000
Aloysius Sarsfield	P1	1											.000
George Woodhead	P1	1											.000

PITCHERS	W	L	PCT	G	GS	CG	SH	IP	H	BB	SO	ERA
Myrl Brown	15	11	.577	28		20	2	195	195	76	108	3.51
Francis Karpp	13	12	.520	34		17	2	219	221	93	85	4.27
Fred Carts	10	9	.526	33		16	3	196	213	78	64	4.00
Charles Bender	8	13	.381	30		15	1	183	172	33	88	**2.41**
Al Schacht	5	6	.455	16		6	2	107	116	23	15	3.20
Myles Thomas	2	8	.200	27		6	0	134	151	92	67	5.37

SYRACUSE
Stars

7th   64-102   .386   -50.5   Frank Shaughnessy

BATTERS	POS-GAMES	GP	AB	R	H	BI	2B	3B	HR	BB	SO	SB	BA
Jim Bottomley	1B119	119	460	78	160	94	29	15	14	36	27	13	.348
Sam Barnes	2B130,OF1	136	512	58	147	57	18	5	2	28	15	11	.287
Walt Keating	SS128,2B20,3B1,OF1	150	550	90	149	40	16	4	0	90	45	29	.271
Irvin Wimer	3B105,SS8,1B1,2B1,OF1,P1	121	381	37	93	35	14	3	2	35	14	7	.244
Howard Jones	OF155	159	591	115	174	81	27	7	13	58	42	27	.294
Robert Taggert	OF				(see multi-team players)								
Art Smith	OF				(see multi-team players)								
Charles Niebergall	C112,OF3	124	390	51	113	51	20	7	10	28	33	6	.299
Jean Dubuc	OF56,P26,3B12,2B2	124	313	51	110	52	23	6	2	47	38	12	.351
Henry Vick	C40,1B19	64	194	22	62	33	6	2	2	15	7	3	.320
Robert Edgar	OF27,3B13,2B10,SS1	56	120	12	25		5	0	0			2	.208

SYRACUSE (cont.)
Stars

BATTERS	POS-GAMES	GP	AB	R	H	BI	2B	3B	HR	BB	SO	SB	BA
Howard Freigau	SS26,OF10,2B9,3B9	52	169	21	40		15	1	2			4	.237
Les Montgomery	P39,OF2,2B1	45	58	6	11		3	0	0			1	.190
Walt Stewart	P39	44	95	10	20		3	1	3			3	.211
Charles Steen	OF33,P3	39	110	26	27		6	4	3			16	.245
Lester Sell	P38	38	77	9	16		3	4	0			0	.208
George Makin	3B35,SS2	37	121	15	34		4	0	3			1	.281
Mike Kircher	P28	33	71	5	14		3	0	0			1	.197
HarryMcCurdy	1B24,C9	32	108	17	34		10	2	2			4	.315
Edwin Dyer	OF12,P9,1B2,SS1	29	70	16	15		4	0	0			2	.214
Walt Schulz	P28	28	37	4	9		0	0	0			0	.243
James O'Rourke	3B13,2B3,SS1	23	46	17	13		1	0	0			2	.283
John Mohardt	OF21	21	65	4	12		2	1	0			4	.185
Art Reinhart	P14	15	34	3	10		1	1	1			0	.294
John Stuart	P15	15	27	1	5		2	0	0			0	.185
Frank Shaughnessy	1B3	12											.235
Ray Ryan	C6	10											.267
Art Ryan	OF8	8											.375
Edwin Sperber	1B4,OF3	8											.364
Earl Wagner	OF7	8											.000
Sam Carter	2B3,3B1,SS1,OF1	7											.333
Matt Kirley	P7	7											.200
Lester Bell	SS7	7											.150
William Barnes	P7	7											.100
Warwick Comstock	OF6	6											.250
Robert Burman	C3	6											.250
James Riley	OF6	6											.167
Milton Dixon	P4	4											.600
Rafield Perry	P4	4											.000
Fred Gadsby	OF3,SS1	4											.000
William Stewart	P3	3											.200
Sidney Benton	P2	2											.000
James Duffy	P1	1											.000
Fred Lynch	P1	1											.000
John Leddy	OF1	1											.000

PITCHERS	W	L	PCT	G	GS	CG	SH	IP	H	BB	SO	ERA
Walt Stewart	14	16	.467	39		24	3	263	275	91	97	3.73
Mike Kircher	10	14	.417	28		13	0	178	202	59	40	3.99
Lester Sell	10	18	.357	38		15	1	238	233	103	77	3.40
Jean Dubuc	8	9	.471	26		13	1	166	176	60	65	4.77
Art Reinhart	5	7	.417	14		7	0	87	76	56	42	3.73
John Stuart	4	5	.444	15		4	0	72	74	34	48	4.00
Walt Schulz	4	10	.286	28		5	1	104	119	63	47	5.37
Les Montgomery	4	14	.222	39		8	1	157	225	60	50	7.05

NEWARK   8th   54-112   .325   -60.5   William Clymer
Bears

BATTERS	POS-GAMES	GP	AB	R	H	BI	2B	3B	HR	BB	SO	SB	BA
John Walker	1B87,C61	152	532	67	153	66	27	5	4	29	37	9	.288
Ed Mooers	2B82,SS42,3B20	143	519	50	127	43	19	6	0	31	49	9	.245
Joe Benes	SS70,2B62,3B5,OF1	138	472	40	115	40	13	2	1	29	43	4	.244
William Webb	3B114,OF10,2B2	127	456	65	139	47	31	1	0	57	46	13	.305
Frank Wigglesworth	OF121	121	453	47	133	52	19	7	2	27	22	4	.294
Fred Brainerd	OF128,2B21,1B15,3B5,P2,SS1	164	629	74	175	65	34	8	8	24	60	34	.278
Jesse Altenburg	OF102	105	385	55	120		18	5	0			6	.312
Michael Devine	C	(see multi-team players)											
Dean Barnhardt	OF42,P36	95	266	31	76	37	14	8	3	12	37	2	.286
Wade Lefler	1B47,OF8,C2	58	228	26	59		7	4	0			3	.259
Ben Filishifter	P40	43	90	4	18		2	2	1			0	.200
Chet Fowler	OF18,SS12,3B7,2B2	42	146	11	35		4	0	0			2	.240
Howard Baldwin	P36	41	102	9	25		7	1	0			0	.245
Luther Barnes	P40	41	88	5	9		0	0	0			1	.102
Rudolph Kneisch	P33	33	76	6	16		4	0	0			0	.211
George Knothe	SS25,3B1	26	86	14	27		3	2	0			0	.314
Robert Kinsella	OF21	23	78	8	15		4	2	1			2	.192
Harry Manning	C15	15	44	5	11		0	0	0			0	.250
Alfred Young	1B13	13											.317
Frank Mueller	OF11,1B2	13											.154
Peter Krumenaker	1B9	11											.379
Frank Loftus	P10	10											.190

NEWARK (cont.)
Bears

BATTERS	POS-GAMES	GP	AB	R	H	BI	2B	3B	HR	BB	SO	SB	BA
Vance Graber	OF3	7											.400
Carl Deetjen	P5,OF1	6											.364
Thomas Walsh	OF4	6											.111
Atwood Gordy	P5	5											.400
Sam Wilson	C4	4											.100
Fred Ross	PH	3											.500
Al Swingler	C3	3											.400
Harry Kane	OF3	3											.167
Finley	P2	2											.000
Charles Fitzberger	2B1	2											.000
Elmer Howe	P2	2											.000
Ken Lavin	OF1	2											.000
Harry O'Neill	P2	2											.000
Mike Kehoe	P1	1											1.000
Cuningham	OF1	1											.500
Ed Hock	OF1	1											.400
Edgar Albans	SS1	1											.250
William Gillies	P1	1											.000
Fawcett	P1	1											.000
William Clymer	PH	1											.000
McDonagh	PH	1											.000
Rekap	P1	1											.000
Clyde Russell	P1	1											.000
Whitney	P1	1											.000
Charles Whitehouse	P1	1											.000
Willard Poole	SS1	1											.000
Thomas DeNoville	1B1	1											.000
Muller	OF1	1											.000
Earl James	P1	1											.000
Stirper	OF1	1											.000
O'Grannigan	C1	1											.000
Ed Williams	OF1	1											.000
Tubbert	C1	1											.000

PITCHERS	W	L	PCT	G	GS	CG	SH	IP	H	BB	SO	ERA
Ben Filishifter	12	11	.480	40		18	1	233	231	120	49	4.21
Dean Barnhardt	10	22	.313	36		30	0	287	296	74	67	3.67
Luther Barnes	10	23	.303	40		23	2	254	255	94	100	3.86
Howard Baldwin	12	21	.364	37		22	2	251	288	87	87	4.48
Rudolph Kneisch	6	20	.231	33		19	2	223	227	106	65	4.44
Frank Loftus	1	8	.111	10		7	0	66	60	29	19	4.23

MULTI-TEAM PLAYERS

BATTERS	POS-GAMES	TEAMS	GP	AB	R	H	BI	2B	3B	HR	BB	SO	SB	BA
Robert Taggert	OF141	NE48-SY96	144	557	88	149	53	19	9	8	39	40	11	.268
Joe Kelly	OF128,1B5	RE46-TO94	140	530	77	160	80	21	7	21	85	8		.302
Henry Haines	OF135,1B3	JC13-RE125	138	504	89	160	68	31	15	2	66	66	45	.317
Art Smith	OF126,1B5	SY95-RO42	137	469	73	140	67	20	12	9	51	46	20	.299
Michael Devine	C125,3B7,1B1	TO59-NE77	136	503	63	150	56	24	3	2	34	17	10	.298
Thomas Ray	SS115,2B4	NE22-JC97	119	400	42	88	47	17	1	1	46	45	3	.220
Fred Fisher	C84	SY27-TO71	98	302	28	72	36	6	0	4	18	35	0	.238
Gus Sandberg	C78,1B1	TO28-RO64	92	262	40	74	34	5	3	3	30	28	8	.282
Charles Babington	OF72,3B3	RE38-BU53	91	294	58	92		17	4	1			18	.313
Pat Martin	P33	TO8-BU25	33	73	2	10		2	0	0			0	.137
Ray Gordinier	P21,OF2	RE13-RO13	26	39	3	12		1	1	0			1	.308
Walter Kopf	2B23,SS5	NE1-RE22	23	79	8	18		3	2	0			2	.228
Otto Scheck	C22	JC7-NE16	23	62	5	11		1	0	0			0	.177
Al Woods	3B13,SS8	NE14-JC7	21	82	9	23		7	1	0			1	.280
Dewey Hill	C14	TO7-BU10	17	37	4	7		0	2	0			1	.189
Clarence Wanner	P13	SY8-NE9	17	8	1	2		0	0	0			0	.250
Ross Swartz	P11	RE10-NE1	11											.235
Emery Ketcham	P8	BU6-NE3	9											.412
John Mercer	SS3,2B2	BU2-JC3	5											.333
Marcus Jackson	P5	BA4-NE1	5											.143
W. Schott	1B2	RE1-NE1	2											.250

PITCHERS		TEAMS	W	L	PCT	G	GS	CG	SH	IP	H	BB	SO	ERA
Pat Martin		TO8-RE25	12	15	.444	33		17	3	215	211	92	90	3.68
Ray Gordinier		RE11-RO10	5	10	.333	21		8	2	117	117	67	58	4.69

MULTI-TEAM PLAYERS (cont.)

PITCHERS	TEAMS	W	L	PCT	G	GS	CG	SH	IP	H	BB	SO	ERA
Ross Swartz	RE10-NE1	3	5	.375	11		6	1	67	81	49	21	6.18
Clarence Wanner	SY8-NE5	0	0	----	13		0	0	23	21	14	7	4.30

TEAM BATTING

TEAMS	GP	AB	R	H	BI	2B	3B	HR	BB	SO	SB	BA
BALTIMORE	169	5755	991	1734	864	281	77	112	573	503	114	.301
ROCHESTER	168	5692	993	1721	828	242	86	39	622	536	175	.302
BUFFALO	168	5533	909	1547	600	258	81	54	695	566	172	.280
JERSEY CITY	167	5429	821	1480	702	256	77	52	652	704	154	.273
TORONTO	165	5466	820	1532	716	234	75	92	613	567	163	.280
READING	167	5488	780	1522	639	259	88	25	557	566	184	.277
SYRACUSE	166	5608	811	1574	679	256	81	74	562	506	176	.281
NEWARK	166	5544	625	1491	545	245	51	26	375	562	101	.269
	668	44515	6750	12601	5573	2031	546	474	4649	4510	1239	.283

1923
LEFTY GROVE

In 1920, the Baltimore Orioles introduced a new pitcher to the International League. This new pitcher proved nearly unhittable as he mowed down batter after batter via the strikeout. The new player was Robert Moses Grove. Since he threw from the port side, most of his colleagues called him Lefty.

At the tender age of twenty, Lefty Grove joined the Martinsburg team of the Blue Ridge League. Catching the notice of Baltimore owner Jack Dunn, Grove joined the pitching staff of the vaunted Orioles in 1920. During his first International League campaign, Grove compiled a 12–2 record, meanwhile making a name for himself in the strikeout department as he whiffed 88 men in only 123 innings.

In 1921, Lefty Grove reached maturity. Pitching a full season, Grove won 25 games. More impressively, he struck out 254, while holding opposing batsmen to a puny .196 batting average—both league-best efforts. In 1922, Grove continued to baffle batters as he fanned 205. In 1923, Lefty Grove would turn up the heat another notch.

The Baltimore Orioles won their fifth straight flag in 1923 as they bested another 100-win Rochester club. Reading jumped to third, while Toronto and Buffalo finished in a virtual tie for fourth. Syracuse, Newark, and Jersey City finished in the last three spots. The circuit-topping hitter was Clarence Pitt (.357), who played for Rochester and Baltimore. Buffalo's William Webb and Baltimore's Max Bishop poled the most home runs (22), while Fred Merkle of Rochester won his second straight runs batted in title (166). Baltimore pitcher Jim Parnham won 33 (the league's best twentieth century mark), while Joseph Lucey of Jersey City posted the lowest earned run average (2.73).

Lefty Grove, to the surprise of none, won his third straight strikeout crown. This time, Grove sent 330 men benchward as he shattered the league's season strikeout record set 35 years before.

After the 1923 season, Lefty Grove won one more International League strikeout crown before joining the major leagues in 1925. Pitching for the Philadelphia Athletics, Grove ripped off seven 20-win seasons on his way to a 300-win career. Of additional note, he won the American League strikeout crown his first seven years in the league.

Lefty Grove's International legacy is one of a blazing fastball. In five short years he struck out over 1,100 batters. Although that mark is just short of the career strikeout record, Grove's 330 total for the 1923 season remains the International League's best. In no other year has any other pitcher come within 100 strikeouts of the total.

BALTIMORE Orioles   1st   111-53   .677   Jack Dunn

BATTERS	POS-GAMES	GP	AB	R	H	BI	2B	3B	HR	BB	SO	SB	BA
James Walsh	1B109,OF38	151	564	107	188	134	41	5	15	63	32	14	.333
Max Bishop	2B159	159	537	117	179	109	35	10	**22**	86	44	7	.333
Joe Boley	SS160	160	615	110	188	104	29	12	9	46	34	7	.306
Fritz Maisel	3B93,2B1	99	364	64	100	44	19	6	6	49	20	15	.275
Merwin Jacobson	OF160	160	606	127	199	106	26	11	11	93	45	36	.328
Otis Lawry	OF151	151	585	137	175	57	19	7	8	83	44	**41**	.299
Dick Porter	OF74,3B68,SS8,2B6	155	617	117	195	111	27	12	18	41	32	9	.316
Joe Cobb	C	(see multi-team players)											
William Styles	C49,1B32,3B10,OF6	106	358	60	113	78	23	5	16	34	15	2	.316
Lefty Grove	P52	52	109	10	17		2	0	1			0	.156
John Ogden	P47,OF1	50	89	15	26		4	0	3			1	.292
Harry Frank	P49	49	60	8	15		1	0	0			0	.250
Jim Parnham	P44	48	136	14	36	26	6	0	2	10	30	2	.265
Alphonse Thomas	P45	45	80	8	16		1	0	2			0	.200
Clayton Sheedy	1B31	34	103	36	37		6	2	1			8	.359
Sewell Dixon	OF15,3B1	24	48	6	12		3	1	0			0	.250
Charles Bender	P18	18	35	2	11		1	0	1			0	.314
William Henderson	P8	8											.368
Joseph Bird	C1	3											.000
Harold Clarke	OF2	2											.333
Norm McNeil	C2	2											.200
Paul Lowder	P2	2											.000
James Clarke	P2	2											.000
Joseph Lance	P1	1											.000

PITCHERS	W	L	PCT	G	GS	CG	SH	IP	H	BB	SO	ERA
Jim Parnham	**33**	7	**.825**	44		28	3	323	294	99	115	3.18
Lefty Grove	27	10	.730	**52**		24	**6**	303	223	**186**	**330**	3.11
John Ogden	17	12	.586	47		17	2	239	255	81	67	4.02
Alphonse Thomas	15	12	.556	44		13	0	222	214	89	142	2.95
Harry Frank	9	2	.818	49		5	2	179	227	54	67	4.68
Charles Bender	6	3	.667	18		5	0	93	109	30	44	5.03

ROCHESTER Tribe   2nd   101-65   .608   -11   George Stallings

BATTERS	POS-GAMES	GP	AB	R	H	BI	2B	3B	HR	BB	SO	SB	BA
Fred Merkle	1B165	165	630	138	217	**166**	**54**	13	19	94	38	27	.344
Cliff Brady	2B156	157	569	107	154	57	23	5	0	90	40	11	.271
John Jenkins	SS142,3B1	149	515	74	159	65	19	14	2	26	28	8	.309
Harry Lunte	3B167	**167**	624	88	191	86	33	5	1	47	21	4	.306
Maurice Archdeacon	OF162	162	638	**162**	**228**	55	29	15	2	89	44	31	.357
John Command	OF114	124	427	63	129	68	23	9	1	36	33	12	.302
Clarence Pitt	OF	(see multi-team players)											
Harry Lake	C122	127	418	41	116	47	20	6	3	28	35	1	.278
Sam Barnes	OF62,SS28,2B13	117	391	69	111	55	15	7	2	37	13	3	.284
Art Smith	OF61,1B2	77	256	43	73	65	12	6	4	23	29	5	.285
John Wisner	P45	45	129	13	31		5	1	0			0	.240
Walt Beall	P42	42	83	14	21		1	0	2			0	.253
John Miljus	P32,OF3	38	81	17	21		3	1	3			0	.259
William Moore	P37	37	81	11	18		3	1	0			0	.222
James Keenan	P31	31	56	5	15		3	1	0			0	.268
Perry Payne	OF14,1B1	16	60	5	17		1	2	0			0	.284
Cicero Littrell	P15	15	22	1	7		2	0	0			0	.318
James Allen	P13	13											.400
Guy Dunning	OF11	11											.419
Sidney Womack	C3	8											.250
Walt McQuinn	C8	8											.200
Herman Schwartje	P5	5											.000
Burney Griffin	PH	3											1.000
Harold Yordy	OF2	2											.500
Harold Drew	OF2	2											.444
John McCafferty	P2	2											.000
Alex Peterson	P1	1											.333
Walter Miller	P1	1											.000
Irvin Wilhelm	P1	1											.000
Carl Meador	P1	1											.000
Henry Thompson	P1	1											.000
Marvin Steggerda	P1	1											.000
Fred Morris	PH	1											.000
Martin O'Malley	OF1	1											.000

ROCHESTER (cont.)
Tribe

PITCHERS	W	L	PCT	G	GS	CG	SH	IP	H	BB	SO	ERA
John Wisner	26	15	.634	45		33	3	338	352	113	167	3.04
William Moore	18	12	.600	37		17	1	214	205	116	121	3.20
Walt Beall	15	9	.625	42		13	2	227	198	109	143	2.81
John Miljus	12	9	.571	32		11	0	180	229	67	61	5.09
James Keenan	9	4	.692	31		7	3	146	142	74	62	4.32
James Allen	1	2	.333	13		1	0	40	48	20	16	5.63
Cicero Littrell	1	4	.200	15		3	0	62	75	24	11	4.06

READING   3rd   85-79   .518   -26   Spencer Abbott
Keystones

BATTERS	POS-GAMES	GP	AB	R	H	BI	2B	3B	HR	BB	SO	SB	BA
Raymond Bates	1B109,3B19,OF1	140	479	71	146	61	24	5	5	63	31	6	.305
Roy Washburn	2B82,1B56	142	494	103	145	84	26	12	11	76	79	9	.294
Charles Ward	SS90,3B5	97	326	27	81	30	11	2	1	37	22	2	.248
Fred Thomas	3B85,SS63	146	537	80	137	66	15	17	10	49	51	17	.255
Thomas Connelly	OF158	161	565	143	178	92	30	9	21	139	76	26	.315
Joseph Lightner	OF138	150	480	75	149	77	19	5	6	108	31	7	.310
Bill Barrett	OF95,2B6,P1	105	407	86	137	70	19	12	8	35	52	23	.337
Byrd Lynn	C103	105	373	48	114	63	24	2	2	29	32	3	.306
Ralph Miller	2B80,3B55,SS17	149	583	95	195	111	49	9	9	49	19	12	.334
Justin Clarke	C69,1B3,OF1	84	250	31	74	36	17	1	1	15	20	0	.296
Hugh Ormand	OF58	64	210	37	63		13	3	1			0	.300
Frank Gilhooley	OF51	56	223	45	66		10	3	0			7	.296
Walt Smallwood	P47	47	97	9	14		3	0	0			1	.144
Pat Martin	P35	35	85	13	19		3	0	0			0	.224
Al Mamaux	P31	32	81	9	23		2	2	2			1	.284
Fred Carts	P28	28	44	3	4		0	0	0			0	.091
Elsworth Hughes	P20	23	35	4	7		0	0	0			0	.200
Oliver Eyrich	P14	14											.222
Phede Lambke	P13	13											.214
Thomas Comiskey	3B6	6											.294
Warren Heller	P6	6											.250
Alvin Julian	C6	6											.200
John Keating	C2	3											.333
Pat Flaherty	P2	2											.333
Tom Kay	OF2	2											.222
Al Schacht	P2	2											.000
Elmer Strauss	C1	1											.400
Frank Hummer	P1	1											.000
Hammond Lieppe	P1	1											.000
Carl Johnson	PH	1											.000
Booker	P1	1											.000

PITCHERS	W	L	PCT	G	GS	CG	SH	IP	H	BB	SO	ERA
Al Mamaux	17	10	.630	31		19	5	217	213	59	141	3.40
Pat Martin	14	14	.500	35		20	0	235	223	78	115	3.79
Walt Smallwood	14	15	.483	47		16	1	265	356	57	61	4.72
Fred Carts	6	10	.375	28		6	0	136	177	51	49	5.63
Elsworth Hughes	5	4	.556	20		4	0	90	117	34	22	5.20
Oliver Eyrich	1	2	.333	14		0	0	32	43	24	14	5.91
Phede Lambke	1	3	.250	13		4	0	47	56	20	12	4.40

TORONTO   4th   81-79   .506   -28   Dan Howley
Maple Leafs

BATTERS	POS-GAMES	GP	AB	R	H	BI	2B	3B	HR	BB	SO	SB	BA
Ed Onslow	1B127	127	455	63	158	93	29	7	11	68	17	10	.347
Otis Miller	2B74,SS19,1B1	101	321	43	77	35	16	2	0	32	20	8	.240
Frank O'Rourke	SS139,2B8,1B4	150	598	103	192	68	41	5	7	45	40	16	.321
Ramon Gonzales	3B112,SS6	120	388	48	109	60	10	2	1	70	32	2	.281
Joe Kelly	OF159	159	591	96	186	95	32	8	16	56	53	22	.315
Al Wingo	OF122	122	455	97	160	85	25	11	20	69	30	8	.352
George Maisel	OF87,1B20,3B14	120	470	85	151	41	15	3	1	48	16	12	.321
Michael Vincent	C114,1B5,3B4,2B1	125	422	51	111	54	16	5	4	29	52	6	.263
Adelbert Capes	2B64,OF51,3B12,SS3	129	458	75	122	38	15	5	0	59	30	21	.266
Edwin Eayrs	OF63,P1	66	213	33	63		4	1	1			7	.296

TORONTO (cont.)
Maple Leafs

BATTERS	POS-GAMES	GP	AB	R	H	BI	2B	3B	HR	BB	SO	SB	BA
Dewey Hill	C49	54	138	16	37		6	2	1			3	.268
Jesse Doyle	P32,1B8,OF5,3B1	52	140	18	41		3	3	0			2	.293
Eusebio Gonzales	2B26,3B21	46	185	29	46		5	0	0			4	.249
Myles Thomas	P37	37	92	11	18		2	0	0			0	.196
William Taylor	P34	34	82	2	20		1	0	0			0	.244
Norm Glaser	P33	33	86	10	18		4	0	1			0	.209
Ed Reis	P15,OF11,1B1	33	70	7	23		3	1	1			0	.329
Art Reynolds	P21,OF1	23	52	3	8		0	1	0			0	.154
William Kenyon	C14	20	53	7	18		2	1	0			0	.340
Don Summers	P19	19	24	2	5		2	0	0			0	.208
William Fullerton	P16,3B3	18	25	0	3		1	0	0			0	.120
Lore Bader	P7	7											.176
Fred Lynch	P4	4											.000
Mike Prendergast	P3	3											.500
Richard Collins	P1	1											.000
George Artus	C1	1											.000

PITCHERS	W	L	PCT	G	GS	CG	SH	IP	H	BB	SO	ERA
Norm Glaser	16	12	.571	33		18	2	221	245	62	46	3.87
Jesse Doyle	15	13	.536	32		23	0	249	277	93	82	3.57
Myles Thomas	13	15	.464	37		22	2	238	272	104	84	3.97
William Taylor	13	16	.448	34		21	2	237	267	58	73	3.41
Art Reynolds	11	5	.688	21		12	1	146	155	52	30	3.88
Ed Reis	3	6	.333	15		5	0	82	87	66	22	4.39
William Fullerton	1	3	.250	16		1	0	51	56	36	11	4.59
Donald Summers	1	5	.167	19		2	0	62	65	31	22	4.35

BUFFALO   5th   83-81   .506   -28   George Wiltse
Bisons

BATTERS	POS-GAMES	GP	AB	R	H	BI	2B	3B	HR	BB	SO	SB	BA
William Kelly	1B164	164	620	123	217	128	49	9	15	68	74	8	.350
Art Butler	2B104	111	381	71	97	38	18	1	3	67	20	18	.255
John Sheehan	SS138	138	472	87	147	52	27	3	2	76	39	9	.311
William Webb	3B121	122	447	105	140	73	33	5	22	75	39	14	.313
Cecil Dye	OF155	155	619	133	197	87	40	13	16	84	52	29	.318
Frank Kane	OF123	124	455	71	127	74	23	11	10	45	49	12	.279
Joe Burns	OF118	130	455	83	128	37	29	8	1	74	24	7	.281
Luke Urban	C104,3B1	106	203	33	63	27	14	1	1	29	15	2	.310
Wescott Kingdon	2B65,3B41,SS29,OF4	144	475	66	126	56	31	9	5	60	67	4	.265
Vern Spencer	OF108	116	400	72	122	54	22	9	4	42	29	11	.305
Harry Heitman	P35,OF5,1B3	62	114	19	29		5	0	1			1	.254
Clarence Fisher	P47	47	88	8	14		1	0	1			1	.159
George Mohart	P44	44	88	10	13		5	0	3			0	.148
Joseph Reddy	P39	39	71	8	18		2	0	2			0	.254
Edgar LePard	P38	38	76	12	15		6	0	1			0	.197
Harry Vanderbach	C30	31	85	9	19		4	1	2			0	.224
Frank Werre	P29	29	61	9	10		2	0	1			0	.164
Graeme Snow	C21	23	68	9	17		3	0	0			0	.250
Atwood Gordy	P17	18	29	5	5		2	0	0			0	.172
Ed Anfinson	C12,3B2	15	44	3	11		2	0	0			0	.250
Murray Boland	P14	14											.000
Ed Marsh	C7	9											.143
Garrett Stearns	C8	8											.208
Roy Akins	C5	6											.000
John Hewitt	P5	5											.333
John Weinecke	P5	5											.333
James Brice	P2	2											.000
George Wiltse	1B2	2											.000
Napolean Ladouceur	P1	1											.000
Frank Dunkle	P1	1											.000

PITCHERS	W	L	PCT	G	GS	CG	SH	IP	H	BB	SO	ERA
Joseph Reddy	16	12	.571	39		20	3	215	235	69	75	3.43
George Mohart	16	15	.522	44		15	0	263	306	119	73	3.56
Edgar LePard	14	12	.538	38		12	1	216	257	92	82	4.87
Clarence Fisher	13	15	.464	47		12	0	242	292	108	76	5.06
Frank Werre	11	9	.550	29		16	0	173	205	64	45	4.01
Harry Heitman	7	6	.538	36		4	1	148	173	64	32	4.68
Atwood Gordy	4	4	.500	17		4	0	75	89	35	18	5.52
Murray Boland	2	4	.333	14		0	0	39	49	17	7	3.92

SYRACUSE
Stars

6th   73-92   .442   -38.5   Frank Shaughnessy

BATTERS	POS-GAMES	GP	AB	R	H	BI	2B	3B	HR	BB	SO	SB	BA
John McCarty	1B77,OF41	127	451	81	144	77	25	10	13	32	32	7	.319
Gard Gislason	2B117	120	388	48	109	59	10	2	1	52	7	2	.281
Walt Keating	SS98,2B44,OF6	151	504	71	134	54	18	6	0	59	54	13	.266
George Makin	3B165	165	565	86	164	87	28	8	2	88	39	3	.290
Robert Taggert	OF146	149	544	100	174	78	31	9	7	64	48	10	.320
Melvin Silva	OF136,3B2,2B1	136	565	99	173	59	30	15	5	53	37	30	.306
Roscoe Holm	OF76,SS56,3B2,1B2	134	482	80	151	76	24	5	3	43	20	4	.313
Charles Niebergall	C123	133	407	65	118	65	19	5	12	41	45	4	.290
Raymond McKee	C55,1B37	106	327	50	96	56	22	5	7	29	21	1	.294
Art Reinhart	P43,OF14	74	150	14	33		3	0	0			1	.220
Jean Dubuc	OF42,P14,1B3	70	177	26	42		7	2	2			0	.237
Adolph Pierotti	P39,OF4	55	105	11	24		5	2	0			0	.229
Thomas DeNoville	1B41	42	151	13	38	29	7	0	1	17	4	2	.252
Vern Parks	P37	41	64	6	10		1	0	1			0	.156
Elmer Hill	P33,OF1	36	51	6	14		4	0	0			0	.275
George Krahe	SS13,2B7,OF4,3B4	31	82	13	22		3	1	0			1	.268
Fred Frankhouse	P23,OF1	31	47	5	15		1	0	0			0	.319
William Ward	P27	28	40	5	7		2	0	0			0	.175
Hubert Mason	OF21	22	66	11	19		3	0	0			1	.288
Don Peden	OF19	22	58	9	14		2	0	0			1	.241
Cliff Jackson	P19	19	12	1	1		0	0	0			0	.083
George Swartz	P16	17	26	0	0		0	0	0			0	.000
Floyd Dougherty	C7,OF4	16	26	4	4		0	0	1			0	.154
Art Riviere	P15	15	14	0	2		0	0	0			0	.143
Wilbur Swansboro	1B13	13											.460
Seymour Bailey	P13	13											.100
William Duryea	OF5,1B2	10											.296
Robert Kinsella	OF9	10											.192
Inal Moheney	P7	9											.250
Quinn	SS6,OF2	8											.211
Al Bool	OF7	8											.125
James Long	C7	7											.267
Lester Bell	SS2,OF1,2B1	7											.263
Homer Burch	C2	5											.200
Edgar Clough	P4	4											.333
William Barnes	P3	3											.000
Ernest Jeanes	OF2	2											.143
Wilford Shupe	P2	2											.000
Frank Shaughnessy	PR	1											.000

PITCHERS	W	L	PCT	G	GS	CG	SH	IP	H	BB	SO	ERA
Art Reinhart	19	19	.500	41		24	0	292	307	147	101	3.66
Adolph Pierotti	17	12	.586	40		18	2	219	278	74	56	4.23
Vern Parks	9	10	.474	36		11	1	176	216	61	49	4.35
Elmer Hill	7	11	.389	33		7	0	145	189	68	39	5.52
Fred Frankhouse	6	11	.353	23		7	1	112	139	58	45	5.22
Jean Dubuc	5	2	.714	14		6	1	64	66	29	26	2.81
William Ward	4	9	.308	27		4	1	125	144	60	36	4.25
George Swartz	3	4	.429	16		4	0	74	73	30	35	4.86
Cliff Jackson	2	5	.286	19		3	0	54	72	31	25	5.50
Art Riviere	0	2	.000	15		2	0	53	62	42	15	5.26
Seymour Bailey	0	4	.000	13		0	0	47	55	17	24	2.68

NEWARK
Bears

7th   60-101   .373   -49.5   Michael Devine -
Fred Brainerd

BATTERS	POS-GAMES	GP	AB	R	H	BI	2B	3B	HR	BB	SO	SB	BA
Ed Miller	1B126,2B24,SS1	149	502	77	120	49	19	3	0	50	60	36	.239
Fred Brainerd	2B107,SS31,OF20,1B1,P1	151	569	86	181	114	31	9	17	44	41	32	.318
Eugene Sheridan	SS107,3B20,P1	127	439	49	110	52	17	3	0	25	17	10	.251
Andy Anderson	3B112,2B19,SS6,OF1	144	447	58	132	61	24	10	5	73	45	16	.295
Hobart Whitman	OF132	134	502	63	142	45	15	4	1	45	17	15	.283
Frank Wigglesworth	OF115	119	419	56	131	60	22	8	7	33	24	8	.313
Bill Zitzmann	OF69,3B34,SS16,1B6,2B1,P1	125	428	108	139	53	21	11	7	71	51	25	.325
Michael Devine	C109,1B4,P4,2B3,3B2,OF2,SS1	132	382	50	111	42	13	1	3	51	12	14	.291
Otto Greenae	C69,1B13,OF2	97	249	31	69	38	12	1	5	34	50	2	.277
John Honig	OF62	73	228	35	65	26	12	2	1	17	22	6	.285
Ben Filishifter	OF46,P18	63	183	17	39		8	1	0			1	.213
Charles See	OF48,P8	55	199	33	55		10	3	1			19	.276
Howard Baldwin	P46,OF1	49	117	6	21		5	2	0			1	.179

NEWARK (cont.)
Bears

BATTERS	POS-GAMES	GP	AB	R	H	BI	2B	3B	HR	BB	SO	SB	BA
Leland Ellis	P48,OF1	49	105	7	16	0	0	1	1			0	.152
James McGarry	P27,OF1	31	50	5	6	0	0	0	0			0	.120
Charles Schlester	P29	29	46	3	4	0	0	0	0			1	.087
Stan Schupka	P17,OF3	21	24	1	5	0	0	0	0			0	.208
James Duffy	1B17,OF1	18	61	3	14	1	1	0	0			0	.230
Charles Nossett	P17	18	26	4	5	2	2	1	0			1	.192
George Knothe	2B8,SS2,OF1	12											.189
Paul Sherman	P10,OF1	11											.080
Jesse Altenburg	OF10	11											.150
Joe Benes	2B6	10											.292
Rudolph Kneisch	P9	9											.233
Henry Grampp	P7	7											.000
George Woodhead	P5,OF1	6											.333
Lyman Sowder	P4	5											.200
Edward Manley	C2	5											.167
J. McComas	3B3,OF1	4											.222
Raymond Harriman	P2	2											.000
Lloyd Brown	P2	2											.000
Schroll	P1	1											1.000
John Connolly	1B1	1											.333
Tom Glass	P1	1											.000
Coacher	P1	1											.000
Osborne	P1	1											.000
Vincent Haley	P1	1											.000
Stucker	P1	1											.000
Tagg	C1	1											.000
Keay	P1	1											.000
Staylor	C1	1											.000
Festus Higgins	PH	1											.000
Faussler	P1	1											.000

PITCHERS	W	L	PCT	G	GS	CG	SH	IP	H	BB	SO	ERA
Howard Baldwin	21	15	.583	46		29	2	308	347	97	113	3.74
Leland Ellis	16	18	.471	48		20	0	291	370	98	69	4.29
Ben Filishifter	7	10	.412	18		7	0	112	132	49	30	4.90
Charles Schlester	5	12	.294	29		5	0	132	151	67	23	5.18
Paul Sherman	3	7	.300	10		8	1	69	88	39	17	4.82
Charles Nossett	2	6	.250	17		6	1	89	86	52	22	4.15
Stan Schupka	1	6	.143	17		1	0	50	77	49	9	7.56
James McGarry	1	13	.071	26		9	0	131	175	80	25	5.56

JERSEY CITY   8th   61-105   .367   -51   Ben Egan
Skeeters

BATTERS	POS-GAMES	GP	AB	R	H	BI	2B	3B	HR	BB	SO	SB	BA
James Holt	1B157	162	573	83	188	128	45	9	17	77	48	9	.328
Thomas Ray	2B74,SS54,3B2	126	362	32	80	37	10	1	0	49	34	4	.221
Wally Wolf	SS75,2B9,OF5,3B2	91	358	54	93	32	10	0	1	21	33	5	.260
Gus Getz	3B90,2B53	143	547	58	151	65	23	8	0	18	18	8	.276
Don Donelson	OF165	165	648	104	185	48	23	7	4	79	57	12	.285
John Jacobs	OF155,2B1	156	568	102	187	78	38	10	12	71	79	23	.329
Art Wagner	OF51,3B33,2B29,1B1	113	397	49	107	39	14	6	0	24	43	7	.270
Otto Freitag	C125,1B1	135	419	56	124	47	23	8	2	52	29	5	.296
Dean Barnhardt	P31,OF10	79	162	12	39		12	1	0			1	.241
Joseph Lucey	P30,OF17,1B9	69	170	24	39		7	4	2			1	.229
Frank McCrea	C56,1B1	59	152	13	38		3	3	0			1	.250
Peter Gallupe	OF47	50	154	23	25		3	0	0			2	.162
Earl Hanson	P39,OF2	50	113	13	29		2	2	2			0	.257
Irvin Wimer	3B44,SS5	49	187	20	49		5	1	1			6	.262
Reid Zellars	P40,OF4	49	114	17	28		4	1	0			2	.246
Al Woods	OF22,2B10,SS3	32	103	13	28		4	5	1			1	.272
Robert Tecarr	P25	25	44	5	9		2	0	0			0	.205
Ted Musante	P24	24	50	1	5		2	0	0			0	.100
Julian Graveson	OF14	16	46	6	9		0	0	0			1	.196
George McNamara	OF7	10											.211
Thomas Moran	2B9	9											.214
Robert Tomlinson	P2	2											.000
William Garvey	OF1	1											.250
W. Butler	PR	1											.000
Ben Egan	C1	1											.000

JERSEY CITY (cont.)
Skeeters

PITCHERS	W	L	PCT	G	GS	CG	SH	IP	H	BB	SO	ERA
Reid Zellars	16	19	.457	40		26	1	271	272	144	84	3.78
Dean Barnhardt	14	12	.538	31		22	2	229	250	65	55	3.26
Earl Hanson	12	22	.353	39		24	4	267	277	133	62	3.61
Joseph Lucey	11	13	.458	29		20	3	198	198	102	75	2.73
Robert Tecarr	4	9	.308	25		7	1	113	146	41	17	5.58
Ted Musante	1	13	.071	24		10	0	126	150	84	32	5.28

MULTI-TEAM PLAYERS

BATTERS	POS-GAMES	TEAMS	GP	AB	R	H	BI	2B	3B	HR	BB	SO	SB	BA
Clarence Pitt	OF150	RO82-BA73	155	582	130	208	70	26	9	7	76	32	19	.357
Joe Cobb	C81,OF26,2B1	JC32-BA83	115	397	72	127	80	19	12	15	46	55	8	.320
James McAvoy	C101	BA42-RO65	107	314	43	97	54	15	5	7	36	29	4	.309
Joseph Faber	SS40,2B3,OF1	BA2-JC42	44	120	9	22		2	2	0			1	.183
Francis Karpp	P37,OF2	RE26-RO18	44	64	9	12		2	0	0			0	.188
John Enzmann	P32	TO5-RE28	33	78	9	20		2	1	0			1	.256
Ralph Judd	P30	RO20-RE12	32	66	6	12		6	1	0			0	.182
John Lynch	P29	JC28-BA2	30	61	3	11		0	1	0			1	.180
Bob Carruthers	P9	NE2-JC8	10											.000

PITCHERS		TEAMS	W	L	PCT	G	GS	CG	SH	IP	H	BB	SO	ERA
John Enzmann		TO5-RE27	16	11	.593	32		17	1	220	240	79	69	3.96
Francis Karpp		RE20-RO17	15	9	.625	37		11	1	180	214	75	50	4.30
Ralph Judd		RO20-RE10	15	9	.625	30		12	1	164	167	66	62	3.67
John Lynch		JC27-BA2	3	13	.188	29		8	0	155	184	112	49	3.77

TEAM BATTING

TEAMS	GP	AB	R	H	BI	2B	3B	HR	BB	SO	SB	BA
BALTIMORE	166	5638	1069	1747	962	277	85	141	641	482	157	.310
ROCHESTER	167	5637	970	1723	803	276	95	41	582	441	112	.306
READING	165	5463	905	1601	777	277	84	77	689	537	115	.293
TORONTO	163	5330	803	1575	682	233	57	64	603	423	124	.294
BUFFALO	166	5469	954	1566	734	328	71	90	709	558	117	.286
SYRACUSE	168	5582	869	1587	758	270	80	61	602	502	89	.284
NEWARK	161	5160	711	1396	527	218	62	48	522	483	185	.271
JERSEY CITY	166	5541	728	1494	644	240	75	44	522	584	82	.270
	661	43820	7009	12689	5887	2119	609	566	4870	4010	981	.290

1924
NOT QUITE

In 1920, after many years of intermittent play, the Little World Series began to be scheduled on a regular basis, pitting the International League champion against the American Association's best in a five-of-nine series. During the early 1920s, the series consisted of the underdog American Association champion serving as cannon fodder for the heavily favored Baltimore Orioles during their seven-year pennant run. But as it turned out, the favorite didn't always come out on top. In 1921, the Association's Louisville Colonels stunned the Orioles by taking a 5–3 decision. Two years later, in 1923, Kansas City edged Baltimore five games to four.

In 1924, the International League's Baltimore team continued its winning ways as the Orioles strolled to their sixth straight flag. Toronto, which finished 19 games off the pace, and Buffalo in third were the only other teams to cross the .500 barrier. Rochester dropped to fourth, while Newark, Syracuse, Reading, and Jersey City rounded out the standings. The Orioles' Dick Porter won the batting title (.364), while William Kelly of Buffalo hit the most home runs (28) and knocked in the most runs as well (155). On the hill, it was Lefty Grove from Baltimore who finished with the most wins and strikeouts (26 and 231). Walt Beall from Rochester had the lowest earned run average (2.76).

The Baltimore Orioles' opponent in the 1924 Little World Series was a familiar foe, the St. Paul Saints. In two previous series, 1920 and 1922, the Orioles had bested the Saints easily. However, the third meeting would be different.

The 1924 Little World Series opened on October 2 in Baltimore. In the opener, the Orioles pushed across two runs in the ninth to wrest a 4–3 decision from the Saints. In game two, the Saints retaliated with a 6–0 calcimining to even the series. Following a thirteen-inning 6–6 tie, the Orioles won the next two, 6–4 and 10–1. On October 9, the series venue switched to St. Paul, where the home team took a 5–2 decision. The next day, the Orioles won 4–0 to take a commanding lead of four games to two. But the Saints weren't finished. In game seven the Association champions squeaked out a 3–2 win. In game eight, the Saints knotted the series at four with a 3–1 win. In the deciding game, the demoralized Orioles fell into a 5–0 hole by the seventh inning. They rallied, but couldn't make up the difference and fell short 6–3, leaving St. Paul to take the series five games to four.

The Baltimore Orioles dominated the International League for the first half of the 1920s, but they couldn't do the same to their Association foes in the Little World Series. Here, Baltimore's record was decidedly mediocre: They won only three of six series, proving that reputation and reality don't always coincide.

BALTIMORE Orioles

1st   117-48   .677   Jack Dunn

BATTERS	POS-GAMES	GP	AB	R	H	BI	2B	3B	HR	BB	SO	SB	BA
Clayton Sheedy	1B165	165	618	105	184	99	37	8	16	46	67	28	.298
Dick Porter	2B129	129	509	116	185	125	36	14	23	50	17	13	.364
Joe Boley	SS157	157	574	110	167	100	32	9	4	52	30	10	.291
Fritz Maisel	3B152	153	588	134	180	88	22	8	20	77	36	26	.306
Merwin Jacobson	OF152	154	552	108	170	97	32	4	18	66	33	24	.308
Thomas Connelly	OF	(see multi-team players)											
John Jacobs	OF	(see multi-team players)											
Joe Cobb	C98	104	347	75	111	84	16	4	22	51	50	6	.320
Harold Clark	OF54	59	192	39	65	39	13	3	9	14	23	4	.339
Ed Tomlin	P31	59	143	24	33	20	2	1	5	5	19	3	.231
Lefty Grove	P47	49	94	15	23	8	5	1	2	6	27	2	.245
John Ogden	P44	48	75	15	11	10	2	1	2	7	26	1	.147
Lew McCarty	C45	47	146	22	45	22	8	0	4	10	14	1	.308
Alphonse Thomas	P43	43	101	15	18	11	4	1	3	2	34	0	.178
Cliff Jackson	P36	36	72	12	22	16	1	1	3	4	18	0	.306
Otto Greenae	C31	32	92	7	20	13	3	0	1	12	19	4	.217
Sewell Dixon	OF21	31	91	13	22	5	2	0	0	6	15	0	.242
Frank Kane		30	78	12	20	7	3	0	0	7	5	0	.256
William Henderson	P21	21	39	4	8	4	0	0	1	0	8	0	.205
Jim Parnham	P18	19	42	8	11	8	2	0	3	4	6	1	.262
George Earnshaw	P13	13											.417
Larry Fischer		11											.355
Tony West	P11	11											.211
John Alberts		7											.000
George Brown		4											.100
Bill Plate		1											1.000

PITCHERS	W	L	PCT	G	GS	CG	SH	IP	H	BB	SO	ERA
Lefty Grove	26	6	.813	47		19	5	236	196	108	231	3.01
John Ogden	19	6	.760	44		9	0	206	210	77	89	3.63
Cliff Jackson	16	8	.667	36		12	3	193	204	80	73	3.92
Alphonse Thomas	16	11	.593	43		16	4	254	241	96	171	4.08
Ed Tomlin	11	2	.846	31		4	0	152	172	55	57	3.61
William Henderson	8	2	.800	21		4	0	86	80	46	56	4.19
George Earnshaw	7	0	1.000	13		4	1	64	56	33	49	3.38
Jim Parnham	6	5	.545	18		7	1	106	134	35	28	4.84
Tony West	3	4	.429	11		3	0	52	51	24	25	5.37

TORONTO Maple Leafs

2nd   98-67   .594   -19   Dan Howley

BATTERS	POS-GAMES	GP	AB	R	H	BI	2B	3B	HR	BB	SO	SB	BA
Ed Onslow	1B145	146	489	96	162	88	25	9	12	86	13	21	.331
Ray Boll	2B149	151	504	95	149	85	25	6	5	91	32	10	.296
Frank O'Rourke	SS102	104	426	100	137	72	35	5	6	31	34	10	.321
Adelbert Capes	3B82	115	373	59	102	39	18	3	0	41	27	20	.273
Frank Gilhooley	OF147	148	576	119	187	47	25	4	3	87	24	13	.325
Joe Kelly	OF138,1B17	155	573	106	201	117	32	12	24	61	47	15	.351
Herman Layne	OF129	134	496	96	169	111	23	11	12	49	46	17	.341
Oscar Stanage	C92	96	322	31	81	44	8	1	1	22	31	2	.252
George Maisel	OF70,3B49	126	453	71	144	75	8	7	4	42	28	10	.318
Otis Miller	SS60,3B32	100	344	52	113	58	17	6	1	19	27	3	.328
Frank Sullivan	C70	72	197	37	55	43	12	3	4	25	43	2	.279
Jesse Doyle	P41	54	134	15	32	15	6	1	0	12	11	2	.239
Claude Satterfield	P26	43	91	9	33	9	3	0	0	9	5	0	.363
Walt Stewart	P39	40	118	19	26	23	4	3	2	13	25	0	.220
Myles Thomas	P39	39	81	6	18	4	0	0	0	5	7	0	.222
Norm Glaser	P36	36	69	9	21	4	4	0	0	4	8	0	.304
Art Reynolds	P28	34	45	11	14	2	3	0	0	3	11	0	.311
Michael Vincent	C17	25	68	11	20	13	3	0	4	9	10	3	.294
Norm McNeil		1											.333
Jess Spring		1											.200

PITCHERS	W	L	PCT	G	GS	CG	SH	IP	H	BB	SO	ERA
Walt Stewart	24	11	.686	39		31	4	307	319	90	130	3.52
Jesse Doyle	19	14	.576	41		27	2	280	298	81	117	3.75
Myles Thomas	16	12	.571	39		15	1	220	246	107	95	4.17
Norm Glaser	13	11	.542	36		10	3	178	199	33	46	3.54
Claude Satterfield	11	9	.550	26		15	1	169	177	45	54	3.83
Art Reynolds	8	5	.615	28		6	1	118	145	30	28	4.81

BUFFALO
Bisons

3rd   84-83   .503   -34   George Wiltse -
                                                       William Webb

BATTERS	POS-GAMES	GP	AB	R	H	BI	2B	3B	HR	BB	SO	SB	BA
William Kelly	1B165	165	629	108	204	**155**	40	9	**28**	55	80	3	.324
Fred Thomas	2B50,SS28	83	279	43	73	28	9	3	1	35	31	6	.262
Westcott Kingdon	SS140,2B28	168	546	78	152	71	24	8	7	86	63	4	.278
William Webb	3B167	167	584	110	181	95	40	13	14	90	45	25	.310
Cecil Dye	OF164	164	650	114	202	75	43	7	10	57	52	20	.311
Andy Anderson	OF145	148	509	120	171	101	43	6	23	**109**	71	26	.336
Vern Spencer	OF132	138	512	92	147	40	35	3	3	80	34	9	.287
James McAvoy	C92	102	325	42	88	50	9	2	4	20	31	7	.271
Dewey Hill	C81	95	279	38	86	51	21	5	6	23	26	0	.308
Joseph Burns	OF46	68	187	31	50	18	13	2	0	24	19	4	.267
Joe Hamel	OF29	52	117	24	32	24	6	3	5	19	22	1	.274
Harry Biemiller	P41	46	69	7	11	11	2	0	1	9	17	0	.159
Clarence Fisher	P44	44	88	12	22	10	2	1	2	2	13	0	.250
Edgar LePard	P41	41	89	4	17	4	0	0	0	2	14	0	.191
Peter Rodwin	2B35	40	119	18	26	10	5	0	3	9	16	0	.218
Eurie Proffitt	P32	39	75	12	19	4	5	0	0	5	16	1	.253
Joseph Reddy	P37	38	98	18	21	7	4	1	1	15	20	0	.214
Ed Williams	P36	36	38	6	3	3	0	0	1	2	5	0	.079
Harry Vanderbach		15	28	3	9	9	0	1	1	2	3	0	.321
Frank Werre		9											.000
James Price		7											.250
William Clark		5											.250
Mickey Welsh		2											.000

PITCHERS		W	L	PCT	G	GS	CG	SH	IP	H	BB	SO	ERA
Joseph Reddy		21	9	.700	37		24	2	255	305	61	104	4.27
Clarence Fisher		16	13	.552	44		15	0	233	246	93	78	4.48
Edgar LePard		15	14	.517	41		19	2	220	266	84	110	4.52
Harry Biemiller		10	14	.417	42		13	1	203	230	126	94	5.41
Eurie Proffitt		9	13	.409	32		12	0	178	218	80	69	4.25
Ed Williams		2	8	.200	36		3	0	128	158	50	34	5.20

ROCHESTER
Tribe

4th   83-84   .497   -35   George Stallings

BATTERS	POS-GAMES	GP	AB	R	H	BI	2B	3B	HR	BB	SO	SB	BA
Fred Merkle	1B151	153	559	123	196	138	37	9	22	82	42	17	.351
Eusebio Gonzales	2B126	133	500	89	139	57	21	7	0	51	43	14	.278
John Jenkins	SS80	82	293	39	87	58	15	5	4	26	21	6	.297
Harry Lunte	3B169	**169**	622	87	180	90	35	5	2	90	50	2	.289
John Conlan	OF165	165	**666**	135	**214**	64	44	15	12	93	41	28	.321
Burney Griffin	OF117	122	478	89	138	73	16	15	8	24	28	9	.289
K. Kirkham	OF	(see multi-team players)											
Harry Lake	C122	128	404	49	125	49	20	8	2	29	29	4	.309
J. Runser	SS60	60	230	40	56	21	5	3	4	19	42	4	.243
George Quellich	OF45	50	153	35	52	42	11	4	10	24	21	1	.340
Al Head	C38	50	108	18	33	20	5	6	3	1	5	1	.306
Francis Karpp	P46	49	64	14	12	2	1	1	0	11	20	0	.188
John Wisner	P48	48	101	8	28	15	3	1	1	5	15	0	.277
Robert Munn	C40	47	101	12	34	21	8	0	1	13	20	1	.337
Harold Drew	OF33	46	128	26	41	12	11	1	0	19	8	1	.320
Walt Beall	P41	41	115	8	20	9	5	1	0	10	27	1	.174
Harry Heitman	OF16	41	96	18	29	18	6	0	0	10	11	1	.302
William Moore	P40	40	86	7	18	10	3	0	0	4	14	0	.209
Doug Walker	3B20	25	98	12	22	9	3	3	0	10	13	1	.224
Berlyn Horne	P20	22	42	6	9	5	3	0	0	1	7	0	.214
Thomas Osborne	2B21	21	75	8	21	9	2	1	1	4	7	2	.280
Alex Peterson	P21	21	18	1	2	0	0	0	0	2	9	0	.111
Frank Wotell		17	50	7	9	5	2	1	0	4	9	0	.180
John Matthews		16	20	1	3	1	0	0	0	0	8	0	.150
Robert Reece		11											.429
Ray Blossom	P11	11											.000
Marvin Steggerda		9											.167
George Terhune		8											.333
Charles Gressett		8											.222
Warwick Comstock		8											.133
Ed Burke		7											.333
Fletcher Hodges		6											.000
Alvin Crowder		5											.167
Joseph Dwyer		4											.167

ROCHESTER (cont.)
Tribe

BATTERS	POS-GAMES	GP	AB	R	H	BI	2B	3B	HR	BB	SO	SB	BA
Joseph Stryker		3											.000
Stan Johnson		2											.500
George Horan		2											.000
Dash		1											.000

PITCHERS		W	L	PCT	G	GS	CG	SH	IP	H	BB	SO	ERA
Walt Beall		25	8	.758	41		27	2	**310**	279	101	227	**2.76**
John Wisner		18	13	.581	48		21	1	275	315	103	92	4.58
William Moore		16	14	.533	40		15	4	248	219	104	178	3.45
Francis Karpp		13	16	.448	45		12	3	196	222	64	65	4.55
John Matthews		3	4	.429	16		2	0	66	94	26	31	5.73
Berlyn Horne		3	11	.214	20		8	1	112	127	51	30	4.58
Alex Peterson		2	4	.333	21		2	0	74	94	31	17	6.30
Ray Blossom		0	2	.000	11		1	0	38	48	21	20	2.13

NEWARK   5th   80-83   .491   -36   Fred Brainerd
Bears

BATTERS	POS-GAMES	GP	AB	R	H	BI	2B	3B	HR	BB	SO	SB	BA
William Styles	1B110,OF16	141	514	51	156	73	22	6	8	42	32	11	.304
Fred Brainerd	2B81,3B18	152	559	75	173	112	28	12	15	50	52	18	.309
John Sheehan	SS147	150	542	110	166	55	30	8	3	96	52	24	.306
George Knothe	3B62	75	258	27	57	21	5	3	2	12	32	12	.221
Frank Kane	OF151	154	586	117	204	112	36	13	15	34	49	25	.348
Hobart Whitman	OF142	146	567	82	202	120	21	6	7	35	11	21	.356
Bill Zitzmann	OF104,3B44	145	548	137	197	50	37	6	8	65	60	34	.359
Michael Devine	C118	123	420	61	136	73	19	12	4	46	15	8	.324
George Hammen	1B45	59	168	16	38	18	4	4	2	9	18	2	.226
Leland Ellis	P45	59	120	26	33	16	4	3	2	12	27	1	.275
Floyd Dougherty	C37	52	117	14	27	13	5	1	2	9	18	1	.231
Myrl Brown	P42	47	95	7	21	11	1	1	0	4	24	0	.221
John Enzmann	P29	42	76	7	20	5	4	1	1	3	16	1	.263
John Martin	2B32	38	139	10	36	15	6	0	0	7	8	1	.259
George Mohart	P34	34	71	6	14	4	2	0	1	3	22	0	.197
Ted Musante	P29	29	41	2	3	0	1	0	0	1	22	0	.073
John Lynch	P21	26	56	4	13	5	0	1	0	3	10	0	.232
James Murray		22	49	3	12	5	4	2	0	4	9	0	.245
Charles Swaine	P21	21	29	3	5	1	1	0	0	2	18	0	.172
Ed Hackbarth		13											.150
Robert Shrimer		6											.250
Ray Radonitz		6											.000
Conroy		2											.250
Art Gardiner		2											.000
Alton Scott		1											.000
James Flowe		1											.000

PITCHERS		W	L	PCT	G	GS	CG	SH	IP	H	BB	SO	ERA
Leland Ellis		20	11	.645	46		23	3	272	322	59	61	4.83
Myrl Brown		15	18	.455	42		21	1	251	280	108	104	4.45
John Enzmann		10	8	.556	29		10	0	143	147	45	48	4.34
George Mohart		10	13	.435	34		14	0	198	237	63	57	4.59
John Lynch		8	9	.471	21		6	1	115	113	47	48	4.45
Charles Swaine		7	5	.583	21		5	1	87	88	16	25	4.04
Ted Musante		5	6	.455	29		6	0	110	146	52	38	5.94

SYRACUSE   6th   79-83   .488   -36.5   Frank Shaughnessy
Stars

BATTERS	POS-GAMES	GP	AB	R	H	BI	2B	3B	HR	BB	SO	SB	BA
Wilbur Swansboro	1B149	150	575	93	156	58	34	10	11	53	64	27	.271
Gard Gislason	2B163	163	651	97	173	69	23	5	5	62	41	21	.266
Tommy Thevenow	SS140	140	495	57	134	46	23	9	0	43	35	12	.271
George Makin	3B146,SS16	162	601	90	161	80	28	10	11	70	46	10	.268
Frank Wetzel	OF145	149	522	88	167	81	27	17	12	48	32	23	.320
Robert Taggert	OF144	146	516	77	165	58	26	8	5	53	36	9	.320
William Holden	OF117	119	444	67	126	82	22	5	14	34	36	6	.284
Ray McKee	C94	112	292	40	88	55	20	3	4	47	25	1	.301

SYRACUSE (cont.)
Stars

BATTERS	POS-GAMES	GP	AB	R	H	BI	2B	3B	HR	BB	SO	SB	BA
Carl Mitze	C86	93	271	30	70	41	12	3	5	40	26	1	.258
George Krahe	OF25,3B22,1B20	91	246	27	68	42	10	8	5	21	31	3	.276
Art Reinhart	P48	70	134	21	45	23	3	3	0	7	15	0	.336
Fred Frankhouse	P40	49	83	7	17	10	3	1	0	6	10	1	.205
Henry Meine	P36	47	100	8	19	8	4	1	1	5	13	1	.190
Vern Parks	P37	39	82	6	14	0	1	0	0	13	16	0	.171
Adolph Pierotti	P25	26	39	3	6	4	1	0	0	1	5	0	.154
Harvey Freeman	P25	25	42	4	3	1	0	0	0	8	15	0	.071
Al Grabowski	P25	25	38	3	6	1	1	1	0	2	10	0	.158
Don Thomas	OF24	24	86	12	31	12	4	1	1	4	9	1	.360
Joe Fortier		9											.350
Art Oeschler		9											.087
William Hollahan		8											.000
William Barnes		6											.500
Les Montgomery		6											.000
William Ward		6											.000
Harmon Minetree		6											.000
Wilford Shupe		3											.000
Hubert Mason		1											1.000
Elmer Hill		1											.000
John Wakefield		1											.000
John Sheridan		1											.000
Frank Shaughnessy		1											.000

PITCHERS		W	L	PCT	G	GS	CG	SH	IP	H	BB	SO	ERA
Henry Meine		17	10	.630	36		19	0	252	269	92	87	3.93
Art Reinhart		17	18	.486	48		18	3	263	281	123	98	4.31
Vern Parks		15	11	.577	37		17	1	265	288	74	81	3.77
Fred Frankhouse		15	17	.469	40		16	1	203	227	86	62	4.70
Al Grabowski		6	2	.750	25		6	1	108	110	36	45	2.67
Harvey Freeman		6	13	.316	25		7	0	138	140	57	28	4.83
Adolph Pierotti		3	7	.300	25		3	0	102	146	43	19	6.63

READING   7th   63-98   .391   -52   Spencer Abbott
Keystones

BATTERS	POS-GAMES	GP	AB	R	H	BI	2B	3B	HR	BB	SO	SB	BA
Howard McLarry	1B88	88	332	64	111	63	25	3	5	36	28	10	.334
Raymond Dowd	2B61	61	230	43	60	21	12	2	0	20	17	8	.261
Jay Boggs	SS62	63	193	34	44	17	5	1	2	28	30	7	.228
Joseph Brown	3B116,2B28	152	568	74	181	59	31	8	2	49	30	14	.319
Hugh Ormand	OF107	118	406	63	128	54	25	3	11	44	31	11	.315
Joseph Horan	OF63	63	242	36	91	46	25	2	6	27	15	2	.376
Melvin Silva	OF	(see multi-team players)											
Byrd Lynn	C90	100	315	33	70	26	15	4	0	23	33	2	.222
Thomas Comiskey	SS44,3B29,OF26	114	389	47	107	72	20	7	5	14	52	10	.275
Pat Haley	C81	104	308	36	85	45	21	3	3	28	19	2	.276
Ralph Miller	2B60,3B17	77	301	28	86	35	21	0	1	11	13	3	.286
Al Elliott	SS59	62	214	38	53	28	10	4	2	35	21	3	.248
Dick Hoblitzell	1B58	58	237	44	80	32	15	3	5	19	10	1	.338
Walt Smallwood	P42	46	103	12	22	9	3	0	2	2	23	1	.214
Joseph Lightner	OF38	41	137	13	34	18	7	1	2	16	4	2	.248
John Jeffries	OF16	35	111	9	28	17	3	3	0	3	16	1	.252
Pat Martin	P29	31	81	4	13	6	1	0	0	5	11	0	.160
Oscar Tuero	P28	28	50	1	11	1	0	0	0	3	7	1	.220
Al Mamaux	P19	23	49	9	10	8	1	0	1	9	6	0	.204
Joseph Zubris	P15	15	34	1	4	1	1	0	0	0	20	0	.118
Phede Lambke	P14	15	22	4	2	0	0	0	0	8	8	0	.090
Reynolds Kelly	P11	11											.300
Fred Blackstock		11											.229
Harry Harper		6											.182
George Valentine		2											.000
Sweigert		1											.000
Warren Heller		1											.000
John Finneran		1											.000

PITCHERS		W	L	PCT	G	GS	CG	SH	IP	H	BB	SO	ERA
Al Mamaux		11	6	.647	19		10	2	130	123	39	67	3.05
Pat Martin		11	14	.440	29		22	3	215	223	87	111	2.97
Walt Smallwood		11	18	.379	42		22	0	260	319	59	69	4.85

READING (cont.)
Keystones

PITCHERS	W	L	PCT	G	GS	CG	SH	IP	H	BB	SO	ERA
Oscar Tuero	5	11	.313	28		10	1	150	196	64	38	5.64
Reynolds Kelly	4	5	.444	10		7	0	70	84	41	29	4.89
Phede Lambke	3	4	.429	14		4	0	70	95	29	16	5.79
Joseph Zubris	3	5	.375	15		6	0	84	83	50	39	4.77

JERSEY CITY 8th 53-111 .323 -63.5 Patsy Donovan
Skeeters

BATTERS	POS-GAMES	GP	AB	R	H	BI	2B	3B	HR	BB	SO	SB	BA
James Holt	1B164	164	616	100	204	126	57	14	16	61	60	9	.331
Ed Miller	2B		(see multi-team players)										
Thomas Ray	SS82	106	335	30	72	34	9	3	1	28	30	2	.215
Eugene Sheridan	3B		(see multi-team players)										
James Walsh	OF135	143	536	89	163	78	37	4	9	71	37	18	.304
Don Donelson	OF133	138	503	70	128	42	22	3	1	54	36	15	.255
Otis Lawry	OF		(see multi-team players)										
Otto Freitag	C134	140	460	46	138	80	32	3	7	76	30	6	.300
Reid Zellars	P52	73	129	17	35	6	2	1	1	8	15	3	.271
Irvin Wimer	3B69	72	253	12	56	18	9	2	1	20	8	2	.221
Dean Barnhardt	P42	60	107	6	16	4	4	0	1	2	26	0	.150
Joseph Lucey	P24,OF21	57	134	13	32	16	4	0	0	13	22	4	.238
Mike Konnick	C40	56	124	7	29	18	2	1	0	12	15	0	.234
Joe Shannon	OF37	40	135	13	32	13	6	5	1	6	18	1	.237
Harold Hadden	OF31	35	93	11	20	8	0	5	1	5	32	1	.215
Philip Neher	SS30	31	108	10	24	3	2	0	0	9	14	3	.222
Walt Keating	SS31	31	102	12	22	2	0	0	0	17	10	2	.216
Sid Agnew	OF24	27	95	8	20	10	4	0	0	8	8	4	.211
William Denike	P19	19	29	1	4	2	0	0	0	1	11	0	.138
Art Wagner		9											.304
John Newell		8											.167
Bayes		7											.238
Jack Henzes		7											.217
Paul Carter		6											.412
Henry LaPlante		6											.091
Weingold		3											.333
Oscar Nossett		3											.000
David Price		3											.000
Frank McCrea		2											1.000
Burroughs		2											.111
Harold Moulton		1											1.000
Mitsche		1											.000
Calvin Davis		1											.000

PITCHERS	W	L	PCT	G	GS	CG	SH	IP	H	BB	SO	ERA
Reid Zellars	14	22	.389	52		27	0	297	349	141	81	3.82
Dean Barnhardt	9	25	.265	42		18	0	261	311	72	45	4.65
Joseph Lucey	7	13	.350	24		11	0	124	142	99	41	4.86
William Denike	2	2	.500	19		2	0	84	104	42	19	3.75

MULTI-TEAM PLAYERS

BATTERS	POS-GAMES	TEAMS	GP	AB	R	H	BI	2B	3B	HR	BB	SO	SB	BA
Thomas Connelly	OF124,2B33	RE45-BA112	157	599	110	187	98	38	10	19	86	62	15	.312
K. Kirkham	OF139	RE10-RO147	157	572	87	189	98	24	10	7	40	8	5	.330
John Jacobs	OF155	JC57-BA98	155	617	94	175	70	33	4	14	56	98	15	.284
Melvin Silva	OF149	SY46-RE108	154	638	107	188	46	22	8	3	37	44	41	.295
Ed Miller	2B148	NE2-JC93-BU55	150	571	106	165	66	20	6	5	55	61	26	.289
Eugene Sheridan	3B135	NE50-JC91	141	523	48	132	53	19	5	3	25	37	13	.252
Otis Lawry	OF84,2B48	BA35-JC100	135	511	91	155	35	18	9	3	55	42	24	.303
Clarence Pitt	OF120	BA53-NE68	121	479	107	148	48	25	4	5	45	29	35	.309
R. Middleton	OF90	SY6-RO16-RE83	105	355	52	119	43	13	4	2	26	12	9	.335
Earl Hanson	P40	JC41-RE3	44	100	8	18	5	3	0	0	3	23	1	.180
Gus Gockel	P32	BA1-NE41	42	73	8	12	4	0	1	0	5	10	1	.164
William Rose	SS19	RO28-JC10	38	110	19	31	17	2	5	3	14	13	2	.282
James Faulkner	P35	TO15-JC20	35	58	5	11	3	2	1	0	1	9	0	.190
Harry Frank	P35	BA8-JC27	35	52	5	9	4	1	0	0	6	21	0	.173
James Clary	P28	RE27-JC4	31	59	5	10	6	3	1	0	2	19	0	.169

MULTI-TEAM PLAYERS (cont.)

BATTERS	POS-GAMES	TEAMS	GP	AB	R	H	BI	2B	3B	HR	BB	SO	SB	BA
Fred Lynch	P28	TO3-NE25	28	58	3	4	2	0	1	0	4	20	0	.069
Ralph Judd	P26	RE14-TO14	28	51	7	15	5	1	0	0	1	9	0	.294
Luther Barnes	P23	NE7-BU16	23	37	4	4	2	0	0	0	6	11	0	.108
Ben Filishifter		JC6-NE2-RO2	10											.111
Atwood Gordy		SY2-BU4	6											.167
Charles Foreman		BA1-NE1	2											.000

PITCHERS		TEAMS	W	L	PCT	G	GS	CG	SH	IP	H	BB	SO	ERA
Ralph Judd		RE12-TO14	7	8	.467	26		9	1	121	149	52	51	5.06
Luther Barnes		NE7-BU16	7	9	.438	23		7	0	120	167	56	42	6.38
Fred Lynch		TO3-RE25	7	12	.368	28		10	0	154	181	41	56	5.20
Gus Gockel		BA1-NE31	6	7	.462	32		4	1	152	182	32	63	4.91
James Faulkner		TO15-JC20	6	8	.429	35		8	0	156	172	70	66	4.21
Harry Frank		BA8-JC27	6	12	.333	35		10	1	159	208	50	42	5.10
Earl Hanson		JC37-RE3	6	22	.214	40		17	1	249	272	127	56	4.12
James Clary		RE24-JC4	5	14	.263	28		11	0	148	193	59	47	5.05

TEAM BATTING

TEAMS	GP	AB	R	H	BI	2B	3B	HR	BB	SO	SB	BA
BALTIMORE	167	5645	**1061**	1692	**929**	289	73	**166**	548	603	157	.300
TORONTO	165	5412	947	1676	852	252	72	77	616	441	131	**.310**
BUFFALO	168	5494	934	1587	797	**312**	68	112	**663**	**610**	118	.289
ROCHESTER	**169**	**5740**	949	**1707**	847	283	**101**	79	551	510	100	.297
NEWARK	163	5522	863	1654	763	250	84	74	479	556	**187**	.300
SYRACUSE	164	5480	768	1504	686	249	88	76	536	382	120	.274
READING	162	5494	775	1553	684	289	57	59	477	524	123	.283
JERSEY CITY	164	5438	673	1434	609	243	62	50	525	606	125	.264
	661	44225	6970	12807	6167	2167	605	693	4395	4232	1061	.290

1925
HIGHEST BIDDER

During the early days of baseball, most minor league entrepreneurs made money in two ways. The first was through ticket sales. The second was through the sale of ballplayers to teams farther up the minor league ladder. Jack Dunn, owner of the International League's Baltimore Orioles, was a master of this second method of gathering revenue.

As the 1920s unfolded, Jack Dunn had assembled a juggernaut team in Baltimore, festooned with potential major leaguers. Major league owners constantly sought Dunn's Orioles, but they usually had to wait. Dunn wouldn't act until he got the highest possible price for his players, often waiting several years to consummate a deal. For example, after four stellar years with the Orioles, star first baseman and pitcher Jack Bentley was finally sold to the Giants for $72,000 in 1922. The next year, five-year veteran second baseman Max Bishop was purchased by the Athletics for $25,000. Following the 1924 season, Dunn made his best deal yet. For an unheard-of sum of $100,000, the Athletics purchased the International's most dominant pitcher, Lefty Grove.

In 1925, the Baltimore Orioles made it seven pennants in a row. The Toronto Maple Leafs finished only four games back, while third-place Rochester was nineteen games in arrears. The stragglers consisted of Buffalo, Reading, Syracuse, Jersey City, and Newark/Providence. (In late May, because of an inadequate ballpark situation, Newark was transferred to Providence.) Buffalo's James Walsh won the batting title (.357). Joe Kelly of Toronto swatted the most home runs (29), while his near namesake, William Kelly of Buffalo, had the highest runs batted in total (125). Pitcher Alphonse Thomas of Baltimore won two honors (most wins, 32, and most strikeouts, 268). Walt Stewart from Toronto finished with the lowest earned run average (2.51).

After the 1925 season, Jack Dunn continued to sell his players to the highest bidder as Alphonse Thomas was purchased by the White Sox for $15,000. Joe Boley was sold to the Athletics for $65,000 in 1926. Dick Porter (to the Indians) and George Earnshaw (to the Athletics) were peddled for a combined $110,000 following the 1928 season.

The minor league system we know today, in which major league teams control whole empires of minor clubs, was in a fledgling state in the 1920s. The only tried and true method for a minor leaguer to reach the majors was to be sold up the line to the highest bidder. In turn, player sales kept minor league teams afloat—or, in the case of the Baltimore Orioles, prospering.

BALTIMORE Orioles

1st **105-61** **.633** Jack Dunn

BATTERS	POS-GAMES	GP	AB	R	H	BI	2B	3B	HR	BB	SO	SB	BA
Clayton Sheedy	1B158	158	587	107	195	117	28	9	26	47	76	14	.332
Fred Brainerd	2B122,1B4,SS1	125	479	64	146	85	26	8	18	24	45	7	.305
Joe Boley	SS152	152	573	91	189	90	37	10	13	40	32	3	.330
Fritz Maisel	3B158	158	632	141	208	76	38	5	19	95	34	18	.329
John Roser	OF100,P1	117	353	75	107	77	16	4	25	80	37	0	.303
Maurice Archdeacon	OF98	98	364	75	113	29	17	4	1	53	30	20	.310
Clarence Walker	OF97	98	363	66	111	100	21	3	18	42	32	5	.306
Joe Cobb	C106,2B7,3B1,OF1	116	402	64	107	49	13	7	19	47	72	2	.266
Dick Porter	OF88,2B32,SS15,3B6	142	548	107	184	103	33	10	13	45	33	11	.336
Thomas Connelly	OF58,2B1	64	215	43	61	32	14	0	10	46	30	3	.285
John Ogden	P51,OF2	59	129	26	37	13	4	1	3	13	31	2	.287
Alphonse Thomas	P56	56	130	18	24	11	4	0	4	13	31	1	.185
George Earnshaw	P53,OF1	55	135	14	34	21	4	1	5	7	26	0	.252
Cliff Jackson	P42,OF2	44	95	10	20	10	4	0	4	1	20	0	.211
Sherry Magee	OF11,1B5,2B1	21	68	13	14	10	5	1	1	9	11	1	.206
L. Fischer	OF12	18	52	9	13	6	0	1	2	5	8	0	.250
William Henderson	P15	15	10	1	4	1	0	0	0	0	2	0	.400
William Corn	OF7	13											.269
Wood Harwood	P12	12											.077
Davenport	P7	7											.250
Harry Courtney	P4	4											.500
Egbert	P4	4											.250
Milligan	P3	4											.250
Kane	2B4	4											.133
Sewell Dixon	OF2,2B1	4											.000
Poppen	P3	3											.000
Bob Vines	P2	2											.500
Moore	OF1	2											.000
Kulda	P2	2											.000
Andrews	P2	2											.000
Davis	C1	1											.500
Nolan	P1	1											.000
Perry	P1	1											.000
Artigiaus	C1	1											.000
Winkerwerden	P1	1											.000

PITCHERS	W	L	PCT	G	GS	CG	SH	IP	H	BB	SO	ERA
Alphonse Thomas	32	12	.727	56		28	4	354	330	118	268	2.97
George Earnshaw	29	11	.725	53		23	3	332	352	113	200	3.52
John Ogden	28	11	.718	51		28	7	327	322	75	143	3.11
Cliff Jackson	13	14	.481	42		8	1	216	248	109	86	4.50
Wood Harwood	0	1	.000	12		1	0	32	34	29	8	3.94
William Henderson	0	5	.000	15		1	0	34	43	24	16	6.09

TORONTO Maple Leafs

2nd **99-63** **.611** **-4** Dan Howley

BATTERS	POS-GAMES	GP	AB	R	H	BI	2B	3B	HR	BB	SO	SB	BA
Minor Heath	1B123	123	365	55	82	46	18	4	3	70	61	5	.225
Charlie Gehringer	2B154	155	633	128	206	108	38	9	25	37	49	8	.325
Otis Miller	SS134	134	488	61	126	50	18	3	3	37	25	6	.258
Andy Harrington	3B93,SS19,OF1	117	427	58	132	77	13	6	4	26	17	6	.309
Frank Gilhooley	OF161	162	654	128	206	64	29	3	5	77	32	10	.315
Cleo Carlyle	OF122	130	422	86	139	78	15	5	17	66	47	4	.329
Joe Kelly	OF112,1B26	140	514	97	175	117	22	6	29	57	35	5	.340
Clyde Manion	C138	138	490	82	156	93	28	4	7	54	40	4	.318
Herman Layne	OF98	110	374	63	129	51	17	5	6	33	23	9	.345
Adelbert Capes	3B45,OF10,SS9,2B1	81	219	34	76	24	6	4	0	14	12	9	.347
Myles Thomas	P47	47	113	9	23	14	4	0	0	7	11	2	.204
George Smith	P45	45	103	14	24	7	4	1	1	3	19	0	.233
Claude Satterfield	P28,OF1	42	80	15	25	14	3	2	3	9	7	0	.313
Sam Gibson	P39	39	98	14	35	6	7	0	1	1	9	1	.357
Walt Stewart	P38	38	88	10	22	13	3	1	1	16	17	0	.250
Norm Glaser	P27	27	24	5	7	3	1	0	0	1	3	0	.292
George Maisel	3B15,OF8,1B1	25	88	10	25	14	4	0	1	4	5	1	.284
Williams	C9	11											.200
William Englishman	P10	10											.500
Grason Standiford	P10	10											.250
Bernard	SS9	9											.179
Erickson	P5	5											.250

TORONTO (cont.)
Maple Leafs

BATTERS	POS-GAMES	GP	AB	R	H	BI	2B	3B	HR	BB	SO	SB	BA
Johnson	P4	4											.000
Hodgett	P1	1											.000

PITCHERS		W	L	PCT	G	GS	CG	SH	IP	H	BB	SO	ERA
Myles Thomas		28	8	.778	47		28	2	322	296	119	100	2.52
Walt Stewart		21	12	.636	38		25	5	265	245	60	99	**2.51**
Sam Gibson		19	11	.633	39		24	2	256	256	88	125	3.20
George Smith		17	15	.531	45		21	2	271	295	**121**	144	3.99
Claude Satterfield		13	8	.619	28		10	0	155	176	70	63	3.89
Grason Standiford		1	0	1.000	10		0	0	28	39	15	7	5.46
William Englishman		0	1	.000	10		0	0	20	32	9	4	7.65
Norm Glaser		0	7	.000	27		0	0	75	101	25	16	5.76

ROCHESTER   3rd   83-77   .519   -19   George Stallings
Tribe

BATTERS	POS-GAMES	GP	AB	R	H	BI	2B	3B	HR	BB	SO	SB	BA
Ed Onslow	1B		(see multi-team players)										
Henry Demoe	2B157	159	628	93	195	75	29	7	1	48	13	8	.311
Al Baird	SS82,1B9,3B4,2B1	101	314	43	89	39	16	4	2	29	42	4	.283
Joseph Rapp	3B110,2B5,SS1,OF1	116	418	59	133	59	19	11	4	41	24	16	.318
Henry Haines	OF142	144	548	104	159	68	24	9	8	87	67	23	.290
John Conlan	OF140	143	544	95	168	69	36	10	6	63	18	20	.309
George Quellich	OF117,1B2	126	386	77	115	72	20	12	19	63	65	5	.298
Harry Lake	C97	100	344	55	96	52	14	0	4	27	43	0	.279
Al Head	C71,OF4	99	264	39	95	54	17	8	4	8	7	2	.360
Harry Lunte	3B41,SS15	56	182	28	40	23	9	1	1	19	12	0	.220
Fred Merkle	1B55	55	215	47	67	37	13	2	6	27	17	6	.312
Berlyn Horne	P40,OF8	55	115	19	29	14	2	2	0	8	20	3	.252
William Urban	SS48	48	160	16	39	21	7	2	0	9	12	1	.244
William Moore	P34	34	89	7	25	8	5	1	0	0	13	0	.281
Herb Thormahlen	P29	30	81	12	20	8	6	0	1	8	25	0	.247
Henry Thormahlen	P27	29	48	6	11	8	1	1	1	3	9	0	.229
Emil Levsen	P27	27	63	6	8	6	3	2	0	7	28	0	.127
Francis Karpp	P23	23	34	1	2	0	1	0	0	4	15	0	.059
William Batch	3B8,SS8	17	45	7	16	5	3	3	0	8	6	1	.356
Carl Yowell	P16	16	42	6	12	3	2	0	0	3	6	0	.286
J. Runser	SS13	13											.205
Gerald Mallett	P12	12											.368
Bedford	3B8,SS2,2B1	11											.226
Charles Gressett	P10	10											.231
Harold Drew	OF4	8											.273
Jacoby	P6	6											.000
Taylor	P4	4											.000
Brottem	C4	4											.125
Tunney	P3	3											.400
Hearne	P3	3											.000
Conners	P2	2											.000
Brown	P2	2											.000
Hardy	C1	1											.000
Army	C1	1											.000

PITCHERS		W	L	PCT	G	GS	CG	SH	IP	H	BB	SO	ERA
William Moore		16	15	.516	34		20	1	235	248	84	101	4.44
Emil Levsen		14	9	.609	27		18	2	185	183	70	64	3.36
Berlyn Horne		13	12	.520	40		20	0	252	282	97	93	3.86
Herb Thormahlen		13	12	.520	29		18	2	232	254	40	100	2.95
Carl Yowell		11	1	**.917**	16		11	1	107	112	41	43	3.20
Henry Thormahlen		6	10	.375	27		6	0	116	154	43	52	6.28
Francis Karpp		5	9	.357	23		7	0	107	128	52	42	5.13
Charles Gressett		2	1	.667	10		0	0	36	57	14	8	5.75
Gerald Mallett		1	1	.500	12		1	0	45	52	22	10	6.20

BUFFALO   4th   78-84   .481   -25   William Webb
Bisons

BATTERS	POS-GAMES	GP	AB	R	H	BI	2B	3B	HR	BB	SO	SB	BA
William Kelly	1B162	162	629	131	200	**125**	28	12	26	74	62	0	.318

BUFFALO (cont.)
Bisons

BATTERS	POS-GAMES	GP	AB	R	H	BI	2B	3B	HR	BB	SO	SB	BA
Ed Miller	2B106	109	397	66	94	35	15	2	4	43	61	12	.237
Wescott Kingdon	SS156,OF2	158	527	80	139	86	25	5	11	84	93	0	.264
William Webb	3B92,OF4	107	348	91	117	73	27	1	19	59	36	12	.336
Vern Spencer	OF162	162	662	128	227	77	43	10	5	101	39	15	.343
James Walsh	OF153,1B1	154	544	120	194	122	34	3	22	91	45	8	.357
Cecil Dye	OF110	125	443	77	130	46	21	7	5	30	26	5	.293
Dewey Hill	C77	96	298	49	85	58	15	2	8	25	17	1	.285
Peter Radwan	3B75,2B10,SS10	102	349	48	110	60	14	4	2	20	25	4	.315
Andy Anderson	OF62,2B36,3B1	99	355	87	114	89	22	1	22	34	29	11	.321
Art Pond	C45	63	167	20	43	25	4	0	3	11	31	0	.257
James McAvoy	C54	60	191	18	52	27	9	1	1	17	20	0	.272
Eurie Proffitt	P46	53	98	15	30	17	5	1	1	1	11	0	.306
Roy Auer	P46	46	47	6	6	1	0	0	0	2	20	0	.128
Joe Maley	P45	45	83	3	12	2	0	1	0	3	21	0	.145
Joseph Lucey	2B26,P10,3B2,OF2	43	118	19	38	16	6	0	5	9	19	0	.322
Joseph Reddy	P36,2B1	42	64	11	18	8	1	0	1	8	17	0	.281
Clarence Fisher	P37	37	81	6	18	10	4	0	0	1	14	1	.222
Edgar LePard	P23	23	41	6	5	0	1	0	0	6	11	0	.122
Gordon Jones	P18	18	15	0	0	0	0	0	0	1	3	0	.000
William Brice	P17	17	16	1	2	1	0	0	0	0	5	0	.125
Tony Murray	OF6	7											.333
A. Applegate	P7	7											.333
W. Hinkle	P4	4											.000
Art Johnson	P3	3											.250
Ed Reis	P1	1											.000

PITCHERS	W	L	PCT	G	GS	CG	SH	IP	H	BB	SO	ERA
Eurie Proffitt	13	12	.520	46		13	0	224	275	96	79	4.78
Clarence Fisher	13	14	.481	37		10	1	194	230	69	66	4.59
Joe Maley	11	18	.379	45		14	2	226	251	83	61	4.86
Edgar LePard	10	9	.529	23		6	0	125	158	59	48	4.54
Roy Auer	9	4	.692	46		3	1	146	147	90	64	4.50
Joseph Reddy	9	14	.391	36		12	0	183	257	53	53	5.85
Joseph Lucey	6	2	.750	10		8	0	79	72	48	47	3.99
Gordon Jones	2	3	.400	18		1	0	49	58	25	11	5.33
William Brice	1	1	.500	17		1	0	49	63	22	11	5.88

READING   5th   78-90   .464   -28   Spencer Abbott
Keystones

BATTERS	POS-GAMES	GP	AB	R	H	BI	2B	3B	HR	BB	SO	SB	BA
Howard McLarry	1B163,OF1	166	600	103	185	95	46	3	14	98	43	10	.308
Henry Scheer	2B99	100	382	55	107	45	19	5	4	22	41	3	.280
Morris Berg	SS168	168	643	91	200	124	36	5	9	36	33	6	.311
Joseph Brown	3B144,P9	145	503	80	138	57	36	9	4	80	32	9	.274
Chick Shorten	OF102	107	372	62	126	58	24	3	2	44	12	4	.339
Hugh High	OF92	94	342	50	105	35	18	0	2	53	12	3	.307
Howard Camp	OF74	75	279	51	82	37	18	7	8	22	18	4	.294
Lew McCarty	C	(see multi-team players)											
Albert Watt	2B67,OF9,3B6,1B3	98	286	41	76	34	12	5	0	19	22	4	.266
Henry Koehler	OF67	71	222	38	61	25	15	3	2	20	6	5	.275
Joseph Smith	C57	63	159	23	39	21	13	0	2	33	27	0	.245
Ralph Fraser	OF47	61	192	40	63	23	13	2	2	22	12	3	.328
Walt Smallwood	P43	44	61	6	13	6	1	0	1	1	18	0	.213
Gomer Wilson	P40	41	91	9	19	8	2	0	1	8	17	0	.209
Fred Hankins	P36	36	63	7	9	4	1	0	2	2	23	0	.143
Steve O'Neill	C29,1B1	34	94	9	25	14	5	0	1	15	6	0	.266
Tim McNamara	P34	34	77	5	15	5	0	0	1	6	23	0	.195
Clyde Schroeder	P29	32	75	9	23	9	5	1	0	1	14	0	.307
Leo Mangum	P26	28	62	6	11	6	1	0	0	5	11	0	.177
Don Seasholtz	C14	19	41	5	8	2	1	1	0	2	6	0	.195
R. Middleton	3B8,OF3,2B1	13											.154
Roberts	P8	9											.333
Meuter	C6	9											.143
John Lynch	P5	5											.286
Graeff	OF2,3B1	3											.375
Joseph Zubris	P3	3											.000
Adams	P3	3											.000
Sam Dailey	P3	3											.000
Andy Rush	P2	2											.000
Palm	OF1	1											.333

READING (cont.)
Keystones

PITCHERS	W	L	PCT	G	GS	CG	SH	IP	H	BB	SO	ERA
Gomer Wilson	16	15	.516	40		22	1	256	310	75	78	4.11
Clyde Schroeder	14	12	.538	29		11	2	173	249	91	59	5.98
Tim McNamara	11	17	.393	34		15	3	208	262	72	66	4.63
Fred Hankins	10	13	.435	36		9	0	176	211	88	48	5.37
Leo Mangum	9	8	.529	26		14	1	165	190	46	53	3.87
Walt Smallwood	9	10	.474	43		8	2	165	201	49	58	4.20

SYRACUSE
Stars

6th   74-87   .460   -28.5   Frank Shaughnessy - Harry Myers

BATTERS	POS-GAMES	GP	AB	R	H	BI	2B	3B	HR	BB	SO	SB	BA
Wilbur Swansboro	1B150,P1	152	550	82	148	100	27	15	16	46	63	22	.269
Gard Gislason	2B161	161	646	101	172	62	26	9	4	59	21	11	.266
Tommy Thevenow	SS112	112	414	62	120	45	18	8	1	32	16	11	.290
George Krahe	3B119,SS16,2B2	138	457	58	138	60	19	6	9	47	5	5	.302
Walt erRoettger	OF115,1B7,3B4	129	447	61	123	58	20	7	8	27	27	4	.275
Robert Taggert	OF112	113	464	72	131	54	23	4	9	38	38	3	.282
Fred Frankhouse	OF64,P29,SS1	104	269	39	89	39	11	1	6	20	30	2	.331
Charles Niebergall	C103	114	358	50	99	43	12	3	14	27	37	3	.277
Bert Griffith	OF64,1B8,3B8	82	312	40	105	63	18	2	7	21	18	4	.337
Roscoe Holm	OF51,3B15	69	254	41	83	39	14	5	4	22	8	6	.327
Harry Myers	OF39,3B4	60	158	24	50	25	8	1	1	6	4	2	.316
Al Grabowski	P42	52	107	6	25	13	6	1	1	7	20	0	.234
Henry Meine	P24,OF20	46	114	15	29	15	4	0	1	9	26	0	.254
Ray Boyd	P40	41	52	5	14	1	2	1	1	5	18	0	.269
James Cooney	SS34	34	132	17	53	17	8	3	0	3	7	5	.402
William Hallahan	P33	33	64	8	9	3	0	1	1	5	31	0	.141
Vern Parks	P29	30	45	2	5	1	0	0	0	0	17	0	.111
Art Reinhart	P19,1B1,OF1	29	59	9	19	9	2	3	0	1	8	0	.322
Clyde Day	P26	26	46	3	11	5	1	0	0	0	12	0	.239
Charles Hafey	OF21	21	84	17	24	8	3	3	2	7	5	3	.286
James Long	C6,3B2,OF2,1B1	20	29	3	8	5	2	0	1	6	6	0	.276
Russ Miller	P13	16	30	4	6	4	3	2	0	4	6	0	.200
Hoke Warner	3B15	15	62	10	21	4	4	2	0	4	4	2	.339
Miller	OF4,1B1,SS1	13											.314
Bliss	OF10,3B1	12											.167
Thomas	OF10	10											.364
Reppy	P9	9											.000
Reece	P6	6											.250
Bauer	P4	4											.000
Foster	P1	1											.000
Thompson	P1	1											.000
Lester Sell	P1	1											.000
Russell		1											.000

PITCHERS	W	L	PCT	G	GS	CG	SH	IP	H	BB	SO	ERA
Al Grabowski	15	12	.556	42		16	2	254	256	93	116	3.51
Henry Meine	10	6	.625	24		9	0	137	171	65	44	4.80
Clyde Day	10	9	.526	26		12	3	139	174	24	43	4.34
William Hallahan	8	15	.348	33		13	1	178	204	114	120	4.25
Ray Boyd	7	14	.333	40		6	1	160	192	59	40	4.95
Russ Miller	6	3	.667	13		5	1	78	84	23	28	4.38
Vern Parks	6	8	.429	29		10	1	134	156	32	42	4.97
Art Reinhart	6	9	.400	19		8	0	120	138	49	59	4.80
Fred Frankhouse	5	9	.357	29		6	0	121	150	69	37	5.30

JERSEY CITY
Skeeters

7th   74-92   .446   -31   Patsy Donovan

BATTERS	POS-GAMES	GP	AB	R	H	BI	2B	3B	HR	BB	SO	SB	BA
James Holt	1B111	118	414	73	139	100	20	3	15	48	36	2	.336
Raymond Dowd	2B140,SS5,3B1	150	594	98	198	84	26	7	6	58	36	38	.333
Lewis Malone	SS117,3b13	129	451	64	122	75	20	2	3	58	44	6	.271
Eugene Sheridan	3B142,SS1	144	527	68	161	83	19	5	3	30	26	7	.307
Merwin Jacobson	OF160	160	623	114	197	90	28	13	8	73	56	10	.316
Aldrik Gaudette	OF119,2B17	142	515	80	160	52	17	3	1	53	30	9	.311
Walt Simpson	OF109,1B1	118	380	71	109	51	22	4	11	60	59	7	.287
Otto Freitag	C142	144	445	57	118	67	16	2	8	62	43	2	.265

JERSEY CITY (cont.)
Skeeters

BATTERS	POS-GAMES	GP	AB	R	H	BI	2B	3B	HR	BB	SO	SB	BA
Robert Unglaub	OF79	89	273	39	87	34	12	4	1	13	17	2	.319
Reid Zellars	P52,OF1	77	107	15	25	10	4	0	0	13	10	1	.234
Ed Shirley	1B48,OF9	59	198	27	58	25	8	8	1	13	27	2	.293
William Urbanski	SS37,3B11,OF2,2B1	56	186	30	50	19	6	1	2	10	11	7	.269
Michael Vincent	C47,1B2,SS1	52	120	8	29	10	1	0	0	9	11	0	.242
James Faulkner	P47,1B2	49	96	9	20	7	1	0	0	6	22	0	.208
Joseph Kiefer	P38	44	86	8	21	7	1	2	0	9	6	0	.244
Cliff Best	P28,OF2	32	55	12	15	11	3	0	1	4	11	0	.273
Guy Cantrell	P30	30	47	7	13	6	2	1	2	2	9	0	.277
Albert Spaulding	P28	28	39	2	5	2	2	0	0	5	16	0	.128
Thomas Sloan	P20,1B2	23	34	4	4	3	1	1	0	3	9	0	.118
James Roberts	P18	18	36	4	10	5	1	0	0	1	10	0	.278
Francis Wilson	OF15	17	49	10	17	2	4	0	0	6	3	0	.348
Miller	OF9	9											.235
Sullivan	C6	9											.200
Garland	SS8	8											.374
Burke	OF4	8											.133
James Clary	P6	6											.067
Blenkiron	OF5	5											.313
Dean Barnhardt	P3	5											.000
Tillman	P3	4											.000
Harold Hadden	OF1	1											.000
McCrehan	P1	1											.000
Pankratz	C1	1											.000

PITCHERS	W	L	PCT	G	GS	CG	SH	IP	H	BB	SO	ERA
James Faulkner	17	17	.500	47		21	2	275	297	106	118	3.60
Joseph Kiefer	14	16	.467	38		22	1	241	268	81	79	2.95
Reid Zellars	14	24	.368	52		21	2	278	346	95	83	4.44
Cliff Best	8	4	.667	28		7	0	131	169	64	45	5.08
Guy Cantrell	5	8	.385	30		4	0	127	141	65	39	4.04
James Roberts	5	9	.357	18		8	0	97	118	49	38	5.10
Thomas Sloan	4	4	.500	20		3	1	87	108	51	35	5.38
Albert Spaulding	4	6	.400	28		4	0	110	158	77	48	5.15

NEWARK / PROVIDENCE   8th   63-100   .387   -40.5   Ed Onslow -
Bears / Grays   Frank Shaughnessy

BATTERS	POS-GAMES	GP	AB	R	H	BI	2B	3B	HR	BB	SO	SB	BA
Harvey Hendrick	1B113	114	434	68	138	74	10	13	8	20	32	7	.318
Ray Boll	2B	(see multi-team players)											
John Sheehan	SS100,2B61	162	564	102	159	71	26	13	7	103	60	15	.282
Frank Sigafoos	3B68,2B34,OF9,SS5	119	380	46	108	55	13	8	3	27	39	2	.284
Hobart Whitman	OF133	136	514	77	169	79	23	5	3	24	3	7	.329
Clarence Pitt	OF131	138	511	78	154	41	14	5	1	49	26	17	.301
Melvin Silva	OF	(see multi-team players)											
Byrd Lynn	C	(see multi-team players)											
Ed Tomlin	P40,3B12,OF7,1B2	91	191	19	51	25	7	5	2	16	25	1	.267
Joseph Faber	SS63,3B13	78	278	52	89	53	16	4	7	25	26	2	.320
Charles Swaney	P54	54	103	9	12	8	4	0	3	5	43	0	.117
Herm Oden	3B41,SS4	44	137	14	36	9	1	2	1	7	20	0	.263
Leland Ellis	P40	43	97	7	23	7	3	2	0	10	24	0	.237
Harold Elliott	C40	42	128	10	33	21	11	1	0	10	5	0	.258
George Trumbower	OF23,P4	42	76	15	19	9	0	1	0	21	14	0	.250
James Fox	C17,OF13,1B3	41	101	12	38	15	6	3	1	11	16	3	.327
George Brown	P35	38	53	5	12	0	3	0	0	2	19	0	.226
Walt Brame	P23	38	50	10	16	3	2	0	1	2	3	0	.320
August Swentor	3B34	35	100	10	27	15	5	2	1	8	22	2	.270
Harold Clark	OF28,3B2	35	92	18	29	17	4	0	2	15	12	3	.315
George Swartz	P32	34	51	8	11	7	0	1	1	2	17	0	.216
Ted Musante	P22	22	25	4	5	2	1	0	0	1	3	0	.200
Brown		11											.385
Cole	C8	8											.300
Murray	P4,1B2	7											.200
Morin	3B2,1B1,C1	5											.375
Charles Schesler	P3	3											.000
Brandell	2B1	2											.333
Walters	3B1	1											1.000
Ruggerio	P1	1											.000

NEWARK / PROVIDENCE (cont.)
Bears / Grays

PITCHERS	W	L	PCT	G	GS	CG	SH	IP	H	BB	SO	ERA
Charles Swaney	14	20	.412	54		20	2	290	385	72	78	5.12
Ed Tomlin	11	14	.440	40		15	1	216	242	107	63	4.54
Leland Ellis	11	18	.379	40		16	1	242	312	82	56	4.87
George Swartz	10	9	.526	32		11	1	160	194	56	57	3.88
Walt Brame	5	3	.625	23		2	0	87	85	75	35	4.66
George Brown	3	13	.188	35		7	0	148	183	71	62	5.29
Ted Musante	2	5	.286	22		1	0	66	69	47	20	4.09

MULTI-TEAM PLAYERS

BATTERS	POS-GAMES	TEAMS	GP	AB	R	H	BI	2B	3B	HR	BB	SO	SB	BA
Frank Kane	OF144	N/P89-RE57	146	525	81	148	72	21	19	7	53	52	16	.282
Ed Onslow	1B130	N/P32-RO99	131	475	73	149	83	21	6	6	51	21	7	.313
William Styles	1B50,C49,3B21,OF5,2B4	N/P55-TO72	127	416	79	122	72	23	3	16	44	30	11	.293
Melvin Silva	OF116,2B1,3B1	RE18-N/P105	123	482	77	162	57	22	8	2	23	26	18	.336
John Jacobs	OF103	BA38-RE73	111	383	60	115	46	18	6	3	29	45	11	.300
Byrd Lynn	C101	RE10-N/P92	102	343	30	96	41	15	0	1	22	35	1	.280
Ray McKee	C90	SY54-BA46	100	293	35	80	31	13	2	6	45	20	1	.273
Lew McCarty	C87	BA11-RE85	96	285	23	84	40	17	3	1	27	29	0	.295
Ray Boll	2B77,3B8	TO21-N/P68	89	317	46	88	35	14	4	6	38	13	1	.278
William McCarren	2B19,SS14,3B12,1B11,OF3	JC51-RE21	72	211	30	65	39	18	2	2	25	16	1	.309
Ed Matteson	P36	RE23-N/P14	37	42	4	5	0	0	0	0	3	7	0	.119
G.eorge Kopshaw	C31	BA14-SY21	35	74	8	16	4	4	0	0	7	19	0	.216
Sam Hyman	P25	RO19-RE7	26	38	7	7	3	1	0	0	4	6	0	.184
Pat Shea	P20	N/P1-BU19	20	28	3	9	3	1	0	0	1	6	0	.321
Ray Young	P17	RO3-RE16	19	17	1	3	0	0	0	0	4	6	0	.176
John Alberts	C8,3B2,2B2	N/P6-BA6	12											.214
Duggan	P7	RO1-N/P7	8											.000
Atwood Gordy	P7	BU3-N/P4	7											.000
McLaughlin	SS3	SY1-N/P1-BA1	3											.333

PITCHERS		TEAMS	W	L	PCT	G	GS	CG	SH	IP	H	BB	SO	ERA
Ed Matteson		RE22-N/P14	8	8	.500	36		8	0	135	156	59	55	4.00
Sam Hyman		RE18-BA7	3	6	.333	25		4	0	103	119	67	56	4.37
Pat Shea		N/P1-BU19	2	6	.250	20		2	0	73	111	33	31	7.40
Ray Young		RO3RE14	1	4	.200	17		0	0	56	70	27	19	5.46

TEAM BATTING

TEAMS	GP	AB	R	H	BI	2B	3B	HR	BB	SO	SB	BA
BALTIMORE	166	5593	980	1682	880	278	69	188	620	624	90	.301
TORONTO	164	5535	921	1690	834	248	54	117	547	458	80	.305
ROCHESTER	162	5344	848	1560	754	262	86	62	586	507	103	.292
BUFFALO	162	5537	990	1649	886	278	50	135	674	644	70	.298
READING	168	5598	832	1598	747	325	61	64	580	500	71	.285
SYRACUSE	162	5446	767	1563	698	244	79	87	444	489	85	.287
JERSEY CITY	167	5537	833	1625	787	223	59	63	569	533	99	.293
NEW/PRO	165	5614	810	1635	730	228	92	61	493	544	93	.291
	658	44204	6981	13002	6316	2086	550	777	4513	4299	691	.294

1926
TOPPLED

In 1925, the Baltimore Orioles won their seventh straight pennant. There were, however, certain signs of slippage. The Orioles managed to win only 105 games, 10 under their average for the last five years. Another difference was that Baltimore no longer enjoyed double-digit game leads over their second-place rivals. In 1925, the Toronto Maple Leafs came within four games of the champions. The Leafs would improve that mark in 1926.

When the Orioles jumped out to their accustomed lead in 1926, most thought the team was well on its way to an eighth straight title. But the Toronto club kept pace. With six weeks to go, the Maple Leafs caught fire. They won 37 of their last 43 games—a torrid pace—to catch and pass the champions. By September 12, they had clinched the pennant, which they won by eight games. After seven years, the Baltimore Orioles finished somewhere other than first.

The Newark Bears, back after their half-season in Providence, jumped up to third, just behind Baltimore. Buffalo finished fourth, while Rochester and Jersey City ended fifth and sixth. The last two spots were occupied by Syracuse and Reading, the latter with the worst twentieth century International League mark. The leading batsmen all came from Buffalo. James Walsh had the highest average (.388). William Kelly set a new home run record (44) and also plated the most runners (151). On the mound, Baltimore's John Ogden won the most games (24), Al Mamaux from Newark had the lowest earned run average (2.22), and his teammate Roy Chesterfield struck out the most batters (141).

Several factors combined to allow the Maple Leafs to topple the Orioles from the top perch. One of the chief factors was changes in personnel. Before the 1926 season, Baltimore owner Jack Dunn had sold several of his stars to major league owners, a practice he had followed for several years. Since Dunn yearly added quality replacement players to the Orioles' roost, no one thought much about it. However, one of the players sold this time was pitcher Alphonse Thomas, a 32-game winner in 1925. There was no replacement of that quality for the Orioles. A second reason for Toronto's success in 1926 was the Maple Leaf pitching staff. Four starters on the staff finished in the top eleven earned run average qualifiers—all four ahead of the top Oriole hurler.

The Baltimore Orioles finished with 101 wins in 1926. During their seven-year string of flags, they had only once finished with a total that low. In those same seven years, there was one team each year that averaged about 101 wins—the second-place team. It seems the 1926 Orioles finished exactly where they should have.

TORONTO Maple Leafs

	1st	109-57	.657		Dan Howley

BATTERS	POS-GAMES	GP	AB	R	H	BI	2B	3B	HR	BB	SO	SB	BA
Minor Heath	1B164	164	537	83	180	115	27	15	10	94	73	19	.335
Carl Schmehl	2B108,SS19	138	406	49	93	38	21	4	1	51	36	11	.229
Otis Miller	SS151	152	536	92	185	120	27	2	7	59	26	15	.345
William Mullen	3B132	134	515	95	184	87	32	5	8	79	33	12	.357
Frank Gilhooley	OF156	156	631	118	193	67	29	8	0	85	22	17	.306
Herman Layne	OF143	148	560	107	196	114	32	16	7	40	33	32	.350
Cleo Carlyle	OF110	122	386	85	117	74	28	8	14	51	43	5	.303
Steve O'Neill	C132	135	435	62	115	69	29	2	3	65	37	5	.264
William Styles	C45,1B18,3B15	89	211	36	66	37	18	1	5	22	25	4	.313
Otis Lawry	2B58,OF22	82	260	49	77	30	13	3	0	28	15	5	.296
Claude Satterfield	P21	70	102	11	36	23	9	0	3	6	6	1	.353
Adelbert Capes	OF18,2B12,3B11	47	132	22	41	16	3	1	1	19	10	2	.311
Owen Carroll	P39	47	86	22	24	8	4	0	1	10	14	1	.279
Jesse Doyle	P33	38	73	15	27	11	3	1	1	5	3	0	.370
James Faulkner	P37	37	95	8	23	2	1	0	0	4	13	0	.242
Walt Stewart	P37	37	89	4	14	3	1	0	0	9	25	0	.157
Andy Harrington	2B10	33	61	10	17	10	3	0	2	2	5	1	.279
Joe Maley	P32	32	45	3	7	5	1	0	0	3	9	0	.156
Carl Hubbell	P31	31	29	2	8	4	1	0	0	1	8	0	.276
Vic Sorrell	P20	20	23	3	5	2	1	1	0	1	8	0	.217
Bill Skiff		5											.273
Ray Hayworth		4											.333
Conacher		3											.000
William Knowlton	P2	2											.000
Phillips	P2	2											.000

PITCHERS		W	L	PCT	G	GS	CG	SH	IP	H	BB	SO	ERA
Owen Carroll		21	8	.724	39		19	1	240	250	120	120	3.56
Walt Stewart		18	9	.667	37		23	6	253	256	48	117	2.99
Jesse Doyle		15	7	.682	33		14	3	185	192	56	67	3.06
James Faulkner		15	12	.556	37		18	1	257	258	87	114	3.50
Vic Sorrell		8	0	1.000	20		4	1	73	52	38	53	3.08
Joseph Maley		8	5	.615	32		8	0	139	145	41	41	3.63
Claude Satterfield		7	6	.538	21		6	1	83	82	29	33	3.90
Carl Hubbell		7	7	.500	31		4	1	93	90	44	45	3.77
Phillips		0	1	.000	2								
Knowlton		0	0	----	2								

BALTIMORE Orioles

	2nd	101-65	.608	-8	Jack Dunn

BATTERS	POS-GAMES	GP	AB	R	H	BI	2B	3B	HR	BB	SO	SB	BA
Pete Monahan	1B101,OF17	124	453	85	140	94	28	10	11	42	44	11	.309
Henry Scheer	2B160	160	584	78	141	80	26	4	7	47	56	10	.241
Joe Boley	SS143	145	526	89	161	117	24	8	19	50	27	7	.306
Fritz Maisel	3B156	158	638	145	201	83	32	10	8	84	35	16	.315
Maurice Archdeacon	OF133	133	530	107	174	66	22	6	5	66	46	19	.328
Clayton Sheedy	OF81,1B72	153	539	117	196	118	45	10	19	72	52	17	.364
George Quellich	OF	(see multi-team players)											
Ray McKee	C91	97	304	45	86	45	18	2	9	49	20	5	.283
Dick Porter	OF53,SS27	95	361	82	116	54	23	3	8	40	20	9	.321
John Ogden	P52	58	106	22	19	9	3	0	2	10	40	0	.179
George Earnshaw	P49	49	110	21	27	9	4	0	2	10	23	0	.245
Cliff Jackson	P40	41	71	9	18	16	2	1	3	6	21	0	.254
Jim Parnham	P34	38	87	13	21	12	3	0	4	2	22	0	.241
William Henderson	P37	37	50	6	8	3	0	0	1	2	12	0	.160
Sherry Magee	OF19	22	59	12	17	11	4	3	4	12	10	1	.288
William Hohman	OF14	14	50	12	13	13	5	0	2	3	7	0	.260
Wood Harwood	P12	12	10	1	2	1	0	0	0	1	2	0	.200
Fred Vincent	P8	8											.056
Art Carlton	P7	7											.083
Blaisdell	P6	6											.250
Cullenberger		6											.182
Jim Tennant	P5	5											.000
Charles Foreman	P5	5											.000
Canavan	P4	4											.333
E. Myers	P4	4											.000
Griffith	P3	3											.000
Brandon		2											.250

BALTIMORE (cont.)
Orioles

PITCHERS	W	L	PCT	G	GS	CG	SH	IP	H	BB	SO	ERA
John Ogden	24	15	.615	52		20	0	281	289	81	123	4.39
George Earnshaw	22	14	.611	49		16	2	267	292	96	99	4.52
Cliff Jackson	16	7	.696	40		2	1	172	206	80	46	5.13
Jim Parnham	13	7	.650	34		11	1	187	217	46	49	5.05
William Henderson	5	10	.333	37		8	1	142	158	85	56	6.21
Fred Vincent	5	0	1.000	8								
Wood Harwood	1	0	1.000	12		1	0	27	36	24	13	8.33
Art Carlton	1	0	1.000	7								
Canavan	1	0	1.000	4								
E. Myers	1	0	1.000	4								
Roy Buckalew	1	0	1.000	1								
Skidmore	1	0	1.000	1								
Charles Foreman	1	1	.500	5								
Blaisdell	0	0	----	6								
Jim Tennant	0	0	----	5								
Griffith	0	0	----	3								
Walker	0	0	----	1								
Siepp	0	0	----	1								
Miller	0	0	----	1								
Poppen	0	0	----	1								

NEWARK
Bears

3rd   99-66   .600   -9.5   Fred Burchell

BATTERS	POS-GAMES	GP	AB	R	H	BI	2B	3B	HR	BB	SO	SB	BA
Nelson Hawks	1B163	163	620	106	184	97	31	10	5	71	43	19	.297
Lew Fonseca	2B143	147	543	127	207	126	40	11	21	61	21	34	.381
Wescott Kingdon	SS		(see multi-team players)										
Joseph Brown	3B159	160	539	98	165	95	44	4	10	97	27	18	.306
George Burns	OF163	163	644	129	194	59	49	5	7	90	36	38	.301
Otis Carter	OF118	134	426	67	133	82	22	16	7	44	56	14	.312
Chick Shorten	OF112	120	407	43	135	66	23	6	2	30	13	3	.332
John Schulte	C101	104	291	44	85	44	13	2	9	72	34	3	.292
George Davis	OF74	78	262	42	76	35	10	2	1	31	11	5	.280
Sam Wilson	C71	78	203	27	50	25	12	1	2	27	23	2	.246
Don Hankins	P37	39	79	7	11	5	1	0	1	2	33	0	.139
Joseph Zubris	P33	36	57	7	7	4	0	0	1	6	23	0	.123
Al Mamaux	P35	35	89	14	23	8	2	3	1	12	20	0	.258
Roy Chesterfield	P34	35	69	3	9	2	1	1	0	2	27	0	.130
Art Decatur	P32	32	65	8	11	13	2	1	0	2	11	0	.169
Ed Tomlin	P16	30	59	4	19	6	2	0	1	6	4	1	.322
Harry Lunte	3B17	26	40	1	7	7	4	0	0	1	4	0	.175
Walt Smallwood	P25	26	32	3	7	5	1	0	0	1	7	0	.219
Edwin Twombley	P23	23	34	1	3	1	0	0	0	5	12	0	.088
Dewey Steffens	OF15	22	72	6	23	14	2	0	0	5	4	3	.319
Harold Gagnon	SS16	18	63	13	13	9	0	1	1	5	15	1	.206
William Batch		13	23	4	8	1	1	0	0	2	2	0	.348
Clyde Schroeder	P11	12	15	1	2	0	0	0	0	2	3	0	.133
Clarke		8											.400
Frank Werre	P6	7											.250
John Lynch	P5	7											.250
McCarty		6											.615
Brady	P5	6											.333
Cressett	P6	6											.000
Torpe	P4	4											.200
Fred Adams	P4	4											.167
Schreiber	P4	4											.000
Dwyer		3											.000
Kennedy		3											.000
Fred Stiely	P2	2											.500
Edgar LePard	P2	2											.333

PITCHERS	W	L	PCT	G	GS	CG	SH	IP	H	BB	SO	ERA
Al Mamaux	19	7	.731	35		24	3	259	222	68	113	2.22
Don Hankins	16	7	.696	37		16	2	210	211	73	68	3.73
Art Decatur	13	6	.684	32		6	2	162	158	55	59	4.28
Roy Chesterfield	13	12	.520	34		13	2	201	191	97	141	3.76
Joseph Zubris	11	10	.524	33		9	0	161	148	97	87	4.30
Edwin Twombly	8	7	.533	23		5	1	118	111	46	30	2.97
Ed Tomlin	7	1	.875	16		8	2	90	94	48	40	2.70
Frank Werre	3	0	1.000	6								

NEWARK (cont.)
Bears

PITCHERS	W	L	PCT	G	GS	CG	SH	IP	H	BB	SO	ERA
Walt Smallwood	3	7	.300	25		4	0	87	100	26	21	6.83
Brady	2	1	.667	5								
John Lynch	1	0	1.000	5								
Fred Stiely	1	0	1.000	2								
Torpe	1	0	1.000	4								
Fred Adams	1	1	.500	4								
Schrieber	1	1	.500	4								
Clyde Schroeder	1	4	.200	11		2	0	43	48	15	8	5.86
Cressett	0	1	.000	6								
Edgar LePard	0	0	----	2								
Jeffcoat	0	0	----	1								

BUFFALO   4th   92-72   .561   -16   William Clymer
Bisons

BATTERS	POS-GAMES	GP	AB	R	H	BI	2B	3B	HR	BB	SO	SB	BA
William Kelly	1B165	165	612	135	202	151	38	7	44	67	67	4	.330
Lafayette Thompson	2B159	159	657	150	217	100	39	8	26	54	40	17	.330
Sam Crane	SS110	110	370	57	102	48	13	3	1	16	31	8	.276
William Webb	3B50	60	154	37	49	20	12	2	4	21	15	2	.318
James Walsh	OF145	147	526	122	204	131	43	3	17	80	36	4	.388
Charles High	OF130	137	482	97	154	82	29	9	13	65	27	5	.320
Andy Anderson	OF80,3B61	152	491	118	159	95	35	6	21	110	76	9	.324
Art Pond	C82	86	235	26	62	45	6	0	8	26	27	2	.264
Peter Radwan	SS73,3B	132	482	69	150	75	26	5	8	28	38	5	.311
Harry Lake	C81	82	227	27	64	46	6	0	7	17	15	1	.282
Vern Spencer	OF40	66	186	32	44	13	8	2	3	26	16	1	.237
Joseph Lucey	OF33,P23	65	161	39	51	34	12	0	6	13	28	3	.317
Bernie Neis	OF43	52	179	34	62	34	13	5	7	15	8	2	.346
Eurie Proffitt	P39	48	94	8	22	8	2	0	1	1	9	0	.234
James Brice	P43	44	38	0	1	1	0	0	0	3	14	0	.026
John Barnes	C33	42	78	10	22	14	2	0	1	6	10	0	.282
Dan Taylor	OF19	34	72	18	22	14	7	1	3	6	10	0	.282
Roy Auer	P32	33	31	4	7	3	1	0	0	1	10	0	.226
Charles Pick		28	53	6	20	8	1	1	1	2	0	1	.377
Walt Leverenz	P28	28	53	7	13	4	2	1	0	3	8	0	.245
Louis Koupal	P24	27	65	9	12	7	1	1	0	1	16	0	.185
Alphonse Kamp	P24	25	43	2	5	1	0	1	0	0	14	0	.116
Sterling Stryker	P21	22	32	2	8	1	0	0	0	0	3	0	.250
Alex Ferguson	P20	20	53	6	12	5	1	0	0	1	16	0	.226
Stuart Bolen	P14	14	27	3	6	2	1	0	0	2	5	0	.222
Harry Bennett	P8	8											.100
Hugh McMullen		5											.381
Walter Kimmick		5											.100
Frank Chase	P2	2											1.000
Dave Keefe	P2	2											.500

PITCHERS	W	L	PCT	G	GS	CG	SH	IP	H	BB	SO	ERA
Eurie Proffitt	15	9	.625	39		15	1	197	247	65	106	5.03
Louis Koupal	13	5	.722	24		10	1	155	169	84	58	4.76
Alex Ferguson	12	6	.667	20		11	2	146	165	51	83	4.01
Joseph Lucey	10	9	.526	23		10	1	136	177	74	51	5.89
Walt Leverenz	9	7	.563	28		9	1	146	144	61	81	3.82
James Brice	6	5	.545	43		3	2	130	153	37	52	5.26
Alphonse Kamp	5	4	.556	24		6	0	114	134	64	34	5.92
Stuart Bolen	5	4	.556	14		3	0	67	69	31	41	4.97
Sterling Stryker	5	9	.357	21		6	0	84	130	41	27	7.50
Harry Bennett	3	1	.750	8								
Roy Auer	3	8	.273	32		3	0	82	101	55	38	7.24
Dave Keefe	0	1	.000	2								
Frank Chase	0	0	----	2								
O'Hare	0	0	----	1								

ROCHESTER   5th   81-83   .494   -27   George Stallings
Tribe

BATTERS	POS-GAMES	GP	AB	R	H	BI	2B	3B	HR	BB	SO	SB	BA
Ed Onslow	1B85	86	332	64	114	59	15	3	1	42	5	11	.343

ROCHESTER (cont.)
Tribe

BATTERS	POS-GAMES	GP	AB	R	H	BI	2B	3B	HR	BB	SO	SB	BA
John Sheehan	2B73,SS33,3B24	128	467	81	137	66	23	6	2	77	36	14	.293
John Jones	SS		(see multi-team players)										
Joseph Rapp	3B62	62	244	43	60	39	15	4	2	13	16	8	.283
John Conlan	OF122	123	497	98	142	49	29	8	3	63	26	11	.286
Melvin Silva	OF110	127	446	70	138	33	20	4	1	29	25	29	.309
Ed Murphy	OF110	111	439	79	156	63	22	7	4	47	22	12	.355
William Devine	C111	119	402	56	126	70	19	2	4	32	15	6	.313
Al Head	C58,3B23,1B15,OF14	129	385	71	135	94	31	4	10	34	10	2	.351
William Rothrock	2B51,SS36	84	315	46	95	35	8	2	2	26	27	5	.302
Berlyn Horne	P42	49	99	8	24	7	3	0	0	8	8	1	.242
William Conroy	3B37,1B10	47	168	26	51	30	8	0	1	18	13	2	.304
Herb Thormahlen	P32	34	103	13	25	19	3	1	3	4	19	0	.243
William McCarren	3B17,1B13	29	100	17	27	12	4	1	0	13	5	4	.270
William Moore	P27	27	52	2	13	5	0	1	0	5	12	0	.250
George Krahe	2B18	24	70	7	19	12	3	0	1	8	8	0	.271
Francis Karpp	P19	23	38	3	3	1	0	0	0	4	18	0	.079
Jim Bagby	P18	22	57	6	12	12	3	1	0	2	6	1	.211
Ray Roberts	P22	22	31	3	7	2	0	1	0	3	6	0	.226
Monroe Mitchell	P21	21	34	5	11	3	1	1	0	1	5	0	.324
Carr Smith	OF17,P2	20	62	11	15	14	2	1	1	6	6	0	.242
Orville Menard	SS13	14	49	3	8	5	3	0	0	1	8	0	.163
William O'Neill		14	21	3	5	1	0	0	0	2	3	2	.238
Harvey Reese	P13	13	19	2	3	1	1	0	0	1	3	0	.158
Clarence Thomas	P12	12	18	2	0	0	0	0	0	2	4	0	.000
Ed Kunesh	OF10	11	37	8	12	0	0	1	0	0	0	0	.324
Ed Shirley		10	30	4	10	5	3	0	0	0	1	1	.333
John Prudhomme	P7	8											.250
Roy Crumpler	P7	7											.200
Brown	P7	7											.000
May	P6	6											.667
McLaughlin	P6	6											.188
Richard Niehaus	P4	6											.000
James McAvoy		5											.282
Lyle		5											.000
Rip Collins	OF	4	16	5	5	1	0	0	1			0	.313
Murphy	P3	4											.250
Forte	P4	4											.000
Weaver	P3	3											.400
Duryea		3											.200
Ed Lennon	P3	3											.000
Starr		3											.000
Shaffner	P2	2											.333
Lee	P2	2											.333
Charles Behan	P2	2											.167
Ed Farber		2											.000

PITCHERS	W	L	PCT	G	GS	CG	SH	IP	H	BB	SO	ERA
Herb Thormahlen	19	11	.633	32		25	2	254	291	36	101	3.37
Berlyn Horne	15	16	.484	42		16	2	241	269	87	111	4.26
Jim Bagby	8	8	.500	18		12	0	142	152	30	54	3.23
Francis Karpp	7	5	.583	19		11	0	110	125	45	33	3.68
William Moore	6	13	.316	27		11	1	159	180	50	69	5.26
Clarence Thomas	5	3	.625	12		5	1	58	63	16	38	3.41
Ray Roberts	5	4	.556	22		5	0	86	117	36	33	6.49
Monroe Mitchell	5	10	.333	21		3	0	90	139	39	35	7.80
McLaughlin	2	1	.667	6								
Harvey Reese	2	3	.400	13		1	0	48	69	23	15	8.06
Forte	1	0	1.000	4								
Weaver	1	0	1.000	3								
Lee	1	0	1.000	2								
John Prudhomme	1	1	.500	7								
Charles Behan	1	1	.500	2								
Roy Crumpler	1	2	.333	7								
May	0	1	.000	6								
Shaffner	0	1	.000	2								
Ed Lennon	0	2	.000	3								
Brown	0	0	----	7								
Richard Niehaus	0	0	----	4								
Murphy	0	0	----	3								
Carr Smith	0	0	----	2								
Spencer	0	0	----	2								
Henry Thormahlen	0	0	----	1								
Whitehouse	0	0	----	1								
Hal Neubauer	0	0	----	1								
McGrew	0	0	----	1								

JERSEY CITY Skeeters

	6th	72-92	.439	-36	Patsy Donovan

BATTERS	POS-GAMES	GP	AB	R	H	BI	2B	3B	HR	BB	SO	SB	BA
Del Bissonette	1B	(see multi-team players)											
Lewis Malone	2B136,3B28	165	624	107	170	116	30	10	19	70	59	19	.273
Charles Corgan	SS165	165	601	74	147	64	21	4	4	77	78	17	.245
William Urbanski	3B118	136	484	61	133	53	13	7	1	25	45	9	.275
Aldrik Gaudette	OF135	141	505	77	154	59	21	2	5	61	35	19	.305
Clarence Twombly	OF112	115	402	70	111	23	14	2	1	75	23	19	.276
Al Moore	OF106	106	410	46	131	52	12	4	4	21	23	20	.320
Thomas Daly	C95	101	318	35	87	37	14	2	0	14	7	2	.274
Bill Rogell	OF33,3B21.2B16,P1	87	248	40	67	42	13	5	2	39	38	7	.270
Guy Cantrell	P53	53	117	13	32	10	0	3	2	0	23	0	.274
Vern Parks	P49	50	101	11	21	6	3	0	0	4	10	1	.208
Robert Unglaub	OF45	48	159	15	36	14	6	2	1	12	14	3	.226
James Holt	1B44	45	152	8	31	10	5	0	0	13	18	0	.204
George Lewis	OF16	36	63	7	17	7	1	0	1	8	9	0	.270
John Manners	P30	31	36	3	6	5	3	0	0	1	8	0	.167
Robert Taggert	OF25	25	90	10	16	10	5	1	1	8	8	0	.178
Roy Hutson	OF20	20	69	10	18	4	4	0	0	16	10	1	.261
Ray Moss	P16	16	34	3	7	1	1	0	0	4	15	0	.206
Frank Smith		16	20	1	1	1	0	0	0	2	9	0	.050
Leon Williams	P8	15	29	3	7	2	0	1	0	1	4	0	.241
Stover		7											.333
O'Neill	P7	7											.000
Albert Spaulding	P4	4											.250
Bill Vargus	P4	4											.000
Thomas Sloan	P3	3											.250
Norm Glaser	P2	2											.333
Sarsfield	P2	2											.000

PITCHERS		W	L	PCT	G	GS	CG	SH	IP	H	BB	SO	ERA
Guy Cantrell		22	19	.537	53		22	3	308	322	179	121	3.07
Vern Parks		19	14	.576	49		23	5	281	287	64	88	2.63
Ray Moss		7	1	.875	16		8	2	90	94	48	40	2.70
John Manners		4	10	.286	30		5	0	119	123	77	41	4.91
Thomas Sloan		1	1	.500	3								
Leon Williams		1	3	.250	8								
O'Neill		1	3	.250	7								
Bill Vargus		0	1	.000	4								
Albert Spaulding		0	2	.000	4								
Norm Glaser		0	2	.000	4								
Frank Smith		0	5	.000	16		2	0	70	73	43	23	5.01
Sarsfield		0	0	----	2								
Bill Rogell		0	0	----	1								

SYRACUSE Stars

	7th	70-91	.435	-36.5	Burt Shotton

BATTERS	POS-GAMES	GP	AB	R	H	BI	2B	3B	HR	BB	SO	SB	BA
Frank Hurst	1B103,OF54	157	562	104	186	129	36	9	18	63	56	10	.331
Pepper Martin	2B88,3B27	129	480	103	144	48	30	8	9	50	54	29	.300
Karl Urban	SS	(see multi-team players)											
Dan Clark	3B107,OF31,2B10	147	535	120	195	110	32	7	31	86	38	12	.364
Walter Roettger	OF126,P1	130	479	73	146	88	27	13	15	23	21	10	.305
Max Flack	OF100	121	391	74	95	38	15	7	7	53	14	3	.243
Howard Williamson	OF95	96	346	56	117	69	13	10	5	20	31	5	.338
Boyce Morrow	C96	104	303	31	92	48	11	3	8	32	14	2	.304
Charles Niebergall	C79	90	253	29	60	28	13	4	3	26	29	7	.237
Fred Frankhouse	P28,OF24	73	151	21	47	15	10	2	3	13	14	3	.311
John Harding	2B25,SS21	52	149	20	40	17	2	0	1	7	12	3	.268
Lyman Nason	OF42	49	176	28	50	27	12	1	2	17	13	4	.284
Guy Froman	1B42	43	140	17	36	21	8	1	3	24	33	0	.257
Edwin Dyer	P23	43	76	9	20	8	4	0	0	8	3	1	.263
Al Grabowski	P33	43	53	8	13	6	1	1	0	4	12	0	.245
Russ Miller	P34	34	75	5	14	5	3	0	0	1	11	0	.187
Roy Boyd	P34	34	37	4	5	4	1	0	0	5	9	1	.135
Leo Dickerman	P26	26	51	4	9	7	1	1	2	2	13	0	.176
Al Kapl	3B23	25	72	8	20	16	3	1	3	9	9	1	.278
Harold Haid	P21	21	53	2	5	1	0	0	0	3	26	0	.094
Louis Benson	SS18	18	71	11	16	8	1	2	0	6	5	0	.225
Carey Selph	2B18	18	65	13	19	13	2	2	0	5	6	2	.292
Paul Johnson	OF12	18	50	9	17	12	5	0	1	4	2	0	.340

SYRACUSE (cont.)
Stars

BATTERS	POS-GAMES	GP	AB	R	H	BI	2B	3B	HR	BB	SO	SB	BA
Wilbur Swansboro	1B10,P1	18	40	4	6	3	1	0	0	0	5	2	.150
Harry Layne	OF15	15	57	16	22	12	1	2	4	2	6	6	.386
Paul Kinney	P14	14	19	1	2	0	0	0	0	1	7	0	.105
Corrigan		11	33	2	4	5	0	0	0	3	6	1	.121
Walter Mails	P10	10	12	1	1	1	0	0	0	3	4	0	.083
Burkett		9											.167
Coggin	P8	8											.333
William Barnes	P8	8											.154
Bogess		7											.217
Ernie Orsatti		6											.286
Cunningham		6											.273
Dudley		5											.571
Lahaie		5											.250
Cuccin		4											.750
Del Gainer		4											.385
Spikes		3											.000
Myers	P2	2											.000
Olsen	P2	2											.000
Waynesburg	P2	2											.000

PITCHERS	W	L	PCT	G	GS	CG	SH	IP	H	BB	SO	ERA
Edwin Dyer	12	6	.667	23		15	3	160	141	54	94	3.09
Russ Miller	12	15	.444	34		14	1	204	236	65	50	3.84
Fred Frankhouse	9	11	.450	28		14	2	166	190	64	74	4.60
Harold Haid	8	9	.471	21		11	1	142	159	43	69	3.87
Al Grabowski	6	11	.353	33		4	0	138	160	55	50	5.23
Paul Kinney	5	1	.833	14		5	1	69	57	34	38	3.13
Leo Dickerman	5	10	.333	26		9	0	135	145	96	63	5.40
Roy Boyd	4	11	.267	34		3	0	121	167	42	47	6.62
Coggin	2	0	1.000	8								
Barnes	2	4	.333	8								
Walter Mails	1	2	.333	10		2	0	44	52	26	17	4.50
Olsen	0	1	.000	2								
Waynesburg	0	0	----	2								
Myers	0	0	----	2								
Martin	0	0	----	1								
Christianson	0	0	----	1								
Wilbur Swansboro	0	0	----	1								
Walter Roettger	0	0	----	1								

READING   8th   31-129   .194   -75   Frank Shaughnessy -
Keystones   Byrd Lynn - George Wiltse

BATTERS	POS-GAMES	GP	AB	R	H	BI	2B	3B	HR	BB	SO	SB	BA
James Keesey	1B144	151	513	61	142	61	22	6	4	62	49	2	.277
Albert Watt	2B	(see multi-team players)											
Frank Sigafoos	SS55,3B51,2B14,OF12	134	507	62	163	74	35	9	8	20	45	10	.321
Jarrell Wright	3B55,OF44,SS27,2B15	152	507	47	131	57	22	1	8	38	94	3	.258
William Corn	OF119	134	473	75	106	36	24	5	9	61	61	6	.224
Hobart Whitman	OF	(see multi-team players)											
Clarence Pitt	OF	(see multi-team players)											
Byrd Lynn	C110	121	345	26	75	32	14	0	2	27	53	0	.217
Andy Phillips	3B36,SS32	73	268	28	72	37	13	2	3	14	23	4	.269
James Marquis	P39,OF20	69	171	16	36	18	11	0	2	8	38	0	.211
John Jacobs	OF53,P1	61	205	26	50	24	10	1	2	22	26	7	.244
Charles Swaney	P47	48	104	6	15	4	1	0	0	20	42	0	.144
Denzel Moore	OF47	47	175	13	36	11	4	2	2	5	42	1	.206
John Beard	P25	29	59	7	9	3	2	1	0	2	19	0	.053
Irwin Krehmeyer	SS20	20	68	6	18	5	2	1	0	10	10	0	.265
Francis Gill	3B17	20	63	7	16	2	1	0	0	4	8	1	.254
Pat Shea	P17	19	43	2	7	1	0	0	0	1	8	0	.163
Joseph Hassler	SS16	16	54	0	10	2	2	0	0	1	13	0	.185
Leon Brock		13	25	1	6	2	0	0	0	0	9	0	.240
Swartz	P7	7											.167
George Durning		6											.222
Hammen		5											.400
Ray Young	P3	5											.333
George Wiltse		5											.143
Ted Musante	P5	5											.143
Holl		4											.083
Rochford		3											.000

READING (cont.)
Keystones

BATTERS	POS-GAMES	GP	AB	R	H	BI	2B	3B	HR	BB	SO	SB	BA
Hummel		2											.000
Hartman		2											.000
Braun	P2	2											.000

PITCHERS	W	L	PCT	G	GS	CG	SH	IP	H	BB	SO	ERA
Charles Swaney	10	29	.256	47		28	0	311	405	69	77	4.75
James Marquis	8	23	.258	39		24	0	261	341	151	74	5.83
John Beard	4	15	.211	25		13	0	140	175	134	55	7.26
Pat Shea	2	12	.143	17		9	0	113	157	44	22	5.50
Swartz	1	1	.500	7								
Ray Young	0	1	.000	3								
Braun	0	1	.000	2								
John Jacobs	0	1	.000	1								
Czerwinski	0	1	.000	1								
Ahrens	0	1	.000	1								
Hartman	0	1	.000	1								
Ted Musante	0	0	----	5								

MULTI-TEAM PLAYERS

BATTERS	POS-GAMES	TEAMS	GP	AB	R	H	BI	2B	3B	HR	BB	SO	SB	BA
Hobart Whitman	OF113,2B38	RE123-BU34	157	610	89	197	78	34	6	8	21	7	12	.323
Del Bissonette	1B156	JC124-RO33	157	566	89	181	132	36	14	15	69	58	9	.320
Wescott Kingdon	SS147	BU2-NE146	148	526	115	157	70	26	4	13	82	51	8	.298
Frank Kane	OF131	NE86-RO52	138	451	76	135	81	25	13	7	47	54	12	.299
Karl Urban	SS102,2B55	RO55-SY73	128	454	53	121	52	24	4	3	33	33	5	.267
Clarence Walker	OF111	BA57-TO62	119	404	95	137	91	21	2	27	71	49	9	.339
Albert Watt	2B99	NE18-RE99	117	388	48	110	38	16	1	0	43	33	10	.284
George Quellich	OF105	RO46-BA67	113	372	71	110	76	16	3	17	50	49	5	.296
John Jones	SS85,2B26	SY49-RO63	112	431	70	142	51	23	6	1	19	14	6	.329
Dewey Hill	C57,OF24	BU19-RE85	104	252	28	72	27	20	0	3	20	14	1	.286
Clarence Pitt	OF94	RE66-BA29	95	364	57	113	33	21	2	2	41	17	7	.310
Otto Freitag	C88	JC56-BA37	93	273	35	61	32	9	1	2	41	26	1	.224
Joe Cobb	C77	BA54-JC33	87	242	40	62	47	9	2	9	40	26	2	.256
Raymond Dowd	2B30	JC38-NE21	59	132	19	24	14	3	2	1	7	10	7	.182
Erv Brame	P42	RE19-JC40	59	117	10	31	10	5	0	1	6	11	1	.265
Cecil Dye	OF48	TO8-BU43	51	181	26	39	20	5	1	1	13	12	3	.215
Andrew Chambers	P42	RE28-BA14	42	93	6	13	5	0	0	0	5	17	0	.140
Leland Ellis	P33	RE24-JC11	35	57	6	10	2	1	0	0	4	14	0	.175
John Schelberg	P34	RE2-SY32	34	33	2	4	2	0	0	0	1	8	0	.121
Jack Slappey	P30	BA19-RE11	30	63	2	7	4	2	0	0	1	28	0	.111
Joseph Reddy	P28	BU7-JC22	29	51	7	11	5	0	0	0	3	6	0	.216
Clarence Fisher	P28	BU14-TO14	28	59	6	11	4	1	0	0	1	11	0	.186
Frank Uzmann	C22	BU3-RE19	22	37	4	5	2	1	1	0	4	6	1	.135
P. O'Brien	OF19	BA11-RE8	19	65	11	24	9	7	2	2	14	4	1	.369
Walt Simpson	OF11	JC15-SY4	19	40	8	6	2	1	0	1	5	5	1	.150
Reid Zellars	P15	JC7-RE11	18	18	4	1	0	0	0	0	2	4	0	.056
E. Ingram		NE3-RE7	10	24	0	6	4	2	0	0	2	3	0	.250

PITCHERS	TEAMS	W	L	PCT	G	GS	CG	SH	IP	H	BB	SO	ERA
Clarence Fisher	BU14-TO14	15	4	.789	28		9	2	150	179	61	57	4.92
Andrew Chambers	RE28-BA14	10	20	.333	42		20	1	252	273	94	101	5.11
Erv Brame	RE7-JC35	9	21	.300	42		16	1	246	243	127	100	3.11
Joseph Reddy	BU6-JC22	8	9	.471	28		8	1	145	168	40	21	4.10
Jack Slappey	BA19-RE11	5	15	.250	30		15	0	172	192	95	40	5.18
John Schelberg	RE2-SY32	4	9	.308	34		5	0	116	144	56	45	5.97
Leland Ellis	RE22-JC11	1	15	.063	33		10	0	172	225	81	32	5.02
Reid Zellars	JC5-RE10	0	6	.000	15		2	0	71	93	35	16	5.50

TEAM BATTING

TEAMS	GP	AB	R	H	BI	2B	3B	HR	BB	SO	SB	BA
TORONTO	166	5519	932	1702	892	299	72	73	667	492	136	.308
BALTIMORE	167	5632	1049	1645	928	288	65	144	644	584	108	.292
NEWARK	167	5476	916	1620	833	311	73	86	682	516	162	.296

TEAM BATTING (cont.)

TEAMS	GP	AB	R	H	BI	2B	3B	HR	BB	SO	SB	BA
BUFFALO	165	5622	1048	**1729**	**957**	305	56	**173**	577	561	68	.308
ROCHESTER	164	5594	896	1680	817	274	66	51	542	425	127	.300
JERSEY CITY	166	5451	718	1437	670	207	58	59	578	567	132	.264
SYRACUSE	162	5372	853	1549	799	253	**80**	116	506	507	108	.288
READING	161	5277	592	1377	534	249	38	54	431	**668**	64	.261
	659	43943	7004	12739	6430	2186	508	756	4627	4320	905	.290

1927
BUFFALO BISONS

In the late 1920s, during the years following the overthrow of the Oriole dynasty, a powerful International League team emerged from upper New York State. As one of the league's oldest members, the team had been in existence for over forty years. In that time, the club had won its share of championships; the year 1927, however, would prove special. The team was the Buffalo Bisons.

After a seven-year run in the National League, the Buffalo Bisons joined the International League in 1886. During the nineteenth century, the team won only one flag, but it did so in style. The 1891 Bison squad finished first by a large margin, with a sparkling .718 winning percentage—one of the league's five best of all time.

After the 1898 season, Buffalo dropped out of the league to join the Western League (later called the American League). When the American League decided to drop the Buffalo franchise, the team gladly rejoined the Eastern League in 1901.

The first decade of the twentieth century saw two pennants fly in Buffalo, and with them the honor of playing in the first two Little World Series (1904 and 1906), both of which the Bisons won. Ten years later, the team won back-to-back titles in 1915 and 1916. In another ten years, the team was poised for more.

When the 1927 season started, Buffalo stampeded to the lead and stayed there. All through the season the team wasn't seriously challenged, and the Bisons ended with a double-digit game lead over the second-place finisher. The team's forte was hitting, as the Bisons led the International League with a lusty .318 average. The key contributor was first baseman Del Bissonette. Loaned to the Bisons from the Brooklyn Dodgers, Bissonette dominated International League batters. He finished the year with the most runs (168), hits (229), runs batted in (167), doubles (46), and triples (20), while finishing second in the batting race (.365). Other Bison batting stars included Andy Cohen (.353, 118 RBI); Clarence Huber (.334); Otis Carter (.331); and, in a part-time role, Al Tyson (.375).

The Syracuse Stars made a huge leap in 1927, moving from seventh to second. The rest of the standings consisted of Newark, Toronto, Baltimore, Rochester, Jersey City, and Reading. Baltimore player Dick Porter won the batting title (.376) while hitting the most home runs (25). Pitcher Al Mamaux of Newark also won two honors as he finished with the most wins (25) and lowest earned run average (2.61). William Hallahan from Syracuse had the highest strikeout total (195).

Buffalo remained in the International League until 1970, winning only two more flags along the way. Although other Bison squads finished with higher winning percentages or better team batting averages, no other Buffalo team has won as many games in one season, which is the true measure of a team's strength.

BUFFALO
Bisons

| | | 1st | 112-56 | | .667 | | | | | | William Clymer | |

BATTERS	POS-GAMES	GP	AB	R	H	BI	2B	3B	HR	BB	SO	SB	BA
Del Bissonette	1B166	166	628	168	229	167	46	20	21	62	69	13	.365
Lewis Malone	2B	(see multi-team players)											
Andy Cohen	SS91,2B54	150	555	90	196	118	34	5	14	22	15	3	.353
Clarence Huber	3B133	135	476	76	159	91	32	13	9	23	26	12	.334
Otis Carter	OF140	140	505	122	167	89	39	4	15	53	72	13	.331
George Fisher	OF98	111	400	62	128	62	21	5	10	28	32	5	.320
Andy Anderson	OF97	112	320	86	105	62	23	2	7	73	30	8	.328
Art Pond	C84	93	245	41	70	37	16	1	4	24	18	2	.286
Ed Taylor	SS82,3B35	122	368	72	106	48	23	4	3	66	23	7	.288
Al Tyson	OF93	93	373	89	140	45	27	10	4	35	21	19	.375
Michael Devine	C83	88	277	31	79	43	11	2	2	19	9	5	.285
Fred Brainard	OF67,2B10	87	319	61	97	53	14	6	9	13	44	9	.304
John Barnes	C27	46	67	6	23	11	4	0	0	8	6	0	.343
Leo Mangum	P35	35	90	12	26	15	6	0	0	1	15	0	.289
Sterling Stryker	P35	35	63	13	19	12	3	1	1	4	7	0	.302
Warren Ogden	P32	34	52	6	16	7	4	0	0	4	3	0	.308
James Wiltse	P32	33	48	1	5	1	1	0	0	0	19	0	.104
John Hollingsworth	P30	32	72	9	11	7	1	0	2	0	20	0	.153
Eurie Proffitt	P31	31	64	7	17	8	0	0	1	3	4	0	.266
Walt Leverenz	P23	23	55	3	9	5	2	0	0	2	21	0	.164
James Brice	P18	18	12	1	1	0	1	0	0	1	5	1	.083
Chet Falk	P10	16	35	12	15	10	3	1	0	0	2	0	.429
Fay Thomas	P12	12	33	3	4	1	1	0	0	1	15	0	.121
John O'Malley		5											.500
John Wight		5											.286
Vince McNamara		1											.000
Ray Pierce		1											.000

PITCHERS		W	L	PCT	G	GS	CG	SH	IP	H	BB	SO	ERA
Leo Mangum		21	7	.750	35		21	5	238	255	40	67	3.34
John Hollingsworth		17	7	.708	30		14	2	199	196	76	106	2.85
Eurie Proffitt		16	7	.696	31		15	2	165	183	33	61	3.60
Sterling Stryker		14	7	.333	35		10	1	173	196	42	46	3.69
Warren Ogden		11	7	.611	32		9	3	146	175	36	59	4.99
James Wiltse		9	3	.750	32		7	2	135	145	28	34	4.07
Walt Leverenz		9	7	.563	23		13	2	143	147	43	50	3.46
Chet Falk		7	2	.778	10		5	1	63	70	13	18	3.71
James Brice		4	2	.667	18		2	1	49	64	14	12	3.65
Fay Thomas		3	5	.375	12		3	0	85	95	28	45	3.91

SYRACUSE
Stars

| | | 2nd | 102-66 | | .607 | | -10 | | | | Burt Shotton | |

BATTERS	POS-GAMES	GP	AB	R	H	BI	2B	3B	HR	BB	SO	SB	BA
Frank Hurst	1B161	162	572	100	185	127	37	10	16	70	36	21	.323
Carey Selph	2B122	129	514	98	159	73	34	4	9	32	23	10	.309
Louis Benson	SS141	144	487	69	142	59	22	5	4	47	36	6	.292
Joseph Brown	3B117,2B48	164	575	125	178	97	34	3	14	89	22	34	.310
Harry Layne	OF161	163	619	138	200	114	29	10	21	84	73	50	.323
Howard Williamson	OF157	157	646	114	211	79	32	18	12	47	48	16	.327
Homer Peel	OF137	140	539	114	177	107	39	8	16	30	33	14	.328
Boyce Morrow	C99	101	318	51	102	51	23	1	5	44	18	5	.321
Gus Mancuso	C60	82	180	28	67	54	9	2	8	25	10	0	.372
Robert Worthington	OF62	73	199	32	52	28	8	3	3	16	14	0	.262
Russ Miller	P36	44	78	12	13	9	2	0	0	6	10	0	.167
Ira Smith	3B40	40	146	22	44	33	11	2	3	8	12	3	.322
William Hallahan	P40	40	87	9	22	16	3	1	1	4	21	0	.253
Del Gainer	1B16,OF10	40	76	18	25	9	4	1	2	11	9	1	.329
Syl Johnson	P36	36	92	9	18	11	2	0	4	3	25	0	.196
Frank Barnes	P33	35	74	8	21	8	2	0	0	4	8	0	.284
Harold Haid	P34	34	66	8	11	6	2	0	1	11	26	0	.167
John Schelberg	P32	32	21	4	5	1	0	0	0	0	8	0	.238
Allyn Stout	P32	32	37	1	5	2	2	1	0	0	11	0	.135
Edwin Dyer		19	25	6	3	5	1	0	0	2	6	0	.120
Karl Urban	SS14	15	38	4	12	7	1	0	0	0	2	0	.316
Joseph Poetz	P15	15	21	3	6	6	0	0	2	0	5	0	.286
Charles Abbott		13	13	2	3	1	0	0	0	4	2	0	.231
Paul Kinney	P10	10	1	0	0	0	0	0	0	0	0	0	.000
Al Grabowski		9											.200
Robert Schang		7											.400

SYRACUSE (cont.)
Stars

BATTERS	POS-GAMES	GP	AB	R	H	BI	2B	3B	HR	BB	SO	SB	BA
Geibert		5											.333
Sam Hamby		4											.333
W. Cohen		3											.000
Stoll		2											.000
Ovid McCracken		2											.000
Warwick		1											.000
Reson		1											.000

PITCHERS	W	L	PCT	G	GS	CG	SH	IP	H	BB	SO	ERA
William Hallahan	19	11	.633	40		18	2	229	221	135	195	3.97
Syl Johnson	18	13	.581	36		22	3	250	231	36	127	3.31
Russ Miller	15	10	.600	36		15	3	208	249	41	60	4.85
Harold Haid	15	11	.577	34		13	2	206	187	84	106	3.84
Frank Barnes	8	6	.571	33		11	0	178	195	35	62	3.69
Allyn Stout	7	4	.636	32		4	0	102	96	40	65	5.21
John Schelberg	7	5	.583	32		1	0	80	84	35	29	4.84
Joseph Poetz	3	2	.600	15		3	0	57	71	25	15	4.26
Paul Kinney	0	0	----	10		0	0	18	17	7	8	7.50

NEWARK   3rd   90-77   .539   -21.5   John Egan
Bears

BATTERS	POS-GAMES	GP	AB	R	H	BI	2B	3B	HR	BB	SO	SB	BA
William Kelly	1B78	78	297	42	86	49	11	4	8	16	19	4	.290
Harold Mackin	2B125	127	477	72	154	63	19	8	4	32	16	3	.323
Wescott Kingdon	SS128,3B30	159	514	82	162	80	26	5	8	68	47	15	.315
William Conroy	3B104,1B11	120	464	73	143	60	22	10	6	40	29	3	.309
Roy Carlyle	OF163	163	629	100	216	122	34	16	18	26	35	9	.343
John Conlan	OF156	157	626	119	201	75	33	11	4	62	28	33	.321
Cliff Lee	OF111	128	432	61	131	71	16	8	7	36	39	11	.303
Bill Skiff	C87	100	303	30	83	27	12	3	1	19	7	4	.274
Leo Casey	OF79	96	299	42	91	49	18	4	3	7	12	6	.305
Al Elliott	SS39,2B25	88	267	53	91	44	14	8	5	24	14	6	.341
Clyde Manion	C74	79	242	41	72	35	11	4	5	29	23	1	.298
Joseph Zubris	P45	48	66	7	11	11	1	1	1	3	30	0	.167
Jack Bentley	P21	45	74	9	20	14	4	2	1	4	5	0	.270
Al Mamaux	P42	42	104	12	24	10	6	1	0	11	12	0	.231
Lloyd Davies	P29	35	70	7	17	4	0	0	0	4	8	0	.243
Fred Myers	3B27	30	103	17	27	12	3	2	1	5	7	0	.262
Don Brennan	P30	30	21	4	3	2	0	0	0	1	7	0	.143
Earl Howard	P28	28	16	4	3	2	0	0	0	3	6	0	.188
William Moore	P25	25	44	4	6	3	0	0	0	6	12	0	.136
Guy Lacey	2B19	19	78	10	20	10	4	0	2	3	3	3	.256
Charles Swaney	P19	19	26	1	4	2	1	0	0	4	12	0	.154
Virgil Cheeves	P14	14	19	0	2	1	0	0	0	1	7	0	.105
Robert Knode		10	34	2	5	6	1	0	0	4	3	0	.147
Edwin Twombly	P10	10	8	0	0	0	0	0	0	2	5	0	.000
Henry Boney		9											.000
James Walkup		5											.000
Warhop		4											.000
Duffy		4											.000
Walt Smallwood		3											.333
Clarke		3											.333
Lind		3											.100
Fred Stiely		3											.000
Fred Adams		2											.000
Shea		2											.000
Carl Fischer		2											.000
Holland		2											.000
Gill		1											.000
Carl Yowell		1											.000
Williams		1											.000

PITCHERS	W	L	PCT	G	GS	CG	SH	IP	H	BB	SO	ERA
Al Mamaux	25	10	.714	42		30	2	318	304	64	141	2.61
Lloyd Davies	14	9	.609	29		15	4	192	193	46	72	3.80
William Moore	13	6	.684	25		12	1	136	140	43	61	3.51
Jack Bentley	11	3	.786	21		9	0	110	113	52	46	4.25
Joseph Zubris	10	18	.357	45		11	1	211	200	102	122	3.88

NEWARK (cont.)
Bears

PITCHERS	W	L	PCT	G	GS	CG	SH	IP	H	BB	SO	ERA
Earl Howard	5	2	.714	28		1	0	78	83	33	25	4.50
Don Brennan	5	3	.625	30		3	0	81	81	47	42	4.56
Charles Swaney	3	5	.375	19		4	0	78	97	19	9	4.62
Virgil Cheeves	3	6	.333	14		4	0	64	73	23	23	6.05
Edwin Twombley	0	3	.000	10		0	0	34	40	27	13	7.15

TORONTO 4th 89-78 .533 -22.5 Lee Fohl -
Maple Leafs Bill O'Hara

BATTERS	POS-GAMES	GP	AB	R	H	BI	2B	3B	HR	BB	SO	SB	BA
Dale Alexander	1B151	153	557	83	188	97	26	11	12	33	45	4	.338
Leslie Burke	2B103,3B29	138	475	61	120	48	15	2	2	31	24	4	.253
Robert LaMotte	SS128	131	464	58	132	73	17	7	5	48	42	12	.285
William Webb	3B86,SS38	125	454	70	127	44	29	3	5	56	57	17	.280
Vern Spencer	OF135	138	539	83	149	53	27	2	2	72	33	11	.276
Merwin Jacobson	OF125	125	471	79	126	58	17	9	6	56	55	24	.268
James Walsh	OF69	69	248	41	80	38	9	2	1	44	9	8	.323
William Hargrave	C124	144	468	80	143	85	31	6	12	49	47	7	.306
Andy Harrington	2B59,3B44	115	393	53	106	48	25	6	2	26	14	2	.270
William Styles	C35,OF11	80	213	28	60	31	14	0	1	29	17	11	.282
George Rensa	C23,OF17	60	136	23	37	20	7	2	0	13	16	3	.272
Claude Satterfield	P28	56	67	6	19	11	4	0	0	5	6	0	.284
James Faulkner	P42	42	107	11	25	14	3	2	2	3	20	0	.234
Vic Sorrell	P32	33	67	8	17	6	1	0	0	2	12	0	.254
Clarence Fisher	P31	31	69	5	15	5	2	0	0	1	9	0	.217
Clarence Walker	OF26	28	100	12	23	12	7	0	1	18	10	0	.230
Jesse Doyle	P27	27	68	6	16	3	0	0	0	9	10	1	.235
Joe Maley	P26	26	50	3	6	2	3	0	0	4	7	0	.120
Minor Heath	1B15	17	40	8	10	4	3	0	2	8	6	0	.250
Erwin Sexton		9											.375
Lucas		8											.167
Noonan		8											.000
Joseph Lucey		7											.333
Don Songer		7											.333
Rudolph Kneisch		5											1.000
Walter Brown		3											1.000
Hogan		3											.333
Walt Beall		1											.333
Holland		1											.000
Joseph Reddy		1											.000

PITCHERS	W	L	PCT	G	GS	CG	SH	IP	H	BB	SO	ERA
James Faulkner	21	10	.677	42		22	2	290	291	82	120	2.86
Vic Sorrell	14	8	.636	32		15	3	190	202	59	93	3.98
Clarence Fisher	14	10	.583	31		13	2	195	192	42	62	3.23
Jesse Doyle	14	10	.583	27		19	4	201	198	32	66	2.82
Claude Satterfield	7	4	.636	28		3	0	93	114	30	37	4.65
Joe Maley	5	14	.263	26		9	1	158	170	32	32	4.16

BALTIMORE 5th 85-82 .509 -26.5 Jack Dunn
Orioles

BATTERS	POS-GAMES	GP	AB	R	H	BI	2B	3B	HR	BB	SO	SB	BA
Clayton Sheedy	1B102,OF33	138	501	90	150	78	30	8	13	31	53	9	.299
William Urbanski	2B98,SS40,3B22	161	574	92	169	71	26	3	9	54	42	8	.294
Everett Scott	SS109	109	409	61	137	69	18	8	11	15	12	4	.335
Fritz Maisel	3B128	136	463	77	136	54	16	4	3	73	16	12	.294
Dick Porter	OF153	155	599	128	225	152	43	18	25	48	29	8	.376
Maurice Archdeacon	OF124	130	473	101	160	30	19	4	2	74	28	22	.338
Frank Brower	OF	(see multi-team players)											
Harry Lake	C121	128	423	39	103	66	20	0	5	25	36	5	.243
Fred Brunier	SS24,3B20,1B19	74	207	14	51	22	9	2	0	18	12	2	.246
Otto Freitag	C52	56	173	10	44	19	6	0	1	12	12	0	.255
George Earnshaw	P46	47	109	8	22	6	1	2	1	3	23	0	.202
James Poole	1B45	45	167	36	56	44	11	4	9	20	12	1	.335
John Ogden	P38	43	86	11	17	5	4	0	0	3	20	0	.198
Fred Vincent	P42	42	53	2	9	1	1	0	0	3	13	0	.170

BALTIMORE (cont.)
Orioles

BATTERS	POS-GAMES	GP	AB	R	H	BI	2B	3B	HR	BB	SO	SB	BA
William Henderson	P36	36	67	6	18	3	1	0	0	2	10	0	.269
Andrew Chambers	P33	33	95	6	16	4	1	0	0	4	16	0	.168
William Hohman	OF25	31	89	11	26	14	3	0	4	8	16	0	.292
Guy Cantrell	P26	27	64	3	15	10	2	0	1	0	7	0	.235
John Beard	P11	12	16	5	7	7	0	0	0	1	3	0	.437
Skidmore		7											.000
G. Miller		6											.000
Phil Voyles		4											.000
Slomy		2											.200
Jim Tennant		2											.000
Wood Harwood		1											.500
English		1											.333
Fred Sackett		1											.000
Rosenberg		1											.000

PITCHERS		W	L	PCT	G	GS	CG	SH	IP	H	BB	SO	ERA
John Ogden		21	9	.700	38		21	3	232	276	49	92	3.72
George Earnshaw		17	18	.486	46		24	1	279	283	108	172	3.77
Andrew Chambers		14	13	.519	33		20	1	232	269	50	101	4.11
Fred Vincent		10	9	.526	42		4	0	141	180	45	31	5.87
Guy Cantrell		8	10	.444	26		11	1	147	172	62	62	4.47
William Henderson		8	12	.400	36		12	0	185	198	82	82	5.21
John Beard		2	4	.333	11		1	0	36	47	25	13	6.25

ROCHESTER   6th   81-86   .485   -30.5   George Stallings -
Tribe   George Mogridge

BATTERS	POS-GAMES	GP	AB	R	H	BI	2B	3B	HR	BB	SO	SB	BA
Ed Onslow	1B92	95	354	50	110	57	15	6	0	39	18	11	.311
Rabbit Maranville	2B75,SS61	135	507	81	151	63	25	10	1	49	39	12	.298
John Jones	SS52	55	176	17	48	21	9	0	2	9	11	1	.273
Henry Groh	3B52	55	182	47	58	18	9	1	1	40	14	2	.319
Ed Kunesh	OF114	128	420	64	136	52	17	7	2	25	25	17	.324
Frank Gilhooley	OF99	102	399	71	138	37	17	7	0	47	12	19	.346
Ed Murphy	OF82	83	305	56	104	52	27	4	1	43	12	7	.341
Al Head	C120	140	481	72	160	102	36	9	4	38	15	11	.333
Joseph Manger	1B76,3B48	144	465	65	141	78	23	7	7	48	40	10	.303
Willard Fleming	OF71	79	265	41	79	24	12	0	1	20	27	4	.298
Richard Ryan	2B48	49	148	12	29	12	4	1	1	7	32	1	.196
Melvin Silva	OF48	65	162	24	46	28	4	1	0	15	12	10	.284
Rip Collins	OF40	45	138	26	34	12	0	4	2	16	18	3	.246
Herb Thormahlen	P36	42	108	13	24	8	2	2	0	6	30	2	.222
Berlyn Horne	P37	42	74	9	21	9	2	1	0	6	6	1	.284
Laverne Costello	SS33	39	110	12	15	15	3	0	1	9	19	1	.136
Milburn Shoffner	P38	39	64	6	11	4	1	0	1	3	23	0	.172
James McAvoy	C35	38	109	4	33	10	6	0	0	2	10	2	.303
Jim Bagby	P30	31	48	6	12	4	4	0	0	1	4	0	.250
Howard Shanks	2B11,OF11	28	102	17	24	13	4	0	1	6	2	1	.235
Hollis McLaughlin	P24	27	47	6	11	8	1	1	1	2	9	0	.234
Sam Wilson	C20	22	53	7	13	5	0	2	0	3	6	2	.245
Art Cousins	P20	20	22	0	1	2	0	0	0	1	5	0	.045
Joseph Himes	P18	18	12	3	3	1	1	0	0	0	6	0	.250
Art Mills	P15	15	28	6	10	6	6	0	0	3	4	0	.357
Hal McCleary	SS12	14	31	3	6	4	0	0	0	5	4	0	.194
Mike Kircher	P14	14	13	0	5	2	1	0	0	2	3	0	.385
John Walsh		13	24	1	3	0	1	0	0	1	1	0	.133
George Martin	SS10	12	43	5	13	5	2	0	0	0	7	0	.302
Elmer Hearn		10	10	1	1	0	0	1	0	0	4	0	.100
Kanip		8											.200
Dana Fillingim		7											.217
Whitehouse		6											.111
Clarence Thomas		6											.000
McHugh		5											.278
Ed Farber		5											.178
D. Jones		5											.400
Baxter		5											.000
George Selkirk		4											.222
Ed Lennon		4											.000
George Mogridge		4											.000
Magholtz		3											.167
Herr		3											.000

ROCHESTER (cont.)
Tribe

BATTERS	POS-GAMES	GP	AB	R	H	BI	2B	3B	HR	BB	SO	SB	BA
Charles Fitzberger		2											.000
Stearns		1											.000
E. Barnes		1											.000

PITCHERS		W	L	PCT	G	GS	CG	SH	IP	H	BB	SO	ERA
Berlyn Horne		18	10	.643	37		15	4	199	212	82	67	4.79
Herb Thormahlen		13	15	.464	36		24	2	268	305	69	105	4.26
Jim Bagby		12	9	.571	30		10	1	138	157	21	33	3.91
Milburn Shoffner		9	14	.391	38		10	2	186	212	97	51	5.13
Hollis McLaughlin		8	7	.533	24		8	0	123	154	33	28	4.98
Art Mills		5	4	.556	15		6	0	88	110	31	22	5.62
Art Cousins		4	8	.333	20		2	0	75	90	34	24	5.04
Mike Kircher		3	0	1.000	14		0	0	35	50	13	5	8.23
Joseph Himes		1	1	.500	18		0	0	39	64	23	14	9.46

JERSEY CITY   7th   66-100   .398   -45   Spencer Abbott
Skeeters

BATTERS	POS-GAMES	GP	AB	R	H	BI	2B	3B	HR	BB	SO	SB	BA
Pete Monahan	1B126	128	434	50	128	59	16	1	8	36	32	6	.295
Harry Collenberger	2B42,SS59,3B27	127	462	55	114	57	15	4	3	21	39	2	.247
Peter Radwan	SS		(see multi-team players)										
John Sheehan	3B28,2B21,SS17	76	289	32	66	19	9	2	0	35	27	2	.228
Al Moore	OF152	153	590	84	189	72	29	6	5	31	41	21	.320
Ernest Nietzke	OF93	97	347	35	98	49	11	4	4	29	33	6	.282
Joe Shannon	OF60,1B37	114	380	57	111	59	22	1	7	16	36	1	.292
Thomas Daly	C98	106	343	25	106	45	11	2	4	16	12	1	.309
Leon Williams	P32,OF19	70	157	19	44	14	5	4	0	13	22	2	.280
Joe Cobb	C48	57	153	16	39	28	7	0	4	19	23	3	.255
Roy Buckalew	P38	38	75	6	7	2	1	0	1	5	33	0	.093
Erv Brame	P33	36	91	6	24	10	5	1	0	8	17	0	.264
Leland Ellis	P31	32	43	2	9	4	2	1	0	4	12	0	.209
John Lehman	3B20	24	64	6	12	8	3	0	0	7	11	0	.162
Richard Smith	C21	22	78	5	16	8	5	0	0	2	13	0	.205
Dick Coffman	P12	12	30	3	4	3	2	0	0	3	10	0	.133
Robert Grody	P10	10	30	4	12	4	0	0	3	2	5	0	.400
James Chaplin	P10	10	18	2	4	2	1	0	1	2	9	0	.222
Snelling		9											.300
Allen		6											.333
Wendell		6											.167
Dyckman		6											.000
Pick		4											.278
Wall		4											.000
Stover		4											.000
Ed Strelecki		2											.333
Carroll		2											.167
Colleran		2											.000
McCormick		2											.000
Robert Unglaub		1											1.000
Casey		1											.000
Beamish		1											.000
Roach		1											.000

PITCHERS		W	L	PCT	G	GS	CG	SH	IP	H	BB	SO	ERA
Erv Brame		18	9	.667	33		23	5	243	260	70	86	3.11
Dick Coffman		9	2	.818	12		9	5	89	84	26	25	1.62
Roy Buckalew		9	16	.360	38		15	1	220	249	43	41	3.11
Leon Williams		9	17	.346	32		20	4	203	217	88	61	3.72
Leland Ellis		8	14	.364	31		10	0	141	169	48	27	3.77
Robert Grody		3	5	.375	10		8	0	79	108	26	16	5.01
James Chaplin		1	6	.143	10		5	1	52	54	15	12	3.29

READING   8th   43-123   .259   -68   Fred Merkle - Fritz
Keystones   Maisel - Harry Hinchman

BATTERS	POS-GAMES	GP	AB	R	H	BI	2B	3B	HR	BB	SO	SB	BA
Nelson Hawks	1B		(see multi-team players)										

READING (cont.)
Keystones

BATTERS	POS-GAMES	GP	AB	R	H	BI	2B	3B	HR	BB	SO	SB	BA
Harry Wilkie	2B95,3B28	128	409	49	94	36	13	4	2	53	47	4	.230
Sam Crane	SS103	113	357	23	70	33	5	1	0	13	20	5	.196
Joseph Rapp	3B	(see multi-team players)											
William Jarrett	OF121	124	462	63	128	44	13	5	4	37	32	4	.277
Dave Barbee	OF108	119	413	47	108	52	20	3	14	20	66	3	.261
George Quellich	OF	(see multi team players)											
Virgil Davis	C106	137	383	50	118	70	17	3	11	44	35	2	.308
Hugh Ferrell	OF32,3B	115	398	47	101	44	16	2	5	17	30	4	.254
Art Oeschler	SS65,2B10	89	270	24	54	19	9	1	1	17	34	1	.200
Thomas Sewell	3B51,2B19	72	273	35	76	23	8	2	0	20	14	1	.278
Floyd Trexler	OF36	60	143	18	39	17	7	3	1	9	15	2	.273
Fred Sinstock	C42	49	124	7	23	9	6	0	0	9	14	1	.185
Dewey Hill	C35	58	113	10	25	11	3	2	2	9	7	1	.221
Neil Dougherty	OF42	43	144	23	47	16	2	0	0	17	15	3	.326
George Davis	OF41	41	150	16	40	10	5	1	0	15	9	3	.267
Fred Merkle	1B26	38	101	13	31	20	3	0	4	14	14	2	.307
Elmer Hansen	P34	34	29	1	4	2	1	0	0	0	8	0	.138
Jack Slappey	P29	30	50	3	8	2	1	0	0	6	18	0	.160
George Maisel	OF26	29	98	10	25	7	3	1	0	7	2	6	.255
Les Rouprich	P25	29	45	2	7	4	1	0	0	0	8	0	.138
Stephen Woodgie	P26	27	44	8	11	1	2	1	0	3	14	0	.250
Fred Carts	P24	25	41	2	5	3	0	0	0	1	3	0	.122
John Watson	P22	22	36	3	2	0	0	0	0	3	11	0	.056
Frank Werre	P18	20	31	3	9	2	1	0	0	2	8	0	.290
Art Carlton	P14	14	10	0	1	0	0	0	0	0	3	0	.100
Clarence Fields	OF12	13	34	2	3	0	0	1	0	2	12	0	.088
John Noble	P11	13	27	1	5	0	1	0	0	0	3	0	.185
Paschal Billings	P10	10	2	1	2	2	0	0	1	1	0	0	1.000
Kerr		6											.000
Cihicki		5											.063
Fallen		5											.000
Silver		4											.077
William Shores		3											.455
Jacoway		3											.000
Hammer		2											.000
Lord		2											.000
Poppen		1											.000
Walker		1											.000

PITCHERS	W	L	PCT	G	GS	CG	SH	IP	H	BB	SO	ERA
John Watson	7	11	.389	22		7	0	112	134	47	26	5.95
Fred Carts	6	11	.353	24		6	2	129	173	42	38	4.40
Stephen Woodgie	5	9	.357	26		10	0	136	174	63	30	5.56
Les Rouprich	3	9	.250	25		7	0	132	171	72	29	5.38
Jack Slappey	3	14	.176	29		8	1	153	182	79	28	5.59
Art Carlton	1	5	.167	14		3	0	39	54	19	8	5.77
Elmer Hansen	1	8	.111	34		4	0	94	136	66	29	6.99
Frank Werre	1	9	.100	18		3	0	78	91	25	17	4.73
John Noble	0	7	.000	11		4	0	46	80	23	11	7.83
Paschal Billings	0	0	----	10		0	0	16	26	9	2	9.56

MULTI-TEAM PLAYERS

BATTERS	POS-GAMES	TEAMS	GP	AB	R	H	BI	2B	3B	HR	BB	SO	SB	BA
Aldrik Gaudette	OF117,3B26	JC95-BA55	150	567	101	165	41	26	1	1	62	47	1	.291
Joseph Rapp	3B148	RE84-RO66	150	522	46	146	50	21	2	2	43	34	20	.280
Lewis Malone	2B131,3B12	JC41-BU108	149	540	61	154	75	21	5	7	36	50	2	.285
Frank Brower	OF143	BA99-JC49	148	517	83	148	93	27	4	20	62	47	1	.286
Hobart Whitman	OF106,2B41	BU38-JC108	146	561	83	173	72	29	9	0	25	12	5	.308
Nelson Hawks	1B115	NE68-RE51	119	393	63	100	49	20	5	3	48	22	4	.254
George Quellich	OF105	BA20-RE96	116	385	69	121	69	36	4	18	54	57	5	.314
Otis Lawry	OF67,2B27	TO28-RO86	114	312	45	99	37	15	4	2	35	11	21	.317
Wilson Fewster	2B78,3B28	JC53-BA59	112	422	73	125	37	21	1	1	47	44	27	.296
Peter Radwan	SS91,3B18	BU1-JC108	109	393	52	108	33	22	6	3	29	28	7	.275
Al Kapl	SS34,3B16,OF10	RO12-SY68	80	230	35	75	43	13	2	7	16	30	0	.326
Fred Bratche	OF66	TO58-BA18	76	247	27	58	32	8	3	5	21	30	2	.235
Charles High	OF62	BU7-TO63	70	191	30	49	31	6	2	4	20	13	3	.257
Roger Nolan	1B53	BU6-RE47	53	151	12	31	10	5	1	2	22	18	1	.205
Nicholas Harrison	P45	RO13-RE33	46	68	6	12	0	0	0	0	13	17	0	.176
Vern Parks	P38	JC31-RE8	39	68	7	8	6	3	0	0	0	7	0	.118
John Prudhomme	P31	RE10-TO21	31	50	7	9	3	0	0	0	5	20	0	.180

MULTI-TEAM PLAYERS (cont.)

BATTERS	POS-GAMES	TEAMS	GP	AB	R	H	BI	2B	3B	HR	BB	SO	SB	BA
Allen Russell	P28	RE17-BU14	31	39	1	6	4	1	0	0	4	18	0	.154
Cliff Jackson	P24	BA13-JC11	24	47	4	9	4	2	0	0	2	13	0	.191
John Schulte	C19	BU1-SY20	21	58	17	19	8	3	0	1	8	1	0	.328
Harry Courtney	P16	RE9-TO12	21	37	4	7	1	3	0	0	2	7	0	.189
William McCarren	3B16	JC16-NE3	19	63	8	12	2	2	0	0	6	8	0	.190
Ray Gordinier	P18	JC12-TO6	18	19	0	4	2	0	0	0	0	3	0	.211
Carl Schmehl		BU7-TO3-RO7	17	32	1	2	0	0	0	0	0	3	0	.063
Jim Parnham	P16	RE11-NE6	17	30	1	5	1	2	0	0	0	6	0	.167
Frank Uzmann	C13	NE14-RE2	16	32	3	6	7	1	0	0	8	9	1	.188
Ralph Head	P14	TO9-RO5	14	18	0	0	0	0	0	0	0	8	0	.000
Elbert Slayback		BA8-BU5	13	28	3	7	3	2	1	0	4	7	0	.250
John Bogart	P10	NE4-RE6	10	14	0	0	0	0	0	0	0	6	0	.000

PITCHERS		TEAMS	W	L	PCT	G	GS	CG	SH	IP	H	BB	SO	ERA
Nicholas Harrison		RO13-RE32	9	16	.360	45		13	0	218	248	119	59	5.33
John Prudhomme		RO10-TO21	8	11	.421	31		9	5	155	147	80	53	4.35
Vern Parks		JC30-RE8	8	19	.296	38		15	0	200	302	41	45	5.22
John Bogart		NE4-RO6	3	4	.429	10		2	2	47	50	24	10	4.60
Harry Courtney		RE5-TO11	3	8	.273	16		5	0	82	95	53	13	5.16
Cliff Jackson		BA13-JC11	3	10	.231	24		8	0	122	121	56	43	4.06
Allen Russell		RE15-BU13	3	12	.200	28		5	1	123	155	47	27	4.24
Ray Gordinier		JC12-TO6	2	3	.400	18		1	0	62	62	30	25	6.23
Jim Parnham		RE10-NE6	2	8	.200	16		2	0	75	104	28	11	6.00
Ralph Head		TO9-RO5	1	3	.250	14		0	0	51	64	18	9	4.76

TEAM BATTING

TEAMS	GP	AB	R	H	BI	2B	3B	HR	BB	SO	SB	BA
BUFFALO	168	5663	**1059**	**1799**	**980**	**340**	79	120	497	528	100	**.318**
SYRACUSE	**170**	5679	1029	1756	955	314	71	**129**	**572**	508	**157**	.309
NEWARK	167	5524	843	1640	787	243	**91**	76	454	430	99	.297
TORONTO	168	5552	793	1532	720	250	57	62	**572**	524	103	.276
BALTIMORE	167	5538	867	1632	776	267	57	102	516	470	90	.295
ROCHESTER	169	5549	790	1612	702	255	70	27	504	494	136	.291
JERSEY CITY	167	5498	656	1512	628	229	45	50	396	508	82	.275
READING	166	5383	609	1349	556	205	38	70	441	**599**	65	.251
	671	44386	6646	12382	6104	2103	508	636	3952	4061	832	.289

1928
FEATHER'S BREADTH

During its first 45 years, the International's family of leagues gained a reputation for tight pennant races. On eight separate occasions, two games or less separated the top two teams. The year 1928 witnessed yet another close finish, with the victor squeezing ahead by the slimmest of margins.

The stage was set for the 1928 pennant race long before the season started. In 1927, the Syracuse Stars became the property of the major league St. Louis Cardinals. Stocked with Cardinals-to-be, the team immediately bounded out of the second division, finishing 1927 second with 102 wins. But when the Stars balked at building a new facility at St. Louis's behest, the Cardinals moved their sponsorship to nearby Rochester. Lacking a mentor, the Syracuse franchise moved to Jersey City, which in turn sold the team to Montreal businessmen.

Blessed with an influx of talent from one of the most powerful National League clubs, Rochester became an immediate contender in 1928. Rechristened the Red Wings, in honor of its Cardinals affiliation, Rochester reached first by mid–July. At the same time, the defending champions, the Buffalo Bisons, were 12 games out of first, residing in seventh. Buffalo then proceeded to turn on the jets. The team won 51 of its next 77 games to pull a game ahead of Rochester with a week to go in the season. During the final weekend, in three consecutive doubleheaders, Rochester won three of the first four. On the final day, Rochester, needing a sweep, won the last pair to take the pennant with a winning percentage of .549, a sliver ahead of Buffalo at .548. There was no difference between the teams in the games-behind category.

The rest of the league did not finish far behind. Third-place Toronto and fourth-place Reading finished less than eight games behind. Montreal and Baltimore tied for fifth, and Newark in seventh finished less than ten games back. Even Jersey City in last was only 26 games off the pace. Dale Alexander from Toronto became the first International Leaguer to connect for the Triple Crown as he had the highest average (.380), most home runs (31), and most runs batted in (141). Reading pitcher Harry Seibold had the most wins (22), Maurice Bream of Jersey City had the lowest earned run average (2.32), and Baltimore's Guy Cantrell struck out the highest number of batters (165).

As it turned out, Rochester's narrow victory hinged on the weather. During the season, four Rochester games were lost to the schedule because of rainouts. With two more wins and losses, Buffalo's winning percentage fell just shy. It is ironic that games not even played could have such a profound effect on the season's most important outcome.

ROCHESTER Red Wings

	1st	90-74	.549		Billy Southworth

BATTERS	POS-GAMES	GP	AB	R	H	BI	2B	3B	HR	BB	SO	SB	BA
Pete Monahan	1B	(see multi-team players)											
George Toporcer	2B86	88	322	59	96	30	17	0	0	34	9	13	.298
Charles Gelbert	SS164	164	573	145	195	116	32	14	21	97	61	30	.340
Joseph Brown	3B134,2B31	164	638	137	200	74	29	11	6	84	21	20	.313
Billy Southworth	OF119	124	438	85	158	81	29	11	6	40	13	10	.361
Harry Layne	OF117	122	439	83	137	56	17	13	6	48	38	26	.312
August Felix	OF	(see multi-team players)											
Boyce Morrow	C117	117	361	51	104	48	24	5	2	55	24	5	.288
Ira Smith	3B33,1B30,OF30	109	370	55	102	66	17	8	4	22	36	6	.276
Karl Urban	2B58	70	213	27	55	25	11	4	1	7	7	1	.258
Tony Kaufmann	OF29,P12	55	112	20	45	30	9	2	0	11	12	1	.402
Del Gainer		52	61	3	20	8	2	1	0	5	5	0	.328
Hank Gowdy	C45	47	127	8	32	22	4	1	3	17	4	1	.252
Harold Smith	P45	45	60	2	5	2	0	0	0	3	25	0	.083
Louis Duncan	OF43	43	147	25	37	25	5	1	0	20	10	4	.252
Herman Bell	P43	43	92	11	13	6	2	2	0	10	28	0	.141
Vic Keen	P34	37	77	2	16	7	0	0	0	4	13	0	.207
Art Decatur	P36	36	63	2	10	7	0	0	0	6	21	0	.159
John Berly	P23	27	28	3	7	3	2	0	0	1	3	1	.250
Ovid McCracken	P25	25	41	2	9	3	1	1	0	4	11	0	.220
Frank Hurst	1B20	20	78	16	24	16	6	2	1	15	4	3	.308
John Schelberg	P19	19	13	1	1	0	0	0	0	0	5	0	.077
Laurence Irvin	P16	16	20	0	5	5	0	0	0	3	3	0	.250
Rip Collins		14	32	5	12	11	0	0	0	4	2	0	.375
Sylvester Heitzman	P10	10	14	2	3	2	0	0	0	1	8	1	.214
Clay Hopper		9											.444
George Hughes		9											.300
Dennis Gearin	P5	9											.125
Anthony Severino		8											.222
Willard Ford	P6	6											.222
William Burkman		6											.300
Edgar Clough	P4	6											.100
William Foreman	P6	6											.000
James Bivin		5											.000
John Bogart	P4	4											.200
Al Grabowski	P4	4											.167
Stephen Toner	P4	4											.000
George Eggert		2											.182
Harry Taylor		2											.000
Guilford Paulsen	P2	2											.000
Ed Baecht	P2	2											.000
Richard Ryan		1											.000
Fancher	P1	1											.000
Bud Stewart	P1	1											.000

PITCHERS	W	L	PCT	G	GS	CG	SH	IP	H	BB	SO	ERA
Herman Bell	21	8	.724	43		22	1	261	269	60	101	3.38
Art Decatur	15	13	.536	36		12	1	190	220	40	61	3.60
Vic Keen	12	11	.522	34		15	0	200	213	91	57	4.05
Harold Smith	9	15	.375	45		10	1	184	211	48	61	4.16
Laurence Irvin	7	1	.875	16		4	3	62	52	43	21	3.05
Ovid McCracken	7	7	.500	25		7	0	121	118	51	25	4.61
John Berly	5	3	.625	23		3	0	87	101	43	32	5.07
Tony Kaufmann	3	2	.600	12		2	0	43	48	26	20	4.40
Sylvester Heitzmann	3	3	.500	10		1	0	50	62	13	15	6.30
Willard Ford	2	2	.500	6								
John Schelberg	1	2	.333	19		0	0	41	62	26	5	9.44
William Foreman	1	2	.333	6								
Edgar Clough	1	0	1.000	4								
Dennis Gearin	1	1	.500	5								
John Bogart	1	1	.500	4								
Stephen Toner	0	0	----	4								
Al Grabowski	0	0	----	4								
Guilford Paulsen	0	0	----	2								
Ed Baecht	0	0	----	2								
Bud Stewart	0	0	----	1								
Fancher	0	0	----	1								

BUFFALO Bisons

	2nd	92-76	.548	-0	William Clymer

BATTERS	POS-GAMES	GP	AB	R	H	BI	2B	3B	HR	BB	SO	SB	BA
William Kelly	1B	(see multi-team players)											

BUFFALO (cont.)
Bisons

BATTERS	POS-GAMES	GP	AB	R	H	BI	2B	3B	HR	BB	SO	SB	BA
Herb Thomas	2B83,SS69	154	571	82	186	89	34	7	10	36	27	6	.326
James Cooney	SS62	65	234	37	84	16	9	2	1	14	3	3	.359
Robert Barrett	3B138	139	525	87	163	100	35	7	19	23	31	2	.310
Al Moore	OF170	170	658	98	215	115	33	13	22	42	37	11	.327
George Fisher	OF138	146	499	90	167	89	30	6	17	56	38	6	.335
Maurice Archdeacon	OF	(see multi-team players)											
John Barnes	C86	99	260	36	86	41	23	6	2	34	14	1	.331
Luke Urban	C43	44	131	19	36	16	5	1	3	11	8	2	.275
Art Pond	C39	39	116	13	28	13	6	0	2	12	21	1	.241
Warren Ogden	P36	38	93	12	26	12	5	0	0	2	9	0	.280
Sterling Stryker	P37	37	43	1	8	2	0	0	0	5	4	0	.186
Ed Taylor	3B22,SS10	34	91	4	22	11	2	1	0	17	8	1	.242
Leon Williams	P29	33	51	6	12	3	1	0	1	2	8	0	.235
Leo Mangum	P30	30	91	11	25	10	4	0	0	2	12	0	.275
Howard Signor	P29	29	40	4	8	6	0	2	0	1	7	0	.200
Eurie Proffitt	P23	25	30	5	9	2	0	0	0	3	5	0	.300
William Marriott	SS21	24	77	13	27	7	4	2	0	8	3	0	.351
Art Mills	P23	23	52	2	7	0	1	0	0	1	6	0	.136
Thomas Nash		17	13	3	1	0	1	0	0	1	1	0	.077
Henry Cullop	OF11	15	45	6	14	6	8	0	0	6	17	1	.311
Henry Wertz	P15	15	39	5	10	8	2	0	2	3	10	0	.256
Frank Pytlak	C13	13	11	1	2	3	1	0	0	2	8	0	.182
James Wiltse	P12	12	18	0	1	0	0	0	0	1	7	0	.056
Earl Chesbro	1B10	11	42	2	11	5	1	0	1	2	12	0	.262
Foster Edwards	P7	7											.200
Emilio Palmero	P7	7											.000
Charles Swaney	P6	6											.333
Bill Dickey		3											.125
James Marquis	P3	3											.000
Hugh Ferrell		3											.333
Joseph Stryker	P2	2											.000
Sutherland Scott	P2	2											.000
James Brice	P2	2											.000
Bill Munday		1											.000
Roth		1											.000
Ernest Evans		1											.000

PITCHERS	W	L	PCT	G	GS	CG	SH	IP	H	BB	SO	ERA
Warren Ogden	21	11	.656	36		22	5	242	281	62	68	3.09
Leo Mangum	15	11	.577	30		22	4	231	263	38	73	2.84
Sterling Stryker	10	7	.588	37		3	0	130	154	48	32	4.29
Leon Williams	9	5	.643	29		5	1	130	147	47	37	4.02
Art Mills	9	7	.563	23		13	1	153	143	51	75	2.82
Henry Wertz	8	4	.667	15		7	1	101	105	27	22	3.74
Howard Signor	8	6	.571	29		6	1	124	145	27	35	3.92
James Wiltse	3	3	.500	12		2	1	52	60	26	8	5.88
Charles Swaney	2	0	1.00	6								
Eurie Proffitt	2	6	.250	23		3	1	80	95	33	25	4.61
Emilio Palmero	1	3	.250	7								
Foster Edwards	0	3	.000	7								
James Marquis	0	0	----	3								
James Brice	0	0	----	2								
Sutherland Scott	0	0	----	2								
Joseph Stryker	0	0	----	2								

TORONTO	3rd	86-80	.518	-4	Bill O'Hara

Maple Leafs

BATTERS	POS-GAMES	GP	AB	R	H	BI	2B	3B	HR	BB	SO	SB	BA
Dale Alexander	1B169	169	621	115	**236**	144	**49**	11	**31**	69	42	15	**.380**
Leslie Burke	2B151	151	519	64	144	58	30	8	1	62	43	4	.277
Warren Cote	SS161	161	565	62	136	61	24	8	3	30	54	6	.241
Fred Bedore	3B90,2B18,SS14	133	433	61	139	58	27	7	1	33	43	6	.321
Clayton Sheedy	OF167	168	633	106	208	90	27	10	8	42	48	17	.329
Joe Rabbitt	OF144	149	552	83	143	51	35	13	8	38	44	**42**	.259
Paul Easterling	OF68	70	210	34	52	20	10	4	6	28	43	4	.248
Ed Phillips	C79	85	262	32	83	45	14	4	6	27	25	8	.317
William Webb	3B89	102	300	46	64	20	13	7	2	39	46	8	.213
William Styles	C75	99	268	33	84	46	15	1	1	27	25	9	.313
Claude Satterfield	OF16,P12	72	115	9	33	14	2	0	0	13	8	1	.287

TORONTO (cont.)
Maple Leafs

BATTERS	POS-GAMES	GP	AB	R	H	BI	2B	3B	HR	BB	SO	SB	BA
Erwin Sexton	OF31	49	90	8	19	7	3	1	1	4	17	0	.211
Jesse Doyle	P34	40	73	8	18	15	3	1	0	7	8	2	.247
Don Hankins	P40	40	67	5	7	0	1	0	0	8	18	0	.104
John Prudhomme	P30	39	105	8	23	14	3	1	3	7	34	0	.219
Ralph Shinners	OF37	37	130	22	41	23	3	2	3	10	12	2	.315
Warren Collins	P33	33	78	9	17	8	2	1	0	11	18	0	.218
Clarence Fisher	P30	30	58	4	11	5	2	0	1	2	9	0	.190
Stephen Martin	P24	24	29	1	7	2	0	0	0	1	2	0	.241
Walt Leverenz	P22	22	48	5	14	5	1	0	2	4	12	0	.292
Don Songer	P20	20	9	3	3	1	0	0	1	1	2	0	.333
Bernard Hungling	C12	12	35	4	6	11	0	1	1	3	8	0	.171
George Rensa		9											.335
Frank Riel	P7	7											.333
Haskell Billings	P6	7											.167
Robert Reece		2											1.000
John Schrey		1											.000
Harry Whitehouse		1											.000
Thompson	P1	1											.000
Walmsley		1											.000

PITCHERS	W	L	PCT	G	GS	CG	SH	IP	H	BB	SO	ERA
John Prudhomme	19	15	.576	38		27	5	277	241	106	84	3.02
Warren Collins	17	9	.654	33		23	4	234	208	94	103	3.38
Don Hankins	12	16	.429	40		15	2	217	250	87	59	4.02
Jesse Doyle	10	11	.476	34		14	0	193	245	57	46	4.48
Clarence Fisher	9	9	.500	30		9	0	166	173	58	56	3.42
Stephen Martin	8	5	.615	24		4	2	89	95	45	44	3.74
Walt Leverenz	7	9	.438	22		11	2	136	149	55	68	3.57
Claude Satterfield	2	0	1.000	12		0	0	31	38	9	5	5.52
Don Sanger	2	2	.500	20		0	0	37	35	23	15	6.81
Frank Riel	0	1	.000	7								
Haskell Billings	0	0	----	6								
Thompson	0	0	----	1								

READING   4th   84-83   .503   -7.5   Harry Hinchman
Keystones

BATTERS	POS-GAMES	GP	AB	R	H	BI	2B	3B	HR	BB	SO	SB	BA
Nelson Hawks	1B166	166	588	102	199	78	34	12	3	65	38	19	.339
Charles Walsh	2B163	163	681	129	224	70	46	12	3	51	38	10	.329
Everett Scott	SS130	131	493	81	156	59	39	6	6	32	21	3	.316
William Conroy	3B120	160	577	99	178	100	42	5	8	70	31	1	.309
John Moore	OF144	146	525	94	172	117	24	18	17	51	31	7	.328
George Quellich	OF134	140	477	85	153	97	33	7	19	58	93	6	.321
Hobart Whitman	OF	(see multi-team players)											
Harry Lake	C81	85	239	29	58	34	10	0	0	22	14	2	.243
Louis Legett	C80	87	269	41	92	46	17	0	11	25	34	4	.342
James Dalrymple	SS44	64	139	16	33	12	4	2	0	15	13	1	.237
Neil Dougherty	OF39	63	143	12	29	17	4	1	0	5	7	2	.203
Nicholas Harrison	P46	46	77	3	10	2	2	0	0	4	20	0	.130
Vern Parks	P40	41	71	10	17	5	2	0	0	3	9	0	.239
Jess Fowler	P40	41	63	2	5	2	0	0	0	3	29	1	.079
Harry Seibold	P38	40	103	15	26	12	4	0	0	7	6	1	.252
John Welch	P32	39	84	11	19	8	5	0	2	2	20	1	.226
Ed Lautenbacher	P36	36	46	2	2	1	1	0	0	3	17	0	.043
Thomas Sewell	3B16	26	65	9	15	7	2	1	0	5	2	0	.231
Frank Kern	OF15	22	54	4	12	5	2	1	0	10	7	2	.222
James McAvoy	C14	15	36	3	5	1	1	0	0	3	7	0	.139
John Wisner	P10	10	20	2	2	0	0	0	0	3	4	0	.100
Nelson Pott	P8	8											.308
Fred Sengstock		8											.208
Charles Schesler	P4	4											.000
John Alberts		4											.000
Les Rouprich	P3	3											1.000
Andrew Moore		1											1.000
Frank Bailey		1											.000
Wallace		1											.000
Fred Carts	P1	1											.000
Henry Schopps	P1	1											.000
Harry Holsclaw	P1	1											.000

READING (cont.)
Keystones

PITCHERS	W	L	PCT	G	GS	CG	SH	IP	H	BB	SO	ERA
Harry Seibold	22	8	.733	38		24	7	270	250	99	98	3.00
John Welch	14	10	.583	32		14	3	182	207	61	76	4.30
Vern Parks	12	14	.462	40		15	5	208	233	48	67	4.37
Nicholas Harrison	11	20	.355	46		11	2	238	255	105	79	4.50
Ed Lautenbacher	10	6	.625	36		10	1	143	163	42	69	4.34
Jesse Fowler	10	13	.435	40		12	2	187	205	76	98	4.24
Nelson Pott	1	2	.333	8								
John Wisner	1	4	.200	10		2	0	53	69	27	14	7.64
Harry Holsclaw	0	1	.000	1								
Henry Schopps	0	1	.000	1								
Charles Schesler	0	0	----	4								
Les Rouprich	0	0	----	3								
Fred Carts	0	0	----	1								

MONTREAL Royals   5th (T)   84-84   .500   -8   George Stallings - Ed Holly

BATTERS	POS-GAMES	GP	AB	R	H	BI	2B	3B	HR	BB	SO	SB	BA
Frank Stapleton	1B117	125	410	58	108	42	26	5	5	46	49	0	.263
Wilson Fewster	2B88	88	338	52	85	48	13	3	1	47	48	12	.252
William Urbanski	SS			(see multi-team players)									
Chet Fowler	3B70	74	259	36	85	38	13	6	2	22	23	11	.328
Henry Haines	OF161	161	589	106	175	81	41	7	6	85	56	39	.297
Thomas Gulley	OF133	134	443	78	143	101	26	6	18	73	48	6	.323
Aldrik Gaudette	OF115,3B27	143	523	93	167	59	35	7	1	77	27	14	.319
Thomas Daly	C96	107	355	34	100	58	20	3	4	21	11	5	.282
Richard Smith	C80	98	298	22	87	46	13	1	0	13	24	2	.292
Joe Shannon	OF73	91	289	34	87	42	17	3	6	16	43	0	.301
James Holt	1B56	71	223	34	52	34	5	1	9	18	26	1	.233
Peter Radwan	SS42,3B17	62	190	29	59	25	13	1	2	30	19	2	.311
William McCarren	2B38	46	155	16	41	14	5	1	0	10	12	2	.265
Elroy Vick	2B12,SS10	45	89	11	22	8	5	0	1	7	21	1	.247
Ed Farber	2B35	35	110	17	28	15	9	1	0	13	11	1	.255
Henry Schreiber	SS34	34	113	8	21	10	4	1	0	4	10	0	.186
Roy Sherid	P34	34	69	4	5	5	1	0	0	3	29	0	.072
Frank Dunagan	P33	33	52	5	9	6	2	0	2	3	16	1	.173
Roy Buckalew	P31	31	60	5	15	4	6	0	0	2	12	0	.250
Chet Falk	P25	30	70	10	12	5	1	1	0	5	11	0	.171
Paul Hopkins	P29	30	57	4	8	3	0	0	0	5	13	0	.140
Don Miller	P30	30	38	2	7	0	0	0	0	1	8	0	.184
Joseph Faber	SS25	25	89	11	19	14	8	0	1	11	8	0	.213
Robert Shawkey	P23	23	56	4	12	4	1	0	0	1	3	0	.214
Bernard Helgeth	3B16	16	49	9	11	6	1	0	2	8	9	1	.224
Rufus Smith	P14	14	19	3	3	3	0	1	0	4	2	0	.158
George Tice		12	26	6	13	6	4	0	1	3	1	0	.500
Seymour Bailey	P12	12	22	1	4	3	0	0	0	2	8	0	.182
Ed Conley	OF10	11	24	6	7	3	3	0	0	5	4	0	.292
Walt Beall	P10	10	16	2	1	1	0	0	0	1	9	0	.063
Waldo Yarnall	P8	8											.500
James O'Neill		7											.263
Chet Nichols	P6	6											.000
George Driscoll		5											.167
James Lyston		5											.000
Robert Grody	P5	5											.000
William O'Hara	P2	2											.000
William Diehl	P2	2											.000
Edgar LePard		1											.000
Arnold	P1	1											.000
Joseph Hyde		1											.000

PITCHERS	W	L	PCT	G	GS	CG	SH	IP	H	BB	SO	ERA
Roy Sherid	15	7	.682	34		13	1	201	223	73	66	3.81
Roy Buckalew	13	8	.619	31		12	1	170	194	69	44	5.14
Chet Falk	10	11	.476	25		15	0	181	197	80	19	4.34
Robert Shawkey	9	9	.500	23		12	1	144	167	50	47	5.62
Frank Dunagan	9	10	.474	33		9	0	142	174	48	32	4.63
Paul Hopkins	7	9	.438	29		5	0	158	190	95	65	5.41
Rufus Smith	4	4	.500	23		3	0	87	101	43	32	5.07
Don Miller	4	7	.364	30		8	1	110	133	54	29	5.73
Seymour Bailey	3	5	.375	12		5	0	60	75	23	21	5.40
Chet Nichols	1	3	.250	6								

MONTREAL (cont.)
Royals

PITCHERS	W	L	PCT	G	GS	CG	SH	IP	H	BB	SO	ERA
Walt Beall	1	5	.167	10		2	0	41	34	49	22	3.73
Waldo Yarnell	0	1	.000	8								
Robert Grody	0	0	----	5								
William Diehl	0	0	----	2								
O'Hara	0	0	----	2								
Arnold	0	0	----	1								
Edgar LePard	0	0	----	1								

BALTIMORE   5th (T)   82-82   .500   -8   Jack Dunn
Orioles

BATTERS	POS-GAMES	GP	AB	R	H	BI	2B	3B	HR	BB	SO	SB	BA
Ed Onslow	1B155	155	570	85	197	114	36	5	7	65	28	21	.346
Ed Mooers	2B105	113	427	65	127	73	25	2	13	36	46	9	.297
Robert LaMotte	SS135	136	466	69	127	72	28	7	7	39	39	9	.273
Dick Porter	3B57,OF80,2B15,SS14	165	618	126	216	97	34	15	12	81	30	15	.350
Frank Brower	OF123	136	467	94	146	108	32	6	21	74	27	7	.313
Dan Clark	OF110,3B26	136	504	120	144	70	24	5	17	84	34	5	.286
Dick Spalding	OF64	64	246	40	84	24	14	1	1	26	32	3	.341
Leo Dixon	C100	102	295	53	79	34	12	3	3	44	29	7	.268
Vince Barton	OF38	63	165	26	47	34	10	0	4	8	23	1	.285
Stuart Bolen	P50	57	118	14	29	15	2	0	3	6	13	2	.246
Fred Coumbe	P44	56	89	15	22	11	5	2	3	12	13	2	.247
Guy Cantrell	P52	53	116	16	33	20	5	1	1	1	16	1	.284
Fritz Maisel	3B43	51	138	29	42	9	6	0	1	16	8	3	.304
William Jacobson	OF12	42	48	4	6	3	0	0	1	0	5	0	.125
Dennis Williams	OF36	39	150	25	47	10	6	2	1	12	8	3	.313
Andrew Chambers	P35	35	73	7	12	5	1	0	0	3	15	0	.164
Russ Johnson	P23	23	37	3	12	8	1	0	0	1	9	0	.324
George Earnshaw	P13	13	24	2	2	1	0	0	0	1	4	1	.083
Fred Vincent	P10	10	3	0	0	0	0	0	0	0	2	0	.000
H. Cates	P8	8											.000
Hawks Hayes	P8	8											.000
Clarence Allen	P6	6											.000
William Shores	P5	5											.167
Beryl Richmond		4											.000
Fred Sackett	P4	4											.000
Duke Herman		3											.143
Ray Walker	P3	3											.000
James Boswell	P2	2											.000
Koenig		1											.000
Harvey Giandomenico		1											.000
L. Walsh		1											.000

PITCHERS	W	L	PCT	G	GS	CG	SH	IP	H	BB	SO	ERA
Stuart Bolen	21	16	.568	50		22	3	288	295	107	161	3.37
Guy Cantrell	19	18	.514	53		19	2	290	309	125	165	4.10
Andrew Chambers	16	12	.571	35		14	1	202	236	50	87	3.92
Fred Coumbe	12	13	.480	44		14	2	215	252	69	64	4.14
Russ Johnson	7	8	.467	23		4	1	103	137	17	37	4.37
George Earnshaw	3	5	.375	13		3	0	60	64	31	47	6.15
Hawks Hayes	1	1	.500	8								
Fred Vincent	0	0	----	10		0	0	15	28	5	7	10.80
H. Cates	0	0	----	8								
Clarence Allen	0	0	----	6								
William Shores	0	3	.000	5								
Fred Sackett	0	0	----	4								
Ray Walker	0	0	----	3								
James Boswell	0	0	----	2								

NEWARK   7th   81-84   .491   -9.5   Walter Johnson
Bears

BATTERS	POS-GAMES	GP	AB	R	H	BI	2B	3B	HR	BB	SO	SB	BA
Jack Fournier	1B141	148	504	87	145	91	26	8	22	83	29	6	.288
Lewis Malone	2B	(see multi-team players)											
Wescott Kingdon	SS162	162	566	106	167	62	32	4	7	83	45	11	.295
Walt Lutzke	3B135	143	482	61	150	78	31	3	6	38	32	7	.311

NEWARK (cont.)
Bears

BATTERS	POS-GAMES	GP	AB	R	H	BI	2B	3B	HR	BB	SO	SB	BA
John Conlan	OF153	154	609	104	183	58	27	9	7	65	29	34	.300
Bill Lamar	OF84	85	328	38	89	50	16	1	7	15	19	5	.271
Dorsey Carroll	OF80	95	270	33	79	25	13	3	1	40	25	5	.293
Joe Jenkins	C79	97	259	32	82	45	15	3	5	19	23	2	.317
Cliff Lee	OF77	94	300	46	74	41	10	4	4	29	32	6	.247
Bill Skiff	C77	87	273	32	79	40	13	2	2	13	11	6	.290
Harold Mackin	2B57,3B17	83	250	24	59	24	6	4	1	11	8	2	.236
Jack Bentley	P22,1B18	67	135	22	42	25	9	2	3	9	6	2	.311
Frank Uzmann	C30	45	63	13	13	8	0	0	1	7	14	1	.206
Don Brennan	P41	41	64	4	5	4	1	0	0	6	27	0	.078
Carl Fischer	P36	39	49	3	6	4	0	0	1	3	10	0	.122
Gerald Fitzgerald	OF23	33	75	11	15	7	2	0	0	6	3	1	.200
William Moore	P27	27	30	3	5	4	0	0	0	2	6	0	.167
Al Mamaux	P25	25	55	3	7	7	0	0	0	5	8	0	.127
Harvey Reese	P24	24	6	1	1	0	0	0	0	0	2	0	.167
Roy Carlyle	OF15	23	71	9	18	12	6	0	1	3	7	0	.259
Harold Goldsmith	P22	22	32	3	6	3	0	0	0	1	3	0	.188
Fred Sheridan	P16	16	16	1	3	1	0	0	0	3	3	0	.188
Hugh McMillan	P14	14	22	1	3	0	1	0	0	1	6	0	.136
Hub Pruett	P13	13	24	2	5	1	1	0	1	1	1	0	.208
Joseph Zubris	P13	13	19	0	3	4	1	1	0	2	4	0	.158
Earl Howard	P11	11	5	0	1	0	0	0	0	0	3	0	.200
Michael Martineck		10	32	6	9	0	1	0	0	5	2	1	.281
George Thomas		8											.276
Walter Johnson	P1	8											.143
Alan Russell	P6	7											.400
Leo Mallonce		7											.350
Fred Adams	P4	4											.250
Joe Brennan		4											.182
Vic Aldridge	P4	4											.154
Earl Mattingly	P4	4											.000
Lloyd Davies	P3	3											.600
Alphonse Kamp	P3	3											.167
Joe Giard	P3	3											.000
Herman Kemner	P1	1											.333
James Lyle	P1	1											.000

PITCHERS	W	L	PCT	G	GS	CG	SH	IP	H	BB	SO	ERA
Al Mamaux	15	8	.652	25		10	2	162	168	34	82	3.33
Carl Fischer	11	8	.579	36		7	1	149	153	80	78	3.62
Don Brennan	10	13	.435	41		8	1	205	205	111	95	3.29
Jack Bentley	6	7	.462	22		8	1	121	113	67	48	4.46
William Moore	5	5	.500	27		1	0	105	109	47	39	3.86
Harold Goldsmith	5	9	.357	22		3	0	99	118	29	30	4.09
Vic Aldridge	4	0	1.000	4								
Hub Pruett	4	3	.571	13		5	1	74	70	45	49	2.92
Hugh McQuillan	3	3	.500	14		3	0	66	85	35	20	4.23
Harvey Reese	2	1	.667	24		0	0	49	64	15	7	4.59
Fred Sheridan	2	2	.500	16		2	1	58	68	26	16	3.57
Earl Howard	2	3	.400	11		0	0	19	17	13	6	6.63
Joseph Zubris	2	5	.286	13		2	0	64	62	25	22	4.36
Earl Mattingly	1	1	.500	4								
Lloyd Davies	1	2	.333	3								
Alan Russell	0	0	----	6								
Fred Adams	0	0	----	4								
Alphonse Kamp	0	0	----	3								
Joe Giard	0	0	----	3								
Herman Kemner	0	0	----	1								
Walter Johnson	0	0	----	1								
James Lyle	0	0	----	1								

JERSEY CITY
Skeeters

8th   66-102   .393   -26   Frank Gilhooley

BATTERS	POS-GAMES	GP	AB	R	H	BI	2B	3B	HR	BB	SO	SB	BA
Jack Smith	1B131	131	465	47	124	57	24	5	1	35	44	9	.267
Joseph Manger	2B101,3B37,1B21	162	534	85	143	68	24	4	6	78	56	8	.268
George Martin	SS137,OF15	159	564	54	131	42	15	4	2	38	52	11	.232
William Calleran	3B73	79	241	25	66	20	8	1	0	30	36	3	.274
James Walsh	OF154	157	543	71	176	90	39	9	3	74	35	6	.324
Frank Gilhooley	OF109	130	426	64	134	33	17	7	1	53	18	12	.315

JERSEY CITY (cont.)
Skeeters

BATTERS	POS-GAMES	GP	AB	R	H	BI	2B	3B	HR	BB	SO	SB	BA
Ed Kunesh	OF88	102	340	53	107	41	19	1	3	24	28	12	.315
Al Head	C106,3B19	148	495	49	136	76	30	7	4	22	10	9	.275
George Selkirk	OF65	82	238	28	62	27	6	4	3	19	43	2	.261
Otis Lawry	2B67	73	281	37	69	21	8	2	1	25	18	9	.246
James Higgins	P28,OF20	50	105	10	22	7	2	1	3	10	15	1	.210
Berlyn Horne	P44	48	84	11	18	4	1	1	0	7	10	0	.214
Bernard McHugh	3B35	42	120	10	25	11	5	0	0	9	11	1	.208
Milburn Shoffner	P38	40	77	8	12	11	2	1	2	2	27	0	.156
Albert Lesko	C32	38	99	9	20	7	2	1	0	8	21	0	.202
Cliff Jackson	P32	33	41	3	7	1	1	1	1	3	12	0	.171
Charles Nalback	SS27	28	113	13	26	10	5	1	1	11	23	3	.230
Maurice Bream	P24	25	50	2	2	1	0	0	0	11	33	0	.040
Art Johnson	P20	20	49	1	8	5	0	0	0	2	11	0	.163
Joseph Himes	P15	15	12	1	2	1	1	0	0	4	7	0	.167
Ted Jourdan	1B14	14	44	9	16	11	7	2	0	9	5	0	.364
Thomas McCarthy		5											.267
Joseph Rapp		4											.200
William Lai		4											.188
Charles Walsh	P3	3											.143
George Starn	P3	3											.000
Ruane		2											.000
William Schulster	P1	1											.000

PITCHERS	W	L	PCT	G	GS	CG	SH	IP	H	BB	SO	ERA
Berlyn Horne	16	17	.485	44		24	3	266	258	**140**	137	3.01
Maurice Bream	10	12	.455	24		15	4	171	181	40	32	**2.32**
Milburn Shoffner	8	17	.320	38		13	1	206	239	102	85	3.80
Art Johnson	7	8	.467	20		7	1	130	145	42	44	3.46
Cliff Jackson	5	13	.278	32		9	1	140	168	68	43	5.27
James Higgins	2	3	.400	28		3	0	110	154	34	19	4.58
Charles Walsh	1	1	.500	3								
William Schulster	0	1	----	1								
Joseph Himes	0	4	.000	15		0	0	45	45	26	12	4.20
George Starn	0	0	----	3								

MULTI-TEAM PLAYERS

BATTERS	POS-GAMES	TEAMS	GP	AB	R	H	BI	2B	3B	HR	BB	SO	SB	BA
Hobart Whitman	OF149	MO11-RE139	150	575	105	200	87	38	10	10	32	3	14	.348
William Urbanski	SS79,2B50,3B18	BA66-MO77	143	528	80	167	68	33	9	6	41	41	17	.316
Maurice Archdeacon	OF133	BA6-BU136	142	511	91	152	27	15	5	1	71	40	11	.297
Lewis Malone	2B110,SS17,3B12	BU28-NE114	142	474	67	145	82	34	2	13	52	28	1	.306
William Kelley	1B136	RO26-BU116	136	473	63	132	73	31	4	18	35	46	3	.279
August Felix	OF128	BU42-RO94	136	467	82	147	94	33	8	9	53	34	9	.315
Merwin Jacobson	OF126	TO61-NE68	129	422	83	119	49	21	1	3	83	40	23	.282
Pete Monahan	1B122	BU34-RO89	123	444	71	125	55	17	5	9	42	28	6	.282
Ed Murphy	OF82	JC47-MO67	114	322	50	98	42	9	2	2	49	13	9	.304
Michael Devine	C105	JC36-BA77	113	330	37	86	50	13	0	1	39	17	2	.261
Al Elliott	2B86	NE17-BU94	111	349	58	101	44	25	3	10	38	17	1	.289
John Mokan	OF77	BU45-RO45	90	297	57	94	63	15	6	8	21	31	9	.317
Willard Fleming	OF51	BA47-JC8-NE5	70	189	40	57	18	7	1	1	26	22	6	.302
Andy Anderson	3B45,OF10	BA50-RO11	61	181	27	47	35	6	0	5	38	17	6	.260
William Henderson	P42	BA15-RE32	47	58	6	8	5	2	0	1	4	17	0	.138
Harry O'Donnell	C39	BU14-RO27	41	95	14	27	15	3	1	0	8	5	1	.284
Otis Carter	OF29	BU8-RE32	40	94	18	21	11	4	3	1	12	14	2	.223
Jim Bagby	P39	JC12-NE27	39	56	9	7	5	0	0	1	7	4	0	.125
John Hollingsworth	P35	BU26-BA12	38	49	4	4	4	0	0	1	8	21	0	.082
Herb Thormahlen	P36	JC20-MO17	37	67	6	15	6	3	0	0	6	18	0	.224
William Jarrett	OF30	JC11-RE24	35	115	16	39	14	6	2	1	14	12	0	.339
Otto Freitag	C28	BA19-TO14	33	59	3	16	10	2	0	1	5	7	1	.271
Wilbert Hubbell	P18	BA6-RE12	18	27	4	8	3	0	0	1	1	7	1	.296
George Maisel		BU9-BA6	15	53	5	14	8	5	0	1	1	2	0	.264
Clayton Madison		TO2-RE13	15	29	2	5	1	0	0	0	5	13	0	.172
Jack Stuvengen	1B14	RO6-BU8	14	44	3	9	7	2	1	1	5	4	0	.205
Ed Mancuso		BU-JC	7											.000
George Milstead	P4	BA-BU	4											.000

PITCHERS		TEAMS	W	L	PCT	G	GS	CG	SH	IP	H	BB	SO	ERA
Herb Thormahlen		JC19-MO17	11	14	.440	36		17	3	223	223	81	98	2.87

MULTI-TEAM PLAYERS (cont.)

PITCHERS	TEAMS	W	L	PCT	G	GS	CG	SH	IP	H	BB	SO	ERA
Jim Bagby	JC12-NE27	11	16	.407	39		10	0	172	222	42	39	4.40
William Henderson	BA11-JC31	9	12	.429	42		8	2	176	201	87	62	4.24
John Hollingsworth	BU23-BA12	8	10	.444	35		12	0	159	169	76	122	3.96
Wilbert Hubbell	BA6-RE12	3	4	.429	18		3	0	69	103	17	22	5.61
George Milstead	BA-BU	0	0	----	4								

TEAM BATTING

TEAMS	GP	AB	R	H	BI	2B	3B	HR	BB	SO	SB	BA
ROCHESTER	165	5419	920	1621	**853**	258	**97**	71	587	485	**143**	.299
BUFFALO	**170**	5539	823	1654	751	297	62	**127**	502	444	52	.299
TORONTO	169	5449	770	1551	725	275	80	80	518	592	138	.285
READING	168	5551	882	**1665**	775	**316**	79	80	508	491	77	**.300**
MONTREAL	**170**	**5556**	797	1553	744	298	54	67	**617**	**617**	119	.280
BALTIMORE	168	5452	**924**	1621	837	279	55	107	612	483	107	.297
NEWARK	166	5358	769	1490	716	261	48	83	539	407	95	.278
JERSEY CITY	168	5424	643	1421	597	235	52	32	534	574	93	.262
	672	43748	6528	12576	5998	2219	527	647	4417	4093	824	.287

1929
FIFTEEN FOR FIFTEEN

As the years pass in any given baseball league, individual games are usually swept aside in favor of the larger picture. Even so, some of these games, even individual pitcher-versus-batter confrontations, can be noteworthy. This was especially true for George Quellich during a few August days in the 1929 International League.

Quellich, an outfielder, joined the International League in 1924 for the Rochester team. After a stint with Baltimore, he moved to the Reading squad during the 1927 season. Quellich remained with Reading in 1928 and 1929, establishing himself as one the team's top batters. In the latter stages of the 1929 season, Quellich would improve his worth, embarking on a streak like none before.

On August 9, 1929, in a game against Toronto, Quellich rapped out three hits in a row—a single, a double, and a home run. The next day, versus Montreal, he reached base with five singles and a home run, followed by two home runs and two singles in the following game. Finally, on August 12, after a home run and a single, Quellich was called out. During the four-game span, George Quellich had come to bat fifteen times and had batted safely in all fifteen—an incredible string.

Leaguewide, Rochester won its second straight flag, this time by a comfortable margin over Toronto. Baltimore and Montreal finished in the next two places, followed by Buffalo, Newark, Reading, and Jersey City. Dan Taylor from Reading won the batting title (.371), while Rochester's Rip Collins swatted the most home runs (38) and runs batted in (134). Montreal pitcher Elon Hogsett finished with the most wins (22), and Newark showcased two titlists: Hub Pruett with the lowest earned average (2.43) and Charles Fischer with the most strikeouts (191).

Led by his batting spree, George Quellich had his finest season in 1929, batting .347, with 31 home runs and 130 runs batted in. After another two solid International League campaigns, George Quellich joined the roster of the Detroit Tigers late in the 1931 season. It would be his only taste of major league life.

Quellich's fifteen-for-fifteen batting streak remains a unique performance not only in the International League, but perhaps in all of baseball. Consecutive hit streaks are not widely chronicled in minor league history, but there is no mention of any that exceeded Quellich's fifteen in a row. Quellich's four games of glory in August 1929 certainly stand as four individual games worth remembering—even down to every at bat.

ROCHESTER
Red Wings

1st 103-65 .613 Billy Southworth

BATTERS	POS-GAMES	GP	AB	R	H	BI	2B	3B	HR	BB	SO	SB	BA
Rip Collins	1B153	154	558	119	176	134	38	12	38	74	74	9	.315
George Toporcer	2B169	169	615	142	161	46	27	14	2	128	28	31	.262
John Sand	SS167	167	557	90	138	101	29	11	14	96	68	5	.248
Joseph Brown	3B155	157	619	116	176	81	27	16	4	79	37	16	.284
Robert Worthington	OF163	163	618	97	202	113	34	15	8	61	34	7	.327
George Watkins	OF135	139	531	110	179	119	28	13	20	40	65	15	.337
August Felix	OF85,1B17	108	354	65	102	56	18	4	5	56	32	4	.288
Paul Florence	C88	94	272	30	72	49	20	2	5	23	31	0	.265
Ray Pepper	OF64	73	245	33	68	35	11	4	3	14	25	2	.278
Boyce Morrow	C68	70	215	28	63	18	9	0	3	23	13	2	.293
James Carleton	P37	41	92	6	12	4	2	0	0	7	34	0	.130
Paul Derringer	P41	41	91	3	14	4	1	0	0	2	24	0	.154
John Berly	P38	40	80	6	22	6	2	2	0	3	15	0	.275
Carlisle Littlejohn	P40	40	48	5	11	3	2	1	0	2	2	0	.229
Gus Mancuso	C36	39	113	18	35	35	5	1	9	20	11	1	.310
Laurence Irvin	P35	39	74	12	17	10	1	2	0	3	14	0	.230
Billy Southworth	OF32	37	106	24	37	25	3	2	4	14	2	2	.349
Ray Blades	OF11	31	48	8	7	2	1	2	0	6	13	1	.146
Ray Lingrel	P31	31	47	9	13	15	2	0	3	1	7	0	.277
Ray Cunningham		26	34	6	7	2	3	1	0	5	5	2	.206
Art Reinhart	P13	25	17	4	5	0	0	0	0	1	2	0	.294
F. Myers	3B12	22	34	9	11	0	0	2	0	7	3	1	.324
Herman Bell	P19	19	44	2	3	1	1	0	0	3	19	0	.068
Willard Ford		15	8	0	1	1	0	0	0	1	2	0	.125
Ovid McCracken	P8	8											.000
Art Jacobs	P3	3											.444
John Burns	P3	3											.000

PITCHERS		W	L	PCT	G	GS	CG	SH	IP	H	BB	SO	ERA
James Carleton		18	7	.720	37		21	2	262	232	108	124	2.71
Paul Derringer		17	12	.586	41		19	1	244	259	96	94	3.91
Carlisle Littlejohn		14	7	.667	40		3	1	145	158	35	52	3.97
Laurence Irvin		14	9	.609	35		14	2	215	203	96	67	3.10
John Berly		12	11	.522	38		13	1	220	241	86	83	3.85
Herman Bell		11	5	.688	19		10	1	122	132	28	50	3.54
Ray Lingrel		9	6	.600	31		3	0	121	144	44	39	4.17
Art Reinhart		3	4	.429	13		1	0	46	60	32	18	6.65
Art Jacobs		2	0	1.000	3								
Willard Ford		2	2	.500	15		1	0	36	46	22	15	7.25
Ovid McCracken		1	0	1.000	8								
John Burns		0	2	.000	3								

TORONTO
Maple Leafs

2nd 92-76 .548 -11 Steve O'Neill

BATTERS	POS-GAMES	GP	AB	R	H	BI	2B	3B	HR	BB	SO	SB	BA
William Sweeney	1B132	135	510	83	171	82	19	13	9	27	24	16	.335
Leslie Burke	2B155	155	551	82	167	79	30	10	3	48	29	4	.303
Warren Cote	SS157	157	547	52	143	68	24	7	3	30	38	11	.261
C. Richardson	3B108,SS12	119	452	59	128	49	17	5	1	35	26	10	.283
Joe Rabbitt	OF168	168	685	128	197	78	36	18	16	46	80	46	.288
Ralph Shinners	OF134	143	495	69	167	81	39	7	12	26	26	13	.337
John Stone	OF79	79	295	53	97	56	19	8	12	28	33	8	.329
Steve O'Neill	C81	93	262	31	84	31	17	1	3	36	14	1	.321
Fred Bedore	3B51,2B14	82	278	36	66	38	7	7	3	11	25	8	.237
Art Ruble	OF55	61	209	30	58	23	11	5	3	26	14	4	.278
Maurice Archdeacon	OF37	60	136	30	36	12	4	0	0	21	15	7	.265
Ed Ainsmith	C35	38	115	12	31	12	3	5	1	14	18	2	.270
Guy Cantrell	P38	38	92	6	16	6	1	1	1	0	24	0	.174
Sam Gibson	P32	33	57	9	20	6	3	1	1	3	3	0	.351
Clarence Fisher	P32	32	45	2	8	3	0	0	0	2	6	0	.178
Joseph Samuels	P27	30	49	7	10	6	2	1	1	4	9	0	.204
Frank Barnes	P27	27	60	8	13	8	2	0	0	3	6	0	.217
Phil Page	P23	23	51	4	10	6	1	1	0	1	10	0	.196
Claude Satterfield	P4	23	22	0	6	4	2	0	0	1	3	0	.273
Walt Leverenz	P19	19	49	3	6	2	0	1	0	1	12	0	.122
Stephen Martin	P20	20	27	3	7	3	0	1	0	1	4	0	.259
Paul Zahniser	P17	17	29	5	8	0	1	0	0	5	14	0	.276
George Rensa	C14	15	45	7	13	1	1	1	0	3	5	1	.289
William Webb	3B12	15	34	5	7	5	3	0	0	6	7	0	.206
Art McHenry	OF13	13	53	6	14	4	1	2	0	3	10	0	.264

TORONTO (cont.)
Maple Leafs

BATTERS	POS-GAMES	GP	AB	R	H	BI	2B	3B	HR	BB	SO	SB	BA
Harry Davis		10	34	6	9	6	2	0	0	1	1	2	.265
Jesse Doyle	P9	9											.071
Roleine Naylor	P8	8											.600
Ray Hayworth		7											.174
Harry Davey		4											.222
Charles Schmidt	P1	2											.000
Regis Lehney	P1	1											.000

PITCHERS	W	L	PCT	G	GS	CG	SH	IP	H	BB	SO	ERA
Guy Cantrell	20	12	.625	38		20	2	248	233	153	154	3.38
Frank Barnes	13	6	.684	27		13	2	177	176	40	60	2.75
Phil Page	10	3	.769	23		9	1	125	125	47	49	3.53
Walt Leverenz	10	5	.667	19		8	0	136	133	60	46	3.44
Joseph Samuels	9	7	.563	27		10	1	139	109	78	55	2.65
Sam Gibson	9	10	.474	32		10	4	164	161	62	71	3.02
Paul Zahniser	6	5	.545	17		6	0	91	108	19	31	4.06
Stephen Martin	5	5	.500	20		2	0	76	86	41	27	6.16
Clarence Fisher	4	9	.308	32		5	0	132	135	45	28	4.50
Roleine Naylor	0	1	.000	8								
Jesse Doyle	0	7	.000	9								
Claude Satterfield	0	0	----	4								
Regis Lehney	0	0	----	1								
Charles Schmidt	0	0	----	1								

BALTIMORE   3rd   90-78   .536   -13   Fritz Maisel
Orioles

BATTERS	POS-GAMES	GP	AB	R	H	BI	2B	3B	HR	BB	SO	SB	BA
John Neun	1B96	96	370	57	122	60	19	2	10	28	20	22	.330
Robert James	2B74	75	277	52	79	40	18	2	6	36	29	16	.285
Joe Benes	SS60	65	212	29	53	14	7	0	2	49	26	5	.250
Robert LaMotte	3B106,SS18	127	407	61	123	51	26	2	5	54	35	8	.302
George Loepp	OF164	164	630	128	197	94	40	6	27	89	57	14	.313
Frank Brower	OF80,1B20	113	351	68	107	61	21	2	15	74	38	4	.305
Harry Layne	OF	(see multi-team players)											
Al Bool	C129	141	540	81	174	130	36	4	31	74	62	10	.347
Ed Mooers	2B72,SS54,3B22	148	529	70	151	76	25	3	14	27	71	5	.285
John Smith	OF64	68	235	35	60	28	14	1	1	28	14	3	.255
Fred Coumbe	P45	53	53	11	15	7	1	1	1	0	11	0	.283
Dan Clark	OF38	51	129	24	31	21	6	0	5	20	6	3	.240
Stuart Bolen	P43	44	93	7	23	12	6	1	2	5	18	0	.247
Joseph Hassler	SS39	41	130	18	30	20	6	2	1	19	12	0	.231
William Clarkson	P39	39	68	5	11	5	2	0	1	8	16	0	.162
William Cronin	C34	37	106	11	28	5	5	3	1	6	5	0	.264
Herm Holshouser	P34	34	60	10	15	5	2	1	0	10	16	1	.250
Del Gainer		33	32	3	11	9	3	1	2	2	3	0	.344
Vic Keen	P33	33	32	1	1	1	0	0	0	2	10	0	.031
Andrew Chambers	P30	30	56	5	11	7	1	0	0	2	17	0	.196
John Hollingsworth	P29	29	46	6	5	2	0	1	1	5	18	0	.106
James Stroner	3B28	28	124	26	37	18	6	1	4	7	15	3	.298
Henry Wertz	P25	25	39	5	10	4	1	0	1	3	13	0	.256
Orell Holland	OF17	22	64	14	19	10	2	1	0	8	7	0	.297
Fred Myers	3B13	16	52	8	17	11	6	2	3	3	6	0	.327
James Dalrymple	2B12	12	47	11	19	3	2	2	0	2	2	0	.404
Fay Thomas	P10	10	8	1	2	0	0	0	0	1	3	0	.250
Ed Wilson		8											.290
Virgil Barnes	P8	8											.222
John O'Connell		7											.421
Ed Walker	P7	7											.250
John Stewart		6											.250
Elmer Hearn	P6	6											.000
John Wisner	P5	5											.500
Cliff Bolton		5											.250
Beryl Richmond	P4	4											.000
Vince Barton		3											.200
Lem Owen	P3	3											.000
Stein Griggs		2											.000
Ed Durham	P2	2											.000
Monte Weaver	P1	1											.000

BALTIMORE (cont.)
Orioles

PITCHERS	W	L	PCT	G	GS	CG	SH	IP	H	BB	SO	ERA
Stuart Bolen	19	14	.576	43		20	4	260	284	109	132	4.29
Fred Coumbe	15	5	.750	45		0	0	132	152	51	38	4.70
William Clarkson	14	13	.519	39		14	1	224	235	95	97	4.26
John Hollingsworth	11	8	.579	29		8	2	136	150	79	96	4.76
Herm Holshouser	9	10	.474	34		4	0	160	182	58	85	5.01
Andrew Chambers	8	10	.444	30		10	1	162	190	44	47	4.83
Vic Keen	6	3	.667	33		5	1	119	138	56	34	5.75
Henry Wertz	3	7	.300	25		1	0	104	128	29	22	5.80
Beryl Richmond	2	0	1.000	4								
Virgil Barnes	1	1	.500	8								
John Wisner	1	1	.500	5								
Elmer Hearn	1	2	.333	6								
Ed Durham	0	1	.000	2								
Monte Weaver	0	1	.000	1								
Fay Thomas	0	2	.000	10		0	0	29	38	20	15	5.28
Ed Walker	0	0	----	7								
Lem Owen	0	0	----	3								

MONTREAL   4th   88-79   .527   -14.5   Ed Holly
Royals

BATTERS	POS-GAMES	GP	AB	R	H	BI	2B	3B	HR	BB	SO	SB	BA
Fred Henry	1B166	166	618	90	174	67	30	11	5	61	63	15	.282
Walt Gautreau	2B137	137	462	50	123	53	18	4	1	66	37	8	.266
William Urbanski	SS167	168	641	98	201	115	39	14	8	50	58	19	.314
J. Fowler	3B161	162	564	72	169	87	24	3	4	55	70	15	.300
Henry Haines	OF149	150	526	103	148	60	29	11	6	108	57	36	.281
Aldrik Gaudette	OF138	143	529	86	171	56	21	9	3	68	35	27	.323
Thomas Gulley	OF124	129	431	76	141	103	24	8	11	85	41	6	.327
Charles Niebergall	C100	106	333	40	91	47	14	7	3	39	34	7	.273
George Tice	OF69	95	220	32	61	36	15	3	1	36	28	5	.277
Ed Conley	OF50	87	194	34	52	23	6	3	3	27	21	4	.268
Thomas Daly	C72	78	252	21	62	27	15	2	0	18	8	0	.246
Peter Radwan	2B44,3B13	68	167	20	47	25	6	1	0	19	14	6	.281
Elon Hogsett	P37	44	111	17	29	7	2	1	3	4	23	0	.261
Roy Buckalew	P38	38	45	1	4	3	1	0	0	8	21	0	.089
Herb Thormahlen	P34	35	88	7	17	10	1	0	3	6	32	0	.193
Chet Nichols	P29	32	64	2	18	9	1	0	0	1	15	0	.281
Elam Van Gilder	P26	30	78	10	22	3	9	0	1	7	11	0	.282
Joseph Hartman	P25	25	28	0	2	1	0	0	0	3	9	0	.071
John Pomorski	P19	19	13	3	2	0	1	1	0	1	2	0	.154
Chet Falk	P10	14	31	2	8	1	1	1	1	0	1	0	.258
William O'Hara	P5	5											.250
James Ripple		4											.500
Peter Beam	P3	3											.000
Frank Dunagan	P3	3											.000
William Hargrove	P3	3											.000
Charles Butler	P2	2											.000
Tony Parquella		1											.000

PITCHERS	W	L	PCT	G	GS	CG	SH	IP	H	BB	SO	ERA
Elon Hogsett	22	13	.629	37		28	2	288	264	94	92	3.03
Herb Thormahlen	16	12	.571	34		18	1	249	253	79	91	4.52
Chet Nichols	13	12	.520	29		16	4	180	172	54	48	3.70
Elam Van Gilder	12	13	.480	26		20	2	199	224	91	80	4.07
Roy Buckalew	11	13	.458	38		10	1	164	188	65	42	4.83
Joseph Hartman	4	4	.500	25		7	2	104	117	26	31	3.81
Chet Falk	3	1	.750	10		2	1	57	69	39	10	6.00
John Pomorski	1	6	.143	19		0	0	46	62	25	15	6.85
Frank Dunagan	0	1	.000	3								
William Hargrove	0	2	.000	3								
William O'Hara	0	0	----	5								
Peter Beam	0	0	----	3								
Charles Butler	0	0	----	2								

BUFFALO   5th   83-84   .497   -20.5   William Clymer
Bisons

BATTERS	POS-GAMES	GP	AB	R	H	BI	2B	3B	HR	BB	SO	SB	BA
Roy Grimes	1B91	104	348	59	88	65	17	3	11	36	58	4	.253
Herb Thomas	2B91	91	385	73	130	64	17	3	14	13	12	6	.338
James Cooney	SS155	155	561	61	164	59	32	5	2	36	10	2	.292
Robert Barrett	3B44	49	183	27	61	32	11	5	2	16	10	0	.333
Al Moore	OF168	168	638	107	218	107	34	16	13	60	40	10	.342
George Fisher	OF150	150	572	119	192	124	28	12	36	74	71	3	.336
Clarence Mueller	OF74	77	288	59	109	59	20	7	10	49	22	3	.378
John Barnes	C85	95	243	32	77	38	23	2	2	29	15	2	.317
Oliver Sax	OF57,3B41,2B16	125	396	95	119	43	22	3	7	92	49	14	.301
Luke Urban	C81	84	236	37	55	22	18	2	3	23	16	5	.233
Leon Williams	P36,OF13	58	110	20	45	11	16	1	0	8	15	0	.409
Art Mills	P39	48	54	7	14	3	2	0	0	3	6	1	.259
James Faulkner	P37	37	98	9	28	8	4	0	1	1	14	0	.286
Leo Mangum	P35	36	82	9	17	7	0	0	0	2	11	0	.207
Warren Ogden	P35	36	54	5	19	1	4	0	0	4	8	0	.352
Baxter Jordan	1B15	33	113	14	19	7	5	1	0	5	4	1	.168
Joseph Bonnelly	P28	31	33	5	8	2	0	0	1	4	9	0	.242
Jesse Barnes	P27	27	43	2	10	3	0	1	0	2	3	0	.233
L. Bettencourt	3B19	20	64	10	15	8	4	0	1	7	8	2	.234
James Buchanan	P19	19	16	1	4	3	2	0	0	0	3	0	.250
Vern Parks	P15	18	16	2	1	0	0	0	0	1	4	0	.063
T. Collins	C13	16	41	5	5	3	1	0	0	11	9	0	.122
Richard Case	P14	14	12	0	1	0	0	0	0	1	10	0	.083
Hugh Ferrell		13	33	5	8	5	1	1	0	0	2	0	.242
Dan Dugan	P11	11	14	0	2	0	1	0	0	1	7	0	.143
Howard Signor	P11	11	9	0	0	0	0	0	0	0	1	0	.000
John Mitchell		9											.200
Leslie Mann		7											.235
John Milligan	P6	6											.250
Alex Ferguson		5											.200
Roy Jacobson		5											.000
Edward Corey		4											.250
Carl Schoof	P3	3											.250
Frank Pytlak		3											.000
James Boswell		2											.000
Joseph Nettles		2											.000
Thomas Kain	P1	1											1.000
Walter Beck	P1	1											.000

PITCHERS	W	L	PCT	G	GS	CG	SH	IP	H	BB	SO	ERA
James Faulkner	16	13	.552	37		19	0	251	300	98	71	4.52
Leo Mangum	15	13	.536	35		15	2	208	263	39	57	4.72
Jesse Barnes	9	5	.643	27		7	1	127	134	39	35	4.75
Leon Williams	9	9	.500	36		8	0	151	184	51	48	4.95
Warren Ogden	9	11	.450	35		7	0	150	174	45	37	4.68
Joseph Bonnelly	8	8	.500	28		4	0	106	106	44	34	3.48
Art Mills	6	12	.333	39		7	0	180	232	58	50	5.35
Dan Dugan	3	1	.750	11		0	0	37	38	23	17	3.89
James Buchanan	3	2	.600	19		0	0	45	51	14	16	4.20
Richard Case	2	1	.667	14		0	0	38	47	13	9	4.26
Vern Parks	2	3	.400	15		1	0	47	55	15	13	5.36
Alex Ferguson	1	4	.200	6								
John Milligan	0	1	.000	6								
Carl Schoof	0	2	.000	3								
Howard Signor	0	0	----	11		1	0	25	40	4	7	7.56
Thomas Kain	0	0	----	1								
Walter Beck	0	0	----	1								

NEWARK   6th   81-85   .488   -21   Tris Speaker
Bears

BATTERS	POS-GAMES	GP	AB	R	H	BI	2B	3B	HR	BB	SO	SB	BA
Wally Pipp	1B116	120	413	63	129	89	30	6	12	48	16	6	.312
Lewis Malone	2B85,3B18	110	367	59	108	40	23	6	2	49	26	6	.294
Robert Stevens	SS166	166	586	73	160	74	25	5	2	48	21	12	.273
Walt Lutzke	3B99	102	343	57	97	55	14	5	9	51	34	6	.283
John Conlan	OF151	160	613	116	186	62	34	13	10	54	22	17	.303
Max West	OF147	153	539	93	179	109	32	5	19	65	15	6	.332
Merwin Jacobson	OF66	83	211	42	59	27	10	4	2	37	25	3	.280
Bill Skiff	C66	70	193	26	58	22	7	1	1	6	16	1	.301

NEWARK (cont.)
Bears

BATTERS	POS-GAMES	GP	AB	R	H	BI	2B	3B	HR	BB	SO	SB	BA
Russ Wrightstone	OF52,1B41,3B20	131	418	78	134	78	27	8	9	63	20	9	.321
Westcott Kingdon	2B84,3B24	118	366	49	84	45	15	1	2	44	29	9	.230
Richard Stahlman	C54	71	163	15	74	21	8	1	4	15	14	2	.331
Gerald Fitzgerald	OF46	64	162	26	42	13	4	0	0	8	7	5	.259
Tris Speaker	OF35	48	138	36	49	20	11	1	5	18	4	2	.355
Al Mamaux	P36	36	98	5	20	10	3	1	0	6	15	1	.204
Albert Harvin	P36	36	45	4	7	5	2	0	0	0	20	0	.156
Charles Fischer	P33	34	91	8	20	12	3	0	0	4	9	1	.220
Hub Pruett	P29	29	69	7	12	4	0	0	1	3	10	0	.174
Lloyd Davies	P25	25	43	5	17	4	0	1	0	3	3	0	.395
Joseph Bush	P7	21	22	6	9	5	3	0	0	5	3	0	.409
John Cummings	C14	18	52	5	14	7	4	1	0	4	8	1	.269
Cliff Lee	OF12	18	40	6	7	2	1	0	1	1	3	0	.175
Harold Goldsmith	P18	18	20	0	1	0	0	0	0	1	5	0	.050
William Moore	P18	18	11	1	2	1	0	0	0	0	4	0	.182
Larry Fischer	OF14	14	52	5	10	5	3	0	0	1	11	1	.192
Jim Bagby	P13	13	12	1	3	3	0	0	0	2	2	0	.250
Ed Fallenstein	P12	12	7	0	0	0	0	0	0	0	1	0	.000
Alvin Bejin	1B11	11	34	3	5	3	0	0	0	6	8	1	.147
Lee Meadows	P10	10	25	4	6	3	3	0	0	2	5	0	.240
Chet Ross	P9	9											.200
Coburn Jones		7											.192
Vic Aldridge	P7	7											.091
Robert Munn		5											.538
Art Johnson	P4	4											.000
Frank Uzmann		4											.000
Charles Ens	P4	4											.000
Jimmy Ring	P3	3											.200
Ken Jones	P3	3											.000
Norm Lehr		2											.333
Don Brennan	P2	2											.000
Harvey Reese	P2	2											.000
James Wiltse	P2	2											.000
Michael Martineck		1											.000
Willard Fleming		1											.000

PITCHERS	W	L	PCT	G	GS	CG	SH	IP	H	BB	SO	ERA
Al Mamaux	20	13	.606	36		22	7	272	291	60	88	2.91
Charles Fischer	18	13	.581	33		21	4	248	239	112	191	3.74
Hub Pruett	16	7	.696	29		18	5	185	193	75	102	2.43
Albert Harvin	8	6	.571	36		4	2	148	149	47	60	3.95
Lloyd Davies	6	10	.375	25		10	0	129	172	36	35	4.67
Joseph Bush	3	3	.500	7								
Ken Jones	2	0	1.000	3								
William Moore	2	2	.500	18		1	1	52	48	18	23	3.63
Vic Aldridge	2	2	.500	7								
Lee Meadows	2	7	.222	10		5	0	68	86	27	16	5.16
Ed Fallenstein	1	2	.333	12		0	0	34	42	19	22	6.35
Harold Goldsmith	1	8	.111	18		3	1	64	84	23	16	6.47
Norm Lehr	0	1	.000	2								
James Wiltse	0	1	.000	2								
Chet Ross	0	2	.000	9								
Jimmy Ring	0	2	.000	3								
Don Brennan	0	2	.000	2								
Jim Bagby	0	5	.000	13		2	0	42	53	7	14	6.00
Charles Ens	0	0	----	4								
Art Johnson	0	0	----	4								
Harvey Reese	0	0	----	2								

READING	7th	80-86	.482	-22	Harry Hinchman

Keystones

BATTERS	POS-GAMES	GP	AB	R	H	BI	2B	3B	HR	BB	SO	SB	BA
Nelson Hawks	1B165	168	640	103	202	77	44	10	10	75	37	12	.316
Charles Walsh	2B141	142	556	73	143	60	23	5	5	52	22	6	.257
Billy Jurges	SS136	142	472	66	121	58	21	3	4	39	62	6	.256
William Mullen	3B	(see multi-team players)											
Hobart Whitman	OF168	169	659	118	230	116	43	5	4	40	14	11	.349
George Quellich	OF159	162	577	97	200	130	36	1	31	74	62	10	.347
Dan Taylor	OF98,3B27	125	426	113	158	90	34	9	18	78	47	36	.371
William Styles	C58	72	178	16	45	24	9	2	1	27	14	1	.253

READING (cont.)
Keystones

BATTERS	POS-GAMES	GP	AB	R	H	BI	2B	3B	HR	BB	SO	SB	BA
Robert Grace	C56	65	192	24	49	33	8	5	8	18	12	0	.255
Everett Scott	SS33,3B20	62	188	27	54	21	18	0	0	15	6	1	.287
Dennis Murphy	C49	55	173	17	55	26	15	1	3	11	8	0	.318
Wallace Hood	OF26	49	112	20	31	12	7	1	3	11	4	3	.277
Jesse Fowler	P44	44	83	6	8	2	1	0	0	6	24	0	.096
William Marriott	3B34	42	168	24	47	14	6	4	1	18	12	6	.280
Nelson Greene	P37	40	78	8	20	7	4	0	0	6	9	0	.256
Sterling Stryker	P37	37	31	3	8	1	2	0	0	2	4	0	.258
John Welch	P34	36	67	4	16	7	2	1	1	1	21	0	.239
Robert Osborne	P31	34	66	9	16	7	0	1	0	3	11	0	.242
Edgar Holly	P31	32	85	10	20	8	5	1	0	2	8	0	.235
Lawton Witt	OF21	30	91	21	30	14	7	1	2	7	5	0	.330
Ed Lautenbacher	P23	23	28	2	5	3	1	0	0	3	6	0	.179
William Jarrett		23	19	4	2	0	0	0	0	1	2	0	.104
Richard Smith	C21	21	52	8	10	3	2	1	0	7	10	0	.192
John Wight		10	30	4	9	5	2	0	0	3	1	1	.300
Harry Lake		8											.000
Clayton Madison		7											.000
Russ Miller	P4	4											.500
Fred Carts	P3	3											.125
Joseph Zubris	P2	2											.000
Robert Murray		1											1.000
Henry Schulster	P1	1											.000
Charles Francis		1											.000
John Balls	P1	1											.000

PITCHERS	W	L	PCT	G	GS	CG	SH	IP	H	BB	SO	ERA
Edgar Holly	18	9	.667	31		18	3	225	242	99	78	3.60
Jesse Fowler	18	12	.600	44		16	2	244	266	102	148	3.95
Robert Osborn	11	14	.440	31		14	1	182	176	79	75	4.10
Nelson Greene	9	12	.429	37		13	3	212	243	52	87	4.50
John Welch	6	15	.286	34		12	0	177	199	76	67	4.22
Sterling Stryker	5	7	.417	37		4	0	105	124	41	23	4.54
Ed Lautenbacher	4	6	.400	23		4	1	93	128	42	37	6.29
Fred Carts	2	1	.667	3								
Russ Miller	0	0	----	4								
Joseph Zubris	0	0	----	2								
John Balls	0	0	----	1								
Henry Schulster	0	0	----	1								

| **JERSEY CITY** | 8th | 51-115 | .307 | -51 | Frank Gilhooley - |
| **Skeeters** | | | | | Ted Jourdan |

BATTERS	POS-GAMES	GP	AB	R	H	BI	2B	3B	HR	BB	SO	SB	BA
Ted Jourdan	1B104	120	373	45	102	33	23	2	3	40	23	7	.273
Wilson Fewster	2B77	80	275	29	64	11	11	2	0	31	36	4	.233
Dan Jessee	SS78	81	270	25	68	24	6	2	5	17	28	3	.252
Julian Wera	3B113	123	460	47	135	65	33	4	5	27	30	6	.293
George Selkirk	OF151	157	548	73	156	65	35	8	13	55	76	6	.285
Ed Kunesh	OF146	151	533	68	148	52	17	16	5	43	48	10	.278
James Walsh	OF121	128	421	55	123	61	26	2	4	70	36	5	.292
Al Head	C75	109	307	29	81	24	10	2	1	16	9	2	.264
Joseph Manger	1B62,2B47	126	396	47	119	75	22	3	13	28	41	4	.301
Arndt Jorgens	C73	84	260	36	72	28	14	0	6	23	27	2	.277
Meredith Hopkins	SS54,2B11	73	220	21	49	17	9	2	1	18	22	1	.223
William Henderson	P40	43	83	9	22	7	2	1	0	3	17	2	.265
Luther Harvel	OF36	41	120	10	30	9	7	0	3	12	11	3	.250
Harold Roberts	P40	40	32	1	4	0	1	0	0	2	7	0	.125
Maurice Bream	P35	35	63	2	5	2	1	0	0	8	28	0	.079
L. Westmoreland	C18	32	66	1	8	4	0	0	1	2	17	0	.121
Gordon Rhodes	P24	25	54	4	9	3	0	0	0	6	22	0	.167
Ernest Sabo	SS10	24	86	9	20	11	5	0	2	9	14	2	.233
Milburn Shoffner	P24	24	52	3	13	6	2	0	1	0	10	0	.250
Frank Gilhooley	OF12	24	55	4	14	2	1	0	0	7	1	3	.255
Jack Hopkins	P21	22	45	1	7	3	1	0	0	2	15	1	.156
George Martin	SS15	21	75	10	15	2	4	0	0	4	12	0	.200
Miller Harris	OF18	19	58	6	17	8	3	0	0	6	8	0	.293
George Grant	P16	16	32	1	5	1	0	0	0	3	11	0	.156
Joseph Glenn	C12	14	49	3	13	4	1	1	0	4	6	0	.265
John Mann		13	29	3	11	2	3	0	0	9	4	0	.379
Verne Underhill	P13	13	22	2	4	3	0	1	0	1	2	0	.182

JERSEY CITY (cont.)
Skeeters

BATTERS	POS-GAMES	GP	AB	R	H	BI	2B	3B	HR	BB	SO	SB	BA
Joe Maley	P11	12	13	3	1	0	0	0	0	3	5	0	.077
Richard Woodward	P5	5											.000
Dick Oliver	P4	4											.143
J. Miller	P3	3											.000
George Manfredt	P3	3											.000
George Starn	P1	1											.000
George Miner	P1	1											.000

PITCHERS		W	L	PCT	G	GS	CG	SH	IP	H	BB	SO	ERA
William Henderson		10	17	.370	40		17	2	246	265	107	118	3.80
Milburn Shoffner		8	10	.444	24		10	2	150	146	63	64	2.82
Maurice Bream		7	20	.259	35		12	0	215	238	74	41	4.56
Gordon Rhodes		6	14	.300	24		13	0	168	184	65	68	4.82
George Grant		4	10	.286	16		9	1	100	129	34	34	5.49
Jack Hopkins		4	14	.222	21		11	0	138	151	77	92	5.09
Harold Roberts		3	11	.214	40		4	0	121	132	69	24	4.69
Joe Maley		2	3	.400	11		3	0	46	60	16	4	4.30
Dick Oliver		1	2	.333	4								
Verne Underhill		1	6	.143	13		2	0	63	66	39	19	5.14
Richard Woodward		0	2	.000	5								
George Manfredt		0	2	.000	2								
J. Miller		0	0	----	3								
George Starn		0	0	----	1								
George Miner		0	0	----	1								

MULTI-TEAM PLAYERS

BATTERS	POS-GAMES	TEAMS	GP	AB	R	H	BI	2B	3B	HR	BB	SO	SB	BA
Harry Layne	OF141	RO2-BA143	145	517	79	157	74	26	8	10	52	42	23	.304
William Mullen	3B92	BU9-RE108	117	393	53	107	40	10	3	3	42	27	4	.272
Dick Spalding	OF89	BU48-RO58	106	316	49	95	29	11	5	1	30	36	2	.301
Clayton Sheedy	1B71,OF25	TO54-BU51	105	362	58	98	44	15	5	5	34	36	3	.271
Bernard Hungling	C74	TO38-NE42	80	241	27	59	36	10	2	6	22	41	0	.245
Joe Kelly	OF69	RE45-JC27	72	254	27	63	29	13	2	4	7	14	2	.248
William Conroy	3B50	JC24-BU46	70	193	25	50	39	10	3	5	41	12	2	.259
Ed Onslow	1B61	BA55-NE12	67	221	37	68	34	10	1	4	18	14	1	.308
James Calleran	2B39,3B10	JC52-RE11	63	170	23	36	13	2	3	1	18	22	2	.212
Joe Jenkins	C32	NE18-BU27	45	96	11	32	24	4	1	3	6	9	1	.333
Don Hankins	P33	TO16-RE17	33	38	4	7	5	0	1	0	2	9	0	.184
Nicholas Harrison	P31	RE17-TO14	31	43	4	8	3	0	1	0	1	10	0	.186
Don Miller	P24	MO9-JC15	24	47	4	12	3	2	1	0	0	5	0	.255
Art Smith	P9	JC3-MO8	11	25	2	5	3	1	0	1	1	2	0	.200
Harry Holsclaw	P3	RE-MO	3											.500
F. Roach		MO-RO	3											.333

PITCHERS		TEAMS	W	L	PCT	G	GS	CG	SH	IP	H	BB	SO	ERA
Nicholas Harrison		RE17-TO14	8	8	.500	31		5	0	124	129	83	46	5.37
Don Miller		MO9-JC15	5	7	.417	24		7	0	118	142	48	23	4.50
Don Hankins		TO16-RE17	5	8	.385	33		4	0	127	176	37	42	6.38
Art Smith		JC-MO	4	0	1.000	9								
Harry Holsclaw		RE-MO	2	0	1.000	3								

TEAM BATTING

TEAMS	GP	AB	R	H	BI	2B	3B	HR	BB	SO	SB	BA
ROCHESTER	169	5591	962	1581	880	273	107	119	682	573	100	.283
TORONTO	168	5554	780	1580	712	254	102	72	412	517	137	.284
BALTIMORE	168	5486	874	1598	811	300	47	147	609	620	113	.291
MONTREAL	168	5454	767	1557	738	260	79	53	666	595	148	.285
BUFFALO	168	5611	896	1680	815	305	75	120	598	506	61	.299
NEWARK	166	5400	822	1538	753	276	62	85	565	399	89	.285
READING	170	5613	850	1638	779	309	56	96	545	458	97	.292
JERSEY CITY	167	5378	598	1400	559	246	51	67	487	608	66	.260
	672	44087	6549	12572	6047	2223	579	759	4564	4276	811	.285

1930
RIP COLLINS

In 1930, one of the International League's glamour batting records was forever shattered by a young veteran entering his seventh season of minor league ball. The record was in the runs batted in category. The record breaker was Rip Collins.

James Anthony Collins, called Rip, played his first pro ball in 1923 for two teams in Virginia and Pennsylvania. After a year off, Collins resurfaced in the Middle Atlantic League, where he played for the Johnstown club. In the latter stages of the 1926 season, after winning the Middle Atlantic's batting (.388), home run (19), and runs batted in (101) crowns, he joined the International's Rochester team. After splitting time between Rochester and lower teams in 1927 and 1928, Collins became the Rochester Red Wings' starting first baseman in 1929. In that year, he led the league in home runs (38) and runs batted in (134).

In 1930, Collins enjoyed his finest season. He finished with a league-best .376 batting mark, accompanied by 40 home runs. Collins also finished with a league-leading 234 hits, setting the stage for his record. Rip Collins used all those hits to knock in 180 runs in 1930, bettering the old mark by nearly 20.

The major beneficiary of Collins' output was his team. Led by their first baseman, the Red Wings claimed their third straight flag, finishing eight over second-place Baltimore. Montreal finished third, followed by Toronto in fourth. Places five through eight were occupied by Newark, Buffalo, Reading, and Jersey City.

In every International League season but one, Rip Collins' 40 home runs would have given him the triple crown. As it turned out, however, he was not the only record smasher in 1930. Baltimore's recently acquired Joe Hauser walloped 63 home runs to obliterate the existing record of 44.

On the other side of the ball, the International's top pitchers both came from Rochester. Paul Derringer won a league-high 23 and struck out 164. Fellow Red Wing John Berly posted the lowest earned run average (2.49)

After the 1930 season, Rip Collins joined the St. Louis Cardinals to start his eight-year major league career. Here, in 1934, he would win runs batted in (135) and home run (34) titles before finishing his career in the Pacific Coast and Eastern Leagues.

Rip Collins enjoyed a career season in 1930, setting an International League runs batted in mark that has never been erased. Unfortunately, his overall performance was upstaged by Joe Hauser's 63 homer barrage—also an all-time league best.

ROCHESTER
Red Wings

1st   105-62   .629   Billy Southworth

BATTERS	POS-GAMES	GP	AB	R	H	BI	2B	3B	HR	BB	SO	SB	BA
Rip Collins	1B167	167	623	165	**234**	**180**	34	**19**	40	86	55	9	**.376**
George Toporcer	2B167	167	622	134	191	61	**49**	5	1	**125**	39	21	.307
Charles Wilson	SS125	142	524	82	157	100	26	18	8	30	51	6	.300
Joseph Brown	3B162	162	661	153	207	68	37	12	10	98	22	17	.313
Pepper Martin	OF124	135	482	121	175	114	33	18	20	51	37	26	.363
Robert Worthington	OF119	123	467	95	175	113	25	12	8	41	26	4	.375
Ray Pepper	OF104	104	412	67	143	78	30	12	4	21	49	4	.347
Paul Florence	C95	100	312	41	93	54	13	4	7	39	16	2	.298
Billy Southworth	OF66	92	276	58	102	58	17	3	6	27	19	5	.370
Clarence Jonnard	C83	85	201	13	47	22	8	1	0	24	22	0	.234
Ira Smith	C14	66	131	14	26	13	3	0	1	4	15	1	.198
James Carleton	P42	47	76	4	14	8	3	0	1	7	25	0	.184
Laurence Irvin	P34	45	64	6	15	11	6	0	2	4	7	0	.234
Paul Derringer	P44	44	119	6	17	12	2	0	0	2	30	0	.143
Howard Williamson	OF38	42	129	20	26	23	7	1	1	6	7	4	.202
George Anderson	SS31	42	92	12	27	14	6	3	1	4	11	0	.293
Fred Lucas	OF32	35	123	23	36	16	13	0	1	8	16	0	.293
John Berly	P30	33	75	9	12	11	4	0	0	4	17	0	.160
Charles Foreman	P33	33	49	4	4	0	2	0	0	2	17	0	.082
Carlisle Littlejohn	P29	29	22	5	4	5	0	0	0	2	2	0	.182
Bob McGraw	P24	24	47	4	8	5	1	0	0	2	21	0	.170
Ed Delker	SS14	21	50	6	18	8	5	1	0	2	7	0	.360
Earl Smith	C18	18	46	4	11	11	1	2	0	7	2	0	.239
Fred Ostermueller	P13	16	17	2	4	0	0	0	0	2	2	0	.235
Gene Bailey	OF11	11	31	2	5	3	0	0	0	3	3	0	.161
Gordon Hinkle		10	28	3	9	3	1	1	0	0	4	0	.321

PITCHERS	W	L	PCT	G	GS	CG	SH	IP	H	BB	SO	ERA
Paul Derringer	**23**	11	.676	44		16	2	**289**	**310**	72	**164**	3.89
John Berly	16	8	.667	30		17	0	210	186	80	81	2.49
James Carleton	13	13	.500	42		15	0	228	251	99	124	5.01
Ira Smith	12	7	.632	35		6	1	156	173	48	53	4.27
Charles Foreman	10	6	.625	33		4	1	134	137	72	54	3.86
Bob McGraw	10	8	.556	24		12	1	129	143	54	45	4.05
Carlisle Littlejohn	8	1	.889	29		0	0	74	95	30	31	4.99
Laurence Irvin	7	4	.636	34		4	0	126	152	62	37	5.71
Fred Ostermueller	2	2	.500	13		2	0	42	53	26	14	6.21
Edwin Chapman	0	0	----	1								

BALTIMORE
Orioles

2nd   97-70   .581   -8   Fritz Maisel

BATTERS	POS-GAMES	GP	AB	R	H	BI	2B	3B	HR	BB	SO	SB	BA
Joe Hauser	1B168	**168**	617	**173**	193	175	39	11	**63**	108	**117**	1	.313
John Stewart	2B	(see multi-team players)											
John Sand	SS164	164	583	101	187	108	35	11	17	77	72	7	.321
James Stroner	3B155	158	584	122	193	130	36	7	27	60	82	1	.331
Frank McGowan	OF168	**168**	661	133	222	113	45	7	21	74	68	4	.336
Vincent Barton	OF147	150	589	143	201	133	38	13	32	58	54	8	.341
John Gill	OF137	148	536	113	174	118	35	6	34	54	71	3	.325
Hugh McMullen	C84	89	292	27	78	45	11	2	3	23	49	1	.267
Julius Solters	OF52	76	215	45	67	48	12	4	6	9	33	4	.312
James Dalrymple	2B44	61	235	38	60	15	7	6	2	14	24	4	.255
James Weaver	P55	55	77	2	13	4	2	0	0	2	32	0	.169
Don Heffner	2B45	51	168	30	42	23	10	2	5	26	27	3	.250
Thomas Padden	C44	46	152	22	45	19	10	0	3	15	22	2	.296
Ike Danning	C40	44	142	17	41	31	6	2	6	14	33	1	.289
Monte Weaver	P39	39	51	7	10	1	3	0	1	1	12	0	.196
Stuart Bolen	P35	38	95	15	25	13	4	1	3	3	12	0	.263
Luther Roy	P33	33	80	12	22	10	1	1	0	5	13	0	.275
Fred Coumbe	P31	32	21	1	1	0	0	0	0	1	8	0	.048
Beryl Richmond	P31	31	48	3	1	0	0	0	0	4	25	0	.021
Foster Edwards	P27	27	42	2	7	1	0	0	0	2	14	0	.167
Tripp Sigman	OF11	16	40	5	13	9	3	0	1	3	8	1	.325
Louis Koupal	P15	16	36	6	11	6	2	0	0	2	3	1	.306
Claude Linton		13	24	1	7	7	1	0	0	1	2	0	.292

PITCHERS	W	L	PCT	G	GS	CG	SH	IP	H	BB	SO	ERA
Stuart Bolen	19	9	.679	35		16	3	235	246	107	124	4.29

BALTIMORE (cont.)
Orioles

PITCHERS	W	L	PCT	G	GS	CG	SH	IP	H	BB	SO	ERA
James Weaver	19	11	.633	55		14	2	236	218	74	142	3.36
Luther Roy	18	9	.667	33		14	3	203	217	91	59	4.17
Louis Koupal	7	4	.636	15		6	0	94	109	37	33	4.21
Foster Edwards	7	7	.500	27		6	0	116	148	33	31	4.81
Beryl Richmond	7	8	.467	31		6	1	146	159	70	74	4.94
Fred Coumbe	5	3	.625	31		0	0	63	91	18	27	6.57
Monte Weaver	4	6	.400	39		3	0	146	171	53	65	4.81
Harry Smythe	2	1	.667	6								
Elmer Hearn	1	0	1.000	9								
J. Hollingsworth	1	1	.500	4								
Martin Lang	0	1	.000	5								
Charles Gumbert	0	1	.000	3								
Charles Hardin	0	0	----	1								

MONTREAL   3rd   96-72   .571   -9.5   Ed Holly
Royals

BATTERS	POS-GAMES	GP	AB	R	H	BI	2B	3B	HR	BB	SO	SB	BA
Fred Henry	1B139	140	495	89	171	82	40	15	8	42	37	6	.345
Walt Gautreau	2B164	164	563	126	166	80	34	7	6	111	43	13	.295
William Urbanski	SS161	162	602	92	190	100	44	10	9	41	58	25	.316
Bernard Helgeth	3B70	71	228	39	61	44	13	4	7	40	42	5	.268
Henry Haines	OF156	158	575	129	158	69	32	9	8	112	70	45	.275
Thomas Gulley	OF148	150	513	80	170	105	30	5	13	87	63	0	.331
James Ripple	OF95,3B20	130	391	79	122	65	18	9	13	30	56	10	.312
Al Head	C114	134	463	74	155	81	36	5	6	21	14	1	.335
Ed Conley	OF80,3B20	119	379	47	97	61	11	5	6	32	55	13	.256
James Calleran	3B37,1B33,2B10	87	244	37	64	31	9	4	2	42	32	5	.262
Charles Niebergall	C57	72	206	23	58	37	14	3	2	16	16	4	.282
Aldrik Gaudette	OF40	54	171	28	58	15	8	3	0	18	15	1	.339
John Pomorski	P37	40	68	8	15	9	3	1	1	4	15	0	.221
Roy Buckalew	P37	37	40	6	8	3	1	0	0	4	18	1	.200
Gowell Claset	P36	36	71	7	10	6	0	0	0	7	22	0	.141
Martin Griffin	P32	34	83	9	15	12	2	0	3	3	25	0	.181
Herb Thormahlen	P28	32	78	9	20	10	3	1	1	6	20	3	.256
Art Smith	P28	29	60	6	14	6	1	0	0	3	12	0	.233
Elam Van Gilder	P17	20	37	2	9	3	3	0	0	1	6	0	.243
Otis Williams	3B18	19	66	9	12	14	1	1	2	8	9	1	.182
Walter Brown	P16	16	20	2	3	2	0	1	0	2	5	0	.150
Harry Holsclaw	P15	15	14	1	3	2	0	1	0	1	4	0	.214

PITCHERS	W	L	PCT	G	GS	CG	SH	IP	H	BB	SO	ERA
Gowell Claset	17	10	.630	36		15	4	217	244	91	94	4.27
Art Smith	14	11	.560	28		13	4	175	193	52	44	4.17
Martin Griffin	14	12	.538	32		18	1	223	234	65	61	3.83
Roy Buckalew	13	4	.765	37		9	1	152	150	54	50	3.61
John Pomorski	13	8	.619	37		12	1	195	190	62	65	3.47
Herb Thormahlen	13	11	.542	28		18	0	215	246	48	65	3.85
Walter Brown	6	2	.750	16		4	0	66	76	33	38	3.95
Elam Van Gilder	3	8	.273	17		7	0	93	115	40	31	5.52
Harry Holsclaw	1	5	.167	15		0	0	50	62	15	35	4.68
Paul Hopkins	0	0	----	1								

TORONTO   4th   87-80   .521   -18   Steve O'Neill
Maple Leafs

BATTERS	POS-GAMES	GP	AB	R	H	BI	2B	3B	HR	BB	SO	SB	BA
Harry Davis	1B115	128	397	43	111	35	20	5	3	27	40	15	.280
Leslie Burke	2B149	154	512	51	137	63	19	2	3	73	21	3	.268
Warren Cote	SS133	135	490	68	130	51	17	5	1	25	35	5	.265
Nolen Richardson	3B140	147	575	71	159	42	38	5	2	39	25	12	.277
Joe Rabbitt	OF147	154	557	86	165	67	28	9	9	36	60	37	.296
Clayton Sheedy	OF143	147	539	81	149	67	15	15	9	51	34	3	.276
Art Ruble	OF94	99	334	42	100	43	15	6	2	33	18	4	.299
Ed Phillips	C109	118	367	53	96	52	21	7	6	43	66	5	.262
Joseph Harris	1B69,OF23	114	345	52	115	82	21	8	11	36	11	5	.333
Steve O'Neill	C58	75	195	26	60	32	10	1	0	27	12	3	.308

TORONTO (cont.)
Maple Leafs

BATTERS	POS-GAMES	GP	AB	R	H	BI	2B	3B	HR	BB	SO	SB	BA
Bill Rogell	SS29,3B19,OF19	68	244	43	77	30	15	5	4	37	33	5	.316
Robert Petrie	OF52	63	174	30	45	22	5	2	3	23	25	3	.259
Nicholas Harrison	P53	53	42	2	11	2	1	1	0	3	14	0	.262
Fred Bedore	2B15,3B15	41	101	14	26	16	2	2	2	7	10	3	.257
Frank Barnes	P38	38	79	10	17	8	0	1	0	6	13	2	.215
Kyle Graham	P35	35	44	2	6	0	0	0	0	0	16	0	.136
John Prudhomme	P35	35	62	7	15	16	4	1	3	11	21	0	.242
Sam Gibson	P33	33	79	9	16	8	3	2	2	0	5	0	.203
Ed Kunesh	OF28	29	107	16	31	13	6	1	1	4	14	2	.290
Guy Cantrell	P28	28	58	6	13	8	0	2	0	1	11	0	.224
Phil Page	P25	26	49	3	9	5	2	1	0	0	9	0	.184
Art McHenry	OF20	21	71	5	17	2	4	0	0	4	9	1	.239
Joseph Samuels	P16	19	13	3	3	0	1	0	0	0	4	0	.231
Clarence Fisher	P18	18	14	1	0	0	0	0	0	1	3	0	.000
Art Herring	P13	15	33	4	9	1	1	0	0	4	2	0	.273
Joseph Shaute	P6	15	22	2	5	3	1	0	0	3	3	0	.227

PITCHERS		W	L	PCT	G	GS	CG	SH	IP	H	BB	SO	ERA
Guy Cantrell		15	5	.750	28		13	2	171	136	69	98	2.68
Sam Gibson		15	11	.577	33		14	3	198	187	79	110	4.00
Frank Barnes		13	12	.520	38		15	4	219	243	49	104	3.99
John Prudhomme		12	14	.462	35		15	3	185	213	50	62	4.52
Kyle Graham		9	4	.692	35		3	0	140	154	71	53	4.50
Nicholas Harrison		8	6	.571	53		2	0	156	139	80	67	4.15
Art Herring		5	7	.417	13		9	0	98	93	35	53	3.85
Phil Page		4	12	.250	25		7	0	133	160	45	33	5.08
Joseph Shaute		3	1	.750	6								
Clarence Fisher		2	3	.400	18		0	0	56	76	11	16	6.27
Joseph Samuels		1	5	.167	16		0	0	38	51	36	15	7.53
Haskell Billings		0	0	----	1								

NEWARK   5th   80-88   .476   -25.5   Tris Speaker -
Bears   Al Mamaux

BATTERS	POS-GAMES	GP	AB	R	H	BI	2B	3B	HR	BB	SO	SB	BA
Willis Windle	1B148	152	537	98	178	103	29	14	12	58	63	23	.332
Robert James	2B94	113	382	70	113	41	15	9	1	27	30	25	.296
Robert Stevens	SS122	123	436	56	131	55	12	14	2	47	20	16	.300
Baxter Jordan	3B51,OF54,1B23	136	475	73	167	75	29	10	9	43	37	11	.352
Harry Layne	OF142	142	568	111	185	85	32	12	20	51	42	25	.326
Bill Zitzmann	OF141	148	533	94	167	71	34	6	9	57	50	21	.313
Ralph Shinners	OF	(see multi-team players)											
Charles Hargreaves	C	(see multi-team players)											
Andy Cohen	3B45,2B39,SS20	106	386	42	100	56	9	4	6	17	10	2	.259
Richard Stahlman	C30	55	103	21	34	19	5	4	1	12	5	1	.330
George Loepp	OF49	50	159	30	41	26	7	2	3	28	19	3	.258
Louis Legett	C39	50	105	12	22	14	5	0	3	16	23	0	.210
Don Brennan	P40	40	43	4	7	1	0	0	0	1	14	0	.163
Al Mamaux	P34	34	55	5	6	8	0	0	0	9	8	0	.109
Albert Harvin	P31	31	52	7	6	9	1	0	2	0	23	0	.115
Charles Fischer	P24	24	50	4	9	0	0	0	0	5	11	0	.180
Henry Boney	P20	20	25	3	5	2	1	0	1	0	6	0	.200
Jesse Petty	P19	19	36	1	6	4	1	0	0	0	12	0	.167
Byron Speece	P19	19	13	1	2	1	0	0	0	0	3	0	.154
Frank Parenti	2B14	18	45	4	8	2	0	0	0	4	1	0	.178
Roy Frazier	OF17	17	70	7	21	7	3	2	0	5	6	1	.300
Myles Thomas	P17	17	33	3	9	0	2	0	0	2	5	0	.273
LeRoy Parmelee	P13	14	26	1	4	2	0	0	0	1	12	0	.154
Tris Speaker		11	31	3	13	3	1	1	0	4	3	1	.419
Ed Fallenstein	P11	11	7	1	2	0	0	0	0	1	2	0	.286

PITCHERS		W	L	PCT	G	GS	CG	SH	IP	H	BB	SO	ERA
Albert Harvin		11	5	.688	31		6	1	148	197	66	76	5.57
Al Mamaux		10	9	.526	34		12	0	184	249	39	66	4.55
Charles Fischer		9	11	.450	24		12	0	147	152	66	92	3.91
Don Brennan		7	5	.583	40		1	0	128	132	85	65	4.78
Jesse Petty		7	5	.583	19		6	0	96	90	23	65	3.84
Myles Thomas		6	6	.500	17		5	0	103	114	49	45	4.54
LeRoy Parmelee		5	4	.556	13		6	0	80	75	64	39	3.81

NEWARK (cont.)
Bears

PITCHERS	W	L	PCT	G	GS	CG	SH	IP	H	BB	SO	ERA
Byron Speece	3	4	.429	19		1	0	48	36	13	29	3.38
Henry Boney	2	3	.400	20		0	0	70	79	33	29	5.27
Clayland Touchstone	1	2	.333	7								
Sterling Stryker	1	3	.250	5								
Ed Fallenstein	0	1	.000	11		0	0	28	38	18	5	9.32
John Cooney	0	1	.000	8								
Edgar Carroll	0	1	.000	7								
Al Jones	0	1	.000	5								
Nick Dumovich	0	1	.000	3								
Ray Lucas	0	2	.000	3								
George Peery	0	0	----	5								
Ted Prichard	0	0	----	3								
Ken Jones	0	0	----	1								

BUFFALO   6th   74-91   .448   -30   William Clymer -
Bisons   James Cooney

BATTERS	POS-GAMES	GP	AB	R	H	BI	2B	3B	HR	BB	SO	SB	BA
Nelson Hawks	1B93	114	385	67	116	67	21	7	9	50	35	4	.301
Herb Thomas	2B		(see multi-team players)										
Oliver Sax	SS80,3B46,2B23	154	602	144	186	81	29	7	12	98	80	15	.309
Robert Barrett	3B		(see multi-team players)										
Al Moore	OF162	162	638	116	221	107	42	13	11	61	41	22	.346
Clarence Mueller	OF155	156	579	113	182	98	39	14	9	81	67	6	.314
Oliver Tucker	OF93	94	356	74	134	76	26	5	18	42	16	4	.376
Frank Grube	C100	104	345	65	120	54	29	4	8	46	37	6	.348
James Cooney	SS69	79	278	40	96	40	14	3	1	16	6	2	.345
Charles Miller	OF44	61	145	23	38	17	12	1	1	21	25	0	.262
Art Mills	P46	53	47	6	11	7	0	1	1	3	8	0	.234
Leon Williams	P32	53	51	9	14	12	5	1	2	4	17	0	.275
Ed Tomlin	1B17,3B12,P10	44	123	23	41	19	5	0	0	10	19	1	.333
Joseph Bloomer	P14	41	31	7	7	3	0	0	0	5	6	0	.226
Fred Fussell	P40	40	72	3	7	3	0	0	0	7	23	0	.097
William Kelly	1B36	39	133	22	34	22	4	1	5	25	36	2	.256
John Wilson	P36	36	64	8	12	7	0	0	0	5	15	0	.188
Jack Henzes	2B31	31	119	12	35	19	6	1	0	9	17	0	.294
Gorham Leverette	P31	31	51	3	9	5	2	0	0	1	16	0	.176
Dave Danforth	P24	24	60	9	7	4	0	0	0	6	24	0	.117
Dennis Murphy	C14	24	49	5	21	10	5	0	1	4	2	0	.429
Hugh Buchanan	P21	21	14	0	1	1	0	0	0	2	3	0	.071
William Ussat	SS18	18	65	6	14	5	2	0	0	5	18	1	.215
Dewey Stover	OF12	18	44	9	20	6	8	0	0	11	7	0	.455
Carl Schoof	P16	16	15	1	2	1	1	0	0	0	1	0	.133
William Batch	3B15	15	62	9	20	16	3	1	2	7	7	2	.323
Elmer Smith		12	16	2	3	1	0	0	0	1	2	0	.188
Vern Parks	P11	12	2	0	0	0	0	0	0	3	0	0	.000

PITCHERS	W	L	PCT	G	GS	CG	SH	IP	H	BB	SO	ERA
Fred Fussell	13	12	.520	40		12	1	212	243	53	83	4.37
Dave Danforth	12	8	.600	24		11	1	161	158	45	161	4.19
John Wilson	12	14	.462	36		8	0	175	224	56	97	5.61
Art Mills	9	8	.529	46		1	0	135	162	51	53	5.47
Joseph Bloomer	6	2	.750	14		7	1	85	115	17	25	4.33
Gorham Leverette	5	12	.294	31		4	0	139	202	52	59	6.80
Leon Williams	3	4	.429	32		2	0	83	113	44	27	7.05
Vern Parks	2	1	.667	11		0	0	17	25	3	8	4.24
Sam Dailey	2	2	.500	9								
Carl Shoof	1	4	.200	16		1	0	50	65	30	29	7.20
Ed Tomlin	1	4	.200	10		1	0	37	55	11	18	6.57
Hugh Buchanan	1	5	.167	20		1	0	54	62	18	16	6.33
Robert Weiland	0	1	.000	5								
Riel Love	0	2	.000	2								
Stan Lucas	0	0	----	3								
Thomas Kain	0	0	----	2								
George Hockette	0	0	----	2								
Jesse Barnes	0	0	----	1								
Baxter Moose	0	0	----	1								
Ben Shields	0	0	----	1								

READING Keystones

7th	68-98	.410	-36.5	Harry Hinchman	

BATTERS	POS-GAMES	GP	AB	R	H	BI	2B	3B	HR	BB	SO	SB	BA
Wilbur Davis	1B153	162	606	95	207	150	32	15	26	51	42	8	.342
Charles Walsh	2B137	147	571	79	157	80	32	3	4	43	34	6	.275
Billy Jurges	SS142	143	532	94	153	57	23	7	6	63	54	9	.288
Robert Jones	3B84	96	301	43	104	47	16	2	1	21	17	5	.346
Hobart Whitman	OF141,P1	143	572	115	182	94	36	9	6	57	9	5	.318
Floyd Scott	OF122	130	455	100	159	109	34	3	32	63	59	5	.349
George Quellich	OF95	97	377	69	122	76	26	6	9	39	43	4	.324
Rodney Whitney	C57	70	173	25	48	14	8	0	0	31	17	1	.277
Earl Grace	OF53,C	137	476	79	154	85	34	6	10	44	24	2	.324
Tony Krasovich	3B49,OF27,SS15	96	319	44	88	37	16	2	8	32	61	2	.276
Richard Loftus	OF64	80	248	49	66	24	7	3	2	40	6	2	.266
LeRoy Herrmann	P39	53	74	10	15	3	1	0	0	3	19	0	.203
Peter Stack	C41	44	137	17	45	18	6	0	1	16	15	0	.328
Nelson Greene	P40	40	57	6	13	5	3	0	0	3	11	1	.228
Ernest Woolfolk	P38	40	22	4	3	1	1	1	0	2	5	0	.136
Ernest Padgett	SS13,3B11	37	94	17	22	11	7	1	0	13	5	1	.234
John Welch	P33	37	65	6	8	7	0	0	1	3	12	0	.123
Henry Grampp	P35	36	37	2	7	3	1	0	0	6	15	0	.189
Lon Warneke	P34	34	75	9	17	8	4	1	0	0	14	0	.227
George Bell	P34	34	74	5	8	3	2	0	0	3	29	0	.108
John Kahn	3B17,2B11	32	98	16	23	12	3	0	1	10	17	0	.235
William McAfee	P21	21	37	8	10	7	2	1	1	2	9	0	.270
John Lehman	3B17	17	54	7	12	4	2	0	0	5	6	0	.222
Fred Carts	P17	17	19	2	2	0	0	0	0	0	2	0	.105
Stanley Ripp	2B13	14	52	11	16	5	3	0	0	3	6	0	.308
Norman Plitt	P13	13	18	2	5	2	0	0	0	3	2	0	.278

PITCHERS	W	L	PCT	G	GS	CG	SH	IP	H	BB	SO	ERA
John Welch	10	13	.435	33		12	2	168	191	69	67	4.82
LeRoy Herrmann	10	14	.417	39		13	0	200	234	75	130	5.45
Nelson Greene	10	15	.400	40		11	0	177	227	43	72	5.54
George Bell	9	11	.450	34		11	0	208	273	110	78	5.63
Lon Warneke	9	12	.429	34		11	1	185	236	68	118	6.03
Henry Grampp	8	3	.727	35		4	1	115	139	70	39	6.10
William McAfee	7	8	.467	21		6	1	97	119	43	31	6.22
Fred Carts	2	5	.286	17		2	0	56	72	33	18	5.14
Norman Plitt	2	5	.286	13		1	0	50	77	18	20	6.30
Ernest Woolfolk	1	4	.200	38		0	0	82	114	37	33	6.80
Kent Greenfield	0	1	.000	3								
Walt Leverenz	0	1	.000	3								
Don Hankins	0	3	.000	5								
Don Miller	0	0	----	3								
Ed Lautenbacher	0	0	----	2								
V. Roberts	0	0	----	1								
Oliver Rohrbach	0	0	----	1								
Edmund Forsberg	0	0	----	1								
Rodney Frey	0	0	----	1								
Hobart Whitman	0	0	----	1								

JERSEY CITY Skeeters

8th	59-105	.360	-44.5	Nick Allen - Joe Tinker	

BATTERS	POS-GAMES	GP	AB	R	H	BI	2B	3B	HR	BB	SO	SB	BA
James Keesey	1B88	89	327	51	85	40	14	6	1	27	35	4	.260
Grant Gillis	2B154	154	578	61	153	68	29	10	4	44	56	6	.265
Clarke Pittenger	SS153	154	612	75	169	55	17	3	3	35	16	15	.276
Julian Wera	3B147	147	548	68	173	90	33	5	9	31	42	6	.316
Max West	OF162	162	601	104	195	96	42	3	16	64	30	7	.324
George Selkirk	OF143	154	500	90	162	88	27	8	16	76	93	2	.324
Fred Walker	OF75	83	325	62	109	41	18	9	7	27	39	9	.335
Arndt Jorgens	C80	82	271	28	71	26	12	3	2	24	20	3	.262
Bobby Veach	OF56	75	219	34	68	35	14	2	5	15	9	1	.311
Maurice Shannon	SS11,1B10	55	117	15	34	13	3	5	1	6	13	0	.291
Thomas Daly	C44	51	126	7	28	15	4	1	0	8	1	0	.222
John Allen	P44	48	72	8	12	5	2	1	2	3	16	1	.167
Maurice Bream	P42	43	65	5	5	2	1	0	0	6	26	0	.077
George Shefflott	C37	39	126	8	30	9	3	1	0	11	18	2	.238
William Moore	P38	38	57	3	8	6	1	0	0	4	9	0	.140
Joseph Manger	1B37	37	123	8	29	11	9	1	1	12	16	1	.236
George Miner	P30	36	56	4	13	6	3	1	0	5	10	0	.232

JERSEY CITY (cont.)
Skeeters

BATTERS	POS-GAMES	GP	AB	R	H	BI	2B	3B	HR	BB	SO	SB	BA
William Outen	OF23	35	90	13	22	15	0	0	5	17	12	1	.244
Jack Hopkins	P26	26	30	3	4	2	1	0	0	2	9	1	.133
George Martin		19	45	5	9	3	1	0	1	5	6	1	.200
William Henderson	P16	19	28	5	6	4	2	0	1	1	6	0	.214
John Pitts	P17	17	24	3	2	1	0	0	0	2	12	0	.083
Harold Yordy		12	29	5	6	3	2	0	2	2	4	0	.207
Joseph Dougherty		12	28	0	5	5	0	0	0	1	3	0	.179
Witt Guise	P11	11	10	2	2	1	1	0	0	0	5	0	.200
Gordon Rhodes	P8	10	13	4	3	0	1	0	0	0	6	1	.231
Don Miller	P10	10	11	0	0	0	0	0	0	3	3	0	.000

PITCHERS	W	L	PCT	G	GS	CG	SH	IP	H	BB	SO	ERA
John Allen	12	16	.429	44		13	2	208	187	115	140	3.98
Maurice Bream	9	22	.290	42		11	4	215	282	49	53	5.48
William Henderson	7	4	.636	16		5	1	88	83	36	44	4.19
William Moore	7	13	.350	38		11	1	175	221	72	78	4.99
George Miner	6	12	.333	30		9	0	155	188	60	65	4.30
Jack Hopkins	5	8	.385	26		3	1	92	102	41	47	6.16
Don Miller	2	2	.500	10		0	0	45	54	14	14	5.20
Robert Walsh	2	2	.500	9								
Gordon Rhodes	1	3	.250	8								
John Pitts	1	6	.143	17		4	0	79	111	35	56	7.06
Witt Guise	0	1	.000	11		0	0	29	26	18	13	4.65
Glenn Liebhardt	0	1	.000	9								
Richard Oliver	0	1	.000	5								
Bobo Newsome	0	1	.000	3								
Jack Doyle	0	0	----	5								
Alfred Noble	0	0	----	1								
Joseph Styborski	0	0	----	1								
Gene Hebert	0	0	----	1								

MULTI-TEAM PLAYERS

BATTERS	POS-GAMES	TEAMS	GP	AB	R	H	BI	2B	3B	HR	BB	SO	SB	BA
Herb Thomas	2B123,SS30,3B15	BU90-NE78	168	677	116	218	131	43	13	19	40	44	6	.322
Ralph Shinners	OF131	NE88-BU47	135	510	89	158	91	39	4	20	33	65	14	.310
Robert Barrett	3B129	BU73-NE58	131	478	70	161	95	28	2	9	48	27	8	.337
John Stewart	2B81	BA96-JC27	123	420	87	113	32	18	9	5	34	46	15	.269
Russ Wrightstone	2B22,1B22,3B22,OF12	NE44-BU63	107	293	52	113	52	14	2	6	40	21	1	.386
Robert Munn	C79	NE54-BU33	87	245	33	65	22	15	2	6	35	53	1	.265
Charles Hargreaves	C75	BU14-NE64	78	246	29	63	31	21	0	2	30	22	1	.256
John Cooney	OF24,1B15	JC46-NE16	61	145	19	39	10	4	3	1	9	12	1	.269
Leo Mangum	P38	BU23-NE19	42	78	10	24	8	6	1	0	4	9	0	.308
George Grant	P39	JC30-RO10	40	70	7	15	2	0	0	1	8	22	0	.214
Henry Wertz	P38	BA22-BU16	38	49	6	12	7	1	0	1	4	5	0	.245
James Faulkner	P35	BU1-NE34	35	54	8	12	5	2	2	0	2	6	0	.222
Harley Boss	1B22	JC18-RE16	34	113	13	29	14	6	0	1	6	11	0	.257
George Susce	C24	BU24-NE5	29	74	12	16	9	2	1	1	11	11	0	.216
Peter Radwan	2B10	MO9-RE13	22	70	4	16	3	1	0	0	4	7	1	.229
Joseph Hartman	P21	RE1-MO20	21	11	2	2	2	0	0	0	1	4	0	.182
Andrew Chambers	P17	BA6-NE11	17	24	3	4	3	1	0	0	0	6	0	.167

PITCHERS		TEAMS	W	L	PCT	G	GS	CG	SH	IP	H	BB	SO	ERA
James Faulkner		BU1-NE34	11	13	.458	35		7	0	153	194	84	40	5.76
George Grant		JC29-RO10	11	14	.440	39		14	0	218	269	84	59	4.58
Leo Mangum		BU22-NE16	10	19	.345	38		11	0	222	287	49	70	5.03
Henry Wertz		BA22-BU16	7	6	.538	38		6	2	156	196	67	46	5.37
Joseph Hartman		RE1-MO20	2	1	.667	21		1	1	49	64	17	12	5.90
Andrew Chambers		BA6-NE11	2	4	.333	17		2	1	65	81	33	23	6.23
Joseph Bonnelly		BU2-RE4	1	2	.333	6								
Myles Hunter		RO1-NE3	0	2	.000	4								

TEAM BATTING

TEAMS	GP	AB	R	H	BI	2B	3B	HR	BB	SO	SB	BA
ROCHESTER	167	5704	1056	1768	993	325	**112**	111	599	528	99	.310
BALTIMORE	168	**5752**	**1115**	1739	**1052**	322	82	**231**	597	**838**	59	.302
MONTREAL	168	5461	912	1597	843	305	84	87	629	661	127	.292
TORONTO	167	5521	730	1528	665	249	81	61	498	530	105	.277
NEWARK	**169**	5663	860	1669	798	281	87	98	514	551	**147**	.295
BUFFALO	165	5699	998	**1787**	926	**335**	76	115	**646**	677	78	**.314**
READING	166	5695	928	1677	870	307	60	109	567	566	53	.294
JERSEY CITY	164	5423	716	1501	662	251	62	78	460	581	66	.277
	667	44918	7315	13266	6809	2375	644	890	4510	4932	734	.295

1931
ROCHESTER RED WINGS

Close on the heels of the seven-year pennant spree of the Baltimore Orioles, another International League dynasty emerged. Located in New York State, it involved one of the league's elder statesmen.

Rochester had been in the International's family of leagues nearly from its onset. The city was a part of the 1885 New York State League, and moved with the league to the International in 1886. In 1890, Rochester left the International to join the major league American Association for one season. For the rest of the nineteenth century, Rochester enjoyed spotty membership in the league, not participating for two years (1893 and 1894) and relocating in two others (1897 and 1898).

Rochester won its first pennant in 1899, followed by another in two years. In the years preceding World War I, the team was the first league franchise to cop three flags in a row. Several lean years followed, ending in a string of three 100-win (second-place) seasons beginning in 1921.

Before the 1928 season, Rochester was purchased by the St. Louis Cardinals to be their top farm team. Blessed with Cardinal largess, the team won the pennant in 1928. It garnered two more first-place finishes in 1929 and 1930.

In 1931, favored to win a fourth flag, Rochester had to work for the bunting. Trailing a strong Newark club, Rochester pulled ahead in the final ten days to win by two games—their fourth straight prize.

The 1931 Rochester Red Wings were sparked by outfielder Ray Pepper. Pepper led the International League in runs (123), hits (233), and triples (20), and just missed the batting title by a whisker (.356). Other stars included George Fisher (.325, 17 HR) and major league veteran George Sisler (.303). Rochester's top pitcher was Raymond Starr, who won 20 and finished with the league's lowest earned run average (2.83).

Behind Rochester and Newark, Baltimore ended up in third, followed by Montreal in fourth. Toronto, Jersey City, Reading, and Buffalo rounded out the standings. Newark's Ike Boone edged out Ray Pepper for the batting title (.356), while Baltimore's Joe Hauser won his second home run crown (31) and James Poole of Reading plated 126 runners. Pitchers Monte Weaver from Baltimore and John Allen from Jersey City/Newark won the most games (21), while Newark's Don Brennan struck out a league-best 143.

Rochester fell to fifth in 1932 as the Cardinals moved their best prospects to another farm team. Though the Red Wings won another half-dozen titles in succeeding years, their legacy lies elsewhere. From their readmittance into the Eastern League of 1895 to the present, Rochester has maintained continuous league participation, a claim no other International League team can make.

ROCHESTER
Red Wings

| | | 1st | 101-67 | .601 | | | | | | Billy Southworth | | |

BATTERS	POS-GAMES	GP	AB	R	H	BI	2B	3B	HR	BB	SO	SB	BA
George Sisler	1B155	159	613	86	186	81	37	5	3	34	17	7	.303
James Jordan	2B		(see multi-team players)										
Ed Delker	SS98	98	333	57	84	37	19	10	1	44	44	3	.252
Charles Wilson	3B117	124	460	63	127	71	25	10	6	32	28	4	.276
Ray Pepper	OF164	165	655	123	233	121	43	20	8	44	64	6	.356
George Fisher	OF110	120	400	77	130	78	24	5	17	59	42	4	.325
Al Moore	OF87	89	331	60	105	58	14	5	0	23	11	3	.317
Paul Florence	C124	125	371	42	101	67	17	3	10	50	24	0	.272
George Puccinelli	OF85	108	299	61	88	73	16	3	18	62	42	5	.294
William Holm	3B55,2B16,OF10	87	281	42	78	30	16	7	1	32	8	2	.278
Clarence Jonnard	C81	81	198	21	58	28	8	0	1	21	14	0	.293
Fred Myers	SS27,2B18	60	169	32	38	15	5	2	3	18	33	3	.225
Billy Southworth	OF34	55	135	22	36	18	11	1	2	15	7	0	.267
Ira Smith	P37	50	74	12	15	9	8	1	0	8	5	0	.203
George Binder	SS43	43	136	15	36	22	4	2	0	16	11	4	.257
Carmen Hill	P37	37	79	9	12	5	1	0	0	3	21	0	.152
Raymond Starr	P37	37	76	10	14	7	3	0	0	5	20	0	.184
Joel Hunt	OF32	36	127	25	32	18	7	2	1	25	21	6	.252
Laurence Irvin	P36	36	30	2	4	2	0	0	0	1	4	0	.133
Herman Bell	P33	33	84	8	16	5	3	0	0	3	22	0	.190
Charles Foreman	P33	33	46	4	5	2	1	0	0	2	9	0	.109
Ralph Judd	P25	30	41	4	8	4	1	0	0	1	7	0	.195
Carlisle Littlejohn	P24	28	17	1	3	2	2	0	0	2	6	0	.176
Jack Bentley	1B11	17	36	5	11	8	0	0	0	5	1	0	.306
Russ Rollings	3B10	16	46	3	9	5	0	1	1	0	3	0	.196
Al Grabowski	P15	15	22	1	5	5	1	0	1	2	6	0	.227
George Anderson		13	27	2	6	1	2	0	0	4	1	0	.222
Ray Moss	P10	10	24	3	4	2	0	0	0	4	4	0	.167
Joe Heving	P5	5											.000
Rose	P2	2											.000
Anderson	P2	2											.000
Tyler		2											.000

PITCHERS	W	L	PCT	G	GS	CG	SH	IP	H	BB	SO	ERA
Raymond Starr	20	7	.741	37		18	1	216	192	102	81	2.83
Carmen Hill	18	12	.600	37		17	5	220	191	61	94	3.03
Herman Bell	16	11	.593	33		18	4	235	239	57	86	3.26
Ira Smith	15	9	.625	37		17	6	204	200	50	60	3.26
Laurence Irvin	7	3	.700	36		2	2	111	124	52	34	4.30
Charles Foreman	7	6	.538	33		4	0	134	141	79	41	4.30
Ralph Judd	7	6	.538	25		4	1	107	120	37	48	5.47
Ray Moss	4	3	.571	10		4	0	64	68	20	20	3.09
Al Grabowski	4	4	.500	15		5	0	64	89	34	31	5.06
Carlisle Littlejohn	2	3	.400	24		0	0	50	50	19	14	3.96
Joe Heving	0	2	----	5								
Rose	0	0	----	2								
Anderson	0	0	----	2								

NEWARK
Bears

| | | 2nd | 99-69 | .589 | -2 | | | | | Al Mamaux | | |

BATTERS	POS-GAMES	GP	AB	R	H	BI	2B	3B	HR	BB	SO	SB	BA
Willis Windle	1B93	117	372	48	100	57	15	4	9	29	37	8	.269
Andy Cohen	2B131	131	539	81	171	65	23	9	10	24	14	2	.317
Herb Thomas	SS75,2B37,3B14	133	479	66	132	49	34	4	6	24	19	0	.276
Robert Barrett	3B141	144	514	61	134	71	25	3	9	29	29	5	.261
Ike Boone	OF124	124	469	82	167	92	33	9	18	63	19	2	.356
Bill Zitzmann	OF108	123	390	59	116	51	15	2	4	35	25	9	.297
Joseph Moore	OF63	79	239	38	83	36	13	4	6	12	19	3	.347
Charles Hargreaves	C124	130	423	48	127	57	22	1	5	39	17	3	.300
Robert Stevens	SS66	77	237	31	54	18	7	3	0	26	16	4	.228
Baxter Jordan	1B71	73	277	48	93	47	18	7	4	18	7	7	.336
George Rensa	C45	60	161	24	50	19	5	1	0	21	8	3	.311
Myles Thomas	P52	54	46	3	8	4	1	0	0	1	5	0	.174
Bill Werber	SS42	52	142	22	30	6	3	0	0	18	17	3	.211
Forrest Jensen	OF51	51	216	35	72	30	9	1	3	8	12	0	.333
Byron Speece	P50	50	26	1	6	3	2	0	0	0	7	0	.231
Don Brennan	P48	48	83	5	14	4	1	0	1	5	19	0	.169
Albert Harvin	P46	46	73	2	9	4	1	0	0	3	25	0	.123
Leo Mangum	P35	36	82	11	22	2	3	1	0	2	0	0	.268
Allen Cooke	OF22	30	67	12	19	7	1	0	0	12	10	2	.284

NEWARK (cont.)
Bears

BATTERS	POS-GAMES	GP	AB	R	H	BI	2B	3B	HR	BB	SO	SB	BA
Al Mamaux	P29	29	28	1	4	3	0	0	0	3	10	0	.143
Hugh Willingham	3B17	27	67	5	13	6	3	1	0	7	12	0	.194
Hub Pruett	P26	26	57	3	11	4	2	0	0	3	5	0	.193
James Moore	OF21	21	77	14	25	15	6	2	2	10	5	2	.325
Harry Rosenberg	OF19	21	67	13	19	6	3	1	0	11	7	1	.284
Benjamin April	C14	21	29	9	6	3	2	0	0	7	6	0	.207
Fred Bennett	OF12	17	42	5	15	6	3	0	2	10	3	0	.357
Gordon Rhodes	P17	17	27	4	5	4	0	0	1	0	10	0	.185
John Milligan	P14	14	18	2	4	1	0	0	0	3	4	0	.222
Harold Bejin		12	23	3	4	1	0	0	0	3	1	0	.174
William McAfee	P10	10	15	0	3	2	1	0	0	2	3	0	.200
Lil Stoner	P10	10	9	1	1	1	1	0	0	0	4	0	.100
McSwain		9											.233
James Faulkner	P8	8											.333
George Loepp		6											.258
Vic Aldridge	P5	5											.000

PITCHERS	W	L	PCT	G	GS	CG	SH	IP	H	BB	SO	ERA
Myles Thomas	18	6	.750	52		1	0	154	143	45	53	3.62
Don Brennan	15	16	.484	48		11	1	250	210	115	143	3.42
Leo Mangum	14	9	.609	35		13	4	225	252	47	55	3.84
Byron Speece	12	6	.667	50		0	0	95	93	37	34	2.84
Albert Harvin	11	9	.550	46		11	2	236	247	90	111	3.97
Al Mamaux	8	1	.889	29		4	2	94	90	19	37	2.20
Hub Pruett	7	10	.412	26		11	1	166	150	74	73	3.36
Gordon Rhodes	6	3	.667	17		5	1	74	69	22	40	3.53
William McAfee	3	1	.750	10		3	0	48	52	15	11	3.56
John Milligan	3	3	.500	14		1	0	58	46	39	35	5.43
Lil Stoner	2	0	1.000	10		1	0	32	38	15	13	5.34
James Faulkner	0	2	.000	8								
Vic Aldridge	0	3	.000	5								

BALTIMORE　　　3rd　　94-72　　.566　　-6　　　Fritz Maisel
Orioles

BATTERS	POS-GAMES	GP	AB	R	H	BI	2B	3B	HR	BB	SO	SB	BA
Joe Hauser	1B143	144	487	100	126	98	20	6	31	100	57	1	.259
William Regan	2B100	101	371	65	119	72	28	4	9	46	59	6	.321
John Sand	SS151	152	553	76	145	74	24	1	14	63	67	2	.262
James Stroner	3B115	128	452	75	125	69	25	6	13	36	53	9	.277
Ralph Boyle	OF154	157	603	116	188	65	36	13	10	101	58	11	.312
John Gill	OF136,1B15	155	613	112	211	124	46	7	23	55	84	9	.344
Dennis Sothern	OF93	101	352	78	115	54	22	6	14	41	54	33	.327
Ike Danning	C57	63	164	25	41	29	9	1	6	19	19	2	.250
Don Heffner	2B72,3B29,SS14	114	384	41	97	53	13	5	12	38	41	0	.253
Frank McGowan	OF65	73	253	39	66	39	13	3	8	38	18	1	.261
Harry Smythe	P52	52	49	8	10	2	4	0	0	3	5	0	.204
Harry Rice	OF44	46	167	29	48	25	4	0	7	21	8	2	.287
Monte Weaver	P40	43	107	14	28	9	3	0	1	2	1	0	.262
Jack Hopkins	P42	42	25	4	5	6	2	0	0	3	7	0	.200
Ken Holloway	P40	40	62	4	9	3	1	0	0	3	8	0	.145
Eugene Hargrave	C37	39	141	27	48	37	8	2	8	11	7	1	.340
Frank Gibson	C34	38	107	12	26	16	4	0	3	10	12	0	.243
Beryl Richmond	P37	37	69	7	6	1	1	0	0	3	41	0	.087
Ed Kenna	C33	35	110	7	34	12	5	1	0	18	8	0	.309
Joseph Cascarella	P31	31	47	2	5	0	1	0	0	2	12	0	.106
Louis Koupal	P25	28	48	8	15	6	1	0	0	1	3	0	.313
Charles Dressen	3B15	23	87	10	19	9	2	2	0	9	7	0	.218
Claude Linton	C18	23	64	7	18	12	4	0	2	9	6	0	.281
Robert James	2B11	22	51	7	9	2	2	0	0	3	7	1	.176
Ray Walker	P17	18	24	1	3	1	0	0	0	2	6	0	.125
Luther Roy	P18	18	22	1	5	1	0	0	0	0	4	0	.227
Fred Eichrodt		15	20	2	4	4	0	0	0	1	4	0	.200
Harry Gumbert	P15	15	11	0	2	0	0	0	0	0	5	0	.182
Russ Scarritt		11	39	5	10	4	0	0	0	3	1	1	.256
Bodgers		7											.444
Tolson		7											.333
Joe Kuhel		6											.296
James Weaver	P5	5											.250
Sheehan	P4	4											.333
Walt Tauscher	P4	4											.250

BALTIMORE (cont.)
Orioles

BATTERS	POS-GAMES	GP	AB	R	H	BI	2B	3B	HR	BB	SO	SB	BA
Ad Liska	P2	3											.000
Prim	P1	1											.667

PITCHERS		W	L	PCT	G	GS	CG	SH	IP	H	BB	SO	ERA
Monte Weaver		21	11	.656	40		20	4	249	253	101	111	3.65
Ken Holloway		15	8	.652	40		11	3	199	214	42	57	4.34
Beryl Richmond		15	8	.652	37		12	1	191	192	72	104	3.63
Harry Smythe		12	10	.545	52		6	0	155	178	58	39	3.60
Louis Koupal		7	8	.467	25		6	0	129	158	51	23	5.51
Ray Walker		5	4	.556	17		1	0	70	68	41	37	4.24
Jack Hopkins		5	5	.500	42		0	0	102	84	44	63	4.32
Luther Roy		5	7	.417	18		4	0	74	108	26	17	6.81
Joseph Cascarella		4	7	.364	31		5	0	142	135	65	60	3.61
James Weaver		3	0	1.000	5								
Sheehan		1	0	1.000	4								
Walt Tauscher		1	2	.333	4								
Ad Liska		0	1	.000	2								
Ray Prim		0	1	.000	1								
Harry Gumbert		0	0	----	15		0	0	37	44	20	9	8.27

MONTREAL   4th   85-80   .515   -14.5   Ed Holly
Royals

BATTERS	POS-GAMES	GP	AB	R	H	BI	2B	3B	HR	BB	SO	SB	BA
Solly Mishkin	1B97	97	304	39	71	34	15	1	3	37	33	0	.234
Walt Gautreau	2B166	166	611	94	170	58	26	2	5	108	40	12	.278
Charles Chatham	SS		(see multi-team players)										
Harry Riconda	3B87	87	314	33	78	32	19	0	3	19	15	4	.248
John Conlan	OF146	149	594	77	178	43	28	6	2	39	22	15	.300
Thomas Gulley	OF141	144	498	72	163	95	40	7	8	76	52	3	.327
James Ripple	OF94,3B33	133	442	77	129	78	38	5	15	49	72	4	.292
Al Head	C114	127	462	58	136	69	19	2	4	21	14	3	.294
Ed Conley	OF90	112	330	47	80	37	13	4	3	19	38	4	.242
Aldrik Gaudette	OF47	94	160	20	41	19	5	1	1	29	16	1	.256
William Urbanski	SS78	78	313	64	106	45	22	6	4	20	31	11	.339
George Martin	3B36,1B23	72	207	15	48	20	9	1	0	8	21	0	.232
Charles Niebergall	C55	59	172	21	32	19	8	0	0	23	22	2	.186
John Pomorski	P46	46	76	5	11	2	1	0	1	3	23	0	.145
Roy Buckalew	P45	45	32	2	6	1	1	0	0	2	12	0	.188
Fred Henry	1B44	44	162	13	37	17	6	2	0	12	7	4	.228
Walter Brown	P37	44	87	5	21	11	3	0	0	5	21	0	.241
Gowell Claset	P43	43	77	6	22	9	8	0	2	3	23	0	.286
Herb Thormahlen	P34	35	69	2	7	5	0	0	1	4	26	0	.101
Jule Long	P32	32	17	0	2	0	0	0	0	1	8	0	.118
Clarence Fisher	P23	23	44	4	8	4	0	0	0	1	11	0	.182
Henry Peploski	3B15	17	52	2	10	6	1	0	0	7	2	1	.192
Sumner Collingwood	P12	12	10	1	3	0	0	0	0	0	2	0	.300
Roy Sherid	P11	11	20	1	1	1	0	0	0	1	5	0	.050
Pat Simmons	P11	11	3	0	0	0	0	0	0	0	2	0	.000
McBride		8											.258
Fred Loftus	P7	7											.000
Joe Malay		6											.455
R. Smith		2											.500
Butler		2											.000
Perkins		2											.000
Falk		2											.000

PITCHERS		W	L	PCT	G	GS	CG	SH	IP	H	BB	SO	ERA
Walter Brown		19	12	.613	37		21	4	237	195	115	133	2.89
John Pomorski		17	9	.654	46		15	3	246	255	72	64	3.33
Gowell Claset		16	14	.533	43		15	2	235	227	121	109	3.52
Herb Thormahlen		11	13	.458	34		10	2	199	233	76	58	4.12
Clarence Fisher		9	6	.600	23		7	0	128	134	46	42	3.73
Roy Sherid		3	5	.375	11		4	0	63	74	25	23	3.71
Roy Buckalew		3	11	.214	45		4	0	118	153	44	31	4.96
Sumner Collingwood		2	0	1.000	12		1	0	31	32	12	10	3.48
Jule Long		2	2	.500	32		0	0	74	84	36	41	6.08
Fred Loftus		0	1	.000	7								
Falk		0	1	.000	2								
Butler		0	1	.000	2								
Pat Simmons		0	3	.000	11		0	0	18	14	21	7	7.00

TORONTO
Maple Leafs

5th   83-84   .497   -17.5   Steve O'Neill

BATTERS	POS-GAMES	GP	AB	R	H	BI	2B	3B	HR	BB	SO	SB	BA
Harry Davis	1B125	133	459	73	144	46	22	11	6	44	37	7	.314
Leslie Burke	2B92	104	317	33	79	39	15	3	2	50	13	1	.249
Bill Rogell	SS116	118	397	83	131	38	22	11	4	68	33	10	.330
Nolen Richardson	3B120	120	455	55	145	56	17	3	4	16	11	12	.319
Joe Rabbitt	OF138	147	528	75	140	69	18	12	13	37	28	30	.265
Ken Strong	OF114	118	438	70	149	80	30	14	9	34	42	12	.340
Ivey Shiver	OF114	115	434	69	134	89	25	14	13	39	80	10	.309
Peter Stack	C98	111	318	37	92	40	14	3	1	26	19	1	.289
Ray Morehart	2B68,OF15,3B12	123	402	50	91	32	14	3	1	40	33	15	.227
Steve O'Neill	C76	89	226	21	51	25	10	0	0	34	16	3	.226
Gerald Walker	OF40	43	160	25	50	20	9	1	1	6	6	8	.313
Louis Brower	SS41	42	139	12	24	11	2	0	1	13	13	4	.173
Frank Barnes	P41	42	87	10	21	8	2	0	0	6	7	0	.241
Guy Cantrell	P41	41	88	8	17	4	1	0	1	0	19	0	.193
Nicholas Harrison	P41	41	54	6	14	2	3	0	0	3	9	0	.259
Art Mills	P27	39	60	4	14	5	2	0	0	4	5	0	.233
Marv Owen	3B35	37	131	18	41	19	9	2	0	13	9	1	.313
Art Smith	P29	31	63	3	10	2	0	0	0	2	15	0	.159
Art Ruble	OF12	25	52	6	11	8	0	2	0	4	5	0	.212
Art McHenry	OF22	23	90	10	22	16	2	1	1	2	12	1	.244
Warren Ogden	P19	19	22	2	6	0	1	0	0	1	5	0	.273
Al Butzberger	P15	15	20	3	4	2	0	1	0	1	4	0	.200
John Mihalic		12	28	2	4	3	1	0	0	4	6	0	.143
James Shevlin		12	23	1	2	3	0	0	1	5	4	0	.087
Elon Hogsett	P11	11	27	1	6	3	0	0	1	0	5	0	.222
Daly		9											.267
Jack Quinlan		6											.273
Novak		6											.238
Robert Shanklin	P5	5											.500
Eberbach	P3	3											.000
Eurie Proffitt	P2	2											.000
McCarren		1											.000

PITCHERS	W	L	PCT	G	GS	CG	SH	IP	H	BB	SO	ERA
Guy Cantrell	17	14	.548	41		15	2	237	243	106	100	4.18
Frank Barnes	15	16	.484	41		20	3	238	278	34	61	3.67
Nicholas Harrison	11	11	.500	41		7	2	164	159	95	65	3.79
Art Smith	6	13	.316	29		14	0	174	214	52	36	4.76
Art Mills	5	6	.455	27		4	1	104	110	44	21	4.24
Warren Ogden	2	2	.500	19		1	0	65	79	22	18	5.12
Al Butzberger	2	5	.286	15		1	0	59	68	30	42	5.03
Elon Hogsett	2	6	.250	11		7	0	72	82	22	28	4.25
Robert Shanklin	0	0	----	5								
Eberbach	0	0	----	3								
Eurie Proffitt	0	0	----	2								

READING
Keystones

6th   79-88   .473   -21.5   Clarence Rowland

BATTERS	POS-GAMES	GP	AB	R	H	BI	2B	3B	HR	BB	SO	SB	BA
James Poole	1B166	166	621	100	190	126	40	4	24	71	61	6	.306
James Partridge	2B165	166	649	119	175	85	27	4	11	83	76	14	.270
James Adair	SS129	130	494	75	141	66	28	4	8	39	29	30	.285
William Conroy	3B129	144	448	58	122	71	39	0	6	63	41	2	.272
Wid Matthews	OF141	145	549	106	172	39	25	5	0	86	15	22	.313
Hobart Whitman	OF135	138	564	88	186	76	42	11	3	31	10	4	.330
George Quellich	OF	(see multi-team players)											
Louis Legett	C124	131	446	53	128	69	30	3	11	37	64	6	.287
Tony Krasovich	3B44,SS39	96	301	32	75	40	12	3	4	11	45	2	.249
Ernest Krueger	C60	83	193	17	56	27	10	1	2	11	24	0	.290
William Barrett	OF37	64	144	24	40	18	7	0	2	19	16	2	.278
Frank Doljack	OF59	59	223	42	64	49	11	5	3	23	36	13	.287
Clay Van Alstyne	P34	40	84	8	19	8	3	0	1	6	9	0	.226
George Kirsch	P38	40	65	7	13	1	3	0	0	8	20	1	.200
John Welch	P31	34	67	9	11	3	4	0	0	11	16	0	.164
Chet Howard	P30	34	60	10	12	8	3	0	0	3	20	1	.200
Frank Mulroney	P33	33	26	2	5	2	1	0	0	3	9	0	.192
Leslie Barnhart	P29	30	47	5	13	1	1	1	0	3	10	1	.277
John O'Keefe	P26	26	13	0	0	0	0	0	0	1	4	0	.000
Charles Willis	P22	22	50	4	9	2	0	0	0	3	10	0	.180

READING (cont.)
Keystones

BATTERS	POS-GAMES	GP	AB	R	H	BI	2B	3B	HR	BB	SO	SB	BA
Nelson Greene	P20	20	11	1	0	0	0	0	0	2	2	0	.000
Sollie Carter	P16	16	11	1	1	0	0	0	0	0	5	0	.091
Kemner	P2	5											.000
Ken Jones	P4	4											1.000
B. Jones		4											.231
Donlan		4											.000

PITCHERS		W	L	PCT	G	GS	CG	SH	IP	H	BB	SO	ERA
Clay Van Alstyne		17	7	.708	34		16	3	215	236	94	64	4.77
John Welch		15	11	.577	31		18	0	202	214	66	86	3.79
Chet Howard		9	10	.474	30		7	1	169	201	75	46	5.43
George Kirsch		8	11	.421	38		12	1	203	243	57	71	4.52
Leslie Barnhardt		6	7	.462	29		6	0	128	131	55	47	3.87
Frank Mulroney		5	4	.556	33		1	0	94	131	24	37	5.74
Charles Willis		5	9	.357	22		9	1	132	167	40	26	4.02
John O'Keefe		3	3	.500	26		1	0	57	76	12	10	6.16
Nelson Greene		3	6	.333	20		1	0	52	81	15	23	7.44
Kemner		2	0	1.000	2								
Sollie Carter		1	3	.250	16		0	0	38	53	13	9	6.39
Ken Jones		0	2	.000	4								

JERSEY CITY   7th   65-102   .389   -35.5   George Toporcer -
Skeeters   Robert Shawkey

BATTERS	POS-GAMES	GP	AB	R	H	BI	2B	3B	HR	BB	SO	SB	BA
John Clancy	1B167	167	625	80	195	93	33	4	13	46	28	6	.312
George Toporcer	2B		(see multi-team players)										.268
Clarke Pittenger	SS75	76	269	21	72	25	17	0	0	15	4	5	.268
Joseph Brown	3B113	130	495	69	151	36	25	2	1	54	17	12	.305
George Selkirk	OF158	159	557	82	173	84	31	6	14	75	63	7	.311
Max West	OF		(see multi-team players)										
Como Cotelle	OF		(see multi-team players)										
Boyce Morrow	C89	104	291	34	74	41	9	0	6	32	21	1	.254
William Hinchman	3B46,SS12	61	184	16	36	16	10	2	3	19	50	0	.196
Jack Shipley	SS49	49	188	25	47	9	3	0	0	18	18	6	.250
Francis Nekola	P38	46	80	9	17	3	2	1	0	7	21	0	.213
Maurice Walsh	C35	43	91	10	17	12	3	0	2	12	14	0	.187
Jimmy DeShong	P38	42	64	4	14	4	2	0	0	4	9	0	.219
Joseph Hartman	P40	40	28	3	3	1	0	0	0	2	5	0	.107
Norm Kies	C34	37	111	6	33	19	8	1	1	4	14	2	.297
Charles Perkins	P33	33	47	1	5	3	2	1	0	3	8	0	.106
Walter Brown	P30	31	75	5	16	5	4	0	0	1	17	1	.213
Grant Gillis	2B13	22	68	9	14	2	3	1	0	8	12	0	.206
Ivy Andrews	P21	22	43	1	3	0	0	0	0	0	2	0	.070
Kenner Graf	P22	22	12	1	2	1	0	0	0	2	3	0	.167
Art Young	OF19	20	66	7	11	7	3	0	0	12	5	1	.167
Curtis Fullerton	P16	16	19	1	2	4	0	0	0	1	4	0	.105
William Dressen	SS12	14	50	4	6	1	2	0	0	3	7	0	.120
George Miner	P13	14	34	1	8	1	1	0	0	0	7	0	.235
Joseph Dugan		12	22	1	3	1	0	0	0	3	2	0	.136
William Outen		11	19	3	7	6	1	1	1	8	1	1	.368
Berlyn Horne	P7	10	15	3	6	1	1	0	0	3	0	0	.400
Robert Shawkey		8											.125
John Pitts	P4	4											.438
Saving		3											.000
Dom Dallessandro		2											.125
Colbert		2											.000
Walsh	P1	1											.000

PITCHERS		W	L	PCT	G	GS	CG	SH	IP	H	BB	SO	ERA
Walter Brown		10	12	.455	30		16	2	203	190	84	118	2.88
Francis Nekola		10	14	.417	38		16	2	210	240	76	65	4.07
Jimmy DeShong		9	18	.333	38		11	3	197	231	85	67	4.84
Ivy Andrews		7	12	.368	21		7	2	130	131	49	45	4.29
George Miner		6	6	.500	13		8	0	87	82	36	32	4.45
Charles Perkins		4	9	.308	33		4	1	147	139	68	56	3.55
Kenner Graf		3	1	.750	22		0	0	57	63	28	17	5.84
Joseph Hartman		3	6	.333	40		0	0	94	89	49	27	3.83
Berlyn Horne		2	4	.333	7								
Curt Fullerton		1	6	.143	16		4	0	63	90	29	17	7.43

JERSEY CITY (cont.)
Skeeters

PITCHERS	W	L	PCT	G	GS	CG	SH	IP	H	BB	SO	ERA
Robert Shawkey	0	1	.000	7								
Walsh	0	1	.000	1								
John Pitts	0	2	.000	4								

BUFFALO   8th   61-105   .367   -39
Bisons

BATTERS	POS-GAMES	GP	AB	R	H	BI	2B	3B	HR	BB	SO	SB	BA
Russ Wrightstone	1B61	65	231	30	64	42	7	2	6	23	14	3	.277
Marvin Olson	2B160	160	596	80	174	68	27	4	1	76	45	6	.292
Warren Cote	SS140	143	524	50	146	54	19	5	3	24	37	5	.279
John Hughes	3B142	143	517	54	133	67	20	4	8	45	57	8	.257
Oliver Tucker	OF152	155	573	103	184	116	33	4	27	77	27	1	.321
Ralph Shinners	OF90	117	386	52	104	58	14	1	15	24	44	2	.269
Oliver Sax	OF86,3B30,SS12	146	507	98	144	36	24	3	6	78	47	19	.284
Clyde Crouse	C103	111	381	54	98	68	20	1	16	37	18	5	.257
Clarence Mueller	OF84,1B56	144	489	65	150	70	27	2	9	69	51	2	.307
Dewey Stover	OF82	124	307	51	80	28	10	5	1	52	26	7	.261
Frank Pytlak	C68	73	222	37	68	26	8	2	4	29	18	5	.306
John Michaels	P47	50	82	6	17	7	0	1	0	6	9	0	.207
John Wilson	P48	48	67	2	14	1	0	0	0	2	7	0	.209
William Gould	P48	48	51	2	7	4	2	0	0	3	17	0	.137
Charles Fitzberger	1B41	41	141	13	34	20	8	1	1	12	14	0	.241
Fred Fussell	P38	39	84	12	14	2	2	0	0	7	20	0	.167
Joseph Bloomer	P31	33	62	6	19	4	2	0	0	1	10	0	.306
Alex Ferguson	P20	20	22	1	5	1	0	0	0	1	5	0	.227
Henry Wertz	P18	18	7	0	0	0	0	0	0	0	2	0	.000
Ollie Carnegie	OF15	15	55	9	19	3	5	2	0	6	9	0	.345
George Grant	P14	14	29	3	3	5	1	0	0	3	13	0	.103
Dave Danforth	P14	14	17	0	2	0	0	0	0	2	13	0	.118
James Cooney	SS10	13	40	1	3	1	0	0	0	2	2	0	.075
Ernest Olsen		10	25	2	6	7	0	0	0	6	5	1	.240
Robert Ledbetter	P10	10	5	0	0	0	0	0	0	1	1	0	.000
Tony Plansky		7											.264
Al Reitz	P6	6											.000
Carl Schoof	P5	5											.308
Art Pfingstler	P5	5											.250
George Ferrell		5											.111
Bolton		5											.000
M. Brown		4											.500
Clarence Hoffman		4											.200
Roy Bergeron	P4	4											.000
Art Sondheim	P1	1											.000
Ruel Love	P1	1											.000
Henry Brewer	P1	1											.000

PITCHERS	W	L	PCT	G	GS	CG	SH	IP	H	BB	SO	ERA
John Michaels	13	8	.619	47		12	1	217	241	36	57	4.40
Fred Fussell	12	17	.417	38		16	2	232	287	76	119	4.81
John Wilson	9	18	.333	48		8	1	208	247	59	92	5.11
William Gould	8	17	.320	48		11	1	177	226	68	41	5.24
Joseph Bloomer	6	16	.273	31		8	0	175	223	62	41	5.55
George Grant	4	7	.364	14		4	1	74	110	35	18	7.30
Dave Danforth	3	6	.333	14		1	0	60	81	17	37	6.45
Al Reitz	1	0	1.000	6								
Carl Schoof	1	1	.500	5								
Henry Wertz	1	4	.200	18		0	0	39	43	19	10	6.00
Alex Ferguson	1	6	.143	20		2	0	68	86	32	37	5.43
Robert Ledbetter	0	1	.000	10		1	0	21	29	10	8	6.86
Ray Bergeron	0	1	.000	4								
Art Pfingstler	0	0	----	5								
Ruel Love	0	0	----	1								
Henry Brewer	0	0	----	1								
Ed Tomlin	0	0	----	1								
Art Sondheim	0	0	----	1								

MULTI-TEAM PLAYERS

BATTERS	POS-GAMES	TEAMS	GP	AB	R	H	BI	2B	3B	HR	BB	SO	SB	BA
James Jordan	2B149	RO80-JC69	149	588	78	162	37	29	4	4	34	21	5	.276
George Quellich	OF138	RE108-NE32	140	532	93	178	111	40	8	20	61	53	3	.335
Max West	OF121	JC117-NE21	138	464	59	113	68	24	2	5	49	23	6	.244
George Toporcer	2B132	JC83-RO53	136	498	81	138	52	25	3	2	63	24	10	.277
Harry Layne	OF98	NE60-JC45	105	369	49	97	38	10	6	2	37	20	21	.263
Charles Chatham	SS101	JC13-MO88	101	343	47	89	43	13	5	5	38	37	6	.259
Como Cotelle	OF80	RO15-JC76	91	306	43	94	44	21	1	5	19	15	4	.307
F. Walker	OF80	JC51-TO29	80	310	40	109	41	17	4	6	12	21	8	.352
Joseph Harris	1B42,OF19	BU9-TO65	74	222	32	69	38	12	5	4	32	15	1	.311
Robert Petrie	OF46,3B10	JC35-RE39	74	214	30	67	35	14	0	6	25	40	0	.313
Rufus Smith	P26	RO7JC33	40	48	3	10	3	0	2	0	3	16	0	.208
Earl Clark	OF31	JC21-NE17	38	119	19	38	11	4	2	0	16	7	2	.319
John Allen	P34	JC8-TO27	35	93	12	22	8	3	1	2	4	11	1	.237
Robert Munn	C30	BU5-BA1-JC26	32	95	6	22	4	5	1	0	10	17	0	.232
Clayton Sheedy	OF22	TO6-JC19	25	74	4	18	10	1	0	2	2	5	0	.243
Glenn Liebhardt	P25	RE1-TO24	25	32	1	5	0	0	0	0	2	12	0	.156
Martin Griffin	P20	MO6-RE14	20	39	5	6	1	1	0	1	2	11	0	.154
George Bell	P20	RE10-BU10	20	23	1	1	0	0	0	0	1	5	0	.043
Henry Grampp	P19	RE2-BU17	19	13	0	1	0	0	0	0	0	4	0	.077
Miller	P4	JC-RE	4											.000

PITCHERS		TEAMS	W	L	PCT	G	GS	CG	SH	IP	H	BB	SO	ERA
John Allen		JC7-TO27	21	9	.700	34		24	3	250	208	101	140	3.02
Martin Griffin		MO6-RE14	8	9	.471	20		7	0	103	141	56	22	6.03
Rufus Smith		RO5-JC21	7	8	.467	26		4	0	120	128	56	50	4.73
Glenn Liebhardt		RE1-TO24	6	5	.545	25		7	1	100	112	31	28	3.96
Henry Grampp		RE2-BU17	1	1	.500	19		0	0	50	70	23	12	6.48
George Bell		RE10-BU10	1	11	.083	20		2	0	83	113	53	30	7.37
Miller		JC-RE	0	0	----	4								

TEAM BATTING

TEAMS	GP	AB	R	H	BI	2B	3B	HR	BB	SO	SB	BA
ROCHESTER	**169**	5690	885	1615	834	298	83	78	556	499	53	.284
NEWARK	168	**5747**	802	**1642**	727	268	60	87	470	410	66	.286
BALTIMORE	168	5609	**899**	1577	**850**	283	60	**166**	**652**	**692**	78	.281
MONTREAL	166	5427	712	1458	642	279	40	54	522	559	70	.269
TORONTO	168	5505	734	1540	674	239	**90**	64	503	485	**122**	.280
READING	167	5661	856	1627	799	**328**	47	94	580	594	109	**.287**
JERSEY CITY	167	5531	659	1471	612	260	31	67	507	479	80	.266
BUFFALO	167	5514	744	1513	695	232	38	98	594	530	65	.274
	670	44684	6291	12443	5833	2187	449	708	4384	4248	643	.278

1932
THE COLONEL STEPS IN

During the 1920s, a new support structure for minor league teams was making its presence felt. This system, which benefited teams both small and large, was called the farm system. Its first master was Branch Rickey of the St. Louis Cardinals.

The farm system worked very simply. The major league team would buy a series of teams located at all minor league levels. The parent major league team could then shepherd its players up the ladder, weeding out the marginal, with only the best reaching the major league pinnacle. In turn, since they were owned outright by the major league team, minor league operators were not left to the vagaries of the baseball public to earn their living. In addition, major league teams could lend their excess talent to their top minor league clubs.

By the late 1920s, the St. Louis Cardinals were reaping the benefits of this system. The team won its first pennant in 1926, followed by more in 1928, 1930, and 1931. None of this was lost on other major league owners.

Colonel Ruppert, owner of the New York Yankees since 1923, had enjoyed phenomenal success as his team won several World Series. But by 1931, the team was suffering a dry spell. Ruppert took a look at the farm system set up by Rickey for the Cardinals and decided to follow suit. For the first link in the chain, Ruppert eyed the closest big city to New York that sported a team. In November 1931, the Yankees boss announced the purchase of the Newark Bears.

For many years, the Bears had been lumbering around in the second division. There had been a few first division finishes, but nothing consistent. This was all to change in 1932. With the addition of a dozen Yankees to the squad, the Newark Bears stormed to the title with their best record to date.

The Baltimore Orioles finished a distant second behind the Bears. Further back were Buffalo, Montreal, Rochester, Jersey City, Albany (who replaced the Reading team on August 6), and Toronto. George Puccinelli from Rochester had the highest average (.391). Oriole Russ Arlett made a serious try for the home run record, finishing with 54, accompanied by a league-best 144 runs batted in. (Note: Arlett twice enjoyed four-run games in 1932, a unique achievement.) Newark pitcher Don Brennan won the most games (26) and finished with the lowest earned run average (2.79). Baltimore's Beryl Richmond struck out the most batters (155).

The Yankees' association with the Newark Bears continued until the late 1940s. During that time, both the Yankees and Bears would prove dominant in their respective leagues, helping each other to nearly 20 titles. The relationship that Colonel Ruppert started in 1931 lived up to his expectations, and certainly proved the value of the farm system.

NEWARK Bears

1st   109-59   .649   Al Mamaux

BATTERS	POS-GAMES	GP	AB	R	H	BI	2B	3B	HR	BB	SO	SB	BA
John Neun	1B156	159	622	126	**212**	57	29	9	2	67	35	**25**	.341
Jack Saltzgaver	2B107	109	396	67	126	88	26	8	13	41	32	9	.318
Red Rolfe	SS145	147	585	96	193	75	36	13	8	36	41	17	.330
Marv Owen	3B	(see multi-team players)											
Jesse Hill	OF149	152	559	130	185	114	39	12	17	66	63	24	.331
Fred Walker	OF141	144	551	107	193	105	30	7	15	56	27	22	.350
Forrest Jensen	OF114	118	438	76	151	71	15	10	7	20	16	9	.345
Charles Hargreaves	C84,1B11	100	321	30	94	40	12	1	0	33	12	0	.293
Robert Barrett	3B83	98	303	39	85	34	11	1	2	29	20	3	.281
James Moore	OF61	68	222	31	65	40	16	1	7	21	17	1	.293
Andy Cohen	2B50	51	216	30	61	26	4	2	4	6	8	1	.282
George Miner	P46	46	29	2	4	2	1	0	0	0	9	0	.138
James Weaver	P44	44	55	5	8	6	1	0	1	3	19	0	.145
Don Brennan	P42	42	96	5	13	5	0	0	0	2	43	0	.135
Ed Phillips	C35	36	104	10	23	14	1	3	2	15	16	0	.221
Harry Holsclaw	P33	33	79	5	13	8	1	0	2	2	23	0	.165
Rufus Meadows	P27	27	55	3	8	2	1	0	0	0	13	0	.145
Norm Kies	C16	24	58	5	14	7	2	2	0	3	11	0	.241
Al Mamaux	P24	24	24	3	4	2	1	0	0	2	2	0	.167
William Brenzel	C22	22	68	4	15	9	2	1	1	4	4	0	.221
John Murphy	P16	21	41	7	7	1	0	0	1	1	15	0	.171
James Welch	P15	20	35	3	13	8	2	1	0	2	4	0	.371
Bill Zitzmann	OF13	18	46	12	11	10	1	0	3	7	1	0	.239
Milburn Shoffner	P9	16	12	1	2	1	0	0	1	0	4	0	.167
Byron Speece	P13	14	8	1	2	0	1	0	0	2	3	0	.250
Joseph Glenn	C10	13	31	3	8	5	0	0	1	7	5	0	.258
James Brillheart	P13	13	7	0	0	0	0	0	0	0	3	0	.000
Pete Jablonski	P12	12	40	6	12	2	1	0	1	0	4	0	.300
Thomas Padden		12	22	4	4	1	0	0	0	3	3	0	.182
Willard Hershberger	C10	11	33	5	7	7	1	1	0	2	4	0	.212
Robert Gibson		7											.250
Floyd Newkirk	P5	5											.250
Roy Sherid	P3	3											1.000
Vito Tamulis	P1	1											.000

PITCHERS		W	L	PCT	G	GS	CG	SH	IP	H	BB	SO	ERA
Don Brennan		**26**	8	.765	42		**21**	6	252	204	104	129	**2.79**
James Weaver		15	6	.714	44		4	1	160	150	80	137	3.83
Harry Holsclaw		14	11	.560	33		14	3	218	237	48	114	3.43
Pete Jablonski		11	1	**.917**	12		9	1	94	94	29	44	3.73
Rufus Meadows		9	6	.600	27		7	1	143	138	74	46	4.53
John Murphy		6	7	.462	25		7	0	122	151	45	43	4.20
Al Mamaux		5	1	.833	24		3	0	81	72	18	40	2.56
George Miner		5	3	.625	46		0	0	111	96	44	68	3.24
James Welch		5	6	.455	15		3	0	83	110	35	47	5.42
Milburn Shoffner		2	0	1.000	9								
Roy Sherid		1	0	1.000	3								
Vito Tamulis		1	0	1.000	1								
James Brillheart		1	1	.500	13		0	0	20	20	11	10	4.95
Byron Speece		1	1	.500	13		0	0	19	28	10	4	8.05
Floyd Newkirk		1	1	.500	5								
MarvinDuke		0	1	.000	1								

BALTIMORE Orioles

2nd   93-74   .557   -15.5   Fritz Maisel

BATTERS	POS-GAMES	GP	AB	R	H	BI	2B	3B	HR	BB	SO	SB	BA
Baxter Jordan	1B118	118	493	98	176	105	31	10	19	35	15	6	.357
William Regan	2B95,3B15,1B14	135	490	93	138	86	35	8	27	44	61	1	.282
John Sand	SS156	157	546	71	152	101	34	3	15	69	61	3	.278
Frank Packard	3B81,OF61	147	528	103	165	98	25	5	28	62	78	5	.313
Frank McGowan	OF162	162	583	131	185	35	31	5	37	112	53	15	.317
Ralph Boyle	OF149	153	617	132	194	62	36	11	9	84	62	7	.314
Russ Arlett	OF133	147	516	**141**	175	**144**	33	4	**54**	112	61	11	.339
Gordon Hinkle	C70	79	257	42	77	42	16	1	7	18	32	0	.300
Don Heffner	2B80,3B17	122	402	85	118	53	20	5	15	44	46	2	.294
Harry Smythe	P53	54	79	8	20	15	4	0	2	5	15	0	.253
Claude Linton	C41	46	145	16	41	20	9	1	4	13	15	0	.283
Walt Tauscher	P44	46	85	12	24	8	5	1	1	0	13	0	.282
Bill Akers	3B36	45	153	25	46	26	8	2	3	27	18	4	.301

BALTIMORE (cont.)
Orioles

BATTERS	POS-GAMES	GP	AB	R	H	BI	2B	3B	HR	BB	SO	SB	BA
Beryl Richmond	P43	43	71	4	4	1	0	0	0	6	37	0	.056
Al Bool	C31	41	121	16	31	19	6	1	3	7	15	1	.256
Ken Holloway	P37	37	69	4	10	6	1	0	0	2	7	0	.145
James Stroner	3B23	35	97	15	31	22	7	1	4	9	8	2	.320
Richard Goldberg	1B26	33	108	13	29	18	4	0	1	8	7	1	.269
Merritt Cain	P30	33	75	6	16	7	1	0	1	5	26	0	.213
Harry Gumbert	P27	27	26	2	5	0	0	0	0	1	9	0	.192
Cliff Melton	P23	23	20	0	2	0	0	0	0	0	7	0	.100
Ed Kenna	C22	22	71	9	15	11	3	0	1	13	7	0	.211
Bruce Cunningham	P11	11	24	6	7	5	2	0	1	3	5	0	.292
Jack Hopkins	P9	9											.083
Swingler		6											.250
Tarr		3											.000
Mattox		2											.400
Ike Danning		2											.250
Taylor		1											.500
W. Moore		1											.000
Murdock	P1	1											.000

PITCHERS	W	L	PCT	G	GS	CG	SH	IP	H	BB	SO	ERA
Harry Smythe	17	12	.583	53		6	2	214	251	72	70	4.88
Merritt Cain	16	5	.762	30		15	2	185	179	85	118	4.18
Walt Tauscher	13	9	.591	44		12	0	216	264	70	61	5.67
Ken Holloway	13	13	.500	37		15	0	204	225	48	52	5.29
Beryl Richmond	12	14	.462	43		10	2	205	223	129	155	5.49
Harry Gumbert	7	4	.636	27		1	0	76	84	37	23	5.33
Bruce Cunningham	6	3	.667	11		5	0	64	70	21	24	5.06
Jack Hopkins	2	0	1.000	9								
Cliff Melton	0	4	.000	23		1	0	60	78	32	46	6.45
Murdock	0	0	----	1								

BUFFALO	3rd	91-75	.548	-17	Ray Schalk

Bisons

BATTERS	POS-GAMES	GP	AB	R	H	BI	2B	3B	HR	BB	SO	SB	BA
John Smith	1B123,2B15	147	575	110	172	51	28	7	3	74	47	8	.299
Otis Miller	2B112	122	447	83	146	70	32	2	10	54	24	6	.327
Bill Werber	SS93	117	422	75	122	62	16	7	17	48	44	24	.289
George Detore	3B155	157	590	132	187	97	39	4	24	89	47	8	.317
Oliver Tucker	OF154	157	585	117	187	120	52	1	21	81	40	1	.320
Ollie Carnegie	OF133	137	508	116	169	140	31	3	36	40	66	1	.333
John Winsett	OF101	109	365	66	128	81	15	6	18	27	64	6	.351
Clyde Crouse	C112	121	374	58	101	48	18	1	15	51	42	4	.270
John Ryan	SS77,2B46	131	455	57	120	55	17	2	10	20	69	9	.264
Clarence Mueller	OF98	124	356	61	102	72	16	1	10	38	34	3	.287
Eugene Hargrave	C65	83	239	43	89	60	21	3	10	30	13	3	.372
John Wilson	P46	47	49	3	9	1	0	0	0	1	7	0	.184
Henry Brewer	P44	44	82	7	17	5	4	1	0	3	33	0	.207
Joseph Bloomer	P35	42	71	8	11	3	1	0	0	4	7	0	.155
Joseph Bartulis	P37	37	42	6	6	2	0	0	0	4	12	0	.143
Fred Fussell	P33	36	63	10	10	5	1	0	0	7	23	0	.158
William Gould	P32	33	62	2	13	6	1	0	0	6	17	0	.210
Hod Lisenbee	P25	25	27	2	7	1	1	0	0	1	6	0	.259
Cecil Caraway	P18	18	28	2	4	0	0	0	0	0	3	0	.143
Roy Bergeron	P17	17	16	2	3	3	1	0	0	6	6	0	.188
George Ferrell	OF11	14	36	6	11	2	4	0	1	1	2	0	.306
Art Pfingstler	P12	13	16	2	4	1	1	0	1	0	7	0	.250
John Hughes		7											.071
Dave Danforth	P4	4											.000
Carl Schoof	P3	3											.000
Joe Rabbitt		2											.000
Ray Schalk		1											.667
Jack Quinlan		1											.000

PITCHERS	W	L	PCT	G	GS	CG	SH	IP	H	BB	SO	ERA
Henry Brewer	17	12	.586	44		11	0	215	266	84	111	4.65
Fred Fussell	15	8	.652	33		17	3	183	207	39	66	4.57
William Gould	13	8	.619	32		14	2	188	188	53	64	4.07
Joseph Bloomer	13	12	.520	35		16	1	214	232	75	51	4.29
Joseph Bartulis	8	4	.667	37		2	1	131	123	71	50	3.57

BUFFALO (cont.)
Bisons

PITCHERS	W	L	PCT	G	GS	CG	SH	IP	H	BB	SO	ERA
John Wilson	7	14	.333	46		3	1	150	170	40	87	4.56
Hod Lisenbee	6	6	.500	25		5	0	88	121	21	53	5.93
Roy Bergeron	4	5	.444	17		4	1	65	78	41	19	6.92
Art Pfingstler	3	0	1.000	12		2	0	38	41	17	18	3.55
Cecil Caraway	2	5	.286	18		1	0	74	88	22	27	3.89
Carl Schoof	1	0	1.000	3								
Dave Danforth	0	0	----	4								

MONTREAL   4th   90-78   .536   -19   Ed Holly -
Royals   Walt Gautreau

BATTERS	POS-GAMES	GP	AB	R	H	BI	2B	3B	HR	BB	SO	SB	BA
Oscar Roettger	1B92	92	360	45	111	61	19	1	7	16	23	1	.308
Walt Gautreau	2B148	151	555	103	173	49	37	7	0	99	34	22	.312
Herb Thomas	SS98,2B24,3B11	142	506	68	155	72	36	7	5	35	25	3	.306
William Walters	3B118	123	405	54	105	50	24	3	10	38	69	9	.259
Ivey Shiver	OF150	152	531	95	166	110	33	16	27	82	87	17	.313
James Ripple	OF148	153	563	99	179	100	35	5	21	59	70	15	.318
John Conlan	OF95	112	353	50	100	31	22	5	2	23	24	11	.283
George Susce	C70	71	231	21	54	32	12	0	3	10	16	0	.234
John Grabowski	C62	67	186	25	39	14	10	0	2	25	30	0	.210
Al Head	C52	64	196	25	50	31	9	3	1	12	7	1	.255
Ed Moore	SS45	48	167	23	49	23	9	0	1	16	7	6	.293
Gowell Claset	P47	47	97	5	13	7	3	2	0	9	35	0	.134
Thomas Gulley	OF32	44	130	15	30	15	4	0	3	9	10	3	.231
John Pomorski	P43	44	57	3	17	3	0	0	0	1	16	0	.298
Walt Brannon	P30	41	51	6	14	8	3	0	2	3	11	0	.275
Clarence Fisher	P37	37	25	1	5	3	0	0	0	2	6	0	.200
Walter Brown	P31	31	67	7	11	9	0	0	0	6	15	0	.164
Shaw Buck	3B18	30	74	5	12	13	0	1	1	2	6	2	.162
William McAfee	P23	28	58	5	12	4	1	0	1	1	17	0	.207
Ed Marshall	SS25	25	100	8	25	12	1	1	0	1	6	3	.250
Leo Mangum	P19	19	50	6	12	4	3	0	0	4	5	0	.240
Roland Gladu		15	17	5	4	4	0	0	1	1	1	0	.235
Peter Beam	P10	10	5	0	1	0	0	0	0	0	4	0	.200
Sumner Collingwood	P8	9											.500
LeRoy Parmelee	P6	9											.105
Paiment		8											.261
Haines		4											.143
Orville Jorgens	P2	2											.00

PITCHERS	W	L	PCT	G	GS	CG	SH	IP	H	BB	SO	ERA
Gowell Claset	23	13	.639	47		16	3	282	280	144	115	3.57
John Pomorski	13	11	.542	43		10	4	166	196	62	61	5.04
Walter Brown	12	11	.522	31		15	2	208	215	94	108	3.68
Leo Mangum	10	7	.588	19		13	1	146	177	25	46	3.51
Clarence Fisher	8	7	.533	37		2	0	92	108	33	35	4.70
Wiliam McAfee	8	9	.471	23		11	0	136	148	51	33	4.70
Walt Brannon	3	5	.375	30		1	0	105	122	47	26	5.57
LeRoy Parmelee	2	3	.400	6								
Sumner Collingwood	1	0	1.000	8								
Peter Beam	0	2	.000	10		0	0	19	19	14	15	3.32
Orville Jorgens	0	0	----	2								

ROCHESTER   5th   88-79   .527   -20.5   Billy Southworth -
Red Wings   George Toporcer

BATTERS	POS-GAMES	GP	AB	R	H	BI	2B	3B	HR	BB	SO	SB	BA
Robert Parham	1B48,OF30	85	262	60	79	39	15	6	5	37	37	7	.302
George Toporcer	2B167	167	655	103	195	77	38	7	1	84	30	15	.298
Charles Wilson	SS113	123	439	73	131	69	27	4	9	25	32	12	.298
Joseph Brown	3B	(see multi-team players)											
George Puccinelli	OF131	133	478	102	187	115	34	8	28	79	60	2	.391
Ray Pepper	OF112	112	457	49	136	85	25	14	9	15	54	5	.298
Leon Riley	OF71	78	257	28	71	36	9	5	6	32	20	8	.277
Paul Florence	C110	115	344	47	88	51	16	0	8	41	27	0	.256
Ira Smith	P36,3B10	64	131	17	38	18	13	2	0	9	11	9	.290

ROCHESTER (cont.)
Red Wings

BATTERS	POS-GAMES	GP	AB	R	H	BI	2B	3B	HR	BB	SO	SB	BA
Al Moore	OF34	59	151	23	47	23	6	0	2	17	11	3	.311
James Shevlin	1B48	57	164	30	45	22	11	3	0	23	11	5	.274
Tony Kaufmann	OF24,P22	52	128	19	32	15	6	2	1	11	13	0	.250
George Fisher	OF48	49	189	34	54	29	15	1	6	16	11	2	.286
Art Teachout	P42	47	82	6	20	3	1	0	0	4	11	1	.244
Delano Wetherell	P45	45	54	6	13	5	2	1	0	1	10	0	.241
James Winford	P41	43	57	8	9	5	1	0	0	7	23	0	.158
Billy Southworth	OF31	42	118	16	26	21	1	2	1	10	5	1	.220
Al Eckert	P42	42	58	7	9	6	0	0	0	13	21	0	.155
Roscoe Holm	OF21,3B17	41	135	22	42	11	8	1	0	19	4	2	.311
George Rensa	C36	39	115	14	23	11	7	0	0	9	4	0	.200
Ed Kunes	3B32	37	130	13	30	10	6	2	2	12	17	0	.231
Minor Heath	1B34	36	116	17	31	18	7	1	7	18	18	1	.267
William Myers	SS29	33	103	14	23	13	2	2	1	12	22	3	.223
William Kluch	SS11	21	65	11	16	4	5	0	0	13	8	0	.246
Colonel Mills	OF14	15	50	9	18	8	3	3	1	2	9	0	.360
Harlan Wysong	P11	13	26	2	5	4	4	0	0	0	5	0	.192
Art Newsome	P11	11	8	0	4	2	1	0	0	0	1	0	.500
Lawrence Barton	1B10	10	31	1	3	1	0	1	0	3	4	1	.097
Nick Cullop	OF	9	30	5	8	4	3	0	1			0	.267
Bill Sherdel	P8	9											.000
Klinger	P6	6											.333
Heise	P6	6											.300
Hubbell		5											.231
Jenkins		4											.235
Dykes Potter	P3	3											.333
Fred Ostermueller	P2	3											.250
Pickett		3											.200
Kirchen		1											.500

PITCHERS	W	L	PCT	G	GS	CG	SH	IP	H	BB	SO	ERA
Ira Smith	16	10	.615	36		14	0	193	232	39	70	4.15
Art Teachout	14	7	.667	42		15	0	221	250	56	85	4.15
Al Eckert	12	12	.500	42		11	1	193	220	73	54	4.66
Delano Wetherell	11	9	.550	45		3	1	154	161	47	49	3.51
Tony Kaufman	10	8	.556	22		9	2	121	131	39	34	4.46
Raymond Starr	9	12	.429	33		7	1	186	186	94	75	5.08
James Winford	8	10	.444	41		8	1	183	169	117	144	3.64
Art Newsome	2	0	1.000	11		0	0	23	23	19	7	6.26
Dykes Potter	2	0	1.000	3								
Harlan Wysong	2	4	.333	11		3	0	57	70	21	25	4.89
Bill Sherdel	1	2	.333	8								
Klinger	0	1	.000	6								
Heise	0	1	.000	6								
Fred Ostermueller	0	0	----	2								

JERSEY CITY   6th   73-94   .437   -35.5   Hans Lobert -
Skeeters   Charles Moore

BATTERS	POS-GAMES	GP	AB	R	H	BI	2B	3B	HR	BB	SO	SB	BA
John Clancy	1B111	111	436	77	134	88	27	3	13	31	18	9	.307
James Jordan	2B95,3B17,P1	131	449	70	131	63	21	5	11	25	37	8	.292
John Warner	SS107	119	422	46	105	45	23	1	4	33	31	7	.249
Robert Reis	3B107	117	386	57	97	63	18	3	11	46	49	7	.251
Ike Boone	OF135	135	491	102	157	95	29	4	16	84	21	9	.320
Clyde Barnhart	OF113	139	429	63	137	78	15	4	6	75	30	9	.319
Len Koenecke	OF88	95	355	80	126	65	15	9	18	48	21	12	.355
William Outen	C96	128	344	66	116	86	17	5	15	76	27	5	.337
Lafayette Thompson	2B51,SS48	102	401	90	120	52	25	9	10	49	18	19	.299
Joseph Moore	OF64	64	266	42	83	37	23	0	6	8	14	6	.312
Albert Cohen	OF52	58	189	36	47	18	13	4	0	34	14	3	.249
George Kelly	1B44	47	153	18	45	31	10	0	6	12	21	1	.294
Charles Perkins	P46	46	93	11	26	11	3	0	2	4	7	0	.280
Dennis Sothern	OF27	38	98	18	26	7	3	0	0	8	14	10	.265
Ed Pipgras	P36	36	47	6	15	4	1	0	1	0	6	0	.319
Art Veltman	C30	32	91	12	16	8	2	0	2	3	4	1	.176
Art Jones	P29	29	37	4	5	3	0	0	0	2	11	1	.135
Clarke Pittenger	SS16	24	55	9	11	9	0	0	2	3	1	1	.200
Earl Mattingly	P23	23	36	1	3	0	0	0	0	1	8	1	.083
Como Cotelle	OF21	22	76	7	19	10	5	2	0	3	4	4	.250
Charles Niebergall	C18	18	52	5	13	3	3	0	0	9	5	0	.250

JERSEY CITY (cont.)
Skeeters

BATTERS	POS-GAMES	GP	AB	R	H	BI	2B	3B	HR	BB	SO	SB	BA
John Krider	P18	18	17	1	1	1	0	0	0	1	5	0	.059
Boyce Morrow		15	29	2	9	2	2	0	0	5	3	0	.310
Russ White	P14	14	13	1	4	1	1	0	0	1	2	0	.308
Laurence Irvin	P13	14	13	0	4	2	1	0	0	0	4	0	.308
Harry Layne	OF11	13	31	2	6	3	0	0	2	1	8	1	.194
Les Sweetland	P10	13	20	0	2	0	0	0	0	0	1	0	.100
William Greene	P5	13	8	1	2	2	0	0	0	0	1	0	.250
Peter Donohue	P11	12	27	1	5	2	1	0	0	0	6	0	.185
Austin Moore	P12	12	26	1	2	0	0	0	0	0	7	0	.077
Phil Gallivan	P11	12	13	0	1	1	0	0	0	0	2	0	.077
Ed Fallenstein	P8	10	9	2	1	1	0	0	0	0	3	0	.111
McCluskey	P3	5											.375
Stryker	P5	5											.000
Lucas	P5	5											.000
Graf	P3	3											.500
Hargrove	P2	2											.000

PITCHERS	W	L	PCT	G	GS	CG	SH	IP	H	BB	SO	ERA
Charles Perkins	14	11	.560	46		11	1	247	276	129	106	5.03
Ed Pipgras	12	6	.667	36		10	2	135	148	30	52	3.67
Art Jones	6	9	.400	29		7	0	116	141	67	47	6.83
Austin Moore	5	4	.556	12		4	0	60	71	28	31	5.40
Earl Mattingly	5	6	.455	23		3	0	103	115	37	26	5.16
Pete Donohue	4	4	.500	11		6	0	70	79	19	25	4.50
Les Sweetland	3	2	.600	10		0	0	38	54	17	10	6.39
Lucas	2	2	.500	5								
John Krider	2	4	.333	18		1	0	51	70	29	16	7.41
Phil Gallivan	2	4	.333	11		1	0	39	58	15	20	7.15
William Greene	1	1	.500	5								
Russ White	1	2	.333	14		0	0	37	42	16	14	5.35
McCluskey	0	1	.000	3								
Hargrove	0	1	.000	2								
Ed Fallenstein	0	2	.000	8								
Laurence Irvin	0	5	.000	13		1	0	36	40	13	7	5.25
Stryker	0	0	----	5								
Graf	0	0	----	3								
Jordan	0	0	----	1								

READING / ALBANY   7th   71-97   .423   -38   Clarence Rowland
Keystones / Senators

BATTERS	POS-GAMES	GP	AB	R	H	BI	2B	3B	HR	BB	SO	SB	BA
Harry Taylor	1B125	125	506	75	150	57	28	5	2	33	34	15	.296
James Partridge	2B132	145	519	84	125	49	19	6	10	65	47	13	.241
Tony Krasovich	SS127	132	447	38	118	68	28	1	4	19	49	4	.264
Lester Bell	3B123	123	465	89	129	94	23	9	19	50	59	5	.277
Hobart Whitman	OF150	158	628	103	203	52	39	8	3	34	5	8	.323
Vince Barton	OF99	105	384	57	113	70	18	4	18	32	34	8	.294
George Quellich	OF94	105	355	51	111	53	26	5	9	31	32	1	.313
Louis Legett	C91	102	313	46	92	52	18	2	14	25	37	3	.294
Ernest Krueger	C82	86	261	25	74	29	14	1	5	22	26	4	.284
Lance Richbourg	OF70	75	272	50	101	44	19	9	3	13	21	9	.371
Emery Zumbro	P47	47	36	4	6	2	1	0	0	2	6	0	.167
Don Curry	SS42	43	135	17	35	15	8	1	0	21	18	1	.259
George Milstead	P38	40	70	7	12	7	1	0	1	9	25	1	.171
Norm McMillan	2B20,3B12	38	130	23	41	20	11	1	2	16	10	2	.315
Charles Willis	P33	37	72	8	16	8	3	0	0	2	15	0	.222
Carroll Yerkes	P35	35	72	0	3	0	0	0	0	2	20	0	.042
Bobo Newsome	P34	34	51	3	7	3	2	0	0	1	10	0	.137
Chet Fowler	3B23	32	103	7	24	8	5	1	0	5	9	6	.233
James Horn	OF14	29	80	15	16	4	3	1	1	14	10	4	.200
Al Shealy	P25	26	57	10	12	10	2	0	2	2	16	0	.211
Clay Van Alstyne	P26	26	49	8	12	7	1	2	1	6	3	0	.245
Paul McCarron	OF11	23	50	9	15	8	4	0	2	6	8	0	.300
Russ Miller	P19	19	18	2	4	1	0	1	1	2	4	0	.222
Herschel Bennett	OF14	17	59	6	14	7	2	3	1	2	4	1	.237
Richard Stahlman		17	31	4	9	6	5	0	0	4	0	1	.290
Merle Campbell	P15	15	28	2	9	2	0	0	0	1	1	0	.321
Charles Gooch	3B11	11	42	7	13	3	1	0	0	6	4	0	.310
Bramhall		8											.200
Adams	P8	8											.000

READING / ALBANY (cont.)
Keystones / Senators

BATTERS	POS-GAMES	GP	AB	R	H	BI	2B	3B	HR	BB	SO	SB	BA
George Kirsch	P6	7											.250
Leslie Barnhart	P5	5											.300
James Wiltse	P5	5											.167
Lawson	P3	3											.000
Ivy Andrews	P3	3											.000
Chet Howard		1											1.000
Charles Schesler	P1	1											.000

PITCHERS		W	L	PCT	G	GS	CG	SH	IP	H	BB	SO	ERA
Al Shealy		11	11	.500	25		13	0	152	165	65	71	4.86
Charles Willis		11	12	.478	33		10	0	179	225	48	35	4.88
George Milstead		10	17	.370	38		14	2	225	269	77	93	4.56
Carroll Yerkes		10	17	.370	35		15	3	210	233	70	65	4.50
Bobo Newsome		7	7	.500	34		4	1	145	454	80	84	5.28
Emery Zumbro		6	5	.545	47		2	0	135	184	48	30	4.87
Clay Van Alstyne		6	11	.353	26		6	0	136	193	74	29	9.26
Russ Miller		5	2	.714	19		1	0	60	76	18	16	5.40
Merle Campbell		4	6	.400	15		5	0	81	79	24	29	3.67
Leslie Barnhart		1	3	.250	5								
Adams		0	1	.000	8								
George Kirsch		0	1	.000	6								
Lawson		0	1	.000	3								
Ivy Andrews		0	2	.000	2								
James Wiltse		0	0	----	5								
Beckman		0	0	----	1								
Chet Howard		0	0	----	1								
J. Boone		0	0	----	1								

TORONTO   8th   54-113   .323   -54.5   Thomas Daly -
Maple Leafs   Lena Blackburne

BATTERS	POS-GAMES	GP	AB	R	H	BI	2B	3B	HR	BB	SO	SB	BA
Fred Henry	1B		(see multi-team players)										
Ray Morehart	2B43	44	144	16	27	9	7	1	0	19	13	2	.188
Stewart Clarke	SS82	82	290	40	63	30	14	9	5	35	44	2	.217
John Michaels	3B68	72	244	26	67	36	11	0	4	19	24	2	.275
Al Wingo	OF78	78	253	26	64	33	11	3	4	45	31	1	.253
Bill Lawrence	OF61	62	236	36	72	18	9	4	0	17	19	8	.305
Murray Howell	OF57	60	237	29	70	36	16	5	6	10	11	2	.295
Richard Smith	C85	96	288	35	71	34	12	1	5	16	32	4	.247
Oliver Sax	3B47,SS21,OF19,2B16	108	366	57	88	20	23	1	0	66	42	6	.240
John Rothrock	OF36,3B23,2B14	79	278	48	91	25	14	3	1	25	19	6	.327
Thomas Daly	C45	60	173	9	38	14	4	0	0	11	7	0	.220
Guy Cantrell	P41	45	101	10	33	18	9	0	2	0	16	0	.327
James Hughes	OF36	37	124	16	35	15	6	3	1	14	12	3	.282
James Calleran	3B23,2B14	37	116	12	14	7	0	1	0	18	14	2	.120
Art Smith	P28	35	73	5	14	5	1	0	0	3	13	0	.192
William Dreeson	2B34	34	125	23	35	12	2	7	1	24	10	0	.280
Earl Cook	P33	33	44	1	1	0	0	0	0	0	9	0	.023
Harold Anderson	OF27	27	100	10	20	6	6	0	1	13	2	2	.200
Art McHenry	OF20	25	73	5	18	7	1	0	1	3	9	0	.247
John Poser	OF15	23	64	2	11	4	2	1	0	5	11	0	.172
Fred Maguire	2B22	22	74	4	16	6	2	2	0	1	3	1	.216
Ray Fitzgerald	OF16	16	57	11	17	6	0	0	1	7	6	2	.298
Rip Sewell	P11	14	22	2	8	3	2	0	0	1	3	0	.364
Jerome Abberbock	P13	13	27	1	4	1	1	0	0	1	10	0	.148
Herb Thormahlen	P12	13	20	3	2	1	0	0	0	0	6	0	.100
William McGill		11	8	1	0	0	0	0	0	4	6	0	.000
Art Mills	P8	9											.000
McKain	P5	6											.077
Al Butzberger	P5	5											.250
Lena Blackburne		5											.167
Hunt		3											.273
John Milligan	P3	3											.000
W. Miller	P1	1											.000

PITCHERS		W	L	PCT	G	GS	CG	SH	IP	H	BB	SO	ERA
Guy Cantrell		14	17	.452	41		20	1	251	319	92	109	4.80
Art Smith		11	13	.458	28		21	3	205	198	61	44	3.64

TORONTO (cont.)
Maple Leafs

PITCHERS	W	L	PCT	G	GS	CG	SH	IP	H	BB	SO	ERA
Rip Sewell	3	6	.333	11		4	1	57	62	21	14	4.42
Herb Thormahlen	3	7	.300	12		4	0	57	63	23	12	5.37
Jerome Abberbock	3	8	.273	13		6	0	79	71	52	35	4.78
Earl Cook	1	8	.111	33		3	0	133	162	52	53	5.75
Art Mills	0	0	----	8								
McKain	1	3	.250	5								
Al Butzberger	0	0	----	5								
John Poser	0	2	.000	5								
Waldo Yarnall	0	0	----	4								
Milligan	0	1	.000	3								
E. Johnson	0	0	----	1								
W. Miller	0	0	----	1								

MULTI-TEAM PLAYERS

BATTERS	POS-GAMES	TEAMS	GP	AB	R	H	BI	2B	3B	HR	BB	SO	SB	BA
Fred Henry	1B161	MO76-TO86	162	569	58	163	77	34	6	6	36	40	8	.287
Marv Owen	3B86,SS66,2B10	TO45-NE115	160	587	103	186	92	38	14	11	55	47	13	.317
Harvey Walker	OF123,3B25	TO49-MO100	149	522	95	136	42	27	10	4	90	74	11	.261
Joseph Brown	3B140	JC38-RO110	148	575	94	159	60	34	6	4	67	23	17	.277
James Poole	1B85	R/A39-BU59	98	300	39	91	64	17	2	15	38	37	1	.304
Fred Bennett	OF84	R/A70-BU24	94	299	52	97	66	26	0	11	43	30	6	.324
George Selkirk	OF84	NE36-TO54	90	310	50	89	61	13	5	11	41	55	11	.287
Claude Jonnard	C74	RO47-JC31	78	198	23	52	25	7	4	1	23	7	0	.263
Bill Hunnefield	2B47,SS20	JC27-R/A19-RO28	74	259	39	69	36	12	1	4	21	19	4	.266
Raymond Fritz	1B58	TO58-MO2	60	232	27	57	39	7	4	7	10	18	8	.246
Peter Stack	C48	TO47-JC12	59	173	11	42	22	6	2	0	13	8	2	.243
Frank Doljack	OF48	TO44-NE12-R/A2	58	174	22	38	26	8	2	6	16	18	6	.218
Willis Windle	1B54	RO36-TO19	55	183	27	41	23	9	0	3	26	15	8	.224
Joseph Cascarella	P42	BA6-JC37	43	50	2	7	2	0	0	0	3	10	3	.140
Charles Foreman	P41	RO9-BA32	41	33	3	8	0	3	0	0	0	8	0	.242
Glenn Liebhardt	P40	TO27-BA13	40	62	1	5	2	0	0	0	2	26	0	.081
Frank Barnes	P39	TO19-MO20	39	55	8	18	11	3	0	0	7	3	1	.327
Robert Stevens	SS29	NE17-TO20	37	109	12	25	12	1	0	1	8	8	5	.229
Jack Shipley	2B25	TO25-JC11	36	117	14	31	10	3	0	0	5	7	0	.265
Warren Ogden	P34	JC17-MO17	34	68	3	13	10	2	0	0	4	9	0	.191
Charles Sullivan	P32	MO11-TO22	33	75	5	14	6	0	0	1	0	13	0	.187
Francis Nekola	P25	TO6-NE19	25	42	4	8	2	0	0	0	1	14	0	.190
Ray Walker	P16	BA2-TO17	19	28	4	11	2	2	0	0	1	4	0	.393
James Chaplin	P16	BA4-JC13	17	29	3	6	4	1	0	0	0	4	0	.207
Nicholas Hanson	P15	BU9-JC6	15	16	1	3	1	0	0	0	2	4	0	.188
Willard Morrell	P12	JC10-BU2	12	18	2	2	1	0	0	0	1	5	0	.111

PITCHERS		TEAMS	W	L	PCT	G	GS	CG	SH	IP	H	BB	SO	ERA
Warren Ogden		JC17-MO17	11	13	.458	34		14	2	205	224	71	73	4.57
Charles Sullivan		MO10-TO22	9	12	.429	32		12	0	161	193	88	62	5.09
Frank Barnes		TO19-MO20	9	14	.391	39		12	3	184	241	47	58	4.94
Glenn Liebhardt		TO27-BA13	7	15	.318	40		8	1	185	234	61	69	5.40
Charle s Foreman		RO9-BA32	6	6	.500	41		0	0	108	139	74	43	7.00
Francis Nekola		TO6-NE19	6	11	.353	25		7	0	122	151	45	43	4.20
Joseph Cascarella		BA6-JC36	4	12	.250	42		4	1	169	197	110	104	5.38
Nicholas Harrison		BU9-JC6	3	2	.600	15		0	0	43	53	19	8	5.86
James Chaplin		BA4-JC12	2	6	.250	16		2	1	73	98	38	18	6.29
Ray Walker		BA1-TO15	2	7	.222	16		6	0	79	90	40	34	5.35
Willard Morrell		JC10-BU2	1	7	.125	12		1	0	62	67	26	21	6.53

TEAM BATTING

TEAMS	GP	AB	R	H	BI	2B	3B	HR	BB	SO	SB	BA
NEWARK	**168**	5726	933	**1740**	856	270	**86**	103	500	517	**132**	**.304**
BALTIMORE	**168**	5663	**1036**	1673	**981**	314	58	**232**	**690**	**693**	59	.295
BUFFALO	166	5693	1010	1705	954	**317**	38	192	619	654	75	.299
MONTREAL	**168**	5521	790	1533	732	306	59	92	545	605	107	.278
ROCHESTER	**168**	5737	861	1630	817	306	75	96	605	546	88	.284
JERSEY CITY	167	5608	902	1583	833	278	51	128	618	456	121	.282
REA/ALB	**168**	5735	821	1606	754	313	60	111	490	554	94	.280
TORONTO	167	5347	626	1328	567	228	63	60	510	591	83	.248
	670	45030	6979	12798	6494	2332	490	1014	4577	4616	759	.284

1933
GOVERNOR'S CUP

In 1892, the Eastern League briefly experimented with a post-season playoff. Coming after a split season, it pitted the two half-season winners, Binghamton and Providence, in a best-of-seven series. More than 40 years later, the International League reinstituted the playoffs, this time using a different format.

To boost sagging attendance caused by the Great Depression, baseball adopted several measures. One idea was a playoff system in which several teams could participate, thus keeping interest in the races for the coveted post-season spots. This idea sparked interest in the International League, no doubt because it was the brainchild of league executive Frank Shaughnessy.

Frank Shaughnessy, general manager of the Montreal Royals, formulated his playoff plan in 1933. The top four teams would meet in a three-of-five playoff series. The winners would then square off for the title using a best-of-seven format.

In the 1933 International League, the playoff plan worked as advertised when a battle royal ensued for the last playoff spot. In the end, Buffalo claimed fourth place by a half-game over Toronto and Montreal in fifth and sixth, and by one over Albany in seventh. Meanwhile, the top three spots were taken by Newark, Rochester, and Buffalo. Only Jersey City, in eighth, finished out of the playoff hunt. Baltimore enjoyed the services of batting and runs batted in champion Julius Solters (.363, 157), as well as home run king Russ Arlett (39). Pitching laurels were bestowed on James Weaver from Newark for wins (25) and strikeouts (175), and on Rochester's Fred Ostermueller for lowest earned run average (2.44).

In the playoffs, Rochester surprised the Newark Bears, besting them three games to one. Fourth-place Buffalo, with a regular season record of 83–85, dusted off Baltimore three games to none. In the finals, Buffalo kept up its improbable good fortune by knocking off Rochester four games to two.

Financially, the playoff plan was a success, as more than 60,000 customers witnessed the Buffalo-Rochester series. But the Newark team cried foul. Seeing their 102-win season despoiled by an early playoff exit, and an under .500 team declared champions in their stead, the Bears tried to throw the Shaughnessy plan out. Instead, the plan was modified. The opening playoff series was lengthened to seven games, using a first-versus-third and second-versus-fourth format.

To honor the International League's playoff champion, the governors of states and provinces containing league cities sponsored a trophy. To this day, the Governor's Cup remains a sought-after prize bestowed on a deserving playoff survivor, even one that finished with a regular season record less than stellar.

NEWARK Bears

1st 102-62 .649 Al Mamaux

BATTERS	POS-GAMES	GP	AB	R	H	BI	2B	3B	HR	BB	SO	SB	BA
John Neun	1B156	158	606	102	187	69	27	10	6	75	50	14	.309
Marvin Olson	2B68	82	244	35	68	27	5	2	3	47	21	3	.279
Red Rolfe	SS153	156	605	113	197	78	40	6	7	65	49	17	.326
Jack Saltzgaver	3B123,2B42	165	620	107	189	100	31	5	11	66	40	24	.305
Myril Hoag	OF145	150	565	86	168	106	31	8	21	39	63	9	.297
John Watwood	OF86,1B13	109	370	51	108	40	17	2	0	43	27	5	.292
Vince Barton	OF	(see multi-team players)											
Norm Kies	C85	96	277	38	80	29	16	1	3	26	28	0	.289
Roy Schalk	2B57,SS15,3B11	96	308	42	80	35	13	2	5	33	35	5	.260
Charles Hargreaves	C78	84	239	23	58	36	7	0	1	31	13	0	.243
John Murphy	P40	41	22	0	4	1	0	0	0	4	10	0	.182
James Weaver	P40	40	85	2	11	6	2	1	0	3	33	0	.129
Jimmy DeShong	P35	36	88	13	12	6	0	0	0	14	15	0	.136
Robert Gibson	3B30	30	97	11	23	13	8	0	1	13	17	1	.237
Pete Jablonski	P22	26	66	10	19	5	2	1	0	4	12	0	.288
Charles Devens	P20	20	44	2	4	3	1	0	0	10	22	0	.091
Allen Cooke	OF19	19	59	11	12	11	1	1	4	14	14	2	.203
Al Mamaux	P18	18	11	2	5	1	0	0	0	2	0	0	.455
Don Brennan	P10	10	30	2	4	3	0	0	0	2	13	0	.133
John Broaca	P10	10	26	2	1	0	0	0	0	3	14	0	.038
William Eisemann		9											.240
Spud Chandler	P7	8											.154

PITCHERS		W	L	PCT	G	GS	CG	SH	IP	H	BB	SO	ERA
James Weaver		25	11	.694	40		22	3	268	233	93	175	2.72
Jimmy DeShong		16	10	.615	35		20	1	269	248	125	116	3.14
Pete Jablonski		13	7	.650	22		13	2	167	159	61	55	3.88
Charles Devens		10	6	.625	20		9	4	143	107	83	92	2.96
John Murphy		9	6	.600	40		1	1	103	86	49	53	2.97
John Broaca		7	2	.778	10		8	1	75	62	32	59	2.04
Don Brennan		6	3	.667	10		5	1	74	62	25	40	3.28
Al Mamaux		2	0	1.000	18		0	0	51	65	16	18	5.12
Spud Chandler		1	4	.200	7								

ROCHESTER Red Wings

2nd 88-77 .533 -14.5 George Toporcer

BATTERS	POS-GAMES	GP	AB	R	H	BI	2B	3B	HR	BB	SO	SB	BA
Minor Heath	1B62	62	226	37	64	42	11	1	9	35	22	4	.283
George Toporcer	2B128	131	471	93	140	40	21	3	1	71	13	18	.297
Thomas Carey	SS165	165	680	93	202	61	31	4	6	24	34	9	.297
Walter Gilbert	3B71	73	263	39	79	32	15	1	2	17	9	6	.300
Ray Pepper	OF142	143	550	73	162	100	32	4	11	24	52	4	.295
Colonel Mills	OF103	104	405	65	125	64	28	8	7	23	38	14	.309
George Puccinelli	OF	(see multi-team players)											
Gordon Hinkle	C93	99	290	43	94	39	19	3	2	26	50	0	.324
Paul Florence	C90	93	257	30	71	40	12	0	9	49	24	1	.277
Robert Parnham	OF63,P1	84	227	30	65	38	12	5	6	31	29	6	.286
Art Shires	1B57	59	195	31	54	24	10	3	2	28	29	2	.277
Charles Wilson	3B33,2B31	63	226	33	52	26	9	4	7	16	10	6	.230
Ira Smith	P32	44	78	13	18	9	6	0	1	6	9	0	.231
Tony Kaufmann	P32	43	92	14	27	11	2	1	1	18	8	1	.293
Fred Ostermueller	P27	43	92	9	29	16	5	0	2	5	10	0	.315
John Mize	1B42	42	159	27	56	32	11	3	8	11	15	1	.352
Estel Crabtree	OF31	40	144	26	43	27	8	1	3	15	8	2	.299
Benny Borgmann	3B20	30	88	20	30	9	4	1	0	11	8	7	.341
Delano Wetherell	P28	28	23	1	1	3	0	0	0	6	8	0	.043
John Goodman	OF12	22	64	12	17	11	3	3	0	4	13	4	.266
Fred Blake	P21	24	56	5	13	6	0	0	0	2	8	0	.232
James Lindsey	P24	24	34	0	5	4	0	0	0	2	4	0	.147
Lloyd Javet		20	59	11	13	2	2	0	1	8	7	0	.220
Edwin Chapman	P18	18	42	2	6	4	0	0	0	6	10	0	.143
William McAfee	P17	17	19	1	2	2	1	0	0	2	7	0	.105
Frank Henry	P15	16	31	4	7	4	2	0	0	0	2	0	.226
Ed Heusser	P15	15	9	1	2	2	0	0	0	1	1	0	.222
James Winford	P14	14	33	3	6	5	0	0	1	3	14	0	.182
Bernie Neis		11	26	3	5	3	1	0	0	1	4	2	.192
James Mooney	P7	8											.286
Al Eckert	P8	8											.000
Lawrence Barton		3											.000
Dykes Potter	P2	2											.000

ROCHESTER (cont.)
Red Wings

BATTERS	POS-GAMES	GP	AB	R	H	BI	2B	3B	HR	BB	SO	SB	BA
William Salmone		1											.000
Heber Newsome	P1	1											.000
Fred Myers		1											.000

PITCHERS		W	L	PCT	G	GS	CG	SH	IP	H	BB	SO	ERA
Fred Ostermueller		16	7	.696	27		21	3	192	177	88	100	**2.44**
Tony Kaufman		13	15	.464	32		18	3	221	233	69	70	4.19
Fred Blake		11	7	.611	21		11	0	143	141	70	61	4.03
Ira Smith		11	11	.500	32		15	2	179	205	52	47	4.58
Edwin Chapman		10	5	.667	18		10	3	134	110	64	85	2.69
Frank Henry		8	4	.667	15		5	0	78	98	38	29	5.42
James Winford		6	3	.667	14		4	0	90	85	60	43	3.60
Ed Heusser		4	5	.444	15		2	0	37	57	18	15	8.51
James Lindsey		3	9	.250	24		5	0	105	110	64	41	5.66
Delano Wetherell		2	2	.500	28		0	0	72	77	35	16	5.00
James Mooney		2	3	.400	7								
William McAfee		1	4	.200	17		3	1	57	72	29	10	5.37
Dykes Potter		0	1	.000	2								
Al Eckert		0	0	----	8								
Heber Newsome		0	0	----	1								
Robert Parnham		0	0	----	1								

BALTIMORE   3rd   84-80   .512   -18   Frank McGowan
Orioles

BATTERS	POS-GAMES	GP	AB	R	H	BI	2B	3B	HR	BB	SO	SB	BA
Del Bissonette	1B101	102	384	65	106	69	21	3	9	47	41	3	.276
Don Heffner	2B164	164	631	122	185	68	37	7	15	72	56	11	.293
George Redfern	SS85	87	322	45	99	46	21	1	2	21	18	7	.307
James Stroner	3B136	139	504	64	148	72	26	3	16	55	72	5	.294
Russ Arlett	OF147,1B11	159	531	**135**	182	146	40	3	**39**	113	61	20	.343
Julius Solters	OF134	147	523	123	190	**157**	46	3	36	37	46	17	**.363**
Frank McGowan	OF120	128	435	91	123	66	11	3	15	83	40	8	.283
Claude Linton	C77	88	263	42	75	42	11	1	14	29	17	0	.285
John Clabaugh	OF67,1B31,3B10	126	372	82	125	82	20	8	16	63	24	14	.336
John Sand	SS55,3B22	84	253	48	56	31	13	1	6	57	36	4	.221
Joseph Sprinz	C72	77	253	26	74	35	8	3	1	22	20	2	.292
Harry Smythe	P54	56	82	10	18	8	2	0	1	4	11	0	.220
Ralph Boyle	OF50	51	195	41	71	16	12	2	2	23	26	6	.364
Cliff Melton	P39	39	96	5	15	7	1	0	0	9	19	0	.156
John Prudhomme	P39	39	64	7	12	9	1	0	3	10	20	0	.188
Earl Mattingly	P35	35	54	2	4	1	2	0	0	0	21	0	.074
Bill Akers	SS24	34	94	14	25	10	4	2	1	14	13	1	.266
Dud Branom	1B29	29	109	11	23	14	3	0	1	6	5	0	.211
Gowell Claset	P28	28	58	4	7	2	1	0	0	4	23	0	.120
Alex Gaston	C20	20	63	4	9	6	3	0	0	6	4	0	.143
Bruce Cunningham	P16	17	29	4	4	2	1	0	1	1	8	0	.138
Beryl Richmond	P13	13	29	5	5	2	1	0	0	2	11	0	.172
Walt Tauscher	P9	9											.375
Clyde Day	P6	6											.000
Joseph Koenig		4											.000
Harvey Thompson	P3	3											1.000
Clarence Pickrel	P3	3											.286
Edgar Carroll	P3	3											.000
Ernest Salamone		2											.250
Merwin Jacobson		2											.000
Carroll Yerkes	P2	2											.000
Harry Gumbert	P1	1											1.000

PITCHERS		W	L	PCT	G	GS	CG	SH	IP	H	BB	SO	ERA
Harry Smythe		21	8	**.724**	**54**		13	0	213	227	60	92	3.97
Cliff Melton		16	10	.615	39		18	1	258	**285**	110	132	4.08
John Prudhomme		12	13	.480	39		11	1	184	210	85	48	5.72
Earl Mattingly		8	11	.421	35		8	1	149	188	74	43	5.80
Gowell Claset		7	10	.412	28		10	0	157	195	82	52	5.96
Beryl Richmond		4	5	.444	13		6	0	87	103	40	47	4.14
Bruce Cunningham		2	5	.286	16		4	0	86	108	38	24	6.38
Harvey Thompson		1	0	1.000									
Clyde Day		1	1	.500	6								
Clarence Pickrel		1	1	.500	3								

BALTIMORE (cont.)
Orioles

PITCHERS	W	L	PCT	G	GS	CG	SH	IP	H	BB	SO	ERA
Walt Tauscher	1	2	.333	9								
Carroll Yerkes	0	1	.000	2								
Edgar Carroll	0	0	----	3								
Harry Gumbert	0	0	----	1								

BUFFALO 4th 83-85 .494 -21 Ray Schalk
Bisons

BATTERS	POS-GAMES	GP	AB	R	H	BI	2B	3B	HR	BB	SO	SB	BA
John Smith	1B152	160	593	101	165	93	27	5	11	66	39	6	.278
Lafayette Thompson	2B	(see multi-team players)											
Greg Mulleavy	SS140,2B14	153	611	127	**206**	65	43	12	7	82	28	19	.337
Gil English	3B	(see multi-team players)											
Len Koenecke	OF159	161	601	113	201	100	36	**15**	8	89	40	30	.334
Oliver Tucker	OF141	152	520	104	168	115	29	2	27	98	32	9	.323
Ollie Carnegie	OF134	147	517	104	164	123	33	6	29	53	75	8	.317
Clyde Crouse	C106	109	322	45	87	57	14	1	12	50	44	3	.270
Clarence Mueller	OF75,1B14	113	313	48	84	50	16	5	2	55	32	0	.269
Roy Tarr	3B42,2B22	76	216	33	58	20	6	0	0	28	21	2	.269
Phil Gallivan	P49	57	98	20	32	16	7	1	2	6	10	0	.327
Harry Danning	C51	55	195	31	68	36	18	3	5	6	13	1	.349
William Gould	P41	41	63	2	11	9	3	0	0	4	15	0	.175
Harold Elliott	P34	34	40	2	8	1	2	0	0	6	14	0	.200
Henry Brewer	P33	33	34	4	10	3	1	0	1	1	11	0	.294
Ray Lucas	P26	26	50	8	10	5	0	0	1	2	17	0	.200
Thomas Kenney	C15	17	53	6	16	12	4	0	0	3	11	0	.302
Cecil Caraway	P11	11	2	0	0	0	0	0	0	0	1	0	.000
Zigmund Broskie		3											.000
Randalph Mineo		1											.000
Ed Fallenstein	P1	1											.000

PITCHERS	W	L	PCT	G	GS	CG	SH	IP	H	BB	SO	ERA
Phil Galivan	15	15	.500	49		13	2	230	279	94	108	5.13
William Gould	14	10	.583	41		13	0	182	226	54	59	4.60
Ray Lucas	9	7	.563	26		8	3	128	145	73	40	4.71
Harold Elliott	9	9	.500	34		5	2	131	142	97	57	5.29
Henry Brewer	2	7	.222	33		3	0	108	137	63	49	6.42
Ed Fallenstein	0	1	.000	1								
Cecil Caraway	0	5	.000	11		0	0	15	20	5	6	8.40

TORONTO 5th 82-85 .491 -21.5 Dan Howley
Maple Leafs

BATTERS	POS-GAMES	GP	AB	R	H	BI	2B	3B	HR	BB	SO	SB	BA
Lu Blue	1B113	113	374	54	97	35	13	4	7	91	24	4	.259
Leslie Mallon	2B167	**167**	624	86	171	78	38	4	4	76	25	11	.274
Nolen Richardson	SS162	162	619	76	162	52	30	2	1	42	23	7	.262
Oliver Sax	3B92,OF17	118	336	61	90	28	10	4	0	61	17	8	.268
Ike Boone	OF156	157	558	100	199	103	36	7	11	89	15	1	.357
Bill Lawrence	OF144	145	536	77	162	74	20	13	3	42	37	5	.302
Murray Howell	OF102	138	449	66	138	69	21	12	6	31	15	4	.307
Wilbur Brubaker	3B62,1B25	92	257	41	66	44	8	1	4	43	56	4	.257
Dave Barbee	OF80	87	287	43	75	45	15	3	5	45	48	1	.261
Robert Smith	C55	76	183	19	41	23	5	4	1	16	34	0	.224
Erv Brame	P31	58	87	6	24	18	3	0	0	8	6	0	.276
Luke Hamlin	P39	42	96	10	13	5	1	0	0	5	27	0	.135
Orlin Collier	P41	42	67	4	6	1	1	0	0	6	21	0	.090
Charles Marrow	P41	41	73	3	9	1	1	0	0	2	17	0	.123
Keith Frazier	P36	36	45	3	6	4	0	0	1	6	9	0	.133
Ralph Birkofer	P30	30	71	5	20	5	3	0	0	2	6	0	.282
Isadore Goldstein	P18	20	53	7	9	3	1	1	0	3	9	0	.170
Earl Cook	P20	20	12	0	3	1	1	0	0	1	3	0	.250
George McQuinn	1B14	14	57	10	20	10	2	2	1	3	3	0	.351
Mayo Smith		13	29	2	3	0	1	0	0	6	6	1	.103
Jerome Abberbock	P4	4											.000
Frank Barnes	P3	3											.667
Ray Walker		3											.154
Searson Wilson	P3	3											.000

TORONTO (cont.)
Maple Leafs

PITCHERS	W	L	PCT	G	GS	CG	SH	IP	H	BB	SO	ERA
Luke Hamlin	21	13	.618	39		23	3	261	261	83	127	3.48
Ralph Birkofer	16	8	.667	30		17	2	196	170	86	114	3.81
Charles Marrow	11	15	.423	41		16	1	217	240	64	57	4.48
Erv Brame	9	7	.563	31		10	1	151	178	39	30	4.59
Isadore Goldstein	9	7	.563	18		11	0	123	118	47	50	4.17
Orlin Collier	9	17	.346	41		11	1	206	241	96	60	5.33
Keith Frazier	4	9	.308	36		3	0	138	135	83	31	4.83
Earl Cook	1	4	.200	20		1	0	53	72	25	15	7.81
Jerome Abberbock	0	1	.000	4								
Searson Wilson	0	1	.000	3								
Frank Barnes	0	1	.000	3								

MONTREAL   6th   81-84   .491   -21.5   Walt Gautreau -
Royals   Oscar Roettger

BATTERS	POS-GAMES	GP	AB	R	H	BI	2B	3B	HR	BB	SO	SB	BA
Oscar Roettger	1B165,P1	165	658	92	201	122	52	2	10	33	31	7	.305
Walt Gautreau	2B128	136	471	72	112	37	20	1	1	91	31	10	.238
Jonah Goldman	SS161	161	547	70	139	35	23	5	0	74	34	16	.254
Urbane Pickering	3B	(see multi-team players)											
James Ripple	OF157	157	602	97	182	84	36	8	11	55	53	7	.302
Ivey Shiver	OF125	145	450	69	140	82	19	6	23	68	82	3	.311
John Winsett	OF85	114	315	47	89	61	14	5	18	51	70	2	.282
Bennie Tate	C114	118	349	31	117	46	17	2	3	37	5	2	.335
John Michaels	P53	68	91	7	19	9	5	1	0	1	11	0	.209
John Grabowski	C57	62	150	11	30	12	6	1	1	14	35	0	.200
Lou Finney	OF63	65	258	43	77	23	16	5	2	17	17	2	.298
Emmett McKeithan	P45	56	56	11	17	7	3	0	1	1	4	0	.304
Clarence Fisher	P54	54	34	2	4	0	0	0	0	3	6	0	.118
Fred Muller	3B27,2B19	49	149	23	36	15	9	1	1	27	19	2	.242
John Pomorski	P38	39	78	5	8	3	1	0	1	8	14	0	.103
William Dietrich	P30	30	54	4	7	8	1	1	0	5	27	0	.130
Warren Ogden	P25	28	53	4	10	10	3	1	1	5	4	0	.189
Roland Gladu		20	21	1	4	2	0	0	1	1	7	0	.190
Ed Grimes	3B11	13	34	5	5	3	3	0	0	6	9	0	.147
Wayne LeMaster	P10	11	17	3	4	2	1	0	1	0	0	0	.235
Les Sweetland	P9	10	13	0	1	2	0	0	0	2	3	0	.077
Joe Genewich	P7	7											.000
Lauri Myllykangas	P6	6											.200
Joseph Samuels	P6	6											.000
Walter Brown	P4	4											.000
Herb Thormahlen	P1	2											.000
Dick McCabe	P1	1											.000

PITCHERS	W	L	PCT	G	GS	CG	SH	IP	H	BB	SO	ERA
John Michaels	17	13	.567	53		16	3	232	244	93	83	4.03
John Pomorski	14	7	.667	38		10	1	226	238	69	53	3.70
William Dietrich	11	14	.440	30		11	2	156	158	104	68	5.19
Clarence Fisher	10	6	.625	54		0	0	124	106	57	32	2.98
Emmett McKeithan	8	6	.571	45		7	0	148	171	82	41	4.80
Warren Ogden	8	6	.571	25		7	1	145	154	48	33	4.47
Wayne LeMaster	2	3	.400	10		2	0	43	57	17	20	5.02
Les Sweetland	1	4	.200	9								
Walter Brown	0	1	.000	4								
Herb Thormahlen	0	1	.000	1								
Lauri Myllykangas	0	2	.000	6								
Joe Genewich	0	4	.000	7								
Joseph Samuels	0	0	----	6								
Oscar Roettger	0	0	----	1								
Dick McCabe	0	0	----	1								

ALBANY   7th   80-84   .488   -22   William McCorry
Senators

BATTERS	POS-GAMES	GP	AB	R	H	BI	2B	3B	HR	BB	SO	SB	BA
Harry Taylor	1B143	144	534	87	165	42	30	3	2	55	30	12	.309
Harold King	2B127	138	456	67	133	79	26	5	3	71	23	3	.292
Ed Marshall	SS	(see multi-team players)											

ALBANY (cont.)
Senators

BATTERS	POS-GAMES	GP	AB	R	H	BI	2B	3B	HR	BB	SO	SB	BA
Stan Hack	3B137	137	515	102	154	64	28	8	6	83	33	17	.299
Mike Kreevich	OF157	162	599	108	175	86	31	12	9	52	63	26	.292
Rupert Thompson	OF112	115	423	60	139	72	17	9	6	24	14	14	.329
James Moore	OF	(see multi-team players)											
Ernest Phelps	C75,1B23	122	368	34	108	70	16	12	10	21	26	2	.293
James McLeod	SS69	71	232	25	64	29	9	1	2	21	22	3	.276
Ned Porter	P31	59	72	16	19	11	4	1	1	7	10	1	.264
Thomas Padden	C53	53	166	23	45	21	7	1	1	25	15	0	.271
Ray Prim	P38	42	71	7	22	12	1	0	0	4	8	0	.310
Gus Dugas	OF38	38	132	24	50	19	9	3	2	15	7	3	.379
Alvin Powell	OF31	37	116	13	29	12	8	2	1	8	14	4	.250
Millard Campbell	P35	35	74	3	14	5	1	0	0	2	16	0	.189
Al Shealy	P32	32	65	9	16	10	2	0	2	4	7	0	.246
Tony Krasovich	2B14,3B13	29	94	9	18	10	4	0	0	9	10	0	.191
Frank Ragland	P26	26	39	2	9	7	0	1	0	2	5	0	.231
Robert Cummings		19	42	2	5	2	0	1	0	6	9	0	.119
Mark Filley	P16	16	30	1	2	2	0	0	0	3	14	0	.067
William Andrus	OF10	17	43	4	8	5	3	0	0	2	5	0	.186
Earl Clark	OF13	14	56	4	11	4	2	1	1	3	9	1	.196
Walt Masters	P12	12	22	1	2	1	0	0	0	0	4	1	.091
Ysmael Moralles		12	19	5	7	6	1	0	1	3	1	0	.368
George Quellich		10	17	1	5	2	2	0	0	1	3	0	.294
Dan Musser		8											.308
Del Young		6											.318
Frank Coleman	P5	5											.000
Charles Willis	P5	5											.000
Zachary Almond		4											.333
Willard Morrell	P4	4											.000
Pat Simmons	P4	4											.000
Emil Reitz		3											.333
Charles Butler	P2	2											.000
William McCorry	P1	2											.000
Clay Van Alstyne	P2	2											.000
Luther Thomas	P1	1											.000
Jack Liddy	P1	1											.000
Lynn Griffith	P1	1											.000
Lester Dodge	P1	1											.000
Robert Edwards	P1	1											.000

PITCHERS	W	L	PCT	G	GS	CG	SH	IP	H	BB	SO	ERA
Ray Prim	14	10	.583	38		13	1	187	198	66	70	3.42
Al Shealy	11	14	.440	32		14	1	176	207	58	82	4.86
Millard Campbell	9	10	.474	35		11	0	208	192	83	76	3.25
Mark Filley	7	4	.636	16		7	0	87	89	41	22	3.31
Frank Ragland	7	8	.467	26		5	0	119	144	63	27	5.07
Ned Porter	4	6	.400	31		2	0	128	149	40	31	4.43
Walt Masters	3	3	.500	12		2	0	59	72	22	17	`5.49
Willard Morrell	2	0	1.000	4								
Charles Willis	2	2	.500	5								
Pat Simmons	0	1	.000	4								
Clay Van Alstyne	0	1	.000	2								
Robert Edwards	0	1	.000	1								
Lester Dodge	0	1	.000	1								
Frank Coleman	0	3	.000	5								
Charles Butler	0	0	----	2								
William McCorry	0	0	----	1								
Luther Thomas	0	0	----	1								
Lynn Griffith	0	0	----	1								
Jack Liddy	0	0	----	1								

JERSEY CITY   8th   61-104   .370   -41.5   Bernard Kelly
Skeeters

BATTERS	POS-GAMES	GP	AB	R	H	BI	2B	3B	HR	BB	SO	SB	BA
John Clancy	1B160	161	605	68	174	90	34	4	6	50	25	2	.288
Loris Baker	2B60,SS27	89	333	33	87	32	12	2	2	19	23	2	.261
Joe Benes	SS50,2B14	76	252	33	72	16	13	5	0	31	25	5	.286
Joseph Brown	3B	(see multi-team players)											
Max Rosenfeld	OF109,2B22	132	484	64	141	70	20	7	9	33	26	8	.291
Ray Fitzgerald	OF78	81	284	44	83	43	16	3	5	31	21	4	.292
Harvey Walker	OF	(see multi-team players)											

JERSEY CITY (cont.)
Skeeters

BATTERS	POS-GAMES	GP	AB	R	H	BI	2B	3B	HR	BB	SO	SB	BA
George Rensa	C106	120	369	39	88	51	14	2	4	41	15	2	.238
Jack Grossman	SS28,3B22,OF15	72	209	21	50	19	7	3	3	14	30	3	.239
Henry Leiber	OF43	44	157	24	47	22	8	1	3	18	13	1	.299
Larry Merville	OF41	41	135	17	35	17	9	2	3	20	13	0	.259
Jeff Emerson	C38	41	99	6	20	13	3	0	0	4	17	1	.202
Dennis Sothern	OF29	38	111	13	28	12	3	0	1	12	18	2	.252
Emile Meola	P36	37	56	3	9	3	1	1	0	2	21	0	.161
Ed Pipgras	P35	36	59	3	6	3	0	0	1	1	11	0	.102
Joseph Coscarella	P33	34	77	5	13	3	0	0	0	1	16	0	.169
Robert Barrett	3B28	28	102	14	25	8	8	0	2	5	8	1	.245
Fred Koster	OF26	27	86	18	19	8	3	0	2	20	13	2	.221
Charles Jamieson	OF20	26	76	9	19	11	2	0	1	8	4	0	.250
James McCloskey	P23	25	49	6	10	0	3	0	0	7	7	0	.204
Ed Strelecki	P24	25	10	2	2	2	0	0	1	2	3	0	.200
Roger Hanlon	P20	20	44	5	8	3	0	1	1	2	9	1	.182
Robert Stevens	SS11	18	45	4	5	3	1	0	0	11	6	0	.111
Val Picinich	C11	16	42	6	13	8	2	0	2	4	3	0	.310
Ray Gardner	SS13	14	37	5	6	6	0	0	1	10	3	2	.162
James Calleran	2B11	11	37	5	8	3	1	0	0	3	4	0	.216
George Savino		9											.214
Robert Hasty	P9	9											.105
James Carrithers	P9	9											.091
Syver Slaavien	P8	8											.067
Howard Grosskloss		8											.067
Paul McCarron		7											.286
Hugh Wise		5											.000
Andrew Spagnardi		4											.455
Carr Smith		4											.000
Laurence Boerner		2											.000
Art Jones	P2	2											.000
Ed Leishman		2											.000
Bill Zitzmann		2											.000
George Simmons		1											.000
John Urbanski	P1	1											.000
William Gerst		1											.000
Charles Cerny	P1	1											.000
Ed Connolly		1											.000

PITCHERS	W	L	PCT	G	GS	CG	SH	IP	H	BB	SO	ERA
Joseph Coscarella	10	16	.385	33		15	1	207	206	85	89	4.09
James McCloskey	8	7	.533	23		9	1	142	145	71	41	3.74
Emile Meola	7	12	.368	36		9	1	160	170	95	68	5.18
Ed Pipgras	7	14	.333	35		8	1	156	185	54	41	5.02
Roger Hanlon	5	10	.333	20		10	0	124	124	55	25	4.57
Ed Strelecki	4	1	.800	24		0	0	49	56	19	10	5.33
Robert Hasty	3	2	.600	9								
James Carrithers	2	2	.500	9								
Syver Slaalien	1	4	.200	8								
Art Jones	0	1	.000	2								
Laurence Boerner	0	1	.000	2								
John Urbanski	0	0	----	1								
Charles Cerny	0	0	----	1								

MULTI-TEAM PLAYERS

BATTERS	POS-GAMES	TEAMS	GP	AB	R	H	BI	2B	3B	HR	BB	SO	SB	BA
Lafayette Thompson	2B152	JC27-BU135	162	622	114	187	95	32	8	12	69	34	35	.301
George Selkirk	OF148	NE82-RO72	154	540	100	165	108	28	15	22	81	82	19	.306
Joseph Brown	3B139	RO24-JC64-BU57	145	533	83	154	48	29	2	3	65	22	18	.289
Harvey Walker	OF133	JC64-MO77	141	453	95	127	48	22	5	11	95	65	17	.280
George Puccinelli	OF136	RO78-NE62	140	511	76	149	92	31	4	15	61	46	8	.292
James Moore	OF125	NE47-AL91	138	456	66	135	78	27	6	5	61	41	3	.296
Urbane Pickering	3B126	MO107-TO28	135	442	56	111	62	28	3	13	47	68	4	.251
Ed Marshall	SS126	BU27-JC3-AL104	134	504	71	132	45	16	4	1	57	26	6	.262
Gil English	3B124	BU76-JC58	134	467	64	130	76	21	4	13	26	41	1	.278
Vince Barton	OF115	AL36-NE82	118	427	55	105	69	18	2	12	33	41	1	.246
William Regan	3B43,2B24,SS15	MO91-BU27	118	310	47	81	35	13	2	12	52	48	5	.261
Herb Thomas	2B44,SS24	AL11-JC63	74	258	32	54	20	19	0	1	21	15	2	.209
Louis Legett	OF48	AL44-BU15	59	171	31	45	16	8	1	4	22	26	3	.263
Peter Stack	OF46	JC17-NE13-MO23	53	152	13	51	21	13	0	1	5	11	1	.336

MULTI-TEAM PLAYERS (cont.)

BATTERS	POS-GAMES	TEAMS	GP	AB	R	H	BI	2B	3B	HR	BB	SO	SB	BA
John Jones	OF48	JC41-AL8	49	175	24	50	27	7	0	8	15	12	0	.286
Art Smith	P38	TO7-MO39	46	62	7	10	6	1	0	0	8	8	0	.161
Joseph Bartulis	P45	BU32-JC14	46	45	2	6	1	2	0	0	4	14	0	.133
John Wilson	P42	JC3-BU41	44	83	8	14	4	2	0	0	5	14	0	.169
Charles Perkins	P41	JC28-BU14	42	79	6	15	7	2	0	0	3	6	0	.190
George Milstead	P41	AL15-BU26	41	58	3	8	1	0	0	1	6	22	0	.138
Hobart Whitman	OF35	AL15-JC22	37	133	16	34	7	2	0	0	11	1	1	.256
Ray Phelps	P35	JC26-MO11	37	74	7	16	4	3	1	0	8	21	0	.216
George Miner	P33	NE12-AL21	33	38	1	7	3	1	0	0	1	8	0	.184
Joseph Bloomer	P31	BU27-JC6	33	30	4	4	4	0	0	0	1	8	0	.133
Vito Tamulis	P26	NE26-AL5	31	49	13	10	8	3	0	1	6	4	0	.204
Marvin Duke	P31	AL1-NE30	31	23	2	1	3	0	0	0	6	8	0	.043
Fred Fussell	P24	BU12-AL13	25	40	4	7	6	1	0	2	6	11	0	.175
John Ogden	P19	RO8-BA16	24	35	6	7	3	2	0	0	4	10	0	.200
Guy Cantrell	P20	TO3-BA17	20	27	3	8	10	1	0	2	0	5	0	.296
Frank Packard	OF11	JC13-BA5	18	49	5	10	8	1	1	2	8	6	0	.204
Robert Munn	C17	BU4-AL10-MO4	18	43	0	6	4	2	1	0	5	12	0	.140
Fred Bennett	OF12	BU7-JC8	15	42	10	13	7	3	1	0	8	4	1	.310
Charles Foreman	P14	BA4-AL11	15	12	0	1	2	0	0	0	0	5	0	.083
Stewart Clarke	SS11	TO9-JC4	13	39	6	10	7	0	0	3	10	6	0	.256
Hod Lisenbee	P10	BU3-JC7	10	8	0	1	1	0	0	0	0	1	0	.125
Glenn Liebhardt	P9	BA7-JC2	9											.286
Lew Krausse	P9	AL3-MO6	9											.250
Charles Sullivan	P6	TO2-JC4	6											.250

PITCHERS		TEAMS	W	L	PCT	G	GS	CG	SH	IP	H	BB	SO	ERA
John Wilson		JC3-BU39	15	6	.714	42		12	0	230	257	63	93	4.11
Ray Phelps		JC24-MO11	13	16	.448	35		11	0	216	237	93	84	4.38
Charles Perkins		JC28-BU13	12	13	.480	41		13	1	225	221	128	148	3.88
George Miner		NE12-AL21	10	8	.556	33		5	1	116	131	47	53	4.66
Fred Fussell		BU12-AL12	9	7	.563	24		12	3	124	122	43	41	3.70
John Ogden		RO6-BA13	7	5	.583	19		8	1	103	87	52	22	3.76
Vito Tamulis		NE21-AL5	7	8	.467	26		7	1	130	155	68	75	5.82
Art Smith		TO2-MO36	7	12	.368	38		5	0	157	210	57	44	6.02
Marvin Duke		AL1-NE30	6	6	.500	31		5	0	105	121	60	54	4.46
George Milstead		AL15-BU26	5	14	.263	41		12	0	187	224	67	69	5.34
Joseph Bartulis		BU31-JC14	4	13	.235	45		6	0	153	199	79	52	6.18
Joseph Bloomer		BU25-JC6	3	9	.250	31		3	0	94	136	44	28	7.09
Glenn Liebhardt		BA7-JC2	2	0	1.000	9								
Charles Foreman		BA4-AL10	2	1	.667	14		0	0	40	33	32	21	4.28
Guy Cantrell		TO3-BA17	2	9	.182	20		5	0	76	93	29	31	6.51
Lew Krausse		AL3-MO6	1	2	.333	9								
Charles Sullivan		TO2-JC4	0	1	.000	6								
Hod Lisenbee		BU3-JC3	0	2	.000	10		1	0	29	41	8	9	5.59

TEAM BATTING

TEAMS	GP	AB	R	H	BI	2B	3B	HR	BB	SO	SB	BA
NEWARK	166	5433	811	1517	758	251	48	91	626	599	93	.279
ROCHESTER	165	5512	833	1591	775	291	58	106	521	496	105	.289
BALTIMORE	166	5463	962	1581	904	290	44	180	680	621	99	.289
BUFFALO	168	5649	980	1667	906	308	59	131	706	546	122	.295
TORONTO	169	5411	740	1475	693	239	60	57	638	464	47	.273
MONTREAL	165	5398	744	1453	679	275	46	105	634	614	71	.269
ALBANY	166	5496	786	1532	715	254	71	56	566	481	97	.279
JERSEY CITY	165	5363	654	1373	596	231	41	66	517	486	55	.256
	665	43725	6510	12189	6026	2139	427	792	4888	4307	689	.279

1934
TO THE LIMIT

Before the 1935 season, minor league baseball executives decided to shorten the Junior (formerly Little) World Series between the International League and the American Association from a best-of-nine format to a best-of-seven. The two leagues were now adopting revenue-generating playoff series of their own, and an extra two games in the Junior World Series only crowded a busy playoff schedule. However, before the demise of the nine-game format, one more dandy classic remained to be played. It would come after the 1934 season.

On the field in 1934, Newark won its third straight pennant. Rochester finished second, while Toronto and Albany ended third and fourth, claiming the final two playoff positions. Buffalo, Montreal, Syracuse (taking the place of Jersey City), and Baltimore finished in the non-playoff positions. Toronto's Ike Boone won his second International batting crown (.372), Woody Abernathy of Baltimore swatted the most home runs (32), and Albany's Fred Sington plated the most runs (147). Hurlers Walter Brown from Newark and Darrell Blanton from Albany won pitching honors. Brown won the most games (20) and posted the lowest earned run average (2.56), while Blanton had the highest strikeout total (165).

In the first round of the playoffs, Rochester cuffed Albany four games to one, while Toronto slipped by Newark four games to three, once more sending the regular season champions home early. In the International League finals, Toronto dominated Rochester four games to one, propelling the Maple Leafs to the Junior World Series. Their opponents would be the Columbus Red Birds, playoff survivors in the American Association.

Columbus, the second-place finisher in the 1934 American Association, was a slight favorite going into the fall classic. True to expectations, Columbus spanked the Maple Leafs 7–1 and 7–4 in the first two games played in Toronto's home park. Toronto rebounded with a 7–2 win in game three before going down once more to the Red Bird attack, 4–0. Trailing three games to one, with the remaining games of the series to be played in Columbus, the picture looked bleak for the Leafs. However, they snapped off a pair of wins (6–4 and 19–9) to pull even. The next two games saw a split as Columbus prevailed 9–8 before Toronto caught up with a 5–1 decision. In the ninth and deciding game, Red Bird hitters pummeled Toronto pitchers 13–8 to win the series by the slim margin of five games to four.

After the Junior World Series was scaled back following 1934, many post-season tilts went the limit. Thrilling as they were, their seven games could not match the excitement of a series that kept pressure building and pulses racing for a full nine games.

NEWARK Bears

NEWARK	1st	93-60	.608	Robert Shawkey

BATTERS	POS-GAMES	GP	AB	R	H	BI	2B	3B	HR	BB	SO	SB	BA
Dale Alexander	1B127,OF14	145	545	89	183	123	35	2	14	72	44	7	.336
Roy Schalk	2B149	150	534	71	138	71	32	0	13	44	54	10	.258
Robert Gibson	SS104	115	380	52	90	56	20	2	14	60	58	1	.237
Fred Muller	3B82	91	297	48	87	64	14	7	16	35	37	2	.293
Jesse Hill	OF154	154	587	104	205	84	30	11	9	75	73	24	.349
Vince Barton	OF146	146	544	97	142	115	32	5	32	55	76	3	.261
George Selkirk	OF105	106	392	105	140	43	23	9	10	68	30	18	.357
Joseph Glenn	C105	115	370	49	98	70	12	5	12	46	52	8	.264
Ed Farrell	3B44,SS37	88	331	57	77	26	10	2	7	36	25	3	.233
John Neun	1B36	77	157	27	40	14	10	0	1	30	9	1	.255
Norm Kies	C55	55	172	16	43	17	5	0	3	13	14	1	.250
Vito Tamulis	P44	54	80	7	17	7	3	1	1	5	11	0	.213
Frank Makosky	P40	40	41	1	7	3	1	0	0	1	6	0	.171
Roy Carlyle	OF34	35	126	19	32	4	5	3	0	17	11	3	.254
Walter Brown	P35	35	89	9	14	7	3	0	1	2	17	0	.157
John LaRocca	P33	33	75	2	10	4	2	0	0	5	31	1	.133
Marvin Duke	P33	33	50	1	10	4	0	0	0	2	7	0	.200
Jack Saltzgaver	3B27	27	100	18	25	11	4	1	2	17	7	4	.250
Charles Devens	P27	27	37	4	6	2	3	0	0	9	12	0	.162
Henry McDonald	P24	25	37	6	9	5	2	0	1	4	11	0	.243
Floyd Newkirk	P24	24	29	6	5	2	0	0	1	3	8	0	.172
James Hitchcock	SS18	18	61	6	15	7	3	0	1	1	4	0	.246
Ernest Koy		11	35	2	5	1	0	0	0	1	6	1	.143
Robert Collins		10	14	4	4	1	0	0	0	3	1	0	.286
Norm McCaskill		3											.333
Floyd Olds	P2	2											.000
Robert Shawkey	P1	1											.000

PITCHERS		W	L	PCT	G	GS	CG	SH	IP	H	BB	SO	ERA
Walter Brown		20	6	.769	35		21	6	239	208	92	130	2.56
Vito Tamulis		13	7	.650	44		14	2	217	206	70	135	2.74
John LaRocca		12	12	.500	33		11	1	207	199	125	155	3.57
Floyd Newkirk		11	4	.733	24		3	0	85	105	46	17	3.81
Frank Makosky		11	6	.647	40		5	0	138	114	70	61	2.80
Marvin Duke		10	6	.625	33		7	2	158	168	55	57	3.59
Charles Devens		9	7	.563	27		3	0	130	128	89	83	4.15
Henry McDonald		6	6	.500	24		3	1	109	105	44	41	4.29
Robert Shawkey		0	1	.000	1								
Floyd Olds		0	0	----	2								

ROCHESTER Red Wings

ROCHESTER	2nd	88-63	.583	-4	George Toporcer

BATTERS	POS-GAMES	GP	AB	R	H	BI	2B	3B	HR	BB	SO	SB	BA
John Mize	1B82	90	313	49	106	66	16	1	17	26	15	0	.339
Benny Borgmann	2B88,3B31	124	427	86	119	42	15	8	1	36	21	18	.279
Thomas Carey	SS142	142	575	74	165	81	28	8	3	19	43	7	.287
James Brown	3B117,SS10	137	530	92	137	41	26	9	1	44	22	5	.259
Ival Goodman	OF139	140	525	117	174	122	31	11	19	65	55	9	.331
John Winsett	OF102	112	343	61	122	74	20	13	21	60	64	3	.356
Lewis Whitehead	OF72	72	268	26	67	34	6	1	2	15	11	6	.250
Bill Lewis	C105	116	382	55	121	69	26	7	3	50	16	2	.317
Estel Crabtree	OF71,1B60	130	485	97	152	89	33	7	15	61	42	6	.313
George Toporcer	2B86,1B26	105	364	59	106	30	20	0	1	36	15	10	.291
Paul Florence	C58	66	173	25	54	25	7	2	5	33	16	0	.312
Colonel Mills	OF63	63	234	35	63	40	9	3	4	22	18	7	.269
John Michaels	P36	43	80	9	15	12	2	0	2	3	9	0	.188
Norbert Kleinke	P25	36	67	13	12	6	1	1	0	12	19	0	.179
Tony Kaufmann	P23	35	52	7	8	6	0	0	0	4	7	0	.154
Ray Harrell	P33	33	70	5	10	4	4	0	0	1	28	0	.143
Ira Smith	P21	32	46	5	12	8	2	1	0	3	7	0	.261
John Berly	P31	31	65	4	11	4	0	0	0	4	16	0	.169
James Winford	P20	21	23	2	7	1	1	0	0	4	5	0	.304
Dykes Potter	P20	20	21	0	3	0	0	0	0	0	8	0	.143
James Moore	OF10	10	32	3	6	4	1	0	0	3	2	0	.188
Howard Moore		8											.250
Virgil Brown	P7	8											.200
Al Sherer	P1	1											.000

ROCHESTER (cont.)
Red Wings

PITCHERS	W	L	PCT	G	GS	CG	SH	IP	H	BB	SO	ERA
Norbert Kleinke	19	7	.731	35		13	0	201	184	104	98	3.27
John Michaels	16	10	.615	36		15	1	199	199	81	94	3.35
John Berrly	14	8	.636	31		12	5	178	186	89	76	3.89
Ray Harrell	12	9	.571	33		7	0	184	165	107	96	4.06
Ira Smith	6	6	.500	21		4	1	82	97	28	45	4.72
Tony Kaufmann	5	7	.417	23		5	0	118	125	53	49	4.04
James Winford	2	7	.222	20		3	0	77	106	68	49	5.96
Virgil Brown	1	1	.500	7								
Dykes Potter	0	4	.000	20		1	0	57	66	45	20	6.00
Al Sherer	0	0	----	1								

TORONTO   3rd   85-67   .559   -7.5   Ike Boone
Maple Leafs

BATTERS	POS-GAMES	GP	AB	R	H	BI	2B	3B	HR	BB	SO	SB	BA
George McQuinn	1B138	138	525	97	174	77	27	13	4	61	40	16	.331
Joe Morrissey	2B137	138	559	104	161	68	19	2	8	40	31	4	.288
Nolen Richardson	SS153	153	557	56	147	74	21	3	1	38	21	16	.264
Harry Rice	3B67,OF24	98	372	65	109	45	13	3	1	53	14	1	.293
Ike Boone	OF135	136	500	87	186	108	32	9	6	82	22	8	.372
Murray Howell	OF120	129	468	65	158	115	36	11	6	47	36	7	.338
Ray Fitzgerald	OF	(see multi-team players)											
John Heving	C65	67	219	15	54	26	3	0	2	19	12	2	.247
Jack Crouch	C57	61	178	26	49	26	6	3	1	28	25	4	.275
Bert Cole	P25	55	110	7	24	13	6	0	0	9	9	1	.218
Charles Lucas	P44	45	42	2	7	3	0	0	0	0	8	0	.167
Walt Hilcher	P37	37	74	9	18	7	3	0	0	1	9	0	.243
Eugene Schott	P33	35	80	10	16	14	3	1	1	3	24	0	.200
Linc Blakely	OF33	33	113	22	26	3	5	2	1	16	15	2	.230
Fred Blake	P30	30	85	7	15	7	0	0	0	6	17	0	.176
Joseph Brown	3B16	28	72	15	24	8	4	0	0	13	2	2	.333
Al Hollingsworth	P25	27	56	4	14	7	3	1	0	2	2	0	.250
James Pattison	P26	27	31	2	4	3	0	0	0	5	7	0	.129
Keith Frazier	P23	24	40	8	12	4	1	0	1	6	5	0	.300
Gordon Hinkle	C12	14	40	7	5	4	1	2	1	6	10	0	.125
Francis Leveque		10	18	2	2	0	0	0	0	2	2	0	.111
Don Brennan	P7	7											.263
Oscar Fuhr	P7	7											.235
Thomas Robello		6											.429
Earl Cook	P6	6											.000
D'Arcy Flowers		4											.000
Malcolm Flowers		2											.143
Jerome Abberbock	P2	2											.000

PITCHERS	W	L	PCT	G	GS	CG	SH	IP	H	BB	SO	ERA
Eugene Schott	18	9	.667	33		17	2	203	217	86	69	3.76
Walt Hilcher	13	11	.542	37		11	0	199	202	108	86	4.43
Fred Blake	13	11	.542	30		18	0	229	235	93	125	4.52
Al Hollingsworth	11	6	.647	25		8	1	149	157	101	96	4.17
Charles Lucas	8	4	.667	44		2	0	129	125	73	73	4.05
Bert Cole	7	4	.636	25		3	0	89	117	38	23	5.16
Keith Frazier	6	11	.353	23		8	1	108	130	51	31	6.17
Don Brennan	3	3	.500	7								
James Pattison	3	5	.375	26		2	0	95	108	50	49	3.88
Oscar Fuhr	2	2	.500	7								
Earl Cook	1	1	.500	6								
Jerome Abberbock	0	0	----	2								

ALBANY   4th   81-72   .529   -12   William McCorry
Senators

BATTERS	POS-GAMES	GP	AB	R	H	BI	2B	3B	HR	BB	SO	SB	BA
Del Bissonette	1B	(see multi-team players)											
Barney Friberg	2B47,3B14	78	186	23	49	24	8	3	1	35	16	1	.263
Bert Delmas	SS	(see multi-team players)											
Wilbur Brubaker	3B135	135	467	66	136	62	32	12	5	63	69	9	.291
Fred Sington	OF149	155	562	123	184	147	32	10	29	75	81	4	.327
Alvin Powell	OF124	137	559	128	202	71	29	7	20	44	65	25	.361

ALBANY (cont.)
Senators

BATTERS	POS-GAMES	GP	AB	R	H	BI	2B	3B	HR	BB	SO	SB	BA
Joe Mowry	OF107,2B10	121	437	77	133	77	33	11	3	59	22	5	.304
Harold Finney	C98	100	344	39	96	37	12	0	2	11	42	3	.279
Gus Dugas	OF41,1B10	57	194	32	72	44	17	5	5	18	16	1	.371
Glenn Chapman	2B33,OF19	53	197	35	65	46	15	4	5	18	19	1	.330
Edwin Chapman	P39	44	72	8	19	8	2	0	0	5	17	0	.264
Elmer Klumpp	C22	34	72	10	16	13	2	3	1	5	14	0	.222
John Milligan	P32	32	50	2	3	2	0	0	0	4	10	0	.060
Joseph Luciano	SS27	29	84	11	25	8	2	1	0	9	9	1	.298
Floyd Young	SS20	28	106	10	22	11	5	0	2	6	20	3	.208
Mark Filley	P28	28	23	2	4	1	0	0	0	3	6	0	.174
Darrell Blanton	P26	27	54	5	10	11	1	0	0	2	8	0	.185
Art Jones	P26	26	36	2	7	1	0	0	0	0	8	0	.194
Ned Porter	P11	24	33	1	6	1	1	0	0	2	8	0	.185
Ray Prim	P23	23	35	5	10	4	1	0	1	4	8	0	.286
Peter Susko	1B22	22	85	12	28	6	2	2	0	5	1	2	.329
William Fold	2B20	22	77	4	21	10	4	1	0	4	20	1	.273
Howard Maple	C21	22	70	9	16	10	3	3	0	9	4	0	.229
Art Herring	P21	22	36	5	12	2	2	0	0	0	7	0	.333
Ed Marshall	SS18	18	70	11	11	4	3	0	0	7	3	1	.157
Ysmael Moralles	OF12	18	47	4	13	4	1	0	1	5	3	2	.277
Clyde Sukeforth	C14	18	40	1	8	2	1	0	0	9	6	0	.200
Richard Barrett	P16	17	22	4	3	1	1	0	0	3	6	0	.136
William Harris	P14	14	40	2	11	3	0	0	0	1	4	0	.275
Robert Edwards	P12	12	16	2	2	0	1	0	0	0	5	0	.125
Walter Beck	P10	11	15	2	4	0	2	0	0	0	1	0	.267
Daniel McGee	SS10	10	37	6	9	4	2	0	1	2	2	0	.243
George Trapp	3B10	10	23	1	5	2	1	0	0	5	2	0	.217
James Carrithers	P10	10	8	0	0	0	0	0	0	0	2	0	.000
William Lambert		8											.308
Ed Pipgras	P7	7											.167
Walt Dunham		7											.000
Ed Phillips		6											.333
Al Shealy	P5	5											.429
Robert Brown	P5	5											.167
Al McNeely		4											.400
Frank Coleman	P4	4											.200
Roberto Estalella		3											.000
Harold Grant		2											.000
John Jackson	P2	2											.000
Henry Cappola	P1	1											.000
William McCorry	P1	1											.000
Del Young		1											.000
Harry Seibold	P1	1											.000
William Prince	P1	1											.000
William Rhea		1											.000
Richard Seibert		1											.000

PITCHERS	W	L	PCT	G	GS	CG	SH	IP	H	BB	SO	ERA
Edwin Chapman	13	11	.542	39		13	2	191	193	121	103	4.43
Darrell Blanton	11	8	.579	26		11	3	147	115	97	165	3.86
John Milligan	10	6	.625	32		5	0	137	123	90	47	4.01
William Harris	9	2	.818	14		8	1	108	81	33	65	2.25
Richard Barrett	6	4	.600	16		5	2	75	65	46	58	2.64
Art Jones	6	5	.545	26		6	1	109	105	47	33	4.29
Robert Edwards	4	2	.667	12		2	0	37	42	23	20	6.57
Mark Filley	4	3	.571	28		3	0	83	91	27	22	4.23
Ray Prim	4	6	.400	23		5	0	89	105	31	45	5.06
Art Herring	4	6	.400	21		5	2	103	118	48	63	4.46
Robert Brown	3	0	1.000	5								
Ed Pipgras	2	3	.400	7								
Walt Beck	2	6	.250	10		3	0	39	43	26	30	7.62
Frank Coleman	1	1	.500	4								
James Carrithers	1	2	.333	10		3	1	35	30	17	12	4.11
Al Shealy	1	2	.333	5								
Harry Seibold	0	1	.000	1								
Henry Capolla	0	1	.000	1								
Ned Porter	0	3	.000	11		0	0	49	48	29	10	3.49
John Jackson	0	0	----	2								
William McCorry	0	0	----	1								
William Prince	0	0	----	1								

BUFFALO Bisons
5th   76-77   .497   -17   Ray Schalk

BATTERS	POS-GAMES	GP	AB	R	H	BI	2B	3B	HR	BB	SO	SB	BA
John Clancy	1B100	108	390	54	105	63	22	6	6	45	28	4	.269
Leslie Mallon	2B83	84	330	70	114	55	22	3	8	40	23	12	.345
Greg Mulleavy	SS154	154	600	131	186	91	38	4	8	81	40	22	.310
Howard Meyers	3B77	80	280	42	77	35	13	2	4	37	19	4	.275
Ollie Carnegie	OF117	120	460	81	154	136	26	5	31	56	77	7	.335
Oliver Tucker	OF113	126	430	81	130	77	34	2	15	69	29	7	.302
Frank McGowan	OF	(see multi-team players)											
Roy Spencer	C77	84	270	30	67	38	9	0	6	31	26	0	.248
John Smith	1B57,3B35	117	376	70	112	58	17	5	8	49	29	5	.298
Fabian Kowalik	P39	49	106	15	25	19	5	1	1	2	14	0	.236
Hod Lisenbee	P48	48	49	3	9	4	1	0	0	2	12	1	.184
Dick Gyselman	3B45	45	155	27	39	8	5	2	1	22	42	1	.252
Clyde Crouse	C41	45	138	23	49	24	7	1	0	20	12	1	.355
John Wilson	P37	38	45	5	4	4	0	0	0	5	11	0	.089
Ken Ash	P36	37	73	11	15	7	3	0	0	2	17	0	.205
Charles Perkins	P31	31	49	6	15	9	1	0	0	3	9	0	.306
George Milstead	P30	30	48	7	3	2	1	0	0	9	20	0	.063
Frank Pearce	P28	28	37	4	10	3	0	0	0	3	12	0	.270
George Connally	P14	14	16	1	1	1	0	0	0	0	5	0	.063
Nick Tremark	OF12	12	46	12	10	8	2	1	1	7	7	0	.217
Lincoln Wasem		12	31	1	10	6	0	0	0	1	3	0	.323
William Gould	P8	8											.000
Leslie Barnhart	P5	5											1.000
Jack White	P4	4											.000
Ken Gordy	P2	2											.000
Edward Honeck	P1	1											.000
Ed Wineapple	P1	1											.000

PITCHERS	W	L	PCT	G	GS	CG	SH	IP	H	BB	SO	ERA
Fabian Kowalik	18	14	.563	39		20	1	229	264	90	82	4.17
John Wilson	11	11	.500	37		8	1	143	162	46	52	4.47
Ken Ash	11	13	.458	36		13	0	201	234	66	79	4.16
George Milstead	10	8	.556	30		6	2	149	179	48	44	4.89
Hod Lisenbee	8	9	.471	48		4	0	165	229	46	49	5.89
Charles Perkins	6	8	.429	31		5	0	130	153	81	72	5.61
Frank Pearce	5	7	.417	28		5	0	105	110	41	42	3.94
George Connally	3	0	1.000	14		2	0	43	52	19	19	5.44
William Gould	0	1	.000	8								
Leslie Barnhart	0	0	----	5								
Jack White	0	0	----	4								
Ken Gordy	0	0	----	2								
Ed Wineapple	0	0	----	1								
Ed Honeck	0	0	----	1								

MONTREAL Royals
6th   73-77   .487   -18.5   Frank Shaughnessy

BATTERS	POS-GAMES	GP	AB	R	H	BI	2B	3B	HR	BB	SO	SB	BA
Oscar Roettger	1B59	59	226	34	64	38	13	3	2	17	16	0	.283
Lafayette Thompson	2B129	135	498	91	155	96	35	8	12	74	38	8	.311
Ben Sankey	SS151	151	564	62	149	76	21	5	0	55	18	4	.264
Harold King	3B126,2B15	142	495	83	144	79	32	3	5	94	39	4	.291
Harvey Walker	OF146	146	515	117	132	45	36	11	7	126	114	33	.256
James Ripple	OF138	142	513	78	137	86	37	7	9	47	61	2	.267
Denver Grigsby	OF133	135	449	56	124	53	26	3	1	78	30	4	.276
Peter Stack	C60	60	182	30	45	30	10	1	4	18	21	0	.247
William Rhiel	OF48,3B20,2B14	103	284	43	83	61	18	4	5	34	39	2	.293
Raymond Fritz	P40,1B18	71	143	23	32	9	4	0	2	15	24	2	.224
Frank Reiber	C42,OF19	70	194	25	47	23	17	1	3	33	17	0	.242
Chad Kimsey	P37	55	95	10	29	14	9	1	2	10	24	0	.305
John Pomorski	P47	51	44	6	7	3	0	0	0	5	8	0	.159
Frank O'Rourke	1B15,3B12	44	98	10	23	14	2	0	0	12	10	3	.235
James Shevlin	1B42	42	145	30	42	18	9	2	1	24	10	1	.290
Lauri Myllykangas	P34	38	32	3	5	2	1	0	0	3	12	0	.156
Orlin Collier	P33	36	35	2	4	4	0	0	0	1	11	0	.114
Harry Smythe	P26	28	44	3	13	6	0	0	0	3	4	1	.295
Bennie Tate	C25	25	83	14	29	11	7	1	1	8	4	0	.349
John Salveson	P19	21	44	6	9	6	1	1	1	2	1	0	.205
Clyde Castleman	P11	11	21	1	4	2	0	0	0	0	6	0	.190
Frank Leach		7											.294

MONTREAL (cont.)
Royals

BATTERS	POS-GAMES	GP	AB	R	H	BI	2B	3B	HR	BB	SO	SB	BA
Clarence Phillips	P7	7											.143
Bevo LeBourveau	OF	5	10	0	1	0	0	0	0			0	.100
Leslie Munns	P5	5											.000
Frank Henry	P4	4											.000
Isadore Goldstein	P3	3											.000
Robert McNamara	P1	1											.000

PITCHERS		W	L	PCT	G	GS	CG	SH	IP	H	BB	SO	ERA
Raymond Fritz		13	12	.520	40		17	3	215	223	103	134	3.81
Chad Kimsey		12	14	.462	37		13	1	201	263	79	63	5.46
John Salveson		11	4	.733	19		10	1	121	126	34	24	3.79
Harry Smythe		8	6	.571	26		5	2	115	121	49	38	4.54
John Pomorski		5	12	.294	47		1	0	147	172	42	47	5.33
Clarence Phillips		4	2	.667	7								
Lauri Myllykangas		4	4	.500	34		2	0	101	115	36	38	4.37
Clyde Castleman		4	5	.444	11		4	0	68	70	27	36	3.84
Orlin Collier		3	4	.429	33		0	0	109	138	54	30	5.78
Leslie Munns		1	1	.500	4								
Frank Henry		0	2	.000	4								
Isadore Goldstein		0	0	----	3								
Robert McNamara		0	0	----	1								

SYRACUSE	7th	60-94		.390		-33.5		Andrew High -				
Chiefs								William Sweeney				

BATTERS	POS-GAMES	GP	AB	R	H	BI	2B	3B	HR	BB	SO	SB	BA
William Sweeney	1B123	123	504	87	169	95	22	6	10	25	26	12	.335
Clarence Blair	2B134,1B20	154	578	63	154	76	22	13	2	44	69	5	.266
Ed Cihocki	SS148	150	516	64	137	53	24	8	3	59	61	3	.266
Andrew High	3B56	56	211	40	66	38	8	3	1	28	6	4	.313
Max Rosenfeld	OF151	151	556	75	158	86	29	4	3	60	23	13	.284
John Watwood	OF143	150	581	112	181	56	28	6	2	88	40	11	.312
John Maruska	OF75	85	271	25	67	21	8	4	1	30	39	2	.247
William Cronin	C94	110	352	26	97	39	14	1	0	19	12	0	.276
James Taylor	C64	80	227	28	52	27	6	1	0	33	20	2	.229
Raymond Combs	P36	60	128	16	34	22	4	2	3	19	15	0	.266
Ed Taylor	3B38,1B16	56	198	19	39	16	7	1	1	14	13	1	.197
James McCloskey	P35	35	57	5	9	4	4	0	0	9	17	0	.158
Fred Fussell	P31	33	56	4	9	2	2	0	0	10	19	0	.161
John Merena	P30	30	53	9	14	7	2	0	1	2	10	0	.264
Emmett McKeithan	P22	25	27	1	6	1	0	0	0	1	4	0	.222
Clarence Pickrel	P24	24	56	1	11	5	1	0	0	4	20	1	.196
Aloysius Murphy	3B19	19	63	7	12	7	2	1	0	3	8	0	.190
Ralph Judd	P10	16	24	4	4	1	1	1	0	3	3	0	.167
John Sherlock	OF14	15	62	9	15	11	5	0	0	6	10	0	.242
Jack Grossman	OF14	15	53	14	16	7	2	1	1	10	10	1	.302
Roger Hanlon	P12	12	16	0	1	0	0	0	0	0	7	0	.063
Joseph Bloomer	P10	10	6	0	1	0	0	0	0	0	1	0	.167
Julius Laviano		8											.118
Andrew Spognardi		5											.111
Al Glossop		4											.154
Bernard Hearn		3											.300
William Gilvary	P3	3											.250
Al Eckert	P3	3											.000
David Hayes		2											.286
John Lyons		1											.333
Oscar Estrada	P1	1											.000

PITCHERS		W	L	PCT	G	GS	CG	SH	IP	H	BB	SO	ERA
Fred Fussell		11	11	.500	31		14	1	178	181	80	62	4.55
Raymond Coombs		10	19	.345	36		19	0	236	282	83	60	4.96
Clarence Pickrel		9	11	.450	24		11	1	154	180	70	41	5.03
John Merena		7	10	.412	30		8	0	145	186	90	54	6.77
James McCloskey		7	14	.333	35		9	0	165	196	102	55	6.44
Ralph Judd		3	2	.600	10		3	0	48	66	16	18	5.25
Emmett McKeithan		3	7	.300	22		5	1	87	104	36	28	6.21
Roger Hanlon		2	2	.500	12		0	0	32	63	13	7	9.56
Joseph Bloomer		1	3	.250	10		0	0	20	33	12	8	10.80
Al Eckert		0	0	----	3								
William Gilvary		0	0	----	3								
Oscar Estrada		0	0	----	1								

BALTIMORE Orioles

| | | 8th | 53-99 | .349 | -39.5 | Frank McGowan - Joe Judge - Guy Sturdy |

BATTERS	POS-GAMES	GP	AB	R	H	BI	2B	3B	HR	BB	SO	SB	BA
Guy Sturdy	1B65	72	229	37	49	26	14	0	2	45	25	10	.214
Irv Jeffries	2B79	79	302	52	91	50	15	2	8	25	25	4	.302
Keith Molesworth	SS144	144	494	70	126	68	23	3	4	73	46	3	.255
John Kroner	3B76,1B26	126	416	73	119	53	22	2	10	73	53	5	.286
George Puccinelli	OF131	133	476	93	169	102	37	6	19	94	46	7	.355
Woody Abernathy	OF126,1B29	151	563	102	174	120	24	9	32	76	93	5	.309
Tom Oliver	OF92	99	370	52	99	36	17	2	3	39	15	6	.268
William Atwood	C79	88	283	30	66	45	11	1	10	22	46	0	.233
Walter Gilbert	3B57	64	241	34	67	34	17	3	0	23	20	3	.278
Robert Asby	C48	62	184	30	54	30	17	2	7	23	51	0	.293
George Granger	P46	47	66	11	14	6	2	0	0	13	15	0	.212
Cliff Melton	P45	45	62	5	7	1	0	2	0	10	15	0	.113
Beryl Richmond	P32	32	41	4	7	2	0	0	0	11	18	0	.171
Euel Moore	P29	31	57	8	18	8	4	0	0	3	10	0	.316
Al Butcher	P31	31	38	3	7	0	0	0	0	6	9	0	.184
George Miner	P22	23	12	1	2	1	0	0	0	3	3	0	.167
Bill Lohrman	P20	21	45	7	12	6	1	1	2	3	7	0	.267
Eddie Mayo	3B15	17	58	12	14	8	5	2	1	8	8	0	.241
Don Robertshaw		17	28	0	5	2	3	0	0	0	2	0	.179
Joe Judge	1B13	15	51	5	10	6	3	0	0	4	4	0	.196
George Darrow	P14	14	40	7	9	6	2	0	0	2	12	0	.225
Richard Goldberg	1B10	10	39	7	11	4	1	0	0	3	7	0	.282
Charles Hargreaves	C10	10	29	4	10	1	0	0	1	2	2	0	.345
Michael Bouza		7											.000
Chris Pickering	P5	5											.000
Herm Holshouser	P4	4											.500
John Krider	P4	4											.000
Beverly Ferrell		2											.000
Arol Fitton	P2	2											.000
A. R. Smith	P2	2											.000
Vic Keen	P1	1											.500
John Ogden	P1	1											.000
Walter Walus		1											.000

PITCHERS	W	L	PCT	G	GS	CG	SH	IP	H	BB	SO	ERA
George Granger	12	14	.462	46		10	1	202	260	99	70	5.48
Euel Moore	8	10	.444	29		8	0	147	159	55	64	4.04
Beryl Richmond	8	12	.400	32		9	2	151	136	98	79	4.47
George Darrow	7	5	.583	14		9	0	110	129	37	41	4.58
Cliff Melton	6	20	.231	45		13	1	209	240	131	90	6.80
Bill Lohrman	5	9	.357	20		10	0	122	134	44	45	4.72
Al Butcher	4	9	.308	31		4	0	107	111	74	42	6.48
Chris Pickering	0	1	.000	5								
Herm Holshouser	0	1	.000	4								
George Miner	0	0	----	22		0	0	44	64	12	11	6.95
John Krider	0	0	----	4								
Arol Fitton	0	0	----	2								
A. R. Smith	0	0	----	2								
Vic Keen	0	0	----	1								
John Ogden	0	0	----	1								

MULTI-TEAM PLAYERS

BATTERS	POS-GAMES	TEAMS	GP	AB	R	H	BI	2B	3B	HR	BB	SO	SB	BA
Del Bissonette	1B143	BA19-AL131	150	538	86	165	111	37	10	11	48	67	6	.307
Marvin Olson	2B123	BA82-BU54	136	484	107	132	62	27	6	8	116	43	8	.273
Bert Delmas	SS77,2B48	MO2-AL119	121	427	82	119	38	17	2	0	73	69	11	.279
Ray Fitzgerald	OF106	TO80-BU41	121	408	59	129	84	13	5	12	36	25	11	.316
Frank McGowan	OF114	BA27-BU88	115	403	92	115	64	21	4	7	104	45	7	.285
William Regan	3B45,2B28,OF21	BU52-TO49	101	331	45	83	45	16	4	9	28	66	3	.251
Joe Benes	3B37,SS17,1B12,2B11	SY-72-AL25	97	270	33	67	20	14	0	1	41	23	2	.248
William Outen	C62	BU47-MO47	94	201	36	56	38	8	1	5	58	17	2	.279
Andrew Moore	OF89	AL5-TO87	92	342	66	85	16	14	4	2	44	55	8	.249
Clarence Mueller	OF79	SY18-BU68	86	275	50	79	33	15	2	2	57	24	5	.287
Earl Clark	OF68	RO6-BA68	74	254	35	62	24	13	3	2	21	22	3	.244
Walt Henline	C53	MO32-BA23	55	165	14	39	16	8	1	1	12	21	0	.236
Ted Norbert	OF50	NE1-BA4-AL5-SY44	54	175	35	53	38	14	4	6	31	17	3	.303
Irv Plummer	OF27,1B24	BU29-MO23	52	164	31	38	30	8	2	4	27	35	3	.232
Clarence Fisher	P48	MO18-SY30	48	43	1	4	2	0	0	0	1	16	0	.093
Ad Liska	P45	RO26-SY26	46	55	4	5	4	0	0	0	7	20	1	.091

MULTI-TEAM PLAYERS (cont.)

BATTERS	POS-GAMES	TEAMS	GP	AB	R	H	BI	2B	3B	HR	BB	SO	SB	BA
Doug Taitt	OF34	SY11-BA34	45	143	20	44	23	12	0	3	17	10	0	.308
Oliver Sax	3B29	TO25-RO15	40	129	25	25	13	1	1	1	24	11	7	.194
Pete Appleton	P39	BA18-RO22	40	73	9	15	7	2	2	0	6	19	0	.205
Robert Smith	C20	TO29-BA2	31	99	10	19	14	2	1	1	3	14	1	.192
Harold Elliott	P30	BU25-SY5	30	36	2	5	4	0	0	1	3	15	0	.139
Warren Ogden	P23	MO16-BA7	23	31	5	7	0	0	0	0	5	5	0	.226
Martin Callaghan	OF13	AL13-SY9	22	57	4	12	3	3	1	0	7	7	0	.211
Spud Chandler	P17	SY6-NE12	18	11	0	2	1	1	0	0	0	4	0	.182
Hormidas Aube	P16	NE3-BA13	16	10	1	0	0	0	0	0	1	5	0	.000
Val Picinich		BA6-TO7	13	27	0	3	1	0	0	0	1	6	0	.111
Clise Dudley	P10	MO8-BA3	11	16	1	2	2	0	0	1	1	5	0	.125
Earl Mattingly	P3	SY2-BA1	3											.000

PITCHERS		TEAMS	W	L	PCT	G	GS	CG	SH	IP	H	BB	SO	ERA
Pete Appleton		BA18-RO21	11	13	.458	39		11	0	208	224	85	93	4.59
Clarence Fisher		MO18-SY30	7	8	.467	48		2	1	136	143	38	35	4.43
Ad Liska		RO19-SY26	6	11	.353	45		6	0	180	216	87	55	4.90
Harold Elliott		BU25-SY5	4	7	.364	30		4	0	107	138	56	40	6.56
Warren Ogden		MO16-BA7	4	8	.333	23		5	1	99	125	29	24	5.00
Spud Chandler		SY6-NE11	2	4	.333	17		0	0	46	55	27	19	6.26
Clise Dudley		MO7-BA3	1	5	.167	10		2	0	49	64	12	7	4.96
Hormidas Aube		NE3-BA13	0	3	.000	16		0	0	37	56	30	18	7.30
Earl Mattingly		SY2-BA1	0	0	----	3								

TEAM BATTING

TEAMS	GP	AB	R	H	BI	2B	3B	HR	BB	SO	SB	BA
NEWARK	154	5096	803	1405	741	249	48	**138**	601	611	90	.276
ROCHESTER	152	**5234**	839	1497	778	252	**73**	94	519	472	73	.286
TORONTO	153	5181	781	1480	724	225	62	48	542	455	**93**	.286
ALBANY	**157**	5232	826	**1514**	770	277	76	86	561	**656**	77	**.289**
BUFFALO	154	5181	**919**	1476	**862**	265	46	119	722	591	86	.285
MONTREAL	153	5042	771	1359	714	**293**	52	57	713	564	65	.270
SYRACUSE	156	5208	690	1399	638	217	56	32	559	505	63	.269
BALTIMORE	153	5094	803	1390	745	270	46	115	**735**	646	54	.273
	616	41268	6432	11520	5972	2048	459	689	4952	4500	601	.279

1935
TRIPLE CROWN

The ultimate individual achievement for any batter is to hit for the highest average, pole out the most home runs, and knock in the most runs—all in the same season. Such an achievement is called the triple crown. It has happened seldom in the history of the International League. Dale Alexander won the first triple crown in 1928. The second crown was awarded in 1935 when a Baltimore outfielder named George Puccinelli rose to the top in all three statistical categories. In addition, he nearly set all-time marks in two of the three.

George Puccinelli started with the San Francisco Seals of the Pacific Coast League in 1927. During the next four years, he bounced to six more teams, making a short visit to the majors with the St. Louis Cardinals in 1930. The following season, he landed in the International League for the first time, playing for Rochester. In 1932, Puccinelli enjoyed a banner year as he battered the ball to the tune of a .391 average, the league's highest in many years. After a couple of brief callups to both St. Louis clubs, he was sent back to the International, this time with Baltimore. Here, Puccinelli would post his finest season.

In 1935, George Puccinelli led the International League in virtually every category. He finished not only with the most runs (135), hits (209), and doubles (49), but also with the highest average (.359), most home runs (53), and most runs batted in (172), thereby clinching the triple crown. His home run and runs batted in totals nearly set league records, both finishing less than ten short.

Montreal won its first pennant in over thirty years, outlasting a gritty Syracuse club, which rose from the depths to finish second. Buffalo and Newark also finished in the first division, while Baltimore, Toronto, Rochester, and Albany finished in the second. Pitching honors were garnered by Montreal's Pete Appleton for most wins (23), Joseph Cascarella of Syracuse for lowest earned run average (2.35), and Buffalo's William Harris for most strikeouts (137).

Buoyed by his 1935 performance, George Puccinelli played for the American League's Philadelphia Athletics in 1936. After one year, he landed back in Baltimore, meandering on to Hollywood and Dallas before his career ended in 1940. Although Puccinelli reached the pinnacle with his triple crown in 1935, nearly setting two records on the way, there is further evidence of his batting prowess. George Puccinelli finished his career in the International League with a career average of .334—the highest in league annals.

MONTREAL Royals

	1st	92-62	.597		Frank Shaughnessy

BATTERS	POS-GAMES	GP	AB	R	H	BI	2B	3B	HR	BB	SO	SB	BA
Del Bissonette	1B140	143	490	76	137	75	24	3	7	56	38	4	.280
Harold King	2B101,3B25	127	408	65	109	57	28	6	9	56	21	5	.267
Ben Sankey	SS155	155	591	86	159	86	33	11	3	44	29	4	.269
Lafayette Thompson	3B123,2B32	155	626	111	194	74	39	9	5	56	41	16	.310
James Ripple	OF155	155	588	97	196	115	41	9	12	74	29	12	.333
Bob Seeds	OF128,1B28	144	562	99	177	58	44	10	4	63	47	13	.315
Gus Dugas	OF123	125	402	79	124	97	29	3	22	56	33	4	.308
Bill Lewis	C81	87	232	27	61	33	10	3	0	31	14	0	.263
Bennie Tate	C77	85	263	33	72	31	14	4	1	21	6	0	.274
Glenn Chapman	OF69	76	229	35	60	29	6	7	2	15	29	2	.262
Ed Montague	2B38,3B19	71	148	25	32	20	6	2	0	22	24	1	.216
William Rhiel	OF49	58	124	22	48	19	10	2	3	13	15	1	.387
Harry Smythe	P45	55	110	9	32	13	5	3	0	8	15	0	.291
Pete Appleton	P41	51	99	16	35	15	8	1	1	3	12	0	.354
Chad Kimsey	P35	49	89	13	25	11	4	1	1	3	17	0	.281
Raymond Fritz	P37	46	75	17	19	7	0	1	2	7	10	0	.253
Lauri Myllykangas	P31	31	46	4	5	4	0	0	0	5	16	0	.109
Leo Mangum	P22	23	42	3	11	7	0	0	0	1	2	0	.262
Peter Stack	C17	17	58	8	17	8	3	0	2	8	2	0	.293
Leon Chagnon	P8	8											.077
Walter Brown	P7	8											.000
Steve Mizerak		4											.333
Clair Forster	P3	3											.000
Eugene Rodgers		2											.500

PITCHERS		W	L	PCT	G	GS	CG	SH	IP	H	BB	SO	ERA
Pete Appleton		23	9	.719	41		23	4	244	211	80	122	3.17
Harry Smythe		22	11	.667	45		23	3	259	280	54	109	3.30
Chad Kimsey		16	7	.696	35		14	1	192	173	71	54	3.14
Raymond Fritz		12	9	.571	37		11	2	185	181	94	121	3.79
Lauri Myllykangas		8	11	.421	31		7	1	147	163	53	59	4.53
Leon Chagnon		4	2	.667	8								
Leo Mangum		3	5	.375	22		3	0	110	128	37	36	5.48
Clair Forster		0	1	.000	3								
Walter Brown		0	2	.000	7								

SYRACUSE Chiefs

	2nd	87-67	.565	-5		Harry Leibold

BATTERS	POS-GAMES	GP	AB	R	H	BI	2B	3B	HR	BB	SO	SB	BA
Glenn Wright	1B46,2B16	64	215	26	54	38	12	1	5	14	21	3	.251
George Toporcer	2B124	125	454	70	121	43	17	6	3	67	21	17	.267
Al Niemiec	SS153	153	569	88	158	70	15	15	3	60	67	12	.278
John Kroner	3B	(see multi-team players)											
Dom Dallessandro	OF105	111	356	80	113	36	20	10	6	72	32	10	.317
Prince Oana	OF87	87	320	46	96	52	21	8	12	16	54	4	.300
James Moore	OF	(see multi-team players)											
George Savino	C89	103	297	29	81	42	9	4	5	19	23	2	.273
Stanley Schino	OF62	86	212	29	45	31	7	5	5	29	33	2	.212
Louis Legett	C69	81	239	24	75	38	14	4	6	12	24	4	.314
Art Graham	OF45	51	139	27	27	18	5	1	3	21	14	7	.194
Raymond Coombs	P40	43	64	8	12	6	1	0	0	9	10	1	.188
Reg Grabowski	P40	40	64	7	15	6	4	1	1	5	21	0	.234
John Watwood	OF35	37	133	22	34	15	3	1	1	16	14	5	.256
Harry Taylor	1B33	34	115	18	27	8	3	0	0	16	7	2	.235
Joseph Mulligan	P34	34	41	0	2	3	0	0	0	2	30	0	.049
Hy Vandenberg	P30	30	59	6	6	2	2	0	0	3	9	0	.102
Clarence Hamel	OF25	26	91	15	30	19	3	6	1	19	12	0	.330
John Maruska	OF19	23	68	11	16	8	3	0	2	3	5	0	.235
John Day	P23	23	18	0	2	0	0	0	0	0	5	1	.111
Joseph Cascarella	P21	22	50	1	5	1	0	0	0	1	18	0	.100
Al Marquardt		21	52	10	12	3	3	0	0	2	5	1	.231
Henry Johnson	P14	21	37	7	7	1	0	2	0	3	8	0	.189
Charles Rhem	P21	21	33	1	5	1	0	0	0	2	8	0	.152
Fred Fussell	P15	15	17	1	2	0	0	0	0	3	3	0	.118
John Wilson	P14	14	22	3	7	0	0	0	0	2	3	0	.318
Clarence Fisher	P9	9											.091
John Merena	P8	8											.000
James McCloskey	P7	7											.333
Jack Grossman		7											.250

SYRACUSE (cont.)
Chiefs

BATTERS	POS-GAMES	GP	AB	R	H	BI	2B	3B	HR	BB	SO	SB	BA
George Hockette	P5	5											.300
William Chamberlin	P3	3											.000
Joseph Cicero		2											.333
Robert Brown	P1	1											.000
Marsh Monroe	P1	1											.000

PITCHERS		W	L	PCT	G	GS	CG	SH	IP	H	BB	SO	ERA
Reg Grabowski		16	11	.593	40		10	3	194	190	42	76	3.99
Hy Vandenberg		13	7	.650	30		11	2	172	158	54	83	3.45
Raymond Coombs		13	11	.542	40		10	0	193	224	60	60	4.80
Joseph Cascarella		11	7	.611	21		11	2	138	115	33	78	**2.35**
Charles Rhem		8	6	.571	21		6	1	104	133	29	51	5.28
Joseph Mulligan		8	8	.500	34		4	0	128	115	82	43	3.59
Henry Johnson		5	2	.714	14		4	0	84	75	34	50	3.64
Fred Fussell		4	2	.667	15		1	0	53	62	16	20	4.75
John Wilson		4	2	.667	14		2	0	71	63	36	40	3.93
George Hockette		2	2	.500	5								
Robert Brown		1	0	1.000	1								
John Day		1	2	.333	23		0	0	65	72	32	27	4.43
John Merena		1	3	.250	8								
Clarence Fisher		0	2	.000	9								
James McCloskey		0	2	.000	7								
William Chamberlin		0	0	----	3								
Marsh Monroe		0	0	----	1								

BUFFALO   3rd   86-67   .562   -5.5   Ray Schalk
Bisons

BATTERS	POS-GAMES	GP	AB	R	H	BI	2B	3B	HR	BB	SO	SB	BA
Richard Seibert	1B136	140	534	93	158	71	30	7	13	36	46	6	.296
Marvin Olson	2B147	147	517	112	169	72	23	9	7	96	42	6	.327
Greg Mulleavy	SS148	150	580	86	169	55	25	11	2	64	37	12	.291
Howard Meyers	3B148	154	581	101	150	62	26	10	6	58	54	8	.258
Ollie Carnegie	OF152	154	583	118	171	153	39	5	37	60	110	6	.293
Ray Fitzgerald	OF138	139	503	95	165	115	29	7	17	64	31	9	.328
Frank McGowan	OF115	124	404	67	120	75	19	7	5	69	34	3	.297
Clyde Crouse	C115	116	347	49	89	44	13	2	5	54	18	1	.256
Howard McFarland	OF63	70	191	23	46	22	11	0	2	22	23	3	.241
Lincoln Wasem	C57	63	140	20	29	17	3	1	3	17	26	0	.207
John Smith	1B22	49	105	3	24	20	5	1	1	8	11	0	.229
Art Jacobs	P45	45	30	2	4	0	0	0	0	6	2	0	.133
Robert Kline	P40	40	83	5	16	12	3	2	0	0	18	0	.193
Hod Lisenbee	P39	39	54	3	7	3	2	0	0	3	21	0	.130
William Harris	P38	38	89	6	23	6	2	1	1	0	9	0	.258
Ken Ash	P36	36	96	8	26	8	4	0	0	5	19	0	.271
Owen Carroll	P27	29	37	3	12	5	2	0	0	3	3	0	.324
Edgar Holley	P23	23	24	1	4	4	3	0	0	1	6	0	.167
John Heving		11	20	0	5	3	0	0	0	3	5	0	.250
John Wilson	P6	6											.000
Dave Lawless	P3	3											.000
Harold Manning	P2	2											.000
Eugene Geary		2											.000

PITCHERS		W	L	PCT	G	GS	CG	SH	IP	H	BB	SO	ERA
William Harris		19	11	.633	38		17	1	242	244	75	137	3.76
Ken Ash		18	11	.621	36		21	0	249	268	63	91	3.80
Robert Kline		17	10	.630	40		15	1	223	265	72	81	4.44
Art Jacobs		9	2	.818	45		2	1	123	140	36	48	4.10
Hod Lisenbee		9	8	.529	39		6	0	168	200	54	57	4.66
Owen Carroll		5	11	.313	27		5	0	105	129	55	26	6.51
John Wilson		3	1	.750	6								
Edgar Holley		3	5	.375	23		2	0	81	110	31	38	7.22
Dave Lawless		0	0	----	3								
Harold Manning		0	0	----	2								

NEWARK Bears

NEWARK Bears	4th	81-71	.533	-10	Robert Shawkey

BATTERS	POS-GAMES	GP	AB	R	H	BI	2B	3B	HR	BB	SO	SB	BA
George McQuinn	1B146	148	563	97	162	77	30	5	11	58	50	7	.288
Don Heffner	2B86,SS17	102	374	53	95	44	14	4	7	42	40	6	.254
Nolen Richardson	SS136	137	542	61	153	68	21	4	6	17	27	6	.282
Merrill May	3B146	147	525	80	156	65	21	4	9	72	25	2	.297
Ernest Koy	OF148	149	566	111	157	88	35	13	16	59	82	33	.277
Dick Porter	OF123	133	458	74	153	74	18	2	8	43	28	6	.334
Fred Walker	OF89	89	317	66	93	67	18	5	17	43	23	1	.293
William Baker	C83	117	317	57	96	61	15	6	7	64	24	3	.303
Willard Hershberger	C71,2B18	107	313	42	97	49	6	4	6	40	18	5	.310
Fern Bell	OF70	81	245	31	66	39	7	4	4	25	23	7	.269
Cecil Spittler	P44	45	57	7	7	0	2	0	0	7	13	0	.123
Ed Leishman	2B33	44	142	27	37	13	4	3	2	17	22	4	.261
Frank Makosky	P42	42	33	1	5	5	1	0	1	1	5	0	.152
Ted Kleinhans	P40	40	72	5	15	5	3	0	0	1	15	0	.208
Kemp Wicker	P35	35	41	8	10	5	2	0	1	4	12	0	.244
Max Rosenfeld	OF23	33	81	9	23	9	6	1	0	6	4	0	.284
John LaRocca	P32	33	58	3	8	6	1	0	0	2	19	0	.138
Marvin Duke	P29	32	57	4	7	5	2	0	0	7	7	0	.123
Daniel Hall	OF17	31	68	13	15	5	1	1	0	15	7	2	.221
Robert Miller	P20	20	15	0	1	0	0	0	0	1	5	0	.067
Roy Schalk	2B15	19	58	11	15	7	3	0	0	12	7	1	.259
Ed Farrell		17	37	6	15	5	1	0	1	5	2	0	.405
Ray White	P14	14	11	2	3	1	0	0	0	1	1	0	.273
James Hitchcock		11	24	2	4	2	0	0	0	2	1	0	.167
Howard LaFlamme	P11	11	18	2	1	1	0	0	1	0	8	0	.056
Steve Sundra	P8	9											.231

PITCHERS	W	L	PCT	G	GS	CG	SH	IP	H	BB	SO	ERA
Ted Kleinhans	17	8	.680	40		18	6	211	190	77	102	2.82
Cecil Spittler	14	11	.560	44		9	1	183	188	99	94	4.03
John LaRocca	11	11	.500	32		12	3	166	159	85	88	5.26
Kemp Wicker	9	9	.500	35		6	0	138	136	47	64	4.04
Marvin Duke	9	11	.450	29		10	0	174	201	42	48	3.93
Frank Makosky	6	7	.462	42		2	0	118	148	42	50	4.96
Steve Sundra	5	1	.833	8								
Robert Miller	3	3	.500	20		1	0	62	60	42	26	4.06
Howard LaFlamme	3	3	.500	11		1	0	56	70	20	15	4.98
Raymond White	0	2	.000	14		1	0	38	47	24	10	6.63

BALTIMORE Orioles

BALTIMORE Orioles	5th	78-74	.513	-13	Guy Sturdy

BATTERS	POS-GAMES	GP	AB	R	H	BI	2B	3B	HR	BB	SO	SB	BA
William Sweeney	1B119	123	490	106	175	75	25	7	13	39	34	19	.357
Irv Jeffries	2B144,3B11	154	638	111	181	68	44	3	19	55	39	15	.284
Robert Gibson	SS126,2B12	143	471	77	128	71	26	5	17	73	92	14	.272
Eddie Mayo	3B130,SS22	154	623	120	162	83	29	10	25	58	44	7	.260
George Puccinelli	OF154	154	582	135	209	172	49	9	53	80	55	4	.359
Woody Abernathy	OF117,1B30	149	544	97	150	110	25	9	31	70	63	12	.276
Vince Barton	OF113	114	381	69	109	85	15	7	27	43	51	8	.286
Roy Spencer	C113	120	405	46	105	44	18	6	4	30	47	3	.259
Walt Cazen	OF96	117	387	70	117	58	24	7	7	23	48	13	.302
Vern Mackie	C15	66	163	12	50	27	8	0	3	10	10	0	.307
Bill Lohrman	P49	56	63	15	16	9	4	0	2	12	30	1	.254
Guy Sturdy		51	63	6	14	9	3	0	0	8	7	0	.222
Harry Gumbert	P46	49	91	7	12	7	1	0	0	1	23	0	.132
Austin Moore	P42	43	51	3	7	3	0	0	0	0	16	1	.137
Fred Blake	P34	37	67	5	9	1	2	0	0	5	13	0	.134
George Darrow	P17	17	31	2	3	3	0	0	0	0	10	0	.097
Alphonse Thomas	P17	17	12	0	0	0	0	0	0	2	3	0	.000
William Atwood		15	42	7	11	5	3	0	0	3	6	2	.262
Dino Chiozza		7											.125
James Mooney	P5	5											.444
Jack Dempsey		1											.500
Charles Dugan	P1	1											.000

PITCHERS	W	L	PCT	G	GS	CG	SH	IP	H	BB	SO	ERA
Harry Gumbert	19	10	.655	46		17	1	245	230	102	114	3.31
Bill Lohrman	14	9	.609	49		3	0	171	180	65	64	5.00

BALTIMORE (cont.)
Orioles

PITCHERS	W	L	PCT	G	GS	CG	SH	IP	H	BB	SO	ERA
Fred Blake	12	12	.500	34		16	4	207	228	91	105	4.57
George Darrow	6	4	.600	17		7	0	86	104	56	31	6.17
Austin Moore	6	11	.353	42		6	2	163	193	57	87	5.30
Alphonse Thomas	3	2	.600	17		0	0	48	78	14	27	6.75
James Mooney	1	4	.200	5								
Charles Dugan	0	0	----	1								

TORONTO   6th   78-76   .506   -14   Ike Boone
Maple Leafs

BATTERS	POS-GAMES	GP	AB	R	H	BI	2B	3B	HR	BB	SO	SB	BA
James Shevlin	1B	(see multi-team players)											
Joe Morrissey	2B99	106	385	55	105	45	21	0	1	30	15	3	.273
Cal Chapman	SS135,2B16	150	577	104	190	77	30	9	12	47	34	18	.329
Lee Handley	3B130	130	452	54	123	49	14	9	6	39	54	6	.272
Wes Shulmerich	OF147	148	517	100	154	106	31	6	17	69	71	7	.298
Tom Oliver	OF144,3B12	154	**645**	102	192	66	24	5	11	51	22	6	.298
Ike Boone	OF124	130	437	82	153	85	23	8	9	68	10	3	.350
Gordon Hinkle	C	(see multi-team players)											
John Peacock	OF27,C25,2B22	92	255	42	74	35	11	2	3	26	22	1	.290
Jack Crouch	C68	77	232	28	63	41	8	9	1	22	17	5	.272
Harlan Pool	OF45,1B20	76	228	34	75	38	8	3	3	19	19	0	.329
James Pattison	P42	49	66	12	18	10	2	4	2	5	15	2	.273
Walt Hilcher	P38	38	83	5	14	8	0	1	0	1	13	1	.169
Stan Lucas	P38	38	24	1	5	2	0	0	0	0	6	1	.208
Junie Barnes	P35	35	75	7	21	8	2	1	0	2	13	0	.280
Joe Vance	P23	34	75	6	14	4	3	1	0	0	15	0	.187
Earl Cook	P33	33	59	6	10	5	1	0	0	0	15	0	.169
Ray Davis	P26	26	49	6	14	5	0	0	0	4	12	0	.286
Edward Miller	SS18	18	65	10	20	12	4	1	0	5	3	0	.308
Tony Piet	2B13	17	71	15	22	6	4	0	1	3	6	4	.310
Frank McCormick		12	51	9	12	7	1	0	2	1	5	2	.235
Francis Nekola	P12	12	20	0	1	1	0	0	0	1	9	0	.050
Raymond Starr	P11	11	18	2	5	1	0	0	0	2	6	0	.278
Frank Coleman	P9	9											.231
Mayo Smith		9											.182
John Pasek		8											.296
Phil Cozad	P7	7											.444
Lloyd Moore	P4	4											.333
John Yelovic	P3	4											.000
Mal Thomas		4											.000

PITCHERS	W	L	PCT	G	GS	CG	SH	IP	H	BB	SO	ERA
Walt Hilcher	19	11	.633	38		17	3	228	236	84	107	4.03
James Pattison	16	8	.667	42		13	1	169	175	55	70	3.73
Earl Cook	11	9	.550	33		12	3	169	166	72	58	4.31
Junie Barnes	8	10	.444	35		9	1	200	204	90	124	4.32
Ray Davis	8	11	.421	26		9	0	142	182	28	51	5.01
Charles Lucas	5	4	.556	38		1	0	84	102	36	33	5.57
Joe Vance	5	8	.385	23		7	0	134	129	55	51	2.55
Raymond Starr	3	4	.429	11		4	1	52	58	37	24	6.06
Frank Coleman	2	2	.500	9								
Phil Cozad	1	3	.250	7								
John Yelovic	0	1	.000	3								
Francis Nekola	0	5	.000	12		3	0	50	56	29	30	4.32
Lloyd Moore	0	0	----	4								

ROCHESTER   7th   61-91   .401   -30   Edward Dyer -
Red Wings   Burt Shotton

BATTERS	POS-GAMES	GP	AB	R	H	BI	2B	3B	HR	BB	SO	SB	BA
John Mize	1B65	65	252	37	80	44	11	1	12	16	15	1	.317
James Brown	2B131,SS16	151	618	73	149	51	20	11	3	37	29	7	.241
Thomas Carey	SS92	92	372	53	112	39	16	7	3	20	14	5	.301
D'Arcy Flowers	3B90,1B11	105	364	59	100	62	16	5	15	47	33	10	.275
Colonel Mills	OF142	149	549	88	172	75	37	13	8	55	52	15	.313
Eugene Moore	OF120	122	445	66	144	81	30	10	16	33	56	8	.324
Estel Crabtree	OF95,3B23,1B20	145	530	83	148	68	21	4	15	69	51	7	.279

ROCHESTER (cont.)
Red Wings

BATTERS	POS-GAMES	GP	AB	R	H	BI	2B	3B	HR	BB	SO	SB	BA
Thomas West	C82,1B13	105	331	34	85	32	12	5	2	18	18	2	.257
Homer Peel	OF71	88	275	35	80	36	17	1	3	21	21	0	.291
Francis Healy	C40,3B13,P1	61	181	21	49	14	10	1	0	11	16	1	.271
Paul Florence	C45	55	153	16	48	24	4	2	4	26	14	0	.314
Charles Wilson	SS44	48	183	13	45	31	5	0	2	4	11	2	.246
Tony Kaufmann	P27	41	90	13	26	12	5	0	2	5	9	0	.289
John Michaels	P40	41	60	6	18	5	1	0	0	1	7	0	.300
Al Fisher	P21	39	79	14	23	18	3	2	4	2	17	0	.291
Hal Epps	OF32	32	112	14	33	7	1	1	1	7	17	1	.295
Ward Cross	P24	29	44	2	11	7	0	0	0	2	6	0	.250
James Irving	1B26	26	96	9	26	7	4	0	0	3	9	1	.271
Lawrence Barton	1B24	26	66	10	13	4	3	1	0	12	17	0	.197
Norbert Kleinke	P24	24	35	3	3	0	0	0	0	0	17	0	.086
Bill Hunnefield	3B14	22	57	4	9	1	1	0	0	3	3	0	.158
Ray Harrell	P20	20	36	1	4	1	0	1	0	1	19	0	.111
Glenn Spencer	P18	19	19	2	4	0	0	0	0	3	7	0	.211
Earl Adams		12	36	4	6	1	1	0	1	5	0	0	.167
Maywood Belcher	P11	11	9	2	3	2	0	1	0	2	0	0	.333
James Lyons	P10	10	13	0	2	0	0	0	0	2	3	0	.154
Michael Posiask	P6	9											.375
Nate Andrews	P8	8											.286
Richard Ward	P7	7											.313
Henry Wayton		7											.000
John Rampola	P6	6											.000
Al Eckert	P6	6											.000
Michael Pellino		5											.154
Max Macon	P5	5											.000
Clarence Heise	P4	4											.500
John Keane		3											.000
Alexander Ivan	P1	2											.000
Sebastian Wagner		2											.000
Howard Krist	P1	1											.500
Rocco Vicino	P1	1											.000
Dykes Potter	P1	1											.000

PITCHERS	W	L	PCT	G	GS	CG	SH	IP	H	BB	SO	ERA
John Michaels	9	10	.474	40		8	0	165	193	63	67	4.42
Tony Kaufmann	8	13	.381	27		13	0	159	166	66	58	4.47
Al Fisher	6	8	.429	21		11	2	127	136	37	55	4.18
Ray Harrell	6	10	.375	20		8	2	103	107	52	51	4.98
Richard Ward	3	3	.500	7								
Glenn Spencer	3	5	.375	18		2	0	72	77	36	36	4.75
Norbert Kleinke	3	9	.250	24		3	0	99	111	53	40	5.00
Michael Posiask	2	0	1.000	6								
James Lyons	2	1	.667	10		3	1	43	44	18	13	4.81
Maywood Belcher	2	5	.286	11		2	0	36	38	18	17	5.25
John Rampola	0	1	.000	6								
Clarence Heise	0	1	.000	4								
Al Eckert	0	2	.000	6								
Nate Andrews	0	0	----	8								
Max Macon	0	0	----	5								
Rocco Vicino	0	0	----	1								
Howard Krist	0	0	----	1								
Dykes Potter	0	0	---	1								
Alexander Ivan	0	0	----	1								
Francis Healy	0	0	----	1								

ALBANY
Senators

8th	49-104	.320	-42.5	Al Mamaux - Johnny Evers			

BATTERS	POS-GAMES	GP	AB	R	H	BI	2B	3B	HR	BB	SO	SB	BA
Oscar Roettger	1B	(see multi-team players)											
Don Kellett	2B73,3B16	87	335	53	84	47	15	4	3	42	39	4	.251
Ed Cihocki	SS153	153	539	60	137	67	26	10	6	36	13	3	.254
Russ Peters	3B68	83	241	34	51	25	12	6	2	28	82	1	.212
Taft Wright	OF125	139	472	73	133	74	22	8	12	44	38	4	.282
Charles Hostetler	OF108	109	429	56	132	43	15	5	1	36	53	9	.308
Ed Boland	OF63	63	243	27	60	33	6	4	3	12	22	1	.247
Frank Hayes	C	(see multi-team players)											
Fred Chapman	C27	34	101	16	35	19	6	2	2	15	6	2	.347

ALBANY (cont.)
Senators

BATTERS	POS-GAMES	GP	AB	R	H	BI	2B	3B	HR	BB	SO	SB	BA
Lewis Wilson	OF50	59	175	30	46	29	9	1	3	44	24	0	.263
Phil Hensiek	P44	46	36	5	7	4	2	0	0	4	13	0	.194
Alex Sparra	2B37	45	151	16	31	5	1	2	0	17	40	3	.205
Murl Prather	1B44	44	149	33	43	21	8	1	2	35	25	1	.289
Charles George	C35	43	138	20	40	14	9	2	0	8	28	0	.290
Edwin Pitts	OF34	43	116	14	27	9	3	0	0	7	24	2	.233
Charles Leiber	P42	43	37	1	6	3	1	0	0	4	13	0	.162
Ed Phillips	C27	34	101	16	35	19	6	2	2	15	6	2	.347
Monte Weaver	P31	31	60	2	12	4	0	0	0	2	9	0	.200
Hugh Mulcahy	P27	30	35	7	8	5	1	1	1	5	8	0	.229
Frank Packard	3B24	29	81	12	21	6	6	1	2	21	18	0	.259
Dan Hafey	OF25	25	100	23	23	23	3	1	6	14	25	1	.230
Peter Susko	1B24	24	95	8	21	11	3	0	0	6	1	3	.221
James Carrithers	P21	21	27	2	2	1	0	0	0	2	5	0	.074
Ed Remorenko		18	52	9	15	10	2	2	1	5	12	0	.288
Raymond Flood	OF16	17	63	13	17	7	4	1	0	6	5	0	.270
Tracy Hitchner	P17	17	8	0	0	0	0	0	0	0	3	0	.000
Mark Filley	P14	16	21	1	1	0	0	0	0	2	9	0	.048
George Caster	P14	15	24	1	6	2	0	0	0	0	7	0	.250
Jack Redmond		14	29	2	7	3	1	0	1	2	3	0	.241
Edwin Chapman	P12	14	10	1	3	1	1	0	0	1	2	0	.300
Joseph Bokina	P13	13	23	3	7	4	1	0	0	1	8	0	.304
Roy Hansen	P12	12	15	2	3	0	0	0	0	1	5	0	.200
William Starr		11	27	2	5	6	0	0	1	1	0	0	.185
Al McNeely		9											.231
Ray Prim	P9	9											.231
Roberto Estalella		9											.100
Jack Plummer		8											.160
Al Mamaux	P6	6											.167
Robert Reeves		6											.136
Allen Benson	P6	6											.000
Len Shires		5											.200
Robert Burke	P5	5											.111
Charles DeLucco	P4	4											.667
Milburn Shoffner	P3	3											.500
Al McLean	P3	3											.000
Orville Armbrust	P3	3											.000
Fred Brickell		3											.000
Robert Edwards	P3	3											.000
Oscar Perrin		2											.250
Carl O'Grady	P2	2											.000
Mike Kash	P2	2											.000
Marlin Stoltz	P2	2											.000
John Rigney	P2	2											.000
Reese Diggs	P2	2											.000
Frank Garrity		2											.000
Harold Elliott	P1	1											.000
Sam Dizenzo	P1	1											.000
George Neslie	P1	1											.000
Joe Krakauskas	P1	1											.000
Ralph Semerad		1											.000

PITCHERS	W	L	PCT	G	GS	CG	SH	IP	H	BB	SO	ERA
Phil Hensiek	8	9	.471	44		2	0	130	125	57	73	4.15
Monte Weaver	7	15	.318	31		8	0	174	226	65	71	5.43
Hugh Mulcahy	4	2	.667	27		1	0	102	117	59	38	5.12
Joseph Bokina	4	2	.667	13		1	0	58	78	29	15	6.98
James Carithers	4	6	.400	21		4	1	80	78	41	27	4.73
Charles Leiber	4	19	.174	42		5	1	141	183	49	38	5.68
Robert Burke	3	0	1.000	5								
Roy Hansen	3	4	.429	12		1	0	45	51	21	12	5.40
Mark Filley	2	3	.400	14		0	0	66	86	30	14	4.91
Ray Prim	2	4	.333	9								
Al McLean	1	1	.500	3								
Allen Benson	1	2	.333	6								
Tracy Hitchner	1	3	.250	17		0	0	43	48	20	10	5.44
George Caster	1	8	.111	14		3	0	80	102	44	35	5.85
Milburn Shoffner	0	1	.000	3								
John Rigney	0	1	.000	2								
Reese Diggs	0	1	.000	2								
Edwin Chapman	0	4	.000	12		0	0	30	44	31	17	12.00
Al Mamaux	0	0	----	6								
Charles DeLucco	0	0	----	4								
Robert Edwards	0	0	----	3								
Orville Armbrust	0	0	----	3								
Mike Kash	0	0	----	2								

ALBANY (cont.)
Senators

PITCHERS	W	L	PCT	G	GS	CG	SH	IP	H	BB	SO	ERA
Carl O'Grady	0	0	----	2								
Marlin Stoltz	0	0	----	2								
Sam Dizenzo	0	0	----	1								
Harold Elliott	0	0	----	1								
George Neslie	0	0	----	1								
Joe Krakauskas	0	0	----	1								

MULTI-TEAM PLAYERS

BATTERS	POS-GAMES	TEAMS	GP	AB	R	H	BI	2B	3B	HR	BB	SO	SB	BA
John Kroner	3B88,1B46,2B17	BA1-SY146	147	554	93	179	112	32	6	15	48	58	6	.323
James Shevlin	1B125	SY4-TO122	126	413	33	114	56	27	3	2	64	31	4	.276
Frank Hayes	C74,1B10	BU5-AL104	109	321	56	94	52	14	6	12	37	58	3	.293
Oscar Roettger	1B93	SY24-AL74	98	346	32	93	37	14	0	3	29	25	1	.269
Oliver Tucker	OF70	BU39-SY56	95	251	36	72	35	14	3	2	38	12	2	.287
Gordon Hinkle	C83	SY15-TO77	92	278	26	64	40	11	3	2	27	46	0	.230
Oliver Sax	3B49,OF10	AL37-SY47	84	197	31	45	16	6	1	1	21	25	6	.228
James Moore	OF67	RO7-SY74	81	234	42	77	40	18	3	4	44	19	4	.329
Julian Wera	3B46	SY40-BU33	73	197	17	44	31	6	0	0	13	11	1	.223
Bert Delmas	2B41,3B11	BU8-AL19-TO37	64	168	31	44	9	3	1	0	17	32	2	.262
John Pomorski	P42	MO13-BU29	42	36	7	8	3	0	0	1	5	11	0	.222
Beryl Richmond	P37	BA11-AL26	37	49	1	4	4	2	0	0	5	25	0	.082
Cliff Melton	P36	NE15-BA21	36	61	2	11	4	0	0	0	7	20	1	.180
George Granger	P30	BA17-MO15	32	54	7	13	9	2	1	1	9	7	0	.241
Frank Pearce	P26	RO9-BA20	29	57	3	9	4	1	0	0	3	16	0	.158
Robert Weiland	P26	AL10-RO16	26	53	5	6	5	0	1	0	3	14	0	.113
John Berly	P22	RO17-BA5	22	39	2	9	7	1	1	0	3	7	0	.231
Robert Smith	C15	AL14-SY4	18	48	5	11	1	2	0	1	1	6	0	.229

PITCHERS	TEAMS	W	L	PCT	G	GS	CG	SH	IP	H	BB	SO	ERA
George Granger	BA16-MO14	9	7	.563	30		6	1	154	176	63	67	5.14
Robert Weiland	AL10-RO16	9	10	.474	26		10	2	164	149	46	112	2.74
Frank Pearce	RO9-BA17	7	9	.438	26		11	3	152	176	48	62	4.68
Cliff Melton	NE15-BA21	7	15	.318	36		10	2	189	194	87	103	4.48
John Berly	RO17-BA5	6	8	.429	22		7	0	109	129	76	50	5.70
John Pomorski	MO13-BU29	4	9	.308	42		2	0	134	168	61	59	5.17
Beryl Richmond	BA11-AL26	3	18	.143	37		4	0	160	217	78	73	6.47

TEAM BATTING

TEAMS	GP	AB	R	H	BI	2B	3B	HR	BB	SO	SB	BA
MONTREAL	155	5242	832	1526	765	306	75	74	548	413	62	.291
SYRACUSE	154	5086	735	1361	677	219	76	74	548	569	87	.268
BUFFALO	154	5096	815	1423	762	242	64	101	590	540	54	.279
NEWARK	152	5040	774	1403	702	212	57	97	547	484	83	.278
BALTIMORE	154	5262	902	1492	845	279	64	202	528	633	101	.284
TORONTO	155	5174	768	1493	709	225	64	72	505	491	64	.289
ROCHESTER	154	5195	681	1425	645	223	69	92	417	511	60	.274
ALBANY	154	5102	671	1290	624	199	60	65	515	855	49	.253
	616	41197	6178	11413	5729	1905	529	777	4198	4496	209	.277

1936
BACK TO JERSEY

Through the early years of the twentieth century, many minor league baseball clubs led an itinerant existence. If owners could not woo fans, they would often uproot the team, seeking more fertile financial fields. Sensing fan indifference, a rival city would sometimes round up some financial backers to tempt an already existing team to relocate. One International League city, Jersey City, had witnessed this process on three separate occasions.

In 1902, the Jersey City Skeeters, located in the New York City metropolitan area, joined the Eastern League. After several second division finishes weakened the club, Baltimore interests, led by Jack Dunn, bought the club in 1916. Undaunted, Jersey City received another franchise in 1918. Nine years later, the club was sold to Montreal businessmen, but without missing a beat Syracuse sold its team to Jersey City, allowing the latter to retain International League membership. Six years later, the situation reversed itself as Jersey City's team was bought by Syracuse interests. Left without a team for the third time, the Jersey City ballpark remained dark for several years. These circumstances would not continue, however, as the city found a new benefactor right on its doorstep.

The 1936 season saw the Buffalo Bisons return to the top seat in the International League after a nine-season absence from that spot. Rochester, Newark, and Baltimore finished as playoff qualifiers, while Toronto, Montreal, Syracuse, and Albany finished out of the money. Smead Jolley of Albany had the highest batting average (.373), Baltimore's Woody Abernathy clubbed the most home runs (42), and Colonel Mills had the highest runs batted in total (134). In pitching, Robert Weiland from Rochester finished with the most wins (23) and most strikeouts (171). Newark's Steve Sundra had the lowest earned run average (2.84)

After the 1936 campaign, the New York Giants of the National League purchased the International's Albany club to start a minor league system of their own. Like the Yankees with Newark, the Giants wanted their team nearby. So they moved the Albany franchise back to nearby Jersey City. In addition, the Giants had a new stadium built to showcase the team. Called Roosevelt Stadium, it served as a fine facility for the Jersey City Giants for many years.

If there was any doubt about Jersey City's love for baseball, it was erased in April 1937. In their first home game, more than 31,000 fans welcomed back the team. Such a display of civic pride was appreciated and noteworthy; to that date it was the largest crowd to witness a contest in all of minor league baseball.

BUFFALO Bisons

BUFFALO Bisons	1st	94-60	.610		Ray Schalk

BATTERS	POS-GAMES	GP	AB	R	H	BI	2B	3B	HR	BB	SO	SB	BA
Elbie Fletcher	1B154	154	599	120	206	85	44	6	17	73	60	9	.344
Marvin Olson	2B148	148	564	86	160	78	31	5	8	70	48	11	.284
Greg Mulleavy	SS149	151	549	96	147	93	32	5	8	59	32	6	.268
Howard Meyers	3B90	104	406	77	122	41	29	5	4	36	44	9	.301
Frank McGowan	OF137	139	522	115	186	111	45	10	23	85	47	3	.356
John Dickshot	OF129	130	482	110	173	112	17	15	17	73	45	33	.359
Ed Boland	OF	(see multi-team players)											
Clyde Crouse	C83	91	287	42	71	43	11	1	5	42	18	1	.248
Ed Phillips	C77	85	264	35	80	51	12	2	10	22	29	2	.303
Ollie Carnegie	OF50	74	193	18	47	34	6	1	4	17	28	1	.244
Art Jacobs	P46	46	28	4	6	1	0	0	0	4	6	0	.214
John Wilson	P41	43	67	4	3	1	0	0	0	4	24	0	.045
Robert Kline	P41	41	73	4	11	8	3	0	0	2	14	0	.151
Eugene Geary	3B27	39	125	23	29	8	5	0	0	17	17	3	.232
Ken Ash	P39	39	66	12	19	10	5	1	2	9	8	0	.288
William Harris	P35	37	80	7	23	16	3	0	0	2	8	0	.288
Rip Sewell	P30	31	67	9	14	10	3	0	1	7	16	0	.209
Joe Mowry	OF23	27	95	18	26	10	7	0	0	6	6	0	.274
Don Ross	3B22	25	85	10	24	13	6	1	0	4	5	1	.282
Charles Fischer	P20	20	51	7	9	2	2	0	0	2	9	0	.176
Gil English	3B19	19	66	6	13	10	2	0	0	8	9	0	.197
Tony Dueker		13	22	6	9	3	1	1	0	6	4	0	.409
Lincoln Wasem		8											.190
John Smith		8											.143
D'Arcy Flowers		8											.111
Hod Lisenbee	P7	7											.000

PITCHERS	W	L	PCT	G	GS	CG	SH	IP	H	BB	SO	ERA
William Harris	15	10	.600	35	31	16	4	201	223	52	110	5.76
John Wilson	14	7	.667	41	22	10	1	193	207	42	82	3.78
Charles Fischer	13	2	.867	20	19	9	3	136	134	38	101	4.10
Ken Ash	13	9	.591	39	28	13	4	205	243	78	74	4.96
Robert Kline	12	10	.545	41	28	9	0	208	255	56	71	4.98
Art Jacobs	11	9	.550	46	1	0	0	108	117	36	44	4.50
Rip Sewell	10	10	.500	30	23	10	2	188	206	75	68	4.55
Hod Lisenbee	0	0	----	7								

ROCHESTER Red Wings

ROCHESTER Red Wings	2nd	89-66	.574	-5.5	Ray Blades

BATTERS	POS-GAMES	GP	AB	R	H	BI	2B	3B	HR	BB	SO	SB	BA
Phil Weintraub	1B101,OF13	115	388	94	144	98	32	10	20	91	63	2	.371
Al Cuccinello	2B136	136	496	87	154	82	31	9	8	54	47	13	.311
James Brown	SS125	133	537	105	166	45	21	7	5	50	49	5	.309
Maurice Sturdy	3B129	130	456	59	132	82	28	5	2	38	42	12	.289
Colonel Mills	OF145	146	550	92	182	134	35	10	18	53	48	23	.331
John Rothrock	OF115	125	468	91	140	51	27	8	5	52	35	7	.299
Lou Scoffic	OF108	115	394	65	126	67	24	2	10	25	65	2	.320
Robert O'Farrell	C102	102	286	30	79	43	20	3	2	24	31	0	.276
Estel Crabtree	OF87,1B42	136	497	96	172	48	24	6	14	65	45	5	.346
Hugh Poland	C86	95	247	30	63	51	7	1	13	21	33	1	.255
Robert Weiland	P55	55	97	5	17	6	1	0	2	7	35	0	.175
Norbert Kleinke	P47	47	73	6	7	1	2	0	0	8	34	0	.096
John Clark	C12	46	59	12	19	9	6	0	1	8	6	0	.322
Raymond Howell	P43	43	75	6	8	7	2	0	3	3	32	0	.107
Tony Kaufmann	P32	41	80	7	21	11	9	2	0	8	13	0	.263
Robert Klinger	P32	33	41	4	4	2	1	0	0	1	7	0	.097
John Michaels	P24	29	13	6	4	1	1	0	0	2	1	0	.308
Lawrence Barton	1B19	28	69	10	17	10	4	0	3	7	14	1	.246
Andrew Doyle	P19	19	14	1	1	1	0	1	0	1	4	0	.071
Louis Bush	2B13	14	52	11	19	8	3	0	1	4	4	1	.365
Frank Doljack	OF13	13	45	6	9	6	2	1	1	3	9	0	.200
Leslie Munns	P12	13	16	3	4	3	0	0	0	0	1	0	.250
Henry Schuble		10	31	5	10	3	3	0	0	2	8	1	.323
Sid Stringfellow		3											.300
Al Fisher	P3	3											.167
Cliff Leahy		3											.000
Norm Isherwood		1											.000
Ed Delker		1											.000

ROCHESTER (cont.)
Red Wings

PITCHERS	W	L	PCT	G	GS	CG	SH	IP	H	BB	SO	ERA
Robert Weiland	23	13	.639	55	29	14	2	265	249	95	171	3.50
Norbert Kleinke	16	12	.571	47	29	10	0	223	258	99	100	4.16
Raymond Howell	14	13	.519	43	34	12	3	212	219	136	153	4.80
Tony Kaufmann	11	9	.550	32	25	11	0	188	209	71	67	4.64
Robert Klinger	7	4	.636	32	9	3	2	109	131	54	51	4.79
John Michaels	4	2	.667	24	1	0	0	49	58	33	14	3.86
Andrew Doyle	1	2	.333	19	5	0	0	46	53	30	20	6.85
Leslie Munns	1	4	.200	12	8	0	0	46	58	29	14	7.04
Al Fisher	0	0	----	3								

NEWARK
Bears

3rd   88-67   .568   -6.5   Ossie Vitt

BATTERS	POS-GAMES	GP	AB	R	H	BI	2B	3B	HR	BB	SO	SB	BA
John McCarthy	1B136,OF15	151	588	94	162	90	33	6	21	35	52	4	.276
Roy Schalk	2B154	154	559	87	148	88	35	4	15	39	49	9	.265
Nolen Richardson	SS153	153	552	80	158	55	21	3	2	38	23	5	.286
Merrill May	3B144	145	529	99	148	63	37	3	10	70	23	5	.280
Ernest Koy	OF139	139	538	87	160	105	24	19	16	46	72	17	.298
Ralph Boyle	OF136	137	513	85	156	70	29	8	14	58	54	6	.304
Dick Porter	OF98	106	343	48	98	43	15	5	4	42	26	6	.286
William Baker	C99	106	335	54	99	59	13	2	9	45	28	3	.295
Max Rosenfeld	OF73	87	234	33	64	33	12	3	1	16	14	3	.274
Frank Makosky	P44	44	27	7	5	4	0	1	0	4	7	0	.185
Spud Chandler	P35	42	82	10	17	5	1	0	2	2	13	0	.207
Francis Hawkins	3B13	40	96	11	19	10	4	2	2	8	15	0	.198
Al Piechota	P38	39	68	8	15	11	3	1	0	4	11	0	.221
Marvin Duke	P35	35	57	5	5	2	0	0	0	7	12	0	.088
Norm Kies	C28	33	96	7	28	16	4	0	0	7	9	1	.292
Kemp Wicker	P33	33	60	2	6	5	1	0	0	4	13	0	.100
Robert Collins	C20	30	93	8	20	12	3	1	1	5	16	2	.215
Steve Sundra	P29	29	72	8	11	5	3	0	1	4	22	0	.153
Raymond Fritz	1B19	24	87	10	27	11	5	1	0	3	12	1	.310
Vito Tamulis	P19	21	40	6	12	3	1	1	0	3	5	0	.300
Howard LaFlamme	P18	18	20	2	3	0	0	0	0	0	2	0	.150
Willard Hershberger	C14	16	54	7	14	12	3	2	1	5	0	0	.259
Robert Miller	P10	10	14	0	1	1	0	0	0	0	5	0	.071
Frank Kelleher		9											.219
Ted Kleinhans	P8	8											.118
Cecil Spittler	P7	7											.167
Don Curry		2											.500
Edward Levy		2											.000
Clyde McCullough		1											.000

PITCHERS	W	L	PCT	G	GS	CG	SH	IP	H	BB	SO	ERA
Spud Chandler	14	13	.519	35	30	14	2	219	231	72	81	3.33
Steve Sundra	12	9	.571	29	26	14	1	187	165	65	103	2.84
Al Piechota	12	10	.545	38	19	9	3	168	160	76	77	3.64
Marvin Duke	11	9	.550	35	26	10	1	189	212	50	55	4.48
Kemp Wicker	11	9	.550	33	25	13	5	191	181	51	85	3.15
Frank Makosky	10	5	.667	44	2	1	0	96	103	37	64	3.19
Vito Tamulis	7	5	.583	19	11	6	2	96	107	30	46	4.69
Ted Kleinhans	4	2	.667	8								
Howard LaFlamme	4	4	.500	18	4	1	0	59	70	27	16	5.19
Cecil Spittler	2	0	1.000	7								
Robert Miller	1	1	.500	10	2	0	0	41	45	32	28	5.92

BALTIMORE
Orioles

4th   81-72   .529   -12.5   Guy Sturdy

BATTERS	POS-GAMES	GP	AB	R	H	BI	2B	3B	HR	BB	SO	SB	BA
Leslie Powers	1B		(see multi-team players)										
Bill Cissell	2B106,SS27	126	493	102	172	78	33	4	15	32	37	11	.349
William Hoffner	SS120	123	420	61	92	27	14	4	3	60	82	5	.219
Joseph Martin	3B121	125	464	81	138	91	36	8	23	28	59	12	.297
Al Wright	OF137	137	535	92	166	130	32	4	24	43	67	8	.310
Woody Abernathy	OF121,2B28	149	554	132	171	127	24	3	42	63	64	11	.309
Glenn Chapman	OF100	123	420	61	92	27	14	4	3	60	82	5	.219

BALTIMORE (cont.)
Orioles

BATTERS	POS-GAMES	GP	AB	R	H	BI	2B	3B	HR	BB	SO	SB	BA
George Savino	C		(see multi-team players)										
Oscar Roettger	1B50	89	233	31	66	34	13	0	5	16	16	0	.283
Paul Florence	C51	68	153	14	31	20	6	0	5	18	22	1	.203
Cliff Melton	P53	53	93	5	19	2	1	0	0	4	18	0	.204
James Bivin	P44	44	40	2	1	0	0	0	0	7	21	0	.025
Fred Blake	P37	38	84	13	20	8	4	0	1	9	18	0	.238
Milton Gray	C28	33	76	13	18	10	4	1	1	11	2	1	.237
Bill Lohrman	P27	29	19	4	3	1	2	0	0	10	9	0	.158
Eddie Mayo	3B26	26	106	18	31	14	2	1	2	13	8	0	.292
Max Bishop	2B20	23	57	14	16	5	4	0	1	18	5	0	.281
Roy Spencer	C19	19	64	7	20	13	1	0	1	8	3	0	.313
Harold Kelleher	P13	15	9	1	2	0	0	0	0	2	3	0	.222
Robert Holland		14	41	3	6	4	2	1	0	2	3	0	.146
Euel Moore	P8	8											.000
Lawrence Benton	P6	6											.000
Frank Anderson	P4	4											.167
James McCloskey	P2	3											.000
Joe Kohlman	P1	1											.000

PITCHERS	W	L	PCT	G	GS	CG	SH	IP	H	BB	SO	ERA
Cliff Melton	20	14	.588	53	32	13	0	271	254	77	158	3.39
Fred Blake	14	16	.467	37	34	18	2	255	307	101	117	4.91
James Bivin	8	8	.500	44	16	6	0	145	177	57	52	5.59
Lawrence Benton	1	1	.500	6								
Frank Anderson	1	1		4								
Harold Kelleher	1	2	.333	13	3	0	0	33	36	27	8	6.55
Bill Lohrman	1	6	.143	27	1	0	0	79	93	20	34	5.58
Euel Moore	0	1	.000	8								
James McCloskey	0	0	----	2								
Joe Kohlman	0	0	----	1								

TORONTO   5th   77-76   .503   -16.5   Ike Boone
Maple Leafs

BATTERS	POS-GAMES	GP	AB	R	H	BI	2B	3B	HR	BB	SO	SB	BA
George McQuinn	1B108	108	410	67	135	61	21	16	9	31	36	6	.329
Lee Handley	2B109	109	390	52	116	48	16	7	6	20	49	18	.297
Edward Miller	SS150	150	546	69	132	59	15	9	8	27	44	1	.242
Julian Wera	3B72	81	265	27	65	38	7	3	1	12	19	0	.245
Tom Oliver	OF147	154	595	94	176	52	25	7	6	61	17	8	.296
Linc Blakely	OF121	130	416	54	114	59	25	10	5	43	59	3	.274
Harlan Pool	OF75	77	278	37	80	33	16	4	2	24	7	1	.288
Thomas Heath	C80	92	274	32	70	32	11	2	5	38	27	1	.255
John Burnett	3B63,2B48	124	421	58	107	45	22	6	5	52	27	3	.254
Henry Erickson	C65	73	204	16	44	16	5	2	0	18	26	1	.216
Ike Boone	OF48	71	169	22	43	22	8	2	3	25	11	3	.254
Adam Comorosky	OF55	61	193	29	50	19	10	2	0	11	10	2	.259
James Pattison	P33	45	55	4	17	9	1	1	1	1	9	0	.309
Les Scarsella	1B42	42	165	24	60	22	10	7	3	8	8	3	.364
LeRoy Herrmann	P36	36	82	3	12	3	1	0	0	1	4	0	.146
Francis Nekola	P34	34	46	4	10	3	0	0	0	2	12	0	.217
Jake Mooty	P32	33	69	8	10	4	2	0	0	3	14	0	.145
Earl Cook	P33	33	43	3	8	1	0	0	0	0	3	0	.186
Silas Johnson	P26	26	50	2	4	3	0	0	0	0	16	0	.080
Art Funk	3B22	22	79	9	25	11	4	0	0	4	5	0	.316
Emmett Nelson	P15	15	16	0	2	0	1	0	0	2	5	0	.125
Robert E. Porter	P1	10	32	2	5	4	1	0	1	0	7	0	.156
Francis Wistert	P10	10	22	2	3	3	1	0	0	1	8	0	.136
William Walker	P6	6											.308
Nelson Potter	P5	5											.333
Walt Purcey	P5	5											.000
Jack Crouch		1											.500
Lloyd Stirling	P1	1											.000

PITCHERS	W	L	PCT	G	GS	CG	SH	IP	H	BB	SO	ERA
LeRoy Herrmann	16	13	.552	36	31	17	2	232	242	96	113	4.31
Jake Mooty	12	8	.600	32	25	7	4	191	180	58	74	3.72
Silas Johnson	10	9	.526	26	18	9	5	155	123	44	82	2.38

TORONTO (cont.)
Maple Leafs

PITCHERS	W	L	PCT	G	GS	CG	SH	IP	H	BB	SO	ERA
James Pattison	9	9	.500	33	15	7	0	119	139	53	57	4.31
Francis Nekola	7	8	.467	34	18	8	2	135	146	51	67	4.87
William Walker	4	2	.667	6								
Earl Cook	4	6	.400	33	13	4	2	116	127	53	52	4.34
Francis Wistert	2	5	.286	10	6	2	0	57	48	43	19	4.26
Walt Purcey	1	0	1.000	5								
Emmett Nelson	1	6	.143	15	7	2	0	52	70	30	33	7.62
Nelson Potter	0	0	----	5								
Robert E. Porter	0	0	----	1								
Lloyd Stirling	0	0	----	1								

MONTREAL	6th	71-81	.467	-22	Frank Shaughnessy -
Royals					Harry Smythe

BATTERS	POS-GAMES	GP	AB	R	H	BI	2B	3B	HR	BB	SO	SB	BA
Del Bissonette	1B77	77	290	36	70	36	13	6	6	30	23	0	.241
Harold King	2B62,3B41	117	359	59	106	63	21	5	12	59	23	0	.295
Ben Sankey	SS145	145	486	52	118	50	19	4	2	36	34	3	.243
Lafayette Thompson	3B77	80	308	41	89	39	22	3	4	26	19	2	.289
Bob Seeds	OF131	131	523	91	166	75	48	13	12	55	38	12	.317
Gus Dugas	OF120,1B12	140	451	82	138	91	26	15	18	73	35	2	.308
William Rhiel	OF88	99	279	40	85	38	16	3	3	20	28	1	.305
Bennie Tate	C68	82	225	17	58	27	7	3	4	17	9	0	.258
Charles Wilson	2B24,OF24,3B21,SS19	110	313	35	82	36	19	3	3	23	18	6	.262
Glenn Myatt	C63	68	182	21	28	17	6	2	0	30	17	0	.154
Hub Bates	OF64	67	247	44	64	28	14	9	1	24	52	3	.259
Minor Heath	1B61	64	213	36	56	34	16	2	3	33	24	0	.263
Dave Harris	OF61	61	220	41	69	34	18	3	4	30	36	6	.314
Harry Smythe	P43	54	82	11	19	4	5	0	0	6	8	0	.232
Henry Johnson	P23	42	82	11	27	14	5	1	2	5	11	0	.329
Lou Polli	P33	40	72	10	14	9	2	0	0	3	14	0	.194
Frank Reiber	C37	41	126	18	38	28	13	0	0	19	12	0	.302
Lauri Myllykangas	P36	36	74	11	17	9	1	1	0	10	20	0	.230
Leon Chagnon	P30	33	58	5	14	5	2	0	0	4	13	0	.241
George Granger	P28	29	43	1	5	1	2	1	0	2	12	0	.116
Phil Hensiek	P25	25	7	0	0	0	0	0	0	2	3	0	.000
Jacob Wade	P24	24	27	4	5	2	0	0	0	2	13	0	.185
Steve Mizerak	2B16	17	52	8	14	6	4	1	0	10	12	0	.269
Chad Kimsey	P8	14	28	7	13	10	1	1	1	2	3	1	.464
Don French	P2	2											.000
Albert Moran	P1	1											.000

PITCHERS	W	L	PCT	G	GS	CG	SH	IP	H	BB	SO	ERA
Lauri Myllykangas	13	12	.520	36	31	18	0	216	230	80	92	4.13
Harry Smythe	12	13	.480	43	19	17	3	189	217	52	79	3.52
Lou Polli	12	14	.462	33	27	15	3	211	225	64	74	3.92
Leon Chagnon	10	10	.500	30	24	11	1	177	212	62	67	4.83
Henry Johnson	9	10	.474	23	21	13	1	163	152	63	93	3.53
Jacob Wade	6	8	.429	24	11	4	2	94	97	45	70	4.88
Chad Kimsey	5	1	.833	8								
George Granger	3	11	.214	28	10	4	0	121	127	51	27	3.79
Phil Hensiek	1	2	.333	25	1	0	0	40	62	22	16	6.83
Don French	0	0	----	2								
Albert Moran	0	0	----	1								

SYRACUSE	7th	59-95	.383	-35	Harry Leibold -
Chiefs					Bernard Kelly

BATTERS	POS-GAMES	GP	AB	R	H	BI	2B	3B	HR	BB	SO	SB	BA
Babe Dahlgren	1B155	155	566	90	180	121	31	21	16	68	66	10	.318
Don Kellett	2B65,3B13	91	292	31	64	28	13	4	1	26	30	9	.219
Len Backer	3B	(see multi-team players)											
Keith Molesworth	SS	(see multi-team players)											
Dom Dallessandro	OF149	151	551	121	177	81	40	13	7	92	46	14	.321
Fred Koster	OF67	75	265	44	72	17	12	4	0	25	35	3	.272
Walt Cazen	OF	(see multi-team players)											
John Heving	C82	89	275	22	73	28	10	4	1	23	19	1	.266

SYRACUSE (cont.)
Chiefs

BATTERS	POS-GAMES	GP	AB	R	H	BI	2B	3B	HR	BB	SO	SB	BA
Louis Legett	C72	89	247	24	57	17	12	3	1	22	22	4	.231
Robert Gibson	2B54,3B26	88	260	28	68	30	14	5	5	39	55	3	.262
John Reder	P29,3B12	66	122	17	33	14	5	1	1	9	27	2	.270
Andrew Pilney	OF33	48	129	10	30	12	7	3	2	6	24	3	.233
Dib Williams	SS25,2B10	44	161	25	41	21	5	1	4	19	10	1	.255
Vince Barton	OF44	44	155	20	37	18	5	8	1	21	19	4	.239
Leo Mangum	P36	36	82	5	18	8	0	1	1	0	16	0	.220
Fred Fussell	P30	33	61	3	12	3	2	1	0	1	23	0	.197
George Hockette	P23	26	30	3	8	0	0	0	0	2	5	0	.267
Emile Meola	P25	25	53	1	4	0	0	0	0	4	15	0	.075
John Maruska	OF20	21	66	5	14	9	2	2	0	7	9	3	.212
Raymond Starr	P20	20	37	2	8	3	0	0	0	4	11	0	.216
John Griffiths	SS13	18	55	11	16	7	3	2	0	3	1	1	.291
Matt Holmes	P17	17	15	0	0	0	0	0	0	1	7	0	.000
John Kerr	3B15	16	46	2	7	6	1	0	0	4	7	0	.152
Aloysius Murphy	3B13	14	51	5	7	6	0	0	1	2	4	0	.137
Stewart Bowers	P14	14	15	0	0	0	0	0	0	4	7	0	.000
Cecil Trent		12	24	2	8	1	0	0	0	2	0	0	.333
Dick Midkiff	P12	12	11	0	2	0	0	0	0	1	6	0	.182
William Humphrey	P10	10	11	0	0	0	0	0	0	1	4	0	.000
Robert Brown	P8	8											.000
John Day	P5	6											.000
Guenther Schmidt	P5	5											.667
Ed Moriarity		4											.000
Merle Coleman	P3	3											.000
Frank Osnato	P2	2											.000
Lewis Grasso		2											.000
Albert Blanche	P1	1											.000
Aubrey Graham		1											.000

PITCHERS	W	L	PCT	G	GS	CG	SH	IP	H	BB	SO	ERA
Fred Fussell	13	11	.542	30	19	10	1	159	161	52	62	3.11
Leo Mangum	10	15	.400	36	27	15	1	222	250	43	71	4.19
Emile Meola	7	10	.412	25	19	11	0	150	167	58	65	4.08
Raymond Starr	6	7	.462	20	17	6	2	121	118	60	52	4.02
George Hockette	4	11	.267	23	16	7	2	102	130	29	27	5.65
John Reder	3	6	.333	29	8	3	0	96	142	51	26	7.88
Stewart Bowers	2	4	.333	14	6	0	0	46	64	23	19	7.24
Dick Midkiff	1	2	.333	12	3	0	0	34	47	18	11	6.88
Robert Brown	1	2	.333	8								
Matt Holmes	1	3	.250	17	5	1	0	52	63	34	18	5.54
William Humphrey	1	4	.200	10	4	2	0	40	54	11	5	5.40
Guenther Schmidt	0	0	----	5								
John Day	0	0	----	5								
Merle Coleman	0	0	----	3								
Frank Osnato	0	0	----	2								
Albert Blanche	0	0	----	1								

ALBANY   8th   56-98   .364   -38   Al Mamaux
Senators

BATTERS	POS-GAMES	GP	AB	R	H	BI	2B	3B	HR	BB	SO	SB	BA
Jake Daniel	1B76	76	259	33	64	47	13	5	10	26	45	2	.247
John Bell	2B134	139	488	85	135	37	14	10	4	62	45	8	.277
Alan Strange	SS133	135	448	35	105	38	18	3	4	49	45	1	.234
Roberto Estalella	3B104	108	410	67	135	61	21	16	9	31	36	6	.329
Smead Jolley	OF155	155	592	109	221	105	52	9	18	72	42	2	**.373**
Robert Loane	OF94,P3	110	369	73	103	46	16	10	9	27	77	5	.279
Howard McFarland	OF		(see multi-team players)										
Jack Redmond	C81	93	286	31	67	53	13	7	4	17	23	2	.234
Jack Peerson	3B33,2B17,SS16	74	198	23	49	28	6	2	3	11	20	3	.247
Wilson Miles	OF66	68	278	53	91	25	16	8	2	6	20	13	.327
Francis Hogan	C45	54	156	17	56	34	15	1	3	18	8	0	.359
Tommy De la Cruz	P50	53	65	6	11	4	3	1	0	1	22	0	.169
Leon Pettit	P41	41	65	5	10	2	0	1	0	10	17	0	.154
Ray Phebus	P33	39	69	7	8	0	1	0	0	9	33	0	.116
Robert Burke	P38	39	62	3	11	5	0	2	0	3	11	0	.177
Alton Benton	P31	31	40	5	10	3	2	2	0	1	16	0	.250
Harry Kelly	P31	31	28	0	2	0	0	0	0	0	11	0	.071
Edward Davis	1B25	27	84	9	20	11	4	0	0	8	15	1	.238
Vern Mackie	C16	23	56	5	16	9	0	1	0	5	0	0	.286

ALBANY (cont.)
Senators

BATTERS	POS-GAMES	GP	AB	R	H	BI	2B	3B	HR	BB	SO	SB	BA
Alvis Veach	P22	22	28	2	4	2	1	0	0	0	9	0	.143
Vern Johnson	OF11	21	46	2	11	1	2	0	0	1	9	0	.239
John Marion	OF19	19	70	4	16	4	2	0	0	6	6	1	.229
Orlin Rogers	P16	19	24	2	10	1	2	0	0	0	2	1	.417
William Starr	C11	18	37	1	6	1	1	1	0	3	4	0	.162
Charles Butler	1B13	16	40	4	9	9	2	1	0	3	6	0	.225
Russ Maxcy	3B14	14	35	3	6	3	2	0	0	3	2	1	.171
Andrew Johnson		11	29	0	6	4	1	0	0	2	3	0	.207
Millard Hayes	P9	9											.556
William McGhee		8											.250
Len Shires	P1	5											.250
Edwin Chapman	P5	5											.231
Paul Dixon	P4	4											.333
Henry Cappola	P4	4											.333
Ramon Cuoto		4											.000
Regino Otero		3											.111
Joseph Bokina	P2	2											.000
John Welaj		2											.000
Rafael Suarez	P1	1											.000
Ivan Woodward	P1	1											.000
Tyrus Wagner		1											.000
Fermin Guerra		1											.000
Harris Gardner	P1	1											.000

PITCHERS	W	L	PCT	G	GS	CG	SH	IP	H	BB	SO	ERA
Ray Phebus	13	12	.520	33	27	15	2	212	185	111	111	3.35
Robert Burke	12	16	.429	38	29	15	3	180	220	73	82	4.65
Leon Pettit	9	22	.290	41	28	12	2	212	237	72	96	4.92
Tommy De la Cruz	6	10	.375	50	16	5	0	187	231	53	85	4.52
Alton Benton	3	11	.214	31	13	3	0	116	134	33	73	4.97
Harry Kelly	3	11	.214	31	11	2	1	93	83	83	52	6.29
Edwin Chapman	2	2	.500	5								
Orlin Rogers	1	2	.333	16	5	0	0	56	78	38	8	7.71
Millard Hayes	1	2	.333	9								
Alvis Veach	1	5	.167	22	8	1	0	83	108	38	31	5.75
Henry Coppola	0	1	.000	4								
Paul Dixon	0	1	.000	4								
Robert Loane	0	0	----	3								
Joseph Bokina	0	0	----	2								
Len Shires	0	0	----	1								
Rafael Suarez	0	0	----	1								
Ivan Woodward	0	0	----	1								
Harris Gardner	0	0	----	1								

MULTI-TEAM PLAYERS

BATTERS	POS-GAMES	TEAMS	GP	AB	R	H	BI	2B	3B	HR	BB	SO	SB	BA
Walt Cazen	OF151	BA32-SY122	154	547	77	165	94	29	11	9	41	84	26	.302
Ed Boland	OF129	AL18-BU124	142	481	83	145	102	28	3	20	46	32	1	.301
Keith Molesworth	SS127	BA20-SY117	137	467	62	121	58	18	7	4	36	45	9	.259
Howard McFarland	OF116	BU20-AL109	129	449	59	116	49	17	4	4	55	31	15	.258
Leslie Powers	1B106	NE1BA104	119	453	109	154	59	27	6	23	29	42	15	.340
Prince Oana	OF110	SY31-BA84	115	418	53	117	66	23	4	7	30	80	5	.280
Irv Jeffries	2B64,3B24	BA40-MO73	113	367	73	115	55	25	4	5	41	20	5	.313
George Blackerby	OF50,1B29	AL73-TO34	107	299	50	98	56	14	6	2	34	23	2	.328
George Savino	C98	AL24-BA82	106	329	37	91	55	10	2	10	28	15	2	.277
Byrne James	2B38,3B24,SS19	SY37-RO54	91	307	52	72	13	15	4	0	31	30	12	.235
Len Backer	3B68	RO17-SY68	85	283	42	76	32	13	2	0	27	21	2	.269
Bernard Snyder	2B20,SS19,3B18	AL49-BA4	53	157	19	41	17	8	1	0	12	6	1	.261
Harry Matuzak	P43	AL15-BA37	52	77	10	9	6	2	1	0	8	23	1	.117
Frank Pearce	P52	BA30-SY22	52	63	8	10	2	1	0	0	6	16	0	.159
George Murray	P50	TO9-RO41	50	59	4	8	4	3	1	0	1	9	0	.136
Hy Vandenberg	P45	SY25-BA20	45	80	6	16	4	2	0	0	4	11	0	.200
Stan Lucas	P41	TO16-BU26	42	24	4	1	0	0	0	0	3	3	0	.042
John Berly	P38	BA21-TO18	39	46	4	11	4	2	1	0	3	7	0	.239
John Pomorski	P31	BU11-TO22	33	16	3	4	1	0	1	0	0	3	0	.250
Clarence Straub	C24	NE2-TO22	24	71	10	23	9	2	1	0	3	7	2	.324
Walt Goebel	C15	BA3-SY13	16	37	6	7	3	0	1	1	6	6	0	.189

MULTI-TEAM PLAYERS (cont.)

PITCHERS	TEAMS	W	L	PCT	G	GS	CG	SH	IP	H	BB	SO	ERA
Harry Matuzak	AL12-BA31	18	10	.643	43	26	14	1	229	258	78	90	4.44
Hy Vandenberg	SY25-BA20	15	17	.469	45	28	17	2	228	248	83	107	4.54
George Murray	TO9-RO41	13	8	.619	50	15	3	0	169	208	68	45	5.38
Frank Pearce	BA30-SY22	13	11	.542	52	24	8	2	196	235	63	73	4.82
John Berly	BA21-TO17	11	12	.478	38	20	7	0	147	149	84	72	4.47
Stan Lucas	TO15-BU26	6	5	.545	41	1	0	0	92	117	40	39	5.28
John Pomorski	BU9-TO22	2	2	.500	31	3	1	1	65	71	28	24	4.43

TEAM BATTING

TEAMS	GP	AB	R	H	BI	2B	3B	HR	BB	SO	SB	BA
BUFFALO	154	**5255**	904	1535	**843**	295	55	117	**610**	521	82	.292
ROCHESTER	155	**5255**	863	**1555**	801	298	69	108	542	657	83	**.296**
NEWARK	155	5146	772	1390	712	248	62	100	453	502	62	.270
BALTIMORE	153	5216	**918**	1470	829	254	44	**184**	508	**669**	89	.282
TORONTO	155	5069	655	1365	588	213	83	56	404	451	52	.269
MONTREAL	152	5049	731	1388	690	**300**	80	76	546	497	39	.275
SYRACUSE	155	5082	671	1341	614	231	**96**	51	502	649	**94**	.264
ALBANY	155	5140	704	1420	661	246	81	81	508	625	62	.276
	617	41212	6218	11464	5738	2085	570	773	4073	4571	563	.278

1937
NEWARK BEARS

Newark made its start in the International League back in 1884. After spotty participation in the nineteenth century, Newark rejoined the league for a long stay starting in 1902. After several years of lackluster performance, highlighted by a flag in 1913, the Bears' fortunes took a sudden upswing. Following the 1931 season, the New York Yankees purchased the team, stocking it with Yankee hopefuls.

The team's upturn was immediate. Enjoying the Yankees' largess, Newark raced to the flag in 1932 with a 109-victory season. Not content with this, the team repeated the feat in 1933 and 1934. After two more first division finishes in the next two years, the curtain was about to rise on the greatest Newark team of them all.

The 1937 Newark Bears obliterated their competition. Finishing an astounding 25 games ahead of second-place Montreal, the team never once looked back, clinching first in mid–August. Their hard-hitting lineup featured many great performances, including outfielder and batting titlist Charlie Keller (.353), third baseman Babe Dahlgren (.340), first baseman George McQuinn (.330, 21 HR), catcher Willard Hershberger (.325), outfielder Bob Seeds (.305, 20 HR, 114 RBI), and second baseman Joe Gordon (26 HR). Pitching was also strong as evidenced by the gaudy records of Joe Beggs (21–4), and Atley Donald (19–2).

Following Montreal in the standings were Syracuse, Baltimore, Buffalo, Rochester, Toronto, and Jersey City (the relocated Albany franchise), who finished in that order. Hitting honors went to Al Wright of Baltimore with his 37 home runs and 127 runs batted in. Pitchers Marvin Duke of Montreal and Joe Beggs of Newark finished with the most wins (21), while Jersey City's Ben Cantwell had the lowest earned run average (1.65) and Norbert Kleinke of Rochester had the most strikeouts (150).

After the regular season, the Bears roared through the International's post-season, trouncing both Syracuse and Baltimore four games to nil. In the Little World Series, after the Association's Columbus squad put them in a three-games-to-none hole, the Bears won the next four in a singular comeback to take the series.

Newark would go on to play many more years in the International League, winning three more titles in the 1930s and 1940s. With attendance plunging, the team was relocated following the 1949 season.

At least eight other teams in International League play have won as many as or more than the 1937 Newark Bears. But all of them had the benefit of playing in a 168-game season. Newark played in only a 154-game season, in which their 109 victories earned them a .717 winning percentage. This mark is among the best winning percentages in International League history.

NEWARK Bears
1st   109-43   .717   Ossie Vitt

BATTERS	POS-GAMES	GP	AB	R	H	BI	2B	3B	HR	BB	SO	SB	BA
George McQuinn	1B114	114	460	95	152	84	30	10	21	38	67	2	.330
Joe Gordon	2B151	151	635	109	178	89	33	6	26	50	70	14	.280
Nolen Richardson	SS153	153	533	53	137	67	18	3	0	36	26	2	.257
Babe Dahlgren	3B85,1B40	125	482	106	164	86	34	12	18	48	42	2	.340
Bob Seeds	OF151	151	568	98	173	114	31	11	20	46	52	4	.305
Charlie Keller	OF145	145	536	120	189	88	34	14	13	71	51	7	.353
Jim Gleeson	OF139	143	560	101	167	79	47	10	16	65	54	6	.298
Willard Hershberger	C85	96	314	54	102	62	15	3	5	33	6	4	.325
Frank Kelleher	3B61,OF13	92	294	47	90	48	15	4	11	25	32	2	.306
Warren Rosar	C61	72	232	32	77	42	15	3	8	18	13	4	.332
Vito Tamulis	P27	35	90	6	28	11	4	0	0	2	13	0	.311
Joe Beggs	P34	35	67	9	11	7	1	0	0	4	19	0	.164
Atley Donald	P28	28	78	6	13	5	1	0	0	3	16	0	.167
Steve Sundra	P27	28	75	13	17	10	4	1	1	10	20	0	.227
Mario Russo	P27	28	44	5	7	2	0	1	0	6	11	0	.159
John Fallon	P25	25	47	3	7	1	0	0	0	1	18	0	.149
Kemp Wicker	P11	11	33	1	3	5	1	0	0	0	10	0	.091
Merrill May		10	34	3	6	2	2	0	0	5	1	0	.176
John Glynn		9											.235
Marv Breuer	P9	9											.167
Bill Yocke	P8	8											.167
Phil Page	P7	8											.100
Tommy Henrich	OF7	7	25	4	11	8	2	2	0			0	.440
Al Piechota	P7	7											.231
John Niggeling	P7	7											.167
Joe Gallagher	OF	6	17	2	6	1	0	0	1			0	.353
Spud Chandler	P4	6											.167
Walter Brown	P5	5											.000
Fern Bell	OF	2	1	0	0	0	0	0	0			0	.000
John LaRocca	P1	1											.000

PITCHERS	W	L	PCT	G	GS	CG	SH	IP	H	BB	SO	ERA
Joe Beggs	21	4	.840	34	18	14	2	179	160	48	57	2.61
Atley Donald	19	2	.905	28	26	17	3	207	189	75	124	3.22
Vito Tamulis	18	6	.750	27	25	16	3	190	217	57	88	3.98
Steve Sundra	15	4	.789	27	25	15	2	201	194	57	105	3.09
John Fallon	9	7	.563	25	13	8	0	132	117	66	61	2.80
Mario Russo	8	8	.500	27	13	5	1	119	129	45	64	3.60
Kemp Wicker	7	2	.778	11	11	8	2	93	83	23	18	2.42
Phil Page	3	1	.750	9								
Al Piechota	3	1	.750	7				34	27	14	12	
Walter Brown	2	1	.667	5								
John Niggeling	2	2	.500	7				31	44	15	11	6.10
Marv Breuer	1	1	.333	9				29	31	11	13	
Spud Chandler	1	2	.333	4				20	20	7	5	4.05
John LaRocca	0	1	.000	1								
Bill Yocke	0	0	----	8								

MONTREAL Royals
2nd   82-67   .550   -25.5   Rabbit Maranville

BATTERS	POS-GAMES	GP	AB	R	H	BI	2B	3B	HR	BB	SO	SB	BA
Bernard Cobb	1B113	113	407	52	123	74	24	4	1	30	16	3	.302
John Bell	2B149	149	583	102	169	58	19	2	9	64	73	15	.290
Ben Sankey	SS149	149	560	60	148	56	23	4	1	33	30	8	.264
Irv Jeffries	3B131	138	500	78	154	65	36	2	6	33	31	11	.308
Dan Hafey	OF129	131	454	74	112	63	13	6	11	55	94	11	.247
Paul Dunlap	OF129	130	487	77	162	75	36	5	5	44	28	9	.333
Dave Harris	OF124	127	433	47	129	76	26	3	18	54	66	6	.298
Norm Kies	C96	96	288	34	69	40	13	1	0	35	31	1	.240
Gus Dugas	OF48,1B37	84	290	48	94	62	28	3	11	42	26	7	.324
Joseph Benning	3B29,OF21	71	158	23	48	20	5	2	0	13	13	2	.304
Harry Smythe	P35	48	99	13	34	20	8	1	0	7	6	0	.343
John Chandler	C41	45	128	18	31	14	7	1	2	20	24	1	.242
Henry Johnson	P27	35	74	10	26	6	7	0	0	5	9	0	.351
Marvin Duke	P33	33	90	7	18	7	2	0	0	0	10	1	.200
Hod Lisenbee	P29	29	42	5	5	5	1	1	0	4	15	0	.119
Lou Polli	P27	28	60	8	12	4	2	0	1	2	18	0	.200
Lauri Myllykangas	P27	27	59	6	6	4	0	1	0	3	12	0	.102
Walter Stephenson	C11	13	21	3	3	2	1	0	0	9	6	0	.143

MONTREAL (cont.)
Royals

BATTERS	POS-GAMES	GP	AB	R	H	BI	2B	3B	HR	BB	SO	SB	BA
Ken Heintzelman	P3	3											.500
John Wasco	P2	2											.333

PITCHERS		W	L	PCT	G	GS	CG	SH	IP	H	BB	SO	ERA
Marvin Duke		21	8	.724	33	29	23	2	235	236	73	70	3.06
Harry Smythe		16	13	.552	35	28	24	0	229	248	53	81	3.46
Henry Johnson		11	7	.611	27	17	10	2	156	147	69	83	3.69
Lou Polli		11	8	.579	27	18	13	2	157	170	69	54	4.36
Lauri Myllykangas		9	10	.474	27	20	10	0	164	200	53	55	5.27
Hod Lisenbee		8	6	.571	29	15	7	1	137	175	37	46	4.93
Ken Heintzelman		0	0	----	3				7	8	8	4	7.71
John Wasco		0	0	----	2								

SYRACUSE   3rd   78-74   .513   -31   Bernard Kelly
Chiefs

BATTERS	POS-GAMES	GP	AB	R	H	BI	2B	3B	HR	BB	SO	SB	BA
Frank McCormick	1B129	129	482	66	155	75	33	6	6	29	28	5	.322
Al Glossop	2B126	130	463	77	116	54	19	6	6	51	59	7	.251
Eddie Joost	SS75,3B56,2B23	151	553	78	149	52	21	12	3	50	71	9	.269
James Outlaw	3B65	65	238	29	73	26	12	4	2	8	25	1	.307
Dick Porter	OF123	126	436	61	137	57	21	6	3	58	20	3	.314
Walt Cazen	OF117	129	429	83	118	56	18	10	6	42	39	14	.275
Harry Craft	OF83	84	312	49	97	55	14	4	10	9	34	4	.311
Dee Moore	C72	85	254	33	67	28	12	4	1	20	32	3	.264
Arnold Moser	OF76	85	310	44	96	47	13	8	2	10	30	2	.310
William Campbell	C69	76	220	27	52	18	6	0	2	35	15	2	.236
Edward Miller	SS74	75	243	25	57	31	7	3	2	20	24	2	.235
Keith Molesworth	3B42	69	172	24	43	18	6	0	0	11	10	1	.250
Lee Gamble	OF47	53	187	36	57	13	13	1	1	13	5	5	.305
Fred Fussell	P35	35	51	3	13	6	3	0	0	7	12	0	.255
Earl Cook	P33	33	43	3	11	6	0	0	0	1	8	0	.256
Frank Pearce	P32	32	37	2	5	2	1	0	0	2	10	0	.135
Robert Loane	OF23	30	66	9	14	14	0	1	1	3	16	0	.212
George Hockette	P26	26	46	4	9	5	0	0	0	2	4	0	.196
Lloyd Moore	P21	21	54	6	12	3	0	0	0	2	12	0	.222
Ray Kolp	P21	21	16	1	2	0	0	0	0	1	4	1	.125
Louis Legett	C14	19	51	11	18	13	4	1	1	3	9	0	.353
John Vander Meer	P17	17	35	1	8	4	0	0	0	0	6	0	.229
John Gee	P16	16	21	0	2	0	0	0	0	0	11	0	.095
John Reder	1B14	15	38	2	7	5	1	0	0	3	13	1	.184
John Campbell	P14	14	4	0	0	0	0	0	0	0	1	0	.000
Dan Cosgrove	1B13	13	31	2	7	4	1	0	0	5	3	0	.226
Jake Mooty	P11	11	23	2	2	0	0	0	0	4	4	0	.087
Virgil Brown	P10	10	12	2	4	4	0	0	0	0	1	0	.333
Eugene Thompson	P10	10	9	1	2	1	0	0	0	0	3	0	.222
Matt Holmes	P8	8											.333
Clyde Chell		8											.200
Russ Arlett	PH	4	4	0	0	0	0	0	0	0			0	.000
Allen Hunt	OF	3	5	1	2	1	0	0	0			0	.400
Wayne Blackburn		3											.333
George Miner	P3	3											.000
Frank Marinette		2											.000
Walt Goebel		1											1.000
Bernard Snyder		1											.000
Robert Brown	P1	1											.000
Miguel Bouza		1											.000

PITCHERS	W	L	PCT	G	GS	CG	SH	IP	H	BB	SO	ERA
George Hockette	11	6	.647	26	18	7	2	132	144	35	35	3.34
Lloyd Moore	11	6	.647	21	17	14	1	142	100	84	149	2.85
Fred Fussell	11	9	.550	35	26	11	1	158	177	47	39	4.44
Earl Cook	9	8	.529	33	18	6	1	134	128	59	76	3.22
Frank Pearce	8	8	.500	32	14	7	2	131	121	37	70	2.82
John Vander Meer	5	11	.313	17	16	11	1	105	82	80	74	3.34
John Gee	4	3	.571	16	7	2	1	62	60	33	30	2.90
Jake Mooty	4	6	.400	11	10	9	1	78	68	37	34	3.69
Virgil Brown	2	0	1.000	10	3	2	1	31	37	11	9	4.07
John Campbell	2	1	.667	14	0	0	0	19	15	15	3	4.74
Ray Kolp	2	2	.500	21	4	0	0	64	73	14	24	4.78

SYRACUSE (cont.)
Chiefs

PITCHERS	W	L	PCT	G	GS	CG	SH	IP	H	BB	SO	ERA
Matt Holmes	1	0	1.000	8								
Eugene Thompson	1	2	.333	10	1	1	0	27	36	18	11	5.33
George Miner	0	2	.000	3								
Robert Brown	0	0	----	1								

BALTIMORE   4th   76-75   .503   -32.5   Guy Sturdy -
Orioles   Clyde Crouse

BATTERS	POS-GAMES	GP	AB	R	H	BI	2B	3B	HR	BB	SO	SB	BA
Leslie Powers	1B146	147	550	96	169	95	28	8	21	56	41	4	.307
Bill Cissell	2B88,SS13	103	412	67	122	51	22	3	5	26	27	6	.296
Chet Wilburn	SS108	109	421	56	108	38	18	3	3	50	39	7	.257
Joseph Martin	3B128	135	467	72	140	72	31	6	22	21	62	4	.300
Al Wright	OF150	150	554	98	169	**127**	44	5	37	42	74	7	.305
Woody Abernathy	OF140	148	546	94	155	71	29	2	21	45	47	3	.284
George Puccinelli	OF139	142	506	96	165	103	34	4	24	87	76	2	.326
Clyde Crouse	C	(see multi-team players)											
Roy Schalk	2B56,3B19	90	320	39	77	33	15	2	8	17	35	4	.241
Milton Gray	C60	64	171	67	38	11	4	1	2	16	15	5	.222
Harry Matuzak	P45	45	54	12	10	4	2	0	0	16	17	0	.185
Bill Lohrman	P41	44	89	17	27	13	8	1	2	10	23	0	.303
Hy Vandenberg	P40	40	86	8	14	5	2	0	0	4	14	0	.163
Pete Sivess	P34	34	54	2	11	5	3	0	0	3	13	0	.204
Gordon Rhodes	P32	32	41	2	8	3	0	0	0	1	9	0	.195
Fred Tauby	OF19	27	82	12	24	7	4	0	1	5	3	0	.293
William Hoffner	SS17	18	54	10	13	1	2	0	0	9	12	1	.241
Ed Remorenko		15	21	1	4	0	0	0	0	0	4	0	.190
Alex Monchak		14	34	4	6	0	1	0	0	5	5	0	.176
Charles Fischer	P13	13	35	4	9	4	0	0	1	1	7	0	.257
Leon Pettit	P13	13	14	1	1	0	1	0	0	1	6	0	.071
Leon Chagnon	P10	10	15	1	2	2	0	0	0	1	2	0	.133
Ed Roetz		8											.222
Henry Winston	P7	7											.200
John Wittig	P4	4											.333
James Kerr	P4	4											.000
Howard Killen	P2	2											.333
Lyle Judy		2											.143
Glenn Chapman		2											.125
Randall Gumpert	P2	2											.000
James Bivin	P2	2											.000
Junie Barnes	P1	1											1.000
James Rego	P1	1											.000
Frank Anderson	P1	1											.000

PITCHERS	W	L	PCT	G	GS	CG	SH	IP	H	BB	SO	ERA
Bill Lohrman	20	11	.645	41	31	22	1	239	233	49	102	3.39
Pete Sivess	15	5	.750	34	12	9	2	163	141	55	100	2.43
Hy Vandenberg	15	17	.469	40	32	17	1	242	**262**	83	111	4.28
Harry Matuzak	11	14	.440	45	25	10	1	198	220	44	107	4.73
Charles Fischer	8	3	.727	13	13	8	1	94	90	31	73	3.93
Gordon Rhodes	5	9	.357	32	18	5	0	124	162	45	55	6.24
Henry Winston	1	1	.500	7								
Leon Chagnon	1	5	.167	10	6	1	0	43	62	18	16	7.12
John Wittig	0	1	.000	4				20	26	6	7	
Howard Killen	0	1	.000	2				7	10	2	3	
Frank Anderson	0	1	.000	1				8	13	5	4	
Leon Pettit	0	3	.000	13	5	0	0	42	45	27	17	4.93
James Kerr	0	0	----	4								
James Bivin	0	0	----	2								
Randall Gumpert	0	0	----	2				7	16	3	3	15.43
James Rego	0	0	----	1								
Junie Barnes	0	0	----	1								

BUFFALO   5th   74-79   .484   -35.5   Ray Schalk
Bisons

BATTERS	POS-GAMES	GP	AB	R	H	BI	2B	3B	HR	BB	SO	SB	BA
Eugene Corbett	1B94	98	316	42	74	21	11	1	3	35	38	4	.234

BUFFALO (cont.)
Bisons

BATTERS	POS-GAMES	GP	AB	R	H	BI	2B	3B	HR	BB	SO	SB	BA
Marvin Olson	2B140	141	489	63	110	45	11	4	6	74	47	13	.225
Greg Mulleavy	SS146	146	539	79	163	48	34	4	4	75	51	11	.302
Tony Dueker	3B85,2B15	107	347	42	89	41	10	5	6	32	29	2	.256
Ollie Carnegie	OF132	134	491	76	151	97	23	6	21	38	70	1	.308
John Tyler	OF107	124	385	70	104	57	21	4	11	43	45	5	.270
Ed Boland	OF98	108	364	53	88	67	10	1	15	25	29	0	.242
Ed Phillips	C81	86	279	31	88	38	11	2	6	16	39	0	.315
Myron McCormick	OF80,1B67	139	498	68	141	57	25	5	3	34	49	14	.283
Howard Meyers	3B77	89	291	45	63	23	6	1	5	30	40	2	.216
Fabian Kowalik	P29	45	70	7	17	10	3	0	1	4	6	0	.243
Art Jacobs	P42	42	38	3	10	0	0	0	0	4	7	0	.263
William Harris	P36	36	91	6	11	8	1	0	0	4	18	0	.121
Frank McGowan	OF28	35	101	12	32	15	7	1	1	8	10	0	.317
Rip Sewell	P31	33	87	11	26	17	5	0	4	8	19	2	.299
Ken Ash	P33	33	61	3	11	5	2	0	0	0	11	0	.180
Norm Hibbs	P32	33	34	3	6	2	1	0	0	4	5	0	.176
Robert Kline	P32	32	68	3	16	11	1	0	0	1	15	1	.235
Ray Pepper	OF25	26	91	10	15	10	2	0	1	8	9	1	.165
Don Ferris	P7	7											.333
Eugene Geary		2											.500

PITCHERS		W	L	PCT	G	GS	CG	SH	IP	H	BB	SO	ERA
Rip Sewell		16	12	.571	31	31	19	6	239	226	86	126	3.31
William Harris		16	16	.500	36	34	20	3	257	262	46	140	3.50
Robert Kline		11	14	.440	32	27	10	2	189	216	40	66	3.67
Ken Ash		11	16	.407	33	25	12	4	177	199	67	71	4.07
Fabian Kowalik		10	10	.500	29	25	16	0	167	182	71	57	4.85
Art Jacobs		5	5	.500	42	3	2	0	114	120	37	56	4.89
Norm Hibbs		3	3	.500	32	5	2	0	109	117	38	58	4.21
Don Ferris		1	2	.333	7								

ROCHESTER   6th   74-80   .481   -36   Ray Blades
Red Wings

BATTERS	POS-GAMES	GP	AB	R	H	BI	2B	3B	HR	BB	SO	SB	BA
Walt Alston	1B61	66	203	20	50	36	6	3	6	22	45	1	.246
Al Cuccinello	2B82	99	284	43	68	30	15	1	6	36	21	1	.239
Marty Marion	SS138	142	479	73	118	37	21	3	4	32	75	4	.246
Jack Juelich	3B140	142	570	93	176	52	25	2	5	43	48	5	.309
John Hopp	OF140	141	527	87	162	69	28	14	9	60	84	33	.307
Estel Crabtree	OF137,3B10	150	508	69	143	86	27	4	15	50	39	3	.281
Lou Scoffic	OF114	127	426	59	139	77	20	3	6	30	50	6	.326
Hugh Poland	C103	113	364	47	88	49	7	5	12	27	57	3	.242
Tony Kaufmann	OF53,P25	95	216	28	61	37	10	2	4	28	13	0	.282
Oscar Roettger	1B58	75	174	10	44	22	8	1	1	8	21	0	.253
Frank Morehouse	2B69	70	255	48	68	17	10	6	3	37	48	1	.267
Robert O'Farrell	C56	70	194	10	45	20	10	0	0	10	24	0	.232
John Watwood	1B52	56	194	18	55	20	7	1	2	18	13	1	.284
Oscar Judd	P34	53	61	9	15	2	2	1	1	3	16	0	.246
Howard Krist	P47	49	72	3	11	7	1	0	1	2	21	0	.153
Norbert Kleinke	P39	39	78	5	8	7	0	0	1	5	25	0	.103
Nate Andrews	P35	36	60	4	6	5	1	1	0	7	20	0	.100
William Walker	P35	35	62	2	4	3	0	0	0	5	26	0	.065
Maurice Sturdy		30	43	8	12	6	1	0	1	5	3	0	.279
Robert Gibson	3B18	25	98	12	23	16	4	1	3	8	13	1	.235
Ira Smith	P23	25	33	4	8	5	3	1	0	1	3	0	.242
Tony Malinosky	SS23	24	73	4	25	10	2	2	0	6	6	0	.342
Truman Connell	OF19	20	45	6	9	4	1	1	0	4	12	0	.200
Frank Myers	OF14	19	31	4	4	1	1	0	0	3	11	0	.129
Herbert Moore	P12	19	12	3	0	0	0	0	0	5	4	0	.000
Andrew Doyle	P17	17	16	0	2	2	0	1	0	0	6	0	.125
Jack Crouch	C10	14	38	4	13	8	1	0	1	1	7	0	.342
Adell White	P11	11	8	0	1	0	0	0	0	0	2	0	.125
Harold Swanson	P7	7											.250
Horace Blair		5											.400
Howard Taylor	P3	3											1.000
Tom Sunkel	P3	3											.000
John Wahonick	P2	2											.000
Gerald Zornow	P1	1											.000
George Waldron		1											.000

ROCHESTER (cont.)
Red Wings

PITCHERS	W	L	PCT	G	GS	CG	SH	IP	H	BB	SO	ERA
Norbert Kleinke	19	8	.708	39	27	14	1	228	235	98	**150**	3.47
Howard Krist	13	15	.464	**47**	29	13	1	232	218	64	100	3.14
William Walker	12	11	.522	35	27	11	2	188	194	83	80	3.93
Oscar Judd	11	11	.500	34	22	8	2	156	159	89	84	5.19
Nate Andrews	9	13	.409	35	23	9	2	184	185	70	100	3.13
Andrew Doyle	3	3	.500	17	3	1	0	49	61	28	16	5.69
Herbert Moore	2	2	.500	12	3	2	0	47	50	18	32	4.02
Ira Smith	2	7	.222	23	10	4	1	92	120	46	37	4.89
Harold Swanson	1	0	1.000	7								
Adell White	1	1	.500	11	3	1	0	30	34	4	14	3.00
Tony Kaufmann	1	6	.143	25	5	2	0	79	91	31	42	4.22
Tom Sunkel	0	3	.000	3								
Howard Taylor	0	0	----	3								
John Wahonick	0	0	----	2								
Gerald Zornow	0	0	----	1								

TORONTO   7th   63-88   .417   -45.5   Dan Howley
Maple Leafs

BATTERS	POS-GAMES	GP	AB	R	H	BI	2B	3B	HR	BB	SO	SB	BA
James Walsh	1B135	135	493	72	135	72	17	5	17	55	81	5	.274
Frank Madura	2B124	124	467	78	124	44	21	8	2	98	27	4	.266
Joseph Gantenbein	SS151	151	564	75	137	60	20	9	7	67	78	5	.243
Don Ross	3B148	149	528	67	161	65	31	3	2	65	35	10	.305
Fred Petoskey	OF142	142	575	68	174	74	23	11	1	35	39	13	.303
Mayo Smith	OF91	99	331	53	97	34	13	3	4	40	23	6	.293
Adam Comorosky	OF86	108	308	35	77	38	18	3	0	46	24	0	.250
Francis Hogan	C63	66	193	10	34	14	5	1	1	39	26	1	.176
Tom Oliver	OF75	102	315	33	85	31	11	6	0	17	10	2	.270
Robert A. Porter	OF81	95	284	38	83	40	11	9	5	35	39	2	.292
Thomas Heath	C58	58	182	25	44	29	9	1	2	41	20	1	.242
John Heving	C49	58	116	11	34	14	4	0	0	23	9	0	.293
Harold Stockman	2B28	53	135	10	27	7	3	1	0	11	19	0	.200
John Berly	P35	38	74	6	12	7	1	1	0	4	12	1	.162
Woodrow Davis	P35	36	68	2	10	2	0	0	0	9	35	0	.147
Francis Nekola	P34	35	36	3	3	1	1	0	0	4	7	0	.083
Joseph Mulligan	P34	34	44	0	3	3	0	0	0	2	21	0	.068
Emile Meola	P33	33	67	5	6	2	0	0	0	8	17	0	.090
Earl Caldwell	P26	27	74	6	16	7	2	1	1	2	14	0	.216
Paul Sullivan	P13	13	7	1	1	0	0	0	0	1	3	0	.143
Richard Henry	1B12	12	51	4	10	3	0	2	0	5	7	0	.196
Ted Horton	P10	10	3	0	2	0	1	0	0	2	0	0	.667
Albert Smith		5											.176
John Upper	P1	1											1.000
Walt Lanfranconi	P1	1											1.000
Walt Klimczak		1											.000
William Honeycutt	P1	1											.000

PITCHERS	W	L	PCT	G	GS	CG	SH	IP	H	BB	SO	ERA
Woodrow Davis	13	13	.500	35	26	12	3	202	199	119	105	4.28
John Berly	11	13	.458	35	23	12	1	197	190	71	111	3.79
Earl Caldwell	10	12	.455	26	25	18	1	193	215	42	66	3.59
Emile Meola	10	17	.370	33	27	17	3	213	234	65	100	4.18
Joseph Mulligan	7	8	.467	34	13	8	0	149	138	92	83	3.26
Francis Nekola	5	6	.455	34	14	5	0	123	155	39	51	4.32
Paul Sullivan	1	4	.200	13	4	0	0	26	44	27	12	11.08
Ted Horton	0	1	.000	10	0	0	0	21	20	9	9	5.57
Walt Lanfranconi	0	1	.000	1				4	11	4	0	
William Honeycutt	0	0	----	1								
John Upper	0	0	----	1								

JERSEY CITY   8th   50-100   .333   -58   Travis Jackson
Giants

BATTERS	POS-GAMES	GP	AB	R	H	BI	2B	3B	HR	BB	SO	SB	BA
Phil Weintraub	1B82	82	275	37	74	41	16	7	5	50	45	0	.269
Harold King	2B		(see multi-team players)										
Otto Bluege	SS109	109	390	32	71	19	9	2	0	47	51	4	.182

JERSEY CITY (cont.)
Giants

BATTERS	POS-GAMES	GP	AB	R	H	BI	2B	3B	HR	BB	SO	SB	BA
Charles Wilson	3B135	137	526	49	140	45	24	3	6	23	18	5	.266
Harold B. Lee	OF148	150	576	69	168	73	35	5	10	41	39	7	.292
Edward Wilson	OF97	107	357	37	83	34	11	3	6	47	58	1	.232
Joseph Dwyer	OF81	88	304	26	80	28	17	2	1	25	9	1	.263
Jack Redmond	C118	126	394	32	86	36	15	5	2	36	28	1	.218
Linc Blakely	OF76	98	272	35	69	28	11	3	4	32	43	4	.259
Ernest Smith	2B32,SS28,3B19	88	259	31	67	18	8	4	0	21	16	4	.259
Jose Gomez	2B55,SS15	69	217	24	50	10	9	4	0	29	27	0	.230
Leroy Anton	1B63	64	221	17	49	19	7	4	1	15	31	4	.222
Elmer Klumpp	C39,OF10	60	156	12	36	15	4	1	1	13	19	1	.231
Glen Gabler	P43	43	74	4	13	4	1	0	0	5	16	1	.176
Tommy De la Cruz	P39	40	30	4	3	1	1	0	0	1	8	0	.100
Rollie Stiles	P36	36	87	7	19	5	3	1	0	4	26	0	.218
John Meketi	P32	32	48	4	3	2	1	0	0	3	32	0	.063
Ernest Sulik	OF17	27	68	5	13	6	4	0	0	8	3	0	.191
Ben Cantwell	P23	24	61	5	9	1	1	0	0	4	6	0	.148
Mitchell Radon	P22	22	21	1	4	2	0	0	0	1	7	0	.190
Don Brennan	P22	22	20	0	1	0	0	0	0	1	11	0	.050
James Asbell	OF14	14	48	5	10	6	2	2	0	6	14	0	.208
Smead Jolley	OF12	12	42	5	14	5	1	0	1	7	0	0	.333
Alvis Veach	P6	7											.167
Ed Madjeski		7											.100
Travis Jackson	SS	6	20	0	5	1	0	0	0			0	.250
John Babich	P6	6											.167
William Gilvary	P4	6											.000
Robert Burke	P4	4											.400
Henry McDonald	P3	3											.250
William Urbanski		3											.000
Charles Matuch	P3	3											.000
Paul Kardow	P3	3											.000

PITCHERS	W	L	PCT	G	GS	CG	SH	IP	H	BB	SO	ERA
Ben Cantwell	12	7	.632	23	20	16	3	175	164	35	50	**1.65**
Glen Gabler	12	**24**	.333	43	30	15	3	231	252	72	60	3.51
Rollie Stiles	8	19	.296	36	32	17	2	193	215	42	66	3.60
John Meketi	5	14	.263	32	24	7	0	157	151	**129**	94	4.93
Don Brennan	4	7	.364	22	5	1	0	71	71	27	31	4.56
Mitchell Radon	3	4	.429	22	7	3	1	83	93	31	20	3.47
Robert Burke	1	2	.333	4								
Tommy De la Cruz	1	5	.167	39	4	1	0	109	128	42	56	4.87
Henry McDonald	0	1	.000	3								
John Babich	0	2	.000	6								
Alvis Veach	0	2	.000	6								
William Gilvary	0	0	----	4								
Paul Kardow	0	0	----	3								
Charles Matuch	0	0	----	3								

MULTI-TEAM PLAYERS

BATTERS	POS-GAMES	TEAMS	GP	AB	R	H	BI	2B	3B	HR	BB	SO	SB	BA
Clyde Crouse	C101	BU16-BA95	111	329	38	84	56	11	2	10	31	21	6	.255
Harold King	2B82	BA26-JC71	97	299	29	74	41	9	1	6	41	26	1	.248
George Savino	C81	BA17-BU72	89	237	26	50	30	9	1	5	35	12	0	.211
George Blackerby	OF65	TO7-BU35-R18-M25	85	236	31	62	24	8	1	1	24	18	2	.263
James Pattison	P31	TO8-MO30	38	55	13	18	9	5	0	1	6	9	0	.327
William Hargrave	C25	NE13-MO19	32	85	7	26	20	3	0	1	4	12	0	.306
Leo Mangum	P29	SY14-JC15	29	47	5	6	0	0	0	0	4	4	0	.128
John Pomorski	P28	TO8-SY20	28	24	3	5	4	1	0	0	1	4	0	.208
Walter Brown	P16	NE5-JC22	27	37	0	11	4	2	0	0	1	6	0	.297
Frank Grube	C22	BA12-BU13	25	55	4	13	1	1	0	0	7	5	0	.236
John Wilson	P22	BU6-TO16	22	30	1	3	0	0	0	0	4	10	0	.100
Chad Kimsey	P11	MO7-BA7	14	14	0	2	1	1	0	0	1	6	0	.143
Edwin Chapman	P8	JC1-MO7	8											.308
Charles Perkins	P7	BU1-BA6	7											.375
Cecil Spittler	P3	NE1-BA2	3											.000

PITCHERS	TEAMS	W	L	PCT	G	GS	CG	SH	IP	H	BB	SO	ERA
James Pattison	TO8-MO23	8	10	.444	31	16	5	1	136	164	61	62	5.23
Leo Mangum	SY14-JC15	7	14	.333	29	22	4	1	132	168	26	42	5.25

MULTI-TEAM PLAYERS (cont.)

PITCHERS	TEAMS	W	L	PCT	G	GS	CG	SH	IP	H	BB	SO	ERA
John Wilson	BU6-TO16	4	8	.333	22	11	5	0	95	124	23	35	5.12
John Pomorski	TO8-SY20	3	6	.333	28	5	1	0	82	106	32	25	6.70
Walter Brown	NE5-JC11	3	6	.333	16	13	4	1	68	81	26	29	4.37
Edwin Chapman	JC1-NE7	1	4	.200	8								
Charles Perkins	BU1-BA6	0	3	.000	7								
Chad Kimsey	MO6-BA5	0	6	.000	11	8	2	0	33	49	31	7	9.82
Cecil Spittler	NE1-BA2	0	0	----	3								

TEAM BATTING

TEAMS	GP	AB	R	H	BI	2B	3B	HR	BB	SO	SB	BA
NEWARK	153	5263	890	1574	843	292	80	141	476	552	48	.299
MONTREAL	149	4920	725	1388	665	257	37	65	470	538	74	.282
SYRACUSE	152	4927	686	1349	605	206	66	46	393	525	20	.274
BALTIMORE	151	5039	777	1398	728	264	37	163	471	577	48	.277
BUFFALO	154	5010	665	1298	605	195	35	91	491	562	59	.259
ROCHESTER	156	5191	685	1377	640	214	53	82	461	720	60	.265
TORONTO	151	4989	613	1298	561	193	64	41	612	564	50	.260
JERSEY CITY	150	4773	467	1142	430	192	47	39	459	534	33	.239
	608	40112	5508	10824	5077	1813	419	668	3833	4572	432	.270

1938
OLLIE CARNEGIE

During the long history of the Buffalo Bisons, 22 home run hitting champions have graced their rosters. Of this group, four won more than one title. First, Jim Murray won a pair of titles in 1907 and 1908. Fifteen years later another Bison slugger copped a duo: William Kelly, in 1924 and 1926. Some ten years later, another Buffalo longball specialist appeared on the scene to nab a twosome. His name was Oliver Carnegie, and when his career was done, his exploits were known league-wide.

Oliver Carnegie, known as Ollie, had his first taste of professional baseball in a seven-game stint for the Flint club in the Michigan-Ontario League in 1922. After eight years outside organized baseball, Carnegie , at the age of 32, reemerged in the New York–Pennsylvania League. Late in the 1931 season, he joined the Buffalo Bisons of the International League.

By 1932, Ollie Carnegie was a mainstay in the Bison outfield. During his first full International League season he cranked out 36 home runs. The next five seasons saw his longball prowess continue as he averaged well over 30 home runs a year.

In 1938, Carnegie was poised for his greatest year. During the course of the campaign he connected for 45 roundtrippers, 17 more than his nearest opponent. He also banged out 136 runs batted in, tops in the International League. As to his average, Carnegie held his own; his .330 ranked sixth overall.

The Newark Bears romped home with their second straight pennant, this time holding a comfortable 18-game bulge over Syracuse. Rochester finished third, followed by Ollie Carnegie's Buffalo Bisons in fourth. The fifth through eighth spots were occupied by Toronto, Montreal, Jersey City, and Baltimore. Newark's Warren Rosar finished with the highest average (.387). (Note: Rosar's teammate Bob Seeds had a memorable two games in May, when he hit seven home runs in ten at bats.) On the hill, Toronto's Joseph Sullivan won the highest total (18), Charles Barrett from Syracuse finished with the lowest earned run average (2.34), and Atley Donald of Newark had the most strikeouts (133).

In the following year, Ollie Carnegie won his second home run title. After two more seasons, he drifted down through the minors. Carnegie returned for a curtain call in Buffalo, serving as a coach and part-time player during World War II.

Although another Bison would win a pair of home run titles in the 1950s, Ollie Carnegie remains Buffalo's supreme slugger. Not only that, he holds the same title in the International League. No one is likely to top Ollie Carnegie's 258 home run and 1,044 runs batted in totals—both International League career records.

NEWARK
Bears

1st   104-48   .717   John Neun

BATTERS	POS-GAMES	GP	AB	R	H	BI	2B	3B	HR	BB	SO	SB	BA
Les Scarsella	1B128	128	508	79	156	89	31	6	14	43	46	11	.307
Herman Schulte	2B134	135	494	86	141	54	27	2	4	72	44	6	.285
Nicholas Witek	SS99,2B17	120	483	90	143	60	15	4	6	53	27	2	.296
Merrill May	3B145	146	519	99	172	108	36	5	12	83	22	6	.331
Charlie Keller	OF150	150	578	149	211	129	36	8	22	108	56	9	.365
Jim Gleeson	OF122	123	487	113	151	81	50	7	16	83	41	7	.310
Frank Kelleher	OF71	77	273	52	77	63	11	1	12	47	29	1	.282
Warren Rosar	C86	91	323	80	125	79	26	2	15	40	10	5	.387
Mike Chartak	OF55,1B22	95	284	75	90	51	14	6	8	76	49	3	.317
William Holm	C55,SS16	78	214	34	58	30	11	2	5	41	48	1	.271
Bob Seeds	OF59	59	230	73	77	95	6	3	28	41	24	2	.335
Lewis Blair	SS42	49	167	15	41	21	7	0	1	6	10	3	.246
Lee Stine	P25	43	77	7	15	9	3	0	0	8	15	0	.195
Phil Page	P35	35	22	2	6	4	1	0	0	1	3	0	.273
John Haley	P34	34	70	5	14	5	2	0	1	2	22	0	.200
Mario Russo	P32	33	73	5	15	7	2	0	0	7	10	0	.205
John Fallon	P31	31	34	2	7	4	3	0	0	2	13	0	.206
Nick Strincevich	P30	30	34	5	4	2	0	0	0	3	7	0	.118
Clyde McCullough	C24	28	93	13	20	13	2	3	2	13	15	1	.215
Atley Donald	P25	25	78	7	18	11	2	0	0	7	19	0	.231
Frank Makosky	P21	21	8	0	0	0	0	0	0	0	1	0	.000
Ernie Bonham	P15	15	33	1	4	4	0	1	0	3	8	0	.121
Norm Branch	P13	15	27	3	9	3	2	0	0	1	4	0	.333
Joe Beggs	P12	13	31	1	2	2	0	0	0	0	10	0	.065
Harry Bassin		12	25	4	7	5	0	0	1	0	2	0	.280
Xavier Rescigno	P7	8											.000
John Lindell	P4	4	6	0	1	1	0	0	0			0	.167
Hi Bithorn	P2	2											.000

PITCHERS	W	L	PCT	G	GS	CG	SH	IP	H	BB	SO	ERA
John Haley	17	2	.895	34	22	10	1	174	160	101	78	3.47
Mario Russo	17	8	.680	32	27	15	1	206	200	73	131	3.15
Atley Donald	16	7	.696	25	25	15	2	192	202	83	133	3.66
Nick Strincevich	11	4	.733	30	9	5	0	102	102	46	44	4.32
Lee Stine	11	8	.579	25	21	13	2	139	159	48	78	5.18
Ernie Bonham	8	2	.800	15	11	2	0	89	105	35	51	4.04
John Fallon	8	4	.667	31	12	4	0	106	113	43	52	4.84
Joe Beggs	6	3	.667	12	10	7	1	76	85	15	45	3.43
Phil Page	5	4	.556	35	2	0	0	68	88	27	23	4.76
Norm Branch	3	2	.600	13	7	3	0	64	71	30	34	4.50
John Lindell	1	1	.500	4				17	18	7	3	
Frank Makosky	1	2	.333	21	0	0	0	35	43	17	19	5.40
Xavier Rescigno	0	1	.000	7				12	14	8	6	
Hi Bithorn	0	0	----	2				9	12	4	2	7.00

SYRACUSE
Chiefs

2nd   87-67   .565   -18   Jim Bottomley -
                                                               Dick Porter

BATTERS	POS-GAMES	GP	AB	R	H	BI	2B	3B	HR	BB	SO	SB	BA
Joe Mack	1B140	142	519	78	148	73	33	9	3	76	59	6	.285
Al Glossop	2B136	144	527	82	135	44	24	6	7	49	63	1	.256
Ashley McDaniel	SS117,3B16	136	461	55	105	47	25	3	2	35	48	6	.228
Howard Meyers	3B		(see multi-team players)										
Ed Longacre	OF143	143	518	60	148	78	19	6	1	35	32	7	.286
Tony Bongiovanni	OF142	142	563	95	181	70	46	4	12	47	28	7	.321
James Outlaw	OF108	114	416	59	141	70	25	9	2	27	38	6	.339
Dee Moore	C126	130	406	66	113	59	25	4	12	56	37	15	.278
Dick Porter	OF37	68	148	17	45	23	7	0	1	26	6	1	.304
Lloyd Richards	C40	50	153	14	29	12	0	3	0	9	25	1	.190
Jake Mooty	P34	35	86	7	23	5	2	1	0	2	3	0	.267
Edward Moore	OF16	34	100	12	24	5	3	0	1	14	6	1	.240
Ted Kleinhans	P33	33	75	7	6	5	1	0	0	5	19	0	.080
John Gee	P32	32	75	1	8	4	1	0	0	4	32	0	.107
Earl Cook	P29	29	66	5	11	5	0	1	0	5	12	0	.167
Charles Barrett	P29	29	56	4	8	4	2	0	0	1	17	0	.143
Reg Grabowski	P23	24	43	1	2	2	0	0	0	5	13	0	.047
Lloyd Russell	SS23	23	103	10	25	4	4	0	0	4	18	1	.243
Ed Remorenko	OF15	21	53	11	15	9	4	1	1	7	8	1	.283
George Miner	P16	18	19	2	5	3	0	1	0	1	3	0	.263
Paul Gehrman	P14	14	21	2	2	1	0	0	0	2	5	0	.095

SYRACUSE (cont.)
Chiefs

BATTERS	POS-GAMES	GP	AB	R	H	BI	2B	3B	HR	BB	SO	SB	BA
James Adair	2B13	13	60	6	11	4	2	0	1	3	8	0	.183
Don Lang	3B,SS	11	32	4	12	5	3	0	0	11	5	0	.375
Jim Bottomley	1B	7	14	0	1	0	0	0	0			0	.071
Bobby Mattick	SS	5	16	1	1	0	0	0	0			0	.063
Irvin Hall	2B	2	7	2	2	0	1	0	0			0	.286
Ray Benge	P9	9											.250
Eugene Thompson	P8	8											.250
Aloysius Murphy		6											.133
Pete Angell		5											.176
Fred Fussell	P4	4											.333
Wayne Blackburn		4											.182
Charles Harig		3											.364
Al Lehman		3											.286
John Leznick		3											.200
Gus Brittain		3											.000
Oliver Hill	P3	3											.000
Robert Wright	P3	3											.000
Emil Hemenway	P2	2											.000
Robert Brown	P1	1											.000
Erling Larsen		1											.000
Steven LeGault	P1	1											.000

PITCHERS	W	L	PCT	G	GS	CG	SH	IP	H	BB	SO	ERA
John Gee	17	11	.607	32	30	18	3	226	200	83	126	2.71
Charles Barrett	16	3	.842	29	15	10	2	154	143	38	52	2.34
Ted Kleinhans	16	12	.571	33	28	17	3	211	206	107	116	2.90
Jake Mooty	11	12	.478	34	27	21	1	232	228	93	110	3.65
Earl Cook	10	12	.455	29	26	12	2	179	171	76	99	3.57
Reg Grabowski	9	6	.600	23	15	8	2	123	136	45	38	3.80
Ray Benge	4	1	.800	9								
George Miner	3	0	1.000	16	1	1	1	55	41	25	28	2.78
Paul Gehrman	1	6	.143	14	9	3	0	72	87	36	21	4.75
Fred Fussell	0	1	.000	4								
Robert Brown	0	1	.000									
Eugene Thompson	0	2	.000	8				13	18	17	6	9.69
Robert Wright	0	0	----	3								
Oliver Hill	0	0	----	3								
Emil Hemenway	0	0	----	2								
Steven LeGault	0	0	----	1								

ROCHESTER 3rd 80-74 .519 -25 Ray Blades
Red Wings

BATTERS	POS-GAMES	GP	AB	R	H	BI	2B	3B	HR	BB	SO	SB	BA
Bernard Cobb	1B81	85	296	29	84	37	16	5	3	27	26	0	.284
Frank Morehouse	2B68,SS36	119	369	68	104	38	18	7	5	55	66	3	.282
Marty Marion	SS109	109	337	32	84	21	15	2	2	14	42	1	.249
Jack Juelich	3B124,2B37	156	591	93	155	60	22	9	2	69	38	4	.262
Louis Vezelich	OF152	152	547	81	156	78	25	10	6	85	52	11	.285
Carden Gillenwater	OF104	111	353	43	98	46	19	1	1	36	51	4	.278
John Hopp	OF97	124	371	73	111	48	21	10	9	60	81	16	.299
Bruce Ogrodowski	C76	80	266	18	57	30	6	2	2	17	10	1	.214
Estel Crabtree	OF96,1B46	136	483	82	145	82	26	4	12	62	26	6	.300
Maurice Sturdy	2B40,1B37,3B36	117	391	65	117	64	22	3	10	47	25	5	.299
Sam Narron	C65	90	241	28	75	49	18	3	7	10	29	0	.311
Oscar Judd	P33	64	77	14	18	11	5	1	0	4	12	0	.239
Ken Raffensberger	P53	53	69	2	8	4	2	0	0	1	32	0	.116
Al Sherer	P47	49	64	8	13	6	2	0	0	5	12	0	.203
Robert Bowman	P48	48	40	1	1	0	0	0	0	8	26	0	.025
Sammy Baugh	SS30	37	71	13	13	11	0	1	1	8	11	0	.183
Silas Johnson	P37	37	60	3	7	3	3	0	0	3	23	0	.117
Norbert Kleinke	P34	34	52	5	4	1	0	0	0	9	19	0	.077
Lou Scoffic	OF29	32	91	12	23	19	1	1	1	23	11	0	.253
Eldon Breese	C27	29	85	2	19	7	0	0	0	6	11	1	.224
Ted Wilks	P27	29	25	3	2	0	0	0	0	3	10	0	.080
Howard Krist	P24	26	43	5	8	0	2	0	0	1	11	0	.186
Tony Malinosky	SS	9	25	0	4	0	0	0	0			0	.160
Floyd Beal		9											.400
Ray Dieffenbach		9											.207
Frank Barrett	P7	7											.000
John Wahonick	P6	6											.333

ROCHESTER (cont.)
Red Wings

BATTERS	POS-GAMES	GP	AB	R	H	BI	2B	3B	HR	BB	SO	SB	BA
Lee Sherrill	P3	3											.250
Robert Doyle	P3	3											.000
Herbert Moore	P2	3											.000
Harold Swanson	P2	2											.250
William Seinsoth	P2	2											.250
Cecil Garriott		2											.000
Archie Templeton	P1	2											.000
Oscar Roettger		1											.000

PITCHERS		W	L	PCT	G	GS	CG	SH	IP	H	BB	SO	ERA
Ken Raffensberger		15	10	.600	53	19	10	4	201	176	72	131	2.91
Silas Johnson		14	11	.560	37	19	13	2	172	160	46	110	3.03
Norbert Kleinke		13	9	.591	34	26	10	3	182	181	60	82	4.05
Robert Bowman		11	7	.611	48	17	3	2	165	152	66	94	3.11
Al Sherer		8	12	.400	47	28	6	0	194	206	105	88	5.20
Oscar Judd		6	5	.545	33	15	2	1	116	121	83	53	4.66
Howard Krist		6	11	.353	24	17	5	0	115	142	44	41	5.09
Ted Wilks		4	2	.667	27	6	2	0	85	80	48	36	3.92
Lee Sherrill		1	0	1.000	3				8	13	13	3	
William Seinsoth		1	0	1.000	2								
John Wahonick		1	1	.500	6								
Robert Doyle		0	1	.000	3								
Herbert Moore		0	1	.000	2								
Francis Barrett		0	4	.000	7				19	19	18	3	
Harold Swanson		0	0	----	2								
Archie Templeton		0	0	----	1				1	0	0	1	0.00

BUFFALO   4th   79-74   .516   -25.5   Steve O'Neill
Bisons

BATTERS	POS-GAMES	GP	AB	R	H	BI	2B	3B	HR	BB	SO	SB	BA
James Oglesby	1B153	153	599	109	191	90	31	2	13	65	28	8	.319
Marvin Olson	2B63	71	254	47	58	23	10	0	3	42	13	3	.228
Greg Mulleavy	SS109,2B38	146	573	98	153	61	34	3	14	59	62	17	.267
Joseph Martin	3B87	105	354	68	117	66	28	6	10	20	30	9	.331
Ollie Carnegie	OF139	142	552	124	182	136	35	3	45	50	98	2	.330
John Tyler	OF132	141	470	88	131	72	23	2	12	61	63	17	.279
Woody Abernathy	OF94	103	375	76	121	74	27	5	21	34	49	3	.323
Ed Phillips	C75	88	262	18	72	43	11	2	4	20	33	1	.275
Ed Boland	OF90	108	317	46	104	67	11	1	14	33	24	4	.328
Dan Carnevale	3B52,SS49	107	375	45	81	25	10	0	4	41	55	1	.216
Mike Tresh	C61	70	200	28	60	24	9	2	3	36	23	0	.300
Tony Dueker	2B51	56	190	28	54	32	2	2	3	29	21	2	.284
Art Jacobs	P50	50	42	8	9	2	0	0	0	3	3	0	.214
Fabian Kowalik	P38	41	85	4	20	10	2	0	0	1	15	0	.235
Robert Kline	P36	36	51	3	7	8	3	0	0	1	12	0	.137
Fred Archer	P32	32	55	5	6	1	1	0	0	2	16	0	.109
Herman Fink	P32	32	52	4	14	7	0	0	1	1	13	0	.269
Norm Hibbs	P29	31	20	1	5	0	0	0	0	2	9	0	.250
Ken Ash	P30	30	67	10	15	1	1	1	0	8	6	1	.224
George Savino	C26	29	88	4	23	11	7	1	0	5	7	0	.261
William Harris	P26	26	50	5	7	4	0	0	0	2	7	1	.140
John Marcum	P10	17	32	4	10	4	2	0	0	1	2	0	.313
Henry Nowak	OF11	16	26	7	8	4	1	0	2	6	5	0	.308
William Howard		11	3	1	1	0	0	0	0	4	1	1	.333
Don Ferris	P7	7											.200
Sal Maglie	P5	5											.250
George Uhle	P2	4											.000
Harold Tyler		3											.000

PITCHERS		W	L	PCT	G	GS	CG	SH	IP	H	BB	SO	ER
Ken Ash		15	8	.652	30	26	15	3	187	192	72	59	3.90
Fabian Kowalik		15	13	.536	38	25	14	1	196	216	83	51	3.77
William Harris		10	6	.625	26	21	8	1	147	161	45	81	5.51
Herman Fink		8	8	.500	32	22	7	0	145	190	59	48	6.02
Robert Kline		8	13	.381	36	23	7	0	145	203	50	31	5.77
Fred Archer		8	14	.364	32	25	10	1	179	206	94	78	4.78
John Marcum		6	3	.667	10	10	5	0	61	72	9	24	4.28
Art Jacobs		6	5	.545	50	0	0	0	124	123	37	70	2.98

BUFFALO (cont.)
Bisons

PITCHERS	W	L	PCT	G	GS	CG	SH	IP	H	BB	SO	ERA
Norm Hibbs	3	3	.500	29	0	0	0	66	81	28	28	4.77
Sal Maglie	0	1	.000	5				12	12	8	4	3.75
Don Ferris	0	0	----	7								
George Uhle	0	0	----	2								

TORONTO   5th   72-81   .471   -32.5   Dan Howley
Maple Leafs

BATTERS	POS-GAMES	GP	AB	R	H	BI	2B	3B	HR	BB	SO	SB	BA
Irving Burns	1B148	148	562	67	156	78	20	7	8	54	25	4	.278
Herman Clifton	2B103	104	331	44	78	24	14	5	2	47	54	5	.236
Charles Sheerin	SS98	119	417	62	103	38	9	3	5	35	56	1	.247
Joseph Gantenbein	3B153	153	598	96	170	67	27	10	9	67	50	4	.284
Robert A. Porter	OF140	140	493	60	132	69	16	7	3	53	58	5	.268
Fred Petoskey	OF128	138	471	61	136	52	22	4	0	44	26	10	.289
Mayo Smith	OF121	133	437	66	119	40	13	7	2	68	37	5	.273
Frank Reiber	C124	138	402	59	105	90	22	4	13	66	40	3	.261
Henry Manush	OF79	81	277	38	86	39	21	5	3	39	19	0	.311
Albert Smith	2B46	72	191	26	46	19	5	2	1	21	31	1	.241
William Urbanski	SS62	68	229	28	54	24	8	1	3	15	18	0	.236
Sam Harshany	C35	68	132	7	30	13	3	0	0	21	13	0	.227
Joseph Sullivan	P37	44	82	7	21	13	0	3	1	2	12	0	.256
Joseph Mulligan	P39	40	49	2	5	2	1	0	0	2	29	0	.102
John Berly	P32	37	53	4	9	3	1	0	0	6	15	0	.170
Ted Olson	P33	33	67	4	11	4	1	0	0	3	22	0	.164
Don Brennan	P33	33	21	0	2	1	0	0	0	0	12	0	.095
Walt Lanfranconi	P26	32	16	4	4	2	1	1	0	1	4	0	.250
Earl Caldwell	P28	30	56	3	8	10	2	1	0	2	18	0	.143
Emile Meola	P27	27	55	7	4	1	1	0	0	8	18	0	.073
Woodrow Davis	P24	25	9	0	2	1	1	0	0	2	3	0	.222
John Wilson	P8	8											.067
George Klivak	P3	3											1.000
Francis Nekola	P2	2											.000
Clarence Straub		2											.000
Walt Klimczak		1											.000

PITCHERS	W	L	PCT	G	GS	CG	SH	IP	H	BB	SO	ERA
Joseph Sullivan	18	10	.643	37	29	16	4	220	242	93	94	3.76
John Berly	11	8	.579	32	19	9	3	155	159	76	69	3.72
Ted Olson	11	13	.458	33	25	10	1	183	185	96	81	3.79
Emile Meola	10	8	.556	27	23	11	1	161	157	78	68	3.75
Joseph Mulligan	8	11	.421	39	14	4	2	146	138	80	69	3.21
Earl Caldwell	8	14	.364	28	24	12	0	160	199	53	48	4.16
Walt Lanfranconi	2	3	.400	26	5	2	0	67	92	41	17	6.58
Don Brennan	2	8	.200	33	6	2	0	85	109	47	42	5.72
John Wilson	1	1	.500	8								
Woodrow Davis	1	5	.167	24	7	0	0	51	64	35	19	6.00
George Klivak	0	0	----	3				5	1	4	1	0.00
Francis Nekola	0	0	----	2								

MONTREAL   6th   69-84   .451   -35.5   Rabbit Maranville -
Royals   Alex Hooks

BATTERS	POS-GAMES	GP	AB	R	H	BI	2B	3B	HR	BB	SO	SB	BA
Alex Hooks	1B155	155	595	83	169	79	25	4	15	57	41	8	.284
John Bell	2B155	155	611	76	156	47	20	4	9	65	47	7	.255
Ben Sankey	SS122,3B17	139	489	63	136	53	22	5	1	46	38	4	.278
Joseph Benning	3B86,P1	108	330	36	95	29	12	7	0	20	32	2	.288
Paul Dunlap	OF112	121	393	56	116	73	15	3	7	64	26	2	.295
Arnold Moser	OF	(see multi-team players)											
Al Wright	OF	(see multi-team players)											
Norm Kies	C71	83	221	23	62	40	11	0	4	37	30	0	.281
William Schuster	3B50,SS37	102	289	49	92	31	13	1	3	53	40	8	.319
Paul Chervinko	C59	64	163	20	39	19	5	1	0	35	18	0	.239
Harry Smythe	P40	59	100	5	31	18	4	1	0	5	10	0	.310
Edwin Chapman	P45	48	73	5	12	10	1	0	1	6	20	0	.164
William Campbell	C40	47	136	22	43	9	7	1	1	22	7	0	.316

MONTREAL (cont.)
Royals

BATTERS	POS-GAMES	GP	AB	R	H	BI	2B	3B	HR	BB	SO	SB	BA
Art Parks	OF39	47	131	18	34	22	5	0	5	20	11	0	.260
Delano Wetherell	P36	40	81	3	17	0	3	0	0	3	14	0	.210
Oadis Swigart	P38	38	35	4	8	2	0	0	0	5	6	0	.229
Robert E. Porter	P35	35	62	4	9	2	2	0	0	2	11	0	.145
Marvin Duke	P34	34	52	4	8	2	2	0	0	1	7	0	.154
Tom Oliver	OF31	32	100	11	29	5	0	1	0	10	2	0	.290
Ken Heintzelman	P24	24	21	5	4	3	0	0	1	3	6	0	.190
William Homan	3B18	21	66	12	19	9	4	0	0	7	6	0	.288
Morris Sands	OF14	18	47	6	6	1	0	0	0	4	6	0	.128
Lou Polli	P7	11	16	2	5	2	2	0	0	2	1	0	.313
Maurice Van Robays	OF	9	25	2	5	2	0	1	1			0	.200
Mercer Harris		8											.280
Clarence Nachand		5											.083
Paul Calvert	P3	3											.400
Ted Duay		2											.250

PITCHERS	W	L	PCT	G	GS	CG	SH	IP	H	BB	SO	ERA
Harry Smythe	16	12	.571	40	25	18	2	215	247	61	86	3.27
Delano Wetherell	11	13	.458	36	24	9	3	183	209	50	62	4.57
Edwin Chapman	9	14	.391	45	21	11	1	196	183	118	99	3.86
Marvin Duke	8	7	.533	34	16	7	0	150	172	48	51	4.98
Robert E. Porter	8	11	.421	35	25	9	1	183	192	48	71	3.63
Ken Heintzelman	4	5	.444	24	9	0	0	69	75	65	43	5.48
Oadis Swigart	4	7	.364	38	8	3	0	120	151	55	44	4.88
Lou Polli	2	1	.667	7								
Paul Calvert	1	1	.500	3				13	8	14	5	4.15
ArnoldMoser	0	0	----	1								
Joseph Benning	0	0	----	1								

JERSEY CITY   7th   68-85   .444   -36.5   Travis Jackson -
Giants   Hank DeBerry

BATTERS	POS-GAMES	GP	AB	R	H	BI	2B	3B	HR	BB	SO	SB	BA
Leslie Powers	1B133	134	509	64	149	54	15	8	5	46	54	6	.293
Mike Haslin	2B101	101	394	56	122	59	17	7	5	22	26	5	.310
George Myatt	SS101,3B15	116	464	82	129	36	17	5	1	54	57	45	.278
Ernie Horne	3B68	70	255	29	67	37	14	1	0	14	18	4	.263
Babe Herman	OF139	145	527	89	171	93	40	5	18	62	37	4	.324
Linc Blakely	OF135	137	497	68	132	53	21	4	7	38	63	11	.266
John Winsett	OF127,P1	132	433	69	112	75	20	7	20	83	88	4	.259
Thomas Padden	C97	101	313	40	87	47	16	2	2	38	30	3	.278
Harold King	3B59,2B34	114	347	32	103	45	13	4	2	43	26	2	.297
Jack Redmond	C67,1B16	93	258	28	56	33	6	3	6	34	22	2	.217
Herschel Honeycutt	SS56	60	204	26	56	22	4	1	1	17	5	2	.275
Kenneth Richardson	2B25	54	143	23	33	13	7	3	1	18	26	1	.231
Harold B. Lee	OF49	50	191	26	44	20	4	2	2	22	17	0	.230
Thomas Baker	P38	48	80	8	25	6	5	0	0	4	16	0	.313
Roy Joiner	P39	47	88	8	20	13	3	0	2	2	29	0	.227
Rollie Stiles	P44	44	80	7	13	5	2	0	0	7	19	1	.163
George Davis	OF38	41	99	12	20	8	4	1	1	8	12	1	.202
Glen Gabler	P40	41	68	1	12	4	1	1	0	4	9	2	.176
Robert Carpenter	P35	35	18	2	3	1	0	0	0	1	3	0	.167
Mitchell Radon	P18	18	6	1	1	0	0	0	0	1	1	0	.167
Hy Vandenberg	P15	15	30	2	8	2	1	0	0	0	4	0	.267
John Hubbell	P15	15	29	4	5	2	0	0	0	0	4	0	.172
William Smith	P14	14	8	1	2	0	0	0	0	0	4	0	.250
Linville Watkins	P13	13	11	2	2	0	0	0	0	0	2	0	.182
Tommy De la Cruz	P10	11	9	2	2	0	0	0	0	0	3	0	.222
Travis Jackson	SS	10	17	0	5	2	1	0	0	2	3	0	.294
Tom Ferrick	P8	9											.250
Alex Gaston		6											.375
George Bausewein	P4	4											.667
John Meketi	P4	4											.125
Charles Murphy		3											.333
Louis Melendez		1											.000
Paul Sullivan	P1	1											.000

PITCHERS	W	L	PCT	G	GS	CG	SH	IP	H	BB	SO	ERA
Rollie Stiles	14	18	.438	44	33	14	5	248	266	74	78	3.74
Glen Gabler	12	11	.522	40	24	11	0	204	218	74	59	3.53

JERSEY CITY (cont.)
Giants

PITCHERS	W	L	PCT	G	GS	CG	SH	IP	H	BB	SO	ERA
Roy Joiner	9	9	.500	39	24	13	0	200	245	66	77	4.05
Thomas Baker	8	22	.267	38	35	16	1	211	196	131	112	4.27
John Hubbell	7	3	.700	15	9	5	1	73	74	29	42	3.70
Hy Vandenberg	5	5	.500	15	10	6	0	85	99	28	38	4.24
Robert Carpenter	5	9	.357	35	8	1	1	87	104	38	30	6.00
Tom Ferrick	4	0	1.000	8								
Mitchell Radon	2	1	.667	18	0	0	0	35	30	21	6	4.11
Linville Watkins	1	3	.250	13	4	2	0	34	38	23	12	4.50
John Meketi	1	3	.250	4								
William Smith	0	1	.000	14	1	0	0	30	41	15	5	6.30
Tommy De la Cruz	0	0	----	10	0	0	0	29	37	10	10	4.03
George Bausewein	0	0	----	4								
John Winsett	0	0	----	1								
Paul Sullivan	0	0	----	1								

BALTIMORE   8th   52-98   .347   -51   Clyde Crouse
Orioles

BATTERS	POS-GAMES	GP	AB	R	H	BI	2B	3B	HR	BB	SO	SB	BA
Eugene Corbett	1B107	107	417	62	125	58	17	5	12	53	38	9	.300
Leo Norris	2B		(see multi-team players)										
Nolen Richardson	SS65	69	257	36	62	26	10	2	0	30	21	2	.241
Joseph Greenberg	3B65,OF17,2B16	108	372	54	106	56	20	3	6	33	29	8	.285
Fred Tauby	OF115	125	473	77	146	81	20	2	16	33	32	9	.309
George Puccinelli	OF52	54	202	40	54	53	11	2	15	32	38	0	.267
Gus Dugas	OF		(see multi-team players)										
Clyde Crouse	C71	96	260	30	69	43	10	1	10	37	29	3	.265
Bill Cissell	3B38,2B29,SS28	97	382	49	112	40	16	5	5	36	21	1	.293
Roy Spencer	C58	71	211	16	57	31	12	0	4	8	29	0	.270
Earl Bolyard	OF42,C13	53	196	26	51	19	7	3	3	12	12	4	.260
Edwin Taylor	SS51	51	203	34	50	10	17	0	3	23	50	1	.246
Henry Schluter	3B44	48	180	14	37	16	7	1	1	7	27	2	.206
Phil Weintraub	1B42	44	139	36	48	26	11	2	7	51	17	1	.345
Harry Matuzak	P37	40	62	8	15	3	3	0	1	7	18	0	.242
John Wittig	P32	33	51	6	5	3	1	0	0	2	22	0	.098
Frank Anderson	P28	29	40	0	6	1	2	0	0	0	7	0	.150
George Sanford	2B25	28	85	6	21	7	2	0	0	11	14	2	.247
Charles Fischer	P26	26	60	6	6	4	1	0	0	3	18	0	.100
Ben Huffman	C14	25	51	7	6	4	1	0	0	15	8	0	.118
Harold R. Lee	OF23	23	79	10	16	5	3	1	1	3	16	1	.203
James Reninger	P19	19	34	1	6	2	1	0	0	3	13	0	.176
Perce Malone	P19	19	27	0	3	2	0	0	0	0	5	0	.111
William Perrin	P19	19	20	1	2	2	0	0	0	0	6	0	.100
Frank McGowan	OF16	16	50	21	21	14	4	0	6	24	1	2	.420
Eugene Geary		16	36	8	8	0	1	0	0	12	5	0	.222
Rogers Hornsby		16	27	2	2	0	0	0	0	6	9	0	.074
Frank Sansotti	P15	16	16	2	5	1	1	0	0	2	4	0	.313
John Ryan		13	44	2	12	7	3	0	0	0	6	1	.273
William McWilliams		13	30	3	4	3	2	0	0	2	9	0	.133
Arnold Heft		11	9	0	0	0	0	0	0	3	3	0	.000
Charles Harris	P9	9											.250
Peter Blumette	P9	9											.125
Syd Cohen	P8	8											.167
Earl Overman	P7	7											.286
Guy Fletcher	P6	6											.286
Peter Stack		5											.286
Raymond Stoviak		5											.000
Chad Kimsey	P3	4											.000
John Swank		3											.500
Stewart Bowers	P3	3											.000
William Ehrensberger	P3	3											.000
Vic Sorrell	P3	3											.000
Marion Semler	P3	3											.000
James Higgins	P2	2											.000

PITCHERS	W	L	PCT	G	GS	CG	SH	IP	H	BB	SO	ERA
Harry Matuszak	11	14	.440	37	23	11	1	198	217	73	88	5.55
John Wittig	10	9	.526	32	19	8	2	143	146	92	99	5.29
Charles Fischer	7	14	.333	26	24	10	0	166	203	68	91	5.26
James Reninger	6	8	.429	19	14	9	1	111	117	58	41	4.95
William Perrin	3	6	.333	19	6	1	0	66	65	34	40	4.09

BALTIMORE (cont.)
Orioles

PITCHERS	W	L	PCT	G	GS	CG	SH	IP	H	BB	SO	ERA
Perce Malone	3	8	.273	19	11	3	1	79	82	49	22	5.24
Frank Anderson	2	9	.182	28	10	4	0	108	135	58	57	6.58
Charles Harris	1	1	.500	9								
Peter Blumette	1	2	.333	9								
Guy Fletcher	1	2	.333	6								
Earl Overman	0	1	.000	7								
Vic Sorrell	0	1	.000	3								
Chad Kimsey	0	1	.000	3								
Arnold Heft	0	2	.000	11	2	1	0	31	36	24	10	5.81
Stewart Bowers	0	2	.000	3								
Syd Cohen	0	3	.000	8				20	20	7	8	
Frank Sansotti	0	4	.000	15	6	1	0	50	69	30	18	6.66
Marion Semler	0	0	----	3								
John Swank	0	0	----	3								
James Higgins	0	0	----	2								
William Ehrensberger	0	0	----	2				5	3	5	0	

MULTI-TEAM PLAYERS

BATTERS	POS-GAMES	TEAMS	GP	AB	R	H	BI	2B	3B	HR	BB	SO	SB	BA
Gus Dugas	OF152	MO56-BA96	152	532	100	167	81	35	5	16	105	52	11	.314
Arnold Moser	OF135,P1	SY10-MO132	142	487	51	143	64	19	6	3	47	33	5	.294
Al Wright	OF135	BA45-MO93	138	479	73	150	85	30	5	15	53	62	8	.313
Howard Meyers	3B136	BU7-SY130	137	529	69	131	53	20	5	2	59	36	2	.248
Leo Norris	2B62	BA61-NE17	78	262	35	72	27	11	2	5	24	37	1	.275
Joseph Dwyer	OF50	JC7-BA49	56	194	19	43	19	8	1	0	11	10	0	.222
Justin Stein	2B37	BA13-RO34	47	117	8	17	6	1	0	0	6	11	0	.145
Orville Jorgens	P35	BA16-MO19	35	46	3	6	2	0	0	0	2	12	0	.130
Ben Cantwell	P29	MO15-BA15	30	43	4	7	1	0	0	0	2	7	0	.163
Hod Lisenbee	P10	MO1-RO9	10	4	0	0	0	0	0	0	0	2	0	.000
Bill Kermode	P2	MO1-BA1	2											.000

PITCHERS		TEAMS	W	L	PCT	G	GS	CG	SH	IP	H	BB	SO	ERA
Orville Jorgens		BA16-MO19	9	9	.500	35	21	5	0	149	178	87	77	5.44
Ben Cantwell		MO15-BA14	4	15	.211	29	20	8	1	125	171	44	38	5.47
Hod Lisenbee		MO1-BA9	0	0	----	10	0	0	0	15	21	4	7	9.00
Bill Kermode		MO1-BA1	0	0	----	2								

TEAM BATTING

TEAMS	GP	AB	R	H	BI	2B	3B	HR	BB	SO	SB	BA
NEWARK	152	5221	1004	1574	934	287	50	147	748	543	57	.301
SYRACUSE	155	5176	676	1352	593	249	54	47	496	542	55	.261
ROCHESTER	156	5101	691	1332	626	227	60	61	560	655	55	.261
BUFFALO	153	5126	833	1456	773	249	31	149	531	605	69	.284
TORONTO	153	4967	647	1283	592	189	60	51	557	567	38	.258
MONTREAL	155	5090	656	1402	609	202	40	63	592	487	50	.275
JERSEY CITY	156	5127	686	1390	639	213	54	73	522	600	93	.271
BALTIMORE	152	5072	712	1354	652	240	34	115	571	640	56	.267
	616	40880	5905	11143	5418	1856	383	706	4577	4639	219	.273

1939
THE FINAL SPOT

The Shaughnessy playoff system was designed to augment the race for first place by allowing the top four teams to compete for playoff positions. Since its institution in the International League in 1933, the plan had worked to perfection. In its first year of use, the playoff system saw Buffalo nose into fourth one game ahead of three other teams. In subsequent years, an average of less than five games separated the last team in and the first team out. In 1939, this average got a whole lot closer.

As the 1939 season started, the main contender for the laurels turned out to be a surprise candidate: Jersey City. The Giants, well stocked with future New York Giants, jumped to the front of the pack and held a slim lead throughout most of the summer. Immediately behind was Rochester, followed by Newark and Syracuse. As the season's final days approached, Jersey City and Rochester locked up the first two playoff spots. This left Buffalo, Newark, and Syracuse neck-and-neck for the final two spots. At season's end, Buffalo finished third. One game behind in fourth, knotted with identical records of 81–73, stood Syracuse and Newark. There would be a one game "run-off" to determine the fourth and final playoff spot.

In the one game test played in Newark, Syracuse jumped out to an early lead. Alas for the Chiefs, the lead could not be maintained. Newark pinch hitter Frank Kelleher walloped a home run in the eighth inning of the contest, leading the Bears to 9–6 victory and a coveted place in the post-season.

In the International League of 1939, the teams out of playoff contention (Baltimore, Montreal, and Toronto) finished in a cluster more than 20 games back. Jersey City's John Dickshot finished as the highest batter (.355), while Ollie Carnegie of Buffalo won his second straight home run (29) and runs batted in (112) crowns. From the mound, Rochester hurler Silas Johnson posted the most wins (22), and Roy Joiner from Jersey City had the lowest earned run average (2.53). John Tising, sharing time with Syracuse and Baltimore, finished with the most strikeouts (144).

In other years, the International League has seen other teams tied for playoff positions. For example, in 1936 an extra game determined the final seeding when Rochester and Newark finished tied for second in the regular season. There was, however, a key difference between 1939, and other playoff ties. In those years, the teams played the run-off games knowing that they would both still be in. There was no such guarantee in 1939, when Newark and Syracuse rolled the dice for nine innings to decide who would go to the playoff party—and who would stay home.

JERSEY CITY 1st 89-64 .582 Bert Niehoff
Giants

BATTERS	POS-GAMES	GP	AB	R	H	BI	2B	3B	HR	BB	SO	SB	BA
Sam Leslie	1B98	112	372	37	117	66	19	1	2	30	16	7	.315
Al Glossop	2B141	144	511	60	132	85	22	3	19	55	49	7	.258
Herschel Honeycutt	SS125	126	491	64	139	36	20	0	3	41	15	10	.283
Tom Hafey	3B76	78	301	49	86	45	13	6	8	17	42	7	.286
John Dickshot	OF152	153	557	100	198	92	26	**16**	8	58	46	8	**.355**
Morris Jones	OF146	148	542	72	167	61	40	4	5	58	50	6	.308
Forrest Jensen	OF86	90	334	48	100	38	16	1	6	24	15	1	.299
Thomas Padden	C92	102	282	43	81	33	15	0	3	60	25	1	.287
Glen Stewart	1B69,3B26,SS19,2B10	133	421	53	122	54	21	5	2	24	36	2	.290
Linc Blakely	OF75	89	242	32	61	18	10	3	1	27	12	6	.252
William Atwood	C81	81	220	20	64	19	10	2	0	28	19	4	.291
Mendel Ramsey	3B54	56	186	20	49	12	8	1	0	15	27	0	.263
Louis Vezelich	OF25	47	96	13	24	8	4	1	1	9	13	1	.250
Roy Joiner	P35	36	85	10	17	4	0	0	0	8	22	0	.200
Hy Vandenberg	P30	34	73	3	12	6	2	1	0	3	9	0	.164
Robert Carpenter	P34	34	52	5	12	4	0	0	0	3	9	0	.231
John Wittig	P33	33	57	4	9	7	3	0	0	2	17	0	.158
Rollie Stiles	P31	31	49	2	3	4	0	0	0	5	14	0	.061
William Harris	P30	30	75	4	13	3	3	0	0	1	5	0	.173
Joe Kohlman	P16	17	4	2	1	0	0	0	0	1	2	0	.250
George Myatt		15	57	12	18	6	2	0	0	5	8	4	.316
John Mihalic	2B	10	17	2	2	1	1	0	0	3	2	0	.118
John Hubbell	P9	9											.000
Linville Watkins	P7	7											.000
John Winsett	OF	3	4	1	1	0	0	0	0			0	.250
Sid Gordon	3B	3	9	1	2	0	0	0	0			1	.222
Herb Anderson	P3	3											.000
John Meketi	P2	2											.000
Lou Chiozza	PH	1	1	0	0	0	0	0	0			0	.000

PITCHERS		W	L	PCT	G	GS	CG	SH	IP	H	BB	SO	ERA
Roy Joiner		21	8	.724	35	32	18	5	235	222	37	91	**2.53**
William Harris		18	10	,643	30	26	16	4	209	196	31	115	2.80
Hy Vandenberg		15	10	.600	30	26	14	3	202	178	55	108	2.72
Rollie Stiles		11	8	.579	31	22	12	3	167	148	36	45	2.86
Robert Carpenter		9	11	.450	34	23	6	1	161	173	51	56	3.80
John Wittig		8	7	.533	33	22	10	0	170	167	85	75	4.02
Linville Watkins		1	0	1.000	7				14	13	8	8	
Joe Kohlman		1	1	.500	16	0	0	0	28	40	8	9	5.14
John Meketi		0	1	.000	2				3	3	5	4	
John Hubbell		0	3	.000	9				23	33	8	7	
Herb Anderson		0	0	----	3				6	3	3	5	

ROCHESTER 2nd 84-67 .556 -4 Billy Southworth
Red Wings

BATTERS	POS-GAMES	GP	AB	R	H	BI	2B	3B	HR	BB	SO	SB	BA
Harry Davis	1B144	145	585	103	174	92	38	7	21	63	47	10	.297
Maurice Sturdy	2B142	145	555	100	174	83	28	11	8	65	34	3	.314
Marty Marion	SS127	128	437	66	119	53	12	5	5	28	61	5	.272
Whitey Kurowski	3B124	124	519	102	151	68	29	8	11	28	44	13	.291
Allen Cooke	OF146	147	532	84	181	74	42	7	4	91	70	2	.340
Estel Crabtree	OF119	133	510	82	172	94	41	7	14	37	21	4	.337
James Asbell	OF104	109	368	46	107	58	15	6	8	42	52	0	.291
Sam Narron	C96	106	358	41	108	62	14	6	9	19	44	2	.302
Carden Gillenwater	OF90	99	314	44	79	28	9	5	3	34	46	2	.252
Floyd Beal	C68	78	236	28	63	36	8	2	4	10	17	0	.267
Dominic Ryba	P37	55	113	9	35	9	8	1	0	7	16	0	.310
Fred Ankenman	SS18	43	105	12	23	14	1	0	0	9	11	0	.219
Ken Raffensberger	P43	43	91	8	19	9	4	0	1	5	31	0	.209
Silas Johnson	P42	42	98	9	18	4	1	0	0	3	28	0	.184
John Grodzicki	P42	42	61	7	21	9	6	1	0	2	9	0	.344
Roy Henshaw	P34	35	54	7	17	3	0	0	0	2	2	0	.315
Preacher Roe	P32	32	38	1	6	0	0	0	0	2	20	0	.158
John Wyrostek	OF22	24	75	17	20	9	3	2	0	6	3	0	.267
Henry Gornicki	P23	23	15	1	1	2	0	0	0	2	9	0	.067
Danny Murtaugh		22	89	13	29	6	3	1	0	14	10	3	.326
John Stopa	3B16	18	58	7	12	10	3	0	0	4	7	0	.207
Herschel Lyons	P15	15	10	1	2	1	0	0	1	0	4	0	.200
John Wahonick	P11	11	6	2	0	0	0	0	0	4	0	0	.000

ROCHESTER (cont.)
Red Wings

BATTERS	POS-GAMES	GP	AB	R	H	BI	2B	3B	HR	BB	SO	SB	BA
Fred Fussell	P7	7											.500
Frank Crespi	SS	5	27	5	7	1	2	0	0			1	.259
Bernard Cobb	1B	1	3	0	0	0	0	0	0			0	.000
Ray Smith	C	1	1	0	1	0	0	0	0			0	1.000
Maynard Snider	P1	1											.000

PITCHERS	W	L	PCT	G	GS	CG	SH	IP	H	BB	SO	ERA
Silas Johnson	22	12	.647	42	35	19	4	252	310	65	129	4.32
Dominic Ryba	18	12	.600	37	28	25	5	251	232	49	123	2.69
Ken Raffensberger	15	15	.500	43	31	16	4	242	257	68	116	3.20
John Grodzicki	8	7	.533	42	18	7	1	166	159	95	90	4.50
Preacher Roe	7	4	.636	32	11	5	2	118	109	62	64	4.35
Roy Henshaw	6	8	.429	34	21	6	1	143	171	50	54	5.41
Henry Gornicki	3	3	.500	23	4	1	0	61	64	30	34	5.16
Fred Fussell	2	0	1.000	7				20	15	9	4	
John Wahonick	2	2	.500	11	2	0	0	28	35	21	14	6.75
Herschel Lyons	1	4	.200	15	3	1	0	43	46	18	20	3.56
Maynard Snider	0	0	----	1				1	1	1	0	

BUFFALO
Bisons

	3rd	82-72	.532	-7.5	Steve O'Neill

BATTERS	POS-GAMES	GP	AB	R	H	BI	2B	3B	HR	BB	SO	SB	BA
James Oglesby	1B144	144	526	92	172	91	32	4	16	59	22	5	.327
Ray Mack	2B115	115	417	56	122	68	29	3	15	37	51	17	.293
Lou Boudreau	SS115	115	481	88	159	57	32	7	17	37	34	6	.331
Joseph Martin	3B129,OF17	149	570	86	183	93	33	3	23	29	42	8	.321
John Tyler	OF153	153	597	124	172	70	30	7	14	66	67	15	.288
Ollie Carnegie	OF131	143	497	84	146	112	25	3	29	51	74	4	.294
Henry Nowak	OF102	116	325	38	83	32	14	3	2	24	34	7	.255
Henry Helf	C85	99	310	46	89	61	16	4	12	21	45	4	.287
Greg Mulleavy	2B39,3B26	96	296	57	93	38	22	2	7	23	41	4	.314
George Savino	C76	83	270	26	71	32	14	1	10	13	23	2	.263
Sam Richmond	OF41	52	158	24	40	19	7	2	5	13	35	5	.253
William Sodd	OF37	41	127	17	26	11	10	0	5	6	34	0	.205
James Webb	SS39	39	147	18	35	12	6	1	4	12	25	4	.238
Sal Maglie	P39	39	35	2	5	1	0	0	0	0	13	0	.143
Clay Smith	P35	35	68	3	7	2	1	1	0	7	31	0	.103
Fabian Kowalik	P30	34	37	1	8	2	3	0	0	1	5	0	.216
Alfred Smith	P31	32	65	8	14	6	1	0	0	1	16	0	.215
Ken Ash	P30	30	66	8	9	5	2	0	0	5	15	0	.136
Raymond Roche	P24	25	12	2	1	0	0	0	0	0	4	0	.083
Earl Cook	P23	24	38	0	6	3	0	0	0	2	6	0	.158
Robert Kline	P22	22	50	4	10	1	2	0	0	0	14	0	.200
Fred Archer	P16	16	8	0	1	1	0	0	0	2	1	0	.125
Art Jacobs	P15	15	11	1	2	3	0	0	0	2	0	0	.182
William Zuber	P13	14	27	4	7	5	1	2	1	0	5	0	.259
Phil Hearn	OF11	11	13	0	2	1	1	0	0	2	4	0	.154
George Uhle	P6	9											.167
Thomas Drake	P8	8											.158
Frank Zubick	C	5	5	1	2	0	0	0	0			0	.400
William Howard	1B	5	3	1	2	0	0	0	0			0	.667
John Tulacz	P5	5											.000
Hal White	P4	4											.000
Norm Hibbs	P4	4											.000
Herman Fink	P4	4											.000
Ernie Talos	PH	1	1	0	0	0	0	0	0			0	.000
Harold Tyler	1B	1	0	0	0	0	0	0	0			0	----

PITCHERS	W	L	PCT	G	GS	CG	SH	IP	H	BB	SO	ERA
Alfred Smith	16	2	.889	31	23	11	3	160	179	49	83	3.26
Clay Smith	13	11	.542	35	24	10	5	199	195	61	85	2.94
Ken Ash	10	9	.526	30	26	12	1	192	235	61	68	3.94
Earl Cook	8	7	.533	23	15	6	0	115	120	41	51	4.07
Fabian Kowalik	6	8	.429	30	16	4	0	108	146	40	31	5.17
Robert Kline	6	10	.375	22	20	8	2	131	138	43	34	3.50
Art Jacobs	5	3	.625	15	1	0	0	37	44	8	19	4.86
William Zuber	5	4	.556	13	10	5	0	75	79	40	34	4.44
Thomas Drake	3	5	.375	8				54	47	31	33	
Sal Maglie	3	7	.300	39	8	0	0	101	102	42	62	4.99

BUFFALO (cont.)
Bisons

PITCHERS	W	L	PCT	G	GS	CG	SH	IP	H	BB	SO	ERA
Raymond Roche	2	1	.667	24	1	0	0	47	56	32	29	4.79
Fred Archer	2	3	.400	16	2	0	0	36	50	24	17	6.75
George Uhle	1	0	1.000	6				11	14	1	5	5.73
John Tulacz	1	0	1.000	5				10	9	8	6	
Herman Fink	1	1	.500	4				4	12	2	3	
Hal White	0	1	.000	4				8	8	5	4	6.75
Norm Hibbs	0	0	----	4				3	6	4	0	

NEWARK   4th   82-73   .529   -8   John Neun
Bears

BATTERS	POS-GAMES	GP	AB	R	H	BI	2B	3B	HR	BB	SO	SB	BA
Edward Levy	1B94	95	348	50	91	47	22	3	11	17	42	5	.261
Herman Schulte	2B138	139	480	81	126	52	30	0	6	60	34	5	.263
Nicholas Witek	SS138,2B20	156	621	100	204	104	39	7	5	35	38	11	.329
Nathan Blair	3B46	51	191	27	60	25	12	2	1	4	12	0	.314
Colonel Mills	OF147	149	541	89	165	82	34	9	7	53	50	5	.305
Walt Judnich	OF144	149	538	95	153	105	23	13	21	66	61	8	.284
Tommy Holmes	OF93	107	386	73	131	55	23	10	4	34	14	3	.339
William Holm	C78	84	221	36	59	38	10	0	7	51	43	2	.267
Frank Kelleher	3B32,OF29	79	223	50	62	38	9	3	12	26	30	0	.278
George Washburn	P32	69	107	13	34	18	1	2	1	4	17	0	.318
Harold Wagner	C60	62	201	26	55	31	8	5	2	19	26	1	.274
Joe Mack	1B58	58	242	38	71	44	13	3	9	22	27	1	.293
Mike Chartak	OF39	53	146	21	50	26	7	2	2	25	26	5	.342
George Barley	P40	47	58	6	13	9	2	0	0	6	21	0	.224
Pete Suder	3B41	42	148	14	35	17	5	3	2	8	14	1	.236
Norm Branch	P41	41	42	4	9	3	1	0	2	0	8	0	.214
Ivy Andrews	P35	35	27	3	4	0	1	0	0	2	9	0	.148
Joe Beggs	P33	33	62	7	7	3	0	0	0	9	17	0	.113
Mark Beddingfield	P33	33	23	0	2	0	1	0	0	3	9	0	.087
John Haley	P32	32	30	1	7	0	1	0	0	0	6	0	.233
Charles George	C25	31	85	7	20	11	1	1	1	9	13	1	.235
Roy Hughes	3B23	29	107	17	40	7	7	1	0	7	8	2	.374
Robert Kahle	3B24	24	84	12	21	6	1	2	0	9	11	3	.250
Nick Strincevich	P20	20	10	1	2	1	0	0	0	0	1	0	.200
Rupert Thompson	OF17	19	65	8	15	9	2	1	2	15	3	0	.231
Hank Borowy	P18	18	37	4	4	5	0	0	0	1	21	0	.108
Joe Gallagher	OF11	11	42	5	8	5	2	0	0	5	4	0	.190
Mario Russo	P10	10	23	2	6	0	1	0	0	0	2	0	.261
Max Macon	P10	10	17	2	7	1	1	0	0	0	0	0	.412
Al Hollingsworth	P8	9											.231
Jimmy DeShong	P6	6											.167
Charles Stanceu	P5	5											.167
Claude Corbitt	SS	5	19	2	2	0	0	0	0			0	.105
Tony DePhillips	C	4	11	0	2	1	0	0	0			0	.182
Russ Bergmann	SS,3B	3	5	1	2	1	0	0	0			1	.400
Art Metheny	OF	1	2	0	2	0	0	0	0			0	1.000
Jack Graham	PH	1	1	0	0	0	0	0	0			0	.000
Steve Peek	P1	1											.000

PITCHERS	W	L	PCT	G	GS	CG	SH	IP	H	BB	SO	ER
George Washburn	13	14	.481	32	30	16	3	196	203	**135**	103	3.95
Joe Beggs	12	10	.545	33	25	12	0	199	228	42	76	3.80
George Barley	10	10	.500	40	20	9	2	174	189	76	71	4.09
Hank Borowy	9	7	.563	18	18	6	0	112	113	64	89	4.82
Norm Branch	8	7	.533	41	8	4	0	119	113	57	92	3.86
John Haley	8	7	.533	32	16	4	1	102	128	44	33	5.38
Ivy Andrews	7	5	.583	35	8	2	0	95	96	24	30	3.13
Mario Russo	5	4	.556	10	8	5	1	64	38	17	28	1.97
Mark Beddingfield	3	1	.750	33	3	0	0	84	91	58	25	4.71
Max Macon	3	1	.750	10	3	1	0	41	46	18	10	3.73
Jimmy DeShong	1	1	.500	6				16	26	13	4	
Nick Strincevich	1	2	.333	20	2	0	0	40	62	28	16	7.20
Al Hollingsworth	1	2	.333	8				34	43	18	16	
Charles Stanceu	0	2	.000	5				22	23	14	18	
Steve Peek	0	0	----	1				2	5	0	1	

SYRACUSE Chiefs

| | 5th | 81-74 | .523 | -9 | Dick Porter |

BATTERS	POS-GAMES	GP	AB	R	H	BI	2B	3B	HR	BB	SO	SB	BA
Ignatius Walters	1B114	114	403	38	113	42	13	1	1	39	26	5	.280
John Kroner	2B125	128	445	53	123	66	14	5	3	39	49	1	.276
Leonard Kahny	SS97,2B26	126	459	64	117	33	9	8	0	41	49	11	.255
Howard Meyers	3B122	125	420	56	121	49	17	8	1	52	30	5	.288
Ed Longacre	OF152	152	589	76	173	58	21	4	2	38	36	10	.294
Dan Taylor	OF122	126	435	56	133	68	21	9	5	53	38	5	.306
Charles Harig	OF89	102	327	35	68	24	10	3	2	32	9	2	.208
John Bottarini	C79	93	268	33	74	43	13	2	5	32	33	2	.276
Dallas Warren	C71	97	284	30	73	42	13	2	7	26	42	1	.257
Irvin Hall	SS28,2B13	44	139	14	30	6	5	2	0	4	19	1	.216
Ted Kleinhans	P35	36	99	5	10	4	1	0	0	2	15	0	.101
John Gee	P35	35	93	6	21	4	2	0	0	5	36	0	.226
Jake Mooty	P27	32	84	3	18	4	3	0	0	3	9	0	.214
Art Jones	P32	32	27	2	4	3	0	0	0	1	5	0	.148
Ray Benge	P30	30	14	0	3	0	0	0	0	0	6	0	.214
Dick Porter	OF	25	35	7	9	6	1	0	0	4	2	0	.257
George Miner	P17	21	5	3	1	0	0	0	0	1	1	0	.200
Charles Moss	OF	6	5	2	2	0	0	0	0			0	.400
Pete Angell	P3	3											.250
Herm Rehbein	P2	2											.000

PITCHERS		W	L	PCT	G	GS	CG	SH	IP	H	BB	SO	ERA
John Gee		20	10	.667	35	34	18	5	240	210	104	153	3.11
Ted Kleinhans		19	12	.613	35	34	19	3	253	248	100	138	3.27
Jake Mooty		12	14	.462	27	27	21	0	216	193	57	97	2.83
Art Jones		3	4	.429	32	2	1	1	91	92	31	26	3.46
Pete Angell		1	0	1.000	3				10	5	11	2	0.00
Ray Benge		1	5	.167	30	0	0	0	58	74	26	38	4.81
George Miner		0	2	.000	17	1	0	0	31	34	20	16	4.06
Herm Rehbein		0	0	----	2				5	0	7	6	4.50

BALTIMORE Orioles

| | 6th | 68-85 | .444 | -21 | Rogers Hornsby |

BATTERS	POS-GAMES	GP	AB	R	H	BI	2B	3B	HR	BB	SO	SB	BA
Nick Etten	1B101	105	384	69	115	65	25	3	14	54	32	5	.299
Eugene Corbett	2B146	153	556	83	138	66	24	6	10	65	60	3	.248
Bill Lillard	SS139	144	482	64	127	73	24	2	9	54	48	3	.263
Baxter Jordan	3B	(see multi-team players)											
Murray Howell	OF146	151	529	97	181	107	39	5	24	81	69	2	.342
Art Graham	OF131	144	500	93	154	80	35	8	12	84	68	0	.308
John Gill	OF63	79	239	33	67	34	11	1	6	25	40	1	.280
Bennie Warren	C96	115	342	63	96	74	12	1	19	43	80	3	.281
Richard West	C55,OF50	108	414	90	133	65	23	9	15	27	62	9	.321
Fred Tauby	OF33	54	130	23	28	16	3	0	5	13	14	0	.215
Harry Matuzak	P47	48	64	7	12	6	1	1	1	9	23	0	.188
Len Gabrielson	1B39	41	146	20	36	19	4	0	2	17	19	2	.247
Roy Bruner	P38	39	36	3	1	1	0	0	0	2	15	0	.028
Leon Riley		38	52	8	11	8	3	0	1	11	11	0	.212
Elmer Burkart	P37	37	19	0	2	1	1	0	0	2	13	0	.105
Charles Glock	3B26	34	103	19	24	12	4	0	1	15	9	1	.233
Edward Moore	3B24	33	102	17	28	12	6	0	0	17	10	6	.275
James Reninger	P28	28	47	7	12	4	1	1	0	2	8	0	.255
Al Mele	OF25	27	96	14	25	13	5	0	0	8	6	0	.260
Gus Dugas	OF13	27	64	10	10	11	2	0	4	10	15	0	.156
James Kerr	P25	25	22	2	4	1	1	0	0	1	12	0	.182
Frank McGowan	OF17	22	56	11	16	12	2	0	2	8	4	2	.286
John Swank	P22	22	2	0	0	0	0	0	0	1	0	0	.000
Italo Chelini	P19	20	32	2	3	0	0	0	0	2	12	0	.094
Peter Naktenis	P18	18	14	0	2	2	1	0	0	0	8	0	.143
Aubrey Sanders		17	15	1	3	3	1	0	0	3	2	0	.200
David Coble	C12	12	31	2	3	0	0	1	0	3	12	0	.097
William Hudson	P10	10	3	1	1	0	0	0	0	0	1	0	.333
Joseph Desmond	P10	10	2	0	0	0	0	0	0	1	0	0	.000
Irving Bartling	3B	9	31	6	9	5	0	0	0			0	.290
William Davis	P8	8											.333
Thomas Hughes	P7	7											.000
Edward Linke	P6	6											.200
Edwin Taylor	3B	5	6	1	1	0	0	0	0	0		0	.167
Alex Monchak	SS	3	6	0	1	0	0	0	0	0		0	.167

BALTIMORE (cont.)
Orioles

BATTERS	POS-GAMES	GP	AB	R	H	BI	2B	3B	HR	BB	SO	SB	BA
Jack Van Orsdol	P3	3											.000
Robert McNamara	SS,3B	2	3	0	0	0	0	0	0			0	.000
Ed Vogel	P2	2											.000
Randall Gumpert	P2	2											.000
Charles O'Hara	P1	1											.000

PITCHERS		W	L	PCT	G	GS	CG	SH	IP	H	BB	SO	ERA
Harry Matuzak		13	16	.448	47	27	10	1	232	262	78	107	4.89
Roy Bruner		11	6	.647	38	15	10	0	144	160	65	49	3.69
James Reninger		10	7	.588	27	22	7	1	147	170	66	62	4.59
Italo Chelini		5	6	.455	19	15	5	0	99	131	26	47	5.45
Edward Linke		2	2	.500	6				22	36	6	5	
James Kerr		2	8	.200	25	10	2	0	77	115	48	29	8.65
Peter Naktenis		2	8	.200	18	9	1	1	56	76	26	34	6.11
Elmer Burkart		2	9	.182	37	5	0	0	97	113	38	41	4.64
John Swank		1	0	1.000	22	0	0	0	38	46	14	14	4.97
William Hudson		1	0	1.000	10	1	0	0	18	31	17	9	9.00
Randall Gumpert		1	0	1.000	2				3	6	2	2	9.00
Charles O'Hara		1	0	1.000	1				1	1	0	0	0.00
Jack Van Orsdol		1	2	.333	3				14	15	8	4	
William Davis		0	2	.000	8				19	30	8	4	
Thomas Hughes		0	2	.000	7				25	29	19	7	6.48
Joseph Desmond		0	0	----	10	1	0	0	21	25	10	5	3.00
Ed Vogel		0	0	----	2				1	3	2	0	

MONTREAL   7th   64-88   .421   -25.5   Burleigh Grimes
Royals

BATTERS	POS-GAMES	GP	AB	R	H	BI	2B	3B	HR	BB	SO	SB	BA
Charles Hasson	1B40	41	131	27	43	29	6	0	6	27	19	0	.328
John Bell	2B144	148	556	83	161	52	21	3	0	72	32	8	.290
Leo Norris	SS		(see multi-team players)										
Don Ross	3B132,SS23	153	549	70	157	81	32	3	2	58	31	9	.286
Lindsey Deal	OF128	134	506	80	160	74	26	6	7	26	30	13	.316
Arnold Moser	OF110,3B24	137	483	74	146	41	18	4	2	49	45	8	.302
Maurice Van Robays	OF91,1B40	136	481	81	154	80	29	8	10	63	35	3	.320
Christian Hartje	C93	116	358	62	106	43	25	5	3	50	45	6	.296
Joseph Becker	C66	93	252	38	77	33	13	3	0	38	23	3	.306
Goody Rosen	OF42,1B38	82	298	52	90	46	18	5	3	50	47	10	.302
Melbern Simons	OF50	72	180	24	52	22	5	0	0	17	7	1	.289
Art Parks	OF63	64	232	46	79	52	11	3	10	44	12	6	.341
Lee Rogers	P43	45	61	6	18	10	1	0	0	7	9	0	.295
Robert E. Porter	P41	41	77	5	9	3	0	0	0	1	13	0	.117
Kemp Wicker	P40	40	77	2	6	5	2	0	0	4	19	0	.078
Marvin Duke	P41	41	57	1	9	4	2	0	0	3	11	0	.158
William Crouch	P36	39	79	8	16	9	2	1	0	8	23	1	.203
Bert Haas	1B34	34	131	14	32	16	4	0	2	13	11	1	.244
Sam Nahem	P24	24	17	0	2	0	1	0	0	0	3	0	.118
Eugene Schott	P14	21	30	1	5	1	1	0	0	1	14	0	.167
Xavier Rescigno	P15	16	12	4	3	2	1	0	1	6	4	0	.250
Norm Kies	C	12	16	1	2	2	2	0	0	2	2	0	.125
Francis Malseed	P11	12	10	0	2	0	1	0	0	2	2	0	.200
William Homan	3B,2B	11	28	6	5	1	1	0	0	4	5	0	.179
Nick Whitiak	SS	8	9	0	1	0	0	0	0			0	.111
Paul Paynick	P7	8											.000
Stewart Hofferth	C	4	13	1	3	1	2	0	0			0	.231
Wayne LaMaster	P4	4											.000
Dykes Potter	P2	2											.000
James Winford	P2	2											.000

PITCHERS		W	L	PCT	G	GS	CG	SH	IP	H	BB	SO	ERA
Robert E. Porter		18	12	.600	41	29	16	1	212	258	38	58	4.08
William Crouch		11	17	.393	36	24	10	1	215	258	85	93	5.02
Kemp Wicker		11	18	.379	40	33	14	3	233	298	53	76	4.25
Lee Rogers		8	12	.400	43	24	5	2	184	209	89	60	4.79
Marvin Duke		6	8	.429	41	20	10	1	182	207	50	52	4.25
Sam Nahem		1	3	.250	24	3	1	0	55	51	35	20	5.73
Xavier Rescigno		1	3	.250	15	3	2	0	52	56	25	28	5.19
Eugene Schott		1	5	.167	14	6	1	0	44	66	21	5	7.77
James Winford		0	1	.000	2				1	5	3	0	

MONTREAL (cont.)
Royals

PITCHERS	W	L	PCT	G	GS	CG	SH	IP	H	BB	SO	ERA
Francis Malseed	0	3	.000	11	6	0	0	32	38	35	15	7.88
Paul Paynick	0	0	----	7				12	20	5	3	
Wayne LaMaster	0	0	----	4				7	8	9	2	
Dykes Potter	0	0	----	2				1	1	0	1	

TORONTO   8th   63-90   .412   -26   Irving Burns -
Maple Leafs   Tony Lazzeri

BATTERS	POS-GAMES	GP	AB	R	H	BI	2B	3B	HR	BB	SO	SB	BA
Irving Burns	1B105	107	386	43	114	61	22	2	11	40	17	11	.295
Emile Dejonghe	2B77,3B50	133	489	58	135	71	27	1	8	13	38	14	.276
William Schuster	SS130	135	483	68	127	46	21	3	4	56	49	19	.263
Herman Clifton	3B104,SS24,2B16	143	544	69	142	38	19	9	1	70	44	22	.261
Mayo Smith	OF143	148	517	78	148	56	21	9	3	77	35	16	.286
Bob Elliott	OF114	115	427	59	140	51	27	8	7	50	14	2	.328
Henry Manush	OF60	66	228	32	55	19	9	3	0	20	27	4	.241
Thomas Heath	C	(see multi-team players)											
Mel Mazzera	1B43,OF41	88	300	36	64	34	13	3	4	28	44	4	.213
Albert Smith	2B51	60	182	19	39	12	5	1	0	25	27	0	.214
John Berly	P52	52	32	1	5	0	0	0	0	2	7	0	.156
Sam Harshany	C39	44	122	14	40	18	5	0	1	26	14	2	.328
Fred Petoskey	OF28	41	125	18	34	20	4	1	2	5	15	2	.272
Tony Lazzeri	2B20,P1	39	97	19	22	20	4	2	1	15	23	3	.227
John Pezzullo	P37	37	61	4	13	4	2	0	0	5	12	0	.213
Ralph McLeod	OF28	36	111	17	27	8	4	2	0	17	13	2	.243
Joseph Mulligan	P35	35	60	3	10	5	1	0	0	2	25	0	.167
Frank Reiber	C25	32	80	10	21	15	1	2	2	11	11	0	.263
Earl Caldwell	P32	32	69	3	15	2	1	1	0	1	13	0	.217
Phil Marchildon	P29	31	34	5	6	3	1	0	0	2	14	0	.176
Anthony Sabol	OF25	29	82	11	17	9	2	0	0	7	10	3	.207
William Weir	P23	26	50	4	9	2	0	1	0	0	8	0	.180
Walt Klimczak	C21	22	59	8	12	3	2	2	0	6	10	0	.203
Walt Lanfranconi	P13	15	14	1	1	0	0	0	0	1	3	0	.071
John Heving	C10	10	28	0	4	0	0	0	0	2	2	0	.143
James Walkup	P9	9											.040
Richard Henry	PH	7	6	1	0	0	0	0	0			0	.000
Don Brennan	P5	5											.000
Joe Walsh	PH	2	1	1	0	0	0	0	0			0	.000
Woodrow Davis	P2	2											.000
Art Kenney	P2	2											.000
George Klivak	P2	2											.000
Russ Van Atta	P2	2											.000

PITCHERS	W	L	PCT	G	GS	CG	SH	IP	H	BB	SO	ERA
John Pezzullo	11	12	.478	37	22	8	1	166	189	88	77	4.12
Earl Caldwell	10	18	.357	32	25	14	4	203	237	53	64	3.68
William Weir	7	11	.389	23	22	6	2	145	171	95	54	5.96
Joseph Mulligan	6	9	.400	35	21	9	0	176	192	63	60	4.30
Phil Marchildon	5	7	.417	29	17	3	0	124	115	92	90	4.50
John Berly	4	5	.444	52	1	1	1	122	102	55	77	2.21
James Walkup	4	5	.444	9				70	79	23	27	
Walt Lanfranconi	3	3	.500	13	6	2	1	48	67	22	21	4.31
Russ Van Atta	0	1	.000	2				3	5	6	2	15.00
Art Kenney	0	1	.000	2				1	3	2	1	
Don Brennan	0	0	----	5				7	11	4	7	
Woodrow Davis	0	0	----	2				2	4	3	1	
George Klivak	0	0	----	2				2	5	2	0	
Tony Lazzeri	0	0	----	1				5	8	3	1	

MULTI-TEAM PLAYERS

BATTERS	POS-GAMES	TEAMS	GP	AB	R	H	BI	2B	3B	HR	BB	SO	SB	BA
Robert A. Porter	OF119	TO38-SY91	129	474	69	133	48	22	5	3	33	48	3	.281
Baxter Jordan	3B71,1B38	SY35-BA76	111	435	72	133	43	10	3	2	27	12	3	.306
Ben Sankey	SS55,3B39	MO17-SY47-BA45	109	324	38	89	21	13	2	0	31	30	5	.275
Leo Norris	SS76	NE10-MO89	99	286	39	71	41	10	2	5	36	51	7	.248
Thomas Heath	C85	SY15-TO71	86	271	20	64	28	10	1	1	40	40	0	.236

MULTI-TEAM PLAYERS (cont.)

BATTERS	POS-GAMES	TEAMS	GP	AB	R	H	BI	2B	3B	HR	BB	SO	SB	BA
Ashley McDaniel	SS70	SY15-MO61	76	231	17	48	23	5	1	0	13	17	0	.208
Doug Dean	OF24,3B16	JC3-SY60	63	147	23	38	15	3	1	0	14	2	2	.259
Reg Grabowski	P56	SY13-MO43	56	41	4	6	2	2	0	0	2	7	0	.146
Frank Pearce	P47	SY4-JC43	47	16	1	3	2	0	0	0	0	7	0	.188
Dick Midkiff	P40	SY9-BA31	40	53	6	4	0	0	0	0	8	21	0	.075
John Tising	P39	BA10-SY29	39	90	4	19	12	1	1	0	1	15	0	.211
Charles Fischer	P35	BA7-TO28	35	83	5	14	7	1	0	0	1	11	0	.169
Emile Meola	P32	TO12-SY20	32	62	2	9	3	0	1	0	6	23	0	.145
Pete Sivess	P23	NE3-BA6-JC16	25	16	2	2	1	0	0	0	0	4	0	.125

PITCHERS	TEAMS	W	L	PCT	G	GS	CG	SH	IP	H	BB	SO	ERA
John Tising	BA10-SY29	19	15	.559	39	30	18	3	**253**	238	76	**144**	3.42
Charles Fischer	BA7-TO28	13	11	.542	35	26	11	3	213	202	85	117	3.13
Emile Meola	TO12-SY20	10	16	.385	32	29	8	0	174	210	85	54	5.17
Reg Grabowski	SY13-MO43	9	11	.450	56	14	1	0	145	175	53	56	4.53
Dick Midkiff	SY9-BA31	9	14	.391	40	29	8	2	174	216	63	69	5.12
Frank Pearce	SY4-JC43	4	4	.500	47	1	0	0	87	95	22	19	3.62
Pete Sivess	NE3-BA6-JC14	3	2	.600	23	7	1	1	60	93	22	13	7.05

TEAM BATTING

TEAMS	GP	AB	R	H	BI	2B	3B	HR	BB	SO	SB	BA
JERSEY CITY	154	5074	663	1443	603	236	44	58	480	468	65	.282
ROCHESTER	153	**5259**	794	**1543**	725	267	**69**	89	482	593	47	**.293**
BUFFALO	154	5192	792	1472	726	**281**	43	**160**	420	657	82	.284
NEWARK	**156**	5207	806	1482	**748**	260	67	96	500	590	55	.285
SYRACUSE	155	5158	611	1364	544	175	51	30	447	500	51	.264
BALTIMORE	155	5051	**816**	1382	738	242	42	126	**604**	**711**	40	.274
MONTREAL	155	5157	745	1455	672	240	44	50	601	512	77	.282
TORONTO	154	5037	618	1301	545	206	53	45	535	560	**103**	.258
	618	41135	5845	11432	5301	1907	413	654	4069	4591	520	.278

1940
SECOND TIME AROUND

Today, the career ladder of a baseball player is a one-way trip. Most players start at the lowest level of the minors, gradually working their way upward in fits and starts. The few that make it to the apex of the major leagues stay there as long as their talent permits. When the day comes that a player can't make the grade in the big leagues, he is cut adrift, his playing days over. Fifty or more years ago, a player's rise to the top of the baseball pyramid was much the same; once their major league services were no longer desired, however, many found second careers back in the minor leagues.

During the first half of the century, the International League was liberally festooned with second career players. A perfect example was Joe McGinnity. After finishing a lengthy major league career, McGinnity joined the minor leagues (including the International League) for an additional fifteen years of playing time. While in the International, Joe McGinnity set several league records, including most innings pitched and most shutouts in a season.

Another fine example of a second career player who sandwiched six years of continuous major league service between two lengthy minor league stints was Dick Porter. Porter joined the International's Baltimore Orioles at the age of 19 in 1921. After eight years and two batting titles, he was sold to the Cleveland Indians. Six years later, sporting a .308 major league average, Porter was deemed no longer suited for the top level of baseball. Undaunted, he rejoined the International League in 1935, this time with Newark. After two years in Newark, Porter joined the Syracuse Chiefs as their player-manager, serving in that capacity for three seasons, ending in 1940.

In the 1940 International League, Rochester cruised to the top over Newark. Jersey City dropped to third, while Baltimore beat out Montreal for the final playoff position. Further back, Buffalo placed sixth, followed by Dick Porter's Syracuse squad, ending with Toronto in eighth. Baltimoreans claimed three top batting prizes: Murray Howell (.359 batting average), Bill Nagel (37 home runs), and Nick Etten (128 runs batted in). Pitching honors fell to Rochester's Dominic Ryba for most wins (24), Buffalo's Hal White for lowest earned run average (2.43), and Newark's George Washburn for most strikeouts (145).

Joe McGinnity, Dick Porter, and other players of yesteryear could take comfort that their trip to the majors didn't result in unemployment once their big league careers were squeezed dry. It was a good feeling to know that in addition to a ladder going to the top, there was one on the other side to help you down.

ROCHESTER Red Wings

1st	96-61	.611	Billy Southworth - Estel Crabtree - Dominic Ryba - Tony Kaufmann		

BATTERS	POS-GAMES	GP	AB	R	H	BI	2B	3B	HR	BB	SO	SB	BA
Harry Davis	1B160	160	588	96	179	101	38	1	17	80	36	10	.304
George Fallon	2B141	142	488	52	133	53	19	5	4	31	51	7	.273
Frank Crespi	SS151	151	544	74	164	80	18	4	6	37	55	7	.301
Whitey Kurowski	3B131	133	520	85	145	73	28	2	15	22	71	13	.279
Gus Bergamo	OF148	149	570	93	163	68	32	7	6	67	50	9	.286
Hal Epps	OF100	107	386	51	118	36	17	8	4	17	24	8	.306
Linc Blakely	OF78	78	254	34	65	22	13	3	1	31	38	3	.256
Ray Mueller	C82	91	279	32	67	34	13	7	5	28	46	5	.240
Robert Scheffing	C73	89	269	34	72	38	14	5	4	28	44	1	.268
Elvin Adams	OF59	63	195	32	37	21	7	5	3	27	49	3	.190
Estel Crabtree	OF57	57	207	34	65	30	13	2	3	37	10	4	.314
Lynn Myers	2B21,SS15	50	106	22	20	10	4	0	2	21	19	5	.189
Gene Lillard	3B28,P17	49	117	14	26	8	5	3	1	11	27	1	.222
Dominic Ryba	P36	49	115	6	27	15	4	0	0	12	15	0	.235
William Brumbeloe	P40	42	75	7	14	2	3	1	0	10	31	0	.187
Henry Gornicki	P41	41	76	8	9	3	3	0	0	11	38	0	.118
Herschel Lyons	P37	37	95	8	17	8	5	0	0	3	14	0	.179
Walt Cazen	OF31	31	104	21	34	33	6	3	4	17	11	7	.327
Preacher Roe	P31	31	40	6	2	1	0	0	0	1	10	0	.050
John Grodzicki	P25	25	24	2	4	3	0	0	0	3	2	0	.167
William Rabe	OF19	23	64	12	16	7	2	1	2	13	15	1	.250
Floyd Beal	C10	10	35	2	7	5	1	0	1	1	3	0	.200
Dain Clay	OF	7	20	4	3	1	1	0	0	2	2	0	.150
James Hitchcock	3B,2B	6	19	2	2	4	0	0	0	3	1	0	.105
William McLaughlin	P6	6	5	2	2	1	1	0	0	0	1	0	.400
William Seinsoth	P4	4	7	0	2	1	0	0	0	0	0	0	.286
Henry Redmond	OF	4	9	0	1	0	0	0	0	0	1	0	.111
Francis Riel	P4	4	6	0	1	0	1	0	0	0	1	0	.167
Harry Walker	OF	3	10	3	3	2	1	0	0	1	0	1	.300
Archie Templeton	P2	2	1	0	0	0	0	0	0	0	1	0	.000

PITCHERS		W	L	PCT	G	GS	CG	SH	IP	H	BB	SO	ERA
Dominic Ryba		24	8	.750	36	34	25	5	272	272	53	125	2.94
Henry Gornicki		19	10	.655	41	36	16	5	244	238	99	127	3.21
Herschel Lyons		19	12	.613	37	33	15	2	256	261	105	124	3.38
William Brumbeloe		18	11	.621	40	30	15	2	230	200	112	77	2.58
Preacher Roe		5	8	.385	31	15	5	0	128	112	58	80	3.94
John Grodzicki		3	3	.500	25	3	1	0	76	80	46	28	3.79
William McLaughlin		1	1	.500	6				15	10	13	9	
Frank Riel		1	1	.500	4				14	17	6	5	
Gene Lillard		1	3	.250	17	2	0	0	43	55	22	21	7.33
William Seinsoth		0	1	.000	4				14	18	11	4	
Archie Templeton		0	1	.000	2				6	10	5	3	

NEWARK Bears

2nd	95-65	.594	-2.5	John Neun	

BATTERS	POS-GAMES	GP	AB	R	H	BI	2B	3B	HR	BB	SO	SB	BA
Edward Levy	1B135	137	536	87	154	87	26	4	20	37	66	19	.287
Alex Kampouris	2B147	147	554	109	151	97	24	4	36	56	136	0	.273
George Scharein	SS132	134	448	46	110	40	11	3	0	31	46	2	.246
Hank Majeski	3B94	105	375	66	121	76	15	4	17	32	36	2	.323
Tommy Holmes	OF162	162	665	126	211	60	33	7	7	66	13	8	.317
Art Metheny	OF145	151	543	82	167	98	27	6	13	62	49	5	.308
Mike Chartak	OF112,1B27	141	440	80	124	74	23	11	20	116	81	14	.282
Thomas Padden	C121	124	361	46	84	45	11	1	9	54	39	4	.233
Lewis Blair	3B70	88	298	39	88	34	12	3	4	14	21	5	.295
Leo Nonnenkamp	OF40	55	143	24	40	22	9	1	4	26	22	3	.280
George Washburn	P35	73	128	12	34	18	7	0	1	4	18	0	.266
Ken Sears	C28	40	104	15	37	27	8	0	5	9	9	1	.356
Norm Branch	P30	36	76	8	18	9	3	0	0	2	13	0	.237
Steve Peek	P36	36	51	1	7	4	2	0	0	1	14	0	.137
John Johnson	P35	35	30	3	8	1	2	0	0	1	5	0	.267
Allen Gettel	P34	34	30	1	5	0	1	0	0	0	2	0	.167
Hank Borowy	P29	32	57	4	11	5	2	0	0	7	24	0	.193
George Barley	P27	30	57	11	10	5	2	0	0	11	22	0	.175
James Shilling	2B15	27	94	11	20	8	3	0	3	9	10	1	.213
Fred Frankhouse	P20	20	4	0	1	0	0	0	0	0	1	0	.250
Tom Reis	P15	16	28	2	4	1	0	0	0	2	7	0	.143
Tommy Byrne	P16	16	24	1	5	1	0	0	0	0	4	0	.208

NEWARK (cont.)
Bears

BATTERS	POS-GAMES	GP	AB	R	H	BI	2B	3B	HR	BB	SO	SB	BA
Russ Bergmann	SS14	15	41	5	13	7	1	0	0	5	3	0	.317
Jack Graham	OF10	13	37	3	6	6	0	0	1	4	9	0	.162
Colonel Mills	OF11	11	41	2	9	7	1	0	1	4	4	2	.220
Sigmund Gryska	SS11	11	31	2	6	3	1	0	0	2	6	2	.194
Mark Beddingfield	P10	10	4	0	0	0	0	0	0	0	3	0	.000
Herb White	C	6	7	0	0	0	0	0	0	0	0	0	.000
Joe Vance	P4	5	11	2	4	1	0	0	0	0	1	1	.364
Harry Bassin	1B	5	6	0	0	0	0	0	0	0	2	0	.000
Edwin Carnett	P4	5	4	1	1	0	0	0	0	0	2	0	.250
George Stirnweiss	SS	4	14	3	6	3	2	1	0	0	1	0	.429
Randall Gumpert	P1	1	1	0	0	0	0	0	0	0	0	0	.000

PITCHERS	W	L	PCT	G	GS	CG	SH	IP	H	BB	SO	ERA
George Washburn	18	8	.692	35	32	20	3	233	197	111	145	3.13
Norm Branch	15	9	.625	30	22	14	4	175	162	62	113	3.09
George Barley	15	9	.625	27	26	14	2	185	196	47	92	4.43
Steve Peek	14	4	.778	36	16	8	1	144	126	65	79	2.69
Hank Borowy	12	10	.545	29	26	12	4	182	168	68	117	3.71
John Johnson	7	6	.538	35	10	2	1	103	103	47	44	3.93
Fred Frankhouse	3	0	1.000	20	0	0	0	25	27	12	7	2.88
Allen Gettel	3	3	.500	34	4	2	0	97	79	41	34	3.43
Tom Reis	4	9	.308	15	13	7	1	87	83	37	36	4.14
Tommy Byrne	2	5	.286	16	8	3	1	69	69	39	35	4.70
Joe Vance	1	1	.500	4				28	29	9	8	
Edwin Carnett	1	1	.500	4				7	9	4	1	10.28
Mark Beddingfield	0	0	----	10	1	0	0	19	15	15	3	5.21
Randall Gumpert	0	0	----	1				3	5	1	1	0.00

JERSEY CITY   3rd   81-78   .509   -16   Bert Niehoff
Giants

BATTERS	POS-GAMES	GP	AB	R	H	BI	2B	3B	HR	BB	SO	SB	BA
James Vernon	1B153	154	569	76	161	65	22	9	9	34	45	13	.283
Del Young	2B90	101	371	51	104	46	13	3	7	19	29	2	.280
Bobby Sturgeon	SS123	124	406	38	95	29	8	1	1	13	18	2	.234
Sid Gordon	3B128	136	501	76	131	39	21	7	5	58	34	7	.261
Allen Cooke	OF142	148	534	70	161	46	21	9	1	47	72	2	.301
John Dickshot	OF132	140	465	87	135	87	25	6	11	76	41	5	.290
Forrest Jensen	OF100	129	421	53	106	45	19	2	8	18	19	7	.252
Rae Blaemire	C102	116	383	33	99	56	21	4	6	21	25	7	.258
Hershel Martin	OF77	89	292	44	82	36	10	6	10	31	32	2	.281
Wayne Ambler	2B48,SS31	83	211	11	46	19	14	0	1	21	12	0	.218
Aubrey Epps	C62	72	203	21	50	38	13	1	2	26	25	0	.246
Glen Stewart	2B27,3B23	55	172	15	43	14	8	0	0	12	20	2	.249
Harold Feldman	P43	43	47	1	11	3	1	1	0	1	9	0	.234
Roy Henshaw	P40	41	58	2	10	5	2	0	0	3	8	0	.172
Alta Cohen	P21	39	38	5	8	7	2	1	0	6	6	0	.211
Thomas Neill	OF31	36	134	20	38	15	6	0	4	7	19	0	.284
William Harris	P36	36	51	3	9	4	1	0	0	0	2	0	.176
Frank Pearce	P34	35	77	2	5	2	0	1	0	1	20	0	.065
Hugh East	P32	32	46	3	12	4	1	0	0	1	15	0	.261
John Wittig	P22	22	51	2	10	4	1	0	0	0	7	0	.196
Louis Roggino	SS20	21	50	7	8	4	1	0	0	13	10	0	.160
Clyde Castleman	P19	19	28	1	4	3	0	0	0	1	12	0	.143
Hy Vandenberg	P17	17	37	1	7	4	0	0	0	1	1	0	.189
Manuel Salvo	P12	12	21	0	2	3	0	0	0	2	8	0	.095
Alejandro Carrasquel	P11	11	7	1	1	0	0	0	0	1	2	0	.143
Rene Monteagudo	P4	6	8	1	4	3	0	0	1	0	0	0	.500
George Myatt	3B	6	8	2	2	0	1	0	0	1	1	0	.250
John Brewer	P4	4	3	0	1	1	1	0	0	0	1	0	.333
Wayne Murdock	1B	2	7	0	1	0	0	0	0	0	0	0	.143
Gil Torres	P2	2	2	1	1	0	0	0	0	0	0	0	.500
Charles Gassaway	P2	2	1	0	0	0	0	0	0	0	0	0	.000
Walter Shinn	PH	1	1	0	0	0	0	0	0	0	0	0	.000

PITCHERS	W	L	PCT	G	GS	CG	SH	IP	H	BB	SO	ERA
Frank Pearce	14	9	.609	34	28	14	4	220	209	44	48	2.78
Roy Henshaw	11	11	.500	40	23	9	0	177	188	54	73	3.15
William Harris	10	9	.526	36	19	12	4	164	142	42	85	2.69
Clyde Castleman	9	4	.692	19	14	6	2	89	98	18	37	3.64

JERSEY CITY (cont.)
Giants

PITCHERS	W	L	PCT	G	GS	CG	SH	IP	H	BB	SO	ERA
John Wittig	9	6	.600	22	16	7	3	128	118	37	72	3.02
Hugh East	7	9	.438	32	16	6	0	144	143	65	68	4.38
Hy Vandenberg	6	8	.429	17	15	8	1	105	117	40	53	4.97
Harold Feldman	5	13	.278	43	11	5	0	141	146	68	73	3.64
Manuel Salvo	4	3	.571	12	9	5	1	60	56	16	17	3.00
Alta Cohen	3	1	.750	21	2	1	0	43	45	22	4	4.19
Alejandro Carrasquel	2	4	.333	11	4	0	0	36	41	14	21	3.75
Rene Monteagudo	1	0	1.000	4				13	9	4	7	
John Brewer	0	1	.000	4				12	17	7	10	9.75
Charles Gassaway	0	0	----	2				4	2	5	1	
Gil Torres	0	0	----	2				8	15	3	4	

BALTIMORE   4th   81-79   .506   -16.5   Alphonse Thomas
Orioles

BATTERS	POS-GAMES	GP	AB	R	H	BI	2B	3B	HR	BB	SO	SB	BA
Nick Etten	1B160	160	576	114	185	**128**	**40**	4	24	82	38	4	.321
Eugene Corbett	2B155	157	589	103	178	82	**40**	5	10	64	42	6	.302
Lamar Newsome	SS145	148	578	75	160	43	39	3	3	35	28	16	.277
Bill Nagel	3B139	145	529	85	142	113	18	3	37	53	112	6	.268
Murray Howell	OF150	152	557	124	200	122	35	4	29	80	56	8	**.359**
Ed Collins	OF141	148	580	87	170	40	26	4	0	53	59	21	.293
Stan Benjamin	OF102	108	404	73	123	59	16	7	11	14	69	10	.305
Joseph Kracher	C88	103	325	44	81	42	12	2	9	32	38	6	.249
Art Graham	OF88	118	339	67	87	54	16	7	15	41	44	5	.265
Jack Redmond	C76	104	263	42	80	60	14	3	15	35	38	1	.304
Ben Sankey	3B24,SS16	76	190	28	58	29	14	3	0	14	12	0	.305
Ken Trinkle	P45	45	32	4	3	1	0	0	0	4	9	0	.094
Italo Chelini	P38	38	55	7	13	6	0	0	1	6	8	1	.236
Thomas Hughes	P36	36	71	3	6	4	2	0	0	0	23	0	.085
Dick Midkiff	P33	33	50	3	9	6	2	0	2	3	23	0	.180
Ted Olson	P20	29	20	2	2	0	0	0	0	0	5	0	.100
Dale Jones	P26	29	17	3	3	0	1	1	0	0	6	0	.176
Roy Bruner	P28	28	39	3	4	2	1	0	0	4	18	0	.103
Orlin Collier	P27	27	59	4	13	6	1	0	0	3	15	0	.220
Elmer Burkart	P22	22	16	0	1	0	0	0	0	0	9	0	.063
Earl Springer	P18	22	10	1	3	1	2	0	0	2	4	0	.300
Danny Litwhiler	OF10	10	31	3	7	2	0	0	0	1	2	1	.226
Charles Lauenstein	P6	6	4	0	0	0	0	0	0	0	2	0	.000
Homer Howell	PH	2	1	0	0	0	0	0	0	1	1	0	.000
Lloyd Gross	P2	2	0	0	0	0	0	0	0	0	0	0	----
Robert Hamilton	PH	1	1	0	0	0	0	0	0	0	0	0	.000
Charles Letchas	PR	1	0	1	0	0	0	0	0	0	0	0	----
Guy Johnson	P1	1	0	0	0	0	0	0	0	0	0	0	----

PITCHERS	W	L	PCT	G	GS	CG	SH	IP	H	BB	SO	ER
Thomas Hughes	14	11	.560	36	26	14	0	192	181	77	86	3.56
Italo Chelini	14	12	.538	38	23	11	1	175	186	41	74	4.47
Orlin Collier	11	12	.478	27	26	14	3	177	188	49	112	4.17
Dick Midkiff	10	12	.455	33	24	9	1	163	200	32	62	4.80
Roy Bruner	7	12	.368	28	21	4	0	143	152	87	58	5.66
Ken Trinkle	5	3	.625	45	4	1	0	117	148	46	54	5.46
Ted Olson	4	7	.364	20	9	2	1	66	100	24	27	6.55
Elmer Burkart	3	3	.500	22	4	1	0	60	63	25	12	4.35
Dale Jones	2	0	1.000	26	2	0	0	60	49	24	29	3.75
Earl Springer	1	2	.333	18	2	0	0	40	47	26	20	4.28
Charles Lauenstein	0	0	----	6				15	17	6	1	
Lloyd Gross	0	0	----	2				2	4	5	1	
Guy Johnson	0	0	----	1				0	2	1	0	

MONTREAL   5th   80-80   .500   -17.5   Clyde Sukeforth
Royals

BATTERS	POS-GAMES	GP	AB	R	H	BI	2B	3B	HR	BB	SO	SB	BA
Gus Suhr	1B119	122	387	63	102	57	22	3	7	71	35	1	.264
John Bell	2B144	148	537	77	146	28	15	3	2	65	19	6	.272
Louis Berger	SS115,2B18	134	436	49	101	50	25	3	6	36	65	4	.232
Don Ross	3B95,SS41	134	487	73	150	76	36	0	7	50	23	5	.308

MONTREAL (cont.)
Royals

BATTERS	POS-GAMES	GP	AB	R	H	BI	2B	3B	HR	BB	SO	SB	BA
George Staller	OF151	151	609	94	187	85	40	12	14	38	74	11	.307
James Ripple	OF109	110	417	56	127	61	27	1	6	29	24	0	.305
George Stainback	OF99	99	418	82	138	44	24	7	9	15	29	6	.330
Joseph Becker	C87	93	272	36	68	20	18	0	1	39	45	0	.250
Bert Haas	3B70,OF37,1B26	138	473	67	128	76	26	4	11	35	52	6	.271
Angelo Giulani	C72	77	233	19	59	40	9	2	0	11	17	0	.253
Charles Gilbert	OF57	57	225	33	65	19	13	5	4	20	15	1	.289
Max Macon	P22	54	75	10	18	4	1	1	2	3	7	0	.240
Steve Rachunok	P40	40	60	3	7	4	2	0	0	2	34	0	.117
Newt Kimball	P34	36	79	10	11	5	1	0	0	8	22	0	.139
Fred Lucas	P13	36	40	1	12	8	1	0	0	3	0	0	.300
William Crouch	P35	35	74	6	14	12	2	0	0	8	18	0	.189
Wayne LaMaster	P23	26	28	4	7	1	0	0	0	0	6	0	.250
Robert E. Porter	P22	22	40	2	5	3	0	0	0	3	7	0	.125
Art Herring	P19	19	10	1	1	1	0	0	0	1	5	0	.100
Ira Hutchinson	P17	17	15	0	1	0	0	0	0	0	3	0	.067
Lee Grissom	P16	16	31	2	3	1	0	0	0	2	9	0	.097
Roy Hughes	2B,3B,SS	13	36	5	12	4	3	0	0	3	3	2	.333
Al Hollingsworth	P8	8	10	3	3	3	0	1	0	0	0	0	.300
Bill Rogell	SS	7	21	1	3	1	1	0	0	3	3	0	.143
Lou Fette	P7	7	6	0	1	0	0	0	0	0	0	0	.167
Richard Bass	P5	5	6	0	0	1	0	0	0	0	1	0	.000
Ray Davis	P4	4	4	0	0	1	0	0	0	0	0	0	.000
Pete Reiser	OF	3	16	2	4	1	1	0	0	0	2	0	.250
Reg Grabowski	P3	3	2	0	0	0	0	0	0	0	1	0	.000
Angelo Scariot	P3	3	0	0	0	0	0	0	0	0	0	0	----
Cal Chapman	PH	2	1	0	0	0	0	0	0	1	0	0	.000
Xavier Rescigno	P2	2	0	0	0	0	0	0	0	0	0	0	----
Paul Chervinko	C	1	1	0	0	0	0	0	0	0	1	0	.000
Manuel Norris	P1	1	0	0	0	0	0	0	0	0	0	0	----

PITCHERS	W	L	PCT	G	GS	CG	SH	IP	H	BB	SO	ERA
Kemp Wicker	18	10	.643	34	32	18	3	232	236	61	97	2.91
William Crouch	14	11	.560	35	30	16	2	209	239	55	86	4.09
Steve Rachunok	13	8	.619	40	21	9	2	182	159	97	115	4.01
Robert E. Porter	8	6	.571	22	19	10	0	134	147	29	20	3.63
Max Macon	7	4	.636	22	10	5	3	99	88	47	29	2.55
Newt Kimball	7	8	.467	18	11	8	3	93	88	28	50	2.61
Lee Grissom	5	4	.556	16	13	5	0	97	103	45	74	4.55
Fred Lucas	2	1	.667	13	3	2	0	47	47	11	8	2.30
Wayne LaMaster	2	7	.222	23	8	2	0	77	93	34	38	5.73
Al Hollingsworth	1	2	.333	8				28	26	24	7	3.53
Lou Fette	1	2	.333	7				17	23	10	6	
Art Herring	1	3	.250	19	1	0	0	40	57	22	29	6.53
Ira Hutchinson	1	7	.125	17	3	0	0	43	63	22	27	6.28
Angelo Scariot	0	1	.000	3				4	4	2	0	9.00
Ray Davis	0	2	.000	4				12	23	4	4	
Richard Bass	0	3	.000	5				21	28	10	8	
Reg Grabowski	0	0	----	3				7	6	5	3	
Xavier Rescigno	0	0	----	2				1	6	2	0	
Manuel Norris	0	0	----	1				1	0	1	0	0.00

BUFFALO   6th   76-83   .478   -21   Steve O'Neill
Bisons

BATTERS	POS-GAMES	GP	AB	R	H	BI	2B	3B	HR	BB	SO	SB	BA
Les Scarsella	1B125	125	439	51	127	55	26	10	10	41	44	5	.289
John Kroner	2B135	136	509	62	121	55	21	2	13	39	66	2	.238
Greg Mulleavy	SS92,2B16	110	360	42	81	31	16	1	0	42	40	6	.225
James Outlaw	3B120,SS18	145	531	85	164	75	32	9	14	31	62	6	.309
Pat Mullin	OF156	157	594	85	162	61	25	11	15	66	63	18	.273
Mayo Smith	OF120	129	456	66	128	51	30	6	6	45	33	5	.281
Ollie Carnegie	OF85	97	331	50	93	64	16	3	15	30	48	6	.281
Clyde McCullough	C145	145	485	69	157	89	21	5	27	42	75	4	.324
Les Fleming	OF78,1B36	122	392	65	100	61	16	1	22	65	75	2	.255
Dan Carnevale	SS57,3B20	78	258	31	58	22	5	0	2	19	38	4	.225
James Trexler	P37	53	60	6	14	12	4	0	0	3	17	0	.233
Earl Cook	P39	39	71	3	11	4	0	0	0	0	11	0	.155
Floyd Gieball	P37	37	85	6	18	9	4	0	1	2	4	1	.212
William Martin	3B23	36	93	9	26	11	3	0	2	3	11	0	.280

BUFFALO (cont.)
Bisons

BATTERS	POS-GAMES	GP	AB	R	H	BI	2B	3B	HR	BB	SO	SB	BA
Hal White	P34	34	66	4	13	4	3	0	1	2	24	0	.197
Lynn Nelson	P18	34	56	5	13	4	3	0	0	2	11	0	.232
Frank Zubick	C20	30	54	7	14	5	2	0	2	6	13	2	.259
Jess Pike	OF20	23	85	9	24	8	1	1	1	12	15	0	.282
Sal Maglie	P23	23	16	0	1	0	0	0	0	0	5	0	.063
Eugene Markland	2B16	22	63	11	15	3	1	1	2	8	14	1	.238
Henry Nowak	OF10	21	41	4	7	1	3	0	0	5	2	2	.171
Joe Rogalski	P17	20	18	5	7	1	2	0	0	0	5	0	.389
Fred Hutchinson	P12	15	41	4	9	2	1	0	0	2	2	0	.220
Art Jacobs	P15	15	7	1	2	2	0	0	0	2	1	0	.286
Quinn Lee	P12	12	21	2	4	0	2	0	0	0	2	0	.190
Walt Ogiego	P9	9	4	0	0	0	0	0	0	0	1	0	.000
William Harnick	OF	7	25	1	9	1	2	0	0	3	8	0	.360
Beryl Richmond	P7	7	1	0	0	0	0	0	0	0	0	0	.000
William Bolton	C	6	15	0	2	0	1	0	0	1	3	0	.133
Pete Angell	P4	4	6	1	2	0	0	0	0	0	1	0	.333
Mike Roscoe	P3	3	5	0	0	0	0	0	0	0	0	0	.000
Raymond Roche	P3	3	1	0	0	0	0	0	0	0	1	0	.333
Clarence Phillips	P2	2	4	0	0	0	0	0	0	0	0	0	.000

PITCHERS	W	L	PCT	G	GS	CG	SH	IP	H	BB	SO	ERA
Hal White	16	4	.800	34	21	15	5	196	165	40	92	2.43
Earl Cook	15	12	.556	39	30	14	4	208	214	51	78	3.85
Floyd Gieball	15	17	.469	37	32	21	4	239	241	82	104	3.73
James Trexler	8	7	.533	37	8	4	0	114	122	54	66	3.95
Fred Hutchinson	7	3	.700	12	11	10	1	94	79	16	57	2.49
Lynn Nelson	5	10	.333	18	15	6	1	109	141	35	65	4.79
Joseph Rogalski	2	5	.286	17	7	1	0	54	95	23	22	8.83
Art Jacobs	1	1	.500	15	0	0	0	33	34	13	16	3.27
Walt Ogiego	1	1	.500	9				20	28	13	6	
Quinn Lee	1	4	.200	12	9	1	0	58	78	22	19	6.67
Beryl Richmond	0	1	.000	7				7	13	8	4	
Raymond Roche	0	1	.000	3				6	3	5	5	
Clarence Phillips	0	1	.000	2				9	15	1	4	
Sal Maglie	0	7	.000	23	5	1	0	54	80	24	22	7.17
Pete Angell	0	0	----	4				13	8	11	0	
Mike Roscoe	0	0	----	3				17	14	3	5	

SYRACUSE   7th   71-90   .441   -27   Dick Porter
Chiefs

BATTERS	POS-GAMES	GP	AB	R	H	BI	2B	3B	HR	BB	SO	SB	BA
Charles Hasson	1B												
Edgar Leip	2B163	163	626	94	143	41	26	6	2	56	58	12	.228
James McLeod	SS85	90	254	22	53	19	5	0	0	27	36	1	.209
Jack Juelich	3B142	143	479	42	110	36	10	7	1	40	30	4	.230
Goody Rosen	OF134,1B10	141	535	78	151	79	27	6	7	64	50	4	.282
Ed Longacre	OF106	123	387	55	110	40	21	7	0	37	19	6	.284
Roy Johnson	OF124	139	432	52	116	57	16	8	9	48	50	9	.269
John Bottarini	C82	104	302	30	83	41	9	5	7	18	46	1	.275
Leonard Kahny	SS66,3B25	89	252	37	68	32	5	4	3	40	32	7	.270
Les Hinckle	P39	45	78	10	14	2	3	0	0	5	8	0	.179
Elmer Rambert	P28	42	74	8	9	6	0	1	0	5	12	0	.122
John Tising	P40	40	91	3	19	5	1	0	0	5	12	0	.209
Ted Kleinhans	P35	40	75	8	10	5	0	0	0	4	12	0	.133
Art Jones	P36	36	20	0	1	0	0	0	0	0	4	0	.050
Lloyd Dietz	P33	34	51	2	6	3	0	1	0	4	23	0	.118
George Barnicle	P20	22	15	4	3	0	1	0	0	0	8	0	.200
William Clemensen	P19	19	19	1	2	0	0	0	0	0	10	0	.105
Ignatius Walters	1B18	18	53	2	11	5	4	0	0	3	0	0	.208
Mervyn Connors	1B10	18	52	0	5	5	2	0	0	1	13	0	.096
Oadis Swigart	P30	31	51	2	12	4	0	0	0	0	2	0	.235
Charles Harig	OF14	18	50	6	13	4	3	0	0	8	3	1	.260
Ace Parker	SS16	16	51	12	20	9	3	0	2	10	6	2	.392
Dick Porter	OF	15	32	7	7	2	2	1	0	3	7	0	.219
Dan Taylor		15	19	1	6	1	1	0	0	3	4	0	.316
Irvin Hall	SS,2B	14	21	3	2	1	0	0	0	0	1	0	.095
Maury Jungman	OF	6	16	2	3	0	1	0	0	2	0	0	.188
Floyd Yount	OF	5	16	1	2	0	1	0	0	0	6	0	.125
Damon Phillips	SS	4	4	0	2	1	0	0	0	1	1	0	.500
James George	SS	4	3	0	1	0	0	0	0	1	2	0	.333

SYRACUSE (cont.)
Chiefs

BATTERS	POS-GAMES	GP	AB	R	H	BI	2B	3B	HR	BB	SO	SB	BA
Lamar Zimmerman	OF	3	6	0	0	0	0	0	0	0	1	0	.000
Darrell Blanton	P3	3	3	0	0	0	0	0	0	1	3	0	.000
Lloyd Richards	3B,C	2	1	0	0	0	0	0	0	0	1	0	.000
Russ Aungst	P1	1	0	0	0	0	0	0	0	0	0	0	----

PITCHERS		W	L	PCT	G	GS	CG	SH	IP	H	BB	SO	ERA
JohnTising		13	16	.448	40	**37**	21	4	269	249	85	137	2.81
Ted Kleinhans		12	**17**	.414	35	32	15	2	229	233	82	112	3.03
Les Hinckle		11	9	.550	39	20	13	0	198	208	50	105	3.82
Lloyd Dietz		9	13	.409	33	21	7	0	158	176	41	60	5.01
Oadis Swigart		8	9	.471	30	21	9	2	137	151	40	71	3.94
Art Jones		7	5	.583	36	0	0	0	68	72	33	30	3.31
Elmer Rambert		7	13	.350	28	21	12	1	160	173	43	48	3.77
George Barnicle		3	1	.750	20	4	1	0	55	51	33	30	4.42
William Clemenson		1	4	.200	19	4	0	0	65	78	35	21	4.85
Darrell Blanton		0	3	.000	3				14	19	7	7	6.43
Russ Aungst		0	0	----	1				1	1	3	0	18.00

TORONTO   8th   57-101   .361   -39.5   Tony Lazzeri
Maple Leafs

BATTERS	POS-GAMES	GP	AB	R	H	BI	2B	3B	HR	BB	SO	SB	BA
Robert Latshaw	1B116	116	401	55	113	57	29	4	4	54	50	4	.282
Dario Lodigiani	2B141	143	494	47	139	78	23	4	7	49	34	7	.281
Fred Chapman	SS118	119	456	85	129	34	21	2	6	41	42	12	.283
Emile Dejonghe	3B99	113	386	38	97	49	10	5	8	5	53	5	.251
Eric Tipton	OF140	143	483	48	136	64	18	9	4	61	55	2	.282
John Tyler	OF137	146	479	64	138	44	22	4	5	54	37	16	.288
Fern Bell	OF130	133	440	40	110	39	18	6	4	51	52	8	.250
Thomas Heath	C75	77	208	17	35	21	2	2	3	38	23	0	.168
Milton Gray	C73	100	240	19	52	18	2	4	0	20	18	1	.217
Herman Clifton	3B35,2B20,SS11	85	242	25	49	4	9	3	0	19	24	4	.203
Hub Bates	OF75	83	281	42	59	23	8	0	8	27	59	7	.210
Carl Fairly	3B29	49	133	7	25	3	4	1	0	11	15	3	.188
John Pezzullo	P46	46	50	4	7	3	0	0	0	6	11	0	.140
Phil Marchildon	P41	42	63	2	13	4	1	1	1	5	14	0	.206
Pat McLaughlin	P42	42	45	2	5	1	1	0	0	3	9	0	.111
Harley Boss	1B41	41	151	19	33	16	4	1	3	14	9	0	.219
Les McCrabb	P35	35	60	2	10	3	1	0	0	0	13	0	.167
Bill Lillard	SS34	34	117	4	25	6	2	0	0	9	11	0	.214
Charles Fischer	P33	33	62	1	10	2	0	0	0	2	12	0	.161
Vallie Eaves	P29	29	47	1	8	2	0	0	0	1	17	0	.170
Walt Klimczak	C26	27	89	8	22	9	2	1	0	9	7	1	.247
James Walkup	P25	25	30	0	4	2	0	0	0	1	10	0	.133
Billy Southworth	OF	15	25	1	7	4	1	1	0	3	4	0	.280
Mel Mazzera	OF	14	30	1	9	0	0	0	0	4	3	0	.300
Tony Lazzeri	OF	13	17	0	3	0	2	0	0	2	3	0	.176
Sam Jones	P8	8	2	0	1	0	0	0	0	0	1	0	.500
James Reninger	P7	7	14	1	1	1	0	0	0	1	5	0	.071
Earl Caldwell	P6	6	10	0	2	0	0	0	0	0	2	0	.200
Richard Hammond	P5	5	8	0	1	0	1	0	0	0	0	0	.125
Ed Watson	P5	5	0	0	0	0	0	0	0	0	0	0	---
Walt Lanfranconi	P4	4	7	0	2	0	0	0	0	0	1	0	.286
Richard Fowler	P1	1	3	0	0	0	0	0	0	0	1	0	.000

PITCHERS		W	L	PCT	G	GS	CG	SH	IP	H	BB	SO	ERA
Charles Fischer		10	12	.455	33	28	11	2	206	186	63	118	2.53
Phil Marchildon		10	13	.435	41	23	9	2	198	164	**116**	135	3.18
Les McCrabb		9	11	.450	35	22	9	2	175	207	53	52	4.58
James Walkup		6	9	.400	25	16	5	2	108	134	30	54	4.08
Pat McLaughlin		5	14	.263	42	15	7	0	175	197	61	56	3.39
Vallie Eaves		5	14	.263	29	18	11	1	148	155	68	90	4.74
John Pezzullo		5	16	.238	46	21	8	0	182	199	92	63	4.50
James Reninger		4	2	.667	7				39	32	22	14	
Sam Jones		1	0	1.000	8				12	12	9	5	
Richard Fowler		1	0	1.000	1				7	10	2	5	
Richard Hammond		1	1	.500	5				21	14	31	9	
Walt Lanfranconi		0	1	.000	4				17	16	11	4	
Ed Watson		0	2	.000	5				3	7	4	1	2.57
Earl Caldwell		0	4	.000	6				27	47	13	7	

MULTI-TEAM PLAYERS

BATTERS	POS-GAMES	TEAMS	GP	AB	R	H	BI	2B	3B	HR	BB	SO	SB	BA
Charles Hasson	1B149	MO22-SY132	154	528	71	132	83	23	4	15	82	89	2	.250
Lindsey Deal	OF122	MO19-SY118	137	438	49	114	46	19	5	4	32	37	13	.260
Christian Hartje	C81	MO18-SY81	99	283	33	79	54	11	8	3	40	25	2	.279
Dallas Warren	C63	SY23-NE38	66	151	12	20	15	5	0	0	28	24	0	.132
John Berly	P51	TO11-RO41	52	21	0	2	1	0	0	0	1	9	0	.095
Floyd Stromme	P30	BU18-BA12	30	61	8	12	3	1	1	0	4	15	0	.197
Willis Norman	OF20	SY4-MO17	21	66	11	21	14	8	1	1	13	10	0	.318
Harry Matuzak	P14	BA12-MO2	14	17	4	4	3	0	0	1	3	5	0	.235

PITCHERS		TEAMS	W	L	PCT	G	GS	CG	SH	IP	H	BB	SO	ERA
Floyd Stromme		BU18-BA12	12	11	.522	30	26	11	3	181	189	55	83	3.88
John Berly		TO11-RO40	5	4	.556	51	1	0	0	88	65	43	48	2.66
Harry Matuzak		BA12-MO2	3	4	.429	14	5	2	0	52	70	22	22	7.10

TEAM BATTING

TEAMS	GP	AB	R	H	BI	2B	3B	HR	BB	SO	SB	BA
ROCHESTER	160	5245	736	1400	661	249	57	78	517	674	85	.267
NEWARK	162	5329	800	1469	749	229	45	141	574	686	69	.276
JERSEY CITY	159	5202	627	1347	582	212	51	66	415	500	49	.259
BALTIMORE	160	5378	884	1539	805	279	46	157	529	679	85	.286
MONTREAL	161	5299	737	1440	660	290	44	76	480	553	44	.272
BUFFALO	160	5227	688	1387	631	241	51	133	473	707	64	.265
SYRACUSE	163	5228	613	1273	554	183	62	47	539	608	62	.243
TORONTO	161	5078	532	1245	487	181	48	53	498	593	70	.245
	643	41986	5617	11100	5129	1864	404	751	4025	5000	528	.264

1941
BATTLE BEFORE THE WAR

In the middle decades of the twentieth century, most of the post-season excitement in the International League revolved around the Junior World Series—the yearly battles with the American Association. Limit-stretching tilts such as the ones in 1924, 1929, 1934, and 1937 were certainly worthy of note. However, before reaching the ultimate matchup with the American Association, International teams had to weather their own playoff cycle. Some of these playoffs proved just as exciting. In 1939, Rochester had to go the full seven games in the semi-finals and the finals to reach the Junior World Series. Two years later, Montreal would have a similar tilt.

The International League playoff system was set in place following the 1933 season. Originally, it pitted the first-place team versus the second, as well as the third-place versus fourth, in a best-of-five format. In 1934, the playoffs were altered to a first-third, and second-fourth alignment, with both series now best of seven. In 1939, a slight tinkering changed the matchups to a first-fourth and second-third in the opening rounds.

The Newark Bears returned to the catbird seat in the 1941 International League season following a two-year absence. Montreal finished ten games in arrears, followed closely by Buffalo and Rochester in the last two playoff spots. Jersey City, Syracuse, Baltimore, and Toronto placed far out of contention. Eugene Corbett, playing for Baltimore and Newark, won the batting title with a mark of .306. Newark's Frank Kelleher hit the most longballs (37) and finished with the most runs batted in (125). Pitching honors were garnered by Buffalo's Fred Hutchinson for most wins (26), John Lindell from Newark for lowest earned average (2.05), and Virgil Trucks of Buffalo for most strikeouts (204).

In the initial round of the International League playoffs, first-place Newark clubbed fourth-place Rochester four games to one. Second-place Montreal had a much more difficult time with third-place Buffalo. Trailing three games to two, the Royals squeaked out a 4–3 decision before rapping the Bisons 11–8 in the final game. In the finals, Montreal led Newark by a three-games-to-one margin before the Bears evened the series with a pair of one-run victories. Not to be outdone, the Royals turned the tables in game seven with a two-run ninth to slide by Newark 4–3, thus claiming the International League championship four games to three.

The Montreal Royals' journey through the International playoffs in 1941 was a rollercoaster ride that ended on top. Unfortunately, from the top of a rollercoaster, the only possible direction is down. Exhausted by the International playoff battle, Montreal lost the war between the leagues—the Junior World Series—four games to two.

NEWARK Bears

NEWARK	1st	100-54	.649		John Neun

BATTERS	POS-GAMES	GP	AB	R	H	BI	2B	3B	HR	BB	SO	SB	BA
Joe Mack	1B75	78	251	41	66	43	9	2	10	53	27	1	.263
George Stirnweiss	2B80,SS20	100	363	50	96	48	9	3	5	39	63	21	.264
George Scharein	SS130	130	419	36	96	39	13	1	2	34	47	4	.229
Hank Majeski	3B108	113	446	74	135	82	16	2	14	37	37	2	.303
Tommy Holmes	OF154	154	630	105	190	59	17	7	9	61	17	12	.302
Frank Kelleher	OF146	151	503	106	138	125	17	4	37	120	116	4	.274
Leo Nonnenkamp	OF126	133	491	88	148	54	22	6	8	58	47	14	.302
Thomas Padden	C87	93	240	30	52	33	8	1	2	50	38	1	.217
Ken Sears	C81	97	306	60	91	51	14	2	18	39	41	1	.298
Fred Collins	1B60,OF16	91	282	33	66	37	12	5	6	26	69	0	.234
Don Lang	3B42,2B32,SS17	90	270	40	80	48	16	5	6	21	33	3	.296
John Lindell	P31	51	114	15	34	9	3	0	0	5	13	0	.298
George Washburn	P23	37	59	5	9	7	2	0	2	4	9	0	.153
Russ Christopher	P31	33	73	11	15	5	2	1	0	8	22	0	.205
Hank Borowy	P31	31	85	6	13	8	2	0	0	6	27	0	.153
Tommy Byrne	P26	27	49	5	13	2	1	0	0	3	4	0	.265
John Johnson	P24	24	22	4	7	5	1	0	0	4	6	0	.318
Edward Levy	1B23	23	86	11	22	11	5	0	1	8	11	2	.256
James Shilling	2B13	20	51	5	12	5	2	0	0	4	6	0	.235
Fred Frankhouse	P14	14	5	1	1	1	0	0	0	1	0	0	.200
Albert Moran	P14	14	2	0	0	0	0	0	0	0	0	0	.000
Walt Stewart	P9	9											.000
James Davis	P8	8											.000
William Johnson	3B,OF	5	16	2	8	1	0	0	0			0	.500
John Haley	P5	5											.000
Steve Peek	P4	4											.400
Mel Queen	P4	4											.000
Stan Andrews	C	3	7	0	0	0	0	0	0	0		0	.000
Rinaldo Ardizoia	P3	3											.000
Louis Berger	SS	2	1	0	1	0	0	0	0	0		0	1.000
Jack Anderson	C	1	1	0	0	0	0	0	0	0		0	.000
Nathan Blair	PH	1	1	0	0	0	0	0	0	0		0	----
James Nicholson	3B	1	0	0	0	0	0	0	0	0		0	----

PITCHERS		W	L	PCT	G	GS	CG	SH	IP	H	BB	SO	ERA
John Lindell		23	4	.852	31		22	3	228	205	59	100	2.05
Hank Borowy		17	10	.630	31		18	1	229	203	65	111	2.91
Russ Christopher		16	7	.696	31		12	3	185	160	77	69	2.82
Allen Gettel		12	9	.571	40		10	3	178	158	64	77	2.98
Tommy Byrne		10	7	.588	26		7	3	129	127	68	75	3.98
George Washburn		9	7	.563	23		8	0	126	122	85	60	4.86
Steve Peek		3	1	.750	4				36	22	12	11	1.50
John Johnson		3	6	.333	24		2	0	74	77	24	32	3.65
Fred Frankhouse		2	0	1.000	14		0	0	26	23	8	6	3.46
Walt Stewart		1	0	1.000	9				20	12	9	12	1.80
James Davis		1	0	1.000	8				18	16	11	7	
John Haley		1	0	1.000	5				15	11	12	3	3.00
Mel Queen		1	0	1.000	4				14	14	8	8	4.50
Albert Moran		1	2	.333	14		0	0	24	24	13	14	4.88
Rinaldo Ardizoia		0	1	.000	3				14	13	8	6	

MONTREAL Royals

MONTREAL	2nd	90-64	.584	-10	Clyde Sukeforth

BATTERS	POS-GAMES	GP	AB	R	H	BI	2B	3B	HR	BB	SO	SB	BA
Paul Campbell	1B154	154	615	86	175	49	19	6	3	41	96	24	.285
Alex Kampouris	2B51,OF39	95	281	31	72	45	18	0	8	38	59	4	.256
Claude Corbitt	SS150	150	593	98	167	52	24	7	0	53	25	18	.282
Roy Hughes	3B106,2B26	137	473	69	143	71	29	5	1	47	29	22	.302
Jack Graham	OF145	146	516	87	152	107	31	3	31	50	58	15	.295
Forrest Jensen	OF138	141	502	58	148	74	33	1	8	38	18	10	.295
Alvin Powell	OF72	72	273	42	72	32	15	2	2	14	23	5	.264
Fred Walters	C66	80	211	24	51	15	8	3	1	19	20	0	.242
Don Ross	3B53,OF28	101	294	41	91	61	24	1	7	43	13	6	.310
George Staller	OF29	53	118	12	31	16	9	0	5	11	15	2	.263
Max Macon	P19,OF11	47	86	8	13	6	3	2	0	2	12	0	.151
Herm Franks	C46	46	120	17	35	18	9	1	4	36	15	1	.292
Al Sherer	P40	45	54	4	14	4	2	0	0	5	5	0	.259
Chester Kehn	P38	44	69	9	9	1	1	0	0	8	10	0	.130
Wes Flowers	P39	39	44	4	6	0	0	0	0	4	6	0	.136

MONTREAL (cont.)
Royals

BATTERS	POS-GAMES	GP	AB	R	H	BI	2B	3B	HR	BB	SO	SB	BA
Ed Head	P32	32	76	6	9	5	0	0	0	4	17	0	.118
Steve Rachunok	P30	30	33	2	3	3	0	0	1	2	18	0	.091
Charles Gassaway	P25	25	18	1	3	1	0	0	1	0	5	0	.167
Charles Gilbert	OF24	24	89	17	27	15	11	2	1	16	4	4	.303
James Carleton	P19	19	17	3	4	1	1	0	0	2	9	0	.235
Van Lingle Mungo	P10	18	24	2	6	5	3	0	0	4	6	0	.250
John Hudson	2B15	15	58	10	17	8	4	0	0	2	4	2	.293
Kemp Wicker	P9	9											.053
Roxie Lawson	P8	8											.250
Elmer Rambert	P8	8											.000
Lou Fette	P2	2											1.000
Spencer Smith	P1	1											.000

PITCHERS	W	L	PCT	G	GS	CG	SH	IP	H	BB	SO	ERA
Ed Head	18	8	.692	32		16	3	209	184	92	149	3.40
Chester Kehn	16	11	.593	38		17	4	210	171	102	101	3.26
Al Sherer	14	9	.609	40		9	0	175	178	58	71	3.65
Wes Flowers	10	7	.588	39		9	1	158	157	59	47	3.65
Steve Rachunok	7	7	.500	30		5	3	120	102	57	53	4.20
Kemp Wicker	6	2	.750	9				65	52	21	25	
Max Macon	5	4	.556	19		3	0	80	80	33	26	3.26
James Carleton	4	4	.500	19		3	1	65	61	37	37	4.71
Van Lingle Mungo	3	1	.750	10		1	0	45	33	28	27	4.00
Charles Gassaway	3	3	.500	25		0	0	60	57	35	29	4.05
Elmer Rambert	0	1	.000	8				18	25	12	7	
Roxie Lawson	0	3	.000	8				25	36	14	8	
Lou Fette	0	0	----	2				5	8	6	1	
Spencer Smith	0	0	----	1				1	3	1	0	

BUFFALO   3rd   88-65   .575   -11.5   Albert Vincent
Bisons

BATTERS	POS-GAMES	GP	AB	R	H	BI	2B	3B	HR	BB	SO	SB	BA
Mike Rocco	1B153	153	545	85	155	79	20	5	21	67	43	9	.284
Lambert Meyer	2B91	91	341	59	104	72	22	3	20	29	50	5	.305
James Levey	SS114,2B12	130	422	62	82	33	11	1	10	26	50	7	.194
Robert Boken	3B111	126	421	56	115	69	20	2	10	32	46	9	.273
Mayo Smith	OF128	134	406	76	106	46	18	6	11	79	26	2	.261
James Outlaw	OF103,3B42	146	511	71	135	47	26	8	2	57	40	8	.264
Robert Harris	OF101	101	385	63	112	41	14	7	8	46	40	6	.291
Ed Parsons	C100	101	327	40	73	60	16	1	14	25	55	0	.224
Robert Patrick	OF93	98	345	50	111	38	23	1	4	19	42	2	.322
Morris Hancken	C71	72	180	10	27	11	2	1	0	18	25	2	.150
Fred Hutchinson	P36	72	148	22	58	23	14	1	2	11	10	4	.392
Ollie Carnegie	OF37	71	148	13	38	25	5	1	7	6	23	0	.257
Eric McNair	2B36,SS28	60	224	25	80	41	15	3	5	11	28	0	.357
Hal White	P36	36	77	4	10	4	2	0	1	5	31	0	.130
James Trexler	P28	36	35	5	7	3	3	0	0	9	7	0	.200
Virgil Trucks	P33	34	64	3	2	2	0	0	0	2	13	0	.031
Charles Fuchs	P27	27	44	1	7	2	0	0	0	4	13	0	.159
Earl Cook	P23	23	35	2	3	2	2	0	0	2	11	0	.086
Mike Roscoe	P23	23	19	3	4	3	0	0	0	4	4	0	.211
Boyd Perry	SS20	20	65	5	18	4	2	1	0	5	6	0	.277
Joseph Martin	3B	18	23	0	5	2	1	0	0	0	3	0	.217
Albert Vincent	3B,2B,SS	17	11	2	1	0	0	0	0	1	0	0	.097
Pat Mullin	OF14	16	56	7	20	6	5	1	2	8	6	1	.357
Richard Korte	SS,2B	13	14	6	2	1	0	0	0	1	0	0	.143
Eugene Markland	2B	9	27	4	7	2	2	0	0			0	.259
Floyd Gieball	P6	6											.444
Leo Pukis	P5	5											.250

PITCHERS	W	L	PCT	G	GS	CG	SH	IP	H	BB	SO	ERA
Fred Hutchinson	**26**	7	.788	36		**31**	3	**284**	241	47	171	2.44
Hal White	16	12	.571	36		16	5	230	229	65	109	2.74
Virgil Trucks	12	12	.500	33		15	1	204	164	76	**204**	3.22
Charles Fuchs	7	13	.350	27		11	1	151	158	61	101	3.40
Mike Roscoe	6	4	.600	23		1	1	76	93	35	16	4.38
James Trexler	6	6	.500	28		4	0	91	90	37	38	4.75
Floyd Gieball	5	1	.833	6				48	41	13	19	1.69
Earl Cook	4	8	.333	23		3	0	115	133	43	45	4.85
Leo Pukis	0	1	.000	5				15	12	8	5	

ROCHESTER Red Wings

ROCHESTER Red Wings	4th	84-68	.553	-15	Tony Kaufmann

BATTERS	POS-GAMES	GP	AB	R	H	BI	2B	3B	HR	BB	SO	SB	BA
Harry Davis	1B149	152	514	84	152	88	29	3	14	104	37	8	.296
George Fallon	2B143	144	513	50	117	51	19	3	4	35	36	9	.228
Lynn Myers	SS54,2B13	83	256	39	78	33	7	3	1	28	29	8	.305
Whitey Kurowski	3B133	142	500	96	144	69	26	11	13	66	87	21	.288
John Wyrostek	OF83	86	298	34	75	39	11	3	3	32	25	4	.252
Gus Bergamo	OF66	72	227	27	62	27	9	3	3	34	16	5	.273
Dain Clay	OF55	61	192	27	45	24	8	2	4	22	20	4	.234
Ray Mueller	C114	116	388	47	93	47	14	8	7	35	37	1	.240
Gene Lillard	SS49,3B24,OF18	99	340	50	89	49	10	4	12	31	71	3	.262
Floyd Young	SS43	63	224	32	59	18	12	2	4	11	35	6	.263
John Berly	P61	61	17	1	5	2	0	0	0	1	1	0	.294
Warren Robinson	C45	56	146	13	32	12	4	1	0	14	34	0	.219
Stan Musial	OF54	54	221	43	72	21	10	4	3	15	21	2	.326
James Ripple	OF51	52	172	29	65	22	14	1	5	20	10	0	.378
Erv Dusak	OF50	51	181	21	55	33	5	1	5	16	27	5	.304
Louis Scoffic	OF48	51	178	23	46	18	6	0	1	22	19	3	.258
Carden Gillenwater	OF34	42	120	18	34	7	9	0	0	16	13	2	.283
Matt Surkont	P38	38	51	5	7	1	2	0	0	5	10	0	.137
Herschel Lyons	P34	34	58	6	16	5	2	1	0	5	9	0	.276
Hy Vandenberg	P28	33	66	4	14	2	1	0	0	2	12	0	.212
Clem Dreisewerd	P33	33	67	6	9	1	1	1	0	9	31	0	.134
Henry Gornicki	P26	26	65	4	8	3	1	2	0	4	33	0	.123
William Brumbeloe	P21	22	20	7	5	0	1	1	0	8	7	0	.250
Roy Bruner	P20	21	19	0	4	1	0	0	0	1	4	0	.211
Steve Mesner	SS15	19	59	9	16	9	6	1	0	10	5	2	.271
Henry Redmond	OF	16	37	4	12	5	6	0	0	2	4	0	.324
Thomas Winsett	OF13	15	50	4	8	3	2	0	0	2	11	0	.160
Bill Curlee	P12	12	16	1	2	0	0	0	0	0	5	0	.125
Ed Wissman	P10	11	29	3	9	0	3	0	0	0	7	0	.310
Carl Doyle	P7	7											.143
Carl Wentz	P4	5											.500
Robert Doyle	P4	4											.000
James Smith	P4	4											.000
Robert E. Porter	P2	2											.000
William Yarewick	P1	1											.000

PITCHERS	W	L	PCT	G	GS	CG	SH	IP	H	BB	SO	ER
Clem Dreisewerd	15	6	.714	33		11	3	198	187	53	79	2.91
Henry Gornicki	12	9	.571	26		12	3	181	170	68	96	2.83
Herschel Lyons	12	11	.522	34		11	1	182	186	80	99	3.96
Hy Vandenberg	11	10	.524	28		11	5	176	162	75	79	3.38
Matt Surkont	10	6	.625	38		7	5	163	139	88	84	3.20
John Berly	6	4	.600	61		0	0	97	77	55	50	3.43
Ed Wissman	4	3	.571	10		4	1	69	68	18	19	2.61
Bill Curlee	4	4	.500	12		2	0	45	48	15	15	4.20
Carl Doyle	3	2	.600	7				22	22	11	8	
William Brumbeloe	3	5	.375	21		2	0	78	80	51	25	4.96
Roy Bruner	3	6	.333	20		3	1	61	59	27	23	5.31
Carl Wentz	1	0	1.000	4				12	10	6	5	
Robert Doyle	0	2	.000	4				6	8	11	2	
James Smith	0	0	----	4				6	13	7	0	
Robert E. Porter	0	0	----	2				5	10	3	2	
William Yarewick	0	0	----	1				2	2	5	0	

JERSEY CITY Giants

JERSEY CITY Giants	5th	74-76	.493	-24	Tony Cuccinello

BATTERS	POS-GAMES	GP	AB	R	H	BI	2B	3B	HR	BB	SO	SB	BA
John McCarthy	1B149,P4	150	569	70	143	79	23	6	12	40	38	2	.251
Nicholas Witek	2B105	105	381	47	109	51	16	10	0	37	13	4	.286
John Davis	SS88,3B46	136	500	72	119	38	18	7	2	70	66	15	.238
Sid Gordon	3B72,SS63,OF17	150	523	69	159	76	15	6	7	80	23	15	.304
Hershel Martin	OF135	140	494	70	133	48	24	2	2	60	40	3	.269
James Maynard	OF98	100	336	52	86	36	18	1	5	53	49	7	.256
Allen Cooke	OF89	99	296	37	82	30	18	4	0	42	31	1	.277
Rae Blaemire	C90	101	323	31	82	41	9	3	5	20	21	2	.254
Tony Cuccinello	2B36,3B20	86	235	24	65	33	15	4	2	29	21	1	.277
William Atwood	C65	78	219	17	42	18	2	0	0	36	26	3	.192
Del Young	3B17,2B15	69	160	15	36	14	5	0	0	12	7	0	.225
Harold Feldman	P39	40	79	7	9	5	3	0	0	4	23	0	.114

JERSEY CITY (cont.)
Giants

BATTERS	POS-GAMES	GP	AB	R	H	BI	2B	3B	HR	BB	SO	SB	BA
Hugh East	P38	38	61	5	9	3	2	1	1	4	16	0	.148
Robert Foxx	OF33	34	117	13	26	7	3	0	0	7	21	2	.222
Roy Henshaw	P33	34	53	1	11	3	1	0	0	1	11	0	.208
Raymond Combs	P33	33	21	2	4	2	0	0	0	2	4	0	.190
James Lynn	P30	31	29	1	4	2	0	0	0	2	4	0	.138
Thomas Neill	OF23	27	88	7	16	7	2	1	0	9	8	2	.182
Reuben Fischer	P24	24	62	4	12	5	2	0	0	2	12	0	.194
William Harris	P23	23	51	2	8	2	0	0	0	4	13	0	.159
Milburn Shoffner	P9	9											.600
Russ Bauers	P7	8											.125
Rene Monteagudo	PH	3	3	0	0	0	0	0	0	0			0	.000

PITCHERS		W	L	PCT	G	GS	CG	SH	IP	H	BB	SO	ERA
Harold Feldman		14	16	.467	39		16	2	237	237	109	104	3.42
Roy Henshaw		13	9	.591	33		11	3	169	137	46	66	2.34
Hugh East		13	10	.565	38		10	1	190	188	89	77	3.60
William Harris		10	5	.667	23		10	2	151	134	26	52	2.62
Reuben Fischer		7	12	.368	24		13	2	175	151	102	84	2.78
James Lynn		6	7	.462	30		4	1	109	111	56	60	4.13
Raymond Coombs		5	5	.500	33		3	0	97	101	28	35	3.53
Russ Bauers		1	1	.500	7				20	18	9	9	2.70
John McCarthy		0	1	.000	4				14	11	6	5	2.57
Milburn Shoffner		0	2	.000	9				18	23	8	3	

SYRACUSE   6th   70-83   .458   -30.5   Benny Borgmann
Chiefs

BATTERS	POS-GAMES	GP	AB	R	H	BI	2B	3B	HR	BB	SO	SB	BA
Charles Hasson	1B137	139	462	54	109	47	23	4	10	81	90	1	.236
Vince Sherlock	2B123	124	460	43	120	44	17	2	1	47	26	8	.261
Woody Williams	SS153	153	547	51	128	52	23	2	0	25	27	2	.234
Bill Nagel	3B62,OF30,1B18,P1	116	401	39	91	59	28	1	13	30	73	3	.227
Goody Rosen	OF154	**154**	558	86	162	54	22	6	7	90	45	11	.290
Ed Longacre	OF109,3B10	133	442	51	116	47	14	4	1	35	29	4	.262
Tony Bongiovanni	OF		(see multi-team players)										
John Bottarini	C96	104	302	27	72	35	10	3	4	50	34	1	.238
Lindsay Deal	OF66	100	252	32	69	21	9	4	0	17	20	2	.274
Jack Juelich	3B31,2B24	58	175	11	34	12	5	1	0	13	13	1	.194
Lin Storti	3B47	56	173	19	41	32	7	0	9	26	35	0	.237
Herm Rehbein	P14	34	7	8	2	2	1	0	0	0	3	0	.286
William Burkhart	P32	32	57	5	11	1	3	0	0	4	17	0	.193
Tom Sunkel	P30	31	82	5	14	3	2	0	0	4	22	0	.171
Frank Secory	OF20	31	79	12	26	15	4	1	4	14	8	0	.329
William Schultz	P29	31	32	1	7	1	1	0	0	0	9	0	.219
Charles Marshall	C24	27	43	5	8	5	0	2	0	14	13	0	.186
Les Hinckle	P26	26	74	4	11	2	1	1	0	2	5	0	.149
Ted Kleinhans	P24	24	15	0	1	0	0	0	0	2	5	0	.067
Eugene Lambert	P21	21	22	1	3	2	0	0	0	1	9	0	.136
Nate Andrews	P15	15	24	2	2	2	0	0	0	6	9	0	.083
Joe Krakauskas	P13	13	29	4	7	0	2	0	0	4	12	0	.241
John Whitehead	P9	9											.083
John Tising	P8	8											.143
Tommy De la Cruz	P5	5											.250
Nathan Pelter	P2	3											.000
Benny Borgmann	3B	2	5	0	0	1	0	0	0			0	.000
Martin Zachar	P1	1											.000

PITCHERS		W	L	PCT	G	GS	CG	SH	IP	H	BB	SO	ERA
Tom Sunkel		15	11	.577	30		16	2	220	183	**119**	135	3.19
Les Hinckle		12	14	.462	26		16	2	200	223	53	86	3.83
William Burkhart		10	10	.500	32		12	3	174	169	64	70	3.05
Nate Andrews		6	5	.545	15		7	0	97	114	36	39	3.43
Joe Krakauskas		5	8	.385	13		7	0	89	83	53	53	3.94
John Whitehead		4	4	.500	9				71	78	16	19	
Eugene Lambert		3	5	.375	21		4	0	74	63	47	28	3.89
Tommy De la Cruz		1	1	.500	5				14	16	8	8	
John Tising		1	2	.333	8				25	37	12	14	
William Schultz		1	7	.125	29		5	0	93	109	51	37	5.13
Ted Kleinhans		1	7	.125	24		3	0	72	85	42	32	5.13
Herm Rehbein		0	0	----	14		0	0	19	19	22	12	4.74

SYRACUSE (cont.)
Chiefs

PITCHERS	W	L	PCT	G	GS	CG	SH	IP	H	BB	SO	ERA
Nathan Pelter	0	0	----	2				3	3	4	3	
Martin Zachar	0	0	----	1				1	1	2	0	0.00
Bill Nagel	0	0	----	1				3	2	4	0	

BALTIMORE		7th	58-94	.382	-41		Alphonse Thomas					

Orioles

BATTERS	POS-GAMES	GP	AB	R	H	BI	2B	3B	HR	BB	SO	SB	BA
Albert Flair	1B147	147	547	72	163	87	24	3	11	54	38	4	.298
Eugene Corbett	2B	(see multi-team players)											
Harold Seiling	SS137	140	567	93	159	46	26	1	11	59	44	13	.280
Tom Hafey	3B74,P4	90	311	45	80	54	17	1	13	22	55	2	.257
Bob Seeds	OF98	108	352	50	93	61	20	2	7	41	54	4	.264
George Honochick	OF97	114	339	56	98	36	18	6	4	57	48	6	.289
Murray Howell	OF66	66	236	36	77	50	10	0	8	43	22	2	.326
Homer Howell	C	(see multi-team players)											
Jack Redmond	C62	94	228	30	57	32	8	1	9	26	34	1	.250
Joseph Kracher	C28,OF23,3B14	77	229	24	51	25	7	4	6	18	31	0	.223
Ben Sankey	3B46,SS13	70	194	17	31	19	6	1	0	23	13	0	.160
Monte Weaver	P53	53	24	2	2	1	0	0	0	1	6	0	.083
Robert Hamilton	OF39	45	147	23	36	20	2	0	3	14	23	5	.245
James Kerr	P43	43	49	4	5	0	1	1	0	3	13	0	.102
Ken Trinkle	P43	43	47	1	3	3	1	0	0	8	20	0	.064
Art Graham	OF38	40	128	23	32	16	3	1	3	21	18	0	.250
Clyde Smoll	P30	31	41	2	4	0	2	0	0	7	22	0	.097
George Polzer	3B20	30	89	9	21	16	4	2	2	11	26	1	.236
Elmer Burkart	P30	30	46	3	6	1	1	0	1	2	18	0	.130
Orlin Collier	P25	25	49	1	4	3	0	0	0	4	20	0	.082
Russ Niller	P20	25	34	3	5	2	1	0	0	5	5	0	.147
Walt Sickles	P21	21	12	1	0	0	0	0	0	0	5	0	.000
Ray Flanigan	P18	18	29	2	2	0	0	0	0	2	13	0	.069
Dick Midkiff	P16	16	2	0	0	0	0	0	0	0	1	0	.000
Floyd Stromme	P14	14	18	3	4	1	1	0	0	0	6	0	.222
Earl Springer	P13	13	7	0	2	1	0	0	0	0	4	0	.286
Ed Vogel	P5	5											.000
Joseph Mueller	P4	4											.333
John Scheidt	1B	4	14	3	3	0	0	0	0			0	.214
Robert Lansinger	OF	1	5	1	1	1	0	0	0			0	.200
Don Richardson	P1	1											.000
Italo Chelini	P1	1											.000
Alphonse Thomas	P1	1											.000
Alex Ronay	P1	1											.000

PITCHERS	W	L	PCT	G	GS	CG	SH	IP	H	BB	SO	ERA
Ken Trinkle	11	15	.423	43		5	0	162	188	54	74	3.78
Elmer Burkart	9	9	.500	30		6	2	133	141	39	42	4.87
Orlin Collier	8	10	.444	25		9	0	152	176	58	72	6.16
Monte Weaver	7	4	.636	53		1	0	117	118	54	62	4.54
Clyde Smoll	5	13	.278	30		8	2	141	168	51	76	4.09
Russ Niller	4	5	.444	20		1	0	101	125	54	34	5.26
Floyd Stromme	4	5	.444	14		3	0	59	74	17	24	6.10
Ray Flanigan	4	10	.286	18		5	1	88	93	37	24	5.73
James Kerr	4	13	.235	43		3	0	155	194	64	73	5.57
Dick Midkiff	1	1	.500	16		0	0	23	35	12	8	7.83
Walt Sickles	1	2	.333	21		1	0	60	74	14	31	4.05
Earl Springer	0	1	.000	13		0	0	27	36	24	13	10.00
Joseph Mueller	0	1	.000	4				14	21	9	3	
Don Richardson	0	1	.000	1				6	8	2	2	6.00
Alex Ronay	0	1	.000	1				2	6	1	1	
Tom Hafey	0	3	.000	4				15	14	7	6	
Ed Vogel	0	0	----	5				5	8	7	2	
Italo Chelini	0	0	----	1				1	1	0	0	0.00
Alphonse Thomas	0	0	----	1				1	2	0	1	9.00

TORONTO   8th   47-107   .305   -53   Lena Blackburne
Maple Leafs

BATTERS	POS-GAMES	GP	AB	R	H	BI	2B	3B	HR	BB	SO	SB	BA
Edwin Morgan	1B118,OF28	146	549	68	126	52	16	3	10	59	48	6	.229
Al Rubeling	2B154	154	556	69	150	83	26	5	14	44	45	3	.270
Len Merullo	SS63	63	255	25	61	17	6	1	1	14	25	4	.239
John Hill	3B129	138	489	46	137	44	11	5	1	40	22	3	.280
Eric Tipton	OF132	136	467	59	123	36	19	9	3	71	53	2	.263
Frank Colman	OF95	113	343	34	101	47	9	2	4	25	28	2	.295
Floyd Yount	OF91	96	307	39	69	34	5	5	4	33	48	3	.225
Robert Garbark	C68	68	237	25	68	33	9	1	0	21	18	2	.287
Joseph Gantenbein	SS33,3B26,OF15	105	306	42	55	27	9	2	5	27	46	4	.180
John Tyler	OF40	50	146	13	30	6	7	0	0	14	22	2	.205
Walt Klimczak	C48	50	123	13	28	13	5	1	0	10	10	0	.211
Herm Besse	P25	44	96	10	20	12	2	1	2	7	17	0	.208
Joe Vance	P41	41	29	1	4	2	1	0	0	1	3	0	.138
Walt Lanfranconi	P34	40	60	5	11	4	0	1	0	1	19	0	.183
Robert Latshaw	1B32	39	119	13	29	24	5	0	1	17	20	0	.244
Bill Lillard	SS31	32	111	12	25	6	3	0	2	18	10	0	.225
George Jumonville	SS30	30	102	7	21	4	4	0	0	0	29	0	.206
Alfred Todd	C30	30	87	8	24	6	7	0	0	13	10	3	.276
Porter Vaughan	P30	30	71	4	10	6	1	1	0	2	21	0	.141
Richard Fowler	P27	27	57	4	14	6	1	1	0	1	16	0	.246
Charles Fischer	P25	25	36	0	7	1	0	1	0	2	8	0	.194
Herman Clifton	3B14	22	53	8	10	0	3	1	0	8	8	3	.189
Vallie Eaves	P21	21	39	2	9	2	1	0	0	0	17	0	.231
Dewey Williams	C19	20	53	3	9	5	2	0	0	4	4	0	.170
Pat McLaughlin	P13	13	11	0	0	0	0	0	0	0	4	0	.000
Ed Selway	P9	9											.143
Richard Hammond	P6	6											.333
James Walkup	P6	6											.250
Al Piechota	P6	6											.111
Art Jones	P2	2											.000
John Leovich	C	1	3	0	0	0	0	0	0	0		0	.000
James Reninger	P1	1											.000

PITCHERS		W	L	PCT	G	GS	CG	SH	IP	H	BB	SO	ERA
Porter Vaughan		12	12	.500	30		17	2	207	186	119	121	3.65
Richard Fowler		10	10	.500	27		11	2	161	152	64	61	3.30
Herman Besse		10	15	.400	25		22	0	203	206	85	110	4.12
Walt Lanfranconi		8	15	.348	34		15	3	177	188	73	47	4.68
Al Piechota		2	2	.500	6				22	26	19	10	
Joe Vance		2	7	.222	41		1	0	112	125	27	41	3.38
Vallie Eaves		2	12	.143	21		5	0	119	141	52	55	5.52
James Walkup		1	4	.200	6				28	48	16	10	
Art Jones		0	1	.000	2				3	3	5	0	
Ed Selway		0	2	.000	9				37	42	18	10	
Richard Hammond		0	2	.000	6				28	28	21	12	
Pat McLaughlin		0	8	.000	13		2	0	42	54	8	19	5.79
Charles Fischer		0	17	.000	25		7	0	125	155	67	51	5.62
James Reninger		0	0	----	1				0	0	4	2	54.54

MULTI-TEAM PLAYERS

BATTERS	POS-GAMES	TEAMS	GP	AB	R	H	BI	2B	3B	HR	BB	SO	SB	BA
Eugene Corbett	2B143	BA119-NE25	144	520	63	159	76	30	2	13	56	41	2	.306
Tony Bongiovanni	OF127	NE26-SY110	136	489	55	126	33	20	4	6	41	15	7	.258
Gil Brack	OF103	BA54-JC61	115	354	64	104	49	16	4	10	47	73	2	.294
John Bell	2B99	MO84-BA30	114	373	60	105	31	13	1	1	48	24	6	.282
Homer Howell	C75	BA74-MO19	93	260	30	58	27	13	0	2	35	33	0	.223
Legrant Scott	OF73	RO10-TO72	82	265	38	79	28	8	0	3	25	14	0	.298
Roy Johnson	OF68	SY7-BA70	77	260	38	78	18	16	2	1	42	41	4	.300
Joseph Becker	C56	MO49-BA12	61	159	23	34	16	5	1	1	23	15	1	.214
Lynn Nelson	P39	BU2-SY37	39	41	1	3	3	0	0	1	2	8	0	.073
John Pezzullo	P28	SY2-BU26	28	29	1	6	6	0	0	0	2	9	0	.207
Frank Pearce	P27	JC16-MO11	27	53	3	6	2	1	0	0	3	13	0	.113

PITCHERS		TEAMS	W	L	PCT	G	GS	CG	SH	IP	H	BB	SO	ERA
Lynn Nelson		BU2-SY37	12	8	.600	39		5	1	138	133	40	57	3.20
Frank Pearce		JC16-MO11	9	12	.429	27		10	3	159	154	30	42	3.34
John Pezzullo		SY2-BU26	5	2	.714	28		1	0	87	107	50	39	4.45

TEAM BATTING

TEAMS	GP	AB	R	H	BI	2B	3B	HR	BB	SO	SB	BA
NEWARK	154	5046	**765**	**1369**	**715**	181	43	**129**	**615**	660	65	**.271**
MONTREAL	**155**	**5051**	702	1359	628	**263**	33	74	501	522	**119**	.269
BUFFALO	153	4916	676	1296	630	222	42	117	478	584	55	.264
ROCHESTER	153	5050	689	1340	595	218	**55**	79	555	652	83	.265
JERSEY CITY	151	4829	583	1217	533	184	49	50	541	489	58	.252
SYRACUSE	**155**	4942	531	1193	485	197	34	56	531	562	43	.241
BALTIMORE	153	4965	666	1282	605	216	28	96	571	**701**	46	.258
TORONTO	154	4957	542	1213	495	157	39	50	460	565	34	.245
	614	39756	5154	10269	4686	1638	323	651	4252	4735	503	.258

1942
DYNASTY

In the long history of the International League, there have been several dynasties (teams winning at least three consecutive pennants) sprinkled through the years. The first dynasty appeared in Rochester, where the team won a trio of flags from 1909 to 1911. Later, the dynastic mantle passed to Baltimore, whose team won an incredible seven straight from 1919 to 1925. Shortly after that, Rochester fielded a quartet of winners from 1928 to 1931. Immediately following, the International witnessed a new championship string. This team never won more than three in a row. However, in addition to that trio, the team won two more pairs of championships shortly thereafter, extending the sequence of domination for more than a decade. This team was the Newark Bears.

Late in 1931, the Bears were purchased by the New York Yankees, the dominant team in the American League. With Yankee help, the team blossomed. In 1932, the Bears routed the competition, finishing more than fifteen games ahead of the field. The team duplicated the feat in 1933 by almost the same margin. The battle was harder in 1934, but Newark once again prevailed to win its third straight flag. The team slumped during the next two years, only to rear like a colossus in 1937 and 1938 to win pennants by a combined total of 43 games. Two more lean years followed before the Bear pennant machine rolled to the top in 1941.

The 1942 version of the Newark Bears proved to be just as powerful as they slapped down the rest of the International League once again. For the second straight year, the Bears finished ten games ahead of Montreal, who finished three and one-half up on Syracuse, and four and one-half ahead of Jersey City. Baltimore, Toronto, Buffalo, and Rochester finished fifth through eighth. Newark player Hank Majeski won two-thirds of the triple crown as he posted the highest average (.345) and most runs batted in (121). Lester Burge from Montreal poled the most home runs (28). On the mound, Syracuse hurler Charles Barrett won the most games (20), Jersey City's Raymond Coombs had the lowest earned run average (1.99), and Jack Hallett from Toronto struck out the most batters (187).

In Newark's seven remaining years in the International League, the team remained largely competitive, finishing in the first division five times. But 1942 would prove to be the end of the line for their domination of the top spot, as the Newark Bears never finished first again.

Newark's 1932 to 1942 teams stack up favorably against other International League dynasties. Although other teams may have won more consecutive pennants than the Newark Bears, none before or since has continued at such a level for eleven years—in itself a remarkable feat.

NEWARK   1st   92-61   .601   Bill Meyer
Bears

BATTERS	POS-GAMES	GP	AB	R	H	BI	2B	3B	HR	BB	SO	SB	BA
Eugene Corbett	1B154	154	546	97	153	75	28	1	8	95	48	18	.280
George Stirnweiss	2B144	144	552	109	149	74	17	10	11	55	67	73	.270
William Johnson	SS153	153	606	111	176	56	23	5	12	76	42	21	.290
Hank Majeski	3B151	151	574	112	198	121	31	6	15	57	38	10	.345
Art Metheny	OF147	148	548	79	162	94	30	3	18	53	53	7	.296
Russ Derry	OF96	112	329	61	92	65	17	4	22	37	58	11	.280
Frank Kelleher	OF88	88	312	79	92	86	15	1	23	62	45	7	.295
Aaron Robinson	C89	100	291	44	83	61	14	3	20	29	23	2	.285
Lloyd Christopher	OF86	93	293	43	72	38	8	5	12	31	60	7	.246
Thomas Padden	C82	86	231	28	48	23	11	0	1	37	34	1	.208
Tommy Byrne	P28	64	125	18	41	12	10	2	2	4	22	0	.328
George Washburn	P30	38	70	9	17	8	1	0	0	5	13	0	.243
Randall Gumpert	P33	37	40	3	12	6	1	0	0	0	9	0	.300
Al Gerheauser	P35	35	72	10	13	6	1	1	1	7	12	0	.181
Joseph Abreu	OF17	30	89	6	21	9	4	1	0	13	11	2	.236
Milo Candini	P29	29	30	1	6	3	1	0	0	1	3	0	.200
Phil Page	P28	28	11	1	0	0	0	0	0	2	3	0	.000
George Stainback	OF23	23	90	12	27	13	2	2	0	2	6	3	.300
Boyd Perry	2B,3B,SS	20	41	6	6	2	0	1	1	7	10	1	.146
Emerson Roser	P20	20	32	0	5	3	1	0	0	0	13	0	.156
Joe Page	P20	20	28	4	4	2	1	0	0	3	11	0	.143
Mel Queen	P16	16	28	3	4	2	0	0	0	0	8	0	.143
Ken Holcombe	P15	15	10	1	2	0	0	0	0	1	6	0	.200
Chet Clemens	OF14	14	42	4	7	4	1	0	0	1	11	2	.167
Jim Turner	P9	11	28	3	6	1	1	0	0	0	2	0	.214
John Babich	P9	9											.115
Leo Intrabartola	C	5	10	2	3	3	0	1	0			1	.300
Frank Silvanic	OF	5	4	0	0	0	0	0	0			0	.000
Larry Guay	P3	3											.000
Walt Stewart	P3	3											.000
Walt Dubiel	P2	2											.000
Alfred Clark	2B	1	3	1	1	0	0	0	0	0		0	.333

PITCHERS		W	L	PCT	G	GS	CG	SH	IP	H	BB	SO	ERA
Tommy Byrne		17	4	.810	28	28	15	2	209	160	145	147	3.10
Al Gerheauser		14	12	.538	35	24	11	2	201	177	76	82	3.24
Randall Gumpert		10	5	.667	33	13	9	2	124	126	43	49	3.77
George Washburn		9	7	.563	30	21	9	2	157	123	139	74	3.96
John Babich		7	1	.875	9				63	68	19	13	
Joe Page		7	6	.538	20	13	5	2	88	71	69	73	4.19
Emerson Roser		6	4	.600	20	8	1	1	86	81	37	56	3.60
Mel Queen		6	5	.545	16	13	3	1	80	79	45	44	5.06
Jim Turner		5	3	.625	9				74	59	15	20	0.97
Milo Candini		4	7	.364	29	15	3	1	95	97	62	38	5.21
Phil Page		3	3	.500	28	0	0	0	51	53	16	26	3.35
Larry Guay		2	0	1.000	3				11	11	6	4	
Ken Holcombe		1	1	.500	15	0	0	0	34	18	21	25	0.26
Walt Stewart		0	2	.000	3				10	9	9	6	
Walt Dubiel		0	0	----	2				4	6	1	2	9.00

MONTREAL   2nd   82-71   .536   -10   Clyde Sukeforth
Royals

BATTERS	POS-GAMES	GP	AB	R	H	BI	2B	3B	HR	BB	SO	SB	BA
Lester Burge	1B152	152	515	75	129	88	26	1	28	92	70	9	.250
Vince Sherlock	2B82	87	256	22	52	19	7	0	0	47	24	8	.203
Stan Rojek	SS144	144	562	90	159	49	21	5	3	46	34	11	.283
Thomas Tatum	3B136,OF19	156	580	95	131	45	24	5	4	94	73	28	.226
Eugene Moore	OF156	156	585	114	184	99	28	12	23	64	51	12	.315
Carl Furillo	OF125	129	445	55	125	51	21	6	3	49	49	13	.281
Jack Graham	OF115	116	431	63	123	93	24	3	25	33	52	7	.285
Cliff Dapper	C87	101	299	38	67	36	12	3	5	37	39	6	.224
Edwin Morgan	OF57	88	210	27	43	28	13	1	7	44	35	1	.205
Charles Gelbert	2B22,SS14,3B14	66	157	12	34	23	7	0	2	30	11	3	.217
Homer Howell	C59	62	170	16	29	17	5	1	1	29	30	1	.171
Alex Kampouris	2B55	55	182	26	50	24	13	1	6	27	38	1	.275
Chester Kehn	P32	40	56	9	15	4	2	0	0	6	6	1	.268
Max Macon	P16	39	68	8	20	7	5	0	0	1	7	0	.294
Les McCrabb	P37	37	43	0	5	2	0	1	0	0	13	0	.116
Jack Paepke	P28	35	30	5	9	0	2	1	1	0	8	1	.300

MONTREAL (cont.)
Royals

BATTERS	POS-GAMES	GP	AB	R	H	BI	2B	3B	HR	BB	SO	SB	BA
Al Sherer	P32	32	51	2	10	3	5	0	0	1	6	0	.196
Ed Spaulding	P31	31	17	0	0	0	0	0	0	1	6	0	.000
John Kraus	P28	28	58	7	10	4	2	0	0	4	21	0	.172
Spencer Smith	P28	28	10	1	0	0	0	0	0	1	5	0	.000
Bob Chipman	P26	26	35	3	6	1	1	0	0	4	16	0	.171
Ed Albosta	P22	22	40	4	8	2	1	1	0	1	12	0	.200
Herm Franks	C15	17	52	2	15	7	4	0	1	8	5	0	.288
Glen Stewart	3B	11	31	3	8	1	2	0	0	5	2	0	.258
Steve Nagy	P4	8											.154
Joseph Hatten	P8	8											.143
Schoolboy Rowe	P3	6											.364
Emile Showfety	OF	5	12	4	2	2	0	1	1			0	.167
Fred Falzone	P1	1											.000

PITCHERS	W	L	PCT	G	GS	CG	SH	IP	H	BB	SO	ERA
John Kraus	12	9	.571	28	25	11	1	169	160	84	74	3.46
Al Sherer	12	10	.545	32	20	10	2	160	144	50	70	2.98
Max Macon	9	4	.692	16	15	9	3	112	84	25	39	2.33
Ed Albosta	9	7	.563	22	17	8	2	130	107	79	69	3.53
Chester Kehn	8	8	.500	32	19	10	1	151	138	85	76	3.46
Les McCrabb	8	11	.421	37	19	7	2	148	157	46	49	3.28
Bob Chipman	6	9	.400	26	18	6	3	116	121	70	51	3.96
Joseph Hatten	4	2	.667	8				36	28	25	22	4.00
Ed Spaulding	4	5	.444	31	3	0	0	72	62	28	34	2.75
Spencer Smith	3	1	.750	28	4	1	0	58	66	34	12	4.97
Jack Paepke	3	3	.500	28	5	0	0	85	86	64	56	4.87
Steve Nagy	2	1	.667	4				24	21	18	14	2.63
Schoolboy Rowe	2	1	.667	3				22	11	5	6	2.05
Fred Falzone	0	0	----	1				0	0	2	0	0.00

SYRACUSE   3rd   78-74   .513   -13.5   Jewel Ens
Chiefs

BATTERS	POS-GAMES	GP	AB	R	H	BI	2B	3B	HR	BB	SO	SB	BA
Ed Shokes	1B149	149	494	66	129	61	18	6	12	61	57	10	.261
Robert Adams	2B111	115	425	53	110	43	30	4	4	33	45	10	.259
Woody Williams	SS153	153	559	61	151	39	20	5	2	37	26	4	.270
Jack Juelich	3B103	116	368	38	88	42	9	2	0	30	20	1	.239
Goody Rosen	OF140	140	502	78	132	42	14	5	3	97	42	13	.263
Al Mele	OF131	137	466	67	123	73	21	6	13	69	29	3	.264
Hank Sauer	OF78	82	291	35	62	44	9	2	11	39	44	1	.213
John Bottarini	C58	60	179	15	42	24	8	2	2	27	44	0	.235
Antonio Rodriguez	3B52,2B13	73	255	28	61	14	8	0	1	26	29	5	.239
Christian Hartje	C55	56	156	21	22	14	4	1	1	38	18	0	.141
Al Lakeman	C48	56	153	19	33	27	7	3	5	17	22	3	.216
Walt Cazen	OF30	47	130	9	36	8	5	1	2	10	17	6	.277
Lindsay Deal	OF30	41	114	13	25	17	6	1	0	10	6	1	.219
Clayton Lambert	P37	39	34	3	6	2	0	1	0	7	19	0	.176
Charles Barrett	P36	36	95	6	14	8	1	0	0	3	16	0	.147
Tommy De la Cruz	P32	33	60	4	10	4	1	1	0	5	12	0	.167
Roland Harrington	2B32	32	118	14	29	10	4	1	1	15	12	1	.246
Clyde Vollmer	OF29	32	117	11	25	9	6	2	1	8	14	2	.214
Nate Andrews	P31	31	75	2	4	3	1	0	0	9	31	0	.053
Ewell Blackwell	P29	29	76	5	8	6	1	0	0	2	28	0	.105
Ben Wade	P25	26	25	3	2	2	1	0	0	0	7	0	.080
Lynn Nelson	P21	24	20	2	2	2	0	0	0	3	9	0	.100
Ed Lukon	OF18	18	68	6	14	7	0	2	2	7	6	0	.206
Les Hinckle	P12	14	18	1	3	1	1	0	0	0	0	0	.167
Earl Harrist	P13	13	1	0	0	0	0	0	0	0	0	0	.000
William Schultz	P5	6											.000
Jim Konstanty	P5	5											.111
Carmel Castle	OF	1	4	0	1	1	0	0	0			0	.250
Wilbur Brubaker	PR	1	0	0	0	0	0	0	0			0	----
Charles Hasson	1B	1	0	0	0	0	0	0	0			0	----

PITCHERS	W	L	PCT	G	GS	CG	SH	IP	H	BB	SO	ERA
Charles Barrett	20	12	.625	36	34	25	7	268	219	60	114	2.05
Nate Andrews	16	12	.571	31	31	21	7	224	202	79	123	2.93
Ewell Blackwell	15	10	.600	29	27	20	4	227	168	79	87	2.02

SYRACUSE (cont.)
Chiefs

PITCHERS	W	L	PCT	G	GS	CG	SH	IP	H	BB	SO	ERA
Tommy De la Cruz	13	14	.481	32	27	11	3	176	161	56	98	3.94
Clayton Lambert	7	3	.700	37	9	7	3	132	110	42	60	1.91
Les Hinckle	2	4	.333	12	5	1	0	47	57	20	21	4.98
Lynn Nelson	2	5	.286	21	4	0	0	56	92	16	21	6.91
Ben Wade	2	11	.154	25	12	3	0	96	82	67	53	5.86
Jim Konstanty	1	0	1.000	5				20	19	14	9	5.85
William Schultz	0	3	.000	5				26	27	17	8	
Earl Harrist	0	0	----	13	0	0	0	26	19	24	18	4.15

JERSEY CITY   4th   77-75   .507   -14.5   Frank Snyder
Giants

BATTERS	POS-GAMES	GP	AB	R	H	BI	2B	3B	HR	BB	SO	SB	BA
Napolean Reyes	1B90,2B13	109	370	48	89	25	11	2	0	24	50	11	.241
Connie Ryan	2B112	112	374	40	91	51	11	5	1	50	37	4	.243
Robert Westfall	SS109	117	365	36	85	40	10	3	2	37	62	9	.233
Joseph Orengo	3B129,2B24	154	537	78	133	50	26	5	10	75	83	13	.248
John Rucker	OF145	148	578	79	165	37	34	5	4	34	64	26	.285
Sid Gordon	OF127,3B12,2B,SS,P1	145	517	68	155	85	17	5	10	61	33	15	.300
Tony Bongiovanni	OF	(see multi-team players)											
Hugh Poland	C120	121	374	33	102	36	19	2	0	36	24	5	.273
Gil Brack	OF61,1B16	88	256	37	75	23	11	3	2	19	35	4	.293
John Kerr	SS55,3B17	78	228	18	43	21	5	0	1	16	12	3	.189
Norm Jaeger	1B55	65	225	26	71	31	5	4	0	19	18	5	.316
Floyd Beal	C54	59	141	8	30	15	2	0	1	13	17	0	.213
Sal Maglie	P50	50	47	3	4	0	2	0	0	5	11	0	.085
Raymond Coombs	P33	36	84	4	13	4	1	0	0	13	12	0	.155
Austin Knickerbocker	OF27	30	101	12	30	12	3	0	4	10	10	0	.297
Hugh East	P29	29	61	1	14	4	3	0	0	3	16	1	.230
John Wittig	P27	28	46	5	10	2	1	0	0	0	8	0	.217
Murray Howell	OF26	26	85	11	24	16	3	0	1	12	16	1	.282
Reuben Fischer	P22	22	34	3	5	3	0	0	1	2	8	0	.147
Warren Pickell	P18	20	21	2	5	5	0	0	0	4	6	0	.238
James Maynard	OF18	18	70	9	23	11	4	1	3	6	5	2	.329
Ken Jungels	P18	18	37	4	7	4	1	0	1	2	7	0	.189
Warren Sandel	P18	18	17	0	1	0	0	0	0	0	9	0	.059
Norbert Barker	OF10	17	40	1	11	2	1	0	0	6	3	0	.275
Frank Stasey	OF13	14	43	3	10	3	0	0	0	6	7	0	.233
Adrian Zabala	P14	14	24	4	7	0	2	0	0	4	6	0	.292
David Koslo	P12	13	23	0	4	1	1	0	0	1	12	0	.174
William Harris	P11	11	15	0	2	2	0	0	0	0	3	0	.133
Jess Danna	P5	5											.200
James Gladd	C	4	7	1	2	0	1	1	0			0	.286
George Bausewein	P3	3											.000
Nick Butcher	P3	3											.000
Rene Monteagudo	P1	3											.000
Sheldon Jones	P2	2											.250
Howard DiMartini	P2	2											.000
Frank Snyder		1											.000

PITCHERS	W	L	PCT	G	GS	CG	SH	IP	H	BB	SO	ER
Raymond Coombs	17	11	.607	33	31	24	6	258	230	50	90	**1.99**
John Wittig	11	10	.524	27	18	9	3	133	98	84	63	3.45
Hugh East	10	10	.500	29	25	15	4	194	165	101	86	2.64
Sal Maglie	9	6	.600	50	7	4	0	165	142	74	92	2.78
Reuben Fischer	8	7	.533	22	19	7	3	108	104	75	66	4.00
Ken Jungels	6	8	.429	18	17	8	0	106	104	54	45	3.65
William Harris	4	3	.571	11	3	3	1	42	41	10	12	3.86
David Koslo	3	2	.600	12	8	2	1	60	53	38	48	3.00
Warren Pickell	3	5	.375	18	9	3	0	74	67	44	33	4.50
Adrian Zabala	3	5	.375	14	10	6	1	75	72	30	25	3.12
Warren Sandel	3	6	.333	18	8	2	0	55	58	50	25	5.40
Jess Danna	0	0	----	4				9	16	10	2	
George Bausewein	0	0	----	3				4	3	5	2	
Nick Butcher	0	0	----	3				11	9	10	7	
Howard DiMartini	0	0	----	2				2	6	2	0	
Sheldon Jones	0	0	----	2				10	9	9	2	1.80
Rene Monteagudo	0	0	----	1				2	2	4	1	
Sid Gordon	0	0	----	1				1	2	1	0	

BALTIMORE   5th   75-77   .493   -16.5   Alphonse Thomas
Orioles

BATTERS	POS-GAMES	GP	AB	R	H	BI	2B	3B	HR	BB	SO	SB	BA
Eddie Robinson	1B143	143	526	83	161	104	21	7	27	52	51	3	.306
Ted Sczepkowski	2B91	106	362	24	83	35	11	3	3	10	50	4	.229
Jack Conway	SS54	54	217	25	51	17	11	4	3	14	12	1	.235
Bob Lemon	3B147	148	596	95	160	80	23	8	21	45	54	7	.268
Henry Edwards	OF137	137	496	82	132	69	18	5	18	68	53	6	.266
George Staller	OF122	129	442	56	125	72	12	2	20	39	54	13	.283
Delbert Jones	OF80	92	294	44	71	30	5	3	0	35	18	9	.242
Joseph Becker	C115	124	358	37	96	32	15	1	4	58	57	3	.268
Sherry Robertson	SS30,OF28,2B,1B,3B	96	248	41	51	38	6	1	14	37	58	4	.206
Harold Sieling	OF43,SS29	86	295	53	79	29	14	0	8	56	30	6	.268
John Bell	2B49	55	173	18	34	9	4	0	0	21	7	0	.197
Ken Trinkle	P47	47	51	4	5	1	0	0	0	10	24	0	.098
Russ Niller	P31	42	35	3	4	1	0	0	0	2	7	0	.114
Ray Flanigan	P37	38	62	3	6	3	0	0	0	5	21	0	.097
Les McGarity	C26	36	85	8	15	7	1	0	0	7	6	1	.176
Elmer Burkart	P36	36	41	3	8	3	1	2	0	1	17	0	.195
Clyde Smoll	P35	35	37	4	3	2	1	0	1	6	19	0	.081
Earl Center	P34	34	68	2	7	3	0	0	0	6	30	0	.103
Joseph Kracher	C17	31	76	6	23	15	8	1	1	7	11	0	.303
Robert Repass	SS30	30	108	15	33	10	8	2	2	8	12	2	.306
Robert Hamilton	OF15	25	57	9	13	7	2	0	0	10	9	1	.228
Steve Gromek	P20	23	22	1	2	1	1	0	0	1	5	0	.091
Joe Krakauskas	P21	21	34	8	6	2	1	0	0	7	9	0	.176
Mike Naymick	P20	20	26	1	2	3	0	0	0	0	7	0	.077
Alex Ronay	P20	20	8	3	1	0	0	0	0	2	5	0	.125
Raymond Roche	P19	19	8	1	2	0	0	0	0	1	3	0	.250
Richard Waldt	P12	12	4	2	1	0	0	0	0	1	3	0	.250
Bob Seeds	OF	11	28	1	4	4	1	0	0	3	3	0	.143
Mike Kardash	SS	9	29	1	4	0	1	0	0			0	.138
Horace Brightman	C	7	15	0	4	1	0	0	0			0	.267
John Langgood	OF,SS	6	8	1	2	0	0	0	0			0	.250
Jim Hegan	C	4	8	1	2	0	1	0	0			0	.250
George Cave	P1	1											.000

PITCHERS		W	L	PCT	G	GS	CG	SH	IP	H	BB	SO	ERA
Ken Trinkle		14	13	.519	47	20	13	0	175	192	47	63	3.81
Earl Center		13	12	.520	34	28	15	1	214	182	103	128	3.70
Ray Flanigan		11	15	.423	37	21	7	1	179	186	78	92	3.72
Clyde Smoll		9	9	.500	35	20	8	2	140	142	54	71	3.86
Joe Krakauskas		8	4	.667	21	18	7	1	104	111	52	63	3.72
Elmer Burkart		6	8	.429	36	10	4	2	123	118	35	42	3.80
Steve Gromek		4	6	.400	20	7	2	0	63	74	24	54	5.14
Raymond Roche		3	2	.600	19	4	2	0	46	45	18	23	5.09
Russ Niller		3	2	.600	31	9	2	1	79	83	56	18	5.47
Mike Naymick		3	5	.375	20	15	2	0	73	62	52	31	5.67
Alex Ronay		1	1	.500	20	0	0	0	45	55	17	14	5.20
Richard Waldt		0	0	----	12	0	0	0	22	34	19	9	9.00
George Cave		0	0	----	1				3	3	3	0	

TORONTO   6th   74-79   .484   -18   Burleigh Grimes
Maple Leafs

BATTERS	POS-GAMES	GP	AB	R	H	BI	2B	3B	HR	BB	SO	SB	BA
Joe Mack	1B	(see multi-team players)											
Burgess Whitehead	2B146	148	528	75	137	46	9	6	1	64	56	26	.259
Edgar Leip	SS105	117	407	56	93	33	11	3	1	54	31	33	.229
Al Rubeling	3B134	136	483	67	123	59	19	7	11	42	42	15	.255
John Wyrostek	OF155	155	562	85	152	79	14	3	18	78	53	17	.270
Frank Colman	OF116	119	413	48	124	62	23	2	7	42	24	18	.300
James Russell	OF61,1B35	99	312	52	92	40	19	2	2	54	35	14	.295
Edward Fernandes	C56	79	167	26	36	18	10	2	4	68	32	5	.216
Floyd Yount	OF28,SS22,C15	86	218	19	47	24	11	1	0	32	39	8	.216
Lee Handley	1B37	69	170	16	36	19	4	2	0	20	12	2	.212
Lynn Myers	SS32,3B19	58	183	21	42	15	5	0	0	17	23	5	.230
Marvin Felderman	C49	53	133	12	29	11	0	0	0	19	14	2	.218
Harry Shuman	P49	49	42	2	2	1	0	0	0	5	17	0	.048
Richard Conger	P49	49	26	2	4	2	2	0	0	1	7	0	.154
Jack Hallett	P38	39	75	4	19	11	2	1	1	2	12	0	.253
William Brandt	P35	36	84	7	17	6	1	0	0	1	5	0	.202
Nick Strincevich	P34	35	67	8	13	4	2	1	0	6	8	0	.194

TORONTO (cont.)
Maple Leafs

BATTERS	POS-GAMES	GP	AB	R	H	BI	2B	3B	HR	BB	SO	SB	BA
Stewart Hofferth	C33	33	102	5	23	13	3	0	0	7	7	1	.225
Nick Gregory	OF28	28	84	11	19	6	2	0	3	7	7	2	.226
Joseph Sullivan	P27	28	43	1	6	0	1	0	0	3	10	0	.140
Robert Bowman	P22	22	5	0	1	0	0	0	0	0	2	0	.200
Robert Latshaw	1B16	19	47	9	14	6	2	1	1	12	11	3	.298
Dewey Williams	C11	16	31	4	5	4	0	0	1	5	5	1	.161
William Jackson		12	26	0	3	1	1	0	0	1	3	0	.115
Emmett O'Neill	P11	11	13	1	2	2	1	0	0	0	6	0	.154
Thomas Drake	P6	6											.000
James Bucher	3B	5	8	0	2	0	0	0	0			0	.250
John Gee	P5	5											.083
Walker Cress	P5	5											.000
James Kerr	P5	5											.000
John Tyler	PH	3	3	0	1	1	0	0	0			0	.333
Mike Haslin	3B	2	5	0	1	0	0	0	0			0	.200
George Gill	P2	2											.000

PITCHERS	W	L	PCT	G	GS	CG	SH	IP	H	BB	SO	ERA
William Brandt	15	11	.577	35	27	13	2	216	225	56	98	3.08
Nick Strincevich	12	10	.545	34	27	14	4	199	191	59	86	2.40
Harry Shuman	12	11	.522	49	18	8	0	170	161	71	108	3.18
Jack Hallett	11	16	.407	38	28	15	3	219	171	72	187	2.88
Richard Conger	6	3	.667	49	5	1	0	114	100	41	71	3.39
Joseph Sullivan	6	14	.300	27	20	8	0	129	122	46	46	3.07
Emmett O'Neill	3	4	.429	11	7	3	0	41	42	27	30	3.73
John Gee	2	2	.500	5				34	32	13	6	
Robert Bowman	2	1	.667	22	0	0	0	36	30	27	16	5.75
James Kerr	1	0	1.000	5				5	10	6	1	
Thomas Drake	1	2	.333	6				34	34	15	4	
Walker Cress	0	1	.000	5				13	16	11	7	6.23
George Gill	0	0	----	2				2	1	1	0	0.00

BUFFALO   7th   73-80   .477   -19   Albert Vincent
Bisons

BATTERS	POS-GAMES	GP	AB	R	H	BI	2B	3B	HR	BB	SO	SB	BA
Mike Rocco	1B103	103	364	61	108	82	9	1	23	53	23	5	.297
Lambert Meyer	2B140	140	488	85	139	89	25	3	20	67	50	12	.285
James Levey	SS147	148	582	81	146	41	24	1	12	43	55	13	.251
James Outlaw	3B121.OF12	136	486	56	128	43	16	2	5	47	37	9	.263
Mayo Smith	OF154	154	549	100	153	63	27	2	11	95	45	16	.279
Ed Kobesky	OF113	121	382	52	111	75	18	1	19	58	28	7	.290
John Welaj	OF100,3B22	130	456	81	141	57	18	4	11	50	40	30	.309
Jack Redmond	C95	100	297	38	80	45	20	0	14	41	25	4	.269
Henry Steinbacher	OF78	91	259	30	64	21	10	0	4	34	34	3	.247
Robert Garbark	C57	72	189	18	45	19	8	0	4	14	6	0	.238
Frank Heller	1B49	65	205	19	54	27	9	2	3	18	18	1	.263
Andrew Sierra	P48	49	68	4	12	8	2	0	1	8	19	0	.176
Rufus Gentry	P40	41	61	3	14	6	1	1	0	2	13	0	.230
Thomas Pullig	P40	41	69	7	10	3	0	0	0	4	25	0	.145
John Tising	P39	39	46	4	10	2	0	0	0	1	12	0	.217
Floyd Giebell	P22	38	69	7	14	5	2	0	0	3	8	0	.203
Lyn Lary	3B11	38	56	6	11	6	2	0	2	4	12	0	.196
Luther Thomas	P30	32	31	1	2	1	0	0	0	1	13	0	.065
Al Ott	P29	31	17	1	2	1	1	0	0	1	10	0	.118
George Barley	P29	30	32	3	3	0	0	0	0	7	17	0	.094
Robert Boken	2B,3B,SS	23	42	4	10	10	1	0	1	7	3	1	.238
Mike Roscoe	P23	23	25	3	6	2	1	0	0	8	6	0	.240
Sam Holbrook	C20	20	54	5	8	5	2	0	1	10	9	0	.148
John O'Neill		15	41	2	5	1	0	0	0	6	4	0	.122
Earl Rapp	OF	9	22	3	4	3	1	0	0			0	.182
Charles Medlar	P7	7											.000
Robert Witt	SS	7	7	1	0	0	0	0	0			0	.000
Albert Vincent	2B,C	6	4	2	0	0	0	0	0			0	.000
John Pollock	PH	1	1	0	0	0	0	0	0			0	.000
Newt Waldstein	P1	1											.000

PITCHERS	W	L	PCT	G	GS	CG	SH	IP	H	BB	SO	ERA
Andrew Sierra	17	11	.607	48	26	16	3	208	188	98	141	3.50
Thomas Pullig	13	11	.542	40	26	11	0	198	219	57	84	4.00

BUFFALO (cont.)
Bisons

PITCHERS	W	L	PCT	G	GS	CG	SH	IP	H	BB	SO	ERA
Rufus Gentry	10	13	.435	40	23	11	1	180	128	122	80	5.65
Floyd Giebell	8	6	.571	22	15	9	2	139	128	75	42	3.69
John Tising	8	14	.364	39	19	5	0	148	165	67	72	4.80
Luther Thomas	7	8	.467	30	16	7	0	115	140	16	30	4.46
Mike Roscoe	5	6	.455	23	10	3	0	85	93	41	23	5.19
Al Ott	3	2	.600	29	5	0	0	66	78	48	24	6.82
George Barley	2	9	.182	29	14	3	0	117	149	44	42	5.38
Charles Medlar	0	0	----	7				11	18	2	2	
Newt Waldstein	0	0	----	1				1	4	1	0	

ROCHESTER   8th   59-93   .388   -32.5   Tony Kaufmann - Estel
Red Wings   Crabtree - Ray Hayworth

BATTERS	POS-GAMES	GP	AB	R	H	BI	2B	3B	HR	BB	SO	SB	BA
Harry Davis	1B127	127	423	58	104	57	23	2	7	76	43	4	.246
George Fallon	2B139	139	524	62	126	49	19	7	2	59	49	8	.240
Robert Blattner	SS87	95	307	47	75	25	7	5	4	63	41	9	.244
Gene Lillard	3B104,P3	107	383	64	100	62	16	2	11	56	66	0	.261
Allen Cooke	OF105	124	380	52	88	33	16	1	2	67	50	2	.232
Erv Dusak	OF80,SS37	122	426	79	126	57	19	6	16	55	63	4	.296
James Ripple	OF	(see multi-team players)											
Warren Robinson	C93	98	302	32	77	36	9	2	3	33	40	2	.255
Ora Burnett	OF51,SS14,3B14	102	344	35	87	35	6	4	3	19	43	5	.253
Hooper Triplett	OF63	71	235	33	64	35	11	1	3	25	32	0	.272
Louis Sakas	P55	55	13	1	2	4	1	0	0	1	5	0	.154
Roy Pfleger	1B27,3B14	46	142	20	40	20	7	1	2	10	9	0	.282
Ed Wissman	P29	44	84	10	23	6	4	1	0	6	14	0	.274
Sam Narron	C37	40	136	11	35	19	6	1	4	7	10	0	.257
Ray Hayworth	C33	35	99	5	19	9	4	0	0	9	8	0	.192
Matt Surkont	P32	32	61	4	11	8	3	0	0	5	14	0	.180
Ira Hutchinson	P31	31	85	3	10	4	0	0	0	3	24	0	.118
Clem Dreisewerd	P31	31	32	0	4	0	2	0	0	2	11	0	.125
Frank Pearce	P24	24	25	1	1	0	0	0	0	0	10	0	.040
Charles Aleno	3B21	23	81	9	22	5	6	0	0	5	3	0	.272
Rolland LeBlanc	OF10	23	45	5	12	4	1	0	0	4	7	0	.267
Joffre Cross	SS16	16	61	10	8	2	0	0	0	8	9	1	.131
Al Jurisch	P14	14	35	1	3	4	0	0	0	4	12	0	.086
Jean Roy	P13	14	30	4	7	4	0	0	1	0	6	0	.233
Michael Clark	P13	13	5	0	1	0	0	0	0	0	1	0	.200
Don White		10	16	4	0	1	0	0	0	2	3	0	.000
Cliff Hopkins	P9	10	15	3	4	1	0	0	0	1	7	0	.267
George Dockins	P9	10	12	0	1	0	0	0	0	1	1	0	.083
Charles Adams	SS	7	25	2	4	0	0	0	0			1	.160
Estel Crabtree	OF	7	15	1	1	1	0	0	0			0	.067
John Clay	P5	5											.500

PITCHERS	W	L	PCT	G	GS	CG	SH	IP	H	BB	SO	ERA
Ira Hutchinson	13	13	.500	31	29	18	2	222	**241**	74	72	3.73
Ed Wissman	10	12	.455	29	23	12	0	186	195	70	71	4.45
Matt Surkont	10	18	.357	32	29	12	0	193	182	107	94	5.04
Louis Sakas	5	3	.625	55	0	0	1	86	84	37	20	2.72
Al Jurisch	4	8	.333	14	14	5	0	101	101	62	65	4.19
George Dockins	3	3	.500	9				43	38	20	14	
Jean Roy	3	5	.375	13	10	5	0	82	73	33	29	3.62
Gene Lillard	1	1	.500	3				16	16	8	13	
Cliff Hopkins	1	3	.250	9				33	33	22	21	
Clem Dreisewerd	1	14	.067	31	15	5	0	111	130	35	46	5.19
John Clay	0	1	.000	5				7	11	5	3	
Michael Clark	0	2	.000	13	3	0	0	23	33	22	6	7.83
Frank Pearce	0	6	.000	24	7	3	0	77	102	22	12	5.73

MULTI-TEAM PLAYERS

BATTERS	POS-GAMES	TEAMS	GP	AB	R	H	BI	2B	3B	HR	BB	SO	SB	BA
James Ripple	OF127	RO78-TO57	135	477	61	119	72	24	1	14	35	37	4	.249
Joe Mack	1B73,OF30	TO79-RO29	108	316	48	73	36	17	2	4	74	48	11	.231
Tony Bongiovanni	OF72	SY7-JC88	95	240	31	44	24	8	3	3	32	8	3	.183

MULTI-TEAM PLAYERS (cont.)

BATTERS	POS-GAMES	TEAMS	GP	AB	R	H	BI	2B	3B	HR	BB	SO	SB	BA
William Rabe	OF83	RO56-BA36	92	275	39	59	41	9	1	11	43	49	6	.215
Bill Nagel	OF29	SY8-TO30	38	118	10	22	11	4	2	3	5	22	0	.186
William Beckmann	P24	TO10-RO14	24	57	2	7	4	0	0	0	5	12	0	.123
Paul Mulach	P15	MO3-TO12	15	7	0	0	0	0	0	0	0	0	0	.000
James Davis	P5	TO2-NE3	5	2	0	0	0	0	0	0	0	2	0	.000

PITCHERS		TEAMS	W	L	PCT	G	GS	CG	SH	IP	H	BB	SO	ERA
William Beckmann		TO10-RO14	11	6	.647	24	22	11	2	149	151	42	53	3.62
James Davis		TO2-NE3	1	2	.333	5				10	13	8	2	9.00
Paul Mulach		MO3-TO12	0	1	.000	15	0	0	0	28	30	15	19	4.82

TEAM BATTING

TEAMS	GP	AB	R	H	BI	2B	3B	HR	BB	SO	SB	BA
NEWARK	154	5070	851	1403	772	219	46	146	583	621	165	.277
MONTREAL	156	4934	687	1242	593	226	43	110	629	628	98	.252
SYRACUSE	153	4845	567	1138	505	176	45	60	556	569	60	.235
JERSEY CITY	157	4959	561	1254	505	182	39	44	489	585	102	.253
BALTIMORE	152	4910	650	1213	597	170	39	128	540	667	64	.247
TORONTO	155	4796	598	1153	530	164	37	65	612	544	166	.240
BUFFALO	154	4906	676	1280	620	197	17	131	582	518	105	.261
ROCHESTER	155	4957	632	1203	562	188	34	70	595	665	41	.243
	618	39377	5222	9886	4684	1522	300	754	4586	4797	801	.251

1943
DEADBALL REDUX

During one season in the 1940s, International League batters seemed to forget how to hit the ball. During this season, only four regulars managed to cross the .300 barrier. On the other hand, a dozen pitchers posted earned run averages under 2.50. This wasn't a nostalgic return to the halcyon days of the deadball era. There was a logical explanation to the hitting downturn, and it had nothing to do with a trend in the game. Instead, it was based on events completely out of baseball's control.

By the early 1940s, the United States and its allies were embroiled in World War II, facing down Germany, Italy, and Japan. Early in the war, the Japanese Empire took control of the East Indies in Southeast Asia. This action deprived the United States and others of several resources native to Southeast Asia. Among these resources was rubber.

Baseballs are made of several different materials. The outer covering is leather. Further in, one finds yarn wrapped around an inner core of cork and rubber. It is the rubber that gives the balls zip and life.

Without a ready supply of rubber, World War II era baseball manufacturers needed to find a substitute. They turned to a substance called balata. This synthetic rubber, used mostly in golf balls, duplicated the feel but did not yield the same results. "Balata balls," as they were known, did not act the same when struck. They did not travel as fast or as far as normal rubber-cored baseballs.

The 1943 International League experienced the full effect of the balata ball. The league as whole batted .245, the lowest total in 35 years. Only 390 International League home runs were struck—half of the usual total. As a result, pitching enjoyed a renaissance, with more than 50 shutouts tossed by league hurlers.

After several moribund seasons, the Toronto Maple Leafs bounced to the top rung in 1943. Newark, Syracuse, and Montreal finished in the other three playoff spots, while Rochester, Baltimore, Buffalo, and Jersey City ended up out of the hunt. Red Schoendienst of Rochester batted .337 to lead International batsmen. Buffalo's Ed Kobesky with 18 home runs and Baltimore's George Staller with 98 runs batted in were the lowest league leaders in 20 years. Ed Klieman from Baltimore pitched the most wins (23), Lou Polli of Jersey City had the lowest earned run average (1.85), and Baltimore's Steve Gromek struck out the most batters (188).

In the latter years of World War II, as rubber became more available, rubber-cored baseballs were gradually reintroduced in the International League, ending the dearth of hitting. In theory, a synthetic rubber baseball should have proved a worthy substitute. In reality, to International League batters, the balata ball was far from satisfactory, not remotely resembling the real thing.

TORONTO
Maple Leafs

1st   95-57   .625   Burleigh Grimes

BATTERS	POS-GAMES	GP	AB	R	H	BI	2B	3B	HR	BB	SO	SB	BA
Harry Davis	1B148	148	477	62	139	64	27	1	6	96	15	18	.291
Charles Letchas	2B141	142	523	81	135	47	14	3	2	55	17	15	.258
Frank Zak	SS148	150	544	101	134	22	9	1	0	104	46	22	.246
Lee Handley	3B84	84	290	35	70	30	11	3	0	26	19	4	.241
James Ripple	OF91	92	317	40	83	52	16	1	8	50	16	2	.262
Maurice Van Robays	OF83	84	308	44	93	51	14	4	4	38	24	7	.302
Lee Gamble	OF65	65	243	29	70	19	7	3	1	11	15	6	.288
Dewey Williams	C89	98	253	27	61	23	6	4	0	26	25	6	.241
Herb Crompton	C89	95	269	15	66	31	13	1	2	22	10	2	.245
James Gruzdis	OF62	95	233	32	60	36	14	0	2	33	25	18	.258
Al Rubeling	3B62,OF31	94	343	42	91	51	14	2	3	44	24	12	.265
Red Kress	P15,3B12,2B11,1B10	67	169	14	45	10	7	1	2	18	15	1	.266
Gus Dugas	OF30	48	113	23	32	27	8	0	3	26	11	4	.283
Ralph Kiner	OF42	43	144	22	34	13	6	2	2	31	25	4	.236
James Tyack	OF41	41	146	20	37	12	5	1	3	18	9	4	.253
James Hopper	P36	36	73	4	11	2	0	0	0	6	17	2	.151
Nick Strincevich	P35	35	77	1	8	5	0	0	0	8	20	0	.104
Al Jarlett	P33	34	54	4	7	5	1	0	0	7	14	0	.130
Frank Colman	OF30	33	109	14	34	19	3	2	3	11	8	0	.312
Luke Hamlin	P31	31	83	5	11	3	2	0	0	3	22	0	.133
Richard Conger	P22	22	53	2	7	2	1	0	0	4	8	1	.132
Harry Shuman	P22	22	13	0	0	0	0	0	0	0	6	0	.000
Lloyd Brown	P17	18	7	1	1	1	1	0	0	1	1	0	.143
Joseph Sullivan	P13	14	33	3	4	2	2	0	0	0	3	0	.121
Ralph McCabe	P13	13	14	1	0	0	0	0	0	0	3	0	.000
Sid Goldstein	P8	8											.000
Woodrow Fair	2B,3B,SS	6	24	3	7	0	1	0	0			1	.292
George Eyrich	P2	2											.000
Joseph Rolla	3B	1	5	1	0	0	0	0	0			0	.000
William Schaedler	OF	1	4	0	0	0	0	0	0			0	.000

PITCHERS		W	L	PCT	G	GS	CG	SH	IP	H	BB	SO	ERA
Luke Hamlin		21	8	.724	31	29	19	8	227	186	46	108	2.14
Nick Strincevich		15	7	.682	35	29	16	6	233	203	47	113	2.47
James Hopper		15	9	.625	36	28	16	4	219	183	101	103	2.63
Al Jarlett		13	7	.650	33	21	9	1	170	159	62	88	2.59
Richard Conger		11	6	.647	22	16	13	0	156	130	47	72	1.96
Joseph Sullivan		6	7	.462	13	12	4	0	91	78	30	27	3.66
Harry Shuman		4	3	.571	22	2	2	1	48	41	22	19	2.06
Red Kress		3	2	.600	15	1	1	0	40	36	15	13	3.15
Ralph McCabe		2	1	.667	13	4	0	0	43	28	41	17	2.73
Lloyd Brown		2	4	.333	17	2	1	1	28	36	17	11	4.50
Sid Goldstein		0	1	.000	8				15	13	6	6	
George Eyrich		0	0	.000	2				2	2	1	0	

NEWARK
Bears

2nd   85-68   .556   -10.5   Bill Meyer

BATTERS	POS-GAMES	GP	AB	R	H	BI	2B	3B	HR	BB	SO	SB	BA
Eugene Corbett	1B151	152	561	77	135	56	22	5	6	68	37	10	.241
Joe Buzas	2B76,3B46,SS26	148	509	50	112	54	11	2	2	29	50	24	.220
Don Savage	SS123,3B21	146	496	72	128	74	21	2	16	47	90	23	.258
Richard Korte	3B67,2B26	100	386	44	104	25	13	5	1	29	25	21	.269
Lawrence Rosenthal	OF145	145	485	79	132	78	29	9	11	98	57	6	.272
Edward Levy	OF138	144	512	75	165	81	31	8	12	59	47	15	.322
Frank Silvanic	OF75	88	225	36	46	33	8	1	6	44	38	1	.204
Mike Garbark	C114	116	326	40	74	40	5	0	6	66	23	5	.227
Joseph Dwyer	OF74	94	252	25	69	14	8	0	3	41	13	1	.274
Charles Marleau	P42	42	14	1	2	2	0	0	0	1	4	0	.143
Ray Viers	2B41	41	144	15	26	11	2	0	0	14	22	2	.181
Russ Derry	OF39	40	153	24	48	19	11	1	6	9	29	2	.314
Walt Dubiel	P26	39	66	9	8	7	1	0	0	3	13	0	.121
Harry Taylor		39	42	6	10	5	1	0	0	7	2	0	.238
Joe Page	P28	32	74	5	16	6	1	0	0	1	20	0	.216
William Cronin	C31	31	75	4	8	3	0	0	0	10	9	1	.107
James Davis	P31	31	68	6	13	10	1	0	2	4	22	0	.191
Frank Hiller	P25	28	60	7	14	6	0	0	0	1	7	0	.233
Jerry Crosby		28	53	9	17	5	1	0	0	8	4	3	.321
Ken Holcombe	P28	28	53	4	10	1	1	0	0	4	12	0	.189
Emerson Roser	P28	28	53	1	7	3	0	0	1	0	14	0	.132

NEWARK (cont.)
Bears

BATTERS	POS-GAMES	GP	AB	R	H	BI	2B	3B	HR	BB	SO	SB	BA
Alfred Clark	2B16,OF10	24	73	2	16	7	1	0	0	5	7	0	.219
Aaron Robinson	C17	19	55	7	15	11	1	0	4	11	3	3	.273
Phil Page	P17	17	4	0	0	0	0	0	0	0	0	0	.000
John Fallon	P16	16	11	1	3	0	0	0	0	0	5	0	.273
William Drescher	C	7	15	2	4	3	0	0	0			0	.267
Stan Platek	OF	4	11	1	3	1	0	0	0			0	.273
Frank Dunlap	C	3	3	1	2	2	0	0	0			0	.667
Clem Hausmann	P2	2											.000
Peter Kunis	P2	2											.000
John Rager	P2	2											.000
Robert Miller	P1	1											.000

PITCHERS	W	L	PCT	G	GS	CG	SH	IP	H	BB	SO	ERA
Walt Dubiel	16	9	.640	26	23	16	6	192	140	64	94	2.02
Joe Page	14	5	.737	28	23	16	3	186	132	119	140	3.05
James Davis	13	11	.542	31	24	13	2	198	178	99	107	2.77
Emerson Roser	12	10	.545	28	26	10	1	162	151	89	94	3.61
Frank Hiller	10	8	.556	25	24	12	1	175	136	77	73	2.67
Ken Holcombe	9	7	.563	28	20	9	0	160	134	97	84	3.66
Charles Marleau	5	5	.500	42	0	0	0	84	85	26	24	2.79
Clem Hausmann	1	0	1.000	2				9	5	1	6	2.00
Phil Page	1	1	.500	17	0	0	0	27	28	9	14	2.67
John Fallon	0	6	.000	16	5	0	0	45	62	20	15	7.80
Peter Kunis	0	0	----	2				1	3	1	1	9.00
John Rager	0	0	----	2				4	3	4	1	1.80
Robert Miller	0	0	----	1				2	2	3	1	

SYRACUSE   3rd   82-71   .536   -13.5   Jewel Ens
Chiefs

BATTERS	POS-GAMES	GP	AB	R	H	BI	2B	3B	HR	BB	SO	SB	BA
Hank Sauer	1B111,OF43	154	571	73	157	75	32	9	12	56	62	8	.275
Roland Harrington	2B133	134	498	70	145	38	21	7	5	36	35	52	.291
Damon Phillips	SS128	129	372	38	76	23	11	3	1	22	27	4	.204
Garton Del Savio	3B120,SS39	148	530	43	127	45	7	4	0	45	29	7	.240
Goody Rosen	OF151	151	565	85	156	46	28	9	5	79	38	15	.276
Al Mele	OF126	132	449	49	113	67	19	2	8	71	22	6	.252
Frank Kelleher	OF108	108	375	49	92	57	16	1	11	58	55	6	.245
Richard West	C89	104	336	36	83	30	26	5	4	28	41	14	.247
Len Rice	C64	75	240	21	57	26	5	0	3	15	14	14	.238
Antonio Rodriguez	3B39,2B24	68	184	14	44	18	2	2	1	17	25	7	.239
Millard Howell	P28	60	115	10	27	11	4	2	2	3	24	0	.235
Walt Cazen	OF35	56	129	9	36	7	6	0	0	12	18	4	.279
Les Goldstein	1B35	42	121	16	29	15	8	1	1	17	14	2	.240
Tommy De la Cruz	P36	37	91	3	15	5	0	0	0	6	26	0	.165
Arnold Carter	P31	35	80	4	14	3	2	0	0	4	17	0	.175
William Schultz	P31	31	68	6	17	1	0	0	0	1	13	1	.250
Jim Konstanty	P29	29	55	4	10	2	0	0	0	1	16	2	.182
Horatio Bartleson	P28	28	48	4	8	3	0	0	0	3	6	0	.167
Milt Stroner	1B10	17	52	3	11	5	3	3	0	2	4	0	.212
Lynn Nelson	P16	16	7	0	2	0	0	0	0	1	0	0	.286
James Blackburn	P13	13	8	1	0	1	0	0	0	2	2	0	.000
Reg Grabowski	P4	4											.000
Como Cotelle	PH	4	4	1	0	0	0	0	0			0	.000
John Lohrey	P2	2											.000

PITCHERS	W	L	PCT	G	GS	CG	SH	IP	H	BB	SO	ERA
Tommy De la Cruz	21	11	.656	36	34	25	6	276	229	66	122	1.99
Arnold Carter	14	12	.538	31	30	21	7	222	195	72	61	2.35
Millard Howell	13	9	.591	28	22	18	4	191	155	123	106	3.11
Horatio Bartleson	12	9	.571	28	18	11	2	154	130	54	51	2.51
William Schultz	11	12	.478	31	27	15	3	208	177	81	85	2.60
Jim Konstanty	8	12	.400	29	21	14	0	166	144	72	45	3.42
Lynn Nelson	3	3	.500	16	0	0	0	28	20	6	12	0.96
Jim Blackburn	0	3	.000	13	2	0	0	39	40	20	11	5.31
Reg Grabowski	0	0	----	4				11	12	2	1	
John Lohrey	0	0	----	2				2	3	0	0	

MONTREAL Royals

4th 76-76 .500 -19 Lafayette Thompson

BATTERS	POS-GAMES	GP	AB	R	H	BI	2B	3B	HR	BB	SO	SB	BA
Alex Hooks	1B96	98	346	40	96	45	16	3	1	26	19	2	.277
Carl Barnhart	2B78,OF18,P1	120	342	47	84	26	10	2	4	34	26	4	.246
Al Campanis	SS103,2B42	148	468	57	97	44	15	1	2	70	71	9	.207
Leighton Kimball	3B134,P1	143	508	67	126	57	26	5	5	48	72	6	.249
Roberto Ortiz	OF152	152	560	85	170	86	40	11	10	44	58	11	.304
Ed Badke	OF110	117	396	45	106	51	16	2	1	48	63	5	.268
Luis Olmo	OF87	89	352	57	111	47	15	12	4	15	22	9	.315
Homer Howell	C103	110	374	47	97	42	14	2	4	43	45	15	.259
Jack Graham	1B51	51	175	42	52	38	11	2	14	35	18	4	.297
Dominic Castro	C34	47	121	6	28	11	5	1	2	4	17	2	.231
Bernard DeForge	P47	47	48	4	9	2	1	0	0	1	11	0	.188
Al Sherer	P42	42	72	1	12	3	2	0	0	7	15	0	.167
Bob Chipman	P35	38	74	12	19	5	3	0	0	9	15	0	.257
Boyd Bartley	SS34	34	107	14	28	10	3	0	0	16	12	1	.262
Wes Flowers	P31	32	78	4	11	5	0	0	0	3	12	0	.141
Gene Mauch	2B16,3B,SS	31	77	5	13	4	1	0	0	11	5	1	.169
John Corriden	OF22	29	84	6	21	7	4	2	0	8	15	2	.250
Max Macon	OF21,1B,P2	26	98	15	34	11	8	0	2	3	7	1	.347
Hal Gregg	P23	26	53	3	8	3	0	0	0	2	14	0	.151
Ed Spaulding	P26	26	19	1	4	1	1	0	0	1	1	0	.211
George Washburn	P7	25	39	6	6	4	0	0	1	2	7	0	.154
Fred Ankenman	2B12	20	73	6	16	6	2	0	0	12	6	0	.219
John Barkley	3B14	18	58	4	12	5	3	0	0	4	13	2	.207
Lou Rochelli	2B12	18	35	6	6	1	1	0	0	4	10	0	.171
Robert Frost	C12,P1	18	31	2	6	2	1	0	0	3	12	0	.194
William Webb	P14	14	23	4	4	1	1	0	0	2	8	0	.174
Robert Dews	C12	13	42	5	9	2	0	0	0	1	2	0	.214
Wayne Collins	P13	13	9	2	2	2	0	0	0	0	3	0	.222
Lloyd Dietz	P10	10	16	1	3	0	0	0	0	0	1	0	.188
James Babcock	SS	8	29	1	4	5	0	0	0			0	.138
Walt Chipple	OF	6	4	0	1	0	0	0	0			0	.250
Rex Barney	P4	4											.000
James Ginley	2B	3	1	0	0	0	0	0	0			0	.000
Norm Koney	OF	2	2	0	0	0	0	0	0			0	.000
Herb Gorman	1B	1	0	0	0	0	0	0	0			0	----

PITCHERS	W	L	PCT	G	GS	CG	SH	IP	H	BB	SO	ER
Bob Chipman	15	7	.682	35	30	16	4	222	196	116	75	3.08
Al Sherer	15	14	.517	42	29	18	2	225	192	68	82	2.76
Wes Flowers	13	13	.500	31	30	15	2	205	183	86	72	2.59
Hal Gregg	11	11	.500	23	19	11	2	145	127	90	66	3.17
Bernard DeForge	6	8	.417	31	8	3	0	109	94	81	35	3.47
William Webb	5	4	.556	14	9	4	1	69	74	18	15	3.65
Ed Spaulding	4	5	.444	26	7	1	0	79	83	42	23	4.44
Wayne Collins	2	2	.500	13	0	0	0	29	29	24	6	5.28
Lloyd Dietz	2	6	.250	10	8	5	0	60	55	22	21	2.85
George Washburn	1	2	.333	7				21	23	36	6	
Rex Barney	0	1	.000	4				22	19	18	18	2.45
Max Macon	0	0	----	2				14	8	4	4	
Leighton Kimball	0	0	----	1				2	4	2	0	
Carl Barnhart	0	0	----	1				1	0	0	0	
Robert Frost	0	0	----	1				0	5	0	0	

ROCHESTER Red Wings

5th 74-78 .487 -21 Pepper Martin

BATTERS	POS-GAMES	GP	AB	R	H	BI	2B	3B	HR	BB	SO	SB	BA
Joe Mack	1B98,OF15	115	354	48	93	51	10	4	9	75	44	4	.263
Steve Mizerak	2B63	92	222	14	47	17	4	2	1	36	32	1	.212
Red Schoendienst	SS136	136	555	81	187	37	21	5	6	38	19	20	.337
William Barnes	3B59,2B19	78	281	43	66	14	8	0	2	24	25	13	.235
Joseph King	OF118	123	398	51	111	32	17	3	0	24	46	8	.279
Earl Naylor	OF117,P1	118	431	63	110	57	15	9	4	42	51	29	.255
Paul Wargo	OF100,P12	116	376	39	102	43	18	3	3	26	71	7	.271
Gerald Burmeister	C110,P1	122	381	36	91	44	17	5	4	43	27	2	.239
Walt Alston	1B66,3B22	115	313	37	75	40	12	2	5	44	37	7	.240
Thomas Koval	OF77	86	273	32	66	37	14	4	5	27	59	4	.242
Del Rice	C59	66	182	14	36	18	5	3	0	6	31	3	.198
Herschel Held	2B31,3B18	51	173	15	39	13	6	2	0	13	17	0	.225
Pepper Martin	OF24,P4	49	82	16	23	12	2	1	1	13	14	5	.280

ROCHESTER (cont.)
Red Wings

BATTERS	POS-GAMES	GP	AB	R	H	BI	2B	3B	HR	BB	SO	SB	BA
Louis Sakas	P44	44	23	2	3	3	0	0	0	1	7	0	.130
William Trotter	P39	39	64	1	5	8	0	0	0	11	34	0	.078
Ira Hutchinson	P37	38	94	5	7	1	0	0	0	5	33	0	.075
Douglas White	3B35	36	117	8	22	13	2	2	2	9	9	3	.188
Kemp Wicker	P35	35	63	5	6	3	0	0	0	8	12	1	.095
Fred Schmidt	P34	34	65	5	6	8	1	1	0	7	25	0	.092
Dain Clay	OF22	32	125	13	33	6	8	2	0	15	8	8	.264
Maurice Sturdy	2B29	29	101	11	24	7	5	1	0	8	7	3	.238
Andrew Timko	2B21	30	57	6	8	12	1	0	0	11	4	1	.140
Syl Donnelly	P29	29	63	2	10	7	1	0	0	7	17	0	.159
Jean Roy	P18	28	23	5	6	2	1	0	0	1	4	0	.261
John Morrow		22	22	4	3	1	0	0	0	3	2	1	.136
Joseph Overman	OF17	20	59	3	11	5	3	0	0	3	8	2	.186
Bert Humphries	P8	8											.000
Francis Bartolomei	SS	6	14	3	2	2	0	0	0			0	.143
Steve Collins	SS	5	10	0	0	0	0	0	0			0	.000
Roy Pinkston	OF	3	7	0	1	0	0	0	0			0	.143
Floyd Beal	PH	2	2	0	0	0	0	0	0			0	.000
James Conboy	P1	1											.000
Robert Vetter	P1	1											.000

PITCHERS		W	L	PCT	G	GS	CG	SH	IP	H	BB	SO	ERA
Syl Donnelly		17	8	.680	29	26	15	5	191	138	116	134	2.40
Ira Hutchinson		17	11	.607	37	32	21	5	265	256	91	88	2.21
Fred Schmidt		13	10	.565	34	21	14	1	201	191	84	99	2.42
William Trotter		12	16	.429	39	30	15	2	226	227	41	77	2.59
Kemp Wicker		10	18	.357	35	29	13	1	216	228	86	70	2.79
Louis Sakas		3	3	.500	44	2	1	0	92	91	43	22	3.33
Jean Roy		2	8	.200	18	10	3	1	61	58	46	22	5.61
Paul Wargo		0	2	.000	12	1	0	0	28	28	18	15	5.46
Bert Humphries		0	2	.000	8				17	26	12	7	
Pepper Martin		0	0	----	4				8	13	10	3	
Gerald Burmeister		0	0	----	1				6	10	4	0	
Robert Vetter		0	0	----	1				2	2	2	1	
Earl Naylor		0	0	----	1				1	0	2	0	0.00
James Conboy		0	0	----	1				1	0	0	0	0.00

BALTIMORE   6th   73-81   .474   -23   Alphonse Thomas
Orioles

BATTERS	POS-GAMES	GP	AB	R	H	BI	2B	3B	HR	BB	SO	SB	BA
Blas Monaco	1B129,SS14	145	497	81	121	42	14	6	6	127	80	41	.243
John Bell	2B153	153	510	53	120	42	10	2	1	80	34	4	.235
Robert Repass	SS82	82	316	51	88	47	22	2	6	35	27	7	.228
Al Tiedemann	3B68,SS68	119	392	48	94	37	8	0	1	44	49	9	.240
George Staller	OF150	153	572	73	174	98	21	3	16	63	59	19	.304
Delbert Jones	OF147	151	550	82	120	45	17	1	0	80	37	23	.218
Felix Mackiewicz	OF80,1B19	109	375	47	90	41	10	3	3	29	53	9	.290
Joseph Becker	C76	81	242	21	56	21	7	0	1	36	30	2	.231
George Honochick	OF71	75	274	37	72	38	11	8	1	30	25	11	.263
Les McGarity	C40	74	144	9	28	18	5	2	0	19	14	0	.194
Ted Sepkowski	3B30,SS17	62	196	15	39	19	5	3	2	16	20	2	.199
Steve Gromek	P46	54	91	9	18	3	2	0	0	11	15	2	.198
John Pare	C43	52	124	13	28	9	6	0	1	33	22	0	.226
Rolland Van Slate	P50	50	66	3	12	3	2	0	1	9	15	0	.182
Burton Swift	P48	48	35	3	8	2	0	0	1	2	14	0	.229
Ed Klieman	P45	45	88	9	17	5	2	0	0	8	15	0	.193
Elmer Burkart	P33	33	40	1	6	3	0	0	1	1	13	0	.150
Harold Sieling	OF22	30	112	21	32	15	3	0	2	15	10	4	.286
Sterling Ecker	P26	26	7	0	0	0	0	0	0	0	3	0	.000
Clyde Smoll	P24	24	38	4	5	2	0	0	0	9	20	0	.132
Paul Calvert	P19	19	29	4	5	3	0	0	0	2	10	0	.172
Sherm Lollar	C12	12	34	3	4	1	0	0	0	7	6	0	.118
John Dornbush		11	13	1	3	1	0	0	0	4	3	0	.231
Al Heuser	P11	11	12	1	0	0	0	0	0	1	7	0	.000
Ed Sudol	PH	8	8	2	1	1	0	0	0			0	.125
Joseph Mueller	P6	7											.000
William Rabe	PH	5	5	1	1	0	0	0	0			0	.200
Mike Kardash	3B	4	11	1	1	0	0	0	0			0	.091
Ned Tryon	1B	3	10	1	3	0	0	0	0			0	.300
John Blum	OF	3	6	2	1	0	0	0	0			1	.167

BALTIMORE (cont.)
Orioles

BATTERS	POS-GAMES	GP	AB	R	H	BI	2B	3B	HR	BB	SO	SB	BA
Grover Roper	P3	3											.000
Sam Lamitina	3B	2	7	0	1	1	0	0	0			0	.143
Milt Stockhausen	C	2	3	0	1	0	0	0	0			0	.333
John Farley	P2	2											.000
Alphonse Thomas	P2	2											.000
Fred Pacitto	OF	1	4	0	0	0	0	0	0			0	.000
John Moesch		1											.000

PITCHERS		W	L	PCT	G	GS	CG	SH	IP	H	BB	SO	ERA
Ed Klieman		**23**	11	.676	45	32	17	2	276	245	103	105	2.84
Steve Gromek		16	13	.552	46	29	21	5	261	240	69	**188**	3.34
Rolland Van Slate		13	17	.433	**50**	29	11	3	238	213	109	131	4.05
Burton Swift		8	11	.421	48	12	4	0	128	140	49	41	3.80
Clyde Smoll		5	5	.500	24	18	5	1	120	121	44	52	3.30
Paul Calvert		4	11	.267	19	16	6	1	87	104	40	38	4.55
Elmer Burkart		3	9	.250	33	16	2	0	118	122	44	39	4.65
Al Heuser		1	2	.333	11	4	2	1	37	55	10	9	6.32
Sterling Ecker		0	1	.000	26	0	0	0	44	48	22	19	5.11
Joseph Mueller		0	1	.000	6				13	8	11	5	
Grover Roper		0	0	----	3				1	2	4	0	
Alphonse Thomas		0	0	----	2				3	2	1	1	
John Farley		0	0	----	2				4	0	5	1	0.00

BUFFALO   7th   66-87   .431   -29.5   Greg Mulleavy
Bisons

BATTERS	POS-GAMES	GP	AB	R	H	BI	2B	3B	HR	BB	SO	SB	BA
Frank Heller	1B86,3B32	122	422	43	102	44	14	2	2	44	32	4	.242
Gerald McNair	2B107,SS11	121	360	38	67	25	12	1	1	42	70	3	.186
Ed Turchin	SS97	97	360	42	77	19	9	1	1	47	35	10	.214
John Bero	3B51	55	199	23	48	27	11	3	3	16	22	5	.241
Mayo Smith	OF136	144	460	68	120	55	16	1	3	96	20	12	.261
Ed Kobesky	OF129	137	479	67	124	88	30	0	18	53	40	10	.259
James Outlaw	OF92,3B41	136	498	76	138	40	35	1	4	43	33	15	.277
Otto Denning	C66,1B17	112	376	52	107	58	17	5	9	49	26	8	.285
Adam Bengoechea	SS45,2B38,3B12	105	324	32	74	21	8	1	3	32	34	8	.228
Norm DeWeese	OF78	100	300	26	87	45	12	1	3	20	35	5	.290
Aloysius Bejma	2B22,3B17	46	133	19	30	8	4	1	1	20	16	1	.226
Al Unser	C43	45	136	19	39	13	4	0	2	21	17	2	.287
John Tising	P43	43	82	2	10	6	1	0	0	1	10	0	.122
Rufus Gentry	P40	42	103	9	17	10	5	0	0	4	19	0	.165
Floyd Giebell	P33	35	90	5	18	5	5	0	1	4	8	0	.200
Mike Rocco	1B32	32	111	12	27	18	4	0	2	22	22	0	.243
Mike Roscoe	P31	31	39	4	4	4	0	0	0	9	4	0	.103
Joseph Roxbury	P31	31	28	3	3	0	0	0	0	6	11	0	.107
Al Ott	P29	29	19	2	3	0	0	0	0	2	9	0	.158
Lyle Parkhurst	P24	25	14	1	0	0	0	0	0	1	5	0	.000
George Barley	P19	20	27	5	3	2	0	0	0	3	11	0	.111
Vic Wertz	OF,P1	18	18	3	4	1	1	0	0	2	2	0	.222
Louis Lorenz		11	13	0	2	2	0	0	0	1	0	0	.154
Murral Hewitt	P10	10	3	0	0	0	0	0	0	0	0	0	.000
Newt Waldstein	P8	8											.000
Elmer Weinschreider	1B	4	5	0	0	0	0	0	0			0	.000
Greg Mulleavy		1											.000

PITCHERS		W	L	PCT	G	GS	CG	SH	IP	H	BB	SO	ERA
Rufus Gentry		20	16	.556	40	**37**	**27**	7	**285**	227	**143**	184	2.65
John Tising		13	20	.394	43	33	16	4	223	241	79	92	4.28
Floyd Giebell		12	17	.414	33	33	20	0	248	252	99	94	3.27
Mike Roscoe		9	10	.474	31	20	7	1	140	164	57	37	4.69
George Barley		6	8	.429	19	13	7	1	100	104	29	41	4.05
Joseph Roxbury		5	7	.417	31	8	3	0	109	94	81	35	3.47
Al Ott		1	3	.250	29	2	1	0	72	84	31	31	4.75
Murral Hewitt		0	1	.000	10	1	0	0	17	24	17	11	6.88
Newt Waldstein		0	2	.000	8				16	14	14	5	
Lyle Parkhurst		0	3	.000	24	4	2	0	63	73	29	14	3.57
Vic Wertz		0	0	----	1				2	2	3	1	

JERSEY CITY Giants

8th	60-93	.392	-34.5	Gabby Hartnett

BATTERS	POS-GAMES	GP	AB	R	H	BI	2B	3B	HR	BB	SO	SB	BA
Everett Robinson	1B101	111	337	23	77	26	11	2	1	27	39	3	.229
John Hudson	2B88	89	300	36	53	12	7	3	0	44	48	8	.177
John Kerr	SS119,3B21	136	435	38	91	22	13	2	0	45	40	9	.209
Jorges Torres	3B94	100	378	38	79	22	12	3	2	21	26	8	.209
Howard Moss	OF113	121	408	40	95	49	16	3	5	23	40	3	.233
Carroll Lockman	OF77	78	271	35	72	18	9	4	0	33	37	6	.266
Daniel Drew	OF76	86	262	23	58	21	6	0	0	19	8	5	.221
James Steiner	C104	112	342	26	77	36	8	1	4	34	17	0	.225
Charles Mead	OF63,2B16	97	310	30	89	40	7	3	0	25	17	3	.287
Murray Howell	OF68	85	237	18	62	25	5	1	1	41	24	3	.262
Andres Fleitas	C53	60	170	16	37	12	2	0	0	6	9	3	.218
Napoleon Reyes	1B29,3B29	58	193	26	66	29	9	2	3	14	13	2	.342
Norm Small	OF49	53	168	21	42	19	10	1	4	20	32	0	.250
Bill Voiselle	P40	40	74	3	14	6	2	0	0	6	19	0	.189
Lou Polli	P35	37	69	5	14	3	1	0	0	8	14	1	.203
Robert Wells	P29	29	42	5	10	3	1	0	1	3	11	0	.238
Jack Maguire	2B13,SS13	26	89	11	25	3	1	0	0	10	18	0	.281
Richard Lajeskie	SS23	24	85	5	12	9	0	2	0	3	23	1	.141
Oscar McClure	2B21	23	82	8	16	4	1	0	0	5	7	1	.195
Ken Trinkle	P23	23	38	0	4	0	1	0	0	10	13	0	.104
Steve Shemo		22	53	3	11	1	0	0	0	1	8	1	.208
Raymond Coombs	P21	21	50	2	14	2	1	0	0	4	5	0	.280
Harold Contini	2B11	20	54	6	13	5	1	0	0	7	7	0	.241
Gordon East	P14	16	31	2	8	4	0	1	0	3	5	0	.258
Gabby Hartnett	C	16	16	0	4	5	1	0	0	3	2	0	.250
Reuben Fischer	P15	15	29	1	4	4	0	0	1	4	11	0	.138
Albert Sima	P11	11	14	1	4	0	1	0	0	0	4	0	.286
Jerome Tiemann	1B	8	25	3	1	1	1	0	0			0	.040
Alvis Shirley	P6	7											.400
Walter Dyche	P7	7											.000
Tim Fiore	P3	4											.250
William Harris	P4	4											.000
Ken Jungels	P3	3											.000
Joe Stephenson	C,PH	2	4	0	0	0	0	0	0	0		0	.000
George Bausewein	P1	1											.000
Richard Kenworthy	P1	1											.000
Phil Oates	P1	1											.000

PITCHERS	W	L	PCT	G	GS	CG	SH	IP	H	BB	SO	ERA
Lou Polli	14	12	.538	35	21	13	4	220	183	59	68	**1.85**
Raymond Combs	10	9	.526	21	19	16	2	151	155	32	46	2.50
Bill Voiselle	10	21	.323	40	32	19	5	238	224	114	124	3.18
Ken Trinkle	7	11	.389	23	16	9	1	145	132	48	50	2.92
Gordon East	4	7	.364	14	13	6	3	95	106	38	49	3.51
Robert Wells	4	11	.267	29	15	11	2	128	137	66	43	4.15
Reuben Fischer	3	9	.250	15	12	7	1	101	89	37	41	2.58
William Harris	1	0	1.000	4				6	9	4	0	
Ken Jungels	1	0	1.000	3								
Albert Sima	1	4	.200	11	6	4	1	46	50	22	11	4.70
Walter Dyche	0	1	.000	7				16	18	13	2	
Tim Fiori	0	2	.000	3				18	18	13	3	
Alvis Shirley	0	0	----	6				16	25	21	5	
Phil Oates	0	0	----	1				2	3	3	1	
Richard Kenworthy	0	0	----	1				1	3	0	0	9.00
George Bausewein	0	0	----	1				1	3	2	0	18.00

MULTI-TEAM PLAYERS

BATTERS	POS-GAMES	TEAMS	GP	AB	R	H	BI	2B	3B	HR	BB	SO	SB	BA
Gil Brack	OF92,1B31	JC68-MO58	126	423	55	120	48	15	11	3	58	71	4	.284
Richard Hahn	C51,1B17	SY2-BU82	84	209	22	57	29	12	0	7	33	42	2	.273
James McLeod	3B73	NE28-BA55	83	282	24	71	25	14	0	0	22	27	3	.252
Thomas Ananicz	P32	NE19-TO13	32	41	3	8	1	1	0	0	3	11	1	.195
Tom Sunkel	P22	JC15-MO8	23	42	2	7	2	0	0	0	3	12	0	.167

PITCHERS	TEAMS	W	L	PCT	G	GS	CG	SH	IP	H	BB	SO	ERA
Thomas Ananicz	NE19-TO13	7	8	.467	32	17	6	1	122	87	76	56	2.95
Tom Sunkel	JC14-MO8	7	9	.438	22	19	11	1	136	110	69	45	2.25

TEAM BATTING

TEAMS	GP	AB	R	H	BI	2B	3B	HR	BB	SO	SB	BA
TORONTO	154	4945	**627**	1244	530	182	29	41	635	413	129	.252
NEWARK	154	4875	613	1211	**555**	171	33	**76**	572	574	119	.248
SYRACUSE	154	4907	542	1220	477	192	47	53	480	487	**143**	.249
MONTREAL	153	4922	620	**1257**	553	**208**	**49**	53	485	636	78	**.255**
ROCHESTER	153	4932	557	1191	486	170	**49**	42	510	**661**	124	.241
BALTIMORE	**157**	**5012**	616	1201	515	157	30	43	**686**	612	137	.240
BUFFALO	153	4821	574	1160	518	198	17	60	585	528	86	.241
JERSEY CITY	154	4848	460	1125	411	135	32	22	456	546	58	.232
	616	39262	4609	9609	4045	1413	286	390	4409	4457	874	.245

1944
A BUCK SHORT

In 1928, International League fans witnessed the closest possible finish between a first- and second-place team as Rochester nosed out Buffalo by a single percentage point. Oddly enough, the scenario duplicated itself 16 years later, augmented by a thrilling dash to the pennant.

On July 6, 1944, the Newark Bears found themselves in the cellar. From this lowly position, the team commenced a laborious climb through the International League standings. By early September Newark had clawed its way into contention. As the league entered its final day of the regular season, the Bears pulled into the lead, one-half game ahead of Baltimore. When the Orioles lost their final game to put the Bears one full game in front, the miracle turnaround seemed complete. All that stood between Newark and the championship was one more regular season doubleheader against the last-place Syracuse Chiefs.

Overconfident, the Newark Bears lost the first game of the twinbill. Stunned, they lost the second game as well, dropping them into an apparent tie with Baltimore. But, since the Orioles had two fewer decisions, their 84–68 record gave them a .5526 winning percentage, one notch better than Newark's .5519 based on an 85–69 record. The Baltimore Orioles had won the pennant by a razor-thin margin.

Behind the two leaders, Toronto and Buffalo finished third and fourth. In the second division followed the rest: Jersey City, Montreal, Rochester, and Syracuse. Buffalo's Mayo Smith won the batting title (.340), while Baltimore Oriole Howard Moss clubbed the most home runs (27) and knocked in the most runs (141). Fellow Oriole Charles Embree took two pitching honors as he won the most games (19) and struck out the most men (225). Wood Crowson from Toronto finished with the lowest earned run average (2.41)

In retrospect, Newark's loss to Syracuse on the season's final day wasn't the huge upset it appeared to be. True, the Syracuse Chiefs were the last-place team in 1944. But they were also the best last-place team in the history of the league, as attested by their .447 winning percentage, which placed them only 16 games behind the leaders. Such information was little solace to the Newark Bears. All they saw was that they had fallen short of an unprecedented last-to-first run by the tiniest of margins.

BALTIMORE Orioles

1st   84-68   .553   Alphonse Thomas

BATTERS	POS-GAMES	GP	AB	R	H	BI	2B	3B	HR	BB	SO	SB	BA
Robert Latshaw	1B114	123	407	60	110	69	21	5	3	78	51	7	.270
Blas Monaco	2B146	147	500	135	147	71	32	8	12	167	79	24	.294
Fred Pfeifer	SS91	107	305	65	53	36	7	2	2	84	40	8	.174
Frank Skaff	3B111	120	421	60	113	74	15	2	17	52	65	9	.268
Howard Moss	OF148	149	581	122	178	141	44	8	27	55	57	14	.306
Al Benjamin	OF119,3B14	133	499	102	150	94	24	8	12	69	70	20	.301
Felix Mackiewicz	OF111,1B35	148	518	103	152	86	27	10	12	101	79	21	.294
Sherm Lollar	C116	126	380	58	95	72	14	2	15	83	52	2	.250
Pat Riley	OF82	100	312	47	78	35	10	3	3	57	22	12	.250
Al Tiedemann	SS44,3B29	72	243	53	70	33	10	5	2	42	38	4	.288
Sam Lowry	P45	46	67	5	16	7	2	1	0	4	2	0	.239
Stan West	P41	42	75	8	13	7	2	0	0	1	12	0	.173
Frank Rochevot	P40	40	25	3	3	1	0	0	0	1	13	0	.120
Ambrose Palica	P37	38	75	6	11	7	3	0	0	6	21	0	.147
Ed Braun	SS35	36	108	9	19	10	1	0	0	11	11	0	.176
Louis Kahn	C24	36	100	9	24	14	4	1	0	11	10	1	.240
Charles Embree	P34	34	79	8	8	5	1	1	0	7	18	0	.101
James Devlin	C16	32	61	7	9	6	2	0	0	10	6	0	.148
Rolland Van Slate	P32	32	45	1	3	4	0	0	0	6	16	0	.067
Harold Kleine	P17	23	32	6	5	7	0	2	0	7	2	0	.156
Elmer Burkart	P16	16	8	0	2	1	1	0	0	1	4	0	.250
Lloyd Shafer		15	22	3	3	4	1	0	0	1	1	0	.136
John Podgajny	P14	15	16	2	3	1	0	0	1	2	3	0	.188
George Hooks	P15	15	13	2	3	2	1	0	1	0	3	0	.231
James Kleckley	P8	11	4	1	2	0	1	0	0	0	0	0	.500
Harry Sollenberger	P5	5											.500
Charles Price	OF	5	9	1	2	1	0	0	1			0	.222
Julius Homokay	P2	2											.000
Alphonse Thomas	P2	2											.000
Harry Imhoff	C	1	2	0	0	0	0	0	0	0		0	.000
Milt Stockhausen	C	1	1	0	0	0	0	0	0	0		0	.000
Guy Coleman	P1	1											.000

PITCHERS	W	L	PCT	G	GS	CG	SH	IP	H	BB	SO	ERA
Charles Embree	19	10	.655	34	28	19	4	225	145	121	225	3.20
Stan West	15	16	.484	41	24	13	2	200	197	94	68	4.28
Ambrose Palica	14	10	.583	37	30	14	1	202	213	113	91	4.01
Sam Lowry	13	8	.619	45	27	11	0	204	215	61	71	4.24
Rolland Van Slate	7	12	.368	32	20	4	0	142	140	89	65	4.12
Frank Rochevot	6	1	.857	40	2	0	0	93	107	51	27	4.74
Harold Kleine	5	4	.556	17	10	2	0	65	72	54	35	5.12
John Podgajny	3	3	.500	14	5	1	0	51	70	22	16	6.35
Elmer Burkart	1	0	1.000	16	1	0	0	31	30	27	12	7.26
George Hooks	1	2	.333	15	2	0	0	41	39	28	15	4.17
Julius Homokay	0	1	.000	2				7	9	6	0	
Guy Coleman	0	1	.000	1				1	5	0	0	
James Kleckley	0	0	----	8				12	16	5	1	
Harry Sollenberger	0	0	----	5				5	4	5	1	
Alphonse Thomas	0	0	----	2				2	4	0	0	

NEWARK Bears

2nd   85-69   .552   -0   Bill Meyer

BATTERS	POS-GAMES	GP	AB	R	H	BI	2B	3B	HR	BB	SO	SB	BA
Roy Zimmerman	1B103	103	378	63	107	69	17	7	4	60	31	14	.283
Joe Buzas	2B104,3B18	125	465	66	138	65	14	8	4	26	24	29	.297
Dan Reynolds	SS145	146	462	67	121	64	19	9	5	62	39	7	.262
Mike Portner	3B92	97	300	47	81	45	7	7	5	55	40	11	.270
William Rabe	OF133	139	463	81	120	58	20	7	6	92	60	26	.259
Steven Kuk	OF95	101	373	82	104	54	20	6	9	52	29	9	.279
Nick Rhabe	OF75	76	276	35	86	31	11	2	0	17	15	3	.312
William Drescher	C118	122	401	50	110	64	15	4	5	49	24	4	.274
Jerry Crosby	2B35,3B35	92	226	35	54	37	8	2	6	39	21	2	.239
Joseph Dwyer	OF42	76	160	24	45	15	7	0	2	29	9	0	.281
Lew Flick	OF59	62	213	37	71	29	5	3	1	21	12	8	.333
Walt Van Grofski	C55	59	134	15	28	17	5	0	2	15	18	5	.209
Eugene Corbett	1B45	47	174	22	49	25	11	0	2	17	13	2	.282
Frank Dunlap	OF29	43	109	17	30	19	5	2	2	18	19	1	.275
Charles Marleau	P41	41	13	0	2	0	0	0	0	2	3	0	.154
Frank Hiller	P29	39	78	18	18	2	1	0	0	3	6	0	.231

NEWARK (cont.)
Bears

BATTERS	POS-GAMES	GP	AB	R	H	BI	2B	3B	HR	BB	SO	SB	BA
Charles Biggs	2B17,3B14	37	119	23	29	13	3	1	2	13	12	3	.244
Ken Holcombe	P33	33	71	8	10	6	1	0	0	7	17	0	.141
Arnold Cohen	OF28	29	100	19	26	1	2	0	0	22	9	2	.260
John Maldovan	P29	29	55	4	11	5	2	0	0	5	9	0	.200
Mel Queen	P24	24	43	3	6	3	0	0	1	0	10	0	.140
Phil Page	P20	20	4	0	0	1	0	0	0	0	0	0	.000
Floyd Bevens	P19	19	53	6	13	4	1	0	2	1	9	0	.245
Robert Reid		19	22	4	7	2	2	0	0	3	3	0	.318
William Sucky	P17	17	12	0	0	0	0	0	0	0	4	1	.000
Robert Miller	P14	14	4	0	0	0	0	0	0	0	2	0	.000
Don Johnson	P12	13	19	0	2	3	1	0	0	2	7	0	.105
Frank Silvanic	OF11	11	31	1	2	1	0	0	0	3	7	1	.065
Joe Page	P9	10	28	1	5	5	0	0	1	3	10	0	.179
Joseph Cicero	OF	9	33	5	8	11	2	0	3			1	.242
Ray Uniak	P9	9											.111
Jack Phillips	3B	7	27	3	7	4	1	0	0			0	.259
Robert Crow	P5	7											.000
Henry Gagain	OF	6	17	0	4	2	1	0	0			0	.235
Karl Drews	P5	5											.000
Bert Singleton	P5	5											.000
Pat Capri	2B	4	7	4	1	1	0	0	0			0	.143
Leo Righetti	SS	4	7	0	1	0	0	0	0			0	.143
Charles Munday	C	4	8	0	0	0	0	0	0			0	.000
Elden Clark	P4	4											.000
Charles Mistos	P4	4											.000
John Rager	P4	4											.000
Harvey Porter	3B,SS	2	7	0	0	1	0	0	0			0	.000
Mike Sperrick	OF	2	4	2	1	0	0	0	0			0	.250
Ray Flanigan	P1	1	1	1	1	0	0	1	0			0	1.000
George Motto	PH	1	1	0	0	0	0	0	0			0	.000
Rudolph Imarata	P1	1											.000

PITCHERS	W	L	PCT	G	GS	CG	SH	IP	H	BB	SO	ERA
Ken Holcombe	17	10	.630	33	28	16	2	205	193	116	123	3.82
Frank Hiller	15	11	.577	29	28	17	6	216	205	79	113	3.08
Floyd Bevens	12	6	.667	19	18	12	3	149	119	65	85	2.96
John Maldovan	10	8	.556	29	25	9	2	165	142	128	147	4.09
Mel Queen	9	7	.563	24	18	10	3	133	101	66	83	3.18
Charles Marleau	7	1	.875	41	0	0	0	79	92	31	27	5.47
Don Johnson	6	2	.750	12	8	4	1	67	66	35	38	4.03
Joe Page	4	5	.444	9				73	53	32	63	2.77
Phil Page	2	2	.500	20	0	0	0	30	26	12	11	2.10
John Rager	1	1	.500	4				17	18	8	11	
Robert Miller	1	2	.333	14	3	0	0	21	25	30	5	9.00
Karl Drews	1	3	.250	5				28	32	27	11	6.43
Robert Crow	0	1	.000	5				10	12	1	3	
Ray Uniak	0	1	.000	5				18	14	18	8	
Elden Clark	0	1	.000	4				9	17	4	3	
Charles Mistos	0	1	.000	4				11	13	8	6	
Rudolph Imarata	0	1	.000	1				4	6	5	2	
Bert Singleton	0	2	.000	5				20	24	9	16	5.40
William Sucky	0	4	.000	17	4	0	0	50	36	55	23	5.22
Ray Flanigan	0	0	----	1				4	8	1	0	

TORONTO   3rd   79-74   .516   -5.5   Burleigh Grimes
Maple Leafs

BATTERS	POS-GAMES	GP	AB	R	H	BI	2B	3B	HR	BB	SO	SB	BA
Harry Davis	1B139	140	458	68	129	57	32	3	6	80	23	10	.282
Tony Castano	2B51,3B44,OF30	123	461	80	141	25	15	2	0	49	31	14	.306
Antonio Ordenana	SS130	132	420	42	96	45	5	3	0	28	23	6	.229
Richard Shoff	3B98,2B48	149	510	58	135	59	25	6	4	32	30	10	.265
John Zontini	OF95,2B18	121	382	63	89	37	15	7	7	58	69	20	.233
James Tyack	OF93	93	309	55	97	54	16	5	7	51	20	15	.314
James Gruzdis	OF58,2B10	72	231	46	60	33	7	2	1	36	15	15	.260
Herb Crompton	C96	101	314	34	88	60	10	3	3	37	12	6	.280
Red Kress	1B14,P12,3B10	70	185	14	48	27	5	3	2	25	12	2	.259
Vernon Thoele	SS24,2B23	64	163	18	37	10	3	1	1	32	18	5	.227
Abe Abramowitz	OF56	56	151	15	43	16	6	2	0	8	4	6	.285
Chet Morgan	OF53	53	187	23	54	19	8	0	1	19	9	2	.289
Alex Mustaikis	P38	51	107	11	28	16	6	0	2	6	12	1	.262

TORONTO (cont.)
Maple Leafs

BATTERS	POS-GAMES	GP	AB	R	H	BI	2B	3B	HR	BB	SO	SB	BA
Dewey Williams	C42	48	150	21	47	20	7	0	1	22	12	6	.313
Al Jarlett	P39	39	78	14	16	11	2	3	1	3	11	0	.205
Luther Knerr	P39	39	65	3	13	3	2	0	0	2	5	0	.200
Wood Crowson	P35	35	53	3	7	1	1	0	0	1	7	0	.132
John Cooney		34	121	12	33	9	2	0	0	15	5	4	.273
Earl Cook	P32	32	21	1	1	0	0	0	0	1	7	0	.048
James Lady	C20	28	69	5	15	6	1	0	0	4	13	0	.217
Harry Jordan	P25	25	43	1	8	1	1	0	0	0	6	0	.186
Dave Lambton	P15	18	20	2	4	3	0	0	0	1	2	0	.200
Thomas Ananicz	P16	16	24	1	5	1	0	0	0	1	3	0	.208
Ralph McCabe	P16	16	6	0	0	0	0	0	0	1	2	0	.000
Orie Arntzen	P9	9											.250
William Mills	C,OF	8	17	3	3	2	1	0	1			0	.278
Juan Monge	OF	7	18	4	3	4	0	0	0			0	.167
William Clayton	2B	3	9	1	0	1	0	0	0			0	.000
Walt Smola	P3	3											.000
Joseph Kania	P2	2											.000
Harry Amato	PH	1	1	0	0	0	0	0	0	0		0	.000

PITCHERS		W	L	PCT	G	GS	CG	SH	IP	H	BB	SO	ERA
Al Jarlett		18	9	.667	39	26	16	3	214	181	85	98	2.78
Alex Mustaikis		17	12	.586	38	24	18	5	214	194	77	89	2.57
Luther Knerr		13	11	.542	39	26	16	2	200	172	85	84	2.97
Wood Crowson		12	6	.667	35	21	12	1	172	146	45	56	**2.41**
Harry Jordan		8	8	.500	25	17	7	1	118	115	48	33	3.36
Earl Cook		3	4	.429	32	4	1	0	76	76	31	27	3.55
Thomas Ananicz		2	4	.333	16	8	2	1	65	71	47	26	5.95
Red Kress		2	6	.250	12	6	5	0	68	69	31	28	4.10
Joseph Kania		1	0	1.000	2				6	7	7	2	
Ralph McCabe		1	2	.333	16	3	0	0	38	41	34	25	4.50
Dave Lambton		1	5	.167	15	8	3	1	49	44	37	15	4.41
Orie Arntzen		1	6	.143	9				41	50	18	15	
Walt Smola		0	1	.000	3				2	8	6	1	

BUFFALO   4th   78-76   .506   -7   Bucky Harris
Bisons

BATTERS	POS-GAMES	GP	AB	R	H	BI	2B	3B	HR	BB	SO	SB	BA
Frank Heller	1B85	85	297	41	83	42	15	2	4	45	16	2	.280
Carl McNabb	2B109	111	375	49	106	30	22	1	1	27	26	3	.283
Les Floyd	SS79	81	269	33	69	36	8	1	0	37	21	10	.256
Robert Maier	3B152	154	588	83	175	78	22	5	1	51	31	25	.298
Mayo Smith	OF149	150	500	123	170	55	30	4	8	149	15	12	**.340**
Ed Kobesky	OF148	148	528	106	173	129	31	2	26	94	42	10	.328
Otto Denning	OF79,1B50,C13	142	527	100	152	99	34	3	21	65	39	16	.288
Andy Seminick	C49,OF37	87	297	57	81	50	8	4	14	40	60	3	.273
Prince Oana	P38	82	137	17	33	23	2	1	4	14	12	1	.241
Al Unser	C44,OF14	63	209	32	46	29	7	3	8	22	22	3	.220
James Levey	SS34,2B28	62	200	16	40	27	5	0	2	18	32	1	.200
Rupert Thompson	OF33	53	100	14	21	10	3	0	1	25	6	0	.210
Ed Borom	SS51	51	166	26	36	9	1	1	1	26	14	6	.217
Carl Sullivan	2B29	43	134	24	35	3	1	2	0	15	19	5	.261
Walt Wilson	P36	38	94	12	24	10	4	1	0	4	17	0	.255
John Tising	P38	38	46	2	5	0	0	0	0	2	9	0	.109
Zeb Eaton	P15	34	66	7	16	17	3	1	5	4	9	0	.242
Mike Roscoe	P30	33	70	7	11	3	1	1	0	7	21	0	.157
Emery Hresko	P32	32	30	3	5	3	0	0	0	1	6	0	.167
Robert Garbark	C31	31	93	8	17	12	1	0	1	12	4	0	.183
James Miller	C23	25	69	3	14	10	1	1	0	10	2	0	.203
Robert Gillespie	P20	20	47	5	7	4	1	1	0	2	27	0	.149
Ed Butka	1B18	18	71	9	18	16	1	2	1	0	7	0	.254
Lewis Fauth	P15	15	7	0	1	0	0	0	0	0	0	0	.143
Forrest Orrell	P14	14	35	4	8	7	0	0	0	0	7	0	.229
Earl Whitehill	P10	10	4	1	1	0	0	0	0	2	1	0	.250
Frank Hamons	P7	7											.167
Thomas Davis	OF	6	6	0	1	0	0	0	0	0		0	.167
William Angstadt	P5	5											.000
John Burrows	P5	5											.000
Dan Radakovich	C4	4	9	1	2	0	0	0	0	0		0	.222
Charles Miller	P3	3											.000
Joseph Roxbury	P3	3											.000

BUFFALO (cont.)
Bisons

BATTERS	POS-GAMES	GP	AB	R	H	BI	2B	3B	HR	BB	SO	SB	BA
Glenn Thomas	P2	2											.000
William Schaeffer	3B	1	1	0	0	0	0	0	0			0	.000

PITCHERS	W	L	PCT	G	GS	CG	SH	IP	H	BB	SO	ER
Walt Wilson	18	14	.563	36	30	18	3	236	251	82	132	3.66
Mike Roscoe	16	10	.615	30	28	17	3	215	217	66	68	3.43
Prince Oana	13	13	.500	38	28	16	6	211	199	103	112	3.63
Forrest Orrell	8	1	.889	14	9	8	0	87	73	24	48	2.90
Robert Gillespie	8	9	.471	20	19	9	1	133	133	82	59	4.26
John Tising	6	10	.375	38	16	9	2	143	180	44	78	4.85
Zeb Eaton	3	4	.429	15	3	0	0	48	46	35	38	5.63
Emery Hresko	3	9	.250	32	14	4	0	96	104	84	28	6.75
Frank Hamons	2	2	.500	7				17	25	16	3	
Lewis Fauth	1	1	.500	15	1	0	0	29	27	28	12	5.90
Earl Whitehill	0	3	.000	10	2	0	0	23	24	14	9	4.30
William Angstadt	0	0	----	5				10	12	4	4	
John Burrows	0	0	----	5				7	10	9	3	
Charles Miller	0	0	----	3				12	18	4	4	
Joseph Roxbury	0	0	----	3				5	8	1	3	
Glenn Thomas	0	0	----	2				1	6	0	1	

JERSEY CITY   5th   74-79   .484   -10.5   Gabby Hartnett
Giants

BATTERS	POS-GAMES	GP	AB	R	H	BI	2B	3B	HR	BB	SO	SB	BA
Mike Schemer	1B106	115	391	58	106	30	9	1	0	59	12	4	.271
John Hudson	2B80	83	260	35	70	30	8	4	0	36	37	1	.269
Roy Nichols	SS84,3B34	116	392	39	86	34	15	1	0	40	23	3	.219
George Souter	3B59,SS19,OF16	98	324	29	86	43	14	3	3	25	32	6	.266
Carroll Lockman	OF136	141	476	81	125	56	18	6	4	77	42	15	.263
Steve Filipowicz	OF110	115	413	52	109	69	25	7	4	30	59	3	.264
Thad Treadway	OF83	84	300	46	88	35	17	3	1	42	14	23	.293
Andres Fleitas	C101	109	338	37	88	34	15	5	2	23	15	1	.260
Russ Wein	SS55,3B20,2B15	96	292	39	62	28	4	2	0	53	23	2	.212
Danny Gardella	OF55	66	212	26	48	42	10	2	6	37	23	0	.226
Battle Sanders	1B42	51	145	37	41	23	6	2	4	46	16	1	.283
Richard Lajeskie	2B47	47	161	24	42	26	7	7	0	19	13	2	.261
Roy Nicely	2B20,3B15	43	123	19	21	11	5	0	0	17	23	0	.171
Ken Miller	P31	43	83	3	12	9	2	2	0	8	22	0	.145
Daniel Drew	OF27	34	135	15	38	14	4	0	0	15	2	1	.281
Francis Rosso	P34	34	62	4	9	8	0	0	0	3	14	0	.145
Robert Henry	P32	32	14	1	3	0	0	0	0	3	3	0	.214
John Toncoff	C28	28	86	8	23	7	4	0	0	12	8	1	.267
Charles Mead	OF22	26	69	9	16	5	4	1	0	12	9	0	.232
Ken Brondell	P24	25	50	7	7	4	1	0	0	5	15	1	.140
Mike Mellis	P24	24	24	1	0	1	0	0	0	1	7	0	.000
Robert Barthelson	P21	21	50	2	11	3	0	0	0	4	12	0	.220
Joe Stephenson	C15	16	46	3	7	3	0	1	0	4	11	0	.152
Andrew Hansen	P15	16	30	2	7	3	2	0	0	4	6	0	.233
Sal Demma	C10	13	25	4	5	1	3	0	0	1	3	0	.200
Lou Polli	P13	13	17	1	4	1	0	1	0	1	1	0	.235
Gabby Hartnett	C	13	11	1	2	6	1	0	0	2	3	0	.182
Ray Curtiss	3B10	12	37	2	5	7	1	0	0	3	5	1	.135
Les Layton	OF11	11	43	6	11	7	2	0	1	3	8	0	.256
Frank Seward	P11	11	23	4	2	0	0	0	0	0	7	2	.087
Walt Ockey	P11	11	8	1	1	0	0	0	0	0	1	0	.125
Robert Comiskey	C10	10	29	3	7	2	0	1	0	3	3	0	.241
Robert Harrison	P6	9											.273
Larry Miggins	3B	8	32	4	5	4	1	1	0			0	.156
Harold Smith	P8	8											.000
Cliff Melton	P7	7											.200
Earl Pugh	OF	6	18	2	3	0	0	0	0			0	.167
Curt Johnson	P6	6											.250
Richard Kenworthy	P6	6											.000
Harry Palmer	P4	4											.125
James McAlarney	P4	4											.000
Saul Rogovin	OF	4	9	1	0	0	0	0	0			0	.000
Frank Cracchiolo	3B	3	10	2	5	2	0	0	0			0	.500
Don Mueller	OF	3	7	1	1	3	0	0	0			0	.143
Juan Montero	P3	3											.000
Gale Pringle	P2	2											.250

JERSEY CITY (cont.)
Giants

BATTERS	POS-GAMES	GP	AB	R	H	BI	2B	3B	HR	BB	SO	SB	BA
George Blasini	3B	1	4	1	1	0	1	0	0			0	.250
John Tramelli	P1	1											1.000
Walter Dyche	P1	1											.000

PITCHERS		W	L	PCT	G	GS	CG	SH	IP	H	BB	SO	ERA
Ken Brondell		13	6	.684	24	18	9	2	140	157	64	40	4.05
Francis Rosso		11	9	.550	34	20	10	1	183	163	100	53	3.34
Ken Miller		10	13	.435	31	25	19	3	204	160	115	58	2.69
Andrew Hansen		8	4	.667	15	11	8	2	100	90	28	31	1.89
Robert Barthelson		8	10	.444	21	18	10	1	144	132	69	46	2.94
Mike Mellis		7	9	.438	24	12	4	1	102	106	25	32	3.44
Lou Polli		4	3	.571	13	4	3	1	50	52	12	20	2.88
Frank Seward		4	6	.400	11	10	4	0	71	83	24	17	3.17
Cliff Melton		3	4	.429	7				45	52	21	14	
Curt Johnson		2	1	.667	6				36	34	17	7	
Robert Henry		2	4	.333	32	6	1	0	74	59	83	26	4.62
Juan Montero		1	0	1.000	3				6	9	3	1	
Harry Palmer		1	3	.250	4				20	28	10	3	
Walt Ockey		0	1	.000	11	4	0	0	27	29	39	8	10.00
James McAlarney		0	1	.000	4				18	21	15	2	
Walter Dyche		0	1	.000	1				2	4	2	1	
Robert Harrison		0	2	.000	6				20	21	30	11	
Gale Pringle		0	2	.000	2				19	12	10	3	
Harold Smith		0	0	----	8				9	8	13	3	
Richard Kenworthy		0	0	----	6				8	8	3	2	
John Tramelli		0	0	----	1				2	5	4	0	

MONTREAL 6th 73-80 .477 -11.5 Bruno Betzel
Royals

BATTERS	POS-GAMES	GP	AB	R	H	BI	2B	3B	HR	BB	SO	SB	BA
Ed Stevens	1B153	153	543	77	147	102	37	4	16	80	76	5	.271
Barney Koch	2B82	82	282	48	71	21	9	2	0	44	35	7	.252
Stan Breard	SS128	128	405	33	77	34	11	4	0	26	47	1	.190
Morris Aderholt	3B138,OF11	150	558	109	161	94	38	5	20	85	45	17	.289
Walt Chipple	OF144	144	528	80	153	83	19	9	4	65	51	8	.290
Elmer Durrett	OF141	142	484	87	141	86	27	9	18	76	81	12	.291
John Corriden	OF138	140	514	102	142	36	25	5	3	63	46	11	.277
Stan Andrews	C141	143	482	63	121	86	25	2	3	50	37	1	.251
Ed Basinski	2B67	68	270	32	66	20	10	1	2	22	24	5	.244
John Cummings	C16	58	77	10	24	22	2	1	1	18	10	0	.312
George Washburn	P15	50	66	10	16	9	4	0	0	15	12	0	.242
Wayne Collins		40	73	7	13	5	2	0	0	3	21	1	.178
John Gabbard	P40	40	67	5	13	4	0	0	0	4	17	1	.194
John Travis	P35	35	32	5	10	3	1	0	0	4	3	0	.313
William Boaz	2B12	32	54	6	7	1	0	0	0	4	6	2	.130
Eugene Dellinger	3B16	28	65	9	12	9	4	1	0	10	16	0	.185
Ed Badke	OF21	25	66	11	12	8	2	0	0	12	12	2	.182
Thomas Warren	P13	23	35	3	8	4	2	0	0	3	6	1	.229
Tom Sunkel	P21	21	51	3	5	6	0	0	0	4	13	0	.098
Ed Spaulding	P21	21	10	2	1	0	1	0	0	2	1	0	.100
Gene Mauch	SS14	14	53	12	15	2	0	0	0	7	2	1	.283
John Banta	P14	14	16	2	3	1	0	0	0	2	4	0	.188
Ralph Branca	P12	12	24	1	2	4	0	1	0	4	7	0	.083
Al Zachary	P11	11	19	1	2	0	1	0	0	1	3	0	.105
Roy Sanner	P10	10	13	1	2	0	1	0	0	0	1	0	.154
Charles Fuchs	P9	9											.400
Mike Ulisney	C	7	20	1	3	2	0	1	0			0	.150
Walt King	SS	6	16	1	5	0	1	0	0			1	.313
Jack Franklin	P6	6											.000
Robert Tart	P6	6											.000
Richard McAtee	C	4	2	0	0	0	0	0	0			0	.000
Harvey Coddle	P4	4											.000
Charles Osgood	P3	3											.000
George Roxborough	P3	3											.000
Duke Snider	PH	2	2	0	0	0	0	0	0			0	.000
Claude Weaver	P2	2											.000
Michael Angelino	P1	1											.000
Karl Krafft	P1	1											.000
Les Zins	P1	1											.000

MONTREAL (cont.)
Royals

PITCHERS	W	L	PCT	G	GS	CG	SH	IP	H	BB	SO	ERA
Wayne Collins	14	15	.483	40	32	14	2	206	214	127	51	4.50
Tom Sunkel	11	7	.611	21	20	11	0	142	120	83	86	2.79
John Gabbard	10	13	.435	40	20	11	0	179	215	80	47	4.42
Warren Thomas	7	2	.778	13	7	5	0	69	52	28	23	1.83
George Washburn	5	6	.455	15	11	4	0	73	84	57	37	5.42
Charles Fuchs	4	3	.571	9				61	63	17	13	
Ralph Branca	4	5	.444	12	11	5	1	71	69	39	37	4.44
John Travis	3	5	.375	35	9	5	0	95	107	50	28	4.64
Roy Sanner	2	3	.400	10	5	2	0	30	34	23	17	6.60
Al Zachary	1	3	.250	11	3	0	0	47	42	27	18	5.74
John Banta	1	4	.200	14	3	0	0	53	55	44	12	4.58
Robert Tart	0	1	.000	6				5	8	7	1	
Ed Spaulding	0	2	.000	21	1	0	0	44	47	30	18	4.91
Jack Franklin	0	0	----	6				11	14	12	4	
Harvey Codde	0	0	----	4				4	10	3	2	
Charles Osgood	0	0	----	3				5	5	4	1	
George Roxburgh	0	0	----	3				4	4	2	1	
Claude Weaver	0	0	----	2				4	7	5	2	
Karl Krafft	0	0	----	1				1	4	0	1	
Michael Angelino	0	0	----	1				1	3	0	1	
Les Zins	0	0	----	1				1	0	1	0	

ROCHESTER   7th   71-82   .464   -13.5   Ken Penner
Red Wings

BATTERS	POS-GAMES	GP	AB	R	H	BI	2B	3B	HR	BB	SO	SB	BA
Maurice Sturdy	1B150	152	537	78	150	68	22	2	3	81	29	39	.279
John Burman	2B76	76	275	28	77	39	11	2	1	24	10	7	.280
Ora Burnett	SS63,2B36	112	447	73	112	36	17	9	4	32	36	41	.251
Herschel Held	3B70,OF51	129	401	61	102	67	14	6	5	71	45	6	.254
Otis Davis	OF106	118	473	60	114	41	18	3	4	24	55	21	.270
Leroy Nichols	OF73	75	276	42	80	26	14	4	2	33	11	13	.290
Earl Naylor	OF69	70	229	35	66	37	9	7	4	47	28	7	.288
Del Rice	C86	92	296	26	78	50	10	3	6	24	40	2	.264
Lugo Lancelotti	3B45,SS22	68	209	17	46	17	8	1	0	27	29	0	.220
James Towns	SS60	62	228	33	67	9	6	2	0	19	7	4	.294
Joseph Overman	OF51	61	184	23	47	23	6	2	0	21	25	2	.255
Ed Malone	C46	52	167	23	45	23	9	2	1	18	9	0	.269
Louis Sakas	P41	41	27	4	7	0	1	0	0	2	5	0	.259
Robert Rausch	2B29	40	122	12	24	7	3	1	0	18	12	1	.197
Vaughn Hazen	OF34	35	120	16	23	6	3	1	0	18	34	1	.192
Francis Cosgrove	C26	34	85	6	17	9	2	0	1	15	13	2	.200
William Emmerich	P34	34	73	5	10	4	0	0	0	7	14	0	.137
Sam Kuipers	P22	34	62	5	11	10	1	0	2	11	20	1	.177
Glenn Gardner	P31	31	66	7	10	2	1	0	0	1	8	0	.152
William Trotter	P31	31	59	1	8	2	0	0	0	11	25	0	.136
Kemp Wicker	P26	26	56	4	11	4	1	0	0	5	13	0	.196
Red Schoendienst	SS25	25	102	26	38	14	3	2	2	13	1	16	.372
Eldred Byerly	P15	16	32	1	5	4	2	0	0	1	9	0	.156
Clair Strommen	P15	15	10	0	1	0	0	0	0	0	4	0	.100
Mike Naymick	P13	13	21	1	2	1	0	0	0	1	11	0	.095
Walt Alston		13	19	2	3	2	0	0	0	5	5	0	.158
Roland Seitz		11	34	1	3	1	0	0	0	2	9	0	.088
Steve Mizerak	2B,SS	7	25	2	6	5	2	0	0			0	.240
Howard Taylor	P7	7											.000
William Trine	P5	5											.000
Fred Strohmeyer	P4	4											.111
George Sumey	P4	4											.000
Lawrence Weldon	P4	4											.000
Thomas Hanrahan	P3	3											.000
Lewis King	OF	2	3	0	0	0	0	0	0	0			0	.000
Nick Ellis	P1	1											.000
Ed Jaworski	P1	1											.000

PITCHERS	W	L	PCT	G	GS	CG	SH	IP	H	BB	SO	ERA
Glenn Gardner	15	14	.517	31	26	15	1	187	186	70	70	3.80
William Trotter	14	12	.538	31	28	18	5	208	198	50	54	2.55
Kemp Wicker	13	9	.591	26	24	13	4	183	173	37	56	2.80
William Emmerich	12	13	.480	34	26	13	2	213	208	76	82	3.17
Louis Sakas	7	3	.700	41	2	0	0	83	95	39	29	4.45
Sam Kuipers	5	6	.455	22	16	7	1	133	128	76	35	4.13

ROCHESTER (cont.)
Red Wings

PITCHERS	W	L	PCT	G	GS	CG	SH	IP	H	BB	SO	ERA
Eldred Byerly	3	9	.250	15	13	8	0	94	83	31	43	3.83
Mike Naymick	1	6	.143	13	8	2	0	61	42	49	40	3.69
Fred Strohmayer	0	1	.000	4				20	14	7	8	
George Sumey	0	1	.000	4				5	10	12	2	
Nick Ellis	0	1	.000	1				4	2	5	2	
William Trine	0	2	.000	5				7	11	4	1	
Clair Strommen	0	5	.000	15	4	1	0	49	51	32	20	4.96
Howard Taylor	0	0	----	7				10	16	10	2	
Lawrence Weldon	0	0	----	4				4	5	4	0	
Thomas Hanrahan	0	0	----	3				4	3	3	0	
Ed Jaworski	0	0	----	1				1	1	1	0	

SYRACUSE   8th   68-84   .447   -16   Jewel Ens
Chiefs

BATTERS	POS-GAMES	GP	AB	R	H	BI	2B	3B	HR	BB	SO	SB	BA
Al Lakeman	1B105	107	383	57	113	71	18	11	8	46	75	1	.295
Ben Geraghty	2B81	84	272	24	61	22	5	2	0	33	22	1	.224
Robert Carson	SS98	98	339	22	83	31	8	1	1	17	43	1	.245
Antonio Rodriguez	3B141	141	542	95	166	45	20	5	2	55	31	19	.306
Al Mele	OF149	150	522	80	153	86	32	5	11	86	21	6	.293
John Tyler	OF104	122	387	56	103	46	19	0	7	51	25	2	.266
Jesus Ramos	OF93,1B15	111	421	60	109	22	8	8	1	28	33	11	.259
Len Rice	C78	82	297	39	86	34	10	4	2	20	22	9	.290
Walt Cazen	OF83	104	340	46	82	40	13	2	7	39	32	16	.241
Herb Moore	SS52,2B19	79	261	22	54	14	1	1	0	30	46	1	.207
Charles Fitzgerald	2B50	71	211	11	39	15	7	0	1	27	61	2	.185
Gilberto Valdivia	C53	60	177	18	40	17	4	1	1	15	17	2	.226
Hod Lisenbee	P34	34	77	5	8	2	2	0	0	8	27	0	.104
John Bebber	P31	34	76	5	10	1	1	1	0	6	20	0	.132
Goody Rosen	OF29	29	105	13	31	20	5	3	2	23	6	2	.295
Les Goldstein	1B28	28	102	4	25	22	4	0	1	16	8	0	.245
Steve Plantz	C22	25	68	6	14	4	0	0	0	9	13	0	.206
George Woodend	P25	25	68	1	13	4	2	1	0	0	14	0	.191
Robert Katz	P23	25	66	3	18	4	3	0	0	2	9	0	.273
Bob Malloy	P24	24	60	8	18	6	1	1	0	2	5	0	.300
Reg Grabowski	P19	19	16	0	4	1	0	0	0	0	8	0	.250
Robert Springer	P13	15	17	0	1	1	0	0	0	0	5	0	.059
Jim Konstanty	P14	14	42	4	7	2	0	0	0	4	9	0	.167
Dick Coffman	P12	12	3	0	0	0	0	0	0	1	1	0	.000
Slobodan Yovanovich	C	10	31	2	8	2	0	0	0	1	4	0	.258
Bill Sisler	P8	9											.200
Dan Phalen	1B	8	23	0	4	0	0	0	0			0	.174
Calvin Brittan	2B,SS	5	5	2	0	0	0	0	0			0	.000
Charles Swart	P4	4											.667
Ed Kalski	P4	4											.500
John Lietz	P1	1											.000

PITCHERS	W	L	PCT	G	GS	CG	SH	IP	H	BB	SO	ERA
Bob Malloy	15	7	.682	24	17	15	2	163	148	81	50	2.76
Hod Lisenbee	15	15	.500	34	32	24	2	248	275	46	58	4.06
John Bebber	11	15	.423	31	27	19	1	224	215	85	86	3.21
Jim Konstanty	8	6	.571	14	13	10	1	115	104	44	38	3.21
Robert Katz	8	13	.381	23	22	16	1	176	193	67	65	4.60
George Woodend	8	14	.364	25	24	15	0	170	183	112	55	5.03
Bill Sisler	1	0	1.000	8				27	25	13	5	
Robert Springer	1	4	.200	13	8	1	0	55	71	18	10	4.75
Reg Grabowski	1	7	.125	19	7	6	0	60	67	17	25	6.45
Dick Coffman	0	1	.000	12	0	0	0	21	23	9	10	5.14
Ed Kalski	0	1	.000	4				13	10	6	2	
Charles Swart	0	1	.000	4				4	7	5	0	
John Lietz	0	0	----	1				1	1	5	0	

MULTI-TEAM PLAYERS

BATTERS	POS-GAMES	TEAMS	GP	AB	R	H	BI	2B	3B	HR	BB	SO	SB	BA
Thomas Astbury	OF126	RO70-TO57	127	460	55	116	42	14	3	4	53	56	22	.252
Jean Roy	P32	RO16-MO46	62	124	15	29	12	5	4	0	13	14	0	.234
Roy Tennyson	P4	TO2-MO2	4											.000

PITCHERS		TEAMS	W	L	PCT	G	GS	CG	SH	IP	H	BB	SO	ERA
Jean Roy		RO5-MO27	12	11	.522	32	24	13	1	192	175	117	112	3.78
Roy Tennyson		MO2-TO2	0	0	----	4				10	12	6	1	5.40

TEAM BATTING

TEAMS	GP	AB	R	H	BI	2B	3B	HR	BB	SO	SB	BA
BALTIMORE	152	4911	**879**	1274	**793**	224	58	**108**	**855**	**683**	123	.259
NEWARK	**154**	4940	745	1298	665	181	**59**	62	636	495	134	.263
TORONTO	153	4791	621	1250	531	175	41	38	541	389	129	.261
BUFFALO	**154**	4895	784	**1351**	704	201	36	98	686	464	98	**.271**
JERSEY CITY	153	4804	615	1167	549	179	50	25	595	506	68	.243
MONTREAL	153	**4951**	731	1261	653	**228**	49	67	617	601	77	.255
ROCHESTER	153	4888	634	1241	540	175	50	38	568	554	180	.254
SYRACUSE	152	4920	587	1256	515	163	46	44	522	564	71	.255
	612	39190	5596	10098	4950	1526	389	480	5020	4256	880	.258

1945
GRAY HEADS AND SMOOTH CHINS

By 1945, World War II was siphoning off virtually all of the able manpower from the United States and Canada to serve in the war effort. As a result of this shortage, a majority of minor leagues shut down for the duration. The International League and several others were able to keep going by utilizing players not eligible for the draft. In some cases, players with chronic physical difficulties who were ineligible for the service could still play ball. In other cases, players were ineligible for war duty because of their age—either too young or too old.

A ballplayer's professional career usually lasts from his early twenties to his mid-thirties. But because players in that age range were prime draft material, baseball leagues needed to stretch the boundaries of age on both ends to fill their rosters.

For instance, Montreal catcher Alfred Todd was one of only two league backstops to catch 100 games in 1945. This was an impressive feat considering the man was 43 years old. Buffalo outfielder Ollie Carnegie was brought back to help out during the manpower shortage at the mature age of 46. In all, more than one dozen players over the age of 40 participated in the International League of 1945.

Conversely, many youngsters under the age of 20 saw International League service. Pitchers Walt Pierce and Art Houtteman both saw action at the age of 17 for Buffalo. Joe Nuxhall pitched in seven September games for the Syracuse Chiefs at the same age. A total of nearly 20 fuzzy-cheeked adolescents participated in International League games in 1945.

After an absence of 10 years, Montreal stepped to the fore in 1945, finishing a half-dozen games up on Newark. Toronto and Baltimore finished over .500 in third and fourth, while Jersey City landed in fifth. Buffalo, Syracuse, and Rochester ended in a near tie at the bottom. Baltimore's Sherm Lollar took the batting average prize (.364), while his teammate Frank Skaff hit the most home runs (38) and knocked in the most runs (126). Montreal pitchers copped the three major awards as Jean Roy posted the most wins (25) and strikeouts (139), while Les Webber finished with the lowest earned run average (1.88).

After the war, many of the International's kiddie corps went on to lengthy playing careers buoyed by their wartime participation. For instance, Joe Nuxhall pitched in the majors until 1966. For the old-timers, the war years saw the end of their playing days. Most, if not all, returned to their interrupted but well-deserved retirement.

MONTREAL Royals

1st	95-57	.621		Bruno Betzel

BATTERS	POS-GAMES	GP	AB	R	H	BI	2B	3B	HR	BB	SO	SB	BA
Ed Stevens	1B110	110	401	64	124	95	19	6	19	72	41	5	.309
Ace Parker	2B148	149	517	83	154	77	38	1	3	87	23	4	.298
Stan Breard	SS133	133	469	63	129	55	23	3	0	40	30	4	.275
Lee Hart	3B69,SS15	93	262	29	67	41	14	0	1	39	33	1	.256
Elmer Durrett	OF130	136	480	119	131	82	17	7	21	110	100	9	.273
Roland Gladu	OF128,3B26	153	603	126	204	105	45	14	12	64	27	14	.338
John Corriden	OF98	102	377	89	118	39	14	6	6	68	59	23	.313
Alfred Todd	C104	114	399	53	109	73	16	5	0	41	23	8	.273
Kermit Kitman	OF82	90	287	53	71	34	6	2	2	54	20	11	.248
Jean Roy	P41	58	132	13	33	22	4	0	1	7	20	3	.250
Frank Powaski	3B50	58	148	20	34	13	8	0	0	14	13	0	.230
Thomas Warren	P31	58	94	22	31	20	5	1	5	7	13	2	.330
Gus Brittain	C42	50	148	26	53	28	5	1	4	14	12	2	.358
Howard Schultz	1B44	44	172	33	57	26	11	4	0	5	10	4	.331
John Gabbard	P42	42	85	6	14	5	4	0	0	3	20	0	.165
Ed Yaeger	OF17	27	75	20	22	2	2	2	0	18	11	3	.293
Ray Hathaway	P24	24	52	1	11	2	0	0	0	3	15	0	.212
John Banta	P24	24	50	3	12	6	1	0	0	2	5	0	.240
Les Webber	P17	21	47	6	15	9	0	1	0	5	5	0	.319
DeWitt Farrell	C16	19	47	8	14	9	0	0	0	10	4	0	.298
Leigh Davis	P14	14	13	2	2	3	1	0	0	6	2	0	.154
Charles Stevenson	P11	11	12	1	3	3	0	1	0	0	1	0	.250
John Colontino	P9	10	2	0	0	0	0	0	0	0	0	0	.000
William Jenkins	P6	8	12	2	5	1	1	0	0			0	.417
Richard Mlady	P7	7											.200
William Tanner	P6	6											.143
Grantham Lambert	P6	6											.000
Harold Kelleher	P5	5											.000
David Danaher	PH	3	3	1	1	0	0	0	0			0	.333
Alfred Ferony	SS,3B	3	1	1	0	0	0	0	0			0	.000
Vic Cegles	OF	2	1	0	0	0	0	0	0			0	.000
Frank Wurm	P2	2											.000
Al Durrett	P1	1											.000

PITCHERS	W	L	PCT	G	GS	CG	SH	IP	H	BB	SO	ERA
Jean Roy	25	11	.694	41	37	29	1	293	277	150	139	3.72
John Gabbard	20	6	.769	42	32	19	4	247	237	64	59	3.32
John Banta	12	9	.571	24	18	10	2	141	125	77	67	4.21
Les Webber	11	3	.786	17	15	14	4	120	99	42	45	1.88
Ray Hathaway	10	8	.556	24	19	8	0	142	135	83	56	4.06
Thomas Warren	9	7	.563	31	15	8	0	148	150	77	38	5.47
Leigh Davis	3	3	.500	14	4	2	0	50	38	36	24	2.88
John Colontino	2	2	.500	9				14	12	14	4	
Richard Mlady	1	0	1.000	7				23	28	14	6	
Wiliam Tanner	1	2	.333	6				23	20	15	13	
Harold Kelleher	1	2	.333	5				20	31	16	10	
William Jenkins	0	1	.000	6				17	21	8	3	
Frank Wurm	0	1	.000	2				1	2	6	0	
Charles Stevenson	0	3	.000	11	1	0	0	32	30	23	7	5.06
Grantham Lambert	0	0	----	6				8	9	6	5	
Al Durrett	0	0	----	1				1	3	1	0	

NEWARK Bears

2nd	89-64	.582	-6.5	Bill Meyer

BATTERS	POS-GAMES	GP	AB	R	H	BI	2B	3B	HR	BB	SO	SB	BA
Roy Zimmerman	1B109	109	404	81	114	81	15	4	32	60	50	19	.282
Clarence Difani	2B47,SS11	72	230	35	63	24	10	1	1	25	22	7	.274
Richard Baker	SS133	135	449	58	122	46	20	3	3	34	52	22	.272
Mike Portner	3B139	143	482	83	132	91	21	9	18	75	78	26	.274
William Rabe	OF142	146	498	110	125	56	19	4	9	102	75	42	.251
Stephen Kuk	OF100	107	338	51	91	39	13	1	7	55	26	15	.269
David Douglas	OF93	94	373	53	120	57	22	4	2	16	17	11	.322
Walt Van Grofski	C74	76	200	21	58	20	7	0	2	21	9	4	.290
Jerry Crosby	OF72,2B31	110	363	46	100	64	17	4	12	31	32	7	.275
Hugh Taylor	C65	71	193	23	43	19	9	0	2	35	12	9	.223
Joe Buzas	2B26,SS19,3B11	61	212	30	54	35	8	2	3	10	9	14	.255
Golden Holt	OF17	55	75	7	20	7	1	0	0	13	5	2	.267
Frank Drews	2B44	44	158	37	45	20	10	2	2	27	10	11	.285
Phil Weintraub	1B39	40	132	28	41	25	10	2	8	26	13	1	.311

NEWARK (cont.)
Bears

BATTERS	POS-GAMES	GP	AB	R	H	BI	2B	3B	HR	BB	SO	SB	BA
Karl Drews	P33	33	86	12	15	9	1	0	0	6	15	1	.174
Ed Mackay	P31	32	63	6	16	6	0	0	0	8	10	0	.254
John Maldovan	P28	30	70	11	17	9	1	2	0	9	14	0	.243
Frank Hiller	P25	29	65	10	16	7	2	0	0	3	9	1	.246
William Steinecke	C27	28	79	9	25	14	2	0	0	10	2	5	.316
Nick Rhabe	OF25	25	91	14	30	7	3	0	0	7	0	1	.330
Phil Page	P23	23	8	3	3	0	0	0	0	0	0	0	.375
Walt Nowak	OF18	22	78	11	22	7	8	1	0	4	10	4	.282
Murray Rothman	OF19	22	70	7	11	11	1	0	0	5	3	2	.157
Jack Farmer	P19	19	12	0	0	0	0	0	0	1	3	0	.000
Frank Makosky	P19	19	9	0	1	0	0	0	0	0	1	0	.111
William Houtz	P14	16	24	7	8	4	3	1	0	3	3	0	.333
William Sucky	P14	14	6	0	0	0	0	0	0	0	4	0	.000
Joseph Dwyer	OF	11	15	0	4	1	1	0	0	2	0	0	.267
Daniel Doy	2B10	10	36	1	4	2	1	0	0	1	8	0	.111
Harry Corbett	P10	10	19	3	4	1	0	0	0	6	2	0	.211
John Moore	P8	9											.188
Otto Meyers	OF	8	16	1	3	3	0	0	0			0	.167
Walt Ockey	P8	8											.000
Jack McKinney	P6	6											.250
Fred Pepper	P5	5											.167
Perry Losey	C	4	12	1	6	2	0	0	0			0	.500
Arnold Cohen	OF	4	6	1	0	0	0	0	0			0	.000
Gene Bearden	P1,OF	3	8	1	3	0	0	0	0			0	.375
Thomas Grace	P3	3											.000
Ted Pfennig	P3	3											.000
Carmine Melignano	P2	2											.000
John Gambol	P1	1											.000

PITCHERS	W	L	PCT	G	GS	CG	SH	IP	H	BB	SO	ERA
Karl Drews	19	9	.679	33	30	24	6	240	193	113	115	2.70
John Maldovan	16	6	.727	28	22	12	3	180	142	148	112	3.95
Frank Hiller	14	8	.636	25	25	13	3	185	169	68	70	2.58
Ed Mackay	12	12	.500	31	25	14	1	194	178	84	86	3.18
Harry Garbett	5	1	.833	10	9	5	0	64	62	57	33	3.80
John Moore	5	2	.714	8				52	36	29	26	
Jack Farmer	4	3	.571	19	2	1	0	44	40	19	13	3.27
William Houtz	4	4	.500	14	9	1	1	56	47	65	32	5.46
Frank Makosky	2	1	.667	19	0	0	0	35	22	14	23	1.80
William Sucky	2	2	.500	14	4	1	0	29	38	25	9	7.14
Fred Pepper	1	2	.333	5				22	30	17	2	
Gene Bearden	0	1	.000	1				8	9	8	1	9.00
Walt Ockey	0	2	.000	8				13	11	14	2	
Thomas Grace	0	2	.000	3				13	9	21	5	
Phil Page	0	4	.000	23	0	0	0	45	63	15	11	4.00
Jack McKinney	0	0	----	6				13	21	15	4	
Ted Pfennig	0	0	----	3				7	7	9	2	
Carmine Melignano	0	0	----	2				5	7	4	1	
John Gambol	0	0	----	1				1	2	2	0	

TORONTO
Maple Leafs

3rd   85-67   .559   -10   Harry Davis

BATTERS	POS-GAMES	GP	AB	R	H	BI	2B	3B	HR	BB	SO	SB	BA
Harry Davis	1B152	152	478	94	125	62	26	1	7	160	34	8	.261
George Ogorek	2B104	112	373	49	82	50	16	4	4	32	43	7	.220
Vernon Thoele	SS143	143	510	93	114	41	18	8	6	117	50	18	.224
Frank Piet	3B81	88	300	27	76	52	11	1	4	26	23	4	.253
Ira Houck	OF152	152	554	101	170	75	17	3	0	73	41	17	.307
Chet Morgan	OF121	121	464	81	138	66	21	4	5	55	12	6	.297
Willis Norman	OF76	76	237	53	69	49	12	4	5	75	18	2	.291
James Pruett	C95	95	331	51	97	65	14	1	8	51	25	7	.293
Tony Castano	3B60,2B53,OF10	120	417	84	125	52	11	4	2	76	19	24	.300
James Lady	C38	62	123	15	29	17	8	1	0	15	16	1	.236
James Reggio	OF39	54	149	19	31	14	2	1	0	28	24	6	.208
Walt Smola	P46	46	36	4	5	3	2	0	1	5	3	0	.139
Harry Jordan	P36	36	64	4	10	4	1	0	0	1	9	0	.156
Al Jarlett	P33	33	32	1	9	3	1	0	0	0	5	0	.281
Luke Hamlin	P30	30	74	6	9	5	1	0	0	10	18	1	.122
James Gruzdis	OF13	30	61	13	13	10	2	1	1	9	5	3	.213
Thomas Crowson	P29	29	59	5	12	10	0	0	0	1	3	0	.203

TORONTO (cont.)
Maple Leafs

BATTERS	POS-GAMES	GP	AB	R	H	BI	2B	3B	HR	BB	SO	SB	BA
Curt Johnson	P26	26	43	3	5	4	2	0	0	1	6	0	.116
Charles George	C24	25	82	16	26	19	5	0	2	14	2	5	.317
Thomas Ananicz	P20	25	41	5	9	1	0	0	0	1	5	0	.220
George Souter	3B15	22	73	10	17	17	3	2	3	10	8	1	.233
Alex Martin	P18	19	42	5	10	4	2	0	0	0	9	0	.238
Les McCrabb	P12	12	32	2	7	2	0	0	0	1	7	1	.219
Francis Cronin	P7	7	6	0	2	0	0	0	0			0	.333
Stan Stenoff	P5	5											.143
Marion Kratzer	C	4	14	2	4	2	1	0	0			0	.286
Max Samuely	P3	3											.333
Irvin Stein	P3	3											.167
Abe Abramowitz	PH	2	2	0	0	0	0	0	0	0		0	.000
Arnold Jarrell	P1	1											.000

PITCHERS		W	L	PCT	G	GS	CG	SH	IP	H	BB	SO	ERA
Luke Hamlin		16	11	.593	30	29	19	0	215	216	53	99	3.32
Thomas Crowson		13	8	.619	29	23	13	1	160	156	61	55	3.54
Harry Jordan		12	11	.522	36	23	8	0	181	206	82	62	4.08
Curt Johnson		9	5	.643	26	15	9	2	117	114	40	31	4.00
Al Jarlett		8	6	.571	33	5	1	0	84	90	50	28	4.71
Alex Martin		8	7	.533	18	16	8	0	106	104	54	32	3.91
Les McCrabb		6	3	.667	12	10	8	0	83	78	28	28	3.25
Walt Smola		6	7	.462	46	8	2	1	131	122	61	58	4.67
Thomas Ananicz		5	2	.714	20	11	4	1	89	86	57	32	3.94
Francis Cronin		1	2	.333	7				16	22	12	4	
Stan Stenoff		0	1	.000	5				15	22	10	4	
Irvin Stein		0	1	.000	3				13	23	2	2	
Max Samuely		0	1	.000	3				4	8	6	1	
Arnold Jarrell		0	0	----	1				3	4	2	0	

BALTIMORE   4th   80-73   .523   -14.5   Alphonse Thomas
Orioles

BATTERS	POS-GAMES	GP	AB	R	H	BI	2B	3B	HR	BB	SO	SB	BA
Robert Latshaw	1B149	149	505	114	146	92	22	10	14	108	49	6	.289
Fred Pfeifer	2B100	112	372	60	84	42	10	1	8	82	34	2	.226
Ken Braun	SS130	130	447	59	102	36	12	5	3	61	42	10	.228
Frank Skaff	3B136	143	520	128	148	126	20	5	38	97	70	4	.285
Joseph Mellendick	OF118	118	420	74	109	67	15	9	11	59	33	4	.260
Louis Kahn	OF97,3B16	121	433	79	128	64	28	8	6	56	38	20	.296
Pat Riley	OF78	81	279	60	64	31	11	3	3	73	26	13	.230
Sherm Lollar	C136	139	464	104	169	111	27	4	34	101	40	5	**.364**
Red Kress	OF25,P19,SS10	85	217	34	58	29	7	1	8	17	25	1	.267
John Podgajny	P66	67	81	7	12	7	2	1	0	6	24	1	.148
Al Barillari	P40,OF11	62	127	15	31	22	7	0	0	11	7	1	.244
James Tropea	OF39	59	142	15	29	16	6	0	0	21	15	2	.204
Tufeck Skaff	2B25,OF15	42	130	18	30	18	3	1	4	11	16	2	.231
George Hocks	P32	34	67	6	17	7	1	0	1	3	8	0	.254
Elmer Weingartner	2B21,SS11	32	124	24	37	32	10	1	5	8	13	5	.298
Harold Kleine	P26	32	57	5	12	4	1	0	0	8	7	1	.211
Frank Rochevot	P28	28	16	2	4	0	0	0	0	1	6	0	.250
Paul Calvert	P24	24	44	5	9	8	0	0	2	4	10	0	.205
Rolland Van Slate	P17	17	27	2	8	8	2	1	0	3	5	0	.296
Walt Jamison	P11	11	8	1	4	1	0	0	0	0	1	0	.500
Jack West	OF	7	12	2	2	0	0	0	0			0	.167
Guy Coleman	P5	5											.182
Dan Henry	P5	5											.000
John Smith	P5	5											.000
Richard Holmes	P3	3											.000
Don Noel	P3	3											.000
Vern Taylor	P3	3											.000
William Skinner	P3	3											.000
Ambrose Palica	P2	2											.000
Paul Smith	P2	2											.000
Ralph Sybert	SS1	1	0	0	0	0	0	0	0			0	----

PITCHERS		W	L	PCT	G	GS	CG	SH	IP	H	BB	SO	ERA
John Podgajny		20	11	.645	**66**	15	7	2	226	256	71	58	3.78
Al Barillari		15	9	.625	40	27	15	1	214	228	99	75	4.04
Harold Kleine		11	9	.550	26	21	13	2	147	138	76	61	4.04

BALTIMORE (cont.)
Orioles

PITCHERS	W	L	PCT	G	GS	CG	SH	IP	H	BB	SO	ERA
George Hooks	10	13	.435	32	27	12	2	183	218	80	68	4.48
Paul Calvert	8	11	.421	24	24	6	1	141	160	69	71	4.40
Rolland Van Slate	6	5	.545	17	13	4	0	75	89	41	30	5.52
Red Kress	5	7	.417	19	9	8	0	89	107	43	21	4.85
Frank Rochevot	2	1	.667	28	1	1	0	59	69	36	18	5.80
Guy Coleman	2	2	.500	5				33	22	23	11	
Walt Jamison	1	1	.500	11	3	0	0	23	31	16	4	7.43
Dan Henry	0	1	.000	5				5	6	7	4	
Don Noel	0	1	.000	3				16	14	5	3	
Richard Holmes	0	1	.000	3				3	6	10	0	
Ambrose Palica	0	1	.000	2				15	13	7	4	
John Smith	0	0	----	5				17	26	6	5	
William Skinner	0	0	----	3				5	5	5	2	
Vern Taylor	0	0	----	3				3	5	5	1	
Paul Smith	0	0	----	2				10	8	5	3	

JERSEY CITY   5th   71-82   .464   -24.5   Gabby Hartnett
Giants

BATTERS	POS-GAMES	GP	AB	R	H	BI	2B	3B	HR	BB	SO	SB	BA
Mike Schemer	1B106	106	403	68	130	46	20	9	5	37	10	4	.323
Richard Shoff	2B93,3B11	106	385	43	100	72	17	4	9	22	25	2	.260
Russ Wein	SS114	121	397	58	102	23	10	1	0	59	24	9	.257
Jorges Torres	3B59,2B14	74	274	44	66	21	8	2	4	36	15	2	.241
George Bennington	OF123	125	451	70	137	66	19	5	2	37	28	18	.304
Charles Mead	OF91,2B10	116	346	53	77	55	12	2	16	67	44	4	.223
Cleston Ray	OF67	76	243	38	60	28	4	4	3	36	25	5	.247
William Clausen	C82	87	259	30	55	31	11	1	0	14	13	1	.212
John Toncoff	C61	62	175	15	34	16	2	1	1	16	24	2	.194
Les Layton	OF54	54	204	46	64	28	10	3	5	20	16	4	.314
William Gardner	3B35,OF13	49	172	16	47	20	4	2	1	7	16	3	.273
Carroll Lockman	OF42	48	126	31	40	28	9	5	4	38	6	8	.317
Ed Kobesky	OF24	40	115	7	24	10	4	0	2	16	14	0	.209
Francis Rosso	P38	38	66	6	12	8	1	0	0	12	15	0	.182
Steve Filipowicz	OF30	37	131	16	39	19	8	3	1	9	6	0	.298
Rex Gardecki	OF25	35	84	4	19	11	4	1	0	9	11	3	.226
Adrian Zabala	P28	32	70	11	19	6	2	1	0	7	9	0	.271
Mike Mellis	P32	32	63	4	11	3	1	0	0	4	19	0	.175
John Piccirillo	P27	30	32	1	9	3	2	0	1	2	5	1	.281
Lou Polli	P25	25	33	7	7	3	0	0	0	9	5	1	.212
Frank Mediamolle	1B20	20	75	17	19	8	3	0	0	7	6	0	.253
James Goodwin	P20	20	25	0	3	0	0	0	0	2	9	0	.120
Ken Brondell	P18	18	32	5	5	1	0	1	0	4	12	0	.156
Dale Matthewson	P13	15	11	0	5	2	0	0	0	2	2	0	.455
William Daues	C13	14	35	3	5	2	0	0	1	2	5	0	.143
Sal Maglie	P14	14	32	4	10	6	0	1	0	1	1	0	.313
John Phillips	P9	9											.273
Joseph Pieson	1B	9	29	3	5	6	0	1	1			0	.172
Don Mueller	OF	8	8	2	2	1	0	0	0			0	.250
Ray Tellier	P8	8										0	.000
Norm Jaeger	1B	7	29	2	6	3	0	0	0			0	.207
Pete Christy	OF	7	17	3	4	3	0	0	0			0	.235
Ray Harrell	P7	7											.188
Andrew Hansen	P5	5	5	0	2	2	0	0	0			0	.400
Jack Shope	P5	5											.000
Al Gardella	1B,OF	4	9	1	3	3	1	0	1			0	.333
Sam Astorini	P3	3	5	0	2	0	0	0	0			0	.400
John Stilwell	P3	3	1	0	1	0	0	0	0			0	1.000
Mel Heiman	P3	3											.000
Frank Holcomb	P2	2											.000
Virgil Abernathy	P1	1											.000

PITCHERS	W	L	PCT	G	GS	CG	SH	IP	H	BB	SO	ERA
Mike Mellis	15	11	.577	32	26	24	2	198	199	76	38	3.86
Adrian Zabala	14	7	.667	28	21	15	1	171	153	75	77	3.21
Francis Rosso	13	15	.464	38	28	25	2	202	211	126	63	4.10
Ken Brondell	7	5	.583	18	15	7	2	100	117	32	27	4.59
Lou Polli	7	8	.467	25	13	6	2	101	116	50	37	4.72
Ray Harrell	4	3	.571	7				52	63	16	12	
James Goodwin	4	6	.400	20	9	3	1	82	94	32	17	4.61
Sal Maglie	3	7	.300	14	9	7	0	88	91	33	41	

JERSEY CITY (cont.)
Giants

PITCHERS	W	L	PCT	G	GS	CG	SH	IP	H	BB	SO	ERA
Dale Matthewson	1	1	.500	13	4	0	0	40	55	37	16	6.98
Ray Tellier	1	3	.250	8				29	30	33	11	
Andrew Hansen	1	3	.250	5				16	25	11	6	7.31
John Piccirillo	1	8	.111	27	6	4	0	98	98	71	34	4.96
Mel Heiman	0	1	.000	3				12	15	4	8	
Sam Astorini	0	1	.000	3				14	10	8	1	
John Phillips	0	3	.000	9				31	31	25	12	
Jack Shope	0	0	----	5				12	7	10	3	
John Stilwell	0	0	----	3				6	8	3	0	
Frank Holcomb	0	0	----	2				1	4	4	1	
Virgil Abernathy	0	0	----	1				2	0	0	0	0.00

BUFFALO   6th (T)   64-89   .418   -31.5   Bucky Harris
Bisons

BATTERS	POS-GAMES	GP	AB	R	H	BI	2B	3B	HR	BB	SO	SB	BA
John McHale	1B77,OF15	92	335	63	105	75	18	6	22	32	37	2	.313
Carl McNabb	2B121	121	471	44	129	32	31	2	0	26	29	3	.274
Pedro Gomez	SS106	108	375	52	101	23	19	2	3	12	75	0	.269
Herschel Held	3B61	75	275	51	81	36	18	4	5	32	26	2	.295
Ed Mierkowicz	OF129	131	498	91	151	94	37	9	21	51	51	9	.303
Ed Boland	OF126	127	469	84	141	111	27	1	23	50	20	5	.301
Elwood Wheaton	OF100,P2	103	390	83	119	34	16	2	2	46	6	7	.305
Ed Mordarski	C91	105	330	37	95	50	13	1	8	20	38	7	.288
Miguel Lastra	SS28,2B25,3B21	83	162	19	32	11	4	1	0	19	21	1	.198
Prince Oana	P31,OF	82	169	22	47	25	6	3	3	15	16	2	.278
Ed Butka	1B56	57	204	26	53	30	13	2	5	21	19	2	.260
Gerard Lipscomb	3B55	56	189	24	58	28	14	0	3	30	13	1	.307
Lloyd Brown	P28	44	82	7	21	20	8	0	0	9	11	0	.256
Milt Welch	C40	41	127	5	23	9	2	0	0	4	15	0	.181
Robert Bowman	P41	41	27	5	3	1	0	0	0	8	15	0	.111
Ollie Carnegie	OF20	39	93	20	28	21	5	1	4	10	6	0	.301
Ed Borom	SS25	35	133	24	32	11	4	0	2	12	8	5	.241
Robert Gillespie	P33	34	56	7	12	6	0	0	1	4	16	0	.214
Dan Radakovich	C31	31	108	11	22	9	0	2	0	7	9	0	.204
Emery Hresko	3B10,P9	22	43	7	19	9	2	5	1	4	3	0	.442
Robert Moyer	1B19	19	69	10	22	13	3	1	2	8	3	0	.319
Quinn Lee	P19	19	32	2	4	3	3	0	0	0	6	0	.125
Mike Roscoe	P17	17	30	0	6	0	0	0	0	3	9	0	.200
Robert Callan	P13	17	30	5	5	3	1	0	0	4	7	0	.167
Walt Pierce	P15	16	33	3	6	2	0	0	1	1	5	1	.182
William Herstek	P16	16	16	1	2	0	0	0	0	1	0	0	.125
Harvey Walker	OF	15	31	7	10	5	1	0	2	7	1	0	.323
Fred Petoskey	OF14	14	55	6	13	3	1	0	0	2	2	0	.236
Lyle Parkhurst	P13	13	18	2	4	3	1	0	0	0	1	0	.222
William Angstadt	P13	13	11	1	3	0	0	0	0	2	4	0	.273
James Scavone	3B10	10	44	8	11	6	3	0	1	3	1	0	.250
Charles Beihl	SS,2B	8	30	0	2	0	0	0	0	0			.067
Joseph Cleary	P8	8											.167
Forrest Orrell	P8	8											.100
Art Houtteman	P6	7											.077
Robert Martin	2B	3	13	0	2	0	0	0	0			0	.154
Lyle Bliss	P1	1											.000

PITCHERS	W	L	PCT	G	GS	CG	SH	IP	H	BB	SO	ERA
Prince Oana	15	14	.517	31	30	24	1	242	260	117	138	4.20
Lloyd Brown	12	9	.571	28	20	16	1	167	169	86	64	4.04
Robert Gillespie	7	15	.318	33	22	9	0	161	165	121	54	5.03
Walt Pierce	5	7	.417	15	13	8	1	83	75	71	57	5.42
Robert Bowman	5	10	.333	41	10	2	0	112	144	67	39	5.79
Quinn Lee	4	3	.571	19	6	4	0	85	88	39	19	3.49
Mike Roscoe	4	11	.267	17	16	4	0	89	129	39	21	6.67
Emery Hresko	3	3	.500	9				23	26	24	7	
Joseph Cleary	3	3	.500	8				41	33	28	16	
Art Houtteman	3	3	.500	6				40	42	15	16	4.05
Robert Callan	1	0	1.000	13	0	0	0	33	52	18	16	8.18
William Herstek	1	1	.500	16	3	1	0	47	63	34	15	6.70
William Angstadt	1	3	.250	12	4	0	0	35	38	37	7	6.94
Lyle Parkhurst	1	4	.200	13	7	1	0	56	84	23	20	7.07
Forrest Orrell	1	4	.200	8				32	41	17	11	
Elwood Wheaton	0	0	----	2				5	8	3	1	
Lyle Bliss	0	0	----	1				5	9	1	2	

SYRACUSE Chiefs 6th (T) 64-89 .418 -31.5 Jewel Ens

BATTERS	POS-GAMES	GP	AB	R	H	BI	2B	3B	HR	BB	SO	SB	BA
Jesus Ramos	1B75,OF14	102	306	41	78	37	7	2	1	28	12	6	.256
Marvin Olson	2B131	139	431	60	115	59	16	0	0	93	15	6	.262
John Dudick	SS94	95	325	57	91	59	18	5	7	46	27	1	.280
Antonio Rodriguez	3B150	153	593	73	156	75	15	5	1	48	32	32	.263
Walt Cazen	OF153	153	620	116	204	68	30	12	6	71	48	74	.329
Al Mele	OF137	138	498	96	149	108	28	8	19	86	18	12	.299
Joseph Beeler	OF132,2B12	148	566	93	168	72	28	7	4	65	44	14	.297
Joe Just	C96	101	374	56	101	34	22	2	4	49	37	6	.270
Jake Daniel	1B73	73	248	44	69	47	11	3	4	55	31	2	.278
Herb Moore	SS58	64	181	29	32	21	2	0	0	51	33	2	.177
Russ Kerns	C48	59	161	24	38	16	3	1	1	39	18	1	.236
Robert Katz	P43	52	120	17	31	19	4	0	0	6	7	0	.258
John Bebber	P38	42	77	10	14	11	2	1	0	7	14	0	.182
John Tyler		37	51	3	8	2	3	0	0	5	9	0	.157
William Blue	P36	36	51	6	13	3	1	1	0	0	12	0	.255
Harold Palmer	C11	34	60	5	13	8	1	0	0	14	4	0	.217
Reg Grabowski	P27	29	31	1	8	4	2	0	1	1	6	0	.258
Mel Bosser	P25	25	45	1	4	4	0	0	0	2	5	0	.089
Francisco Davila	P22	22	47	3	5	6	0	1	0	6	9	0	.106
George Krall	P20	20	10	1	2	0	0	0	0	0	1	0	.200
Herm Wehmeier	P16	16	38	5	7	4	2	0	0	4	7	0	.184
Henry Gagain	OF13	13	43	4	5	1	0	0	0	2	8	0	.116
Ed Kalski	P12	12	13	1	1	0	0	0	0	0	2	0	.077
Bert Humphries	P9	9											.000
Joe Nuxhall	P7	9											.000
Ralph Kraus	2B	7	17	0	1	2	0	0	0			0	.059
Robert Springer	P7	7											.000
Art Simmons	OF	4	14	1	2	1	0	1	0			0	.286
Slobodan Yovanovich	PH	4	4	0	1	2	0	0	0			0	.250
Lloyd Patton	OF	2	9	4	3	3	0	0	0			0	.333
Robert Archer	OF	1	3	0	0	0	0	0	0			0	.000

PITCHERS	W	L	PCT	G	GS	CG	SH	IP	H	BB	SO	ERA
Robert Katz	20	20	.500	43	37	28	3	278	303	122	112	4.05
Francisco Davila	10	6	.625	22	20	12	1	140	147	92	63	4.44
John Bebber	8	20	.286	38	30	11	1	208	225	137	89	5.67
William Blue	7	9	.438	36	14	10	1	149	158	65	65	4.65
Mel Bosser	7	12	.368	25	19	13	2	148	153	82	43	4.20
Herm Wehmeier	4	8	.333	16	14	5	0	102	95	80	30	4.68
Bert Humphries	3	3	.500	9				37	48	20	10	
Reg Grabowski	2	5	.286	27	4	2	0	80	120	22	28	
George Krall	1	1	.500	20	3	1	0	44	42	17	11	3.68
Robert Springer	1	1	.500	7				14	17	6	3	
Ed Kalski	1	2	.333	12	4	0	0	37	32	23	10	5.35
Joe Nuxhall	0	2	.000	7				17	21	21	12	7.94

ROCHESTER Red Wings 8th 64-90 .416 -32 Burleigh Grimes

BATTERS	POS-GAMES	GP	AB	R	H	BI	2B	3B	HR	BB	SO	SB	BA
Ray Baughn	1B84	99	300	43	84	45	14	3	0	54	27	4	.280
Robert Rausch	2B106	141	528	85	171	62	21	5	1	66	23	16	.324
Art Frantz	SS57,P1	58	190	18	40	17	4	2	0	18	19	7	.211
Lugo Lancelotti	3B51	54	186	24	37	18	4	1	0	18	22	3	.199
Leroy Nichols	OF149	151	544	89	165	87	23	10	4	87	41	21	.303
Fred Marsh	OF91	96	341	44	91	32	12	11	0	10	13	13	.267
Joseph King	OF84,3B40	131	455	46	116	68	14	7	1	30	36	15	.255
James Devlin	C	(see multi-team players)											
Frank Bowa	SS36,3B30,2B17	85	258	64	60	32	9	3	0	65	36	10	.233
Charles Baron	1B58	76	235	25	52	33	11	4	3	18	14	4	.221
Don White	OF54	61	186	45	51	23	7	0	6	41	20	4	.274
Norm Shope	P28	53	79	12	18	9	2	0	0	10	12	0	.228
Otis Davis	OF40	52	174	19	34	13	5	1	0	13	21	2	.195
James Payne	OF49	51	182	26	55	34	5	3	1	19	4	3	.302
Louis Sakas	P44	44	28	3	6	2	1	0	0	0	4	0	.214
James Towns	SS29,3B14	42	147	25	37	8	2	0	0	25	7	3	.252
Maurice Sturdy	2B27,1B13	39	141	23	36	17	6	0	0	18	9	6	.255
Eugene Crumling	C36	39	113	9	29	10	3	1	0	9	7	1	.257
George Pratt	C35	38	96	6	23	10	1	1	0	12	6	0	.240
Frank Radler	P33	33	61	6	11	6	1	0	0	4	5	2	.180

ROCHESTER (cont.)
Red Wings

BATTERS	POS-GAMES	GP	AB	R	H	BI	2B	3B	HR	BB	SO	SB	BA
Kemp Wicker	P28	28	57	5	13	9	3	0	0	3	13	0	.228
William Trotter	P25	25	49	6	7	4	1	0	1	8	21	0	.143
Frank Wagner	P24	24	34	2	7	2	1	0	0	2	8	0	.206
Henry Stephenson	SS19	21	52	9	15	6	2	0	2	6	1	1	.288
Glenn Gardner	P20	20	43	4	13	6	3	0	0	1	3	0	.302
Herm Neuberger	P15	18	16	2	4	3	1	0	0	1	3	0	.250
Art Dwyer	P16	16	10	2	3	1	1	0	0	0	3	0	.300
Frank Martin	C11	13	33	3	6	2	1	1	0	3	5	1	.182
Charles Cozart	P13	13	30	2	7	4	1	0	0	1	4	0	.233
Stan Partenheimer	P11	11	18	2	3	2	0	0	0	3	4	0	.167
Clair Strommen	P6	6	1	1	1	0	0	0	0	0			0	1.000
John Pakron	P6	6											.000
Al Pittman	SS	5	7	1	0	0	0	0	0	0		1	.000
George Koby	P5	5											.000
John Cappa	OF	4	7	1	1	1	0	0	0	0		0	.143
Henry Koch	P4	4											.750
Conklyn Meriwether	P3	3	2	1	1	0	0	1	0			0	.500
Odell Creager	SS	2	7	2	2	1	0	0	0	0		0	.286
Joseph Borich	PH	1	1	0	1	0	0	0	0	0		0	1.000
Norm Glick	P1	1											.000
Sam Kuipers	P1	1											.000
Louis Tortora	P1	1											.000
Robert Vetter	P1	1											.000

PITCHERS	W	L	PCT	G	GS	CG	SH	IP	H	BB	SO	ERA
Kemp Wicker	11	12	.478	28	24	11	3	161	176	38	58	4.02
Norm Shope	10	6	.625	28	21	8	1	149	164	83	87	5.07
William Trotter	9	13	.409	25	24	14	1	174	197	32	34	3.83
Glenn Gardner	8	8	.500	20	16	10	0	118	120	36	41	3.58
Frank Wagner	6	4	.600	24	12	6	0	97	99	30	27	3.71
Frank Radler	6	23	.207	33	25	13	1	187	221	64	73	4.91
Stan Partenheimer	4	3	.571	11	7	4	3	51	49	25	26	4.24
Louis Sakas	4	6	.400	44	3	2	0	101	103	30	14	3.65
Charles Cozart	4	6	.400	13	10	3	0	72	84	32	24	4.88
John Pakron	1	0	1.000	6				12	8	9	2	3.00
Herm Neuberger	1	2	.333	15	2	0	0	44	48	25	21	4.50
Clair Strommen	0	1	.000	6				13	15	12	4	
Henry Koch	0	1	.000	4				12	18	10	0	
Art Frantz	0	1	.000	1				0	2	3	1	81.82
Norm Glick	0	1	.000	1				5	5	8	3	10.80
Sam Kuipers	0	1	.000	1				3	5	1	0	
Conklyn Meriwether	0	2	.000	3				5	8	6	2	
Art Dwyer	0	0	----	16	2	0	0	37	38	37	8	5.59
George Koby	0	0	----	5				13	7	14	6	
Robert Vetter	0	0	----	1				0	1	2	0	
Louis Tortora	0	0	----	1				2	0	5	0	9.00

MULTI-TEAM PLAYERS

BATTERS	POS-GAMES	TEAMS	GP	AB	R	H	BI	2B	3B	HR	BB	SO	SB	BA
Roy Nichols	3B68,SS40	JC79-MO33	112	334	45	85	41	13	4	2	44	27	2	.255
Larry Drake	OF92	TO54-BA49	103	354	45	84	48	11	5	8	22	59	5	.237
James Devlin	C88	BA19-RO79	98	259	26	64	29	8	3	4	55	21	1	.247
Al Wright	OF63	BU13-BA62	75	228	35	68	55	12	1	8	25	28	1	.298
Steve Mizerak	2B48	RO9-JC60	69	213	25	53	23	14	0	4	28	25	0	.249
Jack McWeeney	C29	JC14-RO19	33	89	10	18	17	2	2	4	5	21	1	.202
Walt Chipple	OF28	BA1-BU27	28	106	21	32	16	7	2	3	6	10	0	.302
Charles Mistos	P21	NE14-TO7	21	33	3	8	2	0	0	0	10	7	0	.242
Frank Hamons	P6	BU3-SY3	6											.000

PITCHERS	TEAMS	W	L	PCT	G	GS	CG	SH	IP	H	BB	SO	ERA
Charles Mistos	NE14-TO7	6	7	.462	21	15	6	0	118	135	52	41	4.12
Frank Hamons	BU3-SY3	0	1	.000	6				8	13	7	4	9.00

TEAM BATTING

TEAMS	GP	AB	R	H	BI	2B	3B	HR	BB	SO	SB	BA
MONTREAL	153	5007	861	**1443**	766	240	54	74	686	505	95	**.288**
NEWARK	153	4936	772	1327	670	205	40	101	605	510	204	.269
TORONTO	152	4810	771	1243	666	180	37	56	**779**	423	114	.257
BALTIMORE	153	4942	**870**	1317	**793**	202	54	**145**	774	**541**	79	.266
JERSEY CITY	153	4853	671	1246	592	175	51	65	547	432	68	.257
BUFFALO	153	**5118**	750	1404	695	**259**	44	113	458	507	47	.274
SYRACUSE	153	4953	753	1321	665	195	49	48	685	419	157	.268
ROCHESTER	**154**	4916	687	1273	605	168	**59**	26	598	436	120	.259
	612	39535	6135	10574	5452	1624	388	628	5132	3773	884	.267

1946
BARRIERS BROKEN

In October 1945, Jackie Robinson signed a contract to play for the Montreal Royals in 1946. In doing so, Robinson became the first African American in many years to be allowed to participate in organized ball outside the Negro Leagues. Although this was a groundbreaking decision by the Royals, spearheaded by their parent Brooklyn Dodgers organization, Robinson wasn't the first player of his race to grace International League fields. To find the first African American pioneers, one must journey back in time some 60 years earlier.

In mid–1886, a second baseman named Frank Grant joined the Buffalo Bisons after his team in Connecticut folded, thus becoming the first African American to play in the International League. The next year, several other African Americans, including Fleet Walker, George Stovey, and John Fowler, joined Grant in the International. In all, eight African Americans were playing in 1887, spread across six teams.

Unfortunately, racial intolerance soon raised its ugly head. In 1888, at an International League meeting, owners informally decided to sign no more new African American players, though they planned to retain the ones already present. Unwanted, the players drifted out of the International, seeking other leagues. Fleet Walker, catcher for the Syracuse Stars, became the last nineteenth century International League African American player in 1889.

Fifty-seven years later, Jackie Robinson electrified baseball, pushing the Montreal Royals to their second straight pennant. Batting a league-leading .349, Robinson led the Royals to their best record ever, eighteen games ahead of Syracuse. The rest of the teams (Baltimore, Newark, Buffalo, Toronto, Rochester, and Jersey City) finished well back in the standings. Eddie Robinson from Baltimore hit the most home runs (34) and had the most runs batted in (123). Two pitchers, Montreal's Steve Nagy and Jim Prendergast of Syracuse, finished tied for the most wins (17). Buffalo's Art Houtteman struck out the most batters (147), and Herb Karpel from Newark had the lowest earned run average (2.41).

In the years to follow, a trickle of African American players in organized ball quickly turned into a flood. By the mid–1950s virtually every organization was integrated. Jackie Robinson has shown the way for this trend, but the contributions of the nineteenth century African Americans should not be neglected. Robinson led the way to a world of hope and expansion of racial tolerance. Frank Grant and his compatriots could only watch their cause wither and die—a far heavier burden.

MONTREAL Royals

1st   100-54   .649   Clay Hopper

BATTERS	POS-GAMES	GP	AB	R	H	BI	2B	3B	HR	BB	SO	SB	BA
Lester Burge	1B119	124	418	81	119	101	26	8	15	76	58	8	.285
Jackie Robinson	2B119	124	444	**113**	155	66	25	8	3	92	27	40	**.349**
Al Campanis	SS116	127	428	80	126	68	21	6	3	51	50	14	.294
John Jorgenson	3B80,SS30	117	376	79	110	71	21	7	5	58	31	4	.291
Elmer Durrett	OF129	136	464	103	119	97	26	7	17	69	72	8	.256
Marv Rackley	OF122	124	465	102	142	66	20	**14**	4	78	28	65	.305
Earl Naylor	OF104,P1	107	378	74	113	77	20	10	4	50	57	9	.299
Herm Franks	C87	100	289	52	81	67	16	2	14	12	14	3	.280
Thomas Tatum	OF67,1B27,2B23	129	483	93	154	58	27	2	4	49	46	28	.319
Lew Riggs	3B76	90	297	64	90	73	20	5	15	61	23	3	.303
Homer Howell	C75	84	244	46	72	41	14	0	6	31	37	3	.295
Chet Ross	OF38	41	111	23	27	21	5	1	6	22	28	1	.243
Chester Kehn	P34	41	51	10	17	10	3	0	0	10	3	0	.333
Steve Nagy	P30	40	83	20	22	12	3	3	3	12	12	1	.265
John Gabbard	P31	31	29	0	4	2	1	0	0	2	8	0	.138
Cyril Buker	P29	29	52	5	9	5	0	0	0	5	6	0	.173
Glen Moulder	P28	28	55	10	17	7	1	0	0	1	4	0	.309
Jean Roy	P22	27	46	6	8	5	2	0	0	2	6	0	.174
John Banta	P23	23	46	5	6	4	0	1	0	2	6	0	.130
George Shuba	OF18	20	55	18	11	12	0	0	7	23	9	1	.200
Curt Davis	P20	20	26	1	6	2	2	0	0	0	7	0	.231
Stan Breard	SS17	18	60	10	18	10	4	0	0	6	2	0	.300
Paul Schoendienst	1B11	16	47	7	17	10	1	1	0	2	3	0	.362
Armand Cardoni	P11	11	26	1	1	1	0	0	0	0	8	0	.038
Robert Fontaine	P11	11	13	1	1	1	0	0	0	1	4	0	.077
Roy Partlow	P10	10	13	3	2	2	0	0	0	1	3	0	.154
Frank Laga	P7	7											.100
DeWitt Ferrell	C	6	13	3	5	1	0	0	0			0	.385
Ray Hathaway	P6	6											.167
Joe Smolko	P4	6											.143
Joe Gallagher	OF	6	9	0	1	1	0	0	0			1	.111
Bernard DeForge	P6	6											.100
David Pluss	OF	5	11	3	2	2	0	0	0			0	.182
Wayne Collins	P4	4											.000
Otis Davis	OF	4	3	2	0	0	0	0	0			0	.000
Jack Paepke	P4	4											.000
Clarence Groat	OF	3	2	0	1	0	0	0	0			0	.500
Ed Nulty	C	3	2	0	0	0	0	0	0			0	.000
Louis Welaj	SS	2	2	0	1	0	0	0	0			1	.500
John Wright	P2	2											.500
Ben Stansky	OF	2	7	0	1	3	1	0	0			0	.143
Larry Mondorff	P1	1											1.000
Lloyd Fisher	P1	1											.000
William Tanner	P1	1											.000

PITCHERS		W	L	PCT	G	GS	CG	SH	IP	H	BB	SO	ERA
Steve Nagy		**17**	4	**.810**	30	25	17	1	203	188	94	130	3.01
Chester Kehn		12	7	.632	34	11	5	1	130	129	60	71	4.29
Cyril Buker		12	7	.632	29	22	9	1	163	148	77	85	3.81
John Gabbler		11	7	.611	31	12	4	0	104	110	54	31	4.33
Glen Moulder		10	6	.625	28	17	11	2	133	131	56	61	3.25
John Banta		9	6	.600	23	18	7	1	125	140	69	71	5.04
Jean Roy		8	5	.615	22	16	7	1	111	139	77	56	5.59
Curt Davis		5	3	.625	20	8	6	1	75	71	13	30	3.00
Bob Fontaine		3	1	.750	11	5	2	0	44	40	25	20	3.68
Joe Smolko		3	1	.750	4				17	17	13	4	
Armand Cardoni		3	4	.429	11	7	2	0	64	73	15	26	4.36
Ray Partlow		2	0	1.000	10	4	1	0	29	26	16	19	5.59
Bernard De Forge		2	1	.667	6				31	29	10	13	
Frank Laga		1	0	1.000	7				30	23	14	14	
Wayne Collins		1	0	1.000	4				14	14	10	6	
Ray Hathaway		1	2	.333	6				22	22	19	8	
Jack Paepke		0	0	----	4				3	15	1	3	24.00
John Wright		0	0	----	2				6	5	5	3	
Earl Naylor		0	0	----	1				1	1	0	1	0.00
William Tanner		0	0	----	1				5	6	4	2	
Larry Mondorff		0	0	----	1				2	2	2	2	
Lloyd Fisher		0	0	----	1				1	2	0	0	9.00

SYRACUSE Chiefs

2nd   81-72   .529   -18.5   Jewel Ens

BATTERS	POS-GAMES	GP	AB	R	H	BI	2B	3B	HR	BB	SO	SB	BA
Charles Kress	1B145	145	536	100	140	80	23	6	10	64	76	11	.261
Roland Harrington	2B112	114	454	83	122	50	13	4	13	49	29	11	.269
Kermit Wahl	SS109	109	362	52	98	58	15	3	7	57	40	2	.271
Al Rubeling	3B136	145	521	76	144	79	15	12	12	73	47	7	.276
Hank Sauer	OF131	140	517	99	146	90	29	2	21	76	59	13	.282
Al Mele	OF115	117	420	63	122	74	14	3	15	72	19	6	.290
Joseph Beeler	OF103,2B10	114	429	72	124	45	23	2	4	65	52	8	.289
Joe Just	C78	80	245	27	54	41	8	0	6	42	32	3	.220
Dick Sipek	OF78	98	319	35	78	22	14	8	1	26	28	3	.245
Richard West	C73	87	286	47	84	48	10	4	6	34	33	9	.294
John Dudick	SS39	53	156	23	40	22	5	0	3	21	30	1	.256
Millard Howell	P24	52	100	12	19	13	1	1	4	7	22	0	.190
Ken Polivka	P34	34	23	1	3	2	0	0	0	6	3	0	.130
Garton Del Savio	3B15	33	111	9	24	11	2	2	0	5	6	0	.216
Jim Prendergast	P33	33	73	6	18	6	5	0	0	5	20	0	.247
Earl Harrist	P32	32	72	5	12	3	0	0	0	1	17	0	.167
William Schultz	P29	29	46	5	10	4	0	1	0	3	16	1	.217
Ed Heinrich	OF17	27	62	6	14	9	2	0	1	8	10	0	.226
John Wittig	P27	27	20	3	4	0	0	0	0	1	6	0	.200
Len Bobeck	P26	26	16	0	2	0	0	0	0	3	6	0	.125
William Sinton	OF19	24	78	12	18	9	4	2	0	5	11	1	.231
Robert Katz	P22	22	36	6	5	3	0	0	0	1	5	0	.139
Arnold Carter	P14	19	20	6	5	3	1	0	0	1	5	1	.250
Jack Cassini	2B14	15	56	8	9	3	1	1	0	6	4	2	.161
Thad Bosiack	C	11	22	2	6	4	2	0	0	2	4	0	.273
Howard Fox	P7	7											.111
George Burpo	P3	3											.000
John Bebber	P2	2											.000
William Blue	P2	2											.000
Al Korhonen	PH	1	1	0	0	0	0	0	0			0	.000

PITCHERS	W	L	PCT	G	GS	CG	SH	IP	H	BB	SO	ERA
Jim Prendergast	17	10	.630	33	26	12	4	202	228	55	62	3.92
Earl Harrist	15	10	.600	32	29	15	5	212	181	79	105	3.74
William Schultz	11	7	.611	29	15	9	1	144	111	58	80	2.75
Millard Howell	10	14	,417	24	24	19	2	190	191	100	100	3.55
Robert Katz	7	5	.583	22	14	6	0	107	112	58	38	4.96
Ken Polivka	6	6	.500	34	7	2	0	93	99	41	54	4.26
Howard Fox	4	1	.800	7				51	51	36	27	3.71
Arnold Carter	4	3	.571	14	10	4	1	66	61	36	13	3.82
Len Bobeck	2	2	.500	26	4	0	0	74	66	38	35	3.16
John Wittig	1	7	.125	27	5	1	0	71	78	33	52	4.31
George Burpo	0	2	.000	3				12	14	11	7	10.50
John Bebber	0	0	----	2				3	1	4	1	
William Blue	0	0	----	2				2	5	1	0	

BALTIMORE Orioles

3rd   81-73   .526   -19   Alphonse Thomas

BATTERS	POS-GAMES	GP	AB	R	H	BI	2B	3B	HR	BB	SO	SB	BA
Eddie Robinson	1B140	140	528	99	168	123	25	5	34	72	47	3	.318
Al Cihocki	2B151	154	541	69	130	58	19	12	4	41	90	4	.240
Robert Repass	SS151	151	564	96	145	67	21	1	19	61	77	6	.257
Howard Moss	3B130	130	492	90	137	112	21	4	38	42	80	2	.278
Clarence Campbell	OF149	149	520	113	140	43	19	5	8	141	39	8	.269
John Ward	OF131	136	440	74	106	35	17	1	3	78	45	30	.241
Joseph Mellendick	OF125	140	446	62	114	81	18	6	14	55	60	11	.256
Louis Kahn	C76,OF10	102	300	36	83	38	15	3	8	41	35	11	.277
George Staller	OF50	72	201	29	51	26	3	4	2	12	13	7	.254
Sherm Lollar	C62	67	222	37	52	56	6	0	20	40	39	3	.234
John Podgajny	P46	46	45	2	6	3	0	0	0	6	12	0	.133
Al Barillari	P36	40	57	7	11	7	4	0	0	5	7	0	.193
George Hooks	P35	35	37	2	5	2	1	0	0	2	14	0	.135
Stan West	P34	34	71	8	21	14	2	0	0	1	8	0	.296
Ray Flanigan	P34	34	63	8	10	3	0	3	0	8	25	0	.159
Raymond Murray	C23	33	88	7	20	10	0	0	2	4	13	0	.227
Alex Ronay	P31	31	32	4	6	2	0	0	0	7	16	0	.188
Frank Skaff	3B15,1B	25	83	11	13	1	2	0	4	18	21	0	.157
Raymond Poat	P23	23	54	5	5	5	2	0	0	1	22	0	.093
Ed Wodzicki		20	34	2	6	4	1	0	0	8	5	0	.176

BALTIMORE (cont.)
Orioles

BATTERS	POS-GAMES	GP	AB	R	H	BI	2B	3B	HR	BB	SO	SB	BA
George Honochick	OF	13	25	3	7	1	1	0	0	4	3	1	.280
Raymond Roche	P12	12	7	0	2	1	0	0	0	0	4	0	.286
Paul Smith	P12	12	3	0	0	0	0	0	0	0	2	0	.000
Al Tiedemann		10	7	1	0	0	0	0	0	2	3	0	.000
Clyde Smoll	P10	10	3	1	0	0	0	0	0	1	3	0	.000
Vic Badura	P7	7											.000
Phil Seghi	3B	6	18	1	5	2	0	0	0	0			0	.278
John Scheidt	OF,1B	5	9	1	1	0	0	0	0	0		0	.111
Les Webber	P5	5											.154
Burton Swift	P5	5											.000
Robert Latshaw	1B	4	13	2	4	4	1	0	0	0		0	.308
Sam Lowry	P4	4											.000
Joseph Garliss	C	2	4	0	0	0	0	0	0	0		0	.000
Mike Duplinsky	P2	2											1.000
Vic Johnson	P2	2											.000
George Cave	P1	1											.000
Gord Mueller	P1	1											.000

PITCHERS		W	L	PCT	G	GS	CG	SH	IP	H	BB	SO	ERA
Stan West		13	14	.481	34	29	14	2	209	194	100	65	3.96
Ray Flanigan		13	14	.481	34	29	14	3	198	181	112	98	4.09
Raymond Poat		12	7	.632	23	21	9	2	137	127	53	101	4.01
John Podgajny		12	11	.522	46	16	9	3	172	166	52	55	3.40
Al Barillari		11	11	.500	36	21	9	2	155	176	68	68	5.28
George Hooks		7	5	.583	22	14	6	0	120	131	71	64	4.96
Alex Ronay		6	3	.667	31	12	3	0	106	105	68	52	4.75
Les Webber		3	2	.600	5				41	38	21	26	
Raymond Roche		1	0	1.000	12	3	1	0	25	24	14	15	2.88
Sam Lowry		0	1	.000	4				8	9	4	2	
Gord Mueller		0	1	.000	1				3	5	2	2	
Paul Smith		0	0	----	12	0	0	0	15	27	12	7	12.60
Clyde Smoll		0	0	----	10	0	0	0	16	23	9	16	7.31
Vic Badura		0	0	----	7				9	14	12	6	
Burton Swift		0	0	----	5				5	11	3	2	
Mike Duplinsky		0	0	----	2				4	3	1	0	
Vic Johnson		0	0	----	2				3	6	1	2	
George Cave		0	0	----	1				1	3	2	2	

NEWARK   4th   80-74   .519   -20   George Selkirk
Bears

BATTERS	POS-GAMES	GP	AB	R	H	BI	2B	3B	HR	BB	SO	SB	BA
John Hassett	1B105	117	425	67	118	42	23	2	7	65	15	3	.278
Joe Buzas	2B53	62	223	25	52	18	8	2	3	9	17	5	.233
Robert Brown	SS147	148	510	70	174	68	27	4	5	74	19	4	.341
Don Savage	3B66	75	251	38	52	45	6	1	7	45	67	5	.207
Ford Garrison	OF114	115	419	77	121	54	18	3	12	56	34	12	.289
Frank Colman	OF79	84	289	53	88	58	16	8	15	45	23	4	.304
Harold Douglas	OF67	75	278	30	63	39	10	2	3	23	27	1	.227
Yogi Berra	C70,OF10	77	277	41	87	59	14	1	15	16	16	5	.314
John Phillips	3B49,1B37	101	339	51	85	40	12	4	5	51	38	8	.251
Alfred Clark	OF60,3B25	97	352	64	121	70	17	6	14	25	27	2	.344
Joe Collins	OF63,1B	67	243	29	66	31	10	3	6	18	25	4	.272
Mike Milosevich	2B51,3B14	65	192	22	34	17	3	1	2	26	20	4	.177
Milt Byrnes	OF58	58	179	44	46	25	10	2	4	60	20	2	.257
Charles Fallon	C50	54	135	10	27	6	3	0	0	25	7	1	.200
Mike Garbark	C43	48	131	13	27	10	2	0	0	22	13	0	.206
Blas Monaco	2B41	41	129	25	28	17	2	0	5	28	20	3	.217
Herb Karpel	P29	32	64	5	8	3	2	0	0	8	17	0	.125
Duane Pillette	P31	31	62	7	7	2	0	0	0	9	18	0	.113
John Moore	P31	31	45	3	4	6	1	0	0	5	10	0	.089
George Selkirk	OF	31	40	8	12	5	1	0	1	13	9	1	.300
Alex Mustaikas	P29	31	35	3	8	3	0	1	0	1	7	1	.229
Roy Pitter	P16	24	26	3	6	3	0	0	1	2	13	1	.231
Walt Dubiel	P23	23	48	1	7	5	0	0	0	1	13	0	.146
Steve Peek	P19	20	47	6	9	6	1	0	0	5	7	1	.191
Frank Makosky	P20	20	5	0	1	0	0	0	0	0	0	0	.200
Walt Nowak	1B13	18	57	9	13	7	2	0	1	8	13	1	.228
William Houtz	P11	18	15	5	4	2	1	0	0	3	2	0	.267
Wiliam Deininger		16	32	4	6	7	0	0	0	1	5	0	.188
Charles Haag	P13	14	14	2	1	1	0	0	0	1	1	0	.071

NEWARK (cont.)
Bears

BATTERS	POS-GAMES	GP	AB	R	H	BI	2B	3B	HR	BB	SO	SB	BA
Ken Holcombe	P12	13	23	2	4	0	2	0	0	2	10	0	.174
John Haley	P13	13	9	1	2	0	0	0	0	0	2	0	.222
Don Schmidt	P12	12	2	1	0	0	0	0	0	2	1	0	.000
James Tote	P9	10	18	3	2	2	0	0	0	3	9	0	.111
Sal Recca	C	5	9	0	2	1	0	0	0			0	.222
Vic Raschi	P5	5											.333
Richard Korte	2B	4	6	1	0	0	0	0	0			0	.000
Frank Hiller	P4	4											.000
Leon Treadway	OF	2	8	2	2	1	2	0	0			1	.250
Harry Garbett	P2	2											.000
Fred Daniels	PH	1	1	0	0	0	0	0	0			0	.000
Eugene Bergerson	P1	1											.000
Norm Branch	P1	1											.000
James Davis	P1	1											.000
Henry Perry	P1	1											.000
John Robinson	P1	1											.000

PITCHERS	W	L	PCT	G	GS	CG	SH	IP	H	BB	SO	ERA
Herb Karpel	14	8	.636	29	25	18	2	187	167	55	100	**2.41**
Duane Pillette	11	10	.524	31	25	17	2	194	168	96	142	3.66
Steve Peek	10	6	.625	19	18	7	0	136	116	92	50	3.97
Walt Dubiel	9	7	.563	23	21	9	2	125	129	48	69	4.54
John Moore	8	11	.421	31	18	9	0	144	135	68	83	4.31
Alex Mustaikas	7	1	.875	29	0	0	0	84	75	31	44	3.11
Ken Holcombe	6	5	.545	12	12	6	1	76	56	35	29	3.08
Frank Makosky	4	5	.444	20	0	0	0	32	35	17	17	3.09
James Tote	3	4	.429	9				54	50	28	30	
Don Schmidt	2	1	.667	12	0	0	0	21	28	11	10	5.14
Roy Pitter	2	7	.222	16	14	2	1	78	65	48	25	3.81
John Haley	1	2	.333	13	1	0	0	26	24	29	11	4.85
Charles Haag	1	2	.333	13	5	1	0	35	31	17	9	5.66
Willaim Hartz	1	2	.333	11	1	0	0	40	35	29	18	3.60
Vic Raschi	1	2	.333	5				33	32	8	16	3.27
Harry Garbett	0	1	.000	2				7	9	6	2	
Norm Branch	0	1	.000	1				1	1	4	1	
Frank Hiller	0	0	----	4				6	16	4	3	22.50
Henry Perry	0	0	----	1				4	2	3	0	0.00
James Davis	0	0	----	1				1	1	4	0	36.00
John Robinson	0	0	----	1				1	2	2	1	27.00
Eugene Bergerson	0	0	----	1				3	7	3	1	18.00

BUFFALO   5th   78-75   .510   -21.5   Gabby Hartnett
Bisons

BATTERS	POS-GAMES	GP	AB	R	H	BI	2B	3B	HR	BB	SO	SB	BA
John McHale	1B132	133	482	84	130	94	24	4	25	75	83	6	.270
William Radulovich	2B107	117	393	60	116	63	20	5	9	49	30	3	.295
Cornelius Berry	SS136	136	556	93	159	36	21	8	0	61	54	8	.286
John Bero	3B132	134	504	93	140	70	30	3	9	75	60	5	.278
Vic Wertz	OF128	139	478	75	144	91	27	9	19	48	40	2	.301
Coaker Triplett	OF92	101	360	56	109	51	13	4	11	44	19	1	.303
Ed Mierkowicz	OF73,1B21	103	358	53	88	57	20	4	10	39	45	3	.246
Martin Tabacheck	C85	88	255	27	65	18	7	1	0	20	19	0	.255
John Antonelli	2B41,3B23	74	251	37	67	32	14	1	3	24	8	1	.267
Zeb Eaton	P32	73	107	14	31	23	4	0	6	7	14	0	.290
Earl Rapp	OF57	62	204	46	66	38	13	2	5	31	25	8	.324
Walt Chipple	OF47	57	153	28	42	23	5	1	5	23	24	0	.275
Pete Appleton	P36	37	25	1	3	2	1	0	0	2	8	0	.120
Bruce Campbell	OF30	33	107	15	29	13	5	1	2	11	14	1	.271
Art Houtteman	P32	33	78	10	17	6	2	0	0	4	9	0	.218
Chet Wieczorek	OF27	27	103	9	25	15	5	0	4	10	12	0	.243
Ted Gray	P25	26	47	5	8	2	0	0	0	1	13	0	.170
Rufus Gentry	P25	25	60	5	20	8	5	0	1	0	8	0	.333
Les Mueller	P23	23	55	4	12	3	1	0	0	2	16	0	.218
Harold Manders	P20	20	53	5	8	2	1	0	0	0	6	0	.151
Dennis Horton	P19	19	24	0	4	1	1	0	0	2	4	0	.167
Anderson Bush	P19	19	18	2	3	1	0	0	0	3	7	0	.167
Ray Hamrick	SS18	18	65	10	13	2	2	0	0	11	8	2	.200
Vern Curtis	P15	15	14	2	1	0	0	0	0	1	7	0	.071
Walt Pierce	P10	12	19	3	4	3	0	0	0	3	3	0	.211
Louis Kretlow	P11	11	9	1	0	0	0	0	0	1	7	0	.000

BUFFALO (cont.)
Bisons

BATTERS	POS-GAMES	GP	AB	R	H	BI	2B	3B	HR	BB	SO	SB	BA
Ed Boland	OF	10	34	2	9	4	0	0	0	4	1	0	.265
Eugene Markland	2B10	10	32	8	5	4	0	0	1	6	5	0	.156
George Lerchen	OF	9	33	3	8	1	1	0	0			0	.242
Harvey Riebe	C	8	22	2	3	2	1	0	0			0	.136
Stan Rogers	SS,3B	6	20	5	5	1	0	0	1			1	.250
Ray Clark	P3	4	6	1	2	0	0	0	0			0	.333
Frank Heller	PH	2	2	0	0	0	0	0	0			0	.000
Quinn Lee	P2	2											.000
Ernest Andres	3B	1	3	0	1	0	0	0	0			0	.333
Lewis Fauth	P1	1											.000
Robert Hall	P1	1											.000

PITCHERS		W	L	PCT	G	GS	CG	SH	IP	H	BB	SO	ERA
Art Houtteman		16	13	.552	32	**30**	18	4	226	217	75	**147**	4.22
Harold Manders		10	4	.714	20	17	9	1	134	117	68	79	3.90
Rufus Gentry		10	8	.556	25	24	10	2	153	142	**113**	108	5.18
Les Mueller		10	8	.556	23	21	10	1	150	161	79	80	5.04
Pete Appleton		9	5	.643	36	1	0	0	91	89	40	56	3.66
Ted Gray		7	11	.389	25	15	8	0	123	140	82	80	6.22
Dennis Horton		4	3	.571	19	10	4	0	85	70	61	46	4.13
Zeb Eaton		3	4	.429	32	7	3	0	112	126	88	44	7.07
Vern Curtis		3	4	.429	15	8	2	1	57	66	22	27	4.58
Walt Pierce		3	4	.429	10	9	5	0	56	52	44	45	4.50
Anderson Bush		2	7	.222	19	9	3	1	68	70	37	36	5.69
Ray Clark		1	1	.500	3				12	15	12	5	
Louis Kretlow		0	3	.000	11	4	0	0	36	51	33	34	7.25
Quinn Lee		0	0	----	2				4	5	1	2	
Lewis Fauth		0	0	----	1				2	7	2	0	
Robert Hall		0	0	----	1				1	2	0	0	0.00

TORONTO   6th   71-82   .464   -28.5   Harry Davis
Maple Leafs

BATTERS	POS-GAMES	GP	AB	R	H	BI	2B	3B	HR	BB	SO	SB	BA
Bruce Konopka	1B61	61	209	30	59	23	16	1	2	18	16	0	.282
Ben Steiner	2B105	106	386	61	92	22	11	4	3	61	37	13	.238
Fred Chapman	SS86	88	317	38	68	22	7	4	3	32	28	1	.215
Don Richmond	3B107	117	390	38	114	45	22	1	4	23	31	7	.292
Ira Houck	OF143	143	526	67	153	69	18	4	6	53	32	12	.291
Ellis Deal	OF54,P16	90	223	30	55	32	12	4	5	29	50	1	.247
Austin Knickerbocker	OF		(see multi-team players)										
Herb Crompton	C51	52	155	13	36	14	4	2	0	16	5	0	.232
John Wallaesa	SS63	63	202	29	51	24	9	5	6	37	48	2	.252
Henry Biasetti	1B52	56	160	11	32	13	4	1	0	18	7	1	.200
Morris Aderholt	OF44,2B10	54	171	16	41	25	6	3	3	18	21	1	.240
Byron LaForest	3B19,OF17	53	179	25	39	13	6	2	3	25	39	2	.218
Henry Camelli	C46	50	137	12	31	22	5	1	2	26	16	0	.226
Al Brancato	3B33	44	147	20	34	18	8	2	5	20	17	1	.231
Ben Drake	1B28	38	106	12	27	5	4	1	0	13	9	1	.255
Norm Brown	P31	34	27	2	2	1	1	0	0	4	6	0	.074
Otto Denning	1B18,C11	33	120	16	28	19	11	0	2	8	10	0	.233
Chet Morgan	OF24	28	91	12	21	10	5	0	0	7	6	2	.231
Robert Wilkins	2B25	26	82	12	14	3	2	0	0	13	11	0	.171
Vern Benson	OF22	26	71	15	11	8	2	1	3	18	12	4	.155
Joseph Coleman	P26	26	65	6	11	2	1	0	1	7	29	0	.169
Luke Hamlin	P26	26	63	1	11	4	1	0	0	5	12	0	.175
William McCahan	P24	24	51	3	14	3	1	0	0	1	2	0	.275
Herm Besse	P21	22	40	3	6	3	3	0	0	7	7	0	.150
Jim Konstanty	P20	20	44	2	8	6	2	0	0	1	7	0	.182
Dwight Simonds	P20	20	13	0	3	0	0	0	0	0	2	0	.231
Lee Gamble	OF17	19	60	4	12	8	1	2	0	9	2	1	.200
Norm Willis		17	27	4	3	4	0	0	2	9	7	0	.111
Jonas Berry	P16	16	10	0	1	0	0	0	0	0	1	0	.100
Walt Smola	P12	12	7	0	1	1	0	0	0	2	3	1	.143
Harry Davis	1B	11	9	0	4	0	0	0	0	1	2	0	.444
Al Mazur	2B10	10	33	2	6	0	0	0	0	6	9	0	.182
Charles Mistos	P10	10	8	1	4	3	0	0	0	0	3	0	.500
Les McCrabb	P9	9											.067
Harry Jordan	P8	8											.000
Ralph Williams	P3	3											.250
Earl Cook	P3	3											.000

TORONTO (cont.)
Maple Leafs

BATTERS	POS-GAMES	GP	AB	R	H	BI	2B	3B	HR	BB	SO	SB	BA
Marsh Mauldin	OF	2	9	3	4	0	0	0	0			1	.444
Alva Javery	P2	2											1.000
Frank Wagner	P2	2											.000
Joe Astroth	C	1	3	0	0	0	0	0	0			0	.000
William Connelly	P1	1											.000

PITCHERS		W	L	PCT	G	GS	CG	SH	IP	H	BB	SO	ERA
Joseph Coleman		14	10	.583	26	24	17	5	198	187	64	108	2.95
Luke Hamlin		12	10	.545	26	26	17	1	193	209	41	98	3.64
William McCahan		11	7	.611	24	18	13	2	150	149	60	69	2.76
Herm Besse		9	7	.563	21	17	10	2	133	132	48	79	3.86
Ellis Deal		6	6	.500	16	14	6	0	79	88	63	35	5.58
Norm Brown		5	7	.417	31	10	5	1	109	111	60	31	3.63
Henry Jordan		4	3	.571	8				45	44	10	13	
Jim Konstanty		4	9	.308	20	15	8	0	123	135	46	47	3.88
Charles Mistos		2	2	.500	10	4	2	0	34	34	13	8	4.24
Les McCrabb		2	5	.286	9				43	56	20	16	
Walt Smola		1	1	.500	12	0	0	0	30	33	17	11	6.30
Alva Javery		0	1	.000	2				3	9	4	1	
Jonas Berry		0	2	.000	16	0	0	0	37	37	16	28	2.68
Earl Cook		0	3	.000	3				16	19	8	3	
Dwight Simonds		0	6	.000	20	3	2	0	46	41	27	10	3.72
Ralph Williams		0	0	----	3				10	8	5	3	
Frank Wagner		0	0	----	2				5	8	2	0	
William Connelly		0	0	----	1				1	0	4	0	9.00

ROCHESTER   7th   65-87   .428   -34   Burleigh Grimes -
Red Wings   Benny Borgmann

BATTERS	POS-GAMES	GP	AB	R	H	BI	2B	3B	HR	BB	SO	SB	BA
Charles Baron	1B116	118	415	55	118	50	22	5	7	43	30	3	.284
Danny Murtaugh	2B129	139	541	73	174	62	23	4	0	53	46	11	.322
Eddie Joost	SS137	143	493	85	136	101	35	9	19	77	88	5	.276
Vernal Jones	3B67	71	288	49	99	55	16	9	5	12	20	1	.344
Charles Diering	OF141	141	533	84	142	60	22	13	10	80	97	19	.266
Art Rebel	OF138	145	513	84	129	80	25	9	12	63	35	6	.251
Clyde Vollmer	OF87	103	338	38	93	58	20	3	9	30	37	7	.275
Charles Hockenberry	C90	105	252	32	70	21	12	1	2	45	9	6	.278
Robert Detweiler	3B31,1B22,OF19	88	263	31	62	30	9	1	5	21	41	2	.236
Robert Rausch	3B30,2B25	71	186	22	38	9	6	0	0	34	15	3	.204
Leroy Nichols	OF36	51	125	18	29	8	3	1	0	30	12	6	.232
Al Kubski	3B22,OF15	50	156	40	43	12	3	4	1	39	37	7	.275
Charles Marshall	C50	50	106	8	23	9	4	2	0	16	31	1	.217
John Bucha	C34	40	90	6	19	11	2	1	0	12	14	0	.211
Glenn Gardner	P35	35	77	3	13	3	1	0	0	0	12	0	.169
John Mikan	P33	33	66	4	9	9	2	0	0	6	21	0	.136
Paul Wargo	P23	31	34	4	5	3	1	0	0	3	10	0	.147
Walt Bruner	P30	31	26	3	3	3	1	0	0	4	8	0	.115
Eldred Byerly	P29	30	85	5	23	8	4	0	0	5	7	0	.271
William Osborne	P29	30	23	2	6	2	2	0	0	1	6	0	.261
Matt Surkont	P28	28	57	6	9	5	0	0	0	4	4	0	.158
Lloyd Moore	P28	28	20	2	3	0	0	0	0	2	5	0	.150
Ray Yochim	P17	17	28	1	3	1	1	0	0	0	7	0	.107
Warren Robinson	C14	15	40	6	10	2	2	0	0	7	5	1	.250
Bernard Creger	SS13	14	43	5	11	5	1	1	0	3	4	0	.256
Don White	OF,1B	14	30	4	9	4	0	1	0	6	6	0	.300
Ken Johnson	P11	12	18	1	4	1	0	0	0	1	5	0	.222
James Halkard	1B	11	34	1	9	6	2	1	0	2	2	0	.265
Louis Sakas	P10	10	5	1	2	0	0	0	0	0	2	0	.400
Al Cleary	P10	10	5	0	1	0	0	0	0	0	2	0	.200
William Costa	SS	7	18	1	3	0	2	0	0			0	.167
Les Fusselman	C	4	5	0	4	0	0	0	0			0	.800
Roy Huff	OF	4	4	1	0	0	0	0	0			0	.000
Floyd Thierolf	P4	4											.000
Roy Fowler	2B	3	8	1	0	0	0	0	0			0	.000
Eugene Czaplicki	OF	3	6	0	0	0	0	0	0			0	.000
Clint Echols	P3	3											.000
George Koby	P3	3											.000
Joseph DiCecco	P2	2											.000
James Burns	2B	1	4	1	0	0	0	0	0			0	.000
Richard Burgett	OF	1	1	0	0	0	0	0	0			0	.000

ROCHESTER (cont.)
Red Wings

BATTERS	POS-GAMES	GP	AB	R	H	BI	2B	3B	HR	BB	SO	SB	BA
Don Bakkelund	P1	1											.000
Frank Lugos	P1	1											.000

PITCHERS		W	L	PCT	G	GS	CG	SH	IP	H	BB	SO	ERA
Eldred Byerly		15	14	.517	29	29	21	1	213	205	71	63	3.89
Glenn Gardner		14	15	.483	35	30	14	2	208	207	84	72	3.98
John Mikan		10	6	.625	33	21	11	2	183	160	81	98	4.08
Matt Surkont		9	17	.346	28	27	8	0	176	183	109	81	5.47
William Osborne		6	4	.600	29	3	1	0	70	75	39	19	3.86
Ray Yochim		4	4	.500	17	11	5	2	78	80	49	24	3.81
Walter Bruner		3	9	.250	30	9	4	0	102	100	70	24	3.97
Lloyd Moore		2	7	.222	28	8	1	0	81	98	46	30	5.89
Paul Wargo		1	3	.250	23	2	0	0	55	63	38	23	5.07
Ken Johnson		1	4	.200	11	7	3	0	43	45	44	23	5.02
Al Cleary		0	2	.000	10	5	0	0	26	21	25	10	6.23
Louis Sakas		0	2	.000	10	0	0	0	18	30	11	1	12.00
Floyd Thierolf		0	0	----	4				5	5	4	2	
Clint Echols		0	0	----	3				3	9	3	4	
George Koby		0	0	----	3				2	3	2	1	
Joseph DiCecco		0	0	----	2				1	4	1	1	
Don Bakkelund		0	0	----	1				1	0	1	1	0.00
Frank Lugos		0	0	----	1				0	0	1	1	0.00

JERSEY CITY   8th   57-96   .373   -42.5   Bruno Betzel
Giants

BATTERS	POS-GAMES	GP	AB	R	H	BI	2B	3B	HR	BB	SO	SB	BA
Norm Jaeger	1B93	114	358	47	95	45	17	2	11	41	35	3	.265
Richard Lajeskie	2B135	136	464	57	107	56	13	5	9	62	84	2	.231
Robert Westfall	SS93	96	307	53	70	26	12	2	5	69	55	3	.228
Bobby Thomson	3B99,OF45	151	533	93	149	92	12	7	26	51	64	15	.280
Nick Solomon	OF110	124	391	57	107	56	13	5	9	62	84	2	.231
Les Layton	OF108	115	390	44	78	47	12	0	13	52	50	6	.200
Jesse Pike	OF89	96	314	43	81	39	13	0	9	48	47	11	.258
Newt Grasso	C87	106	303	31	69	46	8	0	13	24	43	1	.228
Joseph Lafata	1B42,OF33	85	285	36	85	41	16	6	7	24	34	2	.298
Russ Wein	SS53,2B16	79	193	20	50	12	3	0	0	31	16	4	.259
James Gladd	C44	50	145	13	39	12	4	3	3	13	30	2	.269
Larry Miggins	3B30	37	114	12	29	10	1	1	3	7	22	0	.254
Mike Kash	P36	36	27	0	3	2	0	0	0	2	7	1	.111
Marv Grissom	P34	34	27	4	3	0	0	0	0	9	12	0	.111
Art Fowler	P31	32	40	3	6	3	0	0	0	2	3	0	.150
William Emmerich	P30	30	49	4	10	5	1	0	0	8	13	0	.204
Herb Andrews	P30	30	45	2	4	3	1	0	0	6	11	0	.089
Don Mueller	OF18	28	78	12	28	9	7	0	1	3	3	0	.359
Mike Mellis	P28	28	37	4	5	1	1	0	0	3	8	0	.135
Richard Hoover	P24	24	43	1	3	0	0	0	0	2	13	0	.070
James Maynard	OF20	22	86	14	24	11	6	0	2	11	7	2	.279
George Barley	P22	22	16	1	3	0	0	0	0	3	9	0	.188
Jaime Almendro	SS19	20	58	7	11	2	2	1	0	3	2	0	.190
Robert Barthelson	P18	18	6	1	3	2	0	0	0	0	2	1	.500
Cleston Ray	OF16	17	62	7	14	9	1	0	1	6	6	3	.226
Alex Pecora	3B16	17	48	6	11	6	2	0	0	8	3	0	.229
Mel Harpuder	3B11	17	48	6	9	3	2	1	0	13	10	0	.188
Mike Schemer	1B16	16	61	9	22	5	5	0	0	3	1	0	.361
James Pruett	C13	16	46	3	10	4	1	0	1	5	2	1	.217
Chet Juckno	OF	15	23	1	7	3	1	0	0	0	3	0	.304
Russ Rollandson	C12	14	35	4	9	3	2	1	1	1	4	0	.257
Dan Siracusa	OF11	14	28	3	8	2	1	0	1	5	4	0	.286
Warren Sandel	P12	12	17	0	5	2	1	0	0	1	3	1	.294
Morris Arnovich	OF	10	25	2	5	4	0	0	1	4	2	0	.200
Don Fisher	P9	10	19	1	9	4	4	0	0	0	3	0	.474
Richard Bouknight	C	10	14	0	4	2	1	0	0	2	2	0	.286
George Roholl	P10	10	1	0	0	0	0	0	0	0	0	0	.000
Joseph Becker	C	9	25	2	5	2	1	0	0			0	.200
Harold Swanson	P8	8	6	0	3	2	0	0	0			0	.500
Albert Sima	P8	8											.000
Ken Jungels	P7	7											.000
Phil Oates	P6	6											.250
Joseph Cleary	P6	6											.000
Robert Harrison	P6	6											.000

JERSEY CITY (cont.)
Giants

BATTERS	POS-GAMES	GP	AB	R	H	BI	2B	3B	HR	BB	SO	SB	BA
Jack Maguire	2B,3B	5	15	4	3	1	0	1	0			1	.200
Lou Lucier	P5	5											1.000
Warren Pickell	P4	5											.000
Ervin Austin	OF	4	10	1	3	2	0	0	1			0	.300
Egon Feuker	P4	4											.000
Albert Thomas	P4	4											.000
Everett Robinson	1B	3	7	0	0	0	0	0	0	0		0	.000
Ettore Giammarco	OF	3	4	1	2	0	0	0	0	0		0	.500
Pete Pavlick	2B	3	3	0	1	1	0	0	0	0		0	.333
John Knott	P3	3											.000
Mario Picone	P3	3											.000
John Travis	P3	3											.000
Ray Kennedy	PH	2	1	0	0	0	0	0	0	0		0	.000
Ed Kobesky	C	2	1	0	0	0	0	0	0	0		0	.000
Roger Bowman	P2	2											.000
John Pramesa	C	1	2	1	0	1	0	0	0	0		0	.000
Bennie Warren	PH	1	1	0	0	0	0	0	0	0		0	.000
Steve Denier		1											.000
Phil Popps	P1	1											.000

PITCHERS		W	L	PCT	G	GS	CG	SH	IP	H	BB	SO	ERA
William Emmerich		10	10	.500	30	23	11	2	173	157	79	57	3.74
Richard Hoover		8	11	.421	24	20	10	1	126	142	44	55	3.71
Herb Andrews		7	11	.389	30	17	6	2	143	146	52	43	4.15
Mike Mellis		7	13	.350	28	18	10	0	133	143	57	54	4.26
Art Fowler		4	8	.333	31	13	5	0	118	140	65	55	5.57
Marv Grissom		4	10	.286	34	15	5	2	119	105	81	75	4.16
George Barley		3	3	.500	22	6	1	0	70	73	31	20	3.99
Mike Kash		3	7	.300	36	11	3	0	99	114	40	36	4.09
Harold Swanson		2	0	1.000	8				19	31	6	3	
Robert Harrison		2	1	.667	6				36	26	30	14	
Phil Oates		2	1	.667	6				15	16	10	4	
Don Fisher		2	3	.400	9				47	55	33	12	
George Roholl		1	1	.500	10	0	0	0	11	12	4	5	8.18
Albert Sima		1	3	.250	8				31	32	20	11	5.23
Warren Sandel		1	8	.111	12	9	4	0	47	61	23	28	6.51
Ken Jungels		0	1	.000	7				18	27	14	5	
Joseph Cleary		0	1	.000	6				11	21	8	4	
Warren Pickell		0	1	.000	4				10	11	4	1	
Roger Bowman		0	1	.000	2				3	3	8	2	15.00
Robert Barthelson		0	2	.000	18	1	0	0	29	39	19	8	7.76
Lou Lucier		0	0	----	5				6	10	3	5	
Egon Feuker		0	0	----	4				5	4	4	0	
Albert Thomas		0	0	----	4				8	16	2	2	
John Knott		0	0	----	3				4	7	2	1	
Mario Picone		0	0	----	3				4	7	2	2	
John Travis		0	0	----	3				2	4	1	1	
Phil Popps		0	0	----	1				1	1	0	0	0.00

MULTI-TEAM PLAYERS

BATTERS	POS-GAMES	TEAMS	GP	AB	R	H	BI	2B	3B	HR	BB	SO	SB	BA
Austin Knickerbocker	OF128	JC7-TO123	130	462	66	136	76	19	5	12	42	41	8	.294
Floyd Yount	C85	TO19-BU69	88	242	41	75	52	14	1	10	38	31	0	.310
Joseph Erautt	C69	BU20-TO54	74	176	13	39	15	6	1	3	20	23	0	.222
Ed Collins	OF14	JC37-BU24	61	86	15	25	10	2	0	0	14	6	4	.291
William Rabe	OF30	NE8-TO33	41	100	16	24	14	3	2	3	19	23	2	.240
Floyd Giebell	P17	SY21-BU1	22	29	3	4	3	3	0	0	2	5	0	.138
Paul Calvert	P21	BA16-TO6	22	23	2	2	0	0	0	0	4	5	0	.087

PITCHERS		TEAMS	W	L	PCT	G	GS	CG	SH	IP	H	BB	SO	ERA
Floyd Giebell		SY16-BU1	4	5	.444	17	10	6	1	79	82	38	36	3.65
Paul Calvert		BA16-TO5	4	7	.364	21	9	4	0	75	68	41	32	4.08

TEAM BATTING

TEAMS	GP	AB	R	H	BI	2B	3B	HR	BB	SO	SB	BA
MONTREAL	**156**	5093	**1019**	**1465**	**901**	**260**	**75**	106	**785**	558	**189**	**.288**
SYRACUSE	153	5028	762	1306	685	190	51	103	637	591	79	.260
BALTIMORE	154	4937	771	1251	709	178	44	**156**	656	696	84	.253
NEWARK	154	4976	730	1296	658	195	40	106	673	534	70	.260
BUFFALO	155	**5202**	802	1416	721	237	44	122	608	604	41	.272
TORONTO	155	4885	589	1192	525	189	45	67	572	574	62	.244
ROCHESTER	152	4937	678	1303	616	221	61	70	615	623	73	.264
JERSEY CITY	155	4924	627	1197	578	168	36	114	591	**723**	74	.243
	617	39982	5978	10426	5393	1638	396	844	5137	4903	672	.261

1947
BOTTOM TO TOP

In the first decade of the twentieth century, one Eastern League team did a complete about-face over the space of two years. In 1906, the Toronto Maple Leafs finished last. The very next year, the same team ruled the roost. Forty years later another league team pulled the same trick, adding a new wrinkle to the proceedings.

When the Jersey City International League franchise was resurrected by the New York Giants in 1937, the team soon became competitive. The club won a pennant in 1939, followed by a pair of playoff finishes in 1941 and 1942. During the latter stages of World War II, Jersey City slid into the depths of the second division, finishing last in 1946. However, the Jersey City Giants had a surprise waiting for the International League the next year.

For the previous two years, the Montreal Royals had had their way in the International League. Well infused with talent from the Brooklyn Dodgers, the Royals once again contended in 1947. However, their main competition came from an unlikely source. The Jersey City Giants, the league's most recent tailenders, stayed close to Montreal all summer. During the race's latter stages, the Giants got hot and passed the incredulous Royals to win the International League pennant by one-half of a game.

Behind Jersey City and Montreal, Syracuse and Buffalo finished in the two final playoff spots. Rochester, Newark, Baltimore, and Toronto rounded out the standings. Rochester batter Vernal Jones won the batting title with a mark of .337. In the home run race, Baltimore's Howard Moss outlasted Hank Sauer of Syracuse 53 to 50. Sauer did win the runs batted in race, collecting 141. In pitching, Jim Prendergast of Syracuse won the most games (20), Toronto's Luke Hamlin had the lowest earned run average (2.22), and John Banta from Montreal had the highest strikeout total (199).

Jersey City's up-and-down story was not unique in International League annals, nor in minor league circles. In the early years of the century, minor league teams sold their best players to earn revenue, practically guaranteeing a club's downturn. In post–World War II baseball, the rosters of minor league teams were dictated by the major league teams that controlled them. The makeup of a team could change from day to day as players were shuffled up and down the line. Both of these trends led to wild fluctuations in the standings from year to year. In the International League, more than a dozen teams moved up or down at least four places over the space of a year.

Continuing this trend, Jersey City's stay in the upper echelon of the International League would be brief. The very next year the team plummeted to seventh, nearly completing the circle of feast and famine.

JERSEY CITY 1st 94-60 .610 Bruno Betzel
Giants

BATTERS	POS-GAMES	GP	AB	R	H	BI	2B	3B	HR	BB	SO	SB	BA
John Graham	1B88,OF67	155	592	94	171	121	29	3	34	62	52	12	.289
Burgess Whitehead	2B139	141	447	49	115	40	26	3	0	47	23	6	.257
Thomas Stallcup	SS76	76	308	43	104	67	15	6	15	6	18	4	.338
George Myatt	3B89,SS12	110	383	63	116	50	20	5	1	5	22	11	.303
William Barnacle	OF124	139	468	119	126	63	27	4	12	101	45	4	.269
Les Layton	OF119	125	433	73	125	67	17	2	20	54	54	5	.289
Felix Mackiewicz	OF107	109	399	60	110	77	16	4	17	35	52	5	.276
Newt Grasso	C100	117	388	55	104	52	17	1	16	36	41	7	.268
Sal Yvars	C61	80	208	34	61	43	12	0	8	36	25	6	.293
William Sinram	3B70	72	213	27	48	21	8	0	4	25	26	1	.225
Norm Jaeger	1B67	68	249	28	62	46	11	6	4	40	14	0	.249
Bill Lillard	SS50	62	193	28	51	21	8	1	2	22	18	1	.264
John Corriden	OF43	53	152	32	47	15	8	0	1	21	17	2	.309
Jacob Wade	P32	32	75	7	10	5	2	0	0	5	25	0	.133
Robert Cain	P30	31	37	4	5	5	3	0	0	3	6	0	.135
John Kraus	P29	30	60	10	12	7	2	2	0	7	17	0	.200
Mario Picone	P28	30	27	3	7	0	0	0	0	1	6	0	.259
Richard Lajeskie	SS20	27	79	5	13	2	4	0	0	8	14	0	.165
James Goodwin	P27	27	48	3	4	3	0	0	0	0	10	0	.083
Sheldon Jones	P23	23	45	3	6	3	1	0	0	4	12	0	.133
Herb Andrews	P21	21	40	5	7	5	0	0	0	12	13	0	.175
William Emmerich	P16	17	18	4	8	2	0	0	0	1	3	0	.444
Eugene Thompson	P14	14	11	2	2	2	0	0	0	1	1	0	.182
William Ayers	P12	13	32	3	6	3	1	0	1	1	7	0	.188
Morris Tortoriello	OF	10	18	2	3	1	1	0	0	3	5	2	.167
Stan Shargey	2B,3B	8	22	2	4	0	0	0	0			0	.182
Joe Bracchitta	OF	8	14	4	1	0	0	0	0	0		0	.071
Don Mueller	PH	8	7	2	2	0	1	0	0	0		0	.286
Richard Hoover	P8	8											.000
Roy Bridges	P6	6											.000
Garland Lawing	OF	4	4	0	0	0	0	0	0	0		0	.000
Jack Maguire	2B	4	3	2	1	0	0	0	0	0		0	.333
Mike Kash	P3	3											.000
Robert Harrison	P3	3											.000
William Clausen	PH	2	1	0	0	0	0	0	0	0		0	.000
Robert Hooper	P2	2											.000
Harold Quick	PR	1	0	1	0	0	0	0	0	0		0	----
Hal Breeding	P1	1											.000

PITCHERS		W	L	PCT	G	GS	CG	SH	IP	H	BB	SO	ERA
Jacob Wade		17	5	.773	32	26	18	4	197	188	108	78	2.51
Sheldon Jones		13	3	.813	23	15	10	0	135	123	62	68	3.20
Herb Andrews		13	6	.684	21	19	10	2	148	152	28	44	3.28
John Kraus		12	9	.571	29	24	12	3	177	182	82	78	4.02
James Goodwin		11	7	.611	27	18	9	0	126	132	45	43	3.79
William Ayers		7	4	.636	12	10	7	0	86	94	23	68	4.08
Robert Cain		6	6	.500	30	11	3	0	106	110	58	47	4.92
William Emmerich		4	4	.500	16	10	3	0	59	75	18	14	5.64
Eugene Thompson		3	0	1.000	14	1	1	1	31	24	8	16	1.45
Mario Picone		2	8	.200	28	10	2	0	101	94	67	41	4.19
Mike Kash		1	0	1.000	3				4	4	3	4	4.50
Richard Hoover		0	1	.000	8				19	25	8	7	6.63
Roy Bridges		0	0	----	6				9	9	10	10	9.00
Robert Harrison		0	0	----	3				6	2	4	3	1.50
Robert Hooper		0	0	----	2				8	8	2	4	10.13
Hal Breeding		0	0	----	1				1	0	0	0	0.00

MONTREAL 2nd 93-60 .608 -0.5 Clay Hopper
Royals

BATTERS	POS-GAMES	GP	AB	R	H	BI	2B	3B	HR	BB	SO	SB	BA
Ed Stevems	1B133	133	458	89	133	108	22	4	27	84	76	5	.290
Al Campanis	2B85,SS26	110	363	44	88	40	11	1	0	45	38	7	.242
Louis Welaj	SS127,3B14	141	540	89	136	49	20	4	3	78	37	12	.252
Gil Torres	3B59,2B24,P1	94	323	37	77	34	14	2	0	23	15	1	.238
Richard Whitman	OF137	141	495	90	162	62	28	5	10	54	24	17	.327
Walt Sessi	OF119	130	386	69	101	80	16	3	20	87	55	0	.262
Boris Woyt	OF116,3B17	136	512	98	146	53	22	4	2	36	48	32	.285
Roy Campanella	C126	135	440	64	120	75	25	3	13	66	41	7	.273
Earl Naylor	OF104,P2	129	382	55	104	72	14	3	6	42	42	5	.272

MONTREAL (cont.)
Royals

BATTERS	POS-GAMES	GP	AB	R	H	BI	2B	3B	HR	BB	SO	SB	BA
Mike Sandlock	3B58,C30	101	298	34	66	36	9	2	0	26	11	0	.221
Frank Danneker	2B37,3B10	50	148	16	28	11	6	1	0	20	19	3	.189
John Van Cuyk	P39	39	40	6	3	0	0	0	0	11	25	0	.075
Chester Kehn	P36	38	47	2	10	5	2	0	0	2	3	0	.213
Al Gerheauser	P34	36	81	6	14	8	2	0	0	5	25	0	.173
Ervin Palica	P29	33	67	14	22	8	4	2	0	5	8	1	.328
Joe Smolko	P30	33	46	4	5	3	0	0	1	4	15	0	.109
John Banta	P31	32	74	10	18	6	1	2	0	9	12	0	.243
Ed Heusser	P26	28	61	10	18	9	1	1	2	3	8	0	.295
Louis Ruchser	1B16	16	46	7	10	5	1	0	2	10	6	1	.217
David Pluss	OF12	13	40	5	11	8	2	0	0	11	6	1	.275
Richard Mlady	P10	10	10	1	3	1	0	0	0	0	3	0	.300
Frank Melton	P8	8											.500
Roland Marquardt	P8	8											.125
Leroy Pfund	P6	6											.250
Walter Nothe	P5	5											.000
Homer Matney	OF	2	5	1	2	1	0	0	0			0	.400
Maurice Atwell	PH	2	1	0	0	0	0	0	0			0	.000
Francis Meagher	P2	2											.000
George Brown	P2	2											.000
Jack Lindsay	PH	1	1	0	0	0	0	0	0			0	.000
Walt Olsen	P1	1											.000
Robert Fontaine	P1	1											.000

PITCHERS	W	L	PCT	G	GS	CG	SH	IP	H	BB	SO	ERA
Ed Heusser	19	3	.864	26	22	16	6	165	157	51	53	2.73
John Banta	15	5	.750	31	28	16	7	199	158	81	199	3.17
Al Gerheauser	15	12	.556	34	29	18	4	216	233	53	80	3.54
John Van Cuyk	12	9	.571	39	20	7	1	153	154	56	70	3.53
Ervin Palica	12	10	.545	29	25	12	2	181	164	87	84	4.18
Chester Kehn	9	9	.500	36	15	7	0	146	150	56	60	3.21
Joe Smolko	6	5	.545	30	11	4	1	123	127	49	33	3.66
Walter Nothe	2	1	.667	5				12	8	8	8	1.50
Frank Melton	2	3	.400	8				25	26	17	7	4.68
Leroy Pfund	1	0	1.000	6				16	19	9	4	5.06
Richard Mlady	0	3	.000	10	1	0	0	27	34	15	16	6.33
Roland Marquardt	0	0	----	8				24	18	15	15	4.50
Francis Meagher	0	0	----	2				4	5	2	3	4.50
George Brown	0	0	----	2				4	7	7	1	13.50
Earl Naylor	0	0	----	2				3	8	1	0	9.00
Gil Torres	0	0	----	1				2	3	2	1	0.00
Walt Olsen	0	0	----	1				2	3	1	0	0.00
Robert Fontaine	0	0	----	1				0	0	2	0	0.00

SYRACUSE   3rd   88-65   .575   -5.5   Jewel Ens
Chiefs

BATTERS	POS-GAMES	GP	AB	R	H	BI	2B	3B	HR	BB	SO	SB	BA
Ed Shokes	1B151	153	533	70	141	54	22	3	5	70	48	5	.265
Frank Drews	2B153	153	568	99	148	53	25	3	9	78	54	5	.261
Claude Corbitt	SS134	134	538	84	160	41	19	5	2	54	27	13	.297
Al Rubeling	3B148	148	560	68	153	67	23	7	8	46	45	9	.273
Al Mele	OF148	149	534	90	168	100	27	5	20	82	23	12	.315
Hank Sauer	OF145	146	542	130	182	141	28	1	50	75	74	4	.336
Joseph Beeler	OF118	118	440	62	96	60	22	2	9	55	40	5	.218
Richard West	C84	91	319	35	81	55	15	2	11	18	35	6	.254
Millard Howell	P31	61	122	17	39	23	4	1	4	8	21	0	.320
Al Korhonen	OF34,P1	52	124	18	34	10	3	0	0	9	10	1	.274
Joe Just	C48	49	144	16	25	18	4	0	1	24	17	1	.174
Jim Prendergast	P37	37	89	9	19	12	7	1	2	14	18	0	.213
Howard Fox	P32	32	85	8	16	7	1	0	0	6	14	0	.188
Herm Wehmeier	P28	29	70	6	12	9	1	0	1	2	17	0	.171
William Schultz	P28	28	42	4	14	2	0	0	0	3	8	0	.333
John Bebber	P28	28	27	5	6	4	0	0	0	2	5	0	.222
Thad Bosiack	C25	26	94	13	33	9	3	1	1	5	3	0	.351
Robert Carson	SS20	24	92	11	25	4	2	0	0	2	9	1	.272
Harold Erickson	P22	22	16	2	3	2	0	0	0	0	6	0	.188
Frank Davis	OF19	19	67	9	14	15	0	3	1	13	21	1	.209
William Gates	P19	19	6	0	1	1	0	0	0	0	0	0	.167
John Dudick	3B	11	16	5	3	2	0	0	1	4	2	0	.188
Ed Heinrich	PH	9	9	1	2	0	0	0	0			0	.222

SYRACUSE (cont.)
Chiefs

BATTERS	POS-GAMES	GP	AB	R	H	BI	2B	3B	HR	BB	SO	SB	BA
Arnold Carter	P7	7											.000
Milt Ticco	PH	2	2	0	1	0	0	0	0			0	.500
Terrence Connell	P1	1											.000

PITCHERS		W	L	PCT	G	GS	CG	SH	IP	H	BB	SO	ERA
Jim Prendergast		20	15	.571	37	35	24	3	257	298	60	54	3.08
Howard Fox		19	9	.679	32	27	21	5	225	184	85	83	2.68
Herm Wehmeier		15	8	.652	28	25	15	2	177	150	98	81	4.12
Millard Howell		13	15	.464	31	31	2	4	246	231	126	85	3.59
John Bebber		6	3	.667	28	5	3	0	79	72	38	18	3.19
William Scultz		5	9	.357	28	16	8	0	126	146	48	41	5.50
Harold Erickson		2	1	.667	22	3	1	0	56	62	26	30	4.98
William Gates		1	1	.500	19	2	0	0	33	34	30	14	6.27
Arnold Carter		0	1	.000	7				15	27	7	3	12.60
Al Korhonen		0	0	----	1				3	6	3	0	0.00
Terrence Connell		0	0	----	1				1	0	3	0	0.00

BUFFALO   4th   77-75   .507   -16   Paul Richards
Bisons

BATTERS	POS-GAMES	GP	AB	R	H	BI	2B	3B	HR	BB	SO	SB	BA
James Wasdell	1B120	122	424	75	131	77	33	2	13	39	27	5	.309
John Bero	2B142	148	474	68	107	49	20	3	10	99	72	7	.226
Cornelius Berry	SS123	123	428	64	128	50	20	4	1	59	23	8	.299
Lambert Meyer	3B	(see multi-team players)											.294
Earl Rapp	OF134	137	439	86	129	80	28	3	16	96	56	12	.294
Chet Laabs	OF94	96	338	76	99	76	24	0	22	49	64	4	.293
Coaker Triplett	OF89	107	308	57	97	64	15	0	15	53	14	3	.315
Floyd Yount	C84	101	303	34	81	42	16	2	6	43	38	5	.267
Ansel Moore	OF83,3B33	123	417	74	123	73	15	4	22	46	15	3	.295
Ed Modarski	C46,1B32,OF15	106	283	43	84	57	11	3	9	50	26	8	.297
Lindsay Brown	SS45,3B19,2B15	75	190	23	41	23	8	0	0	16	18	5	.216
Wayne Blackburn	3B46,OF13	73	183	35	52	21	5	1	1	27	15	6	.284
Clint Conatser	OF61	66	222	44	62	30	8	3	9	33	33	5	.279
Paul Richards	C29,1B,3B	47	113	10	28	20	7	1	2	15	11	1	.248
Henry Perry	P38	40	78	12	19	3	3	1	0	6	22	0	.244
Pete Appleton	P36	36	42	4	10	6	0	0	1	2	14	0	.238
Walt Pierce	P28	35	61	1	15	6	3	0	0	0	17	0	.246
Clem Hausmann	P33	33	51	1	11	4	0	0	0	2	10	0	.216
Ted Gray	P33	33	45	0	3	0	0	0	0	5	21	0	.067
Saul Rogovin	P21	31	44	3	9	5	1	0	1	2	12	0	.205
James Kerr	P25	27	26	3	4	1	2	0	1	7	12	0	.154
Louis Kretlow	P18	18	22	3	3	3	2	0	1	2	10	0	.136
Anderson Bush	P14	14	18	1	1	0	0	0	0	1	5	0	.056
Newman Shirley	P11	11	19	2	6	2	0	0	0	0	2	0	.316
Frank Heller	1B	9	29	1	2	3	0	0	1			0	.069
Martin Tabacheck	C	8	22	1	4	2	0	0	0			0	.182
Irvin Hall	2B	7	21	0	5	2	0	1	0			0	.238
Walt Chipple	OF	7	17	1	1	3	0	0	1			0	.059
Adam Bengoechea	2B,3B	5	6	2	1	0	0	0	0			0	.167
Art Houtteman	P5	5											.000
Aaron Silverman	P4	4											.000

PITCHERS		W	L	PCT	G	GS	CG	SH	IP	H	BB	SO	ERA
Walt Pierce		14	8	.636	28	23	12	4	151	127	125	125	3.87
Henry Perry		13	10	.565	38	28	15	0	208	207	104	74	4.07
Ted Gray		11	7	.611	33	22	11	4	150	128	86	138	3.42
Clem Hausmann		8	12	.400	33	20	14	1	184	166	39	88	3.52
Pete Appleton		7	7	.500	36	5	3	0	115	107	55	53	3.68
James Kerr		4	5	.444	25	9	2	0	88	93	51	35	4.50
Art Houtteman		3	1	.750	5				29	24	9	8	1.86
Saul Rogovin		3	4	.429	21	7	1	0	89	90	53	45	4.85
Anderson Bush		3	4	.429	14	6	1	0	60	77	22	39	4.05
Newman Shirley		3	4	.429	11	9	2	1	50	53	34	20	5.22
Louis Kretlow		2	7	.222	18	12	4	0	77	81	62	56	7.01
Aaron Silverman		0	1	.000	4				10	9	9	5	4.50

ROCHESTER   5th   68-86   .442   -26   Cedric Durst
Red Wings

BATTERS	POS-GAMES	GP	AB	R	H	BI	2B	3B	HR	BB	SO	SB	BA
Charles Kress	1B130	130	466	79	131	42	24	4	7	56	58	22	.281
Vernal Jones	2B77,3B30,OF13	118	445	66	150	81	36	12	10	29	24	2	.337
Charles Brewster	SS129	135	457	42	108	58	14	7	4	29	36	4	.236
Claude Wright	3B64,SS27,2B15	107	378	44	96	22	13	4	1	37	47	2	.254
Russ Derry	OF136	143	458	78	123	89	19	9	26	73	88	15	.269
Robert Usher	OF111	119	399	50	101	42	17	4	8	34	41	5	.253
Harold Rice	OF110	120	347	42	86	50	15	1	5	36	41	4	.248
Charles Marshall	C106	112	281	25	64	19	7	5	2	40	57	0	.228
Robert Young	2B68,3B43,SS	118	410	63	129	33	19	11	0	29	23	8	.315
Thomas O'Brien	OF56,3B23	105	297	30	71	42	12	2	5	26	26	1	.239
Vern Benson	OF54	87	186	35	51	30	11	1	6	36	40	3	.274
Dewey Williams	C66	71	149	15	33	10	4	1	0	34	15	2	.221
Lawrence Ciaffone	OF25,C,3B	54	104	6	24	11	4	0	2	4	11	0	.231
John Mikan	P42	42	59	7	10	3	2	0	0	8	25	0	.169
Matt Surkont	P38	39	64	7	15	8	7	0	0	6	14	0	.234
Ray Yochim	P38	38	68	14	15	4	4	1	0	5	16	0	.221
Edwin Green	P36	36	35	0	0	0	0	0	0	2	12	0	.000
Glenn Gardner	P31	31	61	3	11	4	1	0	0	0	10	0	.180
William Reeder	P31	31	45	2	8	5	1	0	0	2	16	0	.178
Howard Krist	P29	31	19	0	2	1	0	0	0	1	7	0	.105
Eldred Byerly	P28	28	46	6	11	5	2	1	1	1	10	0	.239
Charles Baron	1B20	21	74	6	18	5	5	0	0	8	3	0	.243
Herb Moore	P14	14	3	1	1	0	0	0	0	1	0	0	.333
Ed Kazak	3B	12	32	2	4	1	0	0	0	3	4	0	.125
Glenn Nelson	1B	11	18	2	1	2	0	0	0	1	4	0	.056
John Caulfield	SS	6	11	0	2	0	0	0	0			0	.182
Andreas Mohrlock	P4	4											.000
John Gibson	P4	4											.000

PITCHERS		W	L	PCT	G	GS	CG	SH	IP	H	BB	SO	ERA
John Mikan		16	13	.552	42	27	12	1	189	184	127	79	3.90
Matt Surkont		15	10	.600	38	26	12	1	190	163	109	102	3.55
Ray Yochim		14	15	.483	38	29	13	2	227	227	126	103	3.57
Glenn Gardner		8	18	.308	31	27	11	2	192	213	65	64	3.89
William Reeder		5	5	.500	31	14	6	1	130	150	68	55	4.43
Eldred Byerly		5	13	.278	28	20	8	1	129	145	66	26	4.88
Edwin Green		3	7	.300	36	7	2	0	122	103	85	56	4.28
Howard Krist		2	4	.333	29	3	1	0	71	100	25	13	4.94
Andreas Mohrlock		0	1	.000	4				4	6	6	1	9.00
Herb Moore		0	0	----	14	0	0	0	18	16	15	5	6.00
John Gibson		0	0	----	4				10	12	6	0	9.90

BALTIMORE   6th (T)   65-89   .422   -29   Alphonse Thomas
Orioles

BATTERS	POS-GAMES	GP	AB	R	H	BI	2B	3B	HR	BB	SO	SB	BA
Babe Dahlgren	1B149	149	536	62	140	67	22	4	19	49	60	1	.261
Robert Wilson	2B133	143	566	87	159	52	17	4	4	42	40	36	.281
Ralph LaPointe	SS84	85	318	39	88	26	9	0	5	22	17	9	.277
John Antonelli	3B	(see multi-team players)											
Howard Moss	OF136,3B18	152	528	103	142	129	14	5	53	88	95	3	.269
Clarence Campbell	OF129	131	453	74	131	43	12	7	6	95	30	7	.289
Joseph Mellendick	OF103	120	307	39	75	42	9	0	11	42	31	1	.244
Ralph Weigel	C91	110	337	54	95	53	20	4	12	33	45	9	.282
Al Cihocki	3B54,SS48,2B20	123	414	45	105	45	13	4	10	33	39	0	.254
George Staller	OF98	113	371	58	93	50	21	1	10	28	35	10	.251
Dale Lenn	C25	66	130	12	30	11	6	4	0	18	5	1	.231
John Podgajny	P50	53	67	5	7	5	1	0	0	5	22	1	.104
John Wittig	P39	39	51	2	5	2	1	0	1	3	15	0	.098
Lawrence Gast	P33	33	14	0	0	0	0	0	0	4	5	0	.000
Gord Mueller	P31	31	24	1	1	0	0	0	0	0	10	0	.042
Robert Kuzava	P30	30	76	7	19	1	1	0	0	4	19	1	.250
George Hooks	P28	29	38	2	11	2	0	0	0	3	6	0	.289
Ray Flanigan	P29	29	32	1	4	1	1	1	0	0	16	0	.125
Al Heuser	P27	27	17	2	2	0	0	1	0	2	9	0	.118
Raymond Poat	P23	23	58	5	7	3	0	0	1	0	22	0	.121
Chet Ross	OF18	22	57	7	10	8	1	0	3	11	9	0	.175
Robert Repass	SS	9	31	1	3	3	0	0	1			0	.097
Horace Brightman	OF	8	11	0	3	1	0	0	0			0	.273
Earl Center	P8	8											.091

BALTIMORE (cont.)
Orioles

BATTERS	POS-GAMES	GP	AB	R	H	BI	2B	3B	HR	BB	SO	SB	BA
Joseph Pennington	P6	6											.500
George Cave	P5	5											.000
Al Barillari	P3	3											.000
Gene Bearden	P3	3											.000
Gus Zernial	OF	3	4	0	0	0	0	0	0	0		0	.000
Joseph Payne	P1	1											.000
Don Belton	P1	1											.000

PITCHERS		W	L	PCT	G	GS	CG	SH	IP	H	BB	SO	ERA
Robert Kuzava		14	13	.519	30	29	18	3	224	197	76	112	3.17
John Podgajny		13	18	.419	50	25	9	0	213	249	70	44	4.73
Raymond Poat		11	7	.611	23	22	14	1	162	133	58	122	2.44
John Wittig		8	12	.400	39	20	7	0	168	183	64	76	4.71
George Hooks		6	7	.462	28	14	2	0	107	109	52	55	4.54
Al Heuser		3	3	.500	27	5	2	0	74	107	25	20	5.84
Lawrence Gast		3	5	.375	33	4	1	0	75	79	49	37	5.52
Ray Flanigan		3	7	.300	29	11	4	0	98	104	52	49	5.33
Gord Mueller		2	6	.250	31	8	1	0	85	94	41	36	5.40
Al Barillari		1	0	1.000	3				6	4	5	1	0.00
Earl Center		1	3	.250	8				32	34	17	9	5.34
George Cave		0	1	.000	5				7	7	4	6	5.14
Gene Bearden		0	2	.000	3				7	12	1	2	10.29
Joseph Pennington		0	3	.000	6				12	22	9	8	11.25
Don Belton		0	0	----	1				2	4	0	0	9.00
Joseph Payne		0	0	----	1				2	3	2	0	18.00

NEWARK   6th (T)   65-89   .422   -29   George Selkirk
Bears

BATTERS	POS-GAMES	GP	AB	R	H	BI	2B	3B	HR	BB	SO	SB	BA
Joe Collins	1B89,OF12	98	364	52	99	53	10	4	17	39	52	5	.272
Ray Mack	2B136	137	458	57	121	70	12	6	20	66	85	6	.264
John Phillips	SS98,1B20,3B14	122	453	59	135	51	18	11	11	36	37	9	.298
Alfred Clark	3B69,OF47	110	437	79	146	86	27	9	23	37	26	1	.334
Gene Woodling	OF127	128	477	81	138	54	19	8	8	84	27	5	.289
Ford Garrison	OF97	107	370	67	99	35	15	2	11	59	30	6	.268
Ted Sepkowski	OF61	72	244	31	65	28	4	5	9	17	30	1	.266
Sherm Lollar	C102	111	357	56	100	64	9	5	16	50	29	1	.280
Art Metheny	OF55,1B13	79	245	36	65	33	6	4	10	31	13	2	.265
Frank Zak	SS70	76	189	23	39	14	4	0	0	32	31	1	.206
William Deininger	C32	52	118	9	23	9	3	0	1	11	14	2	.195
William Rodgers	OF40	51	170	20	42	6	11	2	1	14	12	2	.247
Nick Etten	1B43	47	145	16	31	17	2	1	7	26	10	0	.214
James Dyck	3B45	46	166	17	48	15	4	0	4	9	10	1	.289
William Drescher	C30	37	113	11	33	22	7	0	2	10	9	0	.292
Herb Karpel	P33	33	61	10	17	12	4	0	0	8	8	0	.279
Frank Colman	OF29	31	102	12	30	14	6	1	4	6	15	0	.294
Art Cuccurullo	P28	29	31	3	8	2	1	0	1	2	7	0	.258
Mal Mallette	P24	24	45	1	7	1	1	0	0	2	25	0	.156
John Maldovan	P24	24	26	0	1	0	0	0	0	2	11	0	.038
George Scharein	2B10	22	59	8	17	5	3	1	0	7	2	0	.288
Richard Starr	P21	22	43	3	7	3	1	0	0	6	13	0	.163
Don Schmidt	P20	20	12	1	0	0	0	0	0	2	7	0	.000
Mario Russo	P15	19	35	2	9	3	2	0	0	3	10	0	.257
Duane Pillette	P18	18	17	2	5	3	1	0	0	3	5	0	.294
John Robinson	P11	16	18	4	4	0	0	0	0	4	6	0	.222
Charles Haag	P13	15	8	0	0	0	0	0	0	0	3	0	.000
James Tote	P13	14	26	2	4	4	2	0	0	0	10	0	.154
Richard Ames	P14	14	19	1	2	1	0	0	0	0	6	0	.105
William Houtz	P9	14	18	2	1	0	0	0	0	4	5	0	.056
Frank Secory	OF	13	34	4	4	2	0	0	1	6	5	0	.118
Frank Bocek	OF	12	35	2	9	3	2	0	0	3	10	0	.257
Ed Basinski	3B10	12	35	2	7	2	1	0	0	3	7	0	.200
Robert Keegan	P11	11	15	2	1	0	0	0	0	1	3	0	.067
Wayne Tucker	2B	7	23	2	3	1	0	0	0			0	.130
Steve Peek	P4	5											.111
Joseph Och	P3	3											.000
Fenton Mole	PH	2	1	1	1	1	0	0	0	0		0	1.000
Carl Ray	P1	1											.000

NEWARK (cont.)
Bears

PITCHERS	W	L	PCT	G	GS	CG	SH	IP	H	BB	SO	ERA
Richard Starr	9	6	.600	21	17	9	1	128	121	58	49	4.01
Herb Karpel	9	11	.450	33	21	10	0	165	181	51	56	4.42
Mal Mallette	6	10	.375	24	20	7	0	129	128	68	68	4.81
Mario Russo	5	7	.417	15	15	7	0	97	115	35	36	3.99
Duane Pillette	4	3	.571	18	11	2	0	63	69	48	25	5.29
John Maldovan	4	4	.500	24	7	2	0	85	101	39	43	4.55
William Houtz	4	4	.500					46	49	29	17	6.26
Richard Ames	3	3	.500	14	8	3	0	64	62	29	29	3.94
Art Cuccurullo	3	6	.333	28	6	1	0	91	100	40	36	4.05
James Tote	3	6	.333	13	9	5	1	70	72	55	27	5.27
John Robinson	2	3	.400	11	5	2	0	56	68	30	12	4.98
Steve Peek	1	1	.500	4				21	22	13	7	4.71
Don Schmidt	1	4	.200	20	1	0	0	56	54	21	23	2.41
Robert Keegan	1	6	.143	11	8	3	0	53	57	22	35	6.11
Charles Haag	0	1	.000	13	1	0	0	32	36	23	3	6.47
Joseph Och	0	1	.000	3				7	9	6	5	6.43
Carl Ray	0	1	.000	1				6	5	3	1	3.00

TORONTO   8th   64-90   .416   -30   Elmer Yoter
Maple Leafs

BATTERS	POS-GAMES	GP	AB	R	H	BI	2B	3B	HR	BB	SO	SB	BA
John Kensecke	1B87	87	289	29	71	27	10	5	3	48	45	3	.246
Roland Harrington	2B150	151	605	84	160	50	19	2	13	42	34	20	.264
Robert Wilkins	SS78	81	226	21	49	11	5	0	0	26	24	3	.217
Oscar Grimes	3B149	154	502	74	137	58	15	7	9	133	79	7	.273
Goody Rosen	OF143	145	485	74	133	58	23	1	7	99	34	2	.274
Austin Knickerbocker	OF103	105	389	41	108	48	13	1	10	28	43	2	.278
George Bennington	OF93	102	259	36	66	11	8	2	1	32	25	7	.255
Matt Batts	C94,OF	110	359	32	94	40	4	2	7	20	36	3	.262
Edward Levy	1B68,OF49	126	425	47	122	71	26	5	13	48	54	7	.287
Ira Houck	OF65	85	238	23	53	19	4	0	2	16	17	1	.223
Fred Chapman	SS71	82	241	21	61	26	12	1	3	19	14	2	.253
Gene DesAutels	C67	75	208	16	39	28	3	1	5	23	18	0	.188
Ellis Deal	P33	71	117	8	24	9	2	0	3	8	25	0	.205
Morris Aderholt	OF41	58	146	18	40	14	2	0	3	19	11	2	.274
Norm Brown	P39	42	67	6	11	3	1	0	0	1	13	0	.164
Don Carter	P38	40	59	3	11	1	1	1	0	2	16	0	.186
Jim Konstanty	P33	34	64	2	9	2	1	0	0	2	9	0	.141
John Thompson	P32	32	42	2	5	0	0	0	0	3	16	0	.119
Luke Hamlin	P24	24	68	3	9	3	0	0	0	5	12	0	.132
Merrill Combs	SS20	22	68	3	14	2	1	0	0	16	8	0	.206
Thomas Fine	P13	16	21	2	5	0	0	0	0	1	3	0	.238
Dwight Simonds	P13	13	6	0	0	0	0	0	0	0	3	0	.000
Anthony Ravish	C	9	18	0	2	1	1	0	0			0	.000
Herm Besse	P8	8											.357
Harry Kimberlin	P6	6											.000
Peter Karpuk	P3	5											.000
John Lanning	P4	4											.500
Mel Deutsch	P3	3											.000
William Kennedy	P2	2											.000

PITCHERS	W	L	PCT	G	GS	CG	SH	IP	H	BB	SO	ERA
Luke Hamlin	15	6	.714	24	24	17	1	195	166	52	99	2.22
Jim Konstanty	13	13	.500	33	26	14	3	197	179	62	78	3.47
Ellis Deal	9	17	.346	33	24	18	1	200	194	88	80	3.42
Don Carter	8	9	.471	38	21	10	3	174	183	85	84	4.24
Norm Brown	7	13	.350	39	21	9	0	173	172	92	46	4.47
John Thompson	6	12	.333	32	17	6	4	135	128	55	69	3.80
Herm Besse	2	4	.333	8				36	49	14	22	6.75
Thomas Fine	2	9	.182	13	9	3	0	66	70	28	23	4.91
Peter Karpuk	1	0	1.000	3				6	3	4	0	6.00
Harry Kimberlin	0	1	.000	6				7	14	3	1	10.29
William Kennedy	0	1	.000	2				6	8	5	6	12.60
Dwight Simonds	0	2	.000	13	0	0	0	31	30	19	12	5.52
John Lanning	0	0	----	4				12	13	3	1	6.00
Mel Deutsch	0	0	----	3				5	5	3	1	3.60

MULTI-TEAM PLAYERS

BATTERS	POS-GAMES	TEAMS	GP	AB	R	H	BI	2B	3B	HR	BB	SO	SB	BA
John Antonelli	3B94	BU3-BA102	105	383	46	114	45	19	1	6	29	19	1	.298
Lambert Meyer	3B86	NE22-BU70	92	337	59	92	43	20	1	10	35	30	2	.273
Warren Robinson	C53	RO11-BA46	57	163	14	28	22	5	0	7	16	20	0	.172
Alex Mustaikis	P41	NE29-SY12	41	39	2	7	2	1	0	0	0	10	0	.179
Russ Wein	2B17,SS13	BA16-MO17	33	92	8	20	5	1	0	0	15	8	1	.217
Mike Mellis	P30	JC27-BA3	30	27	3	1	0	0	0	0	5	11	0	.037
Les Mueller	P28	BU14-NE14	28	54	1	8	0	0	0	0	1	15	0	.148
Robert Katz	P18	SY4-TO14	18	14	1	1	0	0	0	0	0	4	0	.071

PITCHERS	TEAMS	W	L	PCT	G	GS	CG	SH	IP	H	BB	SO	ERA
Alex Mustaikas	NE29-SY12	11	8	.579	41	8	6	1	116	93	51	31	2.79
Les Mueller	BU14-NE14	10	12	.455	28	21	8	0	158	158	77	81	4.33
Mike Mellis	JC27-BA3	5	10	.333	30	12	6	1	118	139	44	42	4.65
Robert Katz	SY4-TO14	2	3	.400	18	5	1	0	53	73	27	23	5.94

TEAM BATTING

TEAMS	GP	AB	R	H	BI	2B	3B	HR	BB	SO	SB	BA
JERSEY CITY	**155**	5006	**772**	1332	**718**	228	37	135	614	549	67	.266
MONTREAL	**155**	4934	758	1294	672	203	37	86	628	529	**93**	.262
SYRACUSE	153	5074	765	**1381**	692	207	34	125	568	512	63	**.272**
BUFFALO	154	4931	778	1326	731	**236**	29	141	**688**	588	75	.269
ROCHESTER	154	4942	630	1267	573	217	**63**	77	502	**634**	69	.256
BALTIMORE	154	5019	667	1280	611	172	36	**149**	539	590	80	.255
NEWARK	**155**	**5095**	692	1352	634	180	60	**149**	588	586	44	.265
TORONTO	154	4932	547	1230	482	152	28	79	597	547	59	.249
	617	39933	5609	10462	5113	1595	324	941	4724	4535	550	.262

1948
MONTREAL ROYALS

After World War II, another dynasty began to wave its colors in International League circles. Continuing in the tradition of the storied Baltimore, Rochester, and Newark eras of domination, this team ruled the league for several years. The name of the team was the Royals. The city where they resided was Montreal.

Montreal first joined the league structure in 1890, fielding two separate replacement teams. Seven years later, the city served as a mid-season replacement for the Rochester franchise. The following year, Montreal joined the league as a permanent member, taking the nickname Royals.

Victory came quickly as the Royals won the 1898 pennant in their first full year of operation. The success did not last, however, and the team floundered around in the second division for 20 years before being relocated following the 1917 season. Eleven years later, the team returned to the International, posting a pennant seven years later in 1935. Three years later, Montreal began an affiliation that would lead them to their years of greatest glory. They signed a working agreement with the Brooklyn Dodgers, shortly to be the premier team in the National League.

In the last year of World War II, this relationship paid off as the Royals finished first. The next year they duplicated the feat with an even stronger team. Following a narrow defeat at the hands of Jersey City in 1947, the Royals were poised to take back their crown in 1948.

The 1948 Royals brushed back the opposition, winning the flag handily. They were led at the plate by Chuck Connors (.307, 17 HR), James Bloodworth (.294, 24 HR, 99 RBI), and Al Gionfriddo (.294, 25 HR). On the hill, John Banta paved the way, winning the most games (19) and finishing with the most strikeouts (193).

In the rest of the league, Newark, Syracuse, and Rochester finished second through fourth, while Toronto, Buffalo, Jersey City, and Baltimore finished fifth through eighth. Buffalo's Coaker Triplett won the batting title (.353), Howard Moss of Baltimore captured his third straight home run crown (33), and Toronto Maple Leaf Ed Sanicki had the most runs batted in (107). William Reeder of Rochester tied Banta with the most pitching wins (19), while Erwin Porterfield from Newark achieved the lowest earned run average (2.17)

Montreal's success continued as the team finished first four times in the next ten years. After the 1960 season, the Dodgers announced they were selling the club, and Montreal left the International League for good. All that was left was a rich lode of memories of one of the International League's greatest dynasties, a team that won five pennants in the space of eight years—a nearly unmatched record.

MONTREAL Royals

1st	94-59	.614		Clay Hopper

BATTERS	POS-GAMES	GP	AB	R	H	BI	2B	3B	HR	BB	SO	SB	BA
Chuck Connors	1B146	147	512	79	157	88	36	5	17	62	50	9	.307
James Bloodworth	2B149	151	557	85	164	99	31	6	24	46	59	3	.294
Robert Morgan	SS151	151	516	92	137	75	28	9	10	89	99	5	.266
Louis Welaj	3B124	129	444	75	115	51	23	1	5	60	23	9	.259
John Simmons	OF129	139	459	64	136	83	21	4	8	51	40	5	.296
Al Gionfriddo	OF119	125	432	88	127	79	18	6	25	68	25	11	.294
Sam Jethroe	OF72	76	292	52	94	25	19	11	1	27	34	18	.322
Cliff Dapper	C104	112	327	46	78	47	11	2	7	63	56	2	.239
Mike Sandlock	C58	79	201	26	53	23	11	0	0	37	18	1	.264
Duke Snider	OF71	77	275	67	90	77	28	4	17	32	44	8	.327
Don Newcombe	P37	42	68	6	18	12	4	0	1	6	12	0	.265
Richard Whitman	OF40	40	151	26	41	20	2	4	3	10	3	2	.272
John Banta	P33	36	88	10	16	14	2	0	0	9	11	0	.182
Clarence Podbielan	P35	36	58	6	11	2	3	0	0	7	13	0	.190
Frank Laga	P33	35	46	6	10	10	4	0	1	3	19	0	.217
John Van Cuyk	P32	32	36	5	3	0	1	0	0	8	19	0	.083
Art Schallock	P24	30	8	2	2	0	1	0	0	3	4	0	.250
Walter Nothe	P28	28	40	0	5	2	1	0	0	2	8	0	.125
Walt Sessi	OF22	22	75	13	21	11	0	0	5	13	4	0	.280
Marv Rackley	OF19	20	74	18	24	13	4	2	3	16	4	4	.324
Clyde King	P18	18	16	2	4	0	0	0	0	1	7	0	.250
Henry Behrman	P14	14	34	2	1	0	0	0	0	2	9	0	.029
Maynard DeWitt	OF	12	24	6	3	1	2	0	0	2	2	4	.125
Al Zachary	P12	12	14	3	2	0	1	0	0	3	2	0	.143
Joe Tepsic	PR	1	0	0	0	0	0	0	0			0	----

PITCHERS		W	L	PCT	G	GS	CG	SH	IP	H	BB	SO	ERA
John Banta		19	9	.679	33	28	20	1	219	184	109	193	3.25
Don Newcombe		17	6	.739	37	27	16	3	189	151	106	144	3.14
Clarence Podbielan		13	8	.619	35	18	9	2	168	168	60	59	2.79
Frank Laga		10	7	.588	33	13	5	0	135	121	87	82	3.80
John Van Cuyk		10	7	.588	32	19	6	1	136	159	59	82	5.63
Henry Behrman		8	2	.800	14	12	7	2	106	87	41	57	2.55
Walt Nothe		6	4	.600	28	15	3	1	119	99	76	79	4.24
Al Zachary		4	3	.571	12	5	2	0	47	48	10	21	4.60
Paul Minner		3	2	.600	6				31	31	8	17	2.90
Art Schallock		2	1	.667	24	1	0	0	50	37	40	33	3.78
Clyde King		2	5	.286	18	6	1	0	53	79	21	15	7.47
Robert Fontaine		0	2	.000	3				11	13	11	3	9.82
Charles Lare		0	3	.000	4				20	30	3	1	5.85
Omar Lown		0	0	----	2				3	5	5	4	12.00
George Brown		0	0	----	1				1	0	3	0	0.00

NEWARK Bears

2nd	80-72	.526	-13.5	Bill Skiff

BATTERS	POS-GAMES	GP	AB	R	H	BI	2B	3B	HR	BB	SO	SB	BA
John Phillips	1B75	75	262	31	65	27	10	5	5	16	22	5	.248
John Lucadello	2B79,3B55	140	480	79	132	56	24	0	12	101	37	0	.275
Jerry Coleman	SS70,2B44,3B33	142	491	65	123	62	26	1	8	54	81	7	.251
Clarence Difani	3B63,OF27	98	323	53	87	54	11	4	14	47	48	15	.269
Ted Sepkowski	OF112,2B28	140	482	67	130	91	13	3	24	27	61	6	.270
Joe Collins	OF86,1B51	139	512	84	140	76	25	6	23	39	67	5	.273
Lou Novikoff	OF70	70	260	43	85	53	14	0	15	18	17	0	.327
Ken Silvestri	C116,1B	129	372	55	81	44	12	3	17	85	62	5	.218
Harry Heslet	OF57,C24	91	252	37	67	43	10	1	9	30	44	3	.266
Henry Workman	OF65	72	212	44	57	38	6	2	16	27	38	3	.269
Ford Garrison	OF66	70	222	32	55	30	10	1	5	27	15	2	.248
Frank LaManna	P30,OF15	68	104	18	27	12	4	0	2	10	19	3	.260
Al Stringer	SS43	44	116	22	30	8	4	0	3	25	18	0	.259
John Wallaesa	SS36	36	127	20	39	24	10	0	6	9	22	5	.307
Richard Starr	P29	32	67	8	9	6	2	0	2	6	21	0	.134
Frank Colman	1B26	29	100	15	28	16	4	1	3	10	8	0	.280
John Maldovan	P28	28	41	3	5	3	0	0	0	2	14	0	.122
Les Mueller	P27	27	21	2	2	2	0	0	0	1	8	0	.048
Erwin Porterfield	P23	25	68	6	10	4	2	0	0	6	18	1	.147
William Holm	C17	24	33	13	9	6	0	0	1	8	6	0	.273
Clarence Marshall	P23	23	57	5	10	5	1	0	0	4	14	0	.175
Ed Little	C17	22	58	7	13	9	1	0	2	4	5	0	.224
William Houtz	P19	21	21	1	4	1	1	0	0	3	4	0	.190

NEWARK (cont.)
Bears

BATTERS	POS-GAMES	GP	AB	R	H	BI	2B	3B	HR	BB	SO	SB	BA
Joseph Seber	P17	19	12	2	3	0	0	0	0	2	4	0	.250
John Mackinson	P17	17	12	2	2	1	0	0	0	1	4	0	.167
Wallace Hood	P14	16	31	3	7	1	0	0	0	1	7	0	.226
Robert Keegan	P16	16	27	5	8	2	0	1	0	4	5	0	.296
Edwin Ehlers	3B12	13	44	3	11	5	0	0	1	4	6	0	.250
Ralph Brown	OF10	12	38	7	10	1	3	0	0	2	2	1	.263
Otis Strain	SS	9	26	2	4	1	0	0		1			0	.154

PITCHERS	W	L	PCT	G	GS	CG	SH	IP	H	BB	SO	ERA
Erwin Porterfield	15	6	.714	23	22	20	6	178	144	51	133	2.17
Richard Starr	14	9	.609	29	28	14	2	199	181	101	158	4.21
Clarence Marshall	9	7	.563	23	20	10	2	155	147	87	77	3.66
John Maldovan	8	7	.533	28	17	6	0	128	111	87	73	3.94
Clarence Mueller	6	5	.545	27	8	4	0	80	74	35	34	4.16
Wallace Hood	6	5	.545	14	12	5	1	86	77	59	48	4.19
Robert Keegan	4	5	.444	16	14	4	0	85	98	34	40	5.51
Frank Lamanna	4	6	.400	30	0	0	0	73	53	38	45	2.84
James Tote	2	0	1.000	4				26	31	19	8	4.50
Mal Mallette	2	2	.500	5				33	22	16	17	2.45
Joseph Seber	2	3	.400	17				38	37	33	23	6.39
John Mackinson	2	4	.333	17	3	1	0	46	43	31	31	4.89
William Houtz	2	6	.250	19	8	2	0	71	70	54	37	6.08
Carmine Melignano	1	0	1.000	8				23	25	17	14	4.30
Joseph Och	1	0	1.000	5				8	6	12	4	5.63
Don Johnson	1	3	.250	6				29	34	15	15	5.28
Joe Valenzuela	0	1	.000	1				9	9	1	2	2.00
Jack McKinney	0	1	.000	1				4	4	0	1	4.50
Ray Schmidt	0	2	.000	3				4	5	3	4	9.00
Elmer Stepanovsky	0	0	----	3				6	8	7	4	0.00
Floyd Bevens	0	0	----	2				8	9	6	0	2.25
Ed Gysen	0	0	----	1				4	2	3	2	4.50
Fred Wolff	0	0	----	1				4	5	0	1	9.00

SYRACUSE   3rd   77-73   .513   -15.5   Jewel Ens
Chiefs

BATTERS	POS-GAMES	GP	AB	R	H	BI	2B	3B	HR	BB	SO	SB	BA
Ed Shokes	1B150	150	501	95	129	62	22	2	10	117	56	5	.257
Frank Drews	2B144	144	520	86	151	65	28	9	9	106	54	5	.290
Harry Donabedian	SS91	95	338	53	84	32	15	0	3	69	39	6	.249
Kermit Wahl	3B81,SS60	141	498	92	127	95	20	2	20	93	77	9	.255
Clyde Vollmer	OF121	122	440	86	127	104	24	3	32	62	61	1	.289
Austin Knickerbocker	OF120	128	452	56	115	70	18	4	16	36	56	4	.254
Frank Davis	OF106	117	343	57	81	43	12	4	11	74	77	6	.236
Richard West	C78	80	258	40	62	24	10	0	3	30	23	6	.240
Al Rubeling	3B66,OF22	103	338	30	78	54	10	3	7	37	48	0	.231
Joseph Beeler	OF81	88	276	39	58	33	10	0	10	48	49	1	.210
Millard Howell	P30	82	146	15	38	17	4	2	2	9	28	0	.260
Thad Bosiack	C76	79	245	18	51	13	3	2	0	24	14	0	.208
John Bebber	P32	32	54	3	9	2	0	0	0	1	8	0	.167
Frank Fanovich	P29	30	64	4	14	5	1	0	0	3	4	0	.219
Frank Seward	P30	30	13	2	1	0	0	0	0	3	8	0	.077
Ed Erautt	P29	29	75	5	9	3	0	0	0	5	20	0	.120
Harold Erickson	P29	29	9	1	0	0	0	0	0	0	5	0	.000
John Hetki	P25	25	53	5	13	7	2	0	0	1	4	0	.245
Alex Mustaikas	P22	22	23	3	4	3	1	1	0	1	6	0	.174
Robert Usher	OF14	14	48	4	8	6	0	0	0	5	7	0	.167
James Wallace	P13	13	21	4	7	3	0	0	0	3	6	0	.333
John Dudick	SS,3B,2B	11	21	6	6	3	1	0	2	6	1	0	.286
Robert Carson	3B	3	11	1	3	2	0	0	0			0	.273
William Schultz	P2	2	3	1	2	2	0	0	0			0	.667
Ed Lynk	PH,PR	2	1	1	0	0	0	0	0			0	.000
Woody Williams		1	0	0	0	0	0	0	0			0	----

PITCHERS	W	L	PCT	G	GS	CG	SH	IP	H	BB	SO	ERA
Millard Howell	17	12	.586	30	30	27	2	247	231	91	101	3.72
Ed Erautt	15	7	.682	29	26	17	3	215	202	61	141	2.97
John Bebber	10	8	.556	32	22	8	2	157	147	74	47	4.30
Frank Fanovich	9	13	.409	29	25	13	2	181	179	110	120	4.08
John Hetki	8	12	.400	25	19	14	1	143	139	49	69	3.78

SYRACUSE (cont.)
Chiefs

PITCHERS	W	L	PCT	G	GS	CG	SH	IP	H	BB	SO	ERA
Frank Seward	6	2	.750	30	0	0	0	70	74	28	10	4.37
James Wallace	4	5	.444	13	10	3	0	69	82	32	35	5.35
Alex Mustaikis	3	8	.273	22	9	5	0	74	94	26	17	5.35
Thomas Hughes	2	2	.500	7				33	31	13	8	2.45
James Ayres	1	0	1.000	3				14	19	6	8	8.36
William Schultz	1	1	.500	2				8	2	2	4	0.00
Harold Erickson	1	3	.250	29	2	1	0	54	60	23	29	6.17

ROCHESTER   4th   78-75   .510   -16   Cedric Durst
Red Wings

BATTERS	POS-GAMES	GP	AB	R	H	BI	2B	3B	HR	BB	SO	SB	BA
Glenn Nelson	1B141	142	485	68	147	63	29	12	7	70	42	11	.303
Robert Young	2B125	126	488	87	131	38	12	12	4	51	39	4	.268
Bernard Creger	SS98	100	336	30	77	36	10	4	0	21	46	3	.229
Ed Kazak	3B140	142	508	72	157	85	24	5	12	41	35	6	.309
Charles Diering	OF147	149	546	91	146	61	31	11	5	71	79	11	.267
Harold Rice	OF143	146	536	80	172	73	36	13	7	47	52	9	.321
Russ Derry	OF90	108	274	51	59	42	5	2	16	51	74	9	.215
Charles Marshall	C91	94	231	32	48	34	8	0	6	63	51	1	.208
Frank Gravino	OF83	116	321	53	89	74	15	6	18	34	98	2	.277
Vern Benson	SS46,OF,1B,3B,2B	97	228	39	56	38	12	2	4	53	44	5	.246
Richard Cole	2B37,SS30,3B10	91	226	33	57	22	11	0	4	25	21	7	.252
John Bucha	C50	54	132	20	40	24	6	1	2	23	20	1	.303
Les Fusselman	C42	50	116	18	27	15	6	4	1	11	20	1	.233
Matt Surkont	P38	38	81	5	14	7	3	0	2	5	19	0	.173
William Reeder	P37	37	82	5	7	2	1	0	0	3	34	0	.085
John Mikan	P36	36	55	4	7	10	2	0	0	6	21	0	.127
Ed Blake	P34	35	37	1	7	3	1	0	0	5	9	0	.189
George Copeland	P33	33	30	2	4	1	0	0	0	2	7	0	.133
Steve Gerkin	P29	29	12	1	1	0	1	0	0	0	4	0	.083
Ken Johnson	P17	24	42	6	8	1	2	2	1	3	13	0	.190
Edwin Green	P19	19	18	2	3	0	0	0	0	1	6	0	.167
Glenn Gardner	P14	14	16	2	3	0	1	0	0	3	2	0	.188
Richard Burgett	OF	13	32	5	13	7	7	0	0	3	4	0	.406
Steve Bilko	1B12	12	41	5	6	3	1	0	0	8	11	0	.146
Al Papai	P12	12	24	3	3	3	1	0	0	4	9	0	.125
Lawrence Ciaffone	PH	8	8	0	1	0	0	0	0			0	.125
Ted Herder	OF	6	11	2	2	1	0	0	1			0	.182
Alex Patterson	P3	3	5	1	2	0	0	0	0			0	.400

PITCHERS	W	L	PCT	G	GS	CG	SH	IP	H	BB	SO	ERA
William Reeder	19	12	.613	37	33	15	5	247	219	98	126	3.17
Matt Surkont	15	11	.577	38	32	14	0	240	229	109	142	4.16
John Mikan	9	9	.500	36	24	8	1	163	157	110	86	4.47
Ed Blake	7	6	.538	34	7	1	1	123	113	68	59	3.88
Ken Johnson	6	9	.400	17	14	4	2	100	78	82	78	4.23
George Copeland	5	3	.625	33	7	3	0	101	73	76	59	2.94
Al Papai	5	6	.545	12	12	7	1	70	62	42	29	4.37
Steve Gerkin	4	4	.500	29	0	0	0	51	54	10	14	3.35
Octavio Rubert	2	0	1.000	6				20	26	11	7	4.05
Glenn Gardner	2	4	.333	14	5	2	0	53	61	28	16	5.09
Edwin Green	2	5	.286	18	8	2	1	57	57	42	27	6.16
David Thomas	1	0	1.000	5				7	11	10	3	9.00
Ray Yochim	1	4	.200	9	6	3	0	45	47	40	28	6.40
Alex Patterson	0	2	.000	3				13	20	6	5	6.23
John Yuhas	0	0	----	4				4	6	5	1	15.75

TORONTO   5th   78-76   .506   -16.5   Eddie Sawyer -
Maple Leafs   Dick Porter

BATTERS	POS-GAMES	GP	AB	R	H	BI	2B	3B	HR	BB	SO	SB	BA
Henry Biasetti	1B148	148	496	82	132	89	16	3	21	109	36	6	.266
Roland Harrington	2B83,SS19	105	403	63	97	46	17	0	8	38	29	8	.241
Vic Barnhart	SS		(see multi-team players)										
Willie Jones	3B118	118	443	69	122	58	22	9	6	45	45	5	.275

TORONTO (cont.)
Maple Leafs

BATTERS	POS-GAMES	GP	AB	R	H	BI	2B	3B	HR	BB	SO	SB	BA
Ed Sanicki	OF154	154	526	82	124	107	19	4	21	81	87	3	.236
John Welaj	OF150	152	543	97	171	69	29	10	6	75	58	18	.315
Bernard Lutz	OF108	118	482	72	148	49	25	6	0	38	43	2	.307
Stan Lopata	C97	110	337	59	94	67	20	8	15	45	58	4	.279
Vince Plumbo	C68	86	235	29	65	37	11	0	6	19	27	0	.277
Harold Albright	SS36,2B29	65	212	26	50	21	7	2	3	32	34	1	.236
George Bennington	OF29	60	118	24	31	11	7	0	0	9	12	2	.263
Oscar Judd	P23	52	83	13	29	26	6	0	3	12	15	0	.349
Jim Konstanty	P46	46	45	2	10	2	0	0	0	2	4	0	.222
Emory Church	P33	40	42	7	7	3	0	0	1	3	13	0	.167
Louis Possehl	P38	39	63	3	12	4	1	0	0	0	17	0	.190
John Thompson	P32	33	66	8	15	6	3	1	0	2	22	0	.227
Jesse Levan	OF29	31	106	14	28	22	3	0	3	19	18	3	.264
Al Porto	P31	31	45	4	13	0	3	0	0	2	5	0	.289
James Ackenet	3B26	30	93	8	13	8	1	0	0	14	12	0	.140
William Johnson	2B27	30	88	11	24	11	5	0	0	15	9	0	.273
Nick Strincevich	P24	24	36	3	8	5	0	0	0	5	11	0	.222
Luke Hamlin	P21	21	46	3	6	5	0	0	0	4	14	0	.130
Aloysius Hodkey	P11	11	7	0	1	0	0	0	0	1	4	0	.143
Robert Green	P10	10	7	0	2	2	0	1	0	1	1	0	.286
Al Lakeman	1B,C	9	26	3	6	2	1	1	1			2	.231

PITCHERS	W	L	PCT	G	GS	CG	SH	IP	H	BB	SO	ERA
Oscar Judd	14	8	.636	23	22	13	2	156	182	63	67	4.79
John Thompson	12	8	.600	32	24	10	1	161	166	93	92	5.09
Louis Possehl	11	11	.500	38	24	9	1	174	180	80	83	4.50
Jim Konstanty	10	10	.500	46	14	7	3	162	163	59	73	4.06
Nick Strincevich	9	7	.563	24	16	7	1	109	110	26	47	3.39
Al Porto	8	5	.615	31	9	4	1	115	107	61	61	4.62
Luke Hamlin	6	10	.375	21	20	10	0	147	161	28	69	3.86
Emory Church	5	9	.357	33	13	3	1	119	119	78	39	5.52
Stephen Ridzik	1	0	1.000	8				34	40	27	15	7.41
Richard Koecher	1	1	.500	5				6	7	2	5	9.00
Don Carter	1	2	.333	9				40	58	19	18	7.88
Paul Calvert	0	1	.000	4				4	9	2	1	18.00
Aloysius Hodkey	0	3	.000	11				36	45	18	13	6.25
Robert Green	0	0	----	10				24	31	20	8	7.50

BUFFALO   6th   71-80   .470   -22   Paul Richards
Bisons

BATTERS	POS-GAMES	GP	AB	R	H	BI	2B	3B	HR	BB	SO	SB	BA
Lawrence Barton	1B116	116	392	64	115	78	22	0	18	74	65	2	.293
John Bero	2B97,SS41	134	437	89	104	35	18	5	10	104	71	12	.238
Manuel Hidalgo	SS62	69	177	19	34	15	2	2	3	6	10	1	.192
Seymour Block	3B94	103	341	50	93	41	15	3	5	32	41	12	.273
John Groth	OF150	150	586	124	199	97	37	16	30	54	75	7	.340
Coaker Triplett	OF113	126	399	87	141	83	32	3	19	58	27	12	.353
Chet Laabs	OF86	89	298	68	88	81	13	1	29	52	63	1	.295
Martin Tabacheck	C79	88	259	25	69	28	7	0	2	29	19	3	.266
Ed Modarski	C78,1B11	105	292	40	75	37	13	1	5	51	32	4	.257
Ansel Moore	OF68,3B21	104	350	62	108	68	13	2	23	33	29	0	.309
Carl Cox	2B49,SS17	72	279	41	76	34	12	3	5	23	25	1	.272
Troyce Cofer	3B22,OF14,2B12	67	155	22	31	24	5	0	0	20	15	3	.200
William Serena	3B21,OF,SS	63	182	43	47	32	8	2	13	49	48	3	.258
Lindsay Brown	SS57	63	138	16	30	18	6	0	1	13	22	7	.217
Saul Rogovin	P31	57	94	16	22	15	2	1	5	9	21	0	.234
Clem Hausmann	P37	37	65	5	9	8	1	0	0	10	17	0	.138
Aaron Silverman	P37	37	40	1	8	5	0	0	0	1	8	0	.200
Anderson Bush	P32	32	33	0	7	1	1	0	0	4	12	0	.212
Jacob Wade	P29	31	48	5	9	3	2	0	1	1	12	0	.188
Henry Perry	P30	30	56	1	4	2	0	0	0	1	23	0	.071
William Connelly	P18	27	32	4	7	3	0	0	0	4	8	0	.219
Norm Jaeger	1B23	23	80	8	19	12	2	0	5	13	8	0	.238
Rufus Gentry	P22	22	28	1	5	4	1	0	0	2	3	0	.179
Newman Shirley	P9	17	18	2	3	2	0	0	0	1	6	0	.167
Paul Richards	C,1B	13	24	2	8	7	1	1	0	7	4	0	.333
Lewis Fauth	P12	12	3	0	0	0	0	0	0	2	1	0	.000
William Radulovich	2B	9	16	0	1	3	0	0	0			0	.063
Ted Wyberanec	P2	2	2	0	1	0	0	0	0			0	.500

BUFFALO (cont.)
Bisons

PITCHERS	W	L	PCT	G	GS	CG	SH	IP	H	BB	SO	ERA
Clem Hausmann	14	11	.560	37	27	14	1	200	207	58	100	3.92
Saul Rogovin	13	7	.650	31	20	10	2	172	170	66	109	3.92
Henry Perry	8	11	.421	30	23	10	2	148	150	81	50	4.50
Jacob Wade	8	11	.421	29	18	10	1	136	153	54	55	5.10
Anderson Bush	6	6	.500	32	8	1	0	118	129	56	56	.4.50
Aaron Silverman	6	7	.462	37	6	2	1	127	132	54	67	4.04
William Connelly	4	5	.444	18	10	0	0	58	69	60	22	6.52
Newman Shirley	3	3	.500	9	9	2	0	52	53	34	17	4.15
Rufus Gentry	3	9	.250	22	13	3	1	86	89	71	48	5.65
Lewis Fauth	0	1	.000	12				21	29	19	12	6.86
Russ Meers	0	1	.000	4				9	20	10	5	18.00
Rafael Rivas	0	0	----	9				12	15	5	3	4.50
Ted Wyberanec	0	0	----	2				5	3	4	0	7.20
Joaquin Gutierrez	0	0	----	2				5	5	7	2	10.90
Pete Appleton	0	0	----	1				1	4	1	0	18.00

JERSEY CITY 7th 69-83 .454 -24.5 Bruno Betzel
Giants

BATTERS	POS-GAMES	GP	AB	R	H	BI	2B	3B	HR	BB	SO	SB	BA
Jack Harshman	1B150	150	511	89	125	76	20	2	24	104	92	1	.245
Burgess Whitehead	2B77	79	278	44	79	22	9	2	1	33	16	3	.284
William Jennings	SS152	152	540	83	135	62	21	7	8	61	93	7	.250
Robert Blattner	3B79,2B24	104	344	60	95	53	20	2	11	63	35	3	.276
Lloyd Gearhart	OF132	139	500	69	144	79	23	5	11	60	68	10	.288
Harold Bamberger	OF126	128	484	77	135	60	21	8	9	41	56	5	.279
Don Mueller	OF98	99	400	67	131	52	17	4	10	31	14	3	.328
Sal Yvars	C111	132	409	67	123	88	17	4	16	65	43	1	.301
William Milne	OF89	111	360	57	99	48	14	5	11	37	55	14	.275
John Pramesa	C58	81	216	25	61	39	12	0	4	16	15	0	.282
William Sinram	3B46,2B15	67	171	12	32	22	4	3	1	24	20	1	.187
Sam Webb	P37	54	106	13	35	9	5	0	0	2	5	1	.330
Andrew Tomasic	P37	40	75	12	17	6	4	0	1	10	15	1	.227
John Kraus	P33	38	83	9	13	9	3	0	0	8	29	0	.157
Jack Maguire	2B33	33	108	18	25	10	3	1	0	18	17	1	.231
Luther Knerr	P29	29	22	1	4	2	2	0	0	0	2	0	.182
Wes Bailey	P28	28	55	4	4	3	0	0	0	4	18	1	.073
Robert Callan	P27	27	20	2	4	3	0	0	1	2	8	0	.200
George Bamberger	P25	25	13	2	1	0	1	0	0	5	3	0	.077
Nicholas Witek	2B11,3B11	22	84	13	25	6	4	0	0	9	4	0	.298
Robert Cain	P17	20	22	0	5	5	1	0	0	2	2	0	.227
Richard Hoover	P16	16	9	0	1	0	0	0	0	2	2	0	.111
Herb Andrews	P14	14	26	3	3	2	0	0	0	4	8	0	.115
Dick Kimble	3B11	11	35	4	8	4	1	0	0	6	3	1	.229
Alex Konikowski	P11	11	7	0	0	0	0	0	0	2	5	0	.000
David Garcia	3B,2B	7	14	2	3	3	2	0	0			0	.214
Nick Solomon	OF	6	4	1	1	0	0	0	0			0	.250
Roger Bowman	P5	6	2	1	1	0	0	0	0			0	.500
Frank Trechock	SS	3	5	0	1	0	0	0	0			0	.200
Joe Bracchitta	PH	3	1	1	0	0	0	0	0			0	.000

PITCHERS	W	L	PCT	G	GS	CG	SH	IP	H	BB	SO	ERA
Sam Webb	18	15	.545	37	34	17	5	230	227	104	65	4.15
John Kraus	13	15	.464	33	32	16	2	223	234	102	98	4.56
Andrew Tomasic	11	16	.407	37	30	16	2	228	195	106	170	4.18
Wes Bailey	7	11	.389	28	20	7	0	149	163	87	95	5.13
Herb Andrews	5	6	.455	14	13	7	0	88	106	27	33	4.50
Luther Knerr	4	3	.571	29	1	0	0	69	72	51	34	7.04
Alex Konikowski	3	0	1.000	11				32	33	15	25	5.34
Robert Callan	3	5	.375	27	3	1	0	67	48	32	44	4.03
George Bamberger	2	2	.500	25	7	1	0	65	83	42	28	6.37
Richard Hoover	2	4	.333	16				36	45	17	17	6.75
Robert Cain	1	5	.167	17	6	0	0	58	53	53	28	6.21
Roger Bowman	0	1	.000	5				6	8	12	8	12.00
Michael Thomas	0	0	----	2				4	2	4	2	6.25

BALTIMORE   8th   59-88   .401   -32   Alphonse Thomas
Orioles

BATTERS	POS-GAMES	GP	AB	R	H	BI	2B	3B	HR	BB	SO	SB	BA
Edward Levy	1B113	121	408	56	99	79	19	5	22	41	44	1	.243
Al Cihocki	2B96,3B33	136	426	50	110	54	14	9	12	39	54	3	.258
Robert Wilson	SS93	117	415	55	105	25	15	7	6	26	37	15	.253
Lew Riggs	3B115	124	387	54	108	52	20	3	15	60	33	0	.279
Howard Moss	OF131	131	451	93	136	94	14	2	33	63	74	3	.302
William Martin	OF124	135	463	67	118	49	13	3	17	37	44	9	.255
William Barnacle	OF		(see multi-team players)										
Warren Robinson	C85	98	266	20	59	24	8	4	5	34	40	4	.222
Ken Mapes	OF57	78	191	19	40	20	4	0	8	17	36	0	.209
Milt Stockhausen	C62	69	197	16	43	24	7	1	3	16	22	0	.218
Ken Braun	SS58	62	201	17	43	6	4	2	0	10	23	3	.214
Roberto Avila	2B50,OF	56	182	18	40	12	9	0	0	23	11	6	.220
John Podgajny	P40	42	34	2	3	1	0	0	0	2	5	0	.088
John Wittig	P33	33	59	5	7	1	2	0	0	3	25	0	.119
Ernest Groth	P29	32	67	6	11	3	1	0	1	3	14	0	.164
Henry Ruszkowski	C10	31	53	5	13	4	1	0	3	9	13	0	.245
Fred Wollpert	P31	31	33	3	4	1	1	0	0	7	7	0	.121
Robert Kuzava	P30	30	59	3	8	1	2	0	0	8	23	0	.136
Mike Mellis	P30	30	11	0	1	0	0	0	0	0	3	0	.091
Herb Conyers	1B28	28	108	5	25	15	4	0	1	2	16	2	.231
James Wasdell	OF25	25	89	11	30	8	1	0	1	14	4	0	.337
George Hooks	P24	25	19	1	4	0	1	0	0	0	7	0	.211
George Anderman	P24	24	36	1	4	1	0	0	0	1	8	0	.111
Lyman Linde	P18	18	36	3	2	2	0	0	1	3	17	0	.056
Robert Kline	3B13	18	35	1	4	1	1	0	0	0	10	0	.114
William Hockenbury	3B	3	10	1	1	0	0	0	0			0	.100
Jim Steck	OF	3	4	0	0	0	0	0	0	0		0	.000
William Padden	SS	1	0	0	0	0	0	0	0	0		0	----

PITCHERS		W	L	PCT	G	GS	CG	SH	IP	H	BB	SO	ERA
Ernest Groth		12	12	.500	29	27	15	2	199	210	74	100	4.48
John Podgajny		9	12	.429	40	12	6	1	131	143	43	30	3.44
Robert Kuzava		9	16	.360	30	29	11	3	192	179	113	154	4.83
John Wittig		8	16	.333	33	29	12	1	191	207	83	99	4.81
Fred Wollpert		5	6	.455	31	8	4	0	122	133	55	74	4.72
George Anderman		5	9	.357	24	17	7	0	108	122	69	57	5.58
Lyman Linde		5	9	.357	18	17	8	2	110	122	42	45	4.50
Mike Mellis		3	2	.600	30	1	0	0	56	66	21	22	4.50
Sam McLawhorn		1	0	1.000	3				7	5	14	5	10.29
George Hooks		1	3	.250	24	2	2	1	62	63	36	22	4.79
Ted Wendt		0	0	----	2				6	9	9	1	13.50

MULTI-TEAM PLAYERS

BATTERS	POS-GAMES	TEAMS	GP	AB	R	H	BI	2B	3B	HR	BB	SO	SB	BA
William Barnacle	OF127	JC22-BA113	135	434	57	106	51	20	4	12	84	52	6	.244
Vic Barnhart	SS103,3B20	MO9-TO119	128	441	66	112	44	13	5	4	55	33	5	.254
Oscar Grimes	3B39,2B17,1B10	TO4-MO81	85	218	57	52	32	11	4	6	61	37	2	.239
Lum Harris	P28	JC8-BU20	28	43	7	14	4	1	0	0	1	11	0	.326

PITCHERS		TEAMS	W	L	PCT	G	GS	CG	SH	IP	H	BB	SO	ERA
Lum Harris		JC8-BU20	6	8	.429	28	14	8	0	122	116	55	64	4.20

TEAM BATTING

TEAMS	GP	AB	R	H	BI	2B	3B	HR	BB	SO	SB	BA
MONTREAL	155	4998	837	1367	767	262	59	133	678	606	84	.274
NEWARK	155	4921	736	1254	683	194	28	169	609	705	63	.255
SYRACUSE	151	4768	708	1180	652	182	33	125	731	659	42	.247
ROCHESTER	154	4939	720	1289	652	223	74	90	610	759	70	.261
TORONTO	155	5009	751	1322	692	210	50	98	633	623	58	.264
BUFFALO	151	4872	802	1325	739	214	40	174	661	682	68	.272
JERSEY CITY	153	4978	744	1331	678	207	44	109	626	646	56	.267
BALTIMORE	148	4613	561	1104	521	157	40	139	492	623	52	.239
	611	39098	5859	10172	5384	1649	368	1037	5040	5303	493	.260

1949
STARS IN OTHER FIELDS

Most professional athletes are content to play one sport, relaxing or pursuing other interests in the offseason. However, there were a few baseball players in the International League who preferred to pursue their athletic careers year round—but not always using a bat and glove.

During the 1910s, a Native American baseball player named Jim Thorpe made a name for himself in the International League and other baseball circuits. Fast as the wind, with a powerful physique, Thorpe took full advantage of his athletic abilities to play professional football after the finish of the baseball season. Jim Thorpe excelled in the fall sport and was voted into the Football Hall of Fame.

A few years later, during the 1920s, a baseball player named Cecil Dye patrolled the outfield for the Buffalo Bisons. During baseball's offseason, Dye laced on skates and played for the Toronto club of the National Hockey League. Like Jim Thorpe, Cecil Dye excelled in his non-baseball athletic career, winning two National Hockey League scoring championships on his way to the Hockey Hall of Fame.

Twenty years later, another two-sport star emerged in the International League. In 1948, a first baseman by the name of Chuck Connors joined the roster of the Montreal Royals. Standing over 6'5", Connors spent some of his winters playing professional basketball for the Boston Celtics and other teams.

The 1949 Buffalo Bisons snuck up on the International field to win the bunting by four games over Rochester, and six over Chuck Connors' Montreal Royals. Jersey City and Toronto slid into fourth and fifth, while Syracuse, Baltimore, and Newark ended on the bottom. Montreal's Robert Morgan won batting laurels (.337), Steve Bilko from Rochester had the most runs batted in (125), and Bilko's fellow Red Wing Russ Derry swatted the most home runs (42). On the hill, Baltimore's Al Widmar won the most games (22), Emory Church from Toronto had the lowest earned run average (2.35), and Montreal Royal Dan Bankhead struck out the most batters (176).

At the completion of the 1947-1948 basketball season, Chuck Connors stopped playing professional basketball to concentrate on baseball. However, after three years with the Royals and two more with the Los Angeles Angels, Connors left pro sports altogether to concentrate on a whole new profession: acting.

Two-sport stars are a special breed. Not only do they have the athletic skills to master more than one sport, their love of the game propels them to commit a majority of their year to pursuit of their goals. This dedication is what sets these special athletes apart, making them stars in any field.

BUFFALO Bisons

1st   90-64   .584   Paul Richards

BATTERS	POS-GAMES	GP	AB	R	H	BI	2B	3B	HR	BB	SO	SB	BA
George Byam	1B134	136	482	73	138	106	21	1	19	66	80	9	.286
Eugene Markland	2B80,3B77	151	522	142	159	90	36	4	25	155	79	12	.305
Billy DeMars	SS109	109	378	49	105	56	18	1	6	47	26	3	.278
Seymour Block	3B75,1B2	87	252	48	65	34	16	1	4	37	29	4	.258
Raymond Coleman	OF152	153	555	109	164	113	29	8	23	81	49	10	.295
Ansel Moore	OF123,3B,1B	131	466	72	138	88	32	1	12	57	30	1	.296
Coaker Triplett	OF113	127	419	98	135	102	25	1	22	75	37	6	.322
Martin Tabacheck	C110	116	353	37	84	44	16	0	2	28	18	1	.238
Linus Frey	2B57,SS21,3B13,OF1	93	314	74	94	51	14	1	11	69	34	4	.299
Frank Trechock	2B40,SS34	80	198	32	42	17	9	0	2	42	25	2	.212
Roger Cramer	OF45	65	135	22	37	27	7	0	3	9	4	2	.274
Jack Hussey	1B28,OF18	51	138	22	29	32	2	2	8	26	35	4	.210
Aaron Silverman	P50	50	50	6	6	5	0	0	0	11	17	0	.120
Robert Hooper	P36,1B1	43	66	11	13	2	2	0	0	0	23	0	.197
Lum Harris	P41	41	42	3	6	2	2	0	0	3	11	0	.143
Jacob Wade	P41	41	22	4	4	1	2	0	1	3	9	0	.182
Len Okrie	C38	40	98	13	21	10	3	0	2	15	27	0	.214
Saul Rogovin	P29	39	90	13	24	18	5	0	3	5	17	0	.267
Luis Aloma	P38	38	54	8	6	2	1	0	0	7	21	0	.111
Bennie Warren	C20	37	78	11	17	18	2	0	3	17	22	0	.218
Clem Hausmann	P31	31	43	11	6	3	0	0	0	21	7	0	.140
James Parton	P29	29	37	4	7	1	2	0	1	3	9	0	.182
Alejandro Carrasquel	P12	12	13	2	2	1	0	0	1	1	3	0	.154
Zeb Eaton	P4,PH	5	3	1	1	0	1	0	0			0	.333
William McCahan	P5	5	2		0								.000
Ed March	P5	5	2		0								.000
Raymond Carlson	PR	2	0	1	0	0	0	0	0	0		0	.000
Paul Richards	C,1B	2	1	0	0	0	0	0	0	0		0	.000
Ed Burtschy	P2	2	1		0								.000

PITCHERS	W	L	PCT	G	GS	CG	SH	IP	H	BB	SO	ERA
Robert Hooper	19	3	.864	36	18	9	0	175	176	85	75	3.96
Saul Rogovin	16	6	.727	29	22	19	1	197	188	101	163	3.65
Clem Hausmann	15	7	.682	31	23	11	3	168	176	59	62	4.23
Aaron Silverman	12	11	.522	50	17	4	0	164	189	76	63	5.54
Luis Aloma	10	9	.526	38	22	7	1	180	177	94	115	4.60
Lum Harris	4	7	.364	41	9	2	0	126	137	62	76	4.94
James Parton	4	7	.364	29	20	3	0	111	120	72	44	4.70
Jacob Wade	3	4	.429	41	7	3	0	82	106	43	42	6.70
Alejandro Carrasquel	2	3	.400	12	4	1	0	43	53	15	18	4.18
Ed March	1	0	1.000	5	1	0	0	10	10	4	6	8.10
Zeb Eaton	1	0	1.000	4	1	0	0	7	5	5	4	2.57
William McCahan	0	4	.000	5	4	0	0	13	20	19	5	9.00
Ed Burtschy	0	0	----	2	0	0	0	1	1	3	1	9.00

ROCHESTER Red Wings

2nd   85-67   .559   -4   John Keane

BATTERS	POS-GAMES	GP	AB	R	H	BI	2B	3B	HR	BB	SO	SB	BA
Steve Bilko	1B139	139	503	101	156	125	32	5	34	84	74	1	.310
Richard Cole	2B106,SS35	141	454	64	107	43	16	4	7	71	49	3	.236
Al Stringer	SS101	101	418	67	112	36	32	1	3	69	47	2	.268
Ralph LaPointe	3B78,2B14,SS9	106	399	53	110	35	12	0	3	23	27	6	.273
Russ Derry	OF134,1B10	148	491	120	137	122	19	4	42	134	94	6	.279
Ed Mierkowicz	OF117,1B,3B	128	451	75	132	88	17	7	15	77	36	3	.293
Richard Burgett	OF117	128	441	72	122	54	22	7	4	43	43	0	.277
Jon Bucha	C104	114	329	47	95	47	19	3	8	61	34	2	.289
Don Thompson	OF92	94	355	45	86	42	18	3	3	34	39	6	.242
Charles Marshall	C62	63	181	22	47	22	9	3	3	31	28	0	.260
Erv Dusak	P25,OF	61	83	18	20	15	1	2	4	12	15	0	.241
Thomas Poholsky	P34	44	101	11	22	14	7	0	3	2	22	0	.218
John Yuhas	P35	36	57	7	8	4	1	0	0	2	14	1	.140
George Copeland	P35	35	48	6	17	10	1	0	0	2	11	0	.354
Cloyd Boyer	P31	31	64	7	11	6	2	1	0	5	17	0	.172
Vaughn Hazen		21	38	5	7	3	1	0	1	9	12	0	.184
Vern Benson	SS10,2B,3B	20	54	7	11	10	2	0	1	6	8	1	.204
David Thomas	P16	17	12	0	1	1	0	0	0	0	2	0	.083
Richard Bokelmann	P15	15	19	0	3	0	0	0	0	2	4	0	.158
James Hearn	P13	14	28	7	6	5	0	0	1	6	12	0	.214
John Grodzicki	P13	13	14	0	4	3	0	0	0	1	4	0	.286

ROCHESTER (cont.)
Red Wings

BATTERS	POS-GAMES	GP	AB	R	H	BI	2B	3B	HR	BB	SO	SB	BA
Bernard Olsen	OF	12	21	3	3	3	1	1	0	5	6	0	.143
Jack Collum	P10	10	17	2	3	0	0	0	0	0	2	0	.176
Willis McDonald	P9	9	8		1								.125
Dan Hile	P8	8	4		0								.000
Octavio Rubert	P6	6	1	0	1	1	0	0	0			0	1.000
Lawrence Ciaffone	C	6	15	0	3	1	1	0	0			0	.200
Wilbur McCullough	P5	5	4		1								.250
James Bryant	P3	3	2		0								.000
Wayne McLeland	P1	1	1		0								.000

PITCHERS		W	L	PCT	G	GS	CG	SH	IP	H	BB	SO	ERA
Cloyd Boyer		15	10	.600	31	22	15	3	190	147	110	143	3.13
Thomas Poholsky		14	10	.583	34	25	14	1	222	213	69	116	3.69
George Copeland		11	7	.611	35	19	9	5	143	107	140	103	4.03
Erv Dusak		11	8	.579	25	21	10	0	138	116	104	87	4.57
James Hearn		8	3	.727	13	12	7	2	89	92	36	44	4.25
John Yuhas		8	9	.471	35	27	9	3	174	191	69	84	4.45
Richard Bokelmann		4	4	.500	15	7	3	0	63	65	33	31	4.29
Jack Collum		3	2	.600	10	4	2	0	42	36	23	23	3.86
Octavio Rubert		2	0	1.000	6	0	0	0	8	7	11	2	10.13
John Grodzicki		2	1	.667	13	1	1	0	37	47	19	17	6.81
David Thomas		2	4	.333	16	4	0	0	43	49	37	16	5.44
Wayne McLeland		1	0	1.000	4	0	0	0	4	7	1	0	4.50
Willis McDonald		0	1	.000	9	1	0	0	29	19	26	13	4.34
Wilbur McCullough		0	1	.000	5	1	0	0	18	17	16	7	4.50
James Bryant		0	2	.000	3	1	0	0	5	4	7	1	10.08
Dan Hile		0	0	----	8	0	0	0	13	18	10	6	7.62

MONTREAL
Royals

3rd 84-70 .545 -6 Clay Hopper

BATTERS	POS-GAMES	GP	AB	R	H	BI	2B	3B	HR	BB	SO	SB	BA
Chuck Connors	1B132,OF1	133	477	90	152	108	25	5	20	84	39	6	.319
Lamar Bridges	2B124,SS26	151	504	77	139	73	28	3	7	60	36	8	.276
Robert Morgan	SS131,3B24	154	567	109	191	112	38	1	19	111	67	10	.337
Kermit Wahl	3B104,2B22,SS,OF	134	451	80	129	83	30	5	11	66	60	12	.286
Sam Jethroe	OF151,C,3B	153	635	154	207	83	34	19	17	79	89	89	.326
George Schmees	OF143,1B3	148	564	99	161	118	29	6	22	40	88	17	.285
Al Gionfriddo	OF127	135	403	103	101	62	16	2	9	126	36	29	.251
Steve Lembo	C85	90	306	41	89	21	10	0	2	25	17	1	.291
Dan Bankhead	P38,1B,OF	58	127	21	41	26	7	3	1	6	15	0	.323
Maurice Atwell	C42,OF1	52	145	14	38	22	5	0	0	14	12	5	.262
Charles Thompson	C36	46	126	11	35	13	0	0	0	15	9	2	.278
Clyde King	P43	43	72	7	8	6	0	0	0	5	12	0	.111
Louis Welaj	3B22,2B7	40	88	14	20	11	3	0	2	17	4	1	.227
Charles Lare	P35	35	24	1	1	0	0	0	0	0	11	0	.042
Clarence Podbielan	P33	34	66	5	10	5	1	1	0	2	3	0	.152
Oscar Grimes	2B,1B,OF,3B	33	66	10	13	6	0	0	1	21	16	0	.197
John Van Cuyk	P33	33	42	4	3	2	1	0	0	9	28	0	.071
Ezra McGlothin	P22	24	57	12	15	13	5	0	0	12	8	0	.263
Robert Wakefield	OF20	22	70	10	18	8	1	0	3	6	5	1	.257
Mel Himes	P19	20	18	0	4	1	0	0	0	0	3	0	.222
Sam DiBlasi	OF13,P5	19	47	8	13	7	0	0	0	4	3	3	.277
Omar Lown	P19	19	26	3	5	1	0	0	0	0	7	0	.192
Frank Laga	P18	18	12	0	1	0	0	0	0	1	9	0	.083
Grady Wilson	3B12,SS	17	44	5	12	6	2	0	0	2	7	0	.273
Dee Fondy	1B16	16	56	5	14	4	1	1	1	5	6	6	.250
Gino Cimoli	OF15	15	39	4	9	3	0	0	0	1	9	0	.231
Bob Addis	OF	12	38	10	13	6	2	0	1	5	4	2	.342
Jean Roy	P10	10	9	1	1	1	0	0	0	0	1	0	.111
Nick Andromidas	P6	6	3		0								.000
William Eggert	P6	6	4		0								.000
Don Newcombe	P5	5	9	2	2	1	0	0	0				.222
William Ripken	OF	4	12	0	1	1	0	0	0			0	.083
Karl Morrison	P4	4	0		0								----
Ron Lee	P3	3	6	0	2	1	1	0	0			0	.333
Sam Narron	C	1	4	0	1	0	0	0	0			0	.250
John Hall	P1	1	0		0								----

MONTREAL (cont.)
Royals

PITCHERS	W	L	PCT	G	GS	CG	SH	IP	H	BB	SO	ERA
Don Bankhead	20	6	.769	38	34	18	3	249	192	170	176	3.76
Clyde King	17	7	.708	43	22	13	1	197	201	67	67	4.25
Ezra McGlothin	13	7	.650	22	21	12	2	159	158	75	70	4.02
John Van Cuyk	10	10	.500	33	21	9	1	156	160	58	79	4.09
Clarence Podbielan	9	13	.409	33	23	11	3	174	179	61	73	3.98
Charles Lare	5	5	.500	35	4	1	0	79	90	41	19	5.13
Ron Lee	2	0	1.000	3	1	1	0	16	10	5	6	0.56
Don Newcombe	2	2	.500	5	5	2	2	34	21	16	27	2.65
Frank Laga	2	3	.400	18	4	2	0	43	29	32	14	5.65
Sam DiBlasi	1	0	1.000	5	0	0	0	12	12	13	3	7.50
Jean Roy	1	1	.500	10	4	1	0	25	25	21	8	5.76
Omar Lown	1	7	.125	19	7	2	0	68	57	54	48	3.97
Mel Himes	1	8	.111	19	6	0	0	52	66	33	26	5.54
William Eggert	0	1	.000	6	1	0	0	11	5	14	8	4.09
Nick Andromidas	0	0	----	6	1	0	0	14	24	15	6	9.00
Karl Morrison	0	0	----	4	0	0	0	2	4	8	2	40.45
John Hall	0	0	----	1	0	0	0	5	8	5	1	10.80

JERSEY CITY   4th   83-71   .539   -7   Joseph Becker
Giants

BATTERS	POS-GAMES	GP	AB	R	H	BI	2B	3B	HR	BB	SO	SB	BA
Fred Gerken	1B134,OF,P1	143	494	62	122	69	12	8	8	76	70	21	.247
Pete Pavlick	2B127	132	464	79	125	52	12	3	7	72	46	20	.269
Rudolf Rufer	SS91,3B36	128	432	64	115	53	17	1	4	38	76	14	.266
Jack Lohrke	3B80,2B4	81	315	44	95	58	17	4	10	28	29	4	.302
Joe Bracchitta	OF125,1B4	128	470	77	128	55	14	5	2	106	51	12	.272
William Milne	OF71	73	256	48	79	33	14	3	3	33	43	13	.309
Monte Irvin	OF66	66	204	55	76	52	18	5	9	59	22	14	.373
Rafael Noble	C59	67	189	33	49	29	6	1	7	31	39	1	.259
Neal Watlington	OF52,C49	103	367	48	99	57	16	0	4	29	21	7	.270
Richard Culler	2B33,SS29,3B19,OF1	81	261	28	60	27	9	2	2	27	23	8	.230
Henry Thompson	SS44,OF26,2B1	68	230	53	68	37	14	3	14	62	26	11	.296
Ford Smith	P31,OF	68	114	16	23	12	2	0	2	22	27	0	.202
Wes Westrum	C49	51	169	38	52	59	10	2	15	38	32	7	.308
Gail Henley	OF40	41	136	21	37	13	7	1	5	15	27	3	.272
Roger Bowman	P34	37	74	5	13	11	2	0	0	1	18	0	.176
Andrew Tomasic	P33	33	55	10	14	4	1	0	0	13	9	0	.255
Ray Piano	OF26,1B1	32	61	9	9	2	1	0	0	18	17	0	.148
George Bamberger	P32	32	59	4	8	5	1	0	0	10	17	0	.136
John Uber	P32	32	29	5	8	1	0	0	0	2	11	0	.276
Francis Hardy	P22	24	44	3	4	4	0	0	0	6	16	0	.091
Len Schulte	3B19,2B1	20	80	10	18	8	2	0	1	3	6	1	.225
Roy Drews	C,OF	20	39	3	8	3	1	0	0	2	8	0	.205
Elbie Fletcher	1B19	19	64	13	13	13	4	0	2	17	3	1	.203
Wes Bailey	P19	19	35	4	2	2	0	0	0	5	16	1	.057
Bill Lohrman	P19	19	10	1	5	3	0	1	0	0	4	0	.500
Felix Mackiewicz	OF14	17	49	8	9	8	2	0	2	5	12	0	.184
William Gardner	3B13	17	45	6	11	1	1	0	0	5	7	0	.244
Robert Hansen	P14	16	10	0	0	0	0	0	0	0	4	0	.000
Albert Sima	P12	12	12	1	2	3	1	0	0	0	7	0	.167
Herb Andrews	P12	12	12	0	0	0	0	0	0	0	5	0	.000
Sam Webb	P11	11	19	2	5	3	0	0	0	1	2	0	.263
Larry Drake	OF	6	18	0	2	2	0	0	0			0	.111
Robert Callan	P4	4	3		0								.000
Maurice Cunningham	OF	3	11	3	1	0	0	0	0			0	.091
Joseph Becker	PH	2	1	0	0	0	0	0	0			0	.000
Vince Dilorenzo	P1	1	3	0	1	0	0	0	0			0	.333
Ed Martin	PR	1	0	0	0	0	0	0	0			0	----
Thomas Michael	P1	1	0		0								----

PITCHERS	W	L	PCT	G	GS	CG	SH	IP	H	BB	SO	ERA
Roger Bowman	15	9	.625	34	26	16	2	194	156	90	165	3.39
Andrew Tomasic	14	8	.636	33	23	15	3	198	188	82	136	3.05
George Bamberger	14	11	.560	32	26	13	5	194	193	87	98	4.50
Ford Smith	10	8	.556	31	19	9	2	154	142	106	78	4.15
Wes Bailey	8	4	.667	19	14	6	1	110	101	54	45	4.66
Francis Hardy	8	8	.500	22	18	10	1	141	132	85	60	4.28
Sam Webb	4	4	.500	11	8	4	0	62	68	19	16	3.78
John Uber	3	5	.375	32	3	0	0	94	101	68	42	5.84
Robert Hansen	2	1	.667	14	1	0	0	32	21	22	9	3.94

JERSEY CITY (cont.)
Giants

PITCHERS	W	L	PCT	G	GS	CG	SH	IP	H	BB	SO	ERA
Bill Lohrman	2	2	.500	19	0	0	0	39	45	31	8	5.54
Herb Andrews	2	5	.286	12	8	1	0	44	56	22	24	6.95
Albert Sima	1	3	.250	12	7	0	0	38	50	26	17	6.16
Vince Dilorenzo	0	1	.000	1	0	0	0	8	11	7	1	4.50
Robert Callan	0	2	.000	4	0	0	0	10	8	7	1	4.50
Thomas Michael	0	0	----	1	0	0	0	1	1	1	0	0.00
Fred Gerken	0	0	----	1	0	0	0	1	3	0	2	18.00

TORONTO   5th   80-72   .526   -9   Del Bissonette
Maple Leafs

BATTERS	POS-GAMES	GP	AB	R	H	BI	2B	3B	HR	BB	SO	SB	BA
William Glynn	1B152,OF3	153	559	76	147	98	24	6	23	55	83	14	.263
Al Roberge	2B103,3B18	124	447	45	115	52	14	3	7	28	27	1	.257
Alex Garbowski	SS118,OF11	129	417	71	111	54	21	6	8	74	54	13	.266
Mike Goliat	3B88,2B	95	381	61	109	49	22	5	9	37	52	7	.286
Ed Sanicki	OF153	153	571	105	153	102	19	2	33	77	70	1	.268
John Blatnik	OF123,1B	131	470	77	138	80	23	5	15	51	79	6	.294
John Welaj	OF83	103	357	53	110	37	21	3	7	27	24	15	.308
Harold Wagner	C90	95	262	31	68	26	16	0	4	42	28	1	.260
Louis Heyman	C82	92	239	34	55	32	3	1	10	32	68	1	.230
Vic Barnhart	3B50,OF10,2B,SS,C	83	253	39	67	35	11	2	7	30	24	1	.265
Oscar Judd	P28	71	87	14	27	21	4	0	2	13	11	0	.310
Emory Church	P34	52	74	9	15	9	0	0	0	1	12	0	.203
James Webb	SS24,2B17	49	132	12	27	9	4	0	0	5	17	1	.205
Ralph Caballero	2B29,SS20	48	195	31	62	16	7	0	1	22	4	10	.318
Nick Strincevich	P41	41	59	4	10	2	2	0	0	8	12	0	.169
Ed Wright	P39	39	55	5	12	5	3	0	0	2	3	0	.218
John Thompson	P32	36	50	8	13	4	3	0	2	1	9	0	.260
Max Peterson	P35	35	41	3	2	1	0	0	0	3	12	0	.049
Louis Possehl	P29	34	31	5	8	3	0	0	0	2	1	0	.258
Al Porto	P32	32	29	4	8	1	1	0	0	1	4	0	.276
William Smith	P22,OF5	28	18	2	6	3	2	0	0	0	0	0	.333
Richard Welker	OF12	21	53	10	8	8	1	1	1	11	7	3	.151
Hugh Radcliffe	P9	12	6	3	2	3	0	0	0	0	0	0	.333
Matt Pliszka	C	2	3	0	1	0	0	0	0			0	.333
Phil Paine	P2	2	0		0								----
Del Bissonette	PH	1	1	0	0	0	0	0	0			0	.000

PITCHERS	W	L	PCT	G	GS	CG	SH	IP	H	BB	SO	ERA
Emory Church	15	8	.652	34	25	15	3	211	152	118	132	2.35
John Thompson	14	5	.737	32	16	7	3	145	111	63	121	2.73
Oscar Judd	12	10	.545	28	19	11	1	146	165	53	45	3.95
Ed Wright	11	11	.500	39	23	12	1	179	202	72	56	3.97
Nick Strincevich	11	15	.423	41	26	13	2	202	215	62	63	3.39
Max Peterson	6	4	.600	35	16	3	2	147	133	53	81	3.31
Al Porto	4	5	.444	32	12	2	1	96	98	59	80	6.00
Louis Possehl	4	10	.286	29	13	2	0	106	129	69	56	5.77
William Smith	2	3	.400	22	1	0	0	41	61	29	8	7.46
Hugh Radcliffe	1	1	.500	9	2	0	0	22	13	29	11	6.14
Phil Paine	0	0	----	2	0	0	0	2	4	1	0	4.50

SYRACUSE   6th   73-80   .477   -16.5   Jewel Ens
Chiefs

BATTERS	POS-GAMES	GP	AB	R	H	BI	2B	3B	HR	BB	SO	SB	BA
Ed Shokes	1B145	145	490	97	130	43	21	2	11	149	65	5	.265
Frank Drews	2B93,3B35	127	447	71	108	66	21	1	16	74	33	1	.242
Sam Meeks	SS127	129	447	67	113	82	21	2	20	37	78	2	.253
Al Rubeling	3B77,1B,OF	96	318	52	83	70	17	1	15	43	50	1	.261
Carden Gillenwater	OF153	153	503	86	151	84	22	3	21	104	87	5	.300
Robert Usher	OF142	142	557	87	160	81	35	3	14	44	54	8	.287
Al Mele	OF135	136	494	68	141	86	30	3	15	71	48	7	.285
Ray Lamanno	C91	92	301	27	73	28	13	2	5	35	33	0	.243
Ben Zientara	2B64,3B31,SS9	110	380	52	101	23	14	1	0	54	31	4	.266
Harry Perkowski	P32	49	95	15	18	7	2	0	2	9	32	0	.189
John Pramesa	C43	45	145	11	37	24	4	0	4	16	11	0	.255

SYRACUSE (cont.)
Chiefs

BATTERS	POS-GAMES	GP	AB	R	H	BI	2B	3B	HR	BB	SO	SB	BA
Richard West	OF25,C	41	91	14	20	12	3	0	1	11	13	0	.213
Art Hartley	P36	36	52	4	11	2	1	0	0	3	8	1	.212
John Hetki	P33	33	99	8	25	10	1	0	1	1	5	0	.253
Thomas Tatum	3B18,OF,1B	28	96	14	25	14	4	0	2	10	11	3	.260
Millard Howell	P9,OF1	26	30	3	5	2	0	0	0	1	4	0	.167
Eldred Byerly	P20	23	54	6	10	4	0	0	0	4	10	0	.185
Roman Brunswick	P20	20	10	0	3	3	0	1	0	1	4	0	.300
Claude Corbitt	SS19	19	67	3	8	2	1	0	0	4	3	0	.119
Jim Prendergast	P18	18	38	3	11	3	2	0	1	6	6	0	.289
Ed Madjeski	C16	16	44	2	7	1	0	0	0	5	10	0	.159
Ken Burkhart	P16	16	34	2	11	4	0	0	0	1	8	0	.324
John Bebber	P16	16	17	0	2	0	0	0	0	0	4	0	.118
Frank Seward	P10	10	2	0	0	0	0	0	0	0	2	0	.000
Al Boresh	P6	7	15		2								.133
Robert Wellman	PH	4	4	0	0	0	0	0	0	0		0	.000

PITCHERS		W	L	PCT	G	GS	CG	SH	IP	H	BB	SO	ERA
John Hetki		16	14	.533	33	32	23	3	250	250	86	108	4.03
Harry Perkowski		14	12	.538	32	29	18	2	209	205	88	138	3.70
Eldred Byerly		11	4	.733	20	15	11	1	128	132	53	67	4.15
Art Hartley		9	9	.500	36	16	8	1	160	167	58	58	4.44
Jim Prendergast		7	9	.438	18	18	11	1	113	146	22	27	5.10
Al Boresh		3	1	.750	6	6	2	1	40	47	14	8	4.28
Ken Burkhart		3	9	.250	16	13	5	1	96	110	23	43	3.75
John Bebber		2	5	.286	16	4	1	0	49	49	31	21	6.24
Millard Howell		2	5	.286	9	9	2	1	39	55	24	11	6.23
Roman Brunswick		1	2	.333	20	0	0	0	46	63	22	21	7.29
Frank Seward		0	1	.000	10	1	0	0	15	23	5	0	8.40

BALTIMORE   7th   63-91   .409   -27   Alphonse Thomas -
Orioles   Jack Dunn III

BATTERS	POS-GAMES	GP	AB	R	H	BI	2B	3B	HR	BB	SO	SB	BA
Henry Arft	1B89	101	295	50	66	41	11	1	12	71	47	0	.224
Robert Young	2B		(see multi-team players)										
Robert Repass	SS130,3B4	138	476	50	111	49	19	4	8	46	58	2	.233
Lee Handley	3B93	94	337	35	69	25	8	2	2	26	30	5	.205
Glenn McQuillen	OF152	152	534	85	153	87	21	3	24	78	55	2	.287
Ken Wood	OF122	122	446	79	126	98	21	3	32	44	72	0	.283
Boris Woyt	OF107,3B14	131	500	71	126	40	21	5	7	39	53	18	.252
Frank Mancuso	C103	122	364	45	94	48	10	5	17	41	55	1	.258
George Binks	1B65,OF49	126	447	56	118	64	20	3	13	31	61	4	.264
Al Cihocki	2B59,SS23,3B16,1B1	111	374	49	100	43	15	0	11	23	33	1	.267
Edgar Holton	C43	53	118	22	23	6	2	0	0	22	21	0	.195
Al Widmar	P45	45	101	8	14	4	1	0	0	10	35	0	.139
Ernest Bickhaus	P31	31	37	2	10	2	1	0	0	1	11	0	.270
John Wittig	P31	31	14	0	0	0	0	0	0	2	6	0	.000
Vern Taylor	P30	30	31	1	3	0	0	0	0	2	12	0	.097
Emory Rudd	P30	30	13	0	2	0	0	0	0	1	5	0	.154
John Maldovan	P28	28	51	1	8	4	1	0	0	11	19	0	.157
Joseph Payne	P26	28	30	1	3	3	0	0	0	2	12	0	.100
Joseph Frazier	OF21	23	80	9	14	5	1	1	0	16	8	0	.175
George Elder	OF16	23	59	8	10	8	1	0	0	14	10	0	.169
Irv Medlinger	P22	23	43	3	7	0	1	0	0	2	10	0	.163
Ellis Clary	2B21,3B1	21	79	9	15	6	1	0	0	14	8	2	.190
Bryan Stephens	P11	11	25	2	4	2	1	0	0	4	10	0	.160
Eddie Kasko	SS	5	9	0	3	0	0	0	0			0	.333
Russ Bauers	P4	4	7		4								.571
Warren Robinson	C	4	7	1	3	0	0	0	0			0	.429
Lacy James	P4	4	4		1								.250
John Mikan	P4	4	3		0								.000
John Podgajny	P4	4	0		0								----
Francis Saucier	PH	3	2	1	0	0	0	0	0			0	.000
Richard Koecher	P2	2	2	0	1	0	0	0	0			0	.500
Don Cerniak	P1	1	0		0								----

PITCHERS		W	L	PCT	G	GS	CG	SH	IP	H	BB	SO	ERA
Al Widmar		22	15	.595	45	32	26	3	294	245	98	173	3.03
John Maldovan		6	16	.273	28	25	11	1	162	190	85	81	4.78
Vern Taylor		5	8	.385	30	13	5	2	105	100	79	80	4.20

BALTIMORE (cont.)
Orioles

PITCHERS	W	L	PCT	G	GS	CG	SH	IP	H	BB	SO	ERA
Irv Medlinger	5	14	.263	22	20	9	1	122	134	62	59	6.12
John Wittig	4	1	.800	31	1	0	0	69	63	35	34	4.17
Bryan Stephens	4	5	.444	11	9	4	0	72	80	26	41	4.50
Ernest Bickhaus	4	7	.364	31	15	6	0	118	136	66	51	4.65
Joseph Payne	4	9	.308	26	14	6	0	107	100	70	57	4.46
Russ Bauers	2	0	1.000	4	2	1	1	22	14	4	10	1.64
Emory Rudd	2	2	.500	30	5	0	0	63	75	54	43	6.00
John Podgajny	1	1	.500	4	0	0	0	4	6	3	1	6.75
Lacy James	0	2	.000	4	2	0	0	17	25	9	4	5.29
John Mikan	0	3	.000	4	3	1	0	13	16	9	7	9.69
Richard Koecher	0	0	----	2	0	0	0	4	7	2	0	6.75
Don Cerniak	0	0	----	1	0	0	0	2	1	2	2	0.00

NEWARK   8th   55-98   .359   -34.5   John Hassett
Bears

BATTERS	POS-GAMES	GP	AB	R	H	BI	2B	3B	HR	BB	SO	SB	BA
Fenton Mole	1B100	107	357	48	96	53	17	2	16	44	48	6	.269
Gene Valla	2B83,3B3	88	360	48	92	16	7	1	0	27	36	15	.256
Martin Hansen	SS124,3B,2B	141	488	50	121	43	22	2	3	63	59	8	.248
Edwin Ehlers	3B54,1B48,OF11,SS3	120	404	50	100	60	12	3	16	35	78	4	.248
Harry Heslet	OF70,C54,1B10	140	464	63	106	75	11	4	22	61	94	1	.228
Henry Workman	OF68	68	241	40	73	44	11	1	13	36	34	4	.303
Leon Culberson	OF	(see multi-team players)											
Ed Little	C63	79	215	20	44	19	5	1	6	19	21	0	.205
Lew Riggs	3B38	72	150	17	36	13	2	3	5	29	13	0	.240
Frank LaManna	P45	63	50	8	16	5	5	0	2	2	11	0	.320
Robert Thurman	OF59	59	221	37	70	33	11	2	6	24	35	4	.317
Nicholas Witek	2B46,3B10	59	220	26	68	12	4	0	1	27	13	1	.309
Lou Novikoff	OF56	57	213	35	55	48	8	0	16	23	16	0	.258
Robert Ferris	P49	49	23	0	1	0	0	0	0	4	11	0	.043
James Dyck	OF24,3B23	45	168	22	41	22	6	0	5	6	26	2	.244
William Woop	P44	44	49	4	3	1	0	0	0	9	19	0	.061
Harry Schaeffer	P35	42	44	5	9	9	1	1	0	3	7	0	.205
Earl Taborn	C30	33	97	6	24	6	5	1	0	10	11	0	.247
Joe Valenzuela	P30	32	45	3	13	0	2	0	0	4	8	0	.289
James Greengrass	3B22	29	75	8	18	6	2	0	4	4	18	1	.240
Frank Austin	SS11,2B	19	71	13	20	6	2	0	1	9	7	2	.282
Otis Strain	SS16,3B3	19	59	9	10	3	1	0	1	10	15	1	.169
Duane Pillette	P17	19	30	2	3	3	0	1	0	6	5	0	.100
Luis Marquez	OF18	18	69	13	17	6	3	0	1	7	5	3	.246
Glenn Lierman	P17	17	14	1	1	0	0	0	0	4	9	0	.071
Art Schult	OF12	16	54	7	10	9	1	0	1	2	7	0	.185
Pat Seerey	OF16	16	51	12	15	10	0	0	4	19	16	0	.294
Bruce McKelvey	C13	16	45	3	11	2	0	0	0	3	5	0	.244
Ted Sepkowski	2B15	15	45	3	10	5	0	0	2	4	7	0	.222
Wallace Hood	P15	15	35	3	4	2	0	1	0	4	10	0	.114
Earl Harrist	P15	15	29	0	4	1	0	0	0	6	6	0	.138
Lee Dodson	P15	15	20	2	3	0	0	0	0	0	9	0	.150
Earl Toolson	P12	12	26	0	3	0	1	0	0	0	11	0	.115
Charlie Keller	OF	8	18	1	4	1	0	0	0			0	.222
Thomas Gorman	P8	8	4		0								.000
Richard Crichton	P7	7	2		0								.00
William Rose	P6	6	8	1	4	0	0	0	0			0	.500
Pete Gebrian	P6	6	3		0								.000
Frank Colasinki	3B,2B	5	18	1	3	0	0	0	0			0	.167
Erwin Porterfield	P5	5	4		1								.250
Frank Shea	P5	5	3		1								.333
Al Tefft	P5	5	3		0								.000
Al McEvoy	P2	2	0		0								----
Richard Mitchell	P2	2	0		0								----
William Freese	P1	1	4		0								.000

PITCHERS	W	L	PCT	G	GS	CG	SH	IP	H	BB	SO	ERA
Frank LaManna	9	9	.500	45	5	4	0	103	107	68	41	5.24
Harry Schaeffer	7	9	.438	35	16	8	2	139	128	81	95	4.34
Duane Pillette	6	7	.462	17	16	7	1	109	115	60	43	4.05
William Woop	6	13	.316	44	20	5	1	163	178	128	118	6.18
Earl Toolson	5	5	.500	12	11	2	0	74	86	40	38	4.86
Wallace Hood	5	6	.455	15	15	5	0	95	82	82	50	6.06
Glenn Lierman	4	5	.444	17	6	2	2	61	73	23	24	5.31

NEWARK (cont.)
Bears

PITCHERS	W	L	PCT	G	GS	CG	SH	IP	H	BB	SO	ERA
Joe Valenzuela	4	12	.250	30	17	6	0	136	156	55	41	5.36
Earl Harrist	3	10	.231	15	15	2	0	91	111	54	44	5.93
Lee Dodson	2	6	.250	27	10	3	1	62	38	70	47	6.10
Pete Gebrian	1	0	1.000	6	0	0	0	15	14	16	4	6.00
Erwin Porterfield	1	0	1.000	5	3	0	0	16	16	7	16	5.67
William Freese	1	0	1.000	1	1	1	1	10	7	2	2	0.00
Robert Ferris	1	7	.125	49	8	1	0	106	100	79	67	6.71
Thomas Gorman	0	1	.000	8	1	0	0	20	26	18	6	6.30
Richard Crichton	0	1	.000	7	1	0	0	15	12	13	4	3.00
Al Tefft	0	1	.000	5	1	0	0	12	8	12	6	6.75
William Rose	0	3	.000	6	4	0	0	27	31	17	9	5.67
Frank Shea	0	3	.000	5	4	0	0	17	16	18	5	8.47
Richard Mitchell	0	0	----	2	0	0	0	3	2	2	1	6.00
Al McEvoy	0	0	----	2	0	0	0	2	3	8	0	27.00

MULTI-TEAM PLAYERS

BATTERS	POS-GAMES	TEAMS	GP	AB	R	H	BI	2B	3B	HR	BB	SO	SB	BA
Robert Young	2B120,3B5	RO47-BA81	128	463	61	124	46	14	7	6	46	31	1	.268
Leon Culberson	OF112,3B1	NE78-JC46	124	414	56	98	38	14	3	6	34	40	6	.237
Chet Laabs	OF118	RO55-TO68	123	403	84	109	75	18	4	22	92	107	1	.270
Don Richmond	3B107	BA38-RO78	116	432	70	130	65	14	1	8	43	22	4	.301
Richard Lane	OF59	SY2-NE58	60	201	18	34	18	6	3	1	29	22	1	.169
William Schultz	P38	SY31-RO7	38	48	5	12	4	1	0	0	2	6	0	.250
Ed Blake	P30	RO29-SY8	37	39	4	10	9	1	0	1	2	4	0	.256
James Wilson	P26	BA22-BU10	32	55	4	10	4	2	0	1	7	11	0	.182
Joe Just	C17	SY5-BA12	17	40	3	7	1	2	0	0	14	8	0	.175

PITCHERS	TEAMS	W	L	PCT	G	GS	CG	SH	IP	H	BB	SO	ERA
James Wilson	BA19-BU7	7	11	.389	26	18	10	1	153	167	63	100	3.94
Ed Blake	RO24-SY6	5	4	.556	30	9	3	0	98	106	64	43	4.78
William Schultz	SY31-RO7	4	10	.286	38	9	4	0	138	144	56	58	4.57

TEAM BATTING

TEAMS	GP	AB	R	H	BI	2B	3B	HR	BB	SO	SB	BA
BUFFALO	155	4995	904	1348	853	253	23	157	832	660	58	.270
ROCHESTER	153	5131	819	1377	755	230	44	140	729	637	34	.268
MONTREAL	154	5117	900	1449	805	239	46	116	725	613	191	.283
JERSEY CITY	154	4987	774	1301	696	189	41	100	735	721	143	.261
TORONTO	153	5032	749	1339	693	209	36	140	568	671	72	.266
SYRACUSE	153	4893	702	1267	656	213	18	129	691	624	37	.257
BALTIMORE	154	4968	647	1216	594	175	31	134	563	675	35	.245
NEWARK	154	4960	613	1202	555	156	27	129	568	728	55	.242
	615	40083	6108	10499	5607	1664	266	1045	5411	5329	625	.262

1950
CHOICES

In the late 1930s and early 1940s, Newark and Jersey City routinely drew large crowds to their ballparks. Located within 15 miles of one another in northern New Jersey, both Newark and Jersey City were just across the Hudson River from New York City. Because of this proximity, both teams averaged over 300,000 in annual attendance right after World War II. In addition, Jersey City set several all-time single-date attendance figures, the largest being the crowd of 56,391 on April 17, 1941.

However, by 1947 some slippage was occurring. Newark's attendance dropped to 180,000. In 1948, Jersey City lost half its fan base as well. The year 1949 was even worse as only 88,000 fans visited the Newark Bears. The culprit behind this disappearing act wasn't any complex demographic population shift; it was television.

By the late 1940s, television was making inroads in American society. Instead of leaving the home for entertainment choices like minor league baseball, Americans were finding amusement (including major league broadcasts) right in their living rooms via television—an intoxicating and all but irresistible concept.

Unable to compete with television, the Newark International League franchise gave up the ghost. After the 1949 season, the Yankees sold the team to the Chicago Cubs, who moved the team to Springfield, Massachusetts—the league's first franchise relocation in over a dozen years.

On the field in 1950, the Rochester Red Wings returned to the top roost for the first time in a decade. Montreal, Baltimore, and Jersey City finished in the playoff picture, while Springfield, Syracuse, Toronto, and Buffalo brought up the rear. Rochester's Don Richmond won the batting title (.336), while his teammate Russ Derry won the home run (30) and runs batted in races (102). Chet Laabs, spending time with both Jersey City and Toronto, equaled Derry's mark of 30 home runs. The Red Wings also dominated pitching categories as Thomas Poholsky notched the most wins (18) and finished with the lowest earned run average (2.17). Jersey City's Roger Bowman struck out the most batters (181).

The attendance figures for New Jersey's sole remaining International League club did not improve in 1950. Rather, they grew worse, as Jersey City drew only 63,000 fans—one-fifth of their 1947 figure. In December 1950, the Jersey City Giants, now the property of the Philadelphia Athletics, became the Ottawa Athletics. Canada now had its third International League club.

For years Newark and Jersey City had enjoyed the benefits of their location near New York. But this location did neither team any good once their fan base deserted them for television. It was hard to draw fans to any baseball contest when they could see a game—and many other things—from the comfort of their own couches.

ROCHESTER Red Wings
1st   92-59   .609   John Keane

BATTERS	POS-GAMES	GP	AB	R	H	BI	2B	3B	HR	BB	SO	SB	BA
Steve Bilko	1B89,2B	109	334	71	97	58	18	6	15	56	88	1	.290
Louis Ortiz	2B96,3B12,SS9	115	348	51	79	54	13	4	12	61	48	1	.227
Ed Nietopski	SS87,3B	96	276	31	58	35	7	0	3	28	48	1	.210
Don Richmond	3B138	140	573	126	191	99	31	11	18	67	37	6	.333
Russ Derry	OF131	133	438	95	123	102	20	2	30	110	70	3	.281
Harold Rice	OF113	114	413	87	128	79	21	8	17	67	40	10	.310
Ed Mierkowicz	OF106,2B	114	389	53	114	64	15	8	7	53	34	2	.293
Delbert Wilber	C114,3B	123	440	64	130	80	23	7	11	24	41	2	.295
Richard Cole	SS74,2B69	135	528	93	147	44	17	5	4	76	39	3	.278
Lawrence Ciaffone	OF81,3B	97	321	47	104	53	7	6	10	17	14	3	.324
Don Bollweg	1B69	92	256	61	80	60	18	0	17	42	29	6	.313
Charles Marshall	C61	65	128	20	26	17	6	2	0	39	27	0	.203
Ken Wild	P32,OF	49	56	11	13	10	2	0	0	9	12	0	.232
Jack Collum	P40	40	34	5	11	6	0	0	0	3	1	0	.324
George Copeland	P32	37	52	5	8	2	0	0	0	1	13	0	.154
William Schultz	P31	33	28	3	9	6	1	0	0	8	4	0	.321
John Yuhas	P32	32	84	14	17	13	2	1	2	2	21	0	.202
Roy Broome	OF31	31	118	18	32	21	6	1	1	22	8	2	.271
Thomas Poholsky	P28	31	78	6	15	3	4	0	0	8	16	0	.192
William Reeder	P23	23	44	2	4	2	1	0	0	3	22	0	.091
John Fasholz	P20,OF1	22	33	5	6	6	2	0	1	0	11	0	.182
Joseph Chucka	P21	21	8	0	2	1	0	0	0	0	0	0	.250
Jerome Witte	1B	19	37	6	10	9	2	0	2	3	11	0	.270
Richard Bokelmann	P10	10	6	0	1	0	1	0	0	0	1	0	.167
Thomas Westcott	OF	5	23	5	9	3	3	0	2			0	.391
George Dries	P4	4	0		0								----
Maurice Garlock	P3	3	2	1	1	0	0	0	0			0	.500
William Long	OF	1	3	0	1	0	1	0	0			0	.333
Louis Ciola	P1	1	0		0								----

PITCHERS	W	L	PCT	G	GS	CG	SH	IP	H	BB	SO	ERA
Thomas Poholsky	18	6	.750	28	25	21	5	212	193	59	90	2.17
John Yuhas	15	6	.714	32	29	11	0	204	214	108	95	4.54
Ken Wild	12	1	.923	21	8	2	0	113	118	52	42	4.86
William Reeder	9	8	.529	23	20	8	1	139	148	73	73	4.60
William Schultz	8	5	.615	31	10	5	2	98	100	37	53	4.50
Jack Collum	8	6	.571	40	3	1	0	104	92	52	52	3.03
George Copeland	8	8	.500	32	19	7	0	138	123	115	84	5.35
John Fasholz	5	3	.625	20	12	5	1	96	98	41	28	4.03
Joseph Chucka	1	3	.250	21	3	0	0	35	42	23	16	7.20
George Dries	0	1	.000	4	1	0	0	6	18	7	1	19.50
Maurice Garlock	0	1	.000	3	1	0	0	10	8	6	8	4.50
Richard Bokelmann	0	5	.000	10	5	0	0	30	38	17	13	8.10
Louis Ciola	0	0	----	1	0	0	0	1	1	2	0	9.00

MONTREAL Royals
2nd   86-67   .562   -7   Walt Alston

BATTERS	POS-GAMES	GP	AB	R	H	BI	2B	3B	HR	BB	SO	SB	BA
Chuck Connors	1B114	121	407	69	118	68	26	4	6	69	36	14	.290
Walt Fiala	2B148	148	567	97	163	67	27	5	4	75	34	4	.288
Lamar Bridges	SS149,2B16	153	553	90	155	83	24	9	5	81	32	16	.280
Damon Phillips	3B84,1B36,SS1	126	452	54	121	77	34	2	1	45	45	4	.268
Don Thompson	OF136	142	515	91	160	87	24	8	11	84	43	16	.311
George Schmees	OF82,1B13	98	339	53	86	65	19	5	9	46	40	5	.254
Al Gionfriddo	OF82	97	323	73	100	41	18	0	5	65	21	14	.310
Maurice Atwell	C102,OF1	112	338	48	93	41	13	2	9	65	22	4	.275
Geno Cimoli	OF63	85	218	36	60	11	8	5	1	24	22	3	.275
Jack Lindsay	3B63,SS,OF	79	255	46	67	35	10	1	6	40	46	1	.263
Richard Teed	C46	55	152	17	42	22	9	2	1	14	23	2	.276
Ron Lee	P54	54	25	2	4	1	0	0	0	5	8	0	.160
Al Epperly	P49	49	15	2	2	2	1	0	0	4	4	1	.133
George Shuba	OF39	39	142	25	36	25	7	1	8	23	23	0	.254
Clyde King	P32	38	58	7	10	5	0	1	0	6	14	0	.172
Omar Lown	P29	32	75	11	17	9	2	2	0	6	13	0	.227
Tom Lasorda	P31	32	46	7	8	3	1	0	0	6	10	0	.174
Ezra McGlothin	P19	20	22	1	4	3	0	0	0	4	4	0	.182
John Banta	P19	19	36	6	5	3	1	0	0	1	10	0	.139
Louis Welaj	3B5,2B	19	23	8	8	4	1	1	0	8	3	1	.348
Carl Erskine	P18	18	40	5	9	4	2	0	0	2	6	0	.225

MONTREAL (cont.)
Royals

BATTERS	POS-GAMES	GP	AB	R	H	BI	2B	3B	HR	BB	SO	SB	BA
George Thomas	P18	18	20	2	3	0	1	0	0	1	8	0	.150
James Hughes	P16	16	31	3	7	1	2	0	0	0	4	0	.226
Charles Thompson	C	12	30	6	14	7	2	2	1	4	0	1	.467
Steve Lembo	C	10	24	2	5	2	0	0	0	3	3	0	.208
William McCahan	P10	10	12	0	3	2	0	0	0	0	3	0	.250
Joseph Landrum	P8	9	18		1								.056
Robert Milliken	P4	4	3		0								.000

PITCHERS		W	L	PCT	G	GS	CG	SH	IP	H	BB	SO	ERA
Ron Lee		14	4	.778	54	4	3	0	123	97	61	44	2.20
Clyde King		13	8	.619	32	22	11	3	182	202	56	58	3.12
Omar Lown		13	9	.591	29	28	14	1	209	181	122	104	3.49
Carl Erskine		10	6	.625	18	17	8	5	118	103	61	89	3.74
Tom Lasorda		9	4	.692	31	17	7	0	146	136	82	85	3.70
Al Epperly		8	6	.571	49	1	1	0	98	72	31	39	2.02
James Hughes		7	2	.778	16	10	5	1	86	73	38	38	2.72
Joseph Landrum		4	3	.571	8	7	4	0	56	50	16	24	3.05
John Banta		4	7	.364	19	17	3	0	97	93	87	63	4.92
Robert Milliken		1	0	1.000	4	2	0	0	12	11	10	3	8.25
William McCahan		1	3	.250	10	8	1	0	34	55	25	8	8.47
Ezra McGlothin		1	7	.125	19	12	3	0	74	95	29	30	6.81
George Thomas		1	8	.111	18	8	0	0	75	73	56	27	3.84

BALTIMORE   3rd   85-68   .556   -8   Nick Cullop
Orioles

BATTERS	POS-GAMES	GP	AB	R	H	BI	2B	3B	HR	BB	SO	SB	BA
George Byam	1B156	156	558	74	159	97	29	12	10	78	65	0	.285
Robert Young	2B136	140	539	78	147	41	22	8	3	62	23	4	.273
Eddie Pellagrini	SS124	130	387	69	109	64	21	1	19	78	54	6	.282
Russ Kerns	3B156	156	545	85	149	78	26	10	19	61	59	2	.273
Boris Woyt	OF152	152	625	100	172	57	21	2	12	52	45	12	.275
Ansel Moore	OF111	119	392	74	110	84	19	0	20	67	27	0	.281
Babe Barna	OF107	118	346	85	102	62	11	4	18	118	48	6	.295
Clyde Kluttz	C81	96	282	46	82	56	13	1	11	26	16	1	.291
Al Cihocki	SS40,2B26,OF2	94	257	38	72	50	10	2	15	25	34	1	.280
Al Unser	C79	86	230	20	51	25	7	1	3	39	31	0	.222
Ben Guintini	OF61	69	215	41	49	29	8	3	10	35	40	3	.228
Ray Shore	P55	55	10	0	0	0	0	0	0	0	2	0	.000
Austin Knickerbocker	OF38	43	139	21	36	34	5	1	10	13	23	0	.259
William Kennedy	P42	42	67	5	11	6	0	0	1	7	11	0	.164
Irv Medlinger	P34	34	52	3	10	5	1	0	0	3	8	0	.192
Joseph Payne	P31	34	18	1	1	1	0	0	0	6	9	0	.056
Sal Hernandez	C15	33	47	2	15	6	2	0	0	13	5	0	.319
Raymond Poat	P17	28	47	8	8	5	0	0	0	1	16	0	.170
Russ Bauers	P25	25	71	2	9	3	0	0	0	0	7	0	.127
Frank Raney	P25	25	42	5	8	1	0	0	0	5	17	0	.190
Karl Drews	P22	22	30	2	3	1	1	0	0	3	15	0	.100
Al Piechota	P20	20	5	0	1	1	0	0	0	1	1	0	.200
Thomas Fine	P16	17	30	4	3	1	1	0	0	0	5	0	.100
Ed Klieman	P15	15	4	0	0	0	0	0	0	0	0	0	.000
Lew Riggs	PH	13	10	0	1	1	0	0	0	3	4	0	.100
James Dyck	OF	12	11	2	3	1	0	0	1	5	0	0	.273
Walter Nothe	P12	12	6	1	2	0	0	0	0	0	3	0	.333
Vern Taylor	P10	11	14	1	2	0	0	0	0	1	3	0	.143
Chalmer Harris	P8	8	0		0								----
Francis Saucier	PH	5	5	0	1	1	0	0	0	0		0	.200
Ed Albrecht	P2	2	0		0								----
Grant Dunlap	PH	1	1	0	0	0	0	0	0	0		0	.000
Richard Culler	PR	1	0	1	0	0	0	0	0			0	----
Bryan Stephens	P1	1	0		0								----
Angello Nardella	P1	1	0		0								----
Oliverio Ortiz	P1	1	0		0								----

PITCHERS		W	L	PCT	G	GS	CG	SH	IP	H	BB	SO	ERA
William Kennedy		16	9	.640	42	23	12	5	198	172	89	144	3.73
Russ Bauers		13	6	.684	25	23	16	2	182	199	59	107	3.36
Irv Medlinger		12	12	.500	34	25	7	2	167	143	97	131	4.26
Raymond Poat		9	4	.692	17	17	8	0	107	112	41	52	4.63

BALTIMORE (cont.)
Orioles

PITCHERS	W	L	PCT	G	GS	CG	SH	IP	H	BB	SO	ERA
Thomas Fine	7	5	.583	16	11	7	4	87	91	29	30	2.79
Frank Raney	7	11	.389	25	24	6	1	149	148	102	110	5.92
Karl Drews	6	2	.750	22	10	2	1	92	84	47	42	4.11
Joseph Payne	5	6	.455	31	13	3	2	96	93	68	45	4.22
Ray Shore	4	5	.444	55	1	0	0	84	68	62	47	3.47
Al Piechota	3	3	.500	20	1	0	0	29	40	21	17	8.07
Chalmer Harris	1	0	1.000	8	0	0	0	10	10	12	8	7.20
Vern Taylor	1	4	.200	10	6	1	0	36	38	31	13	7.00
Walter Nothe	0	1	.000	12	1	0	0	28	36	22	16	8.04
Ed Klieman	0	0	----	15	0	0	0	27	34	14	6	5.33
Ed Albrecht	0	0	----	2	0	0	0	2	3	4	1	9.00
Angelo Nardella	0	0	----	1	0	0	0	2	2	1	1	4.50
Bryan Stephens	0	0	----	1	0	0	0	1	2	1	1	63.00
Oliverio Ortiz	0	0	----	1	0	0	0	1	0	1	0	0.00

JERSEY CITY   4th   81-70   .536   -11   Joseph Becker
Giants

BATTERS	POS-GAMES	GP	AB	R	H	BI	2B	3B	HR	BB	SO	SB	BA
Marv Blaylock	1B114	121	393	76	108	70	18	10	19	72	85	5	.275
Pete Pavlick	2B151	151	577	101	156	50	19	3	6	99	40	23	.270
Ziggy Jasinski	SS146	148	523	57	120	41	15	0	3	36	54	7	.229
Stan Jok	3B128,OF,SS	141	469	63	123	77	22	5	17	62	83	6	.263
Joe Bracchitta	OF139	140	496	91	126	44	12	5	3	127	54	19	.254
William Milne	OF55	59	158	20	44	29	9	6	5	31	25	3	.278
Al Mele	OF	(see multi-team players)											
Sal Yvars	C80,3B2	91	291	48	82	53	12	1	8	38	28	3	.282
Neal Watlington	C72,OF27	114	344	46	92	56	11	4	9	34	20	8	.267
Fred Gerken	1B47,OF38	103	294	39	68	38	14	3	11	49	48	2	.231
Napolean Reyes	3B26,OF13,SS,2B	66	171	33	53	29	3	1	9	14	20	2	.310
Francis Hardy	P37	44	68	6	15	1	0	0	0	4	16	0	.221
Andrew Tomasic	P42	42	53	7	4	1	0	0	0	9	16	0	.075
Norm Fox	P42	42	30	3	6	1	0	0	0	4	16	0	.200
George Heller	P33	34	19	3	3	2	0	0	0	1	2	0	.158
Ed Sokol	C20	33	68	5	16	8	5	0	0	6	9	0	.235
Tony West	P33	33	55	5	12	6	2	0	2	6	14	0	.218
Roger Bowman	P31	32	91	3	13	3	3	0	0	2	25	0	.143
Gail Henley	OF30	31	114	16	31	26	6	2	3	8	18	1	.272
George Spencer	P23	23	43	3	6	6	0	1	0	3	16	0	.140
Monte Irvin	OF18	18	51	28	26	33	4	1	10	29	6	2	.510
Raul Lopez	P16	16	18	1	3	2	0	0	0	5	9	0	.167
John Metkovich	OF11	13	21	3	3	2	0	0	1	2	7	2	.143
Ford Smith	P12	13	13	0	2	2	0	0	0	3	5	0	.154
George McDonald	OF,1B	11	20	1	3	1	0	0	0	1	1	0	.150
Robert Klinger	P8	8	0		0								----
Alex Konikowski	P7	7	11		1								.091
William Henry	3B	4	14	2	3	2	0	0	0			0	.214
William Miller	P2	2	3	0	1	0	0	0	0			0	.333
Elmer Corwin	P1	1	2	0	1	0	0	0	0			0	.500
Mario Picone	P1	1	0		0								----
John Uber	P1	1	0		0								----

PITCHERS	W	L	PCT	G	GS	CG	SH	IP	H	BB	SO	ERA
Roger Bowman	16	11	.593	31	30	19	2	233	202	112	181	3.71
Francis Hardy	13	13	.500	37	26	16	1	205	183	83	119	3.95
Andrew Tomasic	12	9	.571	42	19	6	0	181	170	108	130	4.48
George Spencer	11	5	.688	23	17	9	0	129	131	59	37	4.76
Howard Fox	10	5	.667	42	7	2	0	130	98	111	67	3.39
Tony West	8	11	.421	33	23	9	1	173	146	102	69	4.16
George Heller	6	2	.750	33	5	2	0	67	60	52	34	3.36
Ford Smith	2	3	.400	12	5	1	0	45	41	40	20	3.46
Raul Lopez	2	7	.222	16	12	2	0	63	73	70	34	6.57
Alex Konikowski	1	3	.250	7	6	2	1	38	41	31	24	3.32
William Miller	0	1	.000	2	2	0	0	10	5	13	8	4.50
Robert Klinger	0	0	----	8	0	0	0	12	8	5	5	3.75
Elmer Corwin	0	0	----	1	0	0	0	6	5	1	2	3.00
Mario Picone	0	0	----	1	0	0	0	1	5	1	0	45.00
John Uber	0	0	----	1	0	0	0	0	0	3	0	81.00

SPRINGFIELD   5th   74-78   .487   -18.5   Stan Hack
Cubs

BATTERS	POS-GAMES	GP	AB	R	H	BI	2B	3B	HR	BB	SO	SB	BA
Edwin Ehlers	1B93,3B21	120	379	48	86	39	23	1	7	46	89	0	.227
Jackson Hollis	2B151	151	555	91	139	65	25	3	9	73	50	5	.250
John Wallaesa	SS142,3B3	145	547	80	144	86	21	7	25	47	102	1	.263
Ransom Jackson	3B115	117	425	78	134	68	22	5	20	62	41	4	.315
Robert Talbot	OF143	143	541	65	132	43	16	11	2	35	33	7	.244
Robert Thurman	OF141	145	465	68	125	78	26	7	12	77	43	5	.269
Ted Sepkowski	OF81,1B,2B,3B	109	338	47	85	56	14	3	18	33	41	2	.252
Forrest Burgess	C78	88	315	55	103	52	15	10	8	29	23	4	.327
Leslie Peden	C71,1B3	85	268	32	80	41	14	0	8	16	29	0	.299
Carmen Mauro	OF69	69	257	48	76	39	7	5	8	36	36	6	.296
Ben Taylor	1B53	53	198	19	44	25	8	3	4	17	26	1	.222
Lloyd Lowe	3B14,SS10,1B1	48	106	8	27	12	8	0	1	12	20	0	.255
Frank LaManna	P23,OF8	48	72	12	20	9	5	2	1	3	21	0	.278
William Moisan	P31	42	81	13	18	10	3	0	3	5	21	0	.222
Robert Spicer	P35	38	63	10	16	5	5	2	0	7	9	0	.254
Eugene Costello	P37	38	24	3	6	2	0	0	0	4	5	0	.250
Alan Ihde	P34	34	58	3	8	1	0	0	0	7	20	0	.138
Al Porto	P28	29	33	4	2	0	1	0	0	0	3	0	.061
Anthony Jacobs	P22	22	2	0	0	0	0	0	0	0	0	0	.000
Warren Hacker	P20	20	52	3	11	8	2	1	1	0	14	0	.212
Robert Kelly	P19	19	32	4	10	2	2	0	0	3	8	0	.313
Bill Voiselle	P18	18	34	2	6	3	2	0	0	2	7	0	.176
Henry Edwards	OF	17	41	6	11	9	3	0	1	5	10	0	.268
Joe Valenzuela	P11	11	2	0	0	0	0	0	0	0	0	0	.000
George Zoeterman	P9	9	5	2	3	0	0	0	0			0	.600
Milt Byrnes	OF	8	12	3	1	0	0	0	0			0	.083
Paul Schneiders	P7	7	2		0								.000
Robert Borkowski	OF	6	21	2	6	3	3	0	0			0	.286
James Callahan	OF	6	16	1	4	1	0	0	0			0	.250
Robert Dant	C	5	17	3	4	1	2	0	0			0	.235
William Emmerich	P4	4	1		0								.000
Jim Brosnan	P4	4	0		0								----
Eugene Baker	SS	3	9	0	1	0	0	0	0			0	.111
Gale Pringle	P3	3	8		2								.250
John Liptak	OF	3	6	0	1	1	0	0	0			0	.167
William Padgett	P3	3	5		0								.000
James Atchley	P3	3	0		0								----
Carl Ray	P1	1	1		0								.000
Elvin Stabelfield	P1	1	0		0								----

PITCHERS		W	L	PCT	G	GS	CG	SH	IP	H	BB	SO	ERA
William Moisan		12	9	.571	31	22	11	1	178	166	96	53	3.74
Robert Spicer		12	11	.526	35	26	11	1	191	190	69	64	3.44
Alan Ihde		12	15	.444	34	28	10	0	178	164	122	51	4.40
Warren Hacker		11	4	.733	20	19	10	4	137	137	36	61	3.35
Bill Voiselle		9	5	.643	18	13	6	1	106	95	25	53	3.48
Eugene Costello		5	6	.455	37	8	3	0	102	79	94	62	4.50
Al Porto		4	8	.333	28	13	4	0	111	118	55	53	4.46
Robert Kelly		3	6	.333	19	16	3	0	83	91	55	29	5.75
Anthony Jacobs		2	1	.667	22	0	0	0	24	16	19	13	3.38
Frank LaManna		2	4	.333	23	0	0	0	66	66	49	24	4.50
Jim Brosnan		1	0	1.000	4	0	0	0	7	14	7	3	14.14
Gale Pringle		1	1	.500	3	3	0	0	19	33	8	4	7.05
William Padgett		0	1	.000	3	3	0	0	18	17	6	2	3.50
Elvin Stabelfield		0	1	.000	1	0	0	0	1	3	1	0	36.00
Joe Valenzuela		0	2	.000	11	0	0	0	16	19	11	3	10.69
George Zoeterman		0	2	.000	9	0	0		14	11	9	5	5.14
Paul Schneiders		0	2	.000	7	0	0	0	14	14	11	7	5.79
William Emmerich		0	0	----	4	0	0	0	8	10	5	1	5.63
James Atchley		0	0	----	3	0	0	0	4	6	1	0	9.00
Carl Ray		0	0	----	1	0	0	0	3	5	1	1	6.00

SYRACUSE   6th   74-79   .484   -19   Bruno Betzel
Chiefs

BATTERS	POS-GAMES	GP	AB	R	H	BI	2B	3B	HR	BB	SO	SB	BA
Ed Shokes	1B152	152	467	82	108	61	15	6	14	142	66	7	.231
Ben Zientara	2B120,3B1	131	403	47	103	33	16	2	2	86	39	3	.256
Claude Corbitt	SS125	129	459	59	102	42	17	1	2	71	25	5	.222
Al Rubeling	3B117,1B1	133	415	66	98	62	13	3	14	65	47	2	.236
Carden Gillenwater	OF153	153	520	83	147	97	30	3	14	94	71	8	.283

SYRACUSE (cont.)
Chiefs

BATTERS	POS-GAMES	GP	AB	R	H	BI	2B	3B	HR	BB	SO	SB	BA
Fletcher Robbe	OF82	82	283	33	73	31	13	5	6	51	31	4	.258
Russ Burns	OF71	71	262	42	75	36	11	2	2	30	40	0	.286
Myron Hayworth	C81	86	244	18	57	31	9	0	1	16	21	0	.234
Elbert Flint	3B43,SS31,2B2	105	262	38	53	22	7	1	5	40	35	2	.202
Frank Drews	2B36,OF11	91	187	31	47	15	5	2	5	39	42	0	.251
Gerald Burmeister	C72	75	190	19	41	39	3	0	6	24	32	2	.216
Percy Riggan	OF65,C7	72	229	24	53	25	7	0	3	20	32	1	.231
Ed Blake	P31	43	66	10	15	6	1	0	2	4	9	0	.227
Ken Burkhart	P36	36	19	0	1	1	0	0	0	1	7	0	.053
Art Hartley	P35	35	66	7	6	0	0	0	0	6	15	0	.091
David Jolly	P32	35	49	3	9	3	0	0	0	4	6	0	.184
Kent Peterson	P34	34	54	1	6	5	0	0	0	2	12	0	.111
Jim Prendergast	P33	34	51	2	10	1	3	0	0	3	9	0	.196
Robert Sanders	P33	33	21	0	2	0	0	1	0	0	13	0	.095
Elmer Durrett	OF17	32	56	13	9	7	2	0	1	14	17	0	.161
Eldred Byerly	P31	31	84	6	16	5	4	0	0	4	26	0	.190
Ed Little	C23	24	63	0	9	6	1	0	0	3	6	0	.143
James Avrea	P16	16	6	0	0	0	0	0	0	2	3	0	.000
Roman Brunswick	P6	6	1		0								.000
Wilburn Butland	P5	5	0		0								----
Hugh Mulcahy	P2	2	0		0								----
Steve Filipowicz	PH	1	1	0	0	0	0	0	0	0		0	.000
Richard Libby	P1	1	1		0								.000

PITCHERS	W	L	PCT	G	GS	CG	SH	IP	H	BB	SO	ERA
Eldred Byerly	17	12	.586	31	31	19	3	223	212	90	113	3.79
Ed Blake	12	8	.600	31	23	12	2	182	169	91	65	3.51
Art Hartley	12	13	.480	35	30	14	4	211	193	94	94	3.54
Kent Peterson	11	8	.579	34	21	11	0	158	143	67	102	3.82
Jim Prendergast	6	14	.300	33	22	7	1	153	204	46	46	5.53
Ken Burkhart	5	5	.500	36	1	0	0	71	74	24	43	4.06
David Jolly	5	11	.313	32	16	3	0	146	162	76	73	4.32
Robert Sanders	4	6	.400	33	6	1	0	76	90	57	26	6.99
James Avrea	2	1	.667	16	2	0	0	27	38	13	14	7.00
Hugh Mulcahy	0	1	.000	2	1	0	0	2	6	2	0	27.00
Roman Brunswick	0	0	----	6	0	0	0	10	11	5	2	7.20
Wilburn Butland	0	0	----	5	0	0	0	8	15	1	2	10.13
Richard Libby	0	0	----	1	0	0	0	3	4	7	3	6.00

TORONTO 7th 60-90 .400 -31.5 Jack Sanford
Maple Leafs

BATTERS	POS-GAMES	GP	AB	R	H	BI	2B	3B	HR	BB	SO	SB	BA
William Glynn	1B129,OF20	149	521	70	122	88	20	4	25	87	55	6	.234
Al Roberge	2B73,OF10	94	307	31	75	34	12	4	2	15	32	2	.244
Alex Garbowski	SS96,OF,3B	112	330	57	80	24	13	2	4	63	39	9	.242
Milt Rutner	3B114	119	409	57	117	53	20	7	2	57	30	4	.286
John Mayo	OF139	146	484	93	142	58	24	5	12	92	66	2	.294
Ed Sanicki	OF92	100	303	44	64	42	8	0	10	57	47	6	.211
Harry Heslet	OF73,C22	135	429	57	110	71	21	4	21	62	72	2	.256
Ed Oswald	C76	83	260	29	63	29	7	2	5	25	35	3	.242
Ralph LaPointe	SS77,3B11,2B9	110	393	46	93	27	17	0	5	20	23	10	.237
Fred Collins	OF60,1B26	107	312	36	82	52	12	3	5	34	65	1	.263
Vince Plumbo	C63,3B1	67	183	15	38	21	8	0	2	42	28	0	.208
Charles Bowers	P36	45	29	3	3	1	0	0	0	5	12	0	.103
Louis Possehl	P33	43	32	6	3	0	0	0	0	5	3	1	.094
John Thompson	P35	42	83	6	16	9	2	2	0	2	18	0	.193
Ken Trinkle	P40	40	33	1	3	1	1	0	0	5	8	0	.091
Andrew Skurski	OF31	39	96	17	27	9	4	0	2	13	25	0	.281
John Brittin	P39	39	41	1	7	9	0	0	0	5	0	0	.171
Max Peterson	P37	37	41	3	8	1	1	0	0	9	12	0	.195
Paul Stuffel	P25	26	53	4	9	4	3	1	0	4	24	0	.170
Stephen Ridzik	P18	18	38	3	10	5	3	0	1	1	9	0	.263
Don E. Robertson	P15	15	35	2	2	0	1	0	0	5	14	0	.057
Nick Strincevich	P14	14	7	0	0	0	0	0	0	0	4	0	.000
Ed Wright	P8	8	6		0								.000
Vic Barnhart	3B	7	18	1	2	1	1	0	0			0	.111
William Koszarek	P7	7	3		0								.000
Joe Buzas	PH,PR	3	2	1	0	0	0	0	0	0		0	.000
Ralph Brickner	P3	3	0		0								----

TORONTO (cont.)
Maple Leafs

PITCHERS	W	L	PCT	G	GS	CG	SH	IP	H	BB	SO	ERA
John Thompson	10	14	.417	35	26	12	2	201	209	100	115	4.57
Max Peterson	9	11	.450	37	20	9	0	174	182	61	80	4.14
Stephen Ridzik	8	7	.533	18	15	7	1	103	96	57	49	4.02
John Brittin	7	11	.389	39	19	5	0	141	141	97	69	5.43
Paul Stuffel	6	5	.545	25	20	7	0	142	109	133	118	3.99
Don E. Robertson	6	6	.500	15	12	6	0	112	104	58	43	3.13
Louis Possehl	6	9	.400	33	11	3	0	121	108	75	56	4.83
Ken Trinkle	5	11	.313	40	13	6	1	137	154	72	43	3.94
Charles Bowers	2	5	.286	36	8	1	1	101	118	49	41	4.90
Ed Wright	1	4	.200	8	5	1	0	21	26	10	3	6.00
Nick Strincevich	0	6	.000	14	3	0	0	33	38	13	6	4.64
Ralph Brickner	0	1	.000	3	1	0	0	2	5	6	0	27.00
William Koszarek	0	0	----	7	0	0	0	19	24	8	7	6.36

BUFFALO
Bisons

8th   56-97   .366   -37   Frank Skaff - Ray Schalk

BATTERS	POS-GAMES	GP	AB	R	H	BI	2B	3B	HR	BB	SO	SB	BA
Henry Biasetti	1B144	145	485	94	134	66	25	2	18	112	42	2	.276
Eugene Markland	2B114	120	366	81	109	48	30	2	13	111	68	4	.298
Al Stringer	SS	(see multi-team players)											
Seymour Block	3B65	94	252	38	75	31	14	5	7	41	37	3	.298
John Creel	OF126	127	429	58	117	42	17	5	2	60	24	3	.273
Herb Adams	OF75	76	289	38	78	30	7	5	1	41	12	3	.270
George Binks	OF	(see multi-team players)											
Martin Tabacheck	C94	96	283	21	54	26	16	1	0	29	26	0	.191
Fred Hancock	3B46,SS43,2B37	130	457	71	117	69	25	1	10	58	32	0	.256
Charles Wilhelm	3B49,SS11,2B3	88	239	28	47	28	12	1	5	21	33	3	.197
Walt Novick	C74	83	219	25	54	30	7	0	4	33	31	0	.247
Coaker Triplett	OF45	76	187	27	63	37	10	1	2	18	17	0	.337
Robert Wellman	OF71,1B2	73	277	33	68	41	14	1	3	10	35	1	.245
Harry Minor	OF35,C,1B	49	133	17	37	23	4	1	4	15	30	0	.278
Alejandro Carrasquel	P48	48	30	3	8	1	2	0	0	4	12	0	.267
Gerad Scala	OF45	45	161	16	50	23	9	2	0	22	11	0	.311
Lynn Lovenguth	P41	43	57	6	15	3	2	0	0	7	8	0	.263
Charles Harris	P36	36	58	2	7	4	3	0	0	3	12	0	.120
Aaron Silverman	P33	33	60	2	10	6	2	0	1	4	22	0	.167
Harold Wood	P27	29	51	4	9	5	1	0	1	2	6	0	.176
Jacob Wade	P26	26	33	2	4	2	1	0	0	2	14	0	.121
Clem Hausmann	P23	24	23	7	6	4	0	0	0	9	5	0	.261
Sanford Silverstein	P23	23	35	1	3	1	1	0	0	3	8	0	.086
Harry Byrd	P21	21	43	3	11	5	1	0	0	2	7	0	.256
Frank Trechock	2B14	16	34	7	7	2	0	0	0	12	5	0	.206
Alfred Burch	P8	14	3	2	0	0	0	0	0	0	0	0	.000
Robert Stewart	SS	7	24	0	4	2	2	0	0			0	.167
Ed Burtschy	P7	7	6		1								.167
Phil Marchildon	P5	5	6		0								.000
Franklin Robinson	P5	5	4		0								.000

PITCHERS	W	L	PCT	G	GS	CG	SH	IP	H	BB	SO	ERA
Aaron Silverman	10	14	.417	33	25	12	1	183	199	85	85	5.02
Charles Harris	8	14	.364	36	20	5	0	169	197	70	57	4.95
Jacob Wade	7	6	.538	26	13	7	3	107	111	58	34	4.96
Lynn Lovenguth	7	9	.438	41	16	8	0	170	154	108	94	4.13
Alejandro Carrasquel	6	3	.667	48	1	0	0	110	122	51	36	5.48
Clem Hausmann	6	8	.429	23	14	8	1	94	102	47	36	4.69
Harold Wood	5	16	.238	27	23	10	1	149	146	104	75	4.77
Harry Byrd	4	9	.308	21	15	5	0	108	134	65	66	6.75
Sanford Silverstein	3	10	.231	23	18	5	0	110	133	66	44	5.56
Ed Burtschy	0	1	.000	7	2	0	0	21	24	13	9	3.86
Alfred Burch	0	2	.000	8	2	1	0	18	29	16	11	11.50
Phil Marchildon	0	4	.000	5	5	0	0	23	26	24	13	7.43
Franklin Robinson	0	0	----	5	0	0	0	12	11	16	3	3.00

MULTI-TEAM PLAYERS

BATTERS	POS-GAMES	TEAMS	GP	AB	R	H	BI	2B	3B	HR	BB	SO	SB	BA
Al Mele	OF114	SY85-JC43	128	412	59	113	77	22	3	10	73	37	1	.274
John Welaj	OF99	TO18-MO109	127	426	59	125	82	24	3	10	31	38	13	.293
Chet Laabs	OF117	TO18-JC99	117	386	80	109	87	15	3	30	74	60	3	.282
Robert Rhawn	2B73,3B25	MO4-TO109	113	375	55	105	51	12	5	5	26	25	2	.280
Al Stringer	SS88,OF,3B	RO3-BU99	102	333	46	101	24	23	3	0	29	37	2	.303
George Binks	OF84,1B8	BA1-BU100	101	331	30	71	43	12	0	8	37	39	1	.215
John Wittig	P31	BA5-RO26	31	41	3	10	0	0	1	0	3	10	0	.244
Jack Hussey	OF12	BU10-RO3	13	44	8	11	11	3	0	4	8	13	1	.250

PITCHERS		TEAMS	W	L	PCT	G	GS	CG	SH	IP	H	BB	SO	ERA
John Wittig		BA5-RO26	8	6	.571	31	16	6	0	120	150	54	63	5.48

TEAM BATTING

TEAMS	GP	AB	R	H	BI	2B	3B	HR	BB	SO	SB	BA
ROCHESTER	152	5106	885	1430	832	222	62	152	708	631	42	.280
MONTREAL	153	5096	816	1414	746	255	53	76	709	515	97	.277
BALTIMORE	156	4985	769	1316	713	197	45	152	706	571	34	.264
JERSEY CITY	152	4910	759	1262	702	176	46	139	736	693	88	.257
SPRINGFIELD	153	4991	711	1305	661	228	60	128	540	671	35	.261
SYRACUSE	153	4717	620	1114	566	172	28	83	773	637	36	.236
TORONTO	153	4932	650	1200	592	193	39	103	645	673	52	.243
BUFFALO	154	4937	668	1267	614	242	30	83	696	602	24	.257
	613	39674	5878	10308	5426	1685	363	916	5513	4993	408	.260

1951
ROOKIE OF THE YEAR

After the 1932 season, the International League issued an award honoring the year's best player. Called the Most Valuable Player award, and chosen by sportswriters from league cities, it became an annual honor. Later, the league started a new award. Differing from the Most Valuable Player, which recognized a veteran player's noteworthy season, this award honored the league's newcomers.

In 1947, major league executives created the Rookie of the Year award to honor the majors' best first-year player. Its first recipient was Brooklyn Dodger Jackie Robinson. In 1950, the International League followed suit.

During the 1950 season, Springfield third baseman Ransom Jackson batted .315 and clubbed 20 home runs. These numbers, though solid, didn't qualify as the year's best. However, they were the best for any first-year league player in 1950. Logically, International League sportswriters voted Ransom Jackson the league's first Rookie of the Year.

In 1951, the Montreal Royals returned to their pennant-winning ways, besting Rochester by eleven games. Syracuse finished ˙third, while Buffalo slipped into the final playoff spot one game ahead of Toronto. Baltimore, Ottawa (which took the place of Jersey City), and Springfield filled the last three slots. Rochester's Don Richmond won his second batting title (.350), Marv Rickert of Baltimore poled the most home runs (35), and Buffalo's Archie Wilson knocked in the most runs (112). Pitcher John Hetki from Toronto posted the most wins (19), Ottawa's Alex Konikowski had the lowest earned run average (2.59), and Syracuse Chief William Miller struck out the most batters (131).

Also during the 1951 season, Ransom Jackson became the starting third baseman for the major league Chicago Cubs. During his ten-year major league career, he performed capably for six different clubs, warranting his selection as the inaugural Rookie of the Year player in the International League.

Through the years since, the Rookie of the Year award has been annually given in the International League. Many recipients have gone on to become solid stars in the International as well as other leagues. In 1950, it certainly took foresight for league executives to create an award that honored not only a player's achievement, but also his potential.

MONTREAL Royals

1st	95-59	.617		Walt Alston

BATTERS	POS-GAMES	GP	AB	R	H	BI	2B	3B	HR	BB	SO	SB	BA
George Byam	1B136	141	485	63	130	71	24	6	10	65	46	1	.268
Jim Gilliam	2B92,OF64,3B1	152	565	117	162	73	22	9	7	117	47	15	.287
Robert Morgan	SS155	155	575	84	156	75	33	3	9	74	67	6	.271
Hector Rodriguez	3B151	153	609	105	184	95	28	10	8	56	31	26	.302
Al Gionfriddo	OF134	141	510	95	137	56	27	2	9	101	33	12	.269
James Russell	OF97	110	346	55	99	67	25	4	9	78	57	6	.286
John Welaj	OF97	109	323	50	70	34	12	3	4	38	31	13	.217
Maurice Atwell	C114,OF1	122	395	58	92	45	18	0	9	64	24	4	.233
Walt Fiala	2B71,1B16	106	316	33	90	40	7	1	0	45	18	1	.285
George Shuba	OF84	92	281	54	87	83	25	2	20	70	34	3	.310
George Pfister	C49	60	158	20	39	16	10	2	0	20	9	1	.247
Bill Voiselle	P47	47	27	0	3	4	1	0	0	0	7	0	.111
Tom Lasorda	P31	38	62	7	18	11	5	0	1	5	13	1	.290
Robert Alexander	P32	32	67	7	13	6	2	0	0	8	16	0	.194
Mal Mallette	P25	30	48	7	11	2	2	0	0	3	9	0	.229
Hampton Coleman	P30	30	40	4	6	5	1	0	0	3	8	0	.190
James Hughes	P27	28	36	2	6	3	0	0	0	1	5	0	.167
Joe Black	P26	27	39	2	8	6	1	0	0	4	11	0	.205
Ross Grimsley	P26	27	20	2	3	4	0	0	0	1	5	0	.150
Chris Van Cuyk	P24	24	58	3	11	7	3	0	0	0	8	0	.190
Dan Bankhead	P10,OF	14	22	3	8	2	0	0	1	2	0	0	.364
Bert Haas	1B,OF,3B	13	49	3	6	5	1	0	0	1	3	1	.122
Clarence Podbielan	P9	10	28	5	8	4	0	1	0	0	5	0	.286
Ray Moore	P7	7	12		3								.250
Al Epperly	P5	5	1		1								1.000
Don Hoak	3B	2	10	1	1	1	0	0	1			0	.100
Gino Cimoli	OF	2	7	4	2	0	0	0	0	0		0	.286
Glen Cox	P1	1	2	0	2	3	0	0	0			0	1.000

PITCHERS		W	L	PCT	G	GS	CG	SH	IP	H	BB	SO	ERA
Robert Alexander		15	8	.652	32	27	15	2	216	201	70	97	3.58
Tom Lasorda		12	8	.600	31	21	11	1	165	145	87	80	3.49
Chris Van Cuyk		11	4	.733	24	20	11	2	146	127	48	106	2.84
Mal Mallette		10	2	.833	25	16	7	1	141	113	47	70	2.30
James Hughes		10	4	.714	27	13	5	2	105	92	52	51	3.69
Hampton Coleman		9	5	.643	30	13	6	0	128	125	39	59	3.59
Joe Black		7	9	.438	26	13	3	1	110	106	37	49	3.85
Clarence Podbielan		6	3	.667	9	9	6	1	71	57	17	22	2.92
Bill Voiselle		5	5	.500	47	3	1	0	101	100	38	66	3.48
Ross Grimsley		4	1	.800	26	6	2	0	68	66	28	52	4.37
Al Epperly		2	0	1.000	5	0	0	0	8	8	2	3	2.25
Ray Moore		2	3	.400	7	5	3	0	36	26	37	29	3.75
Dan Bankhead		2	6	.250	10	8	0	0	46	50	26	16	3.91
Glen Cox		0	1	.000	1	1	0	0	3	5	3	0	15.00

ROCHESTER Red Wings

2nd	83-69	.546	-11	John Keane

BATTERS	POS-GAMES	GP	AB	R	H	BI	2B	3B	HR	BB	SO	SB	BA
Steve Bilko	1B73	73	273	41	77	50	14	6	8	37	51	0	.282
Louis Ortiz	2B151	152	498	64	122	50	24	4	7	71	61	2	.245
William Hardin	SS138,3B4	143	577	88	151	48	17	8	1	52	48	4	.262
Don Richmond	3B103	105	412	71	144	49	31	5	5	33	29	4	.350
John Blatnik	OF106	126	376	60	102	60	22	6	11	62	56	0	.271
Russ Derry	OF99	116	337	59	84	53	17	3	19	68	68	2	.249
Jay Van Noy	OF91	97	361	60	81	38	13	0	14	37	73	3	.225
John Bucha	C100	110	349	39	91	45	17	4	3	40	25	1	.261
Rolland LeBlanc	C56,OF,3B	76	206	19	39	16	5	3	2	4	26	1	.189
Ed Mierkowicz	OF53,1B11,SS,3B	74	230	35	66	35	13	0	5	27	23	0	.287
Charles Kress	1B69	71	249	47	65	42	16	3	12	32	32	3	.261
Dan Lynch	3B25,OF15,SS,2B	65	153	21	42	15	8	3	1	20	14	3	.275
Harold Rice	OF54	54	209	30	69	36	10	8	12	17	18	0	.330
Lawrence Ciaffone	OF42,3B3	53	175	24	42	28	7	1	5	9	8	0	.240
Jack Collum	P33	43	83	9	15	16	1	1	4	12	6	0	.181
Ken Wild	P33	42	28	4	5	0	0	0	0	5	4	0	.179
John Yuhas	P34	35	58	3	7	4	1	1	0	1	19	0	.120
John Fasholz	P35	35	55	2	6	6	2	1	0	4	18	0	.109
Robert Tiefenauer	P35	35	54	2	6	4	0	0	0	3	12	0	.111
Fred Hahn	P34	34	37	2	4	1	0	0	0	3	13	0	.108
Robert Habenicht	P31	32	54	5	12	4	5	0	0	4	13	1	.222

ROCHESTER (cont.)
Red Wings

BATTERS	POS-GAMES	GP	AB	R	H	BI	2B	3B	HR	BB	SO	SB	BA
Vernal Jones	3B18,1B	23	95	15	29	24	5	1	5	7	5	0	.305
Kurt Krieger	P20	20	29	2	4	3	1	0	0	0	11	0	.138
John Wittig	P19	19	8	0	2	1	1	0	0	0	2	0	.250
Luis Arroyo	P15	18	8	2	3	1	0	0	0	1	2	0	.375
Walt Fassler	SS,3B	12	35	5	4	0	2	0	0	4	4	0	.114
Ellis Deal	OF8	9	26	3	6	4	2	1	2			0	.231
Roy Huff	OF	7	16	1	3	1	2	0	1			0	.188
Ron Coman	C	5	11	0	5	3	2	0	0			0	.455
Glen Moulder	P5	5	7		2								.286
Don Boring	3B	4	9	0	1	0	1	0	0			0	.111
Joseph Brunacki	OF	4	8	1	2	1	0	0	0			0	.250
Elwood Clear	P4	4	1		0								.000
Delbert Friar	C	3	9	0	2	2	0	0	0			0	.222
William Reeder	P3	3	0		0								----
George Copeland	P1	1	1		0								.000
Greg Masson	C1	1	0		0								----
Harland Coppman	P1	1	0		0								----

PITCHERS		W	L	PCT	G	GS	CG	SH	IP	H	BB	SO	ERA
Jack Collum		15	8	.652	33	25	14	0	222	211	87	108	2.80
John Yuhas		13	11	.542	34	25	9	5	169	163	81	87	3.04
John Fasholz		12	9	.571	35	22	14	1	177	159	67	71	3.41
Robert Habenicht		11	6	.647	31	19	8	1	152	145	80	69	4.33
Robert Tiefenauer		9	9	.500	35	20	9	1	176	167	55	79	2.66
Fred Hahn		7	8	.467	34	16	4	0	134	117	79	84	3.83
Kurt Krieger		6	6	.500	20	15	4	3	89	100	59	34	5.66
Ken Wild		6	8	.429	33	6	2	0	94	107	36	30	3.64
John Wittig		4	2	.667	19	0	0	1	38	32	27	13	2.84
Glen Moulder		0	1	.000	5	3	0	0	22	28	10	6	6.55
Elwood Clear		0	1	.000	4	0	0	0	5	3	4	2	0.00
Luis Arroyo		0	0	----	15	1	0	0	31	41	29	18	7.55
William Reeder		0	0	----	3	0	0	0	4	3	7	2	9.00
George Copeland		0	0	----	1	0	0	0	3	4	2	3	9.00
Harland Coppman		0	0	----	1	0	0	0	1	5	1	2	18.00

SYRACUSE   3rd   82-71   .536   -12.5   Bruno Betzel
Chiefs

BATTERS	POS-GAMES	GP	AB	R	H	BI	2B	3B	HR	BB	SO	SB	BA
Ed Shokes	1B110,OF3	121	376	37	89	45	17	0	6	64	35	1	.237
Frank Drews	2B73,3B13	103	284	31	74	39	13	1	5	57	44	3	.261
Claude Corbitt	SS133	135	479	72	134	55	19	3	2	63	25	2	.280
Loren Babe	3B143,SS12	153	595	88	162	56	32	1	8	84	35	4	.272
Carden Gillenwater	OF147	148	483	71	130	75	24	5	9	126	67	6	.269
Percy Riggan	OF78	100	264	37	56	36	5	1	5	34	44	4	.212
Vic Power	OF73,1B42	129	439	62	129	56	22	5	6	32	25	12	.294
William Baker	C94	103	270	27	63	34	19	1	3	46	18	0	.233
Ben Zientara	2B56,OF15,SS8	100	250	45	55	27	7	2	1	59	23	2	.220
Henry Foiles	C68	85	211	27	45	14	8	2	5	23	41	0	.213
Gus Bergamo	OF11,1B10	62	82	6	17	20	1	0	2	19	7	0	.207
Charles Weathers	OF56	60	196	27	48	14	9	2	0	32	43	1	.245
Henry Workman	OF56	56	205	29	52	40	9	0	9	24	23	0	.254
John Robinson	P38	41	61	7	9	0	2	0	0	3	20	0	.148
Eugene Markland	2B37,SS3	39	126	22	25	12	5	0	2	38	19	0	.198
John Griffore	P37	37	79	5	21	5	4	0	0	2	19	0	.266
Art Hartley	P37	37	57	3	5	5	0	0	0	5	18	0	.088
William Miller	P35	35	74	2	6	4	0	0	0	8	33	0	.081
William Tanner	P33	33	12	0	1	0	1	0	0	0	6	0	.083
Robert Keegan	P29	31	63	4	14	14	2	0	0	7	7	0	.222
William Houtz	P27	31	27	0	3	1	0	0	0	5	10	0	.111
Myron Hayworth	C18	23	40	1	7	1	2	0	0	4	6	0	.175
Mizell Platt	OF20	20	73	7	17	8	2	0	1	6	7	0	.233
Saturnino Escalera	OF15	20	55	7	13	3	2	0	0	9	8	0	.236
Alonzo Perry	1B	9	18	3	5	3	0	0	0			0	.278
Carmine Melignano	P6	6	0		0								----
Malcolm Mick	OF	5	4	1	2	0	0	0	0			0	.500
James Tote	P5	5	0		0								----
Roman Brunswick	P4	4	1		0								.000
James Vitter	P4	4	1		0								.000

SYRACUSE (cont.)
Chiefs

PITCHERS	W	L	PCT	G	GS	CG	SH	IP	H	BB	SO	ERA
William Miller	16	10	.615	35	30	14	4	225	204	118	131	2.96
John Griffore	14	10	.583	37	30	14	4	225	215	64	97	3.64
Robert Keegan	13	9	.591	29	21	13	1	177	162	69	86	3.51
Art Hartley	13	11	.542	37	27	12	0	197	203	75	73	3.20
John Robinson	7	15	.318	38	23	6	0	188	184	75	53	3.73
William Houtz	5	5	.500	27	13	3	1	87	86	80	36	4.76
William Tanner	2	3	.400	33	5	1	0	68	55	49	15	2.78
Carmine Melignano	1	0	1.000	6	0	0	0	8	10	3	5	4.50
Roman Brunswick	0	1	.000	4	0	0	0	5	8	3	0	9.00
James Tote	0	0	----	5	0	0	0	5	4	5	2	5.40
James Vitter	0	0	----	4	0	0	0	12	12	11	2	6.00

BUFFALO   4th   79-75   .513   -16   George Toporcer -
Bisons   Coaker Triplett

BATTERS	POS-GAMES	GP	AB	R	H	BI	2B	3B	HR	BB	SO	SB	BA
Henry Biasetti	1B146	149	446	52	109	56	16	0	13	83	30	1	.244
George Moskovich	2B139	142	462	52	101	51	18	1	9	55	71	6	.219
Al Stringer	SS113,3B1	119	392	61	94	27	18	4	2	57	61	1	.240
Fred Hancock	3B152	152	596	85	141	50	28	4	11	82	44	2	.237
Archie Wilson	OF151	151	605	96	191	112	39	7	28	32	39	7	.316
Wally Post	OF109	111	422	78	129	65	17	5	21	40	61	11	.306
Frank Carswell	OF103,1B29,2B1	124	444	59	134	79	37	3	9	32	28	4	.302
Hobart Landrith	C90	98	288	20	55	28	13	3	3	34	25	1	.191
Robert Wellman	OF98	111	383	49	112	47	20	1	5	25	48	3	.292
Jennings Edwards	SS56,2B23	95	281	37	76	19	16	3	0	28	40	4	.270
Coaker Triplett	OF12	62	72	6	25	22	6	2	0	13	4	1	.347
Walt Novick	C50	59	152	19	40	16	9	1	0	25	13	1	.263
Lynn Lovenguth	P37	48	52	6	14	2	2	0	0	8	7	0	.269
Morris Savransky	P30	41	66	8	15	2	5	0	0	4	14	0	.227
Martin Tabacheck	C34,1B1	36	79	6	16	5	5	0	0	7	6	0	.203
Aaron Silverman	P31	35	66	3	8	2	0	0	0	1	20	0	.121
Thomas Simpson	P35	35	41	1	5	3	2	0	0	1	14	0	.122
Rudolph Minarcin	P33	34	85	9	19	11	3	0	0	10	13	0	.224
Thomas Acker	P31	31	69	1	7	1	0	1	0	5	32	0	.101
Charles Barrett	P28	28	11	0	0	0	0	0	0	0	5	0	.000
Franklin Robinson	P27	27	18	0	2	0	0	0	0	1	5	0	.111
Alejandro Carrasquel	P16	16	5	0	1	2	0	0	0	0	2	0	.200
Clem Hausmann	P12	12	7	1	1	0	1	0	0	0	2	0	.143
James Curley	P7	7	3		1								.333
William Scott	P4	4	0		0								----
Frank Trechock	2B	3	2	0	0	0	0	0	0			0	.000
Carl Lindquist	P3	3	2		0								.000

PITCHERS	W	L	PCT	G	GS	CG	SH	IP	H	BB	SO	ERA
Rudolph Minarcin	16	12	.571	33	31	17	4	242	198	106	111	3.20
Aaron Silverman	12	11	.522	31	29	10	3	175	192	77	78	4.11
Morris Savransky	11	11	.500	30	28	10	1	185	175	104	78	2.92
Thomas Acker	10	13	.435	31	29	11	2	200	166	112	111	3.69
Thomas Simpson	8	6	.571	35	14	5	1	138	118	60	68	3.78
Lynn Lovenguth	7	8	.467	37	14	6	0	133	118	78	89	3.79
Charles Barrett	5	1	.833	28	0	0	0	55	62	21	38	3.60
Franklin Robinson	3	6	.333	27	6	1	0	69	78	40	24	5.22
Clem Hausmann	2	2	.500	12	0	0	0	32	36	31	13	7.59
Alejandro Carrasquel	1	1	.500	16	0	0	0	28	27	13	13	3.21
James Curley	0	0	----	7	0	0	0	16	12	5	5	5.06
William Scott	0	0	----	4	0	0	0	4	5	6	3	2.25
Carl Lindquist	0	0	----	3	0	0	0	7	5	9	2	2.57

TORONTO   5th   77-76   .505   -17.5   Joseph Becker
Maple Leafs

BATTERS	POS-GAMES	GP	AB	R	H	BI	2B	3B	HR	BB	SO	SB	BA
Les Fleming	1B129	135	445	68	119	79	28	3	17	82	33	1	.267
Charles Grant	2B146	149	543	79	143	77	29	5	19	53	73	1	.263
John Sullivan	SS153	153	565	76	131	38	17	1	2	95	64	5	.232
Robert Rhawn	3B67,2B7	78	295	46	89	35	13	1	6	24	20	5	.302
Lewis Morton	OF145	147	538	90	127	70	17	4	21	72	53	3	.236

TORONTO (cont.)
Maple Leafs

BATTERS	POS-GAMES	GP	AB	R	H	BI	2B	3B	HR	BB	SO	SB	BA
Grover Bowers	OF107	119	395	58	115	37	22	2	7	68	32	6	.291
John Ostrowski	OF93,3B29	127	377	40	61	56	15	2	13	58	86	0	.215
Ferell Anderson	C	(see multi-team players)											
Frank Colman	OF91,1B28	126	438	50	125	66	26	0	12	34	31	3	.285
Harry Heslet	OF46	80	187	23	48	27	3	1	6	27	31	2	.257
Vince Plumbo	C68	76	198	18	47	25	8	2	4	25	17	0	.237
Charles White	3B59,SS1	60	230	31	65	27	10	2	4	16	31	5	.283
Ray Shore	P55	55	25	4	6	2	0	0	0	1	5	0	.240
John Hetki	P37	41	97	8	21	6	3	0	0	5	4	0	.216
Hal Hudson	P39,OF1	39	57	7	10	4	0	1	0	0	10	0	.175
Cliff Fannin	P23	32	43	6	5	4	1	1	0	5	8	0	.116
Daniel Balch	C27	31	91	10	23	8	2	1	1	8	13	0	.253
Irv Medlinger	P28	31	48	6	5	1	0	0	0	4	9	0	.104
Russ Bauers	P29	29	68	4	11	3	0	0	0	0	8	0	.162
John Crocco	P24	25	11	1	2	0	0	0	0	0	2	0	.182
Max Peterson	P21	21	27	0	2	1	0	0	0	4	5	0	.074
Leon Day	P14,OF	20	27	5	7	1	1	0	0	2	5	0	.259
Robert Stewart	3B11,2B	19	41	5	9	4	0	1	0	3	7	0	.220
Don E. Robertson	P10	14	13	3	2	0	0	0	0	3	5	0	.154
Fred Collins	1B	13	15	2	1	2	0	0	1	1	5	0	.067
Elmer Singleton	P10	11	15	0	2	0	0	0	0	0	3	0	.133
Jack Bruner	P7	7	1		1								1.000
Charles Harris	P5	5	3		0								.000
Vern Taylor	P5	5	0		0								----
Ed Hrabczak	P3	3	2		1								.500
Frank Raney	P2	2	1		0								.000
Frank Barnes	P2	2	0		0								----
Ernest Bickhaus	P1	1	0		0								----

PITCHERS		W	L	PCT	G	GS	CG	SH	IP	H	BB	SO	ERA
John Hetki		19	10	.655	37	32	17	4	256	215	75	97	2.85
Hal Hudson		16	5	.762	39	24	9	3	181	155	85	90	3.08
Ray Shore		10	8	.556	55	0	0	0	107	72	64	77	2.94
Irv Medlinger		10	10	.500	28	21	6	2	143	157	62	72	3.90
Russ Bauers		9	13	.409	29	28	15	3	195	200	50	128	3.00
Cliff Fannin		6	8	.429	23	20	8	2	130	126	37	72	4.36
Max Peterson		3	5	.375	21	10	3	0	94	104	25	28	3.64
Don E. Robertson		2	3	.400	10	6	1	0	45	48	28	15	4.60
Leon Day		1	1	.500	14	1	1	0	40	33	28	20	1.58
John Crocco		1	2	.333	24	1	0	0	52	56	34	10	4.67
Charles Harris		0	1	.000	5	1	1	0	14	18	8	4	3.86
Ed Hrabczak		0	1	.000	3	2	0	0	9	11	5	5	5.00
Frank Raney		0	1	.000	2	0	0	0	2	1	6	2	18.00
Frank Barnes		0	1	.000	2	0	0	0	1	2	8	1	45.00
Jack Bruner		0	2	.000	5	0	0	0	7	10	7	3	11.57
Elmer Singleton		0	5	.000	10	5	0	0	39	53	9	15	7.15
Vern Taylor		0	0	----	4	0	0	0	6	10	5	2	7.50
Ernest Bickhaus		0	0	----	1	0	0	0	0	2	2	0	108.00

BALTIMORE   6th   69-82   .457   -24.5   Nick Cullop
Orioles

BATTERS	POS-GAMES	GP	AB	R	H	BI	2B	3B	HR	BB	SO	SB	BA
William Glynn	1B142	143	488	67	122	53	19	6	15	74	57	10	.250
Al Cihocki	2B80,3B,SS,OF	117	362	42	85	35	16	2	8	29	45	0	.235
Damon Phillips	SS123,3B14	139	497	46	114	40	20	2	8	46	44	0	.229
Russ Kerns	3B133,2B1	137	485	61	140	83	31	3	17	50	49	2	.289
Marv Rickert	OF139,1B13	152	546	106	175	104	29	3	35	92	57	4	.321
John Mayo	OF115	126	450	76	122	47	22	7	11	69	72	2	.271
Howard Moss	OF	(see multi-team players)											
Ed Oswald	C79	88	259	27	58	33	6	4	1	34	37	0	.224
Ansel Moore	OF74,2B,3B	103	264	36	71	53	11	2	14	38	16	0	.269
Mike Goliat	2B74	74	284	47	80	27	15	4	7	33	35	2	.282
Ken Trinkle	P53	53	28	4	1	0	0	1	0	2	10	0	.036
Boris Woyt	OF44	51	159	19	36	13	4	1	4	9	14	2	.226
Karl Drews	P38	46	90	12	14	6	1	1	1	7	34	0	.156
Clarence Hicks	SS28,2B3	41	130	18	29	11	2	1	3	22	10	1	.223
Jacob Schmitt	P36.OF1	39	59	2	13	3	3	1	0	1	8	0	.220
Stan Lopata	C31	38	102	12	20	6	6	1	1	19	22	0	.196
Louis Possehl	P34	38	52	5	8	2	2	0	0	5	10	0	.154

BALTIMORE (cont.)
Orioles

BATTERS	POS-GAMES	GP	AB	R	H	BI	2B	3B	HR	BB	SO	SB	BA
Stephen Ridzik	P31	33	41	2	6	3	4	0	0	1	8	1	.146
Stan Hollmig	OF28	29	105	14	26	17	3	5	2	15	24	4	.248
Syl Donnelly	P25	26	40	5	5	3	2	0	0	6	8	0	.125
Jack Tanner	C18	25	67	3	16	8	4	0	2	2	19	0	.239
John Brittin	P25	25	54	3	7	0	0	0	0	5	14	0	.130
Leo Cristante	P24	25	19	1	2	1	2	0	0	0	4	0	.105
Andrew Hansen	P19	19	10	0	2	0	0	0	0	0	2	0	.200
Joseph Payne	P11	12	3	0	0	0	0	0	0	0	1	0	.000
Ernest Groth	P10	10	3	0	0	0	0	0	0	0	2	0	.000
Paul Stuffel	P5	5	8		1								.125
Niles Jordan	P2	2	0		0								----
Richard Young	PH	1	0	0	0	0	0	0	0			0	----

PITCHERS		W	L	PCT	G	GS	CG	SH	IP	H	BB	SO	ERA
Karl Drews		17	13	.567	38	29	21	3	253	211	89	127	2.85
Louis Possehl		10	8	.556	34	21	8	3	176	148	78	81	3.38
Jacob Schmitt		10	14	.417	36	26	11	2	189	205	80	116	4.05
Syl Donnelly		7	6	.538	25	20	9	1	137	132	49	79	4.07
John Brittin		7	10	.412	25	21	11	3	156	161	72	67	4.44
Ken Trinkle		6	7	.462	53	6	1	1	118	113	52	42	3.43
Stephen Ridzik		5	11	.313	31	15	5	1	133	133	76	86	4.20
Leo Cristante		4	8	.333	24	7	1	0	72	76	27	31	4.75
Andrew Hansen		1	1	.500	19	0	0		38	40	26	14	5.45
Joseph Payne		1	1	.500	11	3	0	0	19	23	16	4	5.68
Paul Stuffel		1	2	.333	5	5	1	0	18	21	26	25	9.50
Ernest Groth		0	1	.000	10	1	0	0	19	25	14	7	7.58
Niles Jordan		0	0	----	2	0	0	0	2	9	1	2	31.50

OTTAWA   7th   62-88   .413   -31   Hugh Poland
Athletics

BATTERS	POS-GAMES	GP	AB	R	H	BI	2B	3B	HR	BB	SO	SB	BA
Fred Gerken	1B63,OF11,P6	97	270	26	59	29	13	0	6	35	47	3	.219
Robert Hoffman	2B72	72	263	36	72	29	13	1	2	22	23	0	.274
Ziggy Jasinski	SS136	138	418	33	92	30	10	0	0	36	36	12	.220
William Gardner	3B150	150	555	56	128	37	19	6	3	47	72	13	.231
Stan Jok	OF143,3B1	145	502	53	133	56	26	5	3	66	74	13	.265
Harvey Gentry	OF128	128	468	68	121	38	20	7	6	65	72	11	.259
John Metkovich	OF112	114	312	30	65	20	12	7	0	18	73	4	.208
Neal Watlington	C104	116	366	33	87	39	7	4	1	31	21	5	.238
Lorenzo Davis	2B48,1B20,OF14,3B2	78	278	18	73	32	10	3	3	13	20	7	.263
Phil Tomkinson	C59	71	197	14	54	15	12	1	0	19	33	2	.274
Marv Blaylock	1B60	69	218	21	42	11	4	1	3	23	51	3	.193
Mylon Vukmire	2B37,SS27	67	156	9	25	10	4	2	1	22	33	0	.160
Al Mele	OF32	66	141	10	37	24	6	2	2	10	14	0	.262
George Heller	P32	36	20	4	4	2	1	0	0	3	7	0	.200
Milt Joffe	OF30	32	66	8	9	9	1	2	1	16	25	3	.136
Lorenzo Cabrera	1B17	31	72	8	17	7	5	2	0	4	5	0	.236
Alex Konikowski	P30	30	50	2	5	1	0	0	0	3	13	0	.100
Ed Wright	P21	27	36	4	10	4	1	0	0	1	6	0	.278
George Bamberger	P26	26	54	1	6	3	1	0	0	3	25	0	.111
Raul Lopez	P19,3B1	26	20	1	1	0	0	0	0	4	13	0	.050
Elmer Corwin	P21	24	34	4	9	2	1	1	0	0	5	0	.265
Walt Cox	P24	24	7	0	0	0	0	0	0	0	1	0	.000
Andrew Tomasic	P21	21	22	1	2	1	0	2	0	0	10	0	.091
Harry Nicholas	P15	16	25	0	4	0	0	0	0	3	10	0	.160
Francis Hardy	P13	15	25	1	3	1	0	0	0	1	10	1	.120
Peter Karpuk	OF10	13	41	4	8	0	0	1	0	2	11	2	.195
Paul Mauldin	OF12	12	42	5	9	3	1	2	0	8	7	0	.214
Gerald Fahr	P11	11	26	0	4	0	0	0	0	0	9	0	.154
Frank Fanovich	P8	8	14		2								.143
William Metzig	2B,SS	7	16	2	4	4	0	0	2			0	.250
Roger Bowman	P5	5	12		1								.083
Charles Bishop	P4	4	6		1								.167
Pete Burnside	P4	4	5		2								.400
Hugh Oser	P3	3	0		0								----
Artie Wilson	OF	2	7	2	2	0	1	0	0			1	.286
Ed Sokol	C	2	2	0	0	0	0	0	0			0	.000

OTTAWA (cont.)
Athletics

PITCHERS	W	L	PCT	G	GS	CG	SH	IP	H	BB	SO	ERA
George Bamberger	11	11	.500	26	25	12	4	174	158	57	68	3.36
Alex Konikowski	8	7	.533	30	19	10	5	170	144	63	102	**2.59**
Francis Hardy	6	5	.545	13	10	5	2	79	58	30	44	2.05
Gerald Fahr	5	4	.556	11	9	5	1	78	66	18	22	1.96
Andrew Tomasic	5	5	.500	21	10	3	1	78	71	42	49	4.62
Ed Wright	5	6	.455	21	13	7	3	89	79	45	18	3.54
Harry Nicholas	5	6	.455	15	10	5	1	78	76	41	28	4.04
George Heller	4	7	.364	32	9	3	1	85	75	68	49	4.45
Elmer Corwin	2	4	.333	21	8	4	1	91	64	51	51	2.47
Frank Fanovich	2	5	.286	8	7	2	0	46	37	27	30	3.72
Raul Lopez	2	8	.200	19	8	2	0	78	86	46	60	4.96
Fred Gerken	1	0	1.000	6	0	0	0	14	13	8	5	5.14
Walt Cox	1	3	.250	24	1	0	0	34	31	10	8	3.44
Roger Bowman	1	3	.250	5	4	1	1	34	26	13	24	2.91
Charles Bishop	0	3	.000	4	3	1	0	21	16	16	14	4.71
Pete Burnside	0	3	.000	4	3	1	0	14	16	16	8	7.71
Hugh Oser	0	0	----	3	0	0	0	2	3	0	0	4.50

SPRINGFIELD   8th   63-90   .412   -31.5   William Kelly
Cubs

BATTERS	POS-GAMES	GP	AB	R	H	BI	2B	3B	HR	BB	SO	SB	BA
Fred Richards	1B62	66	194	15	42	18	1	3	2	19	22	0	.216
Emil Verban	2B117	119	490	49	130	29	23	4	0	11	23	0	.265
Ed McDade	SS70,3B,2B	82	247	15	48	9	3	1	0	16	22	2	.194
Eugene Hooks	3B111,SS22	130	507	45	132	45	16	2	2	29	47	5	.260
John Liptak	OF138	141	493	63	110	50	15	8	2	91	39	10	.223
Carmen Mauro	OF133	138	501	87	148	53	21	**11**	9	65	72	9	.295
John Wallaesa	OF93,SS48	139	527	56	156	90	40	3	14	56	89	0	.296
Nelson Burbrink	C100,3B5	112	357	35	88	38	18	4	3	55	45	1	.246
Frank LaManna	P28,OF4	78	93	15	27	17	2	1	5	17	15	0	.290
Raymond Cash	C47	62	171	12	33	23	5	1	5	15	37	1	.193
Ron George	1B61	61	231	18	63	26	8	1	2	21	38	0	.273
Anthony Jacobs	P50	50	19	1	2	0	0	0	0	3	4	0	.105
Charles Teague	2B28,SS1	39	96	14	21	6	5	0	1	17	6	0	.219
Don Swartz	P32,3B3	39	39	2	3	0	2	0	0	5	7	0	.077
William Padgett	P33	34	77	10	16	4	3	0	0	10	24	0	.208
Edwin Ehlers	3B15,1B14,SS5	33	84	5	13	6	0	0	1	6	14	0	.155
Ted Sepkowski	3B16,OF11,2B1	30	100	9	21	12	5	0	3	16	14	0	.210
Alan Ihde	P27	27	52	3	11	4	2	0	0	1	24	0	.212
Ed Plank	SS25	26	64	4	10	1	2	0	0	5	9	1	.156
Luvern Fear	P24	25	44	3	6	2	1	0	0	3	13	0	.136
Stan Spence	1B,OF	23	49	5	10	5	3	1	0	13	3	0	.204
Frank Marino	P19	21	59	3	8	5	0	1	1	2	4	0	.136
James Forbes	1B21	21	51	4	5	4	0	0	1	8	16	0	.098
Don A. Robertson	OF13	21	49	9	5	0	1	0	0	4	13	0	.102
Robert Dant	C,OF	15	27	2	5	1	1	0	0	1	3	0	.185
Walt Dubiel	P14	14	36	2	10	4	1	0	0	0	4	0	.278
Umberto Flammini	P14	14	10	0	0	0	0	0	0	1	2	0	.000
Vern Morgan	2B11	13	31	3	3	2	0	0	0	1	7	0	.097
Paul Rutledge	3B,SS	13	17	1	0	0	0	0	0	4	8	0	.000
Harry Chiti	C	12	32	1	7	3	0	0	0	2	2	0	.219
Robert Schultz	P8	8	15		0								.000
Don Watkins	P8	8	9		2								.222
Wes Carr	P7	7	5		0								.000
Ray Bauer	P6	6	0		0								----
Don Verbic	P4	4	5		0								.000
Andrew Varga	P3	3	2		0								.000
Paul Schneiders	P3	3	2		0								.000
Don Brown	PH	2	2	0	0	0	0	0	0			0	.000
Paul Menking	P1	1	2		0								.000

PITCHERS	W	L	PCT	G	GS	CG	SH	IP	H	BB	SO	ERA
William Padgett	16	13	.552	32	31	17	3	221	**217**	65	88	3.22
Frank Marino	9	8	.529	19	19	11	1	156	147	51	61	3.81
Anthony Jacobs	8	9	.471	50	2	0	0	98	86	57	50	3.12
Alan Ihde	8	9	.471	27	22	7	0	153	159	65	64	3.71
Luvern Fear	8	9	.471	24	19	8	2	135	120	66	71	3.27
Frank LaManna	7	9	.438	28	17	9	1	128	127	55	39	4.36
Walt Dubiel	5	9	.357	14	13	8	1	107	104	38	33	2.69
Robert Schultz	2	4	.333	8	7	3	1	49	48	21	29	5.14

SPRINGFIELD (cont.)
Cubs

PITCHERS	W	L	PCT	G	GS	CG	SH	IP	H	BB	SO	ERA
Don Verbic	0	1	.000	4	3	0	0	16	19	6	8	1.69
Wes Carr	0	2	.000	7	2	0	0	24	25	11	8	3.75
Andrew Varga	0	2	.000	3	2	0	0	6	10	8	4	9.00
Don Swartz	0	4	.000	32	3	0	0	109	109	44	33	3.80
Don Watkins	0	4	.000	8	3	1	0	30	30	25	5	5.10
Umberto Flammini	0	6	.000	14	8	0	0	44	46	35	23	5.11
Ray Bauer	0	0	----	6	0	0	0	7	15	6	2	14.14
Paul Schneiders	0	0	----	3	0	0	0	8	7	9	1	4.50
Paul Menking	0	0	----	1	1	0	0	6	7	5	4	4.50

MULTI-TEAM PLAYERS

BATTERS	POS-GAMES	TEAMS	GP	AB	R	H	BI	2B	3B	HR	BB	SO	SB	BA
Ferrell Anderson	C105	BA37-TO73	110	371	30	112	50	21	1	7	24	22	0	.302
Ed Lavigne	OF88	SY21-SP89	110	327	48	76	34	11	1	6	36	33	1	.232
Howard Moss	OF87,3B1	SP4-BA90	94	321	37	79	54	10	1	16	38	66	0	.246
Eugene Costello	P39	SP10-SY32	42	21	2	1	0	0	0	0	0	4	0	.048
Charles Eisenmann	P36	OT17-SY19	36	26	2	5	2	0	0	0	0	5	0	.192
William Schultz	P34	RO1-BU34	35	10	1	0	0	0	0	0	1	3	0	.000
Richard Libby	P25	SY11-OT15	26	25	0	0	0	0	0	0	2	17	0	.000
John Barrett	OF10	BU11-OTT7	18	42	5	11	6	2	0	0	4	4	0	.262
Sanford Silverstein	P6	BU4-RO4	8	0		0								----

PITCHERS		TEAMS	W	L	PCT	G	GS	CG	SH	IP	H	BB	SO	ERA
Eugene Costello		SP10-SY29	7	3	.700	39	3	0	0	82	61	60	58	3.73
William Schultz		RO1-BU33	4	4	.500	34	0	0	0	49	51	17	24	3.49
Richard Libby		SY11-OT14	4	5	.444	25	9	4	1	83	76	53	21	2.60
Charles Eisenmann		OT17-SY19	4	7	.364	36	7	0	1	97	91	60	66	3.80
Sanford Silverstein		BU2-RO4	0	0	----	6	0	0	0	7	9	11	7	9.00

TEAM BATTING

TEAMS	GP	AB	R	H	BI	2B	3B	HR	BB	SO	SB	BA
MONTREAL	155	5089	785	1356	722	250	43	89	761	495	90	.266
ROCHESTER	152	5037	715	1294	641	240	59	117	570	669	25	.257
SYRACUSE	154	4921	633	1202	572	206	23	65	759	599	36	.244
BUFFALO	154	5086	657	1304	603	256	35	101	550	590	43	.256
TORONTO	154	5041	663	1267	614	204	28	120	607	571	31	.251
BALTIMORE	154	5038	655	1273	611	223	45	145	603	677	28	.253
OTTAWA	152	4799	457	1097	412	169	49	33	458	766	80	.229
SPRINGFIELD	153	5061	532	1197	484	189	42	56	527	676	28	.237
	614	40072	5097	9990	4659	1737	324	726	4835	5043	361	.249

1952
COME FROM BEHIND

In the nearly fifty-year history of the Junior World Series between the International League and the American Association, 20 teams have, at some point, been on the lower end of a three-game-to-one advantage. Of these 20 teams trailing three to one, only three have come from behind to win the series. The first was St. Paul of the American Association, which came back against Baltimore in 1924. The second was Newark, which dug itself out of a three-games-to-naught hole where it had been placed by Columbus in 1937. The third team was Rochester, whose victory happened after the 1952 season.

In the 1952 International League season, Montreal retained its title, winning its second in a row. Syracuse finished second, while Rochester and Toronto nabbed the final two playoff spots. Buffalo, Baltimore, Ottawa, and Springfield ended fifth through eighth. Buffalo's Frank Carswell won two portions of the batters' triple crown as he copped the batting title (.344) and slugged the most home runs (30). However, Carswell fell a dozen runs batted in behind Ed Stevens of Toronto, who netted a league-best 113. Pitchers Robert Keegan of Syracuse, Harry Markell of Toronto, and Ottawa's Marion Fricano finished with the most wins (20), lowest earned run average (2.26), and highest strikeout total (120), respectively.

The International League playoffs saw Montreal edge fourth-place Toronto four games to three. At the same time, third-place Rochester stuffed the Syracuse Chiefs four games to zip. The Red Wings then proceeded to knock off the pennant winners four games to two to reach the Junior World Series.

Rochester's opponents in the series were the Kansas City Blues, the American Association's second-place team in 1952. In the opening trio of games played in Kansas City, the hometown Blues won the first and third games 5–2 and 6–2 sandwiched around a 5–3 loss in game two. When the series resumed in Rochester, Kansas City walloped the Red Wings 9–0 in a five-inning game. Trailing three games to one, with their backs firmly against the wall, Rochester struck back with a 10–5 pasting of the Blues in the fifth game. The Red Wings doubled Kansas City again as they evened the series with an 8–4 win. Riding high, Rochester finished off the Association champions 6–4 in the deciding seventh game to capture the Junior World Series four games to three.

The Junior World Series was played intermittently fifteen more times up through the 1980s. In that time, no other team on either side was able to crawl out of a three-games-to-one pit. Rochester's stunning comeback in 1952 remains the last time a team pulled an improbable victory out of near-certain defeat.

MONTREAL Royals

1st 95-56 .629 Walt Alston

BATTERS	POS-GAMES	GP	AB	R	H	BI	2B	3B	HR	BB	SO	SB	BA
Joseph Lutz	1B95	97	339	56	96	73	13	1	14	62	48	1	.283
Jim Gilliam	2B120,OF36,3B4	151	561	111	169	112	39	9	9	100	18	18	.301
James Pendleton	SS151	151	595	87	173	92	24	14	11	31	79	14	.294
Don Hoak	3B143	144	547	109	160	70	32	15	6	81	58	14	.294
Carmen Mauro	OF138	140	529	107	173	61	24	11	11	62	76	12	.327
Walt Moryn	OF102,1B13	114	402	71	111	70	13	4	16	54	50	3	.276
Frank Marchio	OF95	104	335	43	103	52	17	1	1	31	44	2	.307
Charles Thompson	C109,1B,OF	115	416	62	126	60	28	6	5	34	19	7	.303
Walt Fiala	1B49,2B40,OF1	107	320	35	90	34	14	2	0	47	22	0	.281
Don Thompson	OF67	71	249	42	86	58	9	5	4	32	17	11	.346
Al Ronning	C53,OF7,1B1	70	187	17	47	17	6	0	0	21	9	0	.251
James Hughes	P45	46	22	1	3	0	0	0	0	0	2	0	.136
Art Fabbro	P38	39	18	6	3	2	1	0	0	5	3	0	.167
Ed Roebuck	P28	37	69	11	24	17	6	1	1	5	6	0	.348
Gilbert Mills	P30	36	56	7	8	4	1	0	0	7	16	0	.143
Tom Lasorda	P33	35	59	9	8	7	1	0	0	4	13	1	.136
John Simmons	OF22	26	73	10	15	6	2	0	0	7	6	1	.205
Mal Mallette	P26	26	53	5	8	5	1	1	0	5	15	0	.151
Robert Alexander	P26	26	46	2	6	4	0	0	0	3	17	0	.130
James Romano	P26	26	27	7	6	4	1	0	0	4	9	0	.222
John Podres	P24	25	30	4	7	5	2	0	0	2	1	0	.233
Hampton Coleman	P23	23	57	6	12	2	1	0	0	2	16	0	.211
Dan Bankhead	P5,OF	12	9	2	1	0	0	0	0	3	2	0	.111
Gino Cimoli	OF	6	19	3	7	2	1	0	0			0	.368
Lamar Bridges	3B	5	19	2	7	3	1	0	0			0	.368
Jack Lindsay	PH	3	3	0	0	0	0	0	0			0	.000
Glenn Nelson	1B	2	3	0	1	1	0	0	0			0	.333

PITCHERS		W	L	PCT	G	GS	CG	SH	IP	H	BB	SO	ERA
Tom Lasorda		14	5	.737	33	27	12	5	182	156	93	77	3.66
Mal Mallette		13	2	.867	26	22	9	2	145	156	54	63	3.60
Ed Roebuck		12	8	.600	28	18	11	2	165	139	58	62	2.29
Gilbert Mills		11	6	.647	30	15	3	0	161	142	72	84	2.96
Hampton Coleman		10	5	.667	23	20	8	2	138	123	60	65	3.45
Art Fabbro		9	5	.643	38	5	1	0	98	81	45	46	2.94
James Hughes		9	7	.563	45	0	0	0	95	59	52	67	2.84
Robert Alexander		8	7	.533	26	20	6	1	139	140	77	55	4.34
John Podres		5	5	.500	24	13	5	0	88	76	39	47	3.27
James Romano		4	5	.444	26	10	2	0	82	85	44	46	5.81
Dan Bankhead		0	1	.000	5	1	0	0	13	14	11	7	6.92

SYRACUSE Chiefs

2nd 88-66 .571 -8.5 Bruno Betzel

BATTERS	POS-GAMES	GP	AB	R	H	BI	2B	3B	HR	BB	SO	SB	BA
Fenton Mole	1B128	130	415	64	91	62	21	2	22	83	75	2	.219
Ben Zientara	2B145	146	528	55	125	50	22	3	2	64	30	2	.237
Claude Corbitt	SS125	130	467	59	110	23	10	4	1	57	21	3	.236
Loren Babe	3B125,2B5	130	498	67	152	73	19	6	11	61	25	5	.305
Carden Gillenwater	OF121	135	407	56	88	42	12	2	8	78	68	4	.216
Henry Workman	OF110,1B26	135	465	73	117	69	19	4	21	70	22	11	.252
John Blatnik	OF					(see multi-team players)							
William Drescher	C85	97	302	22	65	37	6	0	5	38	21	1	.215
John Welaj	OF81,3B5	101	310	37	77	43	17	1	7	32	25	7	.248
Robert Keegan	P35	39	104	6	24	7	3	0	0	3	7	0	.231
Thomas Upton	SS32,2B1	38	101	9	21	11	4	0	1	11	16	2	.208
Vince Plumbo	C34	36	63	6	15	3	4	0	0	17	13	0	.161
Arnold Landeck	P30	35	49	9	6	2	0	0	0	5	4	0	.122
Myron Hayworth	C27	31	78	2	19	15	1	1	0	4	8	0	.244
John Griffore	P31	31	62	5	12	5	1	1	0	5	11	0	.194
Robert O'Neal	C25	30	77	8	12	9	2	0	1	7	10	0	.156
Art Hartley	P30	30	56	5	8	3	0	0	0	6	16	0	.143
John Robinson	P30	30	24	1	3	0	0	0	0	0	7	0	.125
Alva Holloman	P26	26	61	6	10	3	0	0	0	4	20	0	.164
Andrew Carey	3B24	24	94	8	24	11	4	2	2	13	12	0	.255
William Woop	P20	20	20	0	4	0	0	0	0	5	7	0	.200
Charles Eisenmann	P19	19	6	1	2	0	0	0	0	0	0	0	.333
Charles Weathers		15	39	1	7	1	2	0	0	4	3	0	.179
Al Pilarcik	OF14	14	52	7	14	8	1	1	1	1	3	0	.269
Charles Bell	SS,2B	13	29	4	5	6	1	0	1	2	9	0	.172

SYRACUSE (cont.)
Chiefs

BATTERS	POS-GAMES	GP	AB	R	H	BI	2B	3B	HR	BB	SO	SB	BA
Jack Cerin	OF	12	27	3	7	0	2	0	0	3	3	0	.259
Frank Drews	3B,2B	11	7	2	3	4	1	0	1	4	2	0	.429
Robert Brady	C	5	10	2	1	1	0	0	0			0	.100
William Houtz	P3	3	3	0	1	0	1	0	0			0	.333

PITCHERS		W	L	PCT	G	GS	CG	SH	IP	H	BB	SO	ERA
Robert Keegan		20	11	.645	35	35	27	7	273	245	85	111	2.64
Alva Holloman		16	7	.696	26	19	12	3	183	123	96	75	2.51
John Griffore		12	10	.545	31	26	13	3	185	184	47	54	3.65
Arnold Landeck		11	9	.550	30	20	9	4	166	170	42	49	2.55
Art Hartley		10	11	.476	39	23	10	1	167	157	42	43	2.86
Joe Page		2	0	1.000	3	3	1	0	16	17	11	9	9.00
Paul Eisenmann		2	2	.500	19	0	0	0	25	32	20	13	5.40
John Robinson		2	4	.333	30	5	0	0	85	73	36	24	4.34
William Woop		2	6	.250	20	11	3	0	76	90	47	32	5.21
Carmine Melignano		1	1	.500	8	1	0	0	20	27	10	10	6.75
William Houtz		0	0	----	3	0	0	0	8	7	5	2	1.13

ROCHESTER   3rd   80-74   .519   -16.5   Harry Walker
Red Wings

BATTERS	POS-GAMES	GP	AB	R	H	BI	2B	3B	HR	BB	SO	SB	BA
Steve Bilko	1B78	82	286	55	92	55	22	5	12	36	40	0	.322
Louis Ortiz	2B138	138	468	60	123	73	19	5	9	63	48	2	.263
Fred McAlister	SS75,2B1	78	235	28	54	21	12	2	3	12	31	3	.230
Don Richmond	3B108,OF39	145	578	91	190	62	40	8	6	62	26	3	.329
Eldon Repulski	OF140	142	521	82	154	65	24	7	13	44	43	10	.296
Lawrence Ciaffone	OF102	109	401	39	112	62	17	4	4	12	17	1	.279
Harry Walker	OF99,1B1,2B1	115	367	80	134	36	22	7	4	72	21	3	.365
John Bucha	C142	144	500	75	142	72	25	8	6	63	47	4	.284
Ray Jablonski	SS63,3B54,1B27,2B15	152	592	82	177	103	27	10	18	43	53	0	.299
Ellis Deal	P29,OF7	85	130	21	36	22	7	0	5	18	16	0	.277
Ed Mickelson	1B52	60	197	19	53	27	9	3	2	13	24	1	.269
John Crimian	P56	56	18	0	2	0	0	0	0	1	0	0	.111
Fred Hahn	P38	38	42	4	5	3	0	0	0	1	13	0	.119
Fred Martin	P36	36	67	3	10	1	1	0	0	3	7	0	.149
Russ Derry	OF26	35	78	7	11	5	1	1	1	20	14	0	.141
Louis Kahn	OF24	34	77	4	21	8	4	0	0	5	11	1	.273
John Fasholz	P31	31	76	10	16	7	1	1	0	4	28	0	.211
Jack Collum	P27	30	54	7	11	6	2	0	2	12	2	0	.204
George Condrick	P29	29	46	7	7	4	0	0	0	3	6	0	.152
Robert Tiefenauer	P27	28	21	3	3	0	0	0	0	1	5	0	.143
Walt Lammers	SS22,3B	22	87	13	25	11	3	1	1	8	9	0	.287
Robert Habenicht	P21	21	11	1	3	1	2	0	0	2	4	0	.273
Charles Kress	1B11,OF10	20	62	5	14	6	0	1	0	7	4	2	.226
Richard Bokelmann	P11	11	0	0	0	0	0	0	0	0	0	0	----
Walt Fassler	SS,2B	10	40	5	7	2	0	0	0	3	6	0	.175
Dan Lynch	SS	10	25	2	7	1	0	0	0	1	1	0	.280
Willard Schmidt	P10	10	8	0	2	1	0	0	0	0	1	0	.250
Ron Curnan	C	6	7	0	1	1	1	0	0			0	.143
Don Swartz	P4	4	1	0	1	0	0	0	0			0	1.000
Jim Dickey	PH	2	1	1	0	0	0	0	0			0	.000

PITCHERS		W	L	PCT	G	GS	CG	SH	IP	H	BB	SO	ERA
John Fasholz		15	8	.652	31	25	11	3	196	199	56	63	3.67
Ellis Deal		14	9	.609	29	26	13	2	200	194	80	91	3.56
George Condrick		10	9	.526	29	20	9	1	148	152	44	55	3.35
Jack Collum		9	10	.474	27	21	13	1	167	160	75	83	3.77
John Crimian		8	3	.727	56	0	0	0	90	72	37	48	2.10
Fred Martin		8	14	.364	36	24	6	0	195	244	56	69	4.25
Robert Tiefanauer		5	4	.556	27	6	2	0	74	79	27	31	4.26
Fred Hahn		5	9	.357	38	17	4	2	134	126	69	79	3.76
Elroy Joyce		2	0	1.000	6	2	1	0	26	26	12	14	3.47
Robert Habenicht		2	1	.667	21	6	0	0	49	63	42	28	5.88
Richard Bokelmann		1	1	.500	11	0	0	0	14	17	16	6	5.78
Willard Schmidt		1	1	.500	10	4	1	0	22	26	12	16	6.96
Don Swartz		0	1	.000	4	1	0	0	7	11	6	3	13.29
Ed Ludwig		0	1	.000	4	0	0	0	4	4	1	6	4.50
Dennis Reeder		0	1	.000	1	1	0	0	2	5	2	1	13.50
Dan Lewandowski		0	2	.000	5	2	0	0	16	17	5	7	6.75

TORONTO   4th   78-76   .506   -18.5   Joseph Becker
Maple Leafs

BATTERS	POS-GAMES	GP	AB	R	H	BI	2B	3B	HR	BB	SO	SB	BA
Ed Stevens	1B155	155	554	87	154	113	31	7	26	75	52	4	.278
Pete Pavlick	2B80	81	291	36	73	22	12	1	3	24	24	6	.251
William Jennings	SS114,2B2	118	354	48	71	41	8	2	6	55	63	3	.201
Billy DeMars	3B90,SS46,2B13	141	524	70	148	45	23	6	4	47	15	10	.282
Lewis Morton	OF146	148	514	84	146	59	17	5	17	73	38	11	.284
Grover Bowers	OF80,3B10,2B3	94	330	38	79	34	13	0	5	46	27	3	.240
Marv Rickert	OF	(see multi-team players)											
Ferrell Anderson	C117	123	385	48	115	68	28	0	11	36	12	1	.299
Mike Goliat	3B49,2B43,OF15,SS8	113	369	53	107	52	17	5	8	49	48	4	.290
Charles White	C26,3B12	72	123	7	32	13	9	0	2	15	12	0	.260
Frank Colman	OF11,1B3	66	86	9	25	10	5	0	1	7	10	0	.291
Ray Shore	P64	64	19	2	5	3	0	0	0	1	1	0	.263
Wilmer Fields	OF46	51	165	24	48	13	10	1	2	15	17	2	.291
Harry Markell	P40	45	68	10	13	9	1	0	0	4	10	0	.191
Vic Lombardi	P29	41	49	10	13	8	1	1	1	7	2	0	.265
John Hetki	P30	38	81	9	20	10	2	1	1	4	5	0	.247
Hal Hudson	P35	38	54	7	9	0	0	0	0	4	7	0	.167
Neill Sheridan	OF22	34	73	10	16	10	6	1	1	8	15	3	.219
Gerald Fahr	P33	33	48	3	6	0	2	0	0	5	16	0	.125
Harold Keller	C26	28	79	9	27	12	6	2	1	12	12	1	.342
Paul Lehner	OF26	27	85	9	21	3	5	0	1	10	9	1	.247
Robert DelGreco	OF21	27	61	14	19	12	5	3	0	17	4	2	.311
Russ Bauers	P24	24	43	2	7	4	0	0	0	0	2	0	.154
Robert Rhawn	2B11,3B6	22	81	11	24	14	2	1	2	4	4	0	.296
Jose Bracho	P17	17	6	0	1	0	0	0	0	1	3	0	.167
Phil Haugstad	P15	15	13	1	2	0	0	0	0	0	2	0	.154
Robert Balcena	OF14	14	50	13	16	3	3	2	0	9	7	1	.320
James Mangan	C	13	29	3	5	5	1	1	0	3	6	0	.172
Charles Grant	2B11	11	41	7	9	8	1	1	2	6	8	0	.220
Allen Van Alstyne	OF10	11	34	4	8	1	0	1	0	1	7	0	.235
Harry Fisher	P5,OF	9	7	1	2	0	0	0	0	0			.286

PITCHERS		W	L	PCT	G	GS	CG	SH	IP	H	BB	SO	ERA
Harry Markell		14	8	.636	40	22	7	1	191	178	74	120	3.49
John Hetki		13	7	.650	30	26	14	2	195	164	54	97	2.91
Hal Hudson		11	8	.579	35	24	8	1	155	136	62	80	3.66
Vic Lombardi		10	8	.556	29	23	4	1	161	171	60	68	3.19
Gerald Fahr		10	13	.435	33	23	10	2	171	184	31	42	3.16
Russ Bauers		9	7	.563	24	19	6	1	128	133	43	60	4.43
Ray Shore		5	7	.417	64	1	0	0	100	87	57	74	2.43
Stubby Overmire		3	2	.600	9	2	1	0	24	22	11	11	4.50
Irv Medlinger		2	5	.286	7	6	2	1	33	30	18	27	3.55
Harry Fisher		0	1	.000	5	3	0	0	12	11	15	6	8.25
Phil Haugstad		0	6	.000	15	4	0	0	41	50	25	23	8.12
Jose Bracho		0	0	----	17	0	0	0	37	46	22	21	4.62
Leon Faulk		0	0	----	3	0	0	0	3	7	4	0	6.00
Frank Barnes		0	0	----	1	0	0	0	2	1	0	4	0.00
Charles Barrett		0	0	----	1	0	0	0	1	3	0	0	9.00
William Tanner		0	0	----	1	0	0	0	1	2	0	0	9.00

BUFFALO   5th   71-83   .461   -25.5   John Tighe -
Bisons   Schoolboy Rowe

BATTERS	POS-GAMES	GP	AB	R	H	BI	2B	3B	HR	BB	SO	SB	BA
Harvey Zernia	1B107	108	406	55	110	46	15	3	7	39	40	4	.271
Al Federoff	2B87,SS6	91	365	55	104	29	14	5	0	35	21	8	.285
Harold Daugherty	SS97,3B2	106	351	48	79	33	16	3	6	30	51	5	.225
David Jaska	3B70,SS2	76	261	25	60	15	13	0	2	20	17	5	.230
Frank Carswell	OF135	141	511	88	176	101	34	0	30	39	34	4	**.344**
Don Lund	OF123,1B11	138	441	83	133	80	32	3	16	70	35	6	.302
John Phillips	OF116,3B2	118	454	73	132	49	19	2	14	30	35	14	.291
Lawrence Ciesielski	C93,1B2	102	292	25	77	32	12	0	4	53	39	2	.264
Robert Mavis	3B40,2B26	84	241	20	58	29	7	1	5	26	11	3	.241
Russ Sullivan	OF59,1B1	72	208	28	55	38	15	4	6	44	14	0	.265
William Tuttle	SS48,OF16,3B5	65	236	30	69	24	7	5	3	11	19	2	.292
George Lerchen	OF44	63	159	21	34	24	7	3	4	23	40	0	.214
Joseph Erautt	C51	54	177	22	50	22	11	0	2	16	16	0	.282
Milt Jordan	P50	51	52	7	6	5	1	1	1	2	21	0	.115
Ralph Poole	P48	48	14	0	2	0	0	0	0	1	7	0	.143
Frank Bolling	2B44	44	164	18	40	14	9	1	1	15	24	1	.244

BUFFALO (cont.)
Bisons

BATTERS	POS-GAMES	GP	AB	R	H	BI	2B	3B	HR	BB	SO	SB	BA
Ed Kazak	3B37	38	146	26	146	16	5	0	6	16	9	0	.315
Al Yaylian	P28	38	71	10	12	11	1	0	2	10	15	0	.169
Richard Marlowe	P35	36	51	1	11	2	2	0	0	0	13	0	.216
Werner Birrer	P33	34	52	5	9	9	1	0	2	3	20	0	.173
Hank Borowy	P30	30	69	2	10	6	1	1	0	4	27	0	.145
Ed Mordarski	C26	30	59	6	10	8	2	0	0	11	15	0	.169
Ralph Atkins	1B27	27	85	14	21	6	2	0	2	23	14	2	.247
Wayne McLeland	P26	26	48	3	7	3	0	0	0	1	25	0	.146
Paul Foytack	P21	21	31	3	5	2	2	0	0	2	4	1	.161
Ken Johnson	P7,OF1	16	25	3	7	8	2	1	0	1	4	1	.280
Bennie Taylor	1B11	14	42	5	11	7	3	1	2	7	4	0	.262
William Humphrey	OF	13	29	3	5	3	1	1	0	1	1	1	.172
George Bullard	SS	10	16	3	4	1	1	0	0	2	5	0	.250
Alex Garbowski	SS	8	17	0	2	0	1	0	0			0	.118
Alex DeLaGarza	SS,2B	7	4	1	0	0	0	0	0			0	.000
Jack Baumgartner	PH	1	1	0	0	0	0	0	0			0	.000

PITCHERS		W	L	PCT	G	GS	CG	SH	IP	H	BB	SO	ERA
Milt Jordan		12	9	.571	50	8	6	1	169	187	52	59	3.46
Al Yaylian		12	11	.522	28	26	15	1	180	193	61	75	3.95
Hank Borowy		10	12	.455	30	28	10	1	189	227	61	56	4.29
Richard Marlowe		10	10	.500	35	17	7	2	148	140	55	56	4.01
Werner Birrer		9	10	.474	33	18	8	0	152	171	45	58	3.91
Wayne McLeland		6	11	.353	26	18	5	1	142	144	45	51	4.25
Paul Foytack		4	5	.444	21	14	2	0	94	110	66	65	5.07
Ken Johnson		3	2	.600	7	7	3	1	40	32	34	38	3.37
Dick Littlefield		1	1	.500	3	3	1	0	20	26	6	9	5.40
Ralph Poole		0	5	.000	48	3	1	0	82	92	39	25	4.06
Alex McNielance		0	0	----	4	0	0	0	9	13	3	3	7.00
John Weiss		0	0	----	2	0	0	0	1	0	0	1	0.00

BALTIMORE   6th   70-84   .455   -26.5   Don Heffner
Orioles

BATTERS	POS-GAMES	GP	AB	R	H	BI	2B	3B	HR	BB	SO	SB	BA
Vernal Jones	1B109,OF3,2B1	117	378	44	83	31	12	2	4	22	14	2	.220
Al Cihocki	2B83,3B18	115	376	34	96	32	13	2	6	19	27	2	.255
John Kerr	SS72,3B2	80	240	23	60	11	7	3	0	33	30	0	.250
Russ Kerns	3B107,OF12,1B3	127	433	52	109	59	9	2	14	51	40	4	.252
Roy Weatherly	OF141	143	547	84	155	73	22	6	26	42	48	2	.283
Gerard Scala	OF136	141	486	61	121	44	20	9	1	76	41	6	.249
Clyde Schell	OF85	96	297	28	69	28	7	5	3	31	18	2	.232
Al Lakeman	C103	108	338	37	79	42	14	2	8	37	48	0	.234
Damon Phillips	SS64,3B32,2B6,1B4	115	352	33	95	42	11	0	5	27	12	1	.270
Marv Rackley	OF61	66	225	25	62	26	5	4	1	19	18	1	.276
Martin Tabacheck	C60	62	143	13	27	10	5	0	1	14	8	0	.189
Roy Hartsfield	2B54	55	219	26	49	17	5	1	2	19	25	4	.224
George Byam	1B35	51	132	13	35	15	6	0	2	12	11	0	.265
John Thompson	P39	47	79	7	9	5	2	1	0	2	23	0	.114
Richard Starr	P44	44	64	7	12	3	2	0	1	7	16	0	.188
Syl Donnelly	P44	44	23	2	5	2	0	1	0	0	2	0	.217
Paul Stuffel	P37	43	65	6	11	5	2	1	0	3	26	0	.169
Kent Peterson	P39	39	46	1	6	3	0	0	0	2	16	0	.130
Richard Young	2B15,3B1	34	78	10	20	4	5	0	0	8	8	2	.256
Robert Miller	P32	33	60	6	14	7	1	2	2	2	15	0	.233
James Atkins	P20	23	36	3	7	1	1	0	0	7	6	0	.194
Sam Meeks	SS11,3B	18	47	4	9	4	3	0	0	6	6	0	.191
Ken Trinkle	P18	18	7	1	0	0	0	0	0	1	4	0	.000
James Command	OF13	17	57	8	14	5	3	0	2	4	9	0	.246
Ed Oswald	C14	15	45	8	12	6	4	0	1	1	4	0	.267
Ted Kazanski	SS11	12	35	5	9	4	1	1	0	9	3	1	.257
Dwain Sloat	P12	12	6	1	0	0	0	0	0	2	3	0	.000
Louis Possehl	P11	12	5	1	0	0	0	0	0	0	1	0	.000
Millard Howell	P5	11	8	0	1	1	0	0	0	3	2	0	.125
Fred Taylor	1B	9	27	1	6	2	0	1	0			0	.222
Bob Greenwood	P7	7	5	1	2	3	0	0	1			0	.400
Tom Casagrande	P2	2	1	0	1	0	0	0	0			0	1.000

BALTIMORE (cont.)
Orioles

PITCHERS	W	L	PCT	G	GS	CG	SH	IP	H	BB	SO	ERA
John Thompson	13	14	.481	39	28	11	2	231	179	80	119	2.49
Robert Miller	12	9	.571	32	22	12	1	184	172	44	68	2.35
Paul Stuffel	11	10	.524	37	29	5	0	182	175	127	116	4.50
Richard Starr	10	10	.500	44	23	5	1	191	184	66	96	3.63
James Atkins	9	7	.563	20	17	4	1	110	107	55	48	4.34
Kent Peterson	8	12	.400	39	18	6	2	156	136	52	84	3.12
Syl Donnelly	5	11	.313	44	4	1	1	96	76	46	55	2.62
Jim Barnhardt	1	0	1.000	2	0	0	0	9	10	6	3	2.00
Bob Greenwood	1	3	.250	7	3	1	0	20	27	15	14	6.30
David Cyrus	0	1	.000	6	0	0	0	4	9	4	2	15.75
John Walz	0	1	.000	2	1	0	0	6	11	2	1	12.00
Louis Possehl	0	3	.000	11	3	0	0	23	29	11	10	6.26
Millard Howell	0	3	.000	5	3	0	0	13	26	9	3	11.08
Ken Trinkle	0	0	----	18	1	0	0	42	46	16	10	4.50
Dwain Sloat	0	0	----	12	0	0	0	26	24	26	11	5.54
Tom Casagrande	0	0	----	2	2	0	0	4	9	7	2	11.25
Leo Cristante	0	0	----	1	0	0	0	5	8	0	2	7.20
John Brittin	0	0	----	1	0	0	0	2	5	3	1	27.00

OTTAWA   7th   65-85   .433   -29.5   Frank Skaff
Athletics

BATTERS	POS-GAMES	GP	AB	R	H	BI	2B	3B	HR	BB	SO	SB	BA
Louis Limmer	1B147	148	540	75	140	87	17	7	23	61	34	12	.259
George Moskovich	2B137	138	473	50	116	44	20	1	7	53	66	4	.245
Jack Littrell	SS126	126	457	58	114	55	27	2	7	50	85	2	.249
Stan Jok	3B102,OF41,1B1	141	506	60	127	69	25	9	10	53	57	5	.251
Thomas Kirk	OF131	137	456	41	108	44	14	4	10	41	72	5	.237
John Metkovich	OF125	126	472	61	112	54	19	3	12	28	76	23	.237
Harvey Gentry	OF120	120	460	63	122	33	18	6	4	60	55	15	.265
Neal Watlington	C114	123	399	44	101	37	12	6	4	43	20	5	.253
John Conway	3B30,SS25,2B	69	221	26	43	20	10	2	3	19	30	1	.195
Al Rubeling	3B24,1B6,2B3	54	124	11	33	16	3	2	0	7	6	0	.266
Joseph Murray	P34	37	35	0	6	0	2	0	0	1	7	0	.171
Russ Swingle	P35	35	33	3	4	1	0	0	0	1	0	0	.121
Marion Fricano	P30	32	62	7	12	3	1	0	0	8	24	1	.194
Vince Gohl	P28	29	60	7	14	4	1	2	0	3	14	0	.233
Robert Wellman	OF27	28	98	9	25	16	11	1	0	5	7	1	.255
Henry Foiles	C25	28	87	16	19	13	1	2	1	9	13	4	.218
Charles Bishop	P27	27	68	7	8	9	3	0	1	3	28	0	.118
Ed Burtschy	P27	27	36	2	8	5	2	0	0	0	10	0	.224
Coaker Triplett	PH	24	29	3	5	4	1	1	0	5	3	0	.172
Jean Roy	P22	23	48	3	5	1	0	0	0	1	3	0	.104
James Brown	C16	19	37	4	6	2	1	0	0	4	5	0	.162
Robert Betz	OF12	16	41	6	7	2	1	1	0	4	8	0	.171
Joseph Coleman	P16	16	28	3	5	0	1	0	0	1	10	0	.179
Robert Gardner	2B,3B,SS	15	45	3	12	4	1	0	0	6	6	0	.267
Walt Novick	C	7	8	0	2	0	0	0	0			0	.250
William Poole	C1	1	4	0	0	0	0	0	0			0	.000

PITCHERS	W	L	PCT	G	GS	CG	SH	IP	H	BB	SO	ERA
Marion Fricano	17	8	.680	30	23	15	2	191	163	64	78	2.26
Charles Bishop	12	10	.545	27	25	13	4	193	170	84	116	3.64
Vince Gohl	9	10	.474	28	22	14	1	181	156	59	52	3.28
Joseph Murray	5	9	.357	34	10	3	0	99	97	39	32	4.46
Russ Swingle	4	5	.444	35	6	1	0	111	111	24	31	3.89
Jean Roy	4	11	.267	21	17	6	0	131	124	67	40	3.99
Ed Burtschy	3	5	.375	27	10	1	0	93	95	67	43	4.45
Joseph Coleman	2	7	.222	16	13	3	0	76	56	67	32	3.32
William Hockenbury	1	0	1.000	6	1	0	0	20	19	13	4	2.70
Ed Hrabczak	1	4	.200	6	5	2	0	29	38	14	10	6.21
Tex Hoyle	0	1	.000	7	3	1	0	18	13	15	8	3.00
John Kume	0	2	.000	5	3	0	0	16	23	17	8	10.13
Frank Fanovich	0	2	.000	3	2	0	0	5	6	9	4	14.40
Harry Desert	0	0	----	4	0	0	0	6	6	2	4	1.50
Clarence Zeiser	0	0	----	1	0	0	0	2	4	1	0	4.50

SPRINGFIELD
Cubs

8th   65-88   .425   -31   William Kelly

BATTERS	POS-GAMES	GP	AB	R	H	BI	2B	3B	HR	BB	SO	SB	BA
Mike Rocco	1B88	89	295	30	76	38	11	4	4	49	31	2	.258
Emil Verban	2B136	138	531	45	127	36	20	7	1	8	20	2	.239
Chris Kitsos	SS111,2B15	131	404	59	101	30	21	2	1	103	61	5	.250
Robert Ludwig	3B102,2B9,SS1	114	382	40	96	37	16	3	3	41	35	1	.251
John Wallaesa	OF135,1B12	149	485	61	112	66	21	4	14	92	91	3	.231
Ted Lotz	OF127	132	394	42	84	39	19	5	8	45	59	1	.213
Glenn McQuillen	OF85	85	299	25	70	40	8	5	5	27	26	2	.234
Nelson Burbrink	C92,3B10	112	320	37	91	26	19	1	0	58	22	0	.284
Eugene Hooks	3B51,SS14	67	226	31	57	15	10	1	2	23	27	8	.252
William Higdon	OF61	65	214	36	63	31	17	4	7	17	34	1	.294
Frank LaManna	P16,OF1	58	61	5	15	10	1	0	0	8	14	0	.246
Anthony Jacobs	P53	53	27	2	6	0	0	1	0	0	4	0	.222
Ralph Rowe	OF46	50	128	9	22	14	1	2	1	20	11	0	.172
Alan Ihde	P41	48	46	5	9	1	1	0	0	4	11	0	.196
Ron George	1B38	40	136	13	31	15	5	0	0	13	28	1	.228
Harold Meek	C18,1B14	38	100	9	20	6	2	1	0	5	13	0	.200
William Hardin	SS32	37	126	8	23	2	1	2	0	4	6	0	.183
Thomas Neill	OF31	36	119	11	26	12	6	1	0	12	5	0	.218
Harry Chiti	C26	35	94	7	27	11	2	0	1	5	3	0	.287
William Padgett	P31	31	72	5	12	5	4	0	0	6	27	0	.167
Luvern Fear	P23	27	48	3	8	3	1	0	0	1	9	0	.167
Thomas Simpson	P27	27	37	1	8	2	2	0	0	1	8	0	.216
John Pramesa	C21	26	89	7	29	11	5	0	1	3	4	0	.326
Herm Besse	P24	24	38	1	3	2	0	0	0	2	7	0	.079
Alfred Lary	P16	21	21	2	6	2	1	0	0	2	3	0	.286
Wes Carr	P19	19	32	2	10	4	2	0	0	1	4	0	.313
John Adkins	P19	19	32	1	4	1	0	0	0	1	11	0	.125
Fred Richards	1B	15	38	1	5	2	0	0	0	1	1	0	.132
Walt Dubiel	P8	12	13	1	3	1	0	0	0	1	5	0	.231
Don Vike	P12	12	4	0	1	0	0	0	0	0	1	0	.250
Ned Folmar	1B,OF	11	17	3	3	0	1	0	0	4	4	0	.176
Henry Nasternak	SS	8	20	5	3	2	0	1	0			0	.150
William Fanning	C	3	5	0	0	0	0	0	0	0		0	.000

PITCHERS		W	L	PCT	G	GS	CG	SH	IP	H	BB	SO	ERA
William Padgett		11	13	.458	31	29	13	1	214	243	60	83	3.74
John Adkins		9	4	.692	19	17	6	3	109	101	37	40	2.81
Herm Besse		8	13	.381	24	22	8	2	149	149	59	53	3.02
Wes Carr		7	6	.538	19	13	6	1	95	105	47	27	4.92
Alan Ihde		7	7	.500	41	17	5	1	147	143	78	61	4.35
Anthony Jacobs		7	11	.389	53	2	0	0	109	111	57	40	3.47
Luvern Fear		6	8	.429	23	19	7	4	137	127	52	42	2.96
Thomas Simpson		3	11	.214	27	15	4	0	120	103	38	40	3.67
Alfred Lary		2	3	.400	16	9	2	0	59	74	38	28	4.88
Frank LaManna		2	3	.400	16	0	0	0	44	58	21	13	5.32
Don Vike		1	0	1.000	12	1	1	1	30	26	14	14	5.40
Frank Marino		1	2	.333	9	3	1	0	23	33	7	9	4.30
Walt Dubiel		0	5	.000	8	7	3	0	40	48	15	7	5.85
Darius Hillman		0	0	----	2	0	0	0	5	4	4	1	3.60

MULTI-TEAM PLAYERS

BATTERS	POS-GAMES	TEAMS	GP	AB	R	H	BI	2B	3B	HR	BB	SO	SB	BA
Marv Rickert	OF128,1B17	BA37-TO111	148	477	61	125	68	17	4	13	69	66	8	.262
John Blatnik	OF127,1B1	RO13-SY119	132	471	70	129	66	24	2	17	55	93	4	.274
Percy Riggan	OF107,C2,2B1	SY27-RO95	122	365	54	96	39	12	3	13	35	57	6	.263
Lynn Lovenguth	P31,OF1	BU19-SY27	46	66	9	16	4	1	0	0	12	10	0	.242
Andrew Dobernic	P36	SP17-TO19	36	9	0	0	0	0	0	0	0	3	0	.000
William George	P34	BA2-OT33	35	35	3	6	3	1	0	0	4	7	0	.171
Aaron Silverman	P22	TO8-SY14	22	13	1	2	0	0	0	0	0	2	0	.154
Eugene Costello	P18	SY9-BU9	18	7	0	0	0	0	0	0	1	4	0	.000
Gord Mueller	P15	OT7-BA8	15	3	0	1	0	0	0	0	0	1	0	.333

PITCHERS		TEAMS	W	L	PCT	G	GS	CG	SH	IP	H	BB	SO	ERA
Lynn Lovenguth		BU15-SY16	12	10	.545	31	21	9	4	166	132	108	65	3.58
William George		BA2-OT32	6	11	.353	34	10	3	1	115	116	55	55	2.41
Aaron Silverman		TO8-SY14	2	4	.333	22	3	0	0	53	58	29	17	4.58
Gord Mueller		OT7-BA8	1	0	1.000	15	0	0	0	20	21	28	4	8.55
Eugene Costello		SY9-BU9	1	1	.500	18	2	0	0	42	45	41	20	6.86
Andrew Dobernic		SP17-TO19	1	3	.250	36	0	0	0	56	58	30	24	4.00

TEAM BATTING

TEAMS	GP	AB	R	H	BI	2B	3B	HR	BB	SO	SB	BA
MONTREAL	151	5043	**815**	1450	**760**	238	**70**	78	611	552	**85**	**.287**
SYRACUSE	154	4986	609	1181	503	178	29	103	**649**	555	44	.236
ROCHESTER	**155**	**5312**	748	**1494**	689	**253**	66	97	539	542	33	.281
TORONTO	**155**	4985	674	1307	616	221	43	105	587	511	61	.262
BUFFALO	**155**	5115	688	1352	626	238	35	**115**	544	594	59	.264
BALTIMORE	154	4999	564	1220	508	165	45	82	486	502	28	.244
OTTAWA	150	4896	566	1166	526	195	49	81	472	**668**	78	.240
SPRINGFIELD	154	4860	507	1151	463	197	44	48	562	588	26	.236
	614	40196	5171	10321	4691	1685	381	709	4450	4512	414	.257

1953
THE MOVE EAST

The traditional route of major league encroachment in the minors has been from east to west. In the American Association, the first two major league usurpers had made the journey this way: Boston to Milwaukee in 1953, and Philadelphia to Kansas City in 1955. Likewise in the Pacific Coast League: Brooklyn to Los Angeles and New York to San Francisco in 1958. But in the International League, the path of major league migration ran from west to east.

For more than 50 years, the Baltimore Orioles had been one of the strongest members of the International League. Regularly attracting in excess of 300,000 fans, Baltimore was a minor league city waiting for something more. Baltimore cinched its attractiveness to major league interests when the city built a fancy new stadium, quite suitable for a major league tenant.

The St. Louis Browns had, for many years, been searching for a new home. Sharing the St. Louis market with the Cardinals, in dilapidated digs, the Browns sought a move to Los Angeles in 1941. Thwarted by World War II, they tried again in the early 1950s, this time to Milwaukee. Unfortunately for them, their fellow major league owners thought the Boston Braves were a more suitable candidate. Undaunted, the Browns turned their view eastward.

In 1953, the Baltimore Orioles finished a respectable fourth. Ahead of them finished Rochester, Montreal, and Buffalo. Behind them trailed Toronto, Ottawa, Syracuse, and Springfield. Montreal Royal outfielder Sandy Amoros won the batting title (.353), while his teammate Glenn Nelson knocked in the most runs (136). John Wallaesa, splitting time between Springfield and Buffalo, poled the most home runs (36). On the mound, Ottawa's Robert Trice won a league-best 21, while Toronto's Don Johnson had the best earned run average (2.67) and most strikeouts (156).

On September 29, 1953, major league owners voted unanimously to relocate the St. Louis Browns to Baltimore. Key to the deal was the financial backing of several Baltimoreans, as well as the new stadium, which was ready for play. The new club honored its city's storied minor league team by taking its name. The new team would be known as the Baltimore Orioles.

The major leagues had finally moved into International league territory, and from a different angle—west to east. However, the direction the newcomers traveled is not the important issue. Relocation had recently occurred in the New York area (in Newark and Jersey City), but no new major league team had moved in. This was not the case in Baltimore. As a result, this event serves as a dividing line in the International League—a line between the old and the new.

ROCHESTER
Red Wings
1st   97-57   .630   Harry Walker

BATTERS	POS-GAMES	GP	AB	R	H	BI	2B	3B	HR	BB	SO	SB	BA
Charles Kress	1B147	147	520	111	165	121	26	10	25	95	55	9	.317
Louis Ortiz	2B149	149	520	67	155	81	28	3	11	65	60	6	.298
John Huesman	SS63,2B18,3B4	89	226	36	46	25	10	1	5	23	34	0	.249
Don Richmond	3B133,OF6	139	552	101	172	89	33	8	15	41	30	9	.312
Tom Burgess	OF118	122	407	85	141	93	18	6	22	64	60	3	.346
Wally Moon	OF114	1131	387	83	119	61	24	8	12	45	43	14	.307
Ed Mierkowicz	OF114	117	379	56	115	53	16	6	9	46	37	3	.303
Vern Rapp	C81	97	282	35	71	30	15	9	1	19	12	1	.252
Harry Walker	OF91	112	304	59	92	37	11	1	7	64	15	7	.303
Alfred Clark	OF60,1B10,3B10	80	265	38	87	43	13	3	7	19	18	4	.328
Ellis Deal	P41,OF5	80	140	23	39	30	7	2	2	13	14	0	.279
John Crimian	P62	62	22	2	3	0	1	0	0	2	9	0	.136
Les Fusselman	C60	61	173	19	43	25	10	1	5	23	34	0	.249
Walt Lammers	SS49	59	161	14	29	19	5	1	1	23	23	3	.180
Vern Benson	SS48,3B7	49	175	44	53	34	12	3	6	47	26	0	.303
Louis Kahn	C25,3B1	42	79	9	22	5	5	0	0	18	6	1	.278
Robert Tiefenauer	P38	41	27	2	3	0	0	1	0	1	10	0	.111
Dennis Reeder	P33	39	50	7	9	5	2	0	0	2	15	1	.180
George Condrick	P30	30	36	4	7	4	0	0	0	6	8	0	.194
John Fasholz	P23	24	46	5	12	2	3	0	0	4	11	0	.261
Fred Hahn	P23	23	26	1	1	2	0	0	0	3	7	0	.038
Hector Soto	SS19	19	48	5	9	6	0	1	1	7	9	0	.188
Niles Jordan	P17	18	37	3	7	2	1	1	0	4	15	0	.189
Floyd Melliere	P17	17	14	1	2	1	0	0	0	1	5	0	.143
Octavio Rubert	P14	14	31	1	6	3	0	0	0	0	5	0	.194
William Killinger	OF	11	25	2	1	1	0	0	0	2	4	0	.040
Dan Baich	C10	10	27	2	5	2	3	0	0	2	1	0	.185
Robert Hoch	P8	8											.182
Don Spencer	3B,SS	7	14	2	1	1	0	1	0			0	.071
Harry Hoitsma	P6	6											.000
Louis Ciola	P4	4											.000
Floyd Wooldridge	P2	2											.000
Ben Downs	PH	1	1	0	0	0	0	0	0	0		0	.000
Al Papai	P1	1											.000
Ralph Beard	P1	1											.000

PITCHERS	W	L	PCT	G	GS	CG	SH	IP	H	BB	SO	ERA
Ellis Deal	16	9	.640	41	18	9	2	218	214	84	84	3.72
Jack Crimian	13	5	.722	62	1	0	0	104	91	43	52	2.85
George Condrick	11	4	.733	30	18	5	2	123	140	36	52	3.88
Dennis Reeder	10	9	.526	32	26	6	2	148	127	73	72	3.22
John Fasholz	10	6	.625	23	21	6	2	134	144	39	41	3.69
Robert Tiefenauer	9	3	.750	38	2	0	0	105	83	42	50	2.31
Niles Jordan	8	1	.889	17	16	7	3	99	102	28	36	3.55
Octavio Rubert	7	4	.636	14	11	5	1	75	77	24	32	2.40
Fred Hahn	5	6	.455	23	14	4	2	99	90	48	57	3.82
Floyd Wooldridge	2	0	1.000	2				16	10	7	8	2.81
Floyd Melliere	2	4	.333	17	8	1	0	47	55	19	10	4.60
Al Papai	1	0	1.000	1				9	6	2	1	0.00
Robert Hoch	1	1	.500	8				31	35	13	10	4.06
Ralph Beard	0	1	.000	1				6	8	5	1	3.00
Harry Hoitsma	0	3	.000	6				19	20	11	5	5.68
Louis Ciola	0	0	----	4				9	16	7	1	10.00

MONTREAL
Royals
2nd   89-63   .586   -7   Walt Alston

BATTERS	POS-GAMES	GP	AB	R	H	BI	2B	3B	HR	BB	SO	SB	BA
Glenn Nelson	1B154	154	542	117	167	**136**	33	9	34	106	37	2	.308
Roy Hartsfield	2B134	135	538	74	125	46	30	8	3	48	67	5	.232
Humberto Fernandez	SS145	145	519	63	128	34	21	2	2	31	51	9	.247
Don Hoak	3B134	138	509	84	137	48	25	8	6	78	54	13	.269
Sandy Amoros	OF149	150	539	**128**	**190**	100	**40**	11	23	96	63	11	**.353**
Ken Wood	OF81	95	277	36	65	45	12	3	8	33	33	2	.235
Frank Marchio	OF80	103	280	30	78	44	12	4	2	30	33	1	.279
Charles Thompson	C102	109	372	59	109	59	13	5	10	39	17	1	.293
Richard Whitman	OF62	73	240	42	76	32	16	4	7	25	11	1	.317
Ernest Yelen	C57	71	211	19	60	23	12	2	1	21	14	0	.284
Richard Williams	OF60	66	230	28	64	33	12	1	2	13	31	1	.278
Stan Rojek	3B23,2B22,SS17	66	198	24	54	31	9	2	1	16	13	0	.273

MONTREAL (cont.)
Royals

BATTERS	POS-GAMES	GP	AB	R	H	BI	2B	3B	HR	BB	SO	SB	BA
Ed Roebuck	P40,OF1	52	81	7	15	6	2	1	1	9	8	0	.185
Walt Moryn	OF41	45	145	19	36	18	6	0	2	21	17	2	.248
Tom Lasorda	P36	37	72	3	17	10	2	0	0	5	2	1	.236
Hampton Coleman	P36	36	42	4	8	9	0	0	0	6	5	0	.190
Earl Mossor	P32	34	65	9	17	12	2	0	3	4	9	0	.262
Ron Lee	P33	33	10	2	1	0	1	0	0	2	4	0	.100
Ken Lehman	P30	31	69	5	17	12	5	0	0	2	4	0	.246
Robert Ludwick	P29,OF1	31	37	2	5	1	1	0	0	4	6	0	.135
Gilbert Mills	P23	25	27	4	7	2	2	1	0	0	6	0	.259
Robert Alexander	P20	21	18	1	1	1	0	0	0	2	4	0	.056
Art Fabbro	P20,OF1	21	7	1	3	1	1	0	0	0	1	0	.429
Calvin Felix	OF10	11	36	6	9	5	0	1	1	4	3	0	.250
Al Epperly	P10	10	5	0	0	0	0	0	0	1	3	1	.000
Glenn Mickens	P3	3											.111

PITCHERS		W	L	PCT	G	GS	CG	SH	IP	H	BB	SO	ERA
Tom Lasorda		17	8	.680	36	29	12	3	208	171	94	122	2.81
Ed Roebuck		15	14	.517	40	26	14	2	220	202	70	83	3.07
Ken Lehman		13	9	.591	30	26	14	2	176	153	68	94	3.84
Earl Mossor		10	9	.526	32	16	5	1	159	165	74	64	3.96
Hampton Coleman		8	4	.667	36	16	7	0	134	144	63	63	4.37
Gilbert Mills		7	5	.583	23	9	3	1	76	70	37	40	3.91
Robert Ludwick		6	6	.500	29	20	5	3	128	110	62	33	3.23
Robert Alexander		5	4	.556	20	7	2	0	70	78	36	30	4.76
Art Fabbro		3	1	.750	20				39	25	23	16	2.54
Glenn Mickens		2	0	1.000	3				20	16	9	7	3.60
Ron Lee		2	3	.400	33	2	1	1	65	78	33	24	4.85
Al Epperly		1	0	1.000	10				17	21	7	2	3.18

BUFFALO   3rd   87-65   .572   -9   John Tighe
Bisons

BATTERS	POS-GAMES	GP	AB	R	H	BI	2B	3B	HR	BB	SO	SB	BA
John Wallaesa	1B	(see multi-team players)											
Ken Chapman	2B85,3B22,OF11,SS10	117	395	64	93	30	14	1	7	70	41	3	.235
Clarence Hicks	SS147	147	562	92	166	56	39	5	5	69	52	6	.295
Ed Kazak	3B121	121	423	65	113	59	20	2	13	51	31	2	.267
William Tuttle	OF153	153	548	67	151	75	24	9	11	38	56	19	.276
Rufus Crawford	OF127,P1	130	454	75	110	70	29	1	18	52	70	2	.242
Frank Carswell	OF104	105	362	60	117	75	28	1	23	36	30	3	.323
Joseph Erautt	C60	62	170	20	44	18	14	0	2	10	16	0	.259
Harvey Zernia	1B76,2B11	113	251	31	67	29	13	3	6	31	38	4	.267
Emil Restaino	OF67,1B1	95	186	27	47	27	4	0	6	24	16	1	.253
Frank Bolling	2B52	57	198	31	63	25	13	1	2	16	20	3	.318
Ken Johnson	P29	42	73	11	21	13	5	0	1	3	8	2	.288
Milt Jordan	P38	39	36	5	6	4	0	0	2	1	9	0	.167
Frank Lary	P38	38	83	10	17	8	3	0	2	1	20	0	.205
Don Coppage	P38	38	11	2	2	0	0	0	0	2	7	0	.182
John Weiss	P34	34	32	0	5	3	1	0	0	0	11	0	.156
Dan Ryan	C31	31	85	10	16	8	4	0	0	14	11	0	.188
Paul Foytack	P29	29	63	7	12	8	3	1	1	1	16	0	.190
William Humphrey	OF17	25	63	3	15	3	2	0	0	0	3	0	.238
Ernest Nevel	P23	23	49	5	11	3	2	1	0	3	11	0	.224
Earl Harrist	P19	19	43	1	8	3	0	0	0	2	11	0	.186
Ray Katt	C16	17	53	7	13	3	3	0	2	7	7	0	.245
Keith Little	1B14	14	46	9	12	17	2	0	6	7	20	0	.261
Jack Baumgartner	3B	10	33	4	7	0	0	0	0	0	6	1	.212
Richard Hocksema	P8	10	6	0	0	1	0	0	0	2	1	0	.000
Ted Kapuscinski	P9	9											.250
Alex McNeilance	P9	9											.143
David Madison	P6	6											.300
Carl Linhart	OF	5	10	1	1	1	0	0	0			0	.100
John Maldovan	P5	5											.000
Lawrence Cieslieski	C	4	7	0	2	0	1	0	0			0	.286
Al Yaylian	P4	4											.000
Jim Bunning	P3	3											.000
Ken Fremming	P3	3											.000
Eugene Costello	P1	1											.000

BUFFALO (cont.)
Bisons

PITCHERS	W	L	PCT	G	GS	CG	SH	IP	H	BB	SO	ERA
Frank Lary	17	11	.607	38	32	14	3	223	231	101	117	4.00
Paul Foytack	13	10	.565	29	23	12	2	177	152	97	140	3.97
Milt Jordan	12	1	.923	38	7	5	1	113	112	43	41	3.10
Ken Johnson	12	13	.480	29	29	10	1	163	166	128	115	5.30
Earl Harrist	9	5	.643	19	16	10	3	122	96	30	99	2.66
Ernest Nevel	9	8	.529	23	19	12	1	125	145	45	46	4.10
John Weiss	5	5	.500	34	8	4	1	99	111	46	37	4.82
Dom Coppage	2	1	.667	38	0	0	0	70	80	26	19	4.63
David Madison	2	1	.667	6				26	24	15	12	3.81
Alex McNeilance	1	1	.500	9				26	31	11	14	7.27
Al Yaylian	1	1	.500	3				13	10	11	4	4.15
Ted Kapuscinski	1	3	.250	9				30	25	12	9	3.00
Ken Fremming	0	1	.000	3				10	8	12	3	3.60
Richard Hocksema	0	0	----	8				17	22	6	4	5.29
John Maldovan	0	0	----	5				5	13	13	5	18.00
Jim Bunning	0	0	----	3				5	6	0	4	1.80
Eugene Costello	0	0	----	1				2	1	4	2	4.50
Rufus Crawford	0	0	----	1				1	3	1	0	0.00

BALTIMORE   4th   82-72   .532   -15   Don Heffner
Orioles

BATTERS	POS-GAMES	GP	AB	R	H	BI	2B	3B	HR	BB	SO	SB	BA
Jack Graham	1B89	99	318	45	78	58	11	2	15	45	33	0	.245
Ralph Caballero	2B129	133	462	54	124	49	25	2	5	60	36	9	.268
Ted Kazanski	SS60	60	217	36	63	12	12	2	3	25	20	0	.290
Russ Kerns	3B111	126	426	52	123	67	12	6	12	37	24	5	.289
Archie Wilson	OF148	150	585	76	176	79	29	6	13	28	52	3	.301
Stan Jok	OF98,3B39	141	487	84	136	91	17	10	20	74	67	6	.279
Roy Weatherly	OF96	113	377	56	101	58	12	2	17	29	33	2	.268
Martin Tabacheck	C87	93	265	20	65	27	10	1	1	34	22	0	.245
Damon Phillips	SS57,2B28,3B14,1B13	118	342	32	81	42	14	0	11	30	29	1	.237
Marv Rackley	OF89	111	363	62	116	28	14	2	3	40	21	3	.320
John Mayo	1B46,OF38	91	322	56	92	32	11	6	4	37	32	2	.286
Joseph Lonnett	C54,OF,1B,2B	77	162	27	25	25	3	0	11	24	41	1	.154
Jack Lohrke	SS41,1B,3B,OF	61	180	17	35	18	10	2	2	9	20	3	.194
Clyde Kluttz	C31	42	99	7	19	4	3	0	1	3	5	0	.192
Thomas Herrin	P40	41	31	2	4	3	1	0	1	1	10	0	.129
Bob Greenwood	P37	38	45	3	7	4	1	0	2	4	20	0	.156
Richard Starr	P37	38	41	3	6	2	0	0	1	9	15	0	.146
Ken Heintzelman	P37	37	28	0	2	1	0	0	0	0	4	0	.071
Howard Fox	P34	35	78	6	13	5	3	0	0	2	16	0	.167
John Sanford	P32	33	68	9	20	5	4	1	0	4	15	0	.294
Ron Mrozinski	P30	31	33	1	2	0	0	1	0	4	15	0	.061
John Thompson	P25	27	58	3	8	5	1	0	0	3	17	0	.138
Kent Peterson	P22	22	17	2	6	0	1	0	0	0	3	0	.353
Charles Bowers	P9	9											.000
Vern Taylor	P6	6											.000
Bennett Flowers	P5	5											.071
Joseph Tesauro	PH	2	2	0	0	0	0	0	0	0		0	.000
Clarence Marshall	P3	3											.000
Louis Possehl	P2	2											.000

PITCHERS	W	L	PCT	G	GS	CG	SH	IP	H	BB	SO	ERA
Howard Fox	15	10	.600	34	29	12	1	204	193	76	90	3.83
John Sanford	14	13	.519	32	30	11	0	200	186	110	128	3.96
Richard Starr	11	11	.500	37	19	7	2	159	148	69	87	4.19
Bob Greenwood	11	12	.478	37	20	4	3	146	141	71	110	4.07
John Thompson	10	4	.714	25	22	7	2	154	142	50	68	3.79
Thomas Herrin	8	4	.667	40	3	1	0	95	91	48	42	2.65
Ken Heintzelman	5	4	.556	39	9	1	1	111	115	35	46	3.32
Bennett Flowers	3	2	.600	5				36	29	13	19	2.50
Ron Mrozinski	2	5	.286	30	7	3	0	118	124	59	65	3.97
Kent Peterson	2	5	.286	22	7	1	0	63	61	24	41	3.43
Charles Bowers	1	0	1.00	9				9	13	8	7	11.00
Clarence Marshall	0	1	.000	3				5	8	11	2	9.00
Louis Possehl	0	1	.000	1				1	4	1	0	18.00
Vern Taylor	0	0	----	6				6	6	6	2	6.00

TORONTO Maple Leafs

5th	78-76	.506	-19	Burleigh Grimes

BATTERS	POS-GAMES	GP	AB	R	H	BI	2B	3B	HR	BB	SO	SB	BA
Ed Stevens	1B146	151	520	82	146	92	20	5	19	69	56	6	.281
Robert Wilson	2B135	136	531	66	146	56	20	9	0	46	49	11	.275
Billy DeMars	SS135,3B16	148	545	69	142	52	23	3	3	45	29	5	.261
Mike Goliat	3B98,OF28,2B5,SS1	135	454	77	127	72	26	6	19	64	80	7	.280
Lewis Morton	OF151,C1	152	570	74	175	83	35	3	16	64	36	3	.307
Robert DelGreco	OF109,3B17	129	379	64	90	48	15	10	6	74	65	9	.237
Bob Addis	OF88	88	283	52	76	38	12	2	7	31	19	2	.269
Joseph Rossi	C73	76	245	32	63	37	12	2	3	27	27	3	.257
Harold Keller	C63	76	201	23	55	26	9	3	4	24	25	0	.274
Ray Shore	P70	70	16	1	1	0	0	0	0	0	3	0	.063
Frank Colman	1B12,OF10	62	98	14	25	14	4	1	4	22	17	3	.255
Robert O'Neal	C37	49	88	8	18	6	2	0	0	21	8	0	.205
Louis Sleater	P25	46	71	9	20	12	5	1	0	7	7	0	.282
Kal Segrist	3B33,2B,SS	42	122	12	24	12	2	0	1	24	16	3	.197
Don Johnson	P41	41	79	1	8	6	1	0	0	4	22	0	.101
Cliff Mapes	OF33	40	109	13	24	8	7	0	2	31	31	3	.220
Vic Lombardi	P29,OF1	34	49	6	9	9	2	0	0	3	3	1	.184
Carlton Post	P31	33	44	8	12	2	1	3	0	7	11	0	.273
Robert Boyd	OF29,1B2	31	120	16	37	12	4	4	3	10	7	1	.308
Robert Hogue	P30	30	49	4	6	3	0	0	0	2	14	0	.122
Gerald Fahr	P30	30	39	2	7	6	0	0	1	1	20	1	.179
Stubby Overmire	P29	30	21	6	5	2	1	0	0	3	4	0	.238
Russ Rosburg	OF27	28	91	14	20	19	5	0	7	12	23	0	.220
Forrest Main	P24	24	9	0	1	0	0	0	0	0	3	0	.111
William Jennings	SS11,2B,3B	22	50	6	8	4	1	0	0	10	11	0	.160
Francisco Campo	OF18,1B1	21	67	10	16	6	0	0	3	7	3	2	.239
Alva Holloman	P13	13	19	3	5	1	0	0	0	3	5	0	.263
Clem Koshorek	SS12	12	36	8	9	4	1	0	1	8	1	2	.250
Harold Hudson	P11	11	18	1	7	2	0	0	0	0	2	0	.389
Phil Haugstad	P3	3											.333
Ramon Rodriguez	C	2	5	0	0	0	0	0	0	0		0	.000
Russ Bauers	P2	2											.000
Peter Naton	C1	1	1	0	0	0	0	0	0	0		0	.000
Frank Repchik	P1	1											.000
Don E. Robertson	P1	1											.000

PITCHERS		W	L	PCT	G	GS	CG	SH	IP	H	BB	SO	ERA
Don Johnson		15	12	.556	41	30	15	3	243	216	73	156	2.67
Vic Lombardi		11	8	.579	29	15	6	0	144	127	44	60	3.31
Carlton Post		10	8	.556	31	22	6	1	142	138	62	67	3.73
Robert Hogue		8	11	.421	30	21	5	0	135	146	41	58	3.60
Gerald Fahr		7	8	.467	30	16	5	0	117	131	24	38	4.23
Louis Sleater		7	11	.389	25	20	7	0	137	138	65	64	4.01
Ray Shore		5	3	.625	70	0	0	0	105	83	61	59	2.83
Forrest Main		4	1	.800	24	1	0	0	48	55	22	20	3.56
Harold Hudson		4	2	.667	11	7	2	0	56	51	31	14	2.89
Alva Holloman		4	3	.571	13	8	1	1	55	53	43	23	5.07
Stubby Overmire		3	6	.333	29	7	3	1	84	91	27	30	4.93
Russ Bauers		0	1	.000	2				4	5	3	2	4.50
Frank Repchik		0	1	.000	1				9	7	2	0	2.00
Phil Haugstad		0	0	----	3				6	11	4	2	10.50
Don E. Robertson		0	0	----	1				2	2	0	0	4.50

OTTAWA Athletics

6th	71-83	.461	-26	Frank Skaff

BATTERS	POS-GAMES	GP	AB	R	H	BI	2B	3B	HR	BB	SO	SB	BA
Louis Limmer	1B129	135	467	68	128	73	22	4	15	57	38	5	.274
Everett Kell	2B128,3B1	132	418	55	97	30	24	5	3	43	22	7	.232
Jack Littrell	SS148	148	551	72	134	43	31	6	7	49	95	4	.243
Walt Rogers	3B94,OF66	154	581	77	150	49	22	8	1	68	51	30	.258
Gerard Scala	OF103	103	373	43	107	35	14	3	2	33	29	5	.287
Taft Wright	OF95	106	331	48	117	56	19	5	7	49	22	2	.353
Joseph Taylor	OF69	70	243	42	76	45	16	3	7	24	26	4	.313
Wilmer Shantz	C99,OF	105	317	21	72	27	9	3	0	15	28	2	.227
Jake Spruill	3B52,OF,SS,1B	103	244	34	68	26	15	2	1	20	21	3	.279
Harold Bevan	2B50,3B20,1B12,SS5	101	296	31	92	50	19	2	3	21	24	0	.311
Fred Gerken	OF69,1B12	84	235	24	58	26	7	2	4	26	35	4	.247
Richard Greco	OF60	64	215	24	54	26	8	4	5	20	49	0	.251
Robert Trice	P38	56	106	21	27	16	5	0	4	4	21	0	.255

OTTAWA (cont.)
Athletics

BATTERS	POS-GAMES	GP	AB	R	H	BI	2B	3B	HR	BB	SO	SB	BA
Neal Watlington	C46	55	155	18	39	20	6	0	3	21	12	1	.252
Ed Burtschy	P50	50	30	4	5	3	0	1	0	7	8	1	.167
Al Pinkston	OF21,1B4	45	101	9	20	9	6	0	1	6	18	0	.198
Ed Hrabczak	P40	40	40	2	3	0	0	0	0	1	23	0	.075
Allen Romberger	P39	39	21	0	1	2	0	0	0	6	11	0	.047
Richard Rozek	P23	35	27	0	0	1	0	0	0	0	12	0	.000
John Mackinson	P29	31	49	4	9	3	0	0	0	6	10	0	.184
John Kume	P31	31	29	0	0	0	0	0	0	2	13	0	.000
Andrew Tranavitch	C21	26	50	8	13	3	2	0	1	3	8	0	.260
Vince Gohl	P21	22	28	2	8	5	0	0	0	1	6	0	.286
William Harrington	P21	21	46	3	10	8	1	0	0	3	6	0	.217
Art Ditmar	P19	19	36	4	8	3	1	0	0	0	4	0	.222
Harry Minor	OF	13	21	1	3	1	0	0	0	2	5	0	.143
Len Matarazzo	P9	9											.000
William Hockenbury	P5	5											.000
John Hofmann	P3	3											.500
Courtney Stemple	P3	3											.000
Joseph Mangini	PH	2	2	0	0	0	0	0	0	0			0	.000
James Bell	P2	2											.000

PITCHERS	W	L	PCT	G	GS	CG	SH	IP	H	BB	SO	ERA
Robert Trice	21	10	.677	38	30	20	4	229	207	84	57	3.10
Ed Burtschy	12	7	.632	50	4	2	1	118	98	59	62	2.82
William Harrington	7	9	.438	21	19	6	0	131	147	47	70	4.53
Ed Hrabczak	7	10	.412	40	16	6	0	130	133	69	64	4.15
John Mackinson	7	10	.412	29	22	5	1	151	179	70	73	5.01
Richard Rozek	5	8	.385	23	15	4	0	93	85	62	47	4.26
Allen Romberger	4	1	.800	39	10	2	1	108	121	40	49	3.50
John Kume	3	4	.429	31	6	1	0	100	97	60	60	4.05
Vince Gohl	3	9	.250	21	12	4	0	78	90	43	34	4.73
Art Ditmar	2	13	.133	19	17	3	1	107	116	59	45	5.30
Courtney Stemple	0	2	.000	3				5	8	13	2	12.60
Len Matarazzo	0	0	----	9				19	21	11	4	3.79
William Hockenbury	0	0	----	5				13	13	12	6	9.69
John Hofmann	0	0	----	3				7	4	7	3	3.86
James Bell	0	0	----	2				3	4	6	2	12.00

SYRACUSE   7th   58-95   .379   -38.5   Bruno Betzel
Chiefs

BATTERS	POS-GAMES	GP	AB	R	H	BI	2B	3B	HR	BB	SO	SB	BA
John Douglas	1B76	77	246	27	52	21	6	3	0	32	35	3	.211
Ben Zientara	2B90	98	299	45	77	36	14	1	3	66	19	0	.258
Jim Brideweser	SS84	84	320	52	87	27	20	6	1	45	30	9	.272
Hector Rodriguez	3B116,SS32	148	527	90	159	62	21	7	4	96	62	12	.302
Carden Gillenwater	OF147	147	506	56	126	75	16	4	4	79	52	9	.249
John Blatnik	OF130	138	463	66	123	76	13	5	18	62	105	1	.266
Henry Workman	OF93,1B17	123	376	53	97	56	23	1	9	43	18	2	.258
Roy Partee	C59	64	185	12	33	17	5	0	1	23	35	1	.178
Art Schult	OF79	86	288	30	70	47	12	2	8	24	31	1	.243
Marv Blaylock	1B67	70	254	37	61	24	10	1	5	30	53	3	.240
Richard Kinaman	C47,3B5	57	168	14	39	20	6	2	1	12	21	1	.232
John Welaj	OF22,3B19	57	131	11	28	8	4	0	0	11	14	1	.214
William Drescher	C35	55	133	12	37	14	9	0	1	16	13	0	.278
Lynn Lovenguth	P34	55	83	11	20	7	3	0	0	11	14	0	.241
Harry Markell	P52	52	86	3	16	5	1	0	0	6	26	0	.186
Arnold Landeck	P45	46	30	3	8	3	0	1	0	7	5	0	.267
Marv Williams	P35	39	42	4	11	4	1	1	0	5	8	0	.262
Art Hartley	P34	34	52	4	9	3	1	0	0	10	10	0	.173
Claude Corbitt	SS17,3B5	31	87	10	19	15	5	0	0	8	9	0	.218
Leon Griffore	P31	31	66	3	14	3	4	0	0	1	10	0	.212
Al Robertson	C26	28	72	15	19	5	2	0	0	15	7	1	.264
Art Dyck	P24	28	27	2	8	1	1	0	0	1	4	0	.296
John Robinson	P26	26	11	0	0	0	0	0	0	1	3	0	.000
Norldan Williams	OF15	17	59	9	12	7	1	1	0	6	16	0	.203
Frank LaManna	3B5,P2	9											.100
Wayne Tucker	2B,3B,SS	7	23	1	3	1	0	0	0			0	.130
Charles Bell	2B,SS	7	10	3	3	3	0	0	2			0	.300
Charles Weathers	PH	3	2	0	0	0	0	0	0			0	.000
Len Okrie	C	2	4	1	1	0	0	0	0			0	.250
James Blackburn	P2	2											.000

SYRACUSE (cont.)
Chiefs

BATTERS	POS-GAMES	GP	AB	R	H	BI	2B	3B	HR	BB	SO	SB	BA
Harley Hisner	P2	2											.000
Leon Griffeth	P1	1											.000
William Woop	P1	1											.000

PITCHERS		W	L	PCT	G	GS	CG	SH	IP	H	BB	SO	ERA
Lynn Lovenguth		11	13	.458	34	25	10	0	179	191	86	87	4.68
Harry Markell		11	17	.393	52	30	11	0	247	258	98	155	3.86
Art Hartley		10	16	.385	34	27	12	2	194	194	54	79	4.08
Leon Griffore		10	16	.385	31	24	13	1	187	210	50	60	4.28
Arnold Landeck		6	9	.400	45	12	4	1	120	137	29	32	4.95
Marv Williams		6	12	.333	35	20	4	0	140	149	93	60	4.89
Art Dyck		2	6	.250	24	8	2	1	65	92	28	19	5.40
Leon Griffith		1	0	1.000	1				1	1	0	0	0.00
John Robinson		1	2	.333	26	2	0	0	51	49	30	12	5.29
Harley Hisner		0	1	.000	2				8	10	4	1	6.75
James Blackburn		0	2	.000	2				12	15	4	4	6.00
Frank LaManna		0	0	----	2				3	7	2	0	12.00
William Woop		0	0	----	1				3	13	2	1	33.00

SPRINGFIELD   8th   51-102   .333   -45.5   Bruce Edwards -
Cubs   John Sheehan

BATTERS	POS-GAMES	GP	AB	R	H	BI	2B	3B	HR	BB	SO	SB	BA
George Freese	1B75,OF38,3B16	132	493	53	131	66	26	2	9	32	43	7	.266
Jackson Hollis	2B80	82	298	39	76	21	20	1	2	30	33	8	.255
Harold Daugherty	SS	(see multi-team players)											
Walt Derucki	3B125,SS21	150	511	50	141	51	25	8	4	43	80	4	.276
Ron Northey	OF145	149	489	59	146	82	22	1	20	82	33	0	.299
Herb Adams	OF130	131	538	59	155	37	12	12	0	36	20	4	.288
Eugene Hooks	OF73,2B71	150	550	60	145	42	20	3	1	41	51	7	.264
Nelson Burbrink	C104,2B1	114	344	27	95	47	22	4	2	42	91	1	.276
Harold Meek	C60,1B29,OF12	104	304	38	64	22	17	4	1	30	61	1	.211
Don Elston	P36	51	87	8	15	3	1	0	0	8	14	0	.172
Paul Schramka	OF36	43	117	6	22	7	4	2	1	6	18	2	.188
Darius Hillman	P32	40	31	5	5	1	0	0	0	8	17	0	.161
Bruce Edwards	1B33	38	112	17	32	13	4	1	1	19	7	0	.286
Robert Ludwig	SS12,3B11,2B5	37	109	12	25	12	5	0	1	16	12	2	.229
Eugene Tarabilda	P35	35	42	4	5	3	2	0	0	3	15	0	.119
Jim Brosnan	P29	34	59	1	9	4	1	2	1	3	18	0	.153
Scott Quackenbush	OF22	30	54	6	9	1	1	0	0	0	9	0	.167
Regino Otero	1B11	30	41	2	7	4	1	0	0	3	1	0	.171
John Pyecha	P29	29	52	1	9	1	1	0	0	3	21	0	.173
Luvern Fear	P22	24	35	0	4	1	0	0	0	0	17	0	.114
Sheldon Jones	P20	20	23	0	4	1	0	0	0	0	5	0	.174
Mike Mellis	P16	16	9	1	1	0	0	0	0	1	3	0	.111
George Long	P13	15	15	1	1	1	0	0	0	0	4	0	.067
Robert Sperry	1B12	14	49	3	9	6	2	2	0	0	4	0	.184
Ted Lotz	OF12	12	37	3	8	2	2	0	1	1	4	0	.216
James Willis	P9	9											.000
Chris Kitsos	SS	8	28	4	3	0	0	0	0			0	.107
Robert Hartig	P8	8											.111
Robert Bortz	PH,PR	6	3	0	0	0	0	0	0			0	.000
Elvin Stabelfield	P4	4											.000
Ned Folmar	OF	2	2	0	0	0	0	0	0			0	.000
Joseph Sabatella	1B	2	1	0	0	0	0	0	0			0	.000
John Liptak	C	1	1	0	0	0	0	0	0			0	.000
Darrell Rothrock	P1	1											.000
Thomas Kerr	P1	1											.000
Wes Carr	P1	1											.500

PITCHERS		W	L	PCT	G	GS	CG	SH	IP	H	BB	SO	ERA
Don Elston		9	17	.346	36	28	20	3	224	224	99	104	3.70
Eugene Tarabilda		7	10	.412	35	18	7	0	150	166	37	50	4.02
John Pyecha		7	11	.389	29	24	9	1	161	147	103	70	4.14
Jim Brosnan		4	17	.190	29	21	10	1	161	180	77	91	4.70
Sheldon Jones		3	5	.375	20	7	1	0	74	68	25	29	3.65
Luvern Fear		3	10	.231	22	14	4	0	114	118	42	30	4.18
James Willis		2	3	.400	9	6	2	0	51	62	25	24	3.71
Darius Hillman		2	12	.143	32	15	5	1	118	122	60	50	4.42
Mike Mellis		1	2	.333	16				41	51	24	24	6.15

SPRINGFIELD (cont.)
Cubs

PITCHERS	W	L	PCT	G	GS	CG	SH	IP	H	BB	SO	ERA
George Long	1	5	.167	13	8	2	0	49	53	40	14	7.35
Robert Hartig	1	5	.167	8				35	41	20	17	5.91
Darrell Rothrock	0	1	.000	1				4	5	3	1	6.75
Wes Carr	0	1	.000	1				4	6	3	1	13.50
Elvin Stabelfeld	0	0	----	4				8	15	6	2	10.10
Thomas Kerr	0	0	----	1				1	0	1	0	0.00

MULTI-TEAM PLAYERS

BATTERS	POS-GAMES	TEAMS	GP	AB	R	H	BI	2B	3B	HR	BB	SO	SB	BA
John Wallaesa	1B95,3B58	SP33-BU114	147	505	91	134	111	16	1	36	88	91	1	.265
Harold Daugherty	SS115,2B8	BU13-SP112	125	447	56	92	40	20	8	3	31	67	1	.206
Al Lakeman	C61	BA4-BU62	66	205	28	66	33	17	5	6	25	43	0	.322
Anthony Jacobs	P50	SP48-RO4	52	29	1	4	7	1	1	0	2	9	0	.138
Kurt Krieger	P33	RO10-SY23	33	18	2	0	0	0	0	0	1	10	0	.000
Bill Voiselle	P30	TO4-BU26	30	19	2	2	3	0	0	0	2	5	0	.105
Joseph Budny	P13	SY4-RO9	13	10	3	3	0	0	0	0	0	2	0	.300

PITCHERS		TEAMS	W	L	PCT	G	GS	CG	SH	IP	H	BB	SO	ERA
Anthony Jacobs		SP46-RO4	12	3	.800	50	0	0	0	113	103	47	62	2.63
Bill Voiselle		TO4-BU26	3	5	.375	30	7	0	0	72	100	16	35	5.63
Joseph Budny		SY4-RO9	1	0	1.000	13				34	42	18	11	5.03
Kurt Krieger		RO10-SY23	1	2	.333	33	4	0	0	94	93	33	38	5.32

TEAM BATTING

TEAMS	GP	AB	R	H	BI	2B	3B	HR	BB	SO	SB	BA
ROCHESTER	154	5017	820	1421	765	246	65	124	672	565	65	.283
MONTREAL	154	5078	768	1390	710	258	62	106	593	506	50	.274
BUFFALO	153	4923	720	1309	676	256	32	148	548	662	46	.266
BALTIMORE	154	5030	654	1303	618	193	43	122	506	564	36	.259
TORONTO	154	4939	680	1283	634	208	52	99	629	604	62	.260
OTTAWA	154	5021	617	1296	558	226	48	64	485	605	68	.258
SYRACUSE	153	4919	627	1222	567	190	39	58	656	652	54	.248
SPRINGFIELD	154	5007	532	1242	486	213	50	48	463	636	36	.248
	615	39934	5418	10466	5014	1790	391	769	4552	4794	417	.262

POSTLUDE
NEW CITIES, NEW COUNTRIES

In the years following Baltimore's excisement from the International League, the circuit continued changing. New cities were added as old cities dropped out. In some cases, the league followed its namesake by expanding beyond United States borders.

In 1954, the International League added two new teams. One of them was in Richmond, to replace the Baltimore team. The other, replacing Springfield, opened a whole new frontier for the league. For the past seven years, a team in Havana, Cuba, had played in the Florida International League. In 1954, Havana's team joined the International League, adding a third country to the circuit. Other changes in the league structure during the 1950s included Columbus taking the place of Ottawa in 1955, and Miami replacing Syracuse one year later.

The year 1960 saw another shakeup in the International League. The political situation in Cuba had become unsettled by the late 1950s. The Junior World Series of 1959, played in Havana, had been disrupted by Castro's revolutionaries. When these same revolutionaries snared all American assets the next year, the International League acted in haste, transferring the Havana club to Jersey City. The next year the International returned to the Caribbean as the Miami franchise was switched to San Juan, Puerto Rico. This proved to be a disaster, and the club was transferred to Charleston, West Virginia, in May 1961. Other new clubs in the 1960s included Atlanta, Jacksonville, Little Rock, Indianapolis, Louisville, Norfolk, and Syracuse (after a five-year hiatus). The 1960s also saw the demise of longtime league members Montreal and Toronto. Montreal left the International following the 1960 campaign, while Toronto followed in 1967. This left the league without a Canadian team for the first time since the 1890s.

Another old friend departed in 1970. The Buffalo Bisons, after years of declining attendance, left for Winnipeg, Manitoba. After two years there, the team moved to Virginia, and later to Memphis. Other new clubs during the decade included Columbus (returning after a six-year absence), Charleston (after eleven years gone), and Pawtucket, Rhode Island.

The years from 1980 to the present day have comprised a prosperous and stable time in the International League. A new team from Maine, which came from Charleston, played for five years before moving on to Scranton/Wilkes-Barre. Two brand-new franchises were awarded in 1993, one to Ottawa and another to Charlotte, expanding the league to ten teams. Future plans include a shifting of teams between the American Association and the International League, thus allowing the Buffalo Bisons (now an Association member) to return to the International for the 1998 season.

During the last 45 years of the International League, several outstanding individual hitting and pitching feats took place. For the hitters, Toronto's Glenn Nelson won a pair of Triple Crowns (1955 and 1958). Shortly thereafter (1959), Frank Herrara from Buffalo accomplished the same feat, followed by Pawtucket's Jim Rice in 1974. Two different pitchers also won the hurlers' version of the triple crown (most wins, lowest earned run average, and most strikeouts). Toronto's Al Cicotte turned the trick in 1960, and 16 years later Dennis Martinez did the same for Rochester.

The story of the International League is a story of longevity and flexibility. Tracing its ancestry back more than 100 years, through a half-dozen name changes, at least three disbandments, and over three dozen cities, the league has followed a continuous (though somewhat circuitous) path to the present. No other minor baseball league can come close to matching this mark. As the next century dawns, the International League remains one of the top three minor league circuits in North America. There is every indication that the league will continue—perhaps for a second hundred years.

SELECTED BIBLIOGRAPHY

ARTICLES

Bennett, Brain. "Rochester, 1928." *The National Pastime*, 1997. Society for American Baseball research.

Chrisman, David. "Howie Moss, Minor League Slugger." *Baseball Research Journal*, 1982. Society for American Baseball Research.

_____. "International League Recollections." *Baseball Research Journal*, 1978. Society for American Baseball Research.

Kermisch, Al. "A Vote for Dunn's Orioles." *Baseball Research Journal*, 1977. Society for American Baseball Research.

Murphy, J.M. "Napolean Lajoie: Modern Baseball's First Superstar." *The National Pastime*, 1988. Society for American Baseball Research.

BOOKS

Bauer, Carlos, ed. *The SABR Guide to Minor League Statistics*. Cleveland: Society for American Baseball Research, 1995.

Bready, James H. *The Home Team*. Baltimore: James H. Bready, 1984.

Brown, William. *Baseball's Fabulous Montreal Royals*. Montreal: Robert Davies, 1996.

Bucek, Jeanine, editorial director. *The Baseball Encyclopedia*. 10th edition. New York: Macmillan, 1996.

Deutsch, Jordan, et al. *The Scrapbook History of Baseball*. New York: Bobbs-Merrill, 1975.

Foster, John B. *A History of the National Association of Professional Base Ball Leagues*. National Association of Professional Base Ball Leagues, 1927.

Ivor-Campbell, Frederick, et al., eds. *Baseball's First Stars*. Cleveland: Society for American Baseball Research, 1996.

James, Bill. *The Bill James Guide to Baseball Managers*. New York: Scribner, 1997.

Johnson, Lloyd. *The Minor League Register*. Durham NC: Baseball America, 1994.

Johnson, Lloyd, and Wolff, Miles, eds. *The Encyclopedia of Minor League Baseball*. 2nd edition. Durham NC: Baseball America, 1997.

Lowry, Philip J. *Green Cathedrals*. Cooperstown: Society for American Baseball Research, 1986.

Mayer, Ronald. *1937 Newark Bears*. East Honover: Vantage, 1980.

BOOKS (cont.)

Nemec, David. *The Great American Baseball Team Book*. New York: Signet, 1992.

Obojski, Robert. *Bush Leagues*. New York: Macmillan, 1975.

Okkonen, Marc. *The Federal League of 1914-1915*. Society for American Baseball Research, 1989.

O'Neal, Bill. *The International League*. Austin TX: Eakin, 1992.

Reidenbaugh, Lowell, ed. *Baseball's Hall of Fame: Cooperstown*. New York: Arlington House, 1988.

Seymour, Harold. *Baseball: The Early Years*. New York: Oxford University Press, 1960.

Sullivan, Neil J. *The Minors*. New York: St. Martin's, 1991.

Thorn, John, and Palmer, Peter, eds. *Total Baseball IV*. New York: Viking, 1995.

Tiemann, Robert, and Rucker, Mark, eds. *Nineteenth Century Stars*. Society for American Baseball Research, 1989.

GUIDES

International League Record Book, 1996.

Players' National League Baseball Guide, 1890.

Reach's Official Baseball Guide, 1885–1938.

Spalding-Reach Official Baseball Guide, 1939–1941.

Spalding's Official Baseball Guide, 1885–1938.

Sporting News Baseball Guide and Record Book, 1942–1954.

Supplemental International League Statistics (Nemec Collection), 1884–1899, 1934–1953.

NEWSPAPERS

The Sporting Life, 1886–1916.

The Sporting News, 1886–1953.

INDEX

Every effort was made to find the first names of all the players. In some cases this was not possible. For the players with no first name, each is given a separate entry in the index.